THE EVERYMAN
HISTORY OF
ENGLISH LITERATURE

THE EVERYMAN HISTORY OF ENGLISH LITERATURE

by
Peter Conrad

J.M. Dent & Sons Ltd
London Melbourne

First published 1985
© Peter Conrad, 1985
First published in paperback 1987

This book is set in 11/12½ Ehrhardt by The Alden Press, Oxford
Printed and made in Great Britain by Cox & Wyman for
J.M. Dent & Sons Ltd
Aldine House, 33 Welbeck Street, London W1M 8LX

British Library Cataloguing in Publication Data

Conrad, Peter, 1948–
   History of English literature.
   1. English literature—History and criticism
   I. Title
   820.9   PR83

   ISBN 0-460-02236-9

Contents

Contents

Preface

To tell the long story of English literature within a single book is a risky business; I have thought it worth attempting because I wanted to show that the works of the more than a thousand years that this narrative covers themselves comprise one indivisible, unending book. This conviction underlies and interconnects my history. Literature seems to me a collaborative—almost a familial—activity, marrying the past with the present and from that union generating the future. I do not believe the past to be a burden or an Oedipal infliction, as contemporary criticism sometimes sees it. Recalled and recapitulated in its entirety by every literary generation, the past enlivens and invigorates the present. The furthest-reaching literary futures in England are often restorations of the remotest past. Shaw's intellectualised Utopia, millenia hence, goes back to Methuselah. In a special and unique sense, the literary history of England is timeless.

That is why I have told its story at once forwards and backwards—as anticipation and as retrospection. It resembles a human life, the first half of which you spend wondering about and rehearsing for what will come, while in the second half you reflect on what has already happened and how it has determined you, aware that the present is, moment by moment, reinterpreting the past. In a similar way, the literature writes its own history.

Thus *Beowulf* is a beginning and also, when Seamus Heaney unearths an echo of Anglo-Saxon song in his peat bog, an end. The first great work of English literature begets a posterity in contemporary America, with John Gardner's novel *Grendel* or the poem 'Beowulf' from Richard Wilbur's 1948 volume *Ceremony*, where the epic hero falls victim to a modern agnosticism and is misconstrued by the survivors: the mourners ride round his pyre 'Singing of him what they could understand'. The ancient epic is presciently up-to-date, battling against our abiding night-fears. The ogre in Wilbur's poem is 'a child, / Grown monstrous'. Analogously, the medieval romance becomes the sovereign spirit of nineteenth-century romanticism, and its questers continue to police our culpable daily reality. Raymond Chandler writes detective fables which are versions of the Grail narrative, Graham Greene anti-heroically revises the *Song of Roland*.

I have concentrated on this activity of transmission and adaptation because it demonstrates the literature's perpetuity. The present rejuvenates the past. Chaucer is translated to the eighteenth century by Dryden, or by Pope whose

Wife of Bath is a coquette like Belinda in *The Rape of the Lock* at the end of her career: 'Now all my conquests, all my charms good night!' she sighs in Pope's 1714 version. In John Gay's play *The Wife of Bath* (1730), Chaucer subdues the rebellious pilgrims by imposing a rule of sentimental sympathy, as if he were Sterne arbitrating disputes in the Shandy household. 'We will all turn mediators', ventures Gay's Chaucer (with more diplomatic finesse than his prototype can ever manage), 'and reconcile differences. . . . Let us lovingly take hands, and agree in a dance.' Discipleship becomes devotion, a religious act of homage to the literary past: thus, among the pre-Raphaelites, Chaucer was promoted to something like sanctity. Venus in the *Confessio Amantis* instructed Gower to pass on her compliments to his colleague Chaucer, 'mi disciple and mi poete'; almost five hundred years later, 'sweet-souled' Chaucer has himself become a god, prayed to by William Morris in *The Earthly Paradise* (1868–70):

> O Master, if thine heart could love us yet,
> Spite of things left undone, and wrongly done, . . .
> Help thou us singers of an empty day!

Morris's Chaucer is still resident in paradise—the 'sunny world', as Morris called it, of an idealised feudalism. T. S. Eliot, in the literature's next invocation of its source in Chaucer, abruptly provokes his fall. The April which lashes *The Waste Land* is not Chaucer's genial, ebullient season but a cruel mockery of new life, and Chaucer's pilgrims have declined into literary triflers, bored socialities who 'read, much of the night, and go south in the winter'.

Spenser is claimed as a colleague by Shelley, Keats and Byron, and Virginia Woolf, in an essay published posthumously in 1948, looks to his primitive imagination to release us in the future from an unquiet, modern, mental consciousness: 'He is not merely a thinking brain; he is a feeling body, a sensitive heart.' Shakespeare migrates beyond the drama. He is for Fielding and Dickens the patron of the English novel, for Coleridge the genie of romantic poetry. Milton seems actually to predestine the writing which follows *Paradise Lost*, and which adds impishly revisionist postscripts to it.

Halfway through my book, literature offers to forget this accumulated past and begin anew. The novel is invented as a denial of literary history. Defoe on his tour of Britain dismisses ancient monuments. Yet what someone said of America also goes for the novel: youth and newness are its oldest traditions. In every generation, it pretends to reject a past it is merely revising. Sterne finds the novel's formal source in Shakespearean tragicomedy, Fielding and Richardson derive it from Miltonic epic, deflected into either easy-going romance or quiescent pastoral; later, the novel's tactic is the renovation of previous novels—of *The Mysteries of Udolpho* in *Northanger Abbey*, of *The Pilgrim's Progress* in *The Old Curiosity Shop*, of *Sir Charles Grandison* in *Daniel*

Deronda, of *Tom Jones* in *Jacob's Room*, of every novel in *Ulysses*, and of *Ulysses* in *Earthly Powers*.

In the book's second half, literature changes from prophesying its future to conserving its past. Its most vitally necessary memory is of itself. In Samuel Johnson's lives of the poets and in William Hazlitt's or Matthew Arnold's theories of poetry, literature sadly commemorates its dead. Romantic poetry is sometimes a whispering gallery of quotations from the expired past; the same remains true of *The Waste Land*. Indeed, in both Wordsworth's *Prelude* and Eliot's *Four Quartets*, one of the poet's purposes is to lay the ghosts of his predecessors.

It would be wrong, however, however, to characterise this sense of the past as a paralysing weight. The great poet of this century, W. B. Yeats, acknowledges no pre-emption and is alive in all of the past at once, now an epic warrior, now a Renaissance prince, now a towering romantic ego. In English literature, as it turns out, the moderns are positively medieval. Ezra Pound in his 1934 *A B C of Reading* called Chaucer 'more compendious than Dante' because his culture was not insular. His name is French, and his mind is consequently 'the mind of Europe, not the mind of an annex or an outlying province'. Samuel Beckett praised the same universality in Joyce, who enlarges English and makes of it a punningly polyglot contemporary Latin. If Joyce is modernism's Chaucer, D. H. Lawrence is its Langland, worrying as fanatically as his precursor in *Piers Plowman* about the letter's fidelity to the spirit, and recurring in *The Rainbow* to the biblical commentary and translation from which, in the Middle Ages, our literature initially grew.

This co-operation between the present and the whole of the past rules out the establishment of an authoritarian canon. Rather than delimiting a select 'great tradition', I have tried—within reason—to include everyone of significance, and to relate them all to each other. Relations between writers matter more here than their relation to the society of which they are members or the political system of which they are subjects. I have not written an external history, aligning the literature with social changes or political events; my aim is to demonstrate how history happens within the literature, which has its own chronology. All its different times overlap in space.

But *where* in space? I have been much concerned with the elusive spirit of place in English literature. It is as if, somewhere, all the books were being written side by side. Thomas Dekker imagined the poets co-existing in an earthly paradise; E. M. Forster three centuries later sits all the novelists together at a table in the British Museum reading room; Virginia Woolf domiciles them in a country house.

Throughout my book, an image of this space where times conjoin keeps on returning. It is the April landscape of Chaucer (and the same scene ghoulishly parodied in *The Waste Land*), Spenser's Garden of Adonis, the Edens of Milton and Marvell, or the 'other Eden' and 'demi-paradise' of England mapped by John of Gaunt in *Richard II*; in its green fields Falstaff was born earlier today, and he rests there until he is resurrected tomorrow. In the eighteenth century it goes into mourning, as Oliver Goldsmith's forsaken village or Thomas Gray's country churchyard; in the nineteenth century it goes into hiding, as Lewis Carroll's wonderland or Frances Hodgson Burnett's secret garden. The twentieth century believes it to be diseased. In Daphne du Maurier's *Rebecca* (1938) it is first the fetidly fragrant Happy Valley at Manderley, dank with azaleas and rhododendrons, then is later diagnosed as the warped interior of Rebecca herself, its malign 'growth . . . deep-rooted', its uterus deformed. W. H. Auden finds a corpse in the garden in his poem about detective stories, while Eliot in 'Burnt Norton' scrupulously refrains from opening the door which would admit him to it. It is a lost paradise of course, but then it always has been, and already is so in Chaucer. The Wife of Bath complains that the friars have unhallowed the land. Orson Welles, situating Falstaff in it, once identified this reclusive Arcady as the English dream of a Golden Age, which 'only the oak trees and the flowering chestnuts remember truly'.

Bill Brandt took photographs of it, for the volume he published in 1951 as *Literary Britain*. He glimpses it in the bent-backed tombstones of Stoke Poges, where Gray wrote his 'Elegy', in the prostrate, rain-slick graves of Haworth Churchyard, where the Brontës are buried, or in the tumuli of Hardy's Stonehenge. But it is a place of birth as much as of interment: to illustrate the Hebridean journey of Boswell and Johnson, Brandt photographed a gull's nest on the isle of Skye. Containing three eggs and a feather as a souvenir of the foraging occupant, it is set beside the sea, which Boswell calls 'that universal medium of connection between mankind'. His phrase could serve equally well for literature. Twenty-five years before Brandt, Stanley Spencer, in his painting 'Resurrection', had located the sacred English imaginative haven by the Thames at Cookham. He sees it as a growing garden planted with memories, where the present is embedded in the past and the past resurges in the present; a country churchyard whose funeral tablets—like the one in the bottom right corner of the picture, on which Spencer himself lolls—are opening books, and whose revenants are readers. This is our literature's family plot, and it can be seen on the cover of this book.

My own experience of the literature has been as happily collaborative as the process I describe in the book. My great good fortune is to have been encouraged by three generous teachers—John Bayley, John Buxton and the late James McAuley—and to have had, in my turn, the chance of learning from the students I have taught during the past decade at Oxford. I am grateful as well to Eileen Sahaddy, Donna Chenail and Rosemary Lane, who typed the manuscript during my year as an Arnold Bernhard Visiting Professor at Williams College, Massachusetts; and to my editor, Peter Shellard, for proposing that I should take on the work in the first place.

THE EVERYMAN HISTORY OF ENGLISH LITERATURE

— 1 —
Epic

In the beginning is the epic. Literature begins there. Epic is the institutional form which caters to the first human need, for—singing of arms and the man, as Virgil announces—it is the poem of force and the poem as force, a study in the power that language affords us over things. The epic antecedent of English literature is *Beowulf*, dating from about the middle of the eighth century and deriving, also conjecturally, from West Mercia, now the West Midlands. It is the first English epic and also perhaps the last, for the literature which follows it revises its values, and the genius of English writing is lodged thereafter in the opposed genre of pastoral, dreamily pacific and meditatively drowsy, in love with secret gardens and floral wonderlands, not with fields of battle. But the successors it lacks at home it has had abroad, for the epic is bequeathed to the English literatures of expatriation, translated to countries where the suppressing of monsters and the architectural fortifying of society must still be carried on. This most ancient poem is also presciently modern. Beowulf migrates eventually to America, whose menacing terrain must be colonised and levelled by the axe of Paul Bunyan, the tree-feller of folklore; the Anglo-Saxon troll-killer has as his heirs Melville's Ahab the whaler, Fenimore Cooper's deerslayer, and Michael Cimino's deer hunter. In the literature of England, however, Beowulf and the epic have no progeny, and this in the event turns out to be the refrain of that literature as it develops, the sign of its anti-classical nature and of its national uniqueness.

The first instinct of literature is epic, because language is power. Words subdue the unfriendly, meaningless world to human uses: names commandeer things. William Hazlitt understood this angry monopolistic rage, this epic urge to self-perpetuation which, like the wrath of Homer's Achilles, protests against time, death and the indifference of nature. In his essay on *Coriolanus* in 1816 he describes imagination as a ravening predator and declares that 'the language of poetry naturally falls in with the language of power'. At that stage in the history of literature, his assertion is a shocking one because, ever since the primal epic subjugation of the world, poetry has been living down its kinship with force; in England in particular, the literary imagination has aspired to renunciatory meekness and pastoral modesty. Hazlitt makes his principle the more rebarbative by enunciating it in the course of a defence of tyranny. Coriolanus the mob-hater is a man germane to poetry, he says. The imagination is no leveller: its sympathies are 'aristocratical', while the more timorous mental faculty of understanding is acceptably 'republican'. As well as being politically offensive, the imagination is a greedy carnivore. Hazlitt nominates as symbolic subjects of poetry those 'lordly beasts' which prey on their democratic inferiors—'a lion hunting a flock of sheep or a herd of wild asses'. His argument is disturbing because it is anachronistic: since Beowulf, or his colleague Byrhtnoth in the fragmentary *Battle of Maldon*, the epic heroes of English literature have been either tyrants—Marlowe's Tamburlaine, Hobbes's Leviathan, and Hazlitt's Coriolanus—or else a devil. Indeed the most superbly defiant of them all is Milton's Satan.

Coriolanus enables us to rejoice, Hazlitt says, in our own power and our entitlement to impose it on others. This is the martial spirit of epic. Man is aggrandised and toughened by arms, fitted out with that 'imposing air of superiority' which Hazlitt relishes. He is similarly augmented by song. When Virgil announces that he will sing of arms and the man, he is claiming for poetry a prerogative like that of the weaponry he extols. Epic words are his means of regimenting phenomena. Language is his armament, literature his mode of self-glorifying action and achievement. The composition of an epic is itself an epic feat, a work of mental if not muscular valour. *Beowulf*'s first word is an exclamation calling the world to attention: 'Hwæt . . . !' William Blake, in *The Marriage of Heaven and Hell*, remembers the initial assignment of names to things which was the literary occupation of Adam, dealing with the plants and animals, in paradise. He questions the prophet Isaiah about the coerciveness of imagination, which lies behind Adam's taxonomy, and asks if 'a firm persuasion that a thing is so, make[s] it so'. Isaiah replies, 'All poets believe that it does, & in ages of imagination this firm persuasion removed mountains.' That mountain-moving virile force animates the epic, which militantly orders nature and subordinates it to men. Machines are extensions of vital human power. The ship in which Beowulf travels to the Scyldings cleaves the water with wind-swollen sail and beaked prow like a bird. The elements, too, are tributaries of human will. The fire which consumes the funeral pyre of Hnaef is the hungriest of spirits. Lyric metaphor attests merely to a frail sympathy—which the nineteenth century knew as the pathetic fallacy—between our subjective existence and the objects in nature; epic metaphor arrogates those objects, and subjects them to us.

Beowulf is thus about both why the human tribe needs, at least at first, a hero to defend it, and about why the human tribe needs, in the longer term, the more abiding defence it finds in literature. Though it is primal there is nothing primitive about it: it is above all a work of artifice, and it proposes the necessity of artifice. We need protective walls and sheltering roofs; language is the sternest of the walls we erect against the unknown, and though invisible (except as script or print) it is the most enduring. The poet who empowers us by delivering to us this upright embattled agency of words has performed a service commensurate to that of Beowulf in exterminating Grendel, his mother and the dragon. Grendel's quarrel is not so much with Hrothgar and his clan as with their work of defensive art, the hall they build in which to feast and conduct their tribal ceremonies. That structure is their stockade, their rampart against the goblin-infested outdoors. But it also has the superfluity and the sumptuary glory of art. Its gables make it the grandest of halls in the world, and this architectural canopy houses other arts, music and literature. The harp sounds there, and the bard sings. He sings, significantly, of that other act of making which all artistic creation seeks to replicate and equal—the Almighty's invention of the earth, his subjugation of the elements to his decree, and his animation of creatures with lives of their own. The hall has god as its creative sponsor.

Grendel is that part of nature, consigned to darkness and cast out from grace, which remains uncolonised by man, unredeemed by imagination. He is associated with the brood of Cain, expelled to the waste land beyond settlement by a punitive god; but actually he, too, may be a malingering product of the imaginations of men, for he is mentioned first as a bold demon goaded to fury by the sound of creative joy in the hall, and is only later awarded a name and an identity by Hrothgar's men. He is the regressive beast in us, whom the apparatus of civilisation seeks to repress. His only talent is for destruction. As well as the antagonist outside the wall, he is the nay-sayer within—Shakespeare's Caliban, the 'thing of darkness' that Prospero acknowledges to be his own. When Hrothgar tries to describe Grendel and his mother, it is as indefinable shapes in the fen. One has the likeness of a misshapen man, the other resembles a woman, but they are incomplete, inchoate, and they symbolise the amorphousness of matter which the mind and imagination have not moulded. All the people in *Beowulf* have triumphal lineages, incorporating them with one another and with the tribal past; so do objects—the hilt of Hrothgar's sword is graven with its own memory, recounting the flood and the extinction of the race of giants. Grendel alone is unauthorised, owned by no society, attached to no past. Though the troll which avenges his death is presumed to be his mother, Hrothgar takes care to dispute his ancestry, leaving Grendel in a condition of nonentity: expelled from another world, an aborted thing unworthy of human form, he is nicknamed Grendel though no one knows who spawned or sired him. His non-existence—since outside human society there can be no meaning—is geographical, too. He and his malformed relative inhabit a non-place, a black pool beyond the edge of human experience. The only thing known about it is its unknowability: no one can tell, Hrothgar reports, how deep it is. Grendel and his mother are, like the place where they lurk, literally indescribable, and thus inimical to literature.

Beowulf deploys against these monsters physical and (when he buckles on his armour and trusts in his linked, impenetrable byrny) mechanical power. His victory over the phantasms is also his overcoming of the limits of human life. As he says when leaving to seek out Grendel's mother, death is certain, so we must gain glory before it supervenes.'At the cost of his own life, the epic hero ensures the perpetuity of his name. Byrhtwold does the same at Maldon, sacrificing himself to lie beside his fallen thane. The deaths of the heroes are countered by their survival in literature, which is the tribe's memory and the medium whereby it becomes conscious of itself. *Beowulf* begins and ends with funerals: rites of commemoration. And the epic serves as another such rite. Hence its methods of repetition and recapitulation. By telling things over and over again, it guarantees that they will not be forgotten, like the old woman at Beowulf's pyre who reiterates her lament for the past and her dire predictions for the future. Its formulaic diction has a similar purpose. Alliterative epithets—Spear-Danes, Ring-Danes, Bright-Danes—both insist on the fixity of objects and celebrate the multiplicity of their qualities. The Danes are unchanging yet always different, always characterised by a different attribute. This is a technique averse to narrative: it wants to prevent things from happening, to arrest a development which can only mean deterioration, and it repeats itself so as to keep up the morale of its talismanic objects, fearful lest they weaken or turn treacherous. In no sense is Beowulf's sequence of exterminations a progress, like the exploratory wandering from one adventure to the next of the questing romance hero. He has one act to perform, and he must do it again and again, because it can never be definitively achieved. There will always be another marauder waiting to ravage the made human world, and thus one more campaign for the enforcer.

The epic society resists narrative and dreads history, which it can foresee only as the degeneration bewailed by the mourning women at Beowulf's obsequies. That surety is the refrain of 'Deor's Lament'. The poet lists anecdotes of distress and affliction, and curtails them before they can unfold as narratives: 'That evil ended. So also may this!' Since the end is imminent and annihilating, our best recourse is to recur to beginnings, shoring-up what we have accumulated—our physical treasure, and our mental recollections—against inevitable loss. After Beowulf has killed Grendel, he persists in retelling the story of how he did so. His motive is not boastful: he wants to keep alive that deed because it is the prototype for all subsequent human actions and a remonstrance to all his fellows. Because it will have to be repeated every few years throughout history, it must outlive him. The stories of himself which Beowulf retails—his account of the swimming contest with Breca for instance—are his own obituary notices, rehearsals, even though they celebrate his bodily vigour, of his death. He is preparing for the day when he will exist only in the memory of others. Literature institutionalises that memory: *Beowulf* is oral poetry, transcribed only later in its career of transmission, so its survival is a feat of salutary and heroic remembering, an act of concentration aided by formulaic repetitions, like that for which Beowulf himself hopes. Print manufactures an instant immortality; before this occurs, every fact is a personal heirloom, passed on from one generation to the next by the bequest of recitation. Our collective past is a jealously guarded hoard, a necropolis of stories.

In the poem there are two analogues for this anxious textual retention. One is the dragon's lair, which a thief plunders; the other is the pyre built for Beowulf, on which are heaped his martial implements. The poem begins with the erection of the hall: art's bid for eternity, its mimicry of the first creation. However, by the end, in the sad old age of the world, with Beowulf himself now fifty years older and the dragon vigilant in its vault for three hundred years, the imperative is not creation but preservation. Life itself cannot be preserved, let alone invented (which is the fond hope of the builders of the hall, Heorot). The alternative is the insurance of objects, and the safekeeping of stories. Every item in the dragon's collection marks a demise. As warriors expire, the ring-warden carries their helmets, bucklers and flagons to the barrow, where he inters them. When no human being remains alive to oversee the collection, the dragon, with a life longer than man's, claims it for his own. His miserly policing of his goods mocks the ambition of literature. Like the epic poet, the dragon wants to keep things as they are, to prevent their alienation from him. It is a desire which elegiacally recognises its own futility.

Beowulf admits the unreliability of memory and the consequent helplessness of art. The ring-warden at the barrow is the spokesman for this perception. Depositing the treasures there, he donates them to an earth from which they were, as minerals, in the first place robbed. Man cannot keep the things he makes. He leaves behind him objects as eternal as the earth, but their perpetuity is to him small consolation. Art is as necessary to us as it is useless. We retrieve riches from the ground and must at last surrender them to the ground again. After Beowulf's death, the earls restore the gems to the grave, where—the poet adds—they still remain, as unavailing to men as they always were. A poem cannot even aspire to this cold, lapidary permanence: paper is more penetrable and more easily dispensed with than precious stones. The poet valiantly trains and exercises his memory, because it is an agency for the fancied resurrection of people and actions. In being remembered, they seem to have a second coming. Thus when Wealtheow presents Beowulf with jewelled tribute after the slaying of Grendel, the poet reviews legendary prehistory and declares that it is the richest treasure he has ever heard tell of, and later, when Beowulf hands over the rewards and his story to Hygelac, the poet testifies to the occurrences not from personal experience but from hearsay, on which as our deputed rememberer he must also rely: he has heard, he says, that Beowulf gave Hygelac four horses and to Hygd three more and also Wealtheow's necklace. Beowulf's dual gifts to posterity are the funeral mound he decrees on the headland in remembrance of himself, and the poem which is his after-life. It is a mournful theory of civilisation and of the art it produces: all we leave behind us is a subterranean museum, a mausoleum of commodities finer and longer-lasting than their human devisers and users.

About a century before *Beowulf*, such an art-burial happened at Sutton Hoo in Suffolk. Unearthed in 1939, its contents are now in the British Museum. Though the grave lacked a body, the absent hero's appurtenances were there—an ornamented and buckled gold belt, a purse-lid with garnets, a harp, a helmet which is, as well as a defence for the face, a hieratic mask for it, briefly conferring on flesh and bone the impermeability of gold and bronze. Sutton Hoo is the remnant of the kind of civilization described in *Beowulf*. Inside the encampment, whose borders are patrolled by the epic hero, beauty can be fabricated. Power makes art possible. The moment in the poem when this becomes clear is the appearance of the gilded queen Wealtheow, who courteously welcomes the visitors and offers to Beowulf the mead-cup. Her mannerly and ornamental grace is the leisured privilege which depends on the hero's constant warfaring. The militancy of epic gives way to the later, more leisurely and aesthetic society of romance, which Wealtheow already inhabits. Romance, however, can establish itself only when the ramparts have been secured, and when the territory beyond them ceases to be a source of fear and can become a mysterious infinity to be travelled through. Beowulf has yet to arrive at this luxury. He knows the battle he is fighting is terminal, and that he will sooner or later lose it. He therefore worries about the disposing of his own ornamental trappings. Though he will die, they must not. Before grappling with Grendel, he calmly imagines the monster tearing him apart, and specifies that when this happens his mail-shirt, worked by Wayland the Smith, must be returned to Hygelac. Yet all the things we own, like art, we hold in temporary trust from the earth. Their eventual destination is the riverside mound at Sutton Hoo.

Long after *Beowulf*, but before the excavation at Sutton Hoo, George Eliot, writing about the domestic 'epos' of a would-be heroine, one of those who 'rest in unvisited tombs', employs an image which recalls this human duty of art and seems to conjure up the mortuary ship: 'In these frail vessels', she says of her characters, 'is borne onward through the ages the treasure of human affection.' The ship is now a person, and the treasure an emotional beneficence not a deposit of gold and gems, but the idea, which so moved Henry James that he adopted it as a justification for Shakespeare's heroines and for his own *Portrait of a Lady*, is the same. The acts of amelioration performed by Dorothea in *Middlemarch* are, as George Eliot acknowledges, 'unhistoric', not apocalyptic victories like those of Beowulf; all the same, she contributes to 'the growing good of the world'. She has willed her life to us as a legacy, and art—especially the art of literature, since it is our story of ourselves—is our general inheritance, entrusted in *Beowulf* to the tribe and in *Middlemarch* to the race. Appropriately enough, the vessel containing the treasure is in George Eliot's *Romola* bibliographical: it is the library of the heroine's father, which she struggles to conserve and protect after his death. Art is the gathering of our last things. Literature's natural tense is the grieving past historic, for it exists precisely to delay the haste of present time in its race towards a future none of us will experience.

This chance union of *Beowulf* with George Eliot is a demonstration of the continuity of English literature. A similar anachronistic overlapping occurs in T. S. Eliot, whose collapsed and fragmented epic, *The Waste Land*, could be equated with the dragon's barrow or the tomb at Sutton Hoo, still unknown when he wrote: 'These fragments I have shored against my ruins.' The pyre, in Eliot's poem, is an anthology of fractured quotes, the diaspora of a library. Beowulf predates literature, for rather than permitting his story to be written down he leaves it in the care of his fellows, who will remember it and tell it aloud; relatively early in the course of written literature, Chaucer in *Troilus and Criseyde* frets about the vicissitudes of his text, its liability to miswriting and misreading, which announce to him his own sad obsolescence; towards the end of literature's history, Eliot's poem exemplifies the accident-proneness and mortality of the text. An oral poem depends on being remembered, but perhaps it is in better care than one consigned to the mediation of script or print.

Armouring, that exterior skeleton, grants Beowulf a mighty impersonality. It is the insignia of his epic status. During his swimming contest with Breca, the golden netting of his corselet saves him from the clutches of the sea-beasts. The hero of an epic is less an individual—which is the solitary mission of the errant romance hero—than a divine average: he embodies social solidarity. Armour therefore, as well as keeping his enemies out, serves to interlink him with his fellows, so that Beowulf's troop advancing to Hrothgar's court resembles a marching wall. Their army is armour on the move, with shining byrnies and clanging chain-mail: an image of society mechanically forged into co-operative strength. When they arrive at Heorot, the herald inquires after their purpose by fusing them with their spears and shields. The men are defined as carriers and adjuncts of those weapons, which extend their bodies into armature. It is therefore a drastic choice of Beowulf's to disarm himself before the combat with Grendel. His proud renunciation of those steely aids announces a primitive regression in the poem. For this fight, Beowulf chooses to be an athletic hero, relying on the strength of his body. In later combats, he develops into the epic hero, who relies on the tools which augment that physical puissance. He kills Grendel's mother with a blade from her underwater hoard, and he iron-clads himself for the battle against the dragon, from whom he expects a bombardment of flame.

Rending Grendel's body, Beowulf is a figure from folk-tale, a physiological prodigy like the monster he assails; accepting technological help, he has arrived at the social condition of epic, which takes place in a world manufactured by humans. Gotthold Lessing in 1766 in *Laokoon* points out that the weapons of Achilles in the *Iliad* qualify as epic properties because Homer not only describes their appearance (as the poet of romance will do) but narrates their making by the gods. The epic is a civilisation of engineering: arms, in a coupling of Virgil's formula with Marshall McLuhan's, are man's extension, because with them he can accomplish feats impossible to a single body. Epic describes the use of those weapons to subdue nature and furnish society, and when epic returns to literature in the American nineteenth century Beowulf's sword mutates into the series of guns after which the Westerns are honorifically named—Winchester 73, Colt 45 or the Gatling gun—and his invincible army of foot-soldiers now conquers space in the shape of a steam-powered iron horse.

Beowulf reflects on the nature of its own society by emphasizing the instrumentality of poetry: it, too, like those armaments, constitutes an acquisition of power. The hero describes his victories both before and after the event because his valour is linguistic. He is declaring human primacy in the world, and issuing orders to the hitherto recalcitrant phenomena of nature. Epic song is an armed coercion of the world; lyric song a more plaintive and abject entreaty to it. In Anglo-Saxon literature, lyric is the province of those who have been disarmed, outcast, denied membership of Beowulf's epic and social confraternity. The two great examples are the laments of 'The Wanderer' and 'The Seafarer', which together define an antithesis to *Beowulf*. Like the epic, they are elegiac, but whereas epic memory in its resumption of the past can admonish the future, so that Beowulf's legatees will stay mindful of him because of that monument on the cliff, all the Wanderer can do is meditate on the detritus of the human world and brood on the legends of fighting men now dead. Remembering will not reactivate them: lyric is the mode of powerless acquiescence. Later, we assume the lyric to be the form expressing empathy with and human incorporation in nature. But it is from this unhoused exposure to nature that epic rescues us, and the Wanderer's plight is that, after his lord's death, he is exiled in an inhospitable landscape. Epic had raised walls against that inclement world. Now storms beat at them, and all earth's foundations falter. Lyric ranks low in the Anglo-Saxon hierarchy of genres because it cannot manage the stern compulsiveness of epic. The lyric protagonist is not a man who does things, but one to whom things happen. In the nineteenth century, romanticism reverses this relation: the characters of its epics—Shelley's Prometheus, Keats's Hyperion, Wordsworth's Wordsworth—forswear activism and martial engagement, and aspire to a lyric state of introverted reverie. The Anglo-Saxon lyrics, however, are negations of epic. Beowulf's men cleave the seas on their journey to Hrothgar; the Wanderer disconsolately stares at a wintry ocean on which he is involuntarily tossed. Speech and song are epic impositions of will for Beowulf; the Wanderer retreats into soliloquy, and is merely overheard, certain that there is no one in the vacated world in whom he can confide. If the epic is a social act, the lyric is a personal testimony. The Seafarer begins by saying that his song's truth is authorised by himself, and that self is unbefriended, sustained by no kinship. The epic, praising architecture, describes our human rooting of ourselves in the earth. On the way to Hrothgar's court, the poet notices that the avenue has been paved with coloured stone: nature levelled and made subservient to men, and to art. But both lyrics deal with the homelessness of men and their banishment from earth—the Wanderer and Seafarer are condemned to the unstable, anchorless element of ocean. They travel despite themselves; ejected from epic, they are not yet reconciled to the different world of romance, where the journey is itself an exhilaration and the arrival does not matter. Chaucer traces the chivalric impetus to its lyrical source in nature at the beginning of *The Canterbury Tales*. When the year renews itself in April, men long to go on pilgrimages. The Anglo-Saxon characters experience that wanderlust only as a drifting through limbo. Lyric signifies their banishment from the comfort of human company: the Wanderer finds no epic or architectural fortitude in the world, and transfers his hope of fastness to heaven; the Seafarer does not trust in epic commemoration, and says that a man will live on only among the angels.

It is one of the odd, incidental signs of a unity in English literature that these anonymous poems should turn up again in revealingly personal versions by two modern poets. Ezra Pound wrote his translation of 'The Seafarer' in 1911, W. H. Auden a correlative to 'The Wanderer' in 1930. Both find in the archaic models a modern temperament. Pound, himself a voluntary exile from America, makes the poem into a praise of rootlessness. His Seafarer defiantly spurns the unselfconscious contentment of the landsmen. His journey is a poetic manifesto, since

> Burgher knows not—
> He the prosperous man—what some perform
> Where wandering them widest draweth.

The misery of the Anglo-Saxon is to Pound a vocation. He has commuted epic, which values above all the holding of the fort and defence of a status quo, into buoyant, voyaging romance: this Seafarer goes on to become the Odyssean hero of Pound's first *Canto*. Like Joyce's Stephen Dedalus quitting Ireland, he has resolved on a poetic policy of 'silence, exile and cunning'. Auden's poem converges with the Anglo-Saxon one only in its central stanza, where it deliberately alters the original. The archaic Wanderer had dreamed of embracing his liege-lord. Auden switches the love-object's sex. His Wanderer pines for the 'kissing of wife under single sheet'. Then, having done so, he inserts another sex-change. When the Wanderer awakes from his reverie, he hears, as well as the Anglo-Saxon sea-birds,

> . . . through doorway voices
> Of new men making another love.

That other love restores the epic cult of blood-brotherhood as a homosexual comitatus, an aristocracy (as E. M. Forster said) of the plucky. The poem ends with a hope of homecoming, but not, perhaps, to a domestic and familial society: rather to the male union of epic prowess exhibited in the mountaineering exploits of Auden's and Isherwood's *Ascent of F6* or in the frustrated accord of Fielding and Aziz at the end of Forster's *Passage to India*. Both Pound and Auden are, paradoxically, more stalwart Anglo-Saxons than their prototypes, since neither of their heroes complains of his lot. For both, homelessness can itself be an epic profession.

The lyrics are the interior of epic. They testify to the vulnerability of the character inside the armour. Even *Beowulf* is in this respect a transitional, synoptic poem, overlaying three phases in the evolution of the hero. Beowulf's origins predate the epic, and within the poem he has almost outgrown it, for he gestures towards the next literary stage, the romance, and its different ethics. As monster-slayer or as doughty swimmer, he is the giant of folk-fable, whose power is that of the unaided body. Buckled into his steel carapace, he has become the hero of epic, a fighting-apparatus invented by society to defend itself and vowed to the holding of the fort, like Byrhtwold in *The Battle of Maldon* who rallies his cohorts by telling them that their own fortitude of mind and heart must grow even as their numbers decrease. But just as the bogeys of the folk-tale have been exorcised by the martial drill of epic, and the ancient fears emerging from Grendel's mere or the dragon's lair have been pacified by the hero's efforts, so the epic itself has been revised and glossed by Christianity, and when this happens Beowulf seems about to metamorphose into the spiritual warrior of chivalric narrative. The epic is a world of fatality, where only the exertion of human will can save a man from inevitable extinction. He may be unable to keep his life, but he can eternalize his name. This is a universe of combative physical forces, where the energies of men contend against the indifference of nature, like the flood tide in the river which determines the battle at Maldon; it has no god to oversee it, which is why the epic hero must act as the divine guardian of his tribe.

Because of this godlessness of epic, the most authentic epic hero in later English literature is a figure who intends, by the mad exertion of will, to unseat God: Milton's Satan in *Paradise Lost*. Yet at one stage in the transmission of *Beowulf*, a god has been interpolated, to whom epic victories are attributed. Success is no longer the result of physiological or technological power, but a gift of grace and a spiritual benison. Often the moralising sounds like an afterthought, as when Beowulf, boasting of his strength, remembers to add that God will decide who is to win when he fights with Grendel, or when Grendel is stigmatised as one of the brood of Cain. Hrunting the sword is an epic accomplice, a veteran stand-by. But it fails Beowulf in the underwater fight and God awards him the use of another weapon, which later dissolves like ice, melted by God's superintendence of the seasons. An epic tool has been superseded by the providential and phantasmal equipment of romance: Hrunting gives way to Excalibur, reclaimed—in Malory's and in Tennyson's chivalric narrative—by the Lady of the Lake.

The folk-hero's might is his own muscular prowess; the epic hero is empowered by society; but the romance hero receives his authority from God and returns it, like the sword, to that immaterial source. The epic hero's posture is necessarily static. He is a bulwark, and he must dig in to abide the onslaught from without. This is the decision of Byrhtnoth at Maldon, when he backs off to position his troops on a slope where they await the advancing Danes. The romance hero is more adventurous and itinerant. Relieved from military duty, he embarks on an exploration of the world which is a tour inside himself. It is therefore perhaps a chivalric initiative of Beowulf's to travel to Heorot: he is volunteering to fight someone else's battle. Because he is locked into a fixed and inflexible stance, the epic hero can afford no inner life. To think, at Maldon, is already a symptom of cowardly wavering. The concern of the soldiers is to transform words into deeds, to be as good as the boasts they made in the mead-hall. If they are unequal to this challenge, like Godrinc and Godwig who decamp from the field, they suffer the epic's fate worse than death, which is shame. Beowulf, however, has begun to suffer from that different emotion which afflicts the protagonist of romance: once he acquires an interior existence, he begins to feel guilt. The dragon's attacks grieve him because he wonders if he might have somehow offended God, who has ordained this punishment. He is about to turn into the disabled Fisher King of the chivalric legends, impurely responsible for the ills of his land.

So Beowulf is the first and last of English epic heroes. Christianity declares him obsolete, since its mode of heroic comportment is sufferingly passive, not a mettlesome fury of will; and except for such suicidal ventures as the charge of Tennyson's Light Brigade in 1854—cued in any case by an administrative blunder—the English literary genius is against him. In English literature, even war poetry is pastoral. Andrew Marvell's reaction to the English Civil War is pastoral reclusion and a mystic distrust of action, and the demise abroad of Rupert Brooke's 'Soldier' in the 1914–18 war fertilizes a foreign soil, pastorally implanting in it

> A dust whom England bore, shaped, made aware,
>> Gave, once, her flowers to love, her ways to roam,
> A body of England's, breathing English air,
>> Washed by the rivers, blest by suns of home.

The Virgilian formula was revised for English literature in 1894 by Shaw's *Arms and the Man*, in which the aggressive swagger and chivalric zealotry of Sergius are mocked by the self-preservative wisdom of the Swiss mercenary Bluntschli. Much earlier, Shakespeare's Falstaff—in many ways the archetypal English character, the indwelling spirit of Englishness—had declared in *Henry IV* the better part of valour to be the discreet safeguarding of one's flesh, which to the fat knight constitutes an idyllic pastoral pleasance.

But America, inventing a new literature for itself in the nineteenth century, has recourse to the ancient and aboriginal form. America industrialises the epic—in the prolific and eugenic printing-presses celebrated by Walt Whitman, in Herman Melville's whaling try-works on the *Pequod*, in the abattoirs which Rudyard Kipling admired in Chicago, or in Hart Crane's steely, tensile Brooklyn Bridge, all images of a technological heroism. The poem of force continues to be the inevitable genre for America, whose heroes, whether western sheriffs or urban detectives, always bear arms. The machine age has its own martial music, orchestrating that percussion of clanging byrnies heard in *The Battle of Maldon* or bardically amplifying the single voice through a loudhailer. The genre's continuity is apparent in John Ford's 1945 film *They Were Expendable*. A PT boat is towing another which has been crippled; its captain says to a crewman, 'Repeat the instruction: if we're attacked, burn your boats and we will try to pick you up.' He passes it on through a bull-horn, but accents it poetically in doing so:

> Íf we're attácked
> búrn your bóats
> and wé will trý
> to píck you úp.

The relay has made it bardic poetry, and an epic remonstrance. The helicopters in Francis Ford Coppola's film *Apocalypse Now* (1979) resound with the equestrian rejoicing of Wagner's Valkyries on their aerial steeds, while the men inside them, in a prudent epic armouring, squat on their helmets to save their testicles from being shot off. The machine age has its own epic rites of burial: in 1946 in William Wyler's film *The Best Years of Our Lives* a demobbed bombardier wanders through an aeroplane junkyard in a cemetery of propellers. The heroic era of Old English literature waits for its sequel in modern America.

When that time comes, the epic warrior is supplanted by the monster, and literature—which can now afford to abandon the confident, consolidating rituals of *Beowulf*—admits its origins in a defensive retreat from outlawed, unknowable reality. Epic exists to keep the monster out; its creator, the creature which provokes that existence, is therefore the monster. Melville's novel is about the whale, not about Ahab. The American novelist John Gardner, in accordance with this logic, in 1971 rewrote *Beowulf* as *Grendel*. Gardner's Grendel is advised by his colleague the dragon (whose slayer will be Siegfried) of his responsibility to Hrothgar and his clan: he goads them to think, frightens them into the invention of poetry, science and religion, teaches them, by his own brutishness, to define themselves as humans. They need him, to test themselves against him. When Unferth's attack on the ogre fails, he implores Grendel to do him the favour of killing him, which will ensure him immortality. Grendel ironically declines, and pities the 'awful inconvenience' of having always to be upstanding and to declaim honourably—all the fatiguing pretences of heroism. The most effective weapon the Scyldings have against Grendel is their art, because it enables them to tell lies about him and to comfort themselves with 'an illusion of reality'. Eavesdropping on the bardic song chanted to the harp by the Shaper (*Beowulf*'s 'scop'), he knows that men are dangerous because, like this poet, they are 'pattern makers'. The patterns they make will misrepresent him, declare him unaesthetic and thus unholy. Their songs are a self-congratulating delusion, as is (in this telling) Beowulf's bogus narrative of his swimming contest with Breca. Grendel alone, unshaped, aborted, understands that 'the world was nothing: a mechanical chaos of casual, brute enmity on which we stupidly impose our hopes and fears.' He notes the absurdity of this trust in art. Hrothgar has converted his mead-hall into a museum. It is so congested with painted shields, ornamented swords and coils of gold that there is no room anymore to live in it, and his soldiers have to move to the outbuildings. Is civilisation then a pile of booty in which we fondly invest a spiritual value? These heroes are mere aesthetes, connoisseurs of tributary baubles. The true creativity rages destructively in Grendel, who learns of his power when he hears a sage inform Hrothulf that 'the total ruin of institutions and morals is an act of creation. A *religious* act.' He exercises that 'monstrous energy' by defying gods, eating priests (though he finds them indigestible), and by coercing the imaginations of the men who think they are armed against him—for what is imagination but our dream of Prospero's 'thing of darkness', our subliminal breeding of monsters? 'I have thought up a horrible dream', says Grendel, 'to impute to Hrothgar.'

Gardner's disorderly American native, 'yawping' barbarically as D. H. Lawrence said Whitman did, or howling like Allen Ginsberg, is the artist as savage, noble or ignoble, resolved on checking what Grendel resentfully calls 'the advance of man'. As that advance proceeds, men devise new ways of intimidating him. They presuppose, as their celestial patron, an Orpheus whose lute can tame bestial nature. Caliban is humbled by the musical voices with which Prospero infuses the island's air; Gardner's Grendel when he hears the song in the hall—an excerpt from *Beowulf*—flees in sick dread, a 'ridiculous hairy creature torn apart by poetry'. Soon, too, the humans make for themselves a surer safeguard than the thane in armour: a fragile, female divinity, cowing us by making us worshippers. Hygmod presents to Hrothgar his sister Wealtheow, whose name Gardner glosses as 'holy servant of common good'. Grendel, moved by her beauty, is once again torn apart, as he had been by the Shaper's song. No wonder, when he returns as Caliban, he recognises that to depose Prospero he must first ravish Miranda. The establishment of Wealtheow as the emblem of commonality—the intersection of all dreams and desires—fatally weakens Grendel. Already in *Beowulf*, epic force surrenders to the interior vulnerability and reverence of romance.

— 2 —
Romance

The heroic age is contradicted by the age of chivalry, and epic is overruled by romance. The advance from one to the other is the first great generic shift in English literature, and since genres are literature's institutions—encyclopaedias of precedent, accumulated in order to prescribe a way of understanding and regulating the world—that displacement augurs a breakdown in the society which the literary forms describe. W. P. Ker described that change in his *Epic and Romance* in 1896. For him, the forms are opposites: epic regiments the world, while romance conducts a leisurely and anecdotal exploration of it; epic defends the walls, while romance ventures beyond them; epic enforces a stern and soldierly impersonality and an aggressive extroversion, while romance can relax its guard and can voyage, at the same as it quits the human settlement, within the hero's vagrant mind. The spirit of epic is fatalistic. It is about the human effort to conquer nature, and to defy with armed might the limitations of our lives. The hero knows that his own striving is doomed to fail, yet he persists, for his death will declare his superb contempt for the sorry perishability of human existence. Dying, he will lend himself to the wall he defends, and his body will acquire an architectural fortitude it never possessed while he lived. Achilles knows that his fate is to perish at Troy, just as Byrthwold knows he will fall at Maldon. Neither falters: their own survival is less important to them than that of the society they embody. An individual demise makes possible eventually a collective life.

Romance has outgrown this besieged despair. Its hero no longer grapples backed up against that symbolic city wall. His society does not monopolise him. Demobilised, he can begin to discover a world which the epic hero was engaged in fending off. He ceases to consider that world inimical: on the contrary, it is replete with marvels, and in savouring them he is, for the first time in literature, permitted to inspect himself. His vocation is an introspective one. The dichotomy is that between the *Iliad* and the *Odyssey*; between assault on a citadel and finding your way, at meandering leisure, back home; between the wrathful Achilles and the wily Odysseus. Ker calls the *Battle of Maldon* the *Iliad* of Old English literature, and nominates *Beowulf*—at least its account of the hero's quixotic 'errand of deliverance' in Denmark—as its *Odyssey*. However that may be, romance is certainly predicated on the completion of the epic endeavour at Troy, which is why *Sir Gawain and the Green Knight*, recapitulating that literary genealogy, begins there, remembering the end of the Trojan siege and successively tracing the descent from Aeneas, Romulus and Felix Brutus to Arthur of Britain: from epic founders and imperial colonisers of terrain to a monarch of romance, whose society at Camelot can dispense with epic's armed guard and devote itself instead to revelry; a society which has exchanged fortification for furniture.

R. W. Southern in *The Making of the Middle Ages* (1953) attempted to be more precise about the ways in which the epic world with its raised battlements opens into the wandering, whimsical universe of romance. The transition from one to the other occurs, he believes, during the Carolingian renaissance of the eleventh and twelfth centuries. Southern contrasts the static drill of Benedictine routine (a monastic version of the epic hero's rigorous discipline: the monk is shut inside the walls which the epic protagonist patrols) with the new appraisals of spiritual life by St Bernard and St Anselm, who describe their relation to God as a solitary and almost secret ecstasy not an institutional observance; and he sets the *Song of Roland*, still cramped in postures of defence, against the romances of Chrétien de Troyes, whose heroes are not requisitioned by action and emergency but have dispersed to engage in immaterial, internal quests. The warrior has become the pilgrim, the crusader, the missionary, all of whom are versions of the dreamer. Erich Auerbach's *Mimesis* (1946) identified the same change in syntactic habits between the *Song of Roland* and Chrétien's *Yvain*. The epic mode, Auerbach says, is paratactic: rather than grammatically articulating its sentences, *Roland* engineers the clash of solid, reiterated, formulaic blocks of language. Its terseness is a military music, like the alliterative clangour of the half-lines in the *Maldon* fragment. The sound of epic poetry is a noise of battle, the violent clatter of consonants. *Yvain*, however, has a syntax to suit the forest of beguilement and vision in which the hero wanders: hypotactic, as Auerbach calls it, which means hypothetical, abounding in periodic complication, both looser and more agile than the back-and-forth footwork of epic. It is a syntax to license the hero's new liberty of conjecture, for the mood of romance is yearningly subjunctive.

The epic hero's preoccupation is a present and immediate danger. The romance hero fancifully goes forth to combat perils which he must first invent. He has a quixotic talent for making himself believe in his fantasies, and the language which describes his chimerical career has to be elusively and imaginatively conditional. There is a fine example in *Sir Orfeo*, based on a Breton *lai* and written about 1300. Orfeo has abdicated in favour of his steward while he follows his wife Heurodis to fairyland. He wins her back, and returns disguised to his kingdom where, to test the steward's probity, he reports that Orfeo is dead. When the steward laments, Orfeo knows him to be a true man. But he does not reveal himself at once. He hints at his identity in a teasing sequence of conditional instalments: if he were Orfeo, and had long suffered in the wilderness, and had won his queen back from fairyland, and had brought her here to town, and had left her at a beggar's home, and if he had come thus poorly to the steward to make assay of his good will, and if he had found him true, then the steward should never regret it; though if he had rejoiced at Orfeo's death, he would at once have been banished. Orfeo is doing more here then keeping the steward in suspense. The elaborate question-begging of his sentence suspends Orfeo himself. It is only as if he were Orfeo, and as if he had come safely home. Those incremental ifs tilt his experience towards wishful thinking, and towards the bolder conjecturing of myth: they make his story both literally implausible and profoundly true, enabling Orfeo to describe his own death and then to recover from it. The classical story of Orpheus is a promise of resurrection. Death may not after all be final. Orfeo contends against death with a success which is only conditional—conditional on our 'willing suspension of disbelief' (as Coleridge called the mental mood which romanticism inherited from the romance) in this exception to a natural decree. The happy ending is sadly precious because we know it to be so unlikely. And it is because of the story's non-verisimilitude that we need the myth which lies beneath it, for the myth explains to us the conditions on which we might regain the paradise we have lost.

When Heurodis is threatened with abduction, Orfeo makes a vow abolishing conditions.

> 'Allas!' quath he, 'forlorn Icham!
> Whider wiltow go, and to wham?
> Whider tho gost, Ichil with the,
> And whider Y go, thou schalt with me.'

She at once insists that that cannot be. But as a romance hero his valour consists in his performing the impossible, and to do that he must commit himself to the realm of the ineffable. His language is querulous because it is questing. He demands to know where she is bound, and then says he will follow her wherever it is. That visionary absolutism, not tragically acquiescing at last in the limits of life as the epic hero does, but protesting against them, is the imaginative valour of romance, the willingness to think about—and thereby experience—the worlds that an if balances in the air. Accomplishing the impossible is the creed of these men, of Orfeo plumbing the underworld, or Malory's knights seeking through supernature for the Grail, and the fables recounting their histories are treatises on imagination, for just as R. W. Southern sees the newly introspective monks exercising their minds to approach God rather than enslaving their bodies to his service, so the chivalric hero elects as his destination a perfection we can dream of but cannot actualize on earth. We may attain it, however, in the alternative, 'iffy' world of art.

The romance is beginning to persuade us to trust in literature as compensation for the harms of life. This is why the harp is so priceless a talisman in *Sir Orfeo*. Though Orfeo disburdens himself of kingly power, he retains his harp, and uses it to enchant the wild beasts in fairyland; when he returns, he tells the steward that he had removed the harp from beside the body of the dead Orfeo. Accompanying him and fancifully outliving him, the harp suggests that Orfeo's immortality is his music. It, rather than the epic hero's deployment of force, has accorded him authority, and he hands it on to the poet who, remembering him here, mimics his miracle of dying and being reborn by resuscitating him with and in music: *Orfeo* begins and ends with references to the poet's own (now symbolic and imagined) harp. He first selects Orfeo's story from among 'the layes that ben of harpyng', and when Orfeo reassumes his throne the melodic rejoicing of his subjects modulates into the musical invention of the Breton harpers, who composed the work which the poem commends—

Gode is the lay, swete is the note.

The Orphic grace has been assumed by poetic language. Poets may no longer be able to make the beasts dance or to resurrect the dead, but they can in compensation imagine doing so. The harper in Heorot has a different purpose. He celebrates an act of making, the compulsory establishment and divine policing of a natural order. Orfeo's instrument is a more wistful placation of nature, securing only temporary armistice. When he stops playing, 'no best bi him abide nold'. He is nearer to Coleridge's 'damsel with a dulcimer' than to Hrothgar's bard. As Orfeo uses it, the harp is briefly coercive or (when it softens the heart of Heurodis's captor) persuasive; when he transmits it to the poet of the *lai*, it is disabled. It can describe things, but cannot make anything happen. As a token of imagination in the romance it resembles the Grail in Malory's *Morte d'Arthur*, which is spirit manifesting itself in and then evanescing from material form: 'Then there entered into the hall the Holy Grail covered with white samite, but there was none might see it. . . . And when the Holy Grail had been borne through the hall, then the holy vessel departed suddenly, that they wist not where it became.'

Because the romance hero seeks a symbol like the unseeable Grail, the epic marshalling of force no longer serves him. Orfeo mistakenly trusts in that obsolete method, and to prevent the capture of Heurodis he arrays a phalanx of 'ten hundred knights . . . y-armed stout and grim', but his infantry is powerless against the magic which ravishes her into invisibility. Arms cannot keep her; he can recover her, however, with music. The Heurodis he brings back says nothing. One of the poem's subtle suppositions is that Orfeo has preserved an image of her and not the reality at all. Having lost her irrevocably, he has conjured up a simulacrum of her. And by the time he returns, he is himself equally a character in a story, dreamed up by others—by the beggar for instance, who recites to him the story of Heurodis's defection and Orfeo's exile. Like all his colleagues in medieval romance, Orfeo anticipates the last of his line, Don Quixote, who only goes into battle against windmills.

Sir Gawain and the Green Knight—the most refined and the most comically acute of these works, provisionally to be dated near the end of the fourteenth century—measures the distance between the protocols of epic and romance, and questions whether romance may not be a luxurious and leisured enfeeblement of the epic from which it derives. Romance has begun slyly to parody the combativeness of epic. The knight errant, no longer required to win wars, can pass the time playing games. The trial of contending powers has lapsed into an antagonism of social prevarication. At the same time, the test of moral rigour and probity becomes a scrutiny of manners and courtly graces. Generically, literary history works as a progressive decline. Each new form, slipping down the hierarchy of esteem, parodies its forebear higher up. As the romance derides the epic, so the novel eventually derides the romance, with Samuel Richardson, in the eighteenth century, naming his gold-digging servant-girl Pamela after one of Philip Sidney's Arcadian princesses, and Henry Fielding carnally mocking the high-minded postponements of courtly love in *Tom Jones*; then, once realism asserts itself as the novel's standard, it too assumes a relative value, and each generation can declare itself to be writing about a life which is more real than that treated by its predecessors.

The romance has already embarked on this degenerative history. Jessie L. Weston in *From Ritual to Romance* (1920) defines it as the diaspora of ritual: myths, no longer understood, are repeated as mere fables or fictions. A universe of significances is now a collection of interchangeable stories, from which the romancer makes an arbitrary and idle choice. *Sir Orfeo* begins by summarising the innumerable types of Breton *lais* before regretfully deciding that 'Y can sum telle, but nought all'; when Gawain rides out to his rendezvous with the Green Knight, he encounters so many incidental marvels en route that the romancer spares himself from having to do more than excerpt from them: 'Hit were to tore for to telle of þe tenþe dole.' Instead of the single, immortalising action which epic strives to preserve in memory, romance deals with a world not of history but of story, and it finds all stories equally beguiling and equally inconsequential.

Where history is no longer attended to, fiction can begin. This is why *Sir Gawain* starts by remotely and circumstantially relating Camelot to Troy. As a society of romance, it is made from the wreckage of epic. Arthur has no actual emergency to deal with. He therefore insists on being entertained by the invention of factitious wonders, and will not eat his Christmas dinner until someone tells him a story. The diversions of his society rehearse the rites of e̦ ̦c, which have been safely emptied of relevance. Not needing to fight battles, the courtiers joust instead. The necessary ranking of epic is mimicked by a deft and considerate social placement at Arthur's feast, with the knights distributed between the members of Arthur's family and divided between the honorific dais and supplementary side tables. Military music is sounded in the court as an accompaniment to eating: the drums and trumpets play to announce the

arrival of the first course. And the poet's own access to the story he tells wittily
alters the oral history of the epic bard. At the end of his second stanza he
promises, when enticing us to listen for a while,

> I schal telle hit astit, as I in toun herde,
>> with tonge,
>> As hit is stad and stoken
>> In stori stif and stronge,
>> With lel letteres loken,
>> In londe so hat3 ben longe.

He is adverting here to the new complication which stories have in an age of
script and print. The text confers ambiguity on them. The oral retrieval of the
bard stamps on his matter the authority of personal recollection. How can the
truth of something which is merely written down be ascertained? It is
interesting that the first printer, Caxton, should be so exercised by the
authenticity of what his machine reproduces. His preface to his 1485 edition of
Malory states his scruples: he will agree to retail this lore only when he has been
reliably assured that Arthur did exist, because he sees print as a mark of
veracity. The *Gawain* poet archly intends to imagine his manuscript in the
same way. He envisages its letters interlocking like the Anglo-Saxon
battle-formation of infantrymen. They are 'lel' in the sense of being epically
loyal, faithful to him, and in Caxton's conscientious sense of being truthful.
What locks them together is of course alliteration: the percussion of
consonants. But is he right to place this epic trust in words? One of the
revelations of *Sir Gawain and the Green Knight* is the slippery truancy of what
we say. Gawain and the lady who circuitously seduces him are both experts in
sophistically saying what they don't mean. As if to intimate these ironic doubts,
the poet, immediately before his reference to transcription, mentions the
ancient mode of oral transmission. What, however, does that tongue portend?

In the society of romance, epic history has become gossipy hearsay, like that
which turns Gawain's shame at the end of the poem into the latest scandalous
tidbit to be circulated at court. The speaking voice in Chaucer goes on to
liberate itself when the Wife of Bath defiantly opposes experience—her own
and that of others she's heard tell about—to the repressive authority written
down in books. She is disputing what Caxton tried defensively to establish, the
legalism of print. The would-be epic poet of the *Gest Hystoriale of the
Destruction of Troy* reproves poets who have

> With fablis and falshed fayned there speche,
> And made more of that mater than hom maister were.

Imagination officially equals perjury. Chaucer's achievement is to find ways of
telling and writing lies—that is, literary truths—while securing himself against

the censures of a pettifogging authority like that invoked in the *Gest Hystoriale*. *Sir Gawain* likewise differentiates itself at the outset from the verbal integrity of epic, where a man's word is his deed or bond. The story he tells will have literature's devious relation to life: unbelievable (in its account of a decapitated knight who picks his head up and neatly replaces it on his shoulders) yet requiring the suspension of disbelief; truer than truth and more real than reality.

Plato forbade the poets citizenship of his republic because they trafficked in mendacity. The first self-conscious literary artists in English, the *Gawain* poet and Chaucer, are therefore the most adept and ingenious liars, and never are they less to be literally accredited than when they are professing to be the blinkered translators of their authoritative sources, for in English literature—right up to the claims of Daniel Defoe and Horace Walpole to be editing for publication manuscripts written by others, or to Thomas Chatterton's forgery of the medieval manuscripts he published as the poems of Rowley—the imagination likes to skulk behind a scholarly alibi. Malory can query the mortality of his once and future king by blaming his sources for not being specific enough: 'Thus of Arthur I find never more written in books that be authorised, nor more of the very certainty of his death heard I never read.' That textual uncertainty, as a breakdown in authority, licenses the imaginative rumour-mongering which at once attributes to Arthur a mythic perpetuity. 'Yet some men say', Malory admits, 'in many parts of England that King Arthur is not dead . . .; and men say that he shall come again.'

Epic is about what is necessary to us: shelter, safety. Romance describes a world of surfeit and surplus. (There is the same disparity between the epic faculty of memory, whereby the poet tells us who we are and how we got here, and the romance's skill in fabulation.) The change is summed up in *Sir Gawain* by the transition from armature to vesture. Beowulf's impediments are the body's aspiration to an impervious and undying strength; Gawain's are decor and adornment, cossetting his body—under the steel he wears fur, and his horse Gringolet is as fashionably caparisoned for the journey as he is. His beauty is useless, an imaginative excess. But in this poem beauty is as precious as it is dispensable. The poem's two crises occur at midwinter. The knight challenges Gawain and Christmas, and a year later Gawain goes to meet him to abide the stroke of his axe. Between those two seasons, the earth briefly greens itself and effloresces, but by the time Gawain sets out on his penitential journey it is again epically grim and gaunt, bristling with rugged cliffs and gnarled stones. The human combat with nature remains as cruel as it is in the epic, and the Green Knight, with his callously indifferent humour and his Danish axe (an epic tool, in contrast with Gawain's courtly equipment), embodies, like Grendel, nature's repudiation of the precarious world that human beings have made for themselves. Yet in *Sir Gawain* the means by which nature is kept out or fended off is no longer force: the romance society places its faith in the frail barricade of art. Thus, although the year allows only a short spell of greenery and floral beauty, the castles of Arthur and Bertilak create an indoor spring or summer at Christmas, and Gawain's costume is important because it is art's competitive improvement of nature. The silken shield of his helmet is a stitched and ornamental landscape, an aviary of preening doves and parrots. Arriving at Bertilak's castle he is re-robed in a garment provided by his host; its florid skirts convince the attendants that spring has returned. If Bertilak is green and fertile nature, Gawain is culture's pictorial imitation of and wishful triumph over that nature.

In another poem of the alliterative revival, more or less coeval with *Sir Gawain*, art's abolition of a fallible, perishable nature envisions a lapidary heaven. This is the devotional dream of *Pearl*. A jeweller mislays a gem, only to discover that it has been transferred to supernature where, anthropomorphised, it shines in a New Jerusalem of crystal and invaluable minerals. The jeweller protests against the implausibility and even the inequity of the translation. Why has his pearl been gratuitously selected as the bride of Christ? How has she merited such spiritual favour? But the award of grace is as mysterious as that of beauty, and the pearl is an image of grace made manifest and immanent as beauty. Her adornments are the insignia of saintly attributes. Still the jeweller, chiding her for her presumption, cannot reconcile himself to having made a thing which he must then forfeit because it—his art-work—is so much better, purer, more perfect and more enduring, than his human nature can ever be. He interprets her ideal perfection as a reproach to him. She tetchily schools him in acceptance, and her explanation of the divine plan is a critique of literal comprehension and a defence of that imagination which begot her. She accuses the jeweller of believing only what he can see. He is implying, she continues, that Christ's promise of resurrection is a lie. Actually it is a supreme fiction. Like art, it is literally inconceivable yet in another sense true. And our capacity to make art—the jeweller's talent, which he possesses but does not properly estimate—enables us to resurrect ourselves without Christ's aid. It is a self-made salvation. Yet it remains painfully unsatisfactory to us, because it confers eternity on an object not on ourselves, and the heaven we can imagine (as, with the intercession of the pearl, the jeweller is able to see the city prophetically imagined by St John at the apocalypse) we are forbidden from entering. All that the jeweller is left with is the rondure of the poem itself, with its circular pattern of echoing words: a setting for an absent pearl.

The heaven of art shimmers miraculously in the air in *Pearl*; in *Sir Gawain* it has been domesticated, since the graces of that poem are socially comely, but it is all the same fragile. The epic was at least a solid world. The romance, however, worshipfully pursues what may be an illusion, like Malory's dematerialising Grail. The change imposes itself on architecture. Bertilak's castle, moated and with drawbridge upraised, is still as sternly fortified and immovable as epic requires its characters and its society to be:

> þe bryge watȝ breme vpbrayde,
> þe ȝateȝ wer stoken faste,
> þe walleȝ wer wel arayed,
> Hit dut no wyndeȝ blaste.

But that stout barbican exists to protect one of romance's chimerae: a skyline of unattainable and insubstantial fantasy glimpsed by Gawain, who sees inside the walls coloured pinnacles and crenellations so delicate that they seem to be cut from paper not carved from stone.

During Gawain's sojourn at the castle, a recapitulation of epic action alternates with an experiment in the new, tenser and more devious posturings of romance. While Bertilak goes out to hunt, Gawain remains at home in bed, where he has to cope with the sexual importunity of his host's wife. Bertilak prosecutes an epic warfare outdoors; Gawain simultaneously conducts indoors a campaign of mental and social manoeuvring according to the etiquette of romance. Bertilak engages in an expenditure of physical energy, while Gawain, immobilised, suffers a trial both of moral constancy and of mannered courtesy. Bertilak's arena is nature, Gawain's society. There is a savage violence to the hunt, for epic is about the annihilation of nature, which is why, when it recurs in modern literature, it still delights in the ritualising of massacre—Ahab's harpooning and carving-up of whales, Kipling's abattoirs, Coppola's fire-breathing choppers. The substructure of the exquisite romance is the unremitting epic vow to exterminate a nature which will otherwise overcome us. Hence Bertilak's triple combat against the deer, the boar and the fox. As an epic hero, he does not seek after an ideal or an illusion: he fights an enemy, or runs a beast to ground. After the kill, he dismembers the quarry. This is an epic interpolated within a romance, so its end is a ceremonious dissection. D. H. Lawrence proposed that you could not know a thing until you had killed it; the same conviction impels Bertilak's men, who—according to custom, as the poet notes—conduct an incisive surgery on the deer they have slaughtered, disembowel the boar and skin the fox. These autopsies are analytic: they study something by taking it to pieces. The Green Knight performs such disassembling playfully. As soon as his head is sliced off, he restores it. But to other creatures the process is lethal. Romance has internalised the violence of epic. Bertilak's mutilations become a self-rending inquest of one's own moral state, and this is what the insinuating lady incites in Gawain. Like Bertilak's men with the heaped-up corpses, she anatomises him.

Her offer of herself exposes the inconsistencies between the edicts of epic and romance. As Bertilak's guest, Gawain is beholden to him. He owes an obligation of loyalty to his temporary lord, and dare not betray that by yielding to the man's wife. Yet as a chivalrous celebrity, he owes another obligation to women, whom he must relieve and succour. To refuse her would be to insult her as well as to besmirch his own reputation. The lady exploits this discrepancy between fealty and courtesy, between morals and manners, and Gawain, gently rebuffing her like the jeweller in conversation with the pearl, learns what fiction means. Society forbids us to use the epic recourse of direct action, so our only safety lies in dissembling, in saying either more or less than we mean. Gawain meets the lady's advances with an imaginative and discursive dexterity. She teases him by saying he cannot possibly be the famously suave Gawain, since he is so remiss in accepting her favours. He feigns not to know her meaning, then when she explains it shifts to the defence of timidity and bashful politeness. He fakes awe of a 'daunger' she certainly does not possess, and she at once claims languishingly to be in awe of a constraining force that he will never of course employ. She tracks him through a syntactic maze of condition and delicate obliqueness, which recreates in language those mazy thickets and woods of error in which romance characters are forever going astray. Detour and whimsical divagation are the narrative temptations of romance. Since, unlike his epic progenitor, the knight has no definite end in view, he can afford to digress.

Gawain, like Chaucer's *Troilus and Criseyde*, localises the landscape of the quest in society and in the mind. Inside their heads all human beings harbour that demon-haunted terrain which the knight traverses; and any erotic conversation is a risky adventure and a nimble battle with an unguessable adversary. After we have completed the epic feat of exterminating the ogres, we are confronted, in the romance, with enemies less palpable—ourselves and one another. The knight's axe merely nicks Gawain's neck. His lasting wound is not a shedding of blood but the suffusion of his face by a blush of shame. The hurts of romance bleed internally.

Flustered by the lady and mocked by the Green Knight, Gawain accuses himself of sinful failure, and on his return to Camelot, no longer worthy of the allegorical pentangle, sports instead the lady's girdle as the mark of his disgrace. His misogynistic remorse reveals that he has even now not understood what has happened to him. For the courtiers disconcertingly convert what he interprets as a tragic misdemeanour into a comic truancy, and transform his mortifying token into a fashion. They laugh at Gawain's recital of his untruth. That mockery humanises both him and the poem. He may have considered himself to be undergoing a rite of passage. His fellows, however, have made the transition from ritual to romance, and his distress to them is no more than an outlandish fable. Their adoption of the girdle signifies as much: they are unconcerned about what it means; they simply fancy the colour and the look of it. They are presiding over that corruption of chivalry hinted at by Southern when he comments on the trifling amateurism of knighthood, which 'without ever becoming religious . . . enjoyed the sanction and colour of a religious setting' and lamented by J. H. Huizinga in *The Waning of the Middle Ages* (1924), who sees the code losing faith in itself.

Huizinga's epitaph for the Middle Ages, referring to the teasing humour which attends the fourteenth century's quests, might be a commentary on the conclusion of *Gawain*: 'thus a blasé aristocracy laughs at its own ideal'. That caste disowns its 'dream of heroism', admits 'that life is not so fine, after all—and smiles'. Huizinga is duty-bound ideologically to think so, for he is writing soon after the suicidal chivalric episode of the 1914–18 war, whose slaughtered troops considered themselves crusaders, and he compares chivalry, as a source of political disaster, with 'nationalism and racial pride at the present day'. But his diagnosis does not suit the spirit of that end to *Gawain*, for while an aristocracy which has romanticised ritual and declared its own beliefs to be fictions may have reneged on religious faith, it has graduated to a new faith in literature and art. The laughter in *Gawain* differs from the weary, despairing smile described by Huizinga. The amusement of the courtiers in the poem is amiable and reconciliatory, though it begs the moral question of Gawain's blameworthiness. George Orwell in 1947 remarked on the inability of the English to think logically. But their illogic, covered by laughter, is a benign acceptance of contradiction and a symptom of disbelief in daunting norms and absolutes like the pentangle. In any case the girdle might be a more treasurable item than the pentangle. That ideogram, delineating virtue as a theorem, exists outside the human world. It renders life allegorically transparent in order to point to the moral and spiritual ideality beyond, and it reduces Gawain himself to a diagram. Superimposing the five points of the star on his body, the poet enumerates the rectitude of his five wits, the reliability of his five fingers, his trust in the multiples of Christ's five stigmata and Mary's five graces, and his practice of the five chivalric virtues. The knight thus constituted is an allegorical robot. Instead of a body he has a prickly skeleton of concept. His interior is an emblem: he has the Virgin's image etched on the inside of his shield, so he can derive courage from the sight of it.

Against the geometric absolutism of the pentangle and the stern legalism of vow and covenant, the poem sets a compromising, accommodating, comfortably imperfect human existence. Gawain is from the first a dualistic creature: within, the warrior of faith who is deciphered by the pentangle; on the outside, the fashionably dressed, averagely sensual worldling. Though he priggishly thinks his tempters have besmirched him, they have in fact educated him into the acceptance of human frailty. They have shown him to be a man not a five-pointed icon; they have inducted him into comedy. His lapse is actually a progress, the girdle (as the courtiers realise when they adopt it) a prize not a forfeit. For if the pentangle is diagrammatic, the girdle is pictorial. The one sees through matter to discern spirit; the other contentedly departs from the high imperatives of spirit, and enjoys the benefits of our material world. So, confounding the allegory imposed by the pentangle, it advances from didactic ministry to literary representation. The courtiers decide not to look beneath or behind the surface. They will interpret a ritual as a romance, a portent as an ornament. Everything now exists to be turned into a story, and story is not history, since there is no guarantee that it ever happened. The Green Knight's final explanation makes it clear that Gawain has been the subject of his ensnaring invention. The force which ordains the events in the poem is imagination: the witchy devisings of Morgan le Fay and the magic powers of Merlin her tutor. And the poet's final authority for the tale is a literary fabrication. The story is vouched for, he says, in 'þe best boke of romaunce' and in 'þe Brutus boke3'.

Jessie L. Weston was anxious to demonstrate, by her anthropological researches, that 'the Grail Story is not . . . the product of imagination'. But it became so: it became indeed a charter of imaginative liberties. First, however, the ritual significances which underlay it had to be forgotten—or, as at the end of *Gawain*, laughed off. This is the process Huizinga too sternly sees as the decadent waning of the Middle Ages. When it occurs (and it is already implicit in *Orfeo*) romance becomes authentically romantic. It overtakes the Grail itself in Malory's *Morte*. Does the Grail stand for spirit's incarnation in matter, or for matter's dream of spirit? Is it a sacrament or a man-made image? Does it belong with the pentangle or with the girdle? Malory vacillates between the two conditions, sometimes expounding his action as allegory and sometimes permitting it to extrapolate itself as romance. As allegory, the Grail counsels reprobation of what Christ, when he offers the holy vessel to Galahad, calls 'deadly life'. It provokes us to seek beyond matter, which is spirit's coffin. That allegorical quest must be consummated in death. Galahad, therefore, having received the sacrament of mass, 'began to tremble right hard when the deadly flesh began to behold the spiritual things'. As soon as he expires, returning his soul to Christ from whom he derived it, the Grail itself is confiscated. A hand with no body belonging to it reaches from heaven and removes it. It is abstracted into the invisibility of spirit: 'Sithen was there never man so hardy to say that he had seen the Sangrail.'

Yet there are those in the *Morte* who protest against this dematerialising of the fleshly world. The antithesis of the unearthly Galahad is the erotic Launcelot who officially dedicates himself to the Grail quest but strays from this professed perfection in his love for Guenever. His 'seeming outward' is contradicted by 'his privy thoughts and in his mind so set inwardly to the queen'. As a knight of faith he serves God; as a courtly chevalier he does obeisance to his mistress. The opposition between inner and outer makes him a perjured symbol. But in another sense he has nimbly escaped from the symbol's regimentation. Malory emphasises his priviness: his privy thoughts, and the privy draughts he hotly quaffs with Guenever. Having slyly played truant from the impersonality of his religious duty, he has acquired the freedom to be an individual; and in doing so he has made the transition from militant ritual to day-dreaming romance, for he becomes the collective fantasy of 'ladies and damosels that daily resorted unto him, that besought him to be their champion'. Instead of doing homage to a religious saviour, he is to play-act as saviour for these doting ladies, collaborating with their imaginative infatuation. The same invidious choice between symbolic propriety and the privy promptings of literature detains Bedevere when the dying Arthur orders him to hurl the sword Excalibur into the water. He falters twice, unable to part with the jewelled object. Arthur berates him as a traitor and accuses him of a mercenary lust for the riches of the pommel and the haft. The third time Bedevere obeys, and an arm—like that which stretches from heaven to reclaim the Grail—reaches from the water to repossess the sword and then vanish: object's evanescence into symbol has been assured. Though Bedevere's hesitation may seem, like Launcelot's ardour, a rebellion against the allegory, it is actually the expression of an imaginative and literary scruple. Like the courtiers attiring themselves in bright green baldrics, he venerates Excalibur for its beauty not for its totemic meaning. He wants to keep it for the human world rather than render it up to its unseen maker.

His motives are amplified by Tennyson in his version of the 'Morte d'Arthur' in 1842: the first time Bedivere cannot part with the sword because it is an image which dazzles him, a miracle of lapidary art, 'with diamond sparks, / Myriads of topaz-lights, and jacinth-work'; the second time he reflects that it is his duty to preserve it in some aesthetic reliquary, where it will act as a check on the forgetfulness of 'aftertime'. History will efface all record of Arthur: he will be kept alive only in story, or in his artistic leavings, lodged in the museum which Bedivere envisages as a palace of art, 'some treasure-house of mighty kings'. Arthur, accusing him of greed for possession or of girlishly 'valuing the giddy pleasure of the eyes', is denouncing art and literature, which entice us into reverencing such riches and pleasures, as sinful recusancy.

He is protesting against romance's evolving romanticism. That evolution is in itself another sign of continuity in our literature, for though the connection may seem superficial—referring only to the antiquarian fads of the late eighteenth century—it does go deeper. Romanticism turns romance inside out: the quester becomes an associative mental adventurer. The introversion is imaged in a redefinition of a prop inherited by the romance, the sheathed sword. When Malory's Merlin awards Excalibur to Arthur, he asks him whether he likes better the sword or the scabbard. Arthur answers unwisely. 'The scabbard', Merlin warns him, 'is worth ten of the swords.' Similarly the sword with which Galahad is presented can be drawn from its scabbard only by the hardiest of men who, having attained it, will thereafter be invincible. The moral of these admonitions is both epic and allegorical. Epically, the sword is an augmentation of the hero's physical power: Hrunting is an extension of Beowulf's arm. The man who can withdraw the sword has joined it indissolubly to himself. But because Malory has allegorised epic, he must insubstantialise the sword, and he does so by emphasising the superior virtue of the scabbard. The sword is not a weapon but a symbol, and the scabbard, which, as Merlin tells Arthur, will preserve him from any wounds, is the object's spiritual emanation, its ghost of significance. Romance has interpreted epic armour spiritually; romanticism goes a stage further and interprets it aesthetically or psychologically. Shelley, in his *Defence of Poetry* (1821), takes the knight's armament and, in aestheticising it, renders it proudly useless. He calls poetry 'a sword of lightning, ever unsheathed, which consumes the scabbard that would contain it'; he means that poetry scorns to serve any specious or polemical purpose—any cause such as those which mobilised Malory's Christian warriors.

That latter-day chivalric wanderer, Byron's Childe Harold, on morbid pilgrimage through the wreckage of epic warfare in Europe, arms himself cerebrally against the onslaught of an inimical world, deeming

> . . . his spirit now so firmly fix'd
> And sheath'd with an invulnerable mind.

But that aloof mental invulnerability is an illusion. Byron's lyric 'So, we'll go no more a roving' admits that the cold scabbard cannot temper or resist the entropic heat of the live, dying creature within it:

> For the sword outwears its sheath,
> And the soul wears out the breast.

And if Byron imagines a sword exhausting the bodily organism in which it is housed, Robert Browning describes the opposite calamity—a hollow man who is all container and no contents. His Duke in 'The Statue and the Bust' rides idly by, 'Empty and fine like a swordless sheath.' The quest in nineteenth-century romanticism is an exploration of a troubled mind. Tennyson's 'Sir Galahad' neurotically acts out the contradictions in Malory's code. He delights in the perfumed tributes of the ladies and their sweet looks, but has sworn himself to continence; he boasts of the epic hardihood of his good blade and tough lance, yet longs for release from this puissant body into a visionary ether, where 'this mortal armour that I wear' will be 'turn'd to finest air'. The Grail for him betokens a lyrical exhalation into death, and an escape from the tormenting passion and violence of the world. Success in the quest means, as Browning's knight realises in 'Childe Roland to the Dark Tower Came', an acceptance of necessary failure. Browning permitted his followers to believe that Roland's chivalry ended triumphally, and that he who endured would be saved; but the poem argues otherwise. The mind is no longer an armature for Roland. It is penetrated by doubts, fears and recreant desires. His enemies are self-engendered, his goal not worth attaining.

W. B. Yeats's aphoristic poem 'Symbols', written in 1927, completes the process. It consists of three couplets:

> A storm-beaten old watch-tower,
> A blind hermit rings the hour.
>
> All-destroying sword-blade still
> Carried by the wandering fool.
>
> Gold-hewn silk on the sword-blade,
> Beauty and fool together laid.

Now the impedimenta of chivalry have been won over from use to beauty. No longer functional, they serve as symbols alone, and can be venerated but not understood. The hermit has no visual knowledge of the world, the fool no consciousness of it. But their dual disqualification is the source of their value—of the wise man's insight, of the itinerant knight's power. The actual has yielded to the symbolic, and to the aesthetic. Yeats's final axiom is a justification of Bedivere's desire for Excalibur in Tennyson's poem: sheathed in silk, the sword's sole duty now is to be beautiful, and in doting on it the fool is closer to truth than the hero who would treat it as his utensil.

Since then, the knight has metamorphosed into a detective or a spy, no saviour but an explorer or confidant of our collective guilt. Raymond Chandler named one of his early detectives Mallory, and sends his private eye Marlowe to negotiate the wasted land of the city, where he encounters sleazy parodies of what once were chivalric protectors: *The Lady in the Lake* (1944) is not Malory's mystic sword-maker but the decomposed corpse of a murdered woman, and the lost love whom Philip Marlowe seeks on Moose Malloy's behalf in *Farewell, My Lovely* (1940) turns out to be a homicidal vixen who, having married a judge, has changed her name to Velma Grayle. The chivalric profession undergoes a further adaptation to the modern world and its disbelief in heroism in Graham Greene's *The Confidential Agent* (1939). The agent, dispatched to England in barter for the coal with which his faction hopes to win a civil war, has been a lecturer in romance languages, and discovered in Berne a manuscript of the *Song of Roland*. Greene invents this version as his angry withdrawal of faith in the manners of romance. Now Oliver, who urges Roland to blow his horn and summon the aid of Charlemagne, deserves the heroic role. In the Berne text he supplants the 'big brave fool' Roland, and slays him in reprisal for the lives he wasted by his vainglorious gesture. Greene's prescription, however, is clear: ideal values are best served these days by a man like his spy—innocuous, astutely weak, keeping so low a profile that he is named only by an initial; a hero gone underground out of dread, who does not sound his horn because he does not dare to.

— 3 —
Chaucerian Epic and Romance

Epic and romance have drastically alternative notions of poetic and of social propriety. Epic engineers a closure of form which is a cohering of society: hence the *Gawain* poet's tribute to the cohort-like interlinking of its alliterative vocabulary. The romance straggles syntactically, like Malory's association-mongering sentences, from 'and' to 'then' to 'so', finding room for detour and digression. Its connections are random, often casually trusting in accident. Launcelot tells Lionel in Malory that 'we too will seek adventures'. Those adventures are bemusing advents. Launcelot's course is serendipitous. He sees a black hound in the forest. 'And therewith he rode after the brachet, and he saw lie on the ground a large fuete of blood. And then Sir Launcelot rode after. And ever the brachet looked behind her, and so she went through a great marsh, and ever Sir Launcelot followed'—and so on indefinitely, the adverbs proposing a causal sequence to the chase which the sentence structure, full-stopping and starting-up again in improvised jerks, belies. The knight makes his life up as he goes along. The narrative does likewise. This digressive indefiniteness was to constitute, for the nineteenth century, the romanticism of romance. Launcelot's 'riding after' becomes a cerebral journey: Thomas Carlyle referred to Schiller's 'chivalry of thought, described by Goethe as '"the Spirit of Freedom", struggling ever forward.' Because no military necessity constrains the knight, he can roam at liberty; and because the romance permits him the freedom of an interior life, it is powerless to resist his dissolution of social bonds. The romance must be about division within the self and within the society, both of which are impossible in epic. The epic phalanx becomes the Arthurian round table, held together not by the martial interdependence of its members but by frail, abstract oaths of fealty endorsing a social contract. The romance cannot preserve that order: its vision is of the circle's sundering.

Thus when assembling the miscellany of *The Canterbury Tales*, which asks whether there is any unity to literature's grab-bag of inherited stories and genres or to society's random assortments of people, Chaucer takes over these alternative forms and considers them in turn as means of imposing cohesion on modern reality with its quarrelsome diversity. As *Troilus and Criseyde* finds a romance embedded within the epic, demonstrating how the stasis of the Trojan siege grants to the characters the time for introspection and for the circuitous, private adventure of love, *The Canterbury Tales* describes a collectively questing society of romance, where everyone embarks for the martyr's tomb in pursuit of a private ideal (whether it is godliness, gain or the acquisition of new sexual partners along the way). But because the ideals are inconsistent, they clash uproariously, calling in doubt both the cohesion of the poem and the continuance of the pilgrimage. Within this fractured romance, Chaucer implants an epic—'The Knight's Tale'—about the compulsory ordering of society. It is an admonition no one heeds. The only means of unification Chaucer can conceive for this world, poetically and socially, is anthological. Literature is a polyphonic din of stories, each piece of biased testimony straining to shout down all the others; society, too, is more like a rabble than a chorus. Malory embodies this encyclopaedic hybrid, mongrelising the chance contents of the world, in the Questing Beast tracked by Sir Palomides, 'that had in shape a head like a serpent's head, and a body like a leopard, buttocks like a lion, and footed like a hart; and in his body there was such a noise as it had been the noise of thirty couple of hounds questing.' The ogres of romance are narratives spawning and coupling out of control: thus the monster Error in Spenser's *Faerie Queene* belches up an indigestible mashed meal of literature—'Her vomit full of bookes and papers was.'

In *The Canterbury Tales*, romance has learned the aggressiveness of epic. In epic all are united against a common adversary; here each individual feuds against all his fellows. It is a brutal poem. Blows are forever being exchanged, and most of its jokes are ersatz missiles.

Romance by contrast ought to be pacific. The temper of its characters is a devotional passivity. When Chaucer's Pandarus suggests that Troilus should abduct Criseyde rather than allow her to be exchanged for Antenor, Troilus indignantly rejects the suggestion: to do so would be to outrage a parliamentary decree. He derives his existence from society, and must abide by its will. Similarly Malory's knights, who derive their existence from God, accept whatever providence allots to them, and do not bestir themselves in self-defence: 'When Launcelot was come to the water of Mortaise, . . . he was in great peril, and so he laid him down and slept and took the adventure that God would send him.' That 'and so', which seems such a non-sequitur, corresponds syntactically to the trusting involuntariness of romance. In *The Canterbury Tales*, the only character who possesses this spirit of acceptance is Chaucer the uncritical, peace-loving pilgrim, to whom everyone's opinion—no matter how outrageous—is good; and he, as an ironist, is only feigning acquiescence. Everyone else is as combative as the wrathful Achilles, and the poem turns out to foment their disagreements rather than, as it purportedly intends, to unite them in the game of tale-telling.

Chaucer has brought up to date the epic emergency. *The Canterbury Tales* begins guilelessly and garrulously as a romance, before almost at once falling backwards into the regressive violence of epic. The reversion of genre is the more jarring because the poem starts in paradise. William Blake, cataloguing his own idyllic, pictorial inventory of the pilgrims in 1809, referred to Chaucer as an innocent Adam in the brave new world of Eden: 'As Newton numbered the stars, and as Linaeus numbered the plants, so Chaucer numbered the classes of men.' His classifications, for Blake, determine 'the physiognomies of lineaments of universal human life, beyond which Nature never steps'. Chaucer is not for long so convinced of nature's beneficence. The first meteorological lines of the Prologue, describing April's incitement of renewed life and inspiration of wandering, seem already to expect the revision of them with which Eliot will start his *Waste Land*. Each new year regenerates the world. The sun at the vernal equinox, Chaucer notes, is rejuvenated, nature has been freshened and fertilised. Its renewal is a biological upsurgence in landscape, and a redemptive summons to men, who long to go on pilgrimage to salute the source of their being. Chaucer deposits himself in this setting with the arbitrariness of the romance hero who, set down anywhere, will at once commence or resume his career of adventure:

> Bifil that in that seson on a day,
> In Southwerk at the Tabard as I lay . . .

But already, unsuspectingly, he has undergone a fall. Ejected from the garden he has arrived in the city. And instead of the successive, unlinked sequels of romance, he is confronted with a disparate human company. He emphasises its randomness—

> At nyght was come into that hostelrye
> Wel nyne and twenty in a compaignye,
> On sondry folk, by aventure yfalle
> In felaweshipe, and pilgrims weren they alle

—which in romance would be an earnest of the buoyancy and resilience of fate, though here it implies otherwise.

How can this chance ensemble be united? All they have in common is the pilgrimage, and that is no ground for community because each of them has undertaken it for a different reason, the Knight (for instance) as the conclusion to a career of crusading warfare, the Prioress because she is a lachrymose fantasist, the Monk because he intends to eat well along the way, the Wife of Bath because she is an inveterate tourist, the Pardoner because he is a travelling salesman touting indulgences. Maybe their only common denominator is Chaucer himself. He it is who convenes their society by addressing them in turn and then by anatomising them:

> And shortly, whan the sonne was to reste,
> So hadde I spoken with hem everichon
> That I was of hir felaweshipe anon.

Yet his good nature can only appeal plaintively to a kinship they may not acknowledge; he is powerless to coerce them into amity or even co-operation.

Indeed his own benevolence might, in Chaucer's characterisation of himself as merely another member of that society, with no special privileges of insight or intervention, be simple imperceptiveness. Chaucer is at pains to establish his own unreliability and the shrewd untrustworthiness of the texts he diffidently authorises. His descriptive protocol restricts him to exterior attributes—he offers to catalogue condition, degree and array—so about anything undeclared on the surface (the Squire's age, for instance) he has to guess. Sometimes he claims not to have the data he needs for a description: 'Sooth to seyn', he remarks of the Merchant, 'I noot how men hym calle.' It is an extraordinary abdication, very significant for the subsequent politics of the work, of the authority which is authorship. If Chaucer invented the Merchant, why cannot he name him?

Blake's compliment is already being subtly refused by Chaucer: the Prologue is about his teasingly professed inability to enumerate or categorise mankind. He proceeds rather by insinuation. Chaucer's ironic idiom gainsays his every statement, because he is dramatising the difference between authorial pontification about character—Mrs Bennet in *Pride and Prejudice* was, Jane Austen decides, 'a woman of mean understanding, little information, and uncertain temper'—and the diplomatic evasions and polite perjuries enjoined by our tense dealings with actual people. Prohibited from telling the truth by the terms of social contract, we confide our meaning to tonal inference. Chaucer has perfected this arch double-speak. His every conjecture is an aspersion. Thus his guess that the Shipman is from Dartmouth carries the unstated suggestion that he may be a pirate, for teams of brigands operated from that port. Chaucer's conversational and textual policy is to accredit what everyone says. In doing so he holds society together (in contrast to the mutual abusiveness of the Miller and the Reeve, or the Wife of Bath and the Clerk) but demonstrates that this can be done only by and in the precarious wishfulness of fiction. The Monk for instance disdains a precept which would restrict him to the cloister. Chaucer promptly seconds his opinion. If the Monk has refuted an official text, Chaucer puts his name to a supplementary, officially bland text which he invites us in our turn to dismiss—does he mean to approve of the Monk's greedy worldliness, or is this just the bad faith of good manners?

Chaucer's poetry has to be imagined orally. The tales are, after all, recitation. The false naivety and nervous ingratiation of the speaking voice, which he so wonderfully catches (almost his first poetic utterance is an apology, in the protestation of incompetence which begins *The Book of the Duchess*), act out the problems of fellowship and affinity central to *The Canterbury Tales*. Jane Austen could think or write down that denunciation of Mrs Bennet. She could never say it, and when Emma makes a much more innocuous remark about Miss Bates she is virtually ostracised. The codes of social conduct forbid truth-telling, just as they veto Pandarus's project for the seizure of Criseyde.

Reading aloud at the court of King Richard II, Chaucer is a hired and unheeded bard. Instead of the *Beowulf* poet's peremptory 'Hwæt!', he must rely on mock-modest disclaimers to justify his presumption in requesting to be heard, so his vocal pacification of the poem's external society, its audience, duplicates his attempt to govern the recalcitrant society within the poem. A painting from the early fifteenth century, now at Corpus Christi College in Cambridge, shows him in the act, propped up in a pulpit reading *Troilus and Criseyde* to a rabble of Richard II's indifferent courtiers, some of whom dotingly prosecute their own love-affairs and use the poem merely as a goad to amorous reverie, while others, bored by the performance, escape outdoors to hunt and hawk. A later painting illustrates how literature has lost this sense of Chaucer's peculiar vocal difficulties, a constraint which he ironically finesses into a unique freedom: it is Ford Madox Brown's representation, painted between 1845 and 1851, of 'Chaucer reading the "Legend of Custance" to Edward III and his court on the anniversary of the Black Prince's forty-fifth birthday'; it now hangs in the Art Gallery of New South Wales. This pre-Raphaelite Chaucer is a moral apostle, exhorting the kingdom in the open air. The painting's triangular composition enthrones him, on his dais, on a level with the king. He has attained the poet's romantic status of unacknowledged legislator, in contrast with the self-effacing civil servant of the Cambridge painting. And he reads with index finger upraised towards the sky, like a didactic saint or ministering angel. The arrival of literature is a kind of annunciation: at the same time, Brown was painting Wycliffe reading his translation of the Bible to John of Gaunt. In its promotion of Chaucer to prophetic intermediary between man and God, a translator like Wycliffe of divine meanings, the painting has conferred on the poem the sanctity of scripture—which is exactly what Chaucer could never claim for it (except, as will be seen, in jesting asides). And though both he and Wycliffe are reading aloud, scripture is a symbol of the trustworthiness of print, and Chaucer's is still an oral poetry, whose meaning lies more in the tonal inflection given to the words than in the words themselves. 'I seyde his opinioun was good' cannot be taken literally. The spirit (or the tone) must correct the letter. Even though Wordsworth called the poet 'a man speaking to men', that speaking, in the nineteenth century, must be done silently, for it is a reading of the thoughts of men, not a conversation with them: Brown's Chaucer is a Victorian serial novelist, monopolising the mental lives of his characters and his auditors. The Cambridge Chaucer is one incident among the social distractions of the court. His position explains the arch apology with which the Prologue to the *Tales* ends. Chaucer entreats his listeners or readers to pardon him for a fault he has not yet been accused of:

> . . . first I pray yow, of youre curteisye,
> That ye n'arette it nat my vileynye,

> Thogh that I pleynly speke in this mateere,
> To telle yow hir wordes and hir cheere,
> Ne thogh I speke hir wordes proprely.

As always, his apology covers the adroit taking of a liberty. He asks forgiveness for a crime he has not committed, which licenses him to commit another yet more audacious crime. He hopes the courteous audience will not consider him ill-bred ('vileyn'), because he is duty-bound to repeat the words the pilgrims have spoken, and dare not palliate their occasional rudeness. Chaucer conceives of that fidelity to sources as a moral or familial bond:

> He may nat spare, althogh he were his brother.

Yet this vow of loyalty is the prelude to a betrayal. Chaucer is seeking in advance the right to inculpate that brother (the '*hypocrite lecteur*' who is acknowledged in the nineteenth century by Baudelaire as '*mon semblable, mon frère*'). He intends to say 'vileyn' things to these courtiers, but, thanks to his escape-clause, will be able to blame the offence on his characters. His claim is to be merely taking dictation from them, but it is a ventriloquistic ploy: after all, who invented them? He has put the words into their mouths, and ghosted their supposedly voluntary confessions.

While seeming to ease his way into this well-mannered society, Chaucer is warning that his poem will be—through no fault, he insists, of his—about that society's breakdown. To bless this subversion, both of his sources and of a social compact, Chaucer astonishingly invokes the authorities of scriptural and philosophical precursors:

> Crist spak hymself ful brode in hooly writ,
> And wel ye woot no vileynye is it.
> Eek Plato seith, whoso kan hym rede,
> The wordes moote be cosyn to the dede.

The first citation demonstrates how the protestation of slavish reliance on precedent and of authorial impotence allows Chaucer, underhandedly, to risk an outrageous blasphemy. Christ has been made the prototype for the disrespectful plain-speakers of the *Tales*, who disdain all authority, even that of scripture. The second reference is one of Chaucer's best jokes and one of his subtlest lies (or fictions). In the 'Whoso kan hym rede' Chaucer characteristically gives away his own game. He could not read Plato, and is actually taking Boethius's word for it. As well, the Boethian idea is an explicit contradiction of all those assurances of literal fealty which have preceded it. In the *Consolation of Philosophy*, which Chaucer had translated, Boethius taxes Philosophy with the circularity of her arguments. She justifies herself by reminding him that the world itself is a turning circle or a rotating sphere whose mover remains immobile; she has been imitating that rhythmic revolution. He should not be surprised, she adds. Plato recommends the use of language related to the subject under discussion. Chaucer's translation makes that relationship familial: 'Nedes the wordes moten be cosines to the thinges of which they speken.' That kinship has an extra significance when reprised in the poem so soon after the oath of loyalty to a brother. Again the sense is the reverse of the official one. Chaucer reads Plato by hearsay; so, too, in telling the tales he will be modifying them.

But the words of his tellers will be cousin to their deeds in a more dangerous way, for those words often threaten angrily disruptive action, which the poem is not always able to prevent. Another of Chaucer's reverent sources, the *Roman de la Rose* (which he also in part translated), provides him with a more flagrant excuse for misrepresentation of the letter. Reason, in Jean de Meun's section of the poem, is accused of linguistic lewdness by the lover, just as Chaucer expects to be charged with 'vileyn' speaking. She responds by translating the genitalia, to which she has been referring, into allegorical tokens. Only a fool, she chides, would have understood her literally: she has been employing carnal matter in order to embody spirit, teaching, as philosophers do, by means of myth and fable. Chaucer adapts her didactic technique to his own more devious purposes. The letter of the text is merely his alibi, enabling him to mean what he dare not say. D. H. Lawrence, combating an intrusive moralism in the novel, made it a rule never to trust the teller, only the tale. Chaucer's formula for the evasion of a facile morality is several degrees more sceptical: never trust the teller (or the innocuous letter, since the literal meaning is there to create a diversion), never even trust the tale—in what sense, for instance, do the Pardoner and the Wife of Bath *mean* their tales, which appear to be told, after the evidence of their personal prologues, against themselves?—and above all, do not trust Chaucer, who, at the end of his life, retracts his own greatest poetry.

If, however, the text is systematically to be mistrusted, there is probably a procedure for arriving at the true and unstated sense. The instructresses of Boethius or Jean de Meun call this fabulation. The letter can be deciphered as an allegory of the invisible spirit. Irony is Chaucer's mode of allegory. He says one thing and means another; the decorous deference of the letter permits the unstated spirit to imply whatever it wishes. All these excuses amount to an arrogant, imaginative manifesto. Apologising for uncouth manners, Chaucer is in fact unrepentantly apologising for poetry. This is the encoded intent of his next self-vindication:

> Also I prey you to foryeve it me,
> Al have I nat set folk in hir degree
> Heere in this tale, as that they sholde stonde,
> My wit is short, ye may wel understonde.

—another subversion humorously passing itself off as fatuity. Chaucer recklessly disorders society while claiming to have done no more than clumsily jumbled it up. Instead of degree with its hierarchical ranking, he nominates as the disorganising principle of his world a ludic randomness. The poem is to be a lottery, with the outcome depending on 'aventure, or sort, or cas'. Chaucer manages this renouncing of responsibility under cover of a persona. Since he cannot or will not assume control, he delegates that function to the Host, who devises the game, supervises the initial lot-drawing and later bullies obnoxious pilgrims back into submission. Chaucer himself, after his inane tale of Sir Thopas is gruffly aborted, is one of the Host's butts. The poem has so controverted itself that the creator can be victimised by his own creation.

That pretence, like all of Chaucer's white lies, shadows a truth. He is forswearing the sublimely easy egotism of literature, that mode of fantasising triumph which enables the artist to reconstruct the world to his own liking and in his own image, with himself as ultimate arbiter. His flustered denials make him the first great exponent of a peculiarly English kind of poetic identity, or nonentity—a poet whose only capabilities are, in the phrase Keats used of Shakespeare, negative; a comically absent god.

This resignation to an amicable impotence becomes one of the definingly idiosyncratic attitudes of English literature. It is Sterne's position, and Coleridge's too. It is also, in a different sense, Shakespeare's. His characters can have wills, but Shakespeare himself has no means of wilfully controlling them. The stage is an arena of freedom and of chance. In contrast, the English tradition contains a single exposition of literature as a kind of power: Hazlitt's praise of Coriolanus.

The Prologue to the *Tales* finds in that questing romance a replica of our hesitant, groping exploration of society. The Host says to Chaucer

> Thou lookest as thou woldest fynde an hare,
> For evere upon the ground I se thee stare.

That mystified, myopic shyness is the wisdom of romance, where the hero finds his way by trial and error through a maze, or in quest of a white rabbit. If the romance here represents a modern society, in *Troilus and Criseyde* it stands for the dubiety of consciousness. The maze or wood of error there is the mind of Criseyde, its every avenue a course of action with whose potentialities she experiments. But Chaucer begins the modernised and collective romance of the *Tales* by writing the condensed epic of 'The Knight's Tale'. His reason has to do with the politics of genre. The tales concern the anarchic individualism of society, which the romance promotes; the Knight's interpolated epic protests belatedly against that defeat. In epic, rules can still be promulgated and legislative decrees enforced. An armistice can be imposed on the combative violence of the elements, which would otherwise eat up the substance of the world. Nowhere else in *The Canterbury Tales* do such enchaining judgements work. From the paradisial hope of new beginnings with which the Prologue opens, the poem abruptly regresses. 'The Knight's Tale', told by the oldest and most-travelled pilgrim, inherited from olden times, populated by sage elders like Egeus and able to recall the long history 'sith the world began', is already a pessimistic epilogue to the Prologue's regenerative confidence. The epic remembers the world as a scarred field of battle, piled with corpses. Men fight up to their ankles in blood, and commandeer women (as Theseus does Ypolita) as the spoils of war. Instead of the trustful pilgrimage on which Chaucer's characters set out in search of healing, Egeus remembers the earth as a place of sad and short-lived transit:

> This world ays but a thurghfare ful of wo,
> And we been pilgrymes, passynge to and fro.
> Deeth is an ende of every worldly soore.

The conflict which maddens Palamon and Arcite—a fury of vital will as if violence were the principle of their being and wrath, as for that epic prototype Achilles, a biological delight—continues beneath and above their human stratum. The four elements are in dispute until separated and assigned to their separate provinces, while the squabbling gods are themselves monsters of raging will, arguing by the exchange of thunderclaps and lightning bolts. Engendering nature, which brings the world to birth in the Prologue, is here overtaken by an automatic physiological determinism. Hence Arcite can be briskly terminated by an analysis of his symptoms:

> Nature hath now no dominacioun.
> And certeinly, ther Nature wol nat wirche,
> Fare wel phisik! go ber the man to chirche!
> This al and som, that Arcita moot dye.

Troilus finds no such incompatibility between the values of epic and those of romance. The consummation of his love emboldens his warfaring: in Chaucer's poem about the besieging of Troy and Criseyde, love and war are alike defensive routines. Criseyde fends off Troilus, as he fends off the Greeks. But for Palamon and Arcite, love is the continuation of war by other means. As well as cousins they are blood-brothers, epically interchangeable and lacking the interior individuality of Troilus; so when they find that they desire the same woman, they can differentiate themselves only by attempting to kill each other. Reviewing this carnage, the poem attempts variously to mitigate it. One way of doing so, of course, is the revision of epic as romance—the staging of the bestial feud, with Arcite a ravening tiger and Palamon a ruthless lion, as a tournament; the redefinition of homicide as chivalry. That attempt to socialise the violence by playing war games receives a supernatural warranty in Theseus's final theodicy. His speech is a political coup which provides itself with a philosophical rationale: decreeing an end to the quarrel, he invents as a sovereign patron of his action the First Mover, who has locked the world into a system of obedience which Theseus, as an afterthought, declares to be loving. Men may be saved from themselves if a god can be manufactured to affright them. Society may be preserved if a political system—as at the Athenian parliament—is fabricated to govern it. The Knight's own telling of the tale is another version of this palliation. Though it is an epic of destructive force, with scratching of cheeks, tearing out of hair and the incineration of battle-scarred bodies, a poem of murderous atavism (the consensus when it is over is that it is mnemonically valuable, for epic is about our historical recollection—the tale is complimented as 'worthy for to drawen to memorie'), the Knight tries graciously to retail it as romance, interesting his listeners in its chivalric trappings or enrolling them, as a diversion, in a court of love by asking all lovers to decide 'who hath the worse, Arcite or Palamon?'

At last the Knight decides on matrimony as an ameliorating end, and insists that Palamon and Emelye live on in settled content. But the later tales suggest that marriage is no securer than an armed truce, and there is the same instability in the society of the pilgrimage, where the only guarantee of peace is the mutuality of weaponry and the deterrent temper of the Host. Though Theseus and the Knight both extenuate the tale—deliberately fictionalising it, so that Emelye the votaress of Diana, who wants neither man, suddenly consents to be a tender wife, while Palamon the lion is tamed and made her gentle servant—an epic belligerence persists in the tales which follow. Group A is a triangular combat. The Miller and the Reeve tell tales against each other, and at the same time concur in telling tales against the knight. The narrative pastime which should have united them has turned into their battle-plan.

Despite this abusive disagreement between the three, the tales in Group A confirm one another. The *fabliaux* are, like the Knight's attenuated epic, about the capsizing of those social formalities which dissuade us from waging perpetual war: they are not coarse anecdotes but, properly, fables concerned with our tightrope-walking above the abyss and our anxious equilibration. The body of Alisoun is described not physiologically but agriculturally, as the lavish terrain on which men prey, or as the nature which they capture and accultivate. She is entrammelled by men: caged by her husband John, railed up like an unruly colt within the bondage of Nicholas's fondling, fed on by Absalon who yearns for her like a lamb for the teat. They all appraise her as property, seeking to confine her fluency and to monopolise her fertility. Power over her will assure them of safety and solidity. Like Theseus's disembodied primal cause, they fasten their universe with a chain they call love. The same obsession opposes John's trade of carpentry to the weltering chaos of the flood astrologically predicted by Nicholas. John has rigged up a home-made world with 'his owene hand'. Like Crusoe on his island or like Hrothgar building Heorot, he places his faith in structure, the human invention which excludes riotous nature. Suspending the tubs from the roof, unfurling ladders and victualling these boats, he is engineering a capsule inside which he and his companions will survive—a leaky and unreliable domestic Nautilus. His fellow-fabricator is the blacksmith Gerveys, who

> ... in his forge smythed plough harneys;
> He sharpeth shaar and kultour bisily,

manufacturing the tools with which men exploit and punish a recalcitrant nature—an iron for Absalon to smite Nicholas with; ploughshares for the violent cultivation or sexual ploughing of that landscape which is Alisoun. These machines are made for disciplining the incontinence of human beings and of earth. But the eruptive body shatters such frail tackle. The stormy rumble presaging the apocalypse is Nicholas's fart,

> As greet as it had been a thouder-dent,
> That with the strook he was almost yblent

—a gaseous thunder and a lacerating lightning, which cues Absalon to scorch Nicholas, and John catastrophically to launch his tub. So the chaos ensuing is a human riot not a natural disaster.

More rigid precautions are taken in 'The Reeve's Tale' against this invading anarchy. Arms are here man's means of guarding his property: the jealous and avaricious Symkyn protects his hoard with the bristling array of blades he carries. Description serves the same purpose of cautious retention. Everything in the tale is exactly placed, affixed to an owner. Its topographic detail and its measuring erect a structure to set things in relation to each other in a hierarchy of shackled objects. The Reeve begins by asserting such an order in the poem's setting (no landscape, like the fecund Alisoun, but a minimal cartographic takeover):

> At Trumpyngtoun, nat fer fro Cantebrigge,
> Ther gooth a brook, and over that a brigge,
> Upon the whiche brook ther stant a melle;
> And this is verray sooth that I yow telle.

Thereafter he shows the same proprietorial ranking at work within Symkyn's family, and his exiguous describing—which allows this tale no lyricism—is itself a husbanding of resources. The Miller's realism is that of Crusoe, industriously constructing the world; the Reeve's is the different realm of Moll Flanders, a panicking catch-as-catch-can appropriation of the world. Symkyn steals things because the more goods he has, the more anchored he will feel himself to be. Hence his pride in his wife's lineage, and hence, too, his tethering of the students' horse so 'it sholde namoore go loos'. The disposition of beds in his house effects the same mercenary regimenting of living space, with the cradle at the base of his bed, his daughter lying ten or twelve feet further off and the students a furlong or so in another direction. The complicated sexual triangle is a geometric theorem, a containment of space. Symkyn despises the Cambridge scholars because they lack his yeoman's respect for space and for the reality of tangible, robbable things. Agreeing to let them pass the night, he sneers that they must fit themselves into his spatial regime, and laughs at their abstract mental geometry which can, in defiance of realism, square circles and, as one of Donne's poems pretends to do, make a little room an everywhere:

> Myn hous is streit, but ye han lerned art;
> Ye konne by argumentes make a place
> A myle brood of twenty foot of space.
> Lat se now if this place may suffise,
> Or make it rowm with speche, as is youre gise.

Time, too, in this numerically constricted world, imitates the abbreviation of space. The events happen during what John calls a 'shorte nyght'. Yet the fable illustrates the failure of this acquisitive rage to get a purchase on the materials of life. For all their determination to anchor, tether and hoard, these are people stumbling about in the dark and straying outside the spatial bounds they have taken such care to establish. If they miss their way back to the bed or strike out blindly in the gloom as Symkyn's wife does with her stave, chaos will punctually come again.

Chaucer's comic encouragement of such affrays—the marital fisticuffs in 'The Wife of Bath's Prologue', the uproarious pursuit of the fox in 'The Nun's Priest's Tale', the babel of bird song into which the *Parlement of Foules* capsizes—is his secret offence against an official medieval aesthetic. The medieval poem longs to be a conspectus, an encyclopaedic synopsising of stories like Gower's *Confessio Amantis* or Lydgate's *Pageant of Knowledge* or the drearily comprehensive inventory of tragedies accumulated by Chaucer's Monk. But in Chaucer the additive structure loses faith in itself. Unless things are harnessed together by a philosophical system (in Theseus's scheme) or tagged and tallied as possessions (as by the Reeve), they will fall apart. Chaucer's comedy incites them to do so, for it is the insurgence of human individuality. The Wife of Bath refuses to be categorised, and adheres to her own libidinal experience against the authority of church, society and poem. Once they become, like her, autonomous characters, Chaucer's people reject the structure which has sought to file and assort them. The pilgrimage therefore undergoes fragmentation, and so does the poem. If the group is no more than a sampling of fractious, dissimilar creatures, then the poetic compendium is not a bibliography or typology of narrative forms but a mass of incomplete or misapplied or irrelevant tales. The pilgrims cannot get to Canterbury; nor can Chaucer complete his own version of their quest, which is the composition of the originally envisioned one hundred and twenty stories. G. K. Chesterton, religiously biased though his judgment is, understands this as the meaning of the unachieved structure: 'Chaucer symbolized something of the change from the medieval balance to the modern march; from the philosophy of the Dance to the philosophy of the Race.' The processional troop of the Prologue is maddened into the rabble of villagers in 'The Nun's Priest's Tale', whose noise reminds Chaucer of the revolt of 'Jakke Straw and his meynee'.

Chesterton, for whom in 1932 Chaucer is an Aquinian God—a solar centre of 'radiant receptivity'—laments the change, and believes that Chaucer does so too. He can thus contend that 'Chaucer was more unmistakably orthodox than Langland'. But the miscarrying of the *Tales*, like the inability of *Piers Plowman* to conclude its pilgrimage, is an assault on all orthodoxies. Langland senses that literature itself will mismanage the ideas he places in its charge. A poem fleshes them out, attires what ought to be allegorical spirit in irrelevant matter; it will make of a pilgrimage merely a narrative, or a trip. And so Langland three times self-accusingly breaks off his work. His subversion is inadvertent, and therefore repented; but Chaucer, under the dual cover of comedy and of his professed incompetence and powerlessness, can plot his own literary equivalent to Jack Straw's uprising. Comedy encourages his people to unyoke themselves from the social hierarchy and the poetic structure. Irony allows Chaucer, who has incited them, to pretend he cannot help it. By absconding into or behind his narrators, Chaucer can begin to imply that the purposes of literature and those of faith can have nothing in common. The orthodox tales of Melibee or of the Parson are in subservient prose; Chaucer reserves his finest and most gratuitous poetry for episodes unregulated by a moral intent—for the agricultural terrain of Alisoun's body, for Chauntecleer's absurdly extravagant plumage, for the seasonal rutting of Januarie and May in their mock-paradisial garden, for the sentimental religiose fantasies of the Prioress. He is seeking for poetry and for insurrectionary imagination a margin of freedom beyond the strict borders of truth. This is why his most skittish and wayward invention gets displaced to the margins of narrative, where it delights in detour, parenthesis and associative improvising—the Wife of Bath's multiplication of her consorts, the teetering edifices of preening pedantry erected by Chauntecleer and Pertelote—or why it flourishes between the tales even more than in them, in those link passages where the Host denounces one teller and rallies another or where interruptions can be permitted, like the arrival of the Canon's Yeoman at Boghtoun under Blee.

The Canterbury Tales mimes epic's defeat by romance. The cohering, coercing power variously extolled by the narrators of Group A proves unavailing. The epic regiment scatters along the open road of romance. But romance is in turn outwitted: the shared ideal and destination, symbolised in Malory by the Grail, is subdivided into fractions. Everyone is engaged in the pursuit of a happiness privately defined, which is why they can never arrive as a group at Canterbury. In its explosion of genre and its toppling of the medieval stock-list of stories, *The Canterbury Tales* is the first of the great English literary chaoses, works which have defined for themselves a value more idiosyncratic and indigenous than the classical one of unity—Spenser's meandering and digressing epic, *The Faerie Queene*; Sterne's diagram of thought as a picaresque journey in *Tristram Shandy*; the loose baggy monsters (in Henry James's phrase) and indifferent wholes which are the novels of Dickens.

— 4 —
Chaucer, Langland
and the Treachery of the Text

The anarchists who instigate the rebellion in Chaucer are the Wife of Bath and
the Pardoner, who might be called the first characters in English literature,
because they are the first to claim autonomy and ungovernability for
themselves. The Wife states the ground of their disaffection in her first defiant
insistence that

> Experience, though noon auctoritee
> Were in this world, is right ynogh for me,

and she goes on to dispute all authorities which pretend to suppress her,
including that of her own author, for her garrulous multiplying of marital
reminiscences and her reluctance to get round to telling the tale assigned to her
suggest that she has a sovereignty over Chaucer like that she maintains over her
menfolk, as if he is obsequiously taking dictation from her. Her scornful
opposition between authority and experience is the overturning of a medieval
literary and religious rule. To the medieval understanding, a thing's meaning
lies in the use authority intends for it, not in its experiential adventures. The
ultimate authority is of course God, and nature, like scripture, is a book
authorised and authored by him. The bestiaries survey nature and treat its
livestock as emblematic exempla. The ape for instance was designed, when it
showed its rump, to betoken devilment; the stag's shedding of his horns
admonishes us to abandon our own antlered pride.

The Wife believes none of this. To her, things are interesting and agreeable
in themselves, and the forbidding significances of the bestiary or of scriptural
precept are no more than devices to keep us from the enjoyment of our own
natural existences. The area in which she chooses to argue her case is that of
sexual freedom, but her contentions amount as well to a literary manifesto. In
deriding the habits of biblical exegetes, she is relieving literature from the need
to model itself on exegesis. For the medieval mind, all stories were inevitably
allegorical, since nature itself and human life were allegorical constructs. The
most innocuous sentence could be expounded in a hierarchy of significances,
and up that ladder experience mounted towards authority: the literal meaning
generated an allegorical one, thence a tropological and at last an analogical or
spiritual one; letter aspires to arrive at spirit. Langland's episode of the good
samaritan in *Piers Plowman* is a case of such fourfold deciphering. All this the
Wife of Bath denies. For her, literature can only begin when authority loosens

its hold on the comically inconsistent accidents of experiences. And her prologue and tale accomplish this slackening. Thus whereas Chaucer, for his own devious ironic purposes, is fond of hiding behind incorrigible texts or sources, the Wife frees herself from their pre-empting by misreading them in order to make them conform to her personal case and her bodily needs.

This is her way with the biblical castigations in her prologue, and it licenses a feckless creativity. The single-minded exemplariness of allegory likewise yields to the diversity of what she calls 'sondry wyse'. Morality generalises about the human predicament; literature on the contrary particularises, demonstrating how different we all are from one another. The scriptural praise of virginity is contradicted by the Wife's generous reproductiveness: the patristic literary régime provides for a strictly controlled multiplication of meanings, but the Wife's joy in 'engendrure' makes her, in literary as well as sexual terms, irrepressibly promiscuous, as abundant verbally as she is physically. She therefore opens wide the gap between moralism and the liberties playfully allowed to literary character. Moralising commentators on Chaucer may brand her as a carnal reprobate, but to any reader responsive to the poem she is an embodiment of love—of that creative love whereby literature performs over again the miracle of Genesis and populates the world anew. Dryden, in the preface to his translation of Chaucer in 1700, saluted this ancestral generativeness in him, calling him 'the father of English poetry' and exclaiming of the *Tales*, 'here is God's plenty'. But it is not a plenty approved of by the God who is the allegorical supervisor of medieval literature. It is an illicit and unauthorised plenitude.

Therefore the Wife's wisdom renounces those prohibitive texts engraved on the tablets of the law and expresses itself in the form of proverbs. 'A likerous mouth moste han a likerous tayl', she says, or, speaking of her own seasonal decay,

> The flour is goon, ther is namoore to telle;
> The bren, as I best kan, now moste I selle.

The proverb begins at the opposite end from allegory, though they meet in the middle: it is not authority conscripting experience but experience deriving authority from its own humble, domestic, particular case. Its truth is not handed down from on high, like allegory's; it grows up from the ground and has not yet lost touch with the enlivening anecdote beneath it. Keeping faith with her proverbial and oral lore, the Wife assaults the pedantry and repressiveness of writing: she vents her most intense ire on the book—a digest of misogynistic tracts—which Jankyn reveres. Her own prologue seems to extend itself inordinately, as if she is loth to resign herself to being the teller, the mere transcriber, or transliterator, of someone else's tale; and when she does consent to commence it, she takes care to define it as her personal possession, not some authorised and literary heirloom. Her pagan and ancestral memory ('I speke of manye hundred yeres ago') connects us with the fairy kingdom suppressed by the friars, while the knight who is dispatched to discover as a forfeit 'what thyng wommen loven most' has been expelled by her from the safely closed world of precept symbolised by Jankyn's book and made to investigate the diversity of actual lives. His romance quest is a research into the relativity and multitudinousness of phenomena, a comic education, and thus a recapitulation of Chaucer's pilgrimage to Canterbury:

> . . . he ne koude arryven in no coost
> Wher as he myghte fynde in this mateere
> Two creatures accordynge in-feere.

The Wife's own irrepressible digressiveness ought to be a model to him. To her everything is of such intrinsic, even if irrelevant, fascination that she is content to be a grammatical vagabond and a cosmic gossip, unauthoritatively passing on the accumulations of the world's experience ('somme seyde. . . . And some seyn. . . . And somme seyn. . . . Ovyde, amonges othere thynges smale, / Seyde . . .'). When the hag who is her deputy provides the knight with the all-purpose answer to his query, it is shown to be paradoxically inept. Though the crone has made propaganda for female sovereignty, she is prepared to surrender it and to serve the knight if he will love her. The Wife of Bath ends with a warning to dominant women, but her tale has already contravened the teller: as her fantasy, it confides more about her than she will admit. Just as the proverb has an experiential truth (which is the illicit veracity of literature) so her tale is an imaginative fable and thus a confession, exempting her from her own shrewish dogmatism.

The Pardoner becomes a character by a yet more complex working of involuntary imagination. He begins by announcing as his perennial theme a precept ('*Radix malorum est Cupiditas*') against which his every subsequent word and action offends. He admits the worthlessness of his holy relics, then goes on to peddle them all the same. He tells a tale which accuses him, yet his only concern is for the grisly verbal virtuosity of his telling. His loquacity might sound like the eager masochism of one of Langland's Deadly Sins. However, it lacks that mad fixity which is the self-scourging condition of allegorical caricature. In Chaucer, it becomes a more troubling dramatic ambiguity. 'The Pardoner's Prologue and Tale' promulgates an impious bill of rights for fictional character. As a performer, proud of his oratory and relishing the grotesque riches of his vocabulary, the Pardoner submits to no extraneous control. Chaucer cannot manage him; he cannot even control himself. He is ecstatically carried away by his own extemporary liberty, and by the charmed moral permissiveness of fiction—for despite the scandal of his indulgence-touting and the virulence of the Host's threat, the Knight astonishingly intervenes to laugh off the conflict: fictional character flourishes in a world where it is unimportant to be earnest, unimpeded by moral edicts, so the Host and Pardoner can kiss in reconciliation and ride merrily on together. The episode testifies to Chaucer's nimbleness in the game of ironic counterfeiting. Within a convention of forbidding necessity he has contrived an exhilarating and unlawful runaway freedom. The Pardoner may sound like a personified vice giving evidence against himself; actually he is a dramatically unguessable performing self, inventing and consuming himself as he goes on, existing only in the impersonation he gives of being the Pardoner. The fault at the end is the Host's, not his. Declaring 'I wol no lenger pleye / With thee', the Host has forgotten that everything is a game, that even identity is a role we assume for social exhibition or mercenary gain. The Pardoner has the recklessness to play that game—which supplies the society of the pilgrimage with its diplomatic code—psychologically.

This is why his recitation is so horribly self-dismembering. The Wife, in her fond speculations about the genital organs, de-allegorises the human body, refusing to see it as a moral diagram and determining to enjoy her residence in it; the Pardoner extols the body as a tabernacle of greedy pleasures, and separates out each of its rampant organs. In turn he expatiates on 'the shorte throte, the tendre mouth', the womb and the belly, 'the golet softe and swoote' and the hissing nose, each with its own ribald delight. He carves up the body and ravens on it in a perverse celebration of communion. It is himself he is ingesting.

He has two images for this fierce gustatory enjoyment of himself, and both capture the savage glee with which he outrages moral taboo. The first describes, while pretending to deplore, the grisly oaths of the Flemish roisterers:

> Oure blissed Lordes body they totere,—
> Hem thoughte that Jewes rente hym noght ynough.

The second deals with the massacre of flesh by the culinary art and makes this out to be a scholastic mutation:

> Thise cookes, how they stampe, and streyne, and grynde,
> And turnen substaunce into accident.

Christ's incarnation was the warrant for medieval allegory, because it housed spirit in the literal. To cannibalise that flesh, as the Pardoner's characters riotously do, is to glut on the letter, to consume and void the spirit; it also means that we can treat the authorised heirlooms of the past—the Pardoner's relics, the sacramental body of Christ, all the reverenced sources to which Chaucer everywhere mimes deference—with a hearty, hungry disrespect like that of the cooks, punishing them until they serve and please us. Scholasticism may criticise the misrepresentation whereby substance is changed into accident, but the imagination exults in the process. From the substance of his sources, Chaucer, by mashing and pulverising them, makes the sublime accident of literature.

The Wife and the Pardoner are his surrogates, but the character in the *Tales* who may be closest to Chaucer's creative identity is one who scarcely exists at all, except fugitively—the Nun's Priest. All we know of him is that he is attached to the Nun. He is not even granted singleness: in the General Prologue he is one of a trio. However the tale he tells is the most ripely characterful in the work. He pervades it despite his absence from it, like god in nature or like the ironist lurking invisibly between the lines of what he writes.

Under cover of its apparent triviality, 'The Nun's Priest's Tale' is a reflection on art. Its own art is inordinately lavished on a story which seems not to deserve it (the fable of the vainglorious cock and the flattering fox), but that is the point. Art equals surplus, affluence, the marginal extravagances of an imagination humans do not need but cannot do without. The irony of the poem is that this imagination, which makes us human, is here the preserve of the sub-human characters. The widow who owns the cock lives morally and minimally. Her rectitude enjoins denial, and the language the Nun's Priest uses of her is grudgingly exiguous. All her attributes are negative:

> N'apoplexie shente nat hir heed.
> No wyn ne drank she, neither whit ne reed;

when she does positively possess something that, too, has a minus sign fixed to it by the narrator's rhetoric—thus (with added italics)

> Thre large sowes hadde she, *and namo*,

or

> Milk and broun breed, in which she foond *no lak*.

Chauntecleer by contrast is an object made for no purpose but decoration, a dazzling ornament and a creature both of aesthetic vanity and of overweening intellect. All his faults are justified by the poem's action, for he evades retribution: he is in the poet's special care. The Nun's Priest, introducing Chauntecleer's learned debate with Pertolete, remarks ingenuously

> For thilke tyme, as I have understonde,
> Beestes and briddes koude speke and synge.

Is he, with typical mock-modesty, proposing himself as a farmyard Orpheus, bestowing a lyrical articulacy on nature? He has already set Chauntecleer's crowing into melodious competition with church music:

> His voys was murier than the murie orgon
> On messe-dayes that in the chirche gon.
> Wel sikerer was his crowyng in his logge
> Than is a clokke or an abbey orlogge.

At the end of his amoral fable, the Nun's Priest does seem belatedly anxious to establish its moral utility:

> . . . ye that holden this tale a folye,
> As of a fox, or of a cok and hen,
> Taketh the moralite, goode men.
> For seint Paul seith that al that writen is,
> To our doctrine it is ywrite, ywis;
> Taketh the fruyt, and lat the chaf be stille.

Yet where is the morality to be winnowed? In invoking the Pauline command to read allegorically, Chaucer is issuing his own instruction to read ironically. The 'chaf' in the tale is all that matters: it is about the superfluity or marginality or excessiveness of art. If read morally, it is trite; if read aesthetically, it is superbly bold. The disparity between the two readings— between the luxury of the letter and the paltriness or meanness of the spirit, as worshipped by the widow—states the incompatibility of art and preaching.

When Chaucer came to his own end, he composed a retraction which is, read allegorically, craven, and at the same time, read ironically, unrepentant: a combination of insurance policy and aesthetic heresy written in the voice of the Nun's Priest, for it quotes his quotation from the gospel. Chaucer proposes here an extreme and unforgiving choice between chaff and fruit. He disowns his profane and vainly worldly works, *Troilus* and 'the tales of Caunterbury, thilke that sownen into synne', while humbly staking his claim to grace on his homiletic commissions and his translation of Boethius. Can he mean it? Yes and no. Yes, because he has been responsible for joyously contriving the failure of the pilgrimage, which to Chesterton portends the collapse of an entire social and religious order; no, because in casting off his greatest poems and clinging to his most derivative works he is merely restating the antimony between art and morality, for throughout the *Tales* it is the lewdest episodes which are most lovingly and delicately written and the tracts (the Monk's tale or Chaucer's own intended tale of Melibee) which are allowed to be unreadable because their doctrine is above or beneath the aid of art. And having assumed blame, Chaucer in this most teasing of his texts simultaneously disavows it by denying his own volition. Whatever he has done which is good he accredits to Christ; everything else is not his fault because of his notorious 'unkonnynge'. Nowhere has his 'wyl' been involved. Is this a genuine abasement or is it the Pardoner's or the Wife's creative involuntariness? Having denied his own will, Chaucer can delegate the responsibility of judgement to the whim of his readers. He beseeches 'hem alle that herkne this litel tretys or rede' to like it or to be displeased by it according to their own lights. This challenges us in advance to correct the evaluation of his work which he goes on to make.

Chaucer perfects this technique of hiding behind the text in his *Troilus*, where it is his literary equivalent to the recourse his characters have to the safety of conventional behaviour. They do everything according to the book, and are constantly correcting emotional impulses to adjust them to the courtly system—Criseyde has to be argued into love, and only consents because Pandarus will busy himself to provide a screen of social preoccupation; Troilus has to let her be exchanged for Antenor because he cannot interfere with a parliamentary decree—but they feel no infliction. Convention is their alibi: once their dues are paid, they can do as they wish. As a symbol of this camouflage, and as a reminder of its similarity to his own creative case, Chaucer often makes them retire behind books or letters. Criseyde, who in her garden listens to a reading from a romance about the Theban siege, learns from romance a way of disclaiming her own emotions, so that when she is excited by her glimpse of Troilus she denies her susceptibility by asking 'Who yaf me drynke?', as if someone had administered a love potion to her and the spasm were involuntary. Troilus sends a letter to her as his erotic ambassador and, at Pandarus's urging, artfully fictionalises it, blotting the lines with tears. She writes back, never saying what she means. Her language is an invisible epic armour for truant thoughts: 'Al covered she the wordes under sheld.' Pandarus, too, pretends to be reading an old romance by the fire in Criseyde's bedroom. Criseyde's ultimate shield in the poem is cliché, and she takes her leave of Troilus in a letter which is a tissue of conventional pleas, impersonal and wounding precisely because its every word is so universally true.

While they in this epistolary poem are writing to one another, Chaucer is writing about them, and doing so in imitation of their arch conventionality. For just as, before every initiative of action or emotional commitment, they take care to pretend that they are merely doing or saying what is proper—Criseyde is paying a solicitous visit to Troilus's sick-bed, not agreeing to an erotic rendezvous, or is spending the night at Pandarus's house to avoid going home in the rain—so Chaucer manages to reinterpret the tale and experientially to question its authority while attesting that he is no more than the obsequious translator of a venerable source. Like his characters, he is equipping himself with alibis, sometimes shielding an over-fond compassion, sometimes conceal- ing the fact that he is an intrusive, creative go-between.

The poem itself is a lover's discourse. It is about Chaucer's baffled and, at the last, unrequited love for his characters; a lover himself, he must work as they do by guileful indiscretion and pregnant hinting. Hence his astute adhesion to sources—except that every time he claims to be following a predecessor he is, on the contrary, inventing something, which gives to the poem's creation and management the guiltily seditious thrill associated with the prosecution of a disallowed love affair. Here are some examples of this lover-like dissembling, whereby Chaucer attends to a conspiracy of his own with the text while Pandarus is conspiring to unite Troilus with Criseyde: he claims to derive the visit to Deiphebus's house from 'bokes olde', though he has made it up himself; he cannot report on Criseyde's reaction to Pandarus's importunities at his house because 'myn auctor' does not provide the information, yet this episode, too, has been added to the source by Chaucer; when Troilus at last siezes her, Chaucer, with a reticent, conventional politeness, declares that she quivers with fear 'as writen clerkes in hire bokes olde', although at this point in Boccaccio's *Filostrato* Criseida does not even bother to feign reluctance and briskly undresses for bed.

Adhesion to a non-existent text enables Chaucer to extend to Criseyde the benefit of a doubt she may not deserve. Like Pandarus he supplies her with textual pretexts for her actions. He is commenting both on the mystery of human motive, and on the utter vacancy and malleability of literary character: on the profundity and the emptiness of his own art. He is also, by his pettifogging consistency with a supposed source, dramatising the learnedness and deliberation of love behaviour, which we assume to be so spontaneous. A love affair, he suggests, is as much a matter of skill and technical dexterity and plausible mimicry as the writing of a poem. Love is not something, like lust, which our bodies do for us; it is an art we must painstakingly acquire by study, and its comedy is the element of necessary dissimulation which this introduces into the furious and impulsive world of passion. In contrast with the lecher, the lover must be an introvert, preoccupied with his symptoms, scrutinising himself perhaps more intently even than the object of his ardour. Is he after all in love with love, taken over by the career of doting adoration? When he writes love-letters, is he too concerned with stylistic flourishes? And has he not purloined the emotions he exhibits from his literary forebears? This suspicion of fatuity attaches, early in the poem, to Troilus; Chaucer has his own creative approximation to it. The lover's dissembling is equalled by the poet's: Chaucer claims to be transcribing Troilus's song in Book I from Lollius (who in any case did not, as an author, exist, being merely the addressee of a Horatian epistle) whereas in fact he is translating a Petrarch sonnet. Poet and character are accomplices here in the comic bad faith of erotic infatuation, just as elsewhere Chaucer and Pandarus collude discreetly to obscure the heroine's movements.

Making himself a comically supernumerary participant in his poem, Chaucer is able to explore the analogy between being in love and writing about it. The affair rephrases his own creative dilemma. Courtly love had been encoded, authorised, its every posture and pretence formulated in advance. How did the prescription match the experience of love? Chaucer reprieves his characters and his poem by providing two kinds of sources for actions. On the one hand there is the elaborate stasis of the courtly prototype—Troilus's prostration and his epidemics of fainting, Criseyde's miming of reluctance, which displays the customary 'daunger'. On the other hand there is the more impatient, demotic wisdom of Pandarus's proverbs, goading the lovers to abandon prevarication. The code is an authority they can hide behind, while the proverbs are the voice of an unauthorised experience. The code enjoins a ritualised delaying of gratification. Courtly love is the protraction of foreplay.

The proverbs are anxious to reach an end, and to do so they invoke a bodily necessity which cannot be ignored. They cover a defeat for the code by suggesting, as the proverb's generality always does, that it cannot be helped: 'The yerde is bet that bowen wole and wynde' or 'ay the ner the fir, the hotter is'. In contrast with the code's fatiguing absolutism, they propose adjustment to immutable facts.

Chaucer's poem attempts such an adjustment, which means the recension of the story as comedy. But the authority he fends off throughout must at last supervene by decreeing an end he cannot change. The poem concludes as a tragedy and, so intimate is Chaucer's entanglement with his characters, it turns out almost to be his rather than theirs. They can avail themselves at last of the safeguard of convention: Criseyde retires behind the evasive clichés of her letter, Troilus behind the facilely contemptuous slogans of his misogyny; Chaucer meanwhile frets to relieve himself of blame for their wretchedness by once more invoking the dictatorial sources. As he does so he finds that he has become, suddenly and bewilderingly, the main character of his poem. He is the lover betrayed by his unaccountably autonomous inventions. Troilus and Criseyde have both resigned from the poem, retiring either laterally (as she does to the Greek camp beyond the walls) or vertically (as he does when removed to the eighth sphere). Only Chaucer is left occupying this evacuated terrain. They both learn again the conventional comfort of indifference: the hyperbolic phrases of her letter stand in lieu of feelings, and are the poem's last and least trustworthy interpolated text; looking down from the sky, he now interprets his tragedy as a comedy, and can laugh at it. Chaucer, however, remains desperately responsible. Yet his frantic, embarrassed dismissiveness, as he paraphrases Troilus's contempt for carnal love and scolds the rascality of pagan gods, covers the grandest of his literary self-justifications: for although the love of Troilus and Criseyde may have been painfully broken off, it has its continuing consummation in the poem Chaucer has written about it; the offspring of his creator's love for all the characters is the incubation of a literary infant, his 'litel bok'.

The poem's end is not his spurned rejection of his characters and their ungodly morality but his fond leave-taking of that book. It is written by a parent not a lover. And, having personified the book, he can make solicitous provision for its survival in the world, commending it, as if to godfathers, to the care of Gower and Strode, and warning it not to allow itself to be miswritten or mismetred in after-time. He has achieved its freedom from its subject and from himself and handed it over to the care of the most extended and the most congenially conventional of families, that of literary history, and he educates it in mannerly respect for the elders and betters it will join:

> . . . subgit be to alle poesye;
> And kin the steppes where as thow seest pace
> Virgile, Ovide, Omer, Lucan, and Stace.

Like Spenser identifying the survival of his epithalamial poem with the proxy immortality he will have in his offspring and in their offspring after them, Chaucer invests a biological faith in the poem, whose safety in posterity will keep him alive, and this enables him to arrive at his own version of Troilus's sarcastic conclusion about the action. Troilus vengefully casts off his life; Chaucer tenderly cuts loose his poem by encouraging it to outlive him. Troilus laughs at the woe of those who mourn for him: from his station of cosmic detachment, his end looks in retrospect like a comedy. He is after all a pagan, who knows neither spiritual resurrection nor the aesthetic self-resurrecting which consoles Chaucer. So when Chaucer appeals for another generic change, and asks that the poem which began as a comedy and collapsed into tragedy should beget in turn another comedy, he imagines the process regeneratively:

> Go, litel bok, go, litel myn tragedye,
> Ther God thi makere yet, er that he dye,
> So sende mygbt to make in som comedye!

That comedy is *The Canterbury Tales*, of course; it is also the diviner comedy of Chaucer's perpetuity in and because of his poem. Chaucer here in this benediction claims much more for literature and for himself than he gainsays in his retraction.

The text's skittish freedom is unambiguously withdrawn in the Scots poems of Robert Henryson near the end of the fifteenth century, which monastically medievalise Chaucer all over again. In Henryson's 'The Cock and the Fox' the fable Chaucer employs so seditiously is returned to orthodoxy: Henryson's beast is a 'feyneit foxe, fals and dissimulate', as ingenious in his evasion as Chaucer; and instead of the devious gloss affixed by the Nun's Priest, Henryson advises that the pretensions of his own work to be a poem should be mistrusted and that it should be exegetically disassembled. His concluding 'Moralitas' interprets the fox as a figuration of ingenious evil, the cock as credulous mankind:

> Now, worthie folk, suppose this be ane fabill,
> And overheillit wyth typis figurall,
> Yit may ye find are sentence richt greabill
> Under thir feyneit termis textuall.

The same word smears the fox and the text. Both are in the business of feigning; both must be warded off, seen through.

Henryson's 'Testament of Cresseid' is likewise less a continuation of Chaucer's poem than a rebuttal of its special pleading. Poetry is specifically assailed by Henryson during the march-past of gods who judge his Cresseid: Mercury is named as the patron of rhetoricians and musicians, and also of thieves and liars. Chaucer's relation to his characters had been subtly mercurial; Henryson by contrast insists on a stern legalism and an inflexible literalism. The letter, so astute an alibi for everyone in Chaucer, must for him qualify as a testament. His Cynthia 'red ane bill on Cresseid . . ., / Contening this sentence diffinityve': a moral sentence of death, against which there is no appeal. Chaucer's weak and needy girl expires as a leprous outcast. Texts, definitive in their sententiousness, entomb her. She writes her own testament before she dies, willing her dissolution; after she dies, Troylus enforces her penalty on a funerary tablet: on a marble tomb he writes 'hir name and superscriptioun . . . In goldin letteris'. Once she has been morally accounted for, she can be dispensed with by Henryson, whose poem's brevity warns of its heroine's 'schort conclusioun'. His final line rebukes Chaucer's fussy partiality, and his garrulous covering of Criseyde's exit, unpunished, from the poem: 'Sen scho is deid, I speik of hir no moir.' Henryson's poem begins in a grim Scots winter. The sun's desertion of the earth, like Cupid's discarding of the heroine who had been his creature, signifies the poet's withdrawing from his characters of that too bounteous Chaucerian love.

Criseyde herself does not matter to Henryson; she is significant only because she exemplifies the eternal perfidy of her sex. Her individual existence is stretched between notoriety and nonentity, and both states are negligible. In the hospice,

> Some knew her weill, and sum had na knawledge
> Of hir, becaus scho was sa deformait.

Her career is a degeneration from one kind of emblematic status to another: from the 'A per se' of Troy to a gruesome admonishment to all 'worthie wemen'. A figural reading of her entails her obliteration as a character. When Shakespeare takes over the story in his *Troilus and Cressida*, all these people have been left with is their names, labels branding them as parodic mimicries of their former selves. Character here means caricature. Shakespeare's Troilus, Cressida and Pandarus wish themselves into typological ill-fame as by-words respectively for true love, faithlessness, and procuring guile. 'What's aught,' asks Troilus, 'but as 'tis valued?', and these figures have been irredeemably devalued. 'Hector is dead; there is no more to say' is Shakespeare's equivalent to Henryson's abrupt dismissal of the wasted Cresseid. Yet though the Trojan epic has reached a dead end, with figuration reduced to a mocking charade, the Shakespearean theatre arranges an extra lease of life for these impugned agents. Questioning their obligation to the narrative—as they do in their challenges to each other ('Is this Achilles?' demands Hector, and his doubt is not entirely allayed by the bluffing reply, 'I am Achilles')—they assume the right to dramatise themselves as they see fit, to trick themselves out as their forebears from the epic. When Troilus sees Cressida betray him, he says 'This she? no, this is Diomed's Cressida.' He might just as well have accused her of being Shakespeare's Cressida: she is only an actress pertly impersonating the worn-out prototype, like Patroclus play-acting the Greek commanders in order to amuse Achilles. Shakespeare may seem to confirm Henryson's sentencing of the characters; in fact he has exculpated them with a nonchalance worthy of Chaucer. In Chaucer's poem the text is their shield. In Shakespeare's play, they can hide behind the roles they assume and the lines they speak, in neither of which they need believe.

No such extenuation is available to Chaucer's great contemporary Langland. *Piers Plowman*, like *The Canterbury Tales*, is about the effort of poetry to regiment and redeem society, but whereas Chaucer impenitently abets the dispersal of his pilgrimage and its relapse into a human comedy, Langland cannot forgive himself for this decline into literature. Irony enables Chaucer to temporise between the taxing ideal and the agreeably fallen reality; Langland's allegory demands that, if he cannot transfigure the reality, he must reject it. And—whereas Chaucer is a constant quiet apologist for literature—this means, to Langland, the rejection of his poem. He could be said to be at the end of medieval literature as Chaucer is at the beginning of modern. Chaucer has accepted and delighted in the discrepancy between imagination and the faith or doctrine it is supposed to serve. Langland cannot accustom himself to his own imaginative treason, and he first revises, then furiously rends the text of his poem. Chaucer is happy that his words should never mean what they say. Langland cannot forgive them, or himself. He is obsessed with the integrity and truthfulness of his text, while Chaucer relishes its mendacity. Allegory for him eschatologically eschews literal or literary significances: it threatens the material world—where Langland's gluttons swill in the tavern, where his argumentative devils raven on deity ('gnawen god with gorge when here guttes fullen'), where religious spirit is institutionalised, misinterpreted and exploited 'for profyt of the womb' by mercenary friars—with abolition, as if realism were a reflex of sin. To describe the world, as literature does, is avariciously to covet it, to be encumbered with what Langland calls 'catel', or else to prefer meretricious fictions to premonitory truth. Thus when Patience, feasting Piers on immaterial food, expounds the meaning of charity, a worldly doctor disdains the teaching as a mere story: 'This is a *Dido*, a dysores tale!' He prefers to understand it as a fable; he subjects the abstract discourse to an embodiment which does not—for Langland—make it literary but merely condemns it as a lie.

It is therefore a point of principle with Langland to abrade or exhaust or disown his text before it can run away from him in the direction of literature, before it can costume itself in flesh and ornament itself with imagery. Hence his periodic arrestings of it, lest it be demoralised by the literalness of literature. The promised joust between a chivalric Christ and militaristic Satan cannot occur, for instance, because that would be to misinterpret the antagonists as men. Medieval allegory derives from the incarnation, when spirit took on a body and a holy ghost of meaning literalised itself, but for Langland the flesh is a malady—a compendium of symptoms, 'cowhes and cardiacles, crampes and toth-aches, / Reumes and radegoundes and roynouse scabbes'—which tries to exterminate the holy word by afflicting it with mortal ailments.

The word's scriptural truth can be saved only if it is unwritten. The poem castigates itself for its very existence. Dame Study reprimands her consort Wit for pandering to the pride of intellect by engaging in the theological inquiries which are the poem's main concern. Ymaginitif scolds Will the poet for meddling with 'makynges', idolatrously writing poems rather than saying his psalter. Piers, taking delivery of a pardon for mankind sent from Truth, performs an act of literary sabotage by angrily tearing it up. He is making that same judgement on the poem, and on himself as a character in it corrupted or enfeebled by it, for as soon as he rejects the document he forswears ploughing and 'my bely ioye' to devote himself to an anchoritic existence of prayers and penance. Ploughing, which at first had been an allegorical and spiritual vocation, allying him with the good shepherd, has become—like literature—a mere profession, tending and cultivating the fickle world. Piers abstracts himself rather than imagining himself. He will not be a ploughman but an idea of one. (Ymaginitif, one of the poem's dialecticians, is the name Langland gives to the antithesis of imagination: the character's purpose is to dissuade Will from persisting with the poem, which he knows will be useless.)

Yet even that redefinition is not final. Langland's poem has three more or less parallel texts, editorially classified A, B and C: dismayed by its own formulatings, which strand the vision in a world too treacherously real, it twice breaks off in order not to rewrite but to unwrite itself. In the B text, Piers ripping the pardon is by implication discarding the errant A text; by the time he gets to the C text Langland has dispensed with that precursor, too, and suppresses B by eliminating both the pardon and Piers's decision to renovate his life, for only by *not* representing it can he preserve intact its meaning. He reroutes the poem by means of a generative grammar of goodness, which, as soon as it arrives at one state, exponentiates another. As in the romance, the poem's goal is forever retreating before it, until—in the aborted endings of Spenser's *Faerie Queene* or Browning's poem about Childe Roland—it finally seems that it is best to give up the thought of arriving at the end and to hope instead for a glimpse of the distant ideal, which remains unpolluted because it is unattainable: the failure of narrative constitutes its own kind of perceptual success. Piers undertakes to lead a pilgrimage to Truth, but before it can begin it is superseded. As a preliminary initiation, the pilgrims must help him plough his half-acre. They never get beyond this stage of training: society cannot be rectified by the agricultural discipline Piers imposes, so—even more precipitately than on the way to Chaucer's Canterbury—the pilgrimage is declared impossible and perjured. Piers himself invokes Canterbury in a moment of (for Langland) self-excoriation. The pilgrims offer him money to guide them to Truth. He swears that 'I ne wol fonge a ferthynge, for seynt Thomas shryne!'

The oath protests against the pecuniary tincture which demeans the pilgrimage by turning the spiritual quest back into a physical journey, the outing so variously enjoyed by Chaucer's characters; it also exemplifies that same corrupting process. The shrine of the martyr in Canterbury is here for Piers a merely verbal and abusive standard. Having resolved on a new future, he announces that he has in mind a new destination, Dowel. This is an ideal beyond character and the dead end of embodiment: it means the performing of good works. Yet even it will not serve for long, and has to unfold superlative versions of itself. The goal is renamed Dobet, and then Dobest.

Ultimately, however, this syntactic spiral, progressively raising the odds, finds itself coiled into a circle, and the poem ends where it began, except that it has now transcendentalised and overcome that beginning. Conscience in its last lines sets off once more, this time to seek out Piers Plowman. Piers the pilgrim has become Piers the goal of pilgrimage: the character has been finally cancelled by this last-minute and perfunctory transformation into an ideal. The dreamer who has envisioned the poem promptly wakes up, which introduces an extra qualification. The whole experience has after all been in parenthesis, a sleeping suspension of life.

Though Langland's poem aspires to render literature and itself obsolete, it has its own literary successors. It must be seen behind *The Pilgrim's Progress*. For Bunyan, too, allegory is a systematic critique of literature and of the vain, worldly-wise, talkative illusion which literature persuades us to call reality. Allegory is a means of thinking ourselves out of the world, of dematerialising it. We read life instead of living it: Christian is dispatched on his journey by a book, and sustains himself spiritually by reading from the parchment roll he carries. But that book is scripture not literature, and Christian indignantly denies its fictionality. When Pliable asks if he thinks the words in it are 'certainly true', Christian replies, 'Yes verily, for it was made by him that cannot lie.' This means that, if the text's moral state must be a literal honesty, Bunyan himself is to some degree suspect: the allegory, as in Langland, refutes itself not because it is too literal but because it is not literal enough, with the insubstantiality of fantasy, so that Bunyan in his apology for his own book describes himself beginning to write a tract and then diverging into this narrative, as if *The Pilgrim's Progress* were, like the journey Piers disallows, a perjured undertaking. He says 'I . . . / Fell suddenly into an allegory.' He does not rise to his poem's height, like Milton in the proem to *Paradise Lost*; he tumbles into it. Allegory is a postlapsarian form of speech.

Langland anticipates this puritan case against literature. He also foreknows a romantic disquiet about the medium. His textual quandary, with each statement erasing a preceding draft only to demand its own redrafting, is a goad to the romantics, who take as their norm what in Langland is idiosyncracy and despairing frustration—the idea of the poem as a thing which is required to go on revising itself indefinitely, because its reference is to the imageless deep truth of Shelley's Demogorgon in *Prometheus Unbound*, and which can reach completion only when (like the human body deserted at last by the tenanting spirit) it is abandoned.

Henry James, writing a preface to his early novel *The American* three decades after its publication, looks back on it as a juvenile romance. The form suits, he thinks, the innocence and liberty of juvenile America, which has not yet undergone a fall into the social state, where existence is circumscribed and conditioned. The romance deals with what James calls 'experience liberated'. His later, wiser characters resist that liberation. When Caspar Goodwood in *The Portrait of a Lady* insists to Isabel that 'the world's all before us—and the world's very big', she opposes to the illimitability of romance the novel's melancholy recognition of necessity, saying 'The world's very small'. She is disproving the romanticism of romance. So is James, in that retrospective preface, because he admits that experience can be liberated only by 'the sacrifice of community', of relatedness. Nevertheless, that is what romance means in Chaucer, and that is why Langland censors it: it is the protest of experience against a prohibitive authority, and without it there could be no modern literature.

— 5 —
Two Versions of Pastoral: Arcady and Faeryland

As Henry James's definition of romance declares, the advance from epic is a movement in the direction of romanticism. This revises the classical literary curriculum, which had nominated epic as the goal of literary ambition and of national prowess. An even more radically unclassical shift of genre was to follow, which determines the course of English literature up to the nineteenth century and beyond. This is the submergence of epic in pastoral. Classically, the pastoral signifies the otium and obscurity of the private life. The poet begins there, as Virgil did, before graduating to the heroic, public exertions of epic. The pastoral is an incident in his education, to be transcended. Romantically, however, the priority is reversed. The poet disdains the challenge of heroic action, signified by epic, and retreats to the salving, contemplative quiet of the pastoral. This is the choice of the English writer—of the novelists, after Richardson's psychological version of pastoral; and of Wordsworth, who withdraws from the strife of the French Revolution and writes instead an anti-epic about his native landscape and about the vegetative growth of his own mind back into that nature.

It is a romantic decision which is implicit already in the poetry of the fourteenth century. Piers Plowman announces by his rustic vocation that Christianity has altered the classical literary ethic: the hero is now not the armed man but the humble husbandman. Christ manifests himself as the good shepherd. Literature itself is pastorally disarmed. The poet must no longer battle to achieve perfection, or urge the nation by his martial song to deeds of glory; Langland's successive resignations from his poem suggest that the ideal is to be contemplated or envisioned only, not attained. Chaucer makes this necessary failure the ground of his remorse in the retraction, and Spenser allies himself with it when retiring from his own projected epic. Rather than striving to reach the millenial kingdom where Arthur will wed Gloriana, he will hope, he says at the end of his 'Mutabilitie Cantos', merely to see that paradise which literature cannot regain. In one sense, *The Canterbury Tales* is about the degeneration of epic into romance. The march-past breaks ranks: the procession turns out to be a comically unruly mob. But in another sense, the poem predicts the epic's after-life in pastoral, pointing beyond the military and political enforcements of Theseus to a spirit of conciliatory patience, the devotional calm of pastoral—Grisilde's humbling of herself in 'The Clerk's Tale', the long faithful vigil of Dorigen in 'The Franklin's Tale'—and conjecturally regaining paradise in such personal gardens of fantasising delight as Januarie's in 'The Merchant's Tale', Dorigen's 'verray paradys', or Chauntecleer's seraglio-like roost.

After Chaucer and Langland, the poem which most irrevocably alters the shape of literary tradition, and anticipates its own romantic future, is Spenser's *Faerie Queene*. It is an encyclopaedia of forms and kinds, yet everything it contains is changed by this hybridising. No genre will ever be the same again, once it has been put through Spenser's vast metamorphic clearing-house. He performs, for instance, a triple dissolution of the epic he is professedly writing—into romance, into pastoral, and into allegory. Spenser begins by wanting to do several incompatible things simultaneously, as he explains in 1596 in his letter to Walter Ralegh. But instead of those contrary aims cancelling each other out, they modify each other. The rigour and singlemindedness of epic are adapted to the vagrant whimsicality of romance; its energy to the repose and indolence of pastoral; its activism to the inner disquisitions of allegory. In Chaucer's miscellany of tales, all the available literary genres meet and quarrel. Spenser reconciles them: his poem is the familial compendium, inter-marrying the opposed genres, dreamed of by Shakespeare's Polonius when he mongrelises the 'pastoral-comical, historical-pastoral, tragical-historical, tragical-comical-historical-pastoral'. That garrulous multiplying is Polonius's homage to an unattainable but very English ideal—the work which confuses and so evades all limiting classical regimentation, the poem as romantically profuse as those novelistic indifferent wholes.

Spenser writes such a poem, and he writes it in a language as synthetic as his form. Ben Jonson, proud of his own classicality, judged that Spenser 'writ no language'. No one language, that is: the poem has to be written in a polyglot idiom—now Latinate, now colloquially English; now rustic, now courtly; now medievally and epically alliterative, now lyrically mellifluous—because it is compounding all genres and all ages in a work of myth-making synthesis. It is as if Spenser were writing not a single literary work but an entire literature, and he is therefore enjoined not to confine himself to a single style but to deploy every possible style as occasion suits. Though Chaucer had already done so, for him the styles were enemies, deriding each other, and he hears the universal sum of stories as a chattering rabble. Instead of this discord, as at the parliament of fowls, Spenser arranges a choral and co-operative peace. All stories have their common denominator in myth, just as all languages have their common denominator in the esperanto of music. George Eliot's Casaubon in *Middlemarch* fails to define a 'key to all mythologies'; Spenser's populous, polyphonic work might be a key to all literatures. It gathers into itself its entire past, from 'the antique Poets historicall' to 'Dan *Chaucer*', and by changing that inheritance it begets the future—for, as is made clear by Richard Hurd's praise in 1762 of its Gothic crookedness and its offence against the strictures of Grecian unity, by Hazlitt's account in 1818 of its 'labyrinth of sweet sounds' or by Coleridge's description in the same year of its mazy disregard of 'all artificial boundary', it is, before its time, a romantic poem.

The first thing that happens in it is a declension from epic to romance. The Red Crosse Knight, his armour enseamed with wounds, looks like a spiritual combatant. But his course has the errant nomadism of wandering Odysseus, not the forthright and propulsive direction of Achilles: he at once loses his way in the wood of Error, entangled by an uncertain, ambiguous syntax and misled by the distracting, detailed plenitude of the world. He is beguiled by the wood because, in the seventh and eighth stanzas of the poem, he numbers its individual trees. His truancy from his mission announces the poem's own detour from its professed design. Unlike the heroes of Langland or Bunyan, Spenser cannot manage to repress the beguiling complication of the world. Rather than marshalling phenomena as tributaries of a single heroic will, which epic aims to do, he is tempted simply and lovingly to list things, delighting in and validating their experiential fruitfulness—trees here, rivers at the end of Book IV, months and seasons in the 'Mutabilitie Cantos'. Epic wants to end history, to arrive at a millenium, which for Spenser would have been Arthur's marriage to Gloriana; but in spite of himself, Spenser accepts the endlessness of history and of nature, which will go on recurring and recreating itself.

The epic propulsion of will relents, and wraps round into the cyclical action of romance. Thus in Spenser nothing can ever definitively be achieved. The deed will at once undo itself, shifting into reverse and awaiting its eventual, cyclical repetition. Guyon in Book II demolishes Acrasia's entrancing Bower of Bliss. The narrative does not end there, however: he must now retrace his steps, leaving the place by the same route he used to enter it, confronting the same obstacles in reverse order. That movement backwards is the allegorical glossing of the experience. Guyon has unthinkingly smashed the bower; now, after the event, he wants to know who its bestial inmates were, and the Palmer, as allegorical explicator, tells him. After action comes the mental inquest. And that retroactive review makes Guyon understand the inadequacy or irrelevance of action. One of Acrasia's brutalised victims, Grill the hog, objects to the resumption of human form. He prefers the sensual fantasy, and Guyon lets him remain there: 'Let *Grill* be *Grill*, and haue his hoggish mind.' His victory has been only partial. In any case, there can be no rest, since his travels and travails must continue, and he engages the Palmer for a sequel, urging 'let vs hence depart, whilest wether serues and wind.' During its development, the poem admits to an ethical conversion resembling that of the truculent Grill. Initially it had wanted to overcome mutability, that earthly instability which deludes the epic combatant. Then gradually it commits itself to what Spenser in the letter to Ralegh calls accidents not intendments, and when it breaks off—for it can never end—it has vindicated mutability by showing it to have an immortality of its own. Nature, the goddess of the poem's final canto, can cope with the threat of her opponent Mutabilitie by demonstrating that beneath change lies recurrence; the poem, too, can derive a metaphysical assurance from its own contingencies, detours and postponements.

The exertions of epic—manifested in the monster-slaying of the Red Crosse Knight, the angry vandalism of Guyon, or the knockabout fisticuffs of Britomart at Malecasta's castle in Book III—relax as the poem goes on into the different mood of pastoral, meditative and even mystically indolent. Within the pastoral, nothing must happen. Francis Bacon, glossing the scriptures, argues that God favours the submissive shepherd Abel over the toiling husbandman Cain. It is the contemplative not the active man who is elected to divine grace. This quietism overtakes the poem in Book VI and, like all Spenser's transpositions, it does so in comedy, which is his means of compromise between the absolutism and idealism of epic and its earthlier sequels. Calepine disburdens himself of his armour and drifts off to sleep in the grass. The ideal will be attained, if at all, in dozing reverie not by feats of arms, and will be vouchsafed not to the courtier Calidore but to the shepherd Colin Clout, who conjures up the dancing Graces at the end of the book. Spenser's own renunciation of the poem in the 'Mutabilitie Cantos' follows this logic. He no longer expects to build the New Jerusalem on England's soil, and pleads only for a brief glimpse of it: 'O that great Sabbaoth God, graunt me that Sabaoth's sight.'

Every stanza of the poem pleads, structurally, for this pastoral retirement. The secret duty of the so-called Spenserian stanza is to impede narrative and to dissipate, in its long full-stopped final line, the energies of epic. That concluding line frustrates onward development, and sends the poem always reflexively backwards or into itself. Spenser is a virtuoso at making it mimic the dilemmas of his characters. In the opening episode, for instance, it apes their ambushed traversal of the encroaching wood, its central comma giving them helpless pause:

> So many pathes, so many turnings seene,
> That which of them to take, in diuerse doubt they been;

it repeats itself to represent the dual obfuscation of Error, who lurks

> Where plaine none might her see, nor she see any plaine;

or it expands more or less indefinitely as it adjectivally and alliteratively enumerates the monster's moral qualities:

> Most lothsom, filthie, foule, and full of vile disdaine.

The stanza works in league with the poem's pictorialism, seeming to frame each image self-sufficiently as an object to be pondered on. Pastoral has in any case pictorialised life by stilling it: a picture is space unmolested by time. An old lady to whom Alexander Pope had been reading *The Faerie Queene* described it as 'a collection of pictures'. As in a gallery, the effort of moving between these blissfully eventless episodes is the viewer's or the reader's. We alone, by wanting to continue, reintroduce time and change into the poem, and as readers we are the agents of mutability. The romantics, appreciating Spenser's lyric prolongation of moments, found in him a resistance to temporal harassment which approached mysticism. Coleridge called it his 'charmed sleep', Hazlitt his mellifluous hypnotism, 'lulling the senses into a deep oblivion of the jarring noise of the world, from which we have no wish to be ever recalled', Leigh Hunt his sensual luxuriation. For this subliminal relapse the stanza is responsible, and the romantics therefore revive it. It is the pattern for the embowering stanza of Keats's odes, where the 'thing of beauty' is harboured in a sacrosanct quietness which is the beatitude of pastoral; Byron adopts it for *Childe Harold's Pilgrimage*, where that trailing final line drags a lamed foot and declares that this is a halting, morose and introspective journey, not a grand tour, for each stanza returns to the predicament of Harold immured—in a parody of the Keatsian bower—within himself:

> He stood unbow'd beneath the ills upon him piled.

Romantic interpreters of the poem have been consistently hostile to the allegory. Hazlitt counselled ignoring it altogether; Yeats in 1902 dismissed it as the officiousness of the 'salaried moralist', cravenly atoning for the sins which had in the first place made him a poet. But the epic's submission to allegory fits with Spenser's other romantic modulations—from war to love in Book III, from court to nature in Book VI, from swaggering epic politics to pastoral rite in Book VII—for allegory turns the epic hero, so implacably extroverted, in on himself. The 'darke conceit' is the shadowy contents of his head. The whole poem becomes a psychomachia, its imperilled ladies and rampaging monsters bred by the reason's sleep. Allegory is the name it gives to fantasy, to the unguarded self-revelations of the mind. Pastoral drowsing has deepened into a therapeutic coma. Hence Coleridge's delight in and terror of the poem, which like a drug detains you inside the alluring, shaming scenario of your own imaginings: 'you neither wish, nor have the power, to inquire where you are, or how you got there.' The decipherment of allegory anticipates the Freudian exposition of dreams. The dark conceit is the automatic writing of id, which the ego rewrites into lucidity.

At first in Spenser's poem the process of interpreting is punitive. To explain is to repress the imagination which dreamed up the bogey. The Red Crosse Knight is an exterminator of fantasies, an armed elucidator; Guyon at the Bower razes a fantasy. But in this respect, too, the poem alters as it proceeds. The allegorical analyst ceases to cure the vision by killing it; the poem grants its characters wondering access to a prohibited visual knowledge, and does not subject these mysteries to analytic exorcism—the generative mound of Venus in the Garden of Adonis, Amoret's exposure to her own acted-out, erotic terrors in the house of the enchanter Busirayne, Calidore's spying on the

Graces over Colin Clout's shoulder, Faunus's peeping at the naked Diana. This grounding in sex connects with the poem's adventure into comedy. After the fanaticism of Red Crosse, its later protagonists are humanly compromised, rendered amiably absurd by their own fleshly weakness. Britomart is a knight on the outside, a timorous and yearning girl within; Calidore, bustling in on the tryst of Calepine and Serena or frightening away the Graces, is judged according to a code of polite manners not the unforgiving edicts of morals.

Allegory first redefines epic as a moral rearmament. It accumulates weaponry for a warfare of spiritual absolutes, such as is prosecuted by the Red Crosse Knight. But since the allegorical foe is an idea, force can be of no avail. Hence the disprofessing, as Spenser calls it, of arms in the poem's later stages—Scudamor's abandonment of helmet, spear and coat of mail, Britomart's discovery at the house of Busirayne that violence will not gain her entry or guard her against the magic fire, Amoret's intervention to stop her from slaughtering the enchanter, the eventual escape of the Blatant Beast. The poem's new ethic of pacifism leads it from allegory towards symbolism. Allegory believes that the citadel can be stormed; the symbol is by its nature unattainable, an indistinct and vanishing mirage—as the Graces are to Colin Clout, as the great Sabbaoth God is to Spenser. In Book VII allegory becomes an affectionate humanising, an incarnation which contradicts the austerity at the house of Holinesse: the bossy termagant who browbeats Jove is less a metaphysical principle than a woman whose name happens to be Mutabilitie, and even the androgyny of Nature, whose sex no one can rightly tell, does not disembody her, for Spenser describes her as portentously outsize, surrounding her with supernumerary troops of servile adjectives—

> . . . (great goddesse) great dame *Nature*,
> With goodly port and gracious Maiesty;
> Being far greater and more tall of stature
> Then any of the gods or Powers on hie

—which fatuously adore her while gossipily speculating that she may be inscrutable because her 'vncouth hew' is too horrid to behold.

No wonder Spenser refers, as he gives up *The Faerie Queene*, to 'old *Dan Geffrey*' and 'his *Foules parley*', for like Chaucer he has contrived the levelling of that vertical, vertiginous ladder which conducts medieval literature from matter up to spirit, and has come to terms with an indiscriminate, incorrigible human life. Epic strays into romance or relaxes into pastoral; it is seen through by allegory, but allegory too must forswear its hierarchical designs on the world. Whatever is is right. Spenser covers his exit from the poem's scheme, in the two stanzas of the eighth canto, by aping a Chaucerian stratagem and agreeing with everyone, first sympathising with Mutabilitie's claim, then reminding himself of Nature's counter-argument. His wisdom is one of comic accommodation, cherishing the settled, low contentment of pastoral.

In contrast with Spenser's romantic declension of classical genres—epic's mitigation as romance and eventually as pastoral—Sidney's *Arcadia*, more ambitious for classical status, proceeds in the opposite direction. It begins as a pastoral pastime, an idle repletion of inertia at Wilton, written between 1577 and 1580 for the entertainment of the Countess of Pembroke. Sidney himself disparages it as a trifle. It has the digressive indolence of pastoral, idyllically eventless. Yet Sidney feels obliged progressively to promote it: first to romance, by deserting the mental abasement and otioseness of the shepherds to pursue the erotic adventures of Basilius's daughters and their princely followers; then, in the revision begun by Sidney in the early 1580s and published by Fulke Greville in 1590, as an epic, a work now in praise of what Gabriel Harvey called 'sage counselling' and 'valorous fighting', an incitement to the active career of political and military engagement, as opposed to the retirement of pastoral. The rewriting was left incomplete when Sidney went off, in fulfilment of his own literary directive, to die on the Earl of Leicester's military expedition to the Netherlands. So the work is indeterminate, temporising between the three graduated genres. There is no resolving the contradictions, and no need to, for the work's richness lies in their coexistence.

The *Arcadia* is an anthology of literary kinds. As a romance, in the first version, it is about the attempt to escape from history and to outrun consequences, as Basilius transfers himself to the country in the hope of evading the future disasters predicted by an oracle. But the retreat from history, and from that imposition of will which is the pride of epic, simply licenses accident and inadvertence, the muddling deities of romance. Thanks to an imbroglio of sexual misunderstandings, each item in the oracle's forecast comes true after all. The epic hero affronts fate; his romance counterpart flees from it, like Gawain or Browning's reluctant Roland. And Basilius's refusal leads him back from the romance into the obscurity of pastoral, where the hero can escape from identity altogether. Thus his encounter with Gynecia occurs in a dark cavern, a recess of occlusion which symbolises the pastoral mood. For both romance and pastoral, events are a mystery, over which the hero can have no control. Basilius is told that he will commit adultery with his own wife, and this happens in the cave. The epic recension changes this involuntariness. Sidney now begins *in medias res*, with the shipwreck of Musidorus and Pyrocles. Their subjugation to the ocean's whim still defines them as the accident-prone characters of romance, but thereafter they exert will: the narrative becomes the annals of their adventures.

Beginning in the middle, as epic prescribes, is Sidney's tribute to the voluntarism of the form. The epic hero is thus able to detach himself from his past, and make the future by his own forceful deeds. Yet the impetuosity of epic cannot be sustained. Sidney's narrative irresistibly diverges and digresses, because it is a work not about action but about the elaborations of language, and it has its own syntactic thickets and rhetorical mazes within which the characters delight to lose themselves. Philoclea is bemused within just such a lexicon, 'in this depth of mazes and diverse sorts of discourses', and Pyrocles, though supposedly an epic warrior, is a vagrantly romancing narrator who apologises that 'the delight of those pleasing sights have carried me too far into an unnecessary discourse'. And just as there is an epic heroism of mettlesome aggression, possessed by the burly Amphialus, so there is a pastoral antiheroism of meek forbearance, figured in the suffering Pamela, whose prayer was adopted by Charles I during his imprisonment. Pastoral is spiritualised, as by Bacon in his commentary on Cain and Abel, into a mental estate of devout humility. Musidorus declares himself satisfied with his bucolic lot because 'the highest point outward things can bring one into is the contentment of the mind'. The shepherd's wisdom is a mental continence, an abstinence from action. Pyrocles despises Anaxius the angry warrior as 'he that disdains to obey anything but his passion (which he calls his mind)'. Heroism is a form of mania. The characters of pastoral aspire to the mystic peace of cessation from effort, to what Dametas calls 'the rest of my toiling thoughts'; but *Arcadia* will never grant it to them.

The work's courtliness is shamed by its pastoralism. Thyrsis, in one of the poetic eclogues, summons Dorus from the prostration of pastoral where 'for want of use thy mind ashamed is', and in their double sestina 'Ye goat-herd Gods' Strephon and Claius march round the perimeters of their pastoral enclosure, signified by those recurring, inescapable line-end words, and object to its repetitive agricultural and metrical routines. Politics, caused by 'the dangerous division of men's minds' and causing 'the ruinous renting of all estates', enters to disrupt Arcadia, but the real civil war is one instigated by Sidney: the uprising of wit and the erectness of intelligence against the lowly constraints of the pastoral. Plangus's stepmother, in Pamela's recitation, goads him to rebellion against his father by urging 'the liberty of his mind, the high flying of his thoughts' and 'that he was not born to live a subject life', which conflicts with Pamela's own later, quietly sheepish submission. Sidney the courtier, for whom literary composition is a mode of action and magnificence, agrees with that temptress, and so does Sidney the warrior. The narrative concludes therefore with Euarchus's judgement on the pastoralists as malefactors, truants from their responsibility as 'public persons': Arcadia has been a culpable indulgence, where 'by making themselves private' they have 'deprived themselves of respect due to their public calling'.

Arcadia begins with a divestiture of epic, only to reassume that title at its end. Palladius encourages his soldiers to pass themselves off as shepherds, 'having no banners, but bloody shirts hanged upon long staves, with some bad bag-pipes instead of drum and fife', muffling their armour: the Arcadian condition is for them mere military camouflage. An Iberian knight arrives at the joust costumed pastorally, his weaponry swaddled in wool. The disguise of Pyrocles is an emblem of epic's counterfeiting as pastoral, and the male's transvestite denying of his heroic nature. Musidorus comes upon him attired as a woman, whose only helmet is the jewelled and feathered coronet in her hair, and who sports instead of armature 'a doublet of sky-colour satin'. Palladius himself, for this assault on Cardamila, arms 'all saving the head', and that omission exempts him comically from epic. The epic hero inside his steel and chain-mail is a body trained to kill; the protagonists of romance and pastoral are thinkers, meditative and undefended heads. Hence the femininity of the work: the quest of Pamela is an introverted and circular one. Cecropia watches her 'walk up and down, full of deep, though patient thoughts.'

Epic, during the rebellion, threatens Arcadia with the desecration both of romance and of pastoral. The 'rich furniture' of chivalry, its gem-studded weapons and flaunted pennons, are 'defiled with dust, blood, broken armours, mangled bodies'. The combat which romance ritualises in the tournament is a massacre after all, and must be sustained by the slaughter of the pastoral economy. Pyrocles comments on the different designs that the shepherd and the butcher have on the sheep, and Geron in the fourth ecologue laments that his herd 'which hitherto have enjoyed your fruitful pasture in such quietness as your wool . . . must become the victual of an army'. At its grimmest, the *Arcadia* reverts to the epic violence of 'The Knight's Tale', with its pile of bones and its warriors wading through gore. It sees the earth as Chaucer's Egeus does, strewn with 'disinherited heads', severed arms and legs, 'trailing guts' and cloven hearts: an abattoir and open grave of men. But romance and pastoral, elsewhere in the work, have their own reinterpretations of this carnage. Romantically, the slaughter is redefined as a virtuoso art. Amphialus, in his long struggle against the forsaken knight, epically deploys force; his opponent, shorter than him, responds with a courtly skill. He survives by nonchalant agility and a display of evasive technique, 'answering mightiness with nimbleness'. Amphialus here is the antedeluvian battler. The other has learned from Castiglione's conduct-book for courtiers how to make 'art follow and not strive with nature', and is expert at fleet-footed evasion. Pastorally, warfare is reprised as a dance, harmless because allegorised. The shepherds in the second ecologue stage a 'skirmish betwixt Reason and Passion'. The contest is choreographed and orchestrated, subdued to an aesthetic order by regimented steps and consorted instruments, and it ends in a musical reconciliation as the two opposing camps of shepherds join to sing a duet.

As in this musical truce, art enters to control and correct the vexatious state of nature. This is the ambiguity of Sidney's Arcadia, in contrast with Spenser's faeryland: more like Spenser's tinselled and nastily gaudy Bower of Bliss than his generative Garden of Adonis, it is a place where art replicates and brilliantly supersedes nature. In Spenser's terms, it is a perjured and fake pastoral, because its naturalness is a coy dissimulation. The coiffure of the cross-dressed

Pyrocles sums up the imposture, its curls disposed 'with such a careless care and an art so hiding art that she seemed she would lay them for a pattern whether nature simply or nature helped by cunning be the more excellent.' Sidney's Arcadia is a Utopia: art's conjecture of how nature might be transcended. It has much in common with the alternative and preternatural worlds of science fiction, like the realm of Swift's rational horses or H. G. Wells's encephalic moon-men, for rather than resolving the complex into the simple—which is William Empson's critical formula for what he calls proletarian pastoral—it unpastorally complicates a world which should be ingenuously simple.

In Sidney's Arcadia, the very shepherds are witty. His is an aristocratic society, not the rough democracy described by Empson. Its shepherds are a mental élite, and its lovers are monopolistic tyrants. Dorus cannot 'be content to give desire a kingdom but that it must be an absolute monarchy'. Arcadia likewise is made from the absolutism of artifice. It is a region sacred to style, like Spenser's Bower where everything is a lavishly affluent simulacrum of the real—ivory waves, vermilion blood, ornamental flowers, golden fruits. Niggardly nature, Spenser remarks of Acrasia's pleasance, is grossly outdone by the expensive beautifications of art. This is how Sidney, without Spenser's moral qualms, describes the garden of Kalander. In it horticulture aspires to the condition of decor, with trees serving the flower-beds as a canopy and the flower-beds paving beneath the trees 'a mosaical floor'. This ambition of dissimulation is gratified by the crystalline pond, which perfects actuality by duplicating it in its mirrored surface. The human body undergoes the same aesthetic reifying: in the statue of a naked Venus the blue streaks of the marbling do duty for the veins of her flesh. In this world aesthetically transfigured, people vainly compete with the images which are their redeemed and better selves. Kalander gazes at the painting of Philoclea, 'whose wonderfulness took away all beauty from her but that which it might seem she gave back again by her very shadow'. The shadow or (in the case of the pool) the reflection have superseded the mortal and organic fact: they are animae, souls divinable only by the art which effects nature's second coming.

The pastoral is Sidney's licence for the abolition of a natural reality. It is not after all incompatible with epic or romance. Epically, Arcadia is a walled city defending a treasury of art, like the cave Zelmane discovers vaulted with marble and floored with gold dust or the underground hoard of wealth deposited by Aristomenes, and the poet has supplanted the epic soldier as the guardian of that fabled pile. Romantically, it is the envisioned ideal pursued by the chivalric seeker: a Grail valued for its 'bijouterie' not its spiritual meaning.

Spenser's great pastoral landscapes—the Garden of Adonis in Book III of *The Faerie Queene*, Mount Acidale where the Graces dance in Book VI, Arlo hill in Book VII—are, however, about the grateful acceptance of natural reality. Epic and romance both submit to the more benign wisdom of pastoral.

The epic hero's pride in his singleness and his rage to immortalise his name are shown to be follies, for to nature we matter only as generic beings (Spenser's Venus and Adonis are not gods but names for the male and female reproductive organs) and we survive only by proxy, in the future life we engender. The romance hero's exhausting quest reaches its term here when he discovers that experience is not linear but biologically cyclical and consolingly repetitive. The Garden of Adonis incorporates its people into the landscape, and into one another. The pairs of lovers on the mound of Venus are interchangeable, all engaged in the same seasonal fructifying. The poem begins to mime the cycling regeneration of this seed-bed, sending its words round and round in circles rather than urging them narratively ahead, as when Spenser mentions the fate of the florally transformed lovers, among them

> Sad *Amaranthus*, made a flowre but late,
> Sad *Amaranthus*, in whose purple gore
> Me seemes I see *Amintas* wretched fate,
> To whom sweet Poets verse hath giuen endlesse date.

The movement of the verse compensates for the metamorphosis. Why the repetition of 'sad *Amaranthus*'? Because the second time around the person has become a flower, and the blood a harmless floral hue. The poetry grants to these characters the same fecund immortality which Venus and Adonis achieve through their littered offspring: Aminta's wretchedness is sweetened by verse, and she is reprieved from death and awarded—by that long final line of the Spenserian stanza, which seems so reluctant to reach an end—a eugenic endlessness. In the Garden of Adonis, nature is reassuringly repetitious; at Mount Acidale, it is gratuitously abundant, extravagantly prolific, luxuriating advantages on the place. The trees bud in winter as in summer, the silvery stream is unmarred with moss or mud, the plain offers itself to be enjoyed. But this is not a Sidneyan pleasure-dome, devised by art. It stands for nature's free and profuse granting of gifts to men, its blessedly lavish love, of which the Graces, who appear to Colin Clout here, are the emblems.

The vision is available only to the shepherd, and when the courtier Calidore intrudes it vanishes: pastoral is a glad democracy of thronging existences, and Spenser's own invention longs to share the multitudinousness and (for grace is a gratuity) the open-handedness and even the indifferent forgetfulness of nature. Hence his fondness for assigning places on his allegorical map to multiple sites in the world outside it, or for making composites of opposed mythologies. The mount of vision can be either the Mount of Olives or Parnassus, the well of life could be Silo and Jordan, Bath, the German Spa or Hebrus, and the Garden of Adonis may be in Paphos, on Cytheron hill, or perhaps in Gnidus: nature teaches him not to discriminate. For the same reason, he is addicted to lists. These are not, for him, epic catalogues marshalling things owned, like the Homeric tally of ships and weapons; they pastorally celebrate the progenitiveness of nature, and the poet dares himself to keep pace with this teeming fertility by adjectivally granting attributes to each item as it rushes past, as in the list of sea nymphs in Book IV. Nature begets the nouns, Spenser more adventitiously bestows the adjectives which animate and anthropomorphise these watery creatures:

> Speedy *Hippothoe*, and chaste *Actea*,
> Large *Lisianassa*, and *Pronœa* sage,
> *Euagore*, and light *Pontoporea*,

and so on, more or less forever. One nymph is actually called after her own multiplicity, like a Spenserian location which can be in many different places at once: 'she that hight of many heastes *Polynome*.'

Even when the indignant Diana deserts Arlo and curses it for Faunus's presumption at the end of the poem, her abdication achieves a freeing of pastoral. No longer the preserve of *rentier* gods, the landscape reverts to its human inhabitants. The pastoral, like Spenser's poem, is simply the hospitable and compendious total of everything that is, whether good or bad, and, when Diana leaves, the final lines of the two stanzas which conclude the first Mutabilitie canto swell out to calculate the plenitude men have inherited

> The richest champian that may else be rid,
> And the faire *Shure*, in which are thousand Salmons bred

and also to nod sadly but sagely over the inhering problems that men, in the absence of gods, must deal with: Diana has infested the place with wolves, and the poem both laments and (in that 'too-too true') gently resigns itself to desecration—

> Since which, those Woods, and all that goodly Chase,
> Doth to this day with Wolues and Thieues abound:
> Which too-too true that lands in-dwellers since haue found.

The legatee of the vengeful, absconded goddess is the pastoral poet. Nature now has been entrusted to him, and he must render it sacred by infusing it with human significances. The gap left by Diana will be filled by the eager, yearning, pathetic fallacy of the romantics.

Whereas Milton begs to be vaultingly lifted above his own human nature in the invocatory proem to *Paradise Lost*, Spenser, as the second canto begins, begs to be left unmolested in his pastoral retirement, fending off the Muse's summons to him to leave 'these woods and pleasing forrests'. He has been roused to give an epic account of heavenly politics, but in doing so he comically humanises the contending deities—brash, nagging Mutabilitie, hen-pecked Jove—and is thus able to keep faith with his conviction that poetry is not a heroic and immortalising ascent from this world but a healing reconcilement with it, a gift not from spurious gods but from nature, to which we gratefully and gracefully return it.

By arriving at this revelation Spenser has determined on pastoral as the abiding English poetic form, which dissociates our literature from classicism. Classically the pastoral is esteemed only as an apprenticeship. The hero, like Marvell's Cromwell, plays at planting the Bergamot, but his ambitions lie elsewhere—in the public domain of epic. English literature undoes this automatic graduation: it urges relapse, retirement, an introspective peace; already in Spenser it is a romantic literature. The generic pattern that Spenser establishes in literature transfers itself later to painting, for the great work of Turner and Constable is made possible by a rearrangement of that same classical hierarchy, which saw landscape as an inferior form and proposed the history painting (the epic tableau of active will in triumph) as the summit of pictorial endeavour. The paintings of Turner and Constable could only be English, because they conceal their epic and historical remonstrances within the obscure and lowly pastoral. Their only heroic figures are the foundering hulk of a ship, or the weathered resilient spire of a cathedral among storm clouds.

Spenser's is a truer Arcady than Sidney's, because it is more than a day-dreaming 'vale of bliss' (to use Basilius's phrase for the pastoral otium of sleep). Luxuriously catering to the aesthete's every whim, Sidney's landscape is a flagrant body. His pastoral is a niche, an off-limits cavity, an erotic declivity: Arcadia is indented with such hiding-holes, like Zelmane's 'little arbour' or Pamela's concave 'place safe, for being both strong and unknown'. The human characters are secretive about their private lairs, but nature does not share their coyness. Pamela and Philoclea, surprised while bathing, hasten to hide 'the beauties whereof Nature was proud and they ashamed'. Sidney's Arcadia is a state of nature only in being an overgrown, unashamed fantasy, where human sexuality is as entangled as foliage. Thus Dametas breaks in on the lovers who, though 'possessed with a mutual sleep', are still knotted in 'viny embracements', as rampant and—in their unconsciousness—as blissfully unthinking as plants. Water is sensuously sentimental: when the bathing girls dry themselves its droplets weep to 'part from such bodies'. The arbours and covert abodes of the pastoral, like that 'prohibited place' where Zelmane spies on the bathers, are the crannied nooks of the female, who carries her paradises secreted within. Dorus sees a shepherdess with a young man ensconced in her lap, 'so wrapped up in that well-liked place that I could discern no piece of his face'; Pamela, observed by Musidorus as she sleeps, testifies to her 'inward sweetness' by a stealthy exhalation of breath, which fears its enforced expulsion from her garden of bodily delights and 'seemed loth to leave his contentful mansion but that it hoped to be drawn in again to that well-closed paradise'. Even the bumptious Mopsa is ventilated with 'hidden parts', her organic arcana.

Ralegh in his 'Passionate Man's Pilgrimage' imagines heaven as an analogy with this sybaritic Arcady: a place where sanctity will be indistinguishable from gluttony, and the soul will imbibe sweetness from 'nectar suckets'. Spenser's faeryland is no such site of instant and carnal gratifications. It is harsher and more arduous, a society of frugal subsistence imperilled (in Book VI) by thieves and cannibals or (in Book VII) by wolves, a state of nature which is rude and rustic—as for the witch's son who in Book III woos Florimell with apples—and a school in self-abnegation. Sidney's shepherds are courtiers in fancy dress; Spenser's are pious and thrifty peasants. Meliboe offers his hospitality to Calidore, admitting that he lives merely at one remove from the wilderness,

> Which though it were a cottage clad with lome,
> And all things therein meane, yet better so
> To lodge, than in the salvage fields to rome.

From the hardships he endures he has learned the pastoral virtue of stoic acceptance. Thieves raid his flocks, and the brigands eventually kill him. Like Adam in Shakespeare's *As You Like It*, whose meek and tranquil goodness makes him to Orlando an image of the probity of the antique world, Meliboe resembles the first Arcadians, described by Polybius as primitive victims of nature's hardships.

The Arcadian tradition conflates two literary landscapes: the wilderness of Polybius's Arcadia, and the lush Sicilian groves and meadows of Theocritus. As Erwin Panofsky demonstrates in his essay on the mournful shepherds of Poussin's 'Et in Arcadia Ego', the two unlike versions of nature are already superimposed in Virgil's Arcady, which despite its summery bounty contains sadness and death. Spenser, too, sees nature both as overwhelmingly fertile (as at Mount Acidale) and starkly abstemious (which is how Meliboe unprotestingly experiences it); his faeryland is at once a prelapsarian garden and the exploited, exhausted nature consequent to the fall. Spenser's is a moralised landscape, and an elegiac one. Paradises are lost in the poem: Guyon demolishes the bower, Diana curses the hill she once favoured. But the desecration of paradise begets that stoic, lowly pastoral which is the common denominator of the poem's genres and the ground of its values. The epic's heroism of martial force and the romance's heroism of ambitious quest succumb to a patient pastoral forbearance. Nature's advice to Mutabilitie is

> Cease therefore daughter further to aspire,
> And thee content thus to be rul'd by me.

Faunus, pursued by Diana's vindictive nymphs, learns the prudent wisdom of disappearing into nature. The poem pacifies conflicts by solemnising elemental marriages—the Thames with the Medway in Book IV, Molanna with Fanchin in Book VII.

The same deference of other genres to pastoral, maybe the profoundest instinct of the English literary imagination, occurs in Shakespearean drama. The truths of history, comedy and tragedy are all to be sought in their pastoral kinship with each other. The kingdom in the history plays is a garden; the second part of *Henry IV* turns aside from politics to the maunderings of the Gloucestershire retirees, as Shallow and Falstaff eat last year's pippin in an arbour of the orchard. As Empson realised, the Shakespearean double plot is a pastoral beneficence. The king may end tragically, but the people will comically continue. Therefore the actions of both comedy and tragedy are referred to and tested against nature, when the courtiers decamp to Arden or the lovers to the wood outside Athens or when Lear unhouses himself, confronts the bareness of the heath and, after this abdication, recrowns himself pastorally with ragged weeds. Nature in Shakespeare is where tragedy and comedy meet and merge, and their simultaneity, commingling in the earth when Hamlet looks down into the jester's open grave, corresponds to the mood of Spenserian pastoral.

Though the *Arcadia* may lack this wise and acquiescent pastoralism, which tolerates individual tragedies because nature presides over a divine and collective comedy, it contains in another sense a precise pastoral significance. This has to do with Virginia Woolf's claim in a 1931 essay that it is latently a novel. Not a novel in itself, it made the novel possible by redefining pastoral as a mental dispensation. Because in the pastoral world nothing can ever happen (as Strephon and Claius complain in their sestina), the purpose of its narrative is to occupy the dreariness of duration. 'Read it then at your idle times', Sidney advised his sister. Its characters are preoccupied with elaborating an idling, digressive, teasingly protracted discourse which will replete their vacant time. The women sit 'devising how to give more feathers to the wings of time'. They delight in tantalising longueurs—Zelmane 'to keep him [Dorus] the longer in speech, desired to understand the conclusion of the matter'—and their postponements of an end are a sexual proviso. The imperative is to delay climax, that small death. The expiring Daiphantus fends off mortality's fell arrest in a series of parentheses, subordinate clauses and interjected afterthoughts, for to keep talking is to go on living. Basilius is 'loth to lose the precious fruit of time', and Zelmane wishes 'not to lose this sought-for commodity of time'. But by their repetitions they convert elapsing time into circling space, and Pyrocles actually refers to 'that space of time'.

Virginia Woolf responds to this ritualising of narrative in the *Arcadia*, whose motive, she says, is 'to escape from the present moment, . . . wilfully flouting all contact with the fact'. Its freedom from time and hustling succession grants to the work a spatial vagabondage. The *Arcadia*, she says, is 'a beautiful garden to wander in now and then'—which is how Hurd describes *The Faerie Queene*, and how Keats interpreted the long poem, which he called 'a little Region to wander in'. This sublime inconsequentiality, physically imaged by Woolf's account of meandering aimlessly through the narrative, has a mental correlative. Abstaining from action, *Arcadia* licenses the mind to ramble as it wishes. Sidney's landscape is an ambling soliloquy: after an encounter with Basilius, Philoclea departs 'with a new field of fancies for her travailing mind'. Woolf can compare Sidney with 'any modern novelist' because the characters of novels do not exert their bodies but, cloistered in pastoral, promenade their minds instead. The first such inactive protagonists occur in the novels of Richardson, who named his servant girl after Sidney's Pamela and warned her, when she attends a masquerade with Mr B., to look after her Musidorus, and who dispatched Harriet Byron in *Sir Charles Grandison* to a masquerade costumed as an Arcadian princess. The novel is for Richardson an Arcadian retreat, a hermitage of mind, and Harriet dresses herself as a dweller in this mental landscape, with 'a chaplet of artificial flowers' and 'a little white feather' on her cap; her hoop is diminutive, for 'they wore not hoops in Arcadia'. Diderot in 1762 described *Clarissa* as a latter-day pastoral, scrupulously anti-social. After Richardson comes Jane Austen's inert Fanny Price, whose meek pastoral vocation is the reading of novels in the library at Mansfield Park, and at last there follow the characters of Virginia Woolf herself, becalmed in a pastoral quietude, minds suspended (like the voices in *The Waves*) in a landscape. Kew Gardens, in an early prose poem, is Woolf's own local Arcadia, a sacred, secret garden of thought. 'Doesn't one always think of the past, in a garden with men and women lying under the trees?' asks a stroller there.

Choosing as his title for *Far From the Madding Crowd* a quotation from Gray's 'Elegy Written in a Country Churchyard', Thomas Hardy reassimilates the novel to the moral solace of classical pastoral. His Wessex is a region which enforces that quietism which is the novel's special piety: the Little Hintock in *The Woodlanders* is a ruminative Arcadia 'where may usually be found more meditation than action, and more passivity than meditation', and Fitzpiers tries to reconcile himself to subsistence there and to sequestration—'The secret of quiet happiness lay in limiting the ideas and aspirations'. In contrast with Dickens, who jeers at pastoral when fabricating an etymology for Staggs's Gardens in *Dombey and Son* (alleging that the slum was formerly a grove patrolled by the antlered herd, commonly known as staggses), or George Eliot, who in *The Mill on the Floss* mocks the form when categorising the produce shipped from St Ogg's ('the well-crushed cheese and the soft fleeces, which my refined readers have doubtless become acquainted with through the medium of the best classic pastorals'), Hardy adopts pastoral as both moral order and narrative practice.

Pastoral comedy means the sheepish affiliation of the human family, huddling together to share warmth and comfort, humbly accepting the collective helplessness of our nature. The deputation of choristers waiting on the vicar (their pastor and spiritual shepherd) in *Under the Greenwood Tree* is likened to 'a flock of sheep'. Sheep are comic characters because their existence is tribal. They pretend to no individuality; everything they do is done in concert, and at someone else's behest. They are the harried human passengers on the Erasmian ship of fools. Bathsheba laments their haplessness in *Far From the Madding Crowd*: 'Sheep are such unfortunate animals!—there's always something happening to them' (but never because of them). There can, however, be such a thing as a 'pastoral tragedy', which is what Hardy calls Gabriel Oak's loss of his flock. As in Gray's poem, where the villagers live mutely, tragedy in Hardy's pastoral induces stoic silence and weary immobility, not the violent exertions Hardy elsewhere described as 'desperate remedies'. Like Wordsworth's Michael undergoing petrification at the sheep-fold, Hardy's characters grow solemnly, heavily inert. Pastoral works on them like gravity, weighing them down, dissuading them from vainly fretful action—Fanny Robin dragging herself along the earth towards Casterbridge, Troy congealed in inertia, the apathy of Bathsheba or her 'temporary coma' after her husband is shot, the seclusion and inactivity of Boldwood. Often this meditative stasis keeps watch, like Poussin's Arcadian shepherds, at a grave: Troy does so at Fanny's, later Bathsheba does so at his, as Marty South does at Giles's resting-place in *The Woodlanders*.

Hardy is fascinated by a motionlessness which is at once a pastoral condition (prohibiting action, as Strephon and Claius complain) and a novelistic state of poise or suspense, interrogating motives so as to undertake—eventually—some new motion. He knows that characters in novels are placed, like Bathsheba, 'beyond the pale of activity'. They exist in order to ponder themselves and their relations with others. Hence the denial of animation to Fanny, who 'stood with that tense stillness which signifies itself to be not the end, but merely the suspension, of a previous motion', or the paralysis of Troy at her coffin. His stillness is a loss of 'motive power'; the emotions which might have moved him are mutually cancelling, 'and there was motion in none'. Response, when it at last occurs, is involuntary, like the sun's descent beneath the horizon or the falling stone's magnetised obedience to the summons of the earth. Characters in Hardy, instead of bestirring themselves to act and to move ahead, simply decline or lapse in accordance with the trajectory of pastoral: Troy, who 'had originally stood perfectly erect', slowly sinks forwards until he is kneeling beside the dead Fanny. The posture is his homage to nature. Genuflection is a morally necessary disablement. In that prayerful tableau Troy is experiencing 'an indefinable union of remorse and reverence'—indefinable and incapable ever of being extroverted in action.

As it deters action, pastoral critically questions narrative. Driving through the rain with Bathsheba, Troy remembers reading in a book that 'wet weather is the narrative, and fine days are the episodes, of our country's history'. It is a brilliant comment, both on meteorology and on English literature. It proposes a narrative as unoccupied as a rainy day, with fine spells as episodes or intermissions between the suspending of that continuum and its resumption.

Hardy does not protest against this world where nothing happens or changes but simply repeats itself. Bathsheba finds the 'steady smack of [rain] drops upon the fallen leaves . . . almost musical in its regularity'.

The routine of a single day recapitulates literary history, which is also cyclically recurrent (like the agricultural chores of pastoral), not eventful. Bathsheba thinks as she walks through the twilight of 'how the time of deeds was quietly melting into the time of thought, to give place in its turn to the time of prayer and sleep'. That ordering of the hours is an ordaining of literature and its inevitable, natural development. The 'time of deeds', the day devoted to work, corresponds to epic, which in Bathsheba's chronology is only a beginning. It is succeeded by two more sedate and spiritual eras of being. The vespertinal 'time of thought' is the dominion of pastoral, that holy time which Wordsworth in his poem about evening called quiet and nun-like. Beyond it lies the resumption of unconsciousness, of subliminal eventlessness, as far as can be from the daylight faith in deeds—the peace of the cows, or of the drunken carousers during the storm, in Bathsheba's barn; the nocturnal calm of Weatherbury, which when asleep resembles Gray's Stoke Poges: 'the village . . . was quiet as the graveyard in its midst, and the living were lying well-nigh as still as the dead.' In a classical literary scheme, time would travel in the opposite route. From the prostration of unconsciousness man awakens, spends his infancy pastorally, then accedes to the active life of epic. Hardy romantically reverses that progress, and in doing so he has described the history of English literature. Pastoral is a meditative epilogue to epic, and also a prologue to the romantic immersion in the unconscious mind and its night thoughts.

— 6 —
The Arcady of the Poem

Despite Virginia Woolf's belated attempt to recruit Sidney for the novel, and to represent his fantasyland as that cerebral and novelistic *hortus conlusus* which Zelmane, bidding Philoclea keep silent, calls 'the paradise of her mind', his Arcadia has another function in literary history: it is a symbol for the proud autonomy of poetry. About the time he was completing the first version of *Arcadia*, Sidney wrote a treatise on poetry, published in 1595 almost a decade after his death and called in parallel editions *The Defence of Poesy* or *An Apology for Poetry*. The posture of defensiveness is important to its argument, for Sidney is toying—in succession to Chaucer's play with the opposed values of authority and experience—with discharging literature from the service of doctrine. Because the case he is advancing is so radical, he argues it equivocally and evasively; but he has already, in the *Arcadia*, unapologetically established the right of poetry to bring to birth a non-existent world which brilliantly surpasses the real one. Whereas the medieval poet can only obsequiously versify the truths promulgated by religion, Sidney impiously awards to poetry a religious power of transfiguration. His theory, hesitantly set out in the essay but boldly elaborated in *Arcadia*, makes possible the ultimate romantic theology of literature expounded by Shelley's *Defence of Poetry* in 1821.

Caxton's preface to his second edition of Chaucer in 1484 is vexed by the problem Sidney audaciously solves: the opposition between literature's official subservience to scripture, and its heretical self-delight. Caxton doubly sees Chaucer as his own Chauntecleer. On the one hand, he casts away 'the chaff of superfluity' so as to isolate the 'picked grain' of sententiousness; he is a scavenger of moral nutriment. (Caxton chooses to ignore the reversed relation between chaff and grain which is the point of Chaucer's ironic citation of the text.) On the other hand, he is himself a superfluous creature, dispensing a 'sugared eloquence', and his achievement is to have ornamented and embellished the language. Chaucer is both the lowly fowl grubbing for didactic grain and the beautiful, vainglorious song-bird. He exists between 'rude speech'—the homiletic, rustic truths of the widow's establishment—and the beauteous ornateness, as Caxton calls it, of fiction. His rhetoric, like Chauntecleer's plumage and his crowing, make him 'a laureate poet', and that laureation, an efflorescence of verbal figures which are the poet's crown of leaves, claims for literature the Arcadian freedom to blossom and flaunt at will.

Poetry is floral in Sidney; in John Lyly's *Euphues* (1578–80) it is the human mimicry of sumptuary, sexually flagrant flowers in fashionable dress. Style is thought's extravagant, excessive clothing. Euphues, a theorist of verbal costume, is obsessed by the sartorial habits of the English and their 'inconstancy of attire', mongrelising French collars and barbarian fleeces, and he interprets both language and human emotion as quests, like the cycle of fashion, for perpetual renewal. He tells Philautus that 'thy friendship . . . is like a new fashion', soon found to be stale and discarded but recycled when all the alternatives have been tried on, for eventually nothing is newer than what is old. Lyly's sophistic quibbles and his periodic cadenzas make Chauntecleer's self-display a rule of linguistic conduct. Literature is language at play, or on show. Matthew Arnold, deploring the ingenuities of the seventeenth century, praised the eighteenth-century Augustans for inventing an economical, workable prose. But the boast of Arcady is inutility, and that of Euphuism is unworkability. When Euphues composes a love-letter, his style is so cunningly complex that the missive is misunderstood. That very failure marks its graceful triumph as art.

Eliminating the meanly real, Virginia Woolf says, the *Arcadia* 'gains another reality'. Its rhetoric encourages the triumphant supercession of the real. Arcadia has value because it is a fiction invented and sustained by the magniloquence of language. Style is a means of sublimation: Sidney demonstrates the linguistic perfectibility of life. Claius overcomes the loss of Urania by embarking with Strephon on a Jacob's ladder of words, each level of which conducts to another above it until the grief they feel has been magicked—by the intercession of language—into delight: 'Let us think with consideration, and consider with acknowledging, and acknowledge with admiration, and admire with love, and love with joy in the midst of all woes.' His tribute to her mounts into a superlative realm where she as a physical being is obsolete, replaced by her image. At every stage, the previous one is cancelled: her eye-lids are first compared with 'two white kids', then declared to be as nothing in comparison with 'the day-shining stars contained in them', her breath is a summer breeze but that, too, is negligible in contrast with the 'honeyflowing speech' freighted on it. She is put through a sequence of metaphoric transubstantiations which end by abstractly declaring her to be a 'flock of unspeakable virtues laid up delightfully in that best-builded fold'. Here the pastoral, by its own insistent exaggeration, renders her holy, and though Claius calls her goodness unspeakable he has—in spite of this Platonic reverence for the bodiless, wordless idea—spoken of it.

Euphues pleads the inexpressibility of Elizabeth, saying that like Zeuxis he must paint her with her back turned; yet he goes on to express her with undaunted hyperbole, wishing that, having been forty years a virgin, she should live on for eighty years as a mother, and hoping that the world will end before her reign does. The loyal Fidus warns Euphues that the sovereign renders rhetoric dumb: 'the Orator holdeth a paper in his hand, for that he cannot utter.' Euphues accepts the challenge, and sets his language to invent appropriate superlatives, for its function is to transcend its subjection. As he tells Eubulus, 'it is the disposition of the thought, that altereth the nature of the thing'. Alliteration assists the transvaluing: Euphuism is a rhyming prose wherein the parity of sound wishes away inequities of sense and hints that all propositions may be sophistically reversible, all impediments levelled by the irresistible pleadings of language. Euphues lectures Livia on the difference between shadow and substance, or on 'the deformed man, with the reformed mind'. In the old hermit's narration, the habit of alliterating begets a symmetry in sentences which stands for a freakishness in nature perhaps marvellous, perhaps monstrous. The hermit Cassande has a twin called Callimachus, alike not yet alike, and their relationship incites a patterned gemination in his speech, which bifurcates to reproduce itself and might potentially go on forever. One child is nurtured in thrift, the other in theft, and as they grow the assonant apportionment of qualities continues—'He grave, I gaysome: he studious, I careless: he without mirth, I without modesty'—so that when their father has to divide his estate between them he is at a loss to differentiate them and gives them two bags, one of wealth, one of writings, leaving them to make the decision. Opposites are not self-cancelling but self-balancing. Moral choice yields to the glib compromise of a verbal quibble. Thus Euphues manages rhymingly to solve the diplomatic problem of preference between Oxford and Cambridge, poising the stateliness and free stones of the one against the sumptuousness and fine streets of the other and resting his case by arranging a symmetrical equation: 'Let this suffice, not to enquire which of them is the superior, but that neither of them have their equal, neither to ask which of them is the most ancient, but whether any other be so famous.'

Romanticism turns Arcady into a nest of singing-birds. The shepherds in Yeats's *The Island of Statues: An Arcadian Faery Tale* (1885) vie to awaken Naschina with their lyrics, and refer to themselves as 'singing things'. They dispute who is 'Arcadia's sweetest tongue', and compete with the birds, called by Almintor 'wood-rhapsodists'. Song is the place's foliage. On the enchanted isle Naschina asks

> What are the voices that in flowery ways
> Have clothed their tongues with song of songless days?

But Sidney's Arcady is a gymnasium of lexical not lyrical skills, an academy of language. His shepherds are angelically lucid intellects, their thoughts raised 'above the ordinary level of the world, so that great clerks do not disdain our conference'. Their dialogues are symposia: Greek 'was their natural language'. They talk in a diction of superb and conceited superfluity made possible (as Kalander says) by learning's augmentation of nature. Their words can resurrect things which, if unaided by language, will successively shrivel and diminish. The sublimation of Urania contrasts with the deduction of

Pyrocles's boat, further defrauded by each revised description: 'a ship, or rather the carcase of the ship, or rather some few bones of the carcase hulling there, part broken, part burned, part drowned'. Death means the disassembling of objects and the disabling of language. The speech of these people is their claim to a self-made immortality, and their ultimate victory comes in the lyrical or oratorical mitigation of their own demises—Helen's 'groan full of death's music', or Pyrocles and Musidorus singing 'like quiet swans . . . their own obsequies' and so fortifying 'their minds against all extremities'.

Arcadia is about the dual transition from thing to word (the object's uprisen self) and from the commerce of speech to the ideal self-reference of song. Facts are subsumed in images, emotions in melody. Sidney is representing a perverse levitation in art, a splendid verbal sacrilege. This is how he treats the death of Parthenia in Book III. The luxury of style so beautifies her suffering that it seems language will not accredit what it is describing and cannot help making her death a verbal ecstasy. Her tremulous lips seem to kiss 'their neighbour death', and the wound is her neck—'a neck indeed of alabaster' Sidney adds, thus rendering her body sculpturally impervious and coolly bloodless—does not mar her loveliness but cosmetically flatters it, 'so as here was a river of purest red, there an island of perfectest white, each giving lustre to the other'. Only 'a grossly conceiving sense' would take these distresses to be 'disgraces', Sidney instructs: his own obligation is to see them aesthetically, as 'apparelling beauty in a new fashion'. Amphialus, therefore, looking at her, cannot but admire her appearance. Parthenia herself is as refinedly conceited, and when she understands that death is inevitable, she addresses it as if it were her choice and with a defiant paradox cancels its power over her: 'O sweet life, welcome', she says, and she refers interchangeably to 'O life, O death.' She is muted when 'Atropos cut off her sentence', but she has already claimed, with the aid of Sidney's languishing description, an aesthetic victory over her fate. As a result, the sundering of soul and body does not issue in the latter's decay. Both parts of her have their separate heavens: the soul its invisible realm, which Sidney's adroit parenthesis allows him to disbelieve in, the body the embalmment of its after-life as an image—'the noble soul departed (one might well assure himself) to heaven, which left the body in so heavenly a demeanour'. God may be able to save souls; only the artist can perfect bodies and dotingly preserve them.

Euphues is about a discursive valour, a trial of verbal hardihood. Euphues the slippery, sophisticating Greek travels first from 'Athens, the nurse of wisdom, to . . . Naples the nourisher of wantonness' and proceeds next to England where by his impenitent example he trains the English language—'which as I have heard is almost barbarous'—in dissimulation. His advice to parents emphasises enunciation, not conduct. Children must be 'trained up in the language of their country, to pronounce aptly and distinctly without stammering'. He proposes the same curriculum for England, whose brawling 'diversities of language' he laments. For Euphues literature is linguistics, and he allegorises the human physique in order to demonstrate that the tongue is formed for honeyed mendacity. Hence its protective portcullis: the mouth is to Euphues the sanctum of imagination—'the cunning and curious work of Nature . . . hath barred and hedged nothing in so strongly as the tongue, with two rows of teeth, and therewith two lips'. The dazing leap from base thing to elevated thought which is the arrogance of literature is seconded by a physiological embargo on speaking what is prompted or ratified by emotion. Euphues points out that nature has located the tongue 'far from the heart, that it should not utter that which the heart has conceived'. The agency which prevents the heart from standing up and answering that it has felt is wit, so versed in guile that it chimes alliteratively with amorality: 'None more witty then Euphues, yet at the first none more wicked'; his reprobate youth evinces how 'the wittiest brain is inveighed with the sudden view of alluring vanities.' The countrymen of Euphues are wily shifters (as Philautus says) like Ulysses, the rhetorical politician of Shakespeare's *Troilus and Cressida* whose example Euphues himself invokes when causing the animadversions of Philautus to ricochet. 'I remember', he says, '. . . how valiantly Ajax boasted in the feats of arms, yet Ulysses bare away the armour.' The duel must therefore turn into a debate.

As a proving-ground for literature, Arcadia is a kingdom of wit, a meritocracy of mind. All people there, Kalander says, 'from high to low' are 'given to . . . sports of the wit', and even the infants versify. Daiphantus is enthroned as a demi-god because it is 'beyond the degree of humanity to have a wit so far over-going his age'. By wit Sidney means more than the glib readiness to make jokes: it is our means of self-salvation, the pride of our mental freedom which disdains all levelling necessities, even (as in Parthenia's case) that of death; our intellectual reascent to godliness. This canonising of intelligence contradicts the ethic of pastoral which, as Book IV puts it, intends that 'human reason may be the more humbled and more willingly give place to divine providence'. In contrast with Spenser's stoic, abiding Meliboe, Sidney's shepherds are brazen rebels against that 'almighty wisdom' because, recognising in language a sign of their difference from the animals they tend and the remnant of their forfeited divinity, they strive to use it so agilely and so pyrotechnically that, through it, they will effect a re-creation of themselves. Theirs is a wit metaphysical in its ambition. Arcadia is a arena for the rehearsal and sportive exercise of this linguistic capacity—in the metrical contests of the second ecologues, with their experiments in Phaleuciacks and Asclepiadiks, or in the oratorical competition at the end.

This explains Sidney's reversion, in revising it, to epic. For just as the epic centre of *Paradise Lost* is less the war in heaven than the parliamentary dispute in hell, so Sidney identifies wit with the prowess and self-divinising rage which are the imperatives of the hero. Euphues shames the bragging of Philautus by downgrading it from epic to pastoral: first Philautus is Ajax, then a hen cackling for a lost chicken. Yet between the two stations of literary degree there is a median compromise, hinted at by Euphues when he is explaining why he will not allow Ephoebus to grow up in Athens. He speaks of a threefold division of life: the active career of civil function, the speculative one of meditation and study, and the epicurean ideal of an existence abandoned to voluptuousness. His dialectic goes to work at once on the triad, arguing that 'if this active life be without philosophy, it is an idle life' and 'if the contemplative life be separated from the active, it is most unprofitable.' Euphuism combines political action with pastoral contemplation by making words the agents of will; it is a mode of literary glory. The problem of *Arcadia* is that no such neat synthesis obtains there. Arcadia ought to be a land without politics, but because wit is a means of power and self-promotion it introduces dissension to paradise. Amphialus begets politics by the dexterity and feint of his conceits. 'Amplified with arguments and examples, did he sow abroad many discourses.' He does combat with armaments forged in language: 'He sharpened his wits to the piercingest point.'

Pastorally, too, and more innocently, Arcadia is a product of wit, since the place is a metaphoric state, and metaphor is an innately linguistic talent whereby we can imagine ourselves elsewhere. Sidney is forever indicating the latency of metaphor in words—for instance, the 'maze of amazement' in which Basilius and Gynecia find themselves when their children disappear. Their emotional quandary is imaged as a landscape. Amazement strands them in a maze, just as Pyrocles is becalmed in 'a wandering muse': they grope through a forest of words, a shrubbery of sentences. Musidorus, too, gets lost in a syntactic pastoral. He considers Pyrocles's narrative about Philoclea, 'but therein he found such intricateness that he could see no way to lead him out of the maze'. This world is affiliated with images, which are words proudly displaying themselves and parading their autonomy. Basilius says that Artesia haughtily peacocks herself. Arcadia is planted by the efflorescence of nature. If flowers, like the peacock's tail, are the extravagances of nature, their equivalents in language are simile, metaphor, conceit, those excessive aesthetic graces which are Sidney's counterparts to the moral and spiritual Graces who dance at Mount Acidale in Spenser's poem.

Pyrocles at first takes Arcadia to be the home of some goddess, 'a plot of the celestial dwellings'. In fact it is 'a heap of pleasures' gratifying humans and imagined by them, for Pyrocles's exploration of it takes the form of a sequence of rhetorical questions aimed at Musidorus, who is thus co-opted to Pyrocles's doting fantasy. Do not the trees, he asks, 'seem to maintain their flourishing old age . . ., being clothed with a continual spring?' That imputation of seeming is his aesthetic willing of a natural impossibility. The grass is likewise described as an ideal pastoral society. Each blade is an individual jewel, but their preening beauty contest is adjudged and censured by the mower who collectively levels and humbles them. 'Do you not see the grass, how in colour they excel the emeralds, every one striving to pass his fellow, and yet they are all kept of an even height?' Nature loses its innocence here: aspiring to the duplicity and self-admiration of art, it has to be forcibly ordered and maintained in submission. Arcadia, Pyrocles implies, is the creation of man not nature. 'And see you not', he goes on, 'the rest of these beautiful flowers, each of which would require a man's wit to know and his life to express?' Again the flowers exist to be known, to be expressed (by that exertion of pressure which distils their essences as perfume). Wordsworth's half-hidden violet or his daffodils tell him something about himself. Pyrocles on the contrary tells the flowers something about themselves, and can do so because his own wit is gaily and gloriously floral, a symptom like them of aesthetic surfeit. Wordsworth's romantic longing is to become like the flowers, to share their unconsciousness and insentience; Pyrocles offers, however, to make the flowers like him by persuading them of their witty and otiose obligation to be decor. Thus, soon after, he refers to 'these flowers'—rhetorical and hyperbolic exchanges—'of new begun friendship' with Musidorus. The image is a flower because it is an ornamental excess, achieving the conversion of emotion into art: the tears of the love-lorn Pyrocles are like 'out-flowing blood'. But not only is the blood metaphoric, so are the tears, for he has no palpable hurt, and Musidorus marvels that 'fancy could have received so deep a wound'.

In Sidney's religion of art, the image has a heretical sanctity, for it is the human mimesis of divinity. Dorus, praising Mopsa, celebrates her attractions as 'ornaments of that divine spark within you . . ., . . . descended from heaven'. But Sidney's is an inverse Platonism. Instead of the idea of goodness stepping down from heaven and manifesting itself on earth as physical beauty, which reduces art to the feeble shadow of its celestial source, he founds in Arcadia a heaven on earth, where the beauty manufactured by art outdoes that ideally reserved on high. Philoclea is acclaimed as 'the ornament of earth, the model of heaven, the triumph of Nature, the light of beauty, the queen of love', and those attributes are an anthem of sanctification: no longer modelled on heaven, she is a model for it. And whereas the Platonic idea unclads and disembodies itself to elucidate naked truth, Philoclea's undress is a prerogative of the image, beguiling the worshipper who wishes to possess her. She is 'so near nakedness as one might well discern part of her perfection, and yet so apparelled as did show she kept best store of her beauty to herself'. The Platonic idea summons the mind to ever higher exploits; the image flirts with and teases the profaner fantasy, and her 'light taffeta garment' is 'enough to have made your restrained imagination have thought what was under it'. At last she manages another transvaluation: her eyes are black, but their obscurity must be the sign of a higher lucidity, like Spenser's dark conceits, as if 'nature so made them that we might be the more able to behold and bear their wonderful shining'; she has in any case reversed the relation between darkness and celestial light, for 'goddess-like' she has worked 'this miracle with herself in giving blackness the price above all beauty'. Pyrocles raptly bows to her as his 'divine lady'. Yet she owes that divinity to art—her own enactment of a miracle and his adoration of it.

Lyly establishes as well an audacious theology of art by equating Eden with imagination and then finding the ideal representation of both in a woman. Euphues is 'brought into a paradise by the only imagination of womens' virtues', and to make it clear that his is a heterodox cult he adds that if all the devils in hell were women he would be sure never to live devoutly. He compliments God as a fellow-fashioner of images and says 'artificers are wont in their last works to excel themselves', so that God reserved the creation of man for his climactic feat, and then proceeded to show that he could improve even on perfection by fabricating woman—just as artificers like Lyly and Sidney go on to achieve superlative enhancements of that divine creation. This is why Elizabeth I, with whose praise *Euphues* ends, is such a gift to Lyly. An 'earthly Goddess', uniting Venus and Vesta, beauty and chastity, and systematically outdoing all the heroines of antiquity, she is raised to that height by Lyly's magnificently self-serving and implausible overstatements: hyperbole is his equivalent to Spenser's mythopoeia.

Arcadia is made by the devout exercise of artifice. Sidney's is a work in praise of writing, which enables the artist to remake the world at will, to substitute a facsimile for an actuality. Lyly's Philautus smuggles a letter to his Camilla by removing the kernels from a pomegranate, enclosing his missive there and replacing the sliced-off top so finely 'that it could not be perceived, whether nature again had knit it . . . or his art had overcome nature's cunning'. Dorus's letter in *Arcadia* fetishises its paper (blessed because it will kiss the hand of his mistress) and its ink (whose blackness will shine when she looks at it); when he steals into Pamela's lodge to deliver another epistle he takes the erotic precaution of kissing her ink-stand, craving of it 'a safe and friendly keeping', and then transferring it, with the letter deposited there, to her bed's head. Paper and ink are to be envied because they have improved an abject life by replicating it. The letter is 'O happy messenger of a most unhappy message': the medium has blithely transcended its message, for writing shuns the emotion of the writer and feels only self-delight, the vanity of artistry. It enjoys an imperturbable superficiality. This is its usefulness to the political characters in *Arcadia*. It enables them to trade in and disseminate untruths. Amphialus, knowing 'how few there be that can discern between truth and truth-likeness, between shows and substance, . . . caused a justification of this his action to be written, whereof were sowed abroad many copies.' Writing for him is a forgery of motives, a shoddy rather than a supreme fiction. He is authorising falsehoods, which he does not write but causes to have written, and then publishes; Dorus is in love with the writing, which he does himself, and he even doubles as his own publisher when he delivers the letter. Amphialus wants to be read literally, which means deceptively: his propaganda relies on 'some glosses of probability', and will 'from true commonplaces fetch down most false applications'. Dorus's hyperboles are truer art because they have no designs on life and no makeshift plausibility. His letter is an autonomous thing, wherein he is a character not an author. He empowers it to speak 'not from him—O no, that were not fit—but of him'. And because he has objectified himself within it and overcome his subjective plaint, the conclusion of the letter can perform his death without demanding that he should indeed die: 'End then, evil-destined Dorus, end; and end thou, woeful letter, end.' Dorus is a truer feigner than Amphialus because less likely to be believed, and therefore a better artist. His emotions are verbal only. 'He dieth: it is most true, he dieth; and he in whom you live, to obey you, dieth. Whereof though he plain, he does not complain. . . . He dies, because in woeful language all his senses tell him that such is your pleasure.' His expiring is a pun, a brief sexual self-obliteration brought about by language.

The difference between the two varieties of writing is made clear by Sidney in the *Defence* when he pleads against Plato's expulsion of the poets from his republic. 'For the poet, he nothing affirms, and therefore never lieth': Dorus's letter is a poem as Amphialus's pamphlets can never be, because his performance refers only to itself and to its exultantly exaggerated words. Whereas Amphialus deals in factual misrepresentation, telling 'what is, or is not', Dorus, like the poet in the *Defence*, takes off from the dull or treacherous terrain of the substantive to write about 'what should or should not be', and that subjunctive mood is the home of metaphor. During one of the battles in *Arcadia*, Sidney recounts an incident which is a parable of the artist's high untruthfulness and sublime fictionality. A painter commissioned to 'counter-feit'—important word—the battle of the Centaurs and Lapithes ventures into the fray for purposes of research. He thinks that if he sees 'some notable wounds' he will 'be able the more lively to express them'. But where he stands there gaping at the carnage, Dorus smites off both his hands, 'and so the painter returned well skilled in wounds, but with never a hand to perform his skill'. That amputation warns the artist against transcription from life. If you worry about having the experience, you will be unequipped for depicting it. Art is a sequel to Genesis, conjuring something out of nothing: all aesthetic inventions should be Arcadias.

This is why love is so useful to Euphues as a school of literary beguilement and simulation. He patronizingly tells Philautus 'he that cannot dissemble in love, is not worthy to live', and cites the shape-changings of the gods in pursuit of the mortals they lusted after. Less exhaustingly, scorning to metamorphose into a swan, a ram, a heifer, or a golden shower, he achieves the same end by a linguistic agility, considering 'both might and malice, deceit and treachery, all perjury, any impiety may lawfully be committed in love, which is lawless'. Or rather, like literature, a law unto itself, speaking itself into authority. This is the bluff of which Philautus accuses Euphues, who creates value as he goes along by manipulating proverbs into untruths, fantasticating both law and religion by the deployment of language: 'There is no coin good silver but thy half-penny, if thy glass glister it must needs be gold, if thou speak a sentence it must needs be law, if give a censer an oracle, if dream a prophecy, if conjecture a truth.' Yet what else is art but the legislative edict of imagination, the prophetic exercise of fantasy—Adam's gratified dream of Eve?

Sidney begins the *Defence* more modestly, alleging that he has 'slipped into the title of a poet' without choosing that vocation. The pose of amateurism and courtly nonchalance covers an extreme argumentative daring, for he here assigns to poetry a supremacy among intellectual pursuits (or what he calls the human sciences) and a parity with scripture. He corrects the classical theory that poetry is a divine gift, an infusion of godly and inspiring breath. That would deprive the poet of credit for what is to Sidney a 'human skill', wherewith he unaided outsoars nature and approximates to godhead, restoring to the mind its rightful 'divine essence'. For this reason he defines the poet as a maker, or rather a reifier, redecorating what has already been drably and usefully made, alchemically altering a brazen world into golden perfection, specialising in a counter-creation: 'Nature never set forth the earth in so rich tapestry as diverse poets have done—neither with pleasant rivers, fruitful trees, sweet-smelling flowers, nor whatsoever else may make the too much loved earth more lovely.' This re-creation is inorganic: a woven, fabricated tapestry. Sidney is describing, as a model for poetry, an Arcadian landscape. It is the same in his commentary on the psalms of David as a 'divine poem' or 'heavenly poesy'.

The debate of Euphues with the unbeliever Atheos ends by proving the divinity of art. Atheos challenges Euphues to prove the literal truth of the scriptures, because without them there is no God. Euphues converts the infidel with an argument whose only authority is his own language—a version of that artistic bluff Philautus quarrels with but capitulates to. He knows, he says, that the scriptures come from God because 'the secret testimony of the Holy Ghost' whispers to us that God speaks in them. He has a colleague's intimacy with the deity's workings, and can declare that 'the scriptures come from the mouth of God, and are written by the finger of the Holy Ghost', because God's business, like his own when he brings his civilising mission to England, is linguistic reform. The purpose of the scriptures is the same as that which Samuel Johnson saw as the duty of poetry, the preservation of language: 'The Hebrew tongue lay not only unesteemed but almost unknown, and surely had it not been God's will to have his religion provided for, it had altogether perished.' *Euphues* and *Arcadia*, correspondingly, seek to be divine advents in English, redeeming it from that changefulness which Chaucer fears at the end of *Troilus and Criseyde*.

When Matthew Arnold in the positivist nineteenth century reconsidered the relation between poetry and faith, he recommended abandoning the theology of the scriptures and clinging only to their lyricism. In that agnostic theory, poetry can have nothing to do with the certainty of faith: its only recourse is a soothing make-believe. But Sidney boldly declares the poet to be 'a passionate lover of that unspeakable and everlasting beauty to be seen by the eyes of the mind, only cleared by faith', so that, discussing David's prosopopeias (or personifications), he awards the poet a god's power to animate nature by means of metaphor: 'he maketh you, as it were, see God coming in His majesty, his telling of the beasts' joyfulness, and the hills' leaping.' The romantic theory of the poetic image is, in contrast with this, a renunciation of that activating verbal energy. Shelley in *Prometheus Unbound* admits that the deep truth is imageless. His poetic language must therefore be sadly blank, or vacantly abstracted: to incarnate the idea would be to perjure and to maim it. The skylark can only remain a spirit if Shelley denies, at the beginning of his poem, that it ever was a bird. The sacred image is by definition unimaginable. Sidney however speaks of the unspeakable and renders visible that which is meant 'to be seen by the eyes of the mind'; and he draws attention to the sacrilege of his definition precisely by his elegant disclaimer of any such motive. Having enlisted David as one of his professional predecessors, he fears that 'I seem to profane that holy name, applying it to Poetry, which is among us thrown down to so ridiculous an estimation.' It has been thrown down; he will return it to the astral heights—he refers later to 'the sky of Poetry'—and he does so by 'that high flying liberty of conceit proper to the poet', which is his 'divine force'.

Spenser called his own allegorical conceits dark: obscured by the imperfection of human understanding; pastorally muddied and lowly. Sidney's imagery is of a conceit which is vertiginous not abased, dazzlingly brilliant not humbly bedimmed. Whereas Spenser in *The Faerie Queene* takes the poetic ideal of heroism, collating the classical, ethical virtues and their Christian, spiritual counterparts, and progressively humanises it in such characters as girlish Britomart and errant Calepine, Sidney, having encouraged poetry to excel nature, then finds the art's 'uttermost cunning' in its overcoming of humanity. Poetic characters have none of the impure admixture of mortality. Nature cannot exhibit 'so constant a friend as Pylades, so valiant a man as Orlando, so right a prince as Xenophon's Cyrus'. The final victory Sidney extols is form's submergence of content, and style's subjugation of moral qualms. 'Those things which in themselves are horrible, as cruel battles, unnatural monsters, are made in poetical imitation delightful.' He everywhere refers to poetry in sumptuary terms, as an apparel or a 'masking raiment', a polished or gilded skin or a sugaring; an immaculate surface, insolently unnatural. He might be describing the aesthetic Arcady imaged in the face of Oscar Wilde's Dorian Gray, an art whose surface is its symbolism.

The initial task of poetry is 'to beautify our mother tongue'. That, too, is an angelically Arcadian responsibility, because 'if *Oratio* next to *Ratio*, Speech next to Reason, be the greatest gift bestowed on mortality', then the perfecting of language will help to raise us towards divinity. Hence the recondite, elaborated loquacity of the *Arcadia*: it is less a narrative than a theoretical treatise, like *Finnegans Wake*, on the evolution of language towards a narcissistic self-sufficiency. This is why Sidney praises language's aspiration both to music, 'the most divine striker of the senses', because melody disdains reference to the real world of things (to which words are still attached), and to oratory, because the proficient rhetorician—like the virtuoso plaintiffs at the end of the *Arcadia*—can argue any case assigned to him, no matter what its merits or his own opinions are, since his talent lies in the 'excellent exercising' of words. Poetry is language off-duty, intellect's gambolling leisure.

Though Hazlitt denounced the *Arcadia* as 'one of the greatest monuments of the abuse of intellectual power upon record', the abuse (a retraction from use) is deliberate and historically provident for literature: Sidney is putting language out to pasture, allowing it to amble, idle and go round in circles. This is why, when he explains the poet's manner of proceeding, he cannot help implying that every poem is an induction into Arcadia. He describes the philosopher's argumentative scenery as the obstacle-strewn terrain of romance, fretted with delays and detours. 'He informeth you . . . of the tediousness of the way, . . . as of the many by-turnings that may divert you from the way.' The poet's itinerary is less arduous. He hedonistically welcomes you into a pastoral, and 'doth not only show the way, but giveth so sweet a prospect into the way, as will entice any man to enter it', alluring you with instant satiations: 'Nay, he doth, as if your journey should lie through a fair vineyard, at the first give you a cluster of grapes, that, full of the taste, you may long to pass further.' The poem is a playground for words and for the titillated senses—a miniature and reclaimable paradise, like Marvell's garden. The notion of the poem as a pastoral recess or hidden garden survives, often underground or behind locked doors, like that which shuts off the pleasance in H. G. Wells's story 'The Door in the Wall' (1911). Keats's bower in *Endymion* paraphrases Sidney's lush vineyard. There is a mental version of this horticulture, erecting houses to protect the fantasy, which lays out the ground-plan of the English novel. Sidney anticipates this indoor or cranial pastoral when he speaks of 'the secretest cabinet of our souls': the revelatory rooms explored by Catherine in *Northanger Abbey* or Lockwood in *Wuthering Heights*; the 'house of thought' assembled, 'in the process of . . . brain-building', by Pater's Florian Dedal in 'The Child in the House' (1878), which resembles an 'airy bird's-nest of floating thistle-down and chance straws', an architecture of association. The mental articulation of Sidney's memory-theatre, envisaging the head as 'a certain room divided into many places well and thoroughly known', is the many-chambered house of fiction, as private as Wemmick's in *Great Expectations* when the drawbridge is raised.

For W. H. Auden the beneficence of pastoral continues to be its purposelessness. Poetry should, as he instructs the dead Yeats in 1939, make nothing happen, and pastoral is the region where nothing can happen—a contented, indifferent rural otium like the Breughel landscape in his 'Musée des Beaux Arts' (1938). In 1933 Auden rewrote the double sestina of Strephon and Claius to illustrate the point. Sidney's shepherds use the poetic form of 'Ye goat-herd Gods' with its recurring, recycled line-end words—mountains, valleys, forests, morning, evening, music—to stand for the physical circumscription and routine of pastoral, and for the elaborately futile game of poetry. The words at the end of the lines are like terminal gods, closing off prospects. The life that Strephon and Claius describe is boring; their art salvages from repetition an ingenious formal freedom. Auden's reply, 'Paysage Moralisé', is an urban pastoral, about the failure of revolution, yet despite its radical disgruntlement there is a conservative consolation built into the form. Revolution does not mean only a climacteric, irrevocable change; it is also a rhythm of rotation, according to which the same things go on happening over and over again. Cheated of the future they cannot bring to pass, Auden's characters retain the dream of it, riding forever on the merry-go-round of the sestina. Sidney has the same sense of poetry as a haven, and when he mentions narrative he takes care to describe the stories that poetry tells unhistorically, as a circuitry of inconsequence like the double sestina, because though we may be reading about people doing things, while we are reading we ourselves are doing nothing. The poet tempts us out of time into a charmed purposelessness like that he has conferred in words. He recounts 'a tale which holdeth children from play, and old men from the chimney corner'. Detaining the children, he is staving off the end of their childhood (or supplying them with an infancy which can be revisited whenever they choose, in imagination); button-holing the elders, he is stalling their drift into death, convincing them to re-embark on the wheel. He has introduced an eternity—called Arcadia—into time, and pastorally instituted a heaven on earth inside a book.

Literature exercises its mythopoeic power by showing England to be that Arcady. Hence Michael Drayton's poetic tour of the country in his *Poly-Olbion* (1612–22), which solemnises literature's blessing of its native land. For poetry is now able to re-invest places with spirits, and the characters of Drayton's work are those local genii—the twin rivers Itchin and Test embroiled in a sisterly dispute over the site of Arthur's headquarters; the two competitive Avons; Salisbury Plain clasped in the embrace of Wansdike's aged arms; the Vale of Evesham queening it over its colleagues and rebuking the presumption of spiteful mountains; the overweening braggart Malvern, convinced he is the king of hills. The landscape is once more animate, vivified by imagination. Poetry works to bring about confluence, the matching and mating of phenomena which would otherwise disperse and elapse. This is why Drayton attends so many watery weddings—Severn's with Wye, Tame's with his bride Isis at Oxford—and is so preoccupied with rillets, riverets and the 'fresher

Springs' he sends his muse to seek out along the Derwent: poetry is itself a source, inexhaustible in its renewals. His journey around England is the leisurely perambulation of a beloved body, whose navel is lodged in Lincolnshire and whose back passage is that tunnel in the Derbyshire Peaks 'named / The *Divels-Arse*'. The language he celebrates is an exhalation or suspiration from that body, its vital breeze. Against the thunderous-tongued Saxons and the recondite harmonies of the Welsh singers, he sets 'the sundry Musiques of England', a concert of woodwinds carved from the land and breathing its air.

He acknowledges the bards as his predecessors. With their 'sacred rage' they possessed an epic power of exhortation, inflaming armies; he pays tribute to their mnemonic skills, for they have kept alive—by their epic drill of repetition—the genealogy of 'great Heroes, else in *Lethe* that had slept'. But his own responsibility is different: not conquest and fortifying of terrain but cultivation of it. He is the poet as agricultural worker, tending nature by encouraging its fruitfulness with his plough. The end of the first section is his rest from labour in the fields:

> Heere I'le unyoke awhile, and turne my steeds to meat:
> The land growes large and wide: my Teame begins to sweat.

He humbly insists that his muse take a walking tour, rather than (as Milton was to do) aspiring to fly. Having made the round of Lancashire, he permits her to 'sit her downe to breath' before proceeding—as always on foot—towards Yorkshire. Epic is enforcement. Ogres like Gogmagog, muscular brutes like the wrestler Corin and self-styled great men like Malvern (who prides himself on being so far-sighted) first assert their power over the land. Drayton, in succession to them, pastorally occupies himself in the industrious tallying and affectionate storage of all the things England contains. The rhythm of his journey, equably steady, slow and calm, establishes a tempo for English poetry. John Denham in *Cooper's Hill* (1642) adjusts his verse to the motion of the Thames, as Spenser had earlier done in his *Prothalamion* (1596). Addressing the river, Denham wishes

> O could I flow like thee, and make thy stream
> My great example, as it is my theme!
> Though deep, yet clear, though gentle, yet not dull,
> Strong without rage, without ore-flowing full.

The analogy between literary decorum and landscape's conduct of itself persists. Yeats, impatient with this pastoral placidity, remarks in 1937 that 'the English mind is meditative, rich, deliberate; it may remember the Thames Valley.' George Orwell, gliding through the Home Counties in a boat-train that same year on his return from combat in Spain, interprets the pastoral as a state of moral and political stupor: the landscape and its people are 'all sleeping the deep, deep sleep of England', and will be awakened only by bombs.

Poetry derives from the place, and repays its debt to geography by spiritualising the sites which are its source. *Poly-Olbion* overlays two mythologies, modes—opposed, but reconcilable—of consecrating reality: classical and Christian. The vernacular location derides its classical forebear, when Malvern boasts that he is not intimidated by '*Olympus*, fayr'st of Hills'. Drayton elaborately rehearses the classical derivation of Britain, contending that the land is named after its founder Brutus. He admits that the lineage has been disputed as 'meerelie fictitious', since the Romans deny the existence of such a Brutus; yet why should the imputation of fictionality matter, if the true author of national identity is literature? Drayton proves his case by adverting to the veracity of the scriptures, 'from heaven' and 'like heaven, divinely pure'. Like Lyly's Euphues in a similar argumentative flourish, he does not so much demonstrate the fundamentalist truth of holy writ as the holy supremacy of those fictions which are an alternative to scripture. The classical nymphs—the metamorphosed daughters of Brecan, for instance—who are first domiciled in the landscape are supplanted by the second wave of mythographers, who christen England and 'are canonized here for Saints'. The new faith has its own protocol for sanctifying locations:

> So *Frithstan* for a Saint incalendred we find,
> With *Brithstan* not a whit the holyest man behind. . . .

Yet the real miracle-worker, the real patron of grace when it descends into nature, is neither the classical god nor the Christian martyr but the poet. Drayton with his 'humane wit' can unearth gardens of perfection etymologically embedded deep within the drabbest places: thus his Peryvale, now an innocuous outer London suburb, is glossed as '*Pure-vale*', and encouraged to exult in the bounty of its wheat-crop, arguing like an unabashed Eden

> Why should not I be coy, and of my Beauties nice,
> Since this my goodly graine is held of greatest price?

Poly-Olbion concludes with Drayton's definitive location of Eden in Westmorland, where there is a 'most beloved Brook' of that name. And his summary of his final song leaves it exquisitely unclear whether Eden's source is the bubbling land or the mellifluous muse, for they are one and the same:

> Of *Westmerland* the Muse now sings,
> And fetching *Eden* from her Springs,
> Sets her along. . . .

This rearrangement of terrain, hallowing our native soil, making our little room an everywhere as Donne proposes, is the highest ambition of literature.

Blake in *Milton* (1804–8) would, if he could, build Jerusalem on England's green and pleasant land.

For the romantics, the problem is that the divinity so lovingly implanted in the land by Drayton or Sidney has once more taken flight. Defoe's *Tour Through the Whole Island of Great Britain* (1724–6) unwrites Drayton and deconsecrates the island over again, valuing commodities not spirits, factories not fictions, clearing the ground for its conquest by realism. Thomas Love Peacock in his *Four Ages of Poetry* (1820) laments the desertion of those gods once propitiated by poetry: 'there are no Dryads in Hyde-park nor Naiads in the Regent's-canal.' E. M. Forster in *Howards End* (1910) wistfully seeks Drayton's assistance. Describing Hertfordshire as 'England at its quietest . . .; . . . England meditative', he wonders how Drayton would now describe its resident nymphs if he could bring up to date 'his incomparable poem'.

Yet the absconded deities might be replaced by the writers who once implored them, and who now are the nation's resident gods and saints. Thus whereas Drayton tours the country in quest of naiads, dryads and earth-spirits whom he actually invents, J. B. Priestley in his *English Journey* (1934) finds the places he visits have become sacred to literary associations. Writers and their characters are the country's 'guardian spirits'—Wordsworth on the brooding northern moors, Fielding in the hearty bustle of Bristol, Tennyson on the downs of the Isle of Wight, Arnold Bennett in the Potteries (among whose industrial wares Priestley reckons Bennett's mass-produced novels.) Olivia and Malvolio are imagined at home in the garden of a Cotswold house, Heathcliff at the door of a square stone farm house in Yorkshire. A commercial traveller promotes a tea shop in Kent 'called . . . the Chaucer Pilgrims. . . . Old style—Tudor, you know', which perishes for lack of American tourists. The grim, impoverished back-streets of Gateshead are named, in a spirit of millenial hope, after Chaucer, Spenser and Tennyson. The artists themselves seem to be named after the landscape which nourishes them. The painters Turner, Girtin, Cotman, Cox, Varley and Bonington sound like villages, or apples. Priestley's is an 'England of the poets, a country made out of men's visions'. At Bath, Drayton reports that the medicinal virtue of the waters is attributed by some to Minerva and by others to Hercules, adding that the spring is also a favourite with Phoebus; for Priestley the local genii, housed in those terraces with their 'perfect façades', are the characters lodged there by Sheridan and Jane Austen. Drayton's Chesterfield expresses itself in a 'hard Vale of Rocks, . . . / By her which is instild', Priestley's in the cheerfully warped lunacy of the spire presiding over it. For Drayton, the region is England's underworld, pitted with hellish hollows and muddied by thick vapours. Priestley, however, declares it a genial literary asylum, and in Chesterfield's 'fortress of pleasant folly' imagines a refuge for such incorrigible eccentrics as Shakespeare's Silence, Sterne's Uncle Toby and Dickens's

Micawber. Books are the city's and the island's insulators, writers the terminal gods who cordon off and defend our idiosyncratic national reality.

The Arcady of the Renaissance is the heaven which art can establish on earth. Priestley, fond as he is of the dream, knows it to be only that, and has a social conscience about its blithe contradiction of actuality. Though the Cotswolds seem 'now so Arcadian', he admits that the pastoral beauty of the region is a poor substitute for the prosperity it has lost: it is in truth 'a depressed industrial area'. And where industrial wealth returns, it befouls the nature literature has beatified. Wedgwood's classical elysium of Etruria is 'by the side of a very dirty canal', and the electrified Midlands resembles a charred and smoking pile of refuse. Of even more painful concern is the imminent forfeiture of the national uniqueness proclaimed by Drayton's spirits or by the writers whose enchanted ground Priestley reverently visits. The country in East Durham, defiled by the mines, is not England at all, but an excerpt from the featureless vastness of Russia or America, 'dropped on to this corner of our island', and the new England of arterial roads, filling stations, cinemas and bungalows and wireless sets—the country from which the deracinated Auden derived his unsettling poetic imagery—is, Priestley concludes, born in and imported from America, 'belonging far more to the age itself than to this particular island'. Arcady has been replaced by technological Utopia, whose location is elsewhere.

— 7 —
The Sonnet: History of a Form

Sidney's defence of his art begins in an equestrian academy—an appropriate school for a Renaissance theory of poetry. Sidney recalls his sojourn at the Emperor's court in Vienna, and the lessons he received there from John Pietro Pugliano, whose praise for his own occupation of horsemanship proves that 'self-love is better than any gilding to make that seem gorgeous wherein ourselves are parties'. Pugliano's vain conviction is that the rider prances above all other human endeavours. Though Sidney teases such self-interest, the quality is a characteristic of the poem, as he goes on to describe it: infatuation with a mirror-image, whose beauty outdoes the reality it replicates. Pugliano is a logical *alter ego* as well in that he teaches technique, and for Sidney poetry is a game of skill, requiring a technical adroitness like Pugliano's control of his mounts. In one of the *Astrophel and Stella* sonnets, Sidney's vaunted 'skill in horsemanship' wins him the tournament; in another he complains that though he is 'a horseman to my horse' he is at the same time 'a horse to Love', ridden and tightly reined-in by his mastering passion. A later romantic aesthetic creed sees the poem as something which grows, with an organic and unsupervised stealth, exfoliating at random. Sidney understands the poem to be something which is made, and conceives of the making as a mode of action, a forceful imposition of self on refractory material, like the riding he learns from Pugliano. When romanticism questions this theory, it revises the equestrian image: instead of the horseman's technical subjugation of his mount, the poem is a horse which rides its supposed master. Of this condition, Byron's Mazeppa is the symbol. Strapped to a wild horse, he must go wherever it madly chooses to take him. Yeats in 'The Fascination of What's Difficult' describes his own creativity as the unbarring of the stable door to release the skittish colt.

The English language, Sidney says in the *Defence*, is 'indeed capable of any excellent exercising'. Yet it requires a virtuoso to subject it to this gymnastic pacing. Literature's function is to be an arena for the exhibitionism of language. Symbolism avows that a poem should not mean but be. The static, self-sufficient being and the discursive meaning are less important for Sidney than the sometimes frenetic, manipulative doing, whereby form trains and disciplines a stubborn content. The most resistant of contents is the experience of love, and the form which strains to rationalise and encapsulate it is the sonnet. The love sonnets of the sixteenth century are therefore studies in the enmity between rampant emotion and poetic dexterity, between feeling and writing. *Arcadia* is about the easy hyperbolic supercession of nature; *Astrophel and Stella*, in 1591 the first sonnet sequence in English, is about the more difficult supercession by the writer of his own emotional nature.

The sonnet, so central a poetic kind to the sixteenth century, has ever since been marginal. The reason has to do with more than the vagaries of literary fashion. The sonnet belongs near the beginning of poetic history because it is a means of technical enablement and a trial of verbal powers. It exists in opposition to the lyric, which surrenders to emotion and offers it no formal impediment: the sonnet takes an emotion and successively formalises it, fitting it into its own economical and incontrovertible shape. That shape is the sonnet's obsessive concern. A lyric accommodatingly reshapes itself at the behest of feeling, but in a sonnet feeling has to suffer the stricture and constriction of form. Though the sonnet is a small and separatist unit, anxious about securing its own closure, it does not want to be lyrically unified within itself. Rather it accentuates internal divisions—the dissension between octave and sestet, or between three quatrains and a concluding couplet, the articulation of argument by complex rhyme-schemes. It is like a Fabergé egg: something which we imagine to be organically indivisible (or divisible only at the cost of breakage) undergoes disintegration and exposes the minute, mechanised ingenuity of its workings. The sonnet cannot grow of its own accord; it must be made. But that technical making is the unmaking of the emotion which is its supposed reason for being.

Astrophel and Stella is about Sidney's erotic attachment to a woman, Penelope Devereux, whom he probably never met. The love is notional. Stella is muse rather than mistress, and the poems are about writing and its vexatious relation with feeling. The sonnet is of use to Sidney because it is pledged to the expulsion of emotion. Very often Stella is admitted in a perfunctory afterthought, just as the sonnet is ending—in the fifth for instance, which accumulates reasons for not loving her and then decides in its last line that she must all the same be loved, or in the forty-first which, after cataloguing the compliments paid to Astrophel's equestrian ability, belatedly attributes his prize at the tournament to an inspiring beam from Stella's eyes. Instead of lyrical self-revelation, the sonnets engage in a worried self-analysis which has as its aim the control of feeling and its therapeutic passage into writing. Insofar as Sidney is able to construct a sonnet, he has arisen from the prostration forced on him by love. The wit is, as the *Defence* proposes, the erectile agency here, and Sidney employs it for self-accusation,

> To make myself believe that all is well,
> While with a feeling skill I paint my hell.

That making believe is the inauthentic mental state of poetry. Coleridge described it as the will's acquiescent and voluntary suspending of disbelief—a temporary irrationality, a narcotic whose effect will pass soon enough. Sidney is less reconciled to the imposture, which to him is an infection of reason. Bullied into love, he says in the second sonnet, now 'I call it praise to suffer tyranny'. *Astrophel and Stella* questions whether the supreme fiction of *Arcadia* might not simply be a lie, a studied self-deception. It is about the queasy self-consciousness and consequent dishonesty of both writing and loving. That dissimulation, Sidney's mistrust of his own creativity, is forced on him by the protocol of the court in which he operates. Castiglione's conduct manual, *The Book of the Courtier*, translated into English in 1561, enjoins a scheming artificiality which maligns the radiant artifice of Arcadia. His artful courtiers take care to appear ingenuously artless. They affect modesty merely to assure their own greater glory (as Astrophel perhaps does in his account of the tournament) and are specialists in nudging others into recognition of their merits while contriving to make their stratagems seem casual and unostentatious. The same feigning is recommended to women: men fear entrapment by their wiles, so they should cultivate a simplicity of demeanour which need not, of course, be natural. Because the courtier's aim is the effortless superiority which Castiglione called *sprezzatura*—fencing, jousting, politicking or writing sonnets with an easy untutored grace, versatilely dodging between roles and skills—sexual craving is to him a particular peril. It impedes him because it is obsessive, and because it is so basely natural. Castiglione's character Fregoso criticises the excessive despair and abjectness of the unrequited wooer, which violates the fine indifference of courtly behaviour. His recourse is simulation, to treat love as an art and a technical accomplishment rather than a lustful impetuosity. Love, Sidney begins to suspect, is in any case an invention of literature.

Assailed by the demands of his courtly society—where he is forever being consulted about foreign policy and required by good manners to answer the 'questions busy wits to me do frame' while thinking distractedly of Stella, or where his air of preoccupation causes him to be charged with arrogance—and by an emotion which, for all its fraudulence, will not let him alone, Sidney turns to the sonnet for aid. It should help him to keep his balance by formalising what he contradictorily feels. Its gift is for the exacerbation and then the resolution of inner tensions. It sets up a small internecine strife between its constituent parts; but its structure can contain those disquiets. Sidney identifies this structural dissent within the poem—one stanzaic segment against other, the clash and consonance of rhymes—with his own psychic civil war: wit's argument with will in the second sonnet, reason's brawling with sense and love inside him in the tenth, virtue's spat with love in the fifty-second. But the therapy of form does not always work. The sonnet's only means of adjudication is to cause the imploding of all these quarrelsome agents into a paradox. Thus virtue is made to fall in love, and reproving reason is outsmarted by a word-play which discovers 'by reason good, good reason her to love'. The paradox achieves a quick closure, as the final couplet of the sonnet requires. It compresses the debate, so that the opposites expire into each other or change places. The emotions have not been sorted out or pacified. Instead they are changed into words, whose meaning can be altered at whim. The imminent end of the sonnet calls for a verbal truce, which is hurriedly arranged by a moral pun ('Then love is sin, and let me sinful be' is Sidney's retort in the fourteenth sonnet to a spiritual critic) or by a frantic repetitive casuistry: the thirty-fifth sonnet, worried about the flattery required of lovers, ends by deciding that

> Not thou by praise, but praise in Thee is rais'd.
> It is a praise to praise, when Thou art prais'd.

Is this a logical checkmate, or only a verbal stalemate? Are poetic words capable of telling the truth? The fifth sonnet considers two incompatible orders of truth: the world-renouncing edicts of Platonic philosophy and Christian religion, and the tug of an instinctual urge. It cannot solve the problem, and can only declare the opposites to be simultaneously correct: it is true that Astrophel should not love Stella, and yet also true that he must.

This concern for the relation between poetry and veracity complicates the Renaissance definition of the truest poetry as the most feigning. It makes poetry a forgery of emotions, and a misuse of words. Hence the sceptical nominalism of the sequence. Sidney is not Astrophel, nor is Penelope Stella. The characters are but names. Astrophel's ink inscribes Stella's name in the nineteenth sonnet, as if hoping to make her real; in the fifty-second he iterates it, for the same self-deceptive reason, seeking to prove 'That Stella (O dear name!) that Stella is/That virtuous soul'; the ninety-second entreats her 'to sweeten my poor name' by deigning to voice it. Poetic assertion cannot be trusted. Astrophel's exultant 'I, I, oh I may say that she is mine' trebles its 'I's in default, because the 'she' in question probably will not respond. Elsewhere Astrophel revokes his own statements and discards them as merely conventional. The forty-seventh sonnet declares 'I love you not' only, in its final line, to renege when 'that eye/Doth make my heart to give my tongue the lie'. Here the inner discord essential to the sonnet occurs between the silently speaking truths of eye and heart and the blabbing loquacity of the tongue (or the scribbling pen): lovers, like poets, are always saying what they do not mean, and what Astrophel feels—if indeed he feels anything—cannot be uttered or transcribed. Words rehearse alternatives of action which exist in grammar but not in active possibility, as in Astrophel's review of his options: 'I may, I must, I can, I will, I do' (yet as it turns out he mayn't, he mustn't, he can't, he won't, and he doesn't) or

> I might (unhappy word!), O me, I might,
> And then would not, or could not, see my bliss,

where the various optatives are cancelled by being consigned to an already deceased past.

Literature in appropriating feelings falsifies them. Astrophel's initial protest that he has rejected convention to look in his heart and write is itself conventional. Love and writing are alike plagiarism:

> .... in Stella's face I read
> What Love and Beauty be, then all my deed
> But copying is, what in her Nature writes

where the copying is a Platonically flimsy thing, the attempt to detain in a mortal form an idea which belongs in heavenly disembodiment. Astrophel regularly accuses his works of betraying his meaning. In the nineteenth sonnet they are 'vainly spent', like the shameful expense of spirit in Shakespeare's sonnet 129; in the twenty-first they are 'bad servants', deputed to satisfy his repressed desires. Sidney's sonnet 34 begins 'Come, let me write', writes itself, but is not satisfied that it has achieved anything thereby. It is not even true that it wants to be written. 'Thus write I while I doubt to write', says Astrophel. Its only reason for being is the punishment of its own literary means: Astrophel vengefully outpours ink not emotion, and glories in its 'poor loss'. Sonnet 35 asks, just as self-rendingly, 'What may words say, or what may words not say . . .?' and answers its own question in that very line, for words, which can do nothing, can only say the same thing over and over with desperately witty syntactic variants. Sonnet 45 determines on a cheating self-fabulation. Stella will feel nothing for Astrophel, but weeps over romances. Herself a fiction, she professionally commiserates with another non-existent being. Astrophel therefore wills himself out of existence and requests to be read, treated as a character in someone else's poems:

> Then think, my dear, that you in me do read
> Of lover's ruin some sad tragedy.
> I am not I: pity the tale of me.

This reads as an almost tragic antithesis to the artistic theology of *Arcadia* and the *Defence*. The *Defence*, for instance, admires art's power to make the horrible—'cruel battles, unnatural monsters'—delightful. Astrophel sees that efficacy of art merely as proof of feeling's inefficacy. 'Oft cruel fights well pictur'd forth do please': we slight the suffering reality by adoring the replica. Shakespeare deals with an entanglement comparable to Astrophel's in his sonnet 138:

> When my love swears that she is made of truth,
> I do believe her, though I know she lies.

Instead of the nauseous making-believe in Sidney, Shakespeare amiably validates the pretence and converts it into a truth. A pun even manages to change mendacity into sexual gratification:

> Therefore I lie with her, and she with me,
> And in our faults by lies we flattered be.

The dramatist is unoffended by the falsities of words: after all he writes fictions which performers as his deputies incarnate as truths, and this is what happens here. Shakespeare's sonnets are about the dramatist's authorisation of his characters, and their sometimes bewildering independence of him; Sidney's are not about the freedom of acting but the regimen of writing, and they harry words which Shakespeare (as in that pun on 'lie') allows to breed double meanings as they please.

The sonnet is Sidney's self-inquisition, his scrutiny of his own poetic veracity. In contrast with these exactions and auto-criticisms, the lyrics distributed through *Astrophel and Stella* suffer no inner discontent. Whereas the sonnets worry about where the poetry is coming from, and condemn themselves for their literary imitativeness, the first song (untroubled by the sonnet's vexed inability to differentiate praise from flattery) can repeat itself without being suspected of protesting too much when it claims that

> To you, to you, all song of praise is due:
> Only in you my song begins and endeth.

And whereas the sonnets acknowledge a disagreement between heart and tongue because words are not to be taken literally, the language of lyricism can be trusted because it never breaks silence: in the eighth song the ears of Astrophel and Stella hunger for language,

> But their tongues restrain'd from walking
> Till their hearts had ended talking,

and when their tongues are incapable of speech, Love utters on their behalf through Astrophel and praises Stella's (silent) voice which 'when it singeth, / Angels to acquaintance bringeth'. Eventually language falters:

> 'Grant, O grant—but speech, alas,
> Fails me, fearing on to pass!—'

but while in a sonnet this would be a self-condemnation, in the lyric it is language's proper resort to music, which is non-referential, and thence to silence. It is the same when Stella takes to words:

> Then she spake; her speech was such,
> As not ears but heart did touch.

Astrophel and Stella, whose existences as characters and fictional *alter egos* is the barbed question of the sonnets, can in the lyrics be unseen, ownerless

[98]

voices making music. In the eleventh song they duet at Stella's window during the night, and—in contrast with the irritable nominalism of the sonnets, always taking names in vain—they do so anonymously. They now have the impersonality of the lyric, and their emotions do not belong to them but to everyone, for the lyric is a song to which (as Johnson said of Gray's 'Elegy') every bosom can return an echo.

Astrophel and Stella is about love as an exercise in language, both spoken and written. And, because of its brilliant manipulation of the sonnet, it is about the ways we wrest (or, to use Astrophel's word in sonnet 34, 'wreak') feelings into form; about the poem as emotional effusion and as structural coercion. Spenser, too, in his *Amoretti* sequence in 1595 employs the sonnet to impose a structure and a graduation on what he feels. The sonnet offers the security of conventionality: for Sidney a means of analysing or repressing outlawed emotion; for Spenser a means of directing it. Sidney's sonnets work by inciting an angry disparity within, Spenser's by using those inner divisions as a hierarchy, up which his argument mounts, setting out from an earthly love but changing it—by the mediation and the meditation of the sonnet's form—into a heavenly devotion. Thus while a Sidney sonnet will seem at the end to have exploded or exhausted itself, its wit manically self-cancelling, each Spenser sonnet serenely begets another. The sequence sacramentally extends upwards when the lady's breasts are complimented as 'sweet fruit of pleasure brought from paradice', or when Spenser's profane love changes into sacred worship; and it also questingly extends forwards. Instead of Sidney's anecdotal, episodic arrangement, with each sonnet a hectic but unsequential instant, the *Amoretti* are organised as a narrative. The seasons pass, and the festivals of the church year. The time which Sidney wishes to accelerate extends for Spenser into a longevity of happiness ('the joyous safety of so sweet a rest') and beyond that into everlastingness:

> Even this verse vowd to eternity,
> shall be thereof immortall moniment.

The movement is that of the 'long . . . race', as Spenser calls it in sonnet 80, of *The Faerie Queene*, and the sonnets of courtship have as their sequel Spenser's account of his marriage in the glorious *Epithalamion*, which in turn has as its sequel his entry into a proxy immortality, guaranteed to him by the 'large posterity' he hopes to generate and by the poem's continuance as 'for short time an endless moniment'. Therefore, like the stanza of *The Faerie Queene*, the sonnet is for Spenser a form in which metamorphosis can happen. All its internal arrests are transitional states in an evolution from matter to spirit. The sestet does not contradict the octave, as so often in Sidney; rather it surmounts it. If the octave anatomises the lady's pride, the sestet will justify that fault as a lofty disdain of the material world. Instead of debate, there is dialectic. Sonnets like the eighth, ninth or twenty-second begin on earth only to end in heaven. Spenser characteristically eases the levitation by erasing those sectional breaks on which Sidney pivots his argumentative reversals. The sestet of Sidney's sonnet 15, for instance, indignantly casts off the octave. But in Spenser there is increment and superlative addition, as one part grows from the other. His first sonnet unfurls in this way, from 'Happy . . . leaues' via 'And happy lines' to 'And happy rymes' until in its last line it can reassemble and compound leaves, lines and rhymes.

The writing which for Sidney is traduction—a pedantic fakery, as he declares in sonnet 15—is for Spenser a transliteration. He has allegorised the sonnet. A poem takes an image, activates it, then explicates it, rewriting its materiality as spirit. The second sonnet, for instance, is about the journey of his sorrowful thoughts from 'the inner part' into the presence of the woman who has provoked them. The allegorical progress leads beyond the sonnet, as it conducts the mind beyond the confines of this world: seeking comparisons for the lady's eyes, sonnet 9 can find an equivalent only in 'the Maker selfe', so it allegorises them as a divine radiance, and the fifteenth translates the mineral spoils which merchants dig from the earth into the impalpable invisible mental glory of the woman—

> . . . that which fairest is, but few behold,
> her mind adornd with vertues manifold.

Allegory is metaphor in motion. The sonnets therefore connect the woman with the gods of Ovid, who transform themselves in the pursuit of love. Though their metamorphosing motives were carnal, they were rectified after the event in medieval moralisings of Ovid, which interpret their shape-changings as an allegory of grace's ubiquity in nature. In sonnet 28 Spenser offers the woman a leaf of laurel, remembering Daphne's transformation into a laurel tree and hoping that the nymph will now change her mind and accept from him the love she refused from Apollo. Elsewhere he mentions Penelope's weaving, Narcissus's self-starving, Arion's riding of the dolphin and Orpheus's musical pacifying of war. Both he and the woman expand or metamorphose into the other characters, and allegory, universalising them, at last makes gods of them. Sidney wants to reject himself and the emotions which plague him by fabricating fictions from them, replacing himself with the impersonal Astrophel ('I am not I'); Spenser wants not to be less than himself but more, to show the love in *Amoretti* as a single manifestation of a force thrilling through all men, through nature and through supernature, as he does in the cosmic biology of the *Epithalamion*, where his wedding-night is overseen by 'glad Genius', protector of the 'geniall bed', the gardener who fertilises the earth in Book III of *The Faerie Queene*. Spenser and his bride are merely the vessels through whom that seed is transmitted: impersonality is their metaphysical bonus, while for Astrophel it is no more than a convenient social and literary evasion.

In both cases the guarantor of this more or less than personal state is the sonnet, which forbids the individual emotings of the lyric. A Sidney sonnet takes an emotion and therapeutically analyses it, breaks it down so it can be got rid of; a Spenser sonnet takes an emotion and step by step transforms it into an idea. Thus, whereas Sidney's sonnets are accompanied by a self-analytic commentary

> (I now have learn'd love right, and learn'd even so
> As who by being poison'd doth poison know),

Spenser's come equipped with an exegesis of the idea at which they have arrived. As allegorical machines, they demand elucidation, and Spenser provides it, admonishing the lady in sonnet 29 for misinterpreting his gift of a bay leaf or likening the lady to a tiger, a storm and an obdurate rock and himself to their victims:

> That ship, that tree, and that same beast am I,
> whom ye doe wreck, doe ruine, and destroy.

Sidney's sonnets are, as he says in sonnet 18, a rational audit of what he resents having irrationally to feel; Spenser's extrapolate from and expound the fury of an irrational love into a higher rationality. The process in Sidney is a self-defrauding, in Spenser a self-magnification. Though Sidney, fearing the treason of his own words, disparages the writing of the sonnets ('As good to write, as for to lie and groan'), because they will be misread as symptoms of love rather than the administering of a cure, Spenser sees the resort to writing as an interpretative necessity: words contain the truth of perishable things, just as the idea is the lucid inside of the image, and if he is unable to write (as he purports in sonnet 3) it is for the same allegorical reason which causes Langland to abort *Piers Plowman*—words will mistranslate the woman's celestial goodness by describing her as a mere pretty face. Like the portraitist of the angel in sonnet 17, he needs a language 'that can expresse the life of things indeed'.

That language is metaphor, the indwelling spirit of things. The writing for Spenser is a sacred trust, the prophetic envisioning or articulating of the unseeable and unspeakable. When the lady throws one of his love letters in the fire, he mourns for the paper which has undergone a martyr's death, perishing because of the dangerous truth inscribed on it; and in sonnet 75 writing is a resurrection, the uprising of the soul after the loved body's decay:

> My verse your vertues rare shall eternize,
> and in the heuens wryte your glorious name.

Likewise a muted reading is in Spenser a communion of understandings, since words are meant not to be declaimed (as by Astrophel: 'Fly, fly, my friends! I have my death wound—fly!') but to be pondered. When Stella in the eighth song speaks silently to the heart rather than the ears it is for a social reason. She is rejecting Astrophel's advances, and wants to do so as tactfully as she can. When Spenser, in a sonnet corresponding to that song, asks 'Shall I then silent be or shall I speake?', he reaches a different conclusion. He schools his heart in speaking silently and trains

> . . . mine eies with meeke humility,
> loue learned letters to her eyes to read.

That exchange of glances is a mental semaphore. Feelings and looks are thus translated into literature, because they are directed towards the understanding. Spenser hopes that the ocular letters he reads to her will be spelled out by 'her deep wit'. She will allegorically uncode his messages and rewrite them as rational language, 'soon conceiue, and learne to construe well'.

The difference of mood and meaning between Sidney and Spenser can be defined by a comparison of sonnet 17 in *Astrophel* with sonnet 16 in *Amoretti*. Sidney's poem describes a spat between Venus, Mars and Cupid. The bow-boy shoots off an arrow in jest, 'and I'—Astrophel says in the poem's final line—'was in his way.' Spenser, gazing raptly at his lady, sees a flock of allegorical cupids encircling her. One of them aims an arrow at his heart, but the lady snaps 'his misintended dart'. The poem ends with Spenser's near-miss:

> Had she not so doon, sure I had bene slayne,
> yet as it was, I hardly scap't with paine.

Sidney's poem is brilliant gossip about marital jealousies in a sensual heaven. Venus requires sexual attentions from the slackening Mars. Both gods berate Cupid for their own discontents or failings. He is a spoiled brat, who has to be comforted by 'his grandam Nature'. Beneath the tittle-tattle, it is constructed, like so many of the *Astrophel* poems, as a debate or combat of wills: an internal dispute which issues not in conciliation but in an anticlimax, when Astrophel strays into Cupid's line of fire. The wit lies in the complicity between the cherub's archery and the poet's archness. Sidney can represent his own emotion as an accident, a jest, an error, for which he is not responsible. But Spenser's woman intervenes to break the arrow. Her initiative is that of the allegorist, again like Langland's intrusion into the various texts of *Piers Plowman*: she stays the dart because it is misintended, ill-aimed, because its target is too physical. By recalling it she is rewriting an earthly love as a heavenly one.

Whereas the antagonists in Sidney's poem are venal, pettish, lustful people despite their demi-deity, Spenser's are intellectuals. He writes about seeing the invisible—about the difference between looking and perceiving, between the 'rash beholder' who ogles the woman and the votary whose concern is insight and the veneration of her 'immortall light'. The poem is obsessed with eyes—the lady's 'fayre eyes', her 'glauncing sight', the 'twincle of her eye', Spenser's gazing and his espying. Ranking these different kinds of looking, it is categorising opposed modes of understanding. Cupid wants a sexual victim; the lady prefers to have a transfixed worshipper. She arrests the image because it will misconstrue the idea, and in doing so saves the integrity of Spenser's small allegory. In contrast, the fashioning of allegory is cleverly mocked by Sidney, who sees it as a manufacture of frivolous intellectual playthings. When Cupid's bow and arrows are broken by the angry Venus, Nature rearranges Stella's face in order to re-arm him: she

> Of Stella's brows made him two better bows,
> And in her eyes of arrows infinite.

Allegory for Sidney is a literary version of cosmetics. Perfect as it is, Sidney's poem refuses to take anything, itself included, seriously. Spenser's, however, treats a flippant convention with high seriousness, deciphering the incident as a mental fable. The sonnet teaches Sidney insouciance. The form attracts him because it is so elegantly trivial. But for Spenser the form inculcates an earnest intellectual drill: within it he must prove a poetic theorem.

Sidney's sonnets are misunderstood if he is lyrically identified with Astrophel and Penelope with Stella, just as in Spenser's the woman is not only the Elizabeth Boyle he married in 1594, for the function of the poems is to disembody and render her divine. Even in the *Epithalamion* she is apprehended with awed indirectness, by way of the metaphors which attend on her. And the purpose of metaphor for Spenser is the allegorical restoration of bodies to their source in spirit: thus having hungrily catalogued his bride's charms, calling her lips cherries and her breast a bowl of cream, he reverses this downward journey of sensual appraisal and consummation and redirects his mind architecturally—

> Her snowie neck lyke to a marble towre,
> And all her body lyke a pallace fayre,
> Ascending vppe with many a stately stayre,
> To honors seat and chastities sweet bowre.

So poetic defloration is corrected by allegorical sanctification. *Epithalamion* is named after the bridal-chamber, but it does not happen there: it uses that private room as an epicentre only and extends outwards, publicising the event and generalising it in the town, the woods, and in the 'high heauens, the temple of the gods'.

Shakespeare's sonnets have the same studied evasiveness. They have of course romantically been claimed as Shakespeare's single self-revelation. With this key, Wordsworth declared, Shakespeare unlocked his heart; and ever since, critical sleuths have busied themselves in tracking down prototypes for the young man, the dark lady and the rival poet, and in making diagrams of Shakespeare's snarled affections. The poems, however, do not abide such questioning. Like all sonnets they exist to frustrate it: it is a form in which intimacy is impossible, and no poet makes more teasing use of this conventionality than Shakespeare. His sonnets sound earnestly or aggrievedly personal, yet the more closely they are inspected the more non-committally impersonal they are. Just as we are about to affix an emotion to Shakespeare, he shrugs it off and slips out of the poem.

To the professional dissimulation of the poet—whose skill, as Sidney knows, lies in feigning, and who for Spenser must allegorically surmount the personal case—Shakespeare adds the yet-subtler escapisms of the actor and the dramatist. The actor does not need to feel the emotion he is representing; indeed, it is better if he does not: he is Sidney's imaginative feint in action, deceiving everyone but himself. The dramatist is even more astutely detached, nothing in himself though—by writing speeches—he confers selves on others. The play is an art-work which does not contain the artist. Shakespeare's sonnets are modelled on this mysterious disappearance. Whereas a Sidney sonnet can say 'I am not I', a Shakespeare sonnet (the eighty-fourth in this case) conversely insists 'You alone are you', and goes on to add that 'you are you'. Sidney achieves the division of himself, Shakespeare the objectification of that self in another, or in a multitude of others. He describes his mode of dramatic creativity in 109, while characteristically denying that he is capable of it:

> As easy might I from my self depart
> As from my soul, which in my breast doth lie.

In truth he manages that departure in every sonnet and in every play. The one begets the many, and lives only through that prolific offspring. The sonnets recur to this paradox. The eighth, for instance, treats it familially, arguing that a concord of sounds resembles

> . . . sire, and child, and happy mother,
> Who, all in one, one pleasing note do sing,

and the fifty-third wonders at the metamorphosing and even trans-sexual versatility of the loved one, who can be alternately Adonis and Helen and who insubstantially exponentiates into 'millions of strange shadows':

> . . . every one hath, every one, one shade,
> And you, but one, can every shadow lend.

Spenser in the *Epithalamion* prays to be allowed such a bounty posthumously. For him it must be biological: he will survive in the 'timely fruit of this same night'. Shakespeare attains it by the dramatist's own mode of self-reproduction, engendering characters who can live on his behalf.

The sonnets are a drama Shakespeare has not bothered to write. Each poem is an emotion in search of a character to belong to, a person who will attach it to a circumstantial and psychological context. 'They that have power to hurt and will do none', for instance, is a moral essay, naming no one in particular, so universally applicable that it can end in a couplet pairing interchangeable proverbs. Interpreting it, we invent a character who can own it—Angelo, perhaps, in *Measure for Measure*—and thus supply the drama which Shakespeare has on purpose omitted: we treat it to an audition. The poem has its own version of *sprezzatura*, an amateurism about emotion which is the dramatist's refusal of responsibility. It allows any use to be made of it, and licenses any reader who, as a putative actor, wants to lend it his or her own emotional inflections, but it will offer no assistance, for having painfully invested it with a personal content we then find that it ends in those blandly collective proverbs—

> For sweetest things turn sourest by their deeds:
> Lillies that fester smell far worse than weeds.

The next sonnet also uses a proverb to cover the sly exit of personal identity: 'The hardest knife ill-us'd doth lose his edge.' The proverb is native, primitive allegory. In Spenser it would signify expansion beyond the individual case; in Shakespeare it marks a cautionary retreat from that individuality. Spenser uses the form of the sonnet hierarchically. Arguing through it, he reaches the mid-air of sacredness, from where he reviews and reinterprets the profane. He ends above the sonnet; Shakespeare's concern is to end, like the dramatist watching his play from among the audience, outside the sonnet. That is the ingenuity of those final couplets. Like Sidney's they gainsay the twelve lines which have preceded them: the coda to 30 perfunctorily cheers itself up, that to 53 returns the polymorph to safe singularity of being, that to 129 dismisses its anguished soliloquy about 'th' expense of spirit' as a commonplace, remarking 'All this the world well knows.' Yet this end in a commonplace, a cliché or a proverb is what makes the sonnets so moving, for Shakespeare seems to find in the inevitability and conventionality of the form a small replica of the individual life's advance from identity to non-existence. The sonnet's fourteen lines are a compression of man's seven ages, and like the life-cycle Jaques summarises in *As You Like It* they reach their term in a row of negatives. Sonnet 15 considers this automatic increase and decrease in nature, as do 60 and 73. Each of these contends that time can be defeated by poetry, but Shakespeare's faith does not lie in the permanence of writing. Rather he describes a revivification which is the miracle of drama. 'So long lives this, and this gives life to thee' refers less to a poem or a painting, which can only elegiacally recollect a defunct existence, than to the re-enactment of an existence by its reincarnation in an actor. This is why Shakespeare insists on the presence of spectators ('So long as men can breathe or eyes can see'), because the rebirth cannot occur without their collaborative midwifery. A child will enable the young man 'to be new made when thou art old',

Shakespeare argues, and in sonnet 37 he casts himself as that father and the young man as his child: characters are the dramatist's heirs, whose independence of him he, like a wise parent, blesses and subsidises.

The plot of the sonnets concerns the dramatist's freeing of his characters from himself. A novelist can never bear to let them go. Decades after his invention of his characters, Henry James returned to repossess them in the prefaces to his novels, shackling them to him with those affectionate diminutives he uses of Isabel Archer or Hyacinth Robinson; Jane Austen with an equally proprietorial love said she had created in Emma a character whom no one but herself would much like. The dramatist must, however, instantly inure himself to his characters' rejection of him. The moment he writes the speech, it belongs to the actor. When Shakespeare says

> Farewell! Thou art too dear for my possessing,
> And like enough thou know'st thy estimate.
> The charter of thy worth gives thee releasing;
> My bonds in thee are all determinate

he could be addressing Hamlet, in whom he no longer has the monopoly. The dramatic character does not even belong to itself. As Cleopatra knows, when she dreads being parodied on stage by squeaking boys, that character is the increment of all its eventual, incompatible performances. The after-life that the characters in the sonnets enjoy is one of enactment, lodged 'where breath most breathes, even in the mouths of men' or pacing forth (as 55 says) into a stage-like room where they are praised 'in the eyes of all posterity'.

The love Shakespeare writes about in the sonnets is the dramatist's love for his often ungrateful characters who, having been freed from him, can turn against him, as happens when the young man and the dark lady begin sexually to collude. The 'civil war', as Shakespeare calls it in 35, which rages within Sidney and within his sonnets, happens here between Shakespeare and his personae. The irony of that antagonism is that though he has created these people, who are parasites on his existence, he comes to be dependent on them, and they grudgingly keep him alive. Thus in 35, authorising the young man's trespass, he acknowledges himself an accessory to 'that sweet thief which sourly robs from me'. His renunciation of power over them entitles them to defraud or dismiss him. His very name—in the sonnets punning on will—issues such a permission by cajoling the lady in 136 to adopt him as her Will, to do with him whatever she likes. That is the titular invitation of the comedies: they, too, ask to be taken *As You Like It*, to have done to them *What You Will*. The dramatist cannot afford to pride himself on volition and intention. What he writes is changed at the whim of performers or spectators; his characters make themselves up as they go along in a series of inspired gratuitous acts. Though Will is Shakespeare's name, the will he refers to in sonnets 134–6 is mortgaged to or exercised by others. Thus his most personal intrusion into the sequence is another proviso for ensuring his impersonality and—since he himself has been rendered involuntary—his irresponsibility.

Love in the sonnets of Sidney and Spenser is an alias for poetry. Writing in Sidney is a formalising of emotion, in Spenser a sublimation of it. In Shakespeare's sonnets, writing about love is a cover for writing about drama, and about the dramatist's unrequited emotion for his characters. The sonnets recurrently complain about Shakespeare's absence from the beloved. In 44 he is persecuted by 'injurious distance', in 97 by a wintry separation, in 98 by a joylessly lonely spring. In 109 he roams 'the wide universe'. The poems are describing not an erotic crisis but a condition of the creative mind—the disconsolate departure of the dramatist, like god, from a nature he has created but can no longer govern. The absent god has endowed his characters with freedom, and must suffer them to use it, treacherously, against him. This is what Shakespeare means by 'the imprison'd absence of your liberty' or by

> Those petty wrongs that liberty commits
> When I am sometime absent from thy heart.

Yet while Sidney and Spenser use the structure of the sonnet to gain power over the object of their love—the power of words to possess her by repeating her name in Sidney, or to elevate her by renaming her in Spenser—Shakespeare's is a love which, perhaps remorsefully, unleashes its object: 'Be where you list' is his helpless gesture of acceptance in the fifty-eighth sonnet. He absconds from the poems in those self-effacing final couplets, and he allows those he loves to do the same. He is demonstrating within the sonnet one of those feats of spatial wizardry at which his dramatic characters are so expert, taking a compressed and incarcerating structure and elasticising it. In Hamlet's terms he is expanding the nutshell into a kingdom of infinite space; or, like Macbeth, he has taken a structure which cabins, cribs and confines him and made it 'as broad and general as the casing air'. The sonnet's form is now a case only as the air is in Macbeth's breath-taking phrase: an invisible sheath, not a deterministic cage.

Shakespeare has freed the sonnet from its self-enclosure and from his own emotions, leaving nothing more to be done with it. Donne's collection of love poems is called *Songs and Sonnets* for the simple reason that it contains neither. The regulatory forms have been broken, and emotions now must grow idiosyncratic, unrepeatable shapes of their own. An emotion which submits to the strait-jacket of a compulsory form must be already defunct, or be in need of ritualising.

The sonnet, therefore, after the sixteenth century, allies itself with the observances of mourning. Its terminal structure makes it seem funereal, as does its fragmentariness. It is a gravestone honouring an extinct feeling. Milton's great sonnets are about his loss of his sight, of his wife, of the slaughtered saints in Piedmont. The proper end of a sonnet is patient paralysis:

'They also serve who only stand and waite.' Funereal and fragmentary, the sonnet in Shelley's 'Ozymandias' is the inevitable memorial for the architectural wreckage in the desert. These shattered pillars are all that remains of Ozymandias's empire; the sonnet is the solitary remnant of the epic he intended as his commemoration. Its singleness is the final insult to his arrogance. The one small poem leads to nothing beyond itself; he has been denied the Elizabethan consolations of sequence and posterity. Those consolations exist in Wordsworth's series of *Ecclesiastical Sonnets*, narrating the history of Christianity in Britain, though for him, too, the sonnet is a legislative form, an entablature or an editorial, concise and authoritarian, the proper medium in which to moralise about the church's rites—baptism, visitation of the sick, commination. The sonnet has turned into a sermon. But despite its new monumentality, it is still aware of its momentariness. This was, to Wordsworth, its political efficacy: it took an instant and engraved it into permanence. The first of his 'Sonnets Dedicated to Liberty and Order' was 'Composed After Reading a Newspaper of the Day'. The paper lasts for a day; the sonnet, extracting a conservative wisdom from its reportage, will last forever. Wordsworth wrote a sonnet justifying sonnets in which the form's virtue is its usefulness as a public address system: in Milton's hands, he says, 'The Thing became a trumpet.'

The Elizabethan cycle has a revival among the Victorians, because it suits their necrophiliac romanticism. Dante Gabriel Rossetti, so reluctant to surrender his beloved Elizabeth Siddall to her grave, values the sonnet because it carves 'in ivory or in ebony' a

> Memorial from the Soul's eternity
> To one dead deathless hour,

and Elizabeth Barrett, debating in her *Sonnets from the Portuguese* (1850) whether she should burden Browning with her debilitated life, employs the sonnet as her own gravestone, building as she says of their first meeting 'Upon the event with marble' or likening herself to Electra tending her sepulchral urn. A change has of course overtaken the form. Its Elizabethan loquacity has been muted. In this new world of novelistic intimation and mental inwardness, the sonnet cannot argue or effuse or banter. 'All is said', says Mrs Browning, 'without a word', and the sonnets of Rossetti's *House of Life* (1868-9) transcribe the silence of understanding: Love

> . . . touched his lute wherein was audible
> The certain secret thing he had to tell,

and is attended by a 'dumb throng' of mourners, 'The shades of those our days that had no tongue.' For similar reasons, those internal divisions which the Elizabethans aggravate must be erased. The sonnet now encapsulates emotion rather than expelling it; the form can offer no hindrance to the feeling. In place of the analytic Elizabethan fission, Rossetti seeks fusion—severed selves are joined in love, individual existences melted down into a composite, and so must be the sonnet's separate parts. They make what Rossetti calls a 'blended likeness'. The sonnet's virtue is, for the Victorians, its indissolubility.

One Victorian sequence, however, retains the sonnet's Elizabethan obsession with the divisibility of and detachability from experience. This is George Meredith's *Modern Love* (1862). Although each of its fifty poems has sixteen lines, Meredith considers them to be sonnets. 'Lady,' the husband sarcastically remarks to his adulterous wife, 'this is my sonnet to your eyes.' The sonnet adapts itself to this account of the recriminatory end of a marriage because it is an inquisition of unwelcome emotion. In this sense, the husband is a Victorian Astrophel. The sonnet is pledged to the examination of its own interior, a structural cross-sectioning; that is also the psychological occupation of Meredith's interrogative, mutually suspicious pair:

> Then each applied to each that fatal knife,
> Deep questioning, which probes to endless dole.

As the sonnet remorselessly bares internal contradictions, so these people are 'betrayed by what is false within'. The formal construction of the sonnet corresponds to their thwarted solitary confinement in consciousness: 'self-caged Passion, from its prison-bars, / Is always watching ...'. Analysing feelings, the sonnet has dismissively shifted them into the past tense, not freeing them (as Shakespeare does, when he enables them to leave the poem and find new owners to belong to) but conducting autopsies on them, like Milton or Rossetti writing of dead loves. The sonnet to Meredith's couple is an empty reliquary, the symbol of what they once felt for each other. The poems abound in images of dead emotions, like Milton's ghosts or saints. In bed together, the pair resemble 'sculptured effigies ... / Upon their marriage-tomb'; the woman is a bodiless phantom, or a marmoreal statue of cold sedateness; between them they conceal a skeleton of guilty misgiving. This ghoulishness matches the elegiac past tense of their mood. They are gloomily shackled to 'the "What has been".' There is one moment of remission—a small inserted lyric about a happy, present instant, interpolated into the backward-and inward-looking sonnet:

> Love, that had robbed us of immortal things,
> This little moment mercifully gave,
> And still I see across the twilight wave
> The swan sail with her young beneath her wings.

But the intermission is temporary. Meredith accordingly revised 'And still I see' to 'Where I have seen', acknowledging that the lyric instant is extinct.

Modern Love modernises the sonnet by adapting it to the age of the novel.

When the wife rejects a French novel about adultery as unnatural, the husband upbraids her hypocrisy—

> . . . . these things are life:
> And life, some think, is worthy of the Muse.

From the novel, these sonnets have learned the art of psychological surmise. In a paraphrase of Sidney's eighth song, Meredith notes 'She will not speak. I will not ask.' They need not articulate; as a novelist he can guess at feelings and eavesdrop on silence. Meredith also brilliantly brings up to date the idea of the sequence by treating the sonnet as the journalism of passion. In the thirty-fourth poem the husband, saying nothing, reads the paper. He pretends to be interested in reports of Niagara and Vesuvius, yet interprets them as portents of marital crisis, 'the Deluge or else Fire!' When she begs for commiseration, he withholds it in a sour parody of Shakespeare's disappearance from the sonnet, leaving behind him a wise, all-purpose commonplaceness: 'With commonplace I freeze her.' The reading of the journal and of the French novel signal the sonnet's new functions—to catalogue and memorialise the instants as they elapse, as journalism with its built-in obsolescence does; to be the confessional of consciousness, as the novel is.

— 8 —

Spenser's Garden

Virginia Woolf's analogy of the seed-bed, wherein all English fiction is latent, would better have suited *The Faerie Queene* than *Arcadia*. It is a truly generative work, and like his own fertile Adonis Spenser is 'the Father of all formes'. His great paternal revelation is of the kinship of those forms: he discovers a relationship between such apparent opposites as epic, romance, pastoral and allegory; he is the benign inter-linker and melder of all stories, tracing their common derivation from the parental source of myth.

The Faerie Queene has an entire literature potentiating inside it. Spenser's trick is to suggest that he is merely summarily extracting from the multitude of events he might have recorded:

> Long so they travelled through wastefull wayes,
> Full many Countries they did ouerronne,
> From the vprising to the setting Sunne,
> And many hard adventures did atchieue; . . . .

He is deterred from all-inclusiveness only by a fear of the poem's possibly infinite length, and apologises that 'long were it to describe' the architecture of the castle Ioyeous or 'long worke it were, and needlesse' to give details of the entertainments there. But having begged leave for an omission, he goes on to give such details anyway. The world—by which he means his imagination, since he is inventing faeryland as he writes about it—is inexhaustible; only the transcribing hand suffers occasional fatigue. Thus he calls off the catalogue of sea-nymphs, pleading the tiredness of his Muse. But his relief is to begin another canto (the twelfth of Book IV), and having done so he finds himself reinvigorated, able to resume the enumeration of endlessness:

> O what an endlesse worke have I in hand,
> To count the seas abundant progeny, ...

He has an affectionate omniscience, and is sad to be unable to tell everyone's story simultaneously. His creative love wishes to be impartial, so that when he is required, in the eighth canto of Book III, to shift from Florimell, now suffering the versatile seductions of Proteus, back to Satyrane, he apologises to her

> It yrkes me, leaue thee in this wofull state,
> To tell of *Satyrane*, where I him left of late

and, to give her in compensation something to be going on with, reels off two extravagant stanzas of praise to her chastity. The element of fluster in that adjustment of the action is perfect for Spenser's persona: he is a slightly befuddled god, trying to cope with a world which is not doubly but multiply plotted, and anxious to reassure every creature under his care of his equal attention.

In all these ways, *The Faerie Queene* stands in contrast to the only other poem of its magnitude in our literature, *Paradise Lost*. The thronging liveliness of Spenser who, like Adonis, 'liuing giues to all', engenders a glad democracy of narrative. Everything alive will sooner or later tell its story, the plants and the elements included. Instead of this creative allowance and abundance, Milton's defining gestures are of denial, and his summaries are deathly. The world's prattling stories are fictions or lies. Recounting the fable of Mulciber's fall to earth onto Lemnos, he savagely cancels it across a scything enjambment:

> . . . . thus they relate,
> Erring; . . . .

The Faerie Queene wants a whole literature to issue from it. *Paradise Lost*, sternly correcting its own literary past and predetermining its own literary future, begets reduced, shame-faced epilogues or defensive parodies. If the poet who comes after *Paradise Lost* wishes to salvage a creative freedom it begrudges him, his only option is the rejection of Milton. But even this is a choice foreseen by the poem: its romantic subverters sentence themselves to continue living inside it, for they have cast themselves as its Satan. Spenser hospitably assumes that we are all living at our ease inside his capacious, hospitable fantasy, and after describing the rocky lair of Merlin he offers touristic advice to the reader:

> And if thou euer happen that same way
> To trauell, goe to see that dreadfull place.

Or he can colaterally attach contemporary life to his ancient fantasy, advising the monarch that he has chosen to consider her a descendant of his Britomart:

> . . . thee, O Queene, the matter of my song,
> Whose lignage from this Lady I deriue along.

Residence in Spenser's poem is, he assumes, the native desire of all creatures, since all have been born from it; Milton's great poem is, on the contrary, a prison from which literary history has ever since been trying to escape.

Spenser's stanzas seem never able to encompass the plenitude they hanker after. There is always an overspill from what he calls 'this so narrow verse'. The long final line is the stanza's plump distension of itself, often sounding slumbrously replete. 'So huge their numbers, and so numberlesse their nation' he says of the spawning waters. (Contrast the 'numbers numberless' of troops futilely paraded by Satan in *Paradise Regain'd*: innumerable and unworthy the enumeration; language again censors its own plenitude.) Each line of Milton's blank verse, on the other hand, resounds with the imminence of an ending. His line-ends are abrupt curtailments, like a guillotine's blade; or else they open gulfs of perdition between one verse and the next, like that into which Adam's wreath tumbles when Eve returns with the news that she has consumed the apple:

> From his slack hand the Garland wreath'd for *Eve*
> Down dropd, and all the faded Roses shed.

This difference in versifying corresponds to a different theory of language. Milton virtually considers the language in which he writes a polluted heritage of original sin. His classical etymologies—'erring' in the anecdote of Mulciber, or the 'mazie error' of the stream through paradise—are accusations of words, extorting from them a confession of guilt; their descent from Latin is a small linguistic lapse, a verbal recapitulation of the fall. But an etymology in Spenser serves to establish a divinity in nature, and restores to words the lost grace of their birthright. Amoret's twin sister is called Belphoebe—'as faire as *Phoebus* sunne', Spenser explains. She is named in homage to a spirit in which she shares, so that when Spenser next, with an apparently conventional phrase, mythologises the dawn—

> The morow next, so soone as *Phoebus* Lamp
> Bewrayed had the world with early light,

—Belphoebe, who is the sun's daughter (for its rays immaculately impregnated her mother Chrysogonee), is sensed there as Phoebus's etymological offspring, making the sun at once a spirit and a character. Spenser feels language to be biologically profuse and genial. He 'writ no language' because he was making one up, inventing words as a gift to created things and unable to deter his words from themselves coupling. His repetition of epithets in the Garden of Adonis is language's imitation of the fecundity it finds there:

> Old *Genius* the porter of them was,
> Old *Genius*, the which a double nature has . . . .;

hence, too, the doubled and reborn Amaranthus, or the multiplying in the account of Cupid's consort and her offspring:

> And his true loue faire *Psyche* with him playes,
> Fair *Psyche* to him lately reconcyld, . . .
> She with him liues, and hath him borne a chyld,
> *Pleasure*, that doth both gods and men aggrate,
> *Pleasure*, the daughter of *Cupid* and *Psyche* late.

Psyche has to be named twice in honour of their reunion, Pleasure has to be named twice because it is the dual possession of gods and men, and also the dualistic merging of its parents. This is language's blithe and unembarrassed self-reproduction. Spenser is Miltonically alert to the dangers in language. The lyric sung in Acrasia's bower ('So passeth, in the passing of a day') betrays itself by a punning slither from efflorescence to defloration when it encourages Guyon to

> Gather therefore the Rose, whilest yet is prime,
> For soone comes age, that will her pride deflowre.

and Guyon combats the mellifluous enchantment by a stern denial of lyricism: the stanza which describes his destruction of the Bower lamely makes its rhymes from feminine endings, refusing the special pleadings of poetry—

> . . . all those pleasant bowres and Pallace braue,
> *Guyon* broke downe with rigour pittilesse;
> Ne ought their goodly workmanship might saue
> Them from the tempest of his wrathfulnesse,
> But that their blisse he turn'd to balefulnesse:
> Their groues he feld, their gardins did deface,
> Their arbers spoyle, their Cabinets suppresse.

This is the poem's one case of linguistic apostasy. For the most part, Spenser's language is a life-giving agency. Even metaphor—in most poets a rescinding of the material existence of things and a verbal illusionism: 'Hail to thee, blithe Spirit! Bird thou never wert'—in Spenser confers solidity and a sometimes comical human truth on moral crises. For instance the simile of the happy landfall made by rejoicing mariners, used to dramatise Una's mistaken joy at finding the Red Crosse Knight (actually Archimago), and its pair, the comparison of Archimago's glee with the merchant's pleasure at the homecoming of his commercial argosy. These metaphors are more real and actual than the moral states they elucidate: a means of anchorage on earth. It is in such associative asides that the protagonists of allegory become characters— the starchy maiden Una shares the boisterous jollity of the sailors, and the sorcerer Archimago smirkingly calculates his spell as an investment which has paid off.

Spenserian allegory is in fact metaphor in motion. It materialises and vivifies words as things, or people. In coiling reptilian Error or preening Pride or in the troops of debilitated erotic symptoms exhibited by Cupid's masque in the house of Busirayne, abstract nouns take on flesh, and with it acquire both the volatility of verbs and the variegated personality of adjectives. Language, in personification, has come alive. It is this which Milton must prevent: his error is an abstract mental condition, misunderstood if used to describe the picturesque divagation of a stream; Spenser's Error is a mobile and (as always in Spenser) rampantly productive character, spewing up books and papers which are her monstrous, wriggling, inky brood. Spenserian allegory celebrates a magic potency in words: parts of speech become organs of generation. Error is a noun set verbally and adjectivally into action. The adjective has been pitied by Roland Barthes as the poorest species of word, a feeble parasite on substantives. But J. R. R. Tolkien, writing in 1938 about fairy stories, calls the adjective a spell, and the instigator of a mythic grammar. A mind which ventures to identify qualities in objects can interchange those qualities and alchemically transform those objects into one another: metaphor is a nascent yearning for metamorphosis. Thus George Puttenham in 1589 called allegory 'translative speech'. This eerie verbal transformation can be studied in the decline of Malbecco who, when his wife cuckolds him with a tribe of satyrs, sickens into an allegory, a morbid feeder on the gall and poison of his humiliation. Eventually in his deformity he forgets 'he·was a man, and Gealosie is hight'. The jealous man becomes Jealousy. Rather than having symbolism thrust upon them, Spenser's characters grow into symbols according to the lineal logic of their passions, and Malbecco's vice, like everything in Spenser, has its own genealogy, perversely nurtured in her breast by Proserpine 'and fostred vp with bitter milke of tine'.

The contriving of family trees for words and for emotions is an obsession in *The Faerie Queene*, and a sign of Spenser's concern for the relatedness of phenomena. All the words in a language are akin if they are traced back to their roots; all men in the beginning had the same ancestor; and all stories likewise are reconciled and reunited in the myths from which they fan out. Myth in Spenser is a genetic code, a fathering form like his Adonis; it germinates the long sequences of history and the jabbering polyphony of stories, all clamouring (as he acknowledges in that desertion of Florimell for Satyrane) to be told at once, like the 'thousand thousand naked babes' thronging at the doors guarded by Genius, demanding 'that he with fleshly weedes would them attire'. Myth's authorship of history is accredited in the chronicle of British kings and elfin emperors in Book II. Guyon reads of them in a book at the house of Alma: their record derives from imagination, and the book impartially recounts historical battles and mythic marvels, like Spenser's eclectic nomination of Prometheus as the progenitor of Faeryland, cross-fertilising classical myth with local English fable. Prometheus's first manikin breeds with a Fay he encounters in the Garden of Adonis, 'Of whom all *Faeryes* spring, and fetch their lignage right.' Prometheus's creative effort—or in Tolkien's terms his sub-creative one, since he has invented an alternative or secondary world, at an angle to the one authored by Jove or the God of Genesis—is solemnised by Spenser's forging of an etymology. 'That man so made, he called *Elfe*, to weet / Quick'—a neat case of the Tolkienian adjectival magic, except that elf is an offshoot of an Old English word, and a relative of the German *alp* for nightmare; but the lexicographic bluff is necessary because to Spenser, himself a Prometheus, the act of creation is linguistic. Prometheus with his homunculus 'stole fire from heauen, to animate / His worke'. The Spenserian animation or gift of life is that quickening adjective, promoted to a naming noun.

Though Spenser slights his poem in comparison with Guyon's annals—

> . . . .it was a great
> And ample volume, that doth far excead
> My leasure, so long leaues here to repeat—

The Faerie Queene is modelled on that archive, and on its synchronism of myth and history. At one point in the register of kings, myth intersects with history as eternity announces itself in time. During the reign of Kimbeline (Shakespeare's Cymbeline) Christ

> . . . . in fleshly slime
> Enwombed was, from wretched *Adams* line
> To purge away the gilt of sinfull crime.

All of Spenser's monarchs are historical characters legitimising themselves by a resort to myth. Specifically they assert their right to govern by claiming descent from Brutus, whose 'sacred progenie' rules the kingdom for seven hundred years. Within history, time eternalises itself—as Spenser's narrative does—by automatic self-prolonging. The land is dynastically passed down through successive generations. This orderly numerical sequence disciplines the liveliness which makes those thousand thousand babes demand incarnation from Genius: Morindus leaves 'fiue sonnes begotten of one wife', each of whom reigns in turn, after which

> Then all the sonnes of these fiue brethren raynd
> By dew successe, and all their Nephewes late,
> Even thrise eleuen descents the crowne retaynd,
> Till aged *Hely* by dew heritage it gaynd.

This is biology as a serene and inexhaustible arithmetic.

Enrolled in the catalogue is Shakespeare's Lear (Leyr to Spenser), whose tragic handicap—in this estimation—is his failure to make provision for primogeniture. Without a male heir to follow him, he is obliged to divide his realm between his three daughters. The episode has significance for Spenser as a fable about inheritance and implantation. The daughters have been trained 'in all that seemed fit for kingly seed', and Lear's test of their affection, in Shakespeare a querulous and desperate exaction, has an almost religious seriousness. If they are to rule, they must possess a holy respect for the past, of which they are—for the time being only, since as Spenser tersely notes of a successor of theirs, '*Donwallo* dyde (for what may liue for ay?)'—the legatees and trustees. Lear, sensing the imminence of his own end, inquires 'which of them most did loue her parentage' because that, in Spenser's poem, is the most important of all moral and political questions. The end of the episode as Spenser relates it is not tragic death, as in Shakespeare, but the divinely comic re-establishment of succession. Cordelia makes war on her sisters and restores to her father the crown they have confiscated,

> In which he dyde, made ripe for death by eld,
> And after wild, it should to her remaine.

The resumption of succession also pastorally ensures that the kingdom will be free from politics, and Spenser's great compliments are that 'Leyr in happie peace long raind' or that Cordelia 'peacably the same long time did weld': the pastoral vision is after all about the earth's seasonal regeneration of itself, and Spenser wants politics to defer to the rhythms of natural, self-replenishing process. His theory is summed up in an apparently innocuous couplet about Aruirage, who has performed the great Spenserian and pastoral task of making peace with Rome ('So all was pacifide'):

> He dyde; and him succeeded *Marius*,
> Who ioyd his dayes in great tranquillity.

Happy kingdoms, like happy families, are those in which, as Spenser sees it, there are no stories to be told.

Everywhere in *The Faerie Queene* procreation and nascence are lauded, and they are indeed the structural principles of the poem. It exists in a continual state of becoming. When Britomart's fantasy lover Artegall is praised by Redcrosse, the words are to her as enlivening as a conception, and she locks them up within herself as lovingly as the mother

> . . . . that nine monethes did beare,
> In the deare closet of her painefull side,
> Her tender babe.

That metaphor is to be willed into fertile actuality when Artegall appears, for from his union with Britomart will be born 'a famous Progenie' of rulers. Spenser treats the allegorical derivation of moral meanings, and the etymological unfolding of verbal meanings, as matters analogous with insemination and parturition. Thus to demonstrate that chastity need not exclude sexual fulfillment he twins Belphoebe and Amoret within the virgin womb of Chrysogonee; and in Book IV Agape delivers herself of emblematic triplets in the mutually complementary Priamond, Triamond and Diamond.

Symbols are not made but grown in Spenser. Allegory, mobilising metaphor as Prometheus instils life into his elf, is akin to human reproduction and also to horticulture, for flowers are the metamorphoses of human existences, people preserved as metaphors. When Venus, in one of the tapestries at Malecasta's castle, sees that the gored Adonis is beyond her aid, she achieves his transmigration into allegory:

> Him to a dainty flowre she did transmew,
> Which in that cloth was wrought, as if it liuely grew,

and Busirayne's arras, describing the shape-changing ubiquity of the lustful Jove, represents two of his victims who are vouchsafed a floral after-life. Hyacint and Coronis

> .... are of thy haplesse hand extinct,
> Yet both in flowres do liue, and loue thee beare,
> The one a Paunce, the other a sweet breare.

The polymorphousness of Jove, who alters his physical form to speed his sexual conquests, restlessly parodies the mutation into symbol which creates Spenserian allegory. The same slippery dodging in and out of a body is practised by Proteus, transforming himself to terrorise Florimell, or by Cupid, 'disguiz'd in thousand shapes, that none might him bewray'. Theirs is a sterile or at least dubious metamorphosing, the monstrous birth of spawning simulacrae; their existences are phantasmagorical. Against the incapacity to rest in a single form, Spenser's poem proposes a return of all thriving forms to the parent form which they have separated, a resolution of the many into the engendering one. His imagination is as bountiful as Shakespeare's, but it works in an opposite way. The Shakespearean irradiation of the one into the freed, uncontrollable many—those 'millions of strange shadows'—makes all his characters different from one another; instead of this pluralism, all Spenser's characters genetically overlap like siblings, and yearn for reunion with each other. The gemini Belphoebe and Amoret are comprised within Britomart, who possesses both the chaste dedication of the one and the sensual fire of the other, and she in turn is reprised in the person of the virginal Queen Elizabeth I.

This enfolding of existences in one another, leading back to a lost ovular unity, explains why there are so many images of sexual merger in the poem. The most divisive duality to be overcome is that between the sexes, which were once (in Plato's fable) the complementary yoke and white of a single egg. Within the pluralist universe of Shakespeare, where individualism is the dramatic duty of character, a sexual interchangeability is sinister (in the case of 'the master-mistress of my passion' in the sonnets) or at least mystically perturbing and emotionally confusing (as is the appearance of Viola's twin Sebastian in *Twelfth Night*). But for Spenser it is a sought-for exit from the alienated and subtracted identity of human character, since in becoming one thing we have separated ourselves from all the other things we might have been. His deities are therefore always androgynous. Venus suspects that Cupid may be camouflaging himself as one of Diana's attendant nymphs, 'for he is faire and fresh in face and guize'; Venus herself, when her temple is deciphered in Book IV, has her genital organs arcanely screened because she too, Spenser says,

> hath both kinds in one,
> Both male and female, both vnder one name:
> She syre and mother is her self alone,
> Begets and eke conceiues, ne needeth other none

which with its flurry of boths and its triple negatives is charmingly over-explicit about something which is a priestly mystery, the most obscure of all dark conceits; and Nature in Book VI temporises between male and female behind her veil. The nearest approach for human beings to such a commuting between genders is transvestism, as when the helmeted and hardy Britomart disarms and releases her golden hair and the frock which she tucks up for riding. The two sexes exist in equipoise in Britomart, who is

> . . . . full of amiable grace,
> And manly terrour mixed therewithall,
> That as the one stird vp affections bace,
> So th' other did mens rash desires apall.

Male and female here confront each other in a stand-off of balanced power, with female arousal checked by male intimidation. Book III ends with Britomart imaginatively overcoming this prudent self-division when she witnesses the reunion, made possible by her, of Amoret and Scudamor. Here a sexual fulfillment is described by Spenser not as androgyny but as hermaphroditism, a floral self-pollenating (which explains Spenser's fascination with and envy of flowers, for like his Venus they have both kinds in one):

> Had ye them seene, ye would haue surely thought,
> That they had beene that faire *Hermaphrodite*,
> Which that rich *Romane* of white marble wrought.

Two have grown together into one: the highest Spenserian bliss. Of this there is a devilish parody—like the infernally trinitarian ménage of Sin, Death and Satan in *Paradise Lost*—in the womb of the earth, on whom Typhoeus incestuously begets a pair of twins, the giants Argante and Ollyphant. They, while still embryos, sexually commingled. Spenser denounces their crime as a lecherous cannibalism: Argante foully devours 'her natiue flesh'. But that is a taboo arbitrarily inserted to censure the workings of the poem's dominant literary ambition—the reconvergence of disseuered selves, a compounding of persons.

Spenser contrives to find the same patterns of kinship between the narratives he interconnects with each other. The elderly Malbecco deprives Hellenore of 'kindly joy', which refers not merely to the satiation she finds among the satyrs but to kindliness and kinship, the solaces of nature; he sins against the imperative of the poem when he 'in close bowre her mewes from all mens sight'. Hellenore pines for commonality, union with and, beyond this, metamorphosis into others. The satyrs welcome her into their pastoral society and gratify her with their rude communism. She milks their goats, makes their cheese, 'and euery one as commune good her handeled'. For this reason her refusal to be rescued is a decision of a different moral status from Grill's bestial desire in Book II to remain one of Acrasia's hogs. The 'iolly *Satyres*' offer her the solace of physical incorporation into others.

The conviction that people need to be akin, to be mated or related to each other, also governs Spenser's management of his poetic structure. His apparent eclecticism is controlled by a disclosure of kinship between unlike stories. The sordid *fabliau* of Malbecco's cuckolding is familially descended from the epic which lies behind the poem, because it is a parodic diminutive of that action, with Paridell a libertine Paris and Hellenore a seamy Helen; and in turn that epic of Trojan siege is lineally connected with the ancient British history which is the poem's immediate past, because, as Guyon learns during his course of study in the house of Temperance, London (or the town built by Lud) is Troynovaunt (or a renovation of toppled Troy). The plots in Book VI are increasingly concerned with parentage, as if to prove the common derivation of all stories from a parental myth or archetype: Calepine's vexation with the baby he saves from the bear and his relieved transfer of it to Matilda, who happens desperately to want a child; Calidore's restoration of Aladine and Priscilla to their respective parents; the rosy birthmark on Pastorella's breast which reunites her with her family; the secretly noble origins of Sir Tristram and the salvage man. The means of amalgam between people and between stories is comedy, with its happy unreality. Those family reunions are all the more benign for their improbability: they are comedy's tender wish for us. Comedy, too, is the agent which creates a loving amity between all the poem's characters by narrowing the distance between gods and men. Long before the mockery of terrorised Jove and termagant Mutabilitie in Book VII, Venus and Diana have been comically rendered human. Diana is haughtily and frigidly sarcastic about the straying of Cupid, while Venus, cosily justifying her own glut of sensual knowledge, takes care to mollify the possibly envious virgin and her nymphs. Despite their differences of vocation, they are after all, as Venus reminds her, sisters.

Structurally the poem insists that there is a unity in its haphazard multiplicity: the same oneness which joins the family of man, and which sees through this succession of anecdotes to a communal mythic source. Spenser has taken an anthology of stories even more miscellaneous than the *Canterbury Tales* and persuaded them into conciliation. The poem's humorous analogy for the concord of histories within myth is cooking. Random ingredients are blended, mashed and, as in a melting pot, dissolved into a composite. Myth is made in the same way as Glauce's potion, meant to assuage Britomart's love-sickness. She

> ... gathered Rew, and Sauine, and the flowre
> Of *Camphora*, and Calamint, and Dill,
> All which she in a earthen Pot did poure,
> And to the brim with Colt wood did it fill,
> And many drops of milke and bloud through it did spill.

Glauce's primitive pharmacology doubles as a poetic theory: like her, Spenser arrives at truth by fomenting a rich confusion, and trusting that the unlike quantities he mixes will find a common denominator. Belphoebe, too, does some rustic cooking to heal Timias's wound, gathering a 'soueraigne weede'—which Spenser variously identifies as 'divine *Tobacco* ..., / Or *Panachoea*, or *Polygony*'—and pounding it between two marbles until she has a bruised essence with which she anoints the lesion. Her herbal lore, transmuting a substance from weed into medicine, works like alchemy, as Spenser's mythic writing also does. Spenser includes a demonic counterpart to this salving cookery, when the Witch confects a glacé double for Florimell, using 'snowe in massie mould congeald' for the bodily framework, tempering it with mercury and wax and mingling with them vermilion for a cosmetically sanguine tint, then twining golden wire to serve as a coiffure. What distinguishes her work from the culinary arts of Glauce, Belphoebe and Spenser is its fancifulness and its expense. Her ingredients are recondite—purest snow gathered on the Riphoean hills, fine mercury, virgin wax, perfect vermily—while theirs are rudely natural. She is making not a myth but a machine, with a ghost inside it to simulate life. She employs one spirit to rotate the lamps which counterfeit eyes, and another 'in the stead / Of life, ... to rule the carkasse dead'. The Spenserian ingredients cohere and congeal by happy accident; the witch's, in a parody of mythic creativity as sinister as Frankenstein's, are scientifically manacled into place.

Spenser's poem is haunted by duplicity, and by the duplication which will later in literature pass—as in the Witch's manufacture of an alternative Florimell—for realism. His own aim is multiplicity, the freedom to mean and be several things simultaneously, possessed by the characters of Renaissance pictures, who vacillate between classical mystery and Christian exegesis and might make themselves at home in any mythological system. The art historian Edgar Wind, x-raying Giorgione's 'Tempesta', found the remnants of a Gothic and chivalric narrative on top of which the painter had added a landscape of classical pastoral. Spenser's poem has the same palimpsest-like complexity, which is why it mistrusts the mere duality of realism. The evil magi of *The Faerie Queene* have undergone a schizophrenic self-division. They are models of neurotic duality: Ate with her split tongue, both parts of which speak and disagree with each other, Doubt with his two faces. In contrast with this fission, those in Spenser who are good long for the re-encounter of sundered pairs, and for the consolidation of a multiple existence: the twinned couples on the mound of Venus are all emanations from Venus and Adonis, who are themselves the two potentialities of a single existence; the hermaphroditic wedding of Scudamor and Amoret; the poem's constant metamorphosing of one thing into many others.

This is why *The Faerie Queene* is much more than an allegory. For allegory speaks, like Ate, with a forked tongue, saying one thing and meaning other. It is a device inured to dualism, convinced—as Langland and Bunyan both are—of the irreconcilability of spirit and fallen, written letter. Spenser's linguistic ideal is to say many things at once, in a Protean speech lost to us since Babel. He wants to create a confluence of languages, a watery merging, in contrast with Milton's censorious Latinate purging of the tribal dialect. Ben Jonson, criticising him for writing no language in particular, was confirming that he wrote multilingually. Reaching the poem's great mythic watershed, the convergence of Thames and Medway, Spenser laments his inability to describe the fluid revelry:

> All which not if an hundred tongues to tell,
> And hundred mouthes, and voice of brasse I had,
> And endlesse memorie, that mote excell,
> In order as they came, could I recount them well.

Yet he does acquire the capacities he says he lacks. He has more tongues and mouths than Shakespeare's prattling Rumour. Shakespearean narrative is content with a double plot; Spenser here and elsewhere in the poem copes with tributary thousands. And the source from which all these freshets and associative streams well is indeed an 'endlesse memorie'. Spenser is telling the story of all things alive, and remembering for us both our dreams and the pre-existence to which those fantasies piningly refer. All his rivers flow out of that inspiriting inland ocean which Wordsworth drily recollects in his 'Immortality Ode'. Hence his deserved election as the poet's poet, or the prince of poets. *The Faerie Queene* is a poem in praise of a sometimes anarchic creativity, both linguistic and biological; a home-made myth.

Myth by its very nature instigates a perpetual re-creation. Keats, for instance, wants to be Spenser reborn, begins his poetic career with a loving pastiche of *The Faerie Queene*, and after the Miltonic labour of *Hyperion* pauses to add a stanza to the close of Spenser's Book V, Canto II. That small interpolation describes a mythic rebirth which has been mechanised by literature. Spenser's giant is resurrected by a Gutenbergian sage called Typographus, who refits his mangled limbs and trains him for a career of godly endeavours by making him 'read in many a learned book'. The nursery of Spenser's Genius is now a fount of type, and print qualifies as eugenics. Literature renovates life, as the Keatsian wise man does, in its own image. This is the magic use Keats makes of Spenser in his initial 'Imitation'. He describes a paradise where things can admire their own reflections, and study to measure up to their ideal selves (as Keats is himself humbly practising to be worthy of his own better self, who is Spenser): his crystalline lake is poetry, reflecting 'woven bowers' and 'a sky that never lowers'; in its mirror the kingfisher and the swan see brilliant or majestic facsimiles of themselves, images which are their immortalisation as art. As the lake reflects the sky, so the sky reflects the idyllic island set in the lake. It looks, Keats says, 'as when on high, / Through clouds of fleecy white, laughs the cœrulean sky'. He is claiming for literature—and for Spenser in particular—the life-giving power possessed by Spenser's Venus, who in *Endymion* returns to revivify Adonis.

The cyclical existence of Adonis, dying each winter to germinate again each spring, stands for the mythological potency of literature, quickening the worn-out types and tropes it inherits, bestowing on them new leases of life. A poem for the Elizabethans has a literal power to infuse vitality, to rejuvenate the world. This is Shakespeare's gift in the sonnets, and Spenser's in the *Epithalamion*. The young man's duty to breed is replicated by Shakespeare's duty to write. Both are modes of perpetuation. The lusty goddess in Shakespeare's *Venus and Adonis* exemplifies this renewal. She is the romantic activation of a classical gene; panting, sweating, amorously wrestling and plucking Adonis from his horse, Venus represents the fecundity of imagination, the energetic bounty of language. Thanks to her, a verbal conjugation is as much a symbol of increase as copulation: 'She's Love, she loves, and yet she is not lov'd.' With an abundance like hers or like that of Spenser's Nature, poetry revitalises nature by the violent injection of metaphor, as when Adonis's horse romps free:

> The bearing earth with his hard hoof he wounds,
> Whose hollow womb resounds like heaven's thunder.

Metaphor not only makes a body of earth but makes a character of the horse. Trampling a womb, it anticipates Coriolanus's punishment of the maternal soil guarded by Volumnia. Even when words are not deployed, physique and gesture are silently eloquent. Acting is action, the collision of bodies not the exchange of speeches, and Shakespeare sees the quarrel between Venus and Adonis as a 'dumb play', uproarious in its muteness.

Mythology generates literature, just as classical culture prompts its own rebirth as the Renaissance. The sponsors of both processes are the gods of procreation, Venus and Adonis. Their joy in increase begets a playful numerosity in literature, which tries to enumerate their innumerable offspring. Mythology is a multiplication table: Adonis therefore imagines Venus possessing 'twenty thousand tongues' (beside which, the quota Spenser requests seems modest); she is borne 'a thousand ways' by 'a thousand spleens'; and for her, echoes are not a word's dying fall, as in the modern elegiac lyricism of Tennyson where the echo is a way-stage between language and deathly silence, but its endless self-magnifying—the caves 'make verbal repetition of her moans', redoubling her passion as they repeat her words, so that

> 'Ay me!' she cries, and twenty times 'Woe, woe!'
> And twenty echoes twenty times cry so.

The bestowal of divinity and immortality in Drayton's 1595 poem *Endimion and Phoebe* is an induction into this schematic heaven of self-adding, self-multiplying numbers. When Phoebe rides in triumph, she permits only the third and ninth of the muses to attend on her, because

> . . . being odd [they] include an unity,
> Into which number all things fitly fall,
> And therefore named Theologicall.

Gawain's pentangle has become a device for playing games of computation, as Drayton does when he extols the fractionalising of hierarchies in thirds as 'the perfect forme of true triplicity'. Spenser's *Epithalamion* has been read as a numerological toy, exactly calculating the proportions of its lines and stanzas in order to summarise inside the poem the balanced equations of planetary and human time which preside over the human coupling and regeneration; if so, the *Epithalamion* is a biological clock, organised (at the behest of Venus) for its own potentially infinite reproduction.

The nineteenth-century romantics adored Spenser because of the unbridled creativity they sensed in him. In 1820 Shelley paid tribute to Spenser in inventing the Witch of Atlas. She practises an arcane numerology, weaving a veil from three threads of fleecy mist and three lines of light, marshalling 'million after million' clouds, superintending the 'many thousand schemes' of lovers. She can reproduce herself in fancy, and fashions an hermaphroditic *imago* from a kneaded blend of fire and snow; more than this, she is a pranksome Venus, busy at the poetic work Coleridge called esemplastic, which Shelley interprets as a melding of bodies. She brings together yearning lovers 'in marriage warm and kind', and reunites dissevered friends. She is what Chaucer or Spenser would call Dame Kind, who, instead of presiding over a barnyard parliament or a harvest festival, disports herself in the upper air. She is imagination romantically, in James's phrase, liberating experience.

Her gleeful games could not long continue. She herself, though a liberator, suffered capture. Imitating Spenser, romantic art exchanges the volatility and growthfulness of narrative for the stasis of the picture, where because nothing is alive nothing can change: when Adonis appears in Keats's *Endymion*, he is embowered in a painting, framed, saved (like the 'thing of beauty') from fruition and decay—

> . . . . safe in the privacy
> Of this still region all his winter-sleep.

Shakespeare's Venus, by contrast, derides her Adonis for a pictorial immovability which she, for whom life lies in energy and sexual combat, can only perceive as sterile:

> 'Fie, lifeless picture, cold and senseless stone,
> Well-painted idol, image dull and dead. . . !'

She cannot forgive him for 'contenting but the eye alone'. For Keats, that is all art is capable of contenting, and Spenser is therefore elected—as he had already been by Pope—a painterly poet. Drayton's Endimion undergoes deification when he yields to the goddess; the Endymion of Keats, rather than being enthroned, shares the fate of the romantic symbol and, like Madeline, Porphyro and the nightingale, simply vaporises:

> Before three swiftest kisses he had told,
> They vanish'd far away!

Enumeration, in those three kisses or in the four kisses the Knight gives to the *belle dame sans merci*, no longer rehearses infinitude, as in the Renaissance poems. On the contrary, it is the countdown to a disappearance or a small death. Romanticism coincides with realism, which sees the world as a place of dualism and duplicity, the realm of Spenser's Duessa. In place of Drayton's sacred triplicity there is the hypocritical manipulation of surfaces by Anthony Trollope's Julia Triplex in *The Way We Live Now*, whose married name is Lady Monogram.

Since Adonis is the godly eternality of poetry, there is a sad irony to Shelley's casting of Keats in that role in the poem he wrote in 1821 to lament his death. In 'Adonais' the classical mythology first resuscitated in the Renaissance undergoes a second romantic return. The boar which killed the hero is barbed, skulking, piggish criticism; Urania, no eager wooer now, is a grieving mother. Though the circuit of 'the revolving year' repeats itself as before, it cannot bring Adonais back to life, and Shelley can only congratulate Keats on his good fortune in having quit so unworthy a world. Even when attending to one of its own, literature finds it has forfeited the mythological bounty it possessed in Spenser. His classicism is an implantation of self-seeding forms, a garden of Adonis where types like the existences cared for by Genius replenish and reproduce themselves for ever; the classicism of the later romantic poets is a museum of sculptural fragments, stonily idealised in death—no garden but a graveyard of art, housing those Elgin marbles which Keats, when he first saw them, interpreted as portents of his own extinction:

> My spirit is too weak—mortality
> Weighs heavily on me like unwilling sleep,
> And each imagin'd pinnacle and steep
> Of godlike hardship tells me I must die.

Miracles, Moralities and Marlowe

Consecrating a circle, the drama stages a rite within it. Dramatic representation begins in England as a humble and naive reincarnation of the initial Christian incarnation, a miming of mystery. The miracle in these fourteenth-century plays is the advent, but also the enactment of it. The theatre is already excitedly aware of its tendency to profanation. Medieval drama emerges from the daily celebration of the mass, to which drama returns in Eliot's *Murder in the Cathedral*. Like Chaucer experientially modifying authority, the drama can develop only by varying, perhaps parodying, the church service lying behind it. The incarnation was a single, unrepeatable, magical interruption of normality; the theatre can better that in the infinite sequence of reincarnations which are its performances. The divine comedy is duplicated—and upstaged—by the impertinences of a human comedy.

This is how the double plot, the quizzical core of Shakespearean drama, originates. In the *Secunda Pastorum*, the shepherd's play from the Wakefield mystery cycle in the early fifteenth century, the presence of this duality warns of the impiety implicit in dramatic re-enactment: it is a kidnapping of divinity, the miracle recast as a stunt or a joke. Mak the sheep-stealer wraps the lamb in swaddling clothes and mockingly imitates the cradling of the infant Christ in the manger at Bethlehem. He is the link between the insurgency of the Wife of Bath or the Pardoner and the comedians in Shakespeare who seize on the pastoral cellarage of the double plot as their home, and conduct from there a campaign against tragedy: Falstaff among the farmers, Hamlet communing with Yorick in the earth, Cleopatra nursing the worm.

The defiance or deviance of comedy in the *Secunda Pastorum* uses the play to upset a social order, and also the order of scriptural pre-emption. Coll grumbles at the oppression the shepherds suffer from their genteel landlords. His discontent is the spirit's rebellion against the pettifogging letter, and he says of the officers deputed by the lords that no one can believe a word they say, 'No letter'. The impish, misbehaving spirit of the theatre animates Mak, who is forever devising parodies of literal normality. Gib says to him, 'Mak, the dewill in your ee!', but the devil—in the form of a disrespectful antic disposition—already inhabits him. Mak is an adept at that conjuration which is the theatre's black magic, the dark side of enlightening Christian miracle, and like Shakespeare's Puck he draws circles in the air to ensure that his colleagues will remain in a sleep, blinded and befuddled, until he has accomplished his larcenous business. He has mastered all the tricks of theatrical dissimulation and can phantasmally (as the other shepherds, terrified, marvel) change his appearance along with his voice. Gill, his wife, learns from him how to exploit the theatre's quick changes. When their theft is found out, she pretends that the lamb is their child who has been abducted by an elf and 'forshapyn'. She responds to Mak's theatrical direction with eagerness, offering to groan piteously while he sings a lullaby over their woolly new-born. Mak's plot, with its systematic travesty, as in a revue, of scripture, is an exercise in that risky hocus-pocus which, in our own time, Antonin Artaud has seen as the theatre's indigenous, defamatory brand of magic: its danger. Coll even opposes to the Christian promise of rebirth and renewal made at the nativity the skill in multiple resurrections deployed by the theatre—by Cleopatra dying a thousand times or Falstaff resuming the performance of his life after his supposed death at Shrewsbury. '*Resurrex a mortruus!*' he growls in mangled Latin when he wakes up, and he goes on to compound the theatrical blasphemy with another curse, '*Judas carnas dominus!*' The Lord, for the purposes of the theatre, can incarnate himself as Judas, or Judas play the Lord. It is no accident that Satan persuades Milton to write *Paradise Lost*, at first, as a drama.

Coll's ostentatiously awful Latin announces the play's linguistic version of the double plot. The comedians ape the sacred rite. They caricature deity, even threaten to cannibalise it. When Coll offers to imitate the angel's song of annunciation, Gib likens his crooning to a dog barking at the moon; Gill, in a more startlingly funny and outrageously premature anticipation of the mass, where Christ's body is symbolically consumed, volunteers as proof of her good faith to eat the child in her cradle. That massacre—the most dangerous (in Artaud's terms) initiative in the play—actually happens when Coll garbles the scriptural tags, or when the biblical edicts are corroded by rustic proverbs, which, as in Chaucer, are accretions of experience, not handed-down authority. When Mak tells Gill he has escaped, she says that the more often the pot goes to water, the surer that it will one day come home broken. As with the Wife of Bath, the proverb's morality is prudential, mean and lowly. Mak complicates this linguistic double plotting when he assumes a smart southern, urban accent to beguile the friends he is robbing and brandishes the elegant pronoun 'Ich' as he pretends to be a yeoman: as well as the parody of Latin by nonchalant misquotation and by the earthly vernacular, English itself is dialectally divided.

The play jests with its responsibility of figuration. Its disfiguring of scripture happens in tandem with an impatient, unhallowed prefiguring. Within the Wakefield cycle, it is a replay of that godly mystery which is repeated annually in the seasons of the church year, yet with an arch and perilous anachronism it claims to foreknow events and to be a rehearsal for them, long in advance of their proper and appointed time. This is the case with Gill's macabre communion. The shepherds, like her, are keen, before the nativity, to arrive at the crucifixion, and project themselves there in their oaths. Scripture might seem to have pre-empted their performance of it; Coll boasts, however, that the play is a self-fulfilling prophecy, since the patriarchs who foretold the coming of this child have been outdone by the shepherds who are the event's impertinent witnesses. 'They ar gone full clene', he says of his typological predecessors; 'That hauve thay lorne.' Prefiguring has already been supplanted by replaying. This is why their language looks ahead to a climax which they are restless to perform. Coll swears by the rood, Daw by Christ's cross, and Mak before ensorcelling the others sneers at them in a tag sacrilegiously appropriated from Luke's gospel: 'Manus tuas commendo, / Pontio Pilato'. When the awaited birth is at last signalled by the angel's hymn, it is almost an afterthought, for the comic playing of it has made it an anti-climax, and Gib in paying homage cannot conceal the fact that he is thinking of the next instalment, for in begging to drink of Christ's cup he is, like Gill with her savage meal, expecting the eucharist. The drama which emerges from the mass has, with a scurrilous confidence, absorbed that ceremony into its repertoire and, even before Tamburlaine and Faustus, has proposed the theatre as a sanctuary for blasphemers.

Mak understands that the essence of a play is playfulness—an unconstrained festivity, like that of Euripides's Dionysians, or Puck with his aphrodisiac spells in the nocturnal forest, or Sir Toby with his riots below stairs. The concurrent medieval dramatic form, the morality, is concerned less with games like Mak's than with perseverance and the moral agent's scrupulous consistency. Everyman—dating from about 1485, and possibly translated from a Dutch text—is about character in preparation for action. It has its own version of Aristotle's definition of drama. This is why it so impressed Shaw, who could not approve the irresponsibility of Mak or the Shakespearean clowns. In the preface to Man and Superman he pays its unknown author the highest of compliments, electing him to equality with Ibsen, or with himself: he 'was no mere artist, but an artist-philosopher'.

The philosophy of Everyman is the morality and the metaphysics of drama. It is as formally self-conscious as Hamlet, also preoccupied with the relation between improvised acting and purposeful action. It debars, for a start, the miscreant disfiguring which is the theatrical life of the Secunda Pastorum. The Messenger demands that his audience 'here this mater with reuerence, / By fygure a morale playe.' Matter should indoctrinate form, as in the Aristotelian science of nature and of literary genre. The first speech of the Messenger is, accordingly, about the moral meanings of dramatic form. The play is a deathly figment or fragment, like life: its brevity exemplifies 'how transytory we be all daye'. Drama is terminal with a vengeance. Aristotle demands its unification in time because it will then expose the crisis, or consequence, of action. Its denouement is the arbitration of a last judgement. The legalistic haste of the form supplies the Messenger with another of his moral principles. Because drama concerns what will happen, inevitably, 'in the ende', it should teach us to hearken to that end even in our beginnings. He redesigns the stage, for Mak a charmed circle within which tricks can be played, as a forum or a court, with auditors or jurors deciding on the fate of Everyman, who has been summoned to 'a generall rekenynge'. Thereafter, how many great theatrical scenes will be public prosecutions—Shylock's, Volpone's, or Vittoria's in *The White Devil*, the petty malefactions dealt with by Escalus in *Measure for Measure*; the trials of Gay's MacHeath in *The Beggar's Opera*, of Ibsen's enemy of the people, of Shaw's Saint Joan or his Dick Dudgeon in *The Devil's Disciple*; at last in 1964 the breakdown of John Osborne's barrister Bill Maitland, and with it the confounding of dramatic justice, in *Inadmissible Evidence*. The tribunal in *Everyman* is presided over by the dramatist's judicial self-image: God.

God sending Death on a mission to Everyman is the dramatist summoning his character for the trial of action. That character is generic, which is why he is called Everyman. Novels may study individual men, but the dramatic subject is man, under the aspect either of comedy or of tragedy. The ancient theatrical mask served to eliminate an irrelevant individuality. Even after they have become individuals, dramatic characters appeal to the generality of Everyman—Lear to 'man's life', Shylock to his 'hands, organs, dimensions, senses, affections, passions'. Death's interrogation of Everyman, when he demands where Everyman is going and whether he has forgotten his maker, asks the metaphysical questions which are the substance of drama, here as in *Hamlet* or in Beckett's *Waiting for Godot*: What is our purpose? Why do we imagine our business to be so important? Are we free? Who is our author?

Called to a reckoning, Everyman bargains for extra time. Again the aesthetic decrees of drama are against him: its imperative is the urgent arrival at an end; the moral foreclosure which is Aristotle's unity of time. Every act in drama is irrevocable, and hastens the advance towards that retribution. When Everyman asks if he can take the pilgrimage and then return to his pleasantly trivial life, Death warns that he may never more come here. This is Macbeth's judgement on himself: tomorrows are illusory in drama; our fate is the past's accumulated case against us. Nor can Everyman take refuge in Mak's play-acting. He must represent himself, and may use no actorly attorney as a surrogate. His performance is to consist in the exhibition of his 'many badde dedes and good but a fewe'. Drama remains a moral inquest on action—Athena's verdict on Orestes, God's on Everyman—until Wordsworth in his play *The Borderers* declares that

> Action is transitory, a step, a blow—
> The motion of a muscle—this way or that,
> 'Tis done. . . .
> Suffering is permanent, obscure and dark,
> And has the nature of infinity.

Here, romantically, the causal link between character and action has been snapped. Consciousness prefers inertia. But the drama demands enactment as an accounting. Words must be made good in deed, even if the deed is writing. Everyman pleads that 'my wrytynge'—the ledger tabulating his faults—is unready; Hamlet calls for his tables and scribbles down the precepts he has learned from his father. Their actions must (according to the dramatic morality against which Hamlet's equivocating later offends) honour their bonds. Promises, as Fellowship acknowledges when Everyman begs for his company on the pilgrimage, are duty.

Hence the onerousness of dramatic choice. The allegorical quantities Everyman encounters are fixed, rooted, incorrigible. Goods cannot help because its loot anchors it, encouraging it to lie low. Good Deeds would like to, 'but I can not stande veryly'. Kindred is unavailing. Man in narrative is buoyed up by kin, goods, fellowship, supported by possessions and relationships; man in drama is alone, and owns only his actions. Goods asks Everyman, 'What, wenest thou that I am thyne?' Everyman had thought so, and was mistaken. He can only lay claim to Good Deeds when Knowledge has upraised those lapsed initiatives, as it offers to do when saying to Everyman, 'I wyll go with the and be thy gyde / In thy moost nede to go by thy syde.' Once this moral self-adhesion happens, character has liberated its own capacity to act (which Hamlet is able to do only too late). Thus Good Deeds lifts itself from the ground, rectified and mobilised by the 'clamorous complaynt' of Everyman's eloquence, and can descend with him into the grave. We take our actions with us to the last judgement which is drama's metaphysical court of appeal, that 'compt' when Othello knows he will surely be damned.

The medieval forms survive in Marlowe, who makes a modern drama from their inversion. *Tamburlaine* is a morality play about a brazenly amoral character. Rather than being charged with his actions and their consequences as is Everyman, Tamburlaine discharges them and will accept no responsibility for their commission. *Dr Faustus* is a morality play whose moralists—those prosy angels—are officious bogeys, and a miracle play whose miracles are necromantic special effects and disparagements of divinity: Faustus's conjurings, his addition of horns to the Knight, his boxing of the Pope's ears.

Speech in *Everyman* must be the unlocking of action. Fellowship reproves those who 'wyll saye and nothynge do'. The initial amorality of Marlowe's drama is its freeing of speech. The printer called the first two parts of *Tamburlaine* 'tragical Discourses'. So they are—experiments in linguistic belligerence, and in the self-imposition of theatrical delivery. Tamburlaine the shepherd renounces the innocuousness of pastoral for an epic destiny, casting off his weeds and arming himself instead. But the epic to which he graduates is a mode of diction only. He threatens the world with his voice and its 'high astounding terms'. He is dramatic character in its most psychologically primal state: a noisy self-exhibitor, demanding that attention be paid to him, like

Hamlet out-ranting Laertes in the grave of Ophelia. Though Marlowe's two plays presume to record his conquests, they eliminate political or military manoeuvring and advance directly from Tamburlaine's wanting something to his acquisition of it. He rules by words not deeds.

Wanting to ride in triumph through Persepolis, Tamburlaine—once he has repeated the phrase a few times—does so metrically, in the measured tread of his accents and in the orotundity of a voice which he describes as like that of thundering Jupiter. Zenocrate like the city is won by the sweetness of his talk. Metaphors are his self-promotions: ultimately they divinise him. Comparing himself with Hector, he reminds the Turkish kings that the simile honorifically flatters them by allowing them to stand in for Achilles; comparing Zenocrate with Helen, he declares that, if she had existed then, she would have supplanted Homer's heroine; comparing himself with God, when he burns the Mahometan books, he nominates himself to supply the vacuum in a timorous, muted heaven. Naming is an arrogation. Imprinting a word on a person or a place is to assert ownership. Tamburlaine subdues the Turkish emperor by the simple arrogance of addressing him as Bajazeth, denying him all ceremonial titles and attributes; he advances across the map acquiring kingdoms by recitation, and promises his consort to confound cartographers in an orgy of renaming,

> Calling the provinces, cities and towns
> After my name and thine Zenocrate.

His obsession throughout is to live up to his name, to earn the adjectives and epithets attached to it, and then, having spoken it, to inscribe it into permanence—he will 'write my self great Lord of Africa', he vows. Totalitarianism means for him a monopoly of speech, and he is advised by Theridamas to bridle the slanging tongues of the humbled rulers who draw his chariot.

If Spenser's language discovers the ordaining magic of the adjective, Tamburlaine discovers and revels in the coerciveness of tenses, which are an exercise in projection, launching the self confidently into a future attainable by assertion. Almost all of his speech is inflected in a masterful subjunctive, 'for Will and Shall best fitteth Tamburlaine', and in the trajectory of a single line he can, by his bullying device of incremental repetition, advance from the present to that future. 'To Babylon, my Lords, to Babylon', he cries, and at once he has arrived, for when the next scene begins, the city's governor is discussing whether to surrender. He utters himself into immortality by transferring his 'place and proper title' to his son, who will keep that name alive.

In this world of vocal zeal, death means a reduction to silence. Cosroe admits himself moribund when, after the battle, the organ of his voice is arrested, and Celebinus, mourning his mother, says that 'sorrow stops the passage of my speech'. Only Tamburlaine knows how to make his silence eloquent and commanding. Even his looks and gestures portentously speak. Thus he physiognomically executes Agydas. This Median lord has been slandering Tamburlaine to Zenocrate. Tamburlaine overhears him, stares wrathfully at him, and after stalking off sends Agydas a dagger. Agydas knows how to translate that ocular commandment into act, and promptly stabs himself. If *Tamburlaine* is a tragedy, it is an exclusively discursive one. Tamburlaine is forced to confront the mortal impotence of words. Language, for all its enraged repetitions of her name, is incapable of resurrecting Zenocrate; Tamburlaine in turn suffers a kind of linguistic entropy, exhausting himself by the necessity of constant thunderous utterance. The death of Zabina is a break-down in linguistic composure. Her mad scene, after she finds that Bajazeth has killed himself, consists of senseless ranting in unmetrical prose: she no longer has the self-possession required by Marlovian poetry, and must thereafter fall silent. The means of death chosen by her and Bajazeth—braining themselves against the bars of the cage—signifies their obliteration of the proud, imagining, orating mind.

Rather than this violent cancellation, Tamburlaine undergoes a slow degeneration. He simply cannot emit forever the verbal energy required to keep himself alive and to maintain all others in subordination. At last his bluster against death is noted by Theridamas as a fatal symptom:

> Ah good my Lord, leave these impatient words,
> Which add much danger to your malady.

His death is an event in language, an asphyxiating loss of voice. He pretends to take responsibility for it by pronouncing it and curing it—his last words are 'For Tamburlaine, the Scourge of God must die', and he makes the 'must' sound as if he was choosing to do so—but it exposes his paltriness and his imposture, for it is an experience he cannot talk his way through. The words others find for it are diagnostic only. The physician, analysing his urine and the condition of his arteries, provides a biopsy in place of a tragic obsequy. Since there are no abiding values, the only virtue lies in cheering yourself up and convincing yourself of your own existence by talking. Once you stop that, you cease to be. Despite his bombast, Tamburlaine might all along have been just a prating nonentity.

The play's reduction to inflatedly self-serving words—though undoing it as tragedy—makes *Tamburlaine* an acute commentary on the theatre, on politics, and on political theatre. Marlowe's atheism extends to his own creation. He shows the theatre to be a home for poseurs. Tamburlaine who is not a man of action (since all he does is talk) is, however, a consummate actor. And whereas the Shakespearean actor treads a stage which is a world, the Marlovian actor is alone with his own shadow and the echo of his voice. The stage narrows to an arena of fantasy, where lusts are gratified. This is the use Marlowe's Faustus makes of his power, with the aid of his procurer Mephistophilis, and

Tamburlaine likewise stages his progress as a sadistic charade, treading on Bajazeth, harnessing the kings as cart-horses, affrighting Damascus with a show of flags or executing the gods by flaunting black streamers. The play is less his armed advance across the world than his retreat into himself and into the self-solicitation of fantasy. Hence its peculiar modernity: it is a theatre of cruelty, trafficking in a deviant magic. For Marlowe the play is a perverse sorcery like that in which Faustus engages. It empowers you, briefly, savagely to act out your repressed greeds and longings. Ultimately Tamburlaine, for all his itineraries of conquest and his call for maps, occupies a space as claustrophobic as Bajazeth, caged in the company of his neuroses.

His vocal pomp makes Tamburlaine a natural candidate for opera, where the voice itself is the sole heroic credential, and Handel in 1724 made him the protagonist of an opera seria (its libretto based on a heroic tragedy by Jacques Pradon, a contemporary of Racine)—with an interesting deduction, for Handel's character is a castrato, the more shrilly venomonous for his ephebic timbre, who has made the highest and most mutilating sacrifice for the exigent voice's sake. Tamburlaine suffers also from Diderot's paradox of the actor. Is he who he says he is, or is he—like Beckett's character in *Krapp's Last Tape* (1958)—merely taking dictation from his own rehearsed, recorded voice?

By contrast, Shakespeare's characters are citizens of their language. Mowbray's greatest grief when he is exiled in *Richard II* is that he will be denied the use of 'my native English'. Speech is a charter of legitimacy: Bolingbroke tells Berkeley he must find its title 'in your tongue', and Richard utters words which are laws, sentences (as he remarks to Aumerle) both legal and grammatical. This trust in a language which joins us to one another is the cue for the play's most touchingly witty scene, when the Duchess of York beseeches Bolingbroke to speak the innocuous phrase which will pardon her son. Mowbray, after studying English for forty years, says he is too old 'to fawn upon a nurse' to learn a new language; the Duchess offers to provide this bossy tutelage to Bolingbroke, saying

> An if I were thy nurse, thy tongue to teach,
> 'Pardon' should be the first word of thy speech.

The Duke advises Bolingbroke to pretend to be clement in French, by saying 'pardonne moy'. That way, with decent obscurity, he can excuse himself from being generous. But the Duchess insists that the vow will be good only if made in the speech wherein they are all united:

> Speak 'pardon' as 'tis current in our land;
> The chopping French we do not understand.

Language is for Shakespeare's people a ground of community and therefore of faith, which reposes in relationship. It is their precious, shared creation; for

Tamburlaine, however, it is a personal megaphone. This is what makes Marlowe's play so astute politically. The dictator imposes himself by his untiring harangues, and by an elaborate scenography. Hitler had a technology of amplification to boost the hysterical voice and to broadcast it; Tamburlaine already possesses the public address system of the Marlovian 'mighty line'. Perhaps the ideal designer for the play would be Hitler's architect and the *régisseur* of the Nuremberg rallies, Albert Speer. Since those staged triumphs of will, drama is no longer permitted such totalitarian power. Marlowe's epic theory has yielded to that of Bertolt Brecht (who in 1923–4 made an adaptation of Marlowe's *Edward II*). Epic for Tamburlaine means the hero's absolute dominion. In the epic theatre of Brecht there can be no authoritarian singleness: everyone is the victim of politics. The Marlovian hero demands our terrorised identification with him, pandering to the tyrant in each of us. That orgy of vicarious emotion is frustrated by the alienation effects that Brecht builds into his drama. Notwithstanding the opposition, there is an agreement between the forms, and Brecht was right to be interested in Marlowe. Within the play, Tamburlaine undergoes an alienating diminution. The demi-god is just a bellowing and strutting actor, whose only powers—despite the title's praise of him as a warrior and a monarch—are vocal and gestural.

When the marauding braggart Pistol erupts into the Eastcheap inn in *Henry IV*, he is given some lines of Tamburlaine's: the threat to the pampered Asians he has reduced to jades and harnessed to his chariot. The quote marks Shakespeare's perception of the hollowness in Marlowe's character and his idiom. The hostess despises Pistol as a cowardly swaggerer. But the parody is affectionate, and it announces Shakespeare's comic and human reclamation of Marlowe, for the two parts of *Henry IV*, modelled on *Tamburlaine*, replace Marlovian politics and the pageantry of egomaniacal vengeance with the recurrences of nature and history, and in the figure of Falstaff they return the would-be epic bravo of Marlowe's plays to his origins in pastoral. Falstaff indeed is Shakespeare's Tamburlaine. The fiend has been comically pacified. Tamburlaine is the state. All others exist only so long as they are tolerated by him. Falstaff similarly is the kingdom, but instead of policing it by intimidation and belabouring it into submission he comfortably and warmingly embodies it, as he explains in his speech about sherry and its inspiring properties. In Falstaff it is not the ego but the flesh which imperially distends and dilates. The embonpoint he nourishes and irrigates so generously and which, at Shrewsbury, he takes care to protect from harm, is the body politic. Self-satisfaction and satiety are in Falstaff blamelessly patriotic emotions. His physical acreage relaxes into a landscape: this is his peace-loving pastoralism, for he belongs among the farmers of Gloucestershire with whom, in the second part, he reminisces about the youth of the earth while feeding on its reliable current riches. A plumped-out contentment with one's own being is the native mood of Shakespearean character. His people relish the bodies they are wrapped in,

whereas those of Marlowe rend and torment theirs—Tamburlaine ostentatiously carving a wound in his flesh, Edward II sodomised by a red-hot poker,
Faustus torn apart by the devils. The Marlovian monsters are rendered sacred
by Shakespeare, who cannot help making this imaginative gift of himself, even
if the intention is parodic.

Another of Shakespeare's Tamburlaines is Henry V, and that play is about
the political and military uses of a rhetoric like Tamburlaine's. Harfleur, for
instance, capitulates to Henry's speech. But Henry's tirades do not hope, like
Tamburlaine's, to terrify all others into abjection and silence. Their purpose is
the salving absorption of others into himself, a desire to make them sharers in
his own abundant life. At Harfleur he pleads with the town to save itself by
allowing him to enter. He has Tamburlaine's command of the epic catalogue,
and loves both roll-calls of names and idylls of quantifying; here as well his
purpose is not elimination of countries and opponents by citing them, but a
solemn and fraternal commemoration, as when, after Agincourt, he names and
numbers the French casualties, and salutes their 'royal fellowship of death'.
His morale-boosting rhetoric rallies and unifies his own fractious troops, and
posthumously convenes a community—a solidarity which is the source of
comedy because it cements kinship—among his slain enemies. The last and
most arduous of his linguistic conquests is therefore a sexual and a comic one:
the bilingual scene of Katherine's wooing.

The same contrast obtains between Marlowe's *Edward II* and Shakespeare's
Richard II. The one is about politics, the other about history. The Marlovian
king when deprived of his throne has been reduced, he says, to a shadow. He is
alive only while he wields power. The Shakespearean character escapes from
monarchy into humanity, into membership of that common mortal fate he
accepts when he sits upon the ground and meditates on the deaths of kings.
Will Ladislaw, the artist in George Eliot's *Middlemarch*, misunderstands
Tamburlaine when he illustrates his progress as propulsion of historical
destiny. Explaining his sketch of the tyrant whipping the conquered kings, he
says, 'I take Tamburlaine in his chariot for the tremendous course of the
world's physical history lashing on the harnessed dynasties.' He is, in this
positivist reading, an agent after all of the march of mind, a Daniel Deronda by
other and more peremptory means. Ladislaw releases him into the open spaces
of history, when his actual habitat is the obtuse enclosure of dreams. Edward's
career also works ingressively, as a retraction into a cell of fantasy. The play
studies the infantile and pathological workings of a temperament like
Tamburlaine's. The power Edward seeks to exercise is the absolutism of the
baby, whose every squalling whim is someone else's command. 'I'll have my
will', he declares in a fit of pique. Gaveston learns the same style of
authoritarian whimsy: 'I must have wanton poets, pleasant wits.' Edward's
abasement occurs when that essential verb is deleted from his vocabulary. He
asks Leicester, 'What shall become of us?' and is told, 'Your majesty must go to

Killingworth.' He dolefully reckons his loss: 'Must! It is somewhat hard when kings must go.' Leicester needs to entice him into captivity by appealing to his day-dreaming hedonism, advising that he has 'a litter ready . . . that waits your pleasure.' Power means for Edward the requisitioning of fantasies, the fending-off of a reproving adult reality. He deploys it like someone playing Tamburlaine in a nursery game. Since titles are the trinkets in a dressing-up kit, he lavishes them on Gaveston so he can join in the game, creating him

> . . . . Lord High-chamberlain,
> Chief Secretary to the state and me,
> Earl of Cornwall, King and Lord of Man.

Gaveston feels himself secure in the impersonation of Tamburlaine for only so long as Edward's indulgence subsidises the pretence:

> . . . . I think myself as great
> As Caesar riding on the Roman street,
> With captive Kings at his triumphal car.

Theirs is a sumptuary fantasy, a spendthrift frolic. They 'riot it', Mortimer calculates, 'with the treasure of the realm.' This is why Edward needs the 'regiment' of which the rebellion strips him: it is the defence mechanism of paranoia, a psychological withdrawal, like the guard with which he promises to protect Gaveston from the envy of mankind; the pornotopia's bastion against reality.

Richard II arrives in his prison at an awareness and acceptance of his own powerless irrelevance. Even his horse has treacherously consented to carry Bolingbroke. Yet his Shakespearean urge is to embrace that indignity, and to overcome his isolation within himself—hence his quizzing of the groom, and his identification of himself with other existences, including the horse's. He craves the amplitude of a peopled world, and attempts to transform his dungeon into an entire society by conceited metaphor:

> I have been studying how I may compare
> The prison where I live unto the world.

Edward however belongs in such solitary confinement. Gaveston had devised a theatre of sybaritic sexual enticement for him in his 'Italian masks by night', with page-boys playing sylvan nymphs; in his dungeon Lightborn, the exotic, imported executioner, devises another, crueller theatre of sadistic tableaux, in which Edward consents to perform. Taking off his crown, Edward asks 'let me be king 'till night.' He enters thereafter a nocturnal, cloacal kingdom of avenging fantasy, under the dominion of a killer named for Lucifer, the devil born from light but expelled to darkness.

Rather than expanding the place of his confinement as Richard does, he contracts it further. His cell is 'the closet of my heart', and the cess-pit where he wallows is his own self-revulsion. He has been sentenced to live inside his own traumas, and to confront the fears which lie on the other side of his desires. The drumming—a neurotic tattoo, internally echoing the martial accompaniment which Tamburlaine is always demanding—keeps him awake because his punishment is to be a hypnotic waking dream. Richard fights against his execution, and manages to kill two of Exton's team; Edward consents to his, having been seduced by it, requesting only from Lightborn a titillating postponement of the climax. At last, when Lightborn will delay no longer, Edward offers (in contrast with Richard's discharge of indignant vital energy) the classic self-justification of the yielding virgin: 'I am too weak and feeble to resist.' Holinshed records that Edward was killed by a hot spit thrust anally into his entrails. Marlowe cannot specify such an act, but he implies it by inventing Lightborn, whose speciality is scenarios of exquisite pain and who interprets death as an intercourse-like invasion of the body. He can, he says, blow powder into the ears of sleepers, or open their mouths and pour in quicksilver. From a fancied union with Gaveston, Edward passes to an inflamed copulation with the skewering Lightborn.

Brecht, though paraphrasing Edward's last speech in his adaptation, gives him another immediately before it which opens up the dark Marlovian cubicle and lets the character out into a Lear-like, tragic generality. Brecht's Edward remembers the rain, the starvation, privations and uncleanliness he has suffered, and finds them good. Lightborn tells him to sleep; he insists on remaining awake, because there is now a heroic virtue in self-consciousness, and the drum which is the insomniac torture of Marlowe's Edward is a moral aid to his counterpart in Brecht, ensuring that death will not creep up on him while he is collapsed and unaware.

Marlowe's determination seems to be to prevent any such tragic admission of responsibility. Edward dies in a posture of compliant, ravished passivity. Mortimer, too, avoids responsibility—guiltily acknowledged in Shakespeare not only by Bolingbroke but by Exton, who at once repents of killing Richard and condemns himself to expiation—by hiring and then instantly exterminating Lightborn. Marlovian characters disown their actions, and enlist language to take the blame for them. Faustus justifies his pact with the devil by quibbling over the import of scriptural texts; Mortimer arranges Edward's death while denying that he has caused it by omitting a comma from a Latin missive. The suppression of that punctuation mark is a classic Marlovian dodge: his characters all lead what Mortimer calls 'unpointed' lives, existentially in suspension, reeling from one gratuitous and irresponsible initiative to the next. Drayton in *Poly-Olbion* can even make Edward's mode of death the warrant for a punning turnabout: he says of the king,

> For that preposterous sinne wherein he did offend,
> In his posteriour parts had his preposterous end.

Preposterous means back-to-front, absurd because reversed, so Edward greets death by prepositing his posterior. *Edward II* is no one's tragedy in particular but everyone's successively. When Edward is despatched, his queen says, 'Now, Mortimer, begins our tragedy.' He is at once drawn and quartered, she is imprisoned by her son to await trial. The tragedy is that of imagining you can make yourself safe in a chaotic and valueless world. Edward at least had insulated himself by his stubborn refusal to quit his fantasy.

Sir Toby's boast in *Twelfth Night* that 'I'll confine myself no finer than I am' is a manifesto for Shakespearean character. To his people, identity is a territorial imperative. The stage is their allotment of living-room, and they are all full enough of and in themselves to replete it. Like Parolles in *All's Well That Ends Well*, they have faith in the world's physical largesse: 'There's place and means for every man alive.' But Marlowe prohibits this enlargement. His heroes want what Barabas in *The Jew of Malta*, crowing over his treasury, calls 'infinite riches in a little room'. The Shakespearean stage is an open, random, overcrowded space where tragedy and comedy jostle and collide; Marlowe's is jealously contracted—a strong-box of avarice, or a torture-chamber of ego. Tamburlaine's spatial realm is not the world he talks about but a miniature of it, the map he calls for when he is dying.

Barabas has the Marlovian fantasy at its most insane. He wants to own everything, and to share it with no one. He manages the play so as to engineer the elimination of all competitors for occupancy of the stage's terrain, turning the Shakespearean double plot—supposedly a permission to other existences, accepting that tragedy and comedy must coexist—into a caustic double-cross. Wanting Mathias and Lodowick dead, he has them obligingly kill each other, and sees to it that the friars appear to do the same. What in Shakespeare would be simultaneity is in Barabas's case subversion: instead of comedy acting as a foundation to tragedy, or tragedy as a hidden depth of potential beneath comedy, in the two tiers of the double plot, Barabas reconstructs the stage so as to mine the drama from below, explaining to the Turkish invaders that the rock on which the city is built is hollow and can be tunnelled through to arrive within the walls, then installing a false stage above a pit into which the banqueting Turks will be plunged. His artifices all depend on the exposure and exploration of emptinesses. He has a single Shakespearean line, removed from its context by T. S. Eliot to serve as an epigraph for his 'Portrait of a Lady'. When Friar Barnardine catechises him, he admits to fornication—'but that was in another country; / And besides the wench is dead.' Shakespearean characters have a fondness for such conjectural self-extensions, either into the past or future. Sir Andrew Aguecheek 'was adored once too', Coriolanus launches himself into 'a world elsewhere'. In contrast with their glad augmenting of their existences, Barabas mentions that other country only to establish its irrelevance, and has no sooner tallied the wench than he has summarily sentenced her to death.

This is what separates him from the corresponding character in Shakespeare, Shylock. Though accused of avarice, Shylock is—at least imaginatively—generous and selfless in ways unintelligible to Barabas. Marlowe's Jew enumerates Abigail among his chattels: 'Spare me, my daughter, and my wealth.' Shylock appears to make the same connection when he bewails the robbery of 'My daughter! O my ducats! O my daughter! . . . My ducats and my daughter!' There is a crucial difference, though. Barabas wants people to serve him as a currency, as auxiliaries to his will, and when Ithamore promises unquestioning subservience, Barabas in recompense affects to adopt him

> . . . . for mine only heir:
> All that I have is thine when I am dead;
> And, whilst I live, use half; spend as myself.

Relationship is for him a cash nexus; people are legal tender. All Marlowe's heroes are anally retentive. Emotional avarice is one of their maiming afflictions. The wonder in Shylock's case is his grandiloquent lack of these very habits of which he is accused by his mercantile rivals. Money to him above all constitutes a value, ordained by imagination. There is a bizarre poetry to currency. We arbitrarily invest minerals with an exchangeable virtue, and in the process are constructing symbols—as Portia's father does with the caskets, as Portia herself does with her ring, as Shylock does with the turquoise (precious to him because of its emotional associations) which Jessica squanders to buy a monkey. Financial transactions are to Shylock sacred trusts, and usury (as he explains when recounting the fable of Jacob's flock) a hieratic mystery, profaned by the impious Christians. He therefore, in the court, spurns profit and demands the worthless flesh of Antonio because of the oath he has sworn. His daughter and his ducats are interchangeable not because he is ludicrously unable to distinguish between their worth but because he knows that both incarnate value, and both have the hieratic potency of symbols. Economic dealings are governed by the same ritualistic edicts which constrain family ties.

Unlike Barabas slavering over his treasure, or Jonson's equally costive Volpone, there is a poetic dream in *The Merchant of Venice* which goes beyond cupidity: an imaginative infatuation with riches as spiritual enhancement, worshipfully preserved from the wastage of use. Heaven to Lorenzo is a mint, its floor 'inlaid with patines of bright gold', just as to Shylock it is a depository for moral promissory notes:

> An oath, an oath! I have an oath in heaven.
> Shall I lay perjury upon my soul?

The mercenariness of these people manifests itself as a charitable disbursement of themselves, a Shakespearean open-handedness evident even in Jessica's purchase of the monkey or Shylock's sarcastic bequeathing of himself to the state when he says, 'Nay, take my life and all, pardon not that.' Their very existence is a boon to and an embracement of others. This is the meaning of Portia's hospitality at Belmont, first to the hordes of suitors, then to the diaspora of Venice. The Shakespearean play has to be populous, whereas Barabas's desire for a monopoly of wealth and power suits the different ambition of the Marlovian play, always contracting into monodrama. He will share it only with those who are his accessories, and they must consent—as he tells Ithamore—not only to a merger with himself but to the loss of human qualities:

> . . . be thou void of these affections,
> Compassion, love, vain hope, and heathen fear;
> Be mov'd at nothing, see thou pity none.

Marlowe's protagonists seek a calculated insensitivity or insentience—the numb incapacity for feeling possessed by Tamburlaine, Lightborn and the callously bland Mephistophilis. Their inability to respond alienates these people from drama, with its community of action and reaction. The monologue, given spatial form by the counting-house which is Barabas's little room or the study which is Faustus's, is their natural habitat. What happens in the play occurs inside not around them: a psychotic scenario of revenge or, in Faustus's case, of self-aggrandisement, acted out by enslaved mental phantoms. *Faustus* is about this theatrical hucksterism, about the prostitution of fantasy. It is a mistake to think of Marlowe's characters as over-reachers or supermen. They are dwarfs primping themselves as giants. Rather than the *Ubermensch*, they suggest beneath their megalomania the meagre lusts of *l'homme moyen sensuel*. Marlowe's theatre represents its own spectacles as meanly factitious, its heroes as covert libertines who day-dream the play in which they perform. Compare his Faustus with the romantic reincarnations of the character by Goethe or Thomas Mann. Goethe's hero is a self-transcender, whose pact with the devil enjoins him to a restless spiritual evolution. He will be damned only when he pauses in self-satisfaction, and reverts from becoming to smug static being. His ambition is to carry his fellow-beings along in this evolution, and he busies himself in humanitarian projects like the land-fill. The *Doktor Faustus* of Thomas Mann's novel in 1947 is a romantic decadent, and can transcend himself only at the cost of his health and sanity. He must condemn himself to infection by the world before he can make music from it. Both characters, as creators, are the necessary rivals of deity. Hence Goethe's rearrangement of geography, and Mann's advance beyond good and evil. By contrast, Marlowe's hero is a zany caricature of Faust—a dessicated academic, feeding the senses he has too long denied; and while Goethe's Faust and Mann's both feel bound to overcome the limits of the artistic form in which they are confined—Goethe in Part II of his *Faust* opening out the drama into metaphysical supernature, Mann expanding the novel into the shape of

Leverkühn's symphony—Marlowe's libertine is happy within his play, because the theatre is his meretricious supplier of erotic treats and vindictive japes, all of them stage-managed by Mephistophilis.

Faustus's unregeneracy is Marlowe's joke against both the morality play on which he appears to be modelling his work and against the tragedy it has often been mistaken for. *Faustus* is a black comedy, and its blackness is a creative atheism, refusing to take seriously either morality or tragedy. It believes only in a flagrant sensationalism, to which the theatre—in 'this show' of devils who caparison Faustus, in Lucifer's infernal cabaret of the sins, in Faustus's travelling carnival with its illusory resurrections of the illustrious dead—also caters.

The motives of this Faust are those of a voluptuary. The opening chorus describes his mental conceit in gustatory terms, as an imperialism of greed and a distemper of taste:

> . . . glutted now with learning's golden gifts,
> He surfeits upon cursed necromancy;
> Nothing so sweet as magic is to him,
> Which he prefers before his chiefest bliss.

He is a gross eater, who invites Cornelius and Valdes to dinner and says they will discuss the black arts 'after meat', and who compliments Lucifer on the banquet of sense laid on by his demons ('O, this feeds my soul!'). Wagner cannot believe he is doomed because he continues to carouse and swill without misgiving. The satiety of appetite—sexual as much as alimentary, since Faustus has only to demand a paramour and is at once served up with a succubus in the likeness of Helen of Troy—is his highest ambition, and he exhibits his power over others by the provision of food for them, when the Duchess requests ripe grapes out of season, or by his teasing denial of it, when he confiscates the dainty dishes over which the Pope is salivating. In *Faustus*, the workings of Tamburlaine's temperament are reductively exposed: that cosmic urge is simply an infantile desire for instant gratification; imagination means only the wish-fulfillment of an overweening fantasy. Mephistophilis is employed to act out Faustus's sadistic or orgiastic demands,

> To slay mine enemies, and aid my friends,
> And always be obedient to my will,

and the partnership between them is a sick symbiosis—id's tutelage of ego, or the sadist's marriage to the masochist. Faustus envies the moral ignorance of animals ('all beasts are happy' he reflects when his nemesis approaches), and is fascinated by the amoral intensity and recondite thrills of a life devoted to sensation. His empire lies here. The dominion coextensive with the mind of man which he speaks of in his first soliloquy is in fact the sensorium of the human body. Thus his only worry about damnation is whether it will hurt. He is curious about pain, and eager to know whether Mephistophilis can experience it; his own end is horrific rather than tragic because Marlowe emphasises not the mind's reflection on itself but the body's torture and travail—the destruction of a human identity by panic and hysteria, which lead to an actual dismemberment by the devils.

The comic middle scenes of the play have been an embarrassment for critics intent on discovering a moral or tragic consistency. But if *Faustus* is seen as a theatrical pandemonium—an exploration of the drama's dangerous power to realise our wishes—these interludes are obscenely appropriate. The cheap tricks played on the Pope or on the horse-courser are Faustian art, a demonic charter for the theatre. All stagecraft is practical joking. Faustus has the dramatist's cynical and nihilistic guile. He knows that what everyone else takes for reality is a mocking fabulation. Since 'hell's a fable', so must heaven be, and the pedantic emissaries of the morality play are viewed by Faustus as Brechtian alienation effects, admonitions to a necessary disbelief. One of them, the Evil Angel, in jeering at the Good Angel's offer of 'contrition, prayer, repentance' defines these as alienatory devices, 'illusions . . . / That make men foolish that do trust them most'. Morality is only machinery, or scenic imposture. Marlowe denies moral consciousness to Faustus.

The tragic hero is a creature of exquisite scruple. Although Macbeth is described as a butcher or a hell-hound by victims and opponents, in his soliloquies he contemplates his own actions with an exacting lucidity, and condemns himself before anyone else can do so. Hamlet shares this vocational self-accusing. The unsettling truthfulness of Marlowe's account of Faustus derives from the character's mental cowardice or frantic evasion of consequences. He blames everyone and everything rather than himself, cursing Wittenberg and offering to burn his books, spending his final scene in a gabbled bartering to obtain a stay of execution. Whereas the tragic hero welcomes a moral reckoning, like Macbeth deploring his own sere, sleep-walking, all-but-posthumous life and forbidding to himself 'honour, love, obedience, troops of friends', Faustus at the last wishes himself into a sub-human existence where he will be unmolested by morality: 'Why wert thou not a creature wanting soul?' The tragic hero at his terminus reviews his past and solemnises his arrival at an end. Othello calls it the 'very seamark of my utmost sail'. Faustus in his final soliloquy still exists in the harried, sensationalist present tense of the libertine. There can be no past for him, because he cannot understand the tragic rule that acts are consequential; he wants only to prolong the luxurious present in a 'perpetual day' and even, with garish inappropriateness, quotes an Ovidian lover who implores the horses of night to slow their pace so he can continue the enjoyment of his mistress.

Lucifer's foreclosure on Faustus provokes a foreshortening of drama here:

with the punctuation of the striking clock, the final scene summarises in a few minutes Faustus's last hour of life; it adopts with a vengeance an Aristotelian unity, and its tormenting implosion indicates the difference between the temporal and spatial mood of Marlowe's drama and that of Shakespeare's. The Shakespearean protagonists defy the Aristotelian rule of haste, and decelerate the plays at their digressive leisure. They will be confined neither by time nor space. This is what lends such amplitude to the existences of Hamlet, Falstaff or Cleopatra. Macbeth is at first hustled and harassed by time, which in accord with the precepts of Aristotle fatally overtakes itself and prematurely actualises the future. That headlong velocity exhausts itself with the murder of Duncan, after which Macbeth and Lady Macbeth spend the rest of the play in retrospection, since the dramatic time in which things happen is now to them a meaningless succession of vacant tomorrows. They do not quarrel with the drama's right to impeach them, indeed they accept its executive impatience. But they gain for themselves a Shakespearean freedom from its abbreviations and its ruthless necessity. They go about their business in the accomplishment of a diurnal, domestic routine, wishing 'to be safely thus', imagining a future of unperturbed security. They are larger than the dramatic form, while Faustus is smaller, and at the end of his play the form itself, like a cell whose walls move in on the prisoner until he is crushed, contrives his extermination. Faustus's study is one of those archetypal rooms of drama from which, as Sartre specified in *Huis-clos* (1944), there is no exit.

After Marlowe, the heroic play can be no more than the echo chamber for a man who is no god at all but just a theatrical braggart. Jaffeir in Otway's *Venice Preserv'd* (1682) wanders the city expecting to meet a devil, but none appears to confirm his status as a tragic apostate. The only available divinity comes from rhetorical surplus, as when Aquilina compliments Pierre as a god-like lover. Other characters boost themselves by adducing classical prototypes, but cannot keep being devalued by them. The conspirators self-congratulatingly compare themselves to the assassins of Caesar, Bedamar salutes Pierre as a Mars, the abused Belvidera calls herself a Lucrece with no one to vindicate her wrongs. When Jaffeir hails her as a Portia she vows that she will deserve the role of Brutus's wife and Cato's daughter. She reneges on the plot, however, and he rescinds the parallel:

> Is this the Roman virtue! this the blood
> That boasts its purity with Cato's daughter's!
> Would she have e'er betrayed her Brutus?

While some are aspiring to verbose godliness, others prefer bestiality. The senator who assaults Belvidera is a rank, stinking fox, and among Aquilina's clients is one who, when roused, randily impersonates a bull and a yapping, disobedient dog. Like Faustus with his scurrilities, these characters know themselves to be frauds. The talent for vociferation passes from what Jonson called 'the Tamerlanes and Tamer-Chams' to the strutting pomp of the verbose dwarf in Fielding's 1730 burlesque play *Tom Thumb* or, later and less articulately, to the gluttonous despot who is Jarry's *Ubu-Roi* (1896). The theatre's miracles are oratorical only, and it has developed a morality all its own: sound and fury now, in contradiction of Macbeth, signify everything.

— 10 —
Shakespeare:
Tragedy, Comedy, Tragicomedy

The formal originality of English literature declares itself in the reordering of relations between the classical genres: epic's demotion, or its merger with romance and pastoral. The drama, too, confounds a classical theory. Aristotle decreed a division between tragedy, dealing with venerable, awesome fates, and comedy, representing the absurd or despicable accidents of the bad or the ugly, who deserve to be ridiculed. Tragic character retires behind a mask of hieratic grief; comic character wears a false face which has been lewdly distorted. There can be no congress between such opposites. Shakespeare's decision to ignore this segregation is the most important thing about his drama. None of his plays can be categorised either as tragedy or comedy. Theirs is the intermediate, paradoxical form of tragicomedy. Every tragic character is, latently at least, a comic dupe or gull; comic characters will remove the opprobious mask and expose a vulnerable interior which makes them—like Sir Andrew Aguecheek declaring he was adored once, too—potentially tragic. This repudiation of rules earned Shakespeare the scorn of classical critics. Jonson attributed it to his ignorance, his 'small Latin and less Greek'. Yet eventually his defiance of classical edicts is seen, by Schlegel, Coleridge and Victor Hugo, as a premature romanticism; and that romantic sense of life as a natural and anarchic continuum (rather than classically fencing off unlike experiences) makes Shakespeare, in the nineteenth century's estimation, the forefather of the most compendiously anticlassical of forms, the novel.

Instead of Aristotle's mutually exclusive tragedy and comedy, Shakespearean drama derives from and constantly returns to history, at first the chronicles of Holinshed, later the mazy, vagrant romances which supply plots for his last plays. History is generically impartial. The plays about kingship find an orderly succession of tragedy and comedy through time. The king is dead, long live the king. Or, rather than an inheriting sequence, they demonstrate (in the *Henry IV* plays) the simultaneity of the two: a tragic king has comic subjects. Political history may approximate to tragedy; social history permits the healing recurrences of comedy. Individual lives end, while the collective life— hymeneally celebrated in Shakespeare's comedies, dynastically rallied in the histories ('for here I hope begins our lasting joy', says Edward IV as he takes over from Henry VI)—resumes, and will have no end.

The consolation requires that the continuity be represented, which drama classically prefers not to do. Aristotle insisted on the unifying of time and place:

drama must be a concentrated excerpt from life, studying the crises of action not its long evolution. Shakespeare outrages both unities. Crites in Dryden's *Essay of Dramatic Poesy* in 1668 complains about the prolific irregularity of the plays: 'the business of a day takes up in some of them an age; . . . and for one spot of ground, which the stage should represent, we are sometimes in more countries than the map can show us.' Shakespeare is flouting not only the prescriptions of classical drama but the needful limits of drama itself. Drama—summarised not synoptic, blocking off alternatives of action rather than exploring them at leisure, as Shakespearean digressors like Hamlet do—has been turned backwards, in his plays, into the different mode of narrative. His characters often profess a contempt for the punctual schedules of drama, detaching themselves from it to extrapolate a mental or novelistic narrative, opening an ampler terrain (temporally unharassed, comfortably spacious) within themselves. This is the introspective liberty from dramatic engagement enjoyed by Hamlet the procrastinator; it is the idyllic idleness of Falstaff, who disbelieves in the urgency of history and therefore in the hustling necessities and impending crises of drama, and whose luxuriation in himself directs the second part of *Henry IV* towards pastoral.

Shakespeare already renounces classical precept in two early plays which look like pedantic homages to classicism—the Plautine *Comedy of Errors*, the Senecan *Titus Andronicus*. Each subtly confounds its prototype and urges an accord between those dissevered halves of the human condition, comedy and tragedy. Classically, comedy need only be a punitively efficient machine; Shakespeare romantically attends to the interior sufferings of characters manhandled and hurt by the machine of farce. The Plautine construction naturalises itself, managing a reunion of families, the reconvening of nature's society. The motive of comedy is the arrival at partnership and pairing, whether sexually reproductive or (as here) the encounter with a lost facsimile of the self, a sundered twin. The ancestral rite reuniting the tribe is also, in *The Comedy of Errors*, a psychological mystery. Antipholus of Syracuse describes himself as a drop losing itself in the ocean to find another drop which is its likeness. The biological reproductiveness of comedy, ending as it does in marriage, goes with the theatre's mystic replicating of the world, holding up (as Hamlet says) a mirror in which we see our heavenly counterparts, the shining ghosts of what we were or might be. Dromio of Ephesus salutes his twin as 'my glass, and not my brother'. In *A Midsummer Night's Dream* this is Helena's sense of her 'union in partition' with Hermia, or Hermia's vision 'with parted eye, / When everything seems double'. The theatre's sacrament achieves that 'mutual joinder' and 'interchangement' of which the Priest so beautifully speaks in *Twelfth Night*. The Friar in *Romeo and Juliet* will incorporate two in one, he says; comedy's solemn magic is the multiplying of one into two, our rebirth as another. Antipholus of Syracuse experiences in comedy the immunity to time, consequentiality and our paltry single identity which is the prerogative of Falstaff, born anew every day and at every performance: 'In Ephesus I am but two hours old.' What Orsino in *Twelfth Night* calls comedy's 'natural perspective, that is and is not', symbolised by the apple cleft in twain or by Helena's double cherry, ordains not only our restoration to the sources of our selves, our parents, when the Antipholi are returned to Aegeon and the Abbess, but a resumption by each existence—sexually or fraternally—of its completing, complementing other half. The comedy rebegets a human wholeness. Its apparent errors are, like Bottom's 'translation' and his bottomless dream, profoundly right and just and true.

Encountering their doubles weans the Dromios and the Antipholi of their insistence on the single, unrepeatable will. Their confusion yields to a transcending wisdom: 'Are you a god? Would you create me new?' Antipholus of Syracuse asks Luciana, and begs her to 'transform me then'. The errors amount to a healing metamorphosis, whereby characters are inducted into ownership of other selves or personae within the same bodies. They undergo that augmentation of being which is the loving, empathetic power—inhabiting another—of Shakespearean drama. The Abbess promises this reinstatement of a lost form, an amplitude of existence within the human family denied when we are locked up in individuality. She will, she says of Antipholus, 'make of him a formal man again'. Aegeon can erase, by seeing himself in his regained son, the 'defeatures' inscribed on him by 'time's deforming hand'. To classicism, form means outline and boundary, and it is here restrictively invoked as such by Luciana when she counsels Adriana to accept her own boundedness and subjection; the morphology of Shakespeare's romantic comedy identifies form with the integration we achieve when we recognise that our identity is plural, not jealously our own.

The formality of language in *The Comedy of Errors* is the antiphonal chiming of selves or wits in concordance, as ritually reassuring as responses in a church service: the question-and-answer routines of masters and servants, Adriana's catechising of Luciana. The boon of acting in Shakespeare is a similar self-enlarging. It enables us to try on again the alternate existences we have forfeited. Because acting is the reclamation of these spirit-selves—the strange shadows which attend on the young man in Shakespeare's sonnets—and our invention for ourselves of characters to perform, the most physically portentous character in *The Comedy of Errors* is one who never needs to appear: the geographically corpulent kitchen-wench, a 'mad mountain of flesh', described by the Syracusan Dromio and made real by his dramatising of her. She is a symbol of Shakespearean and anticlassical physique, who cannot come onstage because she is too big for its corseting, constricting unities. Her body comprises a globe. Dromio, bragging that he 'could find out countries in her', goes on to enumerate them, mapping that same bounteous territory which Dryden's critic sees as the sprawling mass of Shakespearean history.

Shakespeare finds in the Senecan blood-bath, as in the Plautine misunderstandings, a natural wisdom, even something close to the pastoral conciliation of comedy or to that 'very tragical mirth' of the play muddlingly performed at Theseus's wedding: for the generic paradox, 'merry and tragical' as Theseus notes, is—when Gloucester dies smilingly or Cordelia's countenance shows 'sunshine and rain at once'—the profoundest human understanding. *Titus Andronicus* is a play of mythic atavism, whose people are members of, physical extrusions from, their sacred historical soil. Tamora declares herself to be 'incorporate in Rome', Titus donates his offspring to that earth. The play's murders and revenges are corporeal transactions, an intercourse with the succouring but greedy earth in which a pit is opened to consume or enwomb men and to drink their blood. The attack on Lavinia is defloration and defoliation, a lopping and hewing of her tree-like body; the amputation of hands required by the emperor seems to Titus an appropriate harvest, plucking up withered herbs. In the brutality there is a natural justice. Titus slays his daughter lovingly, Tamora so loves her sons that she eats them: they kill with kindness. When Aaron is buried alive or Tamora discarded to be provender for fowls, people aliment an earth on which they have hungrily fed, and are again merged with the substance wherefrom they were made. 'I the earth', as Titus elliptically puts it. The phrase could have been Falstaff's: as he dies, the hostess feels the vital heat ebb from his body, which takes on a geological bulk, 'cold as any stone', stolidly occupying the landscape.

Aaron, by refusing to feel, can interpret the play's horrors as amusements. Beholding the tears of Titus, he laughs heartily. His callous reaction suggests the possibility of the tragedy's revision as primal, savage comedy—for comedy is about our earthiness and our gluttony, about what Cleopatra calls our baser elements, and the cruelty of *Titus* is, similarly, an exploration of soiling physical nature and a gratification of ravening appetite, generously wholesome. Weeping irrigates earth, Alarbus's entrails feed the fire. Titus discharges arrows at the sky in the belief that heaven is sentient, and can be wounded: it is a play of a sanguine animism. The tormented body will not accept defeat, but invents a technology to substitute for its ravaged limbs and organs, as the engineered extensions of man. Marcus teaches Lavinia to write handlessly. The physical creature is heroically, comically indestructible. This is not the pestilential theatre of Artaud, spreading delirium or contagion like Peter Weiss's inmates during their enactment of Marat's assassination; nor is it the necromantic theatre of *Dr Faustus*, during a performance of which the actors were alarmed to count one devil too many on the stage. If it is a saturnalia, then so is comedy. Its climax, appropriately, is a cannibalistic festivity. And its obsession, like *The Comedy of Errors*, is familial love and the analogy between our germinating of offspring and the theatre's duplicating of us—'This my self', says Aaron of his child, 'The vigour and the picture of my youth.' What difference is there between the unhallowed, bloodstained aperture which engorges Quintus and Martius and the chink in the wall so smuttily plugged in

A Midsummer Night's Dream? Both are orifices of earth, entries into its body; Martius, peering into the pit's bowels, compares himself with Pyramus, the role assumed by Bottom.

The Shakespearean forms move irresistibly towards their opposites, reconvening tragicomedy. The history plays effect an even more comprehensive reunion: the concise form of drama repossesses the unedited, wayward ampleness of narrative. History means to Shakespeare the necessary expansion of drama to include a life it has neither time nor space to dramatise. The *Henry VI* trilogy is one of his most ambitious inventions, in its insistence on continuing—on an endlessness which defies drama's concern to speed towards a judicious end (and when this trio is over, it is extended both forward and, when the reigns of Henry IV and Henry V are added, behind)—and in its enlargement of the stage's cramped domain. There is a prodigal multiplying of life in *Henry VI*, a reproof to drama's exiguousness. A messenger gabbles of 'three and twenty thousand' French troops; Lucy enumerates the emblazoned titles of Lord Talbot and magnifies him to occupy an entire realm just as Hume promises to Eleanor of Gloucester the multiplication of her title; Suffolk declares the graces of Margaret to be voluminous, proliferating beyond the meagre stage and requiring a book to chronicle them aright, and when despatched to marry her on Henry's behalf he lists the plenum of witnesses:

> . . . . the Kings of France and Sicil,
> The Dukes of Orleans, Calaber, Bretagne, and Alençon,
> Seven earls, twelve barons, and twenty reverend bishops.

In *Tamburlaine* such numbering would be mere theatrical pomp. In Shakespeare it is the validation of the world elsewhere which the play would like, if it had space enough and time, to have included.

The dilation of drama is not only managed by this populous overspilling; it is a psychological feat. Such self-transcendence or superfluity, growing beyond the confines of allotted dramatic role, is the skill and grace of Shakespearean character. Hamlet possesses it, discovering infinitude within the minute nutshell of the mind or the cramped acreage of the stage, that much-contested plot of ground; Falstaff does, too, except that this emblem for it is not the sovereign state of the mind but the swelling bulk of his belly. The same power is already exercised by the people in *Henry VI*. The dying Mortimer's recital of the dynastic past catalogues the contents of his own ancestral memory; and if he can see before the play, Joan of Arc can see beyond it. As her simile of the circle expanding in water implies, her prophetic gift is a power of enlargement, again overcoming drama. She has the freedom of an untrammelled time, and can narrate what is past and passing and to come. She outstrips drama's restriction to the blinkered present of happening. In a play, such magnifying can only be exercised verbally. The genius of Shakespeare's language is in its excess, in its eloquent capacity to universalise the character through whose single voice it is uttered. His people are benign Tamburlaines, who do not need to conquer lands offstage because dramatic imagination and poetic language can transport them there, like Viola in *Twelfth Night* linguistically erecting that willow-cabin for herself outside Olivia's gate, or inventing that sister who can, on her behalf, die of disappointed love.

Henry VI brilliantly studies the politics of this language. Words are, like the technological staffs in *Titus Andronicus*, the extensions of men, their means of imposition on others. The Countess of Auvergne lures Talbot to her den by sending a messenger to beg for her the chance to behold 'The man/Whose glory fills the world with loud report.' When she captures him, he taunts her by saying she has locked up the shadow of him not the substance. To accommodate that, the stage would have to dismantle and stretch itself to take in the universe:

> . . . . were the whole frame here,
> It is of such a spacious lofty pitch
> Your roof were not sufficient to contain 't.

Spatially flexing beyond drama, he is also measuring the limits of his theatrical role. All the play can show of him is this 'smallest part / And least proportion of humanity'; the truth of the man—his historical complexity—abounds in liberty offstage. Talbot's existence is elastic, mentally illimitable here, heraldically omnipresent when Lucy spends ten lines enumerating his fiefs, but contracted again to the single human body from which these powers have verbally irradiated when Joan diminishes him to a corpse, 'stinking and flyblown . . . at our feet'. Shakespeare is forever tactfully indicating that more might be narrated than he can manage to enact. Suffolk disdains to specify all of Gloucester's treacheries, and contents himself with abbreviation: 'Mightier crimes are laid unto your charge.'

The play is in a minority. But its least proportion admits the pullulation of the life outside it, the nimblest wisdom consists in manoeuvering an escape from the compulsions of the historical and dramatic regime. Comedy means an existence of untroubled irrelevance, an exemption from the history being rehearsed—acted out that is, wearisomely over and over again—on stage. The Mayor of London claims this safety and ignominy for himself in an aside prior to his exit:

> Good God, these nobles should such stomachs bear!
> I myself fight not once in forty year.

It is guaranteed to Sir John Fastolfe by his cowardice, and developed into a convenient philosophy by Falstaff, who is so extra-dramatically alive, and so astutely intent on scheming to stay that way, that he can afford to mock the stage's simulations of life and death, performing his end at Shrewsbury in the first *Henry IV* play and then accomplishing the comic miracle of his own resurrection. Because Falstaff is alive outside the theatre—nourished by the landscape in which he reposes, the eternality of pastoral and of comedy—he cannot be killed by it. When Shakespeare wants to terminate him, it has to be done offstage, in *Henry V*; and even then the report cannot be trusted, because the hostess's malapropism when she sends him to Arthur's bosom, not Abraham's, presages his reappearance, which was Arthur's promise to his kingdom. Falstaff is soon again exhumed by royal command, liberated altogether from the vexatious duties of history, and put out to pasture in Windsor forest. He is even permitted, in his copious inclusiveness, to become his generic other half, when he dresses up as the fat woman of Brainford to escape Ford's persecution.

Jack Cade and the disgruntled peasants in *Henry VI* are rebellious because comic, and their leader has a Falstaffian scepticism about the officiousness of political action and the pettifogging responsibilities of history. His own unpolitical arena is the theatre, where he bears a charmed life. He envisages a democracy of blabber, inventing laws (as the Shakespearean character invents himself) as it goes along: 'Away, burn all the records of the realm! My mouth shall be the parliament of England.' In his most negligent cruelty, there is, as in *Timon*, an inadvertent comic compassion. Sentencing Lord Say to 'be beheaded ten times', he is gesturing towards that talent for reincarnation which Falstaff proves at Shrewsbury or which Cleopatra explores with her connoisseurship of easy ways to die and her orgiastically multiple deaths. In ordering Say to be killed, he is allowing him the charmed immortality of the stage, where death is a feint repeated at every performance. Cade's own death occurs in an extraordinary scene which alternates between his scurrilous prose and the genteel pentameters of Iden who slays him. Civil war is not only the play's subject but a model for its form: tragedy against comedy, poetry against prose. And that contradiction remains here unreconciled. Cade dies in a garden where, famished, he has come 'to see if I can eat grass'. His herbivorous end anticipates Falstaff's babbling of green fields. He seeks a retreat into nature, the low-profiled anonymity of prose. His last words announce the Falstaffian ethic, exhorting 'all the world to be cowards'. He refuses to accept Iden's judgement on him, and claims to have been killed only by hunger. His prose will not believe in the termini of tragedy or the foreclosed, conclusive lines of poetry. Nevertheless Iden executes him in poetry and carves up the body which Cade had hoped to conceal in nature, leaving the trunk to be eaten by crows on the dung-hill and carrying the head back to the king.

The play's irony—and irony, as the romantic commentators on Shakespeare realised, is a means of temporising between tragedy and comedy, having both at once as Sterne does—is that while the comedians are plotting to supplant the king, he, tragically burdened, envies the pastoral lowliness and anonymity of comedy. As Henry says in the scene before Cade's death,

> Was never subject longed to be a king
> As I do long and wish to be a subject.

It is the perennial yearning of the Shakespearean monarch. Henry V play-actingly experiences that subjection when disguised on the eve of Agincourt; so does Lear on the heath. Tragedy seeks the tutelage of comedy, history asks for its own disestablishment.

Tragedy resumes as comedy in *Richard III* when—with that seasonal rhythm which is the beatitude of pastoral—the winter of discontent turns to glorious summer. Richard can, like his accomplice Buckingham, 'counterfeit the deep tragedian', but his instincts are those of the comedian. He acknowledges no necessity of moral character: his is a self as impromptu as Iago's. Though he says 'I am determined to prove a villain', nothing determines him but his whim, and he can dazzlingly persuade others to be responsible for his actions—Anne for his infatuation with her, the Mayor and citizens for his ambition, Queen Elizabeth for his marriage proposal to her daughter. He is a frivolously devilish Falstaff or a murderous Puck, a character who exploits the theatre's timelessness as a conjurer's licence, and who knows—like Antipholus in Ephesus—that in a play you are never more than two hours old, and therefore can accumulate no criminal record. Feigning conciliation, he says he is no more at odds with any man 'than the infant that is born tonight'. The Prince of Wales is impatient to 'live to be a man'. Richard, again invoking that seasonal cycle which mutates dramatic genres, comments that 'Short summers lightly have a forward spring', and saves his nephew from the infliction of maturing by killing him off; when Clarence is imprisoned thanks to his scheming, he explains this, too, as a comic benison, another of the theatre's serial rebirths—perhaps Clarence, whose name offends the king, will be 'new christen'd in the Tower'.

Richard is safe so long as he can keep up the hectic business of performing himself, fending off conscience by denying the past's hold on him, living exclusively in the forgetful present and acting at highest speed so that he will not backslide into moral being: 'Richard loves Richard; that is, I am I.' One of his most daring dodges in his recitation of a history which impedes his enemies—

> Let me put in your minds, if you forget,
> What you have been ere this, and what you are—

but which he urges himself to keep ahead of. Hence his desperate need for the horse at Bosworth. With its aid, he might still outrun consequence. In this play of curses and witchery, of promises (like Richard's to Buckingham, on which he reneges) as spells for control of the future, the surest assault Richard's victims can make on him is to deprive him of his 'cheer of mind', and of the comedian's impudent, ebullient liberty. Their sentence is that he collapse into tragic accountability: 'despair and die!'

Richard III speaks of royalizing his brother's blood, Richard II of monarchizing. Both, as actors and as mortal men, know themselves to be only temporary kings. Royalty means for Richard III the ego's impetuous sovereignty, demanding the whim's instant translation into deed (he wants the princes dead, and 'would have it suddenly performed'; he will not dine until he sees the head of Hastings); for Richard II, to reign is to rain tears on the earth which is not the ego's monopolised stage but our collective grave. Tragedy and comedy have their due succession when Northumberland announces that 'the Duke of Lancaster is dead' and Ross adds, 'And living too; for now his son is Duke', and they sickly change places when Bolingbroke, after Richard's death, admits, 'I hate the murderer, love him murdered'. Richard's renunciation of power is his concession to the comedy of mortality, to a pastoral levelling. Monarchy is the self's conceit, our vain confidence in our perpetuity. Richard wisely abdicates from the duty of being the vertical tragic man and consents to become the horizontal man of comedy: 'For God's sake let us sit upon the ground', since that posture is alone appropriate to the recognition of 'the death of kings'. Abasement is the tendency of everything in the play—the apricots dangling and stooping to earth; Richard saluting his 'dear earth . . . with my hand' in Wales, to atone for the hurt inflicted on it by the hooves of the rebels' horses; Bolingbroke 'on both his knees [kissing] King Richard's hands' and offering to lay down his arms 'at his feet'; the arthritic, bended joints of York and his Duchess as they beg for mercy. Richard's is the humbled posture of genuflection. Such bodily submission embarrasses Bolingbroke, who three times bids his pleading aunt to stand up. The comic homage to earth is an offering of filial piety, since it is our parental source. The Duchess of Gloucester, describing her husband as a hacked, felled tree, tells John of Gaunt he is rooted in the same soil, 'that bed, that womb', and Gaunt, dying, takes the metaphor upon himself and becomes the national landscape of which he speaks, furrowed with age, reaping cares as his harvest. His bardic recall of the past, 'writ in remembrance', and his prophetic foreseeing of the future, make him a genealogical tree. Turning into an emblem of his name, he quibblingly couples comedy and tragedy, the marriage-bed and the charnel:

> Gaunt am I for the grave, gaunt as a grave
> Whose hollow womb inherits nought but bones.

Reunited with this turf, Richard will later call himself 'a long-parted mother' greeting her child. Like Gaunt with his 'teeming womb' and his office as nurse to kings or Falstaff complaining 'my womb, my womb, my womb undoes me', Richard as the king is that earth's solicitous mother. Falstaff can disguise himself both as muffled Mother Prat, that rump-fed ronyon, and as a rutting stag in the forest: the overlapping of genres and genders reclaims the multifoliate oneness which is the heart of nature and of its poet, Shakespeare.

Falstaff, in his versatile, human magnitude, symbolises the common denominator between men. He is a comic imp of mischief and at the same time a tragic, sacrificial victim, his offer of love spurned by the world (for the pair of plays which ends which his rejection begins with Henry's reference to 'those blessed feet' nailed 'for our advantage on the bitter cross', and Falstaff himself with a saviour's twinge of remorse declares that Hal is 'able to corrupt a saint'). Henry IV deplores this commonness, remembering that Richard II was 'sick and blunted with community' and deploring Hal's 'vile participation'. But though Falstaff pretends to agree—'Company, villainous company, hath been the spoil of me'—companionability is his generous gift of life. His extroversion makes a dramatist of him, generating offshoots which flourish independently: he is 'the cause that wit is in other men'. In Falstaff, a bodily version of the great globe itself, all existences can be contained and reconciled. Like Doll Tearsheet, he is a highway for a life which treads him down, a road (in Poins's phrase) 'as common as the way between Saint Albans and London'. Gadshill indirectly understands him when he says to the chamberlain '"homo" is a common name to all men'. That faith is later, when Fielding in *Tom Jones* puns on homo and Homer, the enabling edict of the novel, pledged to the study of a shared human nature and to the abolition of generic discriminations.

Throughout the *Henry IV* plays, unlike existences find themselves at home in Falstaff. He and Hotspur for instance come together as agents of misrule and topsy-turvydom, and his comic risk-taking is a more prudent version of Hotspur's self-destructive, chivalric escapades. The weary king, aspiring to shed his cares and to sleep, envies the sloth and unselfconsciousness of the horizontal man and longs for the shallowness and silence which are Falstaff's realm. He plans a journey to the Holy Land; Falstaff, embedded in an English landscape whose 'latter spring' and 'All-hallown summer' he is, already resides there. And Henry learns, as if from Falstaff, the revocability of death when he awakes from his torpor and finds that his sleep has been supposed his demise. When Hal accedes to the throne, he takes on himself a paternity which he has absorbed from Falstaff, assuring his brothers he will now be a father to them and the Lord Chief Justice that he will 'speak my father's words'. Falstaff is a source for all these lives. He denies dramatic activation only to Prince John: 'I would you had but the wit; 'twere better than your dukedom.' People seem to grow from and on him, for he is the nature in which they thrive and the territory they contest. Hal calls him a 'huge hill', and Falstaff speaks of himself as a tree of knowledge known by its fruit, and of his reasons as a plentiful crop of blackberries.

Mistress Quickly, in spite of herself, blesses his fructifying abundance and inexhaustibility in her attempt to curse and condemn him. Ordering Fang to arrest him for breach of promise, she declares him to be 'an infinitive thing': the infinitive is the verbal first mover, capable of infinite and indefinite predications of itself throughout the world. Before he arrives in Gloucestershire, Shallow and Silence are articulating his meaning in terms of pastoral, where tragedy and comedy meet and every death provokes rebirths. They converse of defunct acquaintances and acknowledge that 'Death, as the Psalmist saith, is certain to all; all shall die', but they secure a reprieve for themselves by retrieving—thanks to Falstaff—a youth stored intact in memory, when they reminisce of their merry nights and of Jane Nightwork (who, as Falstaff testifies, still lives), and as well they pay tribute to an earth whose regeneration cannot be interrupted by single, sorry, human fates: 'How a good yoke of bullocks at Stamford fair?' or 'How a score of ewes now?'

Drama is temporally peremptory, spatially restrictive. Falstaff, elongating and expanding himself, gives the lie to both unities. Though his first speech is a question about the time of day, Hal rightly perceives that he asks it only to assert his own incorrigible timelessness. He does not accept the dramatic tempo of inevitability whereby (as in Macbeth's case) the past impends in our present and predestines our tomorrows. When the Justice—legalistically wanting to establish his age so as to equip him with a record of truancies, defining him as the dramatic character who, like Everyman, is the guilty sum total of his actions—upbraids him for calling himself young, Falstaff replies with seraphic ingenuousness, 'I was born about three of the clock in the afternoon, with a white head and something a round belly.' Instead of being born in the past, he conceives himself in the present. He proposes extemporising a play at the Boar's Head, because to be extemporary is to be extracted from time.

The political characters are menaced by abbreviation. 'O gentlemen', says Hotspur, 'the time of life is short!' They operate according to a moral schedule which is the régime of drama, where the clock ticks towards a high noon of judgement. Warwick believes 'There is a history in all men's lives', and the Archbishop also sees forgetfulness of time as the primal error, condemning those who have not learned the lesson of history to suffer the purgatory of repeating it: 'past and to come seems best; things present, worst'. As the scene ends, an exchange between Mowbray and Hastings indicates their obedience to prescriptive time and their conscientious care for enumeration, also flouted by Falstaff when he multiplies the quantity of foes he overcomes at Gadshill. Mowbray says, 'Shall we go draw our numbers, and set on?' to which Hastings adds, 'We are time's subjects, and time bids begone.' Henry IV sees time erosively and punitively. 'The book of fate' records 'the revolution of the times', whereby mountains are worn level as plains. Foreknowledge would advance a feckless comedy into tragedy: 'the happiest youth', if he consulted that predestining text, 'would shut the book and sit him down to die.' Falstaff accepts no such fatality, and weighed down by tragedies—the pox, the gout and consumption of purses, all incurable—can charm them back into comedies: 'A good wit will make use of anything. I will turn diseases to commodity.'

As it is, *Henry IV* contradicts the remorselessness of that text the King consults. If history is written, it is a mode of tragic determinism, for the book is oracular; if it is performed, enacted, it is brought alive and its characters are freed from its prescriptions, allowed to invent—and thus revive—their pasts. The difference between chronicle and drama corresponds to that between history as dynastic annals and as personal, private recollection. Clarence, who, like all the play's politicians, trusts the scribal testimony on which he relies for his immortality, mocks the alternative of oral and popular fabling: 'the old folk, Time's doting chronicles' look for portents of political change in the erratic behaviour of a river. But it is the reminiscences of such old folk which the play increasingly retails, since theirs is the history of the body or the earth, of an entire community, usually unconsulted, which acquires a voice in many-tongued Rumour—Shallow's maunderings of the days he has seen, or Mistress Quickly's compendiously total recall when, giving evidence for Falstaff's jilting of her, she sets about reciting the entire history of the world as she experienced it: 'Thou didst swear to me upon a parcel-gilt goblet, sitting in my Dolphin chamber, at the round table, by a sea-coal fire, upon Wednesday in Wheeson week, when the Prince broke thy head for liking his father to a singing-man of Windsor . . .' and so on, and on. Her remembering is a re-collecting of disparate data, soon implicating goodwife Keech and her dish of prawns, and, if allowed to continue, it would add up into the sum of everything which ever was. Such a summation—a composite of all human experience in his resistance to time—is Falstaff. Thanks to him, Hal can resume in himself 'all humours . . . since the old days of goodman Adam to the pupil-age of this present twelve o'clock at midnight', and Doll extravagantly but aptly celebrates the incorporation within Falstaff of all his paternity: 'Thou art as valorous as Hector of Troy, worth five of Agamemnon, and ten times better than the Nine Worthies.'

The plays about English history reunite tragedy and comedy in pastoral when Falstaff takes his recruiting campaign to Gloucestershire and relapses into a nature at once enfeebled and dying (in Shallow's dreaming of a long-ago juvenescence) and vigorously reborn (in the valour of Feeble, the womans' tailor). Shakespeare's plays about Roman history are a critique of the classical ethics and aesthetics which this English spirit flouts. A classical art prizes the impersonal moral rectitude of Rome—Brutus in David's painting stoically witnessing the return of the bodies of his sons, Racine's Titus denying himself Bérénice for reasons of state—and sees in its own workmanship a similar victory of formal propriety over sentient content. Classicism chills flesh to stone, as the sculptor Canova does with his gelid Paolina Borghese, or else congeals it, as Dickens suspected, to grisly wax. Mrs Jarley, proprietrix of the waxworks in *The Old Curiosity Shop*, sets herself against this native genius when she deplores the vulgarity of Mr Punch and expels comedy from her 'calm and classical' exhibition, which is 'always the same, with a constant but unchanging air of coldness and gentility'. The ideal of the classical is to reify man as a monument.

Shakespeare's Caesar boasts of his constancy, fixing his foot in the sky like the northern star. Like all Shakespeare's Romans, his marmoreal composure seeks superbly to belie the vulnerable, individual life within; he is the antitype to the meek humane principle which is the Falstaffian flesh, concerned about the invigoration of the blood and calcified only in death. The sacrifice performed by the augurers in *Julius Caesar* stands for this exemplary Roman hollowing of the interior. Disembowelling the offering, 'they could not find a heart within the beast'. The double plot in *Henry IV* encourages the civil war of tragedy and comedy, poetry and prose, warfare and clowning; Brutus, seeing that lively contradictoriness as 'a phantasma', stands on guard against a rebellion inside him which will destroy his classical poise and shamingly humanize him: 'the state of man, / Like to a little kingdom, suffers . . . / The nature of an insurrection'. The Roman plays enforce a dictatorship of style. Classicism's moral esteem goes to characters who stint and sear the craven natural flesh, punishing themselves to apologise for their humanity— Cominius's 'would he had slain my son' in *Coriolanus*, which recalls the stoic choice of David's Brutus; the voluntary wound Portia gives herself to prove she is worthy of Brutus's confidence; the conspirators' planning of butchery as surgery, carving Caesar as a dish fit for the gods since it is not a man they are killing but an idea which they are, with their swords, rebutting.

The seat of Shakespearean identity is in the body, as the rubicund Falstaff or the too solidly fleshly Hamlet, 'fat and scant of breath', proclaim. It became a convention of romantic art criticism to argue that classicism confined itself to line, representing only the skeletal Platonic idea of people, whereas romantic painting used colour to suffuse organisms with blood and the tints of vitality. The line circumscribes the human shape but will not fill it in. Shakespeare's classical characters are demeaned by the infirm, amiable body. In contrast with Richard II's sitting on the ground, Caesar is despised for swooning in the market-place. He has 'the falling sickness', which is humanity. If the Romans cannot upraise the body as a statue, they will cancel it altogether by running on their swords.

The imagery of *Coriolanus* is physiological, but monstrously so. Coriolanus's body is a terror to the nature which bore it. The ground shrinks before his treading, thunder tears the sky's cheeks, and his advance tramples on his mother's womb. Volumnia sups upon herself; ambitious to stand 'as if a man were author of himself / And knew no other kin', Coriolanus excludes himself from that nativity in earth which is the subject of Falstaff's meditations in Gloucestershire or Hamlet's at the graveside. His one natural act, when he succumbs to his mother's entreaty, is therefore promptly the death of him.

More than human existence, he craves the unsubjective objecthood of the outcrop of rock carved into the mere likeness of humanity. Aufidius's most portentous compliment is to call him 'thou noble thing', and Cominius wonders at him as 'a thing / Made by some other deity than nature'. In the tribal, warfaring Rome of *Coriolanus*, he attains that condition sacrificially. The body whose preservation he disdains becomes a bloody monument, its wounds oratorical voices, when he exhibits it in the market-place. The Rome of *Julius Caesar* is a later, changed place—a republic no longer ruled by the force of epic will and musculature like Coriolanus's; in its new political system, characters study to feign an inhuman sternness and steeliness not properly theirs. Cassius mocks the human frailty of Caesar, who presumes to divinity though he is a feeble man. The status of 'thing' is not venerable here, as it was in *Coriolanus*. Cassius refuses 'to be / In awe of such a thing as I myself'. Is there, in his phrase, a memory of the *res* in *res publica*, and a definition of the classical democracy which equates all men but only as things, interchangeable objects not (like authentic Shakespearean characters) incompatible, differentiated subjects, each one 'adored once too'?

Nomenclature is a means of ensuring this classical equal measure. Cassius points out that 'Brutus' and 'Caesar' have the same value:

> Write them together: yours is as fair a name.
> Sound them: it doth become the mouth as well.
> Weigh them: it is as heavy.

He is indirectly justifying the logical impartiality of the mob which slaughters Cinna the poet because he has the same name as one of the conspirators. Cassius refers as well to 'my single self'. The singularity of the self is here its blame not its glory; safety lies in membership of a committee. By the end of the play, personal naming—scorned as too natal and natural by Coriolanus, who will be 'a kind of nothing' until he forges a new name in the fire of Rome—has been overruled by a uniform Romanness. Cassius and Brutus quarrel over that appellation, to which they have an equal right; Portia lays claim to it, apologising for her singleness and, again, for her humanity by pleading her membership of a patriarchy:

> I grant I am a woman; but withal
> A woman that Lord Brutus took to wife.
> I grant I am a woman; but withal
> A woman well reputed, Cato's daughter.

If Antony declares Brutus to have been 'the noblest Roman of them all', it is because he had no personal motive, and killed Caesar to serve 'the common good'. Coriolanus disputed nature's authorship of him. Antony says of Brutus that

> . . . . Nature might stand up
> And say to all the world, 'This was a man!'

but his naturalness is formulaic not idiosyncratic, and a matter of chemistry, because Antony insists on the temperate mixture of elements in him. Throughout the play Brutus contends against an insurrectionary human nature in himself, for instance by so archly disdaining to react to Portia's death. Like *Coriolanus*, *Julius Caesar* demonstrates the fatality of a classical denial of the individual. Coriolanus is destroyed when he obeys a natural impulse, and Caesar is killed because of his premeditated scorn for private causes, his objectifying sense of himself as a third person. He will not heed the warnings of the soothsayer because 'what touches us ourself shall be last heard'.

In the third play of the sequence, republican Rome, stringent and self-enclosed, has been stretched into an empire. Its distension is the surrender of classical dramatic form, intent on its own integration, to a Shakespearean diffuseness; and Antony, when he surrenders to Cleopatra, quits the rigour of classical character for a malleable, impulsively contradictory Shakespearean consciousness. Cleopatra alternates between the shrewish and the sublime, the erotic and the strategic. Instead of the prized single self, she has a repertory of variant selves. She is the eternal woman, of whom Cleopatra is only one manifestation. She so far entices Antony out of the stark delineation of Romanness that she tempts him to the ultimate exploratory imitation, that of gender, when she dresses him in her garments and herself buckles on his sword, and she is able to admit, in her own case, that the eternal woman is played by a squeaking boy. Once she has instructed Antony in the dispensability of a consistent character and the delight of a ludic life which veers and frolics according to momentary pleasure, he can instruct his Roman colleagues in the same revelling joy, during the banquet in Pompey's gallery.

Their genius is, like Shakespeare's, for the dissolution of categories, for a fluency of transition imaged by the water which is Cleopatra's element. Their boldest commuting of tragedy to comedy comes in the leisure and luxury of their dying. Unlike his forebears in *Julius Caesar*, Antony finds it difficult to die. Suicide for the conspirators is a technique and an etiquette. Almost by-passing the body, it entails a necessary muting, the silencing of a character whose life consisted classically in oratory. Brutus, again a third person to himself, remarks that his 'tongue / Hath almost ended his life's history'. Antony, who can persuade no one to dispatch him and merely wounds himself when he falls upon his sword, has lost this proficiency at self-cancellation. He is too embroiled in life and in the body to be able easily to quit it. Hauled up into Cleopatra's monument, he tries to recall the stoic rules for expiring, dispensing sage advice and reverting to typicality as 'a Roman by a Roman/Valiantly vanquish'd', but is overruled by Cleopatra's railing and chiding. She has already killed and resurrected herself, sending word prematurely to Antony of her suicide; now she performs the same comic rite for him, reanimating him as an undying, bountifully seminal deity in her speeches to Dolabella. She understands death corporeally, as the spirit's vanishing-act. Of Antony's corpse she remarks, 'The case of that huge spirit now is cold', and she might be the hostess describing Falstaff.

Tragically, death is final, necessary and exemplary: for Othello, 'my journey's end, . . . my butt'. Comically, it has no such terminal value, and is the absurd, contingent expense of spirit. Cleopatra therefore prepares for it by taking instruction from a clown, who presents the worm to her as her conduit to immortality. 'Those that do die of it', he says, 'do seldom or never recover', but Cleopatra is one of those few. Death is a painless cessation to her, like that romantically dreamed of by Keats, and as in comedy—where the reported ends of Hero in *Much Ado About Nothing* or Helena in *All's Well That Ends Well* signify the character's regeneration—it is a rehearsal for rebirths. Performance to Cleopatra is reincarnation. She predicts her successive returns to life, inaugurated by caricaturists in the Roman triumphs: those 'quick comedians' are to be her preservers. The resuscitation continues with every actress who plays this eternal woman. Before Octavius thinks of preaching the conventional obsequy, he marvels at her wizardry in scenically contriving the spirit's exit from the uninjured flesh (left intact, awaiting her reassumption of it), and is only satisfied when the vent of blood and the aspic's trail are pointed out to him. *The Winter's Tale* grants her an encore: Paulina's vivification of the classical statue which is Hermione is, like everything Cleopatra does, at once a revelation and a stunt.

History homes to pastoral, in Shallow's orchard or the oozy bed of Cleopatra's serpentine Nile; so does Shakespearean comedy, in Navarre or Arden or in the nocturnal wood where Bottom dreams his dream which has no bottom, a subliminal depth which is Pope's slough of bathos or the psychological cellarage from which Freudian jokes reer up. The settings of Shakespeare's last plays are maritime because, like *The Comedy of Errors*, they are concerned with the regrouping of people who are life's flotsam; those of the comedies are afforested because they are about our encounter with our own human nature.

The wood in *As You Like It* is the anticipation in comedy of Lear's heath. For Rosalind, it signifies a retreat into the care of Nature, away from Fortune, the fickle superintendent of court affairs, and her comic resolve and resilience are the impulses of her naturalness, laughing at fortune and so amending it. The wrestling match with which the play begins signifies this vital combat in nature. Though Charles believes that his opponent is 'desirous to lie with his mother earth', the play goes on to show that to be no tragic calamity but a comic conciliation. Earth maternally ensures, in Celia's words, that all worldly gifts will 'henceforth be bestowed equally', since we are all equated in our mortality and in our comic bodily cravings and likings. At first it is Rosalind and Celia, 'bred together', who are 'coupled and inseparable'; later Rosalind's disguise enables her to reunite within herself the sundered sexes, to play-act the mystery of Spenser's androgyne Nature or his hermaphroditic lovers, wooing

Orlando the more subtly by appealing to him as a fellow-male than she ever could have if she had remained conventionally female, and extending her versatile insinuation with men as a woman and with women as a man to the audience in her epilogue; and Orlando, succouring elderly Adam, can refer to himself, a youth, as the old man's mother: 'like a doe, I go to find my fawn / And bring it food.' The play's concern is coupling. To Jaques, its wedding processional looks like an embarkation of all species in advance of another flood. Rosalind and Orlando, before they achieve the union of opposites in marriage, have already experienced it within themselves. Orlando practises versifying as just such a biological grafting, and seems potentially able to make all words fertilisingly rhyme with Rosalinde or Rosalinda, whose name he inscribes on the trees 'at every sentence end', because rhyme for him is a marital accord between words. A play about the state of nature concludes with the advent of heaven on earth, and the establishment of comedy's divinity. Hymen sings of 'mirth in heaven' when earthly things atone together: when two, that is, are made at one. Touchstone is the comic philosopher of this natural condition. As a clown he is a natural, and therefore—marrying the sluttish Audrey—is enrolled among the country copulatives. His antagonist, Jaques, exchanges clowning for railery, comedy for satire. Rather than giving in to nature's instinctive promptings, he exiles himself from a humanity which disgusts him. He is not 'for dancing measures', and will not be paired. The anchoritic solitude of satire, as against a comic gregariousness, awaits him in the Duke's 'abandon'd cave'. That dank cell will become the satirist's hideout, when Pope excavates his grotto at Twickenham or Gulliver takes up residence in his stables.

Because *As You Like It* is a pastoral, it contemplatively arrests drama. Between the initial exile and the final homecoming, nothing happens in it: the forest is a place for meditation and debate, a sanctuary exempt from the disturbances of action. The 'convertites', as Jaques calls them, have brought about a conversion of the play's form. There is no clock in the forest. It is immune to the scheduling of dramatic time. But in its timelessness and eternality, it contains, preserved in hallowing recollection, all the ages of man (narrated by Jaques) and his emotional seasons—since as Rosalind says, 'men are April when they woo, December when they wed: maids are May when they are maids'—and as well all the ages of the world, computed by Rosalind to be 'almost six thousand years old'. Like Hal comprising within himself all humours since Adam, Rosalind can remember back through a sequence of identities to 'Pythagoras' time that I was an Irish rat'. Abiding Arden has a memory as long as that of her body. It is all pastoral pleasances overlaid—first the Eden of biblical myth (the play's opening words are 'As I remember, Adam'), since though people suffer there 'the penalty of Adam' which is nature's inclemency, it is their reward for undergoing a fortunate fall in the wrestling match; then a classical Arcady where time fleets carelessly 'as . . . in the golden world'; later the legendary England of 'the old Robin Hood'; at last the agricultural economy of Shakespeare's own society, for Rosalind acquires her cottage from an absentee landlord. The play is prescient beyond itself. Jaques combines satiric contempt for nature with a sentimental pathos about it which makes him bewail the deer's death: romanticism coincides with the industrial revolution, and nature is worshipped by those who are responsible for despoiling and fouling it. William Hodges in 1790 painted a bile-green landscape for the figure of Jaques (added by George Romney) to grieve in over the wounded stag, curled among the roots of a gnarled oak. The misanthrope is making use of romantic nature's latter-day pastoral to ease his conscience.

Arden is a composite everywhere; Illyria in *Twelfth Night* is a fantasticated erewhon, an interior of illusion, which might have been concocted by the captain in response to Viola's first question. Characters employ it as a standard, Sir Toby calling Sir Andrew 'as tall a man as any's in Illyria' and Sir Andrew claiming to be as good 'as any man in Illyria', but as such it is only the alibi for their own deceptive self-promotions. It is adjacent to reality, the product of the age's geographical revisionism, like 'the new map with the augmentation of the Indies' mentioned by Maria. People import their own local referents of reality to it: Antonio arranges a rendezvous with Sebastian in a transplanted London, 'in the south suburbs, at the Elephant'. Nothing in it can be counted on to be firm, fixed and stable. Feste teases Viola by telling her he lives by the church, situating himself in a setting which he is improvising as he quibbles, and he contradicts Malvolio, imprisoned in the dark room, by expounding the fenestration of Olivia's house. He invokes the detail of a real world only to confound people.

There is here no union of opposites in nature. Character is a self-invented chimera: Viola's disguise, Olivia's unveiling of the picture which is her face, Malvolio practising attitudes to his own shadow. Instead of *As You Like It*'s ark, the play's receptacle is a locker of fantasy, allowing for the interchangeability of these polymorphous people: Sir Toby refers to 'the bed of Ware in ᴇngland'. Where Pythagoras is introduced, during Feste's inquisition of the mad Malvolio, it is not to sponsor the self's migratory extensions, like Rosalind in her heyday as an Irish rat, but as a worker of witchcraft, usurping identity. Malvolio is aghast at the notion that his grandam's soul 'mightly haply inhabit a bird'. Such dispossessions are, however, the unsettling subject of the play. Olivia is 'personated'—which means that she is abrogated in her own person—when Maria forges her handwriting, Malvolio is encouraged to counterfeit himself, Orsino is persuaded to dote upon the eunuch Cesario and Sebastian finds himself captured by the disorienting fantasy of Olivia's infatuation. Love means, as Antonio's imprecations put it, the erection of an image to be idolised; its perfection is a devout self-love, or a worship of the replica of self which is one's twin. As if anagrammatically, Viola, Olivia and Malvolio are contained in one another, and the first words of Antonio's curse on the fickle Sebastian could almost be unscrabbled to spell out those offending, mutating names: 'O, how vile an idol proves this god!' Feste is no touchstone. He, too, is told who he is by others, characterised by his foes as an ass, and when he sings he counterfeits emotions for a fee. He is also a self-inventor, who aggrandises the self by conjuring a sibling for it: like Viola, he pretends to ownership of a sister, and wills her to anonymity—he wishes she 'had had no name'. If the play recalls *As You Like It*'s comic history of the world, it is as a muddled alternation of wind and rain, amounting in the end, as Feste's disconsolate song expresses it, to the sad bereavement of illusion. 'A great while ago the world begun', he says, and adds with wry nihilism, 'But that's all one, our play is done.'

The comedy approximates always to tragedy, in the testing extrusion from shelter and society of the courtiers in *As You Like It*, or in *Twelfth Night*'s deranging demonstration that 'Nothing that is so is so', where comedy means (as ancient tragedy did) the unleashing of pestilence. 'Even so quickly', asks Olivia, 'may one catch the plague?' Theseus in *A Midsummer Night's Dream* explains the drama, like love, as a fit, a lunatic's frenzy. In *Love's Labour's Lost* the feckless performance of a comedy gives way, when death intrudes in the forest, to the penance of tragedy, as Berowne is sent to jest for souls in agony and dying men; in *The Winter's Tale* the solemn terminus of a tragedy yields to the recuperation of comedy. The plays designated as problems are so for the same reason that every Shakespearean play is one: the problem is the inseparability in them of tragedy and comedy. *All's Well That Ends Well* adopts as a title a motto for comedy at the end of its tether. Helena keeps repeating it, long after she despairs of its truth, and derives from it a cynical pragmatism. Ends justify means, no matter how humiliating or duplicitous. Parolles, refusing to be shamed or to die, gives voice to the same basely comic biological determination. Life is a habit, even though it can no longer have any value. Comedy resigns its transformative power. The Abbess can make Antipholus a formal man again, but Rosaline prescribes reformation for Berowne and Antonio condemns Sebastian's deformation, calling him unkind: one who secedes, like Hamlet in his first utterance, from comic kinship.

Measure for Measure is comedy's dead end. The tyranny of carnal needs and fears reduces its people to a minimal existence like that of Barnardine, who is scarcely conscious of being alive yet stubbornly reluctant to die. Any life is better, Claudio pleads, than the nonentity of death. The happy ending here means a cheapening compromise, sacrificing all else to the mere necessity of continuing. This is the point of Mariana's abject, humiliating love for Angelo. Offered money by the Duke to purchase an alternative, she craves 'no other, nor no better man'. The unregeneracy of Falstaff is now tedious folly (as Escalus says to Pompey) or else a criminal incorrigibility, and the tapster assures the bawd that she need not change her trade; the only commonality admitted is a complicity in what Isabella starchily calls 'a natural guiltiness'.

Rosalind's natural magic is supplanted by the legal exaction of redress, as comedy mimics a trial. Angelo hopes Escalus will scourge all the miscreants, the Duke is threatened with a tormenting reformation on the rack, and Isabella cries for 'justice, justice, justice, justice'. When enforced, the comic ending in marriage portends a fate worse than death. Angelo begs for immediate execution but is ordered to wed Mariana first; Lucio must make an honest woman of a bawd and then be whipped, after that hanged. The fertile embraces of Claudio and Juliet are here accounted mortal sin. Rather than coalescing, tragedy and comedy get acrimoniously entangled. The maimed overlapping between them announced by Claudius in *Hamlet*—'mirth in funeral and . . . dirge in marriage'—is not far off.

Claudius indeed advises Hamlet that what he considers a tragedy is closer to comedy, because his fate is not singular: 'Your father lost a father; / That father lost lost his.' The refrain of 'death of fathers' is as common and as consolingly inclusive as Richard II's 'death of kings'. Hamlet is a character at ease in comedy, an ally for Benedick or Berowne, passing the time in word-games, drinking-bouts, casual flirtations and amateur theatricals, who is unadapted to the vindictive role. He ingeniously resists his miscasting in a tragedy of revenge, which requires of him only proficiency in killing and does violence to those agile 'graces' of mind grudgingly admired by Claudius. He manages to free himself from the brutal premise of the form by converting a tragic problem into a comic contrivance; and by growing from tragic misery and self-pity to a comic wisdom of acceptance, taught to him by the gravediggers and (as he remembers) by the infinite jests of Yorick. He dissociates himself from a personal tragedy by making a theatrical tragedy of it when he stages *The Mousetrap*, and though the prologue solemnly introduces that piece as 'our tragedy', Hamlet, designing it as a practical joke, can ask the moment it is called off whether the king liked 'the comedy'. Coleridge thought Hamlet had, like Coleridge himself, a fatal gift of generality. Rather he has a talent for fictionality, a parodic disbelief in himself and in everything else. He does not see the eternity in or behind things, as Coleridge contended, but their flimsiness and fraudulence. An agnostic understanding of the theatre enables him to treat the admonishing ghost as a stage prop, as he laughs at the noise it makes beneath the stage when it is supposed to be dematerialising. He exempts himself from the need to take action by calling into question the meaning and utility of action, and as he does so he redefines the drama.

Classically, character in drama equals action. To action, Hamlet prefers the impromptu bravura of antics, or the experimental pretence of acting. In this he is true to his comic identity: for him, drama is play. This is what Tolstoy complained of in 1906 as the 'unsolved riddle' of the work, and attributed to Hamlet's (and Shakespeare's) moral nullity or lack of character. Tolstoy's puzzlement was right, though his disapproval is wrong. Shakespeare starts from a refusal to write the thriller expected of him, and passes that demur on to

Hamlet, who hands it over to the audience as a problem he needs help with. Who will tell him who he is, and why he cannot do the one thing the play demands of him? By this quizzical tactic, Shakespeare comically humanises a macabre and malicious type of tragedy. But his evasion, when romantically reinterpreted, signifies the possibility of liberation from character and action altogether. Forever devising new personae to frustrate the revenge play's regimentation of him, Hamlet sketches a new kind of character—or rather a self of manifold potentiality, which need never harden into character: Sterne's Tristram Shandy, that virtuoso of associative whim, whose novel is imbued with *Hamlet*; Coleridge, for whom procrastination (Hamlet's comic question-begging) is a tragic affliction; Byron, the romantic ironist who is all things to all men and nothing to himself; the neurotic impotence of Eliot's Prufrock, who qualifies as a modern Hamlet by complaining that he is inadequate for the role.

The method in Hamlet's madness is that of the comic spirit, whose acolyte he is. Though he represents indecision as his tragic ailment, his deceleration of the play, as he sends it off on detours, is a scruple of comedy. He has Falstaff's skill at cheating time with its impending retributions, and what he dreads in death is its punctuality, its refusal to be cajoled into postponements or digressions:

> Had I but time—as this fell sergeant, Death,
> Is strict in his arrest—.

So long as he can keep talking, he has defeated it by delaying it. His soliloquies take what he calls the 'calamity of so long life' and rejoice in it by abetting its elongation. They are not an agonised inquiry into a personal despair, but impersonal essays on a condition which is not Hamlet's. What can he know of all the wrongs he lists as causes for choosing not to be? Oppression, despised love, the law's circumlocution, bureaucratic insolence, the unjust deserts of patient merit are all outside his experience; he adduces them as alibis for his evasion of a duty that is too real for him to relish, and they carelessly fail to fit his own case. He is serious, sententious even, only when joking. The answer to his metaphysical question 'To be, or not to be' is, eventually, the nonchalantly shrugged 'Let be' before the fencing match. Tragedy so humbles itself that Hamlet can now discern 'a special providence in the fall of a sparrow'. He understands death not when meditating on it in moral saws borrowed from Montaigne but when laughing it as a happy, reconciling accident. He at first denies kinship with Claudius, and with anyone else; having killed Polonius he sees that he has granted him a fellowship in earth—compounding his body 'with dust, whereto 'tis kin'—which makes his own end bearable, for everyone he knows has preceded him and awaits him in that state. Like Falstaff or Cleopatra, he understands as well the festivity of death. Our demises satiate nature: 'we fat all creatures else to fat us, and we fat ourselves for maggots.' (No wonder Yeats would later insist, as proof of this mystic gaiety, on Hamlet's corpulence.) Madness is his gift to Ophelia, destroying her by its lucidity when it liberates desire in fantasy and prompts her, in those bawdy rhymes, to sing her distraction. He divides Ophelia, Claudius says, from 'her fair judgement'. Yet overturning that censor licenses her to enact what she is within. The antic disposition should have been a blessing to her. Delacroix in 1839 painted a romantic Hamlet, still in the dandy's mortuary uniform of black and seen from a low, almost subterranean angle, against a lowering sky of overcast thought, teetering on the edge of Ophelia's open grave. The character in the play experiences no such sick fear of cessation. He leaps exultantly in to the trench which Gertrude has already likened to a bride-bed, and volunteers to be 'buried quick' there with Ophelia and—for extra company—Laertes.

Hamlet the comedian is also Hamlet the actor, whose imperative here, as in the scene where he challenges Fortinbras for command of the stage's territory, is a determination not to be upstaged. He will show that he can rant as well as Laertes; if a competitor invokes Pelion, Hamlet will o'ertop him with Ossa. With his charmed and mischievous playfulness, he can be roused to vengeance, as he is by Rosencrantz and Guilderstern, only when someone ventures to play upon him, usurping his theatrical dominion. His most outlandish lie is his contention that 'I know not seems'. He is, on the contrary, a professional seemer and simulator. In him is expressed the theatre's self-delight and self-inculpation: he is Diderot's *comédien*, paradoxically prevented from feeling the emotions he exhibits, because if he allowed that to occur the performance could not continue. It is Polonius's error, when boasting that he 'was accounted a good actor', to become the person he plays, which allows him to be killed (as Hamlet, Falstaff and Cleopatra never can be): 'I did enact Julius Caesar; I was killed i' the Capitol; Brutus killed me.' Though Laertes warns Ophelia against credence, what she reports to Polonius as Hamlet's protestation of love is a gestural dumb show, carefully studied from an Elizabethan acting manual. Hamlet imposes the same rule of theatrical imposture on himself when preparing to upbraid his mother:

> I will speak daggers to her, but use none.
> My tongue and soul in this be hypocrites—.

He is himself misled by the actorly hypocrisy of Claudius, kneeling to pray and emoting a repentance he does not (as he admits when the scene is over) feel, and is humiliated by the crocodile tears of the first player. He scourges Ophelia's cosmetics because they harden her face into a mask, a 'counterfeit presentment' like his picture of his father. Claudius assumes the same false face verbally with his 'painted word' and envies its impenetrability in the mad Ophelia who has become as inexplicable as 'pictures, or mere beasts'. He taunts Laertes by supposing his grief to be the mask's rictus: 'are you like the painting of a sorrow, / A face without a heart?' Hamlet lectures the players on the need for precise fidelity to his text, but is himself anarchically infidel to Shakespeare's, protesting against the revenge play's type-casting and claiming the right to be separated from the actions with which the dramatist would wish accusingly to encumber his character. Hence the breathtakingly insolent bravado of his insistence, in the final scene, that he is not responsible for the destruction of Polonius and Ophelia:

> Was't Hamlet wronged Laertes? Never Hamlet.
> If Hamlet from himself be ta'en away,
> And when he's not himself does wrong Laertes,
> Then Hamlet does it not, Hamlet denies it.
> Who does it, then? His madness.

He proceeds, even more audaciously, to argue that he is in truth the wronged one, victim of a madness which is the dramatist's experimental exploitation of him. Hamlet's enterprises 'lose the name of action', and are redefined as performance.

The old, legalistic, dramatic theory of action persists only in the gossip of the clowns, who scholastically expound an act's three branches. Hamlet declares its irrelevance when he considers the lawyer's skull and asks why it cannot complain of the grave-digger's 'action of battery'. Undetermined by character himself, he behaves as if dramaturgically decreeing characters for others. Thus he decides, confronted by the ghost, that 'I'll call thee Hamlet, / King, father, royal Dane.' Beyond the hero of romantic monodrama, dismissing action like Oswald in Wordsworth's *The Borderers* as a transitory physical spasm, he is the protagonist of a more modern drama: not Pirandello's character in search of an author, but a self without a character, acknowledging no authority except his own histrionic caprice.

Hamlet's dangerous freedom in performance constitutes Macbeth's self-made hell. In Hamlet's case, the judicious compulsion of drama is waived, and the play can be slowed down to accommodate its hero's leisure; Macbeth dreams of Hamlet's liberty from consequence, and in an urgently propulsive play longs for the sanctuary of stasis, of being 'safely thus', but is destroyed by the inexorability of dramatic time and the claustrophobia—'cabin'd, cribb'd, confin'd'—of dramatic space. Hamlet can equivocate forever about being and not being, about action and acting, because he is wittily debating and modifying the metaphysics of drama. Macbeth likewise hopes that the be-all will be the end-all, that a thought will be crowned by an act done instantly. Malcolm urges such reactive immediacy on Macduff, telling him to translate sorrow into words, transform grief into anger. The play abounds in the praise of a bold celerity which might outrun the past: Malcolm's 'shift away', Lady Macbeth's 'go at once'. Macbeth dreams of the past's erasure, and the future's control. It is this fond human delusion which renders him so sympathetic, for instance when he wishes to spare his wife the anxious interim before Banquo's death and tells her to 'be innocent of the knowledge . . . / Till thou applaud the deed'; it is the same tender fallacy which prompts them both to trust in the curative powers of water, sleep or medicine, alike means of forgetfulness and self-renovation. Willing the dagger to appear before him is a tactic for disowning the act he has not yet committed by objectifying it, placing it outside himself.

Despite these evasions, our moral predicament remains: we are our pasts, and what we have done prescribes our futures; drama is here the medium of our damnation. *Macbeth* begins with an energetic anticipation of things to come, with vaulting ambition and Duncan's image of coursing Macbeth at heels to be his purveyor. That future when it arrives is a vacant space, repleted by the condemned routine of repeating the past. Macbeth has his litany of listless tomorrows, Banquo his purposeless riding 'as far . . . as will fill up the time / 'Twixt this and supper.' Hamlet sees re-enactment as his vindication, and therefore deputes Horatio 'to tell my story'. Horatio at once takes up the charge, retailing to Fortinbras a revision of events which pretends that the 'acts' in question were casual not causal, and nobody's fault. For Macbeth and Lady Macbeth, re-enactment can only be a purgatory. The tempo of the play, accelerated by their own impatience, hastens them to a premature extinction. Neither dies onstage at the end because they have died long since, at the moment when they forefate themselves and forfeit their own lives by taking Duncan's. Macbeth grandly requests that extinction when he says, 'Had I but died an hour before this chance', Lady Macbeth mimes it when she faints. Thereafter they are restless ghosts, made to revisit a past from which they cannot be exonerated. Lady Macbeth ritually stalks through the same 'actual performances' as before, scrubbing at her guilt; Macbeth dazedly orders new murders as sequels to his first crime, and acts overtime—'Arm, arm, and out'—so as not to think.

Comedy, in this play of pitiless accountability and terrifying abridgement, can only mean inconsequence and its special immunity from prosecution. This is the porter's gospel. He is guarded from effectuality by drink, his friendly equivocator, which 'sets him on, and . . . takes him off; . . . persuades him, and disheartens him', keeping him from the irreversible kinesis of Macbeth when set on by his wife. Liquor has the power, sought by Macbeth, to undo a deed. The porter says it 'provokes and unprovokes' lechery, because 'it provokes the desire, but . . . takes away the performance'. Macduff owes his invincibility to a similar moral charm. The man not of woman born has escaped the first and perhaps most traumatic of consequences, the travail and anguish of birth. 'Untimely ripp'd' from the womb, he has suffered no initiation like Macbeth's into time and its punishment of us; he is a Falstaff made timeless by Caesarean section.

While Hamlet the comedian fends off the nuisance of conscription by tragedy, Othello is the converse case: he repudiates the sordid imputation of comedy, and kills his way out of it into tragedy. Iago the belittling satirist has a mean-spirited theory of human nature, assuming the viciousness of men and the need for their policing. Offering to Othello the evidence of his shame, he offers as well an acrimonious consolation, which resounds in his jaunty, diminishing couplets on the quay—the sour, comic safety of being among friends in infamy, of being no better than the average. He aims to school Othello in a misanthropy which to Iago himself is a rankling pleasure. All his epigram's are levellers, miniature and dismissive last judgements like Swift's, not bothering to discriminate between human cases because all are tainted. He seeks to make Othello believe of himself no more than he already believes of his own situation: that he is a cuckold. His knowingness slurs Desdemona as one more representative, sister to Emilia, of 'our country disposition'. Armed with this reductive thesis and with a manipulative talent for plotting, Iago is comedy's evil genius, robbing men of their freedom and their conviction of uniqueness, defrauding them as Jonson's engineers do and as Henri Bergson argued that comedy always did (though not, usually, in Shakespeare) by ensnaring them in the constraints of mechanism.

This is the comic vision of a demon, sardonically capitalising on comedy's faith in human equality and interchangeability. Tragedy extols the glories and perils of lonely individuality, the 'intellectual being' prized, for all its pain, by Milton's Belial in hell. As possessors of a body, we are all comically alike; as vessels of spirit, we are each tragically separate. As the former, we have sex (which is the obsession of Iago in his ribald taunting of Brabantio); as the latter, we fall in love. Othello will not accept Iago's smirkingly honest account of him, and against the degraded collectivity of comedy chooses a tragic, fatal singleness. The pain of the play is the gratuitousness of this tragic initiative. Iago's motive is the unseating of his rival Cassio. He complies with Othello's demand for his death, but of Desdemona adds 'let her live'. She must be sacrificed to Othello's rectified sense of himself, though her timorous comic wish is simply to stay alive and she wheedlingly volunteers to die tomorrow, so long as she can survive tonight. It is left to Emilia to relegate Othello finally to the comedy he imagines he has, by his executions, lived down, when she calls him 'O gull! O dolt! / As ignorant as dirt!' This comic indictment denies him the stoic refuge of tragedy. He wants to think Iago a devil yet his feet are not cloven, and Desdemona returns to life for long enough to steal from him his judicial responsibility for her end when she claims that the deed belongs to 'nobody—I myself'. Iago in 'Demand me nothing' allows the action to stand as a purposeless practical joke.

The eighteenth century flinched from the grubbiness of *Othello*, with its horns, handkerchiefs and bed sheets; the competition in it between tragedy and comedy made it incomprehensible to the nineteenth century. Verdi's opera *Otello* in 1887 purges the play of comic reproach and satiric superciliousness. Othello is already operatic in the play, but the prosaic, domestic Desdemona, dispensing nourishing dishes or advice about wearing gloves, and the bantering Iago are not. Accorded the gift of song by Verdi, they are raised to spiritual parity with Othello, for while lyricism in the play is a self-deceiving infatuation with the sound of one's own voice ('Soft you; a word or two before you go'), the opera makes it a credential of soul and—in the heroically arduous '*Esultate!*' Otello sings as he is borne in by a whirlwind—an ecstatic agon. Song deifies Shakespeare's imperfect, terrestrial people. Verdi's Desdemona is an interceding angel, whose post-mortem intervention is not the stubborn contradiction which causes Othello to rail at her as a liar, but a benediction. Iago, for whom the librettist Boïto wrote a satanically inverse credo, is a devil. Othello dies disconsolate, Otello in voluptuous transcendence, kissing Desdemona in a reprise of their earlier love duet. Music pardons him, and permits him to recur to the past without pain.

To Othello, comedy is inimical because it is scurrilous and defamatory. To Lear, it is an enlivening challenge, reanimating a man who, as the play begins, desires to crawl towards death but who is resurgently quickened by the experience which rends him, moved to exult in a biologically comic power of continuance and promising to 'wear out' his tormentors by his stubborn survival. The play aligns itself often with comedy. Edmund cues Edgar's entrance 'like the catastrophe of the old comedy', and Goneril smirks as her sexual intrigue gets tangled, 'An interlude!' The moralists in *King Lear* chant the praises of folly. The truest tragic hero is the clown, martyred by our mockery, slain to save us: Lear's boy, threatened when he tells the truth and mysteriously killed; Edgar in whom the antic disposition demands that he stigmatise himself, excruciating his flesh with 'pins, wooden pricks, nails, sprigs of rosemary'; Kent who signs on for the abasement of the stocks and awaits, like Rosalind and Celia, the mutation of tragic destiny into comic luck—'Fortune, good night; smile once more; turn thy wheel'. Edmund speaks at last of the wheel having come full circle, and Lear considers himself 'bound / Upon a wheel of fire'. That wheel's completed revolution, like the sequence of seasons, returns tragedy to comedy.

The romantics thought *King Lear* a cosmic upheaval. Keats called it a dispute between 'damnation and impassion'd clay'. In fact it is more abrasively worldly than that, more touchingly true in its account of domestic squabbles and its revelation of an evil fostered by banality; closer always to the honest human smallness exposed and pitied by comedy than to the sublime anguish of romantic tragedy. The preoccupation of Goneril and Regan is housekeeping, that of Edmund the conniving of wealth. Those people are plaintive in their inadequacy, and their frank admission of it—Cordelia's grudging, uneffusive 'Nothing', or the homely excuse of the Captain who kills her because 'I cannot draw a cart nor eat dried oats; / If it be man's work I'll do it.' It is a soldierly chore to him, and he dreads being demobbed as a peasant; in that single line, the play understands and extenuates him so completely that, when he is killed in turn by Lear, it is hard not to lament his wasted life.

Lear's tragic abdication of life is disallowed for the same reason that Antony's farcically is. Edgar explains the reason when he stage-manages Gloucester's supposed recuperation from his suicide: 'Thy life's a miracle.' Hence comedy's embargo on squandering that resilient vitality, which is invigorated by torments. On the heath Lear is persuaded by the fool's chattering that preservation of the body—the comedian's obsession with keeping it dry, victualled and (as Falstaff reminds himself in reviewing the honourable corpse of Sir Walter Blount) on the go—takes precedence over the lonely integrity of mind. Tragic pain is a mental affliction, which proudly administers voluntary wounds to the flesh, like Portia swallowing fire or Othello declaring that he 'smote him—Thus'; *King Lear*, rather, concerns the inadvertent, absurd pangs of the body, as meaningless as toothache. Edmund wounds himself to incriminate Edgar, but is noisy not stoical about the mess his sword makes: 'Look, sir, I bleed.' In *Macbeth* by contrast, blood is never gore. Always emblematic, it is to that extent saved from murky reality. Macbeth calls it incarnadine, treating it as a dye, and changes its colour to golden when he describes Duncan's body. Lady Macbeth did not reckon on the moral ordure of a killing: 'who would have thought the old man to have had so much blood in him?' The characters of *King Lear* can be hurt because their living depends on softly pulpy, physical extremities, on limbs or organs too frail and too easily restrained or damaged. 'Put in his legs', says Regan as Kent is locked in the stocks; 'Out, vile jelly!' says Cornwall of Gloucester's eye, 'Where is thy lustre now?' The doctor's prescriptions are unavailing in *Macbeth*; in *King Lear* the body can at least be healed, and perhaps revived. The servants mix flax and egg-whites to staunch Gloucester's bleeding; Lear fussily tests the wetness of Cordelia's tears and her breathing; Edgar, who has reclaimed Gloucester for life, ventures to do the same for Lear when he collapses: 'Look up, my lord.' The play's people are groundlings, attached to earth by the lowering necessity of gravity which transmutes Gloucester's leap into the clown's pratfall. Their recourse is to the floor: Kent is tethered on account of his lusty, unruly legs, and though Lear disdains 'to knee this throne' his command to his overflowing sorrow is 'down, . . . / Thy element's below', which the fool compares to a cook's cudgelling of some wriggling eels, 'Down, wantons, down.'

The ripeness Edgar teaches to Gloucester is the readiness Hamlet speaks of to Horatio. The wise passiveness of pastoral (for Edgar has installed Gloucester to sit out the battle under a tree, which serves as his 'good host') joins with the comedian's patient acceptance that he has no power over a life whose temporary trustee he is. Our death, Edgar advises, as much as our birth, is beyond our choosing. Lear boldly conflates the two when, in a pun worthy of Cleopatra, he says he 'will die bravely, like a smug bridegroom', or when he compares our wailing at birth with our weeping at death. That first cry is as much joyful as dismayed: Gloucester and Cordelia intermingle smiles and tears. Lear's 'kill, kill, kill, kill, kill, kill!' or his 'Howl, howl, howl, howl!' paraphrase the baby's jubilant wailing, because their vocal violence and their indefinite repetitiveness overcome the suffering they express. Death has aroused in Lear an awesome access of new life. The howls are less a threnody than a parentally god-like effort, by expending breath, to reinfuse it in Cordelia. Tragic characters have their famous last words prepared in advance, as Lear did at the outset of the play, and the by-standers interrupt him in the hope of arrival at a terminus. Albany prays for him to 'Fall and cease!' However, he expires when he least expects to, reaching no composed or 'promis'd end' but struggling still to prove Cordelia's revivification.

The wonder, as Kent sees it, is that of endurance, or prolongation. He has been stretched on the rack of the world. Spared by tragedy, he is made to withstand the comedy of succession (which Macbeth denies: for him surcease should be the only success, and he dreads issue, causing Macduff's 'egg' to be killed and himself possessing 'no children'); he must survive into the 'old age' refused to Macbeth, with a longevity which belongs to narrative rather than to curtailed life—Macbeth's 'brief candle'—of drama.

Shakespeare's last plays go on to subsume drama once more in history, from which, in the chronicles, he began. Gower, the most garrulously continuous of medieval narrators, re-arises from ashes to be master of ceremonies for *Pericles*, and consents to dramatise only some of the scenes. The rest, concerned with the tidal fluxes of human vagrancy and the regroupment of families, will not fit on a stage or within that hour Macbeth allots to the poor player, and must be narrated. Gower apologises for his laggard metrics, whose feet plod across an earth which time wings above, but his humble craft evinces Shakespeare's medievalism: resisting the classical reforms of Marlowe or Jonson, he remains true to drama's ancestry in tale-telling and in the idyllic endlessness of romance. Although Ben Jonson considered *Pericles* mouldy or mustily old-fashioned, the plays in its group are recklessly new, discovering a future by their resort to the past. Gower says his play can be used as a restorative. Its biological magic is an impregnation of the present, which conceives a parental past: Pericles calls Marina 'thou that beget'st him that did thee beget', and after the vision of his own paternity—again drama's recalling of existences from ashes—in *Cymbeline*, Posthumus cries

> Sleep, thou hast been a grandsire and begot
> A father to me; and thou hast created
> A mother and two brothers.

The plays grow backwards. *The Winter's Tale* begins as a tragedy, modishly and dissociatively new, studying the pathological temperament and motiveless fixation which fascinate Jacobean dramatists, but continues beyond that tragedy's mourning end (when Leontes vows to eke out the remainder of his life in expiatory tears) as a comedy, reassuringly and healingly old, recalling the May-games, Robin Hood plays, morris dances and rustic wassails which prefigure Elizabethan drama. In conducting the play forward across a generation, Time is both demonstrating that tragedy has comedy as its genetic issue and looping back in a Spenserian circle to show that tragedy also has comedy as its genial ancestor. The future is the past reborn. Perdita, the lost thing here recovered, is the drama's infancy in pastoral, tragedy's birth from the exultant comic spirit.

The Winter's Tale aligns drama with the earth's annual renewal, to which plays, as seasonal celebrations, are propitiary offerings. Its characters amend Edgar's conviction, with which *King Lear* ends: if we that are young live to be old enough, we will be made young again, since comedy is a triumphant outlasting of tragedy. Mamillius 'makes old hearts fresh; they that went on crutches ere he was born desire yet their life to see him a man', and his existence revives the shared childhood of his father and Polixenes who thought

> . . . . there was no more behind
> But such a day to-morrow as to-day,
> And to be boy eternal.

Polixenes loves Florizel because his son, while warning him of his tragic obsolescence, makes him comically eternal in his mutability, so that 'a July's day' spent with him seems 'short as December'—except that the wintry abbreviation of day and life advances the cycle towards the renewal of spring. What Leontes thinks of as a tempo of impatient lust, hastening towards consummation and 'wishing clocks move swift; / Hours, minutes; noon, midnight', may be the acceleration of tragic time, which drives on Macbeth or rapidly uses up Faustus's last hour; but the sooner that end is reached, the sooner there can be a new beginning, a resumption of comedy's lazy, unthreatened timelessness. Autolycus like Falstaff lives in a moral time-warp: 'for the life to come, I sleep out the thought of it'. Florizel's beautiful plea to Perdita is that she should eternalise the instant by doing forever what she is doing just then. This is the spell of Goethe's Faust, delaying time because the moment is so precious, and it is the power ironically invoked by Marlowe's Faustus, too late, in his appeal to Ovid's horses of night. Florizel says

> . . . . When you do dance, I wish you
> A wave o' the sea, that you might ever do
> Nothing but that; move still, still so,

—because although the single wave breaks, it is at once succeeded by another, so its death is undone, and the sea (omnipresent in the last plays as the ocean of our collective being, on which the ship of fools is tempest-tossed) is inexhaustible. Comedy's temporal charm is its amnesia. The present, extended forever, can forget the past, as Macbeth is never able to do. Elizabeth in Jane Austen's *Pride and Prejudice*, caught out falling in love with a man she professed to detest, excuses herself by saying that in such matters a good memory is a distinct hindrance. Such forgetfulness is one of Shakespearean time's benefactions. When Helena in *All's Well* is questioned about her father, she remarks, astonishingly, 'I have forgot him', and Pisanio in *Cymbeline* tells Imogen, as he presides over her mutation into a new life, 'You must forget to be a woman.'

Time, the curative agent which heals our wounds and commutes our tragedies to comedy, is the main character of *The Winter's Tale*, and is beseeched long before he is presented in person. Leontes denounces Camillo as a temporizer, but to wait out time—patiently to attend the wheel's revolution—is an earnest of wisdom. Time is a benevolent midwife, assisting the future's nascence. One of the pregnant Hermione's women says 'Good time encounter her!', and Antigonus assigns Perdita to time's safekeeping: 'Blossom, speed thee well!'

Beaumont and Fletcher had developed tragicomedy into a specious compromise between the opposites which in Shakespeare are compounded or made to overlap. Plays like *Philaster* or *The Faithful Shepherdess* titillatingly exploit the danger but avoid the death; as if lacking the courage to be tragedy, they retract into comedy, and—like Amintor in *The Maid's Tragedy* gratuitously relenting after he mistreats Aspatia—they do not really believe in their own salvation:

> I did that lady wrong. Methinks I feel
> Her grief shoot suddenly through all my veins;
> Mine eyes run; this is strange at such a time.

In Shakespeare the formula of Beaumont and Fletcher is a chemical concoction: Cornelius's potion, of which he says 'There is / No danger in what show of death it makes', and with which the Queen boasts that she has on five occasions redeemed Cymbeline from death. Instead of introducing comedy to mitigate tragedy, *The Winter's Tale* understands how, in the fullness of time, one will succeed to the other. It is therefore two complete plays in one, a tragedy begun again, thanks to Time's intercession, as comedy. 'Exit, pursued by a bear' is Antigonus's obituary, but it is a laughable one, because death comes to him so accidentally and absurdly. The clown comprehends that death as a victualling of nature, when the bear dines on Antigonus as Hamlet had described the worms festively enjoying Polonius. The shepherd at once passes on to the care of 'things new-born' and when, a generation later, Paulina is found to be still grieving over the loss of her partner, Leontes pacifies her by insisting that he will find her another mate. A tragedy which is outgrown in time can also be distanced in space. If you consider your own predicament generally enough, you begin to see the comedy of it. Leontes is able to accept a shaming common lot which Othello indignantly denies. There are cuckolds everywhere in nature, he sees, and there is comfort in its being a bawdy planet. Cloten in *Cymbeline* perceives his personal case with the same expansiveness, aggregating Imogen successively into 'lady, ladies, women'. The same incorporating course is prescribed for Leontes by Paulina when she says that he would not recover the equal of Hermione even 'if, one by one, you wedded all the world'. In his vengeful rage, Leontes still possesses an enlargement of vision which answers to the play's ambition of including a world: 'Why, then the world and all that's in't is nothing; / The covering sky is nothing.' Autolycus the larcenous satirist makes the same admission of affinity or kinship—resisted by Jaques, or by Malvolio lording it over the lesser people and declaring 'I am not of your element'—with the comic and bucolic naturals:

> How blessed are we that are not simple men!
> Yet nature might have made me as these are;
> Therefore I will not disdain.

Individuality is at last melted and merged when the courtiers recount the homecoming of Perdita. Cordelia's 'sunshine and rain' are now a sea of joyful tears, in which the characters (as the third gentleman reports it) wade, and because feelings have been freed into generality, shared with everyone, the dramatic individuals who once owned those emotions can no longer be identified: their countenances are so distracted—as the tragic mask rearranges itself into the physiognomy of the comic—that 'they were to be known by garment, not by favour'. Shakespeare's decision to narrate this crucial scene, not dramatise it, is his last, humblest offering to time, whose medium is after all the ample one of narrative not the unified day which Crites in Dryden's dialogue says should be the modicum of drama. Tale-telling is our bequest from the past and the means, as we impart experience to each other, of turning experience into communion. The scene the gentlemen describe is 'an old tale' which can only properly be told by ballad-makers. Narratives like those Gower tirelessly compiled are an anthology of the human family: begging Mamillius to 'tell's a tale', Hermione requests him to recite to her the stories she has taught him; to double her gift by returning it to her with a new complement of love.

She and Mamillius differ over whether the tale should be 'merry or sad'. (He, with the unripeness of youth, prefers a tragedy.) For the clown, however, the forms have reverted to the primal Shakespearean muddle, to the tragical mirth of Bottom's play or the 'tragical-comical-historical pastoral' hybrid of the players in *Hamlet* with their 'scene individable, or poem unlimited': he loves ballads, 'if it be doleful matter merrily set down, or a very pleasant thing indeed and sung lamentably'. Tragedy achieves its comic renewal in pastoral. From the court, *The Winter's Tale* migrates to nature, whose poet Shakespeare is. The double plot is here the speckled variegation Perdita treasures in flowers which, like the mongrelising of genres listed by Polonius, are derided as 'nature's bastards': the inner contradictoriness of Shakespearean drama is the configuration which Gerard Manley Hopkins was to celebrate in 1877 as the glory of English landscape, a 'pied beauty'. This is an art, as Florizel explains, made by nature in its own image, an 'art [which] itself is nature'. In its reversion to the revelry of 'Whitsun pastorals', *The Winter's Tale* harks back to the native English origins of drama in naive mystery, rejoicing at the quickening of spring; when its twelve satyrs cavort, it swells—with the spatial generosity of Hermione, who before delivering Perdita is 'spread . . . / Into a goodly bulk'—to comprise the entire agenda of those ancient dramatic festivals where, after the completion of a tragedy, a satyr-play was performed.

So incompatible are the classical theories of tragic and comic behaviour that they amount to mutually exclusive dogmas. Dryden's Eugenius notes that among the ancients 'tragedies and comedies were not writ . . . as they are now, promiscuously, by the same person'. Shakespeare is just such a gladly promiscuous creator, and he additionally offends against the classical specialism, in *The Winter's Tale* as always, by writing tragedy and comedy not alternately but simultaneously, within the same play.

— 11 —
Shakespeare's After-Life

Shakespeare was at first rewritten into conformity with classicism. This is the service that Dryden, revering French dramatists for their strict observance of structural punctilios and their 'nicety of manners', provided to him in his version of *Antony and Cleopatra*, *All for Love* (1677), and his revision, made with William Davenant's collaboration, of *The Tempest* (1670). On the fluid, unfixed, ever-metamorphosing Shakespearean characters Dryden imposes a classical regularity. His drama is an exercise in their equilibration. Instead of a reckless, riotous expenditure of energy, they seek a steadying poise—the repose of Newtonian mechanism according to which (in Newton's third law of motion) every action begets and is balanced by an equivalent reaction. This oppositional statis is maintained by Dryden's verse, which even in the absence of rhyme aspires always to the measured antithesis of the couplet. The changes of mood, unexpected in Shakespeare, are here premeditated. When Dryden's Antony hears music and longs for a sylvan escape from duty, it is a statuesque eternity—an ideal motionlessness—which he imagines:

> I lean my head upon the mossy bank,
> And look just of a piece as I grew from it.

For classical character, disequilibrium is a psychological ailment, and both Antony, vacillating between Roman valour and Egyptian luxury, and Cleopatra suffer from it. The unbalanced for him means the irrational, and he acknowledges 'I have lost my reason'; her first words concern her frantic quest for the peace of equipoise: 'What shall I do, or whither shall I turn?' Death for them both is the ideally classical state, a perfected balance which conserves energy rather than (in the Shakespearean way) recklessly disbursing it, and although their prototypes in Shakespeare find it difficult to extricate themselves from the querulous flesh, Dryden's couple die gratefully into the chastened rigor mortis of the marble statue, that icon of classical rectitude. As Antony dies, the women raise him and seat him in a chair. He asks Cleopatra to sit beside him—an extraordinary request, which makes sense only in the upright universe of classicism, where to relax your posture is, as in Racine, a drastic concession to mortality. But Dryden's Antony and Cleopatra turn this enfeeblement into a strength. Seated, they are already fixed in the immobility of sculpture. Cleopatra welcomes the 'heavy numbness' which the asps induce in her. Shakespeare's woman feels death as an exquisite pain, a lover's pinch, and tells the asp to disentangle the difficult intricate knot of her life: dying is not a problem but a pleasure. Dryden's queen feels only her only incapacity to feel. The anesthesia of flesh is transforming her to stone. Instead of the Shakespearean combustibility of life, the burning-off of energy in fire and air, the character in Dryden remains still as if awaiting petrification. Serapion reads the dead pair like a monument:

> See how the lovers sit in state together,
> As if they were giving laws to half the world!

Rearranging *The Tempest*, Dryden and Davenant seek as well to equip it with the classical virtues it lacks. Shakespeare's play is mysteriously negative, stirring up drama only to quell it and to expose its own abstract emptiness: it became, in the nineteenth century, a symptomatic romantic work because of this evacuation into the spirituality of 'air, . . . thin air'. As Wagner said the art-work of the future should, it abandons the earth for worlds unrealised, realisable perhaps only in the invisibility of music. It lies behind Shelley's *Prometheus Unbound*, where drama unbinds itself and, in the fourth act, lyrically evaporates as ether. No work could be further from the equations classicism balances than *The Tempest*.

Dryden and Davenant restore to it the stability of symmetry. In their concern for the antiphonal couplings which are the requirement of the heroic couplet in verse, they invent siblings for Ferdinand (Hippolito) and Miranda (Dorinda). The woman who has never seen a man has her complement in a man, Hippolito, who has never seen woman. The logical resolution of their twinned ignorances is copulation—again the triumph brought about by the couplet. The play is obsessed with dualisms, because these are the automatic product of the couplet's self-duplication. As with the sexes, opposites are pacified and made unanimous by being forcibly wed in the verse. Prospero tells Hippolito that women are 'dangerous enemies of men', and to his daughters preaches vice versa. From these reversals, the couplet sorts out at last a satisfied accord.

The bifurcation of nature, understood but overcome by classicism, goes deep in the play, disposing the admonishment to the sinful courtiers for instance as a dialogue sung in two parts. The duetting voices answer and rhyme with each other in a catechism which suggests that the tablets of the law should proclaim their moral norms in couplets:

> 1. Where does proud *Ambition* dwell?
> 2. In the lowest rooms of Hell.
> 1. Of the damn'd who leads the Host?
> 2. He who did oppress the most.

The sexuality of this symmetry puzzles and disturbs Hippolito who, having been confined on the island by Prospero, does not know that you can only have a single father. When Ferdinand laments that his has been drowned, Hippolito sympathises because Ferdinand, it seems, had just one father and the prejudice, in this orderly universe, runs in favour of two. Nor can Hippolito accept the customary monogamy of love. To Ferdinand's annoyance, he wants to love both Miranda and Dorinda. A single integer is sterile and pitiful; he craves, in everything, the equable companionship of pairing. In one of the play's most curious images, Dryden suggests the schizophrenia which goes with this classical division of the world into matched component parts, and hints at its relation to the symmetrical mirroring of the human body. Ferdinand suspects Miranda of fickleness and sees her as nature not yet trained by art, which would teach her to hide her frailty. He wonders

> Why did I think that any Woman could be innocent,
> Because she's young? No, no, their Nurses teach them
> Change, when with two Nipples they divide their
> Liking.

This teasing dualism, disciplined by the antitheses of Dryden's verse and his stagecraft, is maintained by Samuel Johnson in the preface to his edition of Shakespeare (1765). Here the classical equilibrium is no longer so tense. Johnson permits the contraries, in his defence of Shakespeare's mingled drama, to meet in the middle, and is thus himself halfway between a classical insistence on delimitation of forms and the hybridised natural mayhem which the romantics acclaimed in Shakespeare. Though Johnson's official allegiance is to a classical aesthetic theory (and in his notes to *Othello* he speculates on how it might have been 'a drama of the most scrupulous and exact regularity' if only it had begun in Cyprus and narrated Venetian events in retrospect) he is pragmatically able to admit that 'Shakespeare's plays are not in the rigorous and critical sense either tragedies or comedies', and he refers them outside literature to 'the real state of sublunary nature'. He sees that nature as a 'chaos of mingled purposes and casualties': a confusion which foreshadows the tumult of the romantic Shakespeare. But he steadies and tempers the contradictions in his own measured rhyming prose, which decrees an alternation of tragedy and comedy and sees to it that an embarrassing collision at least looks like a decent co-operation, as when he remarks—to justify Shakespearean tragicomedy— that in our world 'at the same time, the reveller is hasting to his wine, and the mourner burying his friend'. They need not, as they always do in Shakespeare, meet: Johnson's syntax preserves a segregation.

The encounter between mourner and reveller was to become more strident and more violent in romantic critiques of Shakespeare: a coexistence of angel and leering gargoyle in Victor Hugo, a coincidental yoking together of sentimental, hymnal tragedy and a ravening comedy in the double plots of

Dickens. Johnson is not yet prepared to permit this free-for-all. He is uniquely able to describe the wisdom and verisimilitude of the mingled form because it corresponds to his own conviction about the world. It is a tragic place, which we must have the courage and resilience to treat comically; man would be a tragic disaster if he were not so comical a buffoon. This Augustan recension of tragedy as comedy has occurred in Pope's *Essay on Man* (1733-4), which treats the Miltonic fall—safety-netted inside the couplet, with all of those infinite chasms opened by Milton's line-ends closed off—as an over-weening social gaffe. Johnson has his own prosaic and democratised version of Shakespearean tragicomedy: the form of the biography, to which all his writings adhere.

Johnson saw tragedy as omnipresent. Every one of his couplets or sentences has a funereal dying fall. Yet his stoicism convinced him that we should not grieve, but exert ourselves to be of good cheer. Tragedy was the instinctive temptation of his temperament, comedy the skilled and therapeutic resistance of his mind—which is exactly the opposite of what, in the preface's most startling judgment, he contends about Shakespeare: 'His tragedy seems to be skill, his comedy to be instinct.' It is a daring declaration, suggesting the classical pedantry of tragedy as against the easy ebullience of comedy. (Johnson says, wonderfully, of *Henry IV* that 'perhaps no author has ever in two plays afforded so much delight'.) This is very far from the post-romantic cult of tragedy, which exults in Nietzsche's ecstatic suffering, or considers the twentieth century's chief shame the death in it of the tragic conscience. Does it, though, imply a refusal by Johnson to tolerate the excruciations of Shakespeare? He considered the blinding of Gloucester 'too horrid to be endured in dramatic exhibition', and is quick to argue the deaths of Cordelia or Desdemona into moral coherence, thus palliating their pain and their appalling, unjust meaninglessness. Although he has begun to release Shakespeare from the classical stereotype, calling the First Folio's classification of the plays as comedies, histories and tragedies the makeshift convenience of two unlearned actors, the relation between tragedy and comedy remains for him contradictory. He needs to see it as an even-tempered alternation, since its purpose is to fortify consciousness: 'an interchange of seriousness and merriment, by which the mind is softened at one time and exhilarated at another.'

Johnson assists in the transference of Shakespeare from drama to the novel's mental theatre. In 1769 he asserted to Boswell, during a conversation about Garrick, that 'many of Shakespeare's plays are the worse for being acted'. Johnson was interpreting Shakespeare for the first age of novelists, and passing on to them the responsibility of learning from the mingled drama. The novel is of course the ultimate reproof to classical genre, and (despite its hostility to drama) during the nineteenth century it is a formal continuation of Shakespeare. Johnson remarks that 'Shakespeare has no heroes; his scenes are occupied only by men', which explains Fielding's promotion of the anonymous, average Tom Jones to the status previously monopolised by epic warriors or national celebrities. Sterne as much as Fielding populates his novels with Shakespearean characters—Tristram Shandy is a comic Hamlet, whose procrastination is no longer (as in drama) an aberrant motive, since he now has the shapeless entirety of a novel to expand into; Yorick in *A Sentimental Journey* is the exhumed jester from the Shakespearean graveyard, a missionary converting everyone he meets, like Feste or Lear's joker, to his philosophy of sensuous and loving folly.

Johnson's commentary makes possible this migration of Shakespeare from drama to novel. The forms, for instance, have profoundly different notions of character. Johnson, saying that 'in the writings of other poets a character is too often an individual; in those of Shakespeare it is commonly a species', interprets Shakespeare's characters novelistically, replacing the theatrical sleight-of-hand of self-invention with an interior existence which makes these people samples of 'general passions and principles'. Shakespearean characters, however, do possess, to an audacious degree, this actorly proficiency. Antonio in *The Merchant of Venice* begins by saying he knows not why he is so sad. He never finds out, although that melancholy is the play's prime motive. Nor does Hamlet ever find out why he delays. They do not need to, and in any case they cannot: motivation in plays is a blank which the dramatist relies on each actor who steps into the part's cut-out vacancy to fill in. This means that Shakespearean character is an elaborate confidence trickery. Yet we can reclaim these theatrical frauds and feigners by devising speculative novelistic biographies for them. It is appropriate that Johnson's tribute to Falstaff should announce itself as a rhetorical question, unanswerable both because Falstaff is theatrically empty and because he is novelistically inexhaustible: 'Falstaff, unimitated, unimitable Falstaff, how shall I describe thee?'

The describing of Falstaff is a task to which Shakespeare himself is scarcely judged adequate. Character progressively separates itself from creator; Maurice Morgann declared the people of the plays to be 'rather . . . Historic than Dramatic beings', rejoicing in a wholeness of life the drama can never comprise. To describe Falstaff therefore means to supplement and correct the piecemeal impressions of him which are all the play has time for. Morgann's essay on him in 1777 sets about filling in a historic (or novelistic) biography of the man, and argues from this invented evidence that Falstaff was no coward. The process continues, and by the time of Robert Nye's novel *Falstaff* in 1976 the character—for Nye a lubricious fertility god, an 'English Bacchus' conceived on the giant's penis at Cerne Abbas, born in a sacred vent of earth in Somerset and ritually baptised in mud and hot water—has made the drama redundant. He has outlived Shakespeare, and lived on in order to travesty him. In these lusty memoirs, Shakespeare's plays are totted up in winking double-entendres. When his new wife tosses Falstaff off, 'love's labour's lost'; he rounds on her to give her 'measure for measure', spanks her buttocks 'as she liked it', and as they 'die' together, 'all was well that ended well'. Shakespeare's characters are taken over as Falstaff's dupes and doxies. Miranda is his incestuous niece who specialises in fellatio, Desdemona his deliciously fecund pet rat. Perdita commits acts of shame with lambkins and Titania with donkeys, while Beatrice is a leathery disciplinarian 'who liked to whip and be whipped, with the tongue and other instruments of pleasure!'

Already in Fielding the novel pays the drama the tribute of believing in the feint of Shakespearean acting. This happens when Tom Jones and Partridge go to see David Garrick's Hamlet. Like all great actors, Garrick had the art of making technical contrivance look natural. The trauma of fear in which Hogarth in 1745 painted his paralysed Richard III on the eve of Bosworth was one of his famous gestural attitudes, which amounted to a posturing silent vocabulary of emotion. Partridge is taken in by this, but because he does not realise it is acting he slights Garrick by saying he could do it as well himself: 'If I had seen a ghost, I should have looked in the very same manner, and done just as he did.' The episode is a brilliant parable of the drama's migration into the novel. Partridge, once he has 'entered in to the spirit of it', upstages Garrick, volunteering to assume his character. His knees knock more noisily than Garrick's when the ghost appears, and when Hamlet rails at Gertrude, Partridge elects to agree with him: 'If she was my own mother, I would serve her so.' His empathy proves Johnson's point that a Shakespearean character is a species, whose emotions belong to us all, and Jones watches him raptly eliding the actors so he can become first one and then another of the characters. 'During the whole speech of the ghost, he sat with his eyes fixed partly on the ghost and partly on Hamlet, and with his mouth open; the same passions which succeeded each other in Hamlet, succeeding likewise in him.'

The irony is that both the performance and the play itself are ousted by Partridge's conviction of their verity. Wishing on them a reality they do not possess, he has claimed them for the novel. Although Garrick is complimented as 'the best player who was ever on the stage', he is outdone by Partridge, to whose excited commentary the audience is 'more attentive . . . than to anything that passed on the stage'; although Shakespeare is the poet of nature, Partridge is more of a natural man than Hamlet, and his alarmed chatter during the play, with its exclamations and alarmed interrogations and its fretted Sternean punctuation, every perception breathily extended into or suspended by a dash, is a more truthfully impromptu novelistic rewriting of the character's studied, almost essayistic soliloquies. Fielding claims a potentially epic heroism for Tom Jones, despite his bluff, middling nature, since in the novel as in Shakespeare there are 'no heroes', or rather everyone is impartially entitled to heroism. Here likewise he allows Partridge the chance to be, latently at least, a tragic hero. The chapter ends with Partridge's insomniac terror of the ghost. He is a more authentic Hamlet than Garrick even: the actor steps out of the role once the performance ends, but Partridge continues to live it, crying out in the night when he fancies the spectre has appeared to him.

Partridge could be nominated as the first romantic respondent to Shakespeare, in that his observation enjoins enactment. Just as Sterne impersonates Yorick, so Coleridge admits to having a smack of Hamlet in him. The roles become for the romantics variant selves, moodily alternating, since each of us is in potential all of Shakespeare's characters. Byron quotes incessantly from Shakespeare's more audacious psychological deceivers in his letters, enlisting them as surrogates for his own dubious and inauthentic self, and Jane Austen's Henry Crawford gives a virtuoso display of this same unstable, romantic versatility of mind and temper in his one-man performance of *Henry VIII* at Mansfield Park, when he reads all the parts. Even a silent reading, like Keats's of *King Lear* in 1818, becomes an exhausting audition, since Keats does not content himself with simulating the emotions in the play—as the actor does—but is ambitious to share them and to be purgingly consumed by them.

As this romantic appropriation of the characters occurs, the plays are necessarily withdrawn from the stage. Charles Lamb saw it as a romantic interpretive duty to free the characters (subjective spirits, tormented as Ariel is by embodiment) from theatrical impersonation, and he insisted on his own right to see Othello's visage in his mind; nor could Carlyle tolerate the thought of Shakespeare engaging in tawdry theatrical shows. His arena must be within—the invisible and solipsistic theatre of the mind. Partridge had already novelistically relocated the drama of *Hamlet* there, and Hamlet presides over the nineteenth century's introversion of literary form, for he is the character who disdains trappings, suits and shows, and who resigns from the tiresome displays of action. He sponsors the romantic abstraction of drama as poetry, and the later evolution of romanticism into symbolism. The incompetent and laggard revenger changes into a mystic, perplexed by the contradiction between inner truths and their outer vestments. His mystery is the elusiveness of the romantic image, or of the symbol—a secret revelation which dare not be verbalised or trapped in material form, and which must therefore leave him and the work containing him with absences at the centre. Shakespeare's teasing or negligent omission of motive is reinterpreted as an awed homage to the symbolic depth beneath or behind the surface. Thus the modern Hamlet of Eliot grows logically out of Coleridge's. Eliot criticised the play for the precise quality which makes it so symbolically significant: its failure to provide an 'objective correlative' to Hamlet's subjective woe. That supposed failure is the symbolist choice. The allegory proposes an equation between spirit and substance; symbolism despairs of ever matching them, because its spirit is vagrant and insubstantial, like Shelley's skylark or Coleridge's Hamlet in whom (as Coleridge remarks) 'suppression prepares for overflow' or like Prufrock who can never make his body and his feelings correspond.

Thus set free, the Shakespearean characters are readied for a universal proliferation. They are found to be omnipresent, pre- and post-dating their appearances in the plays. Lear for instance, in James Barry's 1786–7 painting of the death of Cordelia, inhabits simultaneously a series of overlaid time-zones, which are historical epochs: he belongs at once in ancient Britain, in the Holy Land, and in classical Arcady. He has the stern demeanour and tempestuous mane of Michelangelo's God creating Adam, and he presides at the same time over the sacrifice of the second Adam. Cradling Cordelia in a role-reversed Pietà, he is a patriarchal Mary with a dead female Christ; Edmund is borne off in another re-enactment of the deposition from the cross. Behind him is a Druidic circle like Stonehenge, but the landscape trails away into a serene Mediterranean bay. Barry's inconsistencies free Lear to occur anywhere and everywhere, with the serial existence of a reborn god.

Turgenev in 1870 derives a typology from him which enables his transference to Russia, still (in the nineteenth century) the feudal kingdom of Shakespeare's Lear. We have all, Turgenev argues, known Hamlets, Othellos, Falstaffs and Lears: the individual characters archetypally engender a world of semblances. Hence his bearish, bellicose Kharlov, who is *A King Lear of the Steppes*. This giant resembling a mastodon thrives in the landscape Lear merely rules on the map, and has been that land's saviour in 1812. Kharlov finds a precedent for his woes in Lear, and another further back in Nebuchadnezzar. He becomes his own ancestry. When he takes to the roof of his daughter's house and, with his primeval strength, tears apart the beams and rafters, he assumes the shape of Lear's own parent as Geoffrey of Monmouth describes him, a magus who had mastered the power of flight and controlled the elements at which Shakespeare's Lear can only rail.

The character keeps on reappearing in the present—in the American south of Tennessee Williams's *Cat on a Hot Tin Roof* (1955), for instance, where he is the incurably ill Big Daddy, whose adored Cordelia is a feminised favourite son and who rules a private kingdom: 28,000 acres of the richest land (in a reference to the biblical back-dating of Lear) west of the Nile, plus an endowment of $10,000,000 in cash. Big Daddy's ailment is a physical correlate of Lear's mental revulsion. His colon, he suspects, has been made spastic by disgust. And he outdoes in his rhetoric the turbulent Shakespearean weather on the heath. His imprecations make more noise, it is said, than has been heard since the occasion of the Vicksburg tornado.

The after-life of characters like Hamlet, Lear and Falstaff, and drama's perpetuation as novel, are abetted by Coleridge. His lecture in 1810 on classical and romantic drama, borrowing from A.W. von Schlegel, sees the modern and romantic genius as 'a chaos . . . of atoms apparently heterogeneous'. Shakespeare exemplifies a thriving biological ferment. His plays are products of romantic cross-breeding, a new species requiring a new denomination, 'in the ancient sense neither tragedies nor comedies, nor both in one, but a different genus . . . —romantic dramas, or dramatic romances'.

This goes much further than Johnson's licensing of a mixed drama. John Gay in 1728 had seen in the double plot an image of class warfare, and of society's moral incoherence. The argument of *The Beggar's Opera* learns its seditions from Falstaff's playlets in the inn at Eastcheap: life below stairs is merely the grubby and parodic replica of the privileged existence above it. Fielding, too, saw in the mixed drama a disruptive, undisciplined radicalism. In *Jonathan Wild* he points out that 'there is a nearer connexion between high and low life than is generally imagined'. Rather than allowing the opposites to change places as Gay and Fielding do, Johnson arranged for them to live side by side in mutual, law-abiding peace. Mourner and reveller agree to differ; disparate extremes arrive at a median compromise. It is a pragmatic formula for coexistence, in contrast with Coleridge's dialectical fusion of tragic thesis and comic antithesis. The double plot has overcome its dualism. Coleridge emphasises, in an 1813 lecture, Shakespeare's 'unity-of-feeling', and connects this with the hospitable unitariness of nature itself, not with the censoring exclusions of the classical unities. The dialectic enables him to switch his definition of the new form back to front.

Romantic drama and dramatic romance are different things, but they amount—in his reasoning—to the same. Coleridge's first phrase recalls Shelley's description of *Prometheus Unbound* as 'lyrical drama', a work in which the terrestrial and bodily gravity of drama is progressively banished by a prophetic, abstracting lyricism. What begins as a play ends as a cosmic symphony; the tortured, manacled character is released into the volatility of spirit. In 1856 Elizabeth Barrett Browning's Aurora Leigh can lyrically insist 'I will write no plays', because drama means a confinement which she has cast off. But the second phrase foresees another, complementary future for Shakespeare. If as romantic drama his work levitates, following *The Tempest* into disembodiment, as dramatic romance it solidifies, elongates and overtakes the world, spreading laterally beyond the drama's confines. In romantic drama the play turns into a poem, in dramatic romance into a novel. Stendhal seconds this narrative exfoliation of the plays in his *Racine et Shakespeare* (1823), which reports a dialogue between a pettifogging academician, still berating Shakespeare for offences against the unities, and a romantic who insists on the spectator's liberty to imagine other worlds, beyond the stage's compass: the illimitable terrain of the novel. The novel's justification is its capacity to tell so much more about people than drama, where no truth can ever be trusted because everyone is performing. Thus Thackeray in *Vanity Fair* chattily supplements *Othello*, claiming 'Desdemona was not angry with Cassio, though there is very little doubt that she saw the lieutenant's partiality for her.' He believes, he adds, 'that many more things took place in that sad affair than the worthy Moorish officer ever knew of'—or, it follows, than Shakespeare knew of, since he could not novelistically interrogate his characters from within.

Shakespeare's novelistic conquest of the earth, chorally urged in *Henry V* as the stage's 'wooden O' dilates into a world, proceeds in parallel with his poetic regaining of the sky. He is now the whole of nature, and of literature. Victor Hugo's 1827 preface to his play *Cromwell* sees him as the indwelling spirit of modern art. Hugo distinguishes three ages of humanity, and assigns to each its appropriate literary form. Primitive man, as yet unsevered from his gods, expresses himself in odes. Antique or classical man already has a past, a history, and writes epic. But ours is the Christian (and therefore the modern and romantic) world, which knows man to be a contradictory compound of soul and body, and the form encapsulating this awareness is the double-plotted Shakespearean drama. The modern imagination must charitably enfranchise the ugly as well as the beautiful, the grotesque along with the sublime. Beauty and beast, sylph and gnome are forced into proximity. Angels consort with gargoyles on Gothic cathedrals, and in the plays of Shakespeare. Ruskin also employs the Shakespearean double plot as a standard for the democratic enlivenment of the art he called Gothic. He argues that Veronese's paintings compel the dwarf to fraternise with the soldier, the negress with the queen, just as 'Shakespeare places Caliban beside Miranda, and Autolycus beside Perdita'; and, commenting on architecture, he sees the same Shakespearean principle—responsible for the Nurse's bawdry in *Romeo and Juliet*, the fool's railing at Lear, the porter's drunken grumbling and the disputes of the grave-diggers—at work on Gothic façades, where decorative effects are enhanced by abrupt and violent contrasts.

For Hugo, too, Shakespeare contains an entire created world. It is he who admits reality to art. Literature has descended by stages from the heavens to the earth, Hugo says; the ideal in the Bible leads to the grandiose in Homer and thence to the real in Shakespeare. The characters of the odes are demi-gods, those of epic giants, those of the drama—at last—mere men; and the realist novel continues this process of democratisation and domestication by subjecting Shakespeare's people to the trials of a world of prose. Goethe's Wilhelm Meister is a vagabond modern Hamlet, Balzac's Père Goriot a dethroned modern Lear.

Though Coleridge had magicked duality into a new unity, Hugo continues to see a fissure within Shakespeare. His study of Shakespeare in 1864 reads the double plot as a morbid symptom: 'the idea bifurcated, the idea echoing itself, ... the action attended by its moon'; a nervous approximation to self-parody. If Shakespeare is to be made into a poet, it is necessary to argue, as Coleridge does, for a unity of feeling. But the novel can tolerate, and indeed encourages, antagonistic disunities, like the Shakespearean alliance of hunchback and gipsy girl in Hugo's *Notre-Dame de Paris* (1831). Dickens, adapting Shakespeare to the novel in *Oliver Twist* (1837-9), finds in his doubleness an unhinged and elating schizophrenia. 'It is the custom on stage, in all good murderous melodramas', he says, 'to present the tragic and the comic scenes, in as regular alternation, as the layers of red and white in a side of streaky bacon.'

That analogy from the butcher's block tells a great deal: Dickens has bleedingly cross-sectioned life, and studies the tragedy as raw meat, the comedy as buffering fat. The double plot performs surgery on us, and lays bare the organic squalor of our innards.

Johnson avoids the embarrassment of making the mourner and reveller meet. They are off to their different destinations 'at the same time', but each has his proper space. Dickens has them collide, because there is no distinguishing them: 'Real life', he says, specialises in accelerated transitions 'from well-spread boards to death-beds, and from mourning weeds to holiday garments.' Boards to beds is more punningly ghoulish than Johnson's measured demarcation, and spread's rhyme with bed speeds the mortifying change. This is the obscenely rapid progress from tragedy to comedy, funeral to marriage, of which Hamlet accuses Gertrude. Comedy is liable at any moment in Dickens to collapse into tragedy, and protects itself by the manic and uncontrollable disrespect of its laughter, jeering at the agony it dreads. Dickens here claims for the novel a seismic and whirligig disunity, the ultimate repudiation of classical order. 'Sudden shiftings of the scene, and rapid changes of time and place, are not only sanctioned in books by long usage,' he declares, 'but are by many considered as the great art of authorship.' The author here is a malign god, persecuting his characters by leaving them suspended in deathly dilemmas at the end of each chapter or forcing them to commute grotesquely between pathos and absurdity. The tragicomic vision belongs to a Manichee.

As such, it cannot for long be tolerated by the rationalist nineteenth century, pledged to the advancement of the march of mind. Shaw therefore decries the moral idiocy of Shakespeare and his unintelligent infatuation with 'instinctive temperaments', querulous big babies who demand the gratification at once of their every whim—Faulconbridge, Coriolanus, Leontes and of course Falstaff. These creatures are all psychological primitives, and so, in Shaw's estimation, is Shakespeare: philosophically a simpleton. The classical critique of Shakespeare here recurs in newly Comtean terms, and Shaw, when connecting Shakespeare with Dickens in the preface to *Man and Superman* as ebullient anarchists incapable of any transcendent wisdom, actually invokes the Aristotelian standards by declaring that both dramatist and novelist 'are concerned with the diversities of the world instead of with its unities'. In that appeal to the unities, now no longer a structural fetish but a guide to the schematic rationality of the world which the artist must expound, classicism joins forces with puritanism. Shaw considered Bunyan morally and intellectually superior to Shakespeare, who (as he said in 1897) 'wrote for the theatre because . . . he understood nothing and believed nothing'.

The Victorian suspicion of the theatre confirms the saving transference of Shakespeare to the novel, where facts can be more readily authenticated and motives accredited, in contrast with the theatre's empty fictionality. A.C.

Bradley's *Shakespearean Tragedy* (1904) interprets the works according to a Hegelian theory of tragedy in which the ethical substance of the universe requires the elimination of a personal good or an anti-social happiness. The Shakespearean cases are for Bradley variants of the tragedy that Hegel considered archetypal, *Antigone*, and, like it, they demonstrate the dialectic at its cruel but necessary work. A consequence of this claim for philosophical seriousness is the shift from the play, where all things can remain as disconcertingly dubious as Antonio's motiveless sadness or Iago's motiveless malignity, to the conscientious ascertainments of the novel. This explains Bradley's much-mocked notes on such conundrums as whether Iago *really* believed Emilia to have betrayed him or whether Lady Macbeth *really* fainted. The insistent 'really' is a reflex of Bradley's belief in the ineluctable reality of tragedy, which to him is a secular version of the Passion. The plays are prototypes of those 'experiments in life' conducted by the Victorian novel, demonstrations of the ways in which what Bradley calls 'the highest existence'—Dorothea Brooke or Isabel Archer or Hamlet—is demeaned and defeated by the material world. Bradley the classicist has made Shakespeare classically respectable, at the cost of the double plot. Shakespearean tragedy is a school of moral enlightenment; his comedy is to Bradley insignificant. Falstaff's rejection becomes one more essential sacrifice to that unyielding ethical substance: 'the realities of life refused to be conjured away by his humour'.

For Shaw the opposite divorce is required. Shakespeare can only be rehabilitated and shown to be capable of classical rationality if the tragedy is discarded and the comedy altogether detached from it. In his criticism of the tragedies Shaw adheres still to the neoclassical pernicketiness of two centuries earlier. Thomas Rymer in his *Short View of Tragedy* (1693) ridicules the impropriety of making a tragedy depend on so dispensably comic an item as a handkerchief. The only moral he can discover in the play is 'a warning to all good wives that they look well to their linen'. Shaw likewise thought that '*Othello* is spoilt by a handkerchief', and in his *Quintessence of Ibsenism* (1891) proposes a metaphysical version of Rymer's objection: he despises the 'manufactured misunderstandings and stolen handkerchiefs' of Shakespeare because tragedy is too cosmically portentous—as also for Bradley—to have truck with mere accidents. Its proper concern is destinies (the world-mind on its implacable march, like Will Ladislaw's Tamburlaine) not mishaps.

Tragedy having degenerated into the vulgarity of the murder mystery, comedy is nominated by Shaw as 'the higher form'. But it, too, must metaphysically divest itself of 'horseplay and fun for fun's sake': for him, comedy inherits the conscience of tragedy, representing the intractability of circumstance, Bradley's 'crushed rocks beneath our feet'. Ibsen accomplishes the dialectical feat of establishing tragi-comedy, Shaw says, 'as a much deeper and grimmer entertainment than tragedy', and the best compliment he can pay to Shakespeare is to allow that he anticipated Ibsen and the analysis of the new woman's struggle against society in his own problem play *All's Well That Ends Well*, whose title, in Shaw's understanding, derides the very possibility of a happy ending.

Shaw's summation is adroit, but there are other variations to the dialectic. Oscar Wilde brilliantly understands the interchangeability of tragedy and comedy, imaged by him in the vacuously perfect dedicatee of Shakespeare's sonnets, about whom in 1898 he wrote *The Portrait of Mr. W.H.* The imagined Willie Hughes, a young actor inclining to effeminacy, seen in an apocryphal miniature to be of 'quite extraordinary beauty', is a benign Dorian Gray. Wilde makes him the good genius of European art, assuming that his visit to Dresden in 1613 to play Juliet inaugurated the new culture there and begot—eventually—the enlightenment, Goethe and the romantic resurrection of Shakespeare. The sonnets, Wilde proposes, celebrate Willie's actorly insincerity, deploying the physique, like Dorian, as a façade. 'He could act love but could not feel it, could mimic passion without realising it.' His face is a conflation of the ancient masks of tragedy and comedy, which hang from a pedestal in the forged portrait of him. To him, agony and ecstasy are alike in their unreality. When Erskine kills himself to 'prove' the validity of his theory about Willie, Wilde's narrator makes the juncture which is the secret of the Shakespearean double plot: 'There was something horribly grotesque about the whole tragedy.'

The grotesque merger between tragedy and comedy incites Wilde himself to laugh, as he recommended, at the death of Dickens's Little Nell, and enables Dorian Gray to participate in what he calls a beautiful Greek tragedy, about which he feels nothing at all. Wilde's story is a small myth, comically challenging Nietzsche's theory of the birth of tragedy and deriving that nativity from Shakespeare not the Greeks. He surmises that Willie lies buried in a vineyard outside Nuremberg, and is pleased by the notion because tragedy and comedy are there vinously blended: 'Was it not from the sorrows of Dionysus that Tragedy sprang? Was not the light laughter of Comedy, with its careless merriment and quick replies, first heard on the lips of the Sicilian vine-dressers?' So Shakespeare's Dionysians are Toby with his cakes and ale, or Falstaff with his 'sherris'.

Gilbert in Wilde's *The Critic as Artist* (1891) rephrases Dickens's account of the double plot, acknowledging the irony of the exchange between its opposites. Of 'poor human life', he says 'there is a grotesque horror about its comedies, and its tragedies seem to culminate in farce.' That means the secret kinship of Hamlet and Falstaff, who apparently represent the mutual exclusiveness of tragic and comic man. Wilde achieves their exchange in *The Decay of Lying* (1891) when he brilliantly notes that 'in Falstaff there is something of Hamlet, in Hamlet . . . not a little of Falstaff.' The fat knight can be melancholy, the prince coarse. The romantics elect to be either Hamlet like Coleridge, or Falstaff like Keats: never both. To the consumptive Keats,

Falstaff represented a hale and hearty beatitude. In 1817 he took over one of Falstaff's Eastcheap sermons, begging for the reprieve not of Falstaff but of the life he exemplifies: 'Right Jack Health, honest Jack Health, true Jack Health—Banish Health and banish all the world.' Near death in 1820, he keeps up the enactment with a magnificent bravery, remarking on his revived gratitude for natural beauty: 'Like poor Falstaff, though I do not babble, I think of green fields.' Next month he submits, allowing 'Death must come at last; Man must die, as Shallow says.'

Wilde, nearer the end of romanticism, can contain these alternatives within himself. Baudelaire saw the dandy as a morose, cerebral Hamlet. For Wilde the dandy is rather an avatar of Falstaff, corpulent, indolent, extravagant. Though Wilde and his wife, promenading through Chelsea in their aesthetic attire, were mocked by urchins as ''Amlet and Ophelia out for a walk', Wilde disparaged the tragic hero, calling his pessimism a narcissistic fiction: 'The world has become sad because a puppet was once melancholy.' His own persona was that of the comic reprobate, idyllically lazy ('I *never* walk' he declared, engaging a hansom to transport him a couple of blocks) and luxuriously improvident. He once accepted £100 as an advance on a play he never wrote. Taxed by his patron, Wilde claimed that the play was already composed in his head but that he could not bestir himself to transcribe it with pen and ink. Like Falstaff with Master Shallow, he admitted 'I owe you a hundred pounds.' The actor-manager, embarrassed, insisted 'Oh, don't worry about that!' to which Wilde returned the Falstaffian assurance, 'I don't!' He kept faith with the role, like Keats, until the end. His downfall, like Falstaff's, was the result of truculence, a comic brinkmanship which persuaded him to quip his way through his trial and—just as Falstaff expects to have the laws of England at his command—to twit the attorney Carson during his cross-examination.

Yeats brings about an even more startling merger between the antitheses of the double plot when he physiologically equates Hamlet and Falstaff, and represents their reunion as a solution to the problem of a demoralised, corrupted intellectual history. Explaining in 1922 his reference in 'The Statues' to

> No Hamlet thin from eating flies, a fat
> Dreamer of the Middle Ages,

he attributes to Hamlet the clown's spiritual grace, 'that has no need of the intellect to remain sane', and identifies him as the medieval 'fool of Faery', as recklessly antic as Puck. This is why he refuses to believe in Hamlet's neurotic thinness. Gertrude fondly describes him as 'fat' and 'scant of breath'. He is not hungrily speculative, like the Renaissance or romantic images of man. Yeats sees him as slumbrously content, his inertia recalling 'Buddha's motionless meditation'. He would have grown backwards, given time, into the fat dreaming knight. In 'Lapis Lazuli' (1938) Hamlet has learned the Wildean wisdom, wearing the face as a mask, the self as a role. Prufrock, T. S. Eliot's Hamlet, is all raw, nervous subjectivity, unable to prepare the objective correlative of an appearance to hide behind in society; Yeats's version of him is all graven or metallic objectivity, like 'handiwork of Callimachus', and has boldly denied the timorous subjectivity within. That is why, for Yeats, 'Hamlet and Lear are gay.'

The players introduce their performance to the court as a tragedy. When it breaks off, Hamlet—as he remarks to Horatio—redefines it as a comedy. That is his technique always, revising tragic duty as comic diversion; and it is his fate in the course of the nineteenth century's commentary on him. The romantic Hamlet is a tragedian of proudly solitary mind. His symbolist successor has turned comically ineffective, disabled and made absurd by his malaise. This new Hamlet, passed on to Eliot, is the invention of Jules Laforgue, whose *Moralité Légendaire* about him in 1885 was praised by Maeterlinck as 'more Hamlet than the Hamlet of Shakespeare'. Laforgue's is a lunar Hamlet, less Yeats's medieval fool than a wry pierrot. He inhabits a symbolist cell like the high room of Maeterlinck's Mélisande or the castle of Villiers de l'Isle Adam's Axel: his 'absolute abode' is a tower above a dank, pestilential lake in the royal park. Hamlet's indecision has given way to a refined lassitude like that of Axel, who resolves (prior to his suicide) to leave living to his servants.

Laforgue's hero rephrases Hamlet's question with a mocking grimace: 'To be—well, to be if one must.' And though he has no choice but to be, he draws the line at having to be a hero. He prefers to be an artist, for that profession prosecutes revenge by other means, in imagination. In his private closet he conceals a pair of wax statuettes, the likenesses of his mother Gerutha and her consort Fengo, whose hearts he childishly pierces with needles. He anticipates the problem Eliot professed to find in the play, and solves it in advance. To perform is to equip yourself with the shield of an objective correlative: 'tonight I must objectify myself. I must act.' When he puts on the false face Prufrock senses the need of, he is for the first time described—immature head, girlish ears, beardless face, pouting mouth, receding chin, lady-like feet—and seen for the 'insignificant little character' he is. He can afford to be innocuous because he is merely one among a legion of fashionable lookalikes, and when Laertes kills him his place is taken by one of his imitators. 'Later on,' he comments presciently, 'I shall be accused of having started a school!'

Shakespeare's characters have in them the potentiality to turn into any or every one of us. Yeats interprets the double plot as an aid to this psychological universalising. Writing in 1903 about the 'emotion of multitude'—the mythic access to a collectivity of unconsciousness—he says that Greek drama taps this in its chorus, while Shakespeare absorbs it from 'the sub-plot which copies the main plot', like a shadow's replication of the body which casts it. Gloucester is

Lear's shadow and, as Turgenev's typology demonstrates, the chain does not end there but engirdles, sooner or later, all men. 'The mind goes on imagining other shadows, shadow beyond shadow, till it has pictured the world.' At last Yeats's own turn arrives, and in 'An Acre of Grass' (1938) he vows to remake himself 'till I am Timon or Lear.' Eliot becomes Hamlet in the very act of making Prufrock deny that he is qualified for the role. (Hamlet's self-doubt is just as afflictive as Prufrock's, who is not Prince Hamlet, nor was meant to be: his 'This is I, Hamlet the Dane' at the graveside is overstated bravado.) The character goes on being recreated by Lawrence in *Twilight in Italy* (1916), and Joyce in *Ulysses* (1922).

Lawrence describes a performance of *Hamlet* in Italian by an incongruous village troupe, and relies on this displacement for two interpretative mutations: the tragedian is restudied as a comic nuisance and a psychological menace, 'a creeping unclean thing', always poking and sniffing; the play is thereby expanded into a novel. Laforgue concedes the necessity of the change. His Hamlet has more on his mind 'than five acts can allow'. Only the novel, according to Lawrence, is capable of telling the unsavoury carnal truths about the character. In an essay in 1925 he contends that Shakespeare can get away with Hamlet because the drama has no way of checking on or disputing the character's self-serving interpretation of events. It is restricted to what its people do or say; there is no formal possibility of analysing them. The novel would expose Hamlet's tragic imposture: 'If you wrote him in a novel, he'd be half comic, or a trifle suspicious . . . like Dostoyevsky's Idiot.'

Lawrence misses the point that Hamlet already is these extra things in the play, but the injustice is guilefully necessary to his argument. He dislocates the play, literally rendering it unintelligible. When it is announced to him that a play called *Amleto* is to be performed, he says he does not know of it, and only once he is told that it is 'una dramma inglese' does he identify it. The Italian players have themselves deconstellated it. For them it is no research into the undiscovered country which is 'the northern infinite of the Not-Self', where Laforgue's man in the moon or the Bostonian Hamlet of Eliot dwell. The 'rolling Italian eyes' of Enrico, the company's Hamlet, announce a gusto and a stout physical hardihood which deride the part he is playing, thus serving Lawrence's attempt to understand the character by removing him from context. 'All the actors alike', he notes with comic glee, 'were out of their element.' The Queen is a dumpy peasant who seems about to box Hamlet's ears, the Ophelia blubbers plumply.

As played by them, *Hamlet* changes from tragedy to farce. Their travesty prompts Lawrence to admit an aversion to the play, and to the self-loathing which (he believes) provoked it. They justify his anachronism, for he proceeds to use *Hamlet*—in a long metaphysical disquisition which runs parallel to the performance—to interpret the degenerative cultural history which lies between it and us, or between it and the equally massacred piece which precedes it in the company's repertoire: *I Spettri*, which is Ibsen's *Ghosts* performed as 'good, crude melodrama'. Ibsen's mother-obsessed, syphilitic Oswald is a Hamlet who in the interim has grown even sicker than his prototype, and Lawrence is pleased to note that again the Italian actor's robust, ruddy physique contradicts the mental emaciation of the role. He goes on to interpret Hamlet as the instigator of spirit's revolt against its own flesh, which commences at the Renaissance, is encouraged by the romantics, and supplies Oswald with his hereditary disease. The world has grown more than sad because of this puppet's melancholy. Yet the irony is that just like Enrico who, despite his constitutional contradiction of the role, becomes the Hamlet he is playing and is infected by the character's perverse nausea, so Lawrence, in the very frenzy of denouncing Hamlet, takes on his mental habits and his raging tone. He adopts Hamlet's mode of generalisation (so admired by Coleridge) and circumnavigates the world, reaching back to Aeschylus and forward to Ibsen, free-associating from the crucifixion to the French Revolution; he even falls into Hamlet's first person, giving voice to the rabid ego which is the portion of Hamlet in himself. Thus Hamlet's regicide is a promotion of 'the greatest conception of the Self, the highest conception of the I', and Lawrence writes his own equivalent to one of this Self's psychotic monologues in the play: 'I shall desire a king, an emperor, a tyrant, glorious, mighty, in whom I see myself consummated and fulfilled. This is inevitable!'

Lawrence checks the self-dramatising Hamlet in himself by remembering that he is after all a novelist, who studies character when it is not on set, and he enlarges the play into a novel by considering what happens before and after its performing, in the audience and backstage. He looks down from his box at the gathered peasants and sees among them the same sex-war which the play acts out—except that it is muted, and must be novelistically intuited by Lawrence. Behind the scenes, too, Lawrence investigates a novelistic plot which happens quietly between the declaimed lines of the play. The local barber informs him of the liaisons among the actors. Laforgue made Hamlet and Yorick brothers, and Joyce was to turn the ghost into Shakespeare, who resurrects his dead son Hamnet to punish the adultery of Anne Hathaway with his brother; Lawrence, too, regroups the characters, further embroiling their relationships. The Hamlet's mistress is the servant from *Ghosts*. The Claudius is married to the Ophelia, and the Gertrude is his mother-in-law, the girl with whom the Hamlet is involved their daughter. The play's cast entwines into the extended and, at the same time, ingrown family of the novel.

The logic of this transforming makes Lawrence humorously vary Partridge's reaction to the ghost of old Hamlet in *Tom Jones*. Lawrence refuses to extend Partridge's empathy to the spectre, making it real by lending it his own emotions. He considers the ghost a failure, 'trivial and unspiritual and vulgar'. He remembers once being as susceptible as Partridge, when in his childhood he saw the play performed by a 'twopenny travelling theatre', whose ghost had an

English north country accent: ' 'Amblet, 'Amblet, I *am* thy father's ghost.' The actor was answered by a sceptic from the audience: 'Why thy arena, I can tell thy voice.' The heckling is Lawrence's cue for the play's reclamation as novel. The ghost may be, theatrically, a cheap illusion. The novel can show how he is in truth resident within us all, as a nihilistic tendency to 'non-being'.

Lawrence liberates the subjective quarrel or sickness within *Hamlet*, baring the novel beneath the play's pretences; Joyce identifies the subjective plot, then triumphantly objectifies it. In terms of Stephen Dedalus's triad of forms—epic, lyric and dramatic—Shakespeare is misrepresented by the romantics as a lyric confessor. Joyce demonstrates his evasiveness (he plays the ghost not the prince) and his dematerialisation within his own creation. He is therefore the one who, as John Eglinton says in *Ulysses*, has after God created most. That disappearance is the absconding of the dramatist, who leaves the actors behind as his surrogates. Stephen acclaims this as the dramatist's gesture of moral abnegation: he exteriorises the self, implants it in others. Biologically, this means that the child fathers the man. Shakespeare plays his own father when performing the ghost, and Stephen invents in Bloom—who appears in the library during the discussion of *Hamlet*, like a discreet ghost with an unobserved walk-on—the father with whom he elects to be reconciled. Yet is not this creative feat, called dramatic by Stephen, actually the generous gift of the novel, which in *Ulysses* achieves the modern revival of the epic? So Stephen's three evolving forms, incorporating Shakespeare, bend into a cycle, and literature recurs to its beginnings.

Though Stephen presents his interpretation of the play as a performance, the twists of its argument as theatrical coups, it is contained within a novel. Mr Best suggests it should be written up as a Wildean dialogue, and Stephen, like a Wildean actor, ironically sheds his role with a scepticism endemic to theatre: 'He laughed to free his mind from his mind's bondage.' As a deductive drama, his theory must remain ingeniously specious, notable mostly for its stagey delivery; in the novel, when he later discovers Bloom to be no ghost but a palpable and forgiving parent, it can come true. Like Wilde unearthing the Dionysia in the death of Mr W.H., Joyce has achieved Hamlet's homecoming, marrying Shakespeare (as Mr Best sagely nods) to 'the old Irish myths'. Criticism's extrapolation into mythology enables Hamlet to generate not only a father but to become the mother who will forgive him: on the previous night an actress has played the part in Dublin, reviving scholarly rumours that 'the prince was a woman'. Within *Hamlet*, all contraries gratefully concur.

Myth reconvenes the many in the one. This is the plurality that Yeats called multitudinousness, which ordained that the emotions of Timon or Lear were no longer dramatically particular: their sorrow is, he said in 1907, 'for all men's fate'. Cleopatra in her death-ecstasy becomes, he remarked in 1937, God or a Mother Goddess. This merger with a collective life—the amalgam of Turgenev's typology—happens in Virginia Woolf by immersion, which means the drowning of personal tragedies in an intermingling fluent comedy of consciousness. 'What's the use', asks the hero of *Jacob's Room* (1922) while yachting off the Scilly Isles, 'of trying to read Shakespeare, especially in one of those little thin paper editions whose pages get ruffled, or stuck together with sea-water?' Soon after, the sail flaps and Shakespeare undergoes that mystic absorption into an elemental multitude which Virginia Woolf elsewhere calls saturation: 'Shakespeare was knocked overboard.' He floats away as merrily on his own Ophelia, and then compliantly drowns.

Because he has undergone this sea-change, he can return from submergence in *Mrs Dalloway* (1925) to reunite dissevered characters in the divine comedy which is, for Virginia Woolf, the body's extinction. He now is what people have in common. Having been dosed with *Antony and Cleopatra* by lectures in the Waterloo Road, Septimus volunteers to fight in the trenches 'to save an England which consisted almost entirely of Shakespeare's plays'. Septimus's mental communion with the other characters happens by way of Shakespeare. He is a substitute for society, invoked by Lady Bruton, who has not even read him, when she babbles of 'England, . . . this isle of men, this dear, dear land.' He is craved as a badge of citizenship and psychological intimacy by Septimus's wife, Rezia: 'Could she not read Shakespeare too? Was Shakespeare a difficult author?' Only a prig like Richard Dalloway excludes himself, opining that 'no decent man ought to read Shakespeare's sonnets'. The plays are full of quotations, and our extracting of them as tags convokes a communal sympathy, making us, like Clarissa Dalloway, 'part of people she had never met'. Clarissa quotes the dirge from *Cymbeline*, 'Fear no more the heat o' the sun', and Othello's 'if it were now to die / 'Twere now to be most happy', which when it echoes again in her mind at the end serves as her elegy for Septimus, whom she never knew. It is significant that, in a novel where death is desired as 'an attempt to communicate', such a thanatalogical use should be made of Shakespeare. The contexts within the plays do not warrant this. The dirge is sung for someone who is not dead at all, and Othello's impatience for a fatal consummation is at once, in the scene on the quay, rebutted by Desdemona, who wants to go on happily and sedately living.

The death which Virginia Woolf derives from Shakespeare is that of the drama, and also that of the novel: it is their dual expiry into lyrical poetry, as once prescribed by the romantic reading of Shakespeare. For it means the abolition of the dramatic person, even of the novelistic consciousness, and demands their loosening into a pantheistic flood whose current is those quotes. Shakespeare cannot, for Septimus, be the poet of nature and of human being. 'How Shakespeare loathed humanity—the putting on of clothes, the getting of children, the sordidity of the mouth and the belly!' He has been suicidally spiritualised. Hence the logic of the apparently random collection of writings that Rezia finds in Septimus's drawer. They are 'about war; about Shakespeare; about great discoveries; how there is no death'—about the war in which

Septimus by mistake did not manage to get himself killed, achieving that membership of the majority envied by Hamlet when he looks down into the grave, and about Shakespeare whose use now is to supply that merciful extermination; about the greatest metaphysical discovery of all, which Virginia Woolf arrives at by way of Shakespeare, that our life is death and our death will be life. Characters plead for obliteration. The song from *Cymbeline* is vocalised all over again by the old woman opposite the Regent's Park tube station who—an Imogen expecting no comic return to life—wails of her own 'high burial place', and longs for 'the pageant of the universe', along with the play, to be over.

The Shakespeare whom Dryden's neoclassical revision sought to fix, stabilise and substantialise has here been put through a last romantic metamorphosis, into shrill, shimmering, annihilating atmosphere.

— 12 —
Prospero's After-Life

Shakespeare bequeaths a problem—the reconcilability of tragedy and comedy, and the intimation (like Polonius's mish-mash of genres) of a unity between all literary kinds—and not a posterity. What English drama there is after him is un- or anti-Shakespearean. The reason is that he is himself a one-man history of drama. He invents it, exploits all its possibilities, and exhausts it. This is the puzzle of *The Tempest*: its renunciation of what Shakespeare has already done, and its prediction of a future for drama in its own cool, controlled, mechanistic image. If Prospero is a dramatist, then he is the opposite of a Shakespearean one. Whereas Shakespeare licenses his characters to improvise both themselves and the play, Prospero manacles all his creatures in supervised subjection, and hastens (when he breaks off the wedding masque) to suppress the rebellious sub-plots which Shakespeare incites. He is the artist as Shakespeare's antithesis, not noisily populating his world but emptying it to occupy it alone in what Henry James, identifying himself with Prospero in 1907, called a 'concert of one', vacantly and despairing rehearsing the virtuosity of his art and then abdicating, as James says, into the 'lucid stillness' or blank silence of his style.

The Tempest begins with what might be a Shakespearean drama in miniature, and in unhinged acceleration. The scene on the wrecked ship has Shakespeare's energetic affray, in its collision of contrary purposes, and the truculent comic reaction to a tragic alarm; above all, it has his gratuitousness: this disturbance in nature is as sudden and inexplicable as Iago's malice, Hamlet's procrastination or Antonio's melancholy. But the violent hugger-mugger spends itself in minutes. It is calmed by Prospero when he reveals himself as its entrepreneurial maker, and the second scene—the long and irritable monologue of retrospection which he confides to Miranda—marks his ownership of all events and persons in the play. Here he narrates, rather than (as he did when he sent Ariel to simulate a tempest) dramatises; hereafter he will not enact events, as drama does, but choreograph their summary re-enactment. Everything which happens on the island shadowily restages the initial usurpation and banishment, which occurred a generation before and an ocean away. The play deals therefore only in illusory fabrications.

Prospero's theatre is not a metaphor for life, as it is when Macbeth calls man a poor player or Jaques calls the world a stage, but merely for itself. Hence the evaporation of the play's visions—the subsiding storm, the vanishing banquet, the silenced voices in the air, the curtailed masque—and of the play itself. The wand Prospero lays down is not the instrument with which Shakespeare verbally quickened the stage and made it resound. It refers to, and in advance disclaims, the theatre of Shakespeare's successors: a specular theatre which, because of the new dependence on illusion once the old open stages were abandoned, is pledged to the exclusive study of psychological deception and to the deployment of spectacular artifice.

The theatre comes to specialise in analysing the theatricality of behaviour and in deciphering our deception of others and ourselves. Personae, our acted lies, are put on trial in Webster, or in the duplicitous skirmishes of Congreve. By the time of Wilde's comedies, theatrical people are the masks they wear. Harold Pinter's *Betrayal* (1978) studies adultery as a theorem in dramatic irony. Its characters are what the Duke in *Measure for Measure* calls 'seemers', experts at the play-acting by which we manage our social and sexual lives. *Betrayal* is about the difference between our knowledge of the characters and theirs of themselves—since it happens backwards, we have foresight about the consequences of what they do, while they must make do with rueful hindsight—and about the gaps in their knowledge of each other. 'I wonder if everyone knew, all the time', says Emma, Robert's wife, of her supposedly secret affair with Jerry. Robert says to Jerry 'I thought you knew. . . . That I knew.' Jerry insists 'You didn't *know*! . . . Then why didn't you tell me? . . . That you knew.' Robert comments, 'You didn't know much about anything, really, did you?' For Pinter, dramatic irony means a total relativism. No one can ever know anything for certain. In the theatre people seem to be artlessly betraying themselves to us when they act, even though they may be betraying one another; but it is we who are being betrayed, since they are deluding us with scripted fictions.

For Ben Jonson, at the outset of this tradition, there can, however, be an absolute and trustworthy knowledge in the theatre. The court masque is the play as the ritualised unmasking of truth, and (when the sovereign is revealed) of power at its source. The masque's indoor theatre of visual conjuring replaces Shakespeare's verbal eloquence. Already this dissociation of drama is implicit in *Antony and Cleopatra*. The poetry has become separable from and incommensurate with the characters, propagating images which, like Cleopatra's rhapsodies to the god-like prodigality of the dead Antony, do not match the scheming, petty actuality exposed by the drama. Because of this separation between dramatic belittlement and the illusory aggrandisements of poetry, Antony and Cleopatra are represented as visual and spectacular beings, cynosures for the eye. 'Behold and see' says Philo, introducing them. The episodes which most definitively characterise them happen elsewhere, and are reported by the spectators—their enthronement in the market place, their gaudy nights and drunken reeling, Cleopatra hopping through the public street or triumphant on her barge. Cleopatra's exit from existence is staged by her as a masque of self-transcendence, in which the escape of her own chimerical being is managed by a poetry celebrating, as Prospero's does, its own aerial and ethereal refinement. Her lowlier elements, given by her 'to baser life', are the comic and prosaic, vixenish and kittenish qualities she possessed as a dramatic character, and their last exercise is in her repartee with the clown; now her 'immortal longings' have made a poetic spirit of her, and the dramatic body must be resolved into 'fire, and air'. Octavius ponders her death as a scenic conundrum: his query is not why but how it was done. And it has appropriately been suggested that Cleopatra owes her conception to a masque, for in the first of the entertainments which Jonson wrote and Inigo Jones designed, *The Masque of Blacknesse* in 1605, the Queen appeared with painted face as one of the daughters of Niger.

In *Henry VIII*, first staged in 1613 and probably Shakespeare's last play, the new theatrical aesthetic of the masque contrives the mutation—perhaps even the abolition—of history, the simultaneous source (when political) of Shakespearean tragedy and (when social) of his comedy. Queen Katherine's death, like Cleopatra's, is the performance of a masque, and her prophetic dream accepts the masque's responsibility to abstract drama: to stage, by mechanical intercession, the invisible, and to achieve the take-off of earthly into heavenly, managed by those engines of Inigo Jones's which lifted James I or Charles I into the sky. What might be dramatic is in *Henry VIII* expelled from the stage and left to be reported. Buckingham, 'my chamber's prisoner' like Prospero in his cell, needs to have the encounter between Guynes and Arde described to him by an eye-witness. The second gentleman, who misses Buckingham's trial, has it related to him by a colleague, and this same officious narrator later reports the removal of Katherine from court. A third gentleman retails the crush inside the Abbey at the coronation. All that is left on stage is a show, mute but symbolically enigmatic, which the spectators must interpret— the masque at Wolsey's party, Katherine's dream, the coronation procession. Character, too, has turned from a wilful, dramatically imposing agency into a puzzle for lookers-on. When Wolsey enters, Buckingham reads his looks, and they eye one another with fraught, silent meaning.

Instead of history, *Henry VIII* has an ocular politics. Like the masque, it happens in a realm of ensnaring, deceptive seeming, and the King is less a father of his people like earlier Shakespearean monarchs than a dramaturge like Prospero, whose absolutism is exercised by his power of surveillance. As Prospero quashes the regicidal subplot of Caliban, so Henry thanks Wolsey for quelling the conspiracy against him. The power of dictators derives from a speaking eye, as does that of actors; Henry can see everywhere or through everyone, like the King who, in the audience at performances of the Stuart masques, was the vanishing-point of all perspectives. The only political fault is a lapse in this executive oversight. Henry for instance does not know of the taxations Wolsey authorises. But when he discovers among Wolsey's papers an inventory of the treasure he has greedily amassed, it is as if he has looked into his subordinate's heart, rendered him transparent and thus—like Prospero elucidating 'this thing of darkness', Caliban—disarmed him. The manner in which Wolsey's disgrace is communicated to him catches this strange abstinence from dramatic confrontation. Ordered to resign, he demands written authority. Suffolk says that his words bear 'the King's will from his mouth directly'. That will no longer manifests itself dramatically in action, or even directly in speech. It entrusts its imprimatur to a narrator, who will, having dramatically defused it, enforce it at second hand. Wolsey's request for a warrant expresses the disorientation of Shakespearean character—grounded in written words which are acted out when spoken—in a play where transactions are conducted by the fiat of a glance and all meaning is visual. Incapacitated for drama, Wolsey retires into narrative, or that lyrical, uneventful stillness extolled in *The Tempest* by Henry James. His death is reported to Katherine by Griffith, and she in turn, unconcerned with the dramatic business of her own dying, nominates him as her post-mortem chronicler.

The masque portends an end of Shakespearean drama because its stage is not a globally capacious empty space filled up with words and deeds but a realm apart governed by its own rational and technical laws, receding in accordance with the laws of perspective as diagrammatically calculated by Inigo Jones, and eventually marked off and separated by the proscenium which frames its illusions. Now instead of being inside the amphitheatrical arena, we sit outside and look in at a fictive room whose fourth wall—as the dramaturgy of the nineteenth century pretended—has been obligingly elided. The play, like the box in which it happens, is a contraption, scientifically ruled and managed.

Coleridge's tribute to the perfect plot of *The Alchemist* notices this inductive and calibrated experimental skill in its working. Face and Subtle are pseudo-scientists, spurious magi promising the conversion of base metals into gold, and they treat the action they manipulate with a pitiless rigour of technique. Their stratagems are their apparatuses, all of which they must simultaneously maintain in running order. By doing so, they are skilfully preventing drama: confrontation—the Shakespearean encounter of opposites, as between the mourner and the reveller—would be their undoing, so they file away each client, as soon as another arrives, in a separate compartment of their house. The machine they inhabit is a device for multiple incarcerations, like the box in which the magician makes people vanish. Tiberius recommends the same policy to the hero of Jonson's *Sejanus* (1603), when he is perturbed by the disaffection of Agrappina and her family. 'Confine 'em,' Tiberius proposes. But internment is effective only in comedy: tragedy, as Sejanus recognises, requires their permanent elimination.

The common denominator of both forms in Jonson is, however, their recourse to the artifice of mechanical management. Brainworm, the intriguer in *Every Man in his Humour* (1598), is complimented as 'An artificer! An architect!', an Inigo Jones whose constructions are intricately linguistic. Edward Knowell calls him 'a weaver of language'. The pathology of the humours automates character, making it predictable and thus manipulable, and this dehumanising is accomplished by language. Each humour has its own madly pedantic idiolect: rather than communicating with words, they are disconnected from each other by them. And the very act of creation imposes a mechanical determinism: Kitely adopts an orphan and makes him his cashier, giving 'him, who had none, a surname, Cash'. Thus foredoomed by his allegorical christening, he is expected always to behave according to type. The Roman politics of *Sejanus* demand a nastier engineering. Livia, planning to corrupt Lygdus, says 'he must be wrought / To th' undertaking, with some labor'd act.' That technological preparation and treatment of people is the specialty of Sejanus and of those he employs as, in Macro's words, his 'dumb instruments'. Silius describes the stratagems of Sejanus as the product of a Vulcanian forge, a factory of patented sleight and guile like the supposedly mystical laboratory of the alchemists:

> This boast of law, and law, is but a form,
> A net of Vulcan's filing, a mere ingine.

The characters of tragedy protest, although unavailingly, against the persecution of this psychic engineering. As the play begins, Sabinus complains to Silius that 'we are no good inginers', unequipped to cope with new circumstances at court; it continues only so long as characters remain whose freedom of action is not forfeit to Sejanus's dramaturgic coercion.

The difference between Jonsonian tragedy and comedy is that whereas the Romans struggle to outwit the encroaching mechanism, the gulls duped by Brainworm, Face and Subtle readily surrender their liberty. They feel safest when enslaved to the engine which mentally regiments them, like people in the Bergsonian theory of comedy whose vital élan has been confiscated. Sir Politic Would-Be in *Volpone* (1606) knows he will not withstand the torture, and says 'I have an ingine'. It is a tortoise-shell, under which he proposes to creep so as to render himself invisible. There in the machine, secure in the renunciation of his humanity, he intends to live happily ever after. In the poem 'To Penshurst', Jonson elaborates an ideal social order based on this same victimisation by the omnipotent machine. Like the alchemist's customers, or the clients for the quackery of Volpone and Mosca, the livestock on the Penshurst estate voluntarily replenishes the lordly table. The partridge, honoured to be eaten, 'is willing to be kill'd', and the fish commit suicide as eagerly as kamikaze pilots: carps run into the net and

> Bright eeles, that emulate them, and leape on land,
> Before the fisher, or into his hand.

The agricultural economy of Penshurst proves the truth of Bergson's comic theory. Things become funny by the sacrifice of liberty and, in the case of these slaughtered creatures, life; they die for the greater glory of the sacrosanct social engine.

The irony of Jonson's career was that it yoked him together with an engineer more ingenious than himself. For the masques, Inigo Jones designed pivoted or shuttered settings which could be transformed, instantaneously relocating an earthly action in heaven. Waves broke on stage, clouds crossed the sky, chariots took to the air, gods commuted vertically between the stratosphere and the floor. After their collaboration had ended, Jonson wrote a poetic 'Expostulacion with Inigo Jones' in which he complains of his own superannuation. Angrily exclamatory, the poem berates the properties of masque which had been the symbolic motives of Jonson's drama—'the Engyne!' he rages—and interprets them as symptoms of a 'Mechanick Age' whose upstart architects have driven out the poets:

> Painting and Carpentry are the Soule of Masque!
> Pack with your pedling Poetry to the Stage!

Jonson's reviling of Jones marks a significant moment in the history of drama, and indeed of imagination. For Jones has stolen from him the coveted title of maker, and rendered meaningless the act of fabrication which Sidney saw as the privilege of the poet. Leonardo had already experienced a similar crisis, in his patenting of inventions and his schemes to construct a machine which, like Jones's, could fly. Artistic creativity could no longer conceive of itself as a mode of manufacture. Henceforth, only engineers would be competent to make things. Poets and dramatists, disqualified as fabricators, must accept the lowlier status of fabulists, dealing in fragile illusions. This is the deconversion which Prospero reaches at the end of *The Tempest*. If his creations must be so tawdry—glistening apparel on a clothes-line to tempt the clowns, mock-tempests and the conscription of over-worked spirits to impersonate goddesses in a masque—then he will abjure them.

The drama hereafter signifies a condition of pretence and simulation, a masking of truth, and as such it is assaulted by the novelists, who retain, they believe, access to a reality which the stage can no longer represent. The court masques of Jonson and Jones gave way in the next century to the social fad of popular and unrehearsed masquerades. Defoe, Fielding and Richardson all comment on these, inaugurating a dispute between the feignings of the theatre and the psychological veracity of the novel which continues with Jane Austen's critique of amateur acting in *Mansfield Park* and Virginia Woolf's of the pageant in *Between the Acts*. Roxana, the 'fortunate mistress' of Defoe's novel in 1724, is commissioned when she sets up shop in London to organise 'shining masquerading meetings'. At one of them she dresses in a Turkish costume, captured from a vessel seized near Constantinople. The vestments both are and are not the truth. Roxana admits that the jewels at the girdle 'were not true diamonds, but nobody knew that but myself'. Yet despite this limitation, the pretence does cover a more illicit truth. When Roxana's companions, attired as Georgian or Armenian ladies, abandon themselves to the dance, they 'really acted to the life the barbarous country from whence they came'. The costume permits their reversion to savagery. Roxana finds that the masquerade is as propitious as darkness for sexual scurrility, and at her entertainment she begins a liaison with 'one of the masks, a tall, well-shaped person, but who had no name, being all masked'—a man whose disguise gives him the lecherous ubiquity of an Ovidian god. He is, she archly hints, King Charles II.

Fielding's Tom Jones experiences the society of London as a teasing masquerade of false faces and cryptic innuendi. The artless novelistic hero cannot accustom himself to the counterfeitings and hypocrisies of the play. With innocent literal-mindedness, he mistakes seeming for being. When he spies a shepherdess at a masquerade, he hopes it will be his adored Sophia. But the bucolic virgin is said—by a lady in a domino outfit—to be a trollop. Jones follows his informant, imagining her to be Sophia's cousin, Mrs Fitzpatrick. She intimates that she is the person he suspects, though she insists on continuing to use her affected voice, 'lest I should be known by others'. Tom is inveigled into leaving with her, and when he prevails on her to unmask, she turns out to be the infamous Lady Bellaston. Working more efficiently under cover, she has picked him up.

The masquerade, like all drama, is a school of deceit. This is why Richardson's Pamela so primly disapproves of these occasions. She attends a masquerade—reluctantly, she claims—dressed as a Quaker, with her consort Mr B. in the habit of a Spanish Don. She is affronted by the brazenness of 'a bold Nun' who addresses Mr B. in Italian, a language which sounds unseemly to Pamela because she does not understand it. Her restiveness goes further than a disgust at immodest manners. She is offended by the fictions the self begets, by the theatrical perjuring of that integrity which is to her, as an ersatz novelist, the inner truth of character. A woman in a feathered gown teases her. She calls the person 'the parti-coloured one': the parti-coloured and multifarious are to her synonyms for the meretricious, and personality itself is a versatile harlotry. The self is a shameless performer. Her revenge is to threaten a disrobing of the company, which will expose not faces but moral natures. She has come, she announces, 'out of curiosity to look into the *minds* of both sexes; which I read in their *dresses*'. A fat monk recoils in horror, crying, 'A general satire on the assemblée, by the mass!' For Pamela the unmasking which satisfies the prurient at the end of the evening will be a moment of novelistic truth, a last judgement calling to account these stripped, uprisen sinners.

After these novelistic reprobations, Prospero and his mechanistic masque recur, much reduced, in Sheridan's 'peep behind the curtain' (as Garrick called it), *The Critic*. During his tenure as manager at Drury Lane in 1777, Sheridan revived *The Tempest*, possibly adding to it two songs of his own; the designer was the painter Philippe Jacques de Loutherbourg, a specialist in inundations and avalanches whose Eidophusikon was a toy theatre which Prospero might have devised, dispensing with actors and exhibiting in miniature such 'natural phenomena' as tempests and conflagrations. Two years later, Sheridan and Loutherbourg collaborated on *The Critic*. The fatuous Puff here rehearses his fustian tragedy on the Armada, assailed by accidents and interruptions, until at last the muddling action is swept away by one of Loutherbourg's elemental panoplies. After the sea-battle, a masque of the Thames and its tributaries compliments Britannia, with Father Time presiding in his crystal car and a dance of river nymphs and godlings, all performed to the strains of Handel. Puff is a Prospero at the end of his tether, a ghost keeping the machine at work by diligent flatulence: he is named after the Aeolian rhetoric of self-advertisement, whose blustering varieties he catalogues—'The PUFF DIRECT—the PUFF PRELIMINARY—the PUFF COLLATERAL', and so on. His stunts are shakily gimcrack, his spirits less competent and less well-rehearsed than those Prospero employs. When he calls in Thames and his watery attendants, explaining 'this is blending a little of the masque with my tragedy—a new fancy you know', he has to annotate his effects, pointing out to Sneer that the two 'gentlemen in green' are the river's banks, 'one crown'd with alders and the other with a villa', though by misadventure the errant Thames has got both its banks on the same side. Prospero has the wit to desert his unavailing creation; Puff loyally stands by his, and bolsters it up with his own applause. But though his drama is no more than nonsensical pilferage, the spectacle which concludes it goes beyond parody: Loutherbourg's pantomime was a mechanical marvel, achieving in earnest what Puff cannot manage. *The Critic* demonstrates the prescience of Jonson's anger. Drama is superseded by scenic engineering.

It is Prospero the machinator rather than Shakespeare with whom the literary future sympathises. Henry James admired *The Tempest* for its exquisite vacuity. To him it was a golden bowl, a flawed vessel harbouring emptiness. Near the end of his own creative life in his 1907 essay, he sees it as Shakespeare's loss of faith in an art which, serenely remote from the unshaped unruliness of the world, can extend no aid to suffering, shabby humanity. It is a work of art which expels the artist: too residually human to be sheltered by it, he is cast out to die back in Milan. This formalistic tragedy is the subject of Auden's commentary on the play, *The Sea and the Mirror* (1944), which has James as its grey eminence. In Auden's epilogue, Prospero lugubriously packs his bags for his journey to death, Ariel evaporates, and the other characters dispute the allocation of fates in Shakespeare's conclusion, predicting the eventual accession of Antonio. The figure who remains to interpret the play is Caliban, and he speaks in the fussily periodic manner of the late James.

Auden studied the Jamesian idiom while writing an introduction in 1946 to *The American Scene*. There he sees James's American tour as a religious quest, the search for a Great Good Place unsullied by drab, shabby, raucous diurnal reality. James found it in Washington Square, or behind the locked doors of exclusive clubs, as Prospero found it on a magic island. Giving to the fastidious master the voice of the monster, Auden sums up the paradox of that quest and the insufficiency of art as a substitute for religion. Caliban is the beast in James's jungle—the soiling physical necessity which he cannot, for all his artistry, discipline; the anarchic mess of a world indifferent to his orderly strictures; the crass America which will not stay outside the genteel perimeters of Washington Square. James had actually seen Dickens's novels as the brood of Caliban. He calls them 'loose baggy monsters' because the monster (as is the case with Grendel) is defined by its being without form and void. When the supercilious artist admits that the thing of darkness lurks within him, that he, too, is a piteous, flabby human, he is condemned to failure, just as the bowl is depreciated by the crack in it. He is now bitterly aware that art cannot save us: redemption must be a gift of grace from without, from above. Prospero and James together represent, to Auden, the fallacy of an aesthete's atheism. They hold up in vain a crystalline mirror (cold and lonely, as Miranda reflects in her beautiful lyric) to a sea which seems to them shapeless and valueless and will soon enough overwhelm their precious meanings.

Nothing in Shakespeare himself could please James, with his hatred of irrelevance, of the messy incompleteness and contingency of life, since Shakespeare adopts that informality as the motto for his plays—as you like it, what you will. But in Prospero he found a self-image: an emblem of the lonely dictatorship of artistic vocation, of the artist's voyeurism and the necessity of his living vicariously through the acts of others.

In the play, Prospero is defeated. The character of Mr Puff is a parodic epilogue to his theatrical shame. The nineteenth century rehabilitates him and restores power to his overthrown charms. For these are the potent spells of the revolutionary romantic dreamer, able to bring the envisioned future to pass; and The Tempest is, in Richard Wagner's phrase, the art-work of that future. De Quincey in 1838 hailed in it 'new modes of life, preternatural, yet far as the poles from the spiritualities of religion'. It had become the imperative of the drama to give an exposition of those new modes of life. The pseudo-scientific contraptions of the masque are preparing it for a mutation into science fiction, and throughout the nineteenth century The Tempest is interpreted allegorically or metaphysically as a parable of prehistory or of the apocalyptic aftermath of history. Victor Hugo took the musical isle to be Eden regained. That reconquest was to be achieved by technology: Hugo's Prospero is scientific man in control of the material world. John Ruskin saw on the island a prescription for a model industrial society, an assertion of the machine's benignity. Prospero is the true governor, Sycorax the demon of slavery; Ariel on his errands represents faithful and imaginative craftsmanship, Caliban the disgruntled and rebellious spirit of enforced labour. As Prospero acquired the status of god, Caliban took up a position as his retrograde, debasing enemy: Daniel Wilson in an evolutionary argument in 1873 defined him as the Missing Link.

Wagner claimed there were two routes open for poetry after romanticism, 'either a complete removal into the field of abstraction, a sheer combining of mental concepts and portrayal of the world by expounding the logical laws of thought, and this office it fulfills as philosophy; or a . . . blending with music, . . . whose inner faculty has been disclosed to us by the symphony of Haydn, of Mozart, and of Beethoven.' Both offices had been discharged already, in the nineteenth century's view, by *The Tempest*. Prospero is the grand abstractor, for whom the characters subordinate to him are mental concepts. His exposition of the play's foregoing action to Miranda in the second scene is his equipping and operation of her mind as an instrument. He is also a philosopher of art, and a critic of its unsatisfactoriness. His transcendentalism, however, is as much musical as scientific. The two are complementary: music, invisibly sounding from the air in the play's songs, is an abstraction of the grossly physical world, and *The Tempest*—on which Mozart considered an opera, for which Tchaikovsky and Sibelius wrote accompanying scores—deserts the stage to play itself out as a symphonic poem.

Shelley, assuming the role of Ariel, describes this transformation in his poem 'With a Guitar, To Jane'. Here he reads the play as a work where drama is sublimated by lyricism; where the Orphic ministry of song unbinds men from the dead end of drama, upraises bodies as spirits, and makes audible again (as in the fourth act of *Prometheus Unbound*) the superhuman music of the spheres. Ariel, giving Jane (who is cast as Miranda) the guitar, is the agent of this change. He is the latent romanticism of Prospero; Caliban, the character who replaces him at the centre in the interpretations of James and Auden, is Prospero's opposite motive—the symptom of a guarded classicism worried about order and structure, both of which Shelley's Ariel denies as he floats, invisibly as music, 'through boundless day'. After romanticism, Ariel comes to seem sinister. Is he not manipulating people even more deviously than Prospero did? Auden said that Shelley's definition of poets as 'the unacknowledged legislators of the world' was better suited to the secret police. And when Ariel is dethroned, Caliban—a responsible being, classically and conservatively held in check by the low opinion he has of himself and of human potentiality—takes over.

Beyond its romantic etherealisation as music, the furthest reach of *The Tempest* into the future is in an art-form made possible, like the masque, by science: the cinema. An American film made in 1956, *Forbidden Planet*, confers on it the ultimate abstraction of removal from earth, transposing it to outer space at the end of the twenty-first century. The Prospero, Dr Morbius, is a physicist and philologist who mans a research station on the off-limits planet. Ariel and Caliban are his mechanised appendages. As his domestic factotum he has manufactured a cybernetic Ariel, Robby the Robot, who resembles an ambulatory juke-box and who, as well as transporting intergalactic visitors across the desert terrain, serves up synthetic meals and can even brew whisky for the dipsomaniac Cookie (the space-ship's Stephano) in his steel bowels. 'Robby is simply a tool', declares Morbius. This is an obedient Ariel, acclimatised to a consumerist world in which he relieves human beings of kitchen chores—'a housewife's dream'. Caliban is a dark and marauding planetary force which tears its human victims apart and then vaporises them. At first the monster is thought to be a self-lubricating engine sunk in the body of the planet, emitting thermonuclear power. But it is revealed at last to be bred by and in the id of Morbius. The ogre, he is told by the skipper of the space-ship which has crash-landed on his fief, is 'your other self', and he is killed by it before the planet, its furnaces overheating, blows up. Even the play's music is a scientific prediction of things to come. Morbius's Miranda, called Altaira, tames wild beasts with an ultrasonic whistle, and the film's credits acknowledge that the noises the air is full of are 'electronic tonalities', a lyricism synthesised in the laboratory. *The Tempest* here has fulfilled its own unearthly prophecy.

— 13 —
The Tragedy and Comedy of Revenge

The alternation of tragedy and comedy maintained by Shakespeare breaks down in the drama of the Jacobeans. The opposites, no longer able to keep their distance, merge in the middle, and their composite is satire. Jacobean tragedy approximates to satire because it is the punitive detection and detention of vice; and the comedy of the period is equally preoccupied with a satiric scourging of its victims.

In both Jacobean tragedy and comedy, the recurrent figure is the revenger. He is ambiguous by nature, vacillating between tragic and comic identities— sometimes Hamlet setting to right the out-of-joint times, sometimes Jaques cleansing the foul and infected world by railing at it and caricaturing its pretensions; wielding sometimes a sword and sometimes a razor-edged tongue. His ambiguity compromises him and makes the plays he dominates quizzically uncertain about themselves, for he is at once less than tragic and more than comic. To qualify for tragedy, he must, like Hamlet, be an inefficient revenger; otherwise he is no more than a killer.

Vindice in *The Revenger's Tragedy* (1607) calls vengeance 'Murder's quit-rent' and 'tenant to Tragedy', but his image betrays the discrepancy: murder is the obsequious means employed by tragedy, and revenge plays deal only with tragedy's instrumentality. Tragic heroes do their slaughtering by proxy—Macbeth (after the first occasion) employing surrogates, Hamlet dispatching Rosencrantz and Guildenstern by jesting indirection—for tragedy is about dying, not killing. Jacobean comedy shares this lethal vindictiveness: it murders in jest. Lussurioso tells Vindice to 'be valiant / And kill thine enemies.' This is the satirist's injunction, to kill by ridiculing an enemy into diminution or abjectness, and it is the motive of Jonson's revenge comedy. Cob in *Every Man in His Humour* wants to acidulate his wits on 'revenge: vinegar and revenge: vinegar and mustard revenge', and Bobadil too seeks to be 'reveng'd, by law'. Bacon called revenge a wild (that is, an unsocialised) justice. So is satire: a summary trial and execution of offenders, a laughing assassination. Revenge is an atavistic craving in men, which society and law conjoin to suppress. Denied the chance to be murderers, we become satirists instead. At the same time, revenge proposes a brutal simplification of dramatic form. If drama is about character in action, then the plots of revenge plays can show how action begets reaction and crime issues in an infinite sequence of reprisals and rejoinders.

Shakespeare has his vengeful satirists—Iago, Jaques, or Thersites—but they never succeed in assaulting the faith either of tragedy or of comedy. The choice in *Othello* between sex and love is a choice as well between satire and tragedy, between Iago's wittily reductive theory that all men and women are the same and Othello's desperate conviction that his own case and Desdemona's are singular. Every epigram of Iago's is a diminishment or devaluation, cheapening people by relegating them to categories. 'I know my price', he tells Roderigo, but like the Wildean cynic his knowledge of prices proclaims his ignorance of values. In overreaching as he does, Othello turns Iago's planned revenge into a rite of sacrifice, solemnly impersonal. He can bestow value even on his errors, as he does in his suicide; Iago meanwhile is reduced to the nullity of the satirist who, void and inadequate and maimed himself, wishes his own nonentity on others: 'From this time forth I never will speak word.'

In *As You Like It* a similar choice obtains between the satire of Jaques and the comedy of Touchstone. Jaques envies the clown's impertinent liberty, and requests a suit of motley for himself. He will wear it like the surgeon's sterilised white coat, as his uniform of satiric disinfection, administering to the world a medicine which will cure its foulness. Touchstone has no such purgative ambitions. His folly is generous and forgiving because it includes himself: like the saint, the clown considers himself the lowliest of creatures. The profession of Jaques, however, is a strutting self-conceit. He can scorn humanity because he exempts himself from it, as he declines to join in the dance at the end of the play. The Duke interprets his sarcasms as morbid symptoms of this thwarted sensuality, a disgorging of his own distempers; in doing so he has moved Jaques from comic ingrate to tragic malcontent. The speech on the seven ages of man is in fact the promulgation of a tragic theory, for though it adopts the comic form of the cycle, returning the old man to his original childishness, it omits the regeneration which is comedy's assurance. It is a case of comedy's union with tragedy or satire, and it proclaims the satiric myth, inherited by Swift and Pope, of time as a protracted and corrupt degeneration. As such it is paraphrased by Knowell in *Every Man in His Humour*. Jaques at least permits a 'strange eventful history' to separate the first from the second childhood. Knowell, aghast at the depravities of his son, more succinctly makes the two overlap, and describes infancy being trained up in vice, imbibing ill customs with its milk. Since time is inevitably bringing all creatures to putrefaction and perdition, the revenger's duty, whether in tragedy or comedy, is to assist it by foreshortening it and violently anticipating the retributive end. Jaques boasts of the fatality of his jokes: he can suck 'melancholy out of a song, as a weasel sucks eggs', and his aim, like the weasel's, is to abort life, to prevent the obscenity before it can be born. Every taunt is a sterilising, prescriptive murder. The hierarchy of the Shakespearean court is amended in Marston's *Parasitaster* (1606), where in a masque the gulls are assigned to a cabin each—the solitary confinement of Jonsonian mania, not the populous congress of Shakespearean drama—on the ship of fools. A clown, Dondolo, shepherds them on board, but the ship is under the captaincy of the satiric intelligencer, Hercules.

Hercules is the satirist as a compromised comedian. Playing the sycophantic fawn, he flatters in order (underhandedly) to scourge, and scurrilously trades in gossip and innuendo. Nymphadoro numbers him among 'those cankers, these mischiefs of society, intelligencers or informers'. The satirist as tragic hero is introduced by Marston in *The Malcontent* (1604). The business of Malevole is defamation. Webster's induction to the play sees its creation as a supposedly medicinal besmirchment of the world: 'Such vices as stand not accountable to the law should be cured as men heal tetters, by casting ink upon them.' This remark, delivered by the actor Burbage, places the censuring wit, like the revenger, outside the law, and makes his prescription—the ink smeared on a skin disease—an excremental curse. Duke Pietro's error is to indulge the disguised Malevole by treating him as an allowed fool, whose abuse is comically harmless. He enjoys the cur's snarling, and gives 'thy dogged sullenness free liberty'.

But Malevole is more than a cankered railer. He intends 'revenge most deep', and for him satire is a more corrosive and mortifying triumph than murder would be:

> He that gets blood, the life of flesh but spills,
> But he that breaks heart's peace, the dear soul kills.

He dreams of perfecting a language so pure in its vitriol that it can perform the service of a weapon or of poison, abrading, flaying, searing, causing flesh to rot. He ridicules the bawd Maquerelle by reminding her that her senescent husband 'will not bite'. She admits that she 'took him with his mouth empty of old teeth'. The purpose of speech for Malevole is to rend and tear; hence this sharpening of dental implements.

Later in the seventeenth century, the verbal malefaction becomes a heroic armament. Jaffeir in Otway's *Venice Preserv'd*, railing against the senators, cries, 'Oh, for a curse / To kill with!', though Pierre advises that 'Daggers, daggers are much better!' In the sick vividness of its images, Malevole's language approaches the sorcery of graphic caricature, which actually inscribes on the faces of enemies the distortions and deformities he can only sketch in words. Vindice carries about with him a skull fantastically adorned, as an emblem of this dangerous satiric witchcraft. Rhetoric aspires to scorch skin away and lay bare the bone, to bore into the harried human creature. Women, already deviously indented, are its inevitable patients. Nymphadoro in Marston's *Parasitaster* calls their sex 'but men turn'd the wrong way outward'.

Though Vindice's unmasking of the decayed head, and Malevole's account of the earth as a promiscuous grave, the muckhill of the heavens with man as 'the slime of this dung-pit', suggest Hamlet pondering in the boneyard, they are Hamlets with a difference. He, as a Shakespearean character, instinctively reclads skulls with skin. He revivifies what is left of Yorick, just as, leaping into Ophelia's grave, he joins Laertes in postponing the ceremony of death, holding off the counterpane of earth so he can fancifully restore her to life by speaking of her. Hamlet founders as a revenger because he animates whatever he touches, even if it is a skull; Vindice and Malevole are infallibly fatal. Their madness, like that of all satirists, is to claim for themselves the omniscience of a god, along with the creator's right of distributing penalties. Otway's Pierre, vowing himself to 'dear Revenge', salutes the vendetta as 'the attribute of gods'. Vindice appeals to divine judgment as a cross-sectioning of bodies for analysis. 'The eternal eye', he says, 'sees through flesh and all.' To the intelligencer, acquiring information is an evisceration. Hippolito describes the inquiries of Lussurioso as an adroit flaying: 'he began / By policy to open and unhusk me.'

The savage unmasking or unhusking of the human skeleton goes with a clinical exposure of the theatre. The key word in Jaques's account of the seven ages is his dismissive contention that men and women are *merely* players. Jacobean tragedy is disgusted by the falsifying pretence of the theatre, which enables people to cavort and parade in proud self-sufficiency like the Duke and his train observed by Vindice. The revenger, who masters these disguises in order to strip them away, sets out ruthlessly to deprive the players of their protective impostures. Everything in a play is necessarily a fraud, as cosmetically beautified flesh misrepresents the decay beneath it. There is a naturalness to the theatricality of Shakespeare's characters. The self is an incorrigible role-player, and its impersonations are rehearsals of truth. Rosalind can speak more frankly to Orlando when in transvestite disguise than she could if she were obliged to play the role of herself. But the acting of Jacobean characters is their lie about themselves, the theatre the infirmary of their delusions. The revenger functions therefore as alienist (in the word used of the first psychoanalysts) or alienator, disassembling the people he analytically cleaves. Gertrude tells Hamlet he has cleft her heart in twain, and Beatrice in Middleton's and Rowley's *The Changeling* in 1623 says that de Flores, after her erotic capitulation, 'has undone me endlessly'. As well he takes to pieces the engineered mousetrap of the play itself, like Hamlet maintaining a critical commentary during *The Murder of Gonzago*. He is the malign practical joker, with the power to stop the game: he knows everyone else is acting, but no one must know that he is acting, too. Hence Hamlet's 'antic disposition', and Malevole's 'affected strain'.

Once more the Aristotelian formula has been complicated. These plays are not about character in action, but about actors acting. When hiring Malevole to murder the Duke, Mendoza asks, 'Wilt enact one thing for me?' and he later commissions, to choreograph his revenge, 'some masquery . . . any quick-done fiction'. For Shakespearean characters, altering identity entails a cost in suffering and frustration. Viola regrets her disguise as a wickedness. For the Jacobeans, it is the only logical response to a truthless world: seeing both through it and through himself, the revenger enjoys the satirist's grim satisfaction, the bliss of being undeceived. Vindice's false front is his alienation from himself. Unlike Viola, he can glibly wish himself out of the incriminating thing he is. He decides 'I'll quickly turn into another', and asks his brother to confirm that he is 'far enough from myself'. Yet his vacating of himself begets its own nausea when he learns the truth of his mother's nature, and he reels 'in doubt / Whether I'm myself or no!' In Webster, this perjury becomes a heroic bravura, the theatre's indigenous mode of moral valour. What Delio in *The Duchess of Malfi* (1613) calls 'integrity of life' is a bold consistency in pretence, like Vittoria's affectation of innocence at her arraignment in *The White Devil* (1612) or the Duchess's proud declaration that, despite her torments, she is Duchess of Malfi still.

Webster's heroines are before all else performers, true only to their roles. Hence the arrogance of their self-reference: 'Am I not thy Duchess?' They have perfected that vacuity which Vindice envies, except that whereas when he departs he leaves behind him a mask, they nominate metaphors to represent them. The habit of evasion has got into their language, and they are expert at camouflaging themselves in imagistic likenesses. Vittoria calls herself a crystal river or a ship in a black storm. Even the Duchess's claim to be Duchess still is a metaphor: she is likening herself with something she both is and is not, fashioning for her own aggrandisement an icon of disdainful steadfastness. The comparison to which they are most addicted is diamantine. Vittoria says that hammering accusations will prove as glass against her 'mine of diamonds', and the Duchess speaks of having her 'throat cut / With diamonds'. The lapidary metaphor has here replaced sentient, vulnerable flesh. These women are as proudly impervious as the minerals they admire. In a characteristic linguistic quibble, they mistake virtue for virtù. The luxurious and aristocratic boast of the diamond is that it cedes only to an equal: 'None cuts a diamond but a diamond', says Marston's Mendoza. Flamineo, applauding the stoic performance of the expiring Vittoria, calls her tough and durable, which is the highest Websterian compliment. She has taken on the radiant transparency of glass without its brittleness. Ferdinand's epitaph for the dead Duchess also responds to her glassiness: 'Cover her face; mine eyes dazzle: she died young.' Again the refining of the metaphor desensitises his language and enables him to speak aesthetically, not emotionally or morally, of the sister he has destroyed.

The undoing of character and of the play's deceits practised by other Jacobean dramatists—as by Webster when he has Ferdinand upbraid Bosola for his evil-doing while remembering that he is merely cursing a good actor for playing a villain's part, and by Jonson when he allows Volpone to appeal against the court's sentence to the audience, which will approve him as a performer, not censure him as a moral agent—is completed here by an unmaking of dramatic poetry. The poetry has loosened itself from the drama. What they say does not express the characters but conceals them. This is why Flamineo, dying, can veer so contradictorily between conceits and proverbs, between wittily fantasticating his fate and sagely moralising over it, between acting his death and experiencing it. The words covet the status of objects or icons, which will take over from their human users. The Duchess feels herself to be doomed, rendered humanly obsolete, by the tableau miming the deaths of her husband and children:

> . . . . It wastes me more
> Than were't my picture, fashioned out of wax,
> Stuck with a magical needle, and then buried
> In some foul dunghill.

She is describing here the black magic of the satiric image: the use of a defiling misrepresentation wishfully to kill its model. Such images are made in Webster by a ruthless surgery, as when the Duchess is forced to clasp and cosset a severed hand or when, in *The Changeling*, de Flores amputates Alonzo's finger to carry to Beatrice the diamond he wore on it as a souvenir of murder. (She orders him to bury the bloody digit but advises keeping the stone; 'the true value / . . . is near three hundred ducats.' Her priorities—perdurable gems not putrefying flesh—are Websterian.) And the Duchess makes such an image of herself, arranging herself to die like a <u>hortatory</u> waxwork and triumphantly reporting her achieved incapacity to feel.

Because language in Webster no longer corresponds with the mental or emotional states it professes to record, it need not even belong to the characters who use it. Since its purpose is ornamental, it can be borrowed for however long the display needs to last, as the distraction of Cornelia in *The White Devil* is plagiarised from Ophelia. This is the ghoulish service of the echo at the fort in Milan, which offers a précis and a regurgitation of the conversation between Antonio and Delio. Antonio says he will not talk with the echo, because 'thou art a dead thing'; it at once says the same of him. Webster's theory of influence and allusion makes these echoes, like Cornelia's madness, acts of necrophilia, congress with the dead. Appropriately Cornelia's echoic mad scene, itself an exhumation of Shakespeare, contains an image of the desecrating robbery of a grave:

> But keep the wolf far thence, that's foe to men,
> For with his nails he'll dig them up again;

and this instance of an undead image returning to the semblance of life is resurrected a second time when Eliot quotes the dirge in *The Waste Land*. Webster's people similarly disown any emotion which may have had the temerity to occur within them. Flamineo detaches himself from his remorse by diagnosing it as an alien growth inside:

> I have a strange thing in me, to the which
> I cannot give a name, without it be
> Compassion;

and the Cardinal exorcises his guilty conscience by seeing it as an armed thing clawing at him with its rake from his fish-ponds.

Their image-worship makes Webster's characters esoteric aesthetes, and they were adopted as colleagues almost three centuries later by Swinburne (who considered Webster the equal of Aeschylus, Dante and Shakespeare), John Addington Symonds and Rupert Brooke. The image, by doing their feeling, ageing and reacting for them, solemnises that transaction which is the victory of decadent art: form's annihilation of content. The Duchess of Malfi's wax picture becomes Basil Hallward's painting of Dorian Gray or, when Swinburne descries in Webster's horrors 'the latent mystery of terror which lurks in all the highest poetry or beauty', turns into the enigmatic Mona Lisa as expounded by Walter Pater.

Oscar Wilde actually provided a decadent sister for the Duchess of Malfi in his own *Duchess of Padua* (1883). The people of Wilde's play are idolators. Finding images is their entire dramatic activity. Guido, infatuated, says that poetic tropes are 'but empty images, / Mere shadows of my love', and he and the Duchess work through all the arts, calling love a sculptor, a singer and a painter. The Duchess wants to cut Guido's image from her heart, which is 'such a stone nothing can reach it / Except the dagger's edge.' Aestheticism eventually contrives the replacement of persons by effigies, which are immortal images. The Duke, warning his wife that one of her predecessors crossed him, says that her monument in red marble now lies in the chapel, 'very beautiful'. Webster's characters at least invent themselves. Wilde's must be fashioned by one another. Hence when Guido demands 'Art thou that Beatrice, Duchess of Padua?' she replies with a revision of the Duchess of Malfi's proud restatement of rank and imperturbable value: 'I am what thou hast made me; look at me well. / I am thy handiwork.' As in Dorian's case, the virtue of character resides in a refusal to react to the stresses of drama. Self-poisoned, the Duchess dies with her face contorted; when the Lord Justice uncovers her body, her expression is now 'the marble image of peace'. Ferdinand has the Duchess's dead face covered because he fears its humanity will accuse him. In Wilde's version, there is no such risk: the uncovering unveils an immaculate art-object.

In their disdain of both motive and emotion, and the proud gratuitousness of their behaviour, Webster's characters created a problem for the dramaturgy of Brecht. Adapting *The Duchess of Malfi* for Broadway in 1949 in collaboration with Auden, Brecht had to supply them with motives, which are a matter of biological and economical determinism. He made Ferdinand revile Antonio because he incestuously dotes on his sister the Duchess, and explained the Cardinal's vendetta by making him want to dispossess the Duchess and sieze her lands. The two, in a neat dialectical theorem, cancel each other out: Brecht adds a scene in which Ferdinand slays the Cardinal. Bosola is now supernumerary.

In Webster, Bosola's torture of the Duchess is his attempt perversely to reclaim her for human being. She asks him, 'Who am I?' and he replies with an anatomy of the weak and obscene flesh. Admitting her own membership of this feeble and humbled company might, if this had been Shakespeare, have made a tragic character of her. But she can interpret Bosola's tutelage only as belittlement, and she opposes to it her own unmoved and emotionless persona. His strategy for instructing her in what he calls mortification is rebuffed. She refuses to be terrified of the cord which will strangle her: she rejects the imputation of native bodily feeling. Her death, so immaculately staged by her, is followed by that of Cariola, which, rather than a passing-over into the fixity and sanctity of an image, is the difficult extermination of a live, protesting thing. Cariola, unlike the Duchess, does not want to die, and pleads with her executioners in a crescendo of hysterical objections—she is contracted to a young gentleman; is unconfessed; is quick with child. Meanwhile she bites and scratches, in parody of the Duchess's self-composure. Her death ought to be an offering of gratitude to the life the Duchess so superciliously resigns, but even Cariola's desperation is suspect. In the Websterian theatre, no statement, no matter what the extremity, can be permitted to be ingenuously true, and to stay alive Cariola bravely but unavailingly mimics the Duchess's deathly fictiona-lising of herself by telling a series of hopeful lies. Her three pleas are as disjunct from one another and from herself as the items of Ferdinand's tripartite obituary for his sister. No necessary truth constrains them. Her excuses and his images could be rearranged in any order. Both are merely making phrases, or reciting in obedience to echoes.

Though the play is not, because of her refusal to countenance it, the Duchess's tragedy, it could perhaps be Bosola's. Yet his gratuitous conversion after her death demonstrates the irreconcilability of revenging satire and tragedy. The revenge play can become a tragedy only by accident, as a liability of its own impure form. Hamlet prefers tragic equivocation (or comic procrastination) to the revenger's speedy satiric efficiency. Revengers who begin to question the propriety of what they do are destroyed not saved by their compunction. Bosola dreads his new sense of responsibility, and wants to disown it: 'These tears, I am very certain, never grew / In my mother's milk.' The lapse into tragedy confounds and disorients these characters. The revenger dreams of an act without consequences. Vindice imagines that he can consume Lussurioso's 'noble poison' without harming himself, and Beatrice believes she can employ de Flores to murder for her and thus escape responsibility both for the deed and to her instrument. The revengers are either moralists betrayed into a gloating violence, like Vindice and Giovanni in Ford's *'Tis Pity She's a Whore* (who, to declare his contempt for social prohibition, first impregnates and then kills his sister), or else amoralists handicapped by the advent in them of morality and loyalty, like Bosola or de Flores.

The theatre is the salving metaphor of these people because it allows them to present all actions as play-acting, graced by the irresponsible liberty which Jonson's intriguers enjoy. Once they cease to be performers and develop a consciousness of what they are and how they have determined their own natures, they cannot survive. De Flores is Beatrice's undoing because he is a moral tutor to her, as Bosola tries to be to the Duchess:

> . . . . settle you
> In what the act has made you; y'are no more now.
> You must forget your parentage to me:
> Y'are the deed's creature.

Rather than tragedy, the penalty of such divisiveness is theatrical disqualification, which makes the deaths of these people tersely anticlimactic. Vindice and Beatrice both accept that they have been ruled out, precluded by their own unwelcome inner complexity from further play. He says ''Tis time to die when we are ourselves our foes', she in paraphrase concludes ''Tis time to die, when 'tis a shame to live.'

The characters of these plays test themselves with horrors, but undramatically pride themselves on their failure to react. The paradox of this dramaturgy is at its most perverse in the anesthesia of Ford's *The Broken Heart*, where a cauterising savagery seeks to nullify the very feelings it torments. The play is about the prevention of emotion and reaction: the ban on Orgilus's love, which leads to his prohibition of Penthea's. Killing is a cure of feeling. As the Laconian warriors brag of breaking off 'one man's head, another's nose, / Another's arms and legs' in the fray, so the jealous Bassanes vows to tear out Philas's throat and rip up his maw if he carries letters to or from Penthea. The purpose of this bestiality is to quell his jealous fits, not to express them. Grausis says of him, 'My lord, to cure the itch, is surely gelded', and Orgilus stabs Ithocles twice so as, he says, to alleviate his pain. The tearing-out of the heart, as by Giovanni in *'Tis Pity She's a Whore*, will secure it from emotion. Ithocles admits that he has 'plucked from thy [Penthea's] bosom / A love-blest heart, to grind it into dust; / For which mine's now a-breaking.' The idolatrous ideal in Ford is the body bled dry, not flayed as in Marston: blanched and—by its rigor mortis—hardened into an insentient image. Kissing Orgilus, the maddened Penthea notes 'he has lost his colour'. The characters are fond of architectural analogies because they aspire to the marmoreal pallor and fixity of classical structure. Tecnicus warns Orgilus to

> . . . . beware
> Of an unsure foundation; no fair colours
> Can fortify a building faintly jointed,

and Bassanes, repenting his abuse of Penthea, says he has pulled down a 'temple built for adoration only'.

Ford's deaths in *The Broken Heart* are classical translations of the body into statuary, or waxworks. Orgilus imprisons Ithocles in a chair to kill him, and Penthea is revealed dead in a chair. In the dance, Calantha—after she has been advised of the three deaths—asks if the motion has 'raised fresh colours on our cheeks', but is assured that the blood has enamelled her whiteness. Later she begs Nearchis to kiss her cold lips. Then, instead of reviving, she quietly and voluntarily dies. Death is the draining of life from a traumatised body which is left behind, now perfect because uninhabited. Orgilus, when allowed to choose his mode of death, chooses bleeding and opens an artery. As he dies he welcomes the 'ice that sit'st about my heart, / No heat can ever thaw thee.' Drained of that vital heat, the gelid corpse is an image of neoclassicism: David's Marat in his cold bath-tub.

The revenger's moral peril is his increasing addiction to violence: his inevitable decline from satirist to sadist. Thus while hounding his enemies he destroys himself. Bacon said that 'a man that studieth revenge keeps his own wounds green', and an obsessed revenger in Thomas Nashe's *Unfortunate Traveller* (1593) gloatingly tells his victim how he has riven his own throat with cursing, ground his teeth to powder with angrily chewing on the name of his prey, and caused his tongue to swell with its horrid threats. He is his own victim. This is why, as Horatio tells Fortinbras, 'purposes mistook' fall 'on the inventors' heads'. The revenger's vocation is a cankered self-loathing. That was the Duke's analysis of Jaques, and it is a definition, too, of the satirist's predicament. He is one who loves to hate, for whom enmity is consummation.

The alliance of Beatrice and de Flores in *The Changeling* studies this snarled contradiction. Their affair acts out the psychopathology of satire. De Flores knows she hates him, yet he 'cannot choose but love her', and he punishes himself by wheedlingly inviting her to rail at him. He loves her because she despises him as much, in his misshapenness, as he does himself. She is beguiled into a loving acceptance of responsibility for him because he represents an aspect of herself which she loathes but cannot be rid of. They are bound by their knowledge that neither is any better than the other. When de Flores argues, 'Nor it is fit we two, engaged so jointly, / Should part and live asunder', he is celebrating that coition of love and hate, carnal craving and the death-wish, which makes satire. Their understanding, symbolised by the kiss, seals a satirist's contract: each undertakes to punish the other for the crime of being human. Beatrice knows that she is to bed down with the antagonist who will accord her a requisite and lawful destruction:

> Was my creation in the womb so cursed,
> I must engender with a viper first?

The scene of their wooing has a religious ardour and a spiritual entrancement because, for all its vileness, it is a rite of conversion, solemnising their dual initiation into the cult of penitence and purgative loathing which is the satirist's profession. De Flores specifies that Beatrice must kiss him zealously. T. S. Eliot remarked of *The Revenger's Tragedy* in 1930 that 'the hatred of life is an important phase—even, if you like, a mystical experience—in life itself.' Beatrice by reviling de Flores and he by proving to her her own whorishness introduce each other to this mystical misanthropy. Samuel Johnson notices the same dutiful scouring in Swift, who, cleansing the flesh rather than vindictively searing or scarring it, 'washed himself with Oriental scrupulosity', the orientalism of the habit suggesting its fanatical spirituality. This abluting erasure of shame and guilt (a muddy complexion in Swift's case, which never looked clear, Johnson adds, despite his lavings of it) could be the affliction of Jaques, who is named excrementally after the privy, or jakes. He and Swift are like oriental holy men, apprenticing themselves to filth. Marston's Hercules shares this abrasive primness. Herod demands why clean linen is such a grace and Hercules replies that it is 'the first our life craves, and the last our death enjoys'. Donna Zoya pardons her husband providing he vows 'to wear clean linen, and feed wholesomely'. Hercules bases his diet on the satirist's disgust, which Olivia (speaking of Malvolio) calls his distempered appetite: 'I'll eat no city herbs, no city roots; for here in the city a man shall have his excrements in his teeth again within four and twenty hours.' The seven ages of man are here brutally abbreviated: the human life-span is an incident in the messily organic food cycle.

As well as a religious devotion, satire is a scientific ministration to mankind. Jaques wants to disinfect the world by dosing it with his medicinal asperity, and in *The Changeling*, too, satire is a regime of pharmaceutical treatment for the malady which is humanity. Like Alibius in the asylum labouring over the cure of his brain-sick patients, Beatrice affects to be concerned about the pustules on de Flores's face and offers to make him a cleansing potion. He, too, is in the business of physic, and keeps a medicine chest stocked with vials and a treatise of experiments for deciphering nature's secrets. His insinuations have worked experimentally on Beatrice's nature, enticing into view what she calls 'that secret' of her fascinated revulsion, and he prescribes specifics for her moral nausea, saying (as he claims her) that 'silence is one of pleasure's best receipts'. De Flores's pharmacology is revenge at work, comically demonstrating the manipulability both of body and mind. His recipes depend on the predictability of the patients. Beatrice tries out his formula for determining virginity on Diaphanta, and the water she administers has the effect of reducing the girl to a puppet of her own involuntary nervous spasms. First she sneezes, then she giggles.

As 'the master of the mystery', de Flores has assumed the diagnostic power over others exercised by Jonson's fake alchemist or by Volpone when he sets up shop as a mountebank doctor vending quack remedies for the catarrh, the spleen, dysentery and melancholy. Under cover of his disguise, Volpone is prosecuting a career which aims to kill rather than cure: the unctions and liquors he offers are placebos, because to be born a fool—indeed to be born at all—is a disease incurable. Though mired in filth and infection, sharing Lovewit's house with the rats and the plague germs, the vocation of Face and Subtle in Jonson's *The Alchemist* is a clinical purifying. Dapper is to be bathed and fumigated before his appointment with the Queen of Faery, and arrayed of course in clean linen, while Surly is dispatched to 'be soak'd, and strok'd, and tubb'd, and rubb'd'. The irony of this scouring is its hopeless attempt, like Lady Macbeth scrubbing her hands, to eradicate a moral stain. The more assiduously Jonson's characters wash, the fouler they are.

The collusion of the satirist with the physician continues throughout the seventeenth century. Wycherley's libertine Horner in *The Country Wife* (1675) uses a quack doctor as his pimp, and in about 1676 the scandalous Rochester, socially disgraced, went into hiding as a mountebank doctor called Alexander Bendo, who touted remedies for scurvy, obstructions in the stomach and complaints of the liver. He also supplied cosmetics, which, from Hamlet's attack on the false painted face with which women misrepresent nature to Pope's account of Belinda's toilet in *The Rape of the Lock*, are an irritation to the revenging satirist. The satirist's aim is the surgical unseaming of bodies, the acceleration of their natural decay; cosmetics frustrate him by aesthetically fortifying the body against its imminent wreckage. Bendo, professing to defend women against this moral laceration, has his equivalents to the healing bath Beatrice promises de Flores—he will remove from his clients 'all spots, freckles, heats and pimples, nay marks of the small-pox'—and he indignantly denies that the beautician is the physician's inferior: 'I take more glory in preserving God's image in its unblemish'd beauty, upon one good face, than I should do in patching up all the decay'd carcasses in the world.' Thus Rochester mordantly allows Bendo to betray him.

When Beatrice opens that physician's closet and scrutinises the manual of chemical inquiry, revenge has been deflected from tragedy to comedy. Laying down his arms, the satirist establishes himself as a learned doctor. Jonson's theory of humours is his physiological patent, certifying the maniacal fixity of temperaments and entitling the dramatist to practise on them as if they were the madmen interned by Alibius in *The Changeling*. Kiteley in *Every Man in His Humour* describes the humour as a mental fever, a pestilence of fantasy, and Cash explains its germination and its contagious ravenings: 'It is a gentleman-like monster, bred in the special gallantry of our time, by affectation; and fed by folly.' In *The Alchemist* it has become epidemic, and plague causes Lovewit to quit London. Comedy is the caustic rectifying of this sickly and stinking body politic.

The body in Shakespeare nurtures identity, affords the self a home; the comic wisdom of his fools pleads for its sheltering and victualling. Lear's fool begs to be guarded from the storm, while Touchstone seeks a mate for his needy organism. In Jonson, that body is a foul warren which must be cleaned out: comedy is our revenge on our own culpable humanity. Instead of the Shakespearean polymorph, made from the merger of the crowd's multitudinous identities, as the third gentleman describes it in *Henry VIII*, Jonson takes the guilty body to pieces. Sejanus's régime universalises his body which, erected in magnification as a statue, also penetrates omnipresently the lives of his victims, sending out appendages like extra, supervisory organs. Agrippina imagines 'all Tiberius's body stuck with eyes' and the ears of Sejanus elongated to invade her inmost closet. Retribution therefore insists on the massacre of that engulfing, octopoid body: the toppling of the statue, and the tearing limb from limb of its model. The multitude, rather than being compressed and compounded 'so strangely in one piece' as in *Henry VIII*, subject Sejanus to a grisly surgery in their quest for souvenirs. Some dig out those eyes which by proxy spied on Agrippina, while

> Others are met, have ravish'd thence an arm,
> And deal small pieces of the flesh for favours;
> These with a thigh; this hath cut off his hands;
> And this his feet; these fingers, and these toes;
> That hath his liver; he his heart: . . .

The very punctuation, in its curtailing semi-colons, assists the anatomical division.

Tragedy demands the body's carving-up; comedy still hopes for its cure. Sejanus employs a physician as his poisoner and admires the subtlety of the man's trade. When he enquires after the health of the women at his court, Eudemus is unforthcoming, refusing to divulge professional confidences. Sejanus objects:

> Why, sir, I do not ask you of their urines,
> Whose smells most violet? or whose siege is best?
> Or who makes hardest faces on her stool?

Improper in tragedy, these are, however, the questions to which comedy demands an answer. *The Alchemist* studies the body as a thing profusely excremental, reposing like the scarab in dung (from which Subtle has retrieved Face) and abundant in its ventilation of wastes. Face calls Subtle 'the vomit of all prisons'; Surly says he will divert Sir Epicure's medicines through a whore's body so she can 'piss 'em out next day' after subjecting them to analysis within;

specimens of faeces and menstrue are studied; poets write about the grandiose expansion of the fart; Drugger lives with cheese and like cheese is mined by vermin, so in Face's diagnosis he suffers from the worms. The equivalent in comedy to the dismembering of Sejanus is Face's minimal definition of human identity as the summary of its own physical residue: 'We are but faeces, ashes.'

Among the body's effluents, perhaps the one most offensive to Jonson is language, the uncontrollable drivelling of the mouth. Corvino notes that Volpone's 'nose is like a common sewer, still running' and calls his mouth 'a very draught'. Mosca suggests stopping it up. That vindictive proposal gets at the self-hatred in Jonson's creativity. Just as the tragic revengers identify dramatic creativity with the devising of murderous machines—what Webster calls 'night-pieces', since the imagination is the mind's morbid and nocturnally shaded underside—so Jonson abhors his own linguistic fluency, which is a symptom not of generous abundance (as in the garrulousness of Shakespearean character) but of the body's incontinence. The humours are a sickness within language. Mr Matthew's melancholia rheumily vents itself in writing: 'I . . . take pen and paper presently, and overflow you half a score, or a dozen, of sonnets at a sitting.' Downright's remedy, like Mosca's, is the closure of the leaky orifice. When Matthew wants to recite his elegy, Downright says 'O, I could sew up his mouth, now.' Face imposes the same penalty on Dapper before his tryst with Dol: to ensure that he maintains a respectful silence, 'we'll put, sir, / A stay in's mouth', choking him with gingerbread.

The language of *The Alchemist* is a prodigal wastage, like the excrement to which it so often refers. The verbal energy of the characters goes into inventing synonyms for execration. They converse in curses and in slanging abuse. The gamey vernacular does not enliven their speech, for they are as pedantically precise about their argot as if it were a dead language, classically regimented. Humourists are grammarians, conjugating an obsession. Subtle assails the syntax of Kastril, and Dol in her ravings has not associatively liberated language from reason, like the mad Ophelia, but prattles of phonetic science,

> . . . . where then a learned linguist
> Shall see the ancient used communion
> Of vowels and consonants——.

During one of their deceptive playlets, Surly and Subtle chatter in Spanish, while Face admires the gallantry of their language and Kastril mistakes it for the learned jargon of law-French.

When Shakespeare writes a scene bilingually, as in Henry V's wooing of Katherine, it is to prove the amicable harmony between languages. Learning the parts of speech from her gentle-woman, Katherine wants first to know the words which denote the parts of the body. Shakespearean language, whether French or English, is an organism, a body in which we are lodged, by and of which we become self-conscious. Katherine's lesson is delightfully and childishly sexy because in discovering those new words for her extremities she is discovering the extremities themselves excitedly anew. Jonsonian Spanish, however, like the idiosyncratic uncommunicative English of his humourists, is language as a jealously and madly introverted system: speech as an antic, accelerated machine. The play is the rubble of Babel, where everyone talks at the same time, with garbled unintelligibility. Face and Dol are directed, during her lunacy, to 'speak together'. There is a corresponding incident in *The White Devil* when Vittoria at her trial objects—in contrast with Kastril's awe at law-French—to the lawyer's pleading in Latin. She understands Latin but will not employ it here, fearing that 'this auditory' will not comprehend. The court is her theatre, and she must ingratiate with her audience, the jury. The lawyer goes in to argue in an English vexed by learned neologisms. Vittoria laughs at his coinages as vomit: he has swallowed an apothecary's bill

> And now the hard and undigestible words
> Come up, like stones we use give hawks for physic.
> Why, this is Welsh to Latin.

Her accuser takes her linguistic ignorance to be proof of her infirm moral nature: she

> Knows not her tropes, nor figures, nor is perfect
> In the academic derivation
> Of grammatical elocution.

As in the polyglot quarrels of Jonson, the point is the un-Shakespearean one of the mutual misunderstanding and suspicion of languages, since each person has his or her own idiolect—the lawyer the fustian rhetoric of morality, Vittoria the imagistic license of poetry which enables her (when she begins comparing herself, in extenuation, with things she does not resemble, like that crystalline river or the diamond mine) to make words mean whatever she pleases. As she says to Monticelso, 'whore' and 'murderess' are but names, words only, uncorrelated with deeds. Jonson's comic idiom is that of Webster's lawyer. There is a legalism to the humour, which speaks exclusively in a professional jargon. Subtle capitulating to Face concedes 'Your humour must be law.'

In their management of the action, Face and Subtle operate on an analogy with the disseverers of Sejanus. They rule by dividing. They distribute their clients throughout the house in a catacomb of separate prisons, each (like Dol's 'withdrawing chamber' or Dapper's privy) corresponding to the character's incarcerating mania. Placement is the defining, delimiting, tyrannically rigorous concern of Jonson's dramaturgy. Drugger consults Subtle in the hope that he will recommend a similar ordination of space for his new corner shop. 'Here's the plot on't', he says, plot meaning, as it does for Jonson's engineers, the diagram of the machine's workings. He wants Subtle to lay out the interior as if it were a stage set, each property anchored immovably:

> Which way I should make my door, by necromancy,
> And where my shelves. And which should be for boxes,
> And which for pots.

The longing of Jonsonian character is for the same enslaved assignment to place or function. Humour enforces such a determinism. Even language is as inescapable as an addiction, like nicotine. When Bobadil descants of the weed, Edward Knowell categorises him according to mania and *métier*: 'This speech would ha' done decently in a tobacco trader's mouth.' That classification is the denial of human individuality, for the character has consented to conscription by a type. Whereas Shakespearean comedy urges people to evolve beyond the straitjacket of the category and to assume (by their disguises) new, enriched selves, Jonson's persecutes such augmentation. To believe in your liberty of action or your independent identity is the most dangerous of mental errors. Tiberius in *Sejanus* speaks of 'my peculiar self': the self in Jonson is peculiar and peccant, a chimera of personal freedom. Volpone indulges it for a while—

> .... What should I do,
> But cocker up my genius, and live free
> To all delights my fortune calls me to?—

before he discovers it to be a mirage, since he, too, is conditioned, snared, constrained by the urgent automatism of his passions.

He admits his own unreality, as a nimble dissimulator, in the scene of his erotic persuasion to Celia, where he proposes that they should act in pornographic playlets based on Ovid's tales of the shape-changing gods. Like Face and Subtle who are forever in harried transit between one assumed persona and another, Volpone exists in metamorphosis: from god (as he imagines) to bull, actually from man to beast. Performance is to Jonson a sinister transmigration of souls. Celia's refusal censures the drama. She objects to the visored, mutable existence of Volpone as the starchy Lady does to the enchantments of Milton's Comus. Moral integrity reproves the disintegrative self of the player. But Celia's resignation is her weakness, for to be yourself is a vain struggle in Jonson. Kitely engages in it with weary defeatism, deciding he 'will once more strive, / . . . myself to be'. Face and Subtle, merely the quota of the impostures in their repertory, have resigned from the battle, even hinting, in their versatile role-playing, at their own nonentity; and they despoil others of the conviction that they, too, are individual and unrepeatable. Hence Face's sarcastic flattering of Dol, who will be ensconced in triumph at supper

> And not be styl'd Dol Common, but Dol Proper,
> Dol Singular: the longest cut, at night,
> Shall draw thee for his Dol Particular.

Dol is named after her commonness, and after the communal way in which she is used. Face pretends to redeem her from that indiscriminateness, conferring on her the perquisites of Tiberius's peculiar self: propriety (or self-possession) and singularity. But his tribute is a cheat, of course. She will continue to be awarded by lot to an overnight owner. She will not be particular in herself, but merely the particle and chattel of whoever wins her. The forfeiture of individuality leads inevitably to the loss of humanity. The sardonic victory of Jonson's plotting is to make men beasts. Dol addresses her colleagues as 'my good baboons', and Volpone calls the legacy-hunters

> . . . . vulture, kite,
> Raven, and gorcrow, all my birds of prey,
> That think me turning carcase.

The double plot in Jacobean drama is a schizophrenic disturbance, setting at odds two hostile identities within a play. It sends the madmen of *The Changeling*'s subplot to maraud through the tragic action, as it makes Lovewit call his house a Bedlam, occupied (as Face suggests) by escapees from St Katherine's 'where they use to keep / The better sort of mad-folks'. In Jonson the subplot harbours the bestial lower half of human being, by which we are all prompted and into which we are all liable to collapse. It exists throughout *The Alchemist* in the invective imagery of the characters; everyone in *Volpone* is shadowed by the animal, bird, or insect from which his name derives, and comedy prompts the transmigration of people into the rapacious creatures who lurk in wait to take them captive. This is the demonism of satire, its black art (which Face accuses Subtle of practising): the caricature is a homicidal spell, guaranteeing that people will turn into the ugly image we make of them or the jeering name we call them. Sir Politic, retiring beneath the tortoise-shell, keeps the low profile which befits the satirist's victim, discreetly retreating into his carapace and retiring from membership of the human race.

The revenge comedy of Jonson is a final repudiation of Shakespeare. Jonson's alchemist is a fraudulent Prospero, devising art-works which are trashy travesties, defiling a nature he claims to be perfecting; and his *Bartholemew Fair* (1614), which in its induction jeers at Shakespeare's 'tales, tempests, and such like drolleries', transfers the rustic revelry which is the native source of Shakespearean comedy to the city, and shows the rituals of magical and festive transformation enacted at midsummer in an enchanted wood or on Twelfth Night to be an institutionalised swindle. Instead of multiplying reality as play—the 'natural perspective, / That is, and is not' of Shakespearean drama—Bartholemew Fair purveys to a credulous public a spoiled substitute for reality: 'stale bread, rotten eggs, musty ginger, and dead honey' (the wares of Joan Trash) not the gormandising cakes, ale and ginger hot in the mouth celebrated by Sir Toby. When the drama resumes at the Restoration, it is Jonson rather than Shakespeare who serves as its prototype.

Wycherley's Horner is the successor to the revenge hero of both Jacobean tragedy and comedy. Tragedy likewise now conceives of itself as machination, like that of Jonson's alchemist or his technocratic masques: Bedamar in *Venice Preserv'd* calls the conspiracy 'the mighty engine' which 'must twist this rooted Empire from its basis.' Tragic fate is envisaged as an infernal machine, engineering torments. Pierre begs Jaffeir to spare him from the indignity of being drawn and quartered, and, pointing to the wheel on which the executioner is about to bind him, says, 'Seest thou that engine?' Beyond the seventeenth century, Jonson prefigures the later tradition of English satire. The anal-erotic bathing of his characters, and their imminent decomposition, announce Swift or Smollett, who is mocked by Sterne as Smelfungus; Jonson's disgusted identification of art with the befouling of paper, and the supercession of men by writing—Matthew 'carries a whole realm, a commonwealth of paper, in's hose!'—predicts Pope and *The Dunciad*.

The humours, more insanely and dictatorially introverted than ever, recur as the monsters of Dickens, who in 1845 played Bobadil in amateur theatricals, and Jonson himself returns in Edward Bond's *Bingo* in 1973. Bond's Jonson visits Shakespeare, retired in disgust and despair to Stratford (and catatonically cured by Bond of his generous loquacity: he spends much of the play in tight-lipped muteness), and taunts him during a drinking-bout, still wanting to know what *The Winter's Tale* was about. 'I hate you', he rages at the unresponding Shakespeare, 'because you smile.' The satirist at last has his revenge on the genial comedian.

— 14 —
Lyrical Nothings

Literary history, while appearing to do no more than relate how one thing happens after another, is actually a mode of polemic or even of myth-making. It is the province of the poets, who use it for their own poetic ends: it is their way of justifying themselves by revising their past or foreordaining their future. To do so, they make myths. Samuel Johnson's *Lives of the Poets* (1779–81) is one such, William Hazlitt's *Lectures on the English Poets* (1818) another, Matthew Arnold's *Essays in Criticism* (1865 and 1888) a third. All three works are genealogies for poetry, narratives of its genesis and its workings in the world.

Johnson's is humanistic: poetry must befriend man and assist him better to enjoy or endure the vicissitudes of his life. This is why its criticism is biographical. The lives of poets must themselves be exemplary and their work is of value insofar as it professes consolation. Thus Johnson reproves John Donne and the seventeenth-century metaphysical poets for not 'representing or moving the affections' and Dryden for being 'not often pathetick'. Humane cares so predominate that Johnson confesses to care less for Gray's poetry than for his life: his existence is his true bequest to us. Hazlitt's myth is religious. Poetry is his substitute for divine immanence. The first poets were the biblical prophets, when the divine breath infused them; the last are Wordsworth and Coleridge, not poets at all in Hazlitt's judgment because they are no longer animated from without by an inspiriting creative joy. All they can do is moodily retraverse their own dejected minds. The god has failed them. Hazlitt's lineage therefore also excludes Donne, whom he described as the author of 'some quaint riddles in verse, which the Sphinx could not unravel'. While Hazlitt describes the sanctified past of poetry—its descent to us from a god—Arnold describes its future, when it will make amends to us for the absence of any god from our firmament. That future will be immense, because poetry must now dispense an ennobling wisdom and engrave its perceptions on stone in a grand style. For Arnold, Milton is the apogee of English poetry, supplying to a culture with 'an inadequate sense for perfection of work' a model of classical 'refining and elevation'. That canonising of Milton requires in recompense the belittling of Donne. Arnold's brother Thomas repeated in 1862 the accusation that Donne is over-analytic and to that extent no poet, since he quibbles over matters which 'a poet of feeling could never stop to elaborate'.

Critical values are relativistic, and the very shape of literary provenance is constantly undergoing change, for history after all does not happen forwards but is written retroactively, as the present looks over its shoulder and imagines how the past must or should have been. If the retrospective aim is to see in English poetry an evolution towards classicality—as it was for Johnson and Arnold—then Donne is marginal. Johnson can deny that the metaphysicals are poets at all, because their art is non-mimetic, copying 'neither . . . nature nor life'. Donne is also exiled by a romantic history which, like Hazlitt's, emphasises the degeneration from an original creative joy. De Quincey calls Donne a rhetorician not a poet, and Leigh Hunt sees him as fanciful rather than imaginative because it was his habit 'to look at nothing as it really is, but only as to what may be thought of it'. Henry Hallam added in 1839 that Donne is scarcely even a versifier, with his 'lines too rugged to seem metre'.

All myths are rationalisations of the fall. In literary terms, Hazlitt dates that fall after Homer and the biblical poet-prophets: all their successors are creatively debilitated, bereft of contact with the god-like source. Johnson allows Dryden—who as he says, referring to Augustus's refurbishment of Rome, found English brick and left it marble—to begin a recuperation from that fall. The modernist theory of literary history advanced by T. S. Eliot in 1921 also begins from the dating of a fall. Eliot places it in the mid-seventeenth century and, believing it to have been a psychological event, calls it a dissociation of sensibility. Now Donne, heretofore minor and trivial, becomes crucial, indeed central, for he is in Eliot's view the last antediluvian poet. Thought and feeling interpenetrate in him; afterwards there are only poets who think unfeelingly (in the eighteenth century) or those who thoughtlessly feel (in the nineteenth). Eliot's rehabilitation of Donne serves as a manifesto for his own neo-metaphysical verse, and his partisanship misrepresents Donne as a symbolist before his time. When Eliot comments that the metaphysical poets were to their credit 'trying to find the verbal equivalent for states of mind and feeling', he is praising them for having solved the problem which perplexes Hamlet in his essay on the play: the definition of what Eliot there calls an 'objective correlative'. Hamlet is a failed symbolist, never able to translate his subjective apprehensions into the objectivity of language or action. Donne and his compeers in fantasticating their conceits were adumbrating the symbol, that linguistic cipher—a word which, unlocked, divulges a thought and in turn gives access to a feeling. The symbolist art is one of equivalence. The sensation of 'the odour of a rose', for instance, has in Eliot's thesis its corresponding intellectual perception, just as Mallarmé equated words with colours or scents or musical tones. Symbolism sponsors what Eliot calls 'a new unity', a correlation between the otherwise disjunct senses. This is what he means by saying in the 1920 poem 'Whispers of Immortality' that Donne is 'expert beyond experience', and finds in the senses the only means of knowledge.

The ingenuity of Eliot's argument is its anachronism. It makes a modern of Donne, contemporary with Prufrock, the monologuists in Virginia Woolf's

The Waves, or Leopold Bloom, all of whom have symbolist consciousnesses: minds, that is, inviolable by ideas (as Eliot magnificently said of Henry James), instruments used as sensuous receivers, and as transliterators into words of the impressions made upon the avid organs. This is why Eliot's praise of Donne sounds so like Virginia Woolf's 1919 manifesto on 'Modern Fiction'. Eliot, for instance, says that 'When a poet's mind is perfectly equipped for its work, it is constantly amalgamating disparate experience; the ordinary man's experience is chaotic, irregular, fragmentary.' Symbolism demands the amalgamation of those fragments: each of the six consciousnesses in *The Waves* complements the others and together they join into an Eliotic 'new unity', an androgynous group-mind experiencing the same things in six different, simultaneously possible ways; the plan of *Ulysses* also calls for the reunion of the three mutually supporting consciousnesses of Stephen, Bloom and Molly. Eliot's own Prufrock is less capable. He shares Hamlet's predicament as Eliot analysed it, and cannot arrive at the symbolic transcription of his inner disquiets. He lacks both the omnicompetence of the Donnean consciousness, and its voracity.

Eliot three times refers to the metaphysical poet as a greedy feeder on life. The ordinary man, he says, 'falls in love, or reads Spinoza, and these two experiences have nothing to do with each other, or with the noise of the typewriter or the smell of cooking; in the mind of the poet these experiences are always forming new wholes.' That olfactory hint is taken up when he adds that the metaphysical sensibility 'could devour any kind of experience', and is more viscerally stated when he requires poetry to look not only into the heart but 'into the cerebral cortex, the nervous system, and the digestive tracts'. The stress on the hunger of sensibility, on consciousness as an appetite, suggests less Donne than Bloom's connoisseurship of smells—the urine-scented kidneys he fries for breakfast, his own pleasant ordure in the privy—or the sacramental meal of boeuf-en-daube served by Mrs Ramsay in Virginia Woolf's *To the Lighthouse*, where the sharing of this food symbolises a truce between hostile intellects.

This is the mission, metaphysical in its way, of novelistic consciousness as Virginia Woolf defines it in her essay 'Modern Fiction'—'to convey this varying, this unknown and uncircumscribed spirit, whatever aberration or complexity it may display. . . .' In an essay on Donne which she included in her second *Common Reader* (1932), she makes the modernist claim of affinity with him, except that he is elected by her an honorary novelist. We resemble Donne, she says on her generation's behalf, 'in our readiness to admit contrasts, in our desire for openness, in that psychological intricacy which the novelists have taught us with their slow, subtle, and analytic prose'. The working of his imagination indeed suggests the bombardment of innumerable atoms which is Virginia Woolf's symbol for the impressionism of mental life in 'Modern Fiction': the mind of Donne is a burst rocket, scattering 'in a shower of minute, separate particles'. Though things explosively fall apart in Donne, Virginia Woolf still insists on the tense, unifying duty of consciousness, 'the energy and power of the whole', which reassembles these shattered atoms.

The problem with this account of Donne is its insistence on unification, for Donne's was a dissociative, dissecting mind. He is the fragmenter of English poetry. Eliot blames Johnson for not understanding that the metaphysical poets, after their analytic decomposition of experience, 'put the material back together again'. Yet this is exactly what they are unable to do. Donne inherits from Spenser a poetic system which does bring together all created things. *The Faerie Queene* is a family of man, and a growing tree of language. Everything in it naturally exfoliates into everything else. Spenser's holiest images are of juncture, the merging of opposites not their violent and enforced coupling (which Johnson criticised in Donne), as in the hermaphroditic embrace of Amoret and Scudamor. Donne's 'new philosophy' scientifically disproves this universal accord. His intellect works by studiously breaking things—people, occasions, objects—down into their component parts, which is the discipline of science.

Johnson points out this tendency to 'dispersion' and a consequent 'littleness', as against the 'aggregation' which begets 'sublimity', and notes 'it is with great propriety that subtlety, which in its original import means exility of particles, is taken in its metaphorical meaning for nicety of distinction.' Exility of particles might also describe the dramatic laboratory of Ben Jonson, where the self feels itself to be particular or peculiar, singled out by the science of the humours for analysis and curative extermination. Donne's subtlety is similarly fracturing. Whereas Spenserian love is the recognition of affinity and then identity between the self and the other, between soul and body or earth and heaven, the experience of love fascinates and perplexes Donne because it is the disjoining of all these partners, the sundering of the whole into its parts. As in the satire of Jonson or Marston, analysis is conducted with the scalpel: 'The Dampe' begins with an autopsy on Donne, using mental instead of surgical instruments—

> When I am dead, and Doctors know not why,
>   And my friends curiositie
> Will have me cut up to survay each part, . . .

Donne's dramatic situations are analytic divorces, like this anatomical sundering. He writes of the parting of lovers because it is a parturition of twinned existences into single entities, and a reminder of that break-up of wholeness which is the metaphysical trauma of his 'First Anniversary'; he writes of death because it is a larger severance, of soul from body. Death therefore invades the love poems, since love punningly mimes the demise it so frantically tries to stave off. In 'The Will' he prepares himself to breathe his last, in 'The Relique' he is exhumed, in 'The Apparition' he returns to haunt the living, in 'The Legacie' he dies serially, in a succession of small orgasmic expiries. The activity, as Donne says in 'The Extasie', is an unperplexing, an unmeshing of the complex (Johnson's aggregation, or Eliot's amalgam) into its particular and contradictory simplicities. Subtlety means an unknitting. Undoing the knot which makes us man, it explains to us what we are by experimentally demonstrating what we are not. The lovers in 'The Extasie' are unknotted by those subtracting nots: their emotion is 'not sexe', they see 'not what did move', and all they know is that 'they know not what'. That nothingness encroaches everywhere in Donne, and with it a terrifying nihilism.

He is the poet of the perilous Cartesian adventure: he thinks, as Descartes put it, therefore he is; he is responsible for his own being, rather than deriving it from some source outside himself (like Spenser, who gratefully cedes his existence to that source at the end of the 'Mutabilitie Cantos'). But if he ceases to think, will he cease to be? That is the fear of Cartesian man—of Marlowe's Faustus and Milton's Satan; of Robinson Crusoe on the desert island of his solipsism. It is ironic that Donne's most famous utterance is his denial in a sermon of man's insularity, because in his poetry man is islanded in the solitary confinement of identity. He may share that solitude, as Crusoe does, but the woman he admits to it must be a mute accessory, like Crusoe's Friday, to his will; and beyond their absolute monarchy is a region as meaningless and null as Satan's limbo or Crusoe's ocean. As 'The Sunne Rising' specifies, 'Nothing else is.' Because all else is void, it can be preyed upon. The ego must assertively colonise the nothingness. Donne, for whom a mistress's body is 'my America! . . . My Empire', lies between Tamburlaine and those later imperial minds, Satan and Crusoe, claiming inert matter as the mind's possession.

Eliot in 1931 proposed that Donne had 'enlarged the possibilities of lyric verse as no other English poet has done'. Again, the bequest is the legacy of a death or a fall, a postlapsarian curse. Donne's fragmentation singles out the lyric as the most valid poetic kind, because it alone is true to the temporariness of experience, as brief and dying as the falling star which cannot be caught in Donne's 'Song', and because it is the plaint or boast of the self in its isolation. Sonnets afford Sidney, Spenser and Shakespeare the relief of a conventional retreat from the vexatious self. Form is a camouflaging uniform. This assuagement of the personal is disallowed by Donne. Eliot praised him for having begun the separation of poetry from 'musical accompaniment'. Music, like convention, tempers and harmonises Elizabethan emotion. When Donne entitles a poem 'Song' he does so sardonically, because its bristling intellectuality makes it quite unsingable. He feels impelled to invent a new stanza for each poem, fearing otherwise the traduction of formality, and his process of formation is a punishment of his matter. Richard II has to hammer out the conceit with which he compares his prison to a world; Donne, too, acknowledges that the forming requires an application of force, a mental bludgeoning which—'like gold to ayery thinnesse beate'—brings his poem as close to nothingness as it can get without ceasing to exist. Hence his poetry's identification with a falling star. The lyric is the image of a short and guttering life, of consciousness's premature ejaculation and end. It begins with a rude abruptness and ends with an equally sudden violence. Its spasm is coital, but also meteoric. It is the angrily intense protest of light in a dying, darkening world. Despair and the postponement of death are its motives, but its febrility and its mental haste merely bring death nearer. Donne begins the association of the poem with expiry which concludes in romantic definitions of its dying into life—Byron called the imagination a lava flow, an excreted violence, and Shelley said the creating mind was a fading coal, shedding heat like Donne's shooting star—and in Edgar Allan Poe's demand that it possess a necessary because mortal abbreviation: Poe denied the very possibility of the long poem, since the poetic spasm is so tragically short-lived.

Donne's own long poems, the two anniversaries of 1611 and 1612 comprising his *Anatomie of the World*, predict this collapse of structure. In the lyrics, his activity is one of contraction, pressing things into the quintessences of which he speaks in 'A nocturnall upon S. Lucies day'—an intensifying and condensing retraction of life to its minimum. Here the mind works differently, by grandiose expansion and hyperbolic inflation. This offended Ben Jonson, who doubted the probity of making a cosmic catastrophe depend on the death of an insignificant girl. The methods of the *Anatomie* are additive and accumulative, like the adhesion of similitudes which constructs Spenser's poetic world, yet what it is describing is the opposite process: the shrinking of our life and time, the shortening of a span to a mere niggardly inch; a deathly fragmentation. Donne attributes to Elizabeth Drury the power of elucidation and coherence, both moral and structural, which are wielded by heroic arbiters like Chaucer's Knight or Spenser's Nature:

> She that should all parts to reunion bow,
> She that had all Magnetique force alone,
> To draw, and fasten sundred parts in one; . . .

The poem's calamity is its loss of this ordering centre. In compensation all Donne can do is to lavish vacuous compliments on the girl who has voided it.

Donne's sanctifying of Elizabeth, along with his unctuous idealising of patronesses like the Countess of Bedford (whom he addressed as 'God's masterpiece'), indicate the crisis of his imagery. He exists in fact halfway between the medieval type and the romantic symbol. Though his conceits fret to associate themselves with the security of the older system, they must accept the frail self-reliance of the modern image, discharging the burden of proof without benefit of clergy. He tries to make Elizabeth, in the old allegorical sense, a type or an emblem, as Spenser's women are. But whereas such identifications are natural and inevitable for Spenser and his forebears, in

Donne they can only be provisional and are liable to seem preposterous, since they derive from Donne's own casuistry, not from the inhering virtues of the subject: she might, he says, have been proved to be a type of the Ark; or perhaps it is a type of her. The allegory he rigs up to explain and elevate her is precarious. From the capsizing of that allegory, however, the symbol is made. The allegorical type expounds itself, like the emblematic pictogram; the symbol, disconnected from the grand system of allegorical relations, is mysterious and enigmatic in its singleness. Since it cannot say what it means, the poet must exert himself to do so. The evaporation of type into symbol occurs already in *The Faerie Queene*, when the Graces to whom Colin Clout is piping disappear. As an entwined emblem of the interchange between God and man, the Graces—at first pagan mysteries, later codified and rationalised by Christianity—are moral portents. But allegory nears its own end in Spenser, and its ministers are in flight from the intruder Calidore. To Colin Clout, the Graces are allegories, whose meaning he knows; to Calidore they can only be symbols of he is not quite sure what, as tormentingly vague and as conceptually unreliable as Keats's fugitive nightingale or Shelley's invisible skylark. The romantic symbol does reattain some of the old allegorical immanence. Wordsworth sees the daffodils first as a crowd, then as a host. When a crowd, they are a random incident in perception; redefined as a host, they have become first a symbol and then an allegorical company, a heavenly host of gilded angels, intercessors (like the objects of medieval typology) between divine meaning and human understanding, able to uplift him in his pensive misery. Wordsworth sees them three times in the poem: as fact, as allegory, and then again—when he re-envisions them 'upon that inward eye / Which is the bliss of solitude'—as an arcanely private and remembered or intuited symbol. That romantic liberty to manufacture symbols is not yet available to Donne. He retains the medieval and Spenserian conviction that meaning is implanted by God; yet God has withdrawn from responsibility for his kingdom of meaning, and permitted its 'disformity of parts'. Unaided, human intelligence must now inductively try to imagine meanings for objects.

The conceit, outlandish and improbable, is the quest for a lost significance; as well, it is the trial of a new utility, like that which Donne envisages for his stiff twin compasses. Toppled, the great chain of being has deposited a rubble of found objects and archeological relics. Donne tries to piece them together. He intends to conduct the enquiry scientifically, but the conditions of his existence militate against the patient effort:

> Alas, we scarce live long enough to try
> Whether a true made clocke run right, or lie.

The untrustworthy clock stands for the conceit itself, and for the poem—a zany engine speeding up time. Donne's chronometry is always alarmed. His own biological clock, by being overwound, will the sooner run down: each orgasm, he calculates in 'Farewell to love', lops a day off his life-expectancy. So the machine he has devised to measure time and regulate it likewise turns against him as a *memento mori*. He hands down that clock to a successor in the line of anxiously witty metaphysical speculation: Sterne begins *Tristram Shandy* with Mrs Shandy's interruption of her husband who is busy with the procreation of Tristram to ask, 'Have you not forgot to wind up the clock?' The Shandyean time-teller, like Donne's, signifies the distractedness and futility of image and imagination.

For George Herbert, Donne's contemporary, it is not yet so. Things still cohere, and no argumentative violence is required to manacle them together. The conceit for Herbert is an impiety, the usurpation of that exegetic right which belongs properly to scripture. His sonnet 'Prayer' lists a witty barrage of definitions of its subject, many referring to the contractions and reversals and mechanistic contrivances of Donne's mental engineering—'Engine against th' Almightie' or 'The six-daies world transposing in an houre'—only to dismiss them in its final phrase, 'something understood'. Being understood, prayer needs no definition. Donne's printer, prefacing the *Songs and Sonnets* with an address 'To the Understanders', warns that the reader will need to act as interpreter, engaged in the same piecemeal assembly of meaning which occupied Donne, re-attaching each 'scattered limbe of this Author' to the sundered body. Since there has been no such dismembering in Herbert, no interpretative re-composure is called for. Understanding can be taken for granted. The sense of contraction, terrifying to Donne and plangently sad to Andrew Marvell (whose microcosm is a drop of dew, containing a world for a moment only), is to Herbert a humbling and comforting security, protecting his own littleness: man 'is in little all the sphere' and, in making him, God has taken 'the worlds riches which dispersed lie' and made them 'contract into a span'. Already in Donne the poem is an aggravation of the mind, the venting of an agitated wit. For Herbert it remains a made thing, handiwork or craft, just as man is the work of God's hands. In his architectural scheme for it, *The Temple* (1633) is a temple, a manual labour of love, disposed in accordance with the church's ground-plan so that we enter at the porch and then confront, ahead of us, the altar; his own constructive skill is a devout mimicry of God's making, hieroglyphically shaping poems into cut-outs of the altar or redemptive Easter wings or the entablature of the squarely paved church floor, because, in literature as in nature as medievally read, meaning—being God's signature—is self-evident and worn on the outside. The world is a habitation built by God so he can dwell in it; poems are the home-made furniture that Herbert offers to that house. His own highest ambition is to be a utensil in this store. A meek domestic utilitarianism makes him wish he were a tree, so 'some bird would trust / Her household to me', or to lament when downcast that 'a blunted knife / Was of more use than I.'

Instead of Donne's implosive microcosms, Herbert has miniatures, small replicas inside the earthly household of the many-mansioned divine plenum: the trinity and incarnation are 'two rare cabinets full of treasure', grace and damnation are dispersed from vials or boxes like cordial or corrosive, nativity is our emergence from an enwombing 'chest of sweets', our guilt is the secretive closeting of our heart, and furious thoughts are a case of sharp, abrasive knives—always the imagery is of domestic reticulation, of things enclosed and encased or bottled up, of meaning indwelling or in storage. Herbert is the housekeeper or, as he puts it in 'Grace', the husbandman who must attend to the care and increase of the wealth entrusted to him. He disdains the mechanical saving of labour, attesting that the altar he rears has been carved from his own obdurate heart and cemented with his tears, 'no workmans tool' having touched it. His obsequious gift is for economy, the rationing of supplies and the stinting of self. Whereas Donne consumes or condemns himself, surgically anatomising the body, Herbert subjects that body to an improving denial: the hieroglyphic outlines of the poems are such attenuations, as rigorously uplifting as a fast. The thin central stem of 'The Altar' is the hard heart, chiselled away by God's power; the triangles of 'Easter-Wings' are the body reduced in training to take on the aerodynamism of spirit.

Fracturing and fragmentation, in Donne the encroachments of nothingness, are in Herbert necessary self-abnegations. The lines of the second 'H. Baptisme' poem are unevenly broken because the aperture admitting man to grace is also 'a narrow way and little gate'. The poem's smallness bespeaks its modesty not, as in Donne, its annihilation. Correspondingly Herbert pleads for a physical diminution, for an arrest in infancy—

> O let me still
> Write thee great God, and me a childe:
> Let me be soft and supple to thy will,
> Small to my self

—or, like Marvell disburdening himself of identity in his gardens, in the puerile innocuousness of pastoral. Herbert wants to be a tree because trees are relieved of noxious mental life, existing only to 'be just', their minimal justness a sober justice; Marvell in 'Upon Appleton House' sees himself as an inverted tree because, turned upside down, his thoughts could take root and lose themselves in earth. The hope in both is for respite from the anxiety of having to be themselves. Herbert wants to inhabit another, to be secured in one of his own aedicular shelters, as when he asks permission to 'roost and nestle' in the roof under which God will hide his soul; Marvell seeks a different safety—the evasiveness of non-being and of non-commitment, an escape from the accusing pressures of the dialectic. The stepped structure of the poem, which in Herbert's baptism piece serves chasteningly to scale down and childishly belittle the poet, becomes in Marvell's 'Horatian Ode' the tactic of a politic evasion, a preserving of self from the incrimination of statement. The octosyllabic line is Marvell's preferred measure because it enables him to get away with saying so little.

Donne, too, sees himself and the poem as 'a little world made cunningly'. Yet while Herbert and Marvell are reassured by that littleness, Donne takes it to pieces. The analytic mind delights in controlled destruction or disintegration. The elements he refers to in the fifth Holy Sonnet are his physical carcase and his 'Angelicke spright'. Those components are at mortal war in him, and at odds structurally in the poem: Donne exacerbates the self-division of the sonnet, making octave and sestet schizophrenically clash. The fifth Holy Sonnet dismembers its structure as it remorsefully draws and quarters Donne. He consigns his sinful parts to their various perditions of water and zealous fire. At the same time he is undoing the sonnet: the octave is about the self's hydroptic swelling to extend into new lands and spheres, the sestet about its vengeful dessication. The structural virtue of the sonnet is the cleanliness of the incision it makes between soul and body. In the sixth poem of the sequence, the octave considers the body's profane earthly incarnation; the sestet consigns it to burial and frees the spirit for flight. The poems exploit the sonnet's lacerating courage of self-contradiction. Since they are about man as a walking paradox, made of both mire and grace, they couple two incompatible and separable poems in a single unit, and the argumentative pivot or turn in the ninth line is always a point of unhinging, which reveals how the deathly, salutary dis- or (as Donne calls it) un-jointing might mercifully be achieved. The seventh makes a portentous noise in its octave to orchestrate the last judgement, and then, having summoned to resurrection these 'numberlesse infinities', decides in the sestet on their quietening and its own more studious quietism: 'But let them sleepe, Lord, and mee mourne a space.'

A technique like this disproves Eliot's account of Donne: his genius is precisely for dissociation. The forensic surgery he performs on poems and his own mental state coincides with the activity of Renaissance science, which is obsessed with analysis as the decomposing or unmaking of bodies. Robert Burton's *Anatomy of Melancholy* (1621) quadruply partitions the organism into its quarrelsome and incompatible humours; Thomas Browne's *Hydriotaphia* (1658), a meditation on urn-burial, ponders the destructive crumbling to dusty essences of that body, and rephrases Hamlet's nauseated wonder in the graveyard as a scientific demonstration: 'How the bulk of a man should sink into so few pounds of bones and ashes, may seem strange unto any who considers not its constitution, and how slender a mass will remain upon an open and urging fire of the carnal composition.' Burton's study of the ossuaries in Norfolk convinced him that man is a fraction, his span amounting to 'not one little finger'. Analysis, encouraging Johnson's subtle exility of particles, encourages this breakdown, and Burton actually uses the word Johnson associated with the metaphysicals, describing our expectation of life as 'the remaining particle of futurity' or commenting that some of the ancients—

oppressed by 'the uncomfortable night of nothing', that exterminating void which everywhere encroaches in Donne—'were content to recede into the common being, and made one particle of the soul of public things'. We can know things only by reducing them to their particular atoms, like Blaise Pascal who saw the human world as no more than 'the abbreviation of an atom'.

There is a small analytic murder even in the literary idea of expression. Donne says alchemically in the 'Nocturnall' that love

> . . . did expresse
> A quintessence even from nothingnesse,
> From dull privations, and leane emptinesse.

To express is to exert a constricting pressure upon something, or to force the venting of its innards. It is a curative technique for Bacon, whose natural history in *Sylva Sylvarum* (1626) experiments with the expulsion of pestilence by vomiting or coughing and interprets love-making as a deathly expenditure of spirits, or for Burton, who calls spirit 'a most subtle vapour, . . . expressed from the *blood*'. Love has equated Donne with that feared nothing, and acquainted him with his own nearing demise. The exiguousness of the process is conveyed by the pressing-out of lyricism from suffixes, those negating appendices to words which are the only rhymes Donne will here allow. Like absence and darkness, which concur in a morbid assonance of suffixes at the end of this stanza, these syllables—not words in themselves but particles of them—are verbal zeroes, 'things which are not'. The making of poetry resembles those emetic expressings Bacon prescribes: it is a voiding of self (rather than Marvell's sly avoidance). Donne's argumentative conclusion in the 'Nocturnall' is his decision that 'I am None.' Having expressed himself in love and verse, he has only nothing left. Rochester in 'An Epistolary Essay' discards his poems as an evacuation, the 'Excrements of my dull Brain'.

The poetry endeavours to get as close as it can to that annihilation without risking its own extinction. Hence Donne's reliance on the monosyllable: verbally it is his equivalent to Browne's fraction, or those 'minute accumulations' which make 'petty sums' out of the days of our lives; the particle or integer which, despite its littleness, must be for harried humans a totality. Browne was terrified by the letter θ, the talisman which put an end to language by standing as the initial of thanatos, the Greek word for death. Its threat is of closure, and with it the numbing and muting of life: it is a circle which has swallowed a straight line. Browne perceives that 'circles and right lines limit and close all bodies, and the mortal right-lined-circle must conclude and shut up all.' Donne's extinguishing zero, paraphrased in superstitious circumlocution by the -nesses of the 'Nocturnall', stands in for Browne's character of death.

θ may also be translated in Donne's verse by the fatal monosyllable of exclamation, the O or oh which is language's and life's surrender of breath, conserved within parentheses by Donne because it betokens the ejaculation of spirit:

> Send home my long strayd eyes to me,
> Which (Oh) too long have dwelt on thee,

he demands in a love poem, and in a religious context, too, the syllable also warns of severance, the poisoned body's sundering from soul:

> . . . black sinne hath betraid to endlesse night
> My worlds both parts, and (oh) both parts must die.

Against this expiring of words into the exhaled breath of the death-rattle, he fortifies other monosyllables. His lyrics depend on the stabilising repetition of two of these, I and all—two words whose orthographic minimum is an epistemological maximum. Donne labours to prove that the I is an all, or the room—the closeted or chambered particularity in which Herbert snugly reposes—an everywhere; if he cannot manage the proof, then the I and the all must both be noughts. The poems which have for so long been mistaken for epistles of love are actually about this dilation or distension of the fractional I, to commandeer first a woman and then the world: they have no interest in the mutuality or requital of love, the partnering or mating which links Shakespeare to his truant master-mistress or Herbert to God; great and astonishing as they are, they do not seem to qualify as love poems at all—though they are perhaps a definitive account of sex and our angry, vital drive to perpetuate ourselves.

Their rhetoric protests against the resignation of the *Hydriotaphia*, and its reminder that our names are forfeit to time. 'The Sunne Rising', for instance, is a poem of the new Galilean philosophy, imperiously reorganising the dislocated universe to make Donne, not the unseated earth, its orienting midpoint. The poem masters those astronomical spaces which terrified Pascal (and which are the turbulent limbo of Milton's airborne Satan) by projecting into them that monopolistic I. Its power is its literal egocentricity. And yet the act of absorption it performs is, by its own admission, an annihilating one:

> She'is all States, and all Princes, I,
> Nothing else is.

The punctuation both aids Donne's microcosmic compressing (in that apostrophe which squeezes she and is together) and resists it, aware of its tendency towards an utter elimination of differences and of otherness. The line needs its interrupting commas to stave off the merger those alls demand. As in the 'Elegie on the Lady Marckham', commas ensure the segregation of objects, elements and beings which frustrates Donne and at the same time—since his aim is to make islanded man a continent—reassure him of his own immitigable singleness: he is arguing that death is a consuming ocean,

> ...and though as yet
> God hath set markes, and bounds, twixt us and it,
> Yet it doth rore, and gnaw, and still pretend,
> And breaks our bankes, when ere it takes a friend.

Here, too, as in the lines quoted from 'The Sunne Rising', the combat is between those cosmological monosyllables I and all, and only the punctuation can guard against their cancellation of each other. In 'The Sunne Rising' I equates itself with all, at the cost of sentencing everything which is not I to death; the elegy tragically concedes that I is eroding earth, all an inundating and submerging ocean. Promiscuity is the aggrandising policy of the ego, with commas crediting each new augmentation to that self's account: as 'The Indifferent' boasts,

> I can love her, and her, and you and you,
> I can love any, so she be not true.

The proviso of that final phrase serves, however, to reinvoke nothingness, and to define it as the poem's real state of indifference (or, as in the poem on Lady Marckham, of undifferentiation).

In this poem the self extends its reign by a casual, electioneering sexuality; in 'The triple Foole' it manages, unassisted, a trinitarian self-reproduction. Then in 'Lovers infinitenesse' the crucial monosyllables, like cardinal numbers, are made to face their indissolubility and apartness: 'Deare, I shall never have Thee All.' They are kept apart by that intruding 'Thee'. Love delights in the existence of another; but for Donne the being of a creature outside himself is an intolerable affront. The more concentrated and impacted his poetry becomes, the more it seems to dispense with any words except its primal monosyllables, from which it derives a nervous, crabbed, exigent lyricism. 'The Anniversarie' begins with a trumpeting sequence of alls, which raise Donne's I to the pomp and solemnity of a royal plural; 'Communitie' repeats the word as if that were a power of geometrical multiplication—'Onely this rests, All, all may use.' Still, 'A Valediction: of weeping' cannot prevent the catastrophe of the word's abutment on its opposite, when cartographers 'make that, which was nothing, *All*' and his lachrymose mistress undoes their work by making an all—her global tear—into a dissolving nothing once more. A similar fate overtakes the proud first person singular, so anxious about the punctuated preservation of its imperative territory that Donne has to delimit for the woman 'my selfe, (that is you, not I,)'.

Some poems allow the I an ocular superintendence, as when 'A valediction: of my name, in the window' punningly identifies it with the eye, but in others an insidious rhyme betrays Donne's assertive naming of himself: I lends its vowels to the verbs of mortal capitulation, sigh and die. Thus 'The Will' begins 'I sigh my last gaspe', and elsewhere the pronoun rhymes with its own nullification—'When I dyed last, and, Deare, I dye' or 'Since I die daily, daily mourne.' This execution of the pronoun leads, in one of Donne's final poems, to the abandonment of the noun for which it stands. The 'Hymne to God the Father' welcomes the poet's death in a pun, beseeching redemption from God and advising him that

> . . . having done that, Thou hast done,
> I feare no more.

Donne the self-promoting, self-immortalising noun is content to retract into a verb, and a verb signifying the dead past.

Donne is the first poet to use the lyric as a protest against the harassment of time, and to associate its shortness with that of life. The baroque poet Andreas Gryphius called man a fantasy of time. Donne's poems are goaded to a desperate speed and urgency by time's impatience. The constancy of woman persists but 'one whole day'; a mortal existence does not last much longer. Spenser called his *Epithalamion* an endless monument of short time since, seen eternally, it had understood the insignificance of duration. Donne's poems lack that confidence: to endless, perpetually ending time, they stand as short and impermanent monuments. They share the dying frenzy of sexual pleasure, or of those astral remonstrances which to Burton were the signs of our world's infirmity—the meteors of 'A Feaver'. Their cerebral flashiness is proof of their self-spending combustibility. Thought and life are both brief agues or 'burning fits'.

This metaphysical alarm drives Donne and his successors into a frenetic sexuality, for in the absence of steadying religious certainty the living body is our only protection against the nothing which soon will claim us. The compasses symbolise the erogenizing of intellect, and the wit's pride in its glad being: instruments of mensuration and knowledge, they are also erectile. In Donne's nineteenth elegy, 'Going to Bed', sex supplants religion as an exponent of truth. Instead of incarnation—the spirit's dressing of itself in a body—it is about desecration. It defies God in an excited unhallowing, divesting the woman rather than investing her with sacramental raiments. As an angel from 'Mahomets Paradise' she is robed in white to perform her sacreligious office. 'Full nakedness' is a mystic revelation. Even here, though, the dialectic switches from sex to its counterpart death, for undressing is parodied by the dispensability of flesh itself:

> As souls unbodied, bodies uncloth'd must be,
> To taste whole joyes.

The poem's exhilaration is checked by the awareness that in speeding life up it has brought death closer.

From Donne emerges a tradition which explores the delighted and desolating mortality of the poem—a tradition almost of pornographic panic, extending through Marvell to the life and writing of Rochester. Its first instalment is Marvell's 'To His Coy Mistress'. Already there has been a loss of Donne's rhetorical coerciveness. In contrast with the planetary rearrangement of 'The Sunne Rising', Marvell 'cannot make our Sun / Stand still'; instead he competitively out-races it. Though Marvell's poem has Donne's habits of dilation into the macrocosm and contraction to the microcosm, they are in him the reflexes of an ironic mental futility. The ironist's intelligence contemplates itself both from inside and outside. Marvell therefore imagines an existence unmolested by time, and in contrast a life terrorised by it. He dilates into the one condition, then protectively contracts into the other. The timeless régime—inconceivable to the lyric, which like Gryphius's man is a fugitive in time—has the longueurs and the safe, slothful, vegetative insentience of pastoral. This is why Marvell allies love there with the affections of the plants. His own love wants to be vegetable-like because this ruminative uneventfulness would free him from the frenzy of a human and mental life. Pastoral means renunciation of the unquiet Donnean ego. Despite its subjunctive absurdity, there is a mystic hope in Marvell's first stanza. His prolongations imagine a reprieve from the spending, dying body: his ritualised protractions suggest the American cultists at Oneida in the nineteenth century, whose method of *coitus reservatus* is extolled by Aldous Huxley in his novel *Island* (1962) as an 'organised attempt to regain . . . paradise'. All Marvell's poems are footnotes to Milton's accounts of paradise lost and regained; for Huxley, paradise might be retrieved by sexual self-denial. Huxley's Ranga specifies that the Eden in question is the state of infancy, when sexuality has not headquartered itself in the genitals but is 'diffused through the whole organism'. The Oneida Yogis reattain that diffusion by holding off the deathly climax of love. For Marvell, too, this is a desired and impossible bliss: the pastoral becalming of that over-eager exerter and achiever, the lusting I; an abatement of Donne's panic.

But the second stanza irresistibly starts up again the movement which the first had stalled. Time resumes, and with it fleshly decay. From those opposed propositions, the third stanza contrives a synthesis. Making love, the characters will devour time rather than suffer its stealthy depredations. Coitus for them will be a suicide pact. Rolling up their strength and sweetness into a volatile ball which rends the iron gates of life, they have composed between themselves one of Burton's comets or a Donnean falling star. The imagery is of the heat-loss which is the star's trajectory of death: the evaporation of the bloom of youth like morning dew, the soul's transpiring 'At every pore with instant Fires.' This instantaneousness is the quick expiry of the lyric, too. Marvell's poem is a crescendo from the inertia of the epochal paradise through the winged haste of the chariot to the self-destructive velocity of the conclusion.

After Marvell, the lyric poem is increasingly haunted by its own impermanence. In the work of Rochester it has been diminished, like existence, to 'this live-long Minute'. Sexual conquest in Rochester's songs lasts for a 'lucky Minute' or 'the happy Minute'; the lyric is equally spasmodic. Rochester's career as a debauchee and his premature, burned-out death are experiments in the short-fused sensual ignition which is Donne's definition of life and poetry. His was a tragedy of combustibility. Bishop Gilbert Burnet considered that 'the natural heat of his fancy' was so 'inflamed by wine' that he was never 'cool enough to be perfectly master of himself', and George Etherege's verdict on him in his play *The Man of Mode* in 1676 is also morosely thermodynamic. As the play begins, the libertine Dorimant—Etherege's study of Rochester—complains of having to perjure himself by writing stale love letters 'in cold blood, after the heat of the business is over!' The writing is a debility of passion, a fatal cooling-off. Dorimant says that it is always in letters that we first expose the extinction of our feelings. When Mrs Loveit rends her fan in her fury at Dorimant he warns her to 'spare your fan, Madam, you are growing hot, and will want it to cool you.' His speciality is the chilling refrigeration of others—'when love grows diseas'd, the best thing we can do is to put it to a violent death; I cannot endure the torture of a lingering and consumptive passion', he says, in paraphrase of Marvell's casuist commending a violent remedy to the coy mistress and disdaining the 'slow-chapt' languid decadence of time—while he remains himself alive, alert and therefore on heat.

The carnal needs of a young woman with an elderly lover in one of Rochester's poems are an inflaming defence against the incursion of an ice age and its numbing death:

> Thy Nobler Parts, which but to name,
> In our Sex wou'd be counted shame,
> By Ages frozen grasp possest,
> From their Ice shall be releast:
> And, sooth'd by my reviving Hand,
> In former Warmth and Vigor stand.

Donne's compasses, bristling like thought, are automatically erectile; Rochester's 'ancient person' needs to be chafed and coddled into revivification. But even so the engendering warmth cannot be sustained. Though Marvell hints at a technique for indefinite postponement, practising a continent self-control as he devotes two centuries to each breast and 'thirty thousand to the rest', Rochester's difficulty is the prematureness of ejaculation, the arrival too soon at an obliterating end. His poem 'The Imperfect Enjoyment' is about this embarrassment, and about the mishap of poetry itself in its transitory effort to convince us, as Rochester says in 'The Mistress', that we are alive and not dreaming, sleeping or already extinct. Sex is again a rush to burning judgement: Rochester is 'inspired with eager fire, / Melting through kindness, flaming in desire'; the woman's tongue is 'Love's lesser lightning', his penis an 'all-dissolving thunderbolt'. But his fulmination happens too early, and after it there is only the abject unfeeling death of impotence:

> Ev'n her fair hand, which might bid heat return
> To frozen age, and make cold hermits burn,
> Applied to my dead cinder, warms no more
> Than fire to ashes could past flames restore.

He has been claimed by that nullity or nonentity which forever menaces Donne. Nothing is a recurrent subject in poetry after Donne, because it is the ultimate challenge to an exacerbated wit, thinking in order to assure itself that it is alive. To make something from nothing ought to imitate the uttering of the world in Genesis; however, art is apt, for these poets, to seem an anti-creation, more a conjuring trick than a miracle. Richard Crashaw in *Steps to the Temple* (1646) reflects on Christ's taciturnity when accused, and interprets it as the negation of that initial replenishment of the world:

> O Mighty *Nothing*! unto thee,
> *Nothing*, wee owe all things that bee.
> God spake once when he all things made,
> He sav'd all when hee *Nothing* said.
> The world was made of *Nothing* then;
> 'Tis made by *Nothing* now again.

Christ's silence is a strength of spirit, like his refusal to reply to Satan's blandishments in *Paradise Regain'd* or engage in debate with him. Crashaw condemns himself by praising Christ's quietude with such witty glibness. Yet what does he succeed in saying? Only the word nothing—which Christ refrained from enunciating—five times over. In his translation of a Senecan chorus, the void or zero which is the neutering of desire in his sexual poems teaches Rochester a stoic composure:

> After Death nothing is, and nothing Death;
> The utmost limits of a gasp of Breath.

That exhalation, no longer sexual, is the tragic hero's rendering up of a spirit on which he knows he has no purchase.

Rochester wrote the definitive poem on the non-subject, and in it celebrated the expunging of an entire tradition of fraught ratiocination. His 'Upon Nothing' has the grace to be nothing in itself. It deals in phrases which oxymoronically attach minus signs to themselves, as in its catalogue of non-existent qualities—'*Hibernian* Learning, *Scotch* Civility' and so on—or in lists of synonyms which are alike only in their common meaninglessness, as in the vain effort of wise men to 'Enquire, define, distinguish, teach, devise.' Language itself becomes a system for cancellation, since all propositions have their parallel denials. Hamlet's question, '*Is*, or *is not*' as Rochester puts it, is merely one such handy-dandy.

The poem dismisses the theology of *Paradise Lost* as contemptuously as Marvell, in his paradisial lyrics, yearningly validates it. It serves as a prologue to Milton's poem, asserting the prior right of its own vacuity: Nothing had 'a Being e're the World was made'. Rochester's offence against Milton is to find a security in nihilism equivalent to that which Milton demonstrates in divine providence, for once we see that nothing matters we are relieved of our fears, 'least unsafe and best', and reprieved from the apocalypse which must terminate Miltonic time. Nothingness is Rochester's world without end, a blank eternity lacking the premature climaxes and postcoital anticlimaxes which beleaguer him elsewhere. It is 'of ending not afraid'; Rochester hymnally praises it because he will 'in thee never end'. As well as belying Milton, it mocks the notion of artistic creation in its reversal of birth: matter, dematerialising, seeks refuge in a return 'to thy hungry Womb'. That intromission is satire's malevolent replica of the way God made the world, and Rochester's poem, after *Paradise Lost*, is his prosecution of Satan's scheme for the ruining of the created earth. It looks back to the annihilations of metaphysical wit and forward to a collective uncreation in the next century, when in *The Dunciad* Pope's Dullness also derides Milton's illumining God and 'Light dies before Thy uncreating word.' Eliot perhaps was right after all to sense an antipathy between Donne (with all his heirs) and Milton. The heroes of metaphysical verse are inductive devils, keen to know what has been prohibited and to assay—like Belial with his intellectual being, or Rochester's 'Fantastick Mind' restless to 'prove / The Torments it deserves to try'—the pain which will unmake them.

15

Milton,
'Author and end of all things'

Milton is the greatest English poet, and the one who is most sceptical about poetry itself. In him a literature which had impenitently freed itself from intimidation by scripture is held to account by a poetry as synoptic and as prohibitive as scripture had ever been. Milton's work is an argued refutation of everything which precedes it, as if intending to terminate the history of its art; when that art continues despite him, its practitioners can do no more than add humbled appendices to his foregone conclusions. Milton's persistent concern is a mistrust of literary imagination, which—in the revelatory stunts of Mak or the conjuring of Faustus, in Sidney's man-made heaven of artifice or Spenser's myths of biological ferment—had begun to rival the creative agency of God. Adam in *Paradise Lost*, disabusing Eve of her dream, categorises fancy and imagination as delusive faculties, properly subordinate to reason. Coleridge called imagination <u>coadunative</u>, uniting opposites: for Adam its nocturnal treachery is its 'misjoyning shapes'. Is it not, Milton asks, a tempter to recusancy and error, beguiling us with images which are caricatures of an invisible truth? Does it not impiously cater to human vainglory? Incapable of knowing or representing God, it must be a legacy of that virtuoso arguer and actor, that genius of epic bravado and dramatic crisis, Milton's Satan. *Paradise Lost* with its angelic condescension—for Raphael is reluctant, in his narrative, to compromise spirits by explaining them 'to human sense' or translating them into 'the Dialect of men'—can be reclaimed for literature only by desecration: the romantics will disestablish it as scripture, and acclaim it as a great poem, by assigning its authorship to the devil.

Each of Milton's works is an iconoclasm, shattering the models which have given it form, rebutting its own history. *Paradise Lost* begins by condemning art as idolatry, when the devils transformatively erect and adorn 'the Image of a Brute' in defamation of 'God thir Creator'; as it ends, Michael warns Adam that 'his Makers Image' has been confiscated, so that metaphor can henceforth only sketch deformity. Images are false gods: Eve's infatuation with her reflection; Satan's coupling with himself in the guise of Sin, who tells him, 'Thy self in me thy perfect image viewing / Becam'st enamour'd.' Milton's hymn 'On the Morning of Christs Nativity' in 1629 casts out the heathen pretenders to divinity who, in Spenser, entered into so convenient an alliance with Christianity and served as mythopoeia's sponsors. It is a poem of deicide, silencing oracles and demolishing temples, which doubts the probity even of its own poetic effusion: in contrast with Spenser's rivery fluency, requesting the sweet Thames to run softly till he ends his song, Milton's hymn tersely breaks off—'Time is our tedious Song should here have ending.' That sudden abstention is Milton's recurrent method for quitting his poems: the swain's departure for 'fresh Woods and Pastures new' in 'Lycidas' (1638), Christ's discreet evasion of the festivities in *Paradise Regain'd* (1671). In orchestrating the mourning for Lycidas, Milton's poem laments the tradition of pastoral elegy, again in a deathly revision of Spenser. Amarantus, whose metamorphosis Spenser recalls in the Garden of Adonis, renewing it with his circling repetition of phrases, is here required to despoil himself of that floral identity. Milton bids '*Amarantus* all his beauty shed'. The poem, like the growing landscape, is mere embroidery. The true eloquence is 'unexpressive', as Milton says of the heavenly song heard by the dead Lycidas—inexpressible, expressive of nothing, inaudible, just as Christ in *Paradise Lost* can be a redeemed and upraised metaphor, 'Divine Similitude', only so long as he is saved from visibility by being left undescribed. Milton's own initiative in 'Lycidas' is the defoliation of pastoral, plucking the berries and tearing the leaves 'before the mellowing year'.

Comus in 1634 is equally suspicious of the masque, and of drama. The evil spirit of both is Comus himself, a masquer because of his proficiency at moral feigning, a dramatic character because of his restless, revelling, infernal energy. Against him, the Lady declines to engage in the masque's dissemblings or in the drama's fretful, wasteful activism. Hers is the saintly restraint of passivity and silence. *Samson Agonistes* in 1671 is also forewarned against its own form. Drama's imperative is, as Samson says, to 'exasperate, exulcerate'; beyond its agony, he seeks purgation and peace—'calm of mind all passion spent'. Classically regular but proudly unperformable, Milton's tragedy reproves the native, Shakespearean theatre. He deplores the double plot as adulteration, or bedevilment: he attacks 'the Poets error of intermixing Comic stuff with Tragic sadness and gravity; . . . brought in without discretion, corruptly to gratifie the people.' While Samson declines dramatic engagement, Dalila is Milton's commentary on the specious allure of theatrical persona. 'Bedeckt, ornate, and gay' like a sailing ship 'with all her bravery on, and tackle trim', she exists midway between Cleopatra on her barge and Millamant flouncing into the park in Congreve's *The Way of the World*, her arrival announced by a parodic recollection of Dalila.

Nor can *Paradise Lost*, once written, remain unqualified. *Paradise Regain'd* is less an epilogue to than a withdrawal from it, fearing that after all *Paradise Lost* might be taken for the epic it meant to criticise. The second poem reduces, recapitulates and superlatively abstracts the first. Christ is no epic antagonist. His meek patience precludes even his reacting to Satan's blandishments. Yet he wins a victory 'not of arms' but 'above heroic'. In contrast with Donne's annihilating negations, the poem cancels earthly terms in order to effect their translation into heavenly ones:

> Think not but that I know these things, or think
> I know them not,

Christ warns Satan, and adds that the wisest Greek sage was the one who professed 'To know this only, that he nothing knew.' Reclusive and inactive, Christ is the negative or antithesis of a hero, and Milton refuses to permit his travails to qualify as history or story. Satan is the inventive anecdotalist, quoting instances 'as story tells'. Milton concentrates on a truth unprofaned by material or literal embodiment. Andrew and Simon are, he points out, 'in Holy Writ not nam'd'. Christ refuses to interpret his reign according to the narrow-minded quota of narrative time, which insists on the beginnings and ends of stories. When Satan urges him to demand succession, he retorts

> If of my reign Prophetic Writ hath told
> That it shall never end, so when begin
> The Father in his purpose hath decreed.

Hence the poem's accumulation of anti-climaxes, culminating in Christ's unobserved exit from it. *Paradise Regain'd* shuns the artful, frail attire of incarnation. When Mary's thoughts are troubled, she clads them, Milton says, in sighs: condemning them to the superficial and mortal condition of clothing and of flesh. Satan is the grand imaginist here, who dreams up the illusory enchantments that men call art. He confects a prop-basket banquet for the starving Christ, who rejects it as 'but a dream', a craving we ought to repress.

When art employs Milton's fable in self-justification, it must necessarily alter Milton's judgement and ally itself with the teeming brain and glib showmanship of Satan. Thus the romantics defined poetry by satanically misreading the Miltonic temptations. Keats in 1817 called it 'Adam's dream—he awoke and found it truth', willing the immediate reward of imagination when he envisions Eve; Milton would have thought it more like the bad dream from which Eve is relieved to awake. Adam counsels her to beware of imagination's promptings, and hopes that what in sleep she abhors to dream she will never, when conscious, consent to do. Leigh Hunt, praising in Keats an avid relish which Milton's Christ scorns to display, sees the poet as a voracious feeder on fantasies, a 'young poetical appetite, obtaining its food'—as Christ in the desert might have done by yielding to Satan—'by the very desire of it'. Keats wondered if 'I eat to persuade myself I am somebody.' Gluttony proves on the palate the reality of our world. Christ will not eat because he does not wish to be somebody, or to be duped into trusting the satisfactions, appetitive or aesthetic, of an unreal world.

Paradise Lost had already performed its own strict revaluation of the tradition preceding it. Though an epic, it is determinedly the last epic, and a prototype for the mock-epics which follow it in the satires and burlesques of the eighteenth century. Milton's Limbo of Vanity, the junkyard of nature's abortions, becomes the neurotic nursery of art when Pope redesigns it as the Cave of Spleen in his *Rape of the Lock* (1714); in 1742, Milton's '*Chaos* and *ancient Night*', whose 'nethermost Abyss' is plumbed by Satan, return as the stupefying Dulness of Pope's *Dunciad*.

After *Paradise Lost* there can only be parodies of what is, in the classical hierarchy of genres, the highest of forms, because Milton has demonstrated epic's perfidy and its obsolescence. Epic for Milton proves incompatible with Christianity. In place of the warfaring man of action—wrathful Achilles, battling Brythnoth—the Christian protagonist offers no armed resistance. Milton's saints are resigned to the quietude of pastoral grace: the taciturn Lady, the unresponding Christ. Beyond his suspicion of epic's heathenism, Milton has misgivings about the action which is in Aristotle's aesthetics the motivating force of epic and of drama. Activity is in Milton a depletion of self. Men are goaded to it, like the convulsive Satan, only by the friction in them of contraries and the tyranny of will. Vaunting aloud but wracked with deep despair, perpetually in motion to conceal from himself the futility of his endeavours, rejoicing in damnation because it at least keeps kindled in him the heat of being which would otherwise cool, Satan suffers from the existential hysteria of Donne or Rochester: thought, sense and action—even if the thoughts are vexed by questions which can have no answers, the senses pained and the actions busily irrelevant—are the flailing death-throes of an organism which, *in extremis*, congratulates itself on still being alive; they are all consequent upon the fall. Goodness, on the contrary, has an ideal inertia. The Lady in *Comus* practises stillness, and prefers not, as she says, to unlock her lips.

Before he writes an epic, Milton has decided on the moral and spiritual falsity of the form. The poem of force is the ultimate conceit of a violent, unbelieving human ego. Raphael censures it, refusing to relate the war in heaven as if it were an epic exchange of arms—he will not name the heroes of the fray, for 'those elect / . . . Seek not the praise of men'—and Michael discounts it when permitting Adam foresight of the race of giants, with their cult of 'Might . . . / And Valour and Heroic Vertu call'd.' Going on to write an epic all the same, Milton publishes his judgement of it by making Satan its hero. All the qualities the epic prized—the rage for self-immortalisation, and the obsession with tribal or national glory—devolve upon the devil. He is the patron of literature's wrongly pre-eminent form. Milton's audacity here has seldom been appreciated. Dryden in 1697 asserted that *Paradise Lost* could have been an epic 'if the Devil had been [its] hero, instead of Adam'; Shelley in 1821 and Blake in 1827 proposed Satan as the rightful hero but believed Milton's admiration for him ruined the poem's moral scheme. Milton is guilty of no such illogic. In according heroic status to Satan, he accuses heroism of being an infernal mania and a usurpation of God.

The 'unconquerable Will' of Satan the chieftain therefore suffers fatigue. Its vocal rallying-power, summoning the legions 'so loud', is depleted by his exertions. The ceremony of arms in Book I with its trumpets and clarions is progressively industrialised: Satan's campaign summarises the development of epic from the exercise of muscular prowess, when Beowulf swims against Breca, to technological craft in Ahab's mechanised massacring of whales. Moloch devises a gunpowder plot, Satan discharges a frown like a black cloud fraught with heaven's artillery, and the touch of Ithuriel's spear is the tindery ignition of nitrous dust. The devils institutionalise epic as a munitions factory. Raphael by contrast points out that the saintly phalanx is made invulnerable by beatitude not by military might. If epic is now the manufacture of extinction, the romance—which in the early history of English literature was epic's mitigation, reconciling it with Christianity—is also disowned by Milton. At Pandemonium he remembers the rout of a '*Panim* chivalry', and in Eden he disdains those 'Court Amours' which in the romance are tolerated as analogies for the soul's adoration of God. Pastoral alone is sacred. The angels are crowned with amarant, which Milton (again in correction of Spenser's more nonchalantly overgrown gardening) uproots from Eden and transplants to the spiritually safer realm of heaven. *Paradise Lost* recollects the great generic shift which shapes English literary form by its mocking relegation of epic pretenders to pastoral. The devils swarm into Pandemonium like bees. Menaced by Gabriel's watchmen, Satan is a field of wheat ripe for shearing by angelic ploughmen, who will perform that punitive winnowing which in Chaucer is the technique of allegorical interpretation,

> Lest on the threshing floore his hopeful sheaves
> Prove chaff.

At the poem's mid-point, Christ appears to conclude the war in heaven by harrying the warriors as if they were an angry shepherd's misbehaving flock; he overcomes them by metaphorically diminishing them to a herd of goats or silly sheep.

The action of epic man, its 'energy and magnificence' so thrilling to Shelley, is Satan's folly. His pride in the possession of character and in the mind's occupancy of 'its own place' where heaven and hell can be transposed is his most vicious illusion. No one else in *Paradise Lost* is a character: that idea, so precious to literature, is another inspiration of the devil's. God and Christ are above the pettiness of the personal; Adam and Eve (until they fall) predate it, content to be a part of one another; Sin and Death, incubi of allegory, are outside it. Satan's individuality is the penalty of his estrangement from God. Refusing to be 'me, whom he created what I was', he ventures to invent himself anew by the rabid insistence of will. Yet though he fuels that renegade, dangerously single self with all his emotive and intellectual power, he cannot prevent its degeneration. He slips through ever lowlier bestial impersonations and ends as a serpentine distortion of himself. In place of the character he had prided himself on creating he is made to enact a caricature. Milton here implies the satanism of drama as well as of epic. At first he planned the work as a play, and traces of this version remain—in Satan's stagey spying on Eve, or Adam's warning that their foe lurks near; above all in Satan's addiction to soliloquy and his echoes of Faustus and the Jacobean revengers. The drama suits Satan because, for Milton, it is the furthest reach of alienation: the dementia of epic glory corresponds to the existential hazard of dramatic character, faking a personality to outface the world for him. Satan at last, in another infidel misreading of Milton, regains the drama where he belongs. Shaw's devil in *Man and Superman* (1901–3) corrects the idea of his expulsion from boring heaven, and attributes the shibboleth to 'a long poem which neither I nor anyone else ever succeeded in wading through'.

The heaven of *Paradise Lost* has superseded both epic and drama; it is a thing unattempted yet in prose or rhyme because it is strictly beyond the capability of literature. God cannot be heroic. Milton's deity is not the brawny grandfather painted on Michelangelo's Sistine ceiling. The poem protects its God from the indignity of a literary anthropomorphism. He remains a luminous blur or a fragrant irradiation, mystically 'invisible to mortal sight'. Even when he argues and interposes, it is not as a character in the satanic sense. Since he is the creating *logos*, Milton must make him loquacious, but his language is—to its credit—abstinently characterless. It is an idiom of divine computation, revolving words and meanings in a perfect and empty circle:

> . . . . if I foreknew,
> Foreknowledge had no influence on their fault,
> Which had no less prov'd certain unforeknown.

Milton's is a god of science fiction, abstracted altogether from human being. The eighteenth century conceived of its God as a meticulous watch-maker; later the imagination apprehends him as a self-operating machine, a brain no longer cased in unreliable flesh: the highbrow Martians of H.G. Wells's *War of the Worlds* (1898), the intergalactic 'emissaries' of Arthur C. Clarke's story 'The Sentinel' (1950), who leave a glittering heliographic pyramid on a mountain of the moon, or—in a denunciation of the Calvinist deity's greed and megalomania—the Swedish financier Krogh in Graham Greene's *England Made Me* (1935), who oversees a multinational empire from a futuristic control-room in the frozen north, commandeering the entire world by means of ticker-tape transmissions and scrutinising share prices in all global capitals simultaneously. Milton's God is the first such cosmic locomotive, and literature's first effort to comprehend the humanly inconceivable. Accordingly he precedes literature: he is a grammar not a person. He animates words as verbs and then solidifies them into substantives in

> To pray, repent, and bring obedience due.
> To prayer, repentance, and obedience due;

he is adjectivally extolled by the angels who call him 'Immutable, Immortal, Infinite'; he is mis-transcribed by the devils, who attach negating affixes to his creation when they seek to 'unimmortal make / All kinds'. Pope in 1737 thought it a fault in the poem to have made God an academic grammarian, and complained that

> In quibbles, angel and archangel join,
> And God the Father turns a school-divine.

On the contrary, this is one of Milton's most austere and subtle decisions. God cannot of course dispute or expound theologically. Acts of God are by definition inexplicable. Theology is the human conjecture at an explanation, adduced after the event. Milton takes these posterior rationalisations by the commentators on Genesis and, when God voices them in Book III, makes them his anterior reasons. Explications, backdated, serve as motives. The machine is its own infallible interpreter. This way, Milton preserves his God's sacrosanctness. He is not traduced by the literal human mind.

As the intercessor between the deity and earth, Christ is allowed to approximate to human form. Whereas God's 'Omnific Word' articulates itself in theorems and in witty, prickly formulae like 'God shall be All in All. But all ye Gods . . .', Christ can make use of that human invention, poetry. To God's self-evident and legalistic propositions, Christ replies in a sequence of plangent lyrical questions, repetitively wringing feeling from words as when he complains that man should 'be from thee farr, / That farr be from thee, Father' in a variation which is almost a mellifluous wheedling. But, like God, Christ is reserved from heroism, and he enters the combat resplendent in his chariot only to secure belligerent epic's subjugation as meek, sheepish pastoral.

God and Christ are generic beings, sources of the life that is in others, and thus immune from the fission into personality which is Satan's fate; unfallen Adam and Eve are saved from it by their biological mutuality. They exist only to complement each other, and the reverent hierarchy of their relationship duplicates the kinship of God and Christ:

> For contemplation hee and valour formd,
> For softness shee and sweet attractive Grace,
> Hee for God only, shee for God in him.

Satan the elocutionary actor is alone with the echo of his voice, experiencing character as a solitary confinement. Adam and Eve are paired, and Milton embeds them in the undifferentiated pastoral of created nature by describing them as growths in a landscape. He allows their hair—the body's extrusion, its foliage or efflorescence—to represent them. Adam's does not conceal his brow, which is his seat of surveillance; Eve's can thrive more rampantly, and extends to her waist in vinous tendrils. Their labour is to tend the garden where, in common with all other creatures, they have grown. When first seen, they are hand in hand, and before the fall their speech is a consonant duetting. Paradise is their membership of each other: they are 'imparadis't in one anothers arms', and when Eve addresses Adam as 'thou for whom / And from whom I was formd flesh of thy flesh', Milton's language pines to return to that polymorphous state, so that the words for, from and form cast off their separateness and lyrically overlap. Satan's words are tetchily singular: 'Me miserable!'; those of Adam and Eve consent to merge. Singleness—symbolised by Eve's reflection, which she studies in the lake—is a condition to be grown beyond. Uniting herself with Adam, she participates (as the self-made Satan refuses to do) in the substance of her own being and through him in God, its ultimate origin. Character, jealously retentive of this distinctness, enters as a casualty of the fall when Adam and Eve, expelled from nature and from incorporation in one another, take to recrimination and disagreement.

Along with character, literature arrives in the world as the fall's bequest. Before it there are the metaphysical certainties retailed to Adam by Raphael or the prognostications of things to come, equally certain, which he glimpses under Michael's tutelage; although Adam calls Raphael a divine historian, his pronouncements are not history but myth. Because they are about God's generation and supervision of the world, they happen along a vertical axis, down which the angels travel on their errands and down which, too, the devils plummet to perdition, up which the voices of Adam and Eve hymnally aspire. The horizontal track of toiling human history does not yet exist. Its inauguration is announced at the very end, with the weary labourer's return from the day's work as Adam and Eve commence their journey: as when Diana quits and curses Arlo in *The Faerie Queene*, the sacred zone of pastoral lapses into an exiguous agricultural terrain.

Praising God before the fall, Adam and Eve deliberately rearrange the tenses of historical time and the median points of narrative, celebrating 'Him first, him last, him midst, and without end'; Milton also, in constructing his poem, models it on an unfallen world where all times are simultaneous. Because in God the beginning and the end are the same, Milton begins in the middle and ends at the beginning. After the fall, when the vertical connection between heaven and earth is withdrawn, time unravels into an indefinite and tiring elongation, the shape of narrative with its interminable sequels and of human (as against Raphael's divine) history. The final line of Book IX hints at this vexatious endlessness. Adam and Eve are squabbling, 'And of thir vain contest appear'd no end.' Milton calls Adam 'Our Author' (though Sin, speaking to Death, acclaims Satan as 'our great Author'); Eve, too, salutes her husband as 'My Author', and God insists on man's authorship of his own disgrace. Authorial Adam is the progenitor of the human race and, by his original sin, of its literature. In the Christian theory the accumulation of stories is a rubble of discontinuous anecdotes repeated through the race's life; at last a stop is put to them when time, at the second coming, reverts to eternity. Michael's digest of tales is, as at the lazar-house, a catalogue of maladies. By foretelling human history on the mount of vision, he and Milton render it redundant before it can have the temerity to occur. Yet Adam and his legatees must trudge through it all the same. Milton reflects on the annals of literature as Macbeth does on life: it serves only to while away a purgatorial time which is eternity's judgement on us. *Paradise Lost* aims almost to be the one poem of which Adam cannot claim authorship. As it ends, it seems to concede to Adam and Eve one of those choices—initiatives of free will—which are the instigators of narrative:

> The World was all before them, where to choose
> Thir place of rest.

But Milton rescinds that liberty as soon as it is offered. Providence, he subjoins, is their guide, so their choice is foreknown. Whichever way they select, the outcome will be the same; and because of its prefiguring on the mount, the world is actually all behind them, not optimistically ahead.

If *Paradise Lost* is not Adam's text—and certainly, despite the romantics, it is not Satan's—then whose is it? Milton has successfully expatriated it from the fallen domain of literature. First he changes it from the tragedy of Adam's loss to a divine comedy; then, reconstructing it between 1667 and 1674, he makes sure that in its apportionment of space it transcends the solitary human case by emphasising the recuperation and redemption which intervene between the crime and its punishment.

To interpret it tragically is to belie it. This was Addison's error in his *Spectator* essays of 1711–12. He thought Book X corresponded to 'the last act of a well-constructed tragedy'; everything thereafter, forced into prominence by Milton in the 1674 edition, was a lustreless anti-climax. Addison the humanist, disturbed by the poem's exemption from humanity—it lies, he says, 'out of nature'—misreads it by fitting it back into Milton's initial, discarded dramatic scheme for it. It troubles Addison because it is not a work, like all other human art, of devout mimesis, but a rival creation. Its characters had 'to be formed purely by [Milton's] own invention'. Johnson in 1779 was disturbed by the same superiority to earthly cares in the poem. Milton shares the patronising tone of his own Raphael, who wonders how he can translate for Adam 'what surmounts the reach / Of human sense'. Johnson notices him stylistically stooping: 'The characteristic quality of his poem is sublimity. He sometimes descends to the elegant, but his element is the great.' His complaint against *Paradise Lost* is that 'it comprises neither human actions nor human manners. . . . The want of human interest is always felt.' Pleading on slighted humanity's behalf, he edges near to the judgment of Shaw's devil, who refutes the poem by refusing to read it. Johnson calls it 'one of those books which the reader admires and lays down, and forgets to take up again. None ever wishes it longer than it is.' From Marvell's prefatory poem in 1674 onwards, the only appropriate response to Milton seems to be baffled, fearful, agnostic awe.

These humane reservations correctly sense the prodigy which is the poem. In the absence of precedents, as Addison notes, *Paradise Lost* performs aesthetically the same miracle it describes theologically; it creates anew heaven, earth and hell, as if it were the poem of a god not a man. The heroic centre occupied neither by Satan nor Adam, nor even by God or Christ, is assumed by Milton himself. The poet here regains his forfeited powers as maker and seer. Milton accomplishes over again the creative feat of his own God, and the interceding, elucidating one of Christ. He bodies forth the world in words as God first did when he spoke it into existence; and in electing to justify God's ways to man he attempts by the arduous endeavour of intellect that same demonstration of meaning in the cosmic scheme which Christ achieved by parable and sacrificial example.

Though *Paradise Lost* disdains the force of arms, it lays claim to two specific styles of heroism belonging properly to God but here deployed by man: the power of language, and the power of mind. Milton's God is an unseeable voice, a word made flesh in Christ, his

> Equal to him begotten Son, by whom
> As by his Word the mighty Father made
> All things.

Invisibility—criticised in the poem by Dryden, who thought that Milton perceived nature through the spectacles of books, or by T. S. Eliot, who in 1936 found his poetry deficient in 'the visual imagination' and blamed his blindness for this disablement—is an unapologetic attribute of God. According to Milton's theory, the obliteration of sight may be a provident imaginative benefit. A visual diction must be a parasite on a world already created, which it catalogues; a language predominantly aural, like Milton's, does not assess words as captions to or pictures of things but as emissions of the divine breath, literal inspirations of life into objects. Visually, words come long after things; aurally, they anticipate and ordain them. In Book VII, God's naming of light and firmament precedes his creating of them. The word as uttered by God is omnific because (like the gate of heaven when Milton in Book III recollects Jacob's visionary insight) it is 'viewless'. Milton craves this same omnipotence for his own poetic speech.

Eliot derides Milton's roll-calls of place-names and dynastic titles, denying that they are 'serious poetry'. No poetry, however, could be more ominously serious: such lists rehearse the oracular potency of words, or the use of vocables as spells and incantations. Milton's language refuses the secondariness of description. Its words are the conscription of things, which is why they can reproduce—as Blake said the aboriginal poet did—Adam's confident naming of the animals and plants. When Milton calls Abbana and Pharphar 'lucid streams' he does not mean the adjective picturesquely but as a moral prescription. Water's translucence is its innocence, unmuddied by the demon Rimmon whose power is established on the banks of those streams. The word's etymology is the guarantor of truth in it: when it comes to mean only clearness, and no longer suggests an admonishing clarity, it has been made opaque by misuse. Eliot says that 'Milton writes English like a dead language.' Not quite. He writes it—in another of those oblique motions which place *Paradise Lost* collateral to the rest of literature—as if it were dead and his task were to quicken it again.

This is the case with the sonorous march-past of substantives in a line like 'Thrones, Dominations, Princedoms, Vertues, Powers.' When God first declaims this sequence, it is as a verbal decree, forbidding revocation. The words are the more compelling because they issue from the invisibility of his brightness. He demands that the angels hear him, and asserts over these lesser fiefdoms a dominion which is a tribute to his linguistic authority. Satan next takes over the line, and delivers it as a specimen of what Milton's detractors call the grand style, hollowly formulaic, merely orotund: these 'magnific Titles', Satan alleges, are 'merely titular'. Abdiel then answers for orthodoxy, and reclaims those triumphal nouns for the precise meaning God intended, recalling that they are names assigned by him to his subjects, which denominate 'Essential Powers'. The repetition is a corrective revising. Milton's descriptive language conducts an assay of its own fallen nature, intimating that the accrual of meanings taints words by making them collude with human uses. Etymology enquires into the original sin of our diction. Thus when Milton says that a river ran through paradise 'with mazie error under pendant shades', the noun, more unforgiving than Spenser's wayward delaying of his characters in Error's wood, reverts from the topographically errant to the morally erroneous and linguistically inserts sin into a world as yet ignorant of it; at the same time his adjective, converted to infernal uses, enables Coleridge to map his own hell of indulgent fantasy—the 'sacred river' in 'Kubla Khan', holy because savage and enchanted, animated by gods other than Milton's, runs 'five miles meandering with a mazy motion', and the alliteration collaborates in the drowsy, hypnotic delusion of the mind. So in describing paradise Milton, who must use a language compromised by the fall, has made possible Coleridge's depiction of a personal inferno. Milton's river irrigates Eden with 'many a rill'; Coleridge's gardens, where the water-courses have begun to snake, are 'bright with sinuous rills'.

Sometimes the stringency of this revisionism requires Milton to sentence polluted words to death, as in the systematic set of negations introducing the landscape of paradise by comparing it to the other places which do not deserve the compliment of the simile—'Not that faire field . . .; nor that sweet Grove . . .; nor that *Nyseian* Ile . . .'—or his exclusion from the bridal bower of

'*Pan* or *Silvanus*', all nymphs and Spenser's prurient Faunus. But more often his purifying of a dialect that the tribe has adulterated results in an augmentation of life. Language is an infusion of breath, a vital sign, and Milton's auditory style can sponsor and act out that process of impregnation which impels things into motion, rather than pictorially observing them in stasis. This is the case with his account of the atmosphere in paradise:

> . . . of pure now purer aire
> Meets his approach, and to the heart inspires
> Vernal delight and joy, able to drive
> All sadness but despair: now gentle gales
> Fanning thir odoriferous wings dispense
> Native perfumes. . . .

The activity of the breezes here is an inspiration, since they are exhaled by God—though they, too, like the paradisial river, undergo romantic revaluation when Wordsworth in 'The Tables Turned' (1798) replaces God with Nature and declares, defying Milton, that

> One impulse from a vernal wood
> May teach you more of man,
> Of moral evil and of good,
> Than all the sages can.

Milton's gales, however, are both climatic and spiritual, and his language can ally itself with their work because it respires as lyrically as they do. A lyric after all is the wind's agitation of a lyre. At the same time Milton refreshes meanings, rendering words superlative and stirring them to exceed themselves, as in 'pure now purer aire'. Later in the description of Eden a pun holds together the two meanings of this divine respiration, the airy and the lyrically aria-like, when Milton notes that

> The Birds thir quire apply; airs, vernal airs,
> Breathing the smell of field and grove, attune
> The trembling leaves. . . .

Adam's awakening of Eve in Book V is a similar fertilisation by breath, a vocal and linguistic recreation of her. At first he looks dotingly at her, but sight can never suffice in Milton and must be transposed into the organic vibrancy of sound:

> . . . . then with voice
> Milde as when *Zephyrus* on *Flora* breathes,
> Her hand soft touching, whispered thus.

He whispers to her of the silently spoken summons from nature: the fresh field calls them. Then, however, he lapses into the pictorial. As humans, their purpose is a vigilant and respectful curatorship, not Miltonic creativity; their duty is 'to mark how spring / Our tended Plants' and to watch 'How Nature paints her colours'. As a god, Milton can energise what they can only deferentially observe.

Though Eliot calls Milton's language obdurate and inflexible, it possesses in fact a kinetic energy which is the unique skill of the auditory imagination. It specialises in the mobilising of masses, in a contentious muscularity and a strenuous syntactic grip. Heroism in Milton is a dialectical mental power. Instead of a great action, his poem possesses a 'great Argument', and in Book IX he insists that the exacting proof of providential logic—achieved by a combination of universal learning and forensic audacity—is matter

> Not less but more Heroic than the wrauth
> Of stern *Achilles*.

Writing is now puissant action and martyring agony.

That stress and strife or mind expresses itself in Milton's verbal architecture. God first conceives the world in thought, then suspends it in space. The poem is much concerned with the engineering of habitations or of causeways above the void—the raising of Pandemonium, or the bridge over Chaos on which Sin and Death labour—and it envisages its own argument as a gravity-defying span, cantilevered over impossibility. Milton's is the poetry of a pontifex. As such it is parodied by the contrivance of Sin and Death, which he calls a 'Pontifice' and attributes to their 'wondrous Art / Pontifical'. He calls Satan its 'Author and prime Architect', and differentiates it from his own vertiginous structures because it is congealed and fastened rather than tensely and resiliently flexing to cope with the pressures which assault it. Death with his mace 'petrific' cements the waters 'with *Gorgonian* rigor not to move' just by looking at them. The flaw in the infernal bridge is precisely its fixity:

> . . . . with Pinns of Adamant
> And chains they made all fast, too fast they made
> And durable.

Milton needs no technology of coercion; he can balance arcs like this in air. His first invocation pleads for divine aid in sustaining the aspirant, unfounded edifice of the poem at its perilous 'highth'. Holding aloft those refractory materials with no visible means of support, Milton's grand style is less an affair of diction (as Eliot believed) than of syntax. The mobility of language is its syntax, and Milton's idiosyncratic grammar makes each utterance a connective outreach, hanging in suspense in the poem's vaulted sky, equilibrated only by Milton's breadth of breath. Each of his verse paragraphs is, as Christ says of God's speech, a 'sovran sentence'. That sovereignty is assured by syntax. At the poem's opening, for instance, the withholding of the verb 'Sing' until the sixth line allows it, when Milton at last supplies it, to marshal into subordination all the previous clauses; thus a verb of supplication or invocation is turned into one of compulsion. The sentence anticipates the heroic demonstration that the poem as a whole will make: completing an arch, that verb arrives at a point of rest, a briefly enjoyed victory prior to the next adventure across empty space. The syntax creates contradiction, because from the friction of opposites it generates resistance and derives energy. Hence Milton's manacling into juxtaposition, in this same paragraph, of 'dark' and 'Illumin' or 'low' and 'raise'. English word-order would keep them diplomatically distant. Milton's Latinism pushes them into conjunction and can thus declare the poem's ambition to dramatise and resolve their antagonism.

Milton's is a spatial syntax. His sentences induce a moral vertigo. Rhyme with its in-built balances is inconsistent with his purpose; blank verse cannot rely on one line's automatic accord with the next, so continuation becomes an exertion of will. The drawing-out of the sense—as the printer in 1668 called it—is a bold traversal of the gulf between verses. Each line juts out into an abyss, a physical declevity (as in Satan's plunge 'down / To bottomless perdition') or an apparently unbridgeable moral gap ('till one greater Man / Restore us'), or else a conceptual chasm like that which yawns between heaven and earth when Adam calls Raphael, across a line-end, 'Divine / Historian'. Only Milton's intrepidity can save the verse from collapsing into those bathetic crevices, like Satan dropping ten thousand fathoms into an air-pocket as he crosses Chaos. The poem's obsessive motions are those of ascent and descent. Satan topples from the summit of the universe to its depth, while Milton struggles to rise up in the opposite direction. This vertical battle, extended through the dizzy scale of Milton's cosmos, happens as well within each line of verse. The divisions of the versification fissure the safe horizontal floor of prose. When Eve eats the apple, a colon measures the incommensurate, unbalanced relation between her innocuous act and its consequences, and the end of the next line marks the paralysis of a nature too aghast—while 'Sighing' is held in reserve—to react as yet:

> Forth reaching to the Fruit, she pluckd, she eat:
> Earth felt the wound, and Nature from her seate
> Sighing through all her Works gave signs of woe. . . .

These typographic apertures between cause and effect can be closed only by the thrustful impetus of Milton's syntax. Every enjambment is a leap of faith into the unknown, like Satan's project to 're-ascend / Self-rais'd' or the proud uplifting of man from the prostration of the beasts to 'erect / His stature'; every run-on line is a suspension bridge over nothingness, and an anchoring repetition is unable to prevent slippage and reclamation by that void, which occurs when Beelzebub bemoans a 'faded bliss, / Faded too soon'. Many of the poem's crucial episodes involve the opening of gates, which stand for the calamitous, consequential apertures in its world and in its verse—Sin's unbarring of hell ('She opend, but to shut / Excelld her power'), Satan's air-sick conviction that 'in the lowest deep a lower deep / Still threatening to devour me opens wide', or the widening of heaven's ever-during doors

> . . . . to let forth
> The King of Glorie in his powerful Word.

Milton in his personal interventions in the poem wields language like the beams and girders of sustaining structure. He knows that words are a creative agency, our means of inventing a world not merely of labelling it. Yet though he restores this confiscated power to poetry, he undertakes elsewhere in *Paradise Lost* a scrutiny of the misuses to which poetic language is subjected once it falls from a possession of God to a tool of men, or of devils. The character of Satan renders Milton's verdict on drama and on its language—the language of so-called 'felt thought' which T. S. Eliot and F. R. Leavis (who credits Donne with a Shakespearean use of English, and adds that one might almost call it an English use of English) tried to establish, by their denigration of Milton, as a norm for poetry. The interfusion of thought and feeling is in Satan an inflammation, a moral distemper, and the Shakespearean or Donnean habits—the nervous spontaneity, the witty quibbling, the self-questionings— are the verbal twitches of an aching and resentful insecurity (as in his rhetorical invective to the sun) or a glibly clever simulation of reasoning (as in his syllogistic persuasion of Eve). The dramatic character's talent is adaptability to circumstances: such malleability, registered in his disguises and in the evasiveness of his idiom, is the torment of Satan.

Satan's stealthy mutability makes him an expert at metaphoric deceit, and through him this resource of poetic beguilement is inspected and condemned by Milton. Metaphor (like the Donnean conceit, arranging incongruous matches between subject and object) is a product of the fall and the disconnection of those correspondences which previously aligned earth and heaven. Though man is created as God's similitude, he is deprived by his crime, as Michael tells Adam, of the divine image; metaphor can only be an approximate and impious attempt to marry things which have been irreparably sundered. Here Milton amends an entire theology of poetry, which values metaphor as a gift from beyond, a relic of paradise. Yeats's spirits visited him, like Raphael on his embassy to Eden, to bestow on him 'metaphors for poetry'; in 'High Talk' (1939) Yeats lists his materials as 'metaphor, Malachi, stilts and all', Malachi the messenger being the alleged author of the last book of the Old Testament. In Milton the image is not fall-out from heaven but a deceptive invention of hell. Satan moves in a mist of semblances which is his world and that of any poetry but Milton's. Metaphor practises on visual illusion and mental delusion, cheating with words by making them (in another offence against auditory imagination) pretend to be pictures.

Satan is described in Book I by the distraction of metaphor with its restless metamorphoses. Because the image cannot clarify, he is never actually seen, but the proliferation of similes and their mutation into each other suggests his dangerous ungraspability and his ubiquity. Words fasten on things, then lose their hold. First Milton cites Satan's ponderously solid shield, then admits that it is behind him, so (unlike the shield of Achilles which is a synonym for epic) it is no mirror of him. He goes on, however, to describe it all the same. Its circumference is likened to the moon, then that planet is diminished to the image of itself in Galileo's telescope and in the process is shown to be an infertile waste, a 'spotty Globe' which is the nocturnal negation of earth. The shield having led to this metaphoric impasse, Milton next embarks on the description of another Satanic prop, the spear. It, too, dissipates in a penumbra of alternately aggrandising and belittling metaphors, elongated to a hilltop pine, then hewn and reshaped as a mast, after that dismissed as a mere wand. This mutancy exhausts and consumes the devils, who are squandered in a pair of similes. Their 'Angel Forms' first suggest autumn leaves in Vallombrosa, then scattered sedge on the Red Sea. But that foliage is nature's waste, so the legions suffer a last shape-changing into the human and mechanical wreckage of the Memphian chivalry drowned in that sea—a scum of 'floating Carcasses / And broken Chariot Wheels'. Each metaphor promises to extend their power, geographically consigning them (for metaphor in Greek is a carrier, a means of transport) to a different sector of the human world which their evil will eventually colonise—to Norway where the pine grows, to Tuscany where Galileo has his observatory, or to Egypt. But every migration weakens them, drains them of being.

The similes of Book I renounce the epic poet's ancient device: instead of merging human will with the impersonal energies of nature, as Homer or the *Beowulf* poet do in their metaphors, Milton causes Satanic will to fritter itself away by encouraging it to succumb to the seduction of likeness. And those tantalising comparisons are either cancelled (as when the devils are compared with 'A multitude, like which the populous North / Poured never from her frozen loins') or else changed into other yet more partial and peripheral similitudes. The devils are leaves, then a cloud of locusts, then a deluge. The indeterminacy indicates a suspicion of the visible world, where devils could take on the appearance of any or all of these things. A poetry which trifles with semi-semblances has already capitulated to that world's fickleness and impermanence.

In opposition, Milton's diction is a lexical conscience, valuing the meaning of words, not their vague visual suggestions. In the same infernal assembly, Milton twice says that there were too many fiends to count: 'to thir Generals Voice they soon obeyd / Innumerable', he notes, then a few lines later adds, 'So numberless were those bad Angels seen.' As well as pointing to the imprecision and innumeracy of description, since all those similes cannot manage to tally the devils, Milton's repetition has a wit peculiar to the auditory imagination, minutely discriminating between divergent sounds and senses. A critic of

Milton's language would say that innumerable and numberless are the same, and call this the bluster of the grand style. But the words are different, and Milton needs both, though not because they tell him anything about how the devils looked. 'Innumerable' comes at the end of a metaphor characterising the flurried bewilderment and insentience of the legions, who as yet neither understand their predicament nor feel its pain: it is the right word here because it implies a deficiency in them. The simile has compared them with drowsing sentinels, 'sleeping found by whom they dread'; 'innumerable' catches their dazed incapacity to enumerate or assess their own hopeless cause, the unthinking automatism of their obedience. 'Numberless' is another matter. The simile preceding it is about the obfuscation of sight when the plague of locusts impends over Egypt like night. Numberlessness refers to the indivisibility of the devils, compounded like insects and working as a team, in contrast with the choiring angels of Book III who comprise 'numbers without number' and are beyond the finite reckonings of human arithmetic. By using words as exactly and as illuminingly as he does, Milton can make the darkness in which the devils converge suddenly visible; though they cannot be numbered, they can be named, which is a surer way of controlling them, since, like words with their etymologies, they carry their genealogies around with them. To name them is to arraign them, and this Milton goes on to do at length. Only a name can detain and accuse them, for it is their extradition from a skulking ignominy: as a penalty for their crime, their names have been erased from heavenly records, and they profit from the obliteration by assuming 'new Names' or 'various Names' on earth; Milton's entitling of them ensures their accountability.

The three realms of the poem are different auditory societies, each with its own vocal order. The devils are abashed by Satan's rhetorical tyranny. At the end of the parliament he forbids dissenting reply, and his detractors 'Dreaded not more th'adventure than his voice / Forbidding', just as when Christ descends to Eden Adam fears less his presence than his voice, and clothes himself in defence against its power to see through him:

> I heard thee in the Garden, and of thy voice
> Afraid, being naked, hid my self.

In heaven the voice quits the body altogether and, unseen, enunciates pronouncements which are law. God in judgement is a voice issuing from a cloud, which translates his words meteorologically and 'amidst, in Thunder utterd'. The Son expresses the Father, as Milton puts it during their dialogue on the punishment of man, because he tempers the voice transmitted through him. In Book III God's logical dogmatism is pacified by Christ's gentler plaintiveness; and in Book X God's sentence—both legal and grammatical—is revised by Christ's different voicing of it when he 'divinely answerd mild'. Those authoritative words can be sounded as music, too: eternity's intersection with human time is signalled by a trumpet blast, blown at the expulsion from Eden and

> . . . . heard in *Oreb* since perhaps
> When God descended, and perhaps once more
> To sound at general Doom.

Because hell is a parody of heaven, it is a place of vocal dissidence not accord: hence the parliamentary hubbub, whose raised voices by the end of the poem are indistinguishable from the malevolent, meaningless sibilation of serpents. The utterance of Satan, not serene in unchallengeable invisibility like God's, has to be wrung from him as a symptom of his anguish. He tries three times to speak, while his hushed sycophants wait, but is silenced by his misery. His words—remnants of the divinity in him, because language is man's means for upraising himself to God—must struggle to escape from the body which imprisons them: 'at last / Words interwove with sighs found out thir way'. The elocutionary orator who emboldens the troops or the agile debater who tells Eve that the fruit first taught him speech ends exiled from language, emitting only noise when 'hiss for hiss returnd with forked tongue / To forked tongue'.

The two graces of language allowed to the humans in the poem are conversation and song. Before the fall, the vocal unison between Adam and Eve corresponds to their biological completion of each other. Adam's first speech makes a punning music from this physical interdependency when he calls Eve 'sole partner and sole part of all these joys'. Later Eve, accepting his account of their duties, says, 'Unargu'd I obey': argument, because it is a severance of minds, is unknown to them. Adam values as one of the blessings of paradise 'our delightful talk', and to Eve their dialogue has a musical power to charm time into acquiescence: 'With thee conversing I forget all time.' Their conversation effortlessly parses itself as song, for lyricism is the breath God invested in them rendered up as praise, and music—'harmonic number', in contrast with the unnumbered, disordered devils—disciplines and thus harmonises duration. Adam's masculine, reasonable apology for their gardening routine 'which were it toilsom, yet with thee were sweet' is answered later in Book IV by Eve's more feminine variation which, deducting Adam, decides that none of the natural delights 'without thee is sweet'. There is a moral and emotional proximity to rhyme here (on which Dryden capitalises in the operatic text he made from *Paradise Lost*): the couplet's beatitude is its celebration of the human couple. Hence the joined voices of their morning orisons. Milton here describes a prelapsarian poetry, explaining that they artlessly vary their thanks to God

> . . . . in Prose or numerous Verse,
> More tuneable than needed Lute or Harp
> To add more sweetness.

He is sketching an atavistic history of lyric, arguing that it comes to rely on the assistance of instrumental music only when the sweetness of sentiment can no longer be trusted. A tortured chromaticism invades the Elizabethan lyric, and in 1606 John Danyel in *Songs for Lute, Viol and Voice* demands

> Can doleful notes to measur'd accents set
> Express unmeasured griefs which time forget?
> No, let chromatic tunes, harsh without ground,
> Be sullen music for a tuneless heart.

Eliot commends Donne for his rejection of tuning accompaniment. Milton—as theoretically critical of lyric as he is of epic or dramatic form—rewrites that development and reinstates in the lyric the Orphic powers it has abandoned. He specifies that the 'fit strains' of Adam and Eve are 'unmeditated'; Shelley, a later Orphic and musical lyricist obsessed with the theism of song, remembers this in his transcription of the skylark's inhuman and therefore religious song, which pours out profuse strains of unpremeditated art. The devotional beauty of the hymn Adam and Eve sing is its plea of inarticulacy. The lyric paraphrases what it cannot know or presume to speak of. Adam and Eve admit that God is invisible to them and 'Unspeakable'; they can know him only through his works, and they transfer to the angels with their 'choral symphonies' the task of vocalising his glory. Onto Milton devolves the task of speaking of God, and of justifying his donation to us of language: *Paradise Lost* in its review and revision of the genres it compounds is about the treason of literature—its weakness for fabulations and fancies, and its metaphoric clinging to a fallen, unreal world—but it also hopes for the resuscitation of that literature, when the language which makes it possible is purged and returned to its origins in God.

It is the ambition of *Paradise Lost* both to end literature as it is, and to begin it anew. That new beginning will have to set out from Milton, who has made God in his own image. God calls himself 'Author of all this thou seest / Above, or round about thee or beneath', and is praised by Adam as 'Author of this Universe'; after his six days of creative labour he rests as 'Author and end of all things'. That primacy, terminating one history and inaugurating another, is shared by Milton's poem. The universe of *Paradise Lost* therefore serves, when its various sectors are disassembled, to house all the literature which follows from it.

Heaven descends again to earth in the visionary benedictions of the lyric—first in the reinterpretation of Milton by Andrew Marvell and Thomas Traherne, later in Gerard Manley Hopkins, who in 1877 sees the world charged again with the grandeur of God. Hell, the deformation of Milton's heaven, situated 'under Earth', is the asylum of eighteenth-century satire, made by what Abdiel vindictively calls the uncreation of the godly plan. The graphic satirists are fascinated by Milton's hell, because it is the place where they wish their victims. Hogarth during the 1730s painted a blowsy, bosomy Sin separating wolf-faced Satan and skeletal Death. Milton's theology prepares for the demonism of caricature. Satan is 'punisht in the shape he sin'd', and Michael explains to Adam that the fall's penalty is sick physical distortion,

> Disfiguring not Gods likeness, but thir own,
> Or if his likeness, by themselves defac't.

As pigmies in Pandemonium, Milton's devils are Swift's insignificant men, the Lilliputians; the insects God creates on the fifth day in Book V, before arrival at 'Man / In our similitude', are the gilded pests of Pope's satire, into which men regress.

Between these two realms, earth emerges as the province of the novel, invented to record the tribulations of Adam and Eve once they leave paradise and the poem. Diving out of his boat, the hero of Meredith's *The Ordeal of Richard Feverel* (1859) lands on a magic island. It is Prospero's domain, where he finds in Lucy a phantasmal Miranda; but it is also a regained Eden. In belated correction of Milton's ending, Meredith says of Richard that 'the world lay wrecked behind him'. Admitted a second time to the garden, Richard recovers paradise in Lucy: 'Is it Adam, his rib taken from his side in sleep, and thus transformed, to make him behold his Paradise, and lose it?' Less optimistically, F. Scott Fitzgerald in 1920 locates the novel *This Side of Paradise* and John Steinbeck in 1952 positions it outside the garden, *East of Eden*. Steinbeck's narrative concerns an American Adam's problems with his rebellious offspring Aaron and Cal, and with an Eve who defects to take up residence in a Californian brothel. 'This one story', Steinbeck said of Genesis, 'is the basis for all human neurosis', chronicling 'the total psychic troubles that can happen to a human.' The purpose of myth is now the analysis of our diseases; in literary history, Milton, too, has become a hereditary ailment.

16

The Lost Paradise of the Lyric

Perhaps paradise had not been lost, but had gone into hiding. Ushering Adam from Eden, Michael assures him of the soul's immortality and tells him that in earning Christ's grace by his good deeds in the world he will come to possess 'A paradise within thee, happier farr'. The garden has been replaced by an image of itself, or by a memory. Michael's moral remonstrance soon becomes a literary motive: paradise can be retrieved by and enshrined in a poem. Peter Sterry, who was Cromwell's chaplain and Milton's colleague during the Commonwealth, remarked that 'as Paradise, so the pure Image of God in the Soul, seems to some not to be lost or destroyed, but hid beneath the ruins of the fall. Thus Knowledge springing in the Soul, seems to be a remembrance of the Life of all good . . . sparkling through the Rubbish, the confusions of the present state.'

Sterry's puritan Platonism could also describe the form of Milton's poem. It begins *in medias res* and gradually advances from darkness into light; from the agitated periphery of hell, where the devils are the flotsam of a spent storm, it moves to the calm and timeless garden, the mid-point of the geocentric universe as of the poem. Then it suffers this idyll to be invaded and overturned, the earth tilted on its axis and paradise parched by the new intemperance of weather in the fallen world. Disposing it in this way, Milton makes the work's shape a replica of the paradise within. Retrieved by imagination, it is sequestered in the centre of his poem. Milton passes on this capacity to recall an original, infantile or pastoral perfection to the poets who follow him: each lyric is a survivor from that ruined garden, for which, like Hopkins in 1880 describing the unleaving of Goldengrove, it mourns.

The first poet to inherit this ambition for the lyric is Milton's protégé, Andrew Marvell, who in 1674 published a poem wondering at (and also discreetly revising) *Paradise Lost*. Because Marvell is a miniaturist—only fragments of paradise are lyrically regainable—his inevitable qualification of Milton is a reduction of the poem's scale. He recoils from the sublime immensities which, as Johnson said, were Milton's element, and worries how such 'a vast expense of Mind' can be furnished. Milton for all his amplitude has already subjected his vision to a comfortable diminishment by enfolding it, as Marvell says, 'in slender Book'; Marvell shrinks that book further by praising it in the rhyming couplets which it refuses. Though Milton can do without the assistance of rhyme, Marvell needs it: the couplet restores to him the harmonic speech of paradise and is indeed, in its insulated enclosure and completeness, a small and still inviolate paradise. Milton's own intended flight had been antigravitational, soaring beyond the earth's lowly grasp. Marvell's most admiring and yet most charmingly impertinent joke is to rescue him from those infinite spaces of the upper air and release him into his own ornithological garden, where Marvell himself (pluming his soul like a bird in another poem) would wish to harbour:

> The *Bird* nam'd from that *Paradise* you sing
> So never Flags, but alwaies keeps on Wing.

And even so, Milton's soaring is seen by Marvell as the consequence of a handicap. The bird of paradise was fabled to have no feet; it therefore had no choice but to be forever in flight. Marvell's own longing is more cosily earthbound: to be housed and nestled, like the bees inside the flowers or the chaste, billetted pearls in 'Upon Appleton House'; his paradises within are more snugly anchored than Milton's, and the treasury which stores them is not (as in Peter Sterry's comment) the rectified mind but the fertile arboretum of the body.

Under cover of his praise for the poem, Marvell has subtly altered Milton's theology and his poetic ambition. He has in fact inverted the Miltonic universe, which is as much a literary polity as a map of the creation. Thomas Hobbes, in his answer to Davenant's theory of epic, divided the world into three regions, 'Celestial, Aerial and Terrestrial'. To these elemental realms correspond the three divisions of mankind, court, city and country. Princes and men of power, Hobbes argues, have 'a lustre and influence upon the rest of men resembling that of the heavens'. City-dwellers, inconstant and vexed in their humours, share the distempers of the intermediate sector, 'the mobility, blustering and impurity of the Aire'. Pastoral is the basement of this universe, and the dull plainness of rural people 'endures comparison with the earth they labour'. This is the hierarchical structure of *Paradise Lost*: heaven is a ceremonious court, hell a populous city, congested in Pandemonium (so that Satan trespassing on earth is an urban cad trying his luck with the credulous bucolic girls), and paradise is an agricultural fief. But Marvell sees the vertical system from upside-down. He does not aspire to the sky; he wants instead to up-end himself and be rooted in earth, entangled with vines and tumbling on grass in 'The Garden', planted head first as 'an inverted Tree' in 'Upon Appleton House', or sharing the antipodean topsyturvydom of the salmon fishers in the same poem who 'shod their *Heads* in their *Canoos*'. So for him the pastoral is the primary existence, and the form most lyrically tenacious of paradise.

Cromwell in Marvell's 'Horatian Ode' (1650) has had the tenacity to quit that garden and to embark upon the sublime, altitudinous career of Milton's aerodynamic Satan. At first he is a rural Adam, reserved in 'his private Gardens' attending to his Bergamot pears; but he is ambitious to exercise an epic heroism, which requires the garden's destruction, or (as when he traps King Charles I in 'Caresbrooks narrow case' or plummets like the falcon onto the territories which are his prey) its conversion into a place of political warfare and carnage. He demands the same desecration from the poet, who must quit the dreaming privacy of the lyric for the public and official pronouncements of the ode. Milton in 'Lycidas' apologises for his premature ravaging of the garden where he had been content to spend his poetic apprenticeship. Marvell is goaded to the composition of the ode by a ruder conscription and must, he says, buckle on his armour.

While Cromwell, lightning-like, recaptures that stratosphere which belongs, in Hobbes's theory, to 'men of conspicuous power, anciently called heroes', the references of Marvell's poem remain obstinately and insidiously pastoral. The terrorised country has taken to camouflage, with Cromwell's victims concealing themselves in the anonymity of landscape. The Pict adopts the shelter of his plaid and parti-coloured mind; King Charles's resignation of life is a grateful submission to pastoral ease, laying his head on the block as if on a bed. 'The Garden', too, finds in the pastoral a relief from the military or political exertions of epic (where men grapple for 'the Palm, the Oke, or Bayes') and the erotic strife of romance. Imparadised in that garden, where the grapes press themselves into his mouth and the peaches are his tempters, Marvell enjoys a life of the gratified and glutted senses. Though he experiments with three different theological rationalisations of his state—mystic in the poem's sixth stanza, Platonic in its seventh, Christian in its eighth—he acknowledges by the facetiousness of his tone the irrelevance of understanding. The garden cannot be interpreted, because to do so is to conspire at its annihilation. Yeats's metonym for the failure of poetic joy is 'The Garden died'. If Marvell persists in trying to comprehend the place, he will be expelled from it. Its only explanation is a self-image: the floral clock, which tells a time of its own, unsynchronised with the exhausting, run-down history of the world elsewhere. And the gardener who devised that dial is Marvell's own self-image, for a poem's responsibility is the horticultural tending of an inner and idiosyncratic paradise—a grotto for Pope with his small sheltering excavation at Twickenham; a bower of quietness, florally binding us to the earth, for Keats in *Endymion*.

Milton must atone for the fall by strenuous argument. Marvell can overcome it by lyrical reverie. In one of his astutest interferences with Milton's myth, he suggests that the fall was caused by the mind's awakening in the hitherto contented and luxuriant body. Rather than enabling us to reach up to our forfeited divinity, the intellect has estranged us from the society of the plants and animals. To regain paradise would be to grow back into that condition of vegetable, vegetative love. This is the body's accusation against the soul in their 'Dialogue'. The soul has persecuted the body in which it lodges and, the more readily to arrive at extrusion from it in death, has betrayed it into sin. The body's argument is nature's protest against culture. We can fall only if we are foolhardy enough to rise:

> What but a Soul could have the wit
> To build me up for Sin so fit?
> So Architects do square and hew,
> Green Trees that in the Forest grew.

'The Mower against Gardens' reads even the Miltonic paradise as a perversion of fallen imagination—man's punishment of nature for his own crime. The horticultural régime of Adam and Eve meddles with nature's irregularity and arranges mixed marriages between the species. They castigate and cut back the pampered boughs of fruit trees, or persuade the vine to wed the elm. It is these seductions or allurements to which the Mower objects, a grafting or miscegenating which teaches nature guile and dissimulation. In gardens, statues deputise for the banished gods; the deities themselves have fled to the wild and still innocent fields beyond their bounds. Only the spiritual conceit of the settlers in 'Bermudas' make them consider their island a heaven on earth for the elect. Marvell's parentheses adroitly frame their satisfaction at their own good fortune

> He cast (of which we rather boast)
> The Gospels Pearl upon our Coast

and beg leave to doubt the efficacy of the thanksgiving song which they send booming first to heaven's vault, that Miltonic acoustic roof, from where it

> . . . thence (perhaps) rebounding, may
> Eccho beyond the *Mexique Bay*.

Meanwhile the Bermudans are misreading Milton to suit themselves. They ornithologise the angels, as Marvell was to do with Milton himself, and instead of ministers have fowls which daily visit them through the air. The apple in this place of luxury is embargoed because of its expense, not because of its symbolic meaning: Bermudan pineapples are 'of such a price, / No tree could ever bear them twice.' Adam and Eve must work to tend their garden and to gather from it the chastely healthful salad they serve to Raphael. The Bermudans need not bestir themselves to earn these benefits, since they are overwhelmed by delicacies:

> He makes the Figs our mouths to meet;
> And throws the Melons at our feet.

This paradise is an extraterritorial version of the Elizabethan banquet of sense—an appetitive orgy catering to the greed of childhood, or of poetry.

　　To rid paradise of the abrasions of adulthood, which must reconcile itself to sharing the world with others, Marvell, in another revision of Milton, specifies that he would prefer to enjoy it alone, with the child's ravenous solipsism, rather than suffer Eve to partition it. He alludes in 'The Garden' to the fable of an adrogynous Adam before the fall. The Spenserian hermaphrodite has grown beyond the polarities into which nature is fissured; the Marvellian androgyne yearns for a condition which precedes that division. Ultimately Marvell longs to escape from humanity and from its mental disquiets into the bliss of the vegetative state: to be a self-fertilising plant, procreating—as the mower complains of the cherry—without a sex. The same reprieve from the toils of identity and the limitations of singleness which the male envisages in the garden is offered to the female at Appleton House. The nuns who convert Isabella Thwaites offer her installation in a conventual garden where (in place of the melons, figs and peaches preferred elsewhere to the succulent male taste) the angels will shower lilies down on her, and where she will couch each night with a virgin likeness of herself. 'What need', as the unctuous Abbess puts it, 'is here of Man?' The more treacherous the persuasion is, the more illicitly desirable the fantasy seems, and Marvell's verse relishes the proscribed delight which it goes on, when Fairfax meets the Cistercians, to condemn.

'The *Nuns* smooth Tongue has suckt her in' has all the Marvellian pleasures in it: language as an oral sensation, a loquacious taste; paradise as an admission to the safe-keeping of the body, an engorgement—along with the pastes which the nuns mould as baits for exquisite palates—which seals one in a humid, tropical, internal garden. Eating, in 'The Nymph complaining for the death of her Faun', is the means of entry to this delicious paradise of shared guilt. The fawn's diet is of roses. It feeds on them 'until its Lips ev'n seem'd to bleed', and then it prints that floral gore on the nymph's mouth to seal their childishly erotic pact. While consuming roses, it beds itself on white banks of lilies. The nymph sees it as ensanguined innards with a blamelessly untainted outer skin, a parable of that corporeal Eden which for Marvell can be both corrupt and (because infantile) innocent—'Lilies without, Roses within'.

Close as he is to Milton, Marvell is encouraging poetry's controversion of him. Rather than a promulgation of religious truth, it will henceforward be a replacement for religion, with its own species of truth and its own definitions of holiness; rather than mapping a pre-existent creation, it will perform the miracle of creation over again. Poetry is our confident human invention of paradises from which no one will be able to expel us. Its gardens are inviolable because imaginary, even though (as Marianne Moore specified, thinking of Satan's disguise when he tempts the sleeping Eve in *Paradise Lost*) they have real toads in them.

Marvell's pastoral, in self-defence, can epically take up arms: Fairfax lays out the gardens at Appleton as a fortification of flowers, with blooms discharging cannonades of intoxicating odour. That regimented guard takes over from the cherubim with flaming swords placed by Milton at the gates of Eden when Adam and Eve are evicted. The Miltonic seraphs are there to keep us out; the Marvellian musketeers serve to police the fantasy's stockade and to keep us unmolested within it. Poetry's purpose, like that of gardening, is to delimit Edens for our own pleasure. Marvell at first sees the island kingdom as such a blessed place, fluvially holding the world at bay:

> Thou *Paradise* of four Seas,
> Which *Heaven* planted us to please.

But that national garden is mown, felled and ravished in the course of 'Upon Appleton House', and by the end of the poem the responsibility of denominating another smaller and safer preserve devolves on Marvell. The world's disorder obliges him to order for himself a 'lesser *World*', and he invests Appleton as

> *You Heaven's Center, Nature's Lap.*
> *And Paradice's only Map.*

His admission that this perfect world must be a lesser one is a significant scruple. After the macrocosm's failure—the unsettling of that domed universe which Milton builds and then consigns to slow perdition—poetry seeks salvation in microcosms, finding eternity englobed in a dew-drop, as Marvell does, or like Blake, even more minutely, in a grain of sand. Marvell's most physiologically comforting images are of such tight-fitting, enswathing fantasies, which close around and consolingly entrammel us, as the body does the soul: the world's cramped planisphere in 'The Definition of Love', the contracted fairy-ring in 'Damon the Mower', the cranial vault of Fairfax's house which corresponds to the low-roofed houses worn by tortoises or the shod heads of the fishermen carrying their canoes. Such diminutions are the wise responses of irony to the scary immensities of the Miltonic sublime. The sublime is our confrontation with the infinite spaces which are not us, that nowhere through which Satan recklessly voyages. The mind's grand expansion to take in that vastness begets an opposite reaction: a recoiling into and reclusion within ourselves, the ironist's glad awareness of our own precious limitedness. Hamlet identifies this sovereign mental terrain with a nutshell, Keats with the snail's horn, Marvell with the tortoise's shell. Sublimity is thrilled and challenged by vacuity; irony dreads it, and wants to fill up that airy nothingness. Edmund Burke also identified smallness and preciosity as qualities of the beautiful, as opposed to the hugeness of the sublime.

This is a law of nature for Marvell. It explains both the power vacuum which Cromwell repletes, because 'Nature . . . hateth emptiness', and the withdrawal of small animals into a world paradisially coextensive with their own organisms:

> No Creature loves an empty space;
> Their Bodies measure out their Place.

It is also an edict of his own poetic art. Poetry is made, as gardens are, by strict acts of enclosure. The danger of Cromwell is his refusal to be so circumscribed. Of the ambitious, Marvell says 'with such to inclose / Is more then to oppose'. The poem's achievement is to have confined him all the same within itself. There he is trapped for inspection and dissected by its tiny lines, a giant seen—in another reversal of the Miltonic and Galilean sublime—through the wrong end of the telescope. Marvell's versification manages these ellipses and elisions for him. For an ironist, whose aim is to minimise statement and maximise implication, less is more. Marvell's normative line therefore is not the pentameter but the tetrameter, and even this can be further abbreviated. The 'Horatian Ode' alternates between lines with four stresses and lines with three, and the shorter couplet always has the effect of tacitly reneging on some of what its predecessor has asserted:

> 'Tis Madness to resist or blame
> The force of angry Heavens flame

wonders at Cromwell as a natural portent; the next lines shift into another register and mutter their consent through clenched teeth—

> And, if we would speak true,
> Much to the Man is due

while the 'if' implies that Marvell has elsewhere been speaking diplomatically and untruthfully. His judgment of Cromwell has disappeared ironically between the lines of the poem, or into the gaps between those pairs of couplets, and it is this encoding of speech in formulae which makes the poem so political: it is about the uses of irony as an immunising ambiguity, since the 'Ode' can equally well be read as a royalist or as a republican work. Here the irony is a worldly diplomacy doling out compliments to both sides in turn. The 'Dialogue between the Resolved Soul and Created Pleasure' also understands the prudence of saying as little as possible. Pleasure is verbose, entreating in quatrains; the Soul, sagely taciturn, answers only in couplets. Its brevity, like Marvell's own, is an ironist's insurance.

As microcosms, the poems covet an intact circularity. Marvell makes mathematical diagrams of this ideal shape and charges his verse with working out the geometer's conundrum by warping straight lines into embracing curves. His metaphysically-argued 'Definition of Love' extends the verses indefinitely until they circumnavigate the world:

> As Lines so Loves *oblique* may well
> Themselves in every Angle greet:
> But ours so truly *Paralel*,
> Though infinite can never meet.

Donne's compasses strain towards erection and reunion; Marvell is happy with this frustrating parallelism, a version of the unconsummated, vegetating idyll of which 'To His Coy Mistress' dreams. His geometry is also a mathematical stratagem of irony. The ironist's statements have an innocuous literal truth and a more insidious life of suggestion, but the two senses need never intersect. The alternating couplets of the 'Horatian Ode' resemble those parallel discourses, the one tamely overt, the other more dangerous but guarded by its inexplicitness; the one praising Cromwell, the other blaming him: thus the poem's penultimate couplet sees him as a spiritual warrior raising his sword's cruciform hilt against bogeys while its terse final couplet, innocently professing unawareness of contradiction, can hint that he is a tyrant and a Machiavel. The thought here engages in a perilous balancing-act, shifting sideways and back and forth to ensure that its weight is equitably distributed.

Despite this politic construction with its lateral and circumspect meanings, Marvell's thoughts are mostly, as he says of the dew-drop with its fragile microcosm, 'circling' and self-enfolded, wrapped round into conciliatory non-sequiturs like that with which 'The Garden'—deciding that the best explanation of the place is not any mental extrapolation but an image made from its own substance, the floral dial—does not so much end as begin all over again. This for him is the appeal of the stanza, another device for a comforting enclosure. Made up of lines with four stresses or eight syllables, possessing perhaps four or eight lines, it is a square, bordered by fences as parallel as the perimeters in 'The Definition of Love'. But within that square Marvell houses a thought which goes round in a circle. Each of the stanzas in 'The Garden' is of this kind, brilliantly proving impossibilities or absurdities and wittily thinking its way to a point where thought is cancelled out in mystic nonsense. Thus lovers carve on trees the names of the trees themselves, not of mistresses, and the metamorphoses of the gods show them to have been infatuated by plants not human bodies. The mind arrives at transcendence and surcease when it finds within itself a replica for everything. Having overcome actuality, it can accomplish a fresh creation, in which mind has been submerged in body while intellect wears a physical camouflage,

> Annihilating all that's made
> To a green Thought in a green Shade.

This cancellation in the eighth stanza, fantasising about the androgynous Adam, performs the sleight-of-hand which is the formula of William Empson's pastoral, resolving the dual into single and the complex into the simple:

> Two Paradises 'twere in one
> To live in Paradise alone.

Marvell can afford in 'Upon Appleton House' to leave to others the chop-logical feat of fitting the circle into the quadrature, for his metrics have already done what mathematics cannot, fitting a circular proposition inside a squared stanza and demonstrating—as the undersized house at Appleton does—that greater things can be contained in lesser without constriction. Self-preservation means the forming of such a circle. The lovers are to make 'one Ball' of themselves in 'To His Coy Mistress', rolling up into it their strength and sweetness and employing it as a small planet to live in (another Edenic microcosm), a cannonade to assault an iron and restrictive existence, and a missile to overtake the sun. Granarying up its riches and fertilely occupying all the space available to it, the plumped-out circle even appears in Marvell's account of the Spanish fleet defeated by Admiral Blake at Teneriffe in 1657: 'Every capatious Gallions womb was fill'd' with plunder from the uterine earth of the New World. Marvell's imagination cannot help delighting in the idea of the enemy's spoils as an embryo, that curled and somnolent ball of nascent life.

The circle lodged in the sanctuary of the square can still expand beyond it. In Marvell there is a constant exchange between the ironic and the sublime, the microcosm and the macrocosm, Hamlet's nutshell and his kingdom of infinite space. 'To his Coy Mistress' begins with the mind's leisurely extension to fill up an eternity, and continues with its urgent retraction to concentrate on the present instant. The house at Appleton is equally versatile: though its straitening and narrowness make it secure and spiritually humbling, requiring genuflection from all who enter, and its whole purpose (like the sanctified enclosure of the nunnish life) is a snug and enwombing or imparadising containment, it can huff and puff to regain its lost magnitude when Fairfax enters:

> . . . where he comes the swelling Hall
> Stirs, and the *Square* grows *Spherical*;

and at the end of the poem the darkening hemisphere, whose alien distances trouble Donne and Pascal and challenge Milton's Satan to defiance, contrariwise contracts, closing over Marvell as shelteringly as the head-gear of the fishermen or the tortoises and sending him back to the yet smaller and more compact mental abode of the house.

Marvell's footnote to Milton is crucial, for after him the regaining of paradise is the mission of English poets, and the medium in which it is achieved is the lyric. Poetry is at once a reversion to Eden, and to infancy. Thomas Traherne, in succession to Marvell, takes over the Miltonic theology and derives from it a theory of imagination. In the world of dismal imperfection we have been thrust into, the poet's service to us is his recollection of what we have lost; he is the only unevicted Adam. Marvell may briefly imagine himself restored to paradise in his gardens, but Traherne seems never to have left it. Most of us desert it when we quit the body, ceasing to feel our lives in every limb, and take up residence in the head. Traherne, who possesses that 'more than usual organic sensibility' which Wordsworth took to be the primary gift of a poet, gives thanks for his tenancy of a body because he knows it to be his personal and unfallen garden.

The lyric is about that body's sensuous exploration of the world—the joys of ear or tongue as he says in 'The Salutation', or in 'The Odour' of smell. Our fall is the lapse into a depleted cerebral existence. As children, Traherne declares in 'Eden', we are granted 'a learned and a happy ignorance'. The poet must take care never to surrender that or outgrow it. He remains 'a little Adam in a Sphere', unconcerned with the obligations of adulthood and recapitulating only 'those Acts which Adam in his Innocence / Performed': seeing, prizing, loving, singing. The occupation of Adam and Eve before the fall has become a metaphor for an act of literary worship. Now, instead of cultivating their garden, they write (or incant) lyric poems. The lyric reads the world with the learned ignorance of Traherne's seraphic child; of Goethe's visionary waif Mignon in *Wilhelm Meister's Apprenticeship* (1796) who in her song 'None but the lonely heart' gazes homesick at the firmament and in another lyric wishes herself in the company of the angels who dwell there; or of Craig Raine's spaceman in 'A Martian Sends a Postcard Home' (1979), a heavenly being who has tumbled out of that beyond and reports back to it in the poem, interpreting water-closets as confessionals of weepy lamentation or telephones as snoring sleepers awoken by being tickled with one finger. Metaphor, branded as a satanic illusion by Milton, is the lyric's hopeful misrepresentation of reality. Traherne in 'Shadows in the Water' calls such verbal figurations sweet mistakes which though false intend a truth, because though they are unfaithful to visual reality—lovers are not compasses, nor toppled devils autumn leaves, nor flowers a volleying militia—they intuitively see into the meanings behind sight. Looking at reflections in the water, Traherne views nature upside down. The sky is beneath his feet, the land floats above him. His comical misapprehension keeps alive the wonder and bemusement of an eye seeing things for the first time.

With metaphor, the lyric renovates a sight grown stale and elderly. Again the origins of this world-view are in Milton: Eve looks down into the lake and sees there, to her amazement, another sky and another self. But Milton characteristically reproves such reflexivity as narcissism. A voice enjoins Eve to stop looking at herself since her shadow is fluctuant and unreliable ('With Thee it came and goes'), and sends her off to join Adam, in whose image she has been made. As the subordinate partner, she is merely a metaphor, a variant of the male; adhering to him and foregoing her admiration for her own image, she will be reattached to reality. The lyric is not so easily dissuaded. What if, it asks, the mirror-image were a higher truth? Then we ought not to leave the surface of the lake but focus our eyes to see through it. This is how Traherne views the world—through a glass, brightly. In childhood, he reports, 'the very Night to me was Bright'.

For Marvell, too, metaphor is an optic glass, a microscope to outwit the

Miltonic telescope, rendering the familiar strange. It is interposed between sight and insight, earth and heaven, throughout 'Upon Appleton House'. Maria is an Eve in love with the mirror's flattering reflection, and the limpid brook has been glazed over so that she can adore her own beauty. The water-meadows, 'as a *Chrystal Mirrour* slick', challenge all gazers with the image's perfecting of reality: nothing knows whether it is inside or out. The imagination conducts a passage through the looking-glass. The grazing cattle have vanished to the other side of this 'Landskip drawen in Looking-Glass' where they are diminished to a pimply size. But the microscope's minuteness opens out, with the customary Marvellian contraction and dilation of mind, into the telescope's interstellar enormities:

> Such Fleas, ere they approach the Eye,
> In multiplying Glasses lye.
> They feed so wide, so slowly move,
> As *Constellations* do above.

Marvell's mirror is an aesthetic apparatus, made for the framing of images. It turns everyone into a Narcissus. Even the sun pines to see itself shining in the water, yet fears (like primitives threatened by a camera) the robbery of its aura. Opaque, the Marvellian glass returns to the world a radiant, uprisen, perfected idea of itself. Traherne, however, values the mirroring water for its transparency. It is a window onto 'Another World', and the images he sees in it are the souls of material beings, trembling and shimmering there just beyond that 'thin Skin' of mortality on the surface: 'Our second Selvs those Shadows be.' The lyric's purpose, and the metaphor's, is to intimate immortality, to see through bodies into spirit, to vitrify what to the prosaic gaze is obtusely solid. As Traherne says in the finest of his *Meditations*, recalling the world's glory in his childhood, 'Som thing infinit Behind evry thing appeared.' That ulterior is the image, flaming through flesh and grime—the dust underfoot is gold, the frolicking children 'moving Jewels'.

'Certainly', Traherne declares, 'Adam in Paradice had not more sweet and Curious Apprehensions of the World, then I when I was a child.' He cites as well Christ's desire to be 'Born again and become a little Child that will enter into the Kingdom of Heaven'. Such second childhood is to him a definition of goodness; to the nineteenth century it is a definition of poetic genius, which according to Baudelaire was the recovery at will of the infant's ecstatic delight in the world. The poet is one who contrives not to grow up, and need never leave Eden. Blake inaugurates romanticism by returning poetry to its origins in the nursery rhyme and lullaby in his *Songs of Innocence* (1789). Traherne pleads for readmission to this inspired pre-existence in 'The Return':

> My early Tutor is the Womb;
> I still my Cradle lov.

Shelley, discussing the resuscitation of art in the classical revival, heretically divinises poetry by describing it as a fruit of paradise regained by a fortunate fall. He says that the poets of the Renaissance created 'a paradise . . . as out of the wrecks of Eden', but implies that they did so by succumbing to temptations, not avoiding them. Thus he quotes—in tribute to these poets—Dante's line about the adulterous compact of Paolo and Francesca da Rimini, seduced by their reading of a chivalric romance: '*Galeotto fù il libro, e chi lo scrisse*'. They fall, according to Dante's Christian dogma, because of an accursed book; in Shelley's romantic estimation, it is the same book which enables them to re-arise and reclaim the 'diviner world' annunciated by poetry.

The lyric quest for a regained infancy turns out, however, to be almost as anguished and disappointed as that for the paradise within promised by Michael. Wordsworth's 'Ode' in 1804 is a tragic report on his inability to rejuvenate himself. He uses the language of the Miltonic or Trahernian heaven—cataracts blow trumpets, the child's head is crowned with an aureole of godliness, the grass dazzles with splendour—but his own words, despite the hortatory power which belongs to an ode, cannot animate a moribund world. In contrast with the blithe Orphic conducting of nature by Milton's Adam and Eve, who can command

> Join voices all ye living Souls, ye Birds,
> That singing up to Heaven Gate ascend,
> Bear on your wings and in your notes his praise,

there is desperation rather than joy in Wordsworth's 'Then sing, ye Birds, sing, sing a joyous song!' since no bird sings at a poet's behest. The glass has clouded over. Wordsworth's nature is visionary only in its bleakness and (as he says in the 'Ode' of the setting sun) its mortal sobriety, which tell of God's withdrawal. Poetry takes up again the duty of accompanying Adam and Eve on their journey to death, and its images, instead of corresponding to eternities in Traherne's other world, have to be invested with a sorrowing human significance, like the 'violet by a mossy stone / Half hidden from the eye' with which Wordsworth compares the unknown and in any case dead Lucy, or 'the meanest flower that blows' with its prescriptions of 'Thoughts that do often lie too deep for tears.'

The search for lost time concludes in Edens of a genteel pastoral pederasty, innocently pre-pubescent. Traherne's cherubs become Lewis Carroll's little girls or J. M. Barrie's little boys. The Wonderland of Carroll's Alice and the Neverland of Barrie's Peter Pan are the secret and perverse gardens of a stunted romantic childhood.

Paradise regained in a country garden is the abiding English myth. In Carroll's entranced Oxford it is always, as he insisted in 1887, 'golden afternoon'. His fairyland of budding girls will remain untainted so long as little boys are excluded from it; conversely, in 1945 the adolescent Arcady of Christ

Church in Waugh's *Brideshead Revisited* recoils from what Charles Ryder calls 'a rabble of womankind' imported for the rowing regattas, 'an original fount of the grossest disturbance'. Carroll and Waugh located their retrievable paradise in Oxford. Barrie exiled his, calling it Neverland, the kingdom ruled by Peter Pan so long as he refuses to grow up. His island is circumnavigated by a crocodile which has swallowed an alarm clock: a ticking symbol of encroaching and retributive time. Inside the secret garden of Frances Hodgson Burnett's 1911 story there is a similar embargo on growth. She imagines the nesting robin's satisfaction in 'knowing that your Eggs were as safe as if they were locked in a bank vault'. These are eggs no fertilising worm will ever reach, testicles forever dissuaded from descending; assets conserved by never risking the expense of their spirit in a waste of shame. At best they will hatch Burnett's precocious prodigy, little Lord Fauntleroy. Barrie's map of the garden is also a prenatal one. He thought, as he said in a preface in 1913 to Ballantyne's *Coral Island*, that 'to be born is to be wrecked on an island': England itself is a floating garden on which we drift forsaken, castaway when forced out of the womb. In his *Peter Pan* novel he argued that we all have personal Neverlands, which are interchangeable. 'On these magic shores children at play are forever beaching their coracles. We too have been there; we can still hear the sound of the surf, though we shall land no more'—a painful paraphrase of Wordsworth's inland ocean, where the beached body yearns to repossess the ideality it enjoyed before its deathly birth into this world:

> Our Souls have sight of that immortal sea
> > Which brought us hither,
> > Can in a moment travel thither,
> And see the Children sport upon the shore,
> And hear the mighty waters rolling evermore.

J. A. Symonds, describing his infatuation with a choir-boy in 1858, notes the insularity of Arcadia: 'My love enisled me in an enchanted garden.' Is Neverland, then, the desert solitude of Crusoe? Symonds's phrase is sadder because its verb recollects Matthew Arnold's 'Yes! in the sea of life enisled' in the poem 'To Marguerite', where the grievingly insulated self yearns for the unifying continent from which it has been sundered: 'with echoing straits between us thrown, / . . . We mortal millions live *alone*.'

The prolonged infancy which to the seventeenth century is a metaphor for goodness, and to the nineteenth for genius, is to the twentieth century the name of a neurosis, and a particularly English one. Cyril Connolly called it the hankering after a permanent adolescence: H. G. Wells therefore debars the garden. The green door in the nondescript Kensington Street in 'The Door in the Wall' is a deathly temptation to Wells's hero, for the arbour behind it is a hide-out of 'translucent unreality'. T. S. Eliot, abstinently scrupulous, declines even to enter the rose-garden in 'Burnt Norton'.

Graham Greene finds that the garden has gone protectively underground. In his story 'Under the Garden' a cancer patient spurns surgery and returns to visit his childhood house. There as a boy he had written a story about a pirate cave on an island in a pond which his trusting imagination believed to be a lake. Exploring the place, he recalls the experience which provoked that fable. Under the garden he had stumbled, through the roots of a gnarled oak, into a catacomb of tunnels where he was held prisoner by a sappy, ageless gnome called Javitt and his consort Maria. These earthy deities, guardians of a mineral hoard, had educated him in the vices. Ensconced on an old lavatory seat, Javitt orated to the boy on the pullulation of his stools, and awarded him a golden chamber-pot to piddle in. His housekeeping, too, was cloacal: in a cess-pit beneath the lavatory seat—a soiled version of Alice's rabbit-hole, referred to by Greene as 'the great hole going down'—he stores tin cans of food, enough for several centuries. Greene acknowledges the extra-territorial situation of fantasy, deeming the imagination an off-shore island, when he says the boy's tale has been influenced by *Treasure Island* and *Coral Island*. But Ballantyne's atoll is launched on a psychic ocean. Could his story, Wildwitch wonders, 'have . . . accumulated year by year, like coral, in the sea of the unconscious around the original dream?' Imagination is a bog or sludge buried deep within us and within the earth, under the garden and under what atheists like Wildwitch's mother complacently call the real world. Wildwitch speaks of himself dredging up sentences as he remembers. This is why the golden po is so precious a trophy. It is the child's seat of imaginative absolutism; it means the same thing as the cradle in Wordsworth's 'Ode' or Fauntleroy's earldom. Its dark contents are the earth's deposit, the riches of an everlasting, gladly incontinent youth. Art is the gilding of our bodily refuse.

The anal bunker pays homage to its source in Milton when Wildwitch reads out from an old newspaper a paragraph about a garden fête and Javitt demands whether it was a good or an evil fate. The boy explains that it was not that kind of fate, but the old man is impenitent: 'This is an undergound fate we suffer from here, and that was a garden fate—but it all comes to the same fate in the end.' The pun gives access to another of Greene's corrupted Edens, the garden fête in the bombed Bloomsbury square where *The Ministry of Fear* (1943) begins. The double meaning of the word is made audible under the novel's first sentence. 'There was something about a fête which drew Arthur Rowe irresistibly', whereas of course it is fates of the oracular kind which are irresistible. The square sequesters an idyll inside its railings: 'The fête called him like innocence.' But it is an innocence already besmirched. The treasure-hunt is no game, and he is soon embroiled in a near-fatal plot. Entering the ludic arena, he steps 'joyfully back into adolescence, into childhood', and therefore into terrors he thought he had outgrown. The Mothers of the Free Nations (or Free Mothers), in aid of whom the event is organised, are not nurturing parents but sorceresses, and one of them—the necromancer Mrs Bellairs, who introduces Rowe to his fate by telling his fortune—pitches her tent in the place of excrement. In anticipation of the sewer-like realm beneath the garden, Greene locates the fortune-teller's booth in a corner of the square, where it can be mistaken for 'an impromptu outside lavatory'. The inculpation of the garden continues in the poems of Auden. The chairs are taken in from it, the football field is deluged, only ruined boys play there, and in 1936 in 'Detective Story' a body turns up in its shrubbery. Yet the whodunits that Auden symbolically located in this cosy landscape are themselves footnotes to *Paradise Lost* and its failed lyric hope: what are detective stories but fables of our guilt and common perdition?

— 17 —
Paradise Lost
and its Predestining

In literary history, Milton functions like his own all-overseeing God. It is as if his successors were his creations, and must either defer to him as believers in and imitators of him or else heretically defy him, though even then, parodying him, they all the same helplessly confirm his pre-emption of them. *Paradise Lost*, which contains and confounds its literary past, also determines its own literary future. It is a predestining poem.

Milton intends nothing less than a theoretical, theological authorising of literature. His *Areopagitica*, an essay of 1644 urging Parliament to abolish the licensing and censorship of books, is not quite the liberal plea it might seem, for it imposes on literature the onerous task of manifesting truth. Literature's development was in fact made possible by the opposite allegiance, to sly mockery of holy writ: the uprising of experience against authority in Chaucer. Milton objects to this association with fiction, fantasy, falsity. For him literature must be scriptural and veracious. Truth embodies itself in print and on paper as Christ did in flesh: she 'came once into the world', Milton says, 'with her divine master.' A book is a tabernacle for the soul, 'the precious life-blood of a master spirit, embalmed and treasured up to a purpose beyond life.' The writer's apostolic responsibility is to keep language and meanings pure, and to resist his form's fallen tendency towards fancy, surmise, the specious virtuosity of error. The reader inherits an equally stern task, since every text he confronts is a potential snare which he must test for its truthfulness and reject if it inclines to 'sin and falsity'. Milton declares in the *Areopagitica* that he 'cannot praise a fugitive and cloistered virtue', but his readers can discharge their obligations as warfaring Christians without quitting cloister or study, since their heroic skills are intellectual. The writer, combating the fallibility of his own medium, has taken over the role of his own epic protagonists. Milton's contemporary, Hobbes, concurs in the estimation that the mental life is a battle for truth. His autobiography describes his disagreements with geometers as passages of arms—'I resolved on fight, and in one moment scattered, slaughtered, routed countless foes'—while in *Leviathan* he bravely assails 'the vain and erroneous philosophy of the Greeks'. In 1650 Hobbes's *Answer to Davenant*, whose abortive epic *Gondibert* acknowledged a debt to him, proclaimed the heroic poet as a philosopher-king, himself 'a venerable and amiable image of heroic virtue'.

Given this power and pre-eminence—with Milton increasingly seen as his own poem's invincible hero—literature can advance only by rewriting him. Interpretation is at least a way of escaping from the authority of scripture by making it mean new things. Milton died in 1674; the same year Dryden prepared an operatic adaptation of *Paradise Lost*, called *The State of Innocence*, which begins English literature's long history of Miltonic revisionism.

Dryden's play invents the Milton who will dominate the eighteenth century: a reasonable theist, arguing from design and finding—in rhyming and self-evident couplets—whatever is to be right. Even while complimenting Milton in couplets, Marvell admits their inappropriateness to *Paradise Lost*. Dryden rewrites Milton into consonance with them. The couplet is his model of cosmic equilibrium, all its antitheses prudently weighed and apportioned. As a result, what is mentally or physically strenuous in Milton's epic is rendered glibly easy by the couplet's automatism, since one line's prophecy is promptly fulfilled by the line which answers it. This is how Lucifer commissions Pandemonium:

> All mines are ours, and gold above the rest:
> Let this be done; and quick as 'twas exprest.

There is a mercantile economy as well to the couplet, which by saving words spares time, money and the effortfulness of Milton. Lucifer has no need of the epic strenuousness of Milton's character, and prides himself on the corner-cutting ingenuity of his competition with God:

> Seducing man, I make his project vain,
> And in one hour destroy his six days' pain.

To the opera's humans, the couplet serves as a remonstrance to dutiful copulation. Adam pleads with Raphael for a partner, complaining that he alone is condemned to 'a barren sex, and single, of no use'; the angel at first hesitates, but Adam's couplets demonstrate that such complementary parity is in the nature of things, and make Raphael's eventual agreement inevitable.

Dryden's conversational casualness in verse is of course a boon, though it takes over English poetry at the expense of Milton's tenser manner. The adaptation is crucial to this transition because in revising Milton's language it sets Dryden's own verbal talent of discursiveness at the centre of Milton's universe and declares it to be the measure of a man. Oddly, considering it is an opera, *The State of Innocence* is a poem in praise of speech not song. It is less lyrical than *Paradise Lost* sometimes is, and also less argumentative. Its language is moderated by the sociability of what it calls 'discourse'. Adam, awakening, identifies himself as Cartesian man: 'that I am / I know, because I think.' The proof of his self-knowledge is his capacity to utter this formulation. Lucifer defines mankind as a talkative creature. Angels can intuit what is; men need to be persuaded, and must tentatively articulate the truths of their situation. Hence God's gift to them of speech. That power is the summit of

Adam's enumeration of his skills: 'I move, I see, I speak, discourse, and know.' Speech, when it is discourse (when rationalised, and readied for sharing with others in dialogue), is knowledge. Adam therefore calls speech 'the effect of reason', and the serpent's craftiest contention in its temptation of Eve is its claim that the apple has granted it the power of speech denied to other beasts. Having eaten, Lucifer says, he 'thought, spake, and reasoned'. In Milton's vertiginous universe, with its engulfing limbos and its leaps of faith, the couplet arrives as a safety-net, ensuring regularity by its imperturbable poise. It saves the poem's conclusion from tragedy by making the restoration of paradise sound as logically convenient and as instantaneous as a law of Newtonian physics: Raphael tells the culpable pair in Dryden's final lines to

> . . . part you hence in peace, and having mourned your sin,
> For outward Eden lost, find Paradise within

and, as with the erecting of Pandemonium, it is no sooner said than done.

The couplet's discursiveness is a polite skill, and it presents the fall of man as above all a social mishap not a metaphysical breach. Milton's characters soar and plummet through an infinite, airy space; Dryden's rise and sink on a social scale. Lucifer and Adam are both restless *arrivistes*. Lucifer speaks of climbing 'to o'erleap the ethereal fence' and despises petty man as 'my upstart rival'. Yet to Eve he speaks of divinity as a rung on a ladder of self-promotion: 'As I gained reason, you shall godhead gain.' Gabriel's exposition of nature points out the orderly necessity of these motions, which are not elemental impulses but personal careers of overweening ambition and backsliding disgrace: 'light things mount, and heavy downward go.' Gravity itself in Dryden's world is a steadying social agency, and the couplet is in league with it, as conservative in its metrics as in its ethics because it seeks the conservation of those energies which Milton bravely puts at risk. *Paradise Lost* is becoming, despite itself, an Augustan poem, and when Raphael surveys the multitudinous miseries of the fallen world the couplet's abbreviation gives him the judicial finality of the eighteenth-century satirist, pondering like Johnson the vanity of human ways and wishes. He has no need of Miltonic vision; he can dispose of mankind by categorising its species of miscreants, and he indicates to Adam

> Those who, by lingering sickness, lose their breath;
> And those who, by despair, suborn their death.

Paradise Lost functions as a surrogate typology—a source for all the literature which follows it, as the scripture had been for the literature preceding it and for Milton's poem itself. The Bible is a store of narrative types which, adumbrated in the Old Testament, are recapitulated in the New and then multifariously recur as the components of all later human stories. *Paradise Lost* in the same way begets sequels, because the story it tells is the prototype for every story, and one of the first works to identify itself as the offspring of

Milton is in fact about the very process of typological procreation. It is Dryden's superb *Absalom and Achitophel* (1681–2), which at once employs the Bible and Milton as the types behind its satiric allegory: Shaftesbury endeavouring to exclude the eventual James II from the royal succession in favour of the Duke of Monmouth is the biblical Achitophel to Monmouth's credulous Absalom, and also an insinuating Satan to Monmouth's Adam.

Concerned as it is with succession, Dryden's poem confronts the promiscuity of typology. Its David—King Charles II, who acknowledged fourteen illegitimate children, among them Monmouth—has spent his seed lavishly and 'scattered his Maker's Image through the Land'. Achitophel argues that ''Tis Nature's trick to Propagate her Kind': our elders fancy they will live on in us. But David knows that offspring are unaccountable, and may well be invidious parodies of their forebears. In talking of his parental dismay at Absalom's treachery, he is discussing the filial relation of *Absalom and Achitophel* to *Paradise Lost*, for just as Milton's heaven is misbegotten in his hell, so Milton's epic is parodied here as satire, and the deicide of the devils is typologically mimicked by the attempted regicide of Dryden's politicians. *Paradise Lost* has been delivered of a litter which disgraces it. Dryden's poem is populated by the spawn of Milton's Pandemonium. During Shimei's tenure of office, he notes, 'the Sons of *Belial* had a glorious Time'. *Absalom and Achitophel* is about a trumped-up and factitious plot (the so-called Popish Plot of 1678–9 to assassinate Charles II) and it sees all plots as a typological progeny, over-abundant and unworthy of their maker, like David's bastards. The plots it criticises—'true or false', they are the necessary fuel for political discontents—are literary as much as political. Is Corah, who from

> His Memory, miraculously great,
> Could Plots, exceeding man's belief, repeat;
> Which, therefore cannot be accounted Lies,
> For humane Wit could never such devise

a tattling schemer or a bardic creator? In a prologue addressed to the University of Oxford, Dryden equates plots with dissidence, as if all narrative were a disfiguring of scriptural type, under the devil's patronage:

> Discord, and Plots which have undone our Age
> With the same ruine, have o'erwhelm'd the stage;

and David might be surveying the babbling abundance of literary actions, all cancelling each other out and all predestined to a bad end, when he describes the plots and treason which threaten him as another parodic progeny, 'Unsatiate as the barren Womb or Grave.'

In the devilish typology which derives from *Paradise Lost*, plots get incestuously entangled like the troilist ménage of Satan with Sin and Death in

Milton's poem. Remembering that triangle, and the tendency of fictions to go on reproducing themselves, David prophesies that the plotters will not rest

> Till Viper-like their Mother Plot they tear:
> And suck for Nutriment that bloody gore
> Which was their Principle of Life before.

Thus literature battens on its own leavings, and its history resembles that of a chain-letter, or a lie more preposterously inflated and multiplied by each person who repeats it. Dryden admits his own parasitism on Milton, and his bastardising of that parental source. This is why, whereas Milton asks his muse to sustain him for no middle flight, Dryden restricts himself to a humbler altitude:

> Here stop my Muse, here cease thy painfull flight;
> No Pinions can pursue Immortal height.

For his purpose is, as he realises, a satiric inversion of Milton's epic one. Epic wants to consecrate names, to engrave them in stone and ensure them immortality. It is a poetic mode of ancestor-worship. But satire is the genre of an absurd ignominy: it wants the names it names to perish, and its catalogue of factious Whigs is 'below the Dignity of Verse' because these creatures are as unmemorable as Pope's dunces. If it keeps someone alive, it is only to prolong forever his obloquy and ill-fame: thus it decides that

> . . . *Corah*, thou shalt from Oblivion pass;
> Erect thyself thou Monumental Brass.

MacFlecknoe (1682) had applied this genealogy to the tradition of English poetry, which in each generation diminishes and trivialises the types it inherits. The poetaster Fleckno is as 'blest with issue of a large increase' as the sexually spendthrift David, but he nominates the dunce Shadwell as his legitimate successor, declaring 'Heywood and Shirley were but Types of thee.'

Even works which precede *Paradise Lost* are awarded by Dryden a backdated cognizance of Milton. As part of his project to supply English literature with a classical curriculum, Dryden was a conscientious translator—of Homer, Virgil, Ovid and Boccaccio, of Shakespeare and Milton (in his adaptations) and of Chaucer. 'The Cock and the Fox', his version of 'The Nun's Priest's Tale' in *Fables Ancient and Modern* (1700), is a work of impudent anachronism, cleverly conflating Chaucer and Milton. For the most part it is meticulously faithful to its source, but a translation whose comic point hinges on a mistranslation—Chanticleer's cocky incomprehension of the Latin tag misogynistically assigning blame for the loss of paradise, '*in Principio, | Mulier est hominis confusio*'—can be assumed to have intentions other than a slavish redaction. Dryden has made of Chaucer's anecdote an essay on man, the essential link between Milton's epic and Pope's treatment of the fall as a fault in manners, a sort of spiritual social climbing whereby men aspire to be angels and angels gods.

Coming after Milton, Dryden's Chaucer cannot help but take him into account. Therefore the fox's invasion of the barnyard, sneaking through the hedge and leaping over the fence into what Dryden Miltonically calls 'the forbidden Ground', inevitably suggests Satan's trespass in Eden, and Reynard's flattery situates Chanticleer in the awesomely vertical and bottomless universe of *Paradise Lost*: he says he took the cock's Orpheus-like crowing for

> The Song as of an Angel in the Yard:
> A Song that wou'd have charm'd th' infernal Gods,
> And banish'd Horror from the dark Abodes.

The beast-fable naturally proposes a critique of man, because it sees him patronisingly from below as God views him from above. Chanticleer, who imagines himself Jove's masterpiece, rearranges the anthropocentric world to suit his own conceit. In a reflection on the beauties of their domain addressed to Dame Partlet, echoing Adam's account of paradise, he smiles to observe 'Man strutting on two Legs, and aping me!' Chaucer's warning against flatterers acquires extra force in this Miltonised context: it is an incitement to the original sin of proud disrespect for deity, and Dryden sees it taking captive

> ... Princes rais'd by Poets to the Gods,
> And *Alexander'd* up in lying Odes.

The fall is our repayment for the vice of reaching too high.

Satire labels this crime our presumption. Pope counselled man to study his own middling condition, and to 'presume not God to scan'. Milton shamelessly accused himself of this sublime importunity, having 'into the Heaven of Heavens . . . presumed, / An earthly guest.' Presumption, in its moral and its chronological senses, is exactly what Dryden's translation of Chaucer is about. For to presume is to be arrogantly over-confident, and also to anticipate. Dryden while reprobating the one in Chanticleer has encouraged the other in Chaucer, whose poem now presumes the eventual existence of *Paradise Lost*; and in order to establish this predictive insight, Dryden expands on Chaucer's learned disquisition about predestination—which worries whether the cock has been fated to encounter the fox by his bad dream—so as to include the theological exposition of the same subject by God in Book III of *Paradise Lost*. He ends with a summation of Milton's poem, and the introduction of that word which is the clue to his own augmentation of it: blaming women for the fall, Dryden asks

> For what the Devil had Their Sex to do,
> That, born to Folly, they presum'd to know,
> And could not see the Serpent in the Grass?

Then, because presumption refers as much to man getting above himself as to narrators getting ahead of themselves, he convicts himself in a pun of Chanticleer's fault and affects to regret the very presumptiveness which his poem, finding Milton latent in Chaucer, has so unexpectedly exhibited:

> But I my self presume, and let it pass.

When Milton's God, irritated beyond endurance by his creation, sends Sin and Death to lick up the filth of a world inured to evil, he gives notice of the punitive deity who is the arbiter of eighteenth-century satire. Swift impersonates Milton's angry God in his poem 'The Day of Judgement', which describes Jove's opening of graves and upbraiding of mankind. But since God is now an irate satirist, he cannot be bothered with the scrupulous allotment of penalties, and he dooms all alike:

> I to such Blockheads set my Wit!
> I damn such Fools!—Go, go, you're bit.

That final monosyllable snaps shut like a guillotine or like the jaws of Saturn devouring his young, and the rhyme is apposite. Wit means the capacity to bite; every joke is an execution. The satiric divinity rules the earth by showering down punishments on it: Swift's Laputans on their floating island, in *Gulliver's Travels* (1726), maintain subservience below by pelting the earth with great stones. Swift's office of satirist entitles him to take over God's prerogative of putting a stop to time and announcing doomsday. Gulliver on Glubbdubdrib summons the dead from their sleep, and with their aid demonstrates the human race's entire recorded history to be a squalid fraud. The Struldbrugs, who cannot die, reveal to him the misery of the deconsecrated world that God deserts in *Paradise Lost*: once sin has infected men, their days are a toilsome agony, from which death—as Michael explains to Adam—will offer merciful reprieve. Since paradise has been lost, its timelessness must be, as it is for the senile Struldbrugs, an incurable disease. Gulliver's shape-changings, too, are a human consequence of the physical and metaphoric mutability of Satan. When the gigantic king of Brobdingnag tells his minister, 'who waited behind him with a white Staff, near as tall as the Main-mast of the Royal *Sovereign*', that humans must be contemptible if they can be imitated by 'such diminutive insects' as Gulliver, Swift must be remembering Satan's spear, first a pine, then a mast, then a wand. Satan dwindles in the course of the poem from swaggering general to hissing serpent. Gulliver suffers the same humiliation, the penalty of human being: a potentate in Lilliput, a flea in Brobdingnag.

Like Milton, Swift fancies himself to have terminated literature, by his disabling parodies, along with history. The hack who writes the *Tale of a Tub* (1710) eschatalogically pretends to the power wielded by Milton, casting out all his predecessors as if they were the discredited gods of the 'Nativity Ode': 'I here think fit to lay hold on that great and honourable Privilege of being the

Last Writer; I claim an absolute Authority in Right, as the *freshest Modern*, which gives me a Despotick Power over all Authors before me.' The last writer's imagination is inevitably apocalyptic. Swift's impotent fury is a foretaste of the retribution which impends—the planetary collision predicted by the Laputan astrologers, the carnage of battle as gloatingly described by Gulliver to the Houyhnhnms. Even the detritus of an urban downpour is, in Swift's poem about a city shower, the leavings of a second Noah's deluge, sent to drown a putrid humanity:

> Sweepings from Butchers Stalls, Dung, Guts, and Blood,
> Drown'd Puppies, stinking Sprats, all drench'd in Mud,
> Dead Cats and Turnip-Tops come tumbling down the Flood.

Rejections of Milton can be effective only if they first adopt him as a model. This is the case with *The Decline and Fall of the Roman Empire*, which Gibbon began publishing in 1776. It is a work pledged to the revision and invalidation of Milton; yet this very ambition elects it as one of *Paradise Lost*'s lineal successors—an epic in which myth has ceded to history, poetry to prose, and providence to jurisprudence; a work in which secular enlightenment takes over from the Miltonic leap of faith into the unknown. Gibbon reads history as a disbeliever, noting that the advance of Bajazet 'was checked, not by the miraculous interposition of the apostle, not by a crusade of the Christian powers, but by a long and painful fit of the gout'. His refusal of faith, however, brings him closer to the ethic of epic heroism that Milton could have approached, for Gibbon's critique of the disintegrating Roman world-order blames the mental servility of Christianity, which has denied authentic epic status to *Paradise Lost*.

Milton's poem anticlassically prefers the pastoral meekness of Christ to Satan's military prowess. Gibbon backdates this choice and sees it as the fatal flaw in the classical system. Demoting the values of epic, the new religion leaves society unable to defend itself, and is responsible for the weakening of empire and the return of barbarism: 'The clergy successfully preached the doctrine of patience and pusillanimity; the active virtues of society were discouraged; and the last remains of military spirit were buried in the cloister.' This otherworldly infirmity means that, as places of truancy from epic preparedness, Milton's Eden is indistinguishable—so far as Gibbon is concerned—from Spenser's decadent Bower of Bliss, and in describing the pleasance of Daphne near Antioch he overlays the two, recalling Milton's garden in his account of the 'thousand streams of purest water' which 'preserved the verdure of the earth and the temperature of the air' and Spenser's in his remark that 'the senses were gratified with harmonious sounds and aromatic odours'. The superimposition is a classical judgement on English literature's romantic confusion of genres and of the moral behests which attach to them. The pastoral is treacherous, as religion is. Gibbon, after recording that girls in the grove shunned 'the folly of unseasonable coyness' (like Acrasia, or like Milton's Eve), notes that 'the soldier and the philosopher wisely avoided the temptation of this sensual paradise; where pleasure, assuming the character of religion, imperceptibly dissolved the firmness of manly virtue.' In a startling rationalisation of Milton, Gibbon blames the idea of paradise—whether in this sexual playground, or in religious retreats where 'the soldiers' pay was lavished on the useless multitudes of both sexes, who could only plead the merits of abstinence and charity'—for the loss of the world.

The romantics continue to use *Paradise Lost* typologically. Wordsworth's *Prelude* attempts to regain paradise in nature without benefit of clergy: the epic's final disappearance into pastoral. Though Milton needed to call on a muse for assistance, he is himself a muse or an enabling, vivifying holy spirit to his romantic successors. Keats, overcome with humbled hot flushes when in 1818 he sees a lock of Milton's hair, wants to become an extension of him as that hair was, a 'vassal of thy power'; Blake's *Milton* (1804–8) narrates the poet's outgrowing of his poem and his inspiriting entry into Blake. Keats senses Milton as an inherited infliction, deadening his own creativity; Blake copes with that pre-emption by a wittily voluntary hallucination. He claimed that he often received visits from Milton, with whom he debated. 'I tried to convince him he was wrong, but I could not succeed.' In 1825, he alleged, Milton had called on him and implored him to correct an error in *Paradise Lost*, 'in a poem or picture'. Blake huffily declined, saying 'I had my own duties to perform.'

Milton is begging him to assist the betrayal of *Paradise Lost*, by refuting its dogma about the sinfulness of sex. Blake, however, had already done the poem this revisionist service in *Milton*. Blake's created cosmos there is a rearrangement of Milton's. Since for Blake Milton was 'of the Devil's party without knowing it', the segregated realms of his universe must be dialectically conjoined: Blake's *Milton* is a marrying of heaven and hell, and in it Milton admits as emanations of himself both Christ (whose redemption of the world Milton re-enacts poetically when he awakens and implants eloquence in somnolent Albion, like the resurrected Arthur on whom Milton had considered writing an epic) and Satan (for Milton's voyage to earth, as Blake describes it, couples the incarnation with the devil's exploratory and subversive sortie). He also licenses Blake as his heir, physically entering him and empowering his song. While retaining the structure of Milton's world, Blake has romantically internalised it. In Blake the amplitude of Milton's baroque space with its aerial perspectives, its telescopic vistas, its yawning gulfs, undergoes a romantic contraction and introversion: the poem all happens within Blake's or Milton's head, and its spatial measure is the microscope, an infinitude of littleness. Blake declares that

> The nature of infinity is this: That every thing has its
> Own Vortex

and he vortically cramps the solid and monumental agents and objects of *Paradise Lost* until they are of a size to get inside him, like Milton himself gaining access to Blake by way of the foot. Blakean space implodes, 'opening interiorly into Jerusalem & Babylon' because those names stand in Blake's mythology not for actual places but for mental and physiological conditions. The geography of the poem is cranial—'It is a cavernous Earth / Of labyrinthine intricacy'—or even uterine: Blake explains that 'the nature of a Female Space' is that 'it shrinks the Organs / Of Life till they become Finite & Itself seems Infinite', and refers to his cosmos as a mundane egg, harbouring like a seed-pod a potential world whose generating Blake assists. Within the body or the head, there is an illimitable region of sensation and thought which Blake assumes as his empire. Leutha hides, she says, 'in Satan's inmost brain', and Blake, too, stands 'in Satan's bosom' and beholds its wastage. The paradise within is an <u>intromitted</u> Eden:

> . . . every Generated Body in its inward form
> Is a garden of delight.

In contrast with Milton's grand exteriorisation, whereby mental initiatives are expressed in an athletic trajectory of bodies (everyone in *Paradise Lost* flies or, like Milton himself, wants to), Blake's poem has a spectral and conceptual insubstantiality. His angels announce themselves to be 'not Individuals but States, Combinations of Individuals', and then—whereas Miltonic angels are housed in bodies, which they feed with vegetarian dinners and use for reproduction—they go on further to abstract themselves by specifying that these are 'States that are not, but ah! Seem to be.' Blake has made an allegory of Milton's poem. *Paradise Lost* itself is averse to allegory. It endeavours to prove things concretely and scientifically. Sin and Death therefore cannot only be ideas, as they would be in Spenser or Blake; they must be personages, too, familially entangled with Satan, and as if to demonstrate their substantiality Milton sets them to labour on the engineering of his cemented universe by making them build that causeway over Chaos—'a work too bulky', Johnson thought, 'for ideal architects'.

Blake anticipates here the problem of Keats's Miltonic imitations, which break off at points of metamorphorsis, when the epic physiques of Miltonic personages have to undergo a romantic mutation into ideas. Keats has no style to represent the abstracting change: *Hyperion* abruptly ends with Apollo's shriek as he gives birth to the prophetic idea of the new gods, and *The Fall of Hyperion* arrives at the same impasse when the ignited Hyperion, aflame with agony of evolution in himself, bursts out of his palace as if quitting the body. Between the two versions, Keats adopted apologetically the evasion more boldly used by Blake, representing the action as a vision conjured up by Moneta: it is as if all of *Paradise Lost* were made to happen on Michael's specular mount, as a dream or a nightmare, not (as Milton the rationalist insists) a verifiable history.

Blake's way is that of disincarnation. His beings are shadowy and notional, dreading the dead-end of embodiment: 'Take not the Human Form', Orc advises. The materiality of human form obscures the higher mission which is

> . . . . in fury of Poetic Inspiration
> To build the Universe stupendous, Mental forms Creating.

Blake aerates the massiveness of *Paradise Lost*, since his aim is to liberate the mental wraith caged, like one of Michelangelo's writhing slaves, inside the prison of stone (or flesh). He attributes this motive to his Milton, who contemplates

> The darken'd Urizen, as the sculptor silent stands before
> His forming image; he walks round it patient labouring.

Character is made sculpturally by deduction, not accumulation; by the systematic erosion of what is solid. It is the penetration of stone, the implantation of mind and of organs, enabling the sons of Ozoth to position themselves 'within the Optic Nerve'. The ultimate goal is entry into the imaginative territory beneath consciousness, and this in Milton's system is a satanic technique, for the devil seduces Eve by infecting her fancy when the reason is dormant. Here, too, Blake has redefined Satan's ploy as a poetic and godly prerogative. His allegory is a visionary creation possible only when reason is laid to sleep: the entire poem is a messianic reverie. The peace of his Edenic Beulah is preserved because it is a kingdom of somnolence, and in dreams contraries can confess, in imagistic couplings, their essential likeness. His allegory resembles somnambulism, or talking in your sleep. It is the mind's vigil in a body apparently inert. He describes Milton as a man who, dreaming, does not know his body is asleep but perceives it uprisen and adventuring with him through the phantasmagoria of speaking shadows.

Other romantics relocate the Miltonic precincts of grace and perdition within the body or the mind. Keats, who imagines heaven to be a regurgitation of earthly bliss, lulls and laps Endymion in a 'paradise of lips and eyes'; de Quincey narcotically transports himself to a hell within the head. That is where he lodges not only Milton but the Bible as well, for he believes 'that the dread book of account, which the Scriptures speak of, is, in fact, the mind itself of each individual'. His mind becomes the tributary for Miltonic evil: interpreting the poem, he is letting it take him over and speak through him. He is uniquely moved, he says, by 'the great harmonies of the Satanic speeches in *Paradise Regain'd*, when read aloud by myself'. Heaven and hell are ready to exchange places in their romantic marriage; de Quincey remembers the psychedelic inferno of opium as an off-limits Eden, its barred gates 'with dreadful faces thronged and fiery arms'. Milton's theology is being reinterpreted—now it is recomposed inside the romantic physique, or the romantic consciousness—as psychology. Beckford's *Vathek*, for instance, infantilises Milton. The loss of paradise is a juvenile trauma, a consequence of weaning. Sutlemene has an alimentary version of the Miltonic curses of work and death, denying meat to the children and condemning them to a diet of rice and fog-moistened bread. The moribund pre-Adamite sultans, who ruled the earth before the arrival of 'that contemptible being ye denominate the father of mankind', devalue and disprove Miltonic history. Beckford's most scurrilous revision of Milton consists in refusing to treat him with the high seriousness of moral adulthood. Satan, when encountered in the person of Eblis, does not even have the decadent refinement of Byron's gentlemanly devil in 'The Vision of Judgement'; he is simply a malign child, not the 'stupendous giant' Nouronihar expects, but a spoiled and satiated youth.

As well as determining the course of poetry, Milton directs the history of the novel. The cautious withdrawal of his characters from the temptation of action and plot defines them as novelistic beings, martyrs to consciousness and its exacting self-inspections. Though named after one of Sidney's Arcadian heroines, Richardson's Pamela is also the Lady from *Comus*, whose moral superiority depends on her refusal to yield to Mr B's enticements. The Lady's virtue is rewarded with celestial enthronement, Pamela's with social advantage and financial enrichment: Richardson has acclimatised Milton to a venal and intrigue-ridden human world. Clarissa's seducer Lovelace, a devil of debilitating energy who, after he has abducted her vows to be henceforth 'regardless . . . of anything but my own imperial will and pleasure', is placed by her within Milton's moral typology: she writes to him, 'you are Satan himself.' When Lovelace throws off his disguise and reveals himself to her at Hampstead, he paraphrases Milton's account of Satan reassuming his proper form when the angels discover him disguised as a toad, insinuating treachery into the mind of the sleeping Eve. By misquoting Milton, he demonstrates that the devil—the arch-patron of literary interpretation?—can cite scripture to his own guileful purpose: 'I unbuttoned . . . my cape, pulled off my flapped, slouched hat; I threw open my great-coat, and, like the devil in Milton [an odd comparison though!]

> I started up in my own form divine,
> Touch'd by the beam of her celestial eye,
> More potent than Ithuriel's spear!—'

He imagines he has divinised himself, enlisting the simile to make him an angel and replacing the retributive spear of Ithuriel, whose 'Touch of Celestial temper' routs him in the poem, with the goddess-like superintendence of Clarissa. But his pastiche of the lines hints at an inadvertent self-damnation. Lovelace would like to believe that, unwrapped, he shows off his 'form divine'; Milton's pretext, however, makes no mention of angelic origins and says instead, 'So started up in his own shape the Fiend.'

In *Sir Charles Grandison* (1753–4) Richardson attempts the most difficult of his homages to Milton—the study of a good man, indeed of Christ. Grandison's ethics are those of the Miltonic saviour, and he exerts a moral force which requires no support from arms. He is a hero of sanctified pastoral, and Harriet Byron reflects on this redemption of epic when she remarks of him, 'How much more glorious a character is that of *The Friend of Mankind*, than that of *The Conqueror of Nations*!' Proposing marriage to her, Grandison speaks with the deference of Milton's Son, reluctant to take on the duty of incarnation and heroic sacrifice which constitutes his debut in the world. 'My chief glory will be', he says, 'to behave commendably in the *private* life. I wish not to be a *public* man: and it must be a very particular call, for the Service of my King and Country united, that shall draw me out into public notice.' Here he adopts as his exemplar Christ's return to his mother's house and its privacy after his combat with the fiend in *Paradise Regain'd*. Harriet establishes Grandison's Christ-like infallibility by contrasting him with another, less austerely good Miltonic character. In a letter reflecting on his emotional attachment to Clementina, she surmises that 'had he been the first man, he would [not] have been so complaisant to his Eve as *Milton makes Adam*'. She imagines a Grandisonian revision of Milton's poem: Sir Charles with his usual superb condescension would have gallantly lamented his spouse's fall then, rather than choosing to share her fate, would have waited for the Almighty to annihilate Eve and supply him with a worthier helpmeet. Richardson's novel makes clear its derivation from Milton in a critical dispute near the beginning. Harriet recalls a debate between her scholarly godfather and a friend, who contended, with the aid of Pope's translation of the *Iliad*, that Homer exceeded Milton in sublimity. Mr Diane, however, convinces the doubter that 'the English poet as much as excelled the Grecian in the grandeur of his sentiments, as his subject, founded on the Christian system, surpasses the pagan.'

Allied as he is with Milton, Richardson himself must undergo romantic revision. Hazlitt in an essay on the insipidity of heroism in romance quotes a friend's squib predicting that 'Richardson would be surprised in the next world to find Lovelace in Heaven and Grandison in Hell'; and since the judgment involves a reappraisal of Milton, Hazlitt concludes his essay by nominating Satan as the true hero of *Paradise Lost*, because he is an energetic, avenging activist.

Grandison's rejection of public honours carries with it a manifesto for the novel. Mme de Staël's *Literature considered in relation to social institutions* in 1800 argues that the novelists have redefined the notions of virtue and responsibility which governed the ancient world and the classical literary genres. Classical man, existing in small communities, was a citizen sharing in the apportionment of power. In literature he therefore appears as a public achiever or actor, in epic or drama. Modern man understands liberty not as the chance to distinguish himself in the public space but as a guarantee of his privacy. The literary form which coincides with this introversion is the novel, and Madame de Staël nominates the English as its masters because as a race they have perfected this domestic cosiness. Cowper makes a mock-epic from his snug reclusion in *The Task* (1785), and replaces the embattled fort with the pampering sofa; English novels are to Mme de Staël works of a new morality, according to which 'obscure virtues and destinies can find grounds for exaltation and create a kind of heroism for themselves'.

In *Mansfield Park* Jane Austen, who made a theatrical version of *Grandison*, creates a devout and placid heroine in the tradition of Milton and Richardson, while George Eliot attempts a latter-day Grandison in her high-minded benefactor and racial liberator, Daniel Deronda. To the agnostic George Eliot, Richardson served as a substitute for Milton, and Deronda is a secular saint. Because the morality of *Grandison*, stressing love and service, is independent of any theological system, George Eliot was able ironically to profess herself a pious believer in the novel: in 1852 she wrote that 'I should hate to be the heathen that did not like that book.' *Grandison* is twice invoked in *Deronda* as a moral touchstone. Gwendolen Harleth on horseback resembles Harriet Byron; but the simile only disengages the two women and brands the serpentine Gwendolen as unfit to be Deronda's consort. Among her circle of female friends, the news of Gwendolen's engagement to Grandcourt makes 'real life as interesting as *Sir Charles Grandison*'. Here, too, an irony lies in wait. Whatever else *Grandison* might be, it is not interesting. Johnson remarked that if you read Richardson for the story you would end by hanging yourself—an appropriate verdict on such mental and spiritual obtuseness. This is what the girls have done: they read *Grandison* as a gossipy chronicle of flirtations, elopements, and duels, as epistolary chit-chat not as an exposition of goodness at its work in the world. It is as if they had insulted Milton by reading *Paradise Lost* as a fable.

As Adam leaves the garden, the cosmos of Milton's poem is dismantled behind him. Now instead of the vertical transactions of myth, permitting a sociable commerce between angels and men, there is only the horizontal track of history, unfurling forever into a bleak distance. Vision is succeeded by narration. Up to the flood, Michael permits Adam to see what will happen; beyond that, when the world is remade, he cannot be trusted to look into the future. Michael relates the rest, enjoining Adam to listen. Narrative alone can encompass the endless travail of history, that 'long succession' which must ensue before the kingdom without end is established. Therefore when Adam quits the garden's immortality he steps out from epic into novel. The 'wandring steps and slow' with which he and Eve embark on their journey set the novel's special, dogged pace—digressive, procrastinating, meandering, extending to fill up the many days which, as Michael explains, God has allotted to Adam as his natural term; for as the German romantic theorist Jean Paul

Richter says, just as the action of a drama cannot be too rapid, so a novel needs to be decelerated, meditatively becalmed.

The novel is the formal sequel to *Paradise Lost* because it is a region, as Georg Lukács remarks, of 'transcendental homelessness', like the world Adam and Eve go out into. Its vast meaninglessness appears to Thomas Hardy as Egdon Heath, to E. M. Forster as the chaotic city of Chandrapore in *A Passage to India*, muddied by a Ganges which 'happens not to be holy there', to D. H. Lawrence as 'the immense night which is roused and stirred for a brief while by the day, but which returns, and will remain at last eternal' and which threatens to consume Paul in *Sons and Lovers*. Most novels begin where Milton ends, with the evicted human creature's tentative advance into the vale of soul-making. Tom Jones, banished by Allworthy, 'began to debate with himself whither he should go. The world, as Milton phrases it, lay all before him.' Johnson in *Rasselas* registers a critique of this newly picaresque Adam: his hero is foolish enough to conspire discontentedly at an escape from paradise. In its happy valley, the prince is protected by 'fortresses of security'; the novel is for Johnson tantamount to a satanic temptation, enticing us into a life of mental restiveness and moral truancy. The loss and regaining of paradise is also the subject of Oliver Goldsmith's *The Vicar of Wakefield* (1766). After the abduction of Olivia, Dr Primrose gathers his remaining family to him as penitential Miltonic time overtakes them. Primrose calls the night 'the first of our real misfortunes'. *Emma* begins with a hustled ejection from paradise. In the familial Eden of Highbury, the heroine, blessed by every gift of nature, has passed 'nearly twenty-one years in the world with very little to distress or vex her'. She is indulged by her father and by Miss Taylor, and remembers still the embraces of her dead mother. Yet a serpent menaces her: wilfulness and conceit are, in Jane Austen's careful phrase, latent 'evils'. The novel starts at the moment when her garden of love has undergone its first, imperceptible fall into the difficult outer world of sexual maturity and divided loyalty. The loss of Miss Taylor to Mr Weston is Emma's first encounter with grief. Her sorrow is gentle, however, and induces no 'disagreeable consciousness'. Later she will pass through a loss of happiness which is the beginning of consciousness. Gloomily repenting her crime at Box Hill, she joins Adam and Eve at the gates of Eden to survey the dreary and deathly mileage ahead: 'she was wretched, and should probably find this day but the beginning of wretchedness.'

Thackeray in *Vanity Fair* situates the epilogue to *Paradise Lost* on the road between Chiswick and the Kensington turnpike. As Becky and Amelia graduate from the virginal haven of Miss Pinkerton's academy, he remarks that 'the world is before the two young ladies'—except that Becky, less innocent than he might be presuming, is not beginning the world at all but beginning it again. Novels amend Milton's chronology and query his eschatology: no end is definitive, nor is any beginning. Characters are forever, in the novelistic view of life, returning to origins and setting out once more, incorrigibly hopeful. When Sedley loses his fortune, he tells his wife 'We've got the world to begin over again, dear.' To such exiles from paradise, whether they are ejected angels or mere bankrupts, the novel offers a satanic counsel. It is cynically wise in advance about the ways of that world the characters must traverse, and Thackeray supplies tips about survival in it to Adamic readers, whom he refers to as 'persons commencing the world'. Milton presides over novelistic ends as well as over the form's false starts. The moving conclusion to *Little Dorrit* paraphrases his final lines as the heroine and Clennam leave the Marshalsea prison, carrying within them the paradise of their happiness. Before they can step out into the street, Dickens has—as if with the benefit of archangelic prophecy—previewed the rest of their careers, and prematurely brought their journey to a close; and when they are released, it is into a world which, as so often in novels, accords no respect to individual cases and in its populousness and preoccupation does not care whether this Adam and Eve live or die. The Marshalsea turnkeys are versions, too, of Spenser's Genius, admitting fledgling existences to an earth where they will germinate and soon enough perish. This is how Dickens foresees the novelistic future into which Dorrit and Clennam are ushered: 'They went quietly down into the roaring streets, inseparable and blessed; and as they passed along in sunshine and shade, the noisy and the eager, and the arrogant and the froward and the vain, fretted and chafed, and made their usual uproar.' Other novels end with the absconding of angels, who retire upwards from a world which does not deserve them—Clarissa; Millie Theale in *The Wings of the Dove*, folding her dove-wings over a guilty earth; Deronda abandoning Gwendolen to her own small realm.

Because *Paradise Lost* has predestined the writers who come after it, more and more of them find its final lines ironic: how can they derive consolation from what lies ahead of them, when Milton lies behind? Thus *Paradise Lost* begins to resemble a literary apocalypse, a premature terminus for the art, defining its last things. That is the use Mary Shelley makes of Milton in her novel *The Last Man* (1826), in which humanity is decimated by a plague and the earth restored to its aboriginal emptiness. The end of the world parodies its beginning (as the romantics, whose self-destructive careers Mary Shelley here reviews, parodied Milton). The last dying humans are free, as were their ancestors, to wander wherever they choose: 'the world is our country now'. The novel is written after the expiring of that long history inaugurated at the gates of Eden, and it recalls 'how supremely great man was. It is all over now. He is solitary; like our first parents expelled from Paradise, he looks backward towards the scene he has quitted. . . . the whole earth is before him, a wide desart.' Is that backward glance responsible for the nostalgic fiction which is the preferred tense of novels, the past historic?—a regaining of the lost past as if, impossibly, it were still the present. In his *Confessions of an English Opium-Eater*, de Quincey recalls lodging rent-free—or rather camping indoors—at a mansion in Soho owned but not inhabited by a dubious attorney. He shelters there with a forlorn girl, and they fabricate a Gothic castle in the middle of the city by playfully deliberating over their 'choice of rooms, or even of apartments'. De Quincey says '"The world was all before us", and we pitched our tent for the night in any spot we might fancy.' The Miltonic new beginning is a dead end. Or an ominous, premonitory obsequy. Jasper, in Dickens's *The Mystery of Edwin Drood*, who kills Drood, looks at him lounging so easily: 'The world is all before him where to choose. A life of stirring work and interest, a life of change and excitement, a life of domestic ease and love.' But will it be? Jasper himself curtails those choices, and murderously foreshortens that life.

The poets alter Milton's language, while the novelists venture apocryphal revisions of his fable. The instinct of competitiveness urges Tennyson to better him in 'Gareth and Lynette', one of the *Idylls of the King*. While Milton describes a landscape where 'th' *Etrurian* shades / High overarcht imbowr', Tennyson declares that the treble range of shields at Camelot 'high-arching overbrow'd the hearth'. Bower becomes brow, and the change allows Tennyson's line to claim that it is higher-browed than Milton's: allusion is contest. Browning adopts the novelistic kind of heresy in *The Ring and the Book*, imputing new motives to Milton's characters and that way disputing Milton's authority. Tertium Quid says Pompilia's tale is Eve's, then adds 'no, not Eve's': the novel must be a secular exception to the archetype. Therefore Tertium Quid contends that Eve remained unfallen because she owned her guilt in saying, 'The serpent tempted me and I did eat.' Her daughters, like Pompilia, are full of sly extenuations and plead instead

> 'Adam so starved me I was fain accept
> The apple any serpent pushed my way.'

If Eve's daughters are a delinquent offspring, then the novel equally is the truant and infidel child of the biblical epic. Thus the novel's heterodoxy provokes Lawrence to ever more daring glosses on Milton, his scriptural antecedent. Assuming that all women are versions of Eve, Paul in *Sons and Lovers* treats each one he encounters as a new occasion for recharacterising that parent. He accuses the coy Miriam of enjoying her guilt, and says he believes Eve obscenely relished it, too, as 'she went cowering out of Paradise'; making love with Clara in a field, he feels a childish fear, but just as Milton's guilt is, in Miriam, dismissed as a puritan hypocrisy, so Miltonic shame is defined now as a 'belief in life'. The fear is wonderment. Paul and Clara resemble 'Adam and Eve when they lost their innocence and realized the magnificence of the power which drove them out of Paradise.' That same power, not repentant renunciation of it, can restore them to the garden: Ursula in *The Rainbow* passes with Skrebensky into 'the pristine darkness of paradise, into the original immortality'. In *Lady Chatterley's Lover*, too, Eden is lost by the advent of moral consciousness, and coitally regained within the body. Dukes reinterprets the fable to propose that 'the mental life'—the knowledge symbolised by the sacrosanct fruit—is itself the enemy, and Mellors, remembering his first woman and her cultured talk, exonerates the phallic insinuator which assaults Eve: 'The serpent in the grass was sex. She somehow didn't have any.' When the impotent Sir Clifford goes riding in his wheel-chair, the crushed bracken, with the impudent insurgency of romantic Satanism, lifts 'its brown curled heads, like legions of young snakes with a new secret to whisper to Eve'. These allegorical confoundings of Milton are Lawrence's renewal of the text, for he sees the typology as a protracted weakening and extermination of a significance divine because biological. 'All the modern lot', says Mellors, 'get their real kick out of killing the old human feeling out of man, making mincemeat out of the old Adam and the old Eve.' Milton's couple are after all only anthropomorphised genitals.

James Joyce joins the two revisionisms—poetic rewriting of Milton's lines, novelistic correction of his mythology. His means of poetic subversion is the pun, which supplies Milton's most officially impeccable statements with a basement of double meaning. The theological categories cave in. Milton's fortunate fall or *felix culpa* undergoes a comic dislocation in *Finnegans Wake*. As 'O, felicious coolpose' it advertises a beauty shop: pulchritude has outgrown its sense of sin. As 'O foenix culprit!' it accuses Earwicker, who has committed a sexual misdemeanour in Phoenix Park in Dublin; but as 'O ferax cupla!' it is merely an amenity in the park itself, and 'Poor Felix Culapert!' is no thunderously admonishing God—rather he is the woebegone spirit-medium introduced by a radio announcer. The purpose of these quibbles is always seditious. Butt, denouncing the military rhetoric deployed at Sebastopol, 'his lewd brogue reciping his cheap cheateary gospels', rewrites the first line of *Paradise Lost* to justify his own and mankind's disobedience, both to God and to Milton: 'Of manifest 'tis obedience and the. Flute!' The note played by that flute is a ribald expletive. Joyce's puns dissemble geographically: Phoenix Park doubles as 'Edenborough', and the Serpentine is, to accommodate the tempter, transferred there from Kensington Gardens. Although Milton notices censoriously the erring of the river in his paradise, Joyce jovially misspells Ireland as 'Errorland' and sees it, in contrast to Milton's severe exclusions, as the homeland of all mythologies, Nordic as much as biblical, housing chivalric paladins along with Adams who are also Eddas: the wall predating the barbarians guarded, he says, 'a garthen of Odin and the lost paladys when all the eddams ended with aves'. If the word-play sounds like baby-talk then that is the point, for romanticism has redefined the loss of paradise as a psychological trauma not a moral fault: it means infancy outgrown. Thus the first fall in *Finnegans Wake* is Humpty Dumpty's, and later Glugg is 'eggspilled' from his home.

Milton's monitory parable changes into a nursery rhyme, and accordingly one of Eden's permutations, via a German pun, is into a zoo, an amusement park where children are taken for treats: the 'teargarten'. The terminal combat between Christ and Satan in *Paradise Regain'd* can therefore be replayed as a football game between adolescent teams from Oxford colleges, 'Christ's Church versus Bellial!' Paradise regained now means childhood recovered.

18

Acting and Being:
Comedy from Wycherley to Sheridan

The drama of the late seventeenth century is a logical though interrupted development from that of Ben Jonson. That development takes almost two centuries to complete itself: the comedy of revenge practised by Jonson's professional extortionists perfects a technique for taking to pieces the pretences on which character and society are fragilely founded, using the play—in a way which declares this tradition's denial of Shakespeare—as a synonym for their lack of truth; gradually, however, it begins to fear the consequences of its analytic exposure. As the drama continues into the eighteenth century its cynicism is checked by a benign and philanthropic sentimentality. Mitigated by the values of a new romanticism, the tradition ends in Sheridan.

Characters like Wycherley's Horner in *The Country Wife* (1675) or Congreve's Maskwell in *The Double-Dealer* (1693) are latter-day vindictive intelligencers, trained by Iago, Volpone and Mosca. Horner's pretended self-neutering is his vendetta against women but also against himself and the obscenity of his own human nature. Like Jaques he is a case-study of the satirist's conversion of love into hatred and (when the profession is taken up by Milton's Satan) of good into evil: 'Since I can't love 'em', Horner says, he will 'be revenged on 'em.' Maskwell's virtuosity at dissimulation makes him the slickly empty epitome of theatrical counterfeit, unable any longer, like Iago improvising motives for his gratuitous malignancy, to discriminate between his emotions and the roles he affects. 'I have the same face, the same words and accents', he reflects, 'when I speak what I do think, and when I speak what I do not think—the very same.' His studied mockery of truth, like Horner's assumed impotence, marks his exemption from humanity: both exchange the life of being, doing and feeling for that of knowing, and they fall therefore under the patronage of Milton's Satan, whose revenge also presents itself as a disinterested pursuit of knowledge. Eve is corrupted when he arouses in her the sensual itch of curiosity. Satan establishes his revenge as an intellectual duty. It means for him the mind's seizure of power over nature. Like Satan, described by Milton as an urban sophisticate practising upon the guilelessness of rural women, Horner offers to the countrified Margery the corrupting bait of knowledge, and Maskwell, too, likes to imagine that he is doing his victims a favour by assisting their lapse from a mindless innocence: 'If they will not hear the serpent's hiss, they must be stung into experience.'

The same infernal aura attends Etherege's libertine Dorimant in *The Man of Mode* (1676). The orange-woman who serves as his procuress reports that a pious gentlewoman dreads him as 'an arrant devil' and, like Othello with Iago, 'should she see you . . . she would look if you had not a cloven foot.' Medley suggests that Mrs Loveit, scorned by Dorimant, has elected him as the devil who must purgatively torment her, and she, besotted, admits that, despite his demonism, 'he has something of the angel yet undefaced in him.' Lady Woodvill adds that 'he has a tongue . . . would tempt the angels to a second fall.'

The Country Wife begins with a scene derived from the Jonsonian and satanic promotion of satire to a course of medical and scientific investigation. Like Volpone vending his placebos or Subtle his alchemical trumperies, Horner consults a quack who, attesting to his venereal injury, will pimp for him. The physician is to be a helper of nature, not healing it but scourging and cauterising it, for Horner's own qualification as satirist is his immunity from emotional infection. He boasts of possessing a cure and 'an antidote for the future against that damned malady, and that worse distemper, love'. The play's language is knowingly pharmaceutical. When Pinchwife pretends that his wife has been stricken with smallpox, Mrs Dainty Fidget sagely boasts, 'I understand the disease.' The quack acknowledges Horner as a colleague, saying that they are both 'operators in physic', and deputes him to experiment with his new treatment—'now you shall be the doctor.'

The medical imposture establishes the naturalism which is Horner's austere ethical code. Edmund in *Lear*, satirically denying all authority except that of wit or appetite, declares his allegiance to Nature as his goddess. He means his own virulent nature, not a shared humanity. Assisting putrid nature as it undergoes the tutelage of the knife, Horner joins in Edmund's priesthood. He is offended by the solemn, pious feignings of society, and curses 'all that force nature, and would be still what she forbids 'em!' The epigrams he is fond of are statements of natural law, defying his victims to pretend that their own cases are exceptional. Pinchwife dreads this verbal habit because he senses in it the scientific and satiric reduction of individuals to categories, and of their predicaments to automatic and repetitious symptoms. When Horner opines that a 'grave circumspection in marrying a country wife, is like refusing a deceitful pampered Smithfield jade, to go and be cheated by a friend in the country', Pinchwife mutters 'A pox on him and his simile!' He rurally trusts the evidence of blood-line: 'At least we are a little surer of the breed there.' But to Horner breeding is a social cant and a pudic concealment of the nature whose venal and salacious instincts his similes propound.

When a character in Congreve attacks the addiction to similes—like Sir Sampson in *Love for Love* (1695) who growls at his son's servant, 'A pox confound your similitudes, sir'—it is because of their fatuity. The simile in Congreve is a character's claim to an emotion he does not deserve and cannot feel. Metaphor falsifies identity, and enables these people to misrepresent themselves. Lady Plyant in *The Double-Dealer* shrills that she has 'preserved myself, like a fair sheet of paper' as yet unblotted; her husband, rather than investigating the truth of the assertion, admires its expression and purrs connubially, 'she shall make a simile with any woman in England.' Horner's speech is not affectation but the denunciation of it. Similes discern shaming relationships between distinct groups of creatures, and make them equally subservient to the power of mind. Horner advises Pinchwife to keep a whore rather than marry because 'women . . . are like soldiers, made constant and loyal by good pay, rather than by oaths and covenants.' Lucy the free-thinking maid seeks to cure Alithea's affectations by applying accusative similes to her case. 'Marrying to increase love is like gaming to become rich', she says, and honour is 'a disease in the head, like the megrim or falling-sickness'. Alithea senses and warms to the treachery of the procedure: 'I find by your rhetoric you have been bribed to betray me.' As well as securing the mind's capitulation to the avid body, the epigrams achieve a systematic decipherment of society and its encoded untruths. Horner's disablement is calculated to effect this revelation: it will permit him to know women by translating their reactions to him. If they recoil from him, he will know them to be sexually susceptible, and will prosecute the advantage he has gained. Verbally he has the same power over all other categories of persons, simply negating the protestations of their social roles to arrive, by translation, at the truth about them. Thus he reasons that trustees or executors are cheats, jealous men are cuckolds, churchmen atheists, and wits bores.

The effect is of desecration and, as if in preparation for surgery, of denudation. Sir Jasper Fidget offers to utter 'the naked truth'; his wife forbids him to use that unseemly word. Mrs Squeamish, fending off the wits, says she would 'as soon look upon a picture of Adam and Eve, without fig-leaves, as upon you'. Horner's seduction of the ingenuous Eve who is Pinchwife's bride works by an exposure of mental as well as physical nakedness. Sex is the extension of her inquiry into the world and its arcane procedures: Pinchwife finds her, to his dismay, 'very inquisitive to know'. One thing she wants to know about is plays, and an essential stage in her defiling education comes when Horner teaches her that she, too, is performing in one and equips her to survive socially by practising deceit. Margery begs to be taken to the play or, failing that, to buy some play-texts from the bookseller in the New Exchange. Pinchwife superstitiously forbids both. The theatre is a school of moral and psychological malpractice. Wycherley puns on the theatrical and gaming meanings of 'play', and shows the theatre, like cards, to be an art of dissembling and bluff, of taking tricks by the ambiguous manipulation of words and faces. Margery is first tempted when a gallant admires her at the play; Sparkish, too, absurdly dreads the theatre as a pillory, where he will be burlesqued and thus cheapened and destroyed. Dorilant asks why, since he commissions pictorial effigies, he so fears a theatrical parody of himself, but Sparkish takes umbrage with good reason. Teaching you to act, as it does Margery, the theatre trains you in techniques for conducting social and marital war. But if you are acted—jeeringly impersonated like Sparkish or like the dancing cuckolds at the end—you have had your human reality stolen from you, and are no better than the buffoonish or bestial caricature you see.

The play is fascinated by signs, and by acting as a sign-language; and Horner (who opens a precise gap between seeming and being) instructs the characters in the unique sorcery of signification. Sparkish gossips of the best new signs on display in London and Margery, when allowed into the streets, marvels at the 'power of brave signs'. She sees what they represent, but does not perceive what they mean. Pinchwife dolefully glosses them: the Bull's Head, the Ram's Head and the Stag's Head, excitedly named by Margery, all denote horned creatures. The beginning of wisdom, however, is to recognise that the signs are cryptograms which mutely enunciate the reverse of what they purport to be advertising. Harcourt dissuades Alithea from Sparkish by arguing that 'marriage is rather a sign of interest than love' and Mrs Squeamish explains to Horner that the coy faces of women in boxes at the play are shields, signalling a readiness for erotic engagement. Once this rule is understood, the characters can fashion devices of their own, verbal and visual, to hide behind. Wycherley's equivalent to the Jonsonian engineer is the designer, the inventor of decorative false fronts. The quack asks Horner 'how fadges the new design?'; he asks the quack's opinion of his 'good design'; and Pinchwife pleads with him not to renew his designs on Margery. Having first stripped people naked, Horner than reclads them in a moral camouflage of his own devising. Thus he arranges for the image to take the place of the reality. He declares this as a visual preference when he consents to kiss Mrs Squeamish only after being bribed by the promise of her portrait miniature: 'I love a woman only in effigy, and good painting as much as I hate them.—. . . I could adore the devil well painted.' He remembers here, perhaps, Webster's devil in crystal, an earlier version of this entirely theatrical morality: in a play you are what you say you are, and what you appear to be; cosmetics or jewellery, like performance, beg the question of your actual, culpable identity. Mrs Squeamish reasons that 'the crime's the less when 'tis not known.' Verbally the same elision occurs in the play's innuendos. Its *double-entendres* are signs pointing to one thing but indicating another, like that precious store of Horner's china over which the women squabble. The danger of this translative idiom is that the metaphor may overtake its deviser or designer. Horner in the play does become what he pretends to be—a lamed satyr rendered sterile by his incapacity to feel; or a trinket mauled and manhandled by the female predators who assail him.

Our very systems of communication and representation condemn us. Hence Pinchwife's holy terror of the play, or Sparkish's condemnation of all books, booksellers and readers. The education of Margery is her downfall. Caliban swears that Prospero has taught him language, and his profit on it is that he knows how to curse; Margery, too, when she comes to London, learns how to speak and is thus emboldened to tell lies, how to write and is thus able to publish them. *The Country Wife* extends its analysis of acting and its frauds to take in the equally misleading sign-language of the words we transcribe. Sparkish correctly fears that 'a little reading or learning' makes women vexatious. When Pinchwife dictates to Margery the letter repulsing Horner, he instructs her in how to use its words against him. At first she cannot bear, she says, to write the filthy words of imprecation on which he insists, and discreetly omits them; in her revision of the letter, she applies them to her husband rather than her seducer. She learns at the same time the silent language of gesture, underhandedly exchanging letters or managing her own disguised delivery to Horner and dismissing her husband from Horner's lodgings by some 'signs with her hand'. Horner contemptuously pities Mrs Squeamish, who has not apprehended the symbolism of the china, for her 'innocent, literal understanding'. Margery's letter gets beyond the innocence of the literal: its two versions are text and subtext, the letter which denies and the spirit which invites. Horner, having received the latter version, can compliment it as if it were the former, telling the quack that it is the first honest and undissembling erotic document that ever was, and can assure Pinchwife that he will 'obey her letter to a tittle, and fulfill her desires, be they what they will'. When her forgery is discovered, Margery has the wit to pass it off as dictation from another: she wrote, she says, at Alithea's behest. The text thus becomes a dramatic speech, disowned by being put into another's mouth. She has learned already how to exploit the theatre's institutionalised truthlessness.

The triumph of the play's corruption of her comes when she discovers how to lie both in word and deed. The acquisition of this skill is her rite of admission to the world of the play, and to society. Pinchwife cannot believe that 'the changeling could . . . invent this lie'; but a lie is Margery's ultimate invention, and it allows her with a superb effrontery to hold together the society of the play by agreeing—after piteously feigning to heed the advice of Lucy and Horner and speak only the truth—with her husband's mistaken notion of her adventure.

The drama can go no further than Wycherley does in the anatomy of its own disingenuousness. The other comedies seem a reaction from *The Country Wife*'s cynical demonstration of the links between society and theatre, or between morals and acting. One symptom of that reaction is a withdrawal from London. Farquhar's *The Recruiting Officer* (1706) takes place in Shrewsbury, his *The Beaux-Stratagem* (1707) in Lichfield. That decampment is a retreat into a nature which Horner detests but which Farquhar finds benevolent and invokes (in contrast to Margery's insidious fictionalising) as the solvent of emotional and social quarrels. Cherry in *The Beaux-Stratagem* admits her father to be a rogue, and ponders the 'good nature' of her free-hearted mother.

Mrs Sullen in the same play, complaining of her enslavement to a boorish husband, dreams—almost like a Shakespearean heroine—of being relieved by the same agency, since 'nature is the first lawgiver'; and indeed a legal reprieve is rigged up in accordance with the promptings of nature, for Mrs Sullen is divorced by consent and freed to marry her suitor Archer.

Everywhere Farquhar attempts an amelioration of the form he inherits. Horner's clinical profession is briefly adopted by Mrs Sullen who, when a countrywoman seeks advice on the healing of her husband's sore leg, obeys Horner's policy of killing to cure and tells the woman to chop it off, fillet it, season and roast it. But her cannibalism is a joke. The woman has come to see Lady Bountiful, who is a sentimental not a satiric physician, prescribing homeopathic remedies. Lady Bountiful's medicaments are the charitable infusions of good nature, miracles which work, as Mrs Sullen suggests, because of the patient's faith in them. Lady Bountiful does not mind the aspersion: 'Fancy helps in some cases.' The spells she dispenses are the redemptive wishes of Shakespearean comedy, and she sends the countrywoman to the pantry to 'get your bellyful of victuals'. Mrs Sullen diagnoses Aimwell's case satirically—'Love is his distemper'—but, telling Dorinda that she must be his physician, admits the possibility of a sentimental and palliative cure. Farquhar's beaux are also mitigations of Wycherley's rake. They are aware of the expense and the destructiveness of unbridling appetite, and see obsessive indulgence as a self-murder: quitting London is their renunciation of Horner's example. In *Love for Love*, too, appetite is less the deranging compulsion of Horner and his women than an early stirring of an eighteenth-century epicureanism, urging all human bodies to claim as their due the right to life, liberty and the pursuit of a mild and civil happiness. Sir Sampson is affronted when his son's servant insists that he possesses the same appetites as his master, and requests funds for their succouring. The disinherited Valentine, asking for his legal patrimony, is simply demanding what a bountiful nature has promised him: 'Fortune was prevalent enough to supply all the necessities of my nature, if I had my right of inheritance.'

Archer's is a rational sensuousness, the good nature of the averagely sensual and sentimental man, midway between Horner and Sterne's Yorick in *A Sentimental Journey*: he wishes to keep all five senses keen, and will dispatch them to parties of pleasure only so long as there is no debility to be feared. Aimwell, less circumspect, suffers from a Shakespearean folly, and is the victim of his emotions. He prefers the country to the town because it is more ingenuously amorous. 'The fool', he tells Archer, 'in that passion shall outdo the knave at any time.' Archer amiably mocks him for a vulnerability which is a disqualification in the social world of Horner but a grace of spirit in the later plays, when comedy has been reconciled with nature and acting is no longer a falsification of self: 'You can't counterfeit the passion without feeling it.'

Archer's feat, impersonating an emotion which remains unfelt, is the devious power of the actor, responsible for the enrichment of Volpone and for the sexual victories of Horner. Shakespeare mistrusts those who are lords and owners of their faces, whose physiognomy is itself a mask. Farquhar's play rescues its characters from the theatrical expediency of dissimulation, and accredits their impostures as truth. Thus at its climax news arrives of the death of Aimwell's brother and his assumption of the title to which, in his masquerade with Archer, he had been only a performing pretender. Dorinda invests him with his new identity in words which close the gap, cruelly measured by Horner, between self and role: 'in short, sir, you are the person that you thought you counterfeited.'

Congreve arrives at the same closure in *Love for Love* where, in contrast with the secret sign-language of Horner and Margery, a lie is merely truth at one or two removes. Tattle, instructing the 'silly awkward country girl' Miss Prue in polite falsehoods, inveigles her into a companionable complicity whereby because each of them knows the other is lying they can converse in cipher. False is made true by a double translation: 'Your words', Tattle advises, 'must contradict your thoughts; but your actions may contradict your words.' Thus when he asks her if she loves him, she will deny it, so he can be sure that she does. Miss Prue, preferring these prevarications to 'our old-fashion'd country way of speaking one's mind', learns how to do the translating in the opposite direction. 'Must not you lie too?' she asks. Tattle agrees that he should, though he adds, 'but you must believe I speak truth.' Valentine's last and most desperate stratagem for the regaining of his fortune and Angelica is to affect a lunatic distraction. But again the pose entails a bold veracity, for in his ravings he speaks as Truth and denounces others for their lying. Forswearing the pretence with Angelica he urges her to 'think of leaving acting, and be our selves'. She concedes that she never loved him until he was mad: only by the cunning of that simulation was she assured of his rationality. His acting has been a tactical version of one of those similitudes in which the language of these plays abounds, and which Brisk in *The Double-Dealer* pedantically corrects in Lady Froth's ridiculous poem—a metaphor for what he frustratedly feels but cannot openly avow.

In Vanbrugh's *Provok'd Wife* (1697) disputes are pacified by the intercession of a clement nature. The satiric penalty is once invoked, as in Mrs Sullen's recommended amputation—Lady Brute commits her sot of a husband to the laving and chastising care of Razor, saying 'scour him clean, with a little soap and sand'—but more often sentiment mediates. When Belinda and Lady Brute fall to exchanging insults, they resolve to forgive each other because 'good nature may do much', and Sir John Brute similarly capitulates to common sense and forgives and forgets the intrigues against him. Performance, no longer a lying defamation of nature as in Wycherley, is the imaginative rehearsal of possible courses of action which nature prompts but reason censures. Lady Brute determines, as a revenge on her husband, 'to play the downright wife, and cuckold him' or to 'play the fool' (as she tells Belinda) 'and jest on, till I make you begin to think I am in earnest'. Playing, however, is her insurance against having actually to cuckold him; jest is the defensive device of an earnest hope for affection and respect. Drama does not mean here a deception of others: it is the reflex of a yearning to be what we are not, to be sentimentally self-deceived, to play-act to the admiring audience reflected in the mirror. Lady Fanciful, seen at first embellishing her image in the glass, is named after this dramatic motive, and all her masked or disguised interventions are trials of a self she exercises while doting on its reflection. Heartfree is wrong, at their rendezvous in St James's Park, to accuse her so sententiously of ingratitude to nature in remaking herself as art, for artificiality is in her case the need (and, when she assumes a false face, the convenient alibi) of an unquiet and palpitating nature. She has already made this clear in a scene of catechism with her French maid. Lady Fanciful debates whether to go to the secret appointment in the park. Nature prompts her to do so, reason holds her back. In an exchange which recalls the temptation and fall of Margery, she reminds herself that curiosity is a wicked devil—the fiendish Horner lured Margery with the offer of a forbidden knowledge—and ruined our first parents. 'Elle a bien diverti leurs enfants', rejoins Mademoiselle. Hustling Lady Fanciful off, she explains her own code, which heeds nature rather than reason because 'my nature make me merry, my reason make me mad'.

Whereas Horner achieves a vindictive unriddling of society, which Margery assists by the initiative of her lie, Congreve in *The Way of the World* (1700) describes a society inextricably interknit, conjoined by kinship, affection and obligation, proof against any such alienating nihilism as Horner's. It is a society closer to that of the novel, where individuals are webbed together in co-operation and fellowship, than to the provisional, acted attachments of the earlier drama, and when the characters invoke the tag which is Congreve's title—as Fainall does wearily but not cynically, declaring himself able to cope with 'the ways of wedlock and this world' or accepting his humiliation as 'all in the way of the world', and as Mirabell does triumphantly when he reminds Fainall that ' 'tis *the way of the world*, sir; of the widows of the world'—they are validating that world and its ways and anticipating the novelistic wisdom of adjusting themselves to it, learning to tolerate its conditions.

Coriolanus's angry boast that there is a world elsewhere is the pride of dramatic character, since any place is a possible stage and can be made a sovereign realm of ego. But no alternative is available to Congreve's people. It is only to quieten the raging Mrs Marwood that Fainall promises her they will 'retire somewhere, anywhere, to another world', and when Lady Wishfort proposes to Mrs Marwood that they should 'leave the world, . . . and be shepherdesses', her companion reminds her that they have an intrigue in hand and lack the leisure to retreat. Even Waitwell's consummation must be adjourned, since Mirabell requires him to dispatch another errand. The characters, no matter how they may resent their mutual indebtedness, are contracted to each other and to the society from which they derive their being. Hence the play's network of overlapping relationships, the ties of family entwining with those of erotic interest. A liaison means admission to a tribe: Fainall warns Mirabell that if he marries Millamant he must own as his cousin Sir Wilfull Witwoud. The play's difficult exposition consists in the unfolding of these pre-existing affinities of kin, multiply attaching each person to every other one. Mentioning Sir Wilfull, Fainall grafts himself onto the same family tree, telling Mirabell 'he is half-brother to this Witwoud by a former wife, who was sister to my Lady Wishfort, my wife's mother.' A pretence, similarly, can be the means of a character's graduation into and ascent within society. Waitwell, impersonating Sir Rowland, marvels to find himself 'married, knighted and attended all in one day!' Though Witwoud affectedly disowns Sir Wilfull, reneging on the loyalty he owes to relations, he is fraternally unseverable from his fellow-fop Petulant, since—almost in the manner of a married couple—they have settled on a method of psychological team-work, completing each other's stories, knowing each other's secrets, and perpetually bickering in order to renew their solidarity and reaffirm their contract by making up. Witwoud explains that their animosity is 'like the falling out of lovers'. For purposes of intrigue, a brotherly compact is improvised between Sir Wilfull and Mirabell, who intend to travel together like Pylades and Orestes, and when Mirabell drops out of the agreement Sir Wilfull invites Witwoud and Petulant together to accompany him.

The vanity of character in Congreve is not an affair between oneself and the mirror but a matter of reciprocal and social affection. Petulant retains a consort of trulls whose job it is to go about bothering him in public places. At other times he will even 'call for himself, wait for himself, nay and what's more, not finding himself, sometimes leave a letter for himself': self-obsession, too, must be a love-affair, requited and certified by being publicly viewed. The characters are instinctive conveners of groups, societies fastened together by the sharing of secrets. The women have their sororities of cabal, the men the clubbable competitiveness of their games, like the cards at which Fainall and Mirabell play. In this already incestuous world of cliques and leagues and complementary associations, the possibility of adultery presents itself as almost the natural affinity of siblings. When Mrs Marwood slanders Mirabell, Fainall perceives that she is implying 'a fellow-feeling between my wife and him'. Married love, too, means a consolidation of friendship, a partnership which has as its purpose an adherence to and extension of families. Millamant longs for a feckless freedom—the liberty, as she says, to choose acquaintances as one does clothes—which can be exercised neither in society nor in love, and Mirabell's moralising aims to persuade her of her obligations to those who surround her. Her beauty, he says, is held in trust. It exists only within the charmed ambit of relationship; a lover awards it to her as a gift, and can despoil her of it by ceasing to admire her.

This is why their courtship ends contractually, with Mirabell's legalistic diminution of her dangerous and irresponsible freedom, and his extortion from her of a promise that she will breed. But for the same reason this understanding between them does not end the play. Another one and a half acts ensue, in which the emotional accord is socially ratified and economically subsidised. Though Mirabell and Millamant spell out the terms on which they will consent to be married, unwritten contracts are forever being exchanged by the characters, tested and revoked, and mercantile dealings, like erotic ones, are managed on a basis of trust and faith which affiances people to each other. Mrs Fainall, having been allocated a husband by Mirabell to conceal their prior attachment, insists that she should 'stand in some degree of credit' with him. That credit is the emotional allowance that others, in this delicate system of owed dues and recalled borrowings, generously make us, and when Lady Wishfort is planning revenge on Mirabell the worst she can think of is to 'spoil his credit with his tailor': to withdraw him from social and emotional currency. Gossip, too, like credit, is a social fund, another of the world's amiable, anthropological ways, since the fact that we are going to be chattered about reminds us of our common membership of the family of man. Mrs Marwood dissuades Lady Wishfort from taking her case against her daughter to the courts, because a worse judgement than the legal one will be the indiscreet communal ownership of the details—they will be bawled about by lawyers, annotated by 'young revellers of the Temple', regurgitated 'in Commons, or before drawers in an eating-house', and hawked by the sellers of scandal-sheets. Though Lady Wishfort dreads this outcome, it shows the play's gregarious world at work, interrelating people by the efficiency with which it makes public property of private distresses.

All the play's lines of familial and financial indebtedness converge on the tentacular matriarch Lady Wishfort, who is kept in reserve Congreve until a third of the way through but who has, in her absence, imposed her jealous sexual and economic will on them all. Beyond breeding as she is (in Mirabell's judgement), she craves a renewal of bodily power. She is the progenitor of the characters, seeing maternity as a reduplication of herself—'my child, bone of my bone, and flesh of my flesh, and as I may say, another me', she addresses Mrs Fainall—and also of the world into which she ushers them. She claims to have been her daughter's mould and pattern, 'after you were brought into the world'. Her phrase is exact: birth is an initiation into society, our debut in the world and our delivery into its ways. A larger world than that of the play's action lives noisily in her speech, which consists mostly (by contrast with the duels in dialogue of the other characters) of haranguing monologues, raucously sounding from the unkempt streets where she found Foible 'washing of old gause and weaving of dead hair, . . . and dining behind a traverse rag, in a shop no bigger than a bird-cage'; a rampant, raging language, the many-tongued voice of an entire society. Lady Wishfort's refurbishment of her face doubles as the renovation of a decrepit social fabric. She is, she moans, 'an old peeled wall' urgently in need of repair: a mouldering *ancien régime*. It is not so much her own sexual superannuation she is protesting against as her imminent decomposition and that of the society she commands. 'As I am a person', she says, as if warding off the day, menacingly near, when she will cease to be one, 'I am in a very chaos to think I should so forget myself.' The final dance is her collapse into obsolescence: 'As I am a person I can hold out no longer.'

At the suckling centre of the play's relationships, she suffers the other characters to cling as parasites to the body which nurtures them. When she pleads with Mrs Marwood to 'stick to me', Mrs Fainall declares that she will do so 'like a leech, to suck your best blood' and drop off when sated. This is how she seeks maternally to bind people to her. Sir Wilfull, thanking his aunt for her attentions, notes that she is not one who fashionably remembers to forget her relations. Later, seeking a favour from Witwoud, she asks it in the name of this hereditary ligature, which glues together the members of society as it cements in place the peeling wall and fissured varnish of her visage: 'You will bind me to you inviolably. . . . You will oblige me to all futurity.' Her aim is nothing less than to coerce an after-time which, as Mirabell pronounces when he declares her pityingly to be 'full of the vigour of fifty-five', must exclude her; and, bribing the future by her retention of the spoils accumulated in the past, she therefore guards with her own body the fortune belonging to Millamant. Mirabell's intrigue against her can only succeed if it breaks her bodily hold on her extended family. Hence her imagery of flaying, of breaking her forms, and her 'mortal terror'. Every initiative of action is a depletion or destitution of her body: 'I have an affair of moment that invades me with some precipitation', she tells Witwoud.

The ravaging of her physical sanctuary is symbolised by the opening of the black box with its archive of territorial deeds and sexual confidences. That coffer secures the memory of society and it is fortified, as Lady Wishfort is not, to outlast the erosions of time. If Margery Pinchwife had opened it, it would have been a Pandora's box of infectious guilt; but in Congreve's play it has an almost sacramental significance, like the Domesday Book of legal precedents consulted by Marwood or the profane Bible (actually Messalina's poems) on which she makes Foible and Mincing swear their oath. It contains the society's charter, the act of constitution regulating relations between people. It is an ark of matrimonial and financial covenants, and it reposes all contracts—like the deed of conveyance disposing of Mrs Fainall's portion—'in trust to Edward Mirabell'. He it is, on production of those parchments, who ousts Lady Wishfort and renews a system she cannot, despite her applications of plaster and Spanish paper, patch up; he ends as society's turnkey and trustee. His partner in achieving this coup is, significantly, the countryman Sir Wilfull, another quasi-parental trustee. Just as Mrs Fainall has placed her estate in Mirabell's care, so the orphaned Witwoud is handed over to the guardianship of his half-brother. 'He had', as Witwoud says, 'the disposal of me then.'

With *The Way of the World*, eighteenth-century comedy begins. Though Mirabell likens Waitwell's role to that of 'Mosca in the "Fox"', in his intrigue the revenger has been disarmed and yields to the good-natured man (after whom Goldsmith named a play in 1768). Comedy is here redefined as a mode of philanthropy—a cure of souls, not a flagellation of bodies. Millamant converses with fools for her health, and Lady Wishfort wants to marry for the same reason. Congreve's preface to *The Way of the World* restricts comedy to the treatment of faults which are affected, not innate, arguing that the incorrigible is 'not proper to the stage'. His new ethic of forgiveness is a by-law of eighteenth-century comic theory, reiterated by Fielding in *Tom Jones* and by Charles Lamb in his essay on the tragic (by which he means sentimental) Malvolio, a sufferer from that 'natural folly' at which, as Congreve pleads, we ought not to laugh, or by Mrs Candour in Sheridan's *The School for Scandal* (1777) when she defends a fat dowager against the slanders of her colleagues by avowing, 'Nay, her bulk is her misfortune!' Sheridan revised Vanbrugh's *The Relapse* (1696) in a spirit of moral reformation, converting the characters from satiric revenge to comic clemency. Sir Tunbelly Clumsey, when duped at the end of Vanbrugh's play, exits damning everyone, including his daughter; Sheridan's character in *A Trip to Scarborough* (1777) growls that he wants reparation for the slights of Lord Foppington, but hits on a way of hurting the fop while pardoning his disobedient daughter. Forgiveness is his revenge: he slights the lord by allowing the girl to marry Young Fashion, and is complimented by Berinthia on having 'done a generous action'. In place of Vanbrugh's curse, Sheridan has him call for dancing and drink and makes him wonder—passing off as whimsy the motiveless change of heart the new dramatist has required of him—'how I came to be in so good a humour'.

This moral leniency points beyond drama to the novel, with Fielding (who migrated from one form to the other) as the point of juncture. By discriminating between the natural and the affected, and limiting drama to the latter, Congreve is declaring his own form peripheral. How can a play represent natural behaviour, which is of necessity untheatrical? Mirabell is compromised by the dissimulations of drama. As a man of sensibility, his only affectation is the indifference he exhibits during the game of cards; his fault, in Fainall's view, is an excess of compunction, a renunciation of feigning. But Mirabell also has to be, for the purposes of the intrigue, a dexterous dramatic manipulator, adept at pretence. Good-natured men like Tom Jones or Tristram Shandy or the Vicar of Wakefield are more at home in the novel, which can vouch from within for their integrity, and the Vicar indeed explicitly defends the form against the ungodly negativity (as he sees it) of the theatre. All the villains in Goldsmith's novel are professional dissemblers, amoral actors—the rake

Thornhill who 'performs' marriages, with a popish priest's assistance, to the girls he fancies; the confidence trickster who outfits himself with false faces and has 'learnt the act of counterfeiting every age from seventeen to seventy'. Primrose's own goodness is evinced by his inability to act—'I could never counterfeit false resentment'—and he is therefore affronted when, among a company of strolling players, someone enquires 'whether I was the real chaplain . . ., or whether it was only to be my masquerade character in the play?' He loses a son to theatrical vice: the boy is recruited by the players, and made to undergo unsettling metamorphoses. While his colleagues test him for parts, he is 'driven . . . from one character to another'. In contrast with this world of simulation, where character means only a temporary and assumed persona, Primrose celebrates the verity of the novel, idyllically characterless because no one in it is performing. He cannot, he says, discriminate the characters of his offspring, because 'a family likeness prevailed through all, and . . . they had but one character'; when he engages a limner to represent them, it is as a group, not as theatrically self-imposing individuals. Since they are a part of one another, novelistically interlocked, 'one frame would serve for all'. Mrs Hardcastle, at the denouement of Goldsmith's *She Stoops to Conquer* (1773), disparages this retirement from play: 'Pshaw, pshaw! This is all but the whining end of a modern novel.'

Farquhar's beaux are set to quit the drama, and have the buoyant opportunism of picaresque heroes in eighteenth-century novels. They are prompted by the highwayman Gibbet, who says, 'I understand the world, especially the art of travelling.' Their itineracy is chivalric. Archer claims, 'We are knight-errants, and so Fortune be our guide.' Arriving at the inn, he expects to have as many adventures there as Don Quixote did at his staging-post (or Tom Jones at Upton). This voyaging energy, restless beyond the bounds of the dramatic unities, carries with it a venturesome mobility of mind. Dorinda, in Mrs Sullen's bedroom late at night, wonders what might happen if Archer were to join them. Mrs Sullen pretends to be shocked. Dorinda sees through her protestations: 'Thoughts are free, sister, and them I allow you.' Her phrase might be a motto for the novel, where Horner's libertinism yields to a liberation of consciousness and a liberality of sentiment. When Mrs Fainall reproves Mrs Marwood as a libertine, the latter attests, 'You see my friendship by my freedom'; the malevolent Scandal in *Love for Love* is defined as a free-speaker, his tattling as 'the liberty of your tongue'. By the time of *The School for Scandal*, these extenuations have become the truth, and to Sir Peter's scheme for the suppression of gossip Lady Teazle replies, 'Would you restrain the freedom of speech?'

In Sheridan's comic society, animadversion—no longer a mortal infliction—resembles the wishful thinking of romanticism. It is a dramaturgy of fantasy. The scandal-monger's qualifications, according to Snake, include a 'bold invention', and Crabtree's lampoons are commended for their improvisatory bravura, 'done in the smack of a whip, and on horseback too!' The economy of *The School for Scandal* is one of impetuous, dreamy inflation. Lady Teazle's necessities are ostentatious luxuries, including jungles of flowers in winter and a monkey to frolic in them; Moses offers instruction in how magically to multiply interest rates; Sir Oliver dotingly alters the bank draft from £300 to £800. Slander works with the same romantic midwifery, encouraging its victims to perform what has been lyingly alleged of them. Ordering Joseph Surface to be shown in, Lady Sneerwell says she does not 'wonder at people giving him to me for a lover': the fabrication is a gift to her. Lady Teazle warns Sir Peter that she will not be suspected without cause. If he is determined to believe her guilty, she will gratify them both by being so. She treats her own slanders as trophies of surfeit, like the monkey or the £200 she demands immediately from her husband. 'I say scandalous things', she explains, 'out of sheer good humour.' Scandal elicits and encourages an innate inclination, acting like wine which, as Charles Surface says in a Falstaffian and romantic aside, draws forth 'a man's natural qualities', or like the bribe which extorts an honest deed from Snake: though Lady Sneerwell has paid him to lie, he confesses that 'I have unfortunately been offered double to tell the truth.' Lying is the existential bravado of drama. Falstaff, Cleopatra and Iago never tell the truth because, as dramatic geniuses, there is none for them to tell. But Sheridan's play is a demolition of theatrical pretence—a toppling of screens, a stripping of surfaces—and its new romantic probity is inaugurated when Lady Teazle, in contrast with Margery Pinchwife's corroboration of Horner's story, is offered a lie by Joseph as an easy way out of her embarrassment and refuses to tell it.

The linguistic follies of Mrs Malaprop in Sheridan's *The Rivals* (1775) also place her beyond satire, in that charmed region envisaged by Lady Teazle where speech is free. Mrs Malaprop is not locked inside a systematic jargon, like Jonson's garrulous monomaniacs. Her malapropisms are extravaganzas of free-association. Like Lewis Carroll's Humpty Dumpty, she proudly exercises a romantic right to make words mean whatever it pleases her that they should. Her most inanely ingenious errors pay tribute to language itself as our homemade means of organising and interpreting the world. She orders Lydia to 'illiterate' a wooer from her memory, or commends her to Captain Absolute as 'an object not altogether illegible'. Syntax is power to her, and commands are conjugations: 'I laid my positive conjunctions on her never to think on the fellow again;—I have since laid Sir Anthony's preposition before her;—but I am sorry to say she seems resolved to decline every particle.' She even interprets faces as phrases made visible. Of Captain Absolute, she enthuses, 'His physiognomy so grammatical!'

Whereas Margery Pinchwife learns, in her letter scene, the treasonous lessons of drama about the scripting and acting of factitious emotions, Mrs Malaprop has no guile. Her lexical fancies are the blithe and instinctive idiom of the comic spirit. They rewrite reality with an inspired nonsensicality, as Dickens's Mrs Gamp in *Martin Chuzzlewit* does when she transcribes Mr Harris's imagined distress by testifying that 'his owls was organs'. Hereafter, the censoriousness of satire can be employed only in defence of meaningless words, the names for nonexistent things. Wilde's nominalist play is malapropristically about the importance of being not earnest but Ernest: comedy has resigned from its equivocal compact with morality, and from its analytic and vindictive assault on society.

19

Swift, Pope
and the Goddess of Unreason

Swift and Pope are not satirists holding the fort of civilisation; nor is theirs an age of reason, classically tutored. Renaissance in England required no secession from the past—the Elizabethans, in the syntactic mazes of Sidney or the riddling emblems of Spenser or the doubly- and trebly-plotted revenge plays, remain true to a native genius which is quizzical, insular, eccentric and defiantly unclassical—and the classical standards which fail to establish themselves in the sixteenth century have no power in the eighteenth either. Far from being a temperate Augustan culture, the first half of the eighteenth century looks crankily irrational, furiously parodic, shattering literary form in its mockeries of sacrosanct classical genres.

Swift in *A Tale of a Tub* and Pope in *The Dunciad* deal with a rivalry between the ancients and the moderns. Officially they grieve over the demise of the classical literary work, butchered and profaned by scribblers, lewdly imitated by dunces; but secretly they are elated by the vices and misuses they berate, and their satire covers an ironic formula for having it both ways, camouflaging as jest propositions they are privately considering in earnest. Unofficially, these maimed or debased classics—Swift's epic of battling books or his *Discourse Concerning the Mechanical Operation of the Spirit*, Pope's learned praise of the art of bad writing in *Peri Bathous*—sketch in advance the odd, self-questioning, romantic literary work, as exampled by *Tristram Shandy, Biographia Literaria* or the many texts of *The Prelude*, all of them prognostications for a later poem Wordsworth never reaches: works taking as their subject their valiant failure to achieve what they intend and analysing the shortcomings of literature and the language it is condemned to use. If there was an age of reason in England, the poets found ways to remain irrational during it.

Swift discovers this disorienting, fracturing irony when his satire breaks down. Despite their accumulation of an arsenal of weaponry—Gulliver's scimitar and pocket-pistols, the reaping-hooks of the Brobdingnagians or the impaling forks they use to eat with, the forty-foot-long sword of execution which beheads the murderer, the barber's razor or the saw with which the Laputans perform occipital surgery (all of these substitutes for the porcupine-like pen-quills discharged by the pedants in *The Battle of the Books*)—Swift's satires prove ineffective. Gulliver misses the point of his experiences, learning disgust for human nature but failing to recognise that his own human nature must be included in that revulsion. He discovers the untrustworthiness of language; yet the language he employs is the most untrustworthy of all. In whatever country he finds himself he takes care to study the speech of the inhabitants and prides himself on his skill in this: literacy after all is the measure of man's superiority to the beast. Or so he thinks. For languages turn out to be tribal possessions, mutually incomprehensible, their vocables Swift's tongue-tied and unwritable coinages: who can pronounce, let alone spell, Brobdingnag or the Houyhnhnms? The dialects of Lilliput and Blefuscu have nothing in common, and the ambassadors of each empire address Gulliver through an interpreter.

Since words are so relative and unreliable in their meanings, how can the truth be uttered or written? Visually, Swift's dwarfs and giants create a disorientation like Hogarth's in his satiric diagrams of false perspective, unsettling our estimation of humankind by confusing our terms of reference and our scale of measurement; verbally, he manages the same critique of human presumption by showing that words are—like the perspective whose conventions Hogarth derides—our unearned privilege, whereby we declare the world subject to us and conceitedly imagine that we have understood it. The Laputan academy puts language through a clinical scrutiny, exiguously rationalising it by shortening polysyllables and omitting verbs and participles. 'In Reality', the professors decide, 'all things imaginable are but Nouns.' The rest of language must be a shadow-play of fictions and false quantities. This radical logic leads to a 'Scheme for entirely Abolishing all Words whatsoever.' The policy is urged for medicinal reasons: utterances are expenditures of breath. But though Gulliver concurs with this scientific propriety, his own habits are still tautologous, using more words than are necessary and copiously dying as he gabblingly speaks. In his account of the scheme, 'entirely', 'all' and 'whatsoever' are supernumerary. Those equine angels the Houyhnhnms converse in a dialect which has been pre-purified. They will not besmirch their language by including in it a word for lying. So when they do not believe Gulliver they have to say, with burdensome circumlocution, that he '*said the Thing which was not*.' Their theory is impeccable yet unworkable. They reason that the purpose of language is to communicate and to assist comprehension. If muddied by misrepresentation, its purpose has been defeated. Such probity required Plato to exclude the poets from his republic, or Rousseau to forbid play-actors in his ideal commonwealth of Geneva. The revelation does not impose on Gulliver or on Swift a cautionary continence, or incline them to silence: their artistic virtuosity lies precisely in their corruption of sense and meaning.

The ironist is a specialist in what the Houyhnhnms decry as false representation, saying things which both are and are not, as when Gulliver, after reporting the Brobdingnagian monarch's abuse of the verminous human race, adds that 'nothing but an extreme Love of Truth could have hindered me from concealing this Part of my Story.' His statement, with its unpretending pretence, is made in bad faith, of course. It is Swift's customary dodge to say something unpalatable or untenable and then revoke it or disclaim responsibility for it by attributing it after the event to someone else—one of those befuddled personae who, like the cannibalistic modest proposer, are his masks and stooges. As Swift interprets Gulliver's disclaimer, 'an extreme Love of Truth' comes to seem incompatible with the possession of a language, either spoken or written: we are perjuring ourselves all the time. Read as an official Augustan work, *Gulliver's Travels* might seem an essay on man, sagely reproving his follies; in its unofficial sense, however, it is a text-book of linguistic error, an encyclopaedia of misunderstanding.

In Glubbdubdrib Gulliver blames 'prostitute Writers' for their misleading of the world and their inditing of propagandistic untruths. Yet Swift is one of them, and the more dangerous for being so ingenious at what he does, an experimenter in the literary deception which is irony. His 'Directions to Servants', for instance, ironically outwits itself: sarcastically advising servants to be insolent and inefficient, it encourages the faults it sets out to criticise. Swift's verses in 1731 on his own death contemplate this predicament with a morbid glee. The poem is an application to his own case of La Rochefoucauld's maxim on the pleasure we take in the misfortunes of our friends. Swift ventures to exempt the epigrammatist himself from the rule: his laws

> . . . argue no corrupted Mind
> In him; the Fault is in Mankind.

Is La Rochefoucauld then not a member of culpable mankind? Men cannot be separated from their statements. Of this Swift's final moral obituary is a test-case: though he attributes it to a just and disinterested friend, he is of course dictating it himself. His account of his own modest goodness stands accused of a falsifying pride. When his friends respond to the news of his imminent demise, their language is literary and rhetorical because dishonest:

> In such a Case they talk in Tropes,
> And, by their Fears express their Hopes.

Swift admits that he has as little control over his literary fate as he does over the wasting of his body. The penalty for his ironic absenting of himself from his statements is that those utterances or writings are then left to the negligence of others, the survivors who will either misread him or not read him at all. Chaucer tries to protect his own investment in the text as his progeny and his future by warning off miswriters of *Troilus*; Spenser is confident of his *Epithalamion*'s monumental everlastingness. But Swift has no faith in the verity or the endurance of texts. Offprinted from himself, they either take him over, sentencing him to ignominy and death while they are praised as if belonging to someone else; or else they are discarded and destroyed. Thus some obituarists '*curse* the *Dean*, or *bless* the *Drapier*', wishing good riddance to the man but venerating one of his characters (the Drapier whose letters protested against the importation into Ireland of English small change). The booksellers meanwhile discard Swift's tomes as rubbish. Since he has departed, '*his Works must follow*.' Writing is no hostage to eternity. The short life of his books bears out the excremental theory of creation in *Gulliver's Travels*, where the Yahoos express themselves by voiding their bowels and the Houyhnhnms discuss the necessity of '*Evacuation* . . . either through the natural Passage, or upwards at the Mouth': writing is our expulsion of pestilence, an emetic or laxative relief. This will be the romantic theory of creativity, and it is also the Freudian one, prescribing in D. H. Lawrence's phrase the shedding of sickness in a book. The romantic artist is hurt into poetry; the Swiftian hack is driven to it by desperation and hunger, as 'The Progress of Poetry' argues, and Pope, too, wondering in the 'Epistle to Dr Arbuthnot' about the congenital ailment which dipped him in ink, explains that he writes 'to help me through this long disease, my Life'.

Pope's self-justification pleads that literature is a madness or an infectious mania. Clerks pen stanzas when they should engross and, deprived of ink and paper, scribble 'with desperate charcoal' on their walls. Matthew Arnold, misjudging Pope by failing to sense his incipient romanticism, called him one of the classics of our prose. No verdict could be less true: Pope knows the irreconcilability of judicious prose and giddy poetry; in his own case as in that of the versifier he derides in the epistle, poetry is 'prose run mad', and though he complains of this fate he was indeed 'born for nothing but to write'. Writing is his substitute for living, poetic imagination his second-best satiation of fantasies and cravings which the meagre prose of his daily existence denies to him.

This theory of literature's sources coincides with the establishment of literature as an industry by the talentless journalists of Grub Street: writing therefore is in Swift's terms one of the mechanical operations of the spirit. In the medieval system of meanings, the immaterial spirit published the letter as its emissary or incarnation in the lower world. The Swiftian letter is a botched and abused publication of spirit, or its expletive excretion like the 'Height and *Orgasmus* of their Spiritual exercise' sexually experienced by the preaching zealots in Swift's discourse—an incarnation only too loweringly carnal. In Pope the spirit inscribes defamed letters as graffiti:

> . . . my Name stood rubric on the walls,
> Or plastered posts, with claps, in capitals;

in Swift it dictates letters which are an hysterical, unintelligible, orgiastic babbling, 'compact' like the sermons of the inspired preachers he mocks 'of insignificant Words, incoherences and Repetition'. *A Tale of a Tub* is Swift's analysis of the literary work's absurd condition, confused, schismatic, ill-executed. It takes the form of a mock-scriptural commentary, allegorising the history of the three brothers so as to describe the history of Christianity, the fragmenting of the church and the mutilation of its teaching: Peter is the Pope, Martin is Luther, and Jack is John Calvin. This enables it to review the procedures of biblical exegesis which, from the patristic glosses on scripture through Langland to Spenser, serve as literature's authorisation, its imprimatur of truthfulness and the means of connecting its human fabulations with divine prophecy. That figural mode has here disastrously broken down. The anecdote is empty of significance, the glosses on it are a crazed editorial intrusion. Swift is declaring an end to a classic and sacred tradition of literary utterance, re-enacting the collapse of the skyscraping tower and its condemnation of our speech to jargon, our language to jaw-breaking neologisms like the place-names in *Gulliver's Travels*. Jack is a devotee of a deity 'by some called *Babel*, by others *Chaos*'. But as well as this conservative intent, the *Tale* acquires after the event a radical relevance. Swift is outlining the nature of the romantic art-work. The masterpieces of a later period—editorially accumulating the fragments which are all that remain of a once evident meaning, disjunct quotations from divinity, tirelessly and vainly interrogating themselves—will be not very different from *A Tale of a Tub*.

Swift designs the narrative as an allegory, but indicates in addition that 'there generally runs an Irony through the Thread of the whole Book.' In this dual characterisation, he is indicating both a link and gap between what he calls the ancients and the moderns. In place of allegory, the ancestral certification of truth, the moderns have irony, which is allegory gone into hiding, concealing its meanings in a double-speak to be translated only by 'the Men of Tast', the covert acolytes of enlightenment. Pope's Scriblerus praises the pun as a means of speaking twice, as with a jackdaw's forked tongue. Irony's skill lies in such duplicity: irony is allegory converted to the purposes of modern conspiracy. Allegory speaks in parallelisms, tracking a correspondence between literal and spiritual, earth and heaven. When that accord can no longer be relied on, irony takes over. It enunciates the spirit by marring or falsifying the letter: stating the opposite of what it means, it makes a fine art and a technique of wisdom from the Houyhnhnm crime of saying the thing which is not. In this sense Swift's hack is of course justified in urging the superiority of the moderns to the ancients. Our literary forefathers were obliged to content themselves with what the author of the *Tale* calls static hieroglyphics. The moderns need not remain 'shut up within the Vehicles of Types and Fables'. Irony enables them to produce works which do not mean one thing or (at best, as in allegories) two, but can mean anything at all—or, better yet, nothing. During the fraternal quarrel over the meaning of the will, Swift has the pedantic Wotton append a footnote explicating the jest: '*the next Subject of our Author's Wit, is the Glosses and Interpretations of Scripture, very many absurd ones of which are allow'd in the most Authentick Books of the* Church of Rome.' In fact that absurdity constitutes Swift's liberty. The *Tale* is a work of infinite interpretability, protected by its irony from ever having to specify what it intends. When the author of the *Discourse* decides to resort to allegory out of prudence, he trusts that 'the judicious Reader, may without much straining, make his Application as often as he shall think fit.' Irony, in which allegory is now subsumed, permits that reader to find in the text whatever he pleases.

The *Tale* licenses this new literary science of unending interpretation or self-seeking misinterpretation. (Swift values misreading as a sovereign mental balm: he calls it 'the sublime and refined Point of Felicity, . . . *the Possession of being well deceived.*' Would he have been pleased by the contented incomprehension which has overtaken his own work, turning *Gulliver's Travels* into a children's book?) When Jack for his own greater gain determines that his father's testament shall be '*deeper* and *darker*' than it seems and more bottomless in its implications, Swift hands over his own text to those who will play transubstantiating games with it, and 'who can make *Shadows*, no thanks to the Sun; and then mold them into Substances, no thanks to Philosophy; whose peculiar Talent lies in fixing Tropes and Allegories to the *Letter*, and refining what is Literal into Figure and Mystery.' He is describing the modern (or at least post-romantic) critic, made by Sterne and Coleridge a collaborator with the creator; and, given the religiosity of his context, he is characterising that critic's practice as a black mass, a profane eucharist. There is no god or meaning inhering in or behind the words. The critic's imaginative skill—like Jack's legalistic sophistry—is his conjuring of non-existent significances. Defining the critic as '*a Discoverer and Collector of Writers Faults*', Swift is acknowledging him as the author's successor, the surrogate who sentences the author to death.

The author's demise has already occurred in the *Tale*. It is a book about nothing. Swift declares this to be the highest aim of modern art, 'to *write upon Nothing*; when the Subject is utterly exhausted, to let the Pen still move on; by some called, the Ghost of Wit, delighting to walk after the Death of its Body': a holy ghost of spectral insignificance. He passed on the ambition to Gustave Flaubert, whose professional dream was (as he confided to Louise Colet in 1852) to write a book without a subject. About nothing, the *Tale* is by no one, published anonymously, the question of its authorship vexed by dedicatory letters from the bookseller and then complicated by that retailer's insistence that the *Battle of the Books* is 'unquestionably of the same Author'. The *Discourse* however is a virgin birth, issuing from no-where. Of it the bookseller testifies, 'the following Discourse came into my Hands perfect and entire. . . . Concerning the Author, I am wholly ignorant.' It is a combustible work, which wants to vanish into the nothingness it emerged from. Its departed author attaches to it a plea that the addressee will 'burn this Letter as soon as it comes to your Hands'—before reading it, does he mean? Ideally vacant, the works are further evacuated by editorial damage. There are 'Chasms' or 'defective

Places' in the manuscript, we are assured: consequences of the author's defection. They have been expanded rather than filled in, since the editor's work consists in the addition of deductions. The 'Whole Scheme of Spiritual Mechanism', that small literary miracle mocking incarnation, is represented by a paragraph of pusillanimous asterisks. 'It was thought neither safe nor Convenient to Print it', the editor explains. But the erasure serves to guard the mystery, to keep the meaning spiritually disincarnate, and such opening-up of holes in the text becomes a mystic scruple of romantic narrative in *Tristram Shandy* or in Henry Mackenzie's *The Man of Feeling*, whose inconsequential pages have been used by a hunting curate to plug his gun; Coleridge adopts the same superstitious Swiftian trick and omits from his *Biographia Literaria* the definition of imagination—his version of spiritual mechanism—which the whole book supposedly exists to elucidate.

Literature for Swift exemplifies the absurdity of committing spirit to mechanism: print is not the prolongation of life but its reduction to perishable paper. Literature is a mere freight of books, asking (like Swift's works in the poem on his death) to be torn up or otherwise disposed of. The monster Error in *The Faerie Queene* vomits books and papers: error is a machine for publishing falsehood. Swift has his own bibliographic allegory, describing Criticism as a malignant goddess feeding on books and requiring her to metamorphose into a book. That shape-changing is a dessication, as the body yields to mechanism: she cramps herself into an octavo format, grows white and arid, 'and split in pieces with Driness; the thick turned into Pastboard, and the thin into Paper, upon which her Parents and Children, artfully strowed a Black Juice or Decoction of Gall and Soot, in Form of Letters.' Jupiter's Book of Fate is also catalogued and appraised as a text empty of spirit, its clasps silver, its covers of turkey-leather and 'the Paper such as here on earth might almost pass for Vellum'. Authors have been overtaken and obliterated by the papery testaments which ought to be their deputies, and the *Battle* takes care to point out this arid literalising: by Virgil it means not the man or the poet but 'only certain Sheets of Paper, bound up in Leather, containing in Print, the Works of the said Poet'. What is the writer for Swift?—a paper-fouler, a dried-up creature staining, like a scatological Yahoo, his own white substance. Peter sells pardons to Newgate felons, dispatching proclamations, quoted by Swift, on 'a Piece of Paper in this Form'. Literature, like law in this case, is worth no more than the paper on which it is written. No wonder Piers Plowman tore up his pardon.

Swift's revulsion declares the terms of a romantic literary tragedy: on the one hand, the writer as the medium between heaven and earth, spirit and letter; on the other, the writer as a mere producer of books, an industrious mechanic like Coleridge toiling over the selling of subscriptions in *Biographia Literaria* or filling up the volume with reprinted journalistic diatribes because his printer had miscalculated the quantity of paper. If print mars an original, abstract silence which does not need to speak or write, then so does human life. Shelley describes it staining with its refracted prismatic colours 'the white radiance of eternity', sullying the bleached page. The romantics plead that their poems are mere transcriptions after the event of a fading vision, which can never be literalised. Finding words to match the experience, as Keats discovers with his 'Forlorn!' in the 'Ode to a Nightingale', is a funeral bell tolling the end of that experience. Swift excuses the necessary inexactness and inadequacy of all his words by blaming them on someone else, or defaming them as parodies. The bookseller (who has a financial investment in believing it) is sure that the *Tale of a Tub* will 'live at least as long as our Language'. Swift knows that will not be long. Art does not outlast nature; like life, literature is a morbid phenomenon.

This is where Swift and Pope diverge. Swift tragically rends his own texts, disbelieving in their worth. Pope agrees with him about the obsession with writing and the frustration of living through print, yet he salvages from the effort a fragile, perhaps untruthful, but briefly consoling sense of value. Art makes beauty out of ordure:

> So morning Insects that in muck begun,
> Shine, buzz and flyblow in the setting Sun.

The difference is evident in their commentary on cosmetics, which for both are prescriptions of art. In Swift, face-painting is an obscene enhancement of putrid flesh; in Pope it is a veneration and protection of that vulnerable flesh, transforming the face into an icon, as delicate and breakable as the China jar in *The Rape of the Lock* or the golden bowl in Henry James's novel. Pope's Belinda at her toilet-table consecrates her body, as the muse at the end of the poem preserves her severed lock by enshrining it as a poetic image; the slattern Corinna in Swift's corresponding poem, 'A Beautiful Young Nymph Going to Bed', does not piece herself together into a nature surpassing artifice like Belinda, whose smile outdoes the sun, but takes herself to pieces. She removes in turn, in a ritual butchery, her hair, an eye, her teeth, her dugs, and attends to the care of her cankers and sores. She has resolved herself into the ordure from which, like Pope's insects, she was made. In the morning she wakes to find that a rat has chewed her plaster, a dog infested her wig with fleas, and a cat has pissed on the plumpers which pad out her toothless cheeks. The 'quick poetic eyes' of Pope's muse mark the levitation of the lock: its robbery from Belinda's body saves it from her mortal fate (predicted by Clarissa) and eternalises it as art. But Swift refuses to describe those 'arts' whereby Corinna reunites her scattered limbs and prosthetic appendages, and he forbids his muse to do so:

> The bashful Muse will never bear
> In such a scene to interfere.

Poetry is disallowed because it, too, would contrive, like cosmetics, a palliative beautification.

The Rape of the Lock is a poem in defence of art and of its perverse, neurotic cost to the artist: a tragic work and a genuinely epic one, no mere mock-epic deriding feminine triviality. All its jokes are defensive measures, as is its very littleness. It is Pope's Lilliput. Swift miniaturises in order to demean: he reverses the sublimity of the telescope (invoked in Milton's Galilean infinite spaces) when Gulliver's 'Pocket Perspective' is produced, and demonstrates the ironic, entomological paltriness of the world examined by the microscope. Pope, however, reduces things in order to adore and treasure them and to render them sacredly, infantilely innocent, like the parts dissevered from wholes venerated in reliquaries. The reduction of size in Swift is man's diminution to 'any little hateful Animal we have a Mind to destroy'. The Brobdingnagians respond to Gulliver as to a toad, a spider or perhaps an aborted foetus. The micro-world is a breeding-ground for vermin. In Pope the same tininess serves to question the scale of rational adulthood, to restore the child's eye-view of the world (in contrast with Swift's adoption of a god's supercilious vantage). The Popean miniature renders things useless, and thus fetishistically lovable. It constructs a world fitted to the dictatorial demands of fantasy: another of Hamlet's kingdoms lodged within a nutshell, like the empires of intricacy disclosed by the opening of a Fabergé egg. Recoiling into itself, making itself small and pretending to be inconsequential, *The Rape of the Lock* guards itself from inspection and reproof. The egg or nutshell has been made habitable: a cranial carapace. Within it, the fantasist can impose his own crazily logical order.

Pope's couplets are models of such small worlds, exercises in illogical absolutism. The Swiftean couplet always sounds summary, recurring to those inescapable words which are sentences of death, like 'bit' in 'The Day of Judgement'. One of his ballads—in which he describes a dean who is to be hanged for a rape—exerts itself to find a different rhyme word in every stanza for the name of the crime. Yet the couplet's closure still enforces an unforgiving, unavoidable end. In Johnson's poem on the death of Dr Levet or his analysis of 'The Vanity of Human Wishes', the couplet's completion suits it to the obituary or the moral verdict. Self-sufficiency in Pope's couplets does not work in this judicial or funereal way: it stands for the intact microcosm of words, withdrawn from parity with things outside the couplet.

A double-take is built into each couplet, as into the composition of the entire poem, and that of *The Dunciad*. At first *The Rape of the Lock* is a joke; when Pope rewrites it and supplies it with the Rosicrucian heaven inhabited by the sylphs, it becomes much more than that. It turns into both the epic and the religious parable it was previously deriding, just as *The Dunciad*, with the belated addition of its fourth book, changes from a journalistic squib to a romantically somnolent, death-wishing hymn. So it is with the couplets: a first reading of

> Here thou, great ANNA! whom three realms obey,
> Dost sometimes counsel take—and sometimes Tea

may notice the hollow discrepancy between counsel and tea, but a second reading, instructed by the couplet's equation of them, will reflect that they are indeed commensurate. In the society Pope is describing, drinking tea is just as insidiously political an activity as debating the affairs of state. Pope himself was said never to take a cup of tea without a stratagem. Nor is there, with this hindsight, a mocking difference between great and small in

> One speaks the glory of the British Queen,
> And one describes a charming Indian screen.

Rhyme is an equaliser: flattery of the monarch may be as decoratively politic, as much a screening of actual motives, as the description of that item of furniture. And is not the monarch herself furniture, and (in Walter Bagehot's constitutional theory) a florid screen for the dull mechanism of government superintended by others? Likewise the alternatives proposed by 'Or stain her honour, or her new brocade.' Pope's subversive reasoning suggests that the former is a less heinous affair than the latter: the sullying of honour is at least invisible, and costs less. Belinda would sooner have tolerated actual ravishment than the metaphoric rape of her lock, and wishes the Baron had seized 'Hairs less in sight, or any hairs but these!' On Belinda's dressing-table, great and small are alliteratively regrouped. As itemised by Pope's language, there is no impropriety in the array of 'Puffs, Powders, Patches, Bibles, Billet-doux', because religion and cosmetics are alike devotional, and the Baron constructs an altar from romances. The line, seeming to indicate a blatant non-sequitur, actually employs its alliterative glibness to smuggle the Bible into comparability with the profane aids it mentions. Hence the plurality of Bibles. The holy book is proudly singular; Belinda has many, no doubt all with different bindings. Interpreting the Bible as a book and therefore as art, Pope is contriving as well a revision of his own poetic line, presenting it—in another modality of miniaturisation—as sound, not sense, a list of consonant, concordant words, not discrepant things.

He likes, too, the idea of making poetry from a sequence of substantives, unhustled by verbs, unexploited by subjects and careless of objects: a species of pure poetry, celebrating the autonomy of words and the habitability of the verbal or bibliographical microcosm. Thus he experiments with the autonomous energy of words and with the wilfulness of things set loose from human users, imagining a lexical kindergarten

> Where wigs with wigs, with sword-knots sword-knots strive,
> Beaux banish beaux, and coaches coaches drive.

Art mournfully pines for such a place, where words need not dully mean but can playfully be. Lewis Carroll, a successor to Pope in this English tradition of nominalist fantasy, invented a special language for that realm in the symbolist baby-talk of 'Jabberwocky'.

The *Rape* is genuinely an epic because what Pope calls its 'Machinery' both exalts and undermines its action, disclosing a stratosphere of levity and grace above the social world and excavating a slough of mental despondency beneath it. In classical epic man immortalises himself by deeds of arms: Pope entrusts that eternalising to art. But the efforts of aesthetic embellishment are doomed, as are those of the battling hero. The odds in Pope's poem are as incommensurate as those in *Beowulf*. Art is a species of psychological warfare. Its dream is of etherealisation, escape from the human body whose diseases and disorders are enumerated by Swift; it longs to spurn gravity to 'sport and flutter in the fields of Air'. That freedom is achieved, though, at the price of moodiness and self-maiming. Imagining those fields of air, the poet has retreated into the earth, entombed himself with his afflictions and separated himself from life: his micro-world is a grotto—Pope's own at Twickenham, or the splenetic cave where Pain and Megrim in the *Rape* have their headquarters. The poet celebrates the blithe empty-headedness of his creations but cannot share it.

Pope admires and envies Belinda for the reason promulgated in his epistle *To a Lady*: 'Most Women have no Characters at all.' That may sound like satiric castigation; in fact it is heartfelt praise. Women—compared here to chameleons, or to children pursuing birds—are the freedom of appetite, instinct and fantasy. Characterlessness is their exemption from the masculine edicts of sober conduct and consistency. They are in themselves immaculate art-works, not so much irrational as supra-rational. The sylphs in *The Rape* serve as their elemental genii, assisting their exhalation into fire, air or water—salamander-like termagants, vaporous coquettes, 'soft yielding minds' as fluent as water—casting off the grossness of matter to take on the insubstantiality of dream or vision. Women have a kinship with imagination; the sylphs are confected from imagination, refined altogether out of existence. The delight of lyricism in Pope is always unbodied, wishing with an almost Shelleyan intensity for the angelic volatility of Ariel: hence his enraptured account of the ballet of weightless and transparent squadrons above Belinda's barge. There are no tragedies among the sylphs. They are saved from pain by their intangibility, and when one of them is truncated by the scissors, the catastrophe is at once remedied: 'airy substance soon unites again.'

Though the *Rape* adores this graced state, disburdened of character and of body, it also describes its morose and discomfited origins within the artist. These creatures who exist above reason are bred beneath it. Conjured up inside the artist's yearning body, they remain penned within his head. Or within the sheltering, imprisoning book, ranked among the vials and vases which contain the extracted wits of beaux, caged like gnats, chained like fleas, dessicated like butterflies—for art vainly dreams of being immortal, and its possessive miniaturising of life makes the artist, in the conclusion of the *Rape*, the heir to the seventeenth-century melancholic, locked in his cell in the company of the rheumy secretions and deposits he investigates.

At its most sceptical, the *Rape* admits art to be one of Swift's mechanical operations of the spirit, a physiological spasm of release like the orgasmic sneeze which undoes the Baron, or a congestion of the head like that induced in him by the intoxicating fumes of the coffee he drinks. Belinda's lock is upraised and redeemed, but she herself, laid in dust, can expect no such special treatment. Art, like the lock, acquires its sanctity at the cost of our deaths. We have been tormented by being given the capacity to imagine a condition we can never experience. All this is confessed by the poem in its excursion to the Cave of Spleen. That recess is the underground of iridescent art, the laboratory of the night-working, insomniac poet. In this hospital ward, 'th' hysteric or poetic fit' are correlatives of each other: the gnome Umbriel proposes in advance a Freudian theory of creativity. The nymphs of the poem's upper air have in their hearts only a mobile toyshop; within the head of the artist, however, there is a mausoleum of deformities and abortions, the congregation of anthropo- morphs, monstrous births, and metaphoric half-lives which haunt the sleep of his reason—living teapots, sighing jars, chattering pies, and the worse casualties of imagination:

> Men prove with child, as powerful fancy works,
> And maids turned bottles call aloud for corks.

One of the *Rape's* exhortations to imagination is to see what is invisible: 'Think what an equipage thou hast in Air.' The poem's two most perceptive interpreters, accordingly, are illustrators—Henry Fuseli during the 1780s, and Aubrey Beardsley in 1896. Both of them understand the poem's gloomy, proleptic romanticism. Fuseli's painting of 'The Dream of Belinda', coloured a bilious and distempered green, has the heroine slumped in the posture of Michelangelo's Night on the Medici tomb. She is thus declared to be a nocturnal occultist, imagining the phantoms which haunt her. Fuseli defended Pope's sylphs against the objections of Johnson, who (as with Milton's Sin and Death) rejected the allegorical resuscitation of 'heathen deities'. In Fuseli's theory, allegory derives its warrant not from an antiquated mythological system but from the mind's misgivings, its pornographic fears and desires. He can therefore represent the *Rape* as a psychomachia—Belinda's, Pope's, and his own. As such, it is a cardinal romantic poem: what difference is there between Belinda's slumbers and the disturbed sleep of Coleridge which issues in 'Kubla Khan'? Beardsley subsequently makes the *Rape* a poem of the romantic decadence by venturing to depict the lower level of its imaginings, which Pope keeps out of sight: its privates, indeed. His view of Belinda in her barge shows what is below the surface. She, coyly disdainful, is obscured at waist-height by the boat's decorated side. But the doodlings with which the wood has been carved are genitalia, the motors both of the barge and of the poem's characters: retentive rose-buds, spurting phalluses, luxuriant growths which might be garlands of pubic hair, and for encouragement a flagellant's paddle. Beardsley's Cave of Spleen is an orgy of perversity. Inside the swollen male jar's belly is curled a malevolent, simian embryo. Positioned at the bottom left corner, the pregnant man or his germinating child might have mentally bred the vicious revelry which erupts above them; but in the vortical centre of the plate Beardsley sets its other sponsor, Pope, who, hunched and unsmiling, presides over his own psychiatric festivity. Beardsley locates him in his own poem, as its suffering hero for whom creation is—as for Belinda binding her locks in 'paper durance' and torturing them with hot irons—a tormentingly purgative discipline.

Max Beerbohm contributed a polemical defence of cosmetics to *The Yellow Book* in 1894. It is a belated justification of Belinda, and it coincides with that 'resurrection of eighteenth-century art' which the essayist Jules de Goncourt claimed as one of his own bequests to the literature of decadence. To paint the face is for Beerbohm to sever surface from soul and thus hieratically to make of oneself a symbol. Thus vindicated, Belinda makes a comeback as Beardsley's depraved, narcissistic Venus, the goddess of aestheticism, in his novel *Under the Hill*, begun in 1894 and published in 1896, the same year as his illustrations of Pope's poem. Being coiffed for the reception of Wagner's Tannhäuser, Venus worships herself at a toilet-table resembling 'the altar of Nôtre Dame des Victoires', and during the orgiastic supper at court her acolytes, goaded by aphrodisiacs, contort themselves into the kinky shapes of Pope's neurotics in the Cave of Spleen: 'Sophie became very intimate with an empty champagne bottle, swore it had made her *enceinte*, and ended by having a mock accouchement on the top of the table; and Belamour pretended to be a dog, and pranced from couch to couch on all fours, biting and barking and licking.' The cave stands exposed as an undercover Augustan mound of Venus.

Posing as the crass hack Martinus Scriblerus in 1727, Pope excavated that vast profound which is the spring and perhaps the cesspool of imagination. The *Rape* calls it the Cave of Spleen, the *Dunciad* the abyss of comatose dullness; Scriblerus in *Peri Bathous*, his treatise on *The Art of Sinking in Poetry*, knows it as the inverse and bottomless sublimity of bathos. His colleague in *A Tale of a Tub* extols an arcane obscurantism, arguing that, since Night is a universal mother, writing is fecund in proportion to its darkness, and likening a writer to a well which can pass for profound even if it is shallow, so long as it is wondrously murky. But the extinction of rational enlightenment issues in a romantic dawn. Romanticism is the reverie of the mind's night-side. Therefore while turning upside down Longinus's theory of the sublime, converting the rhapsodic art of flying into a bathetic nose-diving, Pope's Scriblerus intimates a later theory which derives poetry from the sediment and even—in the monologue of Browning's medium—the sludge at the bottom of the mind, and which encourages the poet to sink down through consciousness into the indolence or drowsy numbness of Keats, the visionary dreariness of Wordsworth, the dejection or pained sleep of Coleridge.

When Scriblerus denies that 'the Rules of the Ancients' have power over 'the Moderns', he is contributing to the long manifesto of anti-classicism which underlies English literature; when he demands whether there is 'an Architecture of Vaults and Cellars, as much as of lofty Domes and Pyramids?' he is exploring the spatial realm of romantic fantasy—Coleridge's cavernous underground river, the haunted cellarage of Walpole's *Castle of Otranto*, the miniaturised interior immensity (the size of a brain-pan) of John Martin's teeming illustrations for Milton's Pandemonium. Kenneth Clark remarks that civilised man has always been obsessed by light, and he instances the dazzling lucidity of Vermeer's rooms. The romantic, however, is obsessed by and enveloped in a tender darkness, that of Keats's verdurous gloom or that welcomed by Wagner's Isolde when she quenches the torch. So Scriblerus is speaking more truly than he knows when he announces that 'Darkness is an essential quality of the Profound.' To him, the aboriginal creative climate, the dunghill from which (as he says) gold is mined, is an obscurity within the head or even within the body. Identifying poetry with minerals ('The Profound of Nature') which are earth's stools, he sees the act of writing as a retrieval of treasures from their burial inside us. Like Swift, he speaks of poetry as the mental equivalent of a bodily discharge, the 'evacuation' of some 'natural or morbid Secretion from the Brain'. If the excretory images he uses seem grotesque, it should be remembered that Byron, too, called poetry the lava-flow of imagination: volcanoes do the earth's vomiting for it. As well as his purgative therapy, Scriblerus diagnoses a compact between the imagination and the pudenda, which with their own mode of automatic writing take dictation from our fantasies. These lower regions he calls the 'most fruitful sources or springs, the very Bathos of the human body'. It is from that unfailing source that the fountain—Coleridge's orgasmic equivalent to Byron's eruption—is forced in 'Kubla Khan'.

At the end of *Peri Bathous*, Scriblerus announces that 'An Epic Poem . . . is the greatest work human nature is capable of.' By now he has of course inverted the epic, translated it from classical literature to romantic England, like Fielding in *Tom Jones* requiring it to adjust to the levelling agencies of comedy and prose. Thus he makes it possible for *The Dunciad* to look like a mock-epic, derisively neoclassical, while venturing a romantic adaptation of the form. *The Dunciad* is Pope's Brobdingnag as the *Rape* was his Lilliput, a realm of portent not preciosity, of the imagination's elephantiasis not its retraction into a microcosm of personal, collectible totems. Scriblerus says that the poem 'celebrateth the most grave and ancient of things, Chaos, Night, and Dulness', and consequently claims for it an antedeluvian status, connecting it with the earliest work of literature: the comic epic supposedly composed by Homer before the *Iliad* and the *Odyssey*. However that may be, *The Dunciad* is about poetry's origins in the cloacal mud where the dunces romp, or in the 'universal Darkness' which resumes at its end. *The Rape of the Lock* had already reconstructed Milton's cosmos, envisaging heaven as a palace of art and hell as the artist's psychic studio. *The Dunciad*, too, revises *Paradise Lost* in order to expound an aesthetic theology of its own. Milton's God creates the world with light. Pope uncreates that reasonable, articulated world with his own umbrageous language, but at the same time creates an alternative to it. Art here remakes the world to suit its grandiloquent and captious whim, decreeing for instance that

> The forests dance, the rivers upward rise,
> Whales sport in woods, and dolphins in the skies

and, like the divinely mad Mathesis, finding the circle to be square; it confounds, in a romantic mayhem, those genres which classicism keeps studiously apart:

> How Tragedy and Comedy embrace;
> How Farce and Epic get a jumbled race.

This is the confusion which Milton at the end of *Paradise Lost* sees as a postlapsarian doom. Pope, however, welcomes it as a condition of irrational freedom, where his words can (as God's once did) ordain changes in things, where description can rectify nature by demanding that, as if in Sidney's poetic Arcady,

> In cold December fragrant chaplets blow,
> And heavy harvests nod beneath the snow.

Swift's hack had been ambitious to write a book about nothing. Pope in *The Dunciad* does so, describing as the creative miracle the conjuration of something out of nullity and non-being. Dulness manufactures, as a prize for the filthy pretenders to wit, the similacrum of a poet, ventilated with emptiness. Hers is a parthenogenic reproduction without flesh, an incarnation more astoundingly holy than that of the bodiless sylphs: 'she formed this image of well-bodied air'. The spectre is the dematerialising romantic symbol, as elusive as Keats's nightingale. The victor reaches out for 'the tall Nothing', but

> A shapeless shade, it melted from his sight,
> Like forms in clouds, or visions of the night.

Pope complies with the goddess by himself writing a poetry of nothingness or (in Scriblerus's diagnostic terms) of evacuation, from which all sense has been banished, leaving only sound. *The Dunciad* aspires to the breezy romantic inspiration of the Aeolian harp, instrumentally versifying the invisible wind and making music from absence. Pope describes the cave of poetry as a vent in nature:

> Keen, hollow winds howl through the bleak recess,
> Emblem of Music caused by Emptiness.

His lordling on the grand tour undergoes a similar aeration. Besotted by Italian opera, where sound has usurped sense, he, too, is abstracted from meaning and from corporeal form and 'last turned *Air*, the Echo of a Sound!' The sirens, too, emit this ideal lyricism, consoling 'empty heads . . . with empty sound'.

Pope delights in the games of the dunces, comparing the arcs of their urine or chronicling their frolics in the sewers, just as he sneakingly admired the frippery of Belinda, because in both he finds correlatives for the solemn, magical game of poetry. Poetry has often dreamed, from Spenser's longing to be multilingual to Lewis Carroll's idiolects or Joyce's Aeolian newspaper office in *Ulysses*, of allowing language to speak for itself, to free-associate and write poems without authorial intercession. Pope overhears this dissonant symphony when Dulness orders her acolytes to experiment with 'the wondrous power of Noise' (uproar being an ur-music), and he manages such feats in lines like 'sons of sons of sons of whores' (a sequence which could be continued indefinitely in a verbal cadenza); or in

> Men bearded, bald, cowled, uncowled, shod, unshod,
> Peeled, patched, and piebald, linsey-wolsey brothers,

where the epithets endlessly contradict each other and are encouraged to do so by the vacuous logic of alliteration; or, most amazingly, in a passage which sees letters as themselves spirits, disputatious ghosts risen up from the silence of print to engage in a chattering argument: the grammarian Bentley admits that

> 'Tis true, on Words is still our whole debate,
> Disputes of *Me* or *Te*, of *aut* or *at*,
> To sound or sink in *cano*, O or A,
> Or give up Cicero to C or K.

Is there anything more bizarrely beautiful and more luxuriantly euphonic in English poetry; anything more aware of what poetry is—a love-affair with language and the sensual pleasure of its pronunciation?

Rather than jeering at epic, *The Dunciad* revises it to accommodate romanticism, and this requires, as always in England, a relapse into pastoral and its mystic inertia. Dulness is idyllically comatose. Pope's poets labour 'sleepless themselves, to give their readers sleep'. The drowsing boredom he describes, which has overtaken top-heavy pine trees and threatens to stupefy 'all the western world', was devoutly besought by the romantics. It is enjoyed by Jane Austen's Lady Bertram in *Mansfield Park* as she meditatively vegetates on her sofa, and induced by Coleridge with doses of laudanum, by Keats with draughts of claret, by Fuseli with midnight snacks of raw pork (which could be relied on, he believed, to give him hallucinatory dreams). In Swift, Pope and later Sterne, the romantic makes his debut as a comedian; in the age of reason, a romantic literature, deftly disguised as satire, already exists. Pope's tenebrous, dozing deity soon enters into her rightful realm. The French revolutionaries, having dethroned God, proposed in substitution a custom-made Goddess of Reason. But romanticism cannot do without irrationality, and in *Ulysses* Joyce nominates the pregnant Mina Purefoy as his 'goddess of unreason', prostrate on an altar-stone, 'a chalice resting on her swollen belly'. The apparition manifests itself in a brothel: Pope's 'uncreating word' has proved imaginatively profligate.

— 20 —
Inventing the Novel: Defoe

The novel is, as its name suggests, a renovation of literature, a return to origins. Richardson's epistolary novels are about the act of writing, which is the sole, obsessive activity of his characters; sending letters is a reflex of their incapacity to communicate. The same desperately diligent toil occupies Defoe's novels after *Robinson Crusoe* in 1719. Enumerating things, his characters profess to own them. Their studious realism derives from the need to anchor themselves in the world by attaching themselves to its solid totems, which they can trust. Sterne's Tristram Shandy believes in no such cementing of the self's infirmity, but his own activity is a similar one: a logical classification of the world's unruly phenomena, in the course of which the character writes (rather than experiences) his own life.

These are novels of a terrifying perceptual primitivism. In them the lonely, suffering, subjective creature contends with a universe of overbearing, brutal, objects—the nefarious hands of Mr B. which assail Pamela as she tries to write (which is her only defence); the 'abundance of such things' which Moll Flanders dismisses when listening to the blandishments of her first beau; the sash window which almost unmans Tristram. There is no society for that imperilled self to belong to. Society is provisional, contingent: a desert island; a plague-depopulated city; a non-place of fickle, farcical transience like Fielding's inns in *Joseph Andrews* (1742) or *Tom Jones* (1749). The novelistic character is an outcast, shipwrecked perhaps, a prisoner either voluntary (like the narrator of Defoe's 1722 *Journal of the Plague Year*) or involuntary (like Richardson's heroines), or, like Sterne's Yorick, a tourist, isolated from the language which is his natural community. Tom Jones, characteristically, is first a foundling, then an exile from his adopted home. The journey, which supplies the narrative form of so many of these novels, is a consequence of this errant unhousing; and when characters cannot travel, like Pamela or Clarissa, their entire longing is to do so. Sometimes the prison of selfhood serves as a refuge, as for Crusoe in his fort. In London Defoe notes with interest 'tolerated prisons' like mad-houses or Chancery gaols, which he calls 'private houses of confinement, . . . little purgatories, between prison and liberty, places of advantage for the keeping of prisoners at their own request.' Though Richardson's women protest at their incarceration, their own art confirms it: each letter is an encapsulation of self, the glassy or papery cell from which the individual cannot break out. Coleridge contrasted the expansive open air of

Fielding with Richardson's unventilated, restraining indoors, but even an entire kingdom lacks room enough for Tom Jones to lose himself in. His fate stalks him with the inexorability of Fielding's coincidences. The novel's manacling plot is indeed Fielding's only means of holding society together.

The novel starts literature over again. In Fielding and Sterne, all other forms have disappeared into it. *Tom Jones* is a work of literary synopsis, containing epic and romance, drama (in the staging of the upsets at Upton) and (in the prefatory essays) critical theory, and compounding all these diverse kinds to make a novel. Fielding's orderly amalgam is in Sterne a hybrid muddle. *Tristram Shandy* is ambitious to be everything—Cervantean narrative and Shakespearean play, the account of a single life and a tour of the world, novel and anti-novel. From now on, the novel will be the touchstone of literature, as the epic once was. It is the form which is more than a form, since all competing genres can be housed in it; the form, too, which solves the ancient riddle of literary history by combining tragedy and comedy, as Fielding does when he commutes the sentence of Tom Jones or as Sterne does when he makes tragedy and comedy the simultaneous aptitudes of Tristram's ironic mind; the form which has no name for itself but its own novelty.

That activity of renovation at once alters epic. Fielding domesticates the ancient song of arms and the man to a modern world of comedy and unheroic prose. Defoe likewise sees as the novel's initial project a reprise of the task of epic—a reckoning of the world's contents which, as in Homer's catalogue of ships or weapons, establishes the centrality of human will and the power of human speech (or in Defoe's case the industrial efficacy of print). In this sense, Defoe's work is as heroic as Homer's or the *Beowulf* poet's, for all its humdrum modesty. Crusoe plans a circumnavigation of his island in the canoe he builds: traversal of his boundaries is a necessary scruple, assuring himself that he is safe within his enclosure. Defoe intended to do the same with Britain, coasting 'the whole circuit' of the island 'by sea, as 'tis said, Agricola the Roman general did'. But he decided against such a hazardous course, and made the assay of the national terrain on land instead.

He undertook a series of radial journeys, beginning from London and always returning there before resuming, which he published between 1724 and 1726 as *A Tour Through the Whole Island of Great Britain*. These expeditions constitute a Crusoesque enterprise: one man's subjugation of a country, making himself monarch by the omniscience of his survey. Communicated 'in familiar letters', they are critical of heroic bravado like that of Agricola. Defoe's is the safer, sager, terrestrial course, disdaining to risk himself as Agricola does. But the ambition remains an epic one. The difference is that the epic poet implants a will or divinity in the heirlooms he describes, anthropomorphising them (like the *Beowulf* poet with the sword, or Pope establishing the patriarchal pedigree of the bodkin that Belinda employs against her foe), whereas Defoe deals with a kingdom which is a totality of useful things, tamed by their reclamation for human uses. He views a nature no longer animistic. No gods are the spirits of the places he visits. England, he says at the outset, consists of 'a luxuriance of objects'; later he contends that 'England . . . is an inexhaustible store-house of timber'—a lumber-room of data, statistics, commodities.

Like Milton putting to flight the perjured pagan deities, Defoe routs the antiquarian fables which prevent the country from renovating itself. His interest always is in seeing 'something new', and to do so he must rout the old. He disbelieves the topographical fancies or etymological follies which honour the genii of locality, rejecting the name of Thamisis for the river as it passes through Dorchester, disallowing Ramsgate's presumption to be a gate for the invading Romans, not caring to enter the dispute between Oxford and Cambridge about their relative antiquity, lamenting always as decay or wreckage the memorials of the past which bestrew the countryside and obstruct the bustling commercial present. The Sheldonian in Oxford 'is not to be equalled by anything of its kind in the world; no, not in Italy itself', and the Monument in London overcomes its classical forebears by a purely numerical arrogation—'it is two hundred and two feet high, and in its kind, out does all the obelisks and pillars of the ancients, at least that I have seen' (that qualification adding Defoe's Crusoesque and Cartesian proviso that a thing probably does not exist if he has not seen it).

Reality no longer attaches to things by reason of what they historically were. It is assigned to them by the mensuration and cataloguing of the modern observer. Realism is that observer's perpetual vigilance: an invigilation of objects, to guarantee their security and their fealty to him by exact representation of them. That representation is an insurance policy, a commercial reproduction of reality's prototypes. Thus Defoe himself, as a manufacturer of writings, participates in the mercantile opulence, 'the increase and extensiveness of its commerce', which to him is the pride of contemporary Britain. Beneath its busy stocktaking, the *Tour* is haunted by a fear which is the motive-force of realism. This is the terror of amnesia and obliteration- -Crusoe's traumatic suspicion that he has been eliminated from the world, forgotten by God, condemned to non-existence. The *Tour* grieves over 'the decay of public things, things of the most durable nature'. The impoverishment and desertion of Dunwich is more alarming to Defoe than the remnants of Carthage or Babylon or ancient Rome. Those cities fell with the dynasties which ruled them. Dunwich has wasted in the normal course of events, as we all will. It is, he says categorically, 'the fate of things' to undergo 'their destruction in the womb of time'.

Realism holds off that decease. It guards against the remissness of time, and against the collapse of our world into meaninglessness. It does so by certifying facts and fortifying those unsteady, collapsing things, as Crusoe builds his stockade, or H.F. strengthens his house against the incursions of the plague, or as Sturbridge Fair near Cambridge self-sufficiently equips itself as if besieged, 'like a well fortified city', prohibiting 'disorder and confusion'. The facts Defoe is so careful to ascertain and order are of course fictions, but he must believe in them or else life is impossible. Realism is the act of imagination whereby we pretend to ourselves that the world cares for and caters to us. The captain in *Robinson Crusoe* bluffs the mutineers into surrendering by telling them that the governor of the island, Crusoe, will take action against them. Crusoe comments that 'though this was all a fiction of his own, yet it had its desired effect'. Crusoe defends himself with such brave pretension, imagining himself to be a lord with a castle and a country place, imagining that the passage of time (which he so scrupulously marks) matters to him, imagining that life has significance. The keeping of his journal is an existential necessity: if his ink runs out, will he go on *being*?

What is often assumed to be mere bourgeois acquisitiveness in Defoe goes much deeper. Describing things is a way of maintaining them, of gaining courage from them, of participating in their tenure of safety and solidity. Moll Flanders in 1722 will only believe in things if she can grasp them. That is why she pilfers. Hers is the tenacity of the realist, adorning her fingers with diamond rings, thrusting her hand in a window to steal some jewellery or manoeuvering it behind her body to take another thief's bundle of booty. 'I had full hold of her watch', she remarks of one of her adventures: fastening on a thing with such ferocity is the realist's dream. Moll earns her living with her hands (though she pretends she would gladly 'have turned my hand to any honest employment'), and in witness of this manual rapacity it is the hands of thieves which—as her mother shows her—are branded on the palm. Writing, which Crusoe would call a mechanic exercise, has value and virtue for Defoe because it, too, like Moll's mode of operation, is a manual labour. Mr Wilson in *Joseph Andrews* works as a hack translator, and 'almost writ myself blind'. He contracts as well 'a distemper from my sedentary life, in which no part of my body was exercised but my right arm'.

With his hands the writer builds a sheltering edifice for himself. The novel is constructed by the same craftsmanlike skill that Crusoe uses in the erection of his solitary castle. That dwelling is an endeavour of imagination: finding a hole in the rock, he resolves to call it his door, and with equal fancifulness he declares a cave his kitchen. It is the first house of fiction. He both builds it and supplies it, making it a department store or 'general magazine of all necessary things'. Crusoe is the artist as *homo faber*. He pieces together a home-made and self-made world, whose novelty is its improvised quality. Crusoe must make the tools with which he works, calling a wooden plank a spade and a tree bough a rake or harrow. His art is what Lévi-Strauss, speaking of the mythic science of the savage mind, calls *bricolage*: a primal engineering which takes the random litter of the world and rigs up from it a structured, mentally habitable set. Crusoe's book is made on an analogy with this assemblage of bric-à-brac. He salvages pens from the wreck of his ship, but when they run out can carve replacements from the quills of birds he has shot; his only failure as an engineer is his inability to make ink. He watches despairingly as his diluted supply dwindles, 'so pale it scarce left any appearance of black upon the paper'. The resuming whiteness is appalling nonentity, against what he can no longer assert himself. He considers it a good, sour joke to demand that his Spanish subordinate bring back an oath of allegiance to him from his fellows, 'put in writing and signed with their hands'. He reflects, 'How we were to have this done, when I knew they had neither pen nor ink, that, indeed, was a question which we never asked.' Should not the Spaniards find a way of making pen and ink with those same dexterous hands?

Thanks to Defoe, the novel defines itself as art in a new mode—as handiwork, and as an item put on sale in a consumer economy; its aesthetics are as industrial as its morality. Fielding argues in *Tom Jones* that poetry demands metrical skill, whereas novels are not art but craft, 'to the composition of [which] nothing is necessary but paper, pens, and ink'. Richardson's heroines as much as Crusoe are the tireless manufacturers of their novels, one-woman cottage industries of scribal labour. The whole drama of those novels derives from their obstacle-strewn quest as *bricoleurs* for the 'universe of instruments' (in Lévi-Strauss's phrase) which they need. Where will they find the quantities of paper and ink they require, or the time in which to write, unsupervised, their immense screeds? And once the article is manufactured, how can it be protected from those who would mar or defile it—Pamela hides her papers in her bosom—and how can it be published, smuggled out of the author's confinement to reach its addressee? Tristram Shandy, too, is a clumsy *bricoleur*, struggling to cope with the refractoriness of his implements: an uncontrollably skittish and graphically doodling (rather than verbally transcriptive) pen, a paper which would rather be blacked out or left blank than covered with a disciplined grid of words. All these works are about the work of being a novelist. Fielding's prefatory chapters to *Tom Jones* adduce a theory of the form as a hastily arisen scaffolding, whose stiffening aid will keep the structure standing up. Like the Crusoesque savage scientist, Fielding takes the practices and procedures forced on him in the course of his work and makes sacrosanct legislative rules from them; and like Crusoe selling to the Negroes such trifles as beads, shards of glass, scissors, hatchets and mirrors, or Moll vending her story, he is concerned with the work of art as a means of subsistence and exchange, chiding antagonistic critics because, in attacking his writings, they are depriving him of his only way to earn a living.

In other ways, too, the desert island is a prototype of what the novel was to become. It is a space of freedom, of novelty. Crusoe can do whatever he pleases, but rather than acting with whimsical purposelessness he decides on rules for his daily life. 'This morning', he reports, 'I began to order my times of work, of going out with my gun, time of sleep, and time of diversion.' His invention of a schedule to regiment the indefinite expanses of time corresponds to the novel's voluntary restraint on its own formlessness. It is a genre outside of genre, a ruleless work; therefore from the first it has felt the need to regulate itself. Hence the nascent theory of realism in Defoe, where the activity of writing is an equivalent to the steadying sense of being 'landed and safe on shore' which Crusoe craves, an anchorage of himself. Though Henry James disapproved of *Robinson Crusoe*, considering it cheap and shoddy as he told H.G. Wells in 1911, the logical problem of the novel was for him the same as Crusoe's problem of how to exist in his vacancy. James said that relations can be extrapolated forever, and stop nowhere. Art must correct life's continuity by introducing beginnings and definitive ends. He is deciding as a proviso of fictional theory what is for Crusoe a diurnal trial: how to limit one's options, to hedge off, fence in and make sense of the bewildering novelty of the world.

One of the cruel jests of *Gulliver's Travels* in 1726 against *Robinson Crusoe* is its derision of the novel's comforting delusion that realism is an absolute standard, confirming our human governance of reality, and that the structures which realism cobbles together can be a water-tight shelter for us. Swift's fable demonstrates the relativity of realism and the perspectival deceit of its vision. Gulliver is a giant in Lilliput but an insect in Brobdingnag. He admits, discomfited, that 'Philosophers are in the Right when they tell us, that nothing is great or little otherwise than by Comparison.' The history of the novel bears out this moral. Each generation of novelists inherits a realism which it discovers to be conventionalised and untrue. Adjusting realism to reality, the novel develops through a succession of parodies, constantly renewing itself: Fielding revises Richardson in *Shamela* as Jane Austen does Mrs Radcliffe in *Northanger Abbey;* Thackeray mocks the novels which gild and flatter an affluent society in *Vanity Fair*; Gwendolen in *Daniel Deronda* is George Eliot's criticism of the small-minded heroine of earlier novels, fussing over the intrigues and tribulations of the private life and ignorant of public destinies— and so it continues until Joyce in *Ulysses* parodies every one of his novelistic predecessors. Naturalism was the late nineteenth century's eventual abandonment of a compromised and specious realism: in the slums of New York, Theodore Dreiser found, he says, a life 'realer' than that represented by the comfortable, factitious realm of his forebears.

Crusoe does not remain safe for long. Swift pummels and drenches the small world in which he cowers. When Gulliver strides through the metropolis of Mildendo the citizens hide indoors to avoid being trampled; but during his escape from Brobdingnag he experiences the same terror when his neatly-outfitted box—a portable, navigable version of Crusoe's island—is hijacked by an eagle and dropped in the ocean. The human settlement and the novelistic structure over which Crusoe labours and in which he trusts are discovered by Gulliver to be the frailest of membranes. As his cell is bombarded by the waves, he notes that 'A Breach in one single Pane of Glass would have been immediate Death.' He counts himself lucky that the windows are reinforced outside with a lattice wire. More paranoid than Crusoe, Gulliver takes studious precautions against an unbalanced reality. In his cabin, the chairs are actually fastened to the floor with screws.

Crusoe, however, outlives the collapsible form in which he castellates himself. Though he may not know it, he is a romantic in advance of his time. He scrupulously avoids introversion, seeking (as do all of Defoe's protagonists) the durability of the object, the sturdy thing which has no inside and thus no capacity for fear and foreboding. Moll in Newgate senses this objectivising of herself—she is petrifying, she says, hardening or turning to stone in order to bear the conditions of the prison. Such is the reification which makes realism. Yet commentaries on Crusoe, unfolding a potential he suppresses, make a subjective being of him, someone suffering from the romantic nightmare of aloneness in the world. This is how he appears in 1782 in William Cowper's poem about Alexander Selkirk, the castaway who was a prototype for Crusoe:

> Oh, solitude! where are the charms
>> That sages have seen in thy face?
> Better dwell in the midst of alarms,
>> Than reign in this horrible place.

Romanticism devises an ontological Crusoe, whom Coleridge names the ancient mariner. The bourgeois pride in individuality and self-reliance which is the enabling strength of Defoe's hero has grown demoralised and afraid. Crusoe's joy—sole occupancy of a world reduced, like the deserted London of the *Plague Year*, to a store of goods with no owners—is the mariner's trauma: the dread of being the only live and agonised thing in a universe which is inert and insentient. Crusoe represents himself as an Adam with additional privileges denied to his predecessor in Eden. He has firearms for instance, and when he discharges his weapon to kill the wild fowl he reflects, satisfied, that this was 'the first gun that had been fired there since the creation of the world'. Like Paul Bunyan hewing the American forests, he industrially induces a fall, and counts it no tragedy but a blessing. Instead of the first man in existence and monopolist of earthly riches, romanticism nominates Crusoe as the last man in a wrecked and unprofitable world, the lonely ego awaiting its own extinction. The last man is the subject of a painting by John Martin after Thomas Campbell's poem, and of a novel by Mary Shelley describing a plague which is universal, not merely (as in Defoe's London) municipal. Crusoe's 'island environed every way with the sea' is our human world or even our personal being seen, from afar, in its puny insignificance.

The consequence of this romantic view is George Moore's proposal in 1911 for a new ending to the novel, whereby Crusoe would be kept on the island to die. In the same year, Joseph Conrad in *Under Western Eyes* reflects that to live alone in a desert one must be a saint. Election to that sanctity romantically honours Crusoe, who passes the test failed by Decoud—the dandy killed by alienation, driven to despairing suicide after a few days of solitude on his island—in Conrad's *Nostromo* (1904). That fate is craved by Birkin in Lawrence's *Women in Love* (1920). Recoiling, as he strips in the forest, from the populousness and congested anthropomorphism which were to Lawrence the afflictions of the novel, Birkin longs to be 'on an island, like Alexander Selkirk, with only the creatures and the trees'. Condemned to the society of creatures and trees, Crusoe pines for other people; Birkin's return to Crusoe's unaccommodated state is his desertion of the novel. Nevertheless the valour of Crusoe is his insensitivity to the quandary in which romanticism sets him adrift. Trollope, for instance, is the novelist as a 'very seldom idle' Crusoe, whose vocation is the manufacture of craftsmanlike wares, an accountancy serving to organise time. With a manual dexterity worthy of Crusoe, Trollope devised steadied tables for himself which allowed him to write on trains or on the decks of ships while traversing the world on bureaucratic errands; and like Crusoe he measures achievements by tabulating profits, concluding his *Autobiography* (1883) with a ledger of earnings from his published inventory.

Rudyard Kipling, too, adopts Crusoe as a model because of the protocol he elaborates for an epic fortification of terrain. He first read Defoe's book while at school and at once began, in imitation, erecting a defensive stockade around himself, using as his apparatus—with the catch-as-catch-can fabricative imagination of the *bricoleur*—'a coconut shell strung on a red cord, a tree trunk, and a piece of packing-case which kept off any other world'. This shaky act of exclusion is, as Kipling acknowledges when he recalls it in *Something of Myself* (1937), the commencement of realism, because it decides which things shall be deemed real: 'Thus fenced about, everything inside the fence was quite real.' Thereafter, whether describing how he singlehandedly built his own house in the wilderness of Vermont, keeping out, with his labour, nature which would otherwise have killed him, or extolling the colonial encampments of the British in India in *Kim* (1901) or of the Romans in Britain in *Puck of Pook's Hill* (1906), his ideal reference is always to an embattled Crusoe, the epic warrior patrolling the perimeter of human settlement as Beowulf once did. The Roman Wall is to Kipling the collaborative perfection of everything Crusoe strove for, a rampart raised against unreality: 'It is *the* Wall,' he says in *Puck of Pook's Hill*, and 'even at the narrowest part of it three men with shields can walk abreast, from guard-house to guard-house'—which is the only walking anyone in Kipling's world, even more spatially curtailed than Defoe's, will dare to do. Outside the wall is a grave. In Crusoe's case, it is littered with the remnants of cannibalised men; in Kipling's it is a ditch 'strewn with blades of old swords and spear-heads set in wood'.

This is a militaristic version of Crusoe. Realism means a state of armed preparedness. But Crusoe has also survived the transition to the twentieth century by acquiring a pacifism foreign to the mentality of Kipling. The chore of enumeration and the transcription of data can seem a calming ritual for a mind assailed by horrors. Frederick Henry in Ernest Hemingway's denunciation of epic, *A Farewell to Arms* (1929), reflects that the pompous values of the hero are debased nowadays, but the numbers of troops or of kilometers between villages remain pure, unpolluted by rhetoric. It has been said that *Robinson Crusoe* is one of the few books which could be read with impunity by survivors of the concentration camps, because (presumably) of its sedative fortification of the mind; and Albert Speer proved a similar point by setting out, in his prison quadrangle at Spandau, on an imaginary walking-tour of the world, conducted in stages during his brief spells of exercise. A global journey within the head or within the prison walls is the routine of a modern Crusoe, on guard now not against savages or looters (as the bourgeois Crusoe was) but against an invading nullity. Virginia Woolf found him therapeutic. His objects—those earthenware pots he makes—are at least solid. His shopkeeper's realism undergoes a change, in her 1932 essay, into an abstract, cubistic reformation of things, cutting out the vast emptiness which terrifies Cowper's Selkirk or the ancient mariner: 'By believing fixedly in the solidity of the pot and its earthiness, he has subdued every other element to his design; he has roped the whole universe into harmony.'

Robinson Crusoe is not Defoe's most darkly prophetic work. The hero cannot afford to look within himself; to him, realism is the rallying of the extroverted view. The *Journal of the Plague Year*, though it poses as documentation, is a fable about the secret terrors and cravings of this realism. The view out of the window now sums up the discrepancy between the subjective life in here, guarded and secure, and the chaos of objects out there. It is a vantage from behind that 'little curtain wall, no higher than a man's neck' on top of Kipling's Roman Wall, which lets you peep out at your enemy, or from within the dark room of Isherwood's camera-like stronghold in *Goodbye to Berlin*, surveying the street through a clenched aperture; Defoe calls it the view out from a compulsory sequestration, since houses in London have been boarded up to prevent communication between the infected and their fellow-citizens. And it is a view opening onto nothing. The London of the *Tour* is populous, a 'great mass of building' and 'a vast collective body of people'. But the city conceived of by the novel is a different place. The house of fiction is a bunker. Privacy and introversion are enforced by a compulsory boarding-up. The narrator of the *Plague Year* protests against this imprisonment, but it turns out later to be customary in the novel—Wemmick's castellated villa in *Great Expectations*, Dr Sloper's impregnably genteel retreat in James's *Washington Square*, or the house in Wickham Place in *Howards End*, a backwater of 'profound silence' separated from the main thoroughfare by a lofty promontory of flats, all follow from it.

Crusoe's solitary subsistence is a rule of conduct even for the city dwellers, and Defoe's hero reports on how he contrives to do without intercession from what Kipling calls 'any other world' outside the walls. He bakes his own bread, and brews beer from his store of malt. One of Defoe's grisliest puns enforces the reasons for secession from society. 'All families retrenched their living as much as possible', he says; then shortly afterwards he opens up the space which is the destination of that retrenchment: the parish officers hustle the plague victims into a 'pit or trench no man could come nigh but at the utmost peril'. Either a life apart and alone, or the sociability of a mass grave. Either the tenancy of a subject, or a waste of dead objects. When London is evacuated by a plague scare in Jonson's *Alchemist*, the purpose is to contrive that concentration which is the spatial imperative of drama: all who remain are conjoined at Lovewit's crowded house. But the novel banishes such overpopulation. Its city is ideally, desolately unpeopled.

Defoe here has intimated one of the tendencies of realism towards the surreal, for his vacated London suggests those fearfully empty places which arrive in art once the régime of bourgeois plenitude ends: the mysterious and melancholy streets of Giorgio de Chirico's paintings, crossed only by fugitive shadows; the uninhabited Paris of Eugène Atget's photographs; the thin, provisional, unsheltered New York painted by Edward Hopper. These are post-mortems for the apparently confident bourgeois world. Even before that world has established and replenished itself, Defoe writes about its alienatory nightmares. In its realist accumulation of goods, it is goaded by a *horror vacui*, a desire to conceal that native emptiness which returns in the *Plague Year*. Here Defoe's statistics are negative and necrological. The numbers he adds up are a grim deduction from the human plenum: the novel opens with the constantly inflating and increasing bills of mortality for the London parishes.

Talking of these sum totals of the dead, Defoe makes them, thanks to another covert pun, synonymous with the art of narrative. The grave-diggers are so busy that they lack 'leisure to take an exact tale of the dead bodies, which were all huddled together in the dark into a pit'. Tale means tally: the words have overlapping etymologies. In this case, a tale for Defoe is a numbering of the dead. Narrative generally connotes a garrulous or inquisitive sharing of experience, sustained by a faith in our common humanity. But in the conditions of the plague, narrative itself is a contagion: the disease is the only ground of community known to London, and its only means of currency or of circulating experience. The plague spreads as stories do, passed on from one person to the next. Its advance would have been exponentiated by literary agencies: H.F. is glad that 'we had no such thing as printed newspapers in those days' because these magnify what they transmit and relay scandal as if it were a malady—they 'spread rumours and reports of things, and . . . improve them by the invention of men'. Likewise commodities, amassed by Crusoe to hold unreality at bay, cannot help and may be fatal. The merchants dread goods as much as people, because 'our woolen manufactures are as retentive of infection as human bodies.' Personal relations and economic dealings are suspended. In this world of self-protective insulation, the only communication is that of the virus. 'Those newly infected persons communicated it in the same manner to others,' Defoe notes, and he warns of love as the sickliest carrier of all. The 'fatal breath' of affection transfers the disease from parents to the children by embrace. Instead of donating life, men are said to be 'breathing death' into their offspring.

The retreat from enmeshing associations into nervous privacy is seconded by the new privation of tell-tale, infectious narrative. The editor of *Crusoe* asserts that a 'private man's adventures' are 'worth making public, and . . . acceptable when published': publication is a life astutely merchandising itself, capitalising on what would otherwise be its uselessness. But the *Plague Year* attests to the opposite motive—the shamefaced and retentive privacy of novelistic documents, as secret as confession or as consciousness itself, which should never be made public. The epistolary convention allows the novel to break this taboo. Opening the letters written by the characters, the reader eavesdrops on their thinking and enters into possession of testimony never spoken aloud. Defoe catches this guilty confidentiality (which novels pretend to respect but of course outrage) in the first anecdote he retails. The first house to be infected endeavours to conceal the plague, 'but as it had gotten some vent in the discourse of the neighbourhood, the Secretaries of State got knowledge of it.' Fielding in the inns or carriages of *Joseph Andrews* salutes what he calls discourse or dissertation as a genial fellowship in narrative. Stories celebrate our kinship, and in telling them we reconvene a family of man. But in Defoe discourse is itself a vent—a leakage which ought to be stopped up, the place of entry for a thief, the lesion through which a disease insinuates itself. Far from being the greatest story every told (which is how the epic likes to consider itself), the novel is the story which should never have been told at all.

H. G. Wells in *The Shape of Things to Come* (1933) derided *Crusoe* for its economic idiocy. No man, he thought, could live so independently; 'Defoe's queer story' deters social change, by inhibiting our co-operation with one another. Nevertheless, the withdrawel from society is Defoe's instinct and that of the novel, whose characters regularly claim for themselves a life outside or above the community. Clarissa, dying, achieves this; so, abstinently, do Fanny Price in *Mansfield Park* or Esther Summerson in *Bleak House*. The character of classical literature is public man—warrior, orator, patriarch or law-giver. His counterpart in modern literature is a recluse, owing no responsibility to anything beyond himself. Defoe's H.F. declares such solitude his constitutional privilege, guarded by the edicts of the novel. Liberty means the freedom to reject the public realm, to remain in unmolested privacy. When H.F. is appointed a parish examiner by aldermanic decree and sent to inspect diseased houses he recoils from the ghastly chore, inventing excuses for his dismissal and eventually securing discharge from 'the dangerous office . . . as soon as I could get another admitted'. He obtains a deputy, he admits, by disbursing a bribe.

The *Plague Year* adumbrates the mental territory of the novel at its paranoid: a consciousness voluntarily imprisoned, recording those sideways glimpses which are its only participation in the world. By contrast, *Moll Flanders* is about the resilience and courage of realism, and about the novel's confident mission to take stock—even if fleetingly—of a world in its entirety. The *Tour* makes much of the organic flux or fluidity of material and commerce. Defoe praises the 'flowing variety of materials' and 'the prodigious conflux of people'. In the *Plague Year*, such fluxes are the symptoms of malady, listed beside 'griping of the guts, surfeits, and the like'. The plague itself is fluent, and must be dammed or iced-over into fixity. It abates during winter but 'would like a frozen river have returned to its usual force and current when it thawed'. The ocean, unstable and untrustworthy, is also the element which betrays Crusoe. But Moll is in herself fluctuant and fluvial. Whenever she has a turbulent sea voyage, she resolves 'to venture it no more upon the water, which had been so terrible to me'; yet she cannot keep to her vow because landed society is just as infirmly liquid. She must learn to live with that groundlessness, with the dubious and the contingent. These, to her, are 'the laws of nature'.

She practises a moral and psychological *laissez-faire*, committing herself to the life-stream and endeavouring to remain buoyant, submitting to the use others make of her if she can in her turn make use of them. She represents everything which alarms Crusoe and H.F., and everything which a creator like Henry James disliked in the novel and excluded from his own works: the accidental, the irrelevant or (as he said of *Crusoe*) the improvised. She is the promiscuity of realism, its easy-going artlessness, its hope not—like Crusoe or H.F.—its demoralised despair. If they are latter-day heroes of epic, keeping watch on the walls (and H.F. actually defines London by specifying 'the city, that is to say, within the walls'), she is a spirit of romance, opportunistic and adrift. She conceives of herself as shop-soiled goods, always in hazard but retaining some value, as against the goods preserved from use or the unexchangable coins which Crusoe accumulates, or the stored property which H.F. defends against the looters of his brother's warehouse. Because her life is in circulation, she understands the slipperiness of commodities and their tendency to reincarnate themselves. Though they may not be yours for long, they will have other lives elsewhere, in other shops or under other auspices, as Moll herself does when she revises her identity, first consenting to be nicknamed Moll Flanders and then telling a judge that it is her misfortune to have been mistaken 'for one Moll Flanders, who was a famous successful thief . . .; but that . . . was none of my name'.

Objects share this subjective revisionism. The portmanteau is first the Dutchman's then Moll's, and no doubt soon after someone else's. Theft merely assists the circulating motion of life. Moll's governess makes it her business to help commodities on their metamorphic way by rendering them liquid: 'she always melted down the plate she bought, that it might not be challenged.' The same coursing vitality or currency is Moll's own aim. One of her financial advisers tells her to open a bank account, and explains to her the difference between deposits—those anal-erotic hoards, never to be spent, on which Crusoe squats—and money which will not amass any interest but can be withdrawn and expended at a moment's notice. This, Moll learns, is called 'running cash': a riverine supply, replenishing the means of life. Her glib fluency, which she calls the 'flux and reflux' of inconsistent emotions, at last ensures her survival. When her colleagues at Newgate are put to death, she reacts by deliquescing, and she reports the same in a sentence as dribblingly successive as her grief. 'As soon as they were gone, I fell into a fit of crying involuntarily, as a mere distemper, and yet so violent, that it held me so long, that I knew not what course to take, nor could I stop, or put a check on it, no not with all the strength and courage I had.' This opening of the sluices convinces the minister who attends her that she is penitent, and should not be executed.

Defoe is no unpretending artisan. He is a considerable artist, but one who sees through his own art, understanding the flimsiness of Crusoe's structural barrages. He knows that fiction means a special kind of mendacity (so that when Moll gives to the minister 'an abridgement of its whole history; . . . the picture of my conduct for fifty years in miniature' we can be sure that she has already glossed, edited and packaged it as if it were a novel); however conscientiously it may profess morality, it is in league with cupidinous, acquisitive fantasy. Near the end, Moll announces her reprobate husband's reformation. She 'could fill a larger history than this', she threatens, with evidences of how God's grace works on such sinners. Yet she is too much of an artist—and as a novelist, her trade is that of the confidence trickster—to risk it: 'I doubt that part of the story will not be equally diverting as the wicked part.' Such asides indicate that Defoe, like all his successors, is at once ingenuous novelist and self-conscious anti-novelist, both in- and outside the convenient convention. The novel, pledged to the renewal of literature, demands of its practitioners a permanent revolution.

— 21 —
Richardson and Fielding: Tragic Pastoral and Comic Epic

The eighteenth-century romantic imagination knew itself to be implicated in the common concealment of truth: Thomas Chatterton with his mock-Gothic ballads and James Macpherson with his bardic *Ossian* are forgers. From the first, the novel has been a party to this fraud. The more studiously Defoe's translators attest that the manuscripts they are editing are historical documents, the more certain we are that they are inventions. *Pamela* (1740) retains its power to shock not because of the heroine's ethical affectations but because she is so aware of and so expert at writing as fiction and, therefore, falsehood. This knowledge is the professional bequest to her of Richardson, scribe and master-printer, who understood that writing is a product of false consciousness, which lacks the unselfconscious actuality of feeling, thought or speech.

Pamela's subject is the novel's manufacture—her assembly of tools (pens, wafers, sealing-wax and ink) and her secreting of them about the house or on her person, so that to read her is to be enticed into raping her, for Mr B is convinced that she conceals her papers in her bosom or ties them about her knees with her gaiters; her insistence on being allowed what she calls 'writing-time', which means that the composition of her journal is her sole employment; her suborning of John and Parson Williams as publishers and distributors of her output; and her sale to us of her packaged fantasy, irradiated by what Mr B sarcastically calls 'the sun-beams of a dangerous affluence'. In her first letter, she grieves over the muddying of her page as tears blot her ink, a besmirchment almost more distressing to her than Mr B's attempted assault. The artistry of Pamela the writer is a species of artfulness. Incriminated by her own words, she introduces to the beginning of the novel's history the equivocations of a form which makes brazen fictions from facts, unrepentantly publicises confidences it declares to be private, and while alleging itself to be art is actually merchandise, a consumer item named after the craving of a bourgeois economy—celebrated by Crusoe and by Pamela as she takes possession of cambric aprons, silk handkerchiefs and shoes with silver buckles—for novelties. She therefore provokes a debate on the probity of that form taken up at once by Fielding and still alive for Upton Sinclair two centuries later.

Fielding condemns her in his *Shamela* (1741) because she trades in what his title-page calls 'falsehoods and misrepresentations' and deploys 'matchless arts'; because, in other words, she is a novelist, and an disarmingly good one. At the end of his parody, Shamela, having heard of Richardson's plan to sanitise and immortalise her, chuckles 'to think I shall see myself in a printed book'. Print, she knows, will grant her exoneration by re-inventing her. The credulous parson who believes in Pamela's virtue is called Tickletext, and Fielding shows the tickling of texts—the cajoling from them of contrary senses—to be an elaborate novelistic skill. Shamela's paramour, Parson Williams, bends scriptural citation to suit his sexual convenience. 'His text was, *Be not righteous over-much*', says Shamela after one of his sermons; 'and indeed he handled it in a very fine way.' She, too, betrays the spirit of the law by wantoning with its letter. As for virtue ('vartue' to her), she cannot even spell it. Though she calls it '*a charming word . . ., rest his soul who first invented it*', it remains for her only a word. Moral infractions are no worse than verbal lapses: Shamela's mother, referring to an earlier fall from grace, warns her about 'digressions', and on another occasion, with commercial gain sneaking into the mis-spelled sexual pun, Shamela reports that 'Mrs Jenkes took a glass and drank the dear *monysyllable*; I don't understand that word, but I believe it is bawdy.' (Monysyllable is a slang term for the bodily part which is Shamela's money-maker and her cash-box.)

Parson Williams, persuading her to stay married to Booby for his wealth while retaining Williams himself as a lover, develops a nicely specious moral justification and at the same time contrives a theory to support the novel's textual double-dealing. He tells Shamela 'that the Flesh and the Spirit were two distinct matters, which had not the least relation to each other. That all immaterial substances . . . such as love, desire, and so forth, were guided by the Spirit; but fine houses, large estates, coaches and dainty entertainments were the product of the Flesh.' He counsels her to keep two husbands, one as overseer of each province. Not only has Williams disjoined the realms, he has reversed them by defining pulchritude as an affair of the spirit. His casuistry serves up as well a code for literary conduct. Spirit and letter (fleshly integument: the 'chaff' of Chaucer's 'Nun's Priest's Tale') need no longer concur. Their divorce sets free an undergrowth of inadvertent or implicit meanings, a subliminal text of fantasy truer in spirit than the timid, innocuous letter. Shamela's ribald puns are rooted in that subterranean region, and the bull which menaces Pamela emerges from there. Here as in *Tristram Shandy*, the novel gives evidence of a liberality about meanings and truths which approaches libertinism. The genii of fiction are André Gide's counterfeiters, *Les Faux-Monnayeurs* (1926).

In 1950 Upton Sinclair's *Another Pamela* awarded Richardson's heroine an extra lease of life in contemporary southern California. She comes there as an impoverished Okie to work as parlourmaid in the household of an oil millionaire, and is assailed by the young master who wears a polo shirt and cohabits with Hollywood floozies. Sinclair attributes to Richardson the invention, in *Pamela*, of the English novel, so in criticising his heroine's naive acquisitiveness he is refuting an entire tradition of fiction which panders to that vice. The corruption of Sinclair's Pamela is (as her radical creator sees it) her rite of passage into society and her introduction to the covetousness which is the motive force of bourgeois realism. She gets by heart the names of the expensive fabrics of her employer's dresses, learns to drive (and eventually spell) her seducer's 'Merseedys', and makes out cheques for her mistress to sign.

Her defilement is definitively accomplished by a novel—specifically by Richardson's *Pamela*. At first she has a religious dread of literature. As an Adventist, she is a literalist about Holy Writ, and catechises a prisoner in San Quentin by sending him scriptural texts to ponder. Her infidel lover outrages her by treating scripture as mere literature: 'He does not accept the Bible as a Holy Book, but says it is Jewish history and legend.' Even before her reading of Richardson, she has, as a letter-writer, begun to practise the duplicity which is the imaginative truancy of literature. She writes an anodyne version of events for her mother, a more scandalous and titillating one for her sister. At first she flinches from the perfidy of fiction. Her church 'does not approve the reading of novels'; however, she is enticed to make an exception for *Pamela*, which pretends not to be one—'I am permitted to read letters.' The book itself appeals to her possessive instincts. When a literary gent presents it to her, she is 'overwhelmed, for it is such a pretty book'. She allows herself to read it in half-hour instalments, followed by doses of her Testament and prayers. Reading awakens the devil of concupiscent fantasy in her. She is tempted to peek at the end to see how Pamela comes off, and begins to model herself on her prototype. By the time of her honeymoon with the young reprobate in New York, she has so far surrendered to the world of entrancing, materially splendid fiction that she agrees to accompany him to picture shows. She compensates by lecturing him from the scripture, but reflects—demoralised—that 'these are stories too, and might be on the screen'.

In Sinclair's theory, the more dangerous betrayer is not Mr B. but Richardson himself. The novel was created, he thinks, to cater to a lustful bourgeois greed. Richardson's 'pretty book' is interchangeable with the cheque-book of Pamela's benefactress. Therefore Sinclair's sequel, which begins in his foreword with the production of 'a new form of literature known as the English novel' and slurs Richardson by saying that the novel made him, like his Pamela, 'a celebrity and the darling of London society', ends in a postscript by signalling Sinclair's rejection of both that affluent society and the literary form which sustains it. His last word is 'This is a work of fiction and is to be read as such'—but his purpose in saying so is simply to protect himself from prosecution by libelled individuals, since he claims as his qualification for writing it his long acquaintanceship with 'the so-called "great families" of America'; his fiction is therefore accusative fact. He retains the puritanical literalism and consequent mistrust of literature which his heroine once possessed, but which she forfeited to a reading of Richardson.

Neither Fielding nor Sinclair should have believed their parodies to be exposés of Richardson, who already understood and brilliantly exploited the qualms about writing and fictional misrepresentation for which they deride him. *Clarissa* (1747–8) is about a vocational martyrdom to literature. Pamela is the writer as a hungry materialist, satiating herself by describing things; Clarissa, however, must choose between living and writing, and, like a nun entering holy orders, she elects the latter course, choosing to be hopelessly isolated until her only contact with society is via the exercise of her pen. That she employs meditatively, not to record events or to validate the fretful diversity of existence but to evacuate her mind, to pass beyond drama or even narrative into the calm of introspection and retrospection. Miss Howe praises, in the very first letter, her 'noble consciousness'; it is the consciousness of the novelist, observing life but duty-bound to refrain from participating in it, consciousness as that aerial perspective which James in 1914 saluted in Joseph Conrad's Marlow—'the prolonged hovering flight of the subjective over the outstretched ground of the case exposed'. Such detachment is a professional habit of the wary, unattached mariner Marlow. Clarissa's attainment of it is harder and more heroic: she removes herself mentally from her tragedy, writing about it rather than continuing to perform in it. This is her religious victory, her suppression of the agitated will and her acceptance of a patient, paralysed involuntariness. It is also her literary virtue, for the more passive she becomes the more actively she writes. She will make any sacrifice except that of her pen, and when her store of writing implements is impounded she has 'recourse to my private pen', guarded in secret. The grasp of that pen signifies the inviolability of the mind.

The composition of a letter comes to mean, for Clarissa, an interdiction, a refusal of relationship or of collusive correspondence. The medium absorbs the messages it is supposed to send: writing is an embargo on human union, as when her brother informs her by letter that she is exiled from the presence of their parents and forbidden even to write to them. Lovelace importunes her during her captivity; but she insists that she must conclude a letter to Miss Howe before she will admit him, and they write letters to each other even when they are both resident in the same house. It is as if Clarissa is atoning for the literary guilts of Pamela, Shamela and Sinclair's reincarnated hoyden, and for writing's complicity with fantasy. Correspondence after all means the desire for reciprocation, for the answering respiration of Wordsworth's 'correspond-ing . . . breeze' in *The Prelude*. A co-respondent is a partner in adultery. At first all letters are promptly replied to; but by the end no one is answering anyone else, and each is writing for his or her own therapeutic purposes, transmitting letters without replying to them. Lovelace on June 26 complains that he has sent three to Clarissa (which he copies out for Belford's perusal) but has had 'not . . . one word . . . in answer'. By August 29, Charlotte Montague, Lovelace's collaborator, is affectedly aping Clarissa's fears and is displeased when a copy of her letter is sent to Belford—'that her handwriting, forsooth! should go into the hands of a single man!' The letter's proper state is now that of the monologue—self-immurement. Epistolary protocol ensures this hermetic privacy, and Clarissa is appalled when her parents send her denunciations which arrive 'without superscription, and unsealed', allowing the impudent Betty to behave as if she had trespassed on their contents.

As well as its letters, the novel scrutinizes other documents and interpretatively ponders them, for it is a school of textual criticism. It begins with the will of Clarissa's grandfather, and ends with her own; between these are her ode and its accompanying music, the marriage licence, her fragmented papers (transcribed for Lovelace's study by Dorcas) where her distracted thought chops up the even temper of prose into stanzaic fits of poetry, the letter forged in her name with unsteady fingers by Lovelace or that written by Clarissa in a similacrum of his handwriting with a pen she has stolen from him. These last two exhibits are the most troubling in the novel, perhaps the real conclusion of the mental match between Lovelace and Clarissa. They hint at the forbidden attraction of writing, which allows you dreamily to exchange your own existence for another, to ventriloquise a new identity. In the exchange of signatures and of voices, the sadist and the masochist solemnise a transfer of power: Lovelace becomes Clarissa's victim, while she assumes the role of his tormenter.

The life of writing (and of its correlative, reading) is in *Clarissa* a shamefully clandestine one, nocturnal and ultimately deathly. Writing is night work. The letter is the negation of action, as night is the photographic negative of day. Clarissa vows to sit up all night to write to Miss Howe. Does this make her scribbling an insomniac watch kept by reason ('Hardly a wink have I slept, ruminating on the approaching interview') or, more seditiously, an equivalent of sleep, the reason's subsidence? Are the letters a noctambulant confession, like Lady Macbeth's? Lovelace's sleeplessness is a recurrent topic in the novel. Mr Fortescue avows that he rests but six hours a day, and he compares himself to Julius Caesar 'who performed great actions by day and wrote them down at night'. He spends one night uncomfortably in the coppice, chafing his chilled and numbed hand to encourage it to go on scrawling. Lovelace, however, is the evil genius of literature, its shaded side. If it takes him a whole night to write down the doings of his day, he must, Miss Howe surmises, have crimes aplenty to relate, and his mastery of shorthand excites a further suspicion—'What inducements could such a swift writer as he have to learn shorthand?'

Speed is no aim of Clarissa's: she writes to decelerate experience. Lovelace's rapid notation warns of his interest in the coercive and compulsive power of writing. He writes as things happen, and to make them continue to happen. His is a romantic principle, wanting to seize the fiery coal before its heat (in

Shelley's phrase for the poetic image) flees from it, or to detain instants (as a later romantic, Walter Pater, recommended) before they are swept on to dissolution. But his volatile instantaneousness—that 'infinite vivacity, . . . - which runs away with me'—is itself a morbid symptom. Though he is writing to forestall his own death (which is why he resents having to sleep), he is all the same urgently advancing it. When it comes, he cannot describe it. That, for Virginia Woolf, who spoke of her death as the one experience she would be prevented from describing, is the writer's despair. Clarissa, less deluded, sees that writing is a resignation from the hasty tempo of living, studies her death in advance, and by pre-ordaining it does describe it and its aftermath, leaving precise instructions about her transference to her coffin.

This could be called her classicism. Apart from life, resisting the seductions of time, she toils over the construction of that most classical of structures, her own funeral monument, and her mortuary preparedness associates her with other casualties of her neoclassical era: the black or blank obituary pages in *Tristram Shandy*, the graves in Gray's churchyard, the exemplary deaths which are the climaxes of Johnson's *Lives of the Poets*. Johnson indeed made one of the shrewdest comments on Richardson's novel when he said that the man who read *Clarissa* for the story would end by hanging himself. Such a misreader would be Lovelace, who demands the consummations of narrative and is teased by Belford with the frustration of a coitus interruptus—'How hast thou tortured me by the designed *abruption*!' he rages when his friend breaks off his account of Clarissa's sufferings. Hanging is where Lovelace deserves to end. Romantically, narrative expires in dejection at its own incompleteness. Madeline and Porphyro vanish; the person from Porlock knocks at the door. The classical wisdom is to teach oneself, in reading, an abstinence like Clarissa's, and to give up wanting the blandishments and diversions of story. Having done so, you will have thought yourself out of life into the ritualised timelessness of reading and writing. It is in this region that Johnson sets his own storyless narratives, *Rasselas* with its 'conclusion, in which nothing is concluded' or 'The Vanity of Human Wishes' telling over again in each Ecclesiastes-like couplet the same dismayingly repeated story of pride and its inevitable fall.

Gradually, writing and living move apart, until they stand in ethical opposition. The 'great defect' of Dorcas's character as far as Clarissa is concerned, and the badge of her wickedness, is her pretended illiteracy. She is said to be unable to read or write. Lovelace instructs her to seek tutelage from Clarissa (just as Clarissa's successor Fanny Price in *Mansfield Park* inducts her sister into the conventual order of readers by making her join the Portsmouth circulating library); but the purpose is one of espionage. The inky-fingered Dorcas has been commissioned, with Sally and Polly as her fellow scribes, to make copies of all Clarissa's papers. Clarissa's mode of writing is blameless because it is the mind's withdrawal from experience: the subjective inquisition James remarked on in Conrad's *Chance*. Thus she disdains story-tellers, like the anecdotal beau Touville who performs his tales with a Sternean or Byronic bravura and delights in his own showy virtuosity; and although she is a professional describer, her province is the inner, novelistic one of feelings not the external realm of appearances, on which a covetous, salacious realism like Pamela's dwells.

She herself is not physically described until her abduction, and then of course the describer is Lovelace. His inventory of her charms is his means of possessing her: like Defoe subjectively asserting that he owns the world of objects he surveys, Lovelace fixes and appropriates her in words. Appropriation leads to publication, and when she escapes he threatens to gazette her as an eloped wife, recording for Belford the 'description of her dress' which he will use as his advertisement. The mind has been trapped in a body, made the property first of Lovelace, then of the entire world, for her beauty (as her *Gazette* entry proclaims) 'commands the repeated attention of everyone who sees her'. Words are of use to Lovelace only as a means of power, writing as the plotting or fulfilment of an action. It is he not Clarissa who takes over Pamela's frantic attempt to write to the moment, closing the gap between the event and its transcription, and in the process he is prepared to dispense altogether with the interceding agency of language. The words he favours are ejaculatory, emissions of vital heat, like the 'What! How! When!—and all the monosyllables of surprise' (remembering Shamela's monysyllable?) with which he greets the news of Clarissa's escape; polysyllables, he tells Belford, are good-for-nothing time-wasters. The same eruptive energy, not pausing to articulate itself, inclines him to typographic malediction. Like Tristram Shandy, he adores the asterisk, and marginally brands a letter from Miss Howe to Laetitia Beaumont with dozens of these. Tristram's coy stars are suggestive erasures; Lovelace's are curses, too fearful to be spelled out—the stab-marks with which he would like to scar Miss Howe.

Henry James's injunction to himself was 'Dramatize! dramatize!' Oddly, it is not a command which the novel often obeys. More usually, the novel trusts to a meditative mesmerism. Rather than dramatically goading characters into action, it values their stasis and renunciation—the immobile Clarissa's disavowal of '*self*, this vile, this hated *self*!', Fanny Price's mousey but saintly timorousness, the transcendence of action by James's dying dove Millie Theale. In *Clarissa*, it is Lovelace who is the dramatist; his rampant theatricality and officious stage-management enable Richardson to define the new methods and purposes of the novel by contrasting them with the devilish aptitudes required in the drama. Lovelace takes Clarissa to a play and is forever quoting tags from other dramatists. He coaches his subordinates in their roles, rehearses an ambush as a pretext for capturing Clarissa, even vows that he will write a play about quarrelsome lovers. Seduction for him is dramaturgy. He introduces the encounter on Hampstead Heath as Act II of his scenario. He is fond, as well, of notating dialogue, like that between himself and Clarissa on May 22 while she readies herself to go outdoors, as if he had magicked the novel into drama, and it suits his manipulative sense of superintendence to append stage-directions, cued by him—on May 28, '*Enter Captain Tomlinson, in a riding-dress, whip in hand*' or '*Enter Dorcas, in a hurry.*' Writing itself is a purgatory, as he complains to Belford. For him, life must vent itself in action, performance. He is assiduous in avoiding, he says, reflective repetitions. Clarissa's solace is the novelist's: to ingurgitate and mentally retraverse experience. Her vocational symbol is her memorandum book. She commands herself to recollect ('Recollection! Heart-affecting recollection! How it pains me!') not to dramatise; and for her a ritually tedious repetition is both a technique of writing and a device of moral meditation.

From Sterne and Richardson through Wordsworth's poetic autobiography to Proust, the novel is a book sacred to memory. Clarissa's fidelity to the form diverges from the theatrical libertinage of Lovelace, incidentally explaining why Fanny Price should so stubbornly have disapproved of the play performed at Mansfield. Thus during the summer, while Clarissa is impounded at Hampstead, Lovelace first scribbles down events as they happen, with the acumen and urgency of the dramatist; then Clarissa returns to relate them all over again in suffering retrospection. The drama's impetuosity is contained within the novel's steadfast, abiding mistrust of action and its preference for a backward-looking review and interpretative revision of experience. Henry James thought that the two principles—which he called the scenic and the pictorial—could be combined in the art of the novel. But the scenic, agitated and accelerating, is the dementia of Lovelace; the pictorial, studying the unperturbed contents of a mind which is to James (who called characters reflectors in both the remembering and the mirroring senses of the word) the novel's commanding centre of intelligence, is the patient omniscience of Clarissa.

Within English literature, the dramatic and the novelistic remain opponents, not alternatives. Virginia Woolf calls her last novel *Between the Acts* because as a novel it is the interim and intermission of drama. The novel's concern is silence not speech. When the play resumes, with its willed social amiability and untruth to the disquiet within—as it does in the last sentences of *Between the Acts*, 'Then the curtain rose. They spoke.'—the novel must end. Novels characteristically begin with the resignation of characters from action. Sinclair Lewis's hero in *Dodsworth* (1929) sells off his car works and goes to Europe to study a cultivated, introspective leisure. In Somerset Maugham's *The Razor's Edge* (1944) the hero Larry Darrell refuses a job in a broker's office and goes off to Paris to, as he puts it, 'loaf'. From there he drifts to the Orient, where loafing becomes a mystic discipline. He is a character, like Clarissa or Fanny Price, for whom the novel is consecrated to meditation. Richardson connects the novel's ethics with its aesthetics in *Sir Charles Grandison* (1753–4). Charlotte breaks off her account of Grandison's wedding by telling Lucy that her account is too sentimental—too solicitously internal, too moodily uneventful—for the English. 'Story, story, story', she complains, 'is what they hunt after.' Richardson's moral abstention from narrative (Grandison refuses to fight a duel with Sir Hargrave Pollexfen) coincides with a repudiation of drama, which is a spectacle of character in exhibitionistic, exhausting action. Grandison deplores masquerades as 'diversions that fall not in with the genius of the English commonality.' The same novelistic decree was repeated by Henry James in 1877. 'The arts of the stage', he thought, 'are not really in the temperament and manners of the [English] people', who are 'too highly moral to be histrionic.' The novel continues to prosecute Charlotte's war against story, as well as against the factitious showdowns of drama: with a sigh of dismay, Forster laments that novelists still have the job of telling a story.

The same antipathy to drama persists in George Eliot, for whom Richardson exemplifies the lofty morality of the novel—except that the Richardsonian sacrament of sentiment has yielded to an agnostic evangelism, and the novel, rather than supplementing scripture, has taken over from it as a primer of moral analysis and spiritual counsel. Daniel Deronda, a secularly sacred Grandison, recoils from Sir Hugo's coarse description of him as 'a kind of Lovelace who will make the Clarissas run after you'. He recoils also from the imputation of theatricality. When Mirah asks him if he is on the stage, he denies it with some indignation. Mordecai, like Rousseau legislating against the establishment of a theatre in the rational republic of Geneva, lectures her on the amoral involuntarism of drama. She has read, he charges, 'too many plays, where the writers delight in showing the human passions as indwelling demons, unmixed with the relenting and devout elements of the soul'. Character in drama is a devil inciting people to unreflective action; in novels, character is a patient, introspective stillness, an angel of contemplation not a restless imp—Fanny Price in the library, the chastened Gwendolen Harleth 'sitting motionless' as she reviews her life's errors. Moral fatuity in *Daniel Deronda* is judged by the stupidity of reading life as a drama, which is equivalent to reading Richardson for the story. The foolish girls at Offendene find 'real life as interesting as *Sir Charles Grandison*', although that novel exists to deplore the very category of interest.

The philosopher Schopenhauer in 1851 elaborates a metaphysics for the novel when he argues—adducing *Don Quixote*, *Tristram Shandy*, *La Nouvelle Héloïse* and *Wilhelm Meister* as examples—that literary works can only be beautiful (tranquilly perceptive, spiritually aloof) if they refuse to be interesting, for the interest of narrative would arouse and irritate a fractious will they wish to quieten. The novel itself becomes a sacred text to be meditated on, a guarantor of pastoral's moral calm. Diderot treats Richardson's mental recesses as openings into landscape: a nature of nuance where, he says, as during spring, no two leaves are of the same green; or else, rather than an arbour, a cave for the sensual monster he calls the hideous Moor.

For Richardson the novel is a hermitage, for Fielding a common ground of sociability, sharing an experience which Richardson's characters, blocked by their intransitive letters, cannot pass on to others. A letter in Fielding is not the recourse of an inalienable privacy and sacrosanct secrecy. It exists in the public domain, as an admonitory lecture.

The lady in the coach in *Joseph Andrews* who wishes to tell the story of the jilted Leonora intends to quote the correspondence between her and Horatio 'which I have got by heart'. Mrs Grave-airs piously objects to hearing the letters, but is out-voted. The publicising of these *billets-doux* is no outrage, because Fielding believes the letter to be a social act, a publication of private feelings which are necessarily overstated or defensively understated, and made to depend on the absurd contingencies of literary manufacture. Tom Jones, as soon as he is 'furnished with the proper materials', can dash off a farewell letter to Sophia which obeys the epistolary rules by saying he writes in too distressed a state to be articulate but which is all the same impressively eloquent; then he finds he has no wax to seal it with.

A letter unsealed in Richardson is tantamount to a violation. But as Tom's sentiments are stoutly and genially conventional and public, why should he worry about the wax? Tom's affair with Lady Bellaston is terminated in an exchange of letters, because it was on both sides a forgery of feelings. The veracity of the letter must be attested to by the body. Since writing is so devious a business, letters in Fielding can be trusted only if they are avidly treated as substitutes for the correspondent's physical presence. Tom reads and kisses Sophia's note of forgiveness a hundred times each, and when Black George brings another missive from her he 'spent three hours in reading and kissing' it. Defoe's writings are the letters which the castaway launches in bottles, trying to believe in the remote chance of his ever finding a reader; Fielding's are, at their sincerest, bodily products, produced by one organism and consumed by another. Tom's letter to Sophia arrives inside a cooked pullet along with, and comparable to, its cache of eggs.

A letter stands for the novelist's presumption to know a character from within. This claim Fielding is too tactful to make. Unlike Richardson, he has no wish to be privy. He will not say what Sophia felt when she read the letter delivered inside the fowl, and adds that she did not reply because 'she had no paper, pen, nor ink'; nor will he interpret her daydream of marriage during her conversation with Mrs Fitzpatrick: 'She never revealed this dream to anyone, so the reader cannot expect to see it related here.' Rather than Richardsonian introversion, which he calls (speaking of Allworthy's ignorance of the liaison between Miss Bridget and Captain Bligh) 'the insight of the devil', Fielding prefers the view from without—interpreting, for instance, the 'visible marks' with which the indignation of Partridge's wife has seared his face, and requesting the reader to 'bear witness', also by visual testimony, that the man is blameless. *Jonathan Wild* in 1754 contains a joke about the Richardsonian (and Crusoesque) régime of suffering in epistolary silence: alone on the boat Wild 'spent his time in contemplation, that is to say', Fielding adds, 'in blaspheming, cursing, and sometimes singing and whistling.' Whereas in Richardson to visualise is to capture and symbolically to kill, so that it is only Lovelace who dares to describe Clarissa's appearance, in Fielding description is a reflex of human solicitude and a means—like kissing letters—of delectation. Fielding lip-lickingly itemises what he calls 'the outside of Sophia', and when characterising her mind can only extrovert it in the sweet-tempered glory of her smile. Mrs Waters, fancying Tom, is even less curious about his interior: 'The beauty of Jones highly charmed her eye; but as she could not see his heart, she gave herself no concern about it.' Lady Bellaston, too, appraises him pictorially, and says he might 'sit for the picture of Adonis'.

Because Fielding's art is the vital physiognomic illustration of feelings, it demands—instead of Richardson's continence of spirit, its eyes averted from the distraction of the real—material satisfaction. Once the lady in the coach has mentioned the arrival in her narrative of Bellarmine, Parson Adams begs to be told 'how this gentleman was drest'. The lady, rapidly improvising, supplies details of the foppish garments which she has been informed (she archly says) he had on. Fielding's pen needs to double as a pencil. He is grateful to Hogarth for having drawn—embodied, that is—his characters in advance, and he pre-assigns people in *Tom Jones* to roles in his friend's engravings. Miss Bridget is the purportedly devout churchgoer in Covent Garden in the plate of a winter's morning, Jenny Jones the maid in the third scene of the *Harlot's Progress*, and Thwackum is defamingly made to inhabit the countenance and the physique of 'that gentleman who, in the *Harlot's Progress*, is seen courting the ladies in Bridewell'. Fielding accepts without misgiving that realism is an art appealing to the lusts of the eye. Miss Blifil inclines towards Square's principles because his 'person was . . . agreeable to her eye, for he was a comely man'. The lecherous divines in *Shamela* have proved to be reliable literary theoreticians.

An interesting scene in *Clarissa* has Lovelace and Clarissa in the same room, each writing but each covertly studying the other's eyes—not in appetitive admiration; only because the eye is the keyhole to the closed, dark room of the mind. When Lovelace feels Clarissa's mesmeric gaze, he writes, 'She looked at me as if she would look through me: I thought I *felt* eyebeam after eyebeam penetrate my shivering veins. But she was silent. Nor needed her eyes the assistance of speech.' He has been subjected to her moral insight, in an ocular rape. The equivalent occasion in Fielding is an exact opposite: a speaking look, instead of Clarissa's mute, disabling speech. Sophia remains silent while her father upbraids her, emitting only a sigh. Squire Western, who 'understood none of the language, or, as he called it, lingo of the eye', demands her spoken assent. In place of the Richardsonian vision which bares souls, Fielding's art strips bodies, and dares his characters not to look at what is flagrantly displayed. The falsely pious female traveller in *Joseph Andrews* is aghast at the hero's nakedness. But while disdaining the sight of him she manages secretly to enjoy it: she 'had the sticks of her fan before her eyes'.

Reading, that obsessive Richardsonian occupation, is also suspect in Fielding, because it is a school of feigning. Sophia is discovered by her aunt reading a novel. She has been blushing and whimpering over its tender sentiments. Her aunt, like Parsons Tickletext and Williams, commends the letter's licentious infidelity to the spirit, telling Sophia, 'You should read books which would teach you a little hypocrisy.' More aware than Richardson of the counterfeitings required by society as well as by a literary form which names itself after its own unfactual untrustworthiness, Fielding concurs with Miss Western. A mild dishonesty is Sophia's only technique for coping with the rivalry and enmity of Lady Bellaston. Fielding comments that 'the elegant Lord Shaftesbury somewhere objects to telling too much truth: by which it may be fairly inferred, that, in some cases, to lie is not only excusable, but commendable.' Though illiteracy is for Clarissa in her judgement of Dorcas a moral failing, to Fielding it is a moral delicacy, an exemption from the deceptive self-consciousness of fiction. During their year apart, Joseph Andrews and Fanny have no correspondence because she 'could neither read nor write'. Nor, Fielding adds, thinking of the scribal voyeurism which had been Richardson's apprenticeship to the novel, would she 'transmit the delicacies of her tender and chaste passion by the hand of an amanuensis'. The gypsy king in *Tom Jones* is allowed positively to boast that 'me . . . can neider write nor read'.

The praise of illiteracy is odd in a literary work, but it connects with Fielding's scheme for the novel, which he sees as a declension of previous genres, including them all but superseding them. The novel is thus a critique of its entire literary past. Epic is deflected into the picaresque, easy-going divagations of romance and then, in Fielding's theory, adjusted to a modern, comic and prosaic definition of reality. Parson Adams in *Joseph Andrews* credits Homer with the parentage of all genres, 'of the drama as well as the epic; not of tragedy only, but of comedy also'. Fielding inherits this multiple progeny and dreams of the novel as a work which will be all genres at once—all, and therefore none.

Jonathan Wild demonstrates that epic can no longer pretend to supremacy in the hierarchy of genres: it is a mere matter of verbal flatulence and craven hyperbole. Wild owes his status as a great man to fawning rhetoric. Fielding corrects the fawning fictitiousness of language by translating downwards, effecting a linguistic demotion. 'Aurora now first opened her casement, *Anglicè* the day began to break', he writes in *Tom Jones*. That rewriting of his own inflated idiom is a democratic concession: thus he remarks that though the reader may imagine 'Lady Bellaston to be a member (and no inconsiderable one) of the great world; she was in reality a very considerable member of the little world.' The graceful descent from great to little carries with it an advance from great men (the roguish Wild, or a braggart like Fielding's bombastic dwarf Tom Thumb, afloat on what Squire Western calls a pompous 'Hanoverian lingo') to ordinary ones—divine averages such as the unexceptional Jones, or legal ciphers like the non-existent John Doe, mentioned in *Jonathan Wild*. Since human nature is of the mixed kind, neither good nor evil, the absolutism of genre must accept compromise and contradiction. Fielding's justification of the novel's reunion of tragic and comic epic (depending on his assertion that Homer composed a lost comic alternative to the *Iliad*) coincides with Johnson's defence of the same reunion achieved by Shakespeare in the drama.

The hybridising does not end here. Fielding combines, as well, the incompatible kinds of drama and essay. Often a theatrical scene (like the 'dialogue matrimonial', with stage directions, between Wild and Laetitia) will be followed by a dissertation on the issues raised, or 'observation on the foregoing dialogue'. At Upton, *Tom Jones* is a theatrical farce; in its prefatory chapters, it is a treatise on its own heterodox form. Though in prose, it contains, in its mock-epic flurries, the poetry it has outdone. It even attempts the inclusiveness of a polyglot idiom, like Sterne in the *Sentimental Journey* translating from English to French and thence to the universal language of the heart. The French lieutenant encountered by Jones in the Jacobite episode has 'been long enough out of France to forget his own language, but not long enough in England to learn ours, so that he really spoke no language at all'. Yet he knows of the Trojan war, having read Homer, Fielding's parent and patron. That is the basis of his identity with his colleagues, even with Northerton who curses Homer for having caused him to be beaten at school but reverently mispronounces him as 'Homo': the creator of *homo sapiens* in literature, the genealogical begetter of every genre.

In its containment of all things, Fielding's novel resembles the newspaper, that impartial digest of modern reality, telling a plethora of stories simultaneously. He acknowledges the likeness himself, calling his history 'a newspaper, which consists of just the same number of words, whether there be any news in it or not', or a stagecoach plying the same route whether empty of full. That epically average, democratic man Whitman said that he contained multitudes; so do Fielding's journals and coaches. The newspaper is more gregariously indiscriminate than even Fielding can afford to be. Introducing Miss Nancy and vouching for her moral qualities, he says that because 'our history doth not, like a newspaper, give great characters to people who were never heard of before, nor will ever be heard of again', it is safe to expect her to reappear; if he had the courage of that journalistic indiscriminateness, he would allow her a character whether he intended to make use of her in his plot or not. To the lusty Mrs Honour he allows something of the impartiality he has to deny himself. When she ingratiates with Tom, Fielding remarks that she views 'all handsome men with . . . equal regard and benevolence', and 'might indeed be called a lover of men, as Socrates was a lover of mankind'; or, it could be added, as Homer is to Netherton Homo.

What then can a work belonging to every genre at once be called? To name it a novel does no more than categorise its novelty. Its proper title, Fielding considers, should be biography, the annals of the tragicomic life of a man who might be Everyman. He elaborates rules for the form in *Joseph Andrews*, arguing that it is truer than history because its fictions have a greater veracity than the pettifogging facts of the chroniclers; and again his theory coincides with that of Johnson, who worked in all genres but, writing like Fielding (in the phrase he uses of Cervantes) 'the history of the world in general', equalises and equates them as biography. Johnson's 'Vanity of Human Wishes' is a dictionary of international biography, and the entries in his dictionary are the biographies of words—accounts of their etymological upbringing, their haphazard careers in the world, and their slow corruption and decay.

To be genuinely democratic, Fielding's theory must include the reader. Tom is therefore 'our hero': proof of our human equality, a standard shared by Fielding and everyone else, the basis of community. Fielding takes Tom as his ideally good-natured man; yet the novelist's dealings with characters and readers are the reflex of his own good nature. His management of the plot is a dispensing of charity. He is as susceptible as his averagely sensual hero. He confesses that Sophia is 'a lady with whom we ourselves are greatly in love', and assumes that his readers will likewise dote on her. When a love scene has gone on long enough to try the patience of his readers, Fielding resolves (he declares) to end it; when the Man on the Hill pauses in his narrative to take breath, Fielding thinks fit to allow the reader the same relief, and therefore curtails a chapter; as Partridge dozes off, Fielding wonders if the reader might not crave the same favour and promptly curtails Book VIII.

The novel is designed as a society or a parliament to which the reader is enfranchised. Fielding hears the novel as a Babel of contending voices and wishes, when describing the hubbub over the bleeding Jones, that he had forty pens and could write with them all together. Richardson can do so, now tenanting the persona of Clarissa, now that of Lovelace; Fielding must convoke a social order, and does so by canvassing the majority opinion. There are disputes between Drs Y and Z over Captain Blifil's death, between Square and Thwackum over human nature, between the exciseman and the puppet-show man. On all contentious matters, Fielding defers to the reader, who is permitted the casting vote. The 'men of intrigue', for instance, are called on to judge whether Lady Bellaston's angry letter or her tender postscript gave Tom the greater uneasiness. Fielding's aim is to inveigle us into partnership in his enterprise. He must rely, as a novelist or a sentimental traveller does, on the kindness of strangers. If we reciprocate his sympathetic care for us, he will literally accommodate us within the novel and extend to us the benefit of its comforting furniture. Thus he offers us the use of one of its travelling rooms: the coach which brings Sophia to Upton belongs, Fielding avows, 'to Mr King of Bath, . . . whose coaches we heartily recommend to all our readers who travel that road. By which means they may, perhaps, have the pleasure of riding in the very coach, and being driven by the very coachman, that is recorded in this history.' Sometimes Fielding ventilates his text with an omission which, as in the case of Sterne's asterisks, we make good. The dawn in *Joseph Andrews* is said to be as nubile as Miss ———, and the reader is instructed in a footnote to imagine her in the person of whomsoever he pleases. But generally the novel is not, as for Sterne, a mental space whose vacancy the reader's fantasy fills in; like that ample coach from Bath, it is a physical amenity in which we are invited to relax.

By the casual improvisation of action, decisions about which are often left to the whims of readers, Fielding is reversing the classical relation between character and plot and establishing the romanticism of the novel. In classical aesthetic theory, character is made for action; people are the deputies of plots, and these are fatalistically unstoppable, whether in tragedy or comedy. The two plots Coleridge thought worthy of comparison with that of *Tom Jones*—*Oedipus Rex* and *The Alchemist*—demonstrate this prescriptiveness. But English is a literature of insubordinate characters, averse to action and restive inside plots—the Wife of Bath or the Pardoner, the dilatory Hamlet, Dickens's unruly Mrs Gamp, the Hardy characters who are likened by D. H. Lawrence to flowers bursting from buds and shattering the pots in which they are planted—and Fielding's novel does not belong in Coleridge's triad. It has learned from romance the nonchalant courage to make itself up as it goes along. The plotters in the Sophoclean tragedy and the Jonsonian comedy are classical *apparatchiks*, devising machines of an infernal efficiency. To run such a plot, you must be a pitiless god (in *Oedipus Rex*) or a rapacious schemer (in *The Alchemist*); if Fielding is a despot, he is at least a benevolent one, genially holding together a ramshackle structure and tolerating its imperfections. A lawyer himself, he amends the legalism of classical dramaturgy with its mandatory penalties for characters who are regarded (whether tragically or comically) as incorrigible. There are numerous magistrates in his work— Squire Western who brings to the office a 'wise demeanour'; Allworthy, who has the power to punish Jenny Jones but chooses not to; the gypsy king, the 'one great magistrate' indistinguishable from his subjects in dress or privilege, just as Fielding, absolute monarch within the novel, claims to be no different from or better than his own Tom or any of his readers. These law-givers teach Fielding a distributive justice, which is employed for settling accounts at the inn on the way to Bristol, and as a protocol for arbitrating the competing claims of parallel narratives: 'Before we proceed any farther with Sophia, we must now look back to Mr Jones.'

While Fielding opens the novel to randomness and the undisciplined eventuality of life, encouraging epic's relaxation into quixotic, wayfaring romance, Richardson's heroines remain sequestered in pastoral. They experience the stasis of Milton's Lady in *Comus* or his *Paradise Regain'd* as a prison and a purgation. Pastoral now connotes a tragic fate; epic, contrariwise, is ameliorated by comedy. The novel keeps its promise of renovation: the ancient genres have been rearranged.

— 22 —
Sterne: Tragedy, Comedy, Irony

Sterne is an outcast from English literature's official history. Considered zanily eccentric, he has been denied the centrality which is his due. But it is hard to see how *Tristram Shandy* is any odder than the works of Defoe, Fielding or Richardson, which are allowed to qualify for normality: like the other novelistic renovators, Sterne is engaged in an inquisition of literature's means and the invention of a new form; like them he writes about writing, and about its vexed parallelism with living. Like them, too, he wants to make a work where life immediately happens, in a harried perpetual present as the pen crosses the page. He opens up, as they do, the third dimension of fiction. Instead of pretending to autonomy, presenting itself as a sealed world where characters go about their business free from interference, *Tristram Shandy*—like *Robinson Crusoe*, *Tom Jones* or *Clarissa*—is about two arcs of relationship which later novels withdraw: one between the novelist and a character, who is his surrogate or self-image; another between the novelist and a reader. To Fielding the reader is a travelling companion, to Richardson a confidant (the addressee of all those letters, and the eavesdropper in the confessional box); to Defoe a customer, a fellow-worker (Crusoe vocationally consults his Bible) and as well another marooned soul, housed within and living through a book, like Crusoe keeping a journal to vouch that he is still alive. Sterne inducts the reader into an even more intimate colloquy and colleagueship. He expects us to help him write his book. ·

Not only is Sterne more closely attached to his contemporaries than has often been admitted, he is perhaps more crucial to literary history than they are. For he is the junction between the age of so-called reason and that of romanticism. His work is about the generation gap between the classic and the romantic. Inside the Shandy family, this is the division which sets the systematic and pedantically uniform Walter, collating and legislatively ordering experience, like Johnson in his epigrams or dictionary entries, against the unformed, antic Tristram, the man of feeling or of humid, vibrant sensibility, who is reluctant to discipline emotion and association. The same antagonistic alliance of forbidding classical father and romantically errant child unites Johnson (who disapproved of *Tristram Shandy*) with Boswell (who, in the journals recording his sexual lapses and in the rhapsodic effusions which Johnson reproved, modelled himself on it). By the time of Jane Austen, sense and sensibility have become siblings. Tristram's defection from the regimented existence planned for him by Walter's *Trista-paedia* is his claim to a romantic career indulging the senses; his offences against the norms of literary structure, in a book written back to front, aerated with gaps, forever questioning its own right to exist and its ability to continue, are his formulation of the exhilarated muddle which is to be the romantic work of art.

Like Pope anticipating in his Dulness the bliss of romantic creativity with its 'drowsy numbness', Sterne has defined in advance and in comedy the consciousness of romanticism, which is to become the querulous and bifurcated modern literary mind. Hegel in 1807 calls it 'the contrite consciousness', wherein the self reflects on its own divided nature, and Friedrich von Schlegel in 1829 names it the 'intrinsic dualism and duplicity' of the ironic intelligence; they might both be describing Tristram. And Tristram accordingly, in the work purporting to be his *Life and Opinions*, delivers himself of a romantic opus, alternately worried by and delighting in its own absurdity, fantasticating rules for itself and wondering whether character, narrative and literature itself may not be mere social conventions and false ideas. August Wilhelm von Schlegel in his 1808 lectures elected Shakespeare as the first romantic, because in his plays the classical categories are merged and daringly confounded in a chaos of opposites. This romantic reformulation of Shakespeare originates in Sterne. Yorick is Sterne's nickname for himself; Tristram is his version of Hamlet, a tragicomedian of consciousness in conflict with itself—sometimes morose or morbid, sometimes foolish and pranksome. The genres which contend in Shakespearean tragicomedy are in Sterne simultaneous and inextricable moods of the ambiguous self: 'My mother declared, these two stages were so truly tragi-comical, that she did nothing but laugh and cry in a breath.' His book is therefore a formal hybrid. It attempts to be everything at once, in the hope that it may 'put an end to all kinds of writings whatsoever', and it extends its dominion beyond literature, sketching an art-work of the future in alliance with music and the visual arts, those aids to incapable words. Constantly revising itself and returning to its beginnings (Sterne is still writing prefaces in Book III of *Tristram Shandy*), it can never be accomplished. Yet its frustration becomes a rule for the romantic panoramas of consciousness, sublimely dilating to contain the world and, as they break off, ironically contracting to contemplate their own littleness—Wordsworth's *Prelude* to a poem he never wrote, Coleridge's biography of a book, Byron's *Don Juan*.

The romantic genius of *Tristram Shandy* lies in its taking nothing for granted. It demands, for instance, what constitutes character. Classically, character is attributed from without. Romantically, it is bred from within: it does not mean relegation to a class or category, as in the classical predictability of Jonson's humours, but is the reflex of an individual's uniqueness. Character is what we impose, caricaturally, on others; none of us are in this sense characters to ourselves. The I is subject only, never object. The eighteenth-century novels therefore contrive our detention within a consciousness we never see objectively as character: Defoe's H.F. has no name and no characteristics; Richardson's epistolary structure ensures he has no exteriorised point of view, so the novel is the sum of its various, mutually uncomprehending subjectivities. Even more radically, Tristram asks whether the individual person is an entity at all. He dates his own inception from the moment when he is conceived and—existing as a homunculus, a romantic creature of infinite, unshaped potentiality—has great difficulty getting himself born. Perhaps the publication of his *Life and Opinions* will attest to his identity; but in a recurrence of his prenatal mishaps, Tristram cannot get that written either. His is a conceptual characterlessness. His psychological freedom derives, like that of Hamlet or the fledgling self in the vale of soul-making of whom Keats wrote in his journals, from his inconsistency. Rather than a being, he is a process of becoming.

This exemption from character goes with a scepticism about narrative and its untruthful consecutiveness. Tristram sympathises with his Uncle Toby's inability to tell the story of the Namur siege straightforwardly. In his own case, he advances sideways, by digressions which are (he argues) progressive, though they also regress, looping backwards to recover childhood and even its antecedents. This decomposition of narrative he passes on to the romantics, who are occultists of the story told backwards or (in the case of Wordsworth's ballad about Simon Lee) of the story not told at all. All testimony is rendered subjective by romanticism, which makes narrative chronically unreliable. Mrs Smith in Jane Austen's *Persuasion* presents one account of Mr Elliot's character and behaviour when she believes Anne is engaged to him; disabused of that notion, she is able then to tell 'the whole story her own way'. When Captain Harville contends that there are innumerable stories of female fickleness, Anne, schooled in the partiality of narrative, can answer that 'Men have had every advantage of us in telling their own story.' Self-scrutinising, romantic novels are less stories than congresses of partial, inconclusive story-telling: the exhumations of the past in *Wuthering Heights* by Nelly and her narrative helpers, the double narrative of *Bleak House*, the multiple and conflicting depositions in *The Ring and the Book*.

For the romantics, as for Sterne, narrative is an experiment in deduction, and can never satisfactorily articulate itself. Sternean muddle turns into romantic mystery—in poetry, that of the symbol, which is an object whose history has been suppressed, requiring its interpreter to become a deductive intuitionist; or in narrative, that of the detective story, invented by Edgar Allan Poe because he felt the symbol to be a badge of culpability, whose origins must be forensically unriddled. The two traditions come together in Coleridge. *Biographia Literaria* is a combination of *Tristram Shandy* and the Gothic novel. Its narrative cannot or stubbornly will not utter itself, and this reluctance, which is its Gothic mystery, has to do with its dread of the very imagination, so secretly ashamed and infectious, whose truths it supposedly exists to propound. Incompleteness is Coleridge's safeguard. He will forsake or deface his text rather than permit it to testify against him.

Though he may inherit Tristram's structural scruples, he is too guilt-ridden to share Tristram's befuddled geniality. *Biographia Literaria* is about the invidious business of book-making, touting subscriptions to periodicals, coping with the perishability of paper (a maid sets the fire with one of Coleridge's productions), filling up space left blank by a printer's miscalculation; beneath its comic mayhem there is a tragic self-accusation. Tristram, too, complains of the labours of literature, and of its arbitrary limits: the obstinacy of words, the dull mechanical fixity of print. Yet by delineating these limits he advances beyond them. This is the triumph of what the nineteenth century was to call his romantic irony, his sense—like Hamlet with the nutshell—of the infinitude of his own littleness. Sublimity contemplates, awestruck, the vastness of nature; irony inverts that perception, studying as if through a microscope the bounty and plenitude of the small, the inexhaustible resource of the world we carry inside our heads. Hence the 'infinity of great and small instruments of knowledge' crowded on Toby's table, or Tristram's qualification of his book as a history 'of what passes in a man's own mind'. Aware that the small is as infinite as the vast, the ironist recreates sublimity in miniature. Yorick in Paris suspects the French sublime has its grandeur '*more* in the *word*; and *less* in the *thing*'. He concedes that the ocean may fill the mind with vast ideas, but his own mind is an expanse larger than any ocean. Similarly, by dwelling on the inadequacy of language, Sterne helps to make it more adequate, enabling words to give vent as directly as musical chords or calligraphic doodles to the emotions which they had formerly to translate and, in the process, traduce. His ironic apologies are covert boasts. Though it fails to be the book it intends, *Tristram Shandy* succeeds in being more than a book: it orchestrates feelings in a symphony of sensibility whose means of musical notation are punctuation marks; and it pictorially illustrates those feelings in its marbled, blank or blacked-out pages, in its diagram of its own narrative as a picturesquely furrowed and peaked landscape or in its transcription of the delighted tracery of energy when Trim flourishes his stick.

Sterne's bibliographic comedy is not despairing, like Swift's in *A Tale of a Tub*. The calamities which befall the text, like those which overtake Parson Adams's volume of sermons or his manuscript of Aeschylus in *Joseph Andrews*, punish the book as an object because it misconstrues and deadens life; it can be brought alive, made subjectively sentient, only if the tyranny of print and the thrall of a deadly past historic tense are overthrown in it. Tristram's father, bibliophile and compiler of that universal lexicon the *Tristra-paedia*, has an ancestral respect for the book as a memorial trophy and as an unalterable tablet of the law. Tristram himself proposes a romantic alternative to this view: the letter can never house the fugitive, inarticulate spirit; the more carelessly the letter is treated, the more unconstrained will the spirit be. He anticipates the literary doubts of the romantics, who were fearful of writing their poems because in doing so they were perjuring the vision which prompted them—Coleridge claims that drugs did the writing for him, Wordsworth subsumes the original act of writing into a palimpsest of rewritings, hoping to edge the words closer to the inexpressible truth.

Writing is to Sterne a grievous discipline, an indentured labour which he does not (like Defoe's manufacturers) relish but wishes to cast off. In the *Trista-paedia* he is sentenced to spend 'a year and a half in learning to write his own name'. He knows the text will be used as evidence against him; he is happy therefore only when he can rescind it, like Yorick cancelling the 'Bravo!' he appends to his sermon on Le Fever, or omit it altogether. Thus the missing chapter, or the pages undefiled by print where the reader can inscribe himself, or the censoring of speech in those serried rows of asterisks. Print seems to him a funerary engraving, the assertion that an experience is past or a life ended: his novel abounds in the commemoration of deaths—Yorick's, Le Fever's, Bobby's, Sterne's own (which he expects to prevent him from completion of the later volumes). Life is present only in motion, in the physical exercise ('curveting and frisking') or travel whose vigour writing should share.

Sterne therefore seeks beyond language and literature for an art which will not inhibit this creative liveliness—a writing from and with the entire body, like song (the body's melodious intake and exhalation of breath) or painting (which to Hazlitt also was an art superior to the poet's, because it required the outdoor exercise of healthy animal spirits). Toby's 'life was put in jeopardy by words'. Music, unembarrassed by the need to mean anything, is free from the argumentation which bedevils language. Toby therefore intones his lament for Bobby, 'vibrating the note back again, like a string in unison', or hums his grief, for to translate it into words would be to render it insincere and pretentious; Yorick annotates his sermons with musical comments—adagio, grave and moderato—as if he were conducting them; Trim hums to find the correct key in which to deliver the recitation about the King of Bohemia; Tristram presents himself as an instrumental virtuoso, tuning up his fiddle in a typographic cacophony and preparing to play a capriccio. Sterne, who admired the spasmodic gestures with which Garrick punctuated his performances of Shakespeare, is expert at deciphering the body's mute but eloquent language, as when Walter lays 'the three first fingers of his right hand in the palm of his left' before expostulating with Toby, or clasps 'his fore-finger betwixt his finger and his thumb'. He reads stance as a bodily speech: the sesquipedality of Dr Slop's girth, the willowy swaying of Trim or the uncoiling flourish of his stick.

In accord with these teetering, trembling or plumply swollen lines, Sterne's sentences scorn regularity and inflect or indent or buckle themselves into those curlicued, rococo shapes which Hogarth considered to be the physiognomy of the beautiful. Their disorderliness and incompleteness indicate the presence of life in them, in stuttering dashes or babbling exclamations. Sterne takes this to be a pictorial tactility as well as a musical attunement, pigmentation as much as intonation: 'How does the *Poco piu* and the *Poco meno* of the Italian artists;—the insensible more or less, determine the precise line of beauty in the sentence as well as the statue! How do the slight touches of the chisel, the pencil, the pen, the fiddlestick, *et caetera*,—give the true swell, which gives the true pleasure!' Even Sterne's punctuation stands for a graphic bliss. Normally punctuation marks are termini, the arrival at points of cessation; Sterne's flout this rule of punctiliousness and punctuality. His favoured dashes are hectic deferments of an end, or else they represent the eager outreach of a hand rebelling against the division of human beings from each other. The straight line, said by Hogarth to occur nowhere in nature, is tolerable to Sterne only if it means this stiffening of desire as it speeds the shortest route to its object, which (like Yorick repenting of his Bravo) it decorously obscures by driving straight through the inflammatory word. This is the case with Yorick's gesture at the end of *A Sentimental Journey*: 'When I stretched out my hand, I caught hold of the fille de chambre's ————.' That dash denotes a collision of bodies; it also, in Sterne's pictorial writing, hopes for a communion of souls. It elongates itself to arrive at union with another sentient creature. It is the lineament of an unsatisfied desire, reaching upwards from flesh to spirit; it is also the equivalent of what Yorick, apologising to the lady with whom he shares the room, calls 'an ejaculation': the body's involuntary overflow, the mind's yearning to overcome its solitary boundaries.

For the same reason, that peculiar convention of eighteenth-century fiction, the novelist's confederacy with his reader, is to Sterne a vital necessity. He treats writing as a synonym for conversation. The epistolary habit lies in the background of his efforts: the novel is a letter inveiglingly addressed to its reader, and a love-letter at that—Sterne's purpose is to ingratiate with and to seduce us, just as Diderot, reading *Clarissa*, imagined the heroine's epistles to be a desperate plea intended for him alone, and recklessly volunteered to save her. The connection between Tristram and his reader is as frail and wayward, as liable to be bedevilled by misunderstanding and defeated by the innate solipsism of both parties, as that between the members of the Shandy family. Tristram therefore exerts himself to placate the reader, cajoling and flattering him. He knows that his book is dependent on that reader's whim and temper. Introducing his father's theory of the predestining power of names, he accepts that choleric readers will hurl the book aside when hearing of it, while those of sour and saturnine disposition will refuse to believe it; he hopes that at least the mercurial will laugh at it. Since interpretation is so contingent, he busies himself to appease all parties. Outside the book—for in common with all his novelistic contemporaries he seeks escape from its solitary confinement—he convenes and maintains a society regulated by his own ethic of sensitive mutual sympathy. The reviewers are too savage for inclusion in this club, and Sterne commends them 'to the protection of that Being who will injure none of us'. Occasionally Tristram's patience with his travelling partners or sociable intimates is not equal to the strain: thus he sends an inattentive female reader back to study a chapter all over again, and puts her through an examination on it when she has done so.

This incorporation of the reader into the novelistic scheme—a literal enticement of bodies into flirtatious, consoling unison—ends with the novelist's abdication in favour of that reader. Tristram arrives at a crisis when three plots unexpectedly converge, and beseeches the 'powers . . . which enable mortal man to tell a story' to help him out: the very conduct of the narration is a picaresque imbroglio. Ultimately, however, that enabling power is possessed by the reader. His obligation in *Tristram Shandy* extends beyond the perusal of a prepared and self-explanatory text. All Sterne has supplied us with is a do-it-yourself kit for a novel; we have to assemble it, with a combination of fellow-feeling and technical adroitness. Tristram enlists us both as friends and as creative deputies.

In his pretended incompetence, he makes an art-work of a quite new kind. His vindication comes with romanticism, which describes his accidental shambles as a visionary surmounting of literature. Schopenhauer, writing about the metaphysics of the beautiful, acclaims Sterne for having overcome the dull, entrammeling interest of narrative. Art can be beautiful, for Schopenhauer, only if it is *not* interesting—if it wisely weans us of this false world with its chronologies and its wilfulness. Tristram has already achieved that feat: 'the hero', Schopenhauer reports, 'even at the end of the book, is only eight years of age.' Rather than growing in and through literary narrative, he has grown out of it. Life for him is not a consecutive march ahead but a cyclical, circular meditation, detached from the banality of mere happenings. Tristram has been romantically canonised, accorded the mystical sanctity of Wagner's Tristan, who learns his renunciation of the world and of drama from Schopenhauer. Sterne's imitator Jean Paul Richter in 1796-7 invents, as his Tristram, the parish advocate Firmian Stanislaus Siebenkäs, a harried man of feeling in whom the double plot of Shakespeare has become a psychological ambiguity: he is tragic and comic at once, sublime and ridiculous by turns, mentally rhapsodic yet physically lamed and belittled. The conjunction of those opposed states—the extremes which A. W. von Schlegel praised Shakespearean drama for bringing into proximity—is romantic irony, and to its German exponents Sterne is the writer who inherits it from Shakespeare.

Instead of the Shakespearean panoply of divergent characters, the King and Falstaff, Hamlet and the gravedigger, Lear and the fool, in Sterne there is an inner infinitude: all these people are simultaneously present within Tristram as facets of himself, inhabitants of the small world, cosmic yet miniature, which is his head (the integrity of which his father zealously protects by taking precautions against the compression of Tristram's cranium during the birth pangs) and also his novel: that 'word *world*' as Tristram calls it, 'a small circle described upon the circle of the great world, of four English miles diameter' inside which his characters dwell; a village which expands to encompass all of created nature when the walls of the Shandy house are elided and Toby, refusing to kill the fly, says, 'The world surely is wide enough to hold both thee and me.'

This vibrant, twangling 'sensorium' of Sterne's world, to which Yorick thrills in *A Sentimental Journey*, is an orchestration of consciousness. His words are commuted into music, better able than they are to express two incompatible emotions at once, and able, too, to transcribe emotion without needing to articulate it. Gustav Mahler was an admirer both of Richter's *Siebenkäs* and *Tristram Shandy*, and set himself to confront, like them, the misery and the festivity of life. Funeral marches in his symphonies are interrupted by tunes on hurdy-gurdies; apocalypse alternates with childish beatitude.

Johnson said the mourner and the reveller collided in Shakespeare. In Sterne and his romantic successors you can no longer tell them apart. Each is the other's potential double. Joshua Reynolds in 1761 painted Garrick hesitating between genres. On a country walk, he is obliged to repeat the choice Hercules had to make between wisdom and pleasure, except that the representatives of these opposed ethical persuasions are dramatic muses. On one side he is tugged by winsome, buxom Comedy, on the other sternly entreated by Tragedy, whose hand, like that of the angelic Agnes in *David Copperfield*, points upwards. His indecision can lead to a specious vacillation between the two alternatives. In the charades at Gaunt House in *Vanity Fair*, Becky Sharp is able to demonstrate a versatility like Garrick's because all her emotions are histrionic affectation: she first performs Clytemnestra, then a flirtatious Marquise. Byron was celebrated for such virtuoso double acts in amateur theatricals. Like Becky he can be tragic or comic at will, because he is neither. Sterne however finds another means of solving Garrick's problem: Tristram and Yorick, mental dialecticians, can be both tragic and comic at once. The novel's merging of dramatic genres corresponds to their own psychological complexity. Shakespearean tragicomedy is redefined as irony, and made a prerogative of the romantic mind.

The tragicomedy of Sterne is also a merger, romantically marrying opposites, between epic and lyric, between the shield of Achilles and the Lady of Shalott's mirror. Friedrich von Schlegel in his *Lyceum der schönen Künste* (1799–1800) challenges romantic poetry epically to catalogue the totality of the age, the proliferation of its objects (like those on Uncle Toby's desk). But it must do so, he says, by retracting to lyric and refracting the world through a single mind. The engraved, emblazoned shield with its diagram of social workings can be seen only as reflected by the mirror. This is a prescription for the romantic epics of a lyrical self-consciousness, *The Excursion*, *Childe Harold's Pilgrimage*, de Quincey's *Confessions*. But it had beforehand been adumbrated by Sterne in his history not of deeds and achievements but of the non-events which happen (or do not happen, as the writing of the novel does not) in one man's mind.

Tristram Shandy contains the theory of such a work; *A Sentimental Journey* in 1768 is its exposition in practice. It is a celestial epilogue to the previous, uncompleted novel. The romantic future is already immanent in it. Other contemporary journeys had been the enforcements of a prejudicial status quo—Defoe's inventory of the contents of British reality; Johnson's disgruntled tour of Scotland, behind which lay a scepticism about the value of romantic and itinerant experience, summed up in his remark to Boswell that the Devil's Causeway may have been worth seeing but was not worth going to see; the grumpy dismissal by Smollett (Yorick's Smelfungus) of French and Italian antiquities in his 1766 tour. Travel romantically disrupts the equilibrated stasis which is the security of classicism: hence Boswell's eagerness for the Hebridean trip and Johnson's reluctance to undertake it. Tristram deviates and detours inside his own mind; Yorick in France embodies this spirit of inquisitive, yearning mobility, symbolised typographically by the dash with which his career, for the moment, concludes. Like the heads painted by Guido, he looks forwards, and towards 'something beyond this world'. His journey ends extra-terrestrially, proceeding from earth to heaven in the sacramental supper he shares with the peasant family. After that, even the physical collision with the *fille de chambre* can qualify as a communion.

Yorick's is a messianic tour, seeking converts to his religion of sensibility, and in leading beyond the world it leads necessarily beyond literature. Again its ideal alternatives to the incomplete explicitness of words are music and painting. Bird-song is the esperanto of joy spoken by the starling, entrapped because it has been sentenced to a single language: its 'song for liberty' is in English, and cannot be understood at Paris. The opera is the appropriate location for Yorick's delicate encounter with the French officer (who extends a mute kindness to him, assuming they lack a common language), because it is notoriously unintelligible; yet the obscurity of its words does not matter, for they are inundated by music, the universal idiom of emotion. Sterne's punctuation hopes to invent for words a system of musical inflection and notation, or to dispense with them altogether. He and the Marquesina dodge each other in a blitz of dashes, which splice them together while they are struggling to disentangle themselves. Asterisks, while signifying an omission of words, vouch for the presence of feelings. They are the equivalent of that most speaking of looks, a blush. As if pictorially, looks do the conversing of Yorick's characters for them. The lady whose hand he clasps disengages it 'with a look which I thought a sufficient commentary upon the text'. The text cannot cope with the susceptibility of Yorick's senses—the pulsation of arteries in his fingers, or the dampened spirits with which he discovers that Father Lorenzo is dead. The heart, as he says after an incident at Amiens, can 'say too much' with impunity because it uses no words. Yorick's probity as a man of feeling enjoins him to resign from writing. Labouring over the letter in Amiens, he is 'in no mood to write', and later in Paris he attempts to write a card but finds his hand too ardently tremulous to hold the pen. Feelings entrusted to paper are in any case placed at risk: the interpolated Rabelaisian tale exists as a fragment only, because La Fleur has used the other sheets to wrap a posy.

In this novel, the tragicomic amalgam of opposites, romantic irony with its dualistic consciousness, exists most intensely in brief transit across the face of the Grisset at the haberdasher's, which must be graphically depicted not verbally described. Her look so blends 'whim, and sense, and seriousness, and nonsense, . . . that all the languages of Babel set loose together could not express them'; her expression is all the Shakespeare plays dissolved into unison, and it captures the paradox which Friedrich von Schlegel thought central to Socratic irony—everything is 'at once a joke and a serious matter, at once ingenuously open and deeply dissembled'. Confronted by it, Yorick as *littérateur* is disempowered.

His journey into a country whose language is not his own teaches him the dispensability of his own art, and he blesses the father of the peasant family for his innocent illiteracy. That reference to Babel indicates Yorick's romantic modesty about his own medium: since language is an inherited impediment, the instrument of man's confusion, the writer's pained duty is to act as translator, hoping to create small mutual contacts and comprehensions within the general muddle and uproar. Tristram occupies himself in translating Slawkenburgius's tale, yet despairs of ever rendering it 'into good English'. He is himself almost a victim of mistranslation when a blunder about his Christian name occurs at his baptism, and his father and uncle have a short Babel-like dispute about whether this ceremony was administered before the Reformation in English or in Latin. Yorick, too, proposes translating the Gothic anecdote about the notary's wife, and remarks that even in London, where he is not troubled by linguistic problems, he walks the streets translating the idioms 'of looks and limbs . . . into [the] plain words' of the physiognomic vernacular.

Richardson's Pamela, whose only employment (according to Mr B) is her scribbling, considers that writing to be transitive and translative, though she is a sly enough literary artist to be capable of adapting texts to suit her own convenience. She prepares a version of Psalm 137 which makes it a commentary on her own persecution. Parson Williams and Mr B compare her gloss with the original, and Pamela's variant is generally preferred. In the novel, personal testimony, subjective and unverifiable, takes precedence even over scriptural authority. When Pamela is married, she begs her consort to induct her into another language: 'The English tongue affords not words . . . to express, sufficiently, my gratitude. . . . Teach me some other language, if there be any, that abounds with more grateful terms.' It is her most cunning request: is she acknowledging the infected duplicity of her own speech, aware that as a consummate fictioneer she can no longer tell the truth? Mr B in any case assures her that her 'language is all wonderful', and that she is most loquacious when most professing inarticulacy. By contrast with Pamela's adroit use of writing in order to fictionalise what she feels, Sterne's art tries to be a direct transliteration of feeling, and is tantalised—as the devious Pamela is not—by the approximateness of its renderings.

As well as the romantic epic of consciousness engorging the world, Sterne anticipates in *A Sentimental Journey* the hope and the pathos of the romantic lyric, vainly venturing to prolong moments (as Yorick strives to extend those casual meetings with strangers, or to fix stray, intersecting glances) and to find words equivalent to emotions. In succession to Yorick, Wordsworth in the 1802 preface to the *Lyrical Ballads* likens the poet to a translator, one for whom any language is foreign simply because it is verbal and vocal and who must deem 'himself justified when he substitutes excellences of another kind for those which are unattainable by him'. Pursuit of *le mot juste* is the most exhausting of romantic quests for an evaporating vision; to Flaubert it became a penitential discipline. And beneath Wordsworth's comment on 'the general inferiority to which he [the translating poet] feels that he must submit' lies the suspicion—cheerfully accepted by Yorick, but a source of despair to his romantic offspring—that poetry consists precisely of what is lost in translation.

Sterne's impractical failures become both the tragedy of romanticism (in its chasing after elusive visions and elapsing words, invisible nightingales and unknowable skylarks) and its divine comedy. Carlyle derives the transcendental philosophy of *Sartor Resartus* (1833–4) from a reading of Sterne, as adapted by Jean Paul Richter: *Tristram Shandy* is the model for Teufelsdröckh's disjointed life and recondite opinions, and he is fond of quoting from 'Yorick Sterne'. The scattiness of Sterne's text is seen now as a mystic opacity: like Teufelsdröckh, Tristram is a professor of chaos, who understands that the substance of the world is mere appearance, the flimsy clothing for the idea behind or beneath; he therefore condemns the letter of what he writes to abstruse inefficacy so that he can hint at the spirit which mere words will misconstrue. Irony is the idiom of his transcendental uplift. Because he sees through the world, despoiling it of its garments, he makes statements which we in turn will see through. To read him is to have overcome him: Teufelsdröckh's pettifogging editor comments, 'His irony has overshot itself; we see through it, and perhaps through him.' The editor is wrong to see this as a fault. It is the highest, most mentally spiralling wisdom of all, and it introduces Tristram to the world of romantic symbolism, with its doubling of significance. 'The wondrous agency of *Symbols*', Teufelsdröckh says, is their benignly bemusing concealment: the more they obscure, the more they reveal. All speech dies into a silence which says more than words can ever do, just as the printed letter expires into the immaterial spirit. Teufelsdröckh positively commends the self-contradiction and self-obfuscation which are the addled stratagems of Sternean irony, saying, 'Let not thy left hand know what thy right hand doeth!' The ardently breathless, gabbling sentimentalist has grown—by one of those metamorphoses Teufelsdröckh extols with such rapture—into a symbolist priest, by his secrecy, his reversions to silence, and his ventilations or evacuations of his text, expounding arcana.

Johnson's *Lives* and Boswell's *Life*

The friendship of Johnson and Boswell stretches across a difference of cultures. Theirs was a partnership of opposites, argumentatively allying two types of character and two theories of literature. They embody the classic and the romantic: art with its ancestral conscience for conserving and remembering, and art with its juvenile, ecstatic momentariness; a régime of sense against a mayhem of enthusiastic sensibility.

Though no classical formalist, as his pragmatic defence of Shakespeare demonstrates, Johnson recalls literature's classic origins in an epic ceremony of commemoration. His aim is to preserve men and their vernacular language from the oblivion of time—the ambition which makes the bards recite their history, venerating literature for its mnemonic security, and which emboldens Spenser to call the *Epithalamion* an endless monument or Shakespeare to erect the sonnets, like an epic bulwark, in defiance of change. On his Hebridean tour with Boswell in 1773, Johnson perused a funerary monument and remarked that 'the inscription should have been in Latin, as every thing intended to be universal and permanent, should be'. Boswell records that proviso, but ignores its gloomy implications, so alert is he to the diversions of the instant: 'This being a beautiful day, my spirits were cheered by the mere effect of climate.'

For Johnson, art's purpose is a solemn mortification (as was that of friendship, for with his genius for companionship and solace he knew that friendship was a contract obliging us, sooner or later, to mourn for our brother); it arrives at a state of rigor mortis like the classical statue or the dictionary entry, fixed in perpetuity. Boswell romantically interprets art as vivification. He is a victim of sentiment, like Tristram Shandy or the distracted, blush-prone, impulsive Harley in Henry Mackenzie's *Man of Feeling* (1771). His own life kindles and excites itself from moment to moment, and so must his art. Mackenzie's novel is published as 'scattered chapters, and fragments of chapters': the feeling man is a mayhem, like his text, of illogical and inconsecutive sensations. He disdains completion and finality, which are to him a death-knell. Therefore he leaves himself, as he leaves his work, unfinished, in the hope that he will stay alive. Boswell's career as libertine, social personality and autobiographer is an extrapolation of that dash which Sterne, at the end of *A Sentimental Journey*, allows to trail off into infinity. Were it ever to reach a full stop, it would have resigned itself to mortality. Instead of classical fixture, the romantic craves an art which will expend energy tirelessly and indefinitely. And the romantic sees his own existence analogous-ly—as process, fluid and potentially dissolute. Johnson possesses character, to Boswell's admiration; all Boswell himself has is the volatility of romantic self. His association with Johnson is perhaps his quest for a certainty and reassurance which his own romanticism has denied to him. Johnson has sturdily proved the substantiality of the world and of his own place in it, and can refute the abstract philosophy of Berkeley by gruffly kicking a stone. Boswell, who lives by the imagination, cannot help wondering whether he might not have imagined himself as well. He adheres to Johnson as the classical solution to his own romantic enigma.

Theirs is the same relationship as that dramatised by Diderot in his dialogue *Le Neveu de Rameau*, written possibly in 1761. Here sage unity of being encounters its romantic antithesis. The encyclopaedist, walking in the park, meets an agile virtuoso, who is the prestidigitating nephew of the composer Rameau. The musician's appendage is himself an orchestra, since thoughts, feelings and physical attitudes are all instruments on which—elasticising his fingers and wreathing his body into those acrobatic S-curves which Hogarth called lines of beauty and evidences of life—he uproariously plays. So nimbly evasive and contradictory is he that this inspired clown appears to the censorious Diderot to be a nothingness: he exists only as the nephew of someone else. He delights in the romantic state of ironic, mobile nonentity which Byron, too, had learned from Sterne. Hegel called the nephew the symbolic modern self, the spirit in self-estrangement. He has jettisoned the adult accord between consciousness and society—that responsibility respected by Diderot as it was by Johnson. Though Diderot rationally disdains the nephew's physiognomic opera, as Johnson castigated Boswell's rash enthu-siasms, they are both observing a future they cannot control. However, the romantic renovation of the self needs the steadying reproof of these parental figures of classical reason: the nephew invites Diderot's criticism as Boswell does Johnson's. They are experimenting with a life of sensations not thoughts, and the prospect alarms them as much as it excites them. The nephew seeks from Diderot the guarantee that he will, despite himself, be always the same, and Boswell, in retreat from his own ambiguous, wayward consciousness, dedicates himself not to being himself but to creating a character for Johnson. If he has any character of his own, he owes it (he believes) to Johnson, whom he thanks 'for having established my principles'.

Despite the disparateness of Johnson's writing, there is a magnificent unity to it. Its mode is always biographical, its mood elegiac. His is biography of the classic kind, Plutarchan and exemplary, rather than the romantic study of a person's unrepeatable singularity. Boswell, ironically, invented that later form with his 1791 *Life* of Johnson, emphasising the man's 'petty habits' and 'particularities which it is impossible to explain': character as mystery, not moral quantity. Johnson insists on the duty of all writing to help man better enjoy life or better endure it. But in the event, writing concedes life's small tragedy—that it is an allotted term which we must get through as best we can. Each piece of writing mimes the shortness of a life. Even the entries in the *Dictionary* are elegiac in their purpose, for etymology is ancestry and usage is the protracted history of a word's endurance, its withstanding of the world's vicissitudes and (unless preserved by the lexicographer) its final decay.

The *Dictionary* is Johnson's necropolis. He could carry it through as an epic labour because it coincided with his deepest imaginative and emotional conviction, that it is our responsibility (as he declares in the seventeenth *Rambler*) to mourn and in doing so to remember. Since the entries are lapidary inscriptions or funerary tablets, the whole language amounts to a family plot. Where 'the exuberance of signification' is too unruly, too prolific an offspring, Johnson recommends the tracing of meanings to their parentage in 'the mother term'. He acknowledges his own derivation—as a live, dying thing—from that community of predeceased words when he composes the brave entry for his own native place, Lichfield in Staffordshire. He exhumes its Anglo–Saxon root: 'lich' means a corpse, and the place is 'the field of the dead, . . . so named from martyred Christians'. Yet having opened the grave inside the word, he goes on gratefully to root himself there, adding, in the language he considered aptest for obituary because most permanent, '*Salve magna parens*'.

No wonder that Becky Sharp's first act of rebellion, as she quits Miss Pinkerton's Academy in Thackeray's *Vanity Fair*, is to hurl away her presentation copy of Johnson's dictionary. Her abandonment of the book advertises her disregard for precedent, and her embarkation on a romantic career where words will lyingly be made to mean whatever it pleases her that they should. Throwing Johnson out of the carriage, she is overthrowing conscience. A similar fate befalls *Rasselas* in a concurrent romantic work, *Jane Eyre*. Helen Burns, Jane's consumptive friend at the academy of the sadistically pious Mr Brocklehurst, finishes reading Johnson's fable the night after her flogging. Does she learn from it her masochistic patience under duress? Jane in any case rejects the book's counsels.

The dying fall which is the career of a Johnsonian word makes even the poetic couplet, as used by him, the précis of a life at its term. The couplet's finality—nonsensical for Pope, who within its curtailment can assert the logicality of the irrational; magisterial for Swift, who employs it as the impatient arrival at a condemnation—is for Johnson elegiac. The relentless metre and the enforcement of the rhyme mark the inescapability of human fate. His 'Vanity of Human Wishes' is a compound of the *Dictionary* and the *Lives of the Poets*, a digest of deaths where each pair of lines enters as if in a ledger another instance of our collective dismay. A sad antithesis sounds beneath Johnson's rhymes. They are arranged, like the definition of Lichfield, to disclose by phonic puns the presence of death in life. 'Breath', the vital force of speaking humanity, inevitably finds its synonym in 'death'; 'pow'r', in a couplet summarising the perils of the lordly, finds itself rewarded with 'the Tow'r'; 'joy' begets almost at once the imperative 'destroy'. Each couplet vainly wishes that there might be some way out of this morbid impasse. But of course there is none. That thanatological certainty palls the jaunty couplets that Johnson improvised on Mrs Thrale's thirty-fifth birthday, for he pointed out to her the lexical doom which lay concealed in them: 'the rhymes', he said, 'run in alphabetical order', from 'alive' to 'wive'. They do not quite reach the expiry of Z, but they get near enough to sound a *memento mori*, as do the verses purportedly congratulating Sir John Lade on his twenty-first birthday. The poem cheerfully prophesies a future of dissipation for the young man and ends with his brusque cessation: 'You can hang or drown at last.'

Nor can the shortness of lives be counteracted by the longevity of art. Johnson's criticism is the elegiac biography of moribund works. His *Lives of the Poets* concern not only their deaths—Addison's 'lingering decay', evinced by 'shortness of breath'; the malodorous rotting of Dryden's corpse—but the demise of their art. Cowley's verses have managed to escape, remarkably, 'the mould of time', though *Paradise Lost* may fall victim to human amnesia. The reader admiringly lays it down, 'and forgets to take [it] up again'. *Tristram Shandy*, Johnson declared with an undertaker's complacent gloom, 'did not last'. His verdicts pronounce funeral orations. Commenting that Buckingham's *The Rehearsal* 'has not wit enough to keep it sweet', he translated his own remark into Latinate orotundity to make more explicit the sentence of death it contained: as revised, his decision was that the play 'has not vitality enough to preserve it from putrefaction'. The critic's responsibility resembles the taxidermist's. He is engaged in the same battle against time and degeneration which prompts the scheme, reported in the *Life*, for the embalmment of Dryden. Johnson's own creativity could be roused only by the fear of death. The journalistic deadline was for him precisely that: the tolling of a bell. Boswell describes him writing his *Ramblers* only when 'the moment pressed', and the porter waited. The circumstances in which *Rasselas* was allegedly composed in 1759 sum up this race between writing and dying. Johnson drafted it 'in the evenings of one week', impelled by a mortal urgency. His aim was to 'defray the expense of his mother's funeral, and pay some little debts which she had left'.

Rasselas coincides with the rest of Johnson's work in its adoption of the foreshortened biographical form. Its terseness is an admonition to the novel. Johnson warns his readers not to 'expect that age will perform the promises of youth, and that the deficiencies of the present day will be supplied by the morrow'—not, that is, to accredit the cajolery of the novelist, who rather than drawing together life's beginning and its end indefinitely extends the middle, turning existence into an adventure. The novel misrepresents time, and conceals its 'dull sameness' (from which Johnson suffered during his period as a school-usher). Narrative delights us because it is more interesting and eventful than life, and its eventuality is its optimism. *Rasselas* therefore declines to be narrative. Stories agitate the mind; Johnson's concern is to pacify it. Imlac quietens his consciousness, accustoming it to the contemplative tedium of the happy valley. He has seceded from the fretfulness of the novel and thus can tolerate the idyllic inactivity of the pastoral.

Rasselas is Johnson's dissertation on what the novel is, and what it ought to be. To wean the form of its querulous craving, he plans it as a sequence of sedative anticlimaxes, leading to an inconclusive conclusion. An ordinary novelist would have fomented suspenseful complications when Rasselas has to persuade Nekayah to accompany him on his jaunt into the wider world. Johnson takes a dismissive short cut, saying only that 'when the time came, [he] with great difficulty prevailed on the princess to enter the vessel.' Political intrigues are also dealt with shortly, as encroaching time requires: 'In a short time the second Bassa was murdered. The Sultan, that had advanced him, was murdered by the Janissaries.' The accident which might have made a novel's meretricious climax is here becalmed by summation. Nekayah, after her exploration of the pyramid, prepares 'a long narrative of dark labyrinths, and costly rooms, and of the different impressions which the varieties of the way had made upon her'. This is the gratuitous long-windedness of the novel—the outdoor vagaries of the picaresque ('the varieties of the way'), the indoor reticulations of the Gothic (those labyrinths, later to be groped through by Ann Radcliffe's Emily at Udolpho, by Catherine Morland at Northanger Abbey, by Lockwood at Wuthering Heights, and by Keats in the catacomb-like brain which he laid out according to the ground-plan of Radcliffean romance). It is a mode of titillation: a postponement of that moment of truth which exposes the fiction. Johnson therefore disallows it. Nekayah has no chance to tell her invented story because a real one takes priority, and it is retailed without story-telling artfulness. Pekuah, she is merely informed, has been abducted by Arab raiders.

The denial of narrative makes *Rasselas* a collection of moral essays—Imlac's theories of art, Nekayah's theses on marriage and the discontents of the human family. Narrative is fictionally irresponsible, unconstrained, as the fourth *Rambler* puts it, by 'historical veracity', and potentially dangerous to those whose minds are 'unfurnished with ideas'. Essays—pondering and predigesting experience rather than chasing its every whim, soberly backward-looking because they despair (as Rasselas, retiring from narrative, does) about 'the prospects of futurity'—supply that furniture and reconcile the mind to a stillness which the novel, voyaging like Tom Jones or Yorick, spurns. Imlac possesses this store of moral supports, and therefore does not resent the eventless valley: 'I have a mind replete with images, which I can vary and combine at leisure.' His thinking is essayistic: within him, no new thing ever happens; he recombines particulars to amass a general truth. The experience of the characters of *Rasselas*, and of its readers, should be to warn them off novels—or, if they persist, to drive them to the frustration of the man imagined by Johnson who read *Clarissa* for the story and ended by hanging himself.

Johnson worried that the life of his friend Richard Savage would be written up as 'only a novel', a compound, that is, of 'romantick adventures, and imaginary amours'. *Rasselas* seeks to cure the novel's addiction to adventures, and even to the amorous, indulgent imagination from which they derive. For Johnson, imagination amounted to superstition. Its danger was that of an infidel faith. The readers of *Rasselas* are warned against 'credulity'; the *Rambler* says that novels inflame the mind with 'incredibilities'. Johnson understood the reason's attraction to its own betrayal, its willingness (encouraged by the aesthetics of romanticism) to suspend disbelief or to be deceived by Keats's cheating elf. He conceded as much when talking to Boswell of ghosts, which to him were analogous with the mind-bred fictions and hauntings of imagination. We still cannot tell whether any spirit of a dead person has ever appeared, he said. 'All argument is against it; but all belief is for it.' The credulity of readers in *Rasselas* irrationally accredits ghosts, pursuing 'with eagerness the phantoms of hope'. Those wraiths were to be the deranging portents of romanticism: Blake's filmy, transparent prophets, Coleridge's imagined demons, the visionary woman with eyes where her nipples should have been who sent Shelley screeching from the room.

On his Scottish tour Johnson, who disparaged the forged bardic poetry of Macpherson's Ossian, lends credence to fictions only when he can anchor them to facts. The desolation of the landscape and the remnants of castles persuade him that 'the fictions of the *Gothick* romances were not so remote from credibility as they are now thought.' He appraises the Hebrides as a region of romantic chimerae, describing with 'incredulity' the freaks and phantasms— the supernatural phenomenon of second sight, for instance—which were the subject of William Collins's 1749 ode 'On the Popular Superstitions of the Highlands of Scotland'. Collins excitedly ventures to believe in the 'airy shows' (as Johnson calls them) of susceptible imagination. Johnson fears such credulity as an idolatrous oppression of intellect. He thought Frenchmen absurdly credulous because the dual despotism of religion and politics 'accustomed [them] to implicit submission', whereas the Englishman has a democratic and inductive freedom, being required to take nothing on trust. In a sturdily mercantile way, Johnson sees belief as an extension of credit. He will not take the risk unless he is assured of a reliable return. He refuses such credit to legends like that of the artificial cascade at Gribon. Boswell comments that 'as, on the one hand, his faith in the Christian religion is firmly founded upon good grounds; so, on the other, he is incredulous when there is no sufficient reason for belief.' His wariness was prescient. The imagination soon erected itself as a god: romanticism is a religion lacking the benefit of clergy or of external evidence; an act of faith reposed—as Johnson would have seen it—in fiction.

Both Johnson and Boswell wrote up their Highland experience, and the two accounts sum up the differences in literary theory between them. Johnson's *A Journey to the Western Islands of Scotland* is, like everything he wrote, elegiac. Both the mode and the emotional temper are pastoral—a meditation, quietistically resigned as pastoral must be, on the tragic penury of nature. Boswell's *Journal of a Tour to the Hebrides* is a picaresque novel, populous and comically busy.

Johnson's vision is retrospective: he sees Scotland as a mortuary whose remnants of life—the mournful ruins of St Andrews, the cairn at Coriatachan—he must preserve by annotation, or even by the exercise of mummifying, stabilising memory. Boswell has Miss Flora MacDonald, one of the characters in his romantic novel of chivalric derring-do, tell the story of having succoured Bonnie Prince Charlie. Her 'recital of the particulars' is to Boswell an inset narrative, like Fielding's of the Man on the Hill in *Tom Jones*. Scotland has dreamed up a romantic revival for itself in Jacobite politics; is Flora—of whom Boswell says, when naming her, 'for so I shall call her', as if she were a character invented by him—also an imaginist and fiction-maker, like the forger of Ossian's poems? Johnson listens to her with what Boswell calls 'placid attention'. That placidity is the wisdom of pastoral, the conviction that time is brief, and narrative, no matter how romantically vivid, a delusion. At the end he says, 'All this should be written down'—to be remembered, preserved and authenticated. The written record is for Johnson the present's testimony about the past, and its relegation to that past: Flora is history, and will soon be ancient history. In the event, no one takes her affidavit. Boswell instead writes the story, mixing her tale together with other versions of the case and sketching in advance a fabricated, fictional history like that of Scott's Waverley novels.

Since Johnson's journey is a meditation, it aspires to a classical immobility; it is reluctant to see things, fearing the eye's distraction of the grave and ponderous mind. In contrast to Boswell's journal—journalistic in its Richardsonian eagerness to keep up with experience, so that in Col he fills his diary and has to go out in search of more paper—Johnson writes a travel book which travels and describes as little as possible. It is an appendix, instead, to 'The Vanity of Human Wishes', whose title affords him the motive for movement: at St Andrews he fills his mind, when he sees the ruined university, with 'mournful images and ineffectual wishes'; but he knows 'sorrow and wishes to be vain', and therefore resolves not to linger. Later at Anoch a young woman paraphrases his journey as a continuation of the moral progress undertaken in the poem when she tells him 'how much I honoured her country by coming to survey it'. Her verb is the directive with which the poem opens:

> Let observation with extensive view,
> Survey mankind from China to Peru.

Such omniscience makes a minute attention to Scotland otiose. Human nature can be relied on to be everywhere dismayingly the same. And the survey in the poem is an ocular superintendence, a god's eye-view of the globe; tramping along the ground, Johnson is obliged to notice only those things which do not matter.

Therefore, while Boswell fusses over such 'minute particulars' as Johnson's oak stick, Johnson tries to retain his judicious, generalised distance. He is on guard against everything which the novel proposes about life, and when he is made to acknowledge novelty he does so with glowering disapproval. Thus he scowls after an argument with a divine, 'This is a day of novelties: I have seen old trees in Scotland, and I have heard the English clergy treated with disrespect.' Exceptions, adduced by Boswell in the hope of rendering experience novel, are bent by Johnson into proofs of his mistrustful, defensive rules. Boswell persuades him to eat some veal, to dissuade him from the received idea that such meat is never good in Scotland. Johnson will not be duped: 'Why, sir, what is commonly thought, I should take to be true. *Your* veal may be good; but that will only be an exception to the general opinion; not a proof against it.' So it is when Boswell sublimely aggrandises a mountain as 'immense'. Johnson's reluctant observation begins with a rebuttal and then retreats to the aerial perspective of that opening couplet: 'No; it is no more than a considerable protuberance'—which is how it would appear from the surveyor's mid-air. The phrase he uses is of course a tag of orotund Johnsonese. Appropriately, words (even when, as here, their purpose is deduction and diminishment) occupy more space than things, which they have supplanted. Johnson's relation with the landscape is conducted through the lexicon.

Grieving as he does over the emigration from the Highlands, which he sees as a symptom of human instability and nature's unkindness, Johnson resists description because its purpose is to replete a world which to him is wasted and derelict. He is left therefore with words for non-existent or expired things. Edinburgh is 'a city too known to admit description': the idea has elided the place; all that remains is a phrase, whose function is to be a memorial. St Andrews is also vacated by meditation, so Johnson's words describe the mood of its non-existence: 'the silence and solitude of inactive indigence, and gloomy depopulation'. When compelled to describe, he grudgingly attaches a negative disclaimer to his words, calling Inch Keith 'not wholly bare of grass', the roads beyond Edinburgh 'by no means incommodious', the valley beyond Anoch 'not very flowery'. Boswell can turn even poverty into plenitude by the garrulous joy with which he names the things which are missing, as in his catalogue—inversely Adamic—of all the creatures that are not in Col, 'no foxes; no serpents, toads, or frogs, . . . no black-cock, muir-fowl, nor partridges.' The only abundance Johnson can allow is of a life too rank in its vitality. Though Inch Keith is nearly destitute of grass, it is 'very fertile of thistles'. In the furthest speculative reach of his journey, he envisages the progress of civilisation as a devastation of the world. Sooner or later everything will be pillaged and denuded like Scotland: 'As the Europeans spread over *America*, the lands are gradually laid naked.'

For Boswell the highlands are a theatre of romantic sentiment, as yet unsettled by reason, where he can entertain imaginative delusions. He frightens himself by thinking of the headless, stalking ghost of Lord Kilmarnock, by fancying that a landlord will murder him for gain, by playing (in his mind) the chivalric knight-errant for the womenfolk at the Duke of Argyle's castle. Johnson, scornful of these self-solicitations, cautions Boswell about the solidity of the world, which cannot be wished or dreamt away. He argues against transubstantiation, which he sees as the imagination's most absurd conceit. As in his refutation of Berkeley, he stands by the irreducible substance of the world: he is an imperturbable object to Boswell's unquiet, irritated, quaking subject. His implacability amazes Boswell, who is forever infecting himself with the psychosomatic ailments of the man of sensibility— spleen, indigestion, superstitious terrors. Johnson has no patience with these qualms because they are a voluntary indulgence, made possible by Boswell's actual health and safety. They are literally feather-bedded: though professing to be thrilled by nature, Boswell is effeminately cushioned from it, and at Glenelg while Johnson wraps himself in his riding coat, 'Mr. Boswell being more delicate, laid himself sheets with hay over and under him, and lay in linen like a gentleman.'

In contrast with the restlessness of Boswell, which provokes the trip in the first place—that mental mobility celebrated by Byron as a value of the romantic mind in *Don Juan*—Johnson seems stoically inert. Boswell finds him 'lazy, and averse to move', or complains 'it was long before we could get him into motion'. His sedentariness is a moral posture. Boswell remarks that Johnson's characterisation of himself as *The Rambler* was inappropriate to his 'grave and moral discourses'. Gravity persuades him, almost gravitationally, to stay anchored where he is; Boswell meanwhile, like Yorick, flatters himself that he is 'completely a citizen of the world', with empathy and inquisitiveness as his passports.

Boswell's is a time of moments, and in his conduct of his journal he is as episodically skittish as Tristram Shandy, inserting fragments of Johnsoniana 'without regard to chronology'; Johnson's is a time of penitential and eroding aeons. Therefore while Boswell rejoices in elongation, in spinning out his narrative, Johnson can only lament the agony of longevity: the drudgery of crossing Skye, where 'a very few miles require hours', or the misery of a life extended to a century, when he visits the cottagers. His equivalent of Boswell's romantic neurasthenia—the reflex of a temperament too agitated for its own good—is boredom, the tragic cost of contemplating the tedium of time. Johnson, with an instinct averse to the novel's absorption in duration, seeks time's terse abridgement. Hence the brevity of his essays, or the contraction of the picaresque in *Rasselas*. This for him also was the rationale of poetry, whose rhyming regularity turned time from a horizontal trek into a circle. He describes the highland reapers being consoled by their harvest songs, since their metrical recurrences beget cheerfulness. For the same reason, in Johnson narrative recoils into the abbreviation of the epigram. Boswell describes him prophesying that all writing, grown 'weary of preparation, and connection, and illustration, and all those arts by which a big book is made', will eventually become aphoristic. The aphorism is narrative seen *sub specie aeternitatis*: a novelistic time-span reduced to an instant; a life's premature arrival at an end.

There is the same aphoristic, end-stopped concentration in the finest, angriest and saddest of Johnson's *Lives*, that in 1744 of the bereft, dissipated Richard Savage. He did not want it to be a novel. It begins indeed by specifically discarding novelty. Its opening protocol declares that the story it tells is the old one of miscarrying ambition and blighted advantages, since all stories are the same. Johnson, as when he adds another couplet to a poem or cements another word in its lexical tomb, is simply appending one more *exemplum* to a general law, writing a supplement to the already innumerable 'volumes ... written ... to enumerate the miseries of the learned'. Those pre-existing books are all acts of graveside homage: 'mournful narratives' Johnson calls them.

The *Life of Savage* demonstrates the generic importance of biography to Johnson. Though disdaining the novel, it seeks to supplant the form which Fielding nominated as the epic of a modern, prosaic and comic reality. Biography is for Johnson tragedy acclimatised to a modern order of prose and humbling fact. It is also tragedy collectivised, rid of its proud egomania. Savage's fate is not singular: it is the lot of every gifted man who has ever been broken by the obdurate world. And in being democratised—as the epic is in Fielding—tragedy is abrogated or overcome. When Savage attempts to write a tragedy, the actual tragedy lies not in the factitious distresses of his chosen hero Sir Thomas Overbury but in his own battle as a writer against the demeaning restrictions of poverty. 'Without lodging, and often without meat', he made up his speeches while tramping the fields or the streets, and had to beg the loan of pen and ink to scribble them on scrap paper he had picked up. Now it is the writer who is unaccommodated man on Lear's heath. Yet if tragedy is Johnson's instinct, he will not allow it to teach him despair. Comedy (in a reversal of his judgement on Shakespeare) remains his hard-won existential skill. Thus he emphasises that Savage's was no doom-laden course of soul-making. His heath is Grub Street: 'having no profession, [he] became by necessity an author'. Throughout, Johnson emphasises the truthful compact with facts which is a virtue of biography, disqualifying *Overbury* because the fictions of the dramatisation offend 'the mind, which ... loves truth'.

All the same, without violating the facts, he makes an allegory of Savage's life and of his own writing of it. Savage was disowned by a haughty mother desperate to conceal the adultery which begot him: as in the Highlands,

Johnson sees this as the grudging meanness of a supposedly maternal nature. Her aim, in one of Johnson's buried metaphors, is to inter her child alive. She has 'a scheme for burying him in poverty'. Savage is lyingly accused of plotting matricide, but a truer revenge is the denial of that ceremony of commemoration which we owe (according to Johnson's theory of biography) to others. When his benefactress Mrs Oldfield dies, he wore mourning 'as if for a mother'. Mourning is the payment of our debt to nature. Johnsonian biography extends that elegiac duty. Johnson told Boswell that 'poets . . . preserve languages' (because poetry, in a repudiation of Sterne's practice in *A Sentimental Journey*, cannot be translated, we must learn a language if we want to know its literature); likewise, biographers preserve men. Or at least they endeavour to do so. All they can actually do is eternalise memory, and even then they are not entirely reliable. The small tragedies of the *Life* are memory-lapses. Johnson fails in his fraternal and filial duty to recall the past and preservatively record it. At his end, Savage makes a nobly repentant speech. Johnson wishes to transcribe it, but can manage to do so only 'as far as it could be retained in memory'. On another occasion he must accuse himself of a sorry remissness. He cannot reward the single relative who did not betray Savage: 'He has mentioned with gratitude the humanity of one lady whose name I am now unable to recollect, and to whom therefore I cannot pay the praises which she deserves for having acted well.'

The suppression of narrative is Johnson's means of pacifying the mind. The 'celestial wisdom' at the end of 'The Vanity of Human Wishes' renounces the hope to which narrative appeals. Pastoral performs the same service: as a stoic self-quietening, it is practised by Imlac during his tedious sea voyage. Boswell, rather than studying stillness, treats his mind as an ungovernable agency, a thing with a will—like the other sense-organs—of its own. The man of humid sensibility is turning into the romantic libertine, Tristram Shandy into Byron's Don Juan. In November 1762 Boswell sits through divine service while 'laying plans for having women, and yet I had the most sincere feelings of religion'. He romantically disclaims responsibility for his moral quandary: 'What a curious, inconsistent thing is the mind of man!'

The proponent of this involuntariness is Rousseau, to whom Boswell went on pilgrimage in 1764, the year before Rousseau began to write his *Confessions*. That volume exposed the truths of a recusant nature, candidly relishing its own original sinfulness. Boswell approaches Rousseau, as he did Johnson, in the hope of being ratified by him, of acquiring identity as the gift of another. From Johnson he longed to inherit character; from Rousseau he expects an infusion of intimate sentiment. But the man he meets is a testy hypochrondriac, not the 'wild philosopher' he has imagined. Boswell begs for validation of his agitated, insecure ego, telling him he comes recommended by 'a man you hold in high regard', pleading with Rousseau to tell him whether 'I answer to the description I gave you of myself', bragging that he too suffers from Rousseau's ailment of depression. But there can be no communion between romantic egotists. Rousseau is preoccupied with himself, especially with the tormenting demands made by his bladder, and rejects Boswell's demand that he accept him as a moral pupil. He even declines to permit further visits. The comedy of the occasion lies in Boswell's distraught self-congratulation. Since Rousseau will not look at him, he must study his own reflection in the mirror: he interrupts the transcript of their interview with a preening account of his own costume. And if Rousseau will not prop him up by telling him who to be, he must try to dupe himself into validating his own bogus persona: 'I had great satisfaction', he notes, 'after finding that I could support the character which I had given of myself.' Personality, for the romantic Boswell as for Yates and the Crawfords at Mansfield Park, is an exercise in amateur theatricals.

Thus the *Life* Boswell wrote of Johnson, though modelled on the classic biographies written by Johnson himself—verdicts on moral character, legalistic distributions of praise and blame—is a work of a very different kind: the romantic autobiography of a self which suspects itself of nonentity and (like Coleridge in the *Biographia Literaria*) is aghast at the mystery of 'the great eternal I AM'; the confession of a man without qualities.

Boswell feels himself to have been invented by Johnson. When Johnson proposes writing the history of the Boswell family, it is as if he is attesting to the literary parentage of his young friend. 'My great Master', as Boswell reverently calls him, is a god and a paterfamilias. When, in the later years covered by the *Life*, Johnson temporarily neglects him, Boswell fusses because he has been disinherited, banished to non-being. He sulks when his letters are not promptly replied to, and charges Johnson with imaginary offences. Yet when Johnson's attention returns to him, his relief is moist with the renewed conviction that he might perhaps, after all, exist: 'My readers will not doubt that his solicitude about me was very flattering.' He is in the dubious state of the romantic character, writing (as David Copperfield puts it) to discover 'whether I shall be the hero of my own life, or whether that station will be held by anybody else'. In Boswell's case it is held by another: the hero of his life is Johnson, who is everything that Boswell is not. Boswell treasures him because his certainty alleviates Boswell's own disquiets of sensibility, his 'wretched changefulness' and 'feeble and tremulous imagination'. Romantically, Boswell's life is a vagary. He refers to his 'wavering state': the same moody indecisiveness which made Scott name his first romantic hero Waverley. Johnson by contrast, when Boswell inquires how he responded to the failure of his tragedy *Irene*, classically boasts of a statuesque immutability and insentience: he felt, he said, 'like the Monument'.

If Boswell, in company with the vacillating Tristram Shandy, resembles the romantic Hamlet, that spirit of oversensitive introspection, then Johnson—whose opinions on spectres are a constant topic in the *Life*—performs a corresponding role in the biography's hidden psychological plot: he is the deathly elder, the admonition of adulthood, Hamlet's father. When Johnson first meets Boswell in a shop in 1763, he is introduced with a quotation from the play. 'Mr Davies . . . announced his awful approach to me, somewhat in the manner of an actor in the part of Horatio, when he addresses Hamlet on the appearance of his father's ghost, "Look, my Lord, it comes!" ' There is an extra complexity to this casting, for Boswell is wishing on Johnson a role from which his mentor had earlier fled. Reading *Hamlet* at the age of nine, Johnson was so disturbed by the apparition of the ghost that he ran into the street and, in his desperation to be sure of the world's solidity, clung to a lamp-post. Johnson was not meant to be Prince Hamlet, let alone his clammy father: such romantic immateriality as theirs is a source of fear and nocturnal dread to him. Boswell, though, relishes the chance to re-enact the play, and in his psychic charade he volunteers to be Hamlet and—unconscious, surely, of his motives—enforces upon Johnson both the role and the condition of the ghost. The part of the romantic Hamlet which Johnson shunned was taken over with a will by Boswell himself: the actress Louisa, who infected him with gonorrhea during his first year in London, was noted for her performance of Gertrude; when Boswell challenges and accuses her, he plays out a version of the closet scene with himself as an incestuous Hamlet who (in a newly perverse involution of the subtext) has been venereally tainted by his mother. As Boswell's better self, Johnson is an enemy to him, rebuking him and meting out (conversationally) what Boswell calls 'hard blows'. Hamlet deals with the imposition of authority by questioning the ghost's status as quizzically as he does his own and asking whether the phantom may not be a delusion. His scepticism permits him to joke with it: 'Well said, old mole! Cans't work i' th' earth so fast?' Instead of being old Hamlet's son, he is the romantic child who fathers the man. This is how Boswell manages the portent of Johnson. He abjectly professes to have been made by Johnson; in fact it is he who has remade Johnson in the romantic image Johnson spurned.

Classical biography studies the probity of public character. Boswell's concern, romantically, is the private man. He treasures the minutiae of Johnson's quirks and gestures and crotchets because of his conviction that a person is an unrepeatable, mysterious individuality, not a specimen to be classically compared (as in Plutarch's parallel lives, or in Johnson's mausoleum of poets) with other examples of the human genus. We may all share interchangeable bodies; but the minds they house are unique. Studying what he calls 'the history of [Johnson's] mind' or 'the progress of his mind', Boswell is midway between the two romantic epics of anarchic, organic consciousness: Sterne's 'history-book . . . of what passes in a man's own mind', disdaining all system and regulation, and Wordsworth's account in *The Prelude* of the 'Growth of a Poet's Mind'. When Boswell describes Johnson's stern demeanour as a schoolboy, he notes a consistency which convinces him that 'the boy is the man in miniature'. This is the classical wisdom, as voiced by

Volumnia when she admires the destructiveness of Coriolanus's son. But the romantic obverse is also true of Boswell's Johnson, or of Wordsworth in *The Prelude*: the man is the boy writ large.

Boswell makes an astounding and justified claim for his version of Johnson. 'I will venture to say that he will be seen in this work more completely than any man who has ever yet lived. And he will be seen as he really was.' Romanticism can make this assertion because it sees character from within, and by doing so dissolves its classical and moral lineaments: Rousseau in the *Confessions*, Goethe in his personae as Werther or Wilhelm Meister, Dickens's David Copperfield in what he calls his *Personal History and Experiences* are not characters to themselves but conundrums, concerts of disparate personae, infinite minds attached to wayward bodies, anthologies of qualities variously inherited or acquired. The more intimately they know themselves, the less sure they are about themselves, and the more estranged from their incompatible fellows. Boswell's own persona in the *Life* has exactly this romantic inauthenticity. Prosecuting his gossiping vendetta against Mrs Thrale or assuring Johnson, 'I am very good now', he has the candour of self-consciousness without the security of self-knowledge. Johnson disapproved of mimicry, telling Boswell that the gift for it had driven mad a lady of his acquaintance; Boswell, like Rameau's nephew, delights in this physical and psychological virtuosity, especially when Garrick performs the role of Johnson, but the exact duplication of 'the gestures and voice of a person' only reminds him that the body is the mind's prison. His Johnson suffers the solitude of consciousness. When Boswell quotes his letters, they have the accents of Cowper's Selkirk or Coleridge's mariner: Lord Chesterfield's patronage is refused as the conceit of 'one who looks with unconcern on a man struggling for life in the water, and, when he has reached ground, encumbers him with help'; Johnson, like Boswell, is a self adrift—'a kind of solitary wanderer in the wild of life, without any direction, or fixed point of view'. Even his lexicography seems the penance of a Crusoe, dissociated from human society and castaway in the waste of language: 'I now begin to see land, after having wandered, according to Mr. Warburton's phrase, in this vast sea of words.'

Exhilarated by wine, susceptible to women, averse to routine, depressively afflicted by a 'diseased imagination', Boswell's Johnson is a creature of romantic whim and Shandyean sensitivity. The last and most disgruntled spokesman of classical prohibition is co-opted as one of the first romantics.

— 24 —
Gothic Follies

The ghosts against whose existence Johnson vainly protested—'he was prone to superstition, but not to credulity', says Boswell—are the chimerae of the romantic imagination. Knowledge might cast doubt on them, but belief compels us (as Johnson reluctantly admitted) to accredit them, and in the process perhaps betrays itself. Carlyle argued that Johnson longed all his life to see a ghost but did not have the imaginative intrepidity required: 'Did he never, with the mind's eye as well as with the body's, look round him . . .; did he never . . . look into Himself?' If he had done so, he would have understood that he was himself a ghost: a spirit briefly apparelled in human form, a walking, talking metaphor.

After Johnson, the imagination sets about freeing itself from the constraints of reason. Walter Scott in his essays on Mrs Radcliffe and Clara Reeve criticised 'an age of universal incredulity', and argued that ghosts must be permitted in Gothic fiction because to exclude them is a slight to the phantasmagorical capacities of imagination. By the end of the nineteenth century, the talent for seeing ghosts at will had become itself a metaphor for imaginative empathy; in defending her own stories of the supernatural, Edith Wharton could then distinguish between ghost-seers and ghost-feelers, 'sensible of invisible currents'. Identifying the creative power with a knack for divining spectres, she says that ghosts have retreated because our imaginings are disparaged by the ethic of materialism.

Before the imagination could establish its prerogative to have visions, it experimented with its powers by telling lies. Self-deception is the late eighteenth century's anticipation in comedy of what the romantics considered to be a state of prophetic illumination. The poems of Chatterton, Gray and Collins are, in company with the Gothic novel, a tentative declaration of imagination's independence, working by solemn make-believe. Chatterton faked the parchments on which Rowley had supposedly written by browning paper over a flame and tanning it in tea; Horace Walpole, who was prepared to believe that a sham ruin erected at Hadley had 'the true rust of the Baron's wars' and devised for himself at Strawberry Hill a Gothic folly as flimsy as paper, passed off *The Castle of Otranto* as a medieval relic; Blake allegorised his subservience to imagination by declaring that he took dictation from spirits. Their purpose is cabbalistic: to mystify creation. The image is now an annunciation. Spirit radiantly infuses this world's literal reality; literature—

which in the medieval period with difficulty overcomes its submission to the authority of holy writ—promotes itself to the status scripture has forfeited. Though romanticism is named after the medieval culture it venerated, it exactly inverts the medieval order. Then, the only creator was God, who made the world as his book; now every poet possesses this fiat, and all poems are home-made Bibles, forged esoteric missals like Chatterton's.

Collins in his 1746 preface to *Odes Descriptive and Allegoric* complains that poetry is circumscribed by moralising and that imagination must be indulged. It gains its liberty in the descriptive form: the answer to the didactic is the pictorial, which incarnates visions. Gray and Collins transform the ode from a public ceremony honouring a moral quality or an exemplary individual—Milton's Christ, Marvell's Cromwell—into a private, excited dance around an image: the 'soft salutary power' of Ignorance, to which Gray addresses a hymn; the peremptory, eruptive passions in Collins's 'Ode for Music'. But their attempts to create a space of awe and worshipful danger around images falter for lack of confidence. They can contrive freedom only by subterfuge. Collins in 1742 pretends that his *Persian Eclogues* are transcribed from originals entrusted to him by a trader in Arabian silks and carpets. Walpole, admitting his deception in the second edition of *Otranto*, pleads that the 'great resources of fancy are dammed up by a strict adherence to common life'. Chatterton has Rowley express the same notion in lines crabbed and prickly with misspellings which hope to wrack words into poetry by decoratively defacing them, as if with mock-Gothic crockets and crenellations:

> Now shapelie poesie hast lost yttes powers,
> And pynant hystorie ys onlie grace; . . .
> Nowe poesie canne meete wythe ne regrate,
> Whylst prose, and herehaughtrie, ryse yn estate.

The orientalism of Collins's eclogues, like these wilful disfigurements, is a style aware of its own imposture. The poems are prefaced with apologies, blaming their figurative luxury on a climate riper and spicier than England's, and confessing to lapses in translation. The romantic sensations they contain turn out to be half-hearted: Hassan the camel-driver lacks the mental courage to confront the desert, and rues the day when he quit the safe, settled encampment of Schiraz, just as John Home is rescued from the numinous Highlands and reclaimed for the society of his friends. The man who lives imaginatively runs the risk of perishing, like the 'luckless swain' seized by the fiends summoned out of reason's sleep in the 'Popular Superstitions' poem; or else, more dismayingly still, he is defrauded, his visions exposed as false conjectures:

> Where'er we turn, by Fancy charmed, we find
> Some sweet illusion of the cheated mind.

Afraid of unleashing imagination, Gray and Collins elect a temperate mediocrity. Gray in 'The Progress of Poesy' accepts that he cannot soar like the Theban eagle. He will daydream instead, and watch the elusive forms glittering in the muse's ray. Collins in his 'Ode on the Poetical Character' anticipates Keats's scheme for graduating from the sensuous laxity of Spenser to the rigour of Milton; yet as it happens, both Spenser and Milton forbid Collins to ally himself with them. The poetic gift is imaged as the girdle of Florimell, found by Satyrane in *The Faerie Queene*. Rather than seizing it, Collins flinches from it, dreading it as a fatal zone which will tear itself loose from candidates it adjudges unworthy. If Spenser proves untenable, Milton is inaccessible, headquartered on a sublime pinnacle which Collins, exhausted, cannot scale. At the end of the ode, the myths of Spenser and Milton combine in an embargo on their successors:

> And Heaven and Fancy, kindred powers,
> Have now o'erturned the inspiring bowers,
> Or contained close such scene from every future view.

The garden of lyricism is both Spenser's seditious bower, its blisses censured by Guyon, and Milton's revoked Eden. Failure of inspiration now seems the punishment for some original, unspecified sin. In his 'Ode to Fear' Collins experiments with the infernal alternative, and offers to deliver himself to the powers of darkness if they will alarm him into a poetic fury. 'Fancy lifts the veil' between him and 'the unreal scene' of imagination: the same unveiling, which lays bare the dangerous revelation of the image, constitutes the denouement of Ann Radcliffe's Gothic novels.

The need to release the image from rational control provokes a merger between poetry and painting. The image is the word made flesh, the verbal visually incarnated. Gray was twice illustrated during this period—embroidered with rococo finickiness by Richard Bentley, in an edition made for Horace Walpole in 1753; hallucinatorily transformed by Blake in the late 1790s. Both are liberators of Gray's cautious, earth-bound words. Bentley extends them into the playful purposelessness of fantasy, while Blake involves them in his own demon-peopled spirit-world. His designs are a growth, and perhaps a malign one, on Gray's innocuous texts, and the vegetative uncoiling of their subconscious wishes: 'Around the Springs of Gray', Blake said, 'my wild root weaves.' Blake encourages in Gray the romanticism which the poet's own words suppress. Gray's 'Ode on the Spring', for instance, is about the poet's envious, frustrated exclusion from the glad fecund society of nature. Bentley houses the poet in a Popean palace of art, twined together from palm fronds, curling tails of monkeys, perukes and laurel wreaths. His consolation, like Pope's in his grotto or Walpole's in the Gothic mousetrap of Strawberry Hill, is residence inside a decorative sham. Bentley confects a similar ruin, elegantly dilapidated, for the 'Elegy Written in a Country Churchyard'.

To Blake, Gray's poet is no flimsy fantasist but an euphoric visionary, hunched over his page with a fierce gleam in his eye, unfurling tendrils, as he lies cradled in a tree's roots, which re-embed him in nature. That nature overtakes Gray's words, mechanically cordorned off from it by print. For the final 'Spring' design Blake cut a block of text from the 1790 edition of Gray and made it a nest for the nurselings both of innocence and experience: spirits use it as a perch or diving-board, a spider as anchorage for its web. Here the text buds and flowers into the landscape, as words like seeds unfurl images; in Blake's design for the 'Elegy' the printed page of text is an incubus, weighing on the poet who vexed vision into words. Gray's demoralised artist cowers in a lower corner of the design, writing beneath the vaults of a church. He has drawn his cloak over his head in self-protection and is bent almost broken-backed. The block of text rests like a tombstone on his head, and thrusts him even further down. Bentley's illustrations are a herbaceous border to the text: a marginalia of fanciful extravagance outside the learned sobriety of the verse, existing innuendo-like between its lines. They have that irrationality which is Pope's only means of unconstraining imagination. Blake, cutting windows in his drawing-paper to fit the pages excerpted from Gray, makes the text a magic casement opening onto the spectral realm of imagery. Or sometimes closed against it: occasionally the text is a blinded eye, averse to the rampant scenes drawn by Blake and hoping to blank them out. The characters in Blake's designs for Gray's northern epic poems—'The Bard', for instance, or 'The Descent of Odin'—use the text as armature, holding it in front of themselves like a banner or shield; in the elegiac poems they stare glumly at it as if at a gravestone. But Blake's desire is to speed the text's take-off, and in the frontispiece of his collection Genius, soaring aloft on a swan, carries the inset page with him to use as ballast.

Gray's metaphors have the indefinite, intermediate status of Johnson's ghosts. They begin, in the 'Ode as a Distant Prospect of Eton College', as an allegorical troop of personified sins, but end by dematerialising into moody chimerae, 'vultures of the mind'. They cannot be properly described or depicted by Gray because they lurk in what Collins, in his ode on 'The Manners', calls 'the dim-discovered tracts of mind'. Blake's genius lies in the simple, literal trust with which he draws such fugitive metaphors, as if from the life. He wills them into visibility. This enables the romantic image, like ectoplasm at a séance, to acquire material form. Coleridge, terrified, writes about this portent in the dream preceding 'Kubla Khan': the words of *Purchas his Pilgrimage* took on physical substance, and almost fiendishly 'the images rose up before him as *things*'.

In Blake's own poetry, the printed word flickers or writhes into life as the painted word. The dead metaphors within language are quickened into resurrection. In 'London' first a street and then the Thames is chartered; the blackness of churches is appalled—rendered pallid, draped in deathly palls, as well as horror-struck—by the cry of the chimney-sweeper; and to mark, meaning merely to observe, becomes the physical addition of a disfiguring mark to the things seen. The same vivification is abetted by Blake's illustrations. The words are illuminated from within: their intensity makes them catch fire, as when those tongues of flame crackle above the account of the angels' lamentation in *America* (1793); or they branch, bifurcate and replete the world with their unpruned growth, as on the title-page to *Songs of Innocence* (1789) or in the choking undergrowth of 'A Little Boy Lost'. The image is the fertilisation and exfoliation of the word. In *The Marriage of Heaven and Hell* (1790) Blake envies the ancient poets their demi-urgic power to animate things, implanting gods or genii in them by the mere act of naming them. A literature of print has squandered that power by mechanising it: in hell Blake visits a printing-house, and deplores its metallic enchaining of life in books and libraries. To the regimen of print, deadening things by formalising or by casting them in immitigable type, Blake opposes the energetic suffusion of paint, which can restore to language the vigour and the power of ordination possessed by those ancient poets.

Print is a grid of hard and wiry lines, signifying rectitude. Blake confounds its severity pictorially: a cross-bar on the initial T of 'The Tyger' sprouts a serpent, an S in 'On Another's Sorrow' sports a streaming mane of hair, from the J of *Jerusalem* there emanates a chrysalis. If paint is the blooming and burgeoning of sterile typography, Blake's other technique of etching signifies an acidulous cleansing of perception: 'printing by corrosives' is, he says, 'salutary and medicinal, melting apparent surfaces away, and displaying the infinite which was hid.' In Blake's line engravings, the acid seems to have rendered bodies transparent to disclose spirit. Hence the ribs and sinews he sees through the crawling hulk of Nebuchadnezzar, or the skeleton-like wings of Elohim, seen creating Adam in another 1795 plate.

Blake's career is about the romantic imagination's gradual and devious escape from the shame and guilt imposed on it by the Newtonian tyranny of what *There is No Natural Religion* in 1788 calls 'Ratio'. As a boy, Blake was punished for possessing imagination. When he reported seeing a tree of angels on Peckham Rye, his father threatened him with a beating. Vision—seeing the invisible by a power of in-sight—was stigmatised as lying. Blake defensively persisted in supporting the untruths of his colleagues. In 1803 he impenitently stated, 'I believe both Macpherson & Chatterton, that what they say is Ancient Is so.' But he remains embroiled in the ethical debate about the rights of imagination which lies behind Johnson's assault on superstition and ghosts. Blake's notes on Lavater deny that superstition is mental error; rather it is a naive form of religious faith and of poetic wishfulness. He disapproved of ghosts, though for reasons different from Johnson's. He argued that they were physical prodigies visiting only common, prosaic men; spirits, however, were mental visions, and to see them required the poet's entranced perception of what is not there—an aptitude for intuiting symbols.

The spectre is another name for imagination, that double or *alter ego* (the filmy 'stranger' of Coleridge's 'Frost at Midnight') roving beyond the confines of our physical existence. Blake claimed to converse daily with his dead brother, and to see him 'in the regions of my imagination'. By symbolising imagination as a revenant, Blake could represent himself as its helpless and blameless victim. It has become an involuntary power, as it is for Wordsworth and (in his dejection) Coleridge, a rainbow which comes and goes regardless of the poet's will. Blake apologised for his tardiness in supplying some designs by telling his client he had been transported by his 'Abstract folly' to 'a Land of Abstraction where Spectres of the Dead Wander', despite his efforts to tether himself to 'the world of Duty & Reality', and said he had written *Jerusalem* at the dictation of spirits, 'even against my Will'. This supposed passivity enables him to boast of his poetic inspiration with impunity, 'since I dare not pretend to be any other than the Secretary; the Authors are in Eternity.' Yet the spirits he enlists as accessories sometimes object to Blake's sly suborning of them. The angel in *The Marriage of Heaven and Hell* rebukes Blake because 'thy phantasy has imposed upon me, & thou oughtest to be ashamed'. This is the romantic image's indignant refusal of poetic procurement; it might be Christabel's objection to Geraldine's invasion of her fantasy, or the leech-gatherer's to Wordsworth, the urn's to Keats who makes it utter his credo, or the skylark's to Shelley who denies it the right ever to have been a bird. The angel is supposed to be Blake's mentor, demonstrating to him his lot in eternity. In fact he is Blake's invention and his surrogate. The shame he incites in Blake is remorse for a too-coercive imagination, which enlists other existences or inanimate objects as symbols of and alibis for itself.

Blake often finds the image restive, like Keats's nightingale or Wordsworth's fading aureoles. This happened with the imaginary heads he drew in 1819–20 for the physiognomist John Varley. The capture of these wraiths—the bloodthirsty ghost of a flea; Varley himself mutating into an elephant—is a graphic equivalent to the romantic poet's difficult art: finding words for the inexpressible; making real the unrealisable. Though Blake was drawing ideas, descrying in objects subjective symbols, Varley is misled by a literal credulity. He is inclined to treat Blake's imaginings as physical facts: 'I felt convinced . . . that he had a real image before him.' Blake would tease him by suddenly breaking off in the course of his transcription, claiming that the spirit he was sketching had moved, or frowned to express disapproval at its likeness, or even (as the devil did on one occasion) disappeared. In these sessions, Blake was acting out, with sly comic guile, the anxiety of the romantic artist, who has surrendered himself to imagination and must tolerate its unreliability. Romantic lyrics end, as Blake's sketching did, in a perplexed admission that the image is unrecoverable—Keats's 'Fled is that vision', or Coleridge's vain effort to revive in himself the song of the damsel with a dulcimer. Annotating the discourses of Sir Joshua Reynolds, Blake rages at critics who say 'he can conceive, but he cannot Execute.' This smarts because it is indeed his problem, and that generally of the romantics. Engendering is all; the execution—translating the vision to paper—is defeat and even betrayal. The vision can be safeguarded only by aborting the text. Blake cannot represent his phantoms: King Saul wore a helmet which he could not see properly. The poets, by the same self-denying protocol, leave their most ambitious works incomplete.

Walpole's first preface to *Otranto* in 1764 apologises for the visionary and miraculous in the work, calling them the products of a credulous and barbarous age. The story is not his, he declares; he has happened upon it in an ancestral library, and dates it 'between 1095, the aera of the first crusade, and 1243'. He is able to quibble over his own faith in it—not bound to believe in its marvels, bound only to make his characters believe. When in the second preface he admits his authorship he again practises on the credulity of his readers by attributing the pretence to diffidence not deceit. The admixture of below-stairs comedy, defended by invoking the example of the Shakespearean double plot, is also an appeasement of rational disbelief. Rather than maddening his characters, the excess of imagination makes them absurd.

Otranto is an essay on the epistemology of that enfevered imagination, forever interrogating the precise status of its visions. Manfred is frantically anxious to know whether the gigantic helmet might be a delusion of superstition, or a necromantic prop. 'Do I dream?' he demands of the moving picture. Is what he sees his own vision, or bedevilment? Isabella, fleeing through the subterranean cloisters, is so nervously susceptible that she terrifies herself, and is pursued only by her own fears: 'She thought she heard a sigh. She shuddered, and recoiled a few paces. In a moment she thought she heard the step of some person.' Bianca, too, needlessly torments herself by fancying the young peasant's voice to be that of a squabbling ghost. The reason fortifies itself with scepticism against these bogus dreads. Manfred derides the mental slavishness of those who believe in goblins; Hippolita, though convinced of the phantom's reality, affects to disbelieve in it to pacify the rabid Manfred. *Otranto* enquires into the probity of the novel, with its necessary lies. The priest scatters false clues, enticing Manfred into a 'visionary intrigue' so as to divert him from his plan to renounce his wife. When the monk discovers that the doomed youth is his son, Manfred disparages this as a ploy to save the peasant's life: truth is suspected of being fiction. As well as considering such ethical questions as these, *Otranto* acknowledges that the imagination will erect an alternative theology, since it has assumed for itself a creative power formerly the preserve of god. Theodore's devotion convinces Isabella that he is no mortal but a guardian angel, and Manfred believes that the phantom knight has an unfair, supernatural advantage over him. He is unsure whether 'these omens' are 'from heaven or hell': the romantic poet also asks himself whether imagination is divinity or—in Coleridge's exorcistic 'holy dread'—demonism.

Reviewing *The Mysteries of Udolpho* on its publication in 1794, Coleridge regretted that Mrs Radcliffe had explained away its supernatural mysteries. To him the Gothic novel betokened a right to have secrets and summon up arcana without the need of rational justification. Hence his obfuscation of 'Kubla Khan', or his refusal to elucidate 'Christabel' by completing it. But Mrs Radcliffe's romanticism is more timorous than Coleridge's, and needs the indemnity of reason.

Udolpho sternly guards against imagination's wantonness. St Aubert disciplines the idle mind, otherwise prone to reverie and wayward fantasy; Emily suffers an 'attack of imagination' as if it were a disease, and her distempered spasm is vanquished only by 'returning reason'. Her interpolated poems are a species of sorcery. One of them, she hopes, will act like a spell to enchant her father's judgement. But her verses are classified by Mrs Radcliffe as indulgences of fancy and segregated from the stricter domain of prose, or else trivialised as an 'escape from serious reflections'. In Mrs Radcliffe's plots, the culprit is always imagination. When a bracelet is lost, Emily guesses that 'the poet, the musician and the thief were the same person', thus footnoting Theseus's analogy in *A Midsummer Night's Dream* between the lunatic, the lover and the poet. Mystery is generated by the rational and moral restraints on imagination—by St Aubert's prohibition concerning the papers, or Emily's reluctance 'to tamper with the integrity of a servant' by ordering the picture uncovered. Denied gratification, imagination guiltily invents lapses which it wishes on others. Emily defends her aunt against Montoni by saying, 'it is impossible, that you could yourself have imagined a crime so hideous.' She blames herself 'for suffering her own romantic imagination to carry her so far beyond the bounds of probability' in suspecting Montoni of depravity and murder, and checks these 'rapid flights' before they extend into 'the misery of superstition' and thence to madness. Explication, for her as for Mrs Radcliffe, means allaying the fears and desires of her dreaming mind. Her imaginings are always much worse than the evidence merits. The bandits are not, as she believes, orgiastically exulting over some new 'barbarous deed', but simply tallying their takings; Montoni is not the captain of banditti which 'Emily apprehended him to be'; the cadaver is wax.

If *Otranto* quizzes imagination with a witty scepticism and *Udolpho* refutes its foolish terrors, *Northanger Abbey* proudly insists on its necessity, and at the same time angrily justifies the art of fiction. Jane Austen's work has often been misinterpreted as a parody of Radcliffean romance. In truth it is a more audacious and unafraid Gothic novel than any of its predecessors, showing that the factitious suppositions of Emily are not half as disquieting as the daily perils of common social life, that fact is stranger than the most lurid fiction and the grubby confidences of the laundry list are more likely to expose the ugly bases of human nature than any of Mrs Radcliffe's trumped-up revelations. Jane Austen converts the Gothic fable into its nineteenth-century successor, the novel concerned with what Dickens in *Bleak House* called 'the romantic side of familiar things', aware of reality as surreal nightmare—the spontaneous combustion of Krook, authenticated by Dickens with medical submissions; the drug-deformed cathedral in *The Mystery of Edwin Drood*; the beasts stalking social jungles or crafting pagodas of decorative deceit (like the one Maggie walks round and round in *The Golden Bowl*) in the novels of Henry James.

Whereas Walpole's Isabella or Mrs Radcliffe's Emily suffer from the intemperate abundance of fancy, Catherine Morland's problem is actually the lack of imagination. She cannot conceive of the motives of others, or of their subtle perfidy. She does not recognise that every person is an insoluble mystery. Her 'bold surmise' about Isabella's affection for James 'comprehended but half the fact'; when Isabella later cools James, Catherine finds this 'unsteady conduct . . . beyond her comprehension'. To survive in the society of Jane Austen's novel, characters must possess a romantic imagination and a capacity for devising and deciphering fictions. Mr Thorpe is a professional imaginist, 'telling lies to increase [his] importance', and Isabella thrives in that realm of suspended disbelief where Johnson's ghosts and Blake's envisioned heads lurk. Told the time, she declares it 'inconceivable, incredible, impossible!' that it should be after three o'clock, and will permit 'no assurance . . . founded on reason or reality'. Catherine's initial disqualification is a loyalty to fact misplaced in a work of fiction—she 'could not tell a falsehood even to please Isabella'—and in a society inured to intricate untruths. When she calls on Miss Tilney, a servant first accepts her card then returns it, declaring himself to have been mistaken, for Miss Tilney is not at home. His 'look . . . did not quite confirm his words'. Catherine has been humiliatingly instructed in the cruel social utility of imagination. As she leaves, she dreams up a scenario of rejection, and irresistibly wishes it into truth. She cannot prevent herself from glancing back at the house, from which she sees the supposedly absent Miss Tilney exit. Determined to have the knowledge which has been prohibited, in that backward glance she effects her own shame—the affliction identified by Blake's angel as the imposition of fantasy. Fact retreats before the advance of supreme, exorbitant fiction. Catherine finds history books dull, although she is convinced that they are all ersatz novels. 'The speeches that are put into the heroes' mouths, their thoughts and designs—the chief of all this must be invention.'

As a dealer in such fictions, Jane Austen allies herself with Catherine the fantasist: she is, in her fierce dissertation on the novel, an unashamed romantic. The subject is introduced after the account of the intimate accord between Catherine and Isabella. Their sorority is cemented by their habit of shutting themselves up together 'to read novels'. The novels they read are exclusively female productions, for Jane Austen names the enemies of the form as men of letters ('the man', for instance, 'who collects and publishes in a volume some dozen lines of Milton, Pope, and Prior, with a paper from *The Spectator*, and a chapter from Sterne'; or the male bookseller who, as her advertisement to the book recalls, purchased the manuscript of *Northanger Abbey* in 1803 but left it unpublished for thirteen years, prudishly suppressing Jane Austen's young and inflamed imagination) while its practitioners, characters and customers are women. This makes the novel almost a sexual premium. The friendship of the girls, warm at first, progressing 'through every gradation of tenderness' until they are inseparable, is consummated in the solidarity between them, the Cecilias, Camillas, and Belindas they read about, and Jane Austen herself. 'Alas!' she says, convening this union of females, 'if the heroine of one novel be not patronized by the heroine of another, from whom can she expect protection and regard?' Her language acquires an erotic urgency: 'Let us not desert one another; we are an injured body.' And that body, corporeally imagined, at once engenders a corporation: 'Although our productions have afforded more extensive and unaffected pleasure than those of any other literary corporation in the world, no species of composition has been so much decried.'

The novel is a body given over to pleasure; a collective female organism of desire, expressing itself in plot-making fantasy. For if the Gothic novel is—once it dispenses with the timidity of Walpole or Mrs Radcliffe—an unbridling of imagination, then it must derive its energy from the yearning, raging libido. The novelist's body, described by Jane Austen as injured, abused and degraded, is the secret subject of Gothic fiction. The mental quandaries of Isabella at Otranto or Emily at Udolpho are already, by 1797, physical travails for the two heroines of the Marquis de Sade's *Justine, ou les Malheurs de la Vertu* and *Juliette, ou les Prosperités de la Vice*. There the lubricious imagination researches sensations which are pleasant and painful at once: Justine's martyrdom, bestialised and flagellated, is to Juliette an orgy of enjoyment; Catherine too, reading *Udolpho*, relishes her terror as a delicious luxury. The same kinship in voluptuous dreaming conjoins Catherine and Jane Austen. The novelist is defined as a discreet female libertine. Jane Austen's most gratuitous coup is the conjuring up, at the end of the novel, of a copy-book husband for Eleanor Tilney. The novelist simply dreams of him, and that suffices to summon him to her: her business is supplying both characters and readers with prompt gratification of their imaginative whims. She does not even need to say who the man is or what he looks like, because she can rely on the fantasies of others to corroborate her mental invocation of him. He is an outline filled in by each reader's exigent, idiosyncratic desire—'Any further definition of his merits must be unnecessary; the most charming young man in the world is instantly before the imagination of us all.'

The novel's Gothic architecture becomes a replica of the ardent body, that house for fictional sensations; so does the book, guiltily thrown aside by the novel-reader with whom Jane Austen remonstrates. Blaize Castle is a place of involution and <u>reticulation</u>, invaded by exploratory desire. 'May we go all over it? may we go up every staircase, and into every suite of rooms?' asks Catherine. Isabella replies, 'Yes, yes, every hole and corner.' Henry, in his speech of imaginative incitation, orders Catherine to brave each retentive orifice at Northanger, to unlock doors, ransack drawers, to finger delicate springs which thrust open inner compartments, to seek out 'a division in the tapestry so artfully constructed as to defy the minutest inspection'. The Gothic mind loves labyrinths, whether they are a cerebral architecture (as in the cranium-like castle explored in 'Christabel') or a bodily cellulation: Catherine's 'imagination . . . hoped for the smallest divisions'. The cavities and crannies felt for must harbour forbidden knowledge, like the cabinet whose sliding panel discloses to Gwendolen Harleth the image of her crime, or the secret drawer in which (with the clicking of a patent lock) Dr Grantly makes haste to hide his copy of Rabelais in Trollope's *The Warden* (1855). Catherine probes 'with anxious acuteness' for false linings in a drawer, hoping to lay bare an interior sensitivity. Her tour of the abbey inducts her into a maze of specialised chambers, like those of the many-mansioned brain mapped by Keats—the 'appropriate divisions' of the kitchen, the 'dark little room' sacred to Henry, the 'narrower passage, more numerous openings, and symptoms of a winding staircase' (which describes the spiral, like James's turning screw, as a morbid phenomenon), the cloistral cells and doors leading nowhere bearing still 'the traces of monastic division'.

The book is a corresponding prison of fantasy, a cell for consciousness. It possesses the cerebral ground-plan which Keats, writing to Reynolds in 1818, derived from Udolpho. From the nursery of maiden-thought, the Keatsian explorer gropes ahead to a cavern of grim revelation, like the inquisitorial torture-chamber in Mrs Radcliffe's *The Italian* (1797). From the centre of the multi-camerate mind, 'many doors are set open—but all dark—all leading to dark passages.' The Gothic plot is for Keats an allegory of spiritual growth. Like Keats advancing 'in a Mist', Catherine undertakes to inspect the grime and mire which are the psychological deposits of Gothic. The inventory of domestic linen is no disappointment. To this 'precious manuscript' has been entrusted the most physically private testimony of all. Among the desiderata of imagination is dirt (along with cobwebs and stained glass)—the seamy residue of the nasty mind, which George Eliot, demanding an art more humanely upright, complained of in a letter to Burne-Jones in 1873. At Blaize, Catherine positively exults in that uncleanliness. Thorpe says he 'never saw so much dirt in my life', and Isabella tells Catherine, 'you cannot form an idea of the dirt'. Northanger satisfies her expectation of stains and psychological soiling. It exposes her to the 'dirty work', as she says when she visits the scullery, which is society's secret. Behind the veil is not a corpse but a mercenary hardness of heart, the solution to the mystery of human nature and of a careless, daily evil; that is the motive for the General's expulsion of Catherine from the house. The curious imagination continues to see itself architecturally long after the Gothic novel expires: the minds of the Meyrick girls in *Daniel Deronda* are 'like medieval houses with unexpected recesses and openings from this into that, flights of steps and sudden outlooks'.

Otranto is a mousetrap, or a riddling box of toys. There are trapdoors with spring locks and a chink in the pavement where the casque drops. This castle has the infinite littleness of Sternean irony. Walpole's central notion is of something too sublimely outsize to fit its snugly beautiful structure: the huge helmet of the Knight who has grown too gigantic to be contained in the castle. His jokes are about such disproportion, about irony as an inverse sublimity. Defending the admixture of comedy, he likens Shakespeare to the Greek sculptor 'who, to convey the idea of a Colossus within the dimensions of a seal, inserted a little boy measuring his thumb'. Mrs Radcliffe's ground-plan is ampler, but too delinquent to be explored with safety. Emily disapproves of the 'roundabout passages' commended by Annette: these are both architectural quirks and moral circumlocutions. Udolpho is structurally untrustworthy. Its vaulted corridors are an apparatus for transmitting rumour and for scandal-mongering. They amplify a cough so it sounds like a cannonade; Lodovico advises Du Pont to whisper or else his voice will echo all round the castle. The cell, Jane Austen's hiding-place of fantasy, connotes for Mrs Radcliffe the danger of a mad estrangement from others. Blanche reviles convents because their windows are closed and bolted.

After *Northanger Abbey*, though, the interior space cramped into miniature by Walpole and fenced off by Mrs Radcliffe dilates. Gothic architecture is a diagram of the romantic mind—in the winding staircases which symbolise for Coleridge the dangerous convolutions of thought—or of the visionary romantic eye, as when Keats looks through those

> . . . magic casements, opening on the foam
> Of perilous seas, in fairy lands forlorn.

The castle stands not only for the impenetrable, fortress-like head; it represents, as the abbey does for Catherine, the concave anatomy through which the romantics adventure, in quest of its recondite, sensual havens. This is the meaning of the baronial pile in Keats's Radcliffean *Eve of St. Agnes*: the castle is the body penetrated by Porphyro, which ejects him along with Madeline and then—overtaken by the chill without, draughtily releasing its vitality as its 'long carpets rose along the gusty floor'—itself gives up the ghost. In miniature, the castle is the dress Madeline has shed, on which Porphyro gazes: an empty dress is a body the spirit has cast off. Christabel takes Geraldine to a room

> Carved with figures strange and sweet,
> All made out of the carver's brain.

Here the Gothic decor is the hollowing-out of a head. Shelley in *Julian and*

Maddalo seeks 'entrance to the caverns of [the madman's] mind', while Keats in *The Fall of Hyperion* attempts Gothically to travel into the 'dark secret chambers' of Moneta's skull, its mysteries curtained behind her planetary eyes. Hyperion himself lives in a palace which, bloodily flushing and nervously aching, is the viscerally arched and domed crypt of a diseased organism; he flares out of it, disembodying himself by force, as the poem breaks off.

Gothic is the architecture ordained by romantic imagination for the worship of its own creativity. Coleridge sets in the centre of *Biographia Literaria* a perverse cathedral, where the angels and gargoyles have sacrilegiously changed places; Victor Hugo saw Shakespeare as the same lively, lawless edifice. The triumph of romantic conceit was the building of such dreams—by Beckford at Fonthill, by Scott at Abbotsford. Beckford's was an infernal abbey, modelled after Milton's Pandemonium. Its tower rose by night like an exhalation, without effort from Beckford himself and as if compelled by his wish. Indoors, too, the place telepathically responded to its creator's desires: a door to the sanctuary opened when Beckford gave the magic password (meanwhile pressing a floor-board with his foot). Scott's novels were an imaginary architecture congruent with Abbotsford, which they subsidised. Fiction may be a lie, but it pays for truths; in any case the ethical issues of credulity and credibility over which Johnson worried, tolerating romance only if it could be authenticated by the ruins he visited in Scotland, no longer trouble Scott. In July 1827, resuming *Chronicles of the Canongate*, he noted in his journal that 'works of fiction, vzy Cursed Lies, are easier to write and much more popular than the best truths.' Scott sees his own creativity as a skill at weightless architectural projection. He remarks that 'I can see . . . castles in the clouds', and reckons himself 'one of the best aerial architects now living'. Yet the purpose of his vertiginous imagining is a return to the solidity of earth. After his bankruptcy, he wrote in order to regain his estate, and calculated financial prospects 'in the manner in which [one] builds schemes and not visions'. The dream can requisition facts. One of Scott's antiquarian curios at Abbotsford testified to the new exigency of romantic imagination, able, like Kubla Khan, to commission compliant reality. In *The Heart of Mid-Lothian* (1818) he describes a riot at the Tolbooth, a turreted Edinburgh prison. The insurgents batter its oak portals with sledge-hammers, crow-bars, plough-shares and fire-brands. But the door abides their assault, and when the prison was torn down it was presented to Scott, who built it into a wing of Abbotsford. His comment on the affair jokes about his own impunity, as a romantic who can make dreams true without the disbursement of energy or money: 'Better get a niche *from* the Tolbooth than a niche *in* it, to which such building-operations are apt to bring the projectors.'

The romantic is on his way to becoming an improvident tycoon, like Scott Fitzgerald's Gatsby or his Monroe Stahr. Coleridge's Kubla Khan will soon enough change—lording it over his hoard of fantasies in an estate in the Florida jungle, which he calls Xanadu—into Orson Welles's Citizen Kane.

Wordsworth, Coleridge
and the Failed God

Wordsworth and Coleridge were both beneficiaries and victims of romantic imagination—first elated by it, then demoralised by its desertion of them. For Wordsworth, the source of poetic joy and liveliness lay without, in physical nature; for Coleridge, it lay not so much above, in supernature (as their division of labour in the 1798 *Lyrical Ballads* proposed), as within, an emanation like the eruptive fountains in 'Kubla Khan' from the poet's own troubled psychological nature. In both cases, it is beyond or beneath rational control. The poet is the helpless medium for the poetry which happens to or through him.

Poems to Wordsworth are accidents, like found objects: he does not and cannot anticipate, when he is 'a Traveller . . . upon the moor', his encounter with the leech-gatherer, or, when he is wandering with a cloud's aimlessness, the visionary apparition of the daffodils. At the mercy of a random experience, an irradiation of the world like the angelic host of daffodils beside the lake, he is bereaved when the aureole fades and the vision is revoked. The composition of a poem is no consolation. For the poem stealthily kills what is poetic in it: the writing is a sad and solitary second best. Nature endows the poet with an athletic grace and gladness, a kinesis of physical pleasure, such as Wordsworth experiences when skating in *The Prelude* or when, among the daffodils, he acknowledges that 'A poet could not but be gay, / In such a jocund company.' The writing happens later, when the dance is ended and the deprived, sedentary man comforts himself with memories. The daffodils make a poem only 'when on my couch I lie / In vacant or in pensive mood.' And just as the man who wandered and floated weightlessly through the landscape has become dejected, invalid, so the daffodils have lost their fluttering, capering glory and have been internalised. They now 'flash upon that inward eye / Which is the bliss of solitude'; the heart now, not the body, dances with them. A poem resembles an epitaph to an experience it has extinguished.

Wordsworth collected such inscriptions on his walking tours, wrote essays about them, and willed his poems into company with them by leaving copies to moulder in the landscape at the places where they were composed, repaying their debt to nature. This post-mortem theory of the poem hides within Wordsworth's definition of his art as emotion recollected in tranquillity—emotion, that is, tranquillised by the meditative discipline of memory, subjected to a small death, like that which overtakes Lucy or even lays to rest London, whose 'mighty heart', in the poem written in 1802 on Westminster Bridge, 'is lying still' at dawn, counterfeiting sleep yet having suffered a collective cardiac arrest. The symbols of tranquillity and retrospection in Wordsworth are figures locked geologically in a rigor mortis like that of the poem itself: the immobile leech-gatherer, or Michael paralysed in his misery.

For Wordsworth, the writing of poems came to seem responsible for his loss of poetic inspiration. He declines, in his own view, into a professional and official versifier. Coleridge has a converse problem. It is not so much that he outlives his gift or perjures it by professionalising it as that the gift torments and betrays him and must for his own moral safety be renounced—or else (as happens with the malign transactions between the ancient mariner and the wedding guest, or Geraldine and Christabel, or Kubla Khan and the narcotically enfevered poet, outcast by a 'holy dread') it must be transferred to and blamed on someone else. Wordsworth loses the imaginative capacity, and dreads this because it portends his loss of life; Coleridge, protecting himself by incriminating another, chooses to relieve himself of it. He actually prays, in 'The Pains of Sleep', to be saved from imagination, with its bad dreams and its trespass upon a prohibited knowledge. Whereas to Wordsworth the composition of a poem is a regretful obsequy, grieving over its inability to prolong the experience which provoked it, or prematurely mortifying that experience— before the 'Ships, towers, domes, theatres, and temples' of his London can be enumerated they must undergo this death, announced by the two adjectives, 'silent, bare'—to Coleridge it is an agony but a necessary step in that prayerful therapy. A poem by Coleridge is a withdrawal symptom (which is how he describes the circumstances of 'Kubla Khan''s making), a penalty of his self-administered cure.

The poetic body goes dead slowly: Wordsworth begins with a conviction of vital force and strength possessed by no other poet. His imagination is a physiological power. Hence that phrase so admired by de Quincey, 'far into his heart', which travels through the body as through a landscape, and the poet's envious wonder at the girl in 'We are Seven' whose limbs are alive, or who feels her life in every limb. But there is a contradiction between the mind and that unreflective, energetic body, between consciousness and sentience. The mother in 'The Complaint of a Forsaken Indian Woman' is already undergoing that loss of the body and the retreat into an elegiac, tranquil mind which is, for Wordsworth, the process of making poetry: when her child is taken from her, it is as if a part of herself is amputated; she now retains only the recollection of the corpse she once inhabited ('I cannot lift my limbs to know / If they have any life or no') and is prepared to surrender that, asking, 'Oh let my body die away!' Only when she is left for dead, because sick, by her companion and bereft of her infant does she require the aid of a poem.

Though Wordsworth set out in his *Lyrical Ballads* to incorporate himself within nature, to speak as a man unselfconsciously to other men, the poems are increasingly about the difficulty of shedding mental identity and his exclusion from the physical life he can describe but no longer share. The very title of the collection hints oxymoronically at the contrary aims which are involved. The ballad is innocently and happily extrovert, the body's narrative jog-trot through the world, like Johnny's cantering on the pony in 'The Idiot Boy'; the lyric meanwhile remains inconsolably introverted, brooding on the body's apparent automatism and angrily questioning the motives for its motion. This is the case with 'We are Seven'. The girl is secure in her conviction that all her family is alive. Her prattling narrative constitutes the ballad, which is lyrically vexed and interrupted by the discontented poet, determined to rob her of that faith and burden her with his own awareness of mortality. The lyric is his attempted appropriation: in

> Her eyes were fair, and very fair,
> —Her beauty made me glad

that conquest slyly occurs, with the 'very' signifying the poet's descriptive seizure of her and the next line signalling his triumph. Her beauty exists only to gladden (and then to dismay) him, as Lucy's death happens only to cause a 'difference to me!' The poem's drama comes from the combat between these opposed wills: the girl's bodily assurance of life's continuity, the poet's mental morbidity. In the same way, the leech-gatherer fends off a poet whose ambition is to make of him a symbolic remedy for literary maladies which the old man can know nothing of. The more deviously the poet plots his capture as a subjective image—'I'll think of the leech-gatherer on the lonely moor!'—the more obstinately the man himself insists on being an impenetrable, obtuse, almost mineral object.

The crisis of this cleavage between nature and the deadly, intrusive poetic mind happens in 'The Idiot Boy'. Here the veritable poet is the idiot, and he for that very reason would never think of divulging the secret of his pantheistic revels; the actual writing of the poem is a chore which recalls to Wordsworth in every stanza his alienation from the boy's experience. In this case, the lyric belongs to Johnny or to the hallooing owlet, and is absurdly, ideally free of verbal meaning, like bird-song or the onomatopoeic 'rap, rap, rap' on the doctor's door, the burr, burr of Johnny's lips or the to-whooing of the cocks in his refrain; the narrative devolves on Wordsworth, who must, as in 'Simon Lee', strive to make a tale out of an inconsequential anecdote which he is prevented, by his intellectuality and by his laboured poetic craft, from understanding. Within the experience, animal spirits rampage in delight, and all language can do is repeat itself with the ecstatic inanity of Johnny himself, as when the poet salutes 'Oh! happy, happy, happy John' or attempts to describe his disabling glee:

> For joy he cannot hold the bridle,
> For joy his head and heels are idle,
> He's idle all for very joy.

Poetry here reverts to the noises of nature, and its wordless synonyms for a biological pleasure—the burbling of Johnny, the curring tune of the owlets, or the audibly growing grass. Words, by contrast, create periphrastic problems, as when Wordsworth's rustics stumble over a polysyllabic noun which even the poet cannot persuade into metrical mellifuousness:

> And Susan's growing worse and worse,
> And Betty's in a sad *quandary*:
> And then there's nobody to say
> If she must go, or she must stay!
> —She's in a sad *quandary*.

Condemned to words and meaning, lacking the idiot boy's gift of divine nonsense, the poet can only protest at his exclusion from the poetic vision. He longs to 'put . . . into rhyme' the anecdote, to fabricate 'a most delightful tale' from it, but the muses repel his suit and leave him (as he laments) bereft and unfriended. He asks questions—'Why are you in this mighty fret?' or 'Who's yon, that, near the waterfall . . . ?'—to which no one will tender answers. What should be a story becomes a mystery, its events inaccessible to reason. The horse has a cogitative metabolism, instead of the poet's complex mental life: he is forever equable and paces slackly because 'he is a horse that thinks!'—but he does his thinking with his stomach. Susan Gale's body also cures itself homeopathically, despite the efforts of the mind to aggravate its condition. 'As her mind grew worse and worse, / Her body—it grew better.' The proof of her victory over agitated intelligence is her restoration to physical vigour: she leaves her sick bed and toddles into the wood to shout a greeting to her friends, and from this communion, too—'Oh me! it is a merry meeting / As ever was in Christendom'—the poet is excluded. He deputes Betty to enquire, on his behalf, about Johnny's nocturnal spree. But the boy responds with an idiotic jingle (which is also the aesthetic paradox of Coleridge's dream architecture in 'Kubla Khan', the 'sunny pleasure-dome with caves of ice!'):

> 'The cocks did crow, to-whoo, to-whoo,
> And the sun did shine so cold!'

The poet, in comic despair, abandons his attempt to comprehend the delirium which evokes this poetry, morosely admiring the halo (the nimbus of light crowning a poet, already obscured in the Immortality Ode) encircling the boy's head:

> —Thus answered Johnny in his glory,
> And that was all his travel's story.

Elsewhere Wordsworth had advised himself of the irrelevance of story, the uncommunicability of lyric revelations like Johnny's, fating his own poetry to sad paraphrase of what it has lost. Oswald in *The Borderers* discounts action as transitory and insignificant, in contrast with the obscure and infinite inner reality of suffering (or, in Johnny's case, of joy); the preface to the narrative poem *The White Doe of Rylstone* disparages the dramatist who congests 'his scene with gross and visible action' and says that the poet must quell drama by concentrating on alteration 'in the world of spirit, . . . fluxes and refluxes of the thoughts'. The great lyric 'Animal Tranquillity and Decay' at first had a narrative coda inquisitively attached to it, supplying the old man, ballad-like, with a destination. He is going, he tells the poet, to Falmouth, where his son is dying in the hospital. But the truth of the poem is its account of the man's inner constitution, the fortitude of a thinking body, like that of Johnny's horse—his settled quiet, the peace of mere organism. Wordsworth accordingly cancelled the anecdotal tag. However, the man's stoic physiognomy still remains somehow beneath characterisation, beyond words. Wordsworth describes him in terms of unreachable negatives—of insensibility, of hardly feeling, of effortlessness; his face and all his limbs share 'one expression', but that is inexpressible. The poem knows that it must expire just at the point when mystic concentration takes over and achieves the disconnection of consciousness.

The old man is another anagram for poetry: purged of emotion, he has only the tranquillity of recollection. His nearness to death enforces the poetic analogy, because the mind's cessation will be the body's reawakening, as it is reabsorbed into the nature of growing grass or hardening rock. Dorothy Wordsworth in her Grasmere journal for April 1802 describes herself chastely cradled with William in a trench under a fence: 'William heard me breathing, and rustling now and then but we both lay still, and unseen by one another. He thought that it would be sweet thus to lie so in the grave, to hear the *peaceful* sounds of the earth and just to know that our dear friends were near.' The sentient corpse, its inanition a state of animation, is the Wordsworthian ideal of being and the Wordsworthian definition of the poem. All subjectivity has decayed away, leaving the satisfied inertia of the enduring object—Michael among the other stones, Lucy absorbed into the earth. When this happens, an extraordinary change occurs in Wordsworth's language. Words, before so anxiously subjective in their attempt to translate feelings, turn as well into objects: monosyllabic monoliths. Perhaps the two most astounding Wordsworthian lines describe this geological mutation, as character dies into the landscape and words return to the insentience of a world which contains all nouns and (remembering Oswald's ban on action) no verbs: the account of Michael's end, when he goes to the sheep-fold

> And never lifted up a single stone,

or that of Lucy, who, deprived of motion and force, neither hearing nor seeing, participates in the earth's revolutions (even profounder than those revolutions in the world of the spirit commended in *The White Doe*) and is rolled round

> With rocks, and stones, and trees.

Because of this reversion of words to things, one of Wordsworth's most poetically invaluable words is that all-purpose blunt instrument, 'thing'. Betty calls Johnny 'a little idle sauntering Thing!', the dead Lucy is 'a thing that could not feel', our mortal nature in the 'Ode' trembles 'like a guilty thing surprised'. Another poet would scorn that word as inspecific; Wordsworth prizes it precisely because it does not specify, because it asserts an irreducible reality—our certainty of the world's abiding objects, which we salute like the ancients touching the earth. It is the foundation of his theology in 'Tintern Abbey', with its 'sense sublime/Of something far more deeply interfused',

> A motion and a spirit, that impels
> All thinking things, all objects of all thought,
> And rolls through all things,

and it enables him here to advance imperiously from modest indefinite articles to abstract nouns and thence to that universally comprehensive, iterated adjective, which soon recurs adverbially and substantively when Wordsworth declares his love for 'all that we behold' and 'all the mighty world / Of eye, and ear' or its infusion 'Of all my moral being.' This passage is about the relation between subject and object, 'What [we] half create, / And what perceive', and its verbal genius is that it finds the same problem acted out in its boldly simple language—its dimly apprehended something and its concrete things; its indefinite articles and its contrastingly definite ones ('the round ocean and the living air, / And the blue sky') or its demonstrative, possessive prepositions ('this green earth', or 'this green pastoral landscape', where the first adjective is objective notation and the second a subjective and literary evaluation). This is a primordial poetry of syntax: a godly grammar, recreating nature by inflecting it. If in those lines about Michael or Lucy words are things pacified, fossilised, or crystallised like rock, slain in order to be metamorphically changed, here they are enlivened by that divine breath which makes 'a living soul' or enables Wordsworth to 'see into the life of things'.

Narrative also in Wordsworth, when it is allowed to work without the frustrations which perplex 'The Idiot Boy' or 'Resolution and Independence' (where the old man will not relate his tale because he knows that the poet does not seek relationship with him, only an assuagement of a personal and professional despondency), has a primitive virtue and sanctity. What matters is not the story, but the act of telling it. It can be told in the absence of its subject, as is the Wanderer's narrative of Margaret and her ruined cottage in *The Excursion* (1814); it can be chronologically disjected and fragmented into stray impressions, occasional quotes from Margaret or glimpses of her husband vacantly whittling, and need reach no conclusion, because it is the narrating which has the value. It constitutes the gift of one life to another, a communion of souls and a ratifying of our common lot. When the narrative ends, the poet blesses the dead Margaret 'in the impotence of grief', and wants to thank the

Wanderer 'for the tale which he had told'. Stories are our proof to ourselves that the whole world is kin.

In this respect, as in many others, Coleridge's contributions to the volume of *Ballads* gainsay those of Wordsworth. The two poets have different responses to nature, and different modes of narrative; so profound was the imaginative disagreement between them that each later felt their association to be fatal—Wordsworth had been dessicated by Coleridge's intellectualising of him, Coleridge depressed by his solipsistic outlawry from 'the one life within us and abroad' available to Wordsworth.

Coleridge describes nature with a detail and subtlety missing in Wordsworth—the tangled underwood in 'The Nightingale', the weeds and matted thorns in 'The Picture', the four seasons in 'Frost at Midnight'—but he does so because he can only see, not feel it. In 'This Lime-Tree Bower My Prison', entrapped within his frail self, he does not even see the landscape which his friends traverse, but must imagine it. 'My eyes make pictures, when they are shut', as he puts it in 'A Day-Dream', and those pictures, for all their topographical acuteness, are of the mind's contents: the splenetic torpor of the sea in 'The Ancient Mariner', the psychic chasms of 'Kubla Khan'. Wordsworth can afford to be visually dismissive, as he is of 'the little Celandine' or (yet more humblingly, in another poem) of 'the lesser Celandine'. He does not need to describe things to persuade himself of their existence. His words are encrustations, vouching for the substance of things. The serial repetitions in 'The Thorn' again and again revert to the gnarled and spiky structure or its adhesions of moss and lichen, hardening it until 'it stands erect . . . like a stone.' Coleridge's words, however, demateralise things. The more he repeats them, the more phantasmagorically do the objects they name turn into subjective phantoms. This happens with the mariner's 'water, water', or with his account of the ice and its disturbed somatic music.

Because Coleridge in his fearful mental loneliness suspects reality of being a hallucination, he seeks nervously to fasten the chimerae of his poems to some safe truth outside what he calls, in 'The Three Graves', the hauntings of the brain. Hence the botanical and ornithological annotations to 'This Lime-Tree Bower'. The green and dripping 'long lank weeds' are a 'most fantastic sight!' because they are a vegetation of fantasy; the thickets of 'The Nightingale' or 'The Picture', like the savage cleft in 'Kubla Khan', are allegorical woods of error. Coleridge therefore ventures to objectify them by identifying the weeds as *Asplenium Scolopendrium* (though the proverbial name of Adder's Tongue only demonstrates, in spite of Coleridge, their devilishness—they are nests for the serpent which always in Coleridge betokens the imagination's attraction to a forbidden knowledge). The same precaution leads him to explain the flying rook whose black wing salutes Lamb at the end of the poem by quoting from the bird-watcher Bartram. Otherwise the bird risks being taken for another albatross, or for a denizen of that 'rooky wood' which is the nocturnal conscience of Macbeth before Banquo's murder.

Coleridge's seeing is done from within an impregnable solitude: a bower which is a prison. Therefore narrative to him means not generous communion with another, as it does for Wordsworth, but an escape from the torments of self. He valued conversation, or rather monologising, for the same reason. In place of the troubled brain's silent reverie, it is a rendering-up of breath, a commerce with (as he described it in his *Table Talk*) 'the open air . . . , . . . without which the sense of power sinks back on itself, like a sigh heaved up from the frightened chest of a sick man.' Yet the escape cannot happen without complicity. He can make his getaway only if he cajoles someone else into replacing him in the accursed cell. Narrative therefore in Coleridge is transference, the transmission of an infection. He relieves himself by passing on his curse to another. To listen to a Coleridgean monologue is, as the wedding-guest discovers, to be bewitched. At the end of the poem, the mariner can depart disburdened because his auditor—hitherto blithe and bland, comfortably ensconced in society, as befits one who is identified merely as a guest at a wedding—has become his double, and has taken on his affliction. He turns from the bridegroom's door, stunned and 'of sense forlorn'.

Instead of the Wordsworthian sacrament of tale-telling, in Coleridgean narrative a malign exorcistic magic is at work. The poem is an education in evil. 'Fears in Solitude' represents Coleridge himself as the mariner. Locked in another cabin of uneasy consciousness, 'a small and silent dell', he is assailed by melancholy. He rids himself of it by angrily discharging it into the national community from which he is shut out. His sermon on the degeneracy of manners and morals is, like the mariner's rhyme or like the nether image of herself which Geraldine unveils to Christabel, the exposure of a knowledge withheld by taboo, and a shedding of sickness:

> I have told,
> O Britons! O my brethren! I have told
> Most bitter truth but, without bitterness.

Restored to health, Coleridge can be reabsorbed by nature and community. As he leaves the dell to go home to Nether Stowey, the opening landscape of fields 'seems like society' in its welcome to him. A small poem called 'The Exchange' is about the demonic exchange of minds happening in the other direction. The poet hugs the girl he loves, and from the embrace absorbs her nature. When he goes to confront her father,

> I strove to act the man—in vain!
> We had exchanged our hearts indeed.

Within 'The Ancient Mariner', a dual conveyancing of proscribed meanings goes on: from teller to hapless auditor, and from the poem to the marginal prose gloss added by Coleridge in 1815–16. The gloss is his exculpation, his own belated escape from the entranced nightmare into a world whose co-ordinates are securely fixed in cartography, meteorology and an official theology. It is a symptom, too, of the strange self-mistrust of the Coleridgean text—the same sense that the words cannot be relied on to be truthful which prompts the interrogations and corrections in 'Christabel':

> Is the night chilly and dark?
> The night is chilly, but not dark.

Read laterally, 'The Ancient Mariner' does not so much disclose new meanings as deny them. Yet a Coleridgean retraction is always an admission of guilt, and the prose serves to conceal what the poem has so unguardedly revealed. As well as being narrated forwards, the tale is interpreted backwards. The enquiry after meaning is a nervous retrospection, a re-reading, like the dread-stricken glance over his shoulder of 'one, that on a lonesome road' tries to outdistance the 'frightful fiend' closing on him from behind. The gloss, while pretending to assist this process, is there to confuse it. Instead of analysing after the event in the right margin, it moralises before the event in the left. It is a palliative misrepresentation masquerading as a synopsis, and Coleridge characteristically called its bluff by asking whether the poem might not have been loaded with too much moral. The killing of the albatross is, in the poem, the motiveless outraging of a sacred law: all knowledge is theft, and its penalty is death. The gloss comfortably moralises the crime, and considers it a mere inhospitability of the mariner. When a spirit visits the ship in dreams, like one of the incubi which terrorised Coleridge, the gloss pedantically expounds a theology to account for such apparitions and—extending across the page between poetic stanzas as if in a sanitary cordon—attributes its invention to 'the learned Jew, Josephus, and the Platonic Constantinopolitan, Michael Psellus'. Poetic speech is for the mariner an auto-cannibalism: 'I bit my arm, I sucked the blood.' About this transaction, the gloss is coyly euphemistic, and remarks that 'at a dear ransom he freeth his speech from the bonds of thirst.'

To the poem's tormented questions—'Is that a DEATH? and are there two?'—the gloss responds with evasive reassurances; to the poem's traumatic images it supplies emblematic captions. Thus the water-snakes, alluringly serpentine, slippery and ingenious and polychrome, suggest imaginative bedevilment until they are classified by the gloss as 'God's creatures'; and the moon, in the poem a somnambulistic ghost prowling the sky and frosting the sea in a parody of sunlight, is rescued by the gloss from this mariner-like vagrancy and installed in an orderly, sociable cosmos, where 'the blue sky' is to the stars 'their appointed rest, and their native country and their own natural homes'. The mariner's reanimation of the corpses is a demonic version of the poet's vivifying of nature. From it there follows the recruitment of a human chorus, and the attunement of the sky. He exercises a heretical and impious creativity. The gloss at once argues his feat back into orthodoxy, treating it as a miracle to which divine grace has consented—the uprisen bodies are 'angelic spirits, sent down by the invocation of the guardian saint'—rather than a parable of the undead poetic mind's prompting of the body.

So 'The Ancient Mariner' indemnifies itself by volunteering a misinterpretation of what happens in it. The poet's necessary psychological martyrdom is passed off as a Wordsworthian fable about an offence against and reconciliation with nature. Killing the albatross is equated with Wordsworth's innocuous ravishment of the tree in 'Nutting'.

In 'Kubla Khan' the same apparatus of prevarication and voluntary misreading tries to forestall the poem. The first of its obfuscations comes in its subtitles: it is trebly qualified and trebly confused by being called 'A Vision in a Dream. A Fragment.' Coleridge's preface adds further disclaimers. In the first place, the poem—so distressingly personal in its account of the neurotic energies of Coleridge's imagination—is impersonalised. The poet is 'the Author', scrupulously treated as a third person and deferentially ceding authorship or authorisation of the poem to another, that 'poet of great and deserved celebrity' who, though unnamed, is Byron. It is he who is credited with or blamed for the poem's publication. Nor will Coleridge accept responsibility for its contents: if Byron (himself something of a Khan, possessing a courage to act out his fantasies which Coleridge denies to himself) is the work's instigator, then another fictitious character must be held to account for its incompleteness. This is that importunate 'person on business from Porlock' who interrupts Coleridge's transcription of his opium dream.

As well as supplying him with these *alter egos*, the preface enables Coleridge to disappear behind his sources. Yet every alibi carries with it a clue to its half-truth, and so it is with Coleridge's manipulation of the source. Quoting it, he misquotes it, and a comparison between his version and the original shows what the poem is stealthily doing. *Purchas his Pilgrimage* describes the poem's wild landscape in the sedate terms of the real estate brochure: 'In Xamdu did Cublai Can build a stately Palace, encompassing sixteene miles of plaine ground with a wall, wherein are fertile Meddowes, pleasant Springs, delightfull Streames, and all sorts of beasts of chase and game, and in the middest thereof a sumptuous house of pleasure.' In Coleridge's quote, teasingly served up as 'words of the same substance', a poetic tattoo of compulsion and urgent fantasy has already begun to beat under Purchas's tame prose: 'Here the Khan Kubla commanded a palace to be built, and a stately garden thereunto. And thus ten miles of fertile ground were enclosed within a wall.' The metrical impulse starts up here, only to be stifled again. When the poem itself delivers a third version of those words in its first lines, that impulse is violently freed, and in being freed it unleashes Kubla's overweening romantic imagination. Purchas has been eroticised: that enclosing wall becomes, in the poem, a girdle, encincturing the seething, volcanic body of earth which explodes orgasmically in the woman's wail, the frothing fountains, or those 'fast thick pants' which are its seismic breathing. The preface maintains a superstitious distance from this revelation of poetry's sources in lust and madness, and its compact (in Kubla's imperative decree) with power; Coleridge who has called the author 'he' appears as 'I' only if he can camouflage himself as editor and medical advisor, annexing to the vision another poem which is an analysis and exorcism of it, 'The Pains of Sleep'.

Within the poem, the same transference of responsibility occurs. Kubla is at first the affluent romantic, who does not need to write poems because like Byron, or like Beckford at Fonthill and Scott at Abbotsford, he can commission others to fulfil his fantasies. Then the poet presents himself as the yearning imitator of that potent will. Kubla orders the place to be built; Coleridge can at least, in his meditation on the damsel with the dulcimer, have a vision of it and rebuild it weightlessly in words. The analogy between Kubla's architecture and Coleridge's creativity is made clearer in the preface—another apologetic refusal of responsibility—added in 1816 to 'Christabel', where Coleridge defends himself against the charge of 'plagiarism or servile imitation from myself'. He does so, as always, only to accuse himself: as knowledge is theft, so poetry is a robbery from the dormant, unaware unconsciousness. What Geraldine shows to Christabel is already present in Christabel's mind. The imagery Coleridge employs to assert that the poem wells up from inside himself alone comes from the topography of 'Kubla Khan': critics, he says, deny 'that there are such things as fountains in the world, . . . and . . . would therefore charitably derive every rill they behold flowing, from a perforation made in some other man's tank.' But the Coleridge who has invaded Kubla's domain and parasitically tapped his source dares not allow the poem to conclude without assuaging this guilt. Therefore, just as the preface moves from the helpless he to the accessory I, so the poem begins with Kubla, introduces an 'I' envious of Kubla and dangerously intimate with him, then ends by re-objectifying that 'I' as a 'he' who must be spurned, punished like the mariner or Christabel for battening on those forbidden fruits which are the nourishment of the poet. It ends with an anathema pronounced on its own uprising from those fonts of desire in the earth or the mind:

> And all should cry, Beware! Beware!
> His flashing eyes, his floating hair!
> Weave a circle round him thrice,
> And close your eyes with holy dread,
> For he on honey-dew hath fed,
> And drunk the milk of Paradise.

Charles Lamb, assuming 'Kubla Khan' to be nonsensical, said it proved the justice of the old saw 'Never tell thy dreams.' But de Quincey, who adopted Coleridge's techniques for licensing and then disowning the irresistible, narcotic imagination in his *Confessions of an English Opium-Eater*, understood that the dreamer enjoyed a unique indemnity from moral reproof: 'If there be anything amiss—let the Dream be responsible. The Dream is a law to itself. . . . The Dream knows best; and the Dream, I say, is the responsible party.'

Nevertheless, Coleridge's poems tell of his dreams against his better judgement. He attempts, in unsuccessful mitigation, to prevent them from doing so. A spell stops Christabel from warning the Baron against Geraldine, and it is able to work because the girl has assumed the 'sins unknown' of the reptilian woman; the demented Ellen in 'The Three Graves' tells the truth emetically in a spasm like that of Kubla's ravening earth. Her heart pants and she feels the words like vomit on her tongue:

> She felt them coming, but no power
> Had she the words to smother;
> And with a kind of shriek she cried,
> 'Oh Christ! you're like your mother!'

This is an infernal version of what Coleridge in 1817 calls in the *Biographia Literaria*, when justifying his raids on the ideas of others, the divine ventriloquism of truth ('I care not from whose mouth the sounds are supposed to proceed').

If your words betray you involuntarily, you can always apostasise them later, as Coleridge did with the weird Jacobin sisters who exult in carnage in his 'Fire, Famine, and Slaughter' (1798). In a preface written two decades after the poem, Coleridge describes a reading of it at the house of a sincerely Christian gentleman (William Sotherby), in the presence of 'an illustrious poet' (Scott) and 'the first in the first rank of [our country's] philosophers and scientific benefactors' (Sir Humphrey Davey). These men represent the official society which the poem assaults. Their 'general wish' prompts its performance. Scott is chosen to read it, because he is the one whose political principles are most averse to it, and who may therefore be presumed to be proof against it—though Coleridge, concealing his authorship, delights in the thought that he has ventriloquistically uttered these vicious sentiments through the person of an 'Anti-Jacobin and Anti-Gallican'. After the reading, the eminences turn on the poem and accuse it of sedition. Coleridge astutely defends it with a quibble, arguing that it is an 'imaginary representation' and endowing it with the Coleridgean liberty not to mean what it is saying. He claims for it that self-disbelief, evidenced in the questions about the weather at the beginning of 'Christabel', which to him is the moral salvation of poetry. In fact the allegorical witches in the poem have already made a similar plea. They allege that they are acting against their wills; their effort, the perpetual one in Coleridge, is the reassignment of responsibility for the poetic mania, which here provokes an orgy. 'Who sent you?' asks Slaughter, and whenever one of the trio brags of her rapine the others demand, 'Who bade you do't?' The answer within the poem, riddlingly hinted at by the hags, is Pitt. But outside the poem the culprit is Coleridge. The sisters, like Geraldine or Kubla or the mariner, are the deputies of his fantasy, of what he calls, again in the idiom of the Khan's terrain, his 'seething imagination', and his 'Apologetic Preface' therefore ends with his abandonment of anonymity and his assumption of blame: 'I must now confess, sir!' he tells his host, 'that I am the author of that poem.'

That authorship is to Coleridge less a creative miracle than a self-betrayal. In 'Frost at Midnight', standing watch over Hartley's cradle, he aligns two kinds of creativity, small human replicas of God's generative making of the world—the father engendering a child, the poet inventing (as he talks to himself) this poem. But the one is a dangerous parody of the other. The infant has its corresponding spectral twin in the poem, in the film of flame dancing on the grate which Coleridge calls the stranger. His imaginative progeny is known to him by its estrangement from him. It is his immaterial offspring, unquiet spirit as opposed to Hartley's gently breathing body; he makes it by the same demonic mental science which enables Frankenstein, in Mary Shelley's novel of 1818, to assemble his monster, taking 'a lifeless thing' and fashioning from it 'a companionable form' by transfusing into it (as Coleridge said in various cancelled versions of the poem) his own pleasures and volition and the wildly playful 'reliques of our childish thought'.

Wordsworth called the child the father of the man. In Coleridge—who wrote three sonnets about Hartley's birth, and composed poems for christenings or for the death of an unbaptised baby—the poem, the man's brainchild, is its parent's bad conscience. It is almost as if he predetermines for Hartley a career of degeneration. *Frankenstein* quotes from 'The Ancient Mariner' when the explorer Walton sets off for 'the land of mist and snow', and ends in the landscape of 'Kubla Khan', trapped by ice yet all the same luridly alight with the 'feverish fire' which 'still glimmers in [Frankenstein's] eyes'. Walton salutes Coleridge as 'the most imaginative of modern poets'; his own narrative is about the neurosis of such uncontrollably procreative imagination. Manufacturing life, Frankenstein has blasphemously taken over the creativity which belongs to God, and at the same time outrages the Miltonic taboo by dangerously acquiring knowledge. The monster is the progeny of his imagination, a deformed mental offspring. He is unable to disown it, as Coleridge does: it returns to taunt and punish him for his begetting of it. And the imagined thing has its own imaginative brood, begotten mentally in spite of Frankenstein's denial to it of a mate. 'My vices', it tells him, 'are the children of an enforced solitude.' When Frankenstein calls the laboratory at the top of the house where he vivisects life or reanimates death 'my workshop of filthy creation', he might be describing the romantic brain. His 'unhallowed arts' are the necromantic practices of Coleridge.

'Christabel' breaks off with the creative infanticide of which Frankenstein, tracking the monster which forever eludes him, is incapable. Sir Leoline has rejected his daughter, as the fiendish mother in 'The Three Graves' betrays hers; Coleridge likewise renounces his poem. It is as filially ungrateful and disobedient to him as he is parentally harsh to it, and in the conclusion he reflects on its childish inconsequence—

> A little child, a limber elf,
> Singing, dancing to itself.

A poem is a mere sprite of fancy, like the child. It ought to be innocent of meaning, especially of the sinful implications which accrue in 'Christabel'. But it inherits these mental vices from its creator, who revenges himself on it, as Leoline and Coleridge do, by aborting it. Coleridge's valediction is a comment on his destructive mistreatment of his texts: 'O sorrow and shame should this be true!'

To create, Coleridge needed an alibi. He must have a dupe on whom that creativity can be blamed. His guile—as a liar, and as a plagiarist—is essential to his genius. Once rational officialdom had been placated, imagination could be unleashed with impunity. Wordsworth has no such glib way out. His problem was not the fierce excess of imagination but its desuetude, and for this he could blame only himself. This is the misery of the 'Ode', a tragic poem because it takes the form synonymous, to eighteenth-century critics like Mrs Barbauld, with the infatuated excitement of inspiration (the ode was an oracular outpouring of pure poetry) and uses it to describe the absence of that very inspiration. Its language is ceremonious and even pompous, as the ode, a public performance, demands. It speaks of trumpeting cataracts, imperial palaces, priestly consecrations and radiant coronets; it concludes with an anthem. In it the child is, as we all are, a deposed monarch, an infantile representative of the statesman, prince or emperor who (as in Marvell's poem on Cromwell) is the subject of an ode's unction. But its splendour and solemnity sound hollow. The birds will not, at the poet's behest, 'sing, . . . sing, sing a joyous song!' despite his tautologous urging. Wordsworth can only 'in thought' join the triumph of nature. Poetry has become for him cognate with the reckoning of loss: a poem is about its own inability to revive the experience it grieves over, and which it memorialises in language. Its reason for being is as a threnody.

Because poetry is a mournful, tranquil recollection, Wordsworth transferred to memory the inquisitorial privileges an older morality had invested in the conscience. He praised dame schools because their obtuse rote-learning 'practised the memory'. In a letter he apologises for forgetting a message because 'both my body and my memory were run off their legs', at once substituting memory for the mind or soul which are conventionally placed in apposition to the body and equipping a mental power with physical advantages by giving the memory legs: remembering is ambulatory, tirelessly walking inside the mind, and those marathon hikes of Wordsworth and Dorothy in the landscape of the Lakes were a vigil kept by consciousness, a small protest against the inevitable amnesia of nature. Dorothy, at Waterloo in 1820, acknowledges the defeat of these tireless efforts, charging 'the course of things' with 'ingratitude' for having removed all traces of the warfare: 'Feeble barriers against its tendency are the few frail memorials erected in different parts of the field of battle, and we could not but anticipate the time, when . . . *these* also should fall; and "Nature's universal robe of green, humanity's appointed shroud", enwrap them:—and the very names of those whose valour they record be cast into the shade.' Correctness of recall is a legalistic duty. Dorothy applied to Walter Scott in 1825 to settle a dispute between William and herself about an incident sixteen years earlier. Scott agreed with William, who assessed his submission as if it were evidence before a tribunal: 'Your testimony though negative only, and inferential, tends to establish the truth of my recollection.' Even mountaineering turns into time-travel. The vertical ascent is for Dorothy a descent into the past, a reclamation of remembered youth. 'The pure air of high places', she says, 'seems to restore all my youthful feelings.'

It follows, since memory sedates experience and meditation ingests it, that, as time went on, Wordsworth was less interested in writing than in rewriting, which is the mind's eventual victory over the event which roused it from its visionary stupor. He speaks of composition as a penance. During the 1820s an inflammation of the eyes relieved him of the noxious task, which he passed on to an amanuensis. He saw the pen as his enemy. 'Southey used to say that his pen was a magic wand,' but 'the touch of it benumbs me.' He retaliates by misusing it, spoiling the text which persecutes him. Francis Wrangham saw his illegible hand as an act of sabotage. Sending an autograph to John Brewster, Wordsworth regrets 'that the penmanship is not a more worthy memorial' of himself. Signing his name should be a promulgation of identity; writing it with such negligence is a revocation of the act.

This dual preoccupation with remembering and with a rewriting which reneges on the initial creativity introduces *The Prelude*, and its various revisionisms. Wordsworth did not give the poem that name. He knew it as a study of the growth of a poet's mind: it existed only to grow, to journey without ever arriving, and was the prelude to a longer poem, 'containing views of Man, Nature, and Society', which never reached an end. It is a synonym for becoming, and that process happens both backwards and forwards.

Generically, it is a crucible reforming form as Spenser and Milton had done. Its initial inflection follows their reversing of the classical relation between epic and pastoral. In Wordsworth, too, the epic phenomena of the age—the French Revolution, or the metropolitan din of London—are forsworn; the poet refuses the offer of a heroic debut in public life and returns to his native place, passing his life in a wise and contented quietude. The pastoral vouchsafes him meditative repose and also mystic insight. The mind whose growth he describes expands and enriches itself almost vegetatively in that landscape.

In the stylistic echo chamber of *The Prelude*, Spenser and Milton are rewritten into conformity with romanticism. They have acquired in Wordsworth an actuality they never previously possessed. For Spenser the pastoral is a moral fable, the shepherd a Christian remonstrance to the courtier who cannot share his abasement of estate. But Wordsworth can literally claim to 'pipe / Among the shepherds.' He is a colleague for Colin Clout, and sees himself romping in the fields in words which paraphrase Spenser's characterisation of himself in *The Shepherd's Calendar*: 'A boy, no better.' Because Wordsworth's landscapes are peopled, as Spenser's were, by spirits, he can imagine Spenser's characters among his own more bodiless 'Presences of Nature' or 'Souls of lonely places', and in the forests of the Loire he thinks he has come upon the 'viewless glade'—invisible except to imagination—where the satyrs entertain Hellenore. His revisions of Milton also localise the lost paradise, and restore the child to residence within it. Imagination after all means the recovery of Eden at will. As *The Prelude* begins, Wordsworth sees that 'The earth is all before me': not the world, which awaits Milton's characters after their expulsion and will wear them down to death, but the earth, succouring and maternal. The Miltonic theology has evaporated into meteorology. Instead of ministering angels, Wordsworth's guide back to paradise is 'a wandering cloud', and since the regaining of the primal garden is within his power he can say that he chooses the guide rather than patiently waiting for God to send it to him. The passage on Helvellyn imitates Milton's account of Eden, said to be more beautiful than any exotic pleasance. But whereas Milton favours an extra-terrestrial perfection, Wordsworth can precisely situate 'the paradise / Where I was reared' on a map of Grasmere.

This earthing of his predecessors is of course the formula for mock-epic. That, too, as the eighteenth-century's mode of comprehending the literature of the past, is an option contained by *The Prelude*. The childhood games of cards are a reprise of the ombre in *The Rape of the Lock*. Wordsworth glances at the class relationships which have been upset by such upstart recensions of epic as Pope's or Gay's in *The Beggar's Opera*, describing

> . . . Some, plebeian cards
> Which Fate, beyond the promise of their birth,
> Had glorified, and called to represent
> The persons of departed potentates.

Wordsworth himself succeeds to the departed potentates of epic: hence the portentousness with which he describes his arrival in Cambridge—'And at the *Hoop* alighted, famous Inn.' But beyond the mockery lies a romantic redefinition of heroism. Other Miltonic mimicries contend that Wordsworth's autobiography is, despite its lack of martial exploits, a 'heroic argument'. Milton declared it a hard task to narrate the war in heaven; for Wordsworth it is an equally arduous matter to analyse a soul. The eighteenth-century's mock-heroic habit issued in that modernising of the epic which is, according to Fielding's theory, the novel. *The Prelude*, making of epic an immersion in consciousness, adapts the form to the Victorian novel. It was published in 1850, the same year as *David Copperfield*, which, like it, superimposes two consciousnesses, the reflective present of the ageing writer and the vital, irretrievable past of the child still secure in his personal Eden, when David sees little Emily dancing on the plank and wishes that her life might have ended that day, or finds the drowned Steerforth 'lying with his head upon his arm, as I had often seen him lie at school'.

As well as revising its literary past and conducting an inquest on its own psychological history, *The Prelude* chronically rewrites itself. Its two consciousnesses are two voices—the poetic agility and joy with which Wordsworth relives the skating episode, the prosaic gloss which soothingly recollects the experience and makes it 'tranquil as a dreamless sleep' by sermonising on it as an incident in a religious education—and also two texts. As ever in *The Prelude*, these texts move hopefully forward and at the same time piningly backwards. The 1850 text is in one sense germinated by that of 1805. Thus the later version completes the account of St John's College by adding those two great lines penetrating the statue of Newton in the antechapel:

> The marble index of a mind for ever
> Voyaging through strange seas of Thought, alone.

With these lines in place, the sequence has fulfilled itself. The passage now summarises the itinerary of the entire poem, travelling from society (the college) through landscape (Wordsworth crouches in his 'nook obscure' of the quad as if in a dell, hears the nearby kitchen noises as a humming of bees, and when the clock tells the hours 'twice over with a male and female voice' he senses in it a mystery like that of Spenser's bisexual Nature) and thence into the mind and its vast solitude. From the earth in which Wordsworth cowers it moves to the marine realm of an oceanic pantheism, and then into the free and featureless outer space of Newton's thinking. But other revisions return to the 1805 text to deplete and abstract it, as when the topographic note in Book VI on an Alpine lodging, 'An inn, or hospital, as they are named', is deprived of this local meaning and monumentally situated, with the aid of new precipitous Miltonic line-ends, astride a visionary (and dreary) emptiness:

> That night our lodging was a house that stood
> Alone within the valley, at a point
> Where, tumbling from aloft, a torrent swelled
> The rapid stream whose margin we had trod.

The rewriting, like the reconcilement in the 'Ode', computes both loss and gain—the slow, sad dissipation of spirit; the understanding (symbolised by this election of the inn to parity with Michael's sheep-fold or the beleaguered thorn) of what, memorially, remains behind.

The romantics distinguished between two kinds of poetic identity. Keats called these the negative capability of Shakespeare and the egotistical sublime of Milton (or Wordsworth). Coleridge described Shakespeare as the 'Spinozistic deity—an omnipresent creativeness' and Milton as 'the deity of prescience; he stands *ab extra*.' One is a self-effacing, the other a self-imposing god. If *The Prelude* is a Miltonic hymn to the sublimity and heroic valour of consciousness, then the corresponding work by Coleridge, *Biographia Literaria*, dramatises the shifting Shakespearean tragicomedy of consciousness: not the mind's triumphant conception of the absolute self on its dread watchtower, which to Coleridge (as he puts it in his poem about *The Prelude*) was Wordsworth's prerogative, but its nagging doubt that it has any self to affirm; not 'the great eternal I AM' of the *Biographia*'s twelfth chapter but the querulous demand of Hamlet—an abrasive but distressingly eternal '*Am* I?'

Wordsworth can absorb Coleridge, whom he nominates in the 1805 *Prelude* as 'a living help / To regulate my Soul', into himself. Coleridge lacks the confidence to assimilate Wordsworth. On the contrary he is creatively and psychologically undone by him, reduced to an appendage of that sublimer ego. The annunciation of Wordsworth is as alarming and as disabling to him as the advent of a god. He describes the publication of *Descriptive Sketches* as a primal sunrise, a reprise of Genesis: 'Seldom, if ever, was the emergence of an original poetic genius above the literary horizon more evidently announced.' But the new world Wordsworth has bodied forth is primevally harsh and unnourishing to mere humans, resembling 'those products of the vegetable world, where gorgeous blossoms rise out of the hard and thorny rind and shell within which the rich fruit was elaborating'. Coleridge owes his notoriety, he says, not to any achievements of his own but to his association with Wordsworth and Southey, or to the attacks on him by anonymous critics. Nor are these jibes a tribute to his personality: his opponents are hostile in principle to his convictions. His own theory of poetic character denies that character to himself. Classically, he says, the poet was a man of sweet and reasonable temper; his modern successor must create out of inner division and a nervous anguish or irritability. If genius is proudly selfless, then Coleridge, who can impersonalise himself only by the suborning of proxies or by the subterfuge and deceit which disown imagination in his poems, is (in his own eyes) a negation and a parody of genius. This suspicion of his nonentity makes the more plangent Coleridge's analysis of Charles Maturin's libertine in the supernumerary twenty-third chapter, for this romantic renegade is a man, Coleridge says, who craves to be loved for himself, not for his qualities (or for any literary attainments). That plea is the climax to *Biographia Literaria*—its emotional secret, just as the contraband theory of imagination in the thirteenth chapter is its intellectual secret.

Formally, the *Biographia* has two sources. One is Sterne, the other is the Gothic novel. It is at once a comedy of vagrant sensibility and a tragedy of errant imagination. Like Sterne's novel, it commences a study of Coleridge's *Literary Life and Opinions*, only to conclude that his life is a chapter of accidents and his opinions mostly the possessions of others—of Milton, Leibnitz, Synesii, Descartes, Kant and Berkeley for instance, all of whom, at the beginning of one section, interpose themselves between Coleridge and the esemplastic theory. Its conduct is as chaotic as that of Tristram's novel. A preface expands into a treatise; the intellectual exposition then straggles off into a memoir. No cogitation can be followed through unless Coleridge, fidgeting over cosmic preliminaries, first solves the problem of the universe by determining 'a holy and intelligent first cause'. The twelfth chapter cannot get itself written until Coleridge has legislated on whether the reader, like the inattentive lady in *Tristram Shandy* who is sent back to study the text more closely, should be obliged to struggle through it. He therefore composes 'A chapter of requests and premonitions concerning the perusal or omission of the chapter that follows.' Since this is a journey which never arrives, he invokes the digressive liberties of picaresque narrative, admitting that he has 'wandered far from the object in view' or describing himself tracking 'the steps of a traveller who has lost his way in a fog or by treacherous moonshine'.

Tristram Shandy is about its author's baffled efforts to write the book with that title; Coleridge's biography of his books is likewise about his failure to produce them, and it wonders whether books themselves may not be irrelevant or absurd. He wishes that they were not the sole test of 'intellectual usefulness', and pleads his success as a lecturer. The literary trade is a demeaning, door-to-door salesmanship. Coleridge reminisces about his tribulations with subscribers to his periodical *The Friend*, and about his unsuccessful tour to promote the magazine. The *Biographia* is a work of bibliographic casualties, treating literature as a ludicrous paper chase: a maid sets the fire with Coleridge's copies of *The Watchman*; the printer Grutch overestimates the number of pages and, to avoid the Shandyean prospect of a second volume with half its sheets blank, has Coleridge fill up the space with an anthology of hastily recycled journalism.

But Shandyean muddle is also Gothic mystification. The false trails of argument of picaresque mazes double, in Coleridge's epigraph from Goethe, as a mental labyrinth, a philosophical Udolpho: he wishes, he says, to spare the young those circuitous paths on which he had lost his own way. The friend (Coleridge himself, of course) who intercedes to ban the definition of imagination envisages the argument as a Gothic scenario. The elisions treacherously reduce it to 'the fragments of the winding steps of an old ruined tower'. The letter written by Coleridge to himself in the friend's name is one of the happened-upon manuscripts which are the textual arcana of Gothic fiction—the Ossian papers, reported by Adam Ferguson to be 'much stained with smoke, and daubed with Scots snuff'; the narrative coffered in an old trunk which Maturin edits as *Melmoth the Wanderer*; the Sibylline leaves assembled by Mary Shelley in a Neapolitan cave and sorted out as *The Last Man*; the indecipherable scraps pieced together into the tatterdemalion self of Teufelsdröckh by Carlyle in *Sartor Resartus*. Those fragments are like relics of a truth too combustible or evanescent for consignment to paper: Carlyle reports that the ink he is deciphering has faded almost into invisibility. The friend's letter is legible, but its purpose is obscurantist. He advises Coleridge not to expose the unhallowed workings of the creative mind.

Imagination becomes the monstrous apparition behind the Radcliffean veil, the ultimate culprit in the Gothic plot. The friend is Coleridge's better half, corresponding to the person from Porlock or the man whom Coleridge, to cure his addiction, once hired to obstruct him if he tried to enter a druggist's; the letter is the reason's emissary to insurgent fantasy. In his conclusion, Coleridge imagines the Christian religion as a temple. Like Herbert arranging his poems into the devout ground-plan of a church, he declares reason to be the outer court, miracles the steps, vestibule and portal, and faith 'the true foundation of the spiritual edifice'. This is the pillared, upstanding house of reason; but the friend's letter interprets imagination as a defamation of that official fane, a Pandemonium of dark and insubstantial dreams. The *Biographia* resembles, he says, 'one of our largest Gothic cathedrals in a gusty moonlight night of autumn', a cranium of shadowy terrors. It is a cathedral infernally reconsecrated, for—in a more satanic version of the Gothic façade which Hugo saw in Shakespeare, where angels and gargoyles riotously commingle, and tragedy and comedy conjoin in the grotesque—the friend notices in its 'pictures and stone-work' an exchange of places between saints and ogres, or between reason and the monsters bred by its anodyne-assisted sleep: 'Those whom I had been taught to venerate as almost super-human in magnitude of intellect I found perched in little fret-work niches, as grotesque dwarfs; while the grotesques, in my hitherto belief, stood guarding the high altar with all the characters of Apotheosis.' Thus warned, Coleridge desists. If Wordsworth outlives his imagination, Coleridge in terror tries to live his down.

— 26 —
Romantic Surfeit

Byron in 1813 remarked that Wordsworth had lost his hair and his good humour; in 1811 he noted, with the indignation of a new romantic hedonism, that Coleridge had made a <u>maundering</u> attack on Thomas Campbell's *Pleasures of Hope* 'and all other pleasures whatever'. The mental empire of his predecessors was to Byron a provincial backwater. He called them not the Lake but the Pond poets. To their successors, Wordsworth and Coleridge were gods who had failed, and who lived on—the one an excise-man, the other a futile, prolix talker—to preside over their own digrace. Hazlitt says that personal acquaintance with poets is an error, because it reveals those we worship to be tainted mortals: 'The splendid vision that in youth haunts our idea of the poetical character, fades upon acquaintance into the light of common day; as the azure tints that deck the mountain's brow are lost on a nearer approach to them.' He and de Quincey have their own versions of the imaginative loss which overtook Wordsworth and Coleridge: their loss of faith in the ageing poets equals the loss, experienced by the poets themselves, of their youthful intimations of immortality. This disillusion forces romanticism to redefine itself, and to exchange the natural supernaturalism of Wordsworth and Coleridge for more palpable gratifications. The romantic henceforth will be a connoisseur of sensation, proving reality on the pulses or the palate.

It is as gods that de Quincey, from afar, revered Wordsworth and Coleridge. They are the first and last men in the world, individuals subsuming and transcending all who have lived before them. Coleridge possesses the 'most spacious intellect . . . that has yet existed among men', and Wordsworth is 'that man whom, of all the men from the beginning of the world, I most desired to see.' Coleridge's talk is world-encircling. Like a god he re-invents the earth, and mysteriously attaches it to 'another world' by metaphysical analogy. His failures to achieve are a divine prerogative: the 'unmoved mover' exists in suspense, foreknowing everything. While Coleridge is a cosmic mind, Wordsworth is a physiologically sovereign deity, luxuriating in his bodily power—the 'unoccupied possession of his own arms' or 'absolute control over his own legs and motions'; Coleridge has circumnavigated the earth in thought, Wordsworth has tramped across it in physical fact, and de Quincey calculates that his prodigious legs have in their time traversed no less a distance than 180,000 miles.

These gods create self-consciousness in de Quincey. *Lyrical Ballads* was 'the greatest event in the unfolding of my own brain'. But the volume is anonymous, and it takes him two years to find out the names of its authors. The quest is tantamount to trying to discover who or what made the universe. Pursuit is pilgrimage: de Quincey is prepared to follow Coleridge to Malta, and when an invitation arrives from Wordsworth he hesitates to accept, saying that the poet's 'very image . . . crushed my faculties as before Elijah or St. Paul'. Recalling Coleridge's belief that if you really saw a ghost you would die, he wonders how he managed to survive the encounter at Grasmere. In fact he narrates it with an overawed obliqueness, not introducing or describing Wordsworth but minutely depicting the interior of his cottage. An invisible omnipresence like god in nature, Wordsworth can be sensed in this domestic neatness, in the fertility of vegetation outdoors, or in the characters of his sister and his wife, intermediaries between him and the human world in which he only half-belongs. To visit and befriend one's gods is, however, a perilous undertaking. When de Quincey did so, he found them to be selfish human creatures. Coleridge withdrew only slowly and reluctantly from his mental enclosure when de Quincey announced himself; that reclusion is a symptom of the obscurantist introversion which, in de Quincey's view, at last renders him powerless. And if Coleridge cannot be roused to acknowledge the existence of others, Wordsworth has a different selfishness, which negligently eliminates others and vandalises their property. De Quincey remembers him cutting the pages of a book he had loaned him with a buttery knife.

Hazlitt in 'My First Acquaintance with Poets' suffers a corresponding deconversion. Wordsworth, commenting on the sunset, utters banalities, while Coleridge laxly digresses, floating on intellectual air or sliding on ice. Reality in Hazlitt's essay is determined by the appetite, and spurns their abstruse philosophising: when Coleridge flatters Hazlitt's judgment, it seems that 'the leg of Welsh mutton and the turnips on the table . . . had the finest flavour imaginable'; and when Wordsworth visits Coleridge he 'instantly began to make havoc of the half of a Cheshire cheese on the table'. Coleridge in a conversation with Hazlitt objects to the earthiness of Wordsworth. Hazlitt's revenge is to demonstrate that these supposedly unfettered spirits are bodies after all, that Wordsworth has a convulsive laughter about the mouth and Coleridge, like a Shandyean narrator, is unable to walk in a straight line.

Their poetry, however, had belied this carnal truth, and Hazlitt's revulsion from their abstractness determines the critical positions he later adopts in his redefining of romanticism—his scorn for the dazzling nothingnesses of Turner's paintings, or his praise for bodily over intellectual feats. He was a connoisseur of prize fights, of Indian jugglers and of the feisty vigour of journalistic controversy; he considered painting a superior occupation to literature because it was not sedentary and ingrown but involved the alfresco exertion of the body. Hazlitt sees it as the duty of romantic art to cater to that greedy body: to dispense pleasure or what he calls gusto. His literary judgements are the dictatorial caprices of hedonism. He prefers the 'sublimated . . . animal existence' of Robert Burns to the primness of Wordsworth's phoney rustics, and he interprets dreaming as a passionate, erotic vent not a visionary faculty, remembering that Coleridge used to mock him for his inability to dream. In his essay on *Romeo and Juliet* he employs the play's sensuality to disparage the chaste platonism of Wordsworth's 'Ode'. The same conviction that art has its sources in the cravings of appetite leads him to argue that we relish the despotism of Coriolanus (and also induced him unregenerately to hero-worship Napoleon). A despot itself, imagination naturally justifies despotism: it is an aggrandising, self-procreating appetite, which thrives on procuring excitements for itself; an unreflective, unrepentant libertine. The brazen cruelty of Coriolanus is merely, to Hazlitt, 'the logic of the imagination and the passions'. Having battened on life, the sated body accepts its own extinction. In his *Table-Talk* in 1821 Hazlitt disparages the fear of death. Our demise will be a holiday-time; non-being must surely have its pleasures. In contrast with the funerary Wordsworth, forever in mourning, Hazlitt offers to inscribe on his own tomb 'GRATEFUL AND CONTENTED'. Wordsworth in the preface to *Lyrical Ballads* had indignantly denied that a 'taste' for poetry could be acquired, like one for sherry. Because to Hazlitt the only critical test is that of appetite, repudiation of a work means literally spitting it out: thus he calls Byron's poetry cancerous, preying on itself and 'disgusted with, or indifferent to, all other things', and in *The Spirit of the Age* (1825) he denounces George Crabbe's tales of East Anglian life in *The Borough* as sickly, distasteful, redolent of slime, mud, tar and bilge-water.

Hazlitt is no longer perplexed, as Coleridge was, about the feignings and fictions of poetry, or by qualms about how willing our suspension of disbelief in it should be. His *Lectures on the English Poets* in 1818 see poetry as reverie, a wishful and mostly libidinal thinking: 'If poetry is a dream, the business of life is much the same. If it is a fiction, made up of what we wish things to be, and fancy that they are, because we wish them to, there is no better reality.' Those commas, seeming to articulate a progress, actually send the sentence round in a circle of celebration. There is no reality anymore, only sensation, more or less violent. Keats in the 'Ode to a Nightingale' does not complain that the fancy is a cheat; he simply grumbles that it is not able to cheat better than it does. Hazlitt grades the four greatest English poets according to the increasing intensity of their subjunctive wishfulness: 'Chaucer . . . describes things as they are; Spenser, as we wish them to be; Shakespeare, as they would be; and Milton as they ought to be.' He accepts that there must be an enmity between poetry and scientific understanding, and regrets that 'experimental philosophy' is rationalising a world which poetry would prefer to keep unknown and voluptuously fearful.

Nevertheless, this poetic instinct for mystery has been betrayed. The *Lectures* describe the history of poetry as a progressive desacralisation of the world, which reaches its sad conclusion in the imaginative lapses of Wordsworth and Coleridge, and has as its forlorn epilogue the denial of sacredness to those two poets when de Quincey and Hazlitt approach them. Hazlitt declares that 'in Homer, the principle of action or life is predominant; in the Bible, the principle of faith and the idea of Providence; Dante is a personification of blind will; and in Ossian we see the decay of life and the lag end of this world.' That is an apocalyptic succession—from the first dawn to the abstractly depleted last things. Homeric heroes abound in exuberant animal spirits, which they share with nature in their epic similes. Homer 'describes the bodies as well as the souls of men'; the Bible in the next historical phase deals only with faith which is necessarily disembodied, praising not vital action but resignation. The withdrawal from earth continues in Dante, who in place of the animistic, peopled universe of Homer must make do with the phantoms conjured up by his will. Ossian, even more debilitated, writes in 'the old age of poetry' and 'converses only with the spirits of the departed; with the motionless and silent clouds'.

This is already the drearily void nature of Wordsworth and Coleridge, a depressed blankness which they can fill up only 'with the moods of their own minds'. Hazlitt found their work fatally deficient in passion. Indeed he thought it, according to his definition, not poetry at all, because rather than achieving the imagination's coition with the external world it declines to believe in that world. A mental egotism has devoured the earth. This is why, for both Hazlitt and de Quincey, Wordsworth's rural characters are so false. Hazlitt contends that country folk are grossly obsessed by getting food, and have no leisure for the genteel luxury of loving nature; de Quincey thought that the Pedlar in 'The Ruined Cottage' should have advised the authorities of Margaret's plight rather than sentimentally grieved over her decline and blessed her expiry. Hazlitt specifically refutes the Wordsworthian theory of memory, that agency whereby the world is tranquilly emptied and deadened: in his essay on 'Why Distant Objects Please' he makes the organs of recollection eager sensual retrievers not cerebral brooders, saying that we remember most effectively with our aptitudes for taste and smell.

It follows that the true poet's duty is to live instinctually. Hazlitt's theory is a justification for a romantic decadence—for the eager sensuality of Keats and the promiscuous sensationalism of Byron, for Shelley's laboratory of blissful self-destruction. The libertine, the hero chosen by Byron in *Don Juan* as the figure fittest for this age of emotional affluence, is a professional avatar of the poet. Coleridge considers the libertine with longing in the *Biographia*, only to reject him; Hazlitt, however, unrepentantly paraphrases Coleridge's dream of being loved for yourself and not for your qualities in an essay linking eroticism, the enjoyment of power and the glory of imagination. He lusts, he says, only after inferiors, like Mozart's Don Giovanni with his peasant-girls and serving maids, because he demands the slavery of his appetite's object: 'She should love me for myself alone. I like myself without any reason. I would have her do so too. This is not very reasonable.' Its irrationality, evidently, delights rather than distresses him. The libertine's demand that the ego should be adored, censored by Coleridge, recurs everywhere in this later phase of romanticism. Keats for instance marvels that Fanny Brawne loves him in the absence of attractive qualities: physically 'I am not a thing to be admired.' Having elected to do so, she enjoys the supremacy over him which Hazlitt had made a prerogative of power-hungry imagination. 'You have ravish'd me away by a Power I cannot resist', Keats tells her, and assures her of her right—if she so wishes—to destroy him. Byron has his own chilly, scornful version of this abjectness. Remarking on his difficulties with a Welsh girl, he blames 'my own vanity in fancying that such a thing as I am could ever be loved'. He pretends on another occasion that he is doing the women he satisfies a favour by putting them out of their misery: 'I could love anything on earth that appeared to wish it.'

Sexual complications are here the working-out of a creative belief. Imagination has been defined as a sensual dictator, which victimises the poet. The muse is a domineering, unmerciful mistress—Keats's Fanny, Byron's Lady Caroline Lamb, Hazlitt's Sarah Walker. Hazlitt proves his theory of sexual pursuit and of imaginative conquest in the story of his infatuation with the teasing servant Sarah, which he wrote up in his *Liber Amoris* (1823). The work's subtitle is *The New Pygmalion*, and it is as much about creativity as it is about sex (for to Hazlitt the two are inseparable). Sarah is an equivalent of Endymion's Diana or Juan's Haidée—a fiction actualised by appetite. She is not, however, a submissive fiction. She first wards off Hazlitt's assaults on her, then jilts him. But her treachery is consistent with the dual logic of passion and imagination. She and Hazlitt are alike victims of his frenzy. He is at once tyrant and slave, sadist and grovelling masochist, for his hedonism teaches him—as he puts it in an 1819 essay on *The Times*—that if there is nothing else to derive pleasure from, men will fall in love with their misery; and elsewhere he commended the pleasure to be had from hating. He is proud of his obsession with Sarah because it gives him 'a kind of rank in the kingdom of love' (which is, like the polity desired by Coriolanus, an absolute monarchy). He wishes only that Sarah might have 'understood its value and pitied its excess', admired his emotion not surrendered to it. Passion as he experiences it is, like imagination, overweening, exorbitant, monopolistic. The proof of its compulsiveness is its interference with other, lower appetites. 'I have lost', the besotted Hazlitt notes, 'the taste of my food.' And he has a terser version of Coleridge's mental dejection: 'I was at Stirling Castle recently. It gave me no pleasure.'

Writing to Wordsworth in 1799, Coleridge decried those who had abandoned revolutionary projects to redeem mankind and turned instead into the creatures of despotic pleasure. Hazlitt was to be one of these. His essay on good nature disputes the optimism of Wordsworth and Coleridge, convinced of a heavenly sequel to 1789, by justifying a well-fed contentment. In the ravenous tyrant of this essay he describes another emblem for the newly omnivorous romantic imagination. The same psychological characterization occurs in Beckford's *Vathek* (1786). Here imagination is a puerile Moloch. The demoted imperial child of Wordsworth's 'Ode' is restored to its palace and permitted to exercise its omnipotence, gaining its food (as Leigh Hunt said young poetical appetite should) by dreaming of it and squallingly demanding it. Petted and pampered by obsequious nurse-maids, Vathek's terrible rages are the tantrums of the cross child. He is titanically petulant, and his fury expresses itself, like a baby's, in a stamping of his foot. 'Give it me instantly!' he insists. This is imagination's ultimatum to the world. Even Vathek's vaunted curiosity is an extension of his bodily greed, not a Faustian intellectual curiosity. He wants to know more in the same way that he wants more to eat. He cuffs, bites or punches those who contradict him. Though his fantasy is expensive to sustain, he can afford to buy off the objections of reality: Babalouk showers with coins the crowd Vathek has bereaved and it is soon appeased. 'Voluptuously reposed in his capacious litter upon cushions of silk, with two little pages beside him ... who were occupied in keeping off flies', he is an infant enthroned in its crib, whose two main occupations seem to be eating and sleeping. He is forever being reprimanded by his mother Carathis, who neither eats (having stayed her stomach's cravings with an opiate) nor sleeps (except to have visions, which are business not pleasure) and who is an enemy both to sloth and to amorous dalliance. She is Vathek's spiritual foe, since hers is the crabbed voice of maturity, the dour injunction to grow up.

In Beckford's brilliant journals of his *Excursion to the Monasteries of Alcobaça and Batalha*, published in 1835 in recollection of a tour made in 1794, he translates himself to Vathek's kingdom of carnal indulgence, here located in an ancestrally and enjoyably corrupt Portugal. Founded for mortification, the monasteries have converted to the new romantic religion of the senses. The wily Cistercians of Alcobaça re-route a trout stream so that it passes through the monastic kitchen. Lazing half-asleep in their perfumed gardens, gorging on macedoine, ortolan and quails of 'celestial fatness'—all of these delicacies unknown 'this side Mahomet's paradise'—Beckford is an oriental potentate like Vathek, a prince of pleasure. On the return journey to Lisbon he takes a detour to the royal palace of Queluz, where there are erotic enticements in the shrubbery to complement the fattening of the body by these gourmandising celibates. Beckford appraises Portugal as a garden of temptations, to each of which he is careful to succumb.

Though Beckford was run out of England after rumours of orgies at Fonthill, his depravities are mostly culinary. He identifies art with eating, as the next romantic poets were to do. Leigh Hunt composed an effusion on cream and called for a poetry of splendid satiety; Keats assessed reality orally, and even described *King Lear*, when preparing to re-read, it as a meal, a 'bitter-sweet . . . Shakespearian fruit'. In a peculiarly innocent and English version of the decadence which sent the later French romantics in quest of drugs and specialised sexual experience, the libertine is rendered harmless by being made into a mere over-eater and an incautious drinker. Mozart's tenebrous, driven Don Giovanni changes into Byron's nurseling Don Juan. Leigh Hunt believed that Mozart had drunk 'at the winy fountain' of vital exuberance in Italy, and 'seems to have been intoxicated ever after with love and delight'. Hazlitt relished the 'scented music' of *Don Giovanni* and its eurhythmic joy, but mostly the Mozartean hero was too predatory and ruthless for the English. Charles Lamb preferred the gentler view of the character in the burlesque play based on Shadwell's *Libertine*, where his faults are Falstaffian and his compulsiveness merely frisky; Hunt, too, felt happier with the 'pleasantly mitigated rogue' of the burlesque who, like the infantile genius of poetry, vindicates 'the eternally renovated youth and fair play of nature'.

In that phrase the Wordsworthian tragedy—the loss of youth, the belief in renovation only after death—has been blithely denied. The future is to be a romantic comedy. Accordingly *Don Juan* comically revises the tragic conclusion to *Don Giovanni*, and questions, as it breaks off, the need ever to arrive at an end and a reckoning. In Mozart's opera, the calcified Commendatore interrupts Don Giovanni's supper with a summons to the retributive hereafter. His grip of stone chills the libertine's glad flesh. The body first coldly shudders at its own mortality, and is then consumed by flames. In Byron's comic epic, the translation happens in the other direction. A door opens 'with a most infernal shriek / Like that of hell.' Juan, however, is not conducted to the pit; and the sable-hooded friar who appears to arrest him turns out to be neither marmoreal nor skeletal. He first appraises its sweet breath, pearly teeth and warm breast, then—rather than being himself deadened by its manacling grasp—he touches Mozart's statue into life and into femininity:

> A dimpled chin, a neck of ivory, stole
>   Forth into something much like flesh and blood.

The spirit turns out to be another impatient sexual victim, Her Grace Fitz-Fulke.

A humorous epicureanism, with a sound digestion, is to Thomas Love Peacock the secret of romantic temperament. In his *Four Ages of Poetry* (1820) he mocked the mental back-sliding of the first romantic generation with its credulous antiquarianism and its homage to childhood. Mr Flosky, representing Coleridge in Peacock's *Nightmare Abbey* (1818), withdraws once his revolutionary hopes are disappointed from the daylight of common sense into the 'central opacity of Kantian metaphysics'. Wordsworth meanwhile is disgraced. Forester in *Melincourt* (1817) equates his imaginative collapse with man's expulsion from paradise—Wordsworth is 'a poet, whose fallen state none can lament more bitterly than I do'. The error of the second romantic generation is a lapse into physiological distemper. Mr Cypress in *Nightmare Abbey*, a parody of Byron, espouses satire, while Scythrop, Peacock's caricature of Shelley, flirts with suicide. Hazlitt had seen Byron's poetry as cancerous; Peacock more simply diagnoses it as bilious, and complained of the 'black bile' which poisoned the fourth canto of *Childe Harold's Pilgrimage*. Peacock's solution to the despairing philosophy of romanticism is a salving retraction into the body. The wise man cultivates his <u>embonpoint</u>. In *Headlong Hall* (1816), while Foster the 'perfectibilarian' clashes with Escot the 'deteriorationist', Jenkinson the 'statuquo-ite' allows their arguments to cancel each other out and satisfies himself with the world as it is. The resident sage is no philosopher but a glutton: the Rev Dr Gaster has composed 'a learned dissertation on the art of stuffing a turkey', and during the argument about animal food, when Foster and Escot adopt fixed positions and Jenkinson proposes the savoury compromise of mixing meat and vegetables in one's diet, Gaster gets down to his breakfast and placidly butters an egg. The quarrelsome thinkers prowl the landscape in peripatetic dispute; Gaster makes himself comfortable in the library and browses in the *Almanach des Gourmands*. At the festive board, the inspirational opiate which intoxicates the poet in 'Kubla Khan' is circulated in bottles, to the accompaniment of a rowdy drinking song: MacLaurel the poet acclaims Burgundy as a paradisial liquor, better than milk or honey. Ideas are vain vexations, keeping the body from its rightful satisfactions. While the competing projectors squabble over their ambitions for mankind, Gaster remarks 'Vanity of vanities' and turns down an empty eggshell.

Nightmare Abbey diagnoses romantic maladies of spirit as physical indispositions. Old Glowry is a misanthrope because martyred to indigestion; when Sythrop proposes that he and Marionetta should open their veins and drink the blood as a pledge of love, she sickens, lacking a strong stomach. Flosky lists tea, late dinners and the French Revolution as the triple calamities of the age—tea shatters the nerves, and late dinners upset the stomach. It is not so much the senses as the alimentary canal which has been systematically deranged. Flosky's appraisal of literature is as gustatory as Hunt's and relies, like Keats sprinkling his tongue with cayenne pepper and pouring claret over it, on the ingenuously decadent imbibing of condiments and stimulants. 'The public', he says, spurns 'the solid food of reason for the light diet of fiction' and 'requires a perpetual adhibition of *sauce piquante* to the palate of its depraved imagination.' He might be describing the delicious, appetitive anguish of Keats's Hyperion, tasting in the incense 'instead of sweets, . . . / Savour of poisonous brass and metal sick', or the exotic menu served to the enraptured knight by La Belle Dame Sans Merci: 'roots of relish sweet, / And honey wild, and manna dew.' Scythrop is saved by his bodily selfishness. He converts a grisly Gothic prop to the service of the corporeal idyll by using an ancestor's skull to swill Madeira from, and when made to choose between eating his dinner and feeling miserable he calls for the boiled fowl and a bottle, not his pistol.

Peacock identifies romanticism with a state of society reposed in economic surfeit, addicted to whatever is not necessary. The imagination is a perquisite of affluence, and its action is inflationary. The fondness for the primitive irritates Peacock because it, too, is a moneyed luxury. These people can afford to mimic barbarism: while one wing of Melincourt Castle is 'fast improving into a picturesque ruin', the other 'was as rapidly degenerating, in its interior at least, into a comfortable modern dwelling.' The symbol of expensive abundance is a candied additive supplied to Peacock's triflers at the cost of slave labour in the plantations. Forester in *Melincourt* is an anti-saccharine campaigner, and he decries sugar as a synonym for a vicious romantic inutility, at once 'economically superfluous' and 'physically pernicious', a taste subsidised by poverty and oppression.

Jane Austen's *Sanditon* represents an entire society overtaken by the compulsions of romantic temperament. Affluence and hedonism beget a speculative dissipation. 'Getting and spending, we lay waste our powers', said Wordsworth: the romantic is a psychological spendthrift, and what he expends is his own physical and emotional substance. Sanditon is created by that dangerous impulse. It is a seaside development, capitalising on the new fad for bathing which had made Brighton (where the libertine Prince Regent erected his pavilion as an erotic rendezvous) a romantic resort. Society is now as migrant, mobile and fluctuant as the elements, restlessly reconvened around a trust in nature. Mr Parker is convinced of the efficacy of saline air and immersion as cures for all ailments. His model town will romantically perfect the world, as the French Revolution, Coleridge's Pantisocratic colonies in America and Shelley's troilist ménages in Italy were all—with diminishing ambition—intended to do. It will be 'precluded by its size from experiencing any of the evils of Civilization'. He moves his family from a valley to a hilltop, boldly affronting the gales. 'Our Ancestors . . .', he says, 'always built in a hole.' But his 'contracted Nook' was at least screened from view, whereas the new house, with romantic blatancy, is naked and unshaded. Instead of sheltering greenery, there are canvas awnings and parasols to shield its inhabitants from the sun. When romanticism ends, the opposite movement occurs, returning to the serenity of the valley: Wuthering Heights yields to the domestic defensiveness of Thrushcross Grange.

Even Parker's economic practices are romantic in their consumptiveness: in contrast with the frugal Lady Denham, who prides herself on keeping control of her fortune just as the Heywoods pride themselves on staying classically stationary in this romantic mayhem, Parker squanders his funds in reckless enterprises, buoyed up by faith. He reproves Lady Denham's love of money because, as a romantic, he values it only when relieving himself of it to purchase fantasies; it is hoped that Clara Brereton will soften the matriarch (who begrudges their inheritance to her relatives), acting as curatively as the Sanditon breezes. In financial matters as well as emotional, romanticism delights in surfeit and in conspicuous waste. Sir Edward expends gratuitous raptures on Charlotte, but only to pique Miss Brereton. The town, like Peacock's sugar, is a monument to this condition. Its houses boast of being empty and useless, advertising 'Lodgings to let' but finding no lodgers; the Miss Parkers suffer from an indolent excess of time and energy, so they busy themselves in being uselessly useful. The economy of Sanditon caters to their craving for unnecessary commodities, trinkets of fantasy. 'Civilization, Civilization indeed!' cries Miss Parker, pointing to shop windows stocked with blue shoes and nankin boots. At the circulating library, Charlotte sees everywhere temptations to expenditure on 'all the useless things in the World that could not be done without'. Art, too, like Sir Edward's emotion, functions as the idealisation of inutility. Two females take their ease in a farmyard, elegantly attired and engrossed in books. The sound of a harp issues from the upper window of a baker's shop.

Illness, in this romantic cult, changes from a bodily inevitability to an imaginative election. Romantic poetry is often ascribed to a voluntary malaise: William Roberts in 1817 accused Byron's *Manfred* of hypochondria, Byron called Keats a poetical bed-wetter, while Lockhart facetiously supposed that, being apprentice to an apothecary, Keats had misappropriated some 'diuretic or composing draught' intended for a patient 'far gone in the poetical mania'. In Sanditon, the twin mental powers that Coleridge called fancy and imagination are now diseases. The psychosomatic ills of the Parker girls are derived on one occasion 'from Fancy', on another from their 'good deal of Imagination'. They distrust doctors, and say 'we must trust to our own wretched Constitutions for any relief.' They do not, of course, want to be cured, and like Keats or Byron they curl up to enjoy their sensations and symptoms. Their invalidism spiritualises them; by contrast their brother Arthur, to whom much 'Earthly Dross' still adheres, complains he cannot eat because of nervous distress, but secretly stuffs himself. Jane Austen was writing *Sanditon* during the period of her own mortal illness, and in her letters she jokingly pretends to be enjoying her disease as the Parkers, amateurs of ailments, do. 'Sickness', she says in March 1817, 'is a dangerous Indulgence at my time of Life', and in May she admits that 'with all the Egotism of an Invalid I write only of myself.' The same frenzy of imagination which prompts Mr Parker's economic speculations goads his sisters to invent excruciations for their bodies. Affliction is afflatus and also, as this society exhausts and uses itself up, inflation.

Classical and romantic theories of economy and energy clash when Lady Denham objects to the intrusion of rich colonial families. They scatter money about so negligently that the price of everything rises, she argues. Mr Parker replies that when demand outruns supply, the resulting prosperity is of benefit to everyone. This is his specious justification of a society which works by internal combustion. Romanticism was the ideology of industrialism, and the steam engine has the attributes of self-destructive romantic heroism, harbouring within itself a dangerous incompatibility between the source of its scalding heat and a protective cooling device. Its operation dices with that thermodynamic tragedy—the annihilation of heat-loss—which is the predicament also of the romantic poem. Wordsworth's definition of poetry emphasises the conservation of energy: hence the discipline of memory. But Shelley called the mind in creation a fading coal, and Byron described imagination as a lava flow. To one, writing formalises the bleeding-away of vital heat, accelerating death; to the other, the disturbed organism suicidally empties itself of the fire which was its life. The Parkers treat their bodies, as Byron and Shelley conceive the poem, as internal combustion engines. Worn out by causeless stresses and strife, they drug themselves, as if topping up their boilers, with herbal tea and strong cocoa. Then they must burn off the energy they have accumulated, instead of (like Wordsworth) retentively storing it. With the emphasis of romantic industrialism—like Hazlitt celebrating animal spirits, or the manufacturer Thornton in Elizabeth Gaskell's *North and South*, who disparages Grecian 'leisure and serene enjoyment' (the conservatism of classicism) and calls himself a Goth, hailing life as 'a time for action and exertion'—the Parkers say that the real aristocracy is an élite of vigour; their brother has too little energy, so makes sure that he always has a warm place by the hearth and plenty of food to keep himself running.

Sir Edward's romantic literary taste sees poets burning up emotion in the same industrial way. When Charlotte objects to Burns's moral irregularities, Sir Edward says 'he felt & he wrote & he forgot', expending emotion with the dismissiveness of Byron's volcano. Hazlitt had also gloried in the 'sublimated . . . animal existence' of Burns and contrasted this lusty virility with the maidenliness c. Wordsworth, which Shelley ridiculed in his parody of 'Peter Bell'. Sir Edward reads bad novels to fuel himself, consuming fake emotions: novels serve, he contends, to 'enlarge the Primitive Capabilities of the Heart', increasing its dynamo-like output of energy.

Jane Austen's word for the causeless kinesis of romanticism is rotation. Everyone must whirl in a circle, 'to the prevalence of which rotating Motion, is perhaps to be attributed the Giddiness & false steps of many', like the overturning of the carriage on a steep, rough lane with which *Sanditon* begins. This frenetic rotation is the mobility of Byron's Juan, or of the flighty Adeline, who acts each and every part by turn and exhibits a versatility which Byron calls

> A thing of temperament and not of art,
>   Though seeming so, from its supposed facility;
> And false—though true; for surely they're sincerest
> Who are most strongly acted on by what is nearest.

Byron himself cultivated such contradictoriness, and saw in it the self's deviance from stern, consistent character. To be everything by turns and nothing long is his affront to the Wordsworthian drill of remorseful remembering: he defines mobility in a note to *Don Juan* as 'an excessive susceptibility of immediate impressions'; a life lived always in the heedless present.

Yet it does not enable the dancing, gymnastic ego to outrun itself. The past, Byron's note adds, can never be lost, and mobility is to its possessor 'a most painful and unhappy attribute'. Expressing a fear of emotion and a nervous discontent, it secretly envies the respite and relaxation of non-being. Keats hints as much when he claims for the poetic identity a negative capability: the cancellation of that imperious and sublime egotism which in Wordsworth stands on guard against experience; a readiness to risk sensations which may be the poet's destruction; a calculated breakdown of the body by overtaxing its sensitivity. Romanticism is an affair as much of the life as of writing, and that affair is consummated—in the aborted romantic careers of Byron, Shelley and Keats—in their wearing-out of literature and their devising of their own exemplary deaths.

— 27 —
Romantic Deaths

In England, romantic imagination enjoins not the systematic exploitation of the senses to which Baudelaire, Rimbaud and Verlaine dedicated themselves but a systematic satiation of those bodily capacities. Writing for Keats surfeits the eager organs, feasting on life; Byron's dissipations make trial of the existential capacity for sensation; Shelley anorexically and Arielly starves the greedy organism to achieve his own evaporation into spirit.

Death is the terminus of Keats's love-affair with the body, and of the quarrel within Byron and Shelley between the body and the spirit it cages. Keats anatomises the onset and progress of his consumptive disease, and tries to savour it as he had done the earlier titillations of appetite—the mistress's eyes on which he wants to 'feed deep, deep', the creamy delicacies which Madeline and Porphyro consume as their consummation in *The Eve of St. Agnes*, *Lear* which Keats, in reading, gobbled up. The life he prized and relinquished with such pain is gratefully cast off by Byron and Shelley. Byron's military adventure in the Greek war against the Turks was a convenient solution to his uncertainty. He could cease to be himself by assuming the role of the Byronic hero, and dying in the performance of it. Shelley's drowning is his longed-for dissolution: his reclamation by the fluent, unfixed element he envied.

In all three cases, the writing is an assistance to suicide. Keats exhausts language, demanding that it describe 'the feel of not to feel it'. All his poems end in a small death. He has a physiological version of Wordsworth's mortal tranquillising of emotion. A poem garners experience and ingests it as a body does food, but must surrender it at last in a premonition of expiring—an ejaculatory spending or an alimentary discharge. Madeline and Porphyro are excreted from the castle and everything left behind in it dies, Hyperion thrusts himself from his palace and from his own metamorphosing body, Lamia vanishes from Lycius's arms and life in turn vanishes from his limbs, the Belle Dame leaves the Knight a withered husk on the hillside. Only the Grecian urn can stay life and secure it; but it can do so because it is funereal, and contains cold ashes.

Since for Byron the writing is a wasting of energy and for Shelley a devaluation of meaning (lost when the image is translated into merely approximate words), they resent the literally deadly verbal routine to which they are condemned. Byron was reconciled to writing only if he could equate it with a physical activity like swimming, just as Scott identified creation with the body's exercise. Counting the pages of his life of Napoleon in 1826, Scott says, 'I am now once more at my oar and will row hard'; the next year he comments, 'I am now at writing as I used to be at riding', slow to start but expeditious when mounted. He is happy to compare himself to a hack. In 1828 he says, 'I am like a spavind horse', lame and stiff at first, capable of 'a pretty good trot' when warmed up. For Byron, too, *Don Juan* could be praised only because it was 'life, . . . *the thing*', not because it was art. The poetry has the sportive verve of a live thing: the rhymes in *Don Juan* put language through a course in acrobatics. It is liable, however, to the depletion and breakdown of life when the energy runs out. Juan may have the athleticism of youth, but the poet has to battle against what he describes as the debilities of wasted age, writing in spite of a hangover and keeping at bay the extra distress of boredom. In *Childe Harold's Pilgrimage* the long final line of the Spenserian stanza is the pace of a limping fatigue, the heaving of a sigh which gives up the ghost. How will the poem—each stanza asks when it reaches its end—find the energy to live down its ennui and continue?

Byron, like Keats, has his own sadly post-coital equivalent to Wordsworth's recollection of emotion. Pleasure, he says in a letter in 1813, is self-obliterating while it lasts, and can be appreciated only in anticipation or in memory, in the repose after satisfaction. In Venice he would have his gondolier row him out onto the lagoon at dawn after a debauched night, so he could meditate on what his body had done, and question what he had learned about himself. The poem, likewise, is in the nature of an inquest. Its mercy to Byron, his anaesthetic correlative to Keats's 'feel of not to feel it', is a safe numbness, spared the necessity of having to respond. His 'Lines on Hearing that Lady Byron was Ill' equate feeling with sickness and seek the cure of nullity:

> Me thought that joy and health alone could be
> Where I was *not*.

He sentences his wife to a hypochondriac sensitivity, charging her with being sick even though he is not there to provoke her distemper. His worst wish for her is that she should never lose the capacity to feel—an extraordinary reversal of the creative logic of Wordsworth, who prayed for the restoration of that same capacity:

> . . . thou shalt feel
> A hollow agony which will not heal.

And that agony will be mocked, additionally, by its hollowness. Valour in Byron is a refusal to be contaminated by emotion, the writing's expulsion of feeling: '*Feels he*, think you?' is a question asked in *The Two Foscari* by the torturers of a body they are wracking into sentience. Jacopo Foscari's stoicism enables him proudly to repudiate the imputation of cowardly feeling. The Byronic poem's boast is the same. It may be a gymnasium for sensations—the dexterous skill of versifying, the elastic management of the *ottava rima*—but can harbour no emotion.

Byron seeks what Keats grieves over: the expulsion of emotion, of life itself. The gladiator in *Childe Harold's Pilgrimage* suffers his life to bleed away because by his consent he stoically conquers the pain which might otherwise unman him:

> And through his side the last drops, ebbing slow
> From the red gash, fall heavy, one by one.

There is a corresponding image in Keats. At the cider-press in 'To Autumn' he watches 'the last oozings hours by hours'—but the dripping is of juice not blood, and it is not allowed to run away but is gathered for later drinking; instead of death, there is fermentation. When Jacopo dies at last, it is Marina's error to insist 'there must be life yet in that heart'. The Doge, Jacopo's father, comments more wisely, 'He's free.' At best, writing will be an efficient automatism, done in the absence of thinking or feeling. 'One must make love mechanically, as one swims', Byron commented; poetry was to be made in the same way. Byron therefore detested what he called the sensual luxuriation of Keats, and the over-loaded richness of his writing. Keats wrote, as he ate, in the hope of persuading himself that he was someone. Byron, a fanatical slimmer, who found the waters at Cheltenham salutary because disgusting, and declared that a woman should never be seen consuming food, wrote for the same reason that he did not eat: to cease being someone. Keats commended his own policy to Shelley, telling his volatile colleague to sit still, furl his wings, embed himself in sensory reality and weigh himself down in earth—'load every rift of your subject with ore.' But to Shelley such advice was tantamount to entombment: it was one of Shelley's horrors to be buried alive, because he regarded life as the spirit's suffocation within the body's grave. The plump Keats, meeting Shelley in 1817, thought him and his poetry thin—abstract, un-nourished, un-vital. As Keats misguidedly tells Shelley to enliven his poetry, Shelley commends Keats for dying and achieving disembodiment. In Shelley's 'Adonais' the Keats who venerated life becomes a seraph, glad to be released from his physical cage.

That freedom entails, for Shelley, a release from the lowly need to write. As a Platonist, he believes that life is a disfiguration of the ideal realm beyond it:

> Life, like a dome of many-coloured glass,
> Stains the white radiance of Eternity.

Similarly, writing inflicts a mortal stain on an otherwise radiantly unsmirched page. Whereas in Byron's *Foscari* the purpose of torture is to purge feeling, in Shelley's *The Cenci* the judge orders it for the macabre Platonic reason that it will cleanse a blotted page and erase the untruths written there:

> Let tortures strain the truth till it be white
> As snow thrice sifted by the frozen wind.

This arctic landscape, like the crystalline lunar degree zero which torments the hero in *Prometheus Unbound*, is an expanse of whiteness immune to writing. The judge, hoping to entrap Beatrice, presents her with an unclean parchment and demands, 'Know you this paper, Lady?' Words are incrimination. Beatrice exempts herself by refusing to 'find a word' for the sexual crime of which her father has made her the victim. The mystic truth in Demogorgon's cave is imageless; in *The Cenci* the shaming truth will remain, as Beatrice says 'expressionless'. By refusing to articulate it, she can disappear into that unwritten white radiance and can claim, 'I am as universal as the light.' The madman in Shelley's *Julian and Maddalo*, remonstrating with the woman who has betrayed him, refers to writing as a useless pollution. His plaint is

> charactered in vain
> On this unfeeling leaf which burns the brain
> And eats into it . . . blotting all things fair
> And wise and good which time had written there.

In agreement with Shelley's image of the fading coal, he describes his words as embers heaped upon a fire (the sparks 'of that which has consumed me') to cool and kill it. Like Beatrice, he gains a philosophical peace from his annihilation of the querulous, story-telling self. He will not write down in indictment the history of his life; Julian, having persuaded Maddalo's daughter to complete that history, will not impart it, and his secession from the garrulous narrative community of Wordsworth—which sacramentally conjoins the annalists in 'The Ruined Cottage'—is a last act almost of euthanasia, granting the madman the quiet of non-being, the inconsequential relief of having no story. As the poem ends he interrogates the daughter:

> I urged and questioned still, she told me how
> All happened—but the cold world shall not know.

Byron's Marina asks Loredano 'how *feel you*?' He answers, impenitently unfeeling, 'As rocks.' Marina adds that these can be blasted and shivered by lightning. Beatrice employs a similar image, saying

> . . . Consequence, to me,
> Is as the wind which strikes the solid rock
> But shakes it not.

Byronic heroism lies in being the rock, Shelleyan heroism in being the wind which, like the light, is universal because unbodied. And that wind provides the model for the Shelleyan poem. It is to be written not on paper (where it can only show what Shelley calls 'the vanity of translation', the failure of correspondence between ideas and their verbal, earthly shadows) but on the wind or, as Keats, in a Shelleyan phrase, said of his own life, on water; a stream of fluid sound, a lyrical voice, never a thing fixed in print; a gift of air, as an aria is—and Shelley in fact composed his 'Indian Serenade' to the music of an aria from Mozart's opera *La Clemenza di Tito*. The wind is a source of poetic song in 'Ode to the West Wind' and in 'A Dirge'. In 'With a Guitar, To Jane' it inheres in the musical instrument. The guitar has an ancestral memory of its previous life as a tree, when winds harmoniously agitated it. (This is Shelley's non-human revision of Wordsworth's belief in the infant's pre-existence.) The felling of the tree was a sleeping, painless death; it is hollowed out so that its emptiness will become resonant. Shelley longs for the same voiding in himself: to be a vessel for that breath which enables nature to make music without human intercession. He begs the west wind to make him its lyre, 'even as the forest is'. Lyricism is the re-incitement of fire in words, the arousing of a verbal conflagration. The wind's service to him is that it will propagate what remains of the ardent flame in Shelley and re-awaken the fading coal:

> Scatter, as from an unextinguished hearth
> Ashes and sparks, my words among mankind!

If the page cannot be mercifully blanked out, as Beatrice or the madman manage to do, it can be cauterised. Words are tinder, which music causes to flare up. In the aerial voice's song from *Prometheus Unbound* Shelley gives lips to the 'Life of Life' and makes them enkindle the breath between them, which spontaneously combusts. Acting out his theories of an incendiary lyricism and an elemental poetry, he so far progressed beyond a faith in the human perpetuity of writing that he made the winds and waves his publishers. At Lynmouth in 1812 he boxed his seditious pamphlets and attached them to fiery air-balloons, or bottled them and floated them out to sea; he coupled the elements—infectious, revolutionary fire and confluent water—and made them together as universal as Beatrice's light in their dissemination of his vocal messages by sailing flaming paper boats on the Serpentine, or on a pond near Primrose Hill in London.

Shelley dreamed, like the tree being gutted to make a guitar or carved into the lyre's transparency, of sloughing the body. Byron nicknamed him 'Snake'. Incarnation is his trauma, and Shelley even interpreted his name as a reference to the fortuitously disposable shell in which he was, for the time being, caged. Waiting for Harriet Westbrook to arrive at Mount Street in 1811 for their elopement, he occupied himself by hurling from the window the shells of the oysters he had breakfasted on, remarking as he did so, 'This is a *Shelley* business!' To Keats, this scorn for the physical world was a blasphemy. His child-like decadence takes the form of delectation. Keats envisages poetic development corporeally. Instead of the encyclopaedic enlargement of the mind prescribed for Wordsworth by Coleridge's learned curriculum, Keats in 1819 tells his brother George that he feels more creatively capable because his circulation is steadier and his metabolism sounder. Whereas Wordsworth walked to think and Coleridge to talk, while Shelley prowled the night like a sleepwalker or a spectre, Keats walked digestively (though he counselled George against 'going the first mile just after dinner'). Though Wordsworthian or Coleridgean weather is mental, corresponding to mood, with the sky as the streamy consciousness of nature, Keats, trusting the curative Italian sun, relies on weather as a determinant of bodily health, and at Winchester located 'a dry chalky down where the air is worth six pence a pint'. Morality and metaphysics were for Keats matters of oral guzzling. He called the heart 'the teat from which the Mind or intelligence sucks its identity'. The imbibing of wisdom is therefore the body's plumping-out of itself. Art gorges on a comestible world, and Keats experiences composition as a feast, squeezing a nectarine down his throat while using the other hand to write with, affectionately smearing a page of a letter to Fanny Brawne with blackcurrant jelly, and choosing to understand painting as a gluttonous repaste of pigment: he told his friend Benjamin Haydon that he expected 'to see your Picture plumped out like a ripe Peach', and would crave a slice of it.

This is the oddity of Keats's play *Otho the Great*, which is about character in salivation not action. Its people do not stand apart in defiance of each other, demarcating the stage between themselves as dramatic beings should; so intimate is their congress that they seem to be feeding on each other. Gersa feels himself to be 'the wondering food / Of all these eyes', Ludolph's palate is nauseated by the sycophantic nobles, and paternal love is experienced by Otho as an appetite, whose craving he wants to breathe into his son's ear. These edible individuals contrast with the incorporeal ideas of Shelley's play. Cenci is an infanticidal deity, exulting in torments he 'can never feel' and, as he puts it, feeding the bodies he tortures 'with the breath of fear / For hourly pain.' His daughter is to him a mere 'specious mass of flesh'. But Beatrice outwits him first by descending to the calorific minimum of Prometheus—'Ah! my blood runs cold'—and then by running mad, which to her means the happy chance of exit from her own physical and mental fate: in her delirium she is able to say, 'I thought I was that wretched Beatrice / Men speak of.' Shelley's characters cannot tolerate their existence in a drama, because they disdain to feel; Keats's are too preoccupied by feeling or by the study of their own physiological symptoms—Sigifrid asks whether Ludolph's disguise as the Arab was provoked by 'opium, / Or the mad-fumed wine?', and Ludolph rages that Auranthe stings him 'even as the worm doth feed upon the nut'—to permit the drama to hustle them into action. They have no dramatic power over each other, because the worst they can do to their antagonists is inflict abstruse pleasures on them. Ludolph, menacing Gersa with its sword, describes murder as a delicious intromission:

> There is no part of it, to the very hilt,
> But shall indulge itself about thine heart!

Eating for Keats ensures the body's familial union with its fellows—he instructs his sister to get stout so they can grow into triple-chinned old folks together—and is the source as well of personal identity. That is why Shelley (who fasted at Oxford and later took up an abstemious vegetarian diet) and Byron spurn it. Keats commented in 1819 that Byron cut a figure but was not figurative. Byron attitudinises, exhibits his body, urges it into action, yet is not at ease inside it, like the drowsing Keats; for this reason he is best seen in silhouette, as the black outlined ghost of a departed presence. Marianne Hunt cut a figure of him out of paper after his daily ride in Pisa in 1822, his spurs still on, his riding crop over his shoulder. All that can be captured is his shadow. Or his image, which is theatrical persona, not human truth—Byron costumed as an oriental pasha on his first Mediterranean tour in the painting by Thomas Phillips, or outfitted in the neoclassical armour he commissioned for his last Greek campaign; Byron remade after the event by Mary Shelley in *The Last Man* as the debased sensualist Raymond; by Benjamin Disraeli as the glamorous worldling, Lord Cadurcis, in his novel *Venetia*; as a foppish contemporary of Wilde by Max Beerbohm, whose caricature shows the poet balletically shaking the English dust from his fashionable shoes; later still, as an international playboy in Auden's 'Letter to Lord Byron', where he is photographed for glossy magazines at Croydon aerodrome or during lunch with a Cochran girl. To be figurative (which Byron dreads) is to be full of yourself. Byron, as Keats perceives, is always seeing through himself. Irony is his quizzical paraphrase of the Coleridgean 'I AM': the subject appraised and dispraised as object; the self as other; character as acted personality.

The body Byron tried to see as if it belonged to someone else Shelley sought to belie. James Hogg describes him in 1810 contradicting his own physique. Though big-boned and strong, he appeared slight; though tall, he controverted his height by stooping (in painful contrast with Keats who, made miserable by his own small stature, is forever dreaming of augmenting it, standing 'tip-toe upon a little hill' or climbing atop a pile of stones on the summit of Ben Nevis so he can seem 'a little higher than old Ben himself'); his voice was shrill, as if trying to get out of its skeletal prison. Keats valued ripeness: the organism's accession to maturity. Shelley begged to be spared that happily conciliatory human fate. With the self-congratulatory gloom of adolescence, he wrote to William Godwin when he was nineteen that 'my physical constitution is such as will not permit me to hope for a life so long as yours', because it was too debilitated by the nervous intensity of his spirit. Southey attempted to argue Shelley out of his radical zealotry by predicting that age would mellow him into conservatism: romanticism is for young men. 'When you are as old as I am', Southey said, 'you will think with me.' Shelley determined to prove him wrong by not living to be that old.

Keats's tragedy is that the body cannot survive the imagination's demands on it. In 1819 he tells Haydon that his throat will not allow him to go out. The body is too feeble 'to support me to the Height'. He means this poetically as well as anatomically. In training for his attempt at an epic, he made a mountaineer of himself, since poetry is a vertical toil, a 'gradus ad Parnassum altissimum'. He struggles up Ben Nevis, wearing out his boots, but cannot withstand the rigours of the highland tour which was his course in heroic hardihood. He catches cold on Mull, and has to be sent back to London. The tuberculosis which destroyed Keats was the disease of his romanticism, which hungered to consume a fleshly, palpable world. It pathologically mocked his creativity: the body consumed itself. His digestive tract became so decayed that food slid straight through him, and the doctors expected him to die of starvation. He was maddened by the pangs of hunger, and entreated Severn—who was nursing him in December 1820—to overfeed him. Keats acknowledged that he could grow only by taxing the body, weaning it of the jocund, carnal pleasures he celebrates in *Endymion* or 'Sleep and Poetry', consigning it to crucifixion by a 'World of Pains and troubles'. But because writing is a toll on his used-up organism, he must sacrifice the only means he has of recovering a meaning from his agony. As the malady progresses, he has to give up writing letters because it provokes palpitations, and the doctor forbids him 'to read poetry much less write it'.

The connoisseurship of sensation—Keats's early poetry calls for women, wine and snuff or for a brimming bowl—turns into a tragic scrutiny of symptoms. When he haemorrhaged in February 1820 he knew, having been a surgeon's assistant and a trainee apothecary, that the blood was arterial, and that he would surely die. Illness meant stinting the flesh he had pampered, 'living', as he said, 'upon pseudo victuals.' Yet with a magnificent courage, Keats insisted on considering his sickness as a posthumous and purgatorial trial, and came to long for death as a resumption of the glad life of sensation. Four days before that happened, he wrote, 'Thank God for the quiet grave—O! I can feel the cold earth upon me—the daisies growing over me.' This is his undauntedly hedonistic revision of Wordsworth's speech to Dorothy about their interment in the trench. Death for Wordsworth is not apprehended physically. It means being laid asleep in body to become a living soul. But for Keats death is his tribute to and enrichment of nature. Earth will be his counterpane; flowers will embed themselves in him. A corresponding statement by Shelley marks his different notions of humanity and mortality. In the Protestant cemetery at Rome, where both he and Keats were eventually to be buried, he sees 'the soil . . . stirring in the sun-warm earth' and concludes that 'one might, if one were to die, desire the sleep [those already entombed] seemed to sleep. Such is the human mind, and so it peoples with its wishes vacancy and oblivion.' The virtue of death in this estimation is impersonal, metaphysical, ontological: it is a graduation into what Mary Shelley called the 'continuity of our species', as indicated by that pullulating soil. Shelley's impersonal 'one' exquisitely demurs on the question of whether it is his own fate he is pondering, or whether he, as a sprite, need bother with such eventualities. 'Such is the human mind' marks his sense of death as the mind's decamping from the outworn body. He sees the cemetery as he did Pompeii (about which he wrote a poem) and as he did the world: a mass grave, populated by the phantasmal simulacrae of life which 'nestle in the stream of the inconstant wind, . . . like the steps of ghosts'. Rather than luxuriating in death as Keats recommended, Shelley demanded that it happen instantaneously. In June 1822 he asked Trelawny to find him a compliant chemist who would brew him a potion of prussic acid; he wished to have the means of suicide always at hand.

Shelley's rage to escape humanity carries with it a punitive campaign against nature. On country walks with Hogg, he set up targets on trees and shot at them with his duelling pistols. Was it the targets he aimed at, or the trees he wanted to cancel, disintegrating them into ideas as, in his poetry, he does even to the stony bulk of Mont Blanc? Shelley was an adept of a devilish experimental science which—in Prometheus's theft of fire, as in the later discovery of atomic fission—understands nature in order to acquire power over it, and attains its highest bliss when it learns by what secret formula of physics the world might be destroyed. The Russian composer Alexander Scriabin wrote in 1909 in homage to Shelley a 'poem of fire' called *Prometheus*, using a colour-organ so as to fill the theatre with illusory flames, and in his *Mysterium*, meant to be performed at the base of the Himalayas, he orchestrated a sequence of cabbalistic accords which when sounded would (he believed) cause time at once to stop and life on earth to cease. Shelley's childhood games rehearse that salving apocalypse. Impersonating a devil, he set fire to a stack of refuse so he might lord it over his own hell. At Syon House he blew up a boundary fence and a desk with gunpowder; at Eton he experimented with electricity while chanting the cauldron song of the witches from *Macbeth*, and told a master who interrupted him that he was raising Satan. This was a Platonic and scientific hocus-pocus, however: an attempt to save the world from the dead end of its materiality. Knowledge had to be seized by violence. On Magdalen Bridge once he snatched a baby from its mother and, acting on Wordsworth's creed, interrogated it about life before the anti-climax of birth. The mother was convinced the manic youth intended to hurl her child into the river. (If he had done so, he would only have been restoring the creature to the conceptual heaven from which it fell.)

He is logically bound to be as contemptuous of his own writings, since they are only the paper remnants of ideas. When Hogg worried that some of his early poems could be easily pilloried, Shelley cheerfully set about wrecking them by making small, defaming changes: self-parody for him as for Byron is a convenient exit from the obloquy of identity. It is our human error to mistake words for things. Shelley denies this validation of the world by words in verse which is metamorphic, a haze of metaphors dissolving into one another like the images in Asia's song from *Prometheus* (where the soul is first an enchanted boat, then a sleeping swan, then an angel, then 'one in slumber bound') or like the skylark, which can be apprehended only by approximate similes of unseeable things—the hidden poet, the maiden in the tower, the embowered rose:

> What thou art we know not;
> What is most like thee?

The skylark's value to Shelley lies in its blithe nihilism, its 'ignorance of pain'. Keats's nightingale cajoles him to forget the human world and its agonies; the skylark loftily ignores them. And just as Turner—when accused of a vaporous negation of painting, making, as Hazlitt said, pictures of nothing—replied that indistinctness was his forte, so Shelley's genius is for describing miracles of elemental dissolution which cannot be seen: earth and sea merged in 'one lake of fire' when the Euganean hills seem a mirage from the Lido; the liquification of landscape in *Prometheus*; the sun which in 'The Cloud' may not be described because, with its 'meteor eyes', it cannot be looked at, or the moon in the same poem, known only by the inaccurate name that mortals (as the cloud superciliously says) give to it. Shelley's words are as fluent as water, as empty as air; a melody, like that of the speaking spirits in *Prometheus*, of echoes.

Shelley's love for music—he is the most strictly lyrical of English poets, the one in whom poetry truly attains the condition of music—corresponds to Keats's loving imitation of painting, in which he was instructed by Haydon and Hazlitt. Music's verity to Shelley is its invisibility: it is the vocalising of the spheres. Painting to Keats means the opposite: an impasto of sensual reality; pigment is nutrient. Part of the problem for Keats in the 'Ode on a Grecian Urn' is that he adopts a Shelleyan theory, and cannot persuade himself of its veracity. He tries to eavesdrop on the sound of revelry on the urn, but can only hear melodies unheard, 'ditties of no tone' intended for the spirit not the senses. In compensation, he renders the urn pictorial. Yet its scenes are of absences, or frigid postponements—a desolate town, an immobilised dance. Its Platonic moral is unavailing to him. The neoclassical Shelley, however, who preferred a skeletal and diagrammatic art of line to one of messy prismatic colour, and whose ideal region is that celestial blankness which the world has polluted, admired sculpture. The statue is an urn: a petrification of the body, but also a representation of the cool, whitened, unencumbered soul, like the dead Shelley himself in the statue by Onslow Ford at University College in Oxford, or like Byron who cynically and classically disavowed romanticism by calling himself 'a walking statue without feeling or failing'. This statuesque mode of being is the strength of Prometheus. Among the glaciers, he is turning into an ice-sculpture, burned into shape by cold; and his consolation is that at this hibernant low temperature he will at last, like the mountains, be granted a respite from having to feel.

To Keats, the statue signifies paralysis of the beloved, pulsating organism.

[439]

In the neoclassical mausoleum of *The Fall of Hyperion*, to become a sculpture is a fate worse than death. The poet is transfixed by the prophetess, and feels himself chilled then benumbed by a palsy: the deathly onset of a classical rigidity, from which he is spared and which Juan, too, nonchalantly reverses when he fondles the ghost at the end of Byron's poem. Shelley by contrast, looking at the Medusa attributed to Leonardo, was happy for it gracefully to turn 'the gazer's spirit into stone'. Keats undoes his own attempts at an epic by rendering its statues sentient. Hyperion is epically outsize, with his 'stride colossal', his stamping foot and his thunderous voice. When he arrives at his palace, he should have the kinetic impetus of Milton's Satan. Keats dutifully notes that, 'He enter'd, but he enter'd full of wrath.' Yet the repetition cannot make the action happen in his verse, and to register the potent advent of force Keats has to consult the trembling nervousness of the nature Hyperion disturbs: his roar 'scar'd away the meek ethereal Hours / And made their dove-wings tremble.' Although Keats's ambition tells him he ought to be magnifying objects, at Fingal's Cave he scales down epic hyperbole by saying that giants seem to have bound together the basalt pillars 'like Bunches of Matches'. At his most self-disparaging, he is shamed by this sensuous style of introversion and reduction. When Severn wanted to exhibit his miniature of Keats at the Royal Academy in 1819, Keats objected, saying, 'What a drop of water in the ocean is a Miniature.' It is he who is minute and innocuous, he feels, not just the image.

The difference between music and painting betokens as well the choice between an art which operates in time and one which subsists in space; between busy motion and metamorphosis (for music, as Wagner said, is the art of transition) and the contented, eternalised stillness of the picture. Shelley cannot see the skylark: it exists only as a song, and while it sings it performs a cartwheeling flight which is imitated by Shelley's brief stanzas. The nightingale is more stationary; Keats wants to entrap it pictorially, to frame and own it, and when it flies off his poem must end. The same discrepancy separates Shelley's breathlessly impatient autumn from that season, glutted and sluggish, as represented by Keats. The 'Ode to the West Wind' is a musical poem because it urges a hectic changefulness. The impulse which makes the wind, the 'numen' of autumn, a singer makes it also a propulsive disseminator of ideas (those winged seeds) and a political revolutionary, speeding the cycle of change. Shelley demands, 'If Winter comes, can Spring be far behind?' Keats defers all thought of a future, asking, 'Where are the songs of Spring?' only to add, 'Think not of them.' It is the incendiary haste of Shelley which Keats above all needs to arrest, and the enchantment of painting in 'To Autumn' is that it can dissuade things from happening, reconciled to a patient, corpulent stasis as it watches 'the last oozings hours by hours'.

The motor of Shelley's verse is its verbs, because like the wind they are the agents of mutability: hence the reiterated pleas of 'hear, oh hear!' In Keats the work is done by substantives because, like the application of paint to canvas, they substantialise. 'To Autumn' is intent on impeding change, because if the cycle continues it will do so without the dying Keats; it therefore experiments with a poetry of nouns without verbs. The only verbs it will, at the beginning, admit are infinitives—'to load and bless . . . To bend . . . And fill . . . To swell . . . to set budding'—because these are evasions of movement, depicting completion rather than accompanying action. The accumulation of nouns is a harvesting of substances ('more, / And still more, later flowers for the bees') which gravitationally weights the verse and steadies it in the present tense of surfeit: those bees

> . . . think warm days will never cease
> For Summer has o'er-brimmed their clammy cells.

But an event in the air signals an end to this earthly poise and the abrupt cessation of the poem, now invaded by a premonition of mortality. The 'gathering swallows twitter in the skies', preparing for departure. Like the nightingale, they represent a life which cannot after all be detained in poetry.

Air by contrast is the arena of Shelley's poetry—a space of free fall, an envelope of bodiless consciousness. At Villa Valsovano he inhabited a glazed, roofed terrace from where he surveyed the Apennines and could watch the advance of storms. His aerial module was a spaceship, a prophecy fulfilled in the science fiction of *The Last Man*, where Verney travels to Scotland in a sailing balloon. It granted to Shelley the lofty irresponsibility of his own cloud, whose laughter is thunder, or of his Witch of Atlas, whose idea of hilarity is to vault on the clouds, sport with lightning-bolts and dance among the fire-balls. In this skylab he wrote *The Cenci*, far above the breathing human passion that the play tries to comprehend. Shelley looked patronisingly down on the earth; Beatrice, maddened by her father's assault on her, can only look yearningly up at the sky from which she has tumbled, commenting—in another paraphrase of Shelley's condemnation of the dome of many-coloured glass—that 'The beautiful blue heaven is flecked with blood.' He wrote *Prometheus* in Rome, among the ruins of the Caracalla baths. Its imagery, he said, was 'drawn from the operations of the human mind', and the location doubled as the cavity of a world-mind. The shell of Caracalla moulders to admit 'the bright blue sky of Rome', as the body, when unbound, will be overtaken by the astral firmament of mind. The archaeological wreckage was to Shelley a platform for take-off into that sky: he admired the 'dizzy arches suspended in air'.

If creativity could not be aeronautic, it must at least be entrusted to that other element of dissolution, water. For Keats water meant the obliviousness of life. It was therefore the ground on which he sadly inscribed his epitaph. But Shelley, confronted by destruction, immersed himself in it. He loved to splash about incompetently in the water, and when sailing with Byron would lie on the bottom of the boat commingling with the air and spray, leaving Byron to manage the craft. Knocked overboard, he compliantly sank through the water and waited for it to claim him; Byron, less mystically intent on inundation, had to save him.

Byron was proud of his own strength as a swimmer, because it advertised his dual victory over his lamed body and over a nature which seemed determined to wash him away. When Byron writes in *Childe Harold's Pilgrimage* of 'Dear Nature' as a 'kindest mother' whose 'bare bosom' suckles him, it is in a half-hearted attempt to persuade himself of its maternal benignity. In truth, a mother was what he least needed. His letters express his relieved sense of having been freed from heredity, enabled to invent himself anew, when he looks at his mother's corpse in 1811. His poetry is an effort to defend his precious, precarious self against family, country and all other collective existences—including nature's—which seek to cancel it; a battle, like that of Huysmans's perverse dandy Des Esseintes in *A Rebours*, against nature. Therefore, whenever sea or ocean appear in *Childe Harold*, it is as elements to be mastered, as Mazeppa's horse is. His soul, Byron says, brooks the turning tide; earth is 'a rolling bark' on which we must stay afloat, or else we will be dashed into eternity—not Coleridge's idle, painted ship, nor Baudelaire's reeling *bateau ivre*, but an infirm platform in whose buoyancy we must trust, a plank balanced on nothingness. The 'deep and dark blue Ocean' is the scornful negligence of nature. Swimming or sailing, man tests himself heroically against it and struggles to stay alive. This is the moral of Juan's survival of the shipwreck, and of Byron's own feat in 1810 when he swam the Hellespont, like Leander on his way to the embraces of Hero. He declared himself prouder of this swim than of any political or poetic glory: poetry had value for him only if it could match the bravura of action, the brio of performance. He reports being set upon by a Bolognese quack in Athens, who wants to experiment on him as an aquatic genius; fighting off the obsessive attentions of Lady Caroline Lamb, he hopes to learn from the swimmer's skill in navigating treacherous currents, saying, 'before I sink I will at least have a *swim* for it, though I wish with all my heart it was the *Hellespont* instead.'

The performing self—extroverting mental life as prestidigitation—has come to delight in its own inauthenticity. Byron is the joker in the pack, apparently a fervent romantic, actually a sceptic about romanticism, briefly affecting its moods and manias but claiming as his own sovereign quality a distanced indifference. He possessed a multitude of personalities which all his life sought unsuccessfully for a character. Harold and Juan are variant selves, opposites who are secretly identical: the misanthropic exile of the one is adapted by the other into a comic philosophy of acquiescence and resilience, learning (like the cuckolded husband in 'Beppo') not to care. Byron has mastered a provisional repertoire of identities which require a theatre in which to play themselves out. He is Keats's chameleon Shakespeare, impartially (and indifferently) relishing Iago and Imogen; or he is Henry Crawford in *Mansfield Park*, who plays all the parts in *Henry VIII* simultaneously, using these personae as surrogates, impersonations of a 'dignity or pride, or tenderness or remorse' he can mimic but not feel. Like the actor, Byron is a negatively capable being, adept at assuming the positive existences of others, and quick to shed them when they have served their purpose.

This is why the letters are so central to his literary production: full of Shakespearean quotation and of enthusiasm for the acting of Kean, they are an endless sequence of playlets; a dramaturgy of consciousness. His description of creativity in *Childe Harold* is, properly understood, a theory of acting:

> 'Tis to create, and in creating live
> A being more intense, that we endow
> With form our fancy, gaining as we give
> The life we image, even as I do now.
> What am I? Nothing: but not so art thou,
> Soul of my thought!

Shelley and Keats pursue elusive images, fleeting visitants—Alastor the spiritual 'Being whom he loves', Endymion the moon. The marriage of subject with object which should beget the symbol must remain unconsummated. Byron chases no such ideals; he clones himself, and by playing the part he writes for himself can companionably mate with this exact replica, whether this is his travelling companion Harold, to whom he dismissively lends his own life ('he himself as nothing'), or that juvenile student of Byronic vice, Juan, or the Greek page-boy Loukas who is the subject of Byron's last love poem. When the vision fades, only the inadequate 'sole self' is left for Alastor or Endymion. But Byron transforms himself into the other, willing the original self to disappear. As an actor, he is most alive when performing. Offstage, reverting to reality, he dims into non-existence.

Byron's correspondents are the fractious community of his selves. The comedy of his love life is his farcical manoeuvring to keep antagonistic identities—Annabella Millbanke and Lady Caroline Lamb, for instance—from encountering; his social versatility is a reflex of the actor's psychological prevarication, skilled, because he is nothing in himself, at making himself mankind's epitome to every man or woman he addresses. After the Hellespont episode, he refracts the incident into a set of variations, recasting himself in each small performance like Hamlet, Falstaff or Iago modulating their acts to ingratiate with new auditors. To his friend Drury, Byron is learnedly lewd about the crossing, while for his agent at Newstead he condescendingly glosses the classical parallel; to his mother he first writes with filial bashfulness, then, in a second letter, dares to be suggestive, though by contrast with the innuendos in the account sent to Drury he chastens the anecdote by specifying that there was no Hero awaiting him. That same lack of a lover recurs in a letter to another friend, Dallas, where it has yet another function. It now purifies the deed by making it gratuitous, like the cadenzas or coloratura of those romantic virtuosi (praised by Byron in 'Beppo'), the Improvisatori: 'my labour was even to be its own reward.'

Like Henry Crawford in *Mansfield Park*, Byron is a one-man Shakespeare. His quotes are ventriloquistic tricks, by which he suddenly turns himself into someone else—a Richard III 'deformed in body and mind', a vaunting Coriolanus 'monstering nothings' to Moore, a Falstaff elaborating in a letter to Hogg a criticism of his contemporaries which recalls the fat knight's denunciation of the teetotal Lancastrians: he doubts that either Wordsworth or Southey have ever been drunk, 'and I am of the old creed of Homer the wine-bibber'. (Keats with a characteristic difference of emphasis thought the bard edible not potable, and remarked in a letter, 'I long to feast upon old Homer.')

Friends are necessary to abet these versatile pretences. The letters are soliloquies begging for the reciprocal sympathy of a painfully remote audience. Byron's anxiety about sustaining the personalities he projected made him demand immediate answers to his letters, and he ceased correspondence with the publisher, John Murray, who was tardy in replying. The correspondent is a collaborator in his fictionalising of himself. Byron, who trades in images, finds it convenient to allow the roles he enacts or the fake trinkets he vends to fill up the vacancy he feels within himself. When Caroline Lamb stole his portrait from Murray's office and extorted from Byron, in payment for its return, a lock of his hair, he sent her instead a snippet from the coiffure of his new mistress Lady Oxford. Such trickery is self-perjuring and thus self-purging. He thought of selling off his title for cash, but demurred when he began to doubt whether his identity would raise much of a sum in ready money. He gets rid of emotions by dramatising them, just as by the same reasoning he can defend himself against the emotions of others, treating Caroline's fits of passion as scenes or performances and choosing to consider a letter from her insincere because it is half in rhyme.

Byron told Thomas Moore that he knew of 'no *im*material sensuality so delightful as good acting'. Its sensuality is clinically safe in its immateriality: it is a copulation with the alter ego. Keats's Adam now dreams, creatively and procreatively, not of Eve but of himself. The utility of the enacted role is that it can be left standing as a hostage to the imperceptive world, which will mistake it for the truth. Byron hinted as much to the courtesan Harriette Wilson, who wished to add him to her list of trophies. 'A writer', he said, 'is in general very different from his productions.' He accepted Madame de Staël's accusation of frigidity as the highest of compliments to his technical gift for simulation. Byron's libertinism is, for the same reason, almost chaste—a system of 'violent exercise' calculated (like reading, boxing, swimming and writing, which he numbers as drills for self-forgetful bodily exertion) to waste and wean the clamorous flesh. His vegetarianism was not an ethical principle like Shelley's but a psychological prescription. To slim is to attenuate one's substance, to shed an old identity—returning to Cambridge in 1807 Byron is delighted that he has to tell everyone his name, because he is now so much taller and thinner that his friends do not recognise him—or approximate, in Byron's equivalent of Shelley's mystic death-wish, to no identity at all: after losing weight Byron marvels how little there now is of him, how residual his existence is. His busy social life is in no way inconsistent with this profession. He believes that his weight is controlled in London, where he cannot take exercise, by the evening crushes at crowded parties. If his discipline of abstinence falters, he hands himself over to the doctors for medical punishment. At Patras he was vomited, purged and clystered; at Missolonghi he was bled by the application of leeches, and killed in the process of being cured.

Travel is a symptom of the same urge to outpace the body and to subtract from the self. Kept on the move, as Harold or Juan are, Byron will be saved from the fate of having to be someone. Byron's internationalism is a reflex of his global indifference. He has his own version of that romantic archetype, the last man: unlike Coleridge he does not grieve over his inability to feel what he sees, and enjoys being a tourist on an earth he disdains to care for; loving no one, he is, he says, solitary, '& so perfectly a Citizen of the World'. His tractability includes the capacity to adapt not only to all persons but to all peoples, to different climes and countries. Ironically dismissing the itinerant sentimentality of Yorick, Byron can manage these feats because he is equally alienated from all the other human creatures he temporarily engages with, and from all the foreign places where he chooses, for the time being, to reside. As a romantic at the end of his tether, he anticipates Meursault, the outsider of Albert Camus's novel, whose entitlement to philosophical wisdom (and the cause of his social outlawry) is, in a reaction Byron analysed in himself, his lack of emotion at his mother's funeral. Writing assists this quest for self-oblivion.

As Byron makes love to be rid of the irritation of desire, so he writes with the hasty, merely manual vigour of self-abuse. Like Wordsworth, he confesses his creative discontent in an aside about his handwriting which, he says, 'depends upon my pens & my humours—*both* as you know none of the best'. Writing is not the signature of the self but the pen's time-killing free-association. He calls rhyming a pastime. He spins words to occupy the tedium of existence: his casual brilliance is a remedy for the spleen of Harold, or the burned-out fatigue of the narrator in *Don Juan*. Byron identifies the virtue of literature with the physical act of making it when he says that 'the end of all scribblement is to amuse'. The idea of art as entertainment always implies a boredom which has to be diverted. That ennui is Byron's name for Wordsworth's visionary conditions of tranquillity or dreariness. But whereas Wordsworth becomes a votary of the past, stultifying into that deathly calm, Byron races away from it by vowing to live and write in a brisk, instantly amnesiac present. Hence the appropriateness of the letter as a form for him: it is a thing dispatched as soon as finished, never to be seen again by its miscreant maker.

His Venetian anecdote 'Beppo' is his highest-spirited and also his saddest commentary on these rules of life and writing which are at once a reckless acceleration of romanticism and a disenchanted renunciation of it. The 'cicisbeo' in the poem frequents the 'Improvisatori', and can himself 'extemporise some stanzas'. Improvisation is here not only Byron's chosen means for conducting the poem, which digresses with Sternean abandon until it is curtailed for being 'exceeding tedious to my mind', but his policy for conducting existence itself: make yourself up as you go, adjust yourself to accidents, take no thought either of yesterday or of tomorrow. When Beppo disappears, Laura replaces him. He meanwhile, instead of pining for her, keeps busy in his new trade as a pirate. When he returns, there is no showdown between himself and the Count. All three characters are blessed by their Byronic cold blood, and do not care enough to make a fuss.

Beneath the facile acrobatics of the verse there is a sagging defeatism. *Sprezzatura* no longer means, as it did for Byron's courtly predecessors in the Renaissance, pretending that he feels less than he does; it enables him to go giddily through the motions of living, writing or (in Laura's garrulous case) of talking while feeling nothing. 'Beppo' is a Lenten poem. Byron explains that the Carnival, during which it is set, means 'farewell to flesh': farewell, too, to that fleshly gusto and carnal intensity which had become the avocations of the romantic. Lent is the season of penance, the terminal winter of the odes by Shelley and Keats. Byron's diet adopts Lent's prohibition on 'solid meats'; his scepticism is also a Lenten verdict on defunct pleasures. But he manages, in this society of pious abstinence, to define his own version of that easeful death dreamed of by Keats and Shelley. This is the bonus of unconsciousness. The atmosphere at Venice panders to a discreet oblivion: 'Night with dusky mantle covers / The skies (and the more duskily the better).' So do the gondolas. Shelley, visiting Byron in Venice, had used one of these as a meteorological command-post, observing a cataclysmic storm above the lagoon from within the cabin. The surface of the water remained unruffled as Shelley glided over it, and he could fancy himself to be directing the elements, like Ariel provoking the tempest on Prospero's orders. For Byron, though, the gondola is not a place to see out of but a place he could not be seen in, another convenience for self-obliteration: crouched within it, 'none can make out what you say or do.' In accordance with the Lenten observances of the poem, and with his own hankering after cessation, Byron sees the gondola as a navigable grave, 'just like a coffin clapt in a canoe': his answer to Shelley's airships and the 'cradle shell' of Keats's 'sea-born Venus' or Endymion's gusting bark.

The insouciance of the characters is shared by Byron, and it prevents him from caring about his poem. He neither knows nor wants to know the heroine's real name, and he will not disclose the identity of another female character. These people are 'nought to me', he attests. The composition of the poem also has to be negated. Byron grimaces at his own incompetence, and pretends to have constant recourse to a rhyming dictionary. He will not, in defiance of Coleridge, even suspend disbelief in his own imagination. As for the tattle about Beppo, he says, 'For stories—but I don't believe the half of them.' Arriving at his anticlimax, he turns out to have had no story to tell. When Wordsworth cannot tell a story, in 'The Idiot Boy' or 'Simon Lee', he at least trusts that the reader will be empathetically able to construct the tale and make good the inadequacies of the poet; Byron here will not tell the story because he cannot be bothered. Writing is in any case an absurd and Sisyphean labour, the occupation of emptiness in life and the covering-up of blankness on the page. Byron is reprieved by the lack of paper, and allowed his own lapse into unselfconsciousness:

> My pen is at the bottom of a page,
>   Which being finish'd, here the story ends;
> 'Tis to be wish'd it had been sooner done.

For Keats the creative imperative was to replete the page, to swell or plump it like the gourd or shell—storage-cavities for life—in 'To Autumn'. He sought in writing a narrative to 'make 4000 Lines of one bare circumstance and fill them with Poetry'. Shelley longed for the page's erasure, for the abstract luminiscence of whiteness. His 'Intellectual Beauty' is an 'unseen Power', intelligible neither visually nor verbally. Byron hastily fills the page, but then at once, having used up the space available to him, tears it up and discards it. In doing so, he has, he hopes, dispensed with romanticism.

— 28 —
Imagination and Fiction

'Did I wake or sleep? Had I been dreaming?' asks Jane Eyre as the fortune-telling gypsy metamorphoses into Mr Rochester. She is paraphrasing Keats's inquisition in 'Ode to a Nightingale', and converting its wistfulness into an edict of the romantic novel. In poetry, the imagination takes as its model Adam's dream of Eve, which he awoke (as Keats said) to find true. A god, however, is necessary as the maker and deliverer of that envisioned Eve, and the poets must wait on the divinity's whim. The rainbow comes and goes, beyond their control. But in the romantic novel characters assume this godly power of creativity, and triumphantly substantialise the shadows of their fantasy. Fiction no longer means mendacity—the specious, unscrupulous freedom to write between the lines of literal truth exploited by Pamela, Shamela, Moll Flanders, and refined by Yorick into an ironic duplicity. It connotes a visionary will, a rite of conjuration whereby ardent fiction abolishes demeaning fact.

Jane Eyre is branded by her aunt and by her persecutors at school as a liar. The accusation recurs: when Rochester calls Jane a fairy, Adèle laughs off the conceit by calling him 'un vrai menteur'; he describes as 'a fiction—an impudent invention' Jane's story of St John's proposal. Though on this occasion she declares that she speaks 'the literal truth', she has earlier admitted to the categorical deceit practised by romantic imagination, which turns to the novel because it cannot tolerate the world as realistically constituted. When Eliza asks if the portrait of Rochester she has drawn represents some acquaintance, Jane candidly states 'Of course, I lied.' It is her professional protest against reality. It is also a covert truth, for her sketch of Rochester is the absent-minded doodling of subconscious desire; her image of him precedes the actuality, and throughout the novel directs the fate of the real being, who is the victim of Jane's libidinal creative drive.

Persuasion is the name that Jane Austen, more gently and insinuatingly, gives to this imperious faculty; but in the novels of the Brontës, imagination, like Frankenstein, generates monstrous births. One of them is called Rochester, another—the inchoate mass of a nobody from nowhere, shaped into identity by the imagining sorcery of the characters who invent, adore and destroy him—is Heathcliff.

In Jane Austen's novels, a talent for imaginative fabulation is essential for the conduct of social life. Lies for Elinor in *Sense and Sensibility* (1811) are daring mental initiatives. Her sister Marianne will not dissemble; Elinor therefore assumes the heroic responsibility of devising and acting out gestures of social palliation. She rouses herself to the imaginative duty 'of telling lies when politeness required it', conscientiously obliging herself to praise people like Lady Middleton whom she despises or venturing—as intrepidly as a Gothic heroine—into a territory of social danger when she visits Mrs John Dashwood.

As Jane Austen sees it, society is itself an insecure fiction, and can be maintained only by a co-operative effort of imagination, like that made by Elinor in studying her attitude to Edward and resolving, despite her resentment, to treat him 'as she thought he ought to be treated from the family connection'. The crassest financial calculations require the same inflation of spirit, since it is imaginary quantities which are being juggled, as by John and Fanny in their conversation about the life-expectancy of Mrs Dashwood and her entitlement to an annuity. Disbursements are a romantic challenge to the mercenary John, sublime aggrandisements of the grudging self, which glories in its dilation: he 'really thought himself equal' to bestowing £1,000 apiece on his sisters. Sums of money are cherished because they license our fantasies and underwrite our fictions. Spending them demands extravagant leaps of imagination. Marianne, awarding herself £2,000 a year, mentally purchases a presumptive existence at Combe Magna, while Edward dreams up budgets for dilettantism—Elinor will commission prints, Marianne collect music and volumes of romantic poetry, he will be blissfully idle. Margaret, too, wishes that 'some body would give us all a large fortune a-piece!' Though she regrets 'the insufficiency of wealth'—that impoverishment of the real, which defrauds the romantic—Elinor approves the harmless fictionality of the hope. Marriages survive thanks to a complicity of fancy. Mrs Palmer abides her husband's boorishness by imagining his jibes to be witty. Just as she has hypothesised a character for him, so he fabricates another for himself. Elinor perceives that he is not genuinely ill-natured or ill-bred, but ambitious of distinction; he affects scorn for others because he believes it to be the demeanour of a lofty Byronic misanthropy.

The novel of society is a domestication of the Gothic, replacing mystery with crafty mystification, the detection of crimes with the intuiting of emotional secrets. Elinor tensely tries to understand the implications of Anne Steele's reference to Edward without betraying herself by asking a question; Mrs Dashwood will not enquire whether Marianne is engaged to Willoughby, confining herself to tactful, baffled speculation. In her own estimation, Elinor is a colleague of Catherine Morland. Perplexed by the intricate deceit of human relationships, she mistrusts her own perceptions, which she knows to be no more than imaginative conjectures. When she corrects Edward's error about Marianne, she says (with my italics), 'I have frequently *detected* myself in such kind of mistakes, in a total misapprehension of character . . .: *fancying* people so much more gay or grave, or ingenious or stupid than they really are.'

The romantic problem is differently resolved in *Pride and Prejudice* (1813). Here the characters are detained by society and by the consequences of their own bad judgements, like Mr Bennet imprisoned in his marriage; however, rather than fantasising their way to freedom as Marianne prodigally does, they detach and distance themselves by the stealthier method of irony, which enables Mr Bennet to insult his wife or Elizabeth to avow that she first loved Darcy when she saw his estates at Pemberley.

Irony is the style of their irresponsibility: the incognito not of the moralist (as Kierkegaard called it) but of the amoralist—of Mr Bennet wishing his wife dead when he says, during a dispute about the entail, that he may yet manage to outlive her, or of Elizabeth, when charged with her contradictory change of heart about Darcy, shrugging off her past and dismissing consistency by arguing that 'in such cases as these a good memory is unpardonable'. This idiom is specifically the romantic irony that Jean Paul Richter venerated in Sterne. Richter saw it as a metaphysical talent. It is an aptitude for self-overcoming, and therefore a miniature replica of the sublime. Acknowledging our littleness, we triumph over it (in the sublimatory ecstasies of the romantic confrontation with landscape) or (in the ironist's subtle palaver) negotiate our way round it. Elizabeth cannot overthrow the dictatorship of Lady Catherine; she can outwit her. Mr Bennet cannot extenuate his failings as a parent, or the follies of his offspring; he decides, though, to delight in them and to pretend that they are of his choosing. He elects the reprobate Wickham as his favourite among his sons-in-law, and determines in advance to find Collins, if unbearable, at least divertingly so.

The pain of irony is that, for all its high-spirited irreverence, it is a confirmation of impotence. And in a sad contradiction of that imperative imaginativeness which motivates the romantic novel and secures Jane Eyre her happy ending, it is an impotence here astringently shared by Jane Austen. The novel's magic, assigning husbands to Eleanor Tilney or Anne Elliot with such happy unreality, cannot assist the novelist. Jane Austen is as beleaguered as her characters are by social contingencies. She looks to the novel to provide her with a fortress of solitude where she can speak her mind—the equivalent of Mr Bennet's sacrosanct library, of Jane's distressed withdrawals upstairs, or of Elizabeth's daily walks at Hunsford. But her power of epigrammatic regimentation, expounding the laws of the sexual mart in the first sentence of the novel, or lethally summing up Mrs Bennet at the end of the initial chapter, is illusory. Mrs Bennet, unharmed by Jane Austen's slights or by her husband's too-subtle barbs, succeeds in making him call on Bingley despite his reluctance, and triumphantly gets rid of her eligible daughters. Nor is the novel allowed to be the citadel of privacy which Fanny Price in *Mansfield Park* (1814), by her reading, makes of it. It must be populated. The novelist has to have the indiscriminate gregariousness of Mrs Bennet, convinced of 'the necessity of constant company for her friends', or the inner insufficiency of Wickham, who *'must* have employment and society'. Irony in Jane Austen's case, as in the romantic Sterne's, is at once comic evasion and tragic capitulation.

Except, that is, in *Persuasion* (1818). Here the mild sigh emitted by Anne, as she thinks that soon Wentworth may be again at Kellynch, anticipates the passionate midnight cry of Rochester which, reverberating across the country, summons Jane to him: it is Wordsworth's correspondent breeze, nature's respiration and the poet's inspiration; an animating breath which insists, like Shelley's west wind, on being heard. *Persuasion* undoes Wordsworth's elegiac sense of poetry as emotion subdued by recollection. It proposes, in magically recalling Wentworth, that emotion can be regained.

Anne at first has the morosely Wordsworthian habit, dreading the renewal of 'former feelings' and the 'recollection' of 'former times'. She quits the room to induce a meditative calm. Poetry is dangerous, she tells the Byronic enthusiast Benwick, too nervously taxing; it must be—as are Wordsworth's spots of time in *The Prelude*, when their lyrical instantaneousness yields to prosaic explication and sermonising—subdued to 'a long application of solitude and reflection'. The Wordsworthian creative process is a painful rule of life for Anne. She exiles herself to the lodge 'in a sort of desolate tranquillity', and even when Wentworth's avowal of love arrives, she can think only of the necessary vigil of solitude which 'might have tranquillised her'. If disruptive poetic emotion is disallowed, there remains in compensation the Wordsworthian mnemonic tour, returning devoutly, like the poet himself to Tintern Abbey or the Wanderer to the ruined cottage or Michael to the sheep-fold, to the grave-sites of interred feeling. Anne and her party intend such a ritual succession of grieving pilgrimages to Lyme: 'These places must be visited, and visited again, to make the worth of Lyme understood.' This is the journey of bereft consciousness through a depleted, depeopled world. The novel begins during autumn, with nature's expiry; Lyme is visited out of season, after its annual life has died out of it. Anne herself seems, like Keats's pallid withering knight, to be the dying year, her bloom gone, her spirits clouded. Her unguarded blushes (symptoms of an 'age of emotion' she wishes she had outgrown) are perhaps the 'last smiles' of that moribund season.

All Jane Austen's novels are weather-wise; still, whereas the characters of *Sense and Sensibility* consult nature for confirmation of their volatile moods, interpreting elemental whims psychologically, like Marianne 'observing the direction of the wind, watching the variations of the sky and imagining an alteration in the air', those of *Persuasion* are eroded and abraded by a nature which sentences them to slow death. This has been the lot of Elizabeth, worn down by 'thirteen winters' revolving frosts', now mourningly bedecked, like a dead tree, with black ribbons in memory of Mr Elliot's wife. Sir Walter's vanity is a terrified scrutiny of facial landscapes for the onset of wintry disfigurement or decrepitude: seamen, he believes, get prematurely reddened and weather-beaten by exposure, and 'a sharp frost' will be fatal to the looks of all but one woman in a thousand. He has a haunted vision of a stricken world, posthumously crowded with those dead leaves that Shelley sees as pestilential multitudes or as harried ghosts. At Bath, he reports, the streets are full of scarecrows. But the Shelleyan winter prophesies a spring. Nature's life is cyclical and serial after all, and this is Anne's salvation. The toil of the farmers announces that they mean 'to have spring again'; like Anne, Mrs Smith is seasonally regenerated, her 'spring of felicity' evident in 'the glow of her spirits'. The Wordsworthian routine of visiting tombs and annotating epitaphs, leaving copies of poems in the places where they were composed so they, too, can decay into earth, is contradicted by a return to life—the recovery of Louisa, given up for dead after her fall on the Cobb; the homeopathic healing of the Musgrove child's dislocated collar-bone; the revitalisation of Anne, whose heart is stirred to beat again 'in spite of herself'; the recuperation she predicts for the lachrymose Benwick, who 'will rally again, and be happy with another'. Anne's is a winter's tale, of Hermione born again as Perdita. The secret of survival is trust in nature. 'The fine wind' at Lyme restores to her 'the bloom and freshness of youth.'

Such wise submission is what Jane Austen means by persuasion. It is the strength of tractability, of bending so as not to break, of acknowledging that life is change; in Anne it is a 'persuadable temper', in Mrs Smith an 'elasticity of mind', the gift of 'Nature alone'. This resilience enables Anne to live through 'the stretch of mind, the war of spirits' she suffers. Wentworth, speaking of Benwick, declines to believe in an emotional rejuvenation. He declares it an obscenity that a man should presume to 'recover from' love for a woman. But his own career has already prepared him to disprove his morbid edict. His masculine equivalent to Anne's patient ductility is called weathering—the sailor's capacity for 'bearing most rough usage, and riding out the heaviest weather'.

Nevertheless, this abiding acceptance is not the novel's whole truth. The happy ending is also willed; it pays tribute to the redemptive agency of romantic imagination, remaking the world, devising its own heaven, as does the word 'Resurgam' inscribed by Jane Eyre on the tablet she places on the grassy mound where Helen Burns is buried. Anne fears imagination as a fond, seductive deceiver, like Keats's elf. 'What wild imaginations one forms, where dear self is concerned!' she says when she learns of Mr Elliot's true motives. Jane Austen, though, exercises that impetuous, probability-scorning imagination on her heroine's behalf, and with it persuades reality to grant her the wish she scarcely dares to utter.

The later romantic novel does not worry, as a concession to the real, about being persuasive; it defiantly insists, as Blake did in his comment on Ossian, that we believe its fabulations to be truth. Imagination is now the incitement of a hallucination. Whether by Anne or for her, Wentworth is a recreation, a memory won back to incarnation in the present. The Brontës attempt something more extreme: an engendering of new life; an imaginative parthenogenesis. This indeed is what *Jane Eyre* and *Wuthering Heights* (both published in 1847) are about. They do in the novel what Frankenstein does in his laboratory.

Charlotte Brontë wrote to Coleridge in 1840 about the excitement of god-like parentage, begetting monsters, which she felt in her fantasies about her imaginary land of Angria. 'It is very edifying and profitable to create a world out of one's brain and people it with inhabitants who are like so many Melchisedecs—without father, without mother, without descent, having neither beginning of days nor end of life.' Carlyle, too, reports on rumours that his Teufelsdröckh is 'a kind of Melchizedek, without father or mother of any kind': a brain-child, in other words. This perversely immaculate artistic conception brings to birth novelistic characters who are, like Blake's tiger, ungovernable automata. Emily makes a declaration similar to her sister's in a poem of 1844, 'O thy bright eyes must answer now.' Like Charlotte speaking of edification, she invokes liturgical usages only to replace them with a new religion of imaginative black magic. The poem is a hymn addressed not to God but to a demon who, begotten by Emily, is the male muse with whom she couples:

> Thee, ever present, phantom thing—
> My slave, my comrade, and my King!

As in the aesthetics of Hazlitt, imagination is a despot. The demon serves Emily as a slave. Yet it is at the same time a king, subjecting her (as Sarah did Hazlitt) to a 'Darling Pain'. Conception means copulation with this demon-lover, who 'by day and night' is 'my intimate delight'. The poem ventures a bold romantic theogeny:

> And am I wrong to worship where
> Faith cannot doubt nor Hope despair
> Since my own soul can grant my prayer?

Because the Brontë novels deal with an unbridled profane creativity, they seek to supplant the book spoken by God about his own creation of the world. Like Blake inflaming words in the illumination of his poems, they are making holy books of their own, texts authorised by a divinity within themselves. Those who wish to oppress Jane Eyre do so with the Bible's aid. It is endlessly quoted at Lowood, dully adhered to by Eliza (who studies the Common Prayer Book for the sake of 'the Rubric'), employed as a curse on Jane by St John when he reads from Revelations. In *Wuthering Heights* likewise Joseph exploits it as a source of animadversion: '"Yah knaw whet t'Scriptures ses." And he began quoting several texts, referring us to chapters and verses where we might find them.' Jane is not daunted. She is determined, with the aid of an ordaining language, to be a creator: 'I learned the first two tenses of the verb *Etre*.' When Bessie cannot say the name of the island to which Jane's uncle disappeared, Jane supplies it, as if Madeira were, like Angria, her own invention; and it is eventually the place from which the wishful fairy gold of her inheritance emerges.

Wuthering Heights proposes a choice between the dictatorial, repressive authority of sermons and citations and the personal, imaginative authorship of one's own dreams and fantasies. Lockwood's eye wanders as he falls asleep 'from manuscript to print'—from Cathy's journal to the pious discourse of Jabes Branderham. Literature, too, has moved in that direction, from script to print, from the voice to the machine, from the Ancient Mariner's confession to the orthodox marginal gloss on it; Emily Brontë reverses this evolution, reanimating the 'faded hieroglyphics' which are Cathy's testimony, spirit not letter or (in Jabes's manic numbering of 'seventy times seven' sins) number, soul not body. Nelly's contempt for the correspondence between Linton and young Catherine makes her scoff, 'Why, it's good enough to be printed!' To prevent this, she insists that the letters must be burned. When this society settles down into the worship and elucidation of print, it has lost its original imaginative frenzy, and instead of living poems is writing or reading them. Heathcliff destroys Catherine's books; she defends herself by teaching Hareton to read and sending him a handsome volume wrapped in white paper and tied with ribbon. The votaress of the book, like Fanny Price, has made the same error which confounds Langland's pilgrimage: mistaking the letter for the spirit behind it, failing to understand that literature is a medium only, through which prophetic messages pass.

Jane Eyre is not guilty of this fault. She scandalises Brocklehurst when she tells him she is fond only of some parts of the Bible—Genesis among them—but not the Psalms, which 'are not interesting': the Bible excites her if God is speaking, not if pious commentators are writing and issuing moral dictation, as they do to Brocklehurst's infant 'who knows six Psalms by heart'. The entranced, mediumistic state, whereby we make ourselves the conduits for truths expressed through us without our interpreting them, a literature which speaks in tongues, is the creative mania of the Brontës. Cathy says 'I *am* Heathcliff!' because he is 'always, always in my mind'. He plans to invade her coffin so he can be absorbed into her corpse and Linton will 'not know which is which'. Jane blazingly paraphrases their necrophiliac fusion when she tells Rochester, 'I am not talking to you now through the medium of custom, conventionalities, nor even of mortal flesh;—it is my spirit that addresses your spirit; just as if both had passed through the grave and we stood at God's feet.' Here the union dispenses even with mediation. It is because imagination uses Jane to articulate itself—borrowing her voice to broadcast the madwoman's laughter, or Rochester's cry—that she must reject St John's profession of service to another deity: she is to be a medium, not a missionary.

Imaginative generation is a travail and an agony in *Wuthering Heights*. Cathy dies in child-birth; the body cannot support the fantasy's insemination of it. No one can be sure who they are because, having so intensely and (as Blake's angel reprimands him) shamingly imagined other people, they intimately possess one another. This is why the novel is narrated recessively, as an interlocking set of subjective testimonies. Even the narrators have been imagined by those about whom they tell the story. Cathy deliriously sees in Nelly a 'withered hag' gathering elf-bolts, and in Lockwood's dream he is cast as the sinner in Joseph's crazed pamphlet. Heathcliff's case states the Melchizedek-like conundrum of imagination and its dangerous demonology: who implants these beings in us, and requires us to deliver them into the world? Nothing is known about Heathcliff; everything must therefore be imagined. The novel begins with Lockwood's inept imagining of him in his own image as a fashionable misanthrope and 'a capital fellow'. But Lockwood can only identify himself as 'Your new tenant, sir.' It is as if he, too, is to be a tributary of Heathcliff and his psychological dependent, the tenant—when inside the house—of Heathcliff's fantasy. When Earnshaw first brings Heathcliff back from Liverpool, he seems to have created him *ex nihilo*, as God did the world. He hints, however, that the child may be progeny of another kind—'you must e'en take it as a gift of God; though it's dark almost as if it came from the devil.' Genealogies are surmised for him. Perhaps he is 'a little Lascar, or an American or a Spanish castaway', perhaps the spawn of the Emperor of China or an Indian queen. Lockwood extrapolates futures for him, wondering if he went on the grand tour, or emigrated to America. Nelly vexes herself 'with imagining some fit parentage for him', and wonders whether he might be a ghoul or a vampire. His parentage is indeed the imaginative incrimination of them all: 'the little dark thing, harboured by a good man', coming from nowhere, is bred—as Prospero acknowledges of Caliban—inside all of us. Isabella denounces Heathcliff as a monster, 'not a human being', and wishes that he might be expunged from creation and from her memory—impossible because it is within her memory and within the reveries or mental undergrowths of everyone in the novel that he was begotten, and these people cannot, as Frankenstein finds, kill off or disown what they have culpably and collectively imagined. Family resemblances are another kind of imaginative incubus.

When Heathcliff reproduces himself, he engenders his own image. He describes Hareton as 'a personification of my youth, not a human being'. A birth is the fantasy's procreation of its spectral replica, which Jane Eyre (sacrilegiously adopting the language of biblical typology) calls its type. 'Hareton's aspect', Heathcliff says, 'was the ghost of my immortal love.' The spirits which prowl these moors—like the dead uncle who terrorises Jane in the red-room or the 'Gytrash' she conjures up in the likeness of Rochester, or like Jane herself worn down by her sufferings into 'a mere spectre!'—are the legatees of a perverse resurrection. 'My soul's bliss kills my body', Heathcliff declares. Once he has cast off that physical case, the imago will metamorphi-cally be set free. Jane, however, is determined to embody the fantasy, to wed it in the flesh, as she does when she announces, 'Reader, I married him.' Isabella denies human being to Heathcliff; when Jane returns, Rochester, who cannot see her, demands reassurance—'You are altogether a human being, Janet?' She can answer, 'I conscientiously believe so', which leaves room for doubt: she is after all a spirit who tends on mortal thoughts and cravings, at the behest of imagination.

In Emily's novel, death is imagination's midwife; in Charlotte's, it is the force of sex which brings the imagination's plotted desires to pass. Brockle-hurst believes Jane to be inhabited by the Evil One. In fact she is commandeered by the 'radiant angel' of Emily's poem, and can exercise the shaping power which Coleridge called esemplastic. She is a spirit of imagination who conjoins not poetic images but human bodies. Brocklehurst's imp of mischief is Jane's creative genie. 'Genius', she says of the beautiful Miss Ingram, 'is said to be self-conscious'; Jane's own is a capacity for unselfcons-ciousness, incarnating fantasies without analysing them. In the course of the novel she renovates herself, deserting the identity she has been assigned. To Brocklehurst she answers, when he demands her name, 'Jane Eyre, sir'; later she advertises for employment using the initials J.E.; Adèle, who cannot say her name, vaporises it by pronouncing it 'Aire'; and she at last renames herself Jane Elliott. While uncreating herself, she is working at the creation of Rochester (and of everyone else, for even the mad laughter of the wife in the attic is a version of Jane's ecstatic, imprisoned creativity). Mrs Fairfax annoys her by being incurious about their employer. 'Mr. Rochester was Mr. Rochester in her eyes.' She lacks Jane's gift for characterising people, which is a mode of invoking spirits, since as soon as she has decided on an image of him he materialises before her to confirm it. Finally she absorbs him into herself, and obliges him, like the voice at the séance, to exist through her mediation. After he is blinded, she supplies him with sight by giving him her verbal transcriptions of the world to look at. But while she is mesmerically watching him, he is causing an equivalent imaginative spell to work on her as he observes her, unseen, from curtained recesses or through doors left ajar. His disguise as the sibyl declares this: he shares her creative power of divination and uses it against her, novelistically intuiting her secrets and seeing into her heart.

Charlotte Brontë's early chronicles of Angria or the Glasstown Confederacy were written with her eyes shut. She envisaged these agoraphobic cities of fantasy, she told Coleridge, 'on the retina of that "inward eye" which is said to be "the bliss of solitude".' Her model was pictorial: the infested, storm-beset Babylon or gas-lit Pandemonium of John Martin's paintings. But this does not make her art simply the description of a pre-existent world; she must invent that world before she can describe it, and the desperation of her writing derives from her awareness of the gap between the vague mental picture and its verbal illustrations, between the vision and the words which traduce it. 'Words cannot depict', she complains of a landscape in the novelette 'Julia'; Zamorna's glowering rage in 'Mina Laury' is 'more easily conceived than described'; and another of the Angrian heroines, Caroline Vernon, has 'something about her . . . which I cannot convey in words'.

These narratives are about the difficulty of reconciling apparition and appearance, the poetic intuiting of a phantasm or a symbol (which can remain unseen like Keats's nightingale or Shelley's even more impalpable intellectual beauty) and the novelistic representation of the real. In her conduct of them, Charlotte Brontë is forever seeking the assistance of a reader to help her form the fantasies, to make them real by sharing her belief in them. Elucidation of her private and dreamily nocturnal fiction is her concession to this other and more scrupulously rational being: 'The reader will ask why [Caroline] had set her heart so fixedly on this point. I'll tell him plainly to make no mystery of it.' Yet in pretending to defer to that reader, she is enlisting him, as Coleridge's narrators do their interlocutors, as an accomplice and a surrogate. Mina passes in her carriage, 'deeply veiled'. Charlotte Brontë will not (because she cannot) describe her: 'You', she says, 'must guess at her features.' Everywhere there are directives to the reader, instructions for visualising the invisible. 'See, there are two gentlemen lounging easily on the porch' or, more imperatively, 'Look! hundreds of cavalry men are washing & watering their horses in that clear river.' Charlotte herself claims to possess the freedom to move unseen through her own creation, visiting it like a revenant, and while Thornton in the council of war pines for his wife the novelist traverses the distance between them and reports, 'I stand by Julia in her chamber, I watch her as she sits alone.'

The novelist is in exactly the position of the dead Cathy in *Wuthering Heights*: a ghostly mind without a body, clawing at the window of the real world and begging for admission to it, yet refused entry and exiled to watch—like the young Cathy and Heathcliff gazing through the casements at Thrushcross Grange—an existence she has created but in which she cannot participate. The problem of the Angrian stories is that the fantasy conjured up by Charlotte will not obey her. It is as skittish and unreliable as the spirits Blake set himself to sketch for Varley. And when the imagined beings dissolve, the novelist, like the ghostly Cathy, dematerialises, too. This is why description is an almost legalistic obsession for her, because a pictorial accounting can anchor the wraiths in bodily substance, detain them in reality. In 'Captain Henry Hastings' description is extorted from the novelist by intimidation. Charles Townshend—the novelist who writes this chronicle, and who supplied Charlotte with a pseudonym for her correspondence with Coleridge—is required by the police to give them details of a Mr Wilson's appearance. This Wilson is the Byronically profligate Hastings. Townshend, who as novelist has invented him, finally agrees to part with the information, and adds 'it shall be done con amore'. In anatomising the miscreant's looks, he lovingly creates him all over again. When Hastings next appears, Townshend is spared the necessity of depiction: 'You remember, reader, what I said of Wilson—I need not paint his portrait anew—for this was Wilson.' Only a vigil of imagination can sustain this world, and when imagination falters or is fatigued, the world itself ends in abrupt evanescence. These are the moments which correspond to Lockwood's blocking the window against the intrusion of Cathy. The novelist's characters escape him, and without them he cannot himself continue to exist. Louisa Dance in 'Passing Events' disappears on an evening walk. 'I know no more,' Charlotte reports, 'but she has not since been heard of.' Townshend's narrative is suddenly consumed by the darkness in which, with those closed eyes, Charlotte is trying so anxiously to realise it. Just as Elizabeth is vanishing into the 'dark passages to the distant kitchen' Townshend himself lapses into non-being: 'My candle is nearly burnt out & I must close the chapter—.'

The opposed motives of visionary insight and literal seeing have a complex iconography in Charlotte Brontë. The difference between them is that between a window and a mirror. Romance is an opening of windows, of Keatsian magic casements; realism is a mere shaming confrontation with mirrors. The poverty of realism is that it can only reflect. Romanticism demands the refraction of the real. The delirious Cathy in *Wuthering Heights* has the looking-glass covered with a shawl because the image it returns to her reminds her of her prosaic confinement to herself and to a bodily fate, whereas she, refusing to believe that she is 'entirely contained here', gazes 'beyond, and far beyond—you would have said out of this world'; Charlotte more drastically smashes those obsequious mirrors. Zenobia has a mirror on the polished toilette in her sanctum. After her quarrel with Northangerland, the remnants of that glass interpret her state: she 'said nothing, she could not speak, but a destructive crack & the splendid fragments of a shivered mirror told what she felt'. Lord Hartford, enraged by a bulletin about the Hastings affair, kicks the cheval-glass in his dressing-room, 'thereby shivering to atoms the noble reflect it was affording'. In 'Passing Events' Charlotte calls her mind 'a prism full of colours but not of forms': better the fragmentation of glass, which impedes and redirects light and in doing so brilliantly disembodies the formal world, than that transparency—the mirror in the roadway—which became the boast of the nineteenth-century novel.

Byron uses the image of the fractured mirror in *Childe Harold's Pilgrimage*, where it stands for the fission of unitary character into the multitude of smithereen-like selves:

> Even as the broken mirror, which the glass
> In every fragment multiplies; and makes
> A thousand images of one that was,
> The same, and still the more, the more it breaks.

From the splinters Byron assembles the kaleidoscope of his identity. His mirror breaks inwards: romanticism introverts the real. That fragmentation is the rule of lyric poetry, dividing the continuity of time into separate, recessive, ecstatic moments. But in the realist novel the mirror rather than collapsing in on itself exponentiates outwards, and instead of Byron's multiplication of facets, all of them puzzling because partial, it systematically extends and expands its view until it can encompass all available realities.

This happens in the Osborne drawing room in *Vanity Fair* (1848), where 'the great glass over the mantelpiece, faced by the other great console glass at the opposite end of the room, increased and multiplied between them the brown holland bag in which the chandelier hung; until you saw these brown holland bags fading away in endless perspectives, and this apartment of Miss Osborne's seemed the centre of a system of drawing rooms'—which of course it is, since in this novel no fate is singular. In Byron the one splinters into the disparate many, which have nothing in common. Thackeray corrects this anarchic romantic individualism. It is the task of the novel to show that the many add up into one, that experience is connected and all lives interdependent. To the onanism of romantic fantasy, realism opposes the biblical injunction, remembered in Thackeray's description, to increase and multiply: it exhibits the plenitude of the world, and assists at its replenishment; it enumerates, with the statistical delight of Defoe, the quantity of realities which compound the real.

Yet this compilation can be in its turn subverted by the romantic awareness that our world is not anchored, but hangs suspended, like sooty Manchester in Carlyle's phrase, over the abyss. Teufelsdröckh is angered by the mirroring myopia of the novel: 'a whole immensity of Brussels carpets, and pier-glasses, and or-molu cannot hide from me that such Drawing-room is simply a section of Infinite Space, where so many God-created Souls do for the time meet together.' Romanticism reminds the novel of its relativity. The furnishings are the deceit of what Schopenhauer called representation; realism is the lie romanticism tells itself to cheer itself up. Reality itself is a fiction. 'Ours', says Carlyle when Louis XV dies, 'is a most fictile world; and man is the most fingent plastic of creatures. A world not fixable, not fathomable! An unfathomable Somewhat, which is *Not we*.'

Unlike Miss Osborne in her look-out, Jane Eyre writes in darkened chambers, mental fortresses sealed against the intrusion of rational light, as is Wuthering Heights with its 'narrow windows . . . deeply set in the wall', or Heathcliff's face, with its eyes withdrawing under their brows—the red-room with its shrouded windows and dimly gleaming mirror, the crib where she shelters with her doll, the room at Thornfield which she is 'glad . . . to find . . . of small dimensions', the mystic cell on the third storey. Apertures for sight are pinnacles for supervision: hidden by the window-curtain, she observes from her shadows the brilliance of the room where Rochester entertains his guests and silently—as unmoved mover and unseen seer—characterises them while they chatteringly caricature her. Rochester himself looks in through a window at his mistress's betrayal of him.

More violently, Emily's characters seek to break through the glazed medium which interposes between dream or desire and truth. They shatter windows, not only mirrors. Heathcliff vows to splinter the 'great glass panes' of Thrushcross Grange to rescue Cathy, and when the door is barred to him at the Heights hurls a stone through a window and enters that way; Catherine escapes through the lattice in her mother's room, and when Heathcliff is ready to die he moves to that chamber with a window 'wide enough for anybody to get through'. The magic casements open onto a feverish brain: Heathcliff's eyes have been called 'the clouded windows of hell', and after he is dead Nelly takes care to occlude that region of fantasy by closing both the windows and his eyes. But he insists on bearing witness, and his eyes, she notes, 'would not shut'.

Nelly's exorcistic shuttering marks an advance from romanticism to realism, from Heathcliff's visionary urgency ('I could *almost* see her, and yet I *could not*! . . . I must open my lids to see') or Rochester's contented blindness to an art which ascertains reality by visual inspection. Sick of shadows, Tennyson's Lady of Shalott in 1832 causes the mirror to crack. Charlotte's Hartford curses the mirror in order romantically to fight off the demeaning encroachment of the real; but the Lady wants to quit fantasy for actuality, and because art and life have become incompatible she is condemned the moment she leaves her hermitage. After this, the mirror's sorry duty is to signify the banality of the real. Wilde at the end of the nineteenth century disqualifies both romanticism and realism as mirrors too flatteringly untrue or too grossly truthful: the one enrages Caliban because it does not show him his warty face, the other sickens him because it does. In opposition to the mirror's artless fidelity Wilde proposes the picture of Dorian Gray, a portrait depicting what cannot be seen. The mirror suffers a final cheapening in Joyce, who in *Ulysses* likens the practice of reflection and representation he has superseded to the cracked looking-glass of a servant.

By the time it was published, *Wuthering Heights* already seemed the relic of an extinct culture. Charlotte had to apologise for what she called its artless rudeness. But the romanticism the Victorians discouraged had its epilogue elsewhere, with *Wuthering Heights* as one of its sacred texts. The painter Balthus was obsessed by it, and liked to dress in the saturnine costumes of Heathcliff; in 1933 he made a series of illustrations for it, concentrating on the feral squabbles between its characters when children. As Balthus represents them, they are sensual savages, contorted inside their straight-laced Victorian costumes: theirs is a tragedy of repression. Antonin Artaud said of Balthus's picture of 'Cathy Dressing' that 'the artist has used reality the better to crucify it'.

That crucifixion or excruciation is the programme of romanticism at its most violent in surrealism, and Luis Buñuel noted that *Wuthering Heights* was a favourite book of the surrealists. He filmed it in Mexico in 1954 as *Abismos de Pásion*, using as his musical score the chromatic anguish and febrile eroticism of *Tristan und Isolde*. He makes the novel, which ends in a Victorian pacification of its own imaginative mania, the sponsor of two later, outlandish and extreme variants of romanticism—German and musical in the quotations from Wagner; Spanish and visual in his own surrealism. Instead of the Victorian compromise with reality, the Wagnerian parallels enable the prohibited love to achieve consummation in death: Alejandro (the Mexican Heathcliff) invades the crypt where Catalina is buried and is shot there by Ricardo, the character who corresponds to Hindley; he subsides, bleeding and ecstatic, onto her corpse. What Buñuel interprets as Emily Brontë's necrophilia is a warrant for his own surrealism. The obsession of surrealism is the wormy metamorphosis of flesh into putrescence; it is a torture of organisms. Buñuel's people are instinctive predators whom society cannot restrain, surreal carnivores. Catalina roams the hills shooting vultures, and offers Alejandro a dagger with which to cut his throat; the Linton character, Eduardo, impales butterflies on pins, while his farm-hands stick and bleed a squealing pig; José (Emily's bigoted Joseph) grills frogs on a brazier; Ricardo feeds a fly to a hungry spider, while one of his gambling cronies boasts of having shot twenty rabbits on a recent hunt—though none of them, he regrets, was pregnant.

In England, romanticism was chastened by the incorrigibility of the real. *Wuthering Heights* ends with Lockwood's denial of his unsettling romantic vision. Having gained control of his own imagination, he pities its infirmity in others and derides its prodigies as superstition. Rochester arrives at the same prosaic certainty when Jane tells him that her uncle in Madeira has left her £500: 'This is practical!—this is real! I should never dream that.' The novel commits itself to the humbling admonishments of fact. Ravenswood chides Lucy in Scott's *Bride of Lammermoor* (1819) for her rhapsodic talk, saying that 'in poetry there is always fallacy, and sometimes falsehood'. It cannot prepare her for the ugly prosaic perils of existence—instead of the 'generous lion' which accompanies Una in *The Faerie Queene*, Lucy is menaced by a rampant bull, bellowing furiously—and it is a cause of her lunacy. A bogey-ridden beldame scares her with 'the old legendary tales'; deranged, she slaughters her husband. In Donizetti's opera *Lucia di Lammermoor* (1835) she is romantically reprieved by music, which treats her madness as a seraphic vocal concert. Scott's heroine has no such lyrical recourse, and dies gibbering not singing. His novel describes a bankrupt nobility holed up in dank sooty dwellings like Ravenswood's Wolf's Crag, meagerly fed by imbecile domestics, no longer able to afford the chivalric luxuries of romance. Lucy is a pawn in the legal and territorial squabbles between two degenerate, impoverished clans.

Jane Austen in *Emma* (1816) makes the declension from the romantic to the real the basis for a social covenant. The reckless individuality of romantic character is censured by Knightley, who compels Emma to understand that people are the clients, even the creations of society, without which they wouldn't exist. Each of us must serve what Rousseau called the general will, and good manners (Emma's duty of charity to the tiresome Miss Bates) or family loyalty (her inability to rid herself of her fretful father) are the penances of citizenship. Ford's, Highbury's principal shop, is the town's forum. Frank Churchill recognises that he will not be granted social membership until he has made a purchase there. Goodness means absorption by the uses and interests of others—the garrulous extroversion of Miss Bates, whose conversation resounds with the beatitude of a social existence; the peripatetic errands of mercy of Dr Perry, talked of incessantly but so busy attending to the sustenance of civilization and the suppression of its discontents that he has no time actually to appear in the novel. Emma marries Knightley in ratification of the social contract, abiding by 'the wishes, the hopes, the confidence, the predictions of the small band of true friends who witnessed the ceremony'.

Here the Victorian novelistic career, apprenticed to reality and therefore to society, begins. It is Charlotte Brontë's prescription for her own later heroines—for Shirley in 1849, who is ejected 'from an enchanted region to the real world' and admonished to 'look Life in its iron face: stare Reality out of its brassy countenance'; for the characters of *The Professor* (1857) who, deprived of Jane Eyre's transforming magic, will be ringed by no 'golden halo of fiction'. Initially there is an ethical fervour to the novel's compromise with social reality. Dorothea in *Middlemarch* (1871–2) adopts it as a course in secular sanctity, and Daniel Deronda vows to serve and save his race. But soon novels record the defeat of people who have not managed to outstare the real: Isabel Archer, 'ground in the very mill of the conventional'; Hardy's Tess, sacrificed to social prejudice.

The novel which stretches between romanticism and that Victorian aftermath when as Carlyle prophesied 'the only genuine Romance for grown persons [will be] Reality' is *Vanity Fair*. Charlotte Brontë in her preface to *Jane Eyre* praises Thackeray's romanticism—his aquiline supremacy of mind, his lightning-like satire. But Thackeray's novel has outlasted the romantic youthfulness which, at a distance of thirty years, it represents. It is about the lapse of romance into the shabby mediocrity of the real; it studies, as the novel's protraction in time enables it to do, the decay of all things. The romantic lyric, in its epiphanies, causes time to halt. Novels are about time's remorseless passing: the dynastic time of history or the aeons of human evolution in Tolstoy and George Eliot; the duration of a single life in Proust; the obliteration of all lives in the central, blacked-out section of *To the Lighthouse*. Thackeray's long perspective is temporal as well as (in the mirrored drawing room) spatial, and he cannot prevent himself remembering how 'some few score of years afterwards' the hopeful dawn of life will be mocked by its elderly debility and corruption.

Written in the middle of the century, beginning 'when the present century was in its teens', *Vanity Fair* is a biography of that century, charting its course from romantic adolescence into grubbily realistic middle age. Though it professes to be 'a novel without a hero', its secret hero is the protagonist of the century, as he is of *War and Peace* and of Stendhal's *La Chartreuse de Parme*—the character about whom Jane Austen said she should perhaps have interpolated an essay into *Pride and Prejudice* but who is already omnipresent in that novel, as the pretext for the military manoeuvres which so excite the Bennet girls: Napoleon. He is always lurking just off-stage in *Vanity Fair*, as the cause of the Sedley bankruptcy, as an invidious parallel to George IV when the monarch has his walk-on at St James's, as the saviour recalled from Elba or as an exile glimpsed by Jos at St Helena. In the novel itself, Becky Sharp is his avatar. If he is its absent and defiled hero—for whereas in Byron's 'Beppo' the romantic cavalier 'to his very valet seem'd a hero', it is one of the tenets of realism that, in Carlyle's phrase, 'no man is a hero to his valet'—then she is its rapacious, imperially ambitious heroine, declared by Pitt Crawley a fit consort for an emperor, determining from Paris 'to make a move upon England' to recover Rawdon's fortune, or pressing a militaristic assault on society with the weaponry of her wit: she is 'never without arms' in her sarcastic trouncing of Mr Wagg. The example of 'the Corsican upstart' is Becky's inspiration. Society is to her a career open to the talents, and even the self, in a parody of the romantic journey through the vale of soul-making, can be invented. 'I must be my own mamma', Becky declares.

Her heroism, as befits an English romantic, is as much digestive as mental, and to impress Jos she eats curry, polishes off an entire chili, and endures the agonies of that Keatsian condiment, cayenne. She also has the role-playing dexterity of the Byronic libertine: hence her triumph in the charades. At her most disturbing, she is a female equivalent to Heathcliff or Frankenstein's monster, an unformed thing, come from nowhere (she is forever devising new parentages for herself), signifying no one knows what, stigmatised as a devil—her laughter at Chiswick is demoniacal; when she says she has no taste for bread and water, Lord Steyne rejoins, 'No more than a certain person for holy water'; her singing voice may be angelic, but Thackeray adds that there are two sorts of angel—because she is beyond society's comprehension and control, with the devil's negative capability for shape-changing and dissimulation.

She cannot even be known by the novelist. Thackeray defines himself by brandishing his comprehensiveness: he is as panoptic as Miss Osborne's room. He has the right, he argues, to probe into the secrets of his characters and overhear their prayers; and exposing the fraud of the worthless trophies of battle Becky sends home to Rawdon's aunt, he avers that 'The novelist, who knows everything, knows this also.' But as the novel develops, it becomes clear that there are areas of experience prohibited to him: Gaunt House, for instance, of which he knows only 'the vast wall in front'. He must rely on rumour and surmise to reconstruct what happens inside it. Imagination no longer suffices. He demands accurate information (for Carlyle had predicted that 'poetry will . . . come to be understood as nothing but higher knowledge'), and must make do with the tittle-tattle of a hanger-on, who is not entirely trustworthy. Becky likewise conceals her culpability from him. 'Was she guilty or not?' She denies it; he cannot tell. Thereafter, if he is to adhere to his self-characterisation as 'I, the present writer of a history of which every word is true' (which he makes good by adducing documentation: Horrocks's copy-book; the school texts, 'extant to this day', which Amelia buys for George; or the unspecified source where 'it is on record' that Dobbin spent an evening at the Haymarket Theatre), he must allow her the benefit of his doubt, archly refusing to believe stories of her picaresque adventures in Europe, either conceding that 'Her history was after all a mystery' or resolving that 'the less that is said about her doings is in fact the better.' In place of the bold fabulations which sustain the characters of the romantic novel, Becky has only the abundance of what Thackeray calls her fibs. She is a Gidean false coiner, required to forge new fictions as the old ones are found out, 'so the stock of [her] lies in circulation inevitably multiplies, and the danger of detection increases every day.' Perhaps the mirrored look-out in Russell Square was only a multiplier of such illusions; when, near the end of the novel, Amelia returns to the house with her child, the apparatus of mimesis has been dismantled: 'They went into the great blank rooms, the walls of which bore the marks where the pictures and mirrors had hung.'

Among the vanities which Thackeray wearily exposes are the twin but contradictory deceptions of his century: its romanticism and its realism. Romanticism is realistically robbed of illusion. Miss Crawley, a radical Rousseauist in her youth, is shown decrepit and without her wig. Realism is an undressing: to his valet Isidor, the wardrobe of the dandified Jos consists in articles to be expropriated for his own use; and Becky, too, in accordance with Carlyle's law, is judged guilty of adultery by 'the *Vehmgericht* of the servants' hall'. Yet what value has the realistic pursuit of knowledge, which prompts these desecrations of decorative appearance, if ultimately nothing can be known? Thackeray's refrain towards the end is a defeated 'I don't think' or 'I don't know.' To be unknown—to share the pious ignominy of old John Sedley, taking up 'a quiet and utterly unknown residence in a churchyard at Brompton'—is, he resolves, the sagest of fates. He comes to question the usefulness of the attempt to understand people and to make sense of life which is the project of the realist novel. Novels may pretend that individuals matter, but 'who is ever missed in Vanity Fair?'

Pride and Prejudice ends with the contradiction of imaginative hope by the inveterate way that things and people are. Jane Austen wishes she could report that Mrs Bennet's sense and temper were improved once her match-making schemes succeeded; but no such bonus should be expected. *Wuthering Heights* ends by laying the perturbed imagination to rest, preferring to trust the secure external routine of the world. Lockwood wonders 'how any one could ever imagine unquiet slumbers for the sleepers in that quiet earth'. *Vanity Fair* ends by resigning both from romance and from reality, since they are equally unavailing: 'Which of us has his desire, or, having it, is satisfied?' The novel, it turns out, is as much of a cheating illusion as the elfin poetic fancy.

— 29 —
Dickens and the Breeding
of Monsters

Before the romantic imagination surrenders to realism, it achieves its wildest, freest and most dangerous expression in Dickens. He represents that demon-infested imagination at its extremity, in a condition where it is impossible to tell hilarity from mania and where comedy and tragedy meet in the uncanny, unbalanced conjunction of opposites which is the grotesque. Dickens's novels are a maelstrom of contradictions, a generic chaos, as disturbed as nature (in the romantic theology of A. W. von Schlegel) or (in Dickens's own thinking) as the turbulent, nightmarish individual mind. Coincidence is the motor of Dickens's plots because, in his imagination, unlike things irresistibly converge and conflict: seraphs and ogres, a circus and a factory, a cathedral close and an opium den, human life and the inanimate, automated gadgetries which mock it. What the novel assumes to be reality is for Dickens a besieged boundary zone between the invading, exterminating angels of the supernatural and the rebellious, uprising depths of the surreal.

He is the unifier, perhaps even the culmination of English literature, comprising its history inside himself as he hybridises its previously distinct forms. He manages to be simultaneously medieval and modern: he has the sensibility of the primitive (or of his ontological deputy, the infant), estranged from the external world by fear and gnostic terrors, combating monsters as Beowulf does, and as well that of contemporary, industrial, urban man, an alien in an intractable world with a mechanical will of its own. Dickens's Gothicism brings the atavistic, bogey-ridden phantasmagoria—dating from literature's origins in spells, runes and riddles, recited to keep at bay a universe of inimical things—to the Victorian city. Villas like Wemmick's in *Great Expectations* (1860–1) are his moated castles, fortresses for neurasthenics like the old lady in *Sketches by Boz* (1836) who never dares to visit beyond the distance of next door but one on either side; railway locomotives, like the one which dismembers Carker in *Dombey and Son* (1846–8), are his fire-breathing Grendels; and he localises the lagoon of nonentity which spawns these witchy births in the Thames, where Gaffer Hexam in *Our Mutual Friend* (1864–5) fishes for dead human flotsam. London, through whose thieves' kitchens and gambling dens Dickens went on nocturnal tours with the police, is an underworld, the dark and matted wood of Dante. Yet in this seamy hell he erects a teetering cathedral, enshrining secular saints: martyred children like Tiny Tim or Nell or Jo the crossing-sweeper. He still sees the world, which the positivism of his century interpreted as a horizon of the flat, levelled real, with the dizzy verticality of romantic spirit, like Dante or Milton or Goethe when describing the ascent of Gretchen at the end of *Faust*. From his subterranean abysses, ladders mount to a paradise which Smike in *Nicholas Nickleby* (1838–9) wonderingly names 'Away'.

He is thus a romantic in both senses, the antique and the up-to-date, commuting between the age of romance (when he archly transmogrifies Dombey's mansion into a woodland castle, more fancifully fearful because of its 'grim reality', or when Mrs Skewton rhapsodises over the picturesque barbarism of Warwick Castle) and his own harder times, with their utilitarian hostility to whatever cannot be analytically pulverised by the mills of Mr Gradgrind or by those pedants whom Carlyle scourged as mechanical gerund-grinders.

He believed, as his vindication of *Bleak House* (1852–3) implies, that he had achieved a matching of the two opposed motives of his age, romanticism and the Gradgrinding enumeration of statistical data and dictionary definitions. In truth he managed much more than that. He is in himself a history of the novel, conducting it from its early days of picaresque opportunism, delighting to discover the world—as the Pickwickians do in the coach to Dingley Dell, or as Nicholas Nickleby does when he trustingly embarks on the road—to a later, despairing régime of structural necessity, where the novel's own form becomes a container and classifier of life, conducting a taxonomic assay of society like Balzac or a medical inquisition of its putrid symptoms like Zola, and assuming that society to be an inescapable fate, held together by the common denominators of epidemic (in *Bleak House*) or (in *Little Dorrit*, 1855–7) of incarceration. He begins as Fielding; he ends, in his establishment of the city as an encyclopaedia where all of life is detained and filed away, each item assigned its ecological niche, as Joyce. Or as Eliot, who affixed to an early version of *The Waste Land* an epigraph from *Our Mutual Friend*, Mrs Higden's account of Sloppy's virtuoso recitations from the newspaper: 'He do the Police in different voices.'

That quotation, like the Aeolian printing presses in *Ulysses*, signals Dickens's epic and bardic conquest of refractory modernity. The newspaper, like the novel, is epic democratised, a ruled and columned chaos where contradictory stories happen (as in the streets of the Dickensian city, or in Dickens's double and multiple plots) in parallel; an uproarious parliament where Dickens can impartially mimic all the speakers. Spenser's wish for a hundred tongues has been granted to the polyphonic Sloppy. It is significant, too, that his specialty is police investigations: the city is a mystery, a random proliferation of clues which we must, by the deductive extrapolation of a logic, connect into an orderly and incriminating pattern. After Dickens, and after the establishment of the detective novel by Wilkie Collins, mystery becomes myth: the secret of culpability which *Ulysses* and *The Waste Land* exclude from themselves is that of mythic origins, and of original sin—the travails of the Homeric hero on his way home, the paralysis of the Fisher King. *Ulysses* is an amplification of the Dickensian novel, requiring a single city on a single day to synopsise the history of the world; *The Waste Land*, at least after Pound had edited it, is the Dickensian novel reduced, its narrative relations severed, leaving only the hubbub of simultaneous, quarrelling voices, or—in homage to Sloppy—the newspaper's loose sheaf of disjected anecdotes and fortuitous incidents.

Not content to work through the novel's history for it, Dickens also calls the novel's phenomenological bluff. Novels have never been entirely assured of the reality they catalogue. Crusoe is a realist because he wants to convince himself that things are real, Moll Flanders is one because she knows they are not. Dickens, in exhibiting the romantic side of familiar things, puts on show their underside, or their inside, gruesomely extroverted. The purpose of metaphor is to deny reality to them. Silas Wegg, with one wooden leg already, appears to be growing another. Metaphor is a poetic sorcery, a malign magic which can warp, buckle and contort objects, representing Mrs Crisparkle and her sister in *The Mystery of Edwin Drood* (1870) as Dresden china ornaments or encouraging decor to inform on its human tenantry, like the insidious cushioned stealth of the upholstery in Carker's villa or the nervous neatness of Mr Tartar's chambers, where 'a slack salt-spoon would have instantly betrayed itself'. A Dickensian mirror is never merely mimetic, unless it be that over the Podsnap sideboard which ponderously 'reflects the table and the company', giving its imprimatur to a crass world where things have value only if they are owned and can advertise wealth. Otherwise his mirrors are an apparatus for deforming the real and spying on the invisible: when the ailing Dombey consults the glass, he sees the brooding, haggard ghost of himself. Septimus Crisparkle boxes at the pier-glass, and his mother fears he will break either it or a blood-vessel. His absurd pugilism answers to the surreal ambition of the Dickensian character— the desire of Wilde's Caliban to get beyond or behind or beneath the real. Metaphor is the phantom which stalks and deracinates reality. After the murder of Nancy, Sikes in *Oliver Twist* (1838–9) is tracked by a ghost he has imaginatively summoned up, and his metaphoric susceptibility threatens to madden him: 'every object before him, substance or shadow, still or moving, took the semblance of some fearful thing.'

Children obsess Dickens because they exist in this state of agonising imaginative grace. Reason has not yet illumined and deconsecrated their world, allaying their terrors. They respond to reality with the exquisite paranoia which is the ecstatic, alarmed sensitivity of poetry. While he is young and afraid, David Copperfield remains in this condition of poetic dread and delight, assailed by the snapping lock on Murdstone's bag, comforted by Peggotty's swelling bosom; when he outgrows his traumas, he advances from nervous poetry to the calm rationality of prose, by which, as a professional literary man, he makes his living. Oliver Twist indignantly rejects Brownlow's suggestion that he should become a writer: that would be too facile an exorcism, a tranquil discipline of recollection laying ghosts to rest. Dickens's genius is precisely his ability to recover at will his own terrified childhood, to re-enact it—as in his public readings he put himself through furious repetitions of climactic episodes, like the psychiatric patient compelled to live out the scenarios of his dream—rather than sedating and controlling it by writing it down.

The Dickensian child is in the position of Bailey at Todgers's in *Martin Chuzzlewit* (1843–4). When he whispers the unhealthy secrets of the kitchen through the keyhole, Mrs Todgers rounds on him as 'the most dreadful child', is afraid that 'nothing but hanging will ever do him any good', and sentences him to go downstairs. His crime is the scandalous one of telling the truth. Oliver when he asks for more commits a similar offence: his is the plaint of romanticism, the greed of what Hunt called young poetical appetite or what Hazlitt called gusto, demanding immediate gratification from the world. Oliver's life is a parable of imagination, greedy, compulsive, with a gift for rousing demons. The novel begins with Dickens's stubborn refusal to specify the 'certain town' where Oliver is born, or even to give it a fictitious name: this obstinacy asserts imagination's prerogatives. To bestow a name would authenticate and realise the place. Dickens will not and cannot do so because the world in which that town is located is to him a grim delusion. This is why Oliver, slow to begin breathing and hovering indecisively 'between this world and the next', is reluctant to enter it. When he does, he is named by the parish functionaries with alphabetical arbitrariness, assigned an ill-fitting, inauthentic label.

This world's service to Oliver—in a repudiation of the ethics of the Victorian novel, with its insistence on the moral benefits of capitulating to reality, of resuming life and its chores (as A. H. Clough said in a critical review of Matthew Arnold's poems) on Monday, or its doctrinal pledge, like Charlotte Brontë's in *Shirley*, to be 'as unromantic as Monday morning'—is to instruct him in its unreal feignings. He learns to affect regret when Bumble expatriates him from the baby farm; his job as a mute at funerals demonstrates to him how easily the survivors recover from the public grief they have advertised. Regretting his initial error in committing himself to life, Oliver wishes himself out of it. His equivalent to that pre-natal, inland ocean of romping infants described by Wordsworth's 'Ode' is the charmed condition of sleep, our daily approximation to death. He spends much of the novel in a 'drowsy state, between sleeping and waking'; he suffers through a feverish unconsciousness, dozes in Fagin's den, faints away after the armed robbery, smiles in his sleep when nursed by Mrs Maylie.

But unlike Keats's Adam, whose paradisial reverie is made true when he awakens, reality is Oliver's bad dream. He awakes to find the monsters he had imagined, not a nubile Eve, before him: he stares at the first wipe-snatching incident 'with his eyelids as wide open as they would go', in a daytime nightmare; he falls asleep and wakes to find Fagin grimacing at him through the window, only to have Harry tell him it must have been a dream. His visionary power is an illness like Sikes's epilepsy, and it condemns him to bear visual witness to the unimaginable—to see Fagin for instance in Newgate before his execution, after which Oliver swoons, gratefully resuming unconsciousness. The events of the novel have no trustworthy reality, and are always being ascribed to an unsettled phantasmagoria. Rose's interview with Nancy has 'more the semblance of a rapid dream than an actual occurrence'. Nancy could be a figment of Rose's vagrant fancy, of those 'wandering thoughts' she tries to collect when their talk is over.

Sleep with its delirious imaginings becomes a recurrent subject of Dickens's novels. Their theatre is a nocturnal and neurotic projection of fantasy. Like Coleridge assailed by the pictures which writhe into life when he closes his eyes; like the child in de Quincey who can summon phantoms in the darkness and who says 'I can tell them to go, and they go; but sometimes they come when I don't tell them to come'; or like the poet Gérard de Nerval welcoming sleep as a death and dreams as a mental reincarnation and walking a lobster on a ribbon through the Palais Royal because it had an occult knowledge of 'the secrets of the deep', Dickens creates from a kind of self-hypnosis. An ever more unquiet slumber overtakes the novels. It is while dozing in the church that Pecksniff hears the conspirators, like voices of conscience, accusing him; Mrs Gamp mutters the name of Mrs Harris in her sleep; Nell's grandfather reveals his vicious secret in his sleep, and Nell, spying on him, might be watching only the shadow-play of her bad dreams; interviewed by the police, Bella Wilfer is 'in the state of a dreamer', and for this reason is instinctively directed towards the truth about her situation. When awake, these people seem to be sleep-walking, like Edith gliding through 'the dead time of night'. If insomniac, they oversee the sleep of others, as Florence does with her sick father or Edith with her dying mother. The mind is a haunted house, thoughts its revenants. In her delirium Mrs Skewton realises this, and cries out, 'My fancy! Everything is my fancy!... Is it possible that you don't see it!' Riderhood tells Bradley Headstone, 'Your face is like a ghost's', to which Bradley replies, 'Did you ever see a ghost?' He has of course seen one, inside himself. Dickens calls Paul Dombey's introverted games with monsters who are the 'arabesque work of his amusing fancy' a capacity to convoke spectres and, like Hamlet, to interrogate them: 'Ideas, like ghosts (according to the common notion of ghosts), must be spoken to a little before they will explain themselves; and Toots had long left off asking any questions of his own mind.' Imagination entails a traffic with spirits.

Dickens's imagination incants a sinister lullaby to the reason. Like the hypnotist's spell, it contrives the resurgence of a stalking unconsciousness. In *Martin Chuzzlewit* he entices a house into this treacherous sleep, and can thus reveal it to be a lunatic asylum, given over to those yearning phantoms which rise with the moon: 'in the quiet hours of the night, one house shuts in as many incoherent and incongruous fancies as a madman's head.' In *A Tale of Two Cities* (1859) he nocturnally enchants an entire city, remarking that London by night is a catacomb of dark secrets. In *American Notes* (1842) he excavates an underground city of fugitive and ashamed bad habits when he visits the oyster bars in New York, situated in cellars because 'the swallowers of oysters . . . [copy] the coyness of the thing they eat', and skulk behind partitions or in curtained booths to indulge their solitary vice.

Surrendered to imagination, Dickens is himself a sleepwalker. He has a romantic need to consider the creative process an involuntary usurpation of reason. He does not fabricate characters; they are presentiments, the uprisen incubi of dream. This is how he explains, albeit benignly, the instigation of *The Pickwick Papers* (1836–7): 'I thought of Mr. Pickwick, and began.' Creation is possible for Dickens only when the awaited visitation from a character happens. It is like Blake preparing himself for the apparition of the spirits he propitiates, or like the entry of the fiend into Susan Nipper, who, to quieten Florence Dombey, invokes the local hobgoblin, tells it to eat the girl alive, and makes 'a horrible lowing' to represent its hungry rampage. This is how characters announce themselves in *Oliver Twist*—as spirits uncannily materialising, as utterances from the beyond. Dickens is in the position of Jenny Wren who, nursing Eugene in *Our Mutual Friend*, serves as a medium and is consulted by Mortimer 'as if she were an interpreter between this sentient world and the insentient man'.

Sikes is at first a growling, railing voice. Only later—when he has acquired a body—is it described. The Gooroo man who terrorises David Copperfield reverts to non-being before he can be described. The advent of character is always an account of gestation: character's sudden and alarming embodiment (as when the dark stranger in the cloak, with whom Oliver collides, falls 'on the ground, writhing and foaming, in a fit'); its routine of sustenance, announcing that it still exists by reminders of its predispositions, like Mrs Micawber asserting whenever she recurs that she will never leave Mr Micawber; its initiatives of reinvention. Toby Crackit, when Sikes calls on him, has to be described first and then named ('for he it was') because he has imagined himself anew since his last materialisation. The same is true of 'the male traveller' on the Great North Road in *Oliver Twist*, who re-assumes identity and turns out to be Noah Claypole ('for he it was', notes Dickens again). But the identification is only temporary. Noah soon mutates into Morris Bolter.

For Dickens the creative state was one almost of demonic possession. Writing about Quilp in *The Old Curiosity Shop* (1841), he would scuttle round his room cackling and muttering, having invited the dwarf into himself. His characters happen through him, not because of him. With an imperious autarchic power, they imagine themselves—like Bumble, when Mrs Mann flatters him as a literary character, allowing 'Perhaps I may be', or Durdles in *Edwin Drood* habitually referring to himself as a third person, or Mrs Billickin presumptively equipping herself with a spouse. Beginning with the fat boy in *Pickwick*, Dickens's people are insatiable gormandisers. Their leering fondness for capons or for Christmas dinners represent a lust for incarnation, for the corporeality of character: they eat in order to be, and it is as if, in the process, they cannibalise their creator Dickens. They are incited to this carnal fury by the world's conspiracy—the enforced rationing of rationality—to destroy them. Bumble says that Oliver's distemper is not Madness but Meat; the bereaved man will not give up his starved wife to the undertaker because she is so wasted she will not feed the worms, which will only torment her. Having achieved their own plump incorporation, like Bumble swelling into what he calls a public character or Mark Tapley institutionalised as 'a Co.' in America or Tigg growing into the impersonal status of the Anglo-Bengalee Disinter- ested Loan and Life Insurance Company or the projectors in *Nicholas Nickleby* immortalising themselves by their scheme for the propagation of muffins and crumpets, they reserve the right to kill themselves. For they alone, not Dickens, wield that power. Hence the gruesomeness of Mr Grimwig's reiterated offer to eat his head. The character who has engorged the world will end by making a meal of himself.

Dickens's fantasies of decapitation have a similar moral. Having assured itself of its body, character sets out to grow a head, to acquire a mind—or to chase one which is teasingly elusive, like Mr Dick with King Charles's head in *David Copperfield* (1849–50). When Tom Pinch is discharged by Pecksniff, the god created by his own deluded worship, he undergoes a symbolic beheading, for what he renounces is a personal godhead: 'There was no Pecksniff; there never had been a Pecksniff.' The dethroned deity is so unreal that he can be referred to only as 'the thing supposed to be that Great Abstraction'. God's death entails the assumption of power by devils, or—for Dickens, a much worse fate—the deconsecration of a world which the nineteenth century could then make into the factory of realism. That deicide has as its image a comically ghastly execution. When Tom announces that he has left Pecksniff, the tollman says 'I should as soon have thought of his head leaving him.' Now that 'Pecksniff had gone out of the world—had never been in it', Tom must accept the consequences of godlessness, and it is 'as much as [he] could do to say his prayers without him'.

No wonder Dickens, like Mme Defarge in *A Tale of Two Cities*, is so elated by the guillotine. The revolution's sundering of heads licenses the ribald, post-mortem cavorting of bodies, able to sprout additions at will, like Silas Wegg technologising the organism by mentally manufacturing a second wooden leg. That appendage, a favourite of Dickens's, symbolises the wilfully self-operating body, headless and unreasoning. Mrs Gamp, recalling her husband, remembers 'a wooden leg . . . which in its constancy of walkin' into wine vaults and never comin' out again 'till fetched by force, was quite as weak as flesh, if not weaker.'

Unstoppable once started into life, these characters romantically mimic the machine, with its creative perpetuity and its tireless dynamism. They are Frankensteins who are their own self-engineered monsters. *Martin Chuzzlewit* abounds in sports of nature, imps and bogeys—the dragon on the inn-sign, the coach addressed by Tom as a predatory 'great monster' carrying off his friends. When Mrs Gamp addresses the Antwerp steamer, the novel industrialises that ogre, hailing the machine as a fiendish progenitor of new life, like Dickens himself. She salutes the smoking vessel, which she confusedly associates with the whale which ate up Jonah, as 'a man's invention': the symbol of a runaway inventiveness, and thus a model for Dickensian character. Mr Boffin admiringly compares his wife with a steam engine, and Quilp, infernally alight, fuelling himself with cigars and draughts from saucepans of boiling fluid, is a furnace of seething amoral creativity like that where Blake's tiger is smelted. Toodle treats the train he drives in *Dombey and Son* as an extension, like Wegg's artificial limb, of himself. The express which carves up Carker merely performs, like the guillotine or like the scribal apparatus which writes its victims to death in the story of the penal colony by Kafka (who so venerated Dickens), a clean, creative surgery. The mind is an abattoir, slaughtering life, sectioning it, then galvanically reactivating it. Frankenstein's 'workshop of filthy creation' becomes the operating-table of surrealism, the scene, in Lautréamont's phrase, of random intercourse between a sewing machine and an umbrella. Dickens has many such establishments: the wax museum in *The Old Curiosity Shop*, which Mrs Jarley believes to have superseded life, or the dolls' dress-shop in *Our Mutual Friend*, run by Jenny Wren who complains of the fertility of her lifeless charges, forever getting married and having babies, to the ruination of their waist-lines.

Mechanically reproducing themselves, Dickens's characters patent their idiosyncracies and derive universal edicts from their personal quirks and quiddities. Spinoza declared that the purpose of nature was to make men uniform. There is no such classical regulation of the species in Dickens. Character for him is romantically autonomous, a freak of nature. Chevy Slyme is defined as 'an individual, of whom it can be said . . . that nobody but himself can in any way come up to him'; Mrs Pipchin boasts that 'there's nobody like me', and Paul Dombey is rather glad of it. Such character is a law unto itself. Bumble exults 'in the full pride and bloom of beadlehood'. But beadlehood is Bumbledom: the deviant self aspires to universality. Mrs Gamp promulgates the same creed when she announces that 'Gamp is my name, and Gamp my nater.' *Martin Chuzzlewit* studies this cult of the self-created individual in Pecksniff and Mrs Gamp. It works differently in each case: Pecksniff's is a malign, manipulative creativity, Mrs Gamp's a midwifery which actually gives birth to a phantom of her brain.

Pecksniff's solace is 'I am perfectly self-possessed.' The self is a possession, a dower, an heirloom, of which he is the disinterested trustee: 'I *have* a character which is very dear to me, and will be the best inheritance of my two daughters.' He pretends in his megalomania to a supreme selflessness. He consents to be deified by the adulation of Tom Pinch, and humbly acquiesces in his martyrdom to the service of a believing world. Thus he covenants fidelity to old Chuzzlewit 'while I continue to be called upon to exist'. Yet while playing at being a man abashedly elected a god by his fellows, he occupies himself in recreating those who have created him, finding Chuzzlewit (again like Coleridge's artist exercising his divine esemplastic power) 'very supple in his plastic fingers', relishing Mary as 'the embodied image of his thoughts', coveting and abrogating the creative power of others, as when he appropriates Martin's architectural design. So far as he sees it, the purpose of men is the suppliant raising of cathedrals to his glory: he prescribes for Martin the labour of piling up a cart-load of bricks 'into any form which would remind me . . . of St Peter's at Rome, or the Mosque of St Sophia at Constantinople.' His aim is a monopoly of feelings, a Uranus-like consumption and elimination of the world. In the coach, he congratulates himself on his warmth by reflecting that many other people are not so warm as he is. The totalitarian ego can tolerate other existences only so long as they are tributaries of itself. Pecksniff's aspiration is to a world of impersonality. He descants to his daughter of 'mankind in general; the human race, considered as a body, and not as individuals'; he is therefore the prophecy horribly fulfilled in the America of the novel, where as in a laboratory experiment a race of men has been turned out who, as Bill Simmons reports to Martin, are all alike. And for this reason the passage to America is a fatal one: the republic is the death-chamber of individuality.

By contrast with Pecksniff, Mrs Gamp is a life-giver. Her most wonderful professional achievement as a midwife is her delivery of herself. She deals as well with the other end of human experience, doubling as an undertaker's assistant, but her death-wishes are affectionate and jovial, since her concern is the commonness of our lot. Her fondest thought for Betsey Prig is 'Wishin' you lots of sickness, my darling creetur', and she feels an artist's love for the sick man Betsey tends, 'her fingers [itching] to compose his limbs in that last marble attitude'. Dotingly she says, 'he'd make a lovely corpse!'

In her exercise of these dual powers—bodying forth conceptions, and ritualistically laying them out—she is a surrogate for Dickens himself: the Dickens whose characters irresistibly demand to be born, like the nascent forms imploring Spenser's gardener Genius; the creator who might say as Slyme does of himself, 'I'm full of genius', meaning that he is both rampantly generative and a master of those tutelary spirits called genies which at his behest enter into and animate the obtuse objects of the world; the Dickens who, having created these people, then with an equal love sets about slaying them, and walks the streets all night in tearful mourning after he has dealt the death-blow to Paul Dombey. Dickens's power, like Mrs Gamp's, is one of life and death. He is both paterfamilias to his multiple offspring, and (latently at least) their mass-murderer. The reason he could not finish *The Mystery of Edwin Drood* is that the denouement would stipulate exposure of himself as the culprit. Mr Sapsea in that novel ponderously determines that 'to take the life of a fellow-creature was to take something that didn't belong to you.' But Edwin's life does belong to Dickens, and can be revoked by him as he pleases. Rosa, suspecting Jasper's guilt, asks herself, 'Am I so wicked in my thoughts as to conceive a wickedness that others cannot imagine?' For Dickens, who lacks Rosa's moral self-reproach, imagination means the uninhibited capacity to conceive and execute wickednesses.

The criminology of *Edwin Drood* is a covert essay on creative psychology. The criminal intellect is 'a horrible wonder apart', irreconcilable with 'the average intellect of average men'. Saying so in parenthesis, Dickens is trifling with the amoral freedom experimentally wielded by Rasknolnikov, a creation of his admirer Dostoyevsky, when he murders the money-lender in *Crime and Punishment*. Yet is the sorcerer's apprentice in control of the mad revel he conducts? Mr Bazzard in *Edwin Drood* is dissuaded from 'pursuing his genius'—a secret avocation of play-writing—because it is feared that his genius will vindictively pursue him, as in Frankenstein's case, and punish him with starvation. Dickens on one occasion represents himself as saviour of his characters, when in 1865 after a railway accident in Kent he clambered back into the wrecked carriage to rescue (in manuscript form) the entire population of *Our Mutual Friend*, who would otherwise have perished; but those characters seem increasingly to have resented his misuse of them and teamed up to exert power over him. He was after all the medium through whom they happened, their mere midwife: what can be the meaning of his compulsion at the end of his life, despite the appeals of his doctors, to give public readings of the scene in which Sikes murders Nancy, exciting himself into a paroxysm like that of Sikes, unless it is a literal haunting? Dead characters re-arise from their graves to torment the creator who destroyed them. In losing his own life by his helpless acquiescence in their rebirth—for these readings helped to bring on his final stroke—Dickens is suffering through an imaginative expiation.

This mental diabolism is of course only hinted at by Mrs Gamp's desire to show off her mortuary finesse, although she has a delight like Dickens's own in the grotesque vivisectioning of bodies, and when she sees the dead Gamp on a slab clutching his wooden leg under his left arm she disposes of his disintegrated parts 'for the benefit of science'. (She, too, would have sympathised with the researches of the romantic creator Frankenstein.) Otherwise she exhibits the Dickensian genius at its most comically miraculous. She is not content merely to be her own executrix; she must beget another

[475]

character, genetically modelled after her own image. She does so in her postulation of and conversation with the absent Mrs Harris. This imagined colleague serves as her extension: almost (given Dickens's infatuation with surgical appliances) her prosthesis; also her sly moral exoneration, enabling her to mention charges or to take a drink with complete impunity, since she does so only at Mrs Harris's behest. Their reported chats are, Dickens says, 'visionary dialogues', exactly analogous to those of Blake with his spirits. Mrs Gamp anathematises Betsey for denying that Mrs Harris exists because such disbelief is a denial of imagination. With the same self-righteousness, Dickens demands that his own most extravagant fictions—Krook's spontaneous combustion, or his contention in the postscript to *Our Mutual Friend* that more bizarre wills have been filed than the one left by Mr Harmon—should be accepted as facts.

Mrs Gamp's daring boast is ultimately made good, for the novel does spy on her in the process of creative fusion and fission. It happens when she is preparing for sleep, that romantic condition when the reason is extinguished. Having improvised a bed for herself and put on a nightcap resembling a cabbage, 'she produced a watchman's coat, which she tied round her neck by the sleeves, so that she became two people; and looked, behind, as if she were in the act of being embraced by one of the old patrol.' Here is creativity *in flagrante delicto*. With the aid of this demon lover, Mrs Gamp unfolds into a pair, and can deliver herself of Mrs Harris. The prodigious boy Bailey effects a similar reproductive marvel. A wimp in appearance, he comports himself like a sporting wiseacre. His 'genius', as Dickens calls it, 'eclipsed both time and space, cheated beholders of their senses, and worked on their belief in defiance of all natural laws.' Paul Sweedlepipe must either go mad himself, or accept Bailey's illusionary feat. The youth has become 'an inexplicable creature; a breeched and booted Sphinx'.

Dredging the sediment of subconsciousness, Dickens returns literature to its origins in the lore of shamanism. The primitive source of the novel is an embarrassment to E. M. Forster, who imagines savages round the camp-fire cheering themselves up by telling a story. Dickens has no such qualms: he knows that to tell a story is to cast a spell. This is why the rapt process of creating is itself the subject of those novels—of *The Old Curiosity Shop*, which begins with the elderly, invalid narrator's conjuring of the fiends and angels which he then leaves 'to speak and act for themselves', pretending that they possess an exterior existence and can be located in this world, not in a nether one, by planting the Quilps on Tower Hill; of *Edwin Drood* with its impetuous, premonitory present tense, where Dickens does not narrate what has already occurred but invents characters on a whim and discards them with equal, cruel lawlessness, like nature (as he supposes) dismissing the malformed Mr Grewgious before he has been completed.

What Dickens creates is something like the dream-visions of medieval literature: a psychic allegory played out in that shop of musty antiquities which is the lumber-room of the head. Nell studies the last such allegory, *The Pilgrim's Progress*, and employs it as a model for her own penitential journey through industrial England. It teaches her that her life is a dream-play, peopled by substantial phantoms (as Sampson Brass calls Quilp) or by the hallucinations of the night-time mind, as when she spies on her grandfather's sleep-walking larcenies. Quilp has power over her because, like the dervishes activated by allegory, he originates within her. He is a figment of her reason's torpor, and for this reason he himself—though often discovered lazing in bed, relaxed in an embowering eroticism—is mysteriously insomniac, able to terrorise his wife with his wakefulness.

Quilp is a gargoyle, the remnant of a ruined Gothic cathedral; Sally Brass likewise is mistaken by the constable for a griffin. Gothically, Dickens sees characters as made not grown, carved and whittled into cranky shapes by the rude inventiveness of nature. The gargoyle is an aborted existence, a foetus of fantasy. The grotesque means to Dickens the sculpting of a rickety, lop-sided, hump-backed imagination, as the toys above the beds in the hospital of *Our Mutual Friend* 'in their innocent grotesqueness and incongruity . . . might have stood for the children's dreams'; it is existence's skulking interior and its ulterior. Good Mrs Brown in *Dombey and Son* has a grotesque *alter ego*, a subliminal equivalent to the fire-light which, casting shadows, deforms her: in Florence's 'childish recollection', with its 'grotesque and exaggerated . . . presentment of the truth', she remains the terrifying abductor of the girl's infancy. And though Quilp, like Hugo's Quasimodo on the façade of Notre Dame, might emerge from the matted foliage of Gothic, he acclimatises himself to the industrial and romantic nineteenth century, for he is a thermodynamic demon, eternally delighting in his own energy and stoking it up with warm firesides and steaming saucepans, cursing his wife by wishing her a frosty nose, only extinguished when quenched by the chill river into which he tumbles. His wife's friends vow to tame and subdue 'the rebellious spirit of man'. But Quilp is irrepressible and, worse, irresistible—disturbingly attractive to the woman he has sexually bewitched, and infectiously, callously funny, inciting us (along with Oscar Wilde) to admit that we would need a heart of stone not to laugh at the death of little Nell. Among Mrs Jarley's waxen effigies is an avatar of Quilp's, 'Jasper Packlemerton of atrocious memory, who courted and married fourteen wives, and destroyed them all, by tickling the soles of their feet when they were sleeping in the consciousness of innocence and virtue.'

Quilp is the secret of malice and bedevilment in everyone. Dickens makes a character by turning it inside out to expose that absconded secret. Quilp's eating habits have the same surrealising tendency. Hence his munching of crustaceans (also much fancied by Salvador Dali), gnawing through the armoured defences they present to the world, or his unpeeling of a potato, slavering as he draws it, Dickens says, from the native element in which it cowers. Houses in Dickens wear their characteristics outdoors, rather than shielding them within: in the mews behind Miss Fox's residence in *Dombey and Son* 'the most domestic and confidential garments of coachmen and their wives and families usually hung, like Macbeth's banners, on the outward walls'. Quilp enjoins his wife to worm her way into Nell's secrets: knowledge is the ultimate penetration and wormy defloration of a body. John Jasper states another version of this sinister Dickensian gift for unmaking the people who have so carefully and evasively constructed portable havens for themselves. When Sapsea calls Durdles 'a character', Jasper sneers, 'A character ... that with a few skillful touches you turn inside out.' This psychological law serves also as a rule of Gaffer Hexam's corpse-fishing trade, for he notes that the tide has a habit of leaving the trouser pockets of his catches empty and inside out. Death goes to work like Dickens, pilfering secrets, analysing by eviscerating.

Yet Nell's death is an enshrinement. Dickens's cathedral contains altars, as well as the crypts to which Durdles relegates his secrets, retiring there to 'sleep off the fumes of liquor', or the befogged, fumy dens frequented by Jasper. The Gothicism of the Victorians is in general industriously devout. Thornton the mill-owner in Mrs Gaskell's *North and South* (1855) contrasts Oxford colleges with Darkshire factories and brags, 'We are of a different race from the Greeks, to whom beauty was everything. . . . I belong to Teutonic blood.' Dickens's Gothicism lacks that masonic fervour. It is the architecture of wayward mental rhapsody, of the amorphousness which Richard Hurd's *Letters on Chivalry and Romance* in the eighteenth century defended in Spenser's case as Gothic not Grecian, or of the bravura flourish, describing Hogarth's unclassically serpentine line of beauty, made by Trim's stick in *Tristram Shandy*. It is also an architecture grotesquely able to combine tragedy and comedy—the intercessory suffering of Nell, the evil glee of Quilp—in ways which English critics found justified in Shakespeare and Hogarth. Charles Lamb, who preferred the bedlam in *The Rake's Progress* to Shakespeare's account of a similar despair in *Timon of Athens*, argued that the illustrator and the dramatist both specialised in contradictory composites, 'twiformed births'. Dickensian tragicomedy is the diagnosis of schizophrenia.

The double plot signifies a double life, like that of Miss Twinkleton who 'as, in some cases of drunkenness, and in others of animal magnetism . . . has two distinct and separate phases of being', a diurnal one as schoolmistress, a nocturnal one as scandal-monger. That dualistic creative temperament inscribes itself on the face of the cathedral in *Edwin Drood*, when the tower of Cloisterham wavers and mutates into a Sultan's minareted palace: the sanctum dissolves into the zone of illicit pleasures inspired by opium; the church is planted in the hungering chasm of Kubla Khan's garden. The romantic poet Heinrich Heine, visiting Amiens with a friend, was asked why such cathedrals could not be built in the nineteenth century. He said the reason was that men in Gothic days had faith, whereas his own contemporaries had only opinions. The disbelieving romantics erect cathedrals merely to lay waste to them. Tintern

Abbey becomes holy when the monks are driven out and it moulders into nature; the Gothic cathedral in *Biographia Literaria* is a moonlit coven, overrun by the 'grotesque dwarfs' who have escaped from their alcoves of subordination; Ruskin in *The Seven Lamps of Architecture* (1849) finds on the portal of St Maclou at Rouen a carved inferno 'whose fearful grotesqueness I can only describe as a mingling of the minds of Orcagna and Hogarth', and which theatens to convert the fane into a mad-house. Impressionism inundated the cathedral and its moral remonstrances: Monet's Rouen is liquified by light, Debussy's *cathédrale engloutie* has been submerged.

The same romantic profanation occurs in Dickens. His characters wear the cathedral as a carapace. Durdles lurks in 'odd nooks'; Jasper has (says Edwin) found his 'niche in life'; the crone who comes in quest of Jasper resembles 'one of the fantastic carvings on the under brackets of the stall seats' or is 'as hard as the big brass eagle holding the sacred books' at the lectern; the acolytes of Nuns' House are cramped in postures of humility by the impending ceilings. The Gothic accoutrements, crockets and crotchets of the place have been sprouted by the people. The architecture unfurls from the inside outwards. Hence its symptomatic morbidity: it is a sickness expressing itself, like the pustule with which Mr Honeythunder is compared—'a Boil upon the face of society, Mr. Honeythunder expanded into an inflammatory Wen in Minor Canon Corner.'

Cloisterham and the opium den are the last imperilled recesses of romantic imagination and of what Dickens calls—remembering perhaps those splintered, mimetically baffled mirrors—its 'scattered consciousness', which 'fantastically [pieces] itself together'. It is because of these romantic mysteries that Trollope, writing about Barchester, pledges himself to the abolition of the cathedral or at least to secularising its cult of imagination. Cloisterham will never be overtaken by the nineteenth century's confident march of mind: at the time of the novel it has no railway; even now, Dickens notes, express trains avoid it. It is a dormitory of dreams, a catacomb of night thoughts. Trollope's purpose in analysing the structures and transmission of power in Barchester is, however, to arouse institutions from their ancestral, opiate stupor. Obadiah Slope complains in *Barchester Towers* (1857) that 'the whole of our enormous cathedral establishments have been allowed to go to sleep,—nay, they are all but dead and ready for the sepulchre!' He sees himself, like George Eliot's Felix Holt or Dorothea Brooke or Deronda, as the rational, reformist awakener, an emissary of enlightenment and of mind's advance against obstinate, immutable matter. In microcosm at Barchester—in, for instance, Dr Grantly's defence of his holy of holies, the hospital, in *The Warden* (1855)—Trollope is studying the world crisis which is George Eliot's subject. Like hers, his are political novels. The cathedral interests him as an encapsulation of special interests, jealously guarded privileges, inherited sinecures. 'Let us call it Barchester', he says, having at first left its name blank;

but it could be any other statistically comparable town. It is not, like Cloisterham, a place summoned up by and profanely sacred to imagination. It does duty for England, and its provincial controversies monitor the state of the nation. The Bishop retains his London residence, so as not to forfeit his connection with and influence on metropolitan politics. The very existence of Trollope's characters depends on their exercise of a mandated power. They deal in preferments and the distribution of favours like the meddling Mrs Proudie. Yet even she holds her power in trust, if not from any electorate then from the constituency of readers: when Trollope overheard two clubmen at the Athenaeum complaining that she had grown tiresome, he killed her off at once, as if in an act of impeachment. In Trollope's rationalised national edifice there will be no place left for the gargoyles which abound in Coleridge's cathedral, or Dickens's: Bertie Stanhope in *Barchester Towers* contends that 'no real artist could descend to the ornamentation of a cathedral' and denies the symbiosis between Dickens's characters and their settings, which makes them outcrops of an inanimate world, when he adds that 'buildings should be fitted to grace the sculpture, not the sculpture to grace the building'.

The realism of the Victorians is a missionary project of realisation: they want to indenture their characters—as Louis Moore tells Shirley, as Deronda exhorts the self-indulgently romantic Gwendolen—to a stern reality. Mrs Gaskell interpreted realism as a severe moral calling. Anne Brontë, she thought, wrote *The Tenant of Wildfell Hall* because 'she had . . . been called on to contemplate' the dissipation of her brother Branwell; she assumed it as her 'duty to reproduce every detail'. Though tormented by the task, 'she must be honest'. Life is real, and therefore earnest. To Dickens it is neither. His novels pronounce the doom of this posivitism and pass beyond it.

Dombey and Son, for instance, demonstrates the futility of the acquisitive motive from which novels begin, and which makes Crusoe or Moll or Pamela want to possess things because then they will be assured of their reality. Realism in Dickens's novel is a tragedy of reification. Dombey appraises the world as an emporium of ownable things. By monopolising them he will, he thinks, immortalise himself and secure his dynastic succession. But, as in the Coketown of *Hard Times* (1854) where horses are dissevered by definitions, to know and grasp a thing is to kill it. The objectifying fetish of realism is a curse on the objects coveted: his father's possessiveness kills Paul. Pamela's novelistic career of expenditure, recapitulated here by Susan's taking 'sharp note of the furniture' or her 'exact inventory of her personal wardrobe', ends in the assembly of a mausoleum. After his wife's funeral, Dombey sentences his accumulated objects to the mourning of disuse and desuetude: tables and chairs wear winding-sheets, and 'every chandelier or lustre, muffled in holland, looked like a monstrous tear depending from the ceiling's eye'. The capitalist broods over a grave of wealth, like Wagner's Fafner, metamorphosed into a dragon to guard his hoard in *Siegfried*. And beyond this retentive watch kept by realism over a world it cannot secure forever lies the inevitable dispersal of those treasured things: the invasion of Dombey's house and its ruining by the bailiffs, auctioneers and bidders, 'looking into . . . and disparaging everything'. Their ravaging of its contents resembles the autopsy on his food conducted by Quilp, or on Hexam's cadavers by the river. After the 'shabby vampires' have cannibalised the premises, Dickens notes, 'There is not a secret place in the whole house.' It is this same demolition of a household which, because it signifies the death of realism, is so satisfying to Virginia Woolf in 'A Haunted House' or *To the Lighthouse* or in the reclamation of Poyns Hall by darkness in *Between the Acts*.

Already in Dickens the demise of a world which the nineteenth century too smotheringly sought to lay hold on is predicted. Objects sour and putrefy. Mrs Muff's bonnet is mortified, her face vinegary. At the church when Florence marries Walter, everything is slowly resolving itself into dust and—after that—into funereal ashes. Realism is the rigor mortis of the real: Dombey's armouring of himself in a cold hardness; Edith's marble face; Mrs Skewton's paralysis. At Warwick Castle the superannuated Mrs Skewton cries, 'We are dreadfully real, Mr. Carker, are we not?' Dickens comments that 'few people had less reason to complain of their reality', since she decays each night and is resurrected each morning at her toilet-table. As a cosmetic fiction, she scarcely retains 'a real individual existence'. But this is why she needs to deplore reality: she knows that it will soon enough expunge her. Realism is the taxidermist's macabre stilling of life, or the sepulture practised by Major Bagstock's native attendant, who so enswathes his employer for a ride to the railway station that he seems to travel 'in a living tomb'. Only little Paul, who in dying prematurely abdicates from a world in whose claim to reality he does not believe, has the wisdom to see the void beneath his father's materialism, and behind the *horror vacui* of Victorian decor. He sits imagining emptiness, 'as if he had taken life unfurnished, and the upholsterer were never coming'.

Dombey and Son is Dickens's refutation of *Robinson Crusoe*, with its shop-keeping routine of realism. The store of maritime instruments patrolled by Solomon Gills hopes for the anchorage which, when he affixes things and banks on their durability by measuring and enumerating them, is Crusoe's obsession: 'Everything was jammed into the tightest cases . . . and screwed into the acutest angles, to prevent its philosophical composure from being disturbed by the rolling of the sea.' Again realism prescribes sepulchral encasement. The shop window is a sarcophagus of objects. Eventually in the development of the novel the emporium, too, is abstracted. James's Bloomsbury curiosity shop, where the golden bowl is purchased, is a 'shop of the mind', and A. L. Coburn photographed it in 1909 for the New York edition of James's novels as a subjective, reflexive, mirroring window for consciousness. Gills battens down his merchandise to save it not so much from the rolling of the sea as from the turbulence of the real, symbolised by the havoc of the railway excavations in Staggs's Gardens. The railway unsettles the real by mobilising it: 'The very houses seemed disposed to pack up and take trips.' At the end of this accelerated career, where things recklessly metamorphose and surreally mate in the 'hundred thousand shapes and substances of incompleteness' magicked into being by the railway, lies extinction.

Paul thinks of death fluvially, as his reclamation by the waves. His father's mercantilism, like the labour of literary realism, seeks foundation in earth, but can achieve it only by a mortuary stultification. When Florence appears at Captain Cuttle's establishment, Paul metaphorically rescues her by placing her 'on dry land'. He is only one of the novel's characters for whom a dwelling—or a mind—is a Crusoesque insular exile: Toots declares 'my heart is a desert island.' Dombey has parched and deadened the world in his ambition to realise it. At the dining-table, he is a Crusoe who has sickened into that solipsist of the doldrums, the ancient mariner. He 'looked down into the cold depths of the dead sea of mahogany on which the fruit dishes and decanters lay at anchor.' When Gills recites his tales of boys who have run away to sea like Crusoe, Dickens reflects on the treachery of narrative and of literature, which in pretending to attach us to reality and circumstance are all the while tempting us to evasion and escape: 'there never was a book written . . . with the object of keeping boys on shore, which did not lure and charm them to the ocean, as a matter of course.' Familiar things and their romantic side have become antagonistic. Familiarisation cages and solidifies them; romanticism, with its oceanic feeling and its conviction of one life within us and abroad, drenches, saturates and washes them away. When Gills disappears, Rob says he has—like Paul floating out of his body—simply 'flowed'. The same fluctuance or flight is the imperative of time, hastening the collapse of things as it speeds them towards death. As Edith's marriage approaches, Dickens watches her hustled exit from reality: 'The week fled faster. . . . The week fled faster.'

Crusoe scribbled to persuade himself of the orderliness of phenomena. The novel was his means for keeping his metaphysical accounts. In the later Dickens, the form has been made aware of its own vain fictionality. Mortimer Lightwood's clerk alphabetically tallies, from Aggs to Gaggs or Alley to Malley, the clients who have appointments with his employer—except that none of them exist. His 'long, thin manuscript volume with a brown paper cover' is a novel because its contents are chimerae. He resembles Wegg, who first colonises Our House by staffing it with a novelistic crew of characters—'those great creatures, Miss Elizabeth, Master George, Aunt Jane, and Uncle Parker'—and then, de-realising his own inventions, kills them off; or perhaps Tennyson, who used entrancingly to chant his own name over and over again, making nonsense of the word while mystically making a nonentity of himself. Tennyson is deriving lyricism from our own blithely musical nothingness; Blight the clerk is deriving the novel from our computation of our own absurd contingency. He could not get on, he says, without the strictures of his system, 'by which he probably meant that his mind would have been shattered to pieces without this fiction of an occupation'.

Maintaining that fiction can be managed, in Dickens's last novels, only with the aid of a secured imprisonment (in *Little Dorrit*) or by the slick lacquering of surfaces practised by the Veneerings. Mrs Gaskell said that Anne Brontë's realism enjoined that 'she must not varnish . . . or conceal'. But to Dickens the fraud of realism is its application of a glossy varnish. It decoratively screens the abysses within or beneath things, and tries to prevent their decomposition into dust on Boffin's mounds, into the viscous residue which is all that is left of Krook, into the sewage which, when Mortimer and Eugene drive through Rotherhithe, discharges itself into the forgetful Thames, into the fog which obscures and mystifies London in *Bleak House*. The parallel narratives of that novel are a yet more frightening joke on the illusoriness of fiction. Esther Summerson's testimony in the first person records her modest attempt, lamed by her imperceptiveness, to arrange her life into a patterned meaning. She creeps timidly along the earth; Dickens, meanwhile, in the chapters of omniscient narration enjoys the dizzy irresponsibility of an aerial perspective, looking down on the confusion and unintelligible entanglement of human existences and responding with a careless laughter. If Esther is a solicitous domestic angel, Dickens—her creator and her persecutor—is the prince of the air; while she fusses to organise experience into the semblance of a realist novel, he, like Shelley's west wind, ravages and metaphorically maddens it, celebrating its anarchic distraction in a surreal poem.

The double plot is here the signature of a divided mind—one side of which prefers to ignore (as in *Edwin Drood*'s analysis of the criminal consciousness) what the other is up to—and of a disintegrative world. Dickens is a cockneyfied and slightly crazed reincarnation of Shakespeare.

— 30 —
The Critical Epic

The romantics could not write the epic towards which they strove. Wordsworth avoids it, withdrawing from political engagement and public heroism in France to the practice of a pastoral virtue, cloistered in landscape; de Quincey psychologically summarises it in his *Confessions*. He mentions Dr Arnold's headmasterly fear of 'tremendous revolution' yet chooses to concentrate on his own single mental travail—researching the subterranean secrets of the plebeian hall at Manchester Grammar School or 'the central darkness of a London brothel'—rather than epically rallying a collective liberation. He submerges the epic, with that classical and scholarly cargo which Coleridge instructed Wordsworth to study. After a shipwreck, de Quincey imagines a 'vast submarine Bodleian' deliquescing in the ocean: he drowns the world's accumulated knowledge within his own mind.

The epic of a concerted and militant human fate, as opposed to the romance of a digressive libertinism, is written on the romantics' behalf by Carlyle. J. S. Mill, reviewing his *The French Revolution* in 1837, said, 'This is not so much a history, as an epic poem.' It is an account at once of history's freeing of itself from the dead infliction of the past, and a prescription for a similar freedom in literature. It completes a romantic revolution in the overturning of ancestral and inherited genre—a process which in English literature does not wait for 1789 but has been inexorably happening since Chaucer, Langland and Spenser. That dialectic now collectivises history and heroism; it merges the battling individuals of epic in the recurrent, biologically revolutionary cycles of pastoral. For Carlyle, revolution is the rotation of nature, 'annual, centennial, millenial!' The historical movement is as irresistible as ferment in organic germination. This law of change justifies the coupling of opposites in Shakespeare's plays: in Carlyle's history, the terminality of tragedy is checked by the burgeoning continuity of comedy which, as he declares of Homeric epic, 'does not conclude, but merely ceases'—or pauses, awaiting resumption at the next spring or after Berowne in *Love's Labour's Lost* has served his internship outfacing tragic pain in a hospital.

Teufelsdröckh contends that humanity means not individuals but the mass. The revolution, according that mass its accession to power, redefines the hero as a divine average. Coleridge's lonely 'I AM' becomes the garrulous, amiable American 'Me myself' of Walt Whitman, eugenically interchangeable with any of its look-alike fellow-citizens. Hazlitt in 1818 had described the history of literature as divinity's disenchanted abandonment of the world; Carlyle, in the lectures *On Heroes, Hero-Worship, and the Heroic in History* which he delivered in 1840, restores divinity to that depleted world, and disseminates it there in everyman. The primordial hero is a god, but godhead has successively democratised itself, taking on flesh in the form of prophet, poet, priest, man of letters and modern revolutionary leader, garbing itself innocuously as—for instance—Carlyle's Shakespeare, 'our poor Warwickshire peasant', who deserves election to the sovereignty the French Revolution abolished ('Here . . . is an English King, whom no time or chance . . . can dethrone'), or his great-souled Johnson, trudging (in his mortal incarnation) across the earth with wet feet in worn-out shoes. Revolution teaches Carlyle that epic largesse and tragic suffering may devolve on any human creature, and since all individuals are portions of divinity no one of them crucially matters. Dispensable, they can be replaced from that bountiful seed-bed: Mirabeau's death is, Carlyle admits, insignificant. In an extension of heroic suffrage which remembers Spenser's consignment of his epic to the care of female characters, Carlyle also enrols an insurrectionary army of women.

He calls the mob 'a genuine outburst of Nature; . . . communicating with . . . the deepest deep of nature'—romantically mobile and therefore anathema to a classically stationary character like Shakespeare's Caesar, fixed in the firmament. A revolutionary society is therefore to Carlyle a romantically turbulent landscape. His Homeric similes conjoin epic and pastoral by universalising heroic energy: pamphlets constitute a hot deluge, flooding Paris; troops are the city's effluence; the Terror is, as Byron called poetry, a volcanic lava-flow, the fit of a collective imagination. That imagination has exploded from underground, for one of the revolution's literary meanings is the eruption of the sub-plot, predicted when Chaucer's rabble gives chase to the fox, when Shakespeare's impudent comedians extend their franchise from Eastcheap to Westminster, when the madmen of *The Changeling* are uncaged, or when Dickens sets his grotesques, like the Gooroo man or that bogey in the Monument (the ugly id absconded inside classicism), on the rampage. Revolution is convulsion from below and from within, the birth of a thought stealthily growing during reason's sleep and forming itself, as Carlyle remarks of Patrollotism, 'under the female night-cap'. It therefore stimulates an excavation of that subliminal realm where de Quincey's galleons and their drowned libraries repose: Carlyle describes the *citoyens* frantically digging up their cellars to supply the Republic with saltpetre. The devils in *Paradise Lost*, inventing gunpowder during their war on heaven, are the evil geniuses of epic with its chant of arms and the man. In Carlyle that epic manufacture of gunpowder is the comically pastoral consequence of husbandry—a manic digging and delving in psychic basements.

By the same generic logic, revolution causes tragedy to founder again into comedy. The rebellion of the women is likened by Carlyle to 'the Saturnalia of

[485]

the Ancients'; the King's debasement is his reduction to the democracy of the 'ludicrous-ignominious', for ignominy follows, in its obliteration of name and of the precious prerogatives of rank and identity, from comedy's demonstration of our human equality. Chaos comes again, and with it formlessness: the morphological mess (exemplified by Falstaff's body) which delighted the romantics in Shakespeare, and from which Dickens kneads misshapen creations like Quilp. Carlyle's revolutionaries are therefore grotesques, Gothic amalgams of epic and pastoral, tragedy and comedy. Marat is a *'lusus* of Nature', mockingly fabricated 'out of her *leavings* and miscellaneous waste clay', pummelled from that 'dim unshaped raw material' of unconsciousness that Carlyle imagines inside the slumbering heads of the fanatics; and in Charlotte Corday, virgin and leering gargoyle are conjoined as on the Gothic façade of Hugo's Notre Dame or inside the seditious cathedral of the *Biographia Literaria*—Carlyle calls her 'angelic-demonic'. Her assassination of Marat, classically represented in David's painting as the body's sculptural eternalisation, drained of blood and hardening in a cold bath, is to Carlyle the contrivance of a romantic dialectic, forcing contraries together as in a Dickensian coincidence. 'In this manner', he says, 'have the Beautifulest and the Squalidest come in collision, and extinguished one another.'

Above all, the revolution is a liberation of language. *The French Revolution* is a Niagara of words, so torrentially inexhaustible and so unconstrained by its committal to paper and its damming-up as literature that Carlyle was able to rewrite it—or re-activate the geyser—when Mill's parlour-maid lit the fire with his original manuscript. It is, in the phrase G. K. Chesterton used of Browning's *The Ring and the Book*, an epic of free speech. Carlyle hears language as an elemental force, an 'immeasurable tide of French Speech'. Revolution, exciting a tindery combustibility or goading rivers into flood, unleashes a natural energy; Carlyle's sparky or overwhelming rhetoric manages the same feat in language. He eloquently restores to words a bardic power they forfeited after their literary demise as print. That power is exercised in his narrative by Mayor Bailly with his electoral harangues, by Mirabeau with his strong bass voice, by the raging and roaring guardsmen at Nancy, by the shrieking populace which bays at the tumbrils.

Carlyle's book is a 'Parlement', like the Constituent Assembly with its 1200 delegates: a convocation of quarrelling voices, indignantly rejecting silence. But increasingly its sound becomes mere noise, passing beyond articulacy and the enunciation of words into detonation and cannonade, the 'outburst of sound from iron to other throats'. Speech gives way to cursing vociferation. At length the revolution begins to consume language, and when this happens literature must be reinvoked to secure that language's conservation. The present does not issue in a millenial future; literature therefore resumes its ancient task of remembering, which means inditing not talking. Carlyle describes journalistic writing as 'Speech conserved'.

His duty at first is to decipher silence by verbalising it, overhearing the bluster of nature and of the inanimate city. 'What unutterable things the stone walls spoke', he says, when hung with babbling placards and bulletins. However, he soon begins to be restive when he punningly discovers revolution to be a disturbance in language, stirring up within it a confusion which literature only learned to accommodate in the newspaper office of *Ulysses* or in *Finnegans Wake*. Thus the King, attending the constitutional debates, is seated in the journalists' box, 'the "*Loge of the Logographe*"' or '*Lodge of the Logographie*'. Words are the cerebral sovereignty of reason, man being an animal who not only speaks but writes 'an incarnated Word'; that headmastery is what the guillotine slices off. Increasingly the revolution prohibits both speech (filling Lally's mouth with a gag, drowning the King's voice with a thunder of drums as he speaks from the scaffold) and the testamentary responsibility of writing: Jeanne-Marie Philipon's request for pen and paper 'to write the strange thoughts that were rising in her' is initially refused. Carlyle's own logorrheal uproar also succumbs to fatigue. 'The hundredth part of the things that were done, and the thousandth part of the things that were projected and decreed to be done, would tire the tongue of History'; he is not after all the multilingual gossip who is Shakespeare's rumour-monging historian in *Henry IV*. His epic ends by renouncing its ambition. He has not brought about that miracle of incarnation—word's investiture as flesh, a god's clothing himself in the appurtenances of the human hero—which he sees as the task of the bard, who can create fraternity by his exercise of language. The reader Carlyle addresses is absent and invisible, not the bard's colleague in arms: 'To me thou wert as a beloved shade, the disembodied or not yet embodied spirit of a Brother.' And after the brawling, belligerent, rumbling noise the revolution makes and which it finally canonises as the multitudinous bellowing of the crowd—the 'universal continuous peal, of what they call Public Opinion'—only a single sound remains, which is the humbled, vale-dictory voice of Carlyle himself, issuing from and returning to silence: 'To thee', he says to the reader, 'I was but as a Voice.'

Dickens admired *The French Revolution*, and thought to imitate it in *A Tale of Two Cities*. His homage, however, reassimilates it to that English tradition of reserved, quiescent pastoral which became the novel's home-grown religion and which also counsels Wordsworth's retreat from the affray of history. Dickens's division of his narrative between two cities is a precaution similar to the bifurcation of narrative in *Bleak House*. The domestic enclave of Soho is the safe realm of Esther; Paris is given over to the mob, which respects no interior sanctum. The revolution institutionalises that omniscience so fiendish-ly employed by Dickens himself in *Bleak House*: it relies on the espionage of Barsard. Now the invasion of mental and domestic secrecy is the preliminary to a denunciation. The collectivity which consumes individuals in Carlyle, and which makes itself heard as the cataract of his rhetoric, has to be refuted by

Dickens. The novel requires its characters to be quirky integers, detached from community, society, history. Even Mme Defarge undergoes this disengagement when she is made to do battle with the patriotic Miss Pross. Theirs is no ideological wrestling-match; it is more like Mrs Gamp's somnolent, groaning struggle with Mrs Harris—the mind's combat with its phantoms. Sydney Carton's sacrifice of himself is also a quixotic emotional gesture, not the political mobilisation it appears to be. The public expenditure of self is always in Dickens a false protestation: Mrs Jellyby's telescopic philanthropy in *Bleak House*, or the unfeeling, theoretical zeal of Chadband. Virtue lurks sequestered in a bunker. Mrs Weller in *The Pickwick Papers* interprets her error with the shepherd as a parable of this: 'If a married 'ooman vishes to be religious, she should begin with dischargin' her dooties at home, and makin' them as is about her cheerful and happy'; she should not gad about to chapel. John Ruskin imposed a comparable division of existence in his 1864 lectures which assigned kings to their treasuries, queens to their gardens. The male may busy himself with the management of the world; women are restricted to housekeeping, an indoor horticulture.

Ruskin also, like Carlyle in his account of the revolution, reactivates the epic ambition of the romantics, who wished to assemble a summation of knowledge by indexing the contents of consciousness. In Ruskin's case, as in Arnold's and Pater's and as in Carlyle's studies of literary heroism, the romantic imagination seeks completion and self-consciousness by evolving into criticism. Instead of making art, the romantic now tends and explicates and worships it. For Wordsworth, nature was a supplementary scripture. For Ruskin, the revelation of God's purpose in the world happens not in nature but in landscape painting. The *Modern Painters* celebrated by Ruskin in the five volumes he published between 1843 and 1860 are latter-day saints, or angels of evangelism. Ruskin exalts the romantic lyric—a fragment of sensation, an experience whose flight cannot be arrested—into the dogmatic sureness of epic. Gods regain the firmament in his *The Queen of the Air* (1869). Romantic poems, in succession to Milton's expulsion of the profaned deities in his 'Nativity Ode', had described their unseating: Keats's moribund Titans; Shelley's Zeus, defrauded of fire. Ruskin restores them to power, seeing Athena in 'the rubies of the clouds' or imagining her at work in the sky, plaiting vapour into 'films and threads of plume', exercising a shaping creativity in the domed vault which is the mind of nature.

Walter Pater, in a more decadent phase of romanticism, considered that all the arts should attain the condition of music; for Ruskin, they aspired to the condition of painting. The romantics faltered in their pursuit of divinity because they used words, which must always lag behind things. Pigment—miraculously iridescent, in contrast with the colourlessness of print—signifies to Ruskin the blaze of grace in the world. It animates objects or divinely sets fire to them. Speaking of noonday in the Campagna as represented by Turner and Poussin, he says, 'I cannot cal! it colour, it was conflagration. Purple, and crimson, and scarlet, like the curtains of God's Tabernacle, the rejoicing trees sank into the valley in showers of light.' He thought, as he puts it in *The Storm-Cloud of the Nineteenth Century* (1884), that industrialism had soiled the world, bled of it glad colour and desecrated it; the painter's responsibility was to re-embellish a polychrome creation. The glaring palette of the pre-Raphaelites boded a return, like Wordsworth's daffodils, to the golden age. God is announced by the vivid ignition of nature: in Hopkins's winged emissaries of light—kingfishers which catch fire, dragon-flies which draw flame—brilliance is both meaning and spiritual function.

The epigraph which Ruskin attached to *Modern Painters* announces his descent from (and advance beyond) Wordsworth. In the passage Ruskin quotes from *The Excursion*, Wordsworth refers to his ordination as a priest, serving Nature and Truth, and objects to the belittling of 'the transcendent universe' as a mirror for 'proud Self-love'. His twin divinities revolt, 'offended at the ways of men', and quit an unworthy world. Ruskin wins them back, by demonstrating the omnipresence of moral truth in nature. He reconstructs, indeed, the medieval emblematic reading of landscape. The vine betokens waywardness, its companion the pine stands up for steadfastness and resolution, the mutual reliance of a plant's several parts is a parable of helpfulness, rocks are a fundament or sediment of law. The 'thousand faculties' and 'ten thousand interests' that Wordsworth discerned in the human soul are no longer dispersed in brief glimpses, symbolic shinings, doubtful intimations. They are regimented by liturgical authority: the sadly open-ended romantic lyric, tantalised by a reach exceeding its grasp, yields to that Victorian project which G. H. Lewes called the 'systematic classification of experience'. Unable to tolerate their Shelleyan vagrancy and amorphousness, Ruskin even (as he said) bottled clouds.

But *Modern Painters* is also a counterpart to the Dickensian novel, and in this sense it is a work of a seditious, rampaging comic grotesquerie. Turner, its hero, is Ruskin's equivalent to Carlyle's Robespierre. Or he is a pictorial Shakespeare, presaging the uprising of the lower tier of the double plot; and he eventually prompts Ruskin's exposition in *The Stones of Venice* (1851) of Gothic architecture with what Dickens describes as its tragicomically streaky bacon.

Like Dickens, Turner is to Ruskin the rhapsodist of chaos—of the world in its romantic abundance, undisciplined by classicism. Ruskin attributes his understanding of nature to his urban boyhood in the mud, débris and filth of Covent Garden market. Turner even refers to the avalanche-strewn St Gothard as 'a litter of stones'. Unlike Giorgione, growing up in the classical Elysium of Castelfranco or awakening to the ethereality of Venice, Turner inhabits a landscape peopled by gargoyles not gods. The 'short waists' of female dress 'modify to the last', Ruskin says, 'his visions of Greek ideal'. But his grotesquerie is compassionate, enabling him to enfranchise the contradictory entirety of experience. Ruskin notes his 'regard for the poor, whom the Venetians . . . despised'. He is sublime in his rowdy vulgarity. The 'curious . . . combination of elements' which Ruskin analyses in his character amount to a psychological double-plottedness. Ruskin's metaphor for this incongruity has a messy tactility appropriate to Turner's dabbling in pigment. It suggests to him less the 'regular alternation, as the layers of red and white' in Dickens's cross-sectioned joint of bacon or William Butterfield's chapel at Keble College in Oxford than the inextricable convolution of high and low, jewels and ordure. He imagines 'a cable . . . woven of blood-crimson silk, and then tarred on the outside. People handled it, and the tar came off on their hands. . . . Was it ochre?—said the world—or red lead?'

This sordid adept of 'animal English enjoyment', the frequenter of barracks and picnics, the consort of nymphs of barge and barrow, is elected by Ruskin to the status of hero and national saviour. Born on St George's Day, Turner arrives in a time where there is 'no St. George any more to be heard of; no more dragon-slaying possible'. Is his an epic combat, or merely a squalid and jocose mock-epic? Maggie Tulliver in *The Mill on the Floss* (1860) must punishingly learn, when she longs to be rescued from the gipsies by a legendary saviour like St George, that 'heroes were never seen in the neighbourhood of St Ogg's—nothing very wonderful ever came there'; and Ruskin's mettlesome youth has to accept, like Dorothea Brooke renouncing her dream of sanctity as a contemporary Theresa, his condemnation to an incorrigibly real world. He 'can only make manifest the dragon, not slay him, sea-serpent as he is'.

Modern Painters ends with a revision of Spenser's insular and idiosyncratic myth. Art, Ruskin says, commemorates great spiritual events. In Athens it acclaimed the triumph of Pallas, in Venice the assumption of the Virgin (as painted by Titian), and in England it celebrates the accession of that unslayable dragon 'whom the English Andromeda, not fearing, takes for her lord'. Beowulf, Gawain and Spenser's knights busy themselves in a frustrated effort to regiment or to exterminate nature. They all fail. After Grendel, there is his mother to kill, and so on indefinitely; the beheaded Green Knight puts himself together again, as recurrent and as resurrectible as the spring; the Blatant Beast escapes. Turner converts those failures of classical control into a romantic victory. Wisdom now counsels surrender to the beast, not armed defiance: 'The fairy English Queen once thought to command the waves, but it is the sea-dragon now who commands her valleys.' This recension of Spenser demands as well a rewriting of Milton, for the transfer of power between angel and demon need not mean perdition. Ruskin rejoices that 'of old the Angel of the Sea ministered to' English terrain, whereas now 'the Serpent of the Sea' (Milton's leviathan-like Satan?) has seized dominion. Only classical landscape, like Giorgione's pleasances, envisions paradise; what Ruskin calls modern landscape is more likely to be inflamed and infernal—the gaseous gloom of the amphitheatre where Satan presides in John Martin's designs for *Paradise Lost* in 1827, Turner's volcanoes, or the Venetian spires in his 1836 painting of Juliet with her nurse which Ruskin likens to 'pyramids of pale fire from some vast altar'.

Ruskin imposes on painting the conscientious research into truth which became the agenda of the Victorian novel. George Eliot works inductively, carrying out experiments in life; Balzac wished to be a doctor of social medicine. To be readied for his new responsibility—art's idealising of real life, which Auguste Comte called its true mission, once it had been unfettered from theology—Turner has to lose his romantic mistiness. He is made an honorary pre-Raphaelite: a meticulous and myopic student of nature. The same scruple leads Ruskin himself to advance from the criticism of painting to that of architecture (and thence beyond art in the 1870s to social reconstruction, when he organized street-sweeping in London and road-building in Oxford). Clouds, for instance, distress him. They are too evanescently pictorial a phenomenon; he can tolerate them only if they are hewn into architecture. When he asks, in *Modern Painters*, 'on what anvils and wheels is the vapour pointed, twisted, hammered, whirled, as the potter's clay?' he is paraphrasing the question Blake addresses to the tiger, which also—superbly self-creative— will not answer. 'By what hands', Ruskin goes on, 'is the incense of the sea built up into domes of marble?' His imaginative aim was to sculpt those romantically mobile elements of air and water into perdurable cathedrals. He achieves it in his astounding description of St Mark's in *The Stones of Venice*, where the sea is, as he requests in his interrogation of clouds, petrified and enskied in marble. The pinnacles of the cathedral look to him like 'breakers . . . frost-bound before they fell, and . . . inlaid . . . with coral and amethyst'. The arches are waves of 'marble foam' which inundate the sky in 'wreathes of sculptured spray'.

In quest of certainty, symbolised by the adamantine 'authority of rock', Ruskin is here overcoming a romantic fear confessed in *Modern Painters*. There he quotes, as a specimen of 'the modern manner', Keats's description of waves breaking 'with a wayward indolence', and contrasts it with the habits of Homeric oceans, classically constituted of salt water and therefore averse to the pathetic fallacy of an attributed human motive and emotion. Seeing waves as psychological agents, Keats is also wishing on them a human mortality: his is a 'short-lived foam', as against the eternity of Homer's wine-dark sea, maintained in changelessness by those reliable epithets. Homer, Ruskin decides, had 'a faith . . . much stronger than Keats's'. Since art for Ruskin can be great only, as he said in an 1853 lecture, if it builds to gods, he is censuring the infirmity of romantic impressionism when he raises his own verbal cathedral in that account of St Mark's. On it, Keats's lazily dying waves are a carved and crystalline architrave.

The aestheticism of Pater can defend the romantic philosophy of consciousness, fluently hedonistic like Byron's sea or Shelley's west wind, by rendering the stern, stubborn granite of Ruskin liquid once more, loosing objects (as he does in the 1873 conclusion to his essays on *The Renaissance*) into impressions and declaring that their apparent solidity is but a deceit practised by language. Ruskin's cathedral begins to drown in Pater, who in his study of du Bellay laments the 'rough ponderous mass' of the Gothic cathedrals with their brutish heaviness. The repudiation of the Gothic is part of a war against matter, and against the fixity of morals: among the Romantic ruins, du Bellay grieves over 'the duration of the hard, sharp outlines of things'.

Pater's Renaissance overturns the Gothic orthodoxy of Ruskin. Ruskin's Giorgione is sustained by an architectural conviction: an alabaster Venice, 'paved with emerald', its senate 'impenetrable, implacable' like human columns, its Alps ethereal but strong. Pater's Giorgione has succumbed to the flux of sensation, and to the airy illusions of music. Trusting in no eternity, he prizes only the moments of sensual bliss which he chooses to paint. That spirit is blamed by Ruskin for the decline of Venice. The Renaissance tempts the city to a false, ornamental classicism. San Giorgio Maggiore is to Ruskin a bad building because it is an impious one, a Christian church contorting itself in its pretence to be a pedestalled Greek temple. Like those lutanists in Giorgione on whom Pater lingers, Ruskin's Venetians sacrifice thought and feeling to 'dexterity of touch', and—as founding faith departs—are 'left to felicitate themselves on their . . . neat fingering'.

The Gothic amalgam, embracing, as Ruskin says of Venetian ornament, 'all vegetable and animal forms', survives after the Renaissance by migrating from architecture to Turner's paintings, and to English literature. The gloomy Gothic aisle leads to 'the shadows of Rembrandt, and savageness of Salvator', then to 'the English school of landscape, culminating in Turner'; perhaps, also, to Keats's description of a classical grove in *The Fall of Hyperion* as a Gothic cathedral of overarching trees. 'We Goths', as Ruskin addresses the audience in his 1883 lectures on English art, find in literature a supplementary cathedral, where sanctity and jest, seraphs and leering griffins, are grotesquely paired. He judges Milton to be less characteristic of the English imaginative tradition than Bunyan, because Satan is too classically conceived. His conception is too 'smoothed and artistical'; emphasising his nobility, Milton has a classical reluctance to represent sin as a deformation of body, or as an obsessive self-caricaturing. He refuses to turn Satan into a hobgoblin like Quilp. The cranky extroversion of inner nature predominates in Spenser, where it can be studied 'without reference to Gothic cathedrals'; in Shakespeare, whose grotesquerie Ruskin notes as intolerable to neoclassical French critics; and in Dickens, in whose 'word-wit' Ruskin sees an expression of a demotic, irreverent humour—'the independent language of the operatives'—which once incised its cheekiness in 'the sculptures of the cathedral'. Blake's tiger, that mysterious maker glanced at by Ruskin in his query about clouds, also runs riot in this capricious and lop-sided temple. Ruskin imagines the Gothic mason 'to have been exactly what a tiger would be, if you could give him love of a joke, rigorous imagination, strong sense of justice, fear of hell, knowledge of Northern mythology, a stone den, and a mallet and chisel.'

Ruskin's advance from painting to architecture, and from criticism to theology, conscripts romanticism (with its life of sensations rather than thoughts) to the march of mind. His tragedy is that, at the end, he falters and reverts to a subjectivity as precarious and wayward as romantic perception—an impressionism of consciousness whose emblem, at the conclusion of *Praeterita* in 1889, is the fireflies remembered at Fonte Branda, 'everywhere in sky and cloud rising and falling, mixed with the lightning, and more intense than the stars'; phosphorescences signifying the elusive, winged, romantic image, and also Ruskin's expiring reason. The career of intuition, trusting as Wordsworth does to inspirational breezes and to the ministrations of vagrant clouds, is here extinguished. The sagacious imperative of the Victorians is to know. Teufelsdröckh rejoices in a world where there are theories of everything, and hastens to supply a much-needed theory of clothes. Matthew Arnold's judgement on the romantics was that they did not know enough. Keats is too mawkishly sensual, Shelley too vaporous: they lack the moral fortitude—which Arnold, as if remembering Ruskin's adherence to the cathedral as a symbol of what romanticism lacked, calls architectonics—of intelligence.

Arnold's criticism recapitulates Ruskin's journey from Turnerian water, the flux of sense, to the quarried ruggedness of building, raised by man, as he puts it in *The Stones of Venice*, to assert empire over the ocean and to found a throne on its sands. After the liquefaction of the romantics, Arnold seeks to impose a classical rigour on English literature. Fluctuance is inimical to him. Though he compliments Chaucer's 'divine liquidness of diction, his divine fluidity of movement', those very qualities keep him from possessing the arid steadfastness of greatness. Arnold's metaphors of approbation are always either geological or architectural. Poems must acquire the impermeability of mineral: hence his critical standard of the touchstone, his praise of Milton's rocky excellence, or of Wordsworth's baldness, worn away into a noble austerity like the peak of a mountain, and his argument that Keats, despite the orgiastic poetry of his youth, 'had flint and iron in him, . . . had character'. Those solidified spars of poetry, specimens of language fossilised into classicism and its energy-conserving inertness (one of Arnold's touchstones is of course Wordsworth's massy line 'And never lifted up a single stone'), serve Arnold as a steadying life-preserver. 'Hold fast' is his injunction. And the conviction we must cling to is a belief in foundation, that 'poetry is at bottom a criticism of life'—that it has a bottom after all. There is an urgent tenacity in Arnold's critical imagery, which makes him emphasise what Bernard Berenson was to call tactile values, treating the poetic extract as a thing graven or embossed, whose truth was to be reckoned by the hands, like a string of rosary beads. 'The tact of the Greeks . . .', he says, 'was infallible.' His insistent italics are a device for imposing this tactility, as if words could be made to jut typographically into high relief, as 'that great and inexhaustible word *life*' is on three occasions profiled in two adjoining sentences in Arnold's 1879 essay on Wordsworth.

The same promotion exalts the poets. If Arnold recommended that the Bible should be read for its poetry not its dogma, he also implicitly proposed that poets should be read as scriptural dogmatists. Criticism is his conferment on them of an official rank and an institutional immortality, like Carlyle's suggested enthronement of Shakespeare, Tennyson's reward of a peerage, and Ruskin's election of Turner to an angel of apocalypse, 'sent as a prophet of God to reveal to men the mysteries of His universe'. Wordsworth's head, in Arnold's essay, wears an aureole: 'his glory crowns him.' But for this to happen he must first die, and Arnold writes at a time when 'Wordsworth has been in his grave for some thirty years'. Critical occasions are solemn entombments, recording the entry of poets into the national and classical mausoleum. Arnold remembers Macaulay collecting subscriptions 'to found a memorial' of Wordsworth; his essay on Milton was spoken in a church at the unveiling of a memorial stained-glass window.

Yet Arnold's critical faith in literature as an instrument of restitution and redemption is weakened by his own poetry. Though he praises the ferrous backbone of Keats, Arnold's poems see iron as the harsh metal of industrial utilitarianism, averse to poetic fancy. Wordsworth's misfortune, he thinks, was to have lived on into the iron time of the toil-worn Victorians, and in 'Resignation' diurnal routine is an 'iron bound' which 'hems us all in'. In an 1880 preface to a poetic anthology, he uses an image opposed to his symbolism of stern, retentive, masonic durability: 'It is the course of one great contributory stream to the world-river of poetry that we are invited to follow. We are here invited to trace the stream of English poetry.' The mental landscape is an inadvertently despairing one. The stream's destiny is to be obliterated in the river, the river's in the ocean. This is the aqueous chaos of Turner, with what Ruskin called the 'deathfulness of the open, deep, illimitable sea', or of Pater in the riverine conclusion to *The Renaissance*. Spenser's wedding of Thames and Medway no longer means immersion in a collective life. It bodes the will-less loss of everything, like George Eliot's flood in *The Mill on the Floss*.

Arnold had already represented in a poem the terrain which the essay surveys as that of poetic history. At the end of his *Sohrab and Rustum*, the epic conflict dies into pastoral. The heat of battle gives way to frosty starlight, the crowded plain to a hushed waste, and the river, Oxus, placidly meanders on, washing away the wreckage of those human existences which have tried to stay it and to reprieve themselves from elapsing time, and loses itself in the sea. On Dover Beach, too, Arnold hears the same casual fatality of waters. The moan of the receding tide is the ebbing of faith. Its withdrawal leaves only stranded consciousnesses, beached egos like those 'in the sea of life enisled' which Arnold speaks of in 'To Marguerite'. Donne denied that man was an island. Literature's purpose, like religion's, was to create community. But Emerson, visiting England in 1847–8, discovered each of the islanders to be an island unto himself—exiled in moated granges like Tennyson's Mariana or moated villas like Dickens's Wemmick—and though Arnold would like to believe that literature is the ocean which connects us, his image in the 1880 preface, like the elegiac epilogue to *Sohrab and Rustum*, makes it a river flowing indifferently between us, as cheerfully oblivious as Tennyson's brook which goes on forever while men come and go, or as Joyce's 'riverrun', that drooling continuum of language which (as against Carlyle's 'tide of French Speech') has deluged all its individual speakers.

Arnold thought that 'the future of poetry is immense'. But that future will require it to turn into criticism, which means into prose. Having, in 'Stanzas from the Grande Chartreuse', rejected an adolescent romanticism—Byron's exhibitionism, Shelley's vain hope—Arnold prescribes a new classicism for the art. He writes an epilogue to Hazlitt's theory of poetry's decline in an elderly, desacralised world, declaring in an 1852 letter that 'the difference between a mature and youthful age of the world compels the poetry of the former to use great plainness of speech as compared with that of the latter.' Macaulay believed that the maturing age would outgrow poetry altogether, leave it behind as a mnemonic, metrical aid on which the savage mind had relied. Arnold agrees: in his critical essays, the great literary achievement of the English seventeenth and eighteenth centuries is the invention of a workable, unpretentious prose, of which (he judges) Dryden and Pope are classics. The twin authorities of prose and classicism demand the devaluation of Shakespeare. 'How ill he often writes!' noted Arnold in 1853, as he began *The Tempest*. The play he chooses to reprove is of course the one that commentators like Shelley and de Quincey had seen as Shakespeare's most romantic: lyrically unweighted to earth, its voices make music in the air; it is exempted from that prosaic terrain George Eliot calls the 'hard unaccommodating Actual'.

Once the novel establishes itself as the conscience of reality, conducted in the 'honest prose' of Scott's Ravenswood, poetry is first exposed as falsification, then improvingly abolished. Gwendolen flatters Mrs Arrowpoint in *Daniel Deronda*, who has written a fictional biography of Tasso, by concurring that 'imagination is often truer than fact'. A romantic faith is here a specious dexterity at lying. The treacherous Lizzie in Trollope's *The Eustace Diamonds* (1873), addicted to Byron, mistakenly feels that 'poetry was life and life was poetry'. But poetry appeals to her because, like any other trinket to be conspicuously consumed, it symbolises luxury, wastefulness, the repudiation of moral economy and necessity: 'Poetry was what her soul craved;—poetry, together with houses, champagne, jewels, and admiration.' A tarnished, truthless poetry can be justified only if it metamorphoses into the higher prose,

THE CRITICAL EPIC

acquiring the incised, upright rectitude of the italicised *life* in Arnold's essay. Victorian poetry is prose ennobled, thought elevated by versification. Instead of intense romantic heat, it is elucidated by 'brightening Reason's lamp', which in George Eliot's *Spanish Gypsy* (1868) beckons humanity 'to higher paths', or the cool illumination of Arnold's wise pronouncements 'that pierce the night like stars'. Poetry has been secularised. It no longer descends from a god and ventriloquistically sings through the poet, since there is no deity in whom it can originate. The agnosticism of the Victorians—of Tennyson in *In Memoriam* (1850) and Browning in the relativist universe of *The Ring and the Book* (1868–9), of Arnold worshipping the guardian angels of humanism in 'Rugby Chapel' (1857) and George Eliot singing in the 'choir invisible' (and inaudible)—covers a deeper doubt about the indwelling god of romantic creativity. Arnold gave up poetry, because he had lost the religious certainty on which he thought it must depend.

In *Empedocles on Etna* (1852) he writes about poetry's innocently unconscious past, and about its self-negating future. The boy Callicles whimsically plays his harp in the fertile valleys, his head full of wine. The poems he chants are fables of an unreflectiveness protectively crouched or embowered in nature, restored to a pantheistic Eden: heroes repose in Elysian fields, Cadmus and Harmonia are rescued from their Theban peril and released into the underbrush as two bright snakes. Callicles is the romantic poet, blithe because ignorant. Like Arnold deciding that the romantics did not know enough, Pausanius calls him 'a boy whose tongue outruns his knowledge'. The philosopher Empedocles has outlawed himself from the verdant lower slopes and, passing beyond the line of afforestation to attain the summit of Etna and its 'hot noon, without a shade', from the easy consolations of poetry. While Callicles sings, Empedocles reasons. It is ironically appropriate that he should do so on Etna. The volcano had been studied, during his term of office at Naples, by Sir William Hamilton, and pictured in eruption by Turner, because it demonstrated the romantic volatility and combustibility of the senses and the imagination; its lava was poetry. Arnold calls it simply 'the heat'. But in his poem it is no longer violently ebullient or effervescent, as it is during Carlyle's revolution. It signifies the intransigence of the world, George Eliot's uningratiating actuality. It signifies, also, insignificance, the nonentity of Empedocles, who discounts himself and his worries:

> Our cry for bliss, our plea,
> Others have felt it too.
> Our wants have all been felt, our errors made before.

Its route to the boiling centre of the earth doubles as that hole in a sky from which God has absconded. Empedocles therefore commits suicide by abruptly hurling himself into the vacuum of the crater. The future of poetry consists in an act of critical autopsy.

— 31 —
The Novel's Natural History

At first, the novel justified its genreless name by its delight in novelties—the objects manufactured by Crusoe, filched by Moll, purchased by Pamela. Its accumulation of properties derived from its campaign to realise the world: to secure it, like Gulliver manacling his furniture to the floor. Is realism, not imperialism, the highest stage of capitalism? So Dickens suspects in *Dombey and Son*. The nineteenth century's ambition is not to fix and fasten the existing world, as Crusoe wished, but to achieve that world's amelioration. The novel therefore takes on a new duty. It becomes a school of revolutionary renovation.

The nineteenth century had mobilised, almost motorised history. Its present was stretched taut between two contending epochs. Alfred de Musset in his *Confessions d'un enfant de siècle* (1864) calls these alternative ages the fossilised past and the liberated future. He is in transit between eras, embarked, as he says, on an Atlantic which connects the old continent to the new. Matthew Arnold described the same time-travel between a dying world and another order of things struggling to be born. Revolution is one midwife employed by history; the novel is another. Scott's Waverley novels are about the temporising—or wavering—between two historical dispensations: the monarchical, chivalric past of Mary Stuart in *The Abbot* (1820), the parliamentary future engineered by Cromwell in *Woodstock* (1826).

Mordecai in *Daniel Deronda* (1876) believes in 'a growth, a passage, and a new unfolding of life whereof the seed is more perfect, more charged with the elements that are pregnant with the diviner form.' The novel is enlisted as a form habituated to the study of growth and rites of passage. From Tom Jones and Tristram Shandy to Stephen Dedalus and Paul Morel, its heroes have been creatures striving for self-definition. The Victorians represent that metamorphic agony as a prerogative of nature and of nations, not just of individuals; and in doing so they restore to the novel the sacredness which, in the eighteenth century, it mock-heroically derides. *Daniel Deronda* achieves the novel's universalisation, and in *The Dynasts* Hardy passes beyond the novel to a supervision of history, managing the restoration of the form to its origin in epic. Why is the loose baggy monster—as Henry James called the voluminous novels of the Victorians—so distended? Because its contents amount to the hardware of Hegelian epic: a totality of objects. But their cataloguer is no longer an artisan building from the ground upwards, like Crusoe. He sees the world from a vertical distance, having surmounted it. Novels extend between past and future, earth and heaven: Gwendolen gaming at Leubronn while Deronda, 'outside and above her', superciliously watches; Tess collapsed and defeated at Stonehenge while the President of the Immortals gloats on high. From this aerial vantage, George Eliot studies the society of Middlemarch webbed into interdependence, and Hardy, when Marty and Giles wander in the mist in _The Woodlanders_ (1887), sees 'their lonely courses' as 'part of the pattern in the great web of human doings then weaving in both hemispheres, from the White Sea to Cape Horn'. The novel's enlarging vision undertakes to be cosmopolitan (in the 'very distant varieties of European type' noticed by George Eliot at Leubronn, or in the global itinerancy of the Jews), then cosmic.

The change in the novel's ambition throughout Europe can be measured by comparing _Vanity Fair_ with _War and Peace_. Thackeray omits Waterloo, as Jane Austen had excluded Napoleon from _Pride and Prejudice_: the novel's concern is private lives, blithely unhistorical. Tolstoy, however, concludes with a learnedly painstaking analysis of Napoleon's Russian campaign and the strategies of national resistance. The novel has assumed a responsibility to comprehend the logic of history. Balzac, by relentlessly collecting and classifying phenomena, and Zola, by clinically inspecting human degeneracy and institutional malaise, had made the novel a science of society. For George Eliot and Hardy, too, it is a species of natural history.

The novel's duty is to correct what G. H. Lewes, in his biography of Goethe, calls 'that brilliant error known as the Romantic School'. Goethe himself criticised his own time as retrograde because it was subjective, and lyric poetry is the voice of this whimpering subjectivity. The hero of Lewes's novel _Ranthorpe_, written in 1842, begins his literary career as a poet, brewing narcotics (as a publisher says). But he rejects poetry because it is morally lax and mentally wayward, its practitioners 'vain, impressionable and luxurious; working by fits and starts . . . and hating all continued toil.' He graduates to a Goethean objectivity and from there to a Comtean exercise in atonement, and this access of wisdom is a prescription for the new authority of the novel as an emissary of mind, 'a glorious sun giving the whole world light'. Mr Thornton, who dissuades Ranthorpe from a Wertheresque suicide, remembers Goethe at Weimar: having mastered 'all the storms of life', he understood 'the divine significance of man's destiny—which is work'. Novels, conscientiously researched, arduously justified, embody for the Victorians (in an aesthetic version of the labour theory of value) this improving industriousness. George Eliot positively boasted of the toil _Romola_ (1862–3) had cost her.

Poetry sought redemption, among the Victorians, by imitating the studious hard work done by the novel: hence such hybrids as Browning's _The Ring and the Book_, his wife's _Aurora Leigh_, Coventry Patmore's _The Angel in the House_. The novel, conversely, later frees itself from the meticulous drudgery of the Victorians by seizing once more the mental irresponsibility of poetry. No one works in the novels of Henry James (who, visiting Newport in 1870, declared an indolent society fitter for the pictorial purposes of fiction than an industrious one); and Virginia Woolf's most insulting judgement on her predecessors, in an *Athenaeum* essay of 1920, is to charge that the novel's literalism has reduced prose to a household chore. 'The novelists put their English to the most menial tasks', and prose, which would rather be wantoning at liberty like poetry, is tethered to domestic routine: it must 'do all the work of the house; . . . make the beds, dust the china, boil the kettle, sweep the floors.'

The first works of Dickens were called sketches, those of George Eliot scenes. Each adopts a pictorial mode, one adapted to the city, the other to the country. *Sketches by Boz* (1836) is about fragmentariness in town, *Scenes of Clerical Life* (1857) about the dutiful relationships and moral regularities of a rural existence. A sketch is swift and incomplete; it makes a provisional graphic scrawl, but accepts the erasure of its own short-lived markings, which stands for the city's obliteration of transitory existences. In one of Boz's anecdotes, an old lady goes off to the seaside, 'and during her absence [the half-pay captain] completely effaced the name from her brass door-plate, in his attempts to polish it with aqua-fortis'. The sketch knows itself to be, like a life, momentary; a scene studies life, and in doing so eternalises it, demonstrating—as George Eliot does in her stories of Shepperton—how people belong to and are sustained by each other, and how their society submits to the tutelage of nature. The landscape is scenic as Dickens's London can never be because it is governed by rhythmic recurrence and necessity (the basis of morals) not by unrepeatable, sketchy glances. It defers, as Ruskin says, to 'the divine laws of seed-time which cannot be recalled, harvest which cannot be hastened, and winter in which no man can work'.

George Eliot's theory of community begins from this scenic reverence, which is the pictorial idiom of pastoral: observation not as Boz's visual agitation but as ritual observance. In 1856 she wrote an essay about W. H. Riehl's sociological account of peasant culture, which she entitled a 'Natural History of German Life'. She praises Riehl for having achieved what English literature has not so far managed: a study of the popular mind. Dickens she discounts because he is limited to 'the external traits of our town population'; he cannot see people from within, intuiting 'their conceptions of life', because he is disjoined from the steadying society of the countryside. He represents an alienated modernity; George Eliot wants to narrate the long history of the race, whose dead end is the Dickensian city. She begins with Riehl's peasants since they are the contemporary vestiges of our mental infancy. They represent the perpetuity of the middle ages, before mind had commenced its march. She advises artists wanting to draw medieval characters to seek models among the peasantry, and explains 'why the old German painters gave the heads of their subjects a greater uniformity of type than the painters of our day: the race had not attained to a high degree of individualization in features and expression.' The country is a nascent condition prior to individual character. George Eliot's own first novels of rural Loamshire are retrospective accounts of this state of nature which she herself—acquiring a mind and with it the capacities for foresight and hindsight, embarked on the rolling pavement of history—has outgrown. Reviewing the past, she sees a world of hallowing and haunted primitivism. Mrs Tulliver or Silas Marner fussing or grieving over their household goods are propitiating household gods, deities tabernacled on the hearth. Domestic transactions, as when Bartle Massey offers a last supper of bread and wine to Adam Bede, are homely sacraments.

George Eliot's novels describe the progressive course of modern history which starts from the death of these omnipresent gods, and in doing so they recapitulate the history of literature. Her first novelistic hero is an Adam, her last, Deronda, is not a man at all (as one of the disputants in Henry James's 1876 debate says of him) but a secular Christ; and between the old Adam and the new, her novels extend from biblical allegory or fairy-tale—the fabulations of what she calls in _Silas Marner_ (1861) 'the peasants of old times', who live still in 'the early ages of the world' and invent literature as a story-telling magic for appeasing the unknown—to the modern rationalisation which enables literature, passing beyond the witchery of Raveloe or Mr Tulliver's attribution of rats, weevils and lawyers to Old Harry, to leave behind the superstitious imagination. Now, in _Daniel Deronda_, the novel graduates to doing the work of science and of religion, explaining the world and thereby saving it.

The novels begin in the consoling repetitiveness of pastoral, frustrating the onward journey of history. Silas's avarice is just such a tediously habitual motive: 'Do we not wile away moments of inanity or fatigued waiting by repeating some trivial movement or sound, until the repetition has bred a want . . .?' If narrative means decisions and choices, it cannot exist in this world: the dog slinks after Godfrey Cass 'perhaps because she saw no other career open to her'. Its only permissible narratives are twice-told tales which arrive routinely at foregone conclusions. George Eliot's rustics 'say over again with eager emphasis the things they had said already anytime that twelve-month'. This is the stalled world of primordial epic, where literature consists in a formulaic, repetitive drill, calculated to prevent things from happening. By contrast Deronda affronts a destiny which envisages a world without end and, leaving for the east, quits the too-terrestrial, middling march of the novel for an epic of mental adventure and humanitarian reconcilement. He embodies that Victorian notion which J.S. Mill called 'the spirit of the age': history as itself a spirit in motion, immaterially, through time.

Mill said that the main intellectual endeavour of the Victorians was that of 'comparing one's own age with former ages'. This studious retrospection, defined as 'Looking Backward' by George Eliot in one of the _Essays of Theophrastus Such_ (1879), is a pastoral vision, because it subdues the past and stills it in a picture. The ploughed, pastured, fenced and hedged landscape of England is, George Eliot says, 'a piece of our social history in pictorial writing'.

Pictorialism is a contemplative consciousness, pondering life (like Deronda scrutinising Gwendolen at the gaming-table) in the hope that fretful action might be raised to the dignity and the poised calm of idea. Redemption means, in this positivist universe, permitting yourself to become an object of knowledge. To be known is to be seen, and that is to be pictorially studied. Gwendolen first resents Deronda's gaze, but is at last grateful for its introversion and pacification of her. She tells him, resigning all hope of possessing him, that it will be better with her for having known him—for having been known by him.

The interiors of *Adam Bede* (1859) are already conceived in the way Deronda ponders Gwendolen: they are bathed in a lambent light of understanding, made radiant by George Eliot's affectionate field-work on them. 'What a fine old kitchen this is!' says the squire to Mrs Poyser. He pictures it condescendingly, in a tone of social patronage; George Eliot herself wants to picture it with the devotional altruism of learning. What she admires in Dutch genre paintings, she says, is their 'rare, precious quality of truthfulness'. Historical truth is made manifest pictorially, slowed down for examination. Or else it can be arrested—by a combination of love and knowledge, which both want to rescue unrepeatable instants from time—in photography: another of George Eliot's standards for truth of perception was 'the delicate accuracy of a sun-picture', in reference to the first photographs of David Octavius Hill and Robert Adamson. Henry James, reviewing an exhibition of Dutch pictures in New York in 1872, acknowledged the same quality of vision in 'the quietly wise De Vries'. This pictorial wisdom counsels the pastoral deceleration of narrative. Hence the chapter in *Adam Bede* entitled 'In Which the Story Pauses a Little'. Such an intermission allows the novel to relax reflectively into picture, essay and excursus. It licenses that withdrawal from particular cases into intellectual generality which is the logical tendency of George Eliot's mind: of Dorothea's marital trial she remarks, 'in such a crisis as this, some women begin to hate'; when Gwendolen intrigues against Lush, her initiative is also scientifically classified: 'we mortals have a strange spiritual chemistry going on within us.'

In the novels of Trollope, pastoral means a genteel denial of time and motion, an embargo on industry and its speeding-up of history. He insists that his Barsetshire is 'purely agricultural'; he argues that England is 'not yet a commercial country', and might 'as well be called feudal England or chivalrous England'. Here pastoral means idyllic ignorance, the shiftlessness of Falstaff. In George Eliot it enjoins awareness. From the bucolic hamlets of the first novels, changeless and therefore scenically able to withstand George Eliot's gaze ('The dairy was certainly worth looking at', she notes in *Adam Bede*), she passes to societies arousing themselves from slumber, acquiring—as history begins to impel them—a consciousness of themselves which is the studious, comprehensive boon of pastoral.

The Renaissance in the Florence of _Romola_ and the Reform Bill in the Treby Magna of _Felix Holt_ (1866) are both passages from the innocence of moral stupidity to an acceptance of conscience and consequence, of history and of morality (for it, too, is a matter of understanding time, the unrepeatability of actions and their causal laws). To the nineteenth century, the Renaissance marked a global advent of consciousness. Jules Michelet in 1855 referred to its dual discoveries—of the world, and of man. Its heroes are explorers, both geographical (Columbus and the other navigators) and psychological (Machiavelli, or the murderous Dukes and sybaritic Bishops who are the adornments of the Italian Renaissance in Browning's monologues). It is the period which invents perspective, and thus allows the precise measurement of significance. Browning's Fra Lippo Lippi delights in this new mental instrument; George Eliot employs it in _Daniel Deronda_ when Offendene, from which Gwendolen decamps, is perspectively revalued and becomes 'picturesque through aerial distance'. In her prologue to _Romola_ George Eliot personifies its _Zeitgeist_. Her 'resuscitated Spirit' of the fifteenth century exists, like Arnold's Victorians, between two worlds, and suffers the pangs of metamorphosis: the perturbation of 'human conscience . . . in the unrest of a new growth'. Industrialisation brings the same mental evolution to the Midlands of _Felix Holt_. An agrarian market-town has been awakened by social and economic change: first a canal, then coal mines, after this a saline spring and a projected watering-place. It must now ready itself to undertake the improving ordeal of mentally renovating itself. Unmoved, George Eliot says, by the French Revolution, the Napoleonic wars, by Tom Paine or Cobbett, it begins in 1832 'to know the higher pains of a dim political consciousness'. And just as a small renaissance occurs in Romola, so Esther suffers through a reformation when exposed to Felix. George Eliot calls this 'the first religious experience of her life'. The nature of the conversion has been altered by the new religion of humanity. It is the acquisition not of grace but of knowledge: Freud's 'Where Id was, Ego shall be', or the resolve of André Malraux 'to transform destiny into awareness'. George Eliot describes Esther's education by Felix as at once an induction into a holy order and a session of psychotherapy. It is 'the first self-questioning, the first voluntary subjection, the first longing to acquire the strength of greater motives and obey the more strenuous rule.'

In Dickens's _Hard Times_, industrialism is a similar education. When Louisa visits Stephen Blackpool, she must face up to the 'individuality' (missing, for George Eliot, from Riehl's peasants) of this Coketown worker. Dickens, however, prescribes for Coketown not the mental apprenticeship of Treby Magna but the fantasticating misinterpretation of metaphor. To the travellers on express trains, the town's factories look 'like Fairy palaces'. His version of pastoral serves up to the industrial toilers the brief forgetfulness of a holiday at Sleary's circus. The romance that Dickens sought out in familiar things was not Carlyle's progressive 'chivalry of thought'; it counselled playful, infantile regression, the hallucinatory abolition of actuality which enables him, in an 1850 *Household Words* article on the Post Office, to see a band of journalists as 'knights-errant in a fairy-tale' and the sorting-room as a venue for 'the ball in "Cinderella"'. Dickens remains romantic (at least according to Arnold's definition) in his brave refusal to know. Pastoral means to George Eliot, on the contrary, an arena of intellect. The Florentine forum possesses a world-encompassing omniscience. The citizens are enclosed within the hills, and then even more tightly girdled about by their ancient walls, yet their political interests like their trade extend 'from Syria to Britain'. Bratti says, 'One may never lose sight of the cupola and yet know the world.' The polity of the city-state is defined as a kind of consciousness, which carries with it the responsibility of engagement: 'Men knew each other as they passed in the street, . . . and were conscious not only of having the right to vote but the chance to be voted for.' The Medici despotism can be considered benevolent because it is an absolute mental superintendence. The Augustinian monk tells the shipwrecked scholar Tito that 'at Rome you will be lost in a crowd'—the Dickensian experience: erasure of self, cancellation of will, descent into the dream which is London's underground river—whereas 'at Florence every corner is penetrated by the sunshine of Lorenzo's patronage'. The same illumining cognisance is assumed by the novelist, who must encyclopaedically know his characters. Henry James once volunteered to sit for an examination on Isabel Archer.

The Florentine forum, tightly self-contained yet all-knowing, 'a narrow scene of corporate action' which universalises itself, is midway between the villages of George Eliot's first novels and the expatriated vagabondage of *Daniel Deronda*. As a sequence, her novels are a resumé of modern society's growth: a supplement to Balzac's stock-taking of social types, or Tolstoy's account of a nation's combat for survival. Their evolutionary urgency makes them dissatisfied, however, with the novel. Middlemarch is less a place than a name for the limited world which the novel has been too busy representing to bother with reforming.

Middlemarch is the Midlands but also middle earth, the downcast terrain of human meanness. It is as well the capital of mimesis: Dorothea and Lydgate are denied the heroic lives they long for, because the novel (born from mock-epic, and comfortably settled, as Henry Tilney tells Catherine, in the middle counties of England) can tolerate only mediocrity. Amos Barton in *Scenes of Clerical Life* exists already in this state. 'He was superlatively middling, the quintessential extract of mediocrity.' Deronda, too, pretends to what he calls 'middlingness', though Gwendolen argues that 'To be middling with me is another phrase for being dull.' Everything in Middlemarch, spotted with commonness, is middling. Mind has here reached midway on its march, stirring the desire for an alternative existence which cannot yet be brought to pass. Dorothea and her kind must tolerate a pastoral innocuousness, and resign themselves to being forgotten. Having 'lived faithfully a hidden life', they are laid to rest in 'unvisited tombs'. Compressed within the word there is also a reminiscence of that mill on the Floss which James was to use as an image for a belittling, reductive reality, when Ralph Touchett tells Isabel she has been ground in the very mill of the conventional—put through, that is, the action of a novel. Hardy employs an image similar to that of the cheapening, reductive mill when Bathsheba in _Far From the Madding Crowd_ (1874) turns Gabriel's grindstone: labouring at a wheel, he says, benumbs the mind in an 'attenuated variety of Ixion's punishment'. But this drowsiness and dreariness—'the brain gets muddled, the head grows heavy'—is in Hardy a mood of gravitational homecoming, tugging the mind down through the body towards the earth where they both belong. The mill can for Hardy induce a state of almost mystic torpor. Nor are his people defiled by commonness, like Lydgate. Instead they share, embedded in the soil of human being, a common imperfection. When Fitzpiers proves unfaithful, Grace in _The Woodlanders_ hopes for 'a sympathetic interdependence, wherein mutual weaknesses were made the ground of a defensive alliance'. Hardy's pastoral, by its very inertia, restores people to their proper membership of nature.

As the puns restive within _Middlemarch_ suggest, this was a time of discontent for the novel. The bulkier and more apparently veracious it grew, the more doubtful it became about the reality it validated. Meredith's _The Egoist_ in 1879 jestingly capsizes the illusion of the real, propped up by the privileges of rank, with which Sir Willoughby Patterne so wilfully patterns unruly experience. Its hero's name brands him as one who subscribes to Schopenhauer's two fallacies: his world is compounded of nagging will and schematic, novelistic representation. Meredith's ludic version of George Eliot's triumphally marching mind is the comic spirit, whose silvery laughter deflates pomposity and our pretence that our lives matter, or have any material substance.

Trollope's _The Way We Live Now_ (1874–5) likewise assaults that way of life and the novels which are its vindication. The novel represents, as its title shockingly proposes, a direct transcription of contemporary reality; yet that reality is compounded of fictions, frauds and forgeries. Though Melmotte is described as 'so great a reality, such a fact in the commercial world', his career is a gigantic bluff. Though the Pacific and Mexican railway scheme is documented with maps and schedules, it, too, is a projection of cheating fancy. The society is a matter of make-believe, except that no one can quite make himself believe in it. Paul Montague tries to do so with the railway extravaganza; Mrs Hurtle urges him to rise above honesty. The traffic in credit—which makes the novel's young reprobates settle gaming debts with worthless paper IOUs—extends into religious affairs, where Trollope exposes a conspiracy of credulousness or incredulity, but can discern no certainty of creed. Bishop Yeld professes the faith without feeling it. 'I doubt', Trollope notes, 'whether he was competent to teach a creed.' Conviction is reserved for those who believe what Trollope accounts, in any case, a lie: of Father Barham he says, 'the fervent Romanists have always this point in their favour, that they are ready to believe.'

In the absence of a god to discern truth and regulate knowledge, *The Way We Live Now* intimates an aesthetic atheism. It cannot bring itself even to believe in the novel. Hence the importance in it—as its vacuous, uncohering centre—of the talentless Lady Carbury, authoress first of inaccurate history, then of unimaginative novels. Fiction is the appropriate vocation for her because she is an embodied falsehood, 'educated in deceit' and 'false from head to foot'. As the novel ends, she is forbidden by her new husband to write more novels. Trollope's fellow-professionals are inveigled into lending reality to society's pretences by attending its festivities and sycophantically celebrating them. When Melmotte entertains the Emperor of China, the poet laureate and 'the second poet' are invited *ex officio*. The novel is dealt with more offhandedly than poetry, though: 'a novelist was invited; but as royalty wanted another ticket at the last moment, the gentleman was only asked to come in after dinner.' Trollope's anonymous colleague grandly refuses—not out of integrity, but out of pique. Novelists are more intimately collusive than anyone else in society's licensing of lies.

At its most despairing, Trollope's novel identifies literature with the papery feigning which makes his gamblers exchange chits when they do not have what Dolly Longestaffe calls 'tin'. The society's financial system is a solemn delusion, agreeing to pretend that value inheres in inherently valueless bits of paper. What else is literature? Lady Carbury reposes in her trashy manuscript the same mistaken trust which the regulars at the Beargarden place in 'unsecured paper': she demands that her publisher lodge it—as if in a bank vault—in a fireproof safe, because 'those scraps of paper, so easily destroyed, apparently so little respected, may hereafter be acknowledged to have had a value greater, so far greater, than their weight in gold!' Is literature merely a flimsy, perishable facsimile of national bullion? Trollope observes literature being made in its native form as letters, and sees it as the papery traduction of feelings. Mrs Hurtle writes to a Paul a letter which takes much time but affects to be dashed off, drafted and then redrafted with 'premeditated erasures'; when Georgiana informs her mother that her fiancé Brehgert is a Jew, she writes 'this last word . . . very rapidly, but largely, determined that there should be no lack of courage apparent in the letter.' If literature is not worth the paper it is written on, people can equally be resolved into the inhuman substances from which they are fabricated. Mrs Hurtle is reckoned attractive because 'the taste for flesh and blood has . . . given place to an appetite for horsehair and pearl powder', while the Emperor is alleged to be 'stuffed with hay, and . . . made up fresh every morning at a shop in the Haymarket'.

Melmotte is at once illiterate, an unscrupulous *littérateur*, and a greedy consumer of literature. Trollope, commenting on his ignorance of the England he maintains is his fatherland, suspects him of never having read a book. His swindling, however, obliges him to study being a writer, as when, with the aid of some tissue paper, he first traces and then forges on 'various documents' the signatures of his daughter and the clerk Croll. (He is rumoured to be the son of a New York coiner—a relative, perhaps, of Gide's aesthetic *faux-monnayeurs*; and his minting of fake currency goes with an aptitude for linguistic sleight-of-hand, for he is also supposed to have begun life as an Irishman with the name of Melmody.) In the novel's most extraordinary scene, he expresses his contempt for the paper transactions which are the obsession of commerce, of law, of journalism and literature—for all the institutions of Trollope's society are houses built on sand, as Paul sees, and houses built, at that, only of paper—by making first a bonfire and then a meal of some incriminating letters and documents. All but one of these he incinerates over a gas-burner, blowing the ashes out through the window (and when he treats himself to a cigar, he exhales 'volumes' of smoke, as if committing more paper to an internal physiological furnace); the one remaining 'he put bit by bit into his mouth, chewing the paper into a pulp until he swallowed it'. It is the logical consequence of the novel's shaming role as a consumer item.

That shame George Eliot seeks to surmount in *Daniel Deronda* by dividing the novel against itself, representing in the career of Gwendolen the form's materialistic recusancy, its infatuation with social gossip and fashionable trivia, while opposing to her a Deronda who high-mindedly revises the form, rendering it philosophically serious and spiritually zealous, changing it from a helpless account of the way we live to a prescription of how we ought to live. By his messianic 'knight-erranting', as Sir Hugo calls it, he restores the novel to the noble source from which, in Cervantes and Fielding, it has shabbily declined: it is to be 'a whole heroic poem of resolve and endurance', attempting a reversal of literature's degenerative history. In a Holborn secondhand bookshop, Deronda surveys 'the literature of the ages . . . from the immortal verse of Homer to the mortal prose of the railway novel'. He sees the declension as Hazlitt did in 1818: literature records man's expulsion of god from the world.

Gwendolen is a prosaic mortal, trapped on a rotating earth whose symbol is the roulette wheel, dreaming of alternative existences elsewhere and casting herself as a heroine in fatuous dramas like those Catherine Morland envisaged. Imagination for her is, as for Meredith's hero, a 'passionate egoism', coercing life into the fictitious service of a self-image. She determines upon dominion in a 'little world', and dissevers herself from 'the historic stream', the collective life of human struggle which Deronda epically and impersonally leaves the novel to lead. Gwendolen gives voice to what might be called the novel's metaphysical provinciality: 'Is the society pleasant in this neighbourhood?' she demands. Even Mrs Meyrick has advanced beyond the novel's local realities, and prefers the global digest of *The Times* to the petty itemisation of 'maidens choosing': 'She was a great reader of news, from the widest-reaching politics to the list of marriages; the latter, she said, giving her the pleasant sense of finishing the fashionable novels without having read them, and seeing the heroes and heroines happy without knowing what poor creatures they were.'

Gwendolen herself is deprived, as the novel goes on, of the diversionary actions she believes the form promises. Like Harriet Byron censuring 'story, story, story', George Eliot forbids the drowning of Grandcourt to happen in the novel: it is reviewed only in retrospect; remembered, then analysed, then absolved. Spiritualised, the novel changes from a theatre of restless activity to a penitential chamber of recollection where life is studied not experienced. This is what Gwendolen learns when she submits herself to Deronda as her confessor; it is what George Eliot all along practises, writing not a novel but a cosmic essay on fiction and on the unalterable facts it glosses over, prefacing her first chapter with an epigraph which denies that narrative beginnings are anything more than 'make-believe' and ending with a quotation from *Samson Agonistes* which denies that death is a significant terminus because it is the paltry individual ego's release into 'the divine Unity'—arguing against the conventional limits of her form so as to surmount them.

Deronda overcomes the novel not so much in 'immortal verse' as in that 'immortal music' made in the world by the 'choir invisible' of George Eliot's humanist anthem. The work's ambition urges it to seek beyond language, too divisively national, for an art capable of unifying the expanded world—stretching from Mirah's childhood in New York throughout England and across Europe to Deronda's kingdom or Lady Hester Stanhope's realm (envied by Gwendolen) in the east—this cosmopolitan novel surveys; for an art as international as Judaism, or Klesmer's Pan-Slavism. That art is music, and specifically the Wagnerian 'music of the future' extolled by Klesmer. Music means to George Eliot the universality of spirit; it is the redemptive re-ascent of the voice, in advance of the soul, to God. One of the participants in Mordecai's colloquium quotes *Prometheus Unbound* (and George Eliot elsewhere praises the musical and scientific perfectibility of Shelley's *Queen Mab*, after whom one of the Meyrick girls is named). George Eliot's hope is to make the novel, like the Shelleyan lyrical drama, an Orphic symphony.

The novel's small, domestic conclaves are symposia of lucid song. Mab is said to incline 'to the opinion of Socrates: "What motive has a man to live, if not for the pleasures of discourse?"' Mordecai, leaning on the parapet of Blackfriars Bridge, hears the clamour of 'world-commerce' on the river as an aerodynamic music, 'a fine symphony . . . which . . . makes a medium that bears up our spiritual wings' (just as Wagner, the year after *Daniel Deronda*'s publication, said that London—as he saw it sailing up the Thames—was his Nibelheim from *Das Rheingold*). Everyone in *Daniel Deronda* has or wants a musical career, because music, as Daniel remarks to Gwendolen, 'answers for all larger things'. Daniel's mother was a great singer, and Sir Hugo believes

Daniel might become one. Gwendolen wants to study singing, Mirah performs at social receptions, and Mrs Glasher, though she plays no instrument, is compared to one: her quick, incisive speech suits her features, 'as the tone and timbre of a violin go with its form'. Music is the downtrodden novel's metaphor for the ideal region it has fallen from. Deronda's boy soprano brings 'an idyllic heaven and earth before our eyes'. Religious ecstasy is therefore a wordless, chordal bliss, a sacramental vocalising. In the Frankfort synagogue Daniel gives 'himself up to that strongest effect of chanted liturgies which is independent of detailed verbal meaning'. Those rhapsodic cadenzas are lispingly paraphrased when Mirah sings a Hebrew hymn she remembers her mother murmuring to her. 'I don't sing real words—only here and there a syllable like hers', says Mirah, who fears the result will seem 'childish nonsense'. But that musical baby talk is also the sound of grace and of goodness.

George Eliot's first novels recall society's slumbrous origins in nature (and literature's source there in proverbs and fables); from this rural past she proceeds to the all-inclusive future of *Deronda*, 'full', as James said, 'of the world'. The dialectic also manages by degrees to make our human institution of literature into a sacrament. Whereas Arnold proposed reading the Bible as poetry, George Eliot recommends reading the novel as poetry, which means as a man-made Bible. One aspect of this reclamation is the overtaking of words by music; another is their supercession by painting, the ideal's arrival on earth, when Hans poses Mirah as Berenice. Both acts of adaptation foster what Deronda calls 'the transmutation of self', and that revolution requires the transmutation of literature.

Hardy's natural history of human life and of the novel extends the form across a time-span just as epochal, though for him the evolution happens in the opposite direction. Rather than rallying a conquest of the future, Hardy presides over the novel's unravelling into a remote and buried past. If George Eliot is concerned with the novel's spiritual predictiveness, Hardy concentrates on its prehistory. Instead of the revolution which lies ahead of history, he stretches it back into the myth which lay before history. Like George Eliot, his novels summarise the growth of consciousness and of art, but they conceive of the sequence very differently. Her positivist advance is atavistic relapse in Hardy.

The injunction which governs his own writing is inscribed on the forest, as a rule of seasonal decay and decline, in *The Woodlanders*. Winter induces a 'change from the handsome to the curious'. Hardy notes that curves give way to angles, lush surfaces to carved reticulations, in a reversion 'from the ornate to the primitive on Nature's canvas, . . . comparable to a retrogressive step from the art of an advanced school of painting to that of the Pacific Islander'. His novels follow that backward course. For him, the novel must be anything but new. It is, in Defoe, the product of an urban industrial society anxious to outstrip the past—the same society which invents, as mechanical persecutions of an agrarian order, the devilish harvester in _Tess of the D'Urbervilles_ (1891) and the seed-drill in _The Mayor of Casterbridge_ (1886). Reacquainting it with a past it imagined it had cast off, Hardy grafts it onto a literary ancestry which originates in myth and fable and creates, as the novel's unacknowledged begetters, the dynastic genres of epic, romance and pastoral. The novel which attends only to surfaces is 'ornate': Hardy's revelation, like the wood's in winter, is of what is beneath the superficiality of the real. His images of carvery and reticulation demonstrate that people are not the factitious inventions of society, like Trollope's straw Emperor or his fraudulently coined Melmotte, but are slowly, wearingly, sculpted into truth by their abiding existence in nature.

The difference between Hardy and George Eliot can be measured in their different uses of the metaphors of music and painting. Whereas George Eliot argues that the old German painters could not represent the difference between one peasant and the next because their society did not recognise the individual's existence, Hardy justifies the prejudices of Mrs Yeobright in _The Return of the Native_ (1878)—who, though ignorant of the great world, intuitively understands it—by saying that she saw communities multitudinously and as from a distance, like the throngs in Flemish canvases: 'vast masses of beings ... whose features are indistinguishable by the very comprehensiveness of the view.' Mrs Poyser's kitchen, on the other hand, is a Dutch picture precisely because it is uncomprehensive and uncomprehending. It stands for life and a phase of history congealed in, immobilised by, paint. Hardy can call _Under the Greenwood Tree_ (1872) 'a rural painting of the Dutch school' with no such misgivings. The forming and framing of the picture is in this case a reflex of the way these people, the happy legatees of nature, accept the conditions of their lives. Grandfather James stoops to form 'a well-illuminated picture as he passed towards the fire-place', Mr Penny in his shop-window is 'like a framed portrait of a shoemaker by some modern Moroni'.

Chiaroscura is the tracing of light to its source in darkness, of human society to its origin in landscape, pictorially blurring single entities so as to aggrandise them. On a spring evening, each of the choir members is 'backed up by a shadow as long as a steeple'. William's titanic shadow extends thirty feet, 'stretching away to the east in outlines of impossible magnitude, his head finally terminating upon the trunk of a grand old oak-tree'. The pictorial distortion tells a heroic human truth. The portentous shadows these people cast are their pedigrees in earth, or their claims (in the steeple simile) to the authority accorded to endurance. The process which, in the wood, Hardy calls reticulation shapes the characters of _Far From the Madding Crowd_, not by elongating and ennobling their shadows but by crafting them into architecture. Beneath the surface—which in this case is perishable, dressed-up human flesh—Troy has the columnar rigidity of the pillars in All Saints' church, Boldwood's body is 'a great tower', and Gabriel's face is a stained-glass window.

Correspondingly, although Mr Spinks tells his fellow-choristers 'strings be safe soul-lifters', the music which provokes the dispute in Mellstock is not George Eliot's sonic forecast of the future. It is an ancient remedy for harmonising the world and soothing its grumbles. The choir laboriously goes the rounds of the large parish, taking care to bestow a carol on every family. They are the creators of social adhesion, and rather than ascending into the sky or descending from there, as do the chants of George Eliot's 'choir invisible', their music describes generously all-embracing, reliably repetitive circles. Those figurations, cycling like the seasons, give the novel its form—the figure of eight into which Fancy will twist the parson; Mrs Crumpler apparently rolling across the dance-floor on castors; the hypnotic gyrations of humming-tops; the 'mathematical circles' of the landlord's rolling eyes. The songs have value because they are eternally returning, like the chairmen on the esplanade at Budmouth who undergo annual reincarnation, restored 'to life for the summer in new clean shirts and revivified clothes'. And because they are 'orally transmitted from father to son', remembered and enjoining memory (like the hymn the choir sings called 'Remember Adam's fall'), the songs take the novel back to the bardic parentage of literature itself.

Hardy's is a music which does not move in and through time, but cancels it by showing it to be a rondel. Myth is a refrain, history its successive reprises. The groaning, creaking, halting clockwork in the church tower dies into silence outside its natal room, raising in 'meditative minds the fancy that here lay the direct pathway of Time': this clock's ageing music does not tell time; it is the sound of timelessness. Fancy Day has 'a pair of green-faced eight-day clocks, ticking alternately', which take in turn two and a half and three minutes to strike twelve. Duplication, with the ticking syncopated so the computations never quite agree, is another metronome-like way of seeing to it that time never passes. Perhaps the most authentic lyricism in Hardy is the music, like the chronological competition in Fancy's house or the wheezing expiry of time in the tower, made by nature itself—the Gregorian chant of the elm boughs which distresses John South, or the tintinnabular symphony of Melbury's sixteen dray horses, wearing bells 'tuned to scale, so as to form two octaves'. _Under the Greenwood Tree_ ends with a transliteration of the noises made in and by nature. Hallooing their joy across the landscape, the revellers elongate their vowels as Hardy had distended their shadows, making the voice an epic megaphone sending out its summons through time. Dick cries out to 'Eno-o-o-o-ch!' that he is 'Just a ma-a-a-a-arried!' and invites him 'to the party to-ni-i-i-i-i-ight!' And the novel's final sound returns to the rapturous onomatopoeia of the owl and the burbling idiot boy in Wordsworth's ballad. A 'loud, musical, and liquid voice' addresses the lovers from a thicket, 'Tippiwit! swe-e-et! ki-ki-ki! Come hither, come hither, come hither!' It is the angelically nonsensical fluting of the nightingale.

Obedience to chronology is a strict moral duty in George Eliot. Deronda, during the search for Mirah's family, misuses the calendar to put off a disagreeable chore. Trollope the chronicler wrote as a slave of Chronos. He worked with a clock on his desk, and set himself to get through two hundred and fifty words every quarter of an hour. Tennyson was another Victorian victim of this temporal ailment: In 'Come not, when I am dead' he claims to be 'sick of time', made sick by its unendurable duration.

Hardy is exempted from this ageing, belated sense of literary history, like Gabriel who can tell the time by the constellations and needs no watch. Even the gold watch that Troy uses to allure Bathsheba is preoccupied not with the onrush of seconds into the future, but with the solemn, bardic commemoration of the past: its aristocratic lineage qualifies it for a ritualistic time-keeping, and Troy says it 'has regulated imperial interests in its time—the stately ceremonial, the courtly assignation, pompous travels, the lordly sleeps.' As if in turn regulated by it, his language metrically regularises itself into blank verse as he speaks. A lie is an irregularity, an offence against the time of nature. Bathsheba's excuse for Troy's apparent absence from church is to Gabriel 'the thirteenth stroke of a crazy clock'. Slipping through the fir plantation at night, Bathsheba is said to be moving as 'covertly as Time', but to say so is again to annihilate time which (like Bathsheba) is invisible, imperceptible. Hence when Hardy calls a thing chronic it is not to charge it with inveteracy or incurability but in tribute to its everlastingness, like myth rendering time eternal. The sheep-bell is to Gabriel 'a chronic sound' and also a musical one, 'like the ticking of the clock to other people', and as Troy beguiles Bathsheba a flushed, excited face is 'little less than chronic with her now'. Jude and Sue complete the process by nicknaming their offspring Father Time.

In Wordsworth, the child is father to the man; Hardy modifies that romantic faith, showing the child to be resident still within the adult, existing just under the surface like the primitively angular life-forms of the wood. Gabriel's face holds within itself, like sediments and deposits overlaid in earth, the remnants of earlier existences—'the hues and curves of youth', and in its 'remoter crannies some relics of the boy'. Night thoughts, like winter in *The Woodlanders*, dredge this submerged mental ancestry up into visibility. When Henchard in *The Mayor of Casterbridge* puzzles over Elizabeth-Jane's parentage, he watches her asleep, which has the effect of a geological dig: 'in sleep there come to the surface buried genealogical facts, ancestral curves, dead men's traits, which the mobility of daytime animation screens.'

This is the oddity of Hardy's characters. They are not single, unrepeatable individuals occurring once in history; typologically ubiquitous, they are mythically seeded throughout time. George Eliot, too, identifies prototypes for her people, yet in her world they suggest affected mimicry—Gwendolen as the actress Rachel or Cecilia, Rex as Napoleon—and the spurious play-acting of characters who resent the belittled identity that life has assigned them. Deronda vows to exhaust all prototypes by equalling them: offered the chance to model his life on the singer Mario, on Porson or Leibnitz, he says he wants to be 'a greater leader, like Pericles or Washington'. Hardy is constantly likening characters to their predecessors in myth, legend and history. Doing so he does not diminish them but demonstrates them to be periodically reborn, indefatigable deities. Henchard is a biblical prophet or, dining at the King's Arms, a Napoleon at Austerlitz; Venn advancing on Eustacia's house is 'the great Frederick making war on the beautiful Archduchess' or 'Napoleon refusing terms to the beautiful Queen of Prussia'; even Gabriel's dog, a sentinel against the sky, can resemble 'Napoleon at St. Helena'. Bathsheba bestraddles Christian and classical theologies. Her tears are a stream as liquid as that of Moses in Horeb, yet she chastely worships Diana. At the same time, she dialectically recomposes within herself the opposites in more recent British history, being 'an Elizabeth in brain and a Mary Stuart in spirit'. Troy slithers between epic similes: he lies like a Cretan, he has the spruce amorality of a Corinthian.

The metaphors come and go contradictorily, and have as their purpose to prevent characters from cohering in the usual way: these are not human moral agents, subjects in a laboratory for one of George Eliot's experiments in life; they are compounds of warring traits and inconsistent impulses, as gratuitous in their actions as gods, as incalculable as animals. They extend indeed between a sky from which they have fallen—like the Olympian Eustacia tumbling into mortality on Corfu, or Clym returning from Paris 'like a man coming from heaven'—and a warm, nestling earth into which, like small furry creatures, they snuggle for shelter: Tess asleep in her clothes like a sunned cat, Bathsheba gliding across the landscape like a kingfisher or a hawk, Eustacia's smile as a passport to the pagan underground, where 'such lip-curves' lurk interred on 'fragments of forgotten marbles'. Since identity is serial and anthological, the result of countless metamorphoses and mutations, naming can never be definitive, unless perhaps it hyphenates contrary existences and begins the work of synthesising, as is the case with Elizabeth-Jane. Tess's name is the invention of a D'Urberville heritage for her, Jude's the obscuring—as with those inglorious, nameless sleepers in Gray's churchyard—of his birthright. Bathsheba teases Gabriel by challenging him to find out her name. Anonymous, she maintains her mystery. Though she names things after herself, branding her lambs B.E., she cannot be limited or known by the affixing of a name. In any case it is a meaningless label, like the back-to-front LAMƎꓭ imprinted on the wagons by Joseph Poorgrass. Gabriel pretends to a namelessness like Bathsheba's when he comes to call, sending word that 'somebody would be glad to speak to her'. Hardy remarks that 'calling one's self merely Somebody, without giving a name' is a reflex of modesty—of a metaphysical reticence perhaps, denying to the name its presumption of making or defining the man, since Hardy's characters are all the time being unmade, rescued from the subtractions of selfhood and sent to wander, like genes or spores, at random through the world.

By this loosening of people from society, Hardy manages to write novels which are about all times and all places at once. The province does not have to be generalised, as George Eliot's version of his country is when she archly claims in *Deronda* that 'nothing is narrated here of human nature generally: the history in its present stage concerns only a few people in a corner of Wessex'. Hardy's Wessex is no such small-minded outpost; it is already an everywhere. Metaphors distribute it throughout space. On the morning when Elizabeth-Jane goes to the graveyard, Casterbridge is as deserted as Karnac. Temporally, too, Wessex is a palimpsest of civilizations—Druidic Stonehenge, the Roman amphitheatre at Casterbridge, Egdon Heath as Eustacia's personal Hades. Zones of time amiably coexist there.

Between the two parts of *The Mayor of Casterbridge*, more than eighteen years seem to have supervened: the gap separates a roistering tribal past of wife-bartering and epic bravado from a circumspect, officious, bourgeois present, in which the past's resurgence is a stalking by spectral revenants. Mrs Henchard is called a ghost by the boys, and when Henchard reads Lucetta's love-letters to Farfrae he listens aghast as 'her own words greeted her . . . like spirits from the grave'. The future lies latent within the present, too, preparing to germinate (or to be unpacked when time is propitious). Boldwood, made to wait by Bathsheba, determines to 'annihilate the six years . . . as if they were minutes'; he purchases the future in anticipation, and locks it in a closet. The wedding gifts he accumulates for her are carefully wrapped and 'labelled "Bathsheba Boldwood", a date being subjoined six years in advance in every instance.' His hopeless love is a seed-capsule, ripening in darkness to its long-deferred consummation.

Everyone has his own coordinates for time-keeping, and the relativity which results provokes a cheerful squabble among the mummers in *The Return of the Native*. Some take the Quiet Woman's ruling as their standard, others Blooms-End, which differs by half an hour, and there are proponents for Grandfer Cantle's watch and the captain's clock, also unsynchronised. Hardy concludes that 'on Egdon there was no absolute time of the day.' The comic diachronism suits the occasion: how could the mummers be expected to keep to historic schedule, when their business is mythic? Their performance of the warfare between Christian and Saracen is no refurbishing revival of a pastime but a 'fossilized survival', indicating that they still live in the past they are representing. A face in Hardy can be a place of chance meeting, like the institution of mumming or the rendezvous in the fuel-house, for divergent times. He hesitates over the description of Clym because—so unaccountable are his characters by the novel's conventional means—he is not sure how far back to date him. He is, like all of us, ageless. A middle-aged person would think him young, a youth would consider him old. Both are right and neither is, for the face conveys 'less the idea of so many years as its age than of so much experience as its store'. Hardy contrasts Clym the 'modern man' with the millenial patriarchs of Genesis: he does not need to live a thousand years, his age being 'measured by the intensity of his history'. All the same, a protracted erosive process is at work in Clym, like that which, over centuries, contours landscape. Thought slowly incises his face from within 'with legible meanings'; consciousness wears down flesh. Maturing is described as a variant of that ageing retrogression, mining beneath the surface, which happens to the plantation in *The Woodlanders*.

The characters of novels generally follow horizontal courses. They are travellers on the road which begins at the barred gate of Milton's Eden. Even George Eliot's saintly Theresa toddles out with her brother on her child-pilgrimage to martyrdom, only to be captured by 'domestic reality . . . in the shape of uncles' and returned to the place where she began. Hardy's, however, move through a vertical world with the freedom Milton permitted to gods or their agents but denied to mortals. Fancy, floating down the school steps 'in the form of a nebulous collection of colours inclining to blue', is a nebular dazzle, the apparition of a cloud-descended divinity; Grace, after being received by Mrs Charmond, looks as if she is de-levitating, with a face like that of 'Moses when he came down from the Mount'; Clym takes over the eminence of Rainbarrow to preach weekly sermons on the mount. Alighting on earth, they recoil into it. This is a theology of a new kind. Chthonic gods do not arise from the ground and take to the air. Rather they are tugged down from their astral heights to burrow and root themselves in it, as its vital growths. Rest and death are capitulations to this gravity, pastoral absorptions in earth. When Clym lies down in a ferny green basin, he is carried back in an instant to 'the ancient world of the carboniferous period', and Eustacia mimes the Turkish knight's 'dogged decline' as a 'gradual sinking to the earth': no 'direct fall from upright to horizontal' but an infinitely gradual deceleration, allowing herself to be stilled and then to be overtaken by the homing impulse below the sod, as characters are when they die in Wordsworth. The Mellstock villagers suspect Mrs Endorfield of witchery, and therefore venerate her as a 'Deep Body, . . . as long-headed as she was high'. The mind is a tunnel travelling through that body's caves into a buried wisdom. Character again is archaeology.

This is why Hardy so often begins his novels with characters on a roadway who instead of travelling along it seem to use it as a rung on a ladder between their native underground and the forfeited air—the old man on Egdon, the Henchards advancing towards Weydon-Priors. Silhouetted on ridges against the browning sky, they are caught in the midst of a process which is not mental evolution (as in George Eliot), reaching towards the illimitable sky of mind, but a biological growth backwards into nature. Hardy even speaks of consciousness as earth: 'the soil of Miss Melbury's mind'. And his eye of imagination moves downwards in obedience to the specific gravity which gives things weight and bulk and therefore reality, like Mr Percombe following 'tall stems of smoke' down, not up, to their 'root on quiet hearthstones'. Things are real in Hardy because they have gone to ground, owned by an earth which will not relinquish them. Thus although Mrs Dollery's van is travelling—a vehicle of novelistic imagination on tour, the mirror advancing down the road—it seems 'rather a movable attachment of the roadway than an extraneous object'. And the level to which it is uncomplainingly fettered is earth as the cranium of nature, not a middlemarch of bodily mediocrity. The highway crosses the woods like a 'head of thick hair bisected by the white line of its parting'. The things which have been briefly allowed to extrude can be reclaimed by that dark, subterranean interior, their reality recoiling in the operation of a metaphor. This happens when Eustacia and Wildeve sink below the sky 'as two horns which the sluggish heath had put forth from its crown, like a mollusc, and had now again drawn in'. Mind's spurning of matter, the high imperative of George Eliot's positivism, can to Hardy signify only an obscene preying upon the body: Mrs Charmond's purchase of Marty South's hair, Fitzpiers's of Grammer Oliver's brain.

For both George Eliot and Hardy, the novel constitutes a natural history of humankind. In her case, it is the annals of man's struggle against confining reality—a mental epic of transcendence. In his case, it describes the opposite course. Surrender to those conditions, in the wise passiveness of pastoral, enables the novel to descend through that reality to the beginnings of literature. George Eliot ushers in the cerebral science which is the novel's epilogue, in the moon-men of H. G. Wells, the psychic engineers of Aldous Huxley, and the mystical astronauts of Doris Lessing; Hardy makes possible its research into a world which predates the modern but still lives beneath it, in the work of the novelist who was his finest critic, D. H. Lawrence.

32

'From Romance to Realism':
Tennyson and Browning

The poetry of Tennyson and Browning begins as a continuation and a revision of romanticism. Tennyson's departure is from Keats, Browning's from Shelley. But the romantic models soon prove unavailing. Keatsian painting loses its gustatory relish in Tennyson, whose pictures are of silenced, deadened landscapes; Shelleyan music changes in Browning to ebullient, intemperate, demotic noise.

In both, the romantic lyric undergoes a mutation into its modern successor, the symbolist mystery. The winged, elusive truths of Keats and Shelley, too fleet for capture in words, are in Tennyson and Browning metaphoric conundrums, riddling clues to a world which means (as Fra Lippo Lippi says) intensely but obscurely; or they are brave, foolhardy attempts to establish significance in a world which—like the waste land of Wimpole Street in *In Memoriam* or the scruffy wilderness Childe Roland gropes through—disowns it. Roland derives from the Byronic pilgrim Childe Harold, as Tennyson's Sir Galahad is a less carnal Endymion; their own heirs, however, are Eliot's J. Alfred Prufrock and Ezra Pound's Hugh Selwyn Mauberley. The confident fantasists of romanticism, who wake and find their dreams immediately come true, yield to the tentative, mystified, deductive questers of symbolism, adrift in a dream where they try to locate truth by what Browning in 1850 in 'Easter-Day' calls 'the mere task of making real', the compulsion 'to realize it'. Reality does not exist: it has to be constructed, always provisionally and always frustratedly, in a poem.

Keats made things real by feasting on them. That is not possible for Tennyson, whose world has meaning only spiritually and spectrally, in its after-life. His images are unsustaining substitutes for the live things they depict. The poet lives, like Mariana or the Lady of Shalott, at second hand. Gareth in *Idylls of the King* (1859) rails at the black knight's 'ghastly imageries, / Of that which Life has done with.' These are the symbolist corpses of Tennyson, in which meaning is defunct—the dying swan, the floating lady who 'singing in her song . . . died', the streets numbed and rendered dumb by snow through which Galahad passes, the ruined shrine in Lyonnesse, the bodies in the hollow in *Maud* (1855). The change is evident already in the 'Saint Agnes' Eve' which Tennyson wrote in 1837, as a corrective to Keats's *Eve of St. Agnes*. The sensual gluttons of Keats's poem have been sanctified, at the cost of their vitality. Madeline is replaced by Agnes herself in her convent,

Porphyro by a frigidly heavenly Bridegroom. The lyric does not feed on life but exhales it in an evaporation of sound:

> My breath to heaven like vapour goes:
> May my soul follow soon!

Keats's poem was a source for the pre-Raphaelites—Holman Hunt illustrated it in 1848, Arthur Hughes in 1856—but they, too, misread it as Tennyson does, representing the flight of the lovers as spirit's decampment from the gross world of matter. For Holman Hunt, the poem was, he said, about sacred love and its superiority to fleshly cravings. John Everett Millais, too, chilled and chastened it when he spent a night shivering in the Jacobean bedroom of a deserted country house in order to study the winter moonlight silvering the breast of Madeline as she undresses. Rossetti paid a similarly mistaken tribute to Keats, calling 'La Belle Dame Sans Merci' the origin for 'all the poetry of my group'. Yet no one could be further from Keats's belle dame than Rossetti's blessed damozel. The Keatsian woman is an earth-spirit, on whose roots and honey the knight can gorge; Rossetti's character is an etherised angel. At the bar of heaven, all that remains of the tactile, edible world is a Shelleyan mirage, souls like 'thin flames', prayers melted 'like a little cloud', song dying into an echo of itself.

Similes are Rossetti's frail bridges across the gulf between earth and heaven, yet they always fall short of that 'endless unity' where 'we two', like tenor and vehicle in the metaphor, were 'one . . . once of old'. That is the plaint of the Tennysonian image, approximating only partially to the ideal, like Arthur's visage—in the report of Bellicent in the *Idylls*—manifesting itself as 'a momentary likeness of the King' in the eyes of his knights. The Keatsian picture is in Tennyson a sad, bereft simulation of the real. When Arthur vanquishes his opponents, 'like a painted battle the war stood / Silenced, the living quiet as the dead'; when Lancelot departs, leaving only the embroidered case of the shield he has carried off as an image and memento of himself, the Lady of Astolat broodingly 'his picture form'd / And grew between her and the pictured wall.' The lover in Rossetti's poem is also aware of how tenuous his metaphoric connection with the eternal must be: his is 'the soul whose likeness with thy soul / Was but its love for thee.'

Instead of Xanadu, that profane and palpable cathedral of romantic desire, Tennyson constructs a wavering illusion: Camelot shining through the mist as Gareth and Lynette approach, then disappearing; or the Palace of Art, where the topography of unmanageable reality is brought indoors and installed in a succession of dioramas, as at a museum. To make a picture is to render life unreal. Tennyson's characters experience their own lives as if they were landscapes outside the window or inside a frame: Œnone, the lotos-eaters and Enoch Arden are the paralysed observers of 'a land where', as in a picture, 'all things always seem'd the same.' Keats's bower of quietness is a neurasthenic prison. Despite occasional rallying-calls to progress—Odysseus's 'Courage!', immediately weakened by a lyrical lassitude; Maud's taunting martial song; the bugle-horn which sounds in 'Locksley Hall'—the pictorial detention of life is Tennyson's deepest need. Yet it is also a source of unease and self-mistrust. The virtue of words, he confesses in *In Memoriam*, is their dulling narcosis and their skill at concealing the truth. The poet, misappropriating Carlyle's theory of clothes, acknowledges himself to be an idolater of appearances, a fabricator of fine surfaces. Meredith described the *Idylls* as elegant haberdashery or fancy gewgaws: 'The lines are satin lengths, the figures Sèvres china.' Certainly the poem is obsessed with fabrics and furnishings, which are its expensive, aesthetic barricade for the exclusion of the real, from the silk pavilion used by Sir Morning-Star as a robing-room to Enid's longing for new clothes of 'silver tissue' or Vivien's 'samite without price', whose immorality (as against the agency of words in *In Memoriam*) lies in its tendency to reveal not conceal: it 'more exprest / Than hid her.' Romanticism is changing into a sumptuary aestheticism. It is this religious use of art which causes the soul to sicken guiltily and resolve to quit its palace of paintings. Beyond Camelot lies Yeats's tower.

Browning's painters are always demoralised by the conditions of their art. They can only slavishly imitate the real, which is itself a misrepresentation; his musicians blithely supersede it. Andrea del Sarto is cursed by his own capacity for perfection; Fra Lippo Lippi, secretly iconoclastic, resolves to be an official iconographer, supplying churches with pretty pictures, because he knows the appearances in which he traffics deceive; Pictor Ignotus resigns from the business of pictorial dissimulation, and wills his frescoes to moulder on their damp walls. The aesthete in Browning is a killer, murderously fixing appearances forever, like the grandee in 'My Last Duchess' who causes smiles to stop but can announce of his victim, 'There she stands / As if alive', or Porphyria's lover and assassin declaring 'all night long we have not stirred'. Art is at best a palatial after-life: the tomb commissioned for himself by the Bishop. Music, however, deals in the impalpable and unseeable, so for Browning, as for Shelley, it is a means of transcribing the soul's motions without the intercession of words. Charles Avison, in Browning's 1887 'Parleying' with him, extols it as man's truest truth, and in token of this the poem ends beyond words, in a quavered and crotcheted page of score.

Elsewhere Browning sets language to compete with music—with its deftness at emotional modulation and mental transition, its stream of consciousness along the keys, in the plaintive thirds, diminished sixths and commiserating sevenths of Galuppi's Toccata; with its fugal uproar, speaking contrapuntally in many tongues at once, in the organ-loft of Master Hugues; with its endless evolvings and resolutions in celestial C Major during Abt Vogler's improvisation. Browning's ideal instrument is the organ, like the one which growlingly emits God's voice in St Peter's in 'Christmas-Eve', because it is a compendious parliament of pipes, an entire orchestra on which one man can multilingually play. Its sound is a cathedral of expressed air: not frozen music (as Goethe called architecture) but a building breathed into life, resonant with energy.

G. K. Chesterton brilliantly called *The Ring and the Book* an 'epic of free speech'. It frees language from literature: the advocate Bottinius imagines print congealed in death; reading his speech he would enliven it 'with many a flower'. Rhetoric for him is a kind of rampant vegetation, like the thickets of decoration in medieval manuscripts which—in contrast with the regularity of script—yearn for a graphic liberty and doodling whimsicality which can now exist only on the margin. Giving voice to words breathes life into them. It also sends them on a jostling, clamorous promenade: speech, in this congested urban poem, is a *flâneur*, and Tertium Quid invites his listeners not to confine truth in the solitude and quiet of the brain but to 'walk it forth by way of tongue'.

Browning's is above all a vocal poetry, and to that extent a more or less than verbal one, since he introduces into it the stammerings, splutterings, mutterings, screeches and eructations of speech, which maul and mangle language. G. M. Hopkins described him as a man talking loudly with a mouthful of bread and cheese. The freeing of speech is music, but it is also noise, and Browning's music is the unlinguistic exclamatory noise his verse makes: the 'Gr-r-r' of the monk in the Spanish cloister, the 'Bang, whang, whang' of the drum and 'tootle-te-tootle' of the fife in an Italian fiesta, the scolding squeak of a chapel's door-hinge, Mr Sludge's keening 'Aie-aie-aie!' or his choked glottal 'Ch-ch!', the dissonant sharps and flats of the marauding (and pestilently rhyming) rats in Hamelin. Language as a system conspires to suppress this plosive din, as Browning's dead grammarian attempted when

> He settled *Hoti*'s business—let it be!—
> Properly based *Oun*—
> Gave us the doctrine of the enclictic *De*,
> Dead from the waist down.

Licentiously rhyming 'fit ally' with 'Florence, Italy', Browning writes in repudiation of rules. Grammar is replaced by metre—the musical pulse which sends his verse galloping on horseback from Ghent to Aix, or thump-thumps and shriek-shrieks in the engine of the train leaving Manchester—because it is a quickening of words.

It therefore follows that Browning's music is not that of Shelley's Ariel but that of Caliban; not an evanescent sighing in the air but a primordial grunting underground. In 'Caliban upon Setebos' the monster romps and grovels in a swamp which is the unarticulated 'much mire' of language before lexicographers or grammarians had regulated it. This is the same 'inordinate muchness' that Henry James wondered at in *The Ring and the Book* and which Browning retrieved in the original book found in the Florentine market, a lump of raw matter as yet unmoulded into form. The 'book in shape' is 'really, pure crude fact': creation for Browning must be recrudescence, relapse to amorphousness and ambiguity.

Prospero exercises power on Browning's island because he can write. He has stitched a book from leaves, whittled a wand for himself, and inscribed words on the parchment. But Caliban's aggression pits speech against scribble, and the lingual against the linguistic. Language is for him a salivating, oral pleasure. He chews on words and regurgitates ideas as he snaps at and crunches fruit, as the long-tongued pie licks up worms, and as the wave with 'its large tongue' idly consumes a fence of wattles. Browning's diction tries to get close to the lapping, slurring, spittle-assisted making of phonemes inside the mouth when Caliban lets his 'rank tongue blossom into speech'. When terror silences him, that cavern of chattering sound is closed off: 'Maketh his teeth meet through his upper lip.' The slovenly rumbling noises Caliban makes are, however, the logical demonstrations of his natural theology. Clumsily learning to talk, he experiments with his power to name things and thus to differentiate himself from everything which is not him; this enables him eventually to imagine god, who in this jungle of bruit is its negation, 'The Quiet', and cannot be named, only superstitiously pointed at or exclaimed over—'there, there, there, there, there . . . !' As well as inventing God, who in 'Easter-Day' lectures Browning as a Voice, he adumbrates Browning's ventriloquistic theory of poetry. Puffing through a home-made pipe in imitation of the jay's scream, he exults

> 'I make the cry my maker cannot make
> With his great round mouth; he must blow through mine!'

Character in Browning constitutes a mouth-piece, a medium like Sludge at his séances, through which spirit can prattle in tongues; a poem is, as Auden says in his elegy for Yeats, 'a mouth'. Browning's eerie skill is not for disembodying his voice, like Shelley in the songs from *Prometheus Unbound*, but for projecting it across space into and through bodies other than his own. This is his poetic theology, commanding things into existence by the act of respiration which inspirits them. Browning identifies his own art with Sludge's fakery (since he is the vocal aperture for 'Milton composing baby-rhymes' and 'Homer writing Greek / In noughts and crosses', for the dictation from spirits involuntarily suffered by Blake) but also with the Holy Ghost's visitations to those through whom it—in Sludge's phrase—vomits truth. Archangelis in *The Ring and the Book* quoting Solomon attributes the sentiment to 'the Holy Spirit speaking by his mouth'. A person is, as Caliban feels himself to be, the speaking-trumpet for the absent deity, or for that equally absconded god (imaged in Caliban's case by the sleeping Prospero), the dramatist. Caliban's theology joins with Browning's theory of creativity in a late poem 'The Names', which begins by invoking Shakespeare and then leaves that name to reverberate in awesome silence. Browning compares its power with that of the nameless name

> . . . the Hebrew reads
> With his soul only: if from lips it fell,
> Echo, back thundered by earth, heaven and hell,
> Would own 'Thou didst create us!'

Utterance is sacrilege, the appropriation of a godly prerequisite. Browning's analogy between Shakespeare and the amplified voice speaking from burning bushes or writing on walls claims for himself that capacity to invade all creation which the romantics celebrated in Shakespeare. The dramatist's plurality is the god's ubiquity. In truth, despite Keats or Browning, Shakespeare is neither Iago nor Imogen. He may play them but he is never—as Browning is—possessed by them. His art is dissimulation, not Browning's shamanistic fit as a character takes him over. There is divinity in Browning's theory, but also demonism.

Browning's art replicates and transliterates the sound of creation: 'God breathes, not speaks', as Guido says. Incarnation was the advent of a word. Struggling to learn language, like Caliban or Archangelis's baby with his lisping Latin conjugations, we are qualifying ourselves, as 'The Names' puts it, to have been created in the god's likeness. For Pompilia, 'strength comes . . . with the utterance' of Caponsacchi's name, after which she leaves a typographical gap of reverent silence. Yet is not this garrulous spending of words (which in *The Ring and the Book* are so loquacious that the street is a public mouth and the confessional a public ear) a pollution of the life whose source, as Guido acknowledges when he checks to see if Pompilia is still breathing, is the mouth? The Pope refers to 'this filthy rag of speech'. Though 'He, the Truth, is, too, / The Word', that vocabulary gift has been contaminated. Most men love language, as the Pope sees, because of its proficiency for lies and slithering evasions. And how can the poet and dramatist know, if he is to value Iago equally with Imogen, whether good or evil spirits have entered into him? Browning likes to treat speech as revivification: the transfusion from his 'live soul' casts out 'the death in things'. His orators and gossips in testifying to 'the puissance of the tongue' are evangelists of joyful regeneration. To the Pope, however, this trick of transmitting voices across space or summoning them from the beyond is a ghoulish exhumation. He therefore begins his judgement with the anecdote of Formosus, hustled out of the grave and propped on the papal throne to be put on trial; and Browning's surrogate in the story is the deacon appointed by Stephen VII to represent Formosus and 'be . . . mouthpiece of the corpse', who, 'emboldened by the Spirit', stammers and blurts legalistic half-truths 'with white lips and dry tongue'.

At its most doubtful, *The Ring and the Book* considers its outpourings to be no more than wastage: 'Mere words and wind!' in Guido's phrase. It allies poetry with verbosity; Tennyson meanwhile identifies it with what Whitman called 'verbalism'. His characters do not vociferate, like Browning's. Their lyricism is a propitiation of silence, and they repeat words in the hope that they will at last die into that musical nothingness. Their spells are the 'ditties of no tone' that Keats overheard on the urn. Verbal music like Tennyson's is, in Browning, an absurd elasticising of language, like Conti's elongation of a vowel during vespers while he is whispering sedition to Caponsacchi: '*in secula/Se-cul/o-o-o-o-rum*', he chants. Or else it is a rehearsal of empty-headed scales, signifying the absence of emotion. The operatic castrato mocked by Guido shrills 'Si, do, re, me, fa' in protestation of all the erotic passion 'the poor bloodless creature never felt'. A lyric can exist only if it is not felt: that is why Browning's love-poems—'By the Fire-Side' for instance—refuse, in their tortuous argumentation and interrogative barrages, to be mellifluous.

For Tennyson, though, musical incantation is useful precisely as a way of arriving at language's destitution of meaning, emptying words into echoes and thus consigning them to silence. The vowels that Conti enjoys hearing resonate in the throat commend themselves in Tennyson because they are vacuous, short cuts to the abyss between or beneath words. Everard Hall reading 'Morte d'Arthur' mouths out 'his hollow oes and aes'. The hollowness goes with his scornful comment that his poem is 'faint Homeric echoes', and its music will fade—'on the mere the wailing died away'—into the silence which after the reading wakens the dozing parson who, like the ideal Tennysonian auditor, has been 'sent to sleep with sound'. Hall at last triumphantly nullifies his own poem: 'There now—that's nothing!' Tennyson was fond of threnodically repeating his own name until he attained this negative bliss, reminding himself that human identity is as arbitrary as the collection of syllables which tag it. Tennyson's lyrical repetitions are not incremental, as music ought to be; they are a serial elimination of words, and this is why they are so often associated with death and ceremonies of interment, for they are the dirge of poetry itself. Examples abound: 'to weep, and weep, and weep / My whole soul out to thee', or 'bury me, bury me / Deeper, ever so little deeper'; 'hollow, hollow, hollow all delight' or 'answer echoes, answer, dying, dying, dying'; the choked, stumbling iteration in the dedication of the *Idylls* to the dead Prince Albert—'I dedicate, / I dedicate, I consecrate with tears— / These Idylls'—or the flatulent pomp of the 1852 burial service for the Duke of Wellington, 'with honour, honour, honour, honour to him, / Eternal honour to his name.' The riddling of the bards serves the same purpose in 'Gareth and Lynette', obfuscating meaning in a music of assonant, inane rhyming:

> 'Confusion, and illusion, and relation,
> Elusion, and occasion, and evasion.'

Browning rings similar changes on words, for instance in Guido's 'Deformed, transformed, reformed, informed, conformed!' There is forensic frenzy here, though, not mesmeric chanting. Guido is describing, in self-extenuation, how he has grown out of and back into manhood, to 'be man indeed / And all man.' Repetition is an inquisition of words and a trial of meanings, as also in his 'Why do things change? Wherefore is Rome un-Romed?' or his suspicion that his visitors are prying 'for truth truer than truth itself'; it is an ex-pressing of significance from language, like the hammering-out of the ring, the punishing of Archangelis's pancake batter, or the wracking and wrenching of Guido himself into truth. Browning's verbal wit is a torture of words, and that excruciation of matter—as when the metal is 'made [to] bear hammer and be firm to file'—is an engineering of art. The Pope says that truth is evolvable from the mess of evidence, but he evolves it by belabouring words and turning them inside out. He does so in characterising Violante:

> Unmotherly mother and unwomanly
> Woman, that near turns motherhood to shame,
> Womanliness to loathing.

In 'Lancelot and Elaine' Tennyson explains his theory of repetition as enchantment or estrangement. Her father gazes bemusedly at Elaine

> As when we dwell upon a word we know,
> Repeating, till the word we know so well
> Becomes a wonder, and we know not why.

As a result, the processions of words, though intended to suggest the hieratic catalogues of epic or the etymological pedigrees of Spenser—for instance the roll-call of predecessors in 'The Coming of Arthur',

> Carádos, Urien, Cradlemont of Wales,
> Claudias, and Clariance of Northumberland,
> The King Brandagoras of Latangor,
> With Anguissant of Erin, Morganore

—end by anticipating the vain saying of mantras at the end of Eliot's *The Waste Land* or the helpless, punning circles inside which words revolve in the *Four Quartets*. Tennyson's spendthrift verbalism is the working of Guido's 'mere . . . wind' which equalises words before volatilely sweeping them away. Wind is indeed a nihilistic singer in Tennyson, wailing that repetitious refrain about hollowness at the end of the *Idylls*, sounding 'shrill, chill, with flakes of foam', or lamenting in an empty, extinguished world when the funeral barge approaches.

In Memoriam worries that its effusions may have been just such an unsignifying, pre-verbal breeze: 'I trust I have not wasted breath.' It boldly reduces its theodicy to that infantile plaint which is, for Tennyson, the source of poetry—a child 'crying in the night / . . . And with no language but a cry.' Shipwrecked, Enoch Arden is also benignly bereft of language, returned to 'muttering and mumbling'. But his inarticulacy is the sound made by Tennysonian nature. The shepherd in *The Princess* entreats the mountain maid to live with him in the lowlands where she will be serenaded by

> The moan of doves in immemorial elms,
> And murmuring of innumerable bees.

The elms are memorials to a dead time, the song of the doves is a moan, and by the second line there is nothing left but muted, inspecific buzzing, not lyricism but the elegiac echo of it. Though the shepherd wants to praise her, he cannot (despite his paraphrase of *Paradise Lost*) keep her alive in this world of intoning vacancy: 'Sweet is every sound, / Sweeter thy voice, but every sound is sweet.' A human voice cannot, as in Browning, pretend to priority, and in contrast to the admonishments of the Voice in 'Easter-Day' Maud is uncreated because apparition is cancelled out by audition. Tennyson's madman commands 'Silence, beautiful voice!' and refuses to listen, because the song is 'Not her, . . . / Not her, not her, but a voice.' Browning's eagerness, however, in the rambunctious chaotic city is for 'Something to see, . . . something to hear . . .!'

As well as muffling voices, Tennyson erases sights. Mariana 'could not look on the sweet heaven, / Either at morn or eventide', and Enoch's wife cannot 'fix the glass to suit her eye' so misses his departing ship. Keeping watch over emptiness, they have at least been spared the Lady of Shalott's curse. To look is fatal, because it is an acquiescence in life, a validation of reality. Simeon Stylites on his column acquires sanctity along with visual and aural immunity. 'Half deaf', he can scarcely hear 'the people hum' far below, and 'almost blind' he 'scarce can recognize the fields I know.' Pater in his lecture on Pico della Mirandola establishes the mysticism of this dual inattention, deriving the world 'mystic' from the Greek for '*shut*, as if to *shut one's lips*, brooding on what cannot be altered', and also 'from the act of *shutting the eyes*, that one may see the more, inwardly.' Arthur, dying, ought to be glad of the infirmity which dismays him: he is 'laid widow'd of the power in his eye / That bow'd the will.' Sedation of the will is one of the mystic's initiatic tasks. Tennyson's landscapes are perceived by 'dying ears' or 'dying eyes': looked at, they are ocular elegies. This is most daringly true of the exotic island where Enoch is cast away and stares at

> The blaze upon the waters to the east;
> The blaze upon his island overhead;
> The blaze upon the waters to the west;
> Then the great stars that globed themselves in heaven,
> The hollower-bellowing ocean, and again
> The scarlet shafts of sunrise—but no sail.

All there is to do is observe. Hence the fatigued reiteration of 'blaze', which cumulatively makes the glare intolerable, the circling-back of 'and again', and the conclusion naming the one prosaic object which, among all these tropical wonders, is desired and therefore unforthcoming.

Enoch watches, but is not interested in poetic description or in verbal equivalences to the visual. These literary activities are games for passing time, recourses of the bored poet, who is himself a stranded man. In any case, sight has already caved in during the description, succumbing first to sound, then to an echo. The waves represent the monotony of lyricism, ebbing from the alliterative drum-beat of 'the league-long roller thundering on the reef' to 'the hollower-bellowing ocean'. Lapsing into a monotone, the thing seen becomes the thing recalled, summoned as a spectre. Tennyson's repetitions are in one sense a means of forgetting, in another a mnemonic drill for treasuring 'the days that are no more'. The poetry which in Browning vivifies, like the lump of stone in Tertium Quid's deposition 'made alive' by the adhesion of moss and weed or the germination of 'worm, and fly, and . . . the free bird', is in Tennyson a necrophile, holding dear 'remember'd kisses after death'. Tennyson sees the mind as a haunted house, whose ghosts are memories. His 'Deserted House' is a dead body; intellect in 'The Two Voices' retires like Yeats to 'a ruin'd tower.' As against this funereal quiet, an empty house in Browning remains vocal. In Guido's Roman dwelling, 'the ghost of social joy' makes mouths at him, he says, 'from empty room / And idle door.' When he arrives at the Castle Perilous, Gareth imitates Browning's Roland, jubilantly announcing himself on his slug-horn, and 'sent all his heart and breath thro' all the horn'. He seems—with the aid of those insistent alls—to have worked Browning's miracle of resuscitation. At the echo, the castle starts into life. But its vitality is a necrotic mockery of life, in 'hollow tramplings', 'muffled voices' or a busy transit of shadows; and it voids a knight who is an impersonation of Death.

Ruskin in 1884 argued that nature had sickened and discoloured during the nineteenth century. Mechanism had sentenced it to death, and against this debility Tennyson's images make a valiant, vain protest. Simile and metaphor are recollections of a spent life, bequests of a meagre vitality. Classical landscape was instinct with gods, alive with energy; though the vale where Œnone wanders is lovely, everything in it droops or creeps or loiters in slow motion because it, too, like Œnone, is expiring: 'they cut away my tallest pines.' The same fatal abstracting can happen in the middle of London, as when Tennyson declares that

> There where the long street roars, hath been
> The stillness of the central sea.

The great (because bravely incongruous) word here is 'central', which clings, as if on a spar, to an urban sense of location—a Victorian and metropolitan conviction of centrality, as in the naming of something like Grand Central Station, grand because central—only to cast that spatial confidence adrift or submerge it, since the ocean is centreless, its dominion an affront to the very idea of anthropocentricity. Tennyson composed a monologue for an oak tree to test the possibility of poetically humanising external nature; he can make it talk, but cannot make it humanly sensitive, since what has kept it alive for five hundred years, like the old yew in *In Memoriam* or the brook which chuckles 'men may come and men may go, / But I go on for ever', is its sturdy insentience and inability, as it says, to be embraced. To such an immortality, Tithonus prefers extinction. He begs the gods to withdraw the gift they have made him; Tennysonian images likewise first give then take away, enlivening only to deplete. His words, like Merlin's beard which is the ashes of his 'youth gone out', or like the 'all but smoulder'd out' Lot who is

> A yet-warm corpse, and yet unburiable,
> No more; nor sees, nor hears, nor speaks, nor knows,

patiently await their quietus. Poetry offers anima in its metaphors, as when the damp hill-slopes are 'quicken'd into green' or Earl Limours is kindled by drink or the ashen Merlin colours, 'like an opal warm'd', in response to the witchy caresses of Vivien. But the regeneration works for only as long as the metaphor lasts. Merlin, post-coitally abject, soon 'in the hollow oak . . . lay as dead'. Even a blush, in Keats the face's fecund blooming, is in Tennyson a mortal wound: on Lynette's forehead, 'shame, pride, wrath / Slew the may-white.'

Tennyson's pictures are death-masks; Browning for this reason rejects in *The Ring and the Book* what he calls 'landscaping', which paralytically pictures nature,

> The land dwarfed to one likeness of the land,
> Life cramped corpse-fashion.

He proposes instead a poetry which keeps up with the variance and changeability of living things. Roland has learned this lesson, abandoning all preconceptions and venturing on a perceptual quest, entrusting himself to the tuition of a world about which nothing can ultimately be known—'solve it, you!' Tennyson studiously paints his landscapes, but he cannot prevent the tinted life from bleeding or fading from them. The Grail's luminescence, when it is revealed to the pale nuns, dyes whiteness and then dies into black. His heroes blanch, too: Arthur is white as the mist on the battlefield, Bedivere weakens into 'the white winter of his age'. And Bedivere's enfeeblement is a commentary, too, on Browning's vocalism: as he tells the story of Arthur's passing, 'the man was no more than a voice'. A monologue in Browning is an ego's trumpet; in Tennyson it is the overheard pining of a mood which dare not speak out, like the first (and more persuasive) of 'The Two Voices', which is called still, small, secret and silent.

Metaphors suffer their own small deaths in Tennyson. Often, being reflections only, they deliquesce. The knights whom Gareth fights are seen inverted in the stream they cross; when he topples the knight whose emblem is

the noonday sun, 'the stream / Descended, and the Sun was wash'd away.'
Isolt's face travels with Tristram like an image disturbed and recomposed
when wind ruffles water, Enid dreams of immersion in a dark pool, Geraint
scatters his foes as if obstructing the light and thus obliterating them: they are a
shoal of glittering fish, 'slipping o'er their shadows', and he is a man on the
brink who lifts 'a shining hand against the sun' and blots them out. Browning
has his equivalent to this image, but in his pool there is no fracture, only
dilation. He compares the structure of *The Ring and the Book* to the concentric
circles vibrating from a stone dropped in a pool. Reflexivity does not prove, in
his case, the image's brittleness, but its extensibility.

Nothing in Tennyson can withstand this metaphoric evanescence in water.
Geraint's biceps, for instance, supposedly trophies of epic fortitude, are
lyrically erased or eroded in a simile which notes that they travel down his arms
'as slopes a wild brook o'er a little stone'. The 'small violence' of Modred's
resentment languishes in transference to a landscape, where it is said to perturb
him like a wind irritating

> A little bitter pool about a stone
> On the bare coast.

The violence, small to begin with, is belittled even further by that
supernumerary 'little'. When Guinevere cries after Arthur, between the
determination and the act there interposes, like a shadow, the life-denying
simile, which suspends her purpose in air. Her voice does not reach him
directly but falters 'as a stream that spouting from a cliff / Fails in mid-air.'
The simile's intercession achieves the failure of action: it operates like the
opiate atmosphere of lotos-land. Browning's poems exist as preludes or
epilogues to a dramatic act, which is very often violent. 'I doubt, I will decide,
then act', says Guido. Caponsacchi, after the event, needs to 'justify an act / Of
sober man'. Tennyson's poems must prevent the action which would be their
undoing. Though Ulysses resolves to exercise the will, he, too, expects a watery
dissolution: 'it may be that the gulfs will wash us down.' Arthur's demand that
Bedivere's voice should 'rise like a fountain for me' contains the same prophecy
of relapse. Prayer can mount from earth to heaven, like Herbert's thunder in
reverse; a fountain only assays that ascent, and weeps its waters haplessly back
to the ground. The Bernini Triton in Browning's market-place is a fountain of
a different kind: a tireless, snorting, spouting talker, conversing in water.

Arthur, as he quits Guinevere, evaporates into a simile. 'The King'
vaporously vanishes into 'the phantom of a giant'. Repetition insubstantialises
him further by noting that inside the mist he is 'gray / And grayer'. At last he
fades into a simile—the mere likeness of a solid thing, 'as mist / Before
her'—which means into a spectre, 'moving ghost-like to his doom'. Yet what is
Arthur, after all, but a metaphor? Malory's Arthur was a historical character, a
real man: the fiction, as Caxton's preface shows, craves the authority of fact.

Spenser's Arthur was a supreme fiction: a recreation of fact, myth's correction of history. Tennyson's, whom he calls 'ideal manhood closed in real man', can be neither. The real man who was his model, Albert, is dead; the ideal cannot be, as it is by Spenser, incarnated. So Arthur must, in Tennyson's concluding address to Queen Victoria, imagistically vaporise: he is 'that gray king, whose name, a ghost, / Streams like a cloud, man-shaped'.

The Round Table's mission is for Tennyson an aesthetic one, the irradiation and revitalisation of reality. Arthur seeks 'power on this dead world to make it live'—the same power Browning exults in when he retrieves life from the inert book and its long-dead characters. In Tennyson's redeemed society, the poet will be sovereign, and currency will be imagery. Ambrosius tells Percivale that he and all his colleagues are 'stamp'd with the image of the King'. But the poem founders when it realises that the ideal will not inhabit the real, nor the image imprint itself on human faces. Symbolism is not illumination, but a pursuit of shadows; it deals in replicas not realities. Arthur, granting Balin permission to paint his shield, admits

> The crown is but the shadow of the king,
> And this a shadow's shadow.

When the Grail appears, it is at once involved in—and de-realised by—this scepticism about the image. Ambrosius calls it 'the phantom of a cup that comes and goes' (like Wordsworth's rainbow); Percivale insists on its actuality: 'what phantom? . . . The cup, the cup itself.' Ambrosius can only apprehend it as 'the holy thing', the nun as 'the Holy Thing'. It is that unpunctual, unfocused, evasive quantity, the romantic symbol. Wordsworth, Keats and Shelley try to snatch it from the air; Yeats finally lays its ghost by exposing it as a mere prop, trotted out for show along with his other exploited 'circus animals'.

Roland, whose business is the decipherment of a symbolically muddled landscape, understands (without, like Tennyson's knights, being dismayed by) the unreliability of the image. Like Browning with the ring, he begins from 'a thing's sign', then advances to guess at 'the thing signified'. He is intellectually challenged by the uncertainties of this deductive procedure, asking 'What bad use was that engine for, that wheel, / Or brake, not wheel . . .?' He knows that metaphor is itself a neurotic symptom, using nature for his own psychic confession, as when he calls the stream a serpent or fancies he has speared a baby in it not a water-rat. Contemplating the raddled horse, he sees through the anthropomorphic comfort of the pathetic fallacy and through language's optimistic offer of life to nature: 'Alive? he might be dead for aught I know.' The dark tower puts an end to the poetic chore of match-making between unlike objects. It is 'without a counterpart / In the whole world'; failing as a metaphor, it can only be a symbol, and Roland calls it 'blind as the fool's heart'.

Sludge is right to see the world as ominous with meaning. He is a charlatan only because, as in his anecdote of the pigeons, he codifies those omens. He interprets life as an allegorical puzzle, not a symbolist enigma. Browning's characters acknowledge that, linguistically, their reach exceeds their grasp, so their tropes are raids on the unknown, which must always fall back into exhilarated inadequacy. Hence Rabbi Ben Ezra's 'That metaphor!' or Blougram's 'A simile!' Both are adumbrations, partial and fleeting, of a truth, snatched at because the characters are greedy for 'any revelation called divine'. Blougram's substitute for the unthinking confidence of dogma is the experimental adventure of symbolism. He is an heir to Teufelsdröckh, disrobing the universe:

> Some think, Creation's meant to show Him forth:
> I say, it's meant to hide Him all it can.

The problem of verity has been solved by irony. 'He believed, say, half he spoke', which is exactly the ironist's allowance, since he employs arguments, masks and personae as his surrogates, making trial of what cannot be ascertained and securing himself the freedom—as in the polyphony of *The Ring and the Book*, or in the Socratic quizzings of Wilde's critical dialogues—to entertain contrary propositions at once.

Tennyson's Pellam cries that Balin 'defileth heavenly Things / With earthly uses!', just as Arthur reprimands Bedivere for treasuring Excaliibur's beauty rather than respecting its heavenly and immaterial meaning. They are repeating a medieval protest against literature's independence. Browning's agnostic churchmen are less conscience-stricken. They authorise art's profanation because, God having disappeared, it is man's duty to make himself a god by becoming an artist and redeploying ecclesiastical emblems as personal symbols. This is why the Bishop covets the chunk of lapis lazuli for his tomb. Between his knees it will poise 'like God the Father's globe on both His hands'. Art's incarnation of spirit in body affords a positively carnal delectation to the Bishop, who fondles the stone which is 'blue as a vein o'er the Madonna's breast'. At his most flagrantly proud, the artist can claim—having admitted a sensual infatuation with the mother of god—to be the inventor and executioner of deity. Thus the Bishop (in succession to those rioters in 'The Pardoner's Tale' who 'our blissed Lordes body . . . to-tere' because the Jews had not rent it enough, and who in cannibalising Christ are advancing literature's assassination of scripture) wants to be installed in St Praxed's where he can listen for centuries to 'the blessed mutter of the mass', now no more than a half-articulate, Browningesque stammer, and, most shockingly, 'see God made and eaten all day long'. The Pope notes wearily that 'of the making books there is no end'. Likewise, it seems, of the making and unmaking of gods.

Henry James thought the Pope's verdict a miscalculation on Browning's part. His is too *ex cathedra* a pronouncement; it is as if Browning, afraid of the poem's relativism, had sought the indemnity of an absolute. But the Pope does not, in fact, have the last word. Guido disputes his decision, Browning himself reserves judgement. Tertium Quid has already pilloried the mechanical, judicial descent of divinity in a play's fifth act. For this reason, the poem's adherence is to the novel not the drama, because novels (at least after Fielding's magistracy) abolish the legalism of dramatic form. Dickens's Lord Chancellor in *Bleak House* is a dotard; Conrad's novels, like *Lord Jim*, are tribunals without an executive president.

The Pope's summary conclusion is seen, inside the poem, as a regression. He, who begins by reading and ends by writing, is himself a book-maker. The poem reverts from speech to print, and thus dies into literature; from its 'rabble-brabble' it reverts by way of what the Pope, scoffing at the faked letters, calls 'just handwriting and mere authorship', to the authoritarianism of the word indited and issued as an encyclical. Guido's mistake was to take up his pen and compose the letters Pompilia is made to trace. This is of course no more than 'mere novel-writing', as Sludge says of his séances, yet Browning's ideal is the novel which need not be written—because writing is forgery—but can, in a union with monologising drama, be uttered. Pompilia's moral safeguard is her illiteracy. 'She never penned a letter in her life / . . . Being incompetent to read and write', and therefore exists outside the circumscription of literature. Guido, too, implicitly repenting his own epistolary crimes, says when he is pleading for his life, 'The letter kills, the spirit keeps alive / In law and gospel.' He might have gone on, as Chaucer does in his citations of St Paul, to extend this liberty from law and gospel to literature, that lawless alternative to holy writ. If so, he would have arrived at Wilde's splendid announcement, anticipated by Browning, that 'writing has done much harm to writers. We must return to the voice.' Or, preferably, to a Babel of simultaneous voices.

Since it must be written, *The Ring and the Book* contrives to overcome the limiting, deadening toll of that transcription by being all things at once. During Archangelis's deliberations, it is written in two parallel languages. The advocate divides his lines between Latin and vernacular translations. The authoritativeness of his classical jargon is mocked by an idiomatic impertinence; the dead language is upraised by its living descendant; the text is revived as a voice. It also finds a way of being both prose and poetry, just as the love-notes Guido manufactures alternate between rankly blossoming verse and terse, prosaic messages: as print, *The Ring and the Book* is prose; as speech it is poetry. The city's hubbub, Browning comments, 'speaks out the poesy which, penned, turns prose'. When Wilde declared that Browning used 'poetry as a medium for writing in prose' he was acclaiming this very dexterity of the work as it commutes between the two.

Because the poem is, in James's phrase, 'so essentially Gothic a structure', conjoining the Madonna with clowns who (as Caponsacchi says) pile up their dung-heap in the sacristy, it amalgamates opposed genres. Like the Professor

in 'Christmas-Eve', it is 'three parts sublime to one grotesque'. The tragedy of
Guido's shame is 'a comedy the town was privy to'; Tertium Quid compares
the events with the doubly-plotted puppet-show in the Piazza Navona where
'what you thought tragedy' recurs as farce—for tragedy is fatal and singular,
and by telling it over and over again Browning is rewriting it as incorrigible
comedy, incapable of learning from its mistakes and bound to repeat them, like
Mrs Micawber insisting, every time she reappears, that she will never desert
her hopeless spouse. If it is anyone's tragedy, perhaps it is that of a
supernumerary character, the victim of circumstance like Duncan's grooms:
Patrizj the policeman gets overheated while pursuing the murderers, catches a
fever and dies of pleurisy. Between tragedy and comedy, Browning's anecdote
occupies the middlemarch of compromise staked out by the novel, which
derives its catastrophes (as James said) from unpaid butchers' bills. It is 'an
episode / In burgess-life', says Tertium Quid: 'why seek to aggrandise, / Idea-
lise, denaturalise the class?' The novel does not mind being spotted with
commonness.

Wordsworth wrote a pastoral prelude to epic; Tennyson writes an elegiac
epilogue to it. 'Morte d'Arthur' is all that remains of Everard Hall's
twelve-book epic on King Arthur: the fragment purports to be Book XI, saved
from the fire by a friend. After this, romanticism turns into a cult of the
aesthetic. The Lady of Shallot returns in *The Picture of Dorian Gray*. Sibyl
Vane, quitting the theatre for the reality she thinks she has discovered in
Dorian, says she is sick of shadows; the decision to abandon her pasteboard
palace of art kills her just her as it did Tennyson's heroine. Dorian, too, before
he stabs the portrait, throws down and breaks a mirror which cannot show him
how he truly looks inside. Mimesis is a superficial imitativeness. Lord Henry is
grateful to music for being the one art left which does not profess to make
pictures. Even ugliness—that of Browning's grotesque clamour and his rowdy,
brawling urban epic—can in this last phase of romanticism be colonised as a
species of the beautiful. Writing to his lover Alfred Douglas from Reading
Gaol in *De Profundis* (1897), Wilde sees his betrayal as the apostasy of the
nineteenth century: Bosie had become nostalgic for the gutter, and 'with very
swift and running feet . . . had passed from Romance to Realism'. Like Dorian
at the moment of his death, he has changed from Ariel to Caliban. Wilde
laments that Shakespeare's uncouthness, obscenity and grotesquerie are 'Life
calling for an echo of her own voice and rejecting the intervention of beautiful
style through which alone should life be suffered to find expression';
Browning's clotted, complicated word-mesh has been replaced by the Lady's
magic web. 'Poor noisy Caliban', as Wilde patronisingly referred to him, must
be outlawed. Browning's gross, ingratiating swamp-monster is forbidden entry
to the citadel of art.

33

Decadence and Nonsense

Decadence manifests itself in England as the renewal of romanticism, not as degeneration. Wilde called it the 'English Renaissance of art', long-delayed; for he believed that, in England, Renaissance had been preceded and thus frustrated by Reformation. Yeats likewise saw Spenser as a casualty of a baffled, officially repressed romanticism: a romantic because a pagan, he was required by the state he served to betray his genius by reforming and allegorically rationalising it. The theorists of aestheticism are therefore proponents of Renaissance. Wilde told Yeats that Pater's *Studies in the History of the Renaissance* was his 'golden book' and 'the very flower of decadence', and saluted in it the arrival of millenium, or perhaps apocalypse: 'the last trumpet should have sounded the moment it was written.'

Browning's Renaissance was the awakening of consciousness; Pater's is the uprising of sensuality. That is why Ruskin condemns the Renaissance and its enfeebling luxury, which beguiles his stern Gothic Venice and makes the church of San Giorgio Maggiore profanely wrest itself into the shape of a classical temple. Another historian of the Renaissance and apologist for decadence, J. A. Symonds, accounts for his infatuation with the marble musculature of classical statuary by saying that these works appealed to 'the Greek in me'. He means the phrase patronymically—his family's name had been Simonides, and he felt himself a spiritual native of 'ancient Hellas'—but also homosexually. In Pater, too, the infidel gods banished from literature by Milton's reformism in the 'Nativity Ode' return to resume power: Leonardo's St John, a smirking sensual enchanter, is one of these disgraced demons 'who, to maintain themselves, after the fall of paganism, took employment in the new religion'. Spenser's dancing Graces are pagan mysteries reformed as Christian virtues. Leonardo's seductive Baptist subscribes to no such allegorical regeneration, and the cross with which he has been issued fades and disappears, Pater notes, in successive copies of the painting; at last he is exposed as a naked Bacchus dressed up as a Christian apostle. Botticelli's Madonnas, conscripted against their will to the service of the new faith, remain agnostically abstracted from it. Pater argues that the pen with which one of them, her hand guided by Botticelli, is inscribing the Magnificat 'almost drops from her hand' since the officious, ceremonious words 'have no meaning for her': in fact he has stolen that pen from her and made it controvert her creed; the painting reaches its completion, and its moral undoing, in his prose-poem about it.

Pater's writing is here a re-writing of scripture, translating the Hebraic back into the Hellenic. He practised criticism as heresy, deftly persuading the works he studies to surrender their secrets. So averse is he, in his praise of 'brilliant sins and exquisite amusements', to the 'rude strength of the Middle Ages' that he even discovers a contraband eroticism within the phalanx of Chaucerian epic, wondering if 'the love of both Palamon and Arcite for Emelya, or of those two for each other, is the chiefer subject of the *Knight's Tale*' and tenderly referring to the scarred veterans as 'the two lads'. When he interferes with the Madonna's writing or makes the warriors fall in love with each other, Pater is inventing a modern criticism which is art's re-creation. The critic had traditionally been a devil: Iago says he is nothing if not critical; Goethe's Mephistopheles is the spirit of negation. That impish denial changes in Pater into an unending revisionism. As Gilbert says in Wilde's dialogue *The Critic as Artist*, 'the one duty we owe to history is to re-write it.'

Pater therefore in 1873 re-writes the Italian Renaissance as an anticipation of the English 1890s. Arthur Symons in 1893 equated, as terms for the movement he called modern, Decadence, Symbolism and Impressionism. The two main branches of decadence were, he thought, the symbolist and the impressionist, and he believed them to be complicitly alike. Neither sought 'general truth' ('the object as it really is' Hebraically scrutinised by Arnold); they inquired after essences, the symbolist attesting to 'the faith of spiritual things to the spiritual vision' while the impressionist reckoned with 'the truth of appearances to the senses, of the visible world to the eyes that see it'. Both procedures originate from Pater.

The predicament of the symbolist is the embodying of the invisible, and it is anticipated by Pater's Leonardo, perplexed by the need for 'the transmutation of ideas into images'. Significances forever elude him. He is obsessed, Pater says, by 'the smiling of women and the motion of great waters'. The enigmatic smile of Mona Lisa dematerialises into the grin of Lewis Carroll's Cheshire cat, the symbol for a body which has absented itself; those waters, swamping the solid world in the cartoons Leonardo made about 1514, become the flux of Pater's impressionism, an elapsing life 'driven in many currents', and of Virginia Woolf's waves. Dissolute, the Arnoldian object disperses into a subjective fantasy. Or, when the idea is triumphantly embraced in a matching image, Pater describes a narcissism like Dorian Gray's as he kisses his portrait: consummated self-love, whereby the subjective phantom marries its objective and correlative twin.

This is the case with the story of the friends Amis and Amile, homo-erotically interpreted by Pater. Their 'entire personal resemblance' betokens 'the inward similitude of their souls'; symbolism licenses their love. The ultimate symbolist mystery is that of the hermaphrodite, expounded in Pater's essay on Winckelmann as 'a moral sexlessness'. The hermaphrodite is the symbol's chaste self-replication. Its genital arrangements act out a principle of Wilde's:

he recommended insincerity as a device for multiplying one's personality and begetting a posterity of images. The 'higher beauty' of these unnatural creatures possesses what Pater extraordinarily calls an 'insignificance of its own'. The symbol's most celestial quality is its refusal to signify, to do duty—as allegory demands—as a sign. (This marks the difference between the allegorical hermaphrodite of Spenser and its symbolist successor in Pater.) Therefore Pater reads paintings and poems as symbolist vacuums, significant only for what they decline to show or say. Giorgione's 'painted poems' refuse to articulate a story and conceive of life as 'a sort of listening', an audition of silence: they preserve the mystery by suppressing narrative and muting music. Du Bellay's lyrics are about sensations roused by a symbol which flees before the poem begins. 'The thing has vanished', Pater says, 'because it was pure effect.'

The symbol's flight leaves behind it only the impression. Pater's Renaissance art disputes that victory of realism over romanticism which Wilde saw as the tragedy of his century and the perfidy of Bosie. It dissolves the real into an imprecise impression. Pater sees Luca della Robbia making atonement for sculpture's tendency to 'a hard realism' by using stone liquidly. Leonardo's smile and his vagrant waters recur as examples of what Pater calls expression, by which he means transitory impression: della Robbia's effigies record 'the passing of a smile over the face of a child, the ripple of the air on a still day over the curtain of a window ajar'. His work protests against its entrapment in matter, against the stolid unspirituality of form; Michelangelo's sculptures and unfinished designs discover a metaphysical freedom from form. Michelangelo is the poet, Pater says, of the amorphousness which life emerges from and dies back into: his body-builders train the organism because, like the nocturnal figures on the Medici tombs, they strive to shed it. That struggle is both their Platonic reascent to symbol and their subsidence into impression. The new body, when they are invested with it, will be insubstantially radiant, 'a passing light, a mere intangible, external effect', for stubborn objects can be loosened into impressions by submergence in water or by the bombardment of light: drowned in Monet's lily-ponds of reverie at Giverny, or ignited by the sun which makes his haystacks shimmer.

While purportedly writing about the past, Pater is prescriptively defining an art for the future. That art will, he hopes, have done away with language, for words fix things into a false concreteness. The word must fragment into pigment ('colour, odour, texture' are, as he specifies in his conclusion, the impression's constituents) or into a musical vibration. Pater argues in the essay on Giorgione that art longs for abstractness, wanting to be rid 'of its responsibilities to its subject or material'. Symons's study of the symbolist movement in 1899 virtually paraphrases him, describing an art 'in which the visible world is no longer a reality, and the unseen world no longer a dream', or applauding the attempts of Stephane Mallarmé and Maurice Maeterlinck 'to spiritualise literature, to evade the old bondage of rhetoric . . . [and] . . . exteriority'.

The Picture of Dorian Gray in 1890 establishes the Renaissance in contemporary England. Pater had written of a 'refined and comely decadence'; Dorian, with his 'gracious and comely form', is its image, and in Basil Hallward's description he is verbally painted as an androgynous version of Pater's witchy Gioconda. She is an undying, migrant goddess, arisen of course beside those waters which are the fluent contents of the impressionist mind and the carriers of spawning symbols: Pater imagines her to be 'a diver in deep seas'. She has an undiscriminating fertility. As Leda, she has begotten Helen of Troy; as St Anne, she has begotten Mary. Dorian, however, transforms her serial lives into costume-changes, and the only reproduction he will engage in is a doting self-reflection. Basil had drawn him 'as Paris in dainty armour, and as Adonis with huntsman's cloak'. He, too, is water-borne, but instead of germinating in it like Pater's woman he appropriates its surfaces as his looking-glasses: in one of Basil's designs he ornaments the prow of Adrian's barge and gazes across the Nile, in another he leans over 'the still pool of some Greek woodland, and [sees] in the water's silent silver the marvel of [his] own face'. This ransacking of the past's wardrobe precedes Basil's decision to paint Dorian as himself, in his own dress. The ubiquitous god at length arrives in the present, to be—as Lord Henry proposes—a 'visible symbol' of the 'new Hedonism'. Dorian, however, is luckier than the Gioconda in that he has found a means of preventing the introspection which, 'wrought out from within upon the flesh', stealthily lining the eyelids and hands, has written her maladies upon her. He knows that the making of his soul will be the marring of his body. He resolves therefore—like Garbo (who longed to play Dorian Gray) at the end of *Queen Christina* emptying and refrigerating her face, or Andy Warhol retiring behind an ashen, moronic blandness—to be an immaculate surface, and thus a symbol gloriously signifying only itself. Axël in Villiers de l'Isle-Adam's fable disdains living and leaves it to his servants; Dorian, even more haughtily, leaves it to his portrait.

Written at and about the *fin de siècle* and nervously anticipating (as Lady Narborough does) the *fin du globe*, Wilde's novel reviews the literary tradition of which it is the terminus, just as Dorian—globally researching exotic sensations and pillaging a cosmopolitan treasury of baubles; systematically working through and discarding every creed and ethic—synopsises within himself 'the whole of history' and treats it 'merely as the record of his own life, not as he had lived it . . . but as his imagination had created it for him'. Sempiternal like La Gioconda, his career comprises the century's.

He extends backwards to the origins of romanticism, and commandeers its left-over trophies: he is offered a frame from Fonthill, which the dealer—alluding to Beckford's profanation of the abbey—says would suit a religious painting. The frame left empty by Beckford Dorian steps into. His country house is located, like Newstead, in Nottinghamshire, so geography makes him a Byron *de nos jours*. When Dorian cries, 'Each of us has Heaven and Hell in him', he assumes the lineage of the romantic superman, in succession to Milton's Satan and in alliance with Nietzsche's Zarathustra. He also lives on into and contemptuously outlives Victorian culture, where romance in its fragile palace of art withdraws from the messy reality of the streets. The Lady of Shalott and Browning's Caliban, the tutelary opposites of that culture, are both present in the novel. Disgusted with the theatre, Sibyl Vane declares she is sick of shadows, and Dorian shatters a mirror. For each, quitting the aesthetic sanctum is fatal. Browning's swamp-ogre recurs in the East End, as the fat oily Jewish entrepreneur who is Sibyl's employer and who blames his five bankruptcies on 'The Bard': Dorian loathes him, feeling 'as if he had come to look for Miranda and had been met by Caliban', but Wilde's point is that the Victorians have reduced romance to an opiate evasion of the real which still relies on reality for a commercial subsidy; so Miranda has quite logically declined into the hired plaything of Caliban. At Oxford, Wilde temporised between the antagonistic influences of Ruskin and Pater. Dorian seditiously achieves their merger when he reads a poem of Gautier's about Ruskin's holy city of Venice. To Gautier, Venice is a flagrant Venus whose body, like La Gioconda's, emerges from the water.

Lord Henry, catechising Gladys, rules that 'romantic art begins with its climax'. Formally, this explains Poe's rejection of all poetry which is not spasmodically and climactically lyric, consisting only of Pater's pure effect, or the post-coital exhaustion already audible in the prelude to Wagner's *Tristan und Isolde*. The only progress a romantic work is permitted is a return from the end to the beginning, like Wagner's immersion of the world in the overflowing Rhine in *Götterdämmerung*. Historically, too, Dorian is the indolent end of romanticism, in whom the beginning is latent. He experiences as well romanticism's epilogue. The portrait is his advance into realism: Basil refers to 'the Realism of [its] method'; it is a romantic remonstrance to the real. From this phase, Dorian graduates to the next, which is naturalism. No longer shunning ugliness, he becomes obsessed by it, because it alone can certify the reality of things. His detours to opium dens and low dives in Whitechapel explore the social orifices unclad by naturalism: Baudelaire's gutter, Zola's stews and sewers. The apostasy is inevitable. The aesthete's craving for sensation demands ever more virulent satiations; the denial of nature by Dorian's model, Des Esseintes in Huysmans's novel *A Rebours*, induces a corresponding lust for the nature which has been prohibited. Symons, who thought Zola filthy, allowed that 'his realism is a distorted idealism'. So Dorian's naturalist slumming is the inversion and the consequence of his romantic faith. Both the romantic and the naturalist cancel the dreaded real, the one by fancying himself an angel, the other by behaving like a beast. Ariel and Caliban are closer colleagues than they seem.

If *Dorian Gray* sums up romanticism's corruption as realism and then as naturalism, representing the history of art and literature as a hereditary disease, it also foretells realism's eventual defamation as surrealism. Dorian's portrait is the first surreal painting—the first to dramatise that morphological calamity which is, in Dali, the calamity of surreal nature: objects rotting, losing shape and inscribing on themselves the inner history of their crimes. When Picasso cruelly abstracted Gertrude Stein's face, he was experimenting with the image's surreal power to put a curse on the actuality which is its model. Stein protested that she did not look like that. 'You will', declared Picasso with a sinister predictiveness worthy of Dorian. The anecdote is the more pertinent because it echoes one told (for a change) against Wilde. Admiring a friend's witticism, he is alleged to have wished that he had said that. 'You will, Oscar, you will', commented one of the company. The predicted plagiarism is a blithe theft, a demonstration of unaccountability; Picasso's remark mandates penalties, as surrealism does. Those who live by the image will at last be trapped inside it.

Generically, *Dorian Gray* is equally comprehensive, and equally paradoxical. It audaciously couples Gothic horror and Grecian symposium; it refuses to be a novel, yet at the same time will not be, in default, a play. It cannot be a novel, because its people are what they wear and how they look. There is nothing behind their faces; Lord Henry's private meditations are not informal consciousness but publishable essays. Being the agent of drab reality, the novel is specifically scorned. Lord Henry defines American novels as dry-goods, and says that if he wrote one—which he never will, of course—it would be 'as lovely as a Persian carpet, and as unreal'. One novel is venerated and worshipfully imitated by Dorian: Huysmans's *A Rebours*. It is neutered, however, by being left unnamed (a symbolist scruple, since absence makes a mystery and a conspiracy of it) and by being qualified as no novel at all—it is called 'a novel without a plot, and with only one character'. The association with counterfeiting which is the novel's shame in *The Way We Live Now* is here its sole aesthetic pride: Dorian, in a new instalment of the rumours about Melmotte, is said to consort with coiners and to have been inducted into the secrets of their trade, while Adrian Singleton, corrupted by Dorian, has forged his friend's name on a bill.

Though its dialogues belong to the drama not the novel, *Dorian Gray* also sees through the tawdry pretences of the theatre, as Dorian does from his seat in the stage-box. Sibyl mocks the silly melodramas in which she has been made to act, yet her brother delivers himself of some 'mad melodramatic words' threatening vengeance. Lord Henry says he loves acting because it is so much more real than life. Still, reality proves inimical to the Wildean theatre. When Sibyl falls in love, she can no longer realise Juliet's passion in her acting. The actor is an ambulatory paradox, feigning emotions he is debarred from feeling: Dorian is a more accomplished professional than Sibyl because, while he acknowledges her death to be a tragedy, it is one that he walks through with cool unresponsiveness. Dorian aims to be, like Des Esseintes or La Gioconda, a world-spirit, the summation of all anterior epochs; whereas his existence is anthological, Sibyl is less even than the sum of the roles—Juliet, Rosalind, Imogen—she plays, and is never herself. The novel's discussion of 'the palmy days of the British Drama' enables Wilde to demolish the romantic Shakespeare, the chameleon who (more speciously versatile than Sibyl) was both Iago and Imogen. That loving empathy celebrated by Keats is just play-acting to Wilde. In the country, Dorian performs in an impromptu *Winter's Tale* as Florizel to the Perdita of the village girl Hetty (though he revises the play by jilting her), and even Hamlet, the patron of romantic introversion and of the subjective, symbolic grief for which there is no corresponding object, is seen as an implacable surface, another unmoved mummer: Dorian says his portrait reminds him of 'those curious lines in some play—*Hamlet* I think' about 'the painting of a sorrow, / A face without a heart.'

Salomé, a play about the aborting of a prophecy, itself possesses a similar literary hindsight and a talent for prognostication. Like *Dorian Gray*, it both describes romanticism's climax and prescribes its sequel. Jokanaan in his cistern anticipates the coming of a god and the renewal of human history; the play, self-consciously positioned at an end to literary history, is written after that divinity's departure, and enjoins its replacement by art.

Wilde inherited his heroine from Des Esseintes, who is fascinated by Gustave Moreau's paintings of her dance. Yet between Huysmans's novel in 1884 and Wilde's play in 1891 a desecrating change has happened. Des Esseintes studies Salomé as an omnipresent spirit, the celebrant of a fertility rite and thus a presence in all religions. He extrapolates from biblical tradition to the theologies of the Far East, and equips her with a lotus, 'the sacred flower of Egypt and India', and the wand of Isis. The palace—or eclectic cathedral—in which she performs is a compound of all architectural orders, as she is the common denominator of all mythologies: with Romanesque columns, it is a basilica built at once in the Moslem and Byzantine styles. In Huysmans's reading, the dethroned god and the decapitated evangelist are replaced by this fecund, hysterical goddess. In Wilde there is no such primordial, anthropological religion. At the play's centre is an echoing emptiness: the baptist is lodged in a hole in the ground. The religious disputes which occupy its characters dissever the sects which Huysmans unites in the world-wide cult of Salomé. Each faction has manufactured its own god: the Pharisees and Saducees quarrel about the existence of angels, the Jews squabble among themselves about Alexandrian heterodoxy and about the perfidy of the Samaritans, the Nubians propitiate their gods with blood-sacrifices while the gods of the Cappadocians have been exterminated by the Romans. The soldier finds all theological arguments laughable.

This death or departure of the gods announces Yeats's 'new dawn' of symbolism. The absurdity of the Jews, who 'worship a God that you cannot see' and indeed 'only believe in things that you cannot see', is the symbolist's warrant. The prophet can only decode signs (Baudelaire called the poet a *déchiffreur*); the symbolist actually encodes them, creating significance in a world which would otherwise have none. The action of Wilde's play consists largely in such a making of metaphors. The moon, for instance, is a nonentity, a pallid disc of borrowed light. Yet everyone seeks to confer an identity on it by seeing it symbolically—to Salomé it is a virgin, to the page a dead woman, to Herod a mad, naked harridan. Symbol-making is a kind of coining (the activity with which Dorian is tainted), imprinting meanings on otherwise valueless objects, and Salomé imparts as much when she says the moon is 'like a little piece of money'. At best these metaphors, last ventures of the pathetic fallacy, are linguistic illusions. Because lunatics are supposed to have looked at the moon, Herod is convinced that the moon itself looks like a lunatic. The reflexivity of *Dorian Gray* ends in a hall of mirrors. It is with metaphors that Salome woos Jokanaan, in her multitudinous similes for his eyes, hair, mouth and body, and her mother's lusts are incited by iconography: hers is a lechery of the eyes, Jokanaan charges, stimulated when she sees 'the images of men painted upon the walls, the images of the Chaldeans limned in colours'. Herodias is often accused of obtuseness for devaluing metaphors when she declares 'the moon is like the moon, that is all', but Gertrude Stein after all made a reputation for modernist percipience by repetitiously saying much the same thing about a rose: objects correspond only to the labels words arbitrarily attach to them; fabricating metaphors, we are only spending and wasting words, or investing in the idols touted beneath that gateway Salomé mentions when she is tempting Narraboth. Jokanaan's cryptic thunderings can be endlessly interpreted, as is symbolism's wont, but no reading is conclusively true. Herodias says he is reciting the doom of Herod; Herod is sure he is referring to 'the King of Cappadocia, who is mine enemy'. Salomé believes his imprecations are directed at Herodias; the soldier scoffs that it is all too obscure for him to understand.

Linguistically expatriated—Wilde wrote it in French, hoping Sarah Bernhardt would perform it; Alfred Douglas translated it back into English—*Salomé* finds language to be a powerless naming of things which no longer respond to denomination. 'I called them by their names', says the Cappadocian of his vanished gods, 'and they did not come. I think they are dead.' A Baptist is an appropriate victim for the play: christening is naming or consecration, and that rite—the initiative of Milton's God, who in speaking the world into existence annunciates all subsequent literary speech—has failed. It can be revived only as solemnly sacrilegious nonsense: Jokanaan's baptismal office is taken over, in 1895, in *The Importance of Being Earnest*, by Canon Chasuble, who anoints the self-counterfeiting of the play's heroes.

But if words have been emptied of meaning, *Salomé* foresees alternatives to literature. The heroine abjures words altogether when she dances, and musically overpowers them when, in Richard Strauss's opera of 1905, set to a German translation of the play by Hedwig Lachmann, she sings. Ballet is her recourse because it solves the problem of correspondence between word and thing which troubles literary symbolism: the dancer, as Yeats says, is inseparable from the dance. Symons in 1898 called the ballerina 'all pure symbol'. Her body as she gyrates does her talking for her. In opera, too, though Strauss's Salomé struggles to pronounce Wilde's text against the subliminal din of the orchestra, she expresses herself voicelessly. The passage which defines her is the orchestral interlude between Jokanaan's return to the cistern and Herod's entrance—silent and therefore non-existent in Wilde, but in Strauss an agonisingly protracted pause—when a series of wrenching modulations changes Salomé's pleas for Jokanaan's mouth into her demand for his head; and for all her verbal efforts, her desires are gratified instrumentally, when tickling arpeggios help her to excite Narraboth, or woodwinds on her behalf ruffle the matted hair of Jokanaan. Once Strauss interceded, it seemed that the play had always been appealing for its own relief by music. The page, in a speech Strauss cuts, hears Narraboth's voice as a flute, and a mistranslation of Hedwig Lachmann's encourages the orchestrating of emotion. Wilde had Salome tell Jokanaan, *'Ta voix m'enivre'*, which Douglas translated as, 'Thy voice is wine to me.' Lachmann, as if already hearing the Dionysia in Strauss's pit, renders the phrase as *'Deine Stimme ist wie Musik in meinen Ohren'*. Literature's words can do no more than yearningly envy the condition of music. In Strauss they attain its nonsensical, sensual grace.

Nonsense is decadence under the frivolous sign of comedy. It is also an English version of symbolism. Symons's study of the symbolist movement began by declaring that 'without symbolism there can be no literature; indeed, not even language' because words are symbolic spells, arbitrary phonemes to which significations are, irrelevantly, applied. Tennyson's keening repetitions and the bruit of Browning approach this truth by their spoliation of meaning from words. After them, it is gloriously proclaimed by Lewis Carroll in his anagrams and acrostics, his alphabet-cipher, castle-croquet and teasing doublets.

Nonsense became, as G. K. Chesterton predicted, the literature of the future, because of its gratuitousness. It is the gay science of Nietzsche, shunning the world of utility where words are the captions for things. Pope's 'mad Mathesis', who spurns 'material chains', has been granted the immateriality which Symons, in his essay on Huysmans, sees as the condition of symbolism: she is the goddess who liberates the novel from the bondage of realism, internalises it 'to a complete liberty'. Art's exhilaration is its recognition that 'it is so absolutely free'. Yet what can that freedom achieve, except the fantastic trickery of Mathesis running round the circle to find it square? Poetry has become a game, the assembly (as Virginia Woolf puts it in *The Waves*) of squares and oblongs, and is becoming what Beckett calls an end-game, aware of its futility and of the obtuseness of its constituents. Following upon the absolute freedom extolled by Symons is the modernist imposition of claustrophobic limits: delight changes to despair when the croquet of the Queen of Hearts is replaced by the word-golf in Nabokov's *Pale Fire*, by Hermann Hesse's glass-bead game, or by William Burroughs's cutting-up of his manuscripts.

But in Carroll, language is still gleefully off-duty. He enjoys its pranks, and the cavortings of numerals, for mathematics (the musical and mystical science of Yeats's Pythagoras in 'Among School Children') is a symbolist purification of language:

> Yet what are all such gaieties to me
> Whose thoughts are full of indices and surds?

$$X^2 + 7x + 53 = \frac{11}{3}$$

When the White Knight in *Through the Looking-Glass* mimes 'Resolution and Independence', he transforms Wordsworth's stoic reverie into agitated mental arithmetic:

> But I was thinking of a way
> To multiply by ten,
> And always, in the answer, get
> The question back again.

The stuttering confusion of the speaker in 'The Three Voices' makes no sense, but at the same time makes lyrical nonsense. The man's agony is a staccato patter-song, emptying the very mind he is fretting to define:

> 'Mind—I believe—is Essence—Ent—
> Abstract—that is—an Accident—
> Which we—that is to say—I meant—'.

This is verbal semaphore, a telegraphic syllogism. Carroll's world is deranged in its excess of reason.

The art of symbolism lies in discerning that what seems to be muddle is in fact a precise and systematic puzzle. The deductive drill of interpretation is expounded in Carroll's treatise (as Dodgson) on *Symbolic Logic*. Here he resolves logic into a fastidious etiquette, as irrationally autocratic as that policed by the Queen of Hearts. The answers to Dodgson's conundrums are laws of social comportment: hedgehogs do not take in *The Times*, neither do engine-drivers live on barley-sugar, kangaroos are to be avoided, and 'No cheque of yours, received by me, is payable to order.' Setting logic to work on language, Carroll could make words perform acrobatic stunts. He had a procedure for converting the word Conservative by a series of regulated steps into its antithesis, Liberal: a symbol contorts itself into its opposite number. His pictograms effected the same vanishing-acts in the visible world, as when he changed an albatross into a penny-postage-stamp. The bird, Coleridge's incubus of imagination, can be exorcised by legerdemain, and transmitted to a surrogate by mail.

Alice's adventures in wonderland happen by virtue of a romantic mood. Her induction is made possible by a torpor like Keats's drowsy numbness. Wonderland itself compounds the architecture and the horticulture sacred to English romanticism: the cerebral Gothic house with its dark halls and small passages; arrived at through it, by the exercise of memory which regains childhood, 'the loveliest garden you ever saw'. Alice gets there by shutting herself up like a telescope. The restoration of infancy happens as a physical retraction: the body packs itself away, leaving only an elongated eye. That optic—a 'camera obscura' for Carroll the photographer—is both Milton's Galilean telescope, trained on the infinite spaces above us, and the microscope through which Fuseli studied an insect world of thronging, invisible diminutiveness; it equates Brobdingnag and Lilliput, the outsize prodigies of the sublime and the infinite littleness which Jean Paul Richter identifies as the realm of the ridiculous.

Though access to the fantasy happens by these traditional routes, the wonder of Carroll's land is that it is not a romantic haven but a symbolist playground for verbal surds. Words there, released into meaninglessness, rampage as things—a mouse's tale lengthens into a coiling tail, a prohibitive not gets snarled into an inextricable knot—or breed to produce the mergers that Humpty Dumpty, explicating 'Jabberwocky', calls portmanteaux. These hold-alls are the punning constituents of *Finnegans Wake*: the Johnsonian dictionary, where words are lodged in separate compartments and arraigned as moral individuals, is communalised as Joyce's lexicon, a language potentially compacted in one versatile, undifferentiated, endless word.

Carroll does not need, like the romantics, to shatter mirrors, because he—or Alice at least—can travel through them; and he is in any case aware that the mirror is not, as the romantics feared, a mimetic enforcement of actuality. The mirror subversively queries reality by reversing it: Tweedledum and Tweedledee deride Alice's complacent conviction that she is real. The looking-glass world, where everything is the same 'only the things go the other way', operates according to the same principle as Dorian's picture. Objects are altered by reflection, which reverses them; Dorian's face is immaculate surface, the portrait is ulterior symbol. Seeing things as mirror images of themselves is in Carroll a formula for rendering them symbolic: he wrote letters back to front, played music boxes backwards, claimed to have begun 'The Hunting of the Snark' at the last line, 'For the Snark *was* a Boojum, you see', and prints the first stanza of 'Jabberwocky' in mirror-writing. The White Queen, refusing ever to allow it to be today, propounds the wisdom of 'living backwards': the mnemonic devotion of romanticism, practised by Sterne, Wordsworth and Proust, all of whom discovered, as the Queen says, that 'one's memory works both ways', as retrospection and as prophetic foresight, since to all of them the child is the predestining parent of the adult and can (as Alice cannot) 'remember things before they happen'.

To accord with this mirror-imaging, the symbolist poem must be written in reverse, like Carroll's 'Snark'. The poet begins with a meaning, which he then meticulously obscures or conceals; deciphering it is the reader's duty. Yet the end he attains when he does so is merely a beginning. He has been cheated by language's sleight-of-hand, which permits Carroll to make the Snark a Boojum after all. Baffled by the Red Queen's reasoning, Alice inadvertently defines the symbolist poem when she says 'it's exactly like the riddle with no answers'. ('What matter that you understood no word!' says Yeats's Ribh after his ecstatic song.) Or the riddle has innumerable speculative and inconclusive answers: Alice's interview with Humpty Dumpty, 'who can explain all the poems that ever were invented—and a good many that haven't been invented just yet', is a seminar on the kind of interpretation modern literature expects—reading as detection, and as a conjurer's trick. In symbolism, interpretation precedes creation (Yeats pointed out that 'Wagner spent seven years arranging and explaining his ideas before he began his most characteristic music'), for the symbol is defined by its inexhaustible, indefinite hospitality to interpretation. Yeats argues that the horns of Michelangelo's Moses are a symbolist mystery not an allegorical attribute because 'a hundred generations might write out what seemed [their] meaning . . ., and they would write different meanings.' The problem must remain, as it is for Alice, insoluble.

Among Humpty's symbolist prerogatives, useful both to poet and to explicator, is his decision that 'when *I* use a word, it means just what I choose to make it mean.' Symons, writing about Mallarmé in 1893, virtually paraphrases him: his poems are 'a sequence of symbols', and 'every word must be taken in a sense with which its ordinary significance has nothing to do.' Humpty's edict also justifies the nonsensical nominalism of *The Importance of Being Earnest*, Wilde's most jokingly decadent work. Pater in *The Renaissance* warms to the seditious antinomianism which disputes medieval orthodoxy; its rebellious heroes are Abelard, or Tannhäuser sojourning in the Venusberg. Wilde takes up this career of sensual recusancy. Dorian, flirting with religion, is titillated by 'the subtle antinomianism of mysticism'; Gilbert in *The Critic as Artist* opines that 'the artistic critic . . . is an antinomian always'; at last in the play the spiritual rebel's avocation of controversy and espousal of antinomies develops into a comic credo, airily juggling with words which no longer correspond to things. It is sublimely unimportant to be earnest, important only—for the name is a rune, an amiable abracadabra—to be Ernest. Gwendolen, whose extravagant nominalism is both musically and mystically rapturous, thrills to the divinity of that cognomen, and neither she nor Cecily will consider marrying a man who has the temerity to be called anything else. Jack and Algernon therefore, in a jesting tribute to those religiously regenerative conversions beloved by the decadents, have themselves rebaptised. Canon Chasuble admits them to a church profaner than that which is the refuge of Marius the epicurean in Pater's novel: a cult not of the Word but of glittering, loquacious, reverberantly empty words.

The characters speak with the authoritarianism of moralists, chattering about 'hard and fast rules' for conduct or lamenting the debasement of the lower classes, yet all that is left of morality is its absolutist cadences. They exercise a dialectic which can reverse relations at will, or if necessary equate anything with its opposite. When Lady Bracknell discovers that Jack's house is on the unfashionable side of Belgrave Square, she avows 'that could easily be altered'. Jack asks if she refers to the fashion or the side. She replies imperiously, 'Both, if necessary.' A speech so elevated and so purged of lowly meaning aspires, as Pater would have wished, to song. Lady Bracknell's ring on the doorbell is Wagnerian, and Edith Evans introduced to the part an octave-vaulting cadenza on the query 'A hand-bag?' The operatic erasure of verbal quantities brings this dulcet chatter near to the condition of Jabberwocky. Jack complains of Algy's paradoxes, a system for perversely depriving words of significance which operates like Mallarmé's symbolic substitutions. 'You never talk anything but nonsense', he says; Algy nonchalantly answers, 'Nobody ever does.'

The dramatic rule that character must be action has been listlessly, elegantly disproved. Wilde described *Dorian Gray* as 'rather like my own life' because it was 'all conversation and no action', and congratulated himself on the uneventfulness of his plays: 'I wrote the first act of *A Woman of No Importance* in answer to the critics who said that *Lady Windermere's Fan* lacked action. In the act in question, there was absolutely no action at all. It was a perfect act.' While drama is annihilated by the paradox of an inactive act, the novel likewise undergoes a decadent change from representation of reality to impotent fabulation. Hence Miss Prism's definition of the brain-child she deposited in the basinette: in her triple-decker 'the good ended happily, and the bad unhappily. That is what Fiction means.' That at least is what the supreme fiction of Christian judgement, the prototype for novelistic dispensations, likes to pretend will come to pass. Until that happens, the Wildean imperative is, as Shaw's Ann tells Jack Tanner in *Man and Superman*, to 'go on talking'. Tanner is aghast at the instruction, because his talk is a prosy second-best for the persuasive song of his archetype, Don Giovanni, and he knows Ann is not listening; but talk is the poised arrogance of Wilde's people. They dandify existence and perfect it by finding words for it. Only once does the bold, vain veneer falter. Cecily, writing down Algernon's proposal as he utters it, stops short at his 'Ahem!', admitting, 'I don't know how to spell a cough.' Control of one's language is a stratagem for survival, since words are already proliferating and misbehaving in that underground of implication that Freud opened up: the speech of Chasuble and Miss Prism is defamed by double meanings—that of 'abandoned', or of the clichéd compliment 'young women are green'—which they are at pains, too late, to correct. Metaphor is the rank concupiscence of language. Miss Prism therefore warns Cecily, when studying her political economy, to omit 'the chapter on the Fall of the Rupee. . . . It is somewhat too sensational. Even these metallic problems have their melodramatic side.'

Wilde overcomes in comedy that duality which is the moral affliction of Dorian and the interpretative problem of the symbol, imperilling (as he warns in the preface to the novel) all who venture beneath the surface. The division between the unblemished face and the guilty image is rationalised in Algernon's policy of 'Bunburying' and Jack's invention of the nonexistent Ernest whom he and Algernon eventually, by the agency of a sacrament, become. Their double lives enable them to be both Dorian and the portrait at different times and in different counties, and to evade altogether consequences Dorian can only defer. Character has been elided by persona, the face by a mask one can hide behind. Wilde disliked André Gide's lips, 'straight like those of someone who has never lied', and offered to teach Gide mendacity so his mouth would twist into the wry semblance of an ancient vizor.

Romanticism had wanted to see through the surface to the spirit, to do away with Shelley's staining prism. Wilde, by rendering it impenetrable, made it into the symbol. Words were no longer forlorn, as Keats said, in their ineptitude at translating thoughts and feelings. So long as they were content to be self-referring (for art, according to *Intentions*, 'never expresses anything but itself'), they could share in the sainted narcissism of the dandy, whose self-love is a life-long affair. Symons in 1901 identified Wilde's artistry with his attitudinising. His achievement was to have imagined himself, to be someone rather than do anything. He had fashioned himself into a venerable, totemic image; without his intercession, the world then refashioned itself into an image of him. Wilde toured America in 1882 in competition with the caricature of himself in Gilbert and Sullivan's operetta *Patience*, and on the train to Sacramento was supplanted by a parodic lookalike; his lecture-audience at Harvard consisted of sixty velveteen clones kitted out in knee-breeches and black silk stockings, with over-ripe sun-flowers in their button-holes. Dorian has multiplied himself in an iconographic offspring, without need for recourse to bodies: 'mirror on mirror mirrored', as Yeats says, 'is all the show.' Thus the image manages its own perpetuation. Wilde's frivolity and effrontery have a devout earnestness after all. The man was a serious joke, and so—since in England it is the point of transition and connection between the romantic and the modern—is decadence.

— 34 —
The Last Romantic?

Yeats in 1931 woefully admitted to being one of the last romantics. He was not that, only the latest: romanticism does not exhaust itself in him. But his conscious location of himself in literary history is very proper, for though situated (as he liked to think) in the aftermath of that history, he remembers back to its sources and revives them within himself. He had a theory of poetic inheritance as elaborated as Eliot's, though very different. Eliot emphasises severance and schism, the fragmentation of poetry into dissociated quotes. Yeats insists on continuity—the perpetuity of what he calls 'the old nation', the ribald and mystic Merry England of Chaucer and Spenser, driven into hiding when Bunyan invents Modern England and puritanically allegorises the old pagan symbols; the subterranean river of Celtic fantasy, which flows from Malory's knights to Shakespeare's fairies and on to Scott's antiquarian highlanders—and he proves that continuity in his own person. His writing has a noble resoluteness, a refusal to swerve from what he sees to be the truth or to time-serve, and for fifty years he adheres to that faith. Symons in 1900 wondered at his 'continuously poetical quality of mind'. He was always himself, and always a poet. He retained that unitary, absolutist self by perpetually renewing it. He can, as he put it in 1937, alter his intellect as easily as altering his syntax, but the intellect—whether it pays its dues to Irish wizardry or Rosicrucian theology, to Neo-Platonism or astrology or the yogic meditative postures of Bhagwān Shri Hamsa—is still inalienably his own: there never was a more sublime or supreme poetic ego.

Nor a more capaciously inclusive one. Eliot, with his theory of the literary past's irrecoverable wholeness, had to interpret influence as a looting of the museum. He often uses metaphors of theft to describe the process, saying that mediocre poets borrow while great ones steal, or calling meaning a decoy, the scrap of meat the robber feeds to the guard-dog so he can effect his entry into the unconscious. Yeats does not see poetry as a raid on the past, or a burgling of the reason. He owns the past, because it is alive in him. A poet reincarnates all his forebears. 'I owe my soul', he said, 'to Shakespeare, to Spenser and to Blake, perhaps to William Morris'; the connection is familial, genetic. Influence is no infliction, like Milton's predestining of his successors, from which the only freedom is parodic denial; influence in Yeats invigorates, and it does so by communion with that reservoir of images—Coleridge's much-perforated tank in the preface to 'Christabel'—which Yeats identifies in

'The Second Coming' as Spiritus Mundi or in 'The Tower' as the Great Memory.

Quotation means companionship, and the transmission of life. In his 1937 poem, 'The Municipal Gallery Revisited', Yeats, as his predecessor's trustee, takes over a line from Spenser, 'No fox can foul the lair the badger swept.' It comes from Spenser's poem on the death of the Earl of Leicester, and Yeats is re-visiting it, too, along with the gallery where his friends are imaged and immortalised: he had already singled it out for its pungency in his essay on Spenser in 1902. Its recurrence here is literally vitalising, for Yeats goes on to characterise himself, Synge and Lady Gregory as acolytes of Antaeus, ritually touching the parental earth and so growing strong and able to sing. Quoting that 'image out of Spenser and the common tongue' is the homage of Antaeus: literature is one of the 'deep-rooted things' Yeats venerates in the gallery. The talisman has a magic potency, repairing the damage of history. Spenser's poem is called 'The Ruins of Time'; Yeats excerpts a line from it to convince both Spenser and himself that time's depredations can be undone, just as his dead friends re-arise on the walls in painted and undying icons. Yeats's infirmity thus changes into fortitude. He grumbles about 'my mediaeval knees', but the adjective, like the Spenserian tag, atones for the very debility which saddens it: the body's elderliness is evidence of tradition's survival, and of rootedness. Yeats's extremities are living relics. His head may be modern; lower down he is primeval. And he can recover from his feebleness by an act of genuflection, again like Antaeus's grounding of himself. His knees only 'lack health until they bend'.

Yeats is of course preoccupied by the injustice of ageing, from the old pensioner who spits in the face of time in *The Rose* (1893) to the wild old wicked man in his 1938 volume, from the withered Queen Maeve of 1903 to the cancer-stricken Mabel Beardsley gaily playing at mortality in 'Upon a Dying Lady'; and, like Dylan Thomas encouraging his father to rage at the imminence of extinction, his concern is both with a human and a literary destiny. Thomas's, too, is an impenitent, incorrigible romanticism: a refusal to mourn, and a refusal (urged on his father) to die. In Yeats the idiot boy yields to frenzied, inspiredly senile elders, to Crazy Jane or the Lear of 'Lapis Lazuli': poetry is not childhood regained but second childhood revelled in. An indecent old age is Yeats's solution to the problem of literary history and its apparent consignment of him to an epilogue. He is fond of doleful pronouncements of an end, like the shepherd's 'The woods of Arcady are dead' or 'Romantic Ireland's dead and gone' or 'The Garden died'; in his early poems the season is Keatsian autumn, as in his elegy for 'The Falling of the Leaves', and the atmosphere one of Tennysonian desolation, with lyricism the keening echo of a sound—the sad shepherd's 'inarticulate moan', the 'wandering music' of the horns or the wailing of the hounds in the foxhunter's ballad. Thereafter Yeats grows steadily, blazingly younger. Hazlitt, who thought romanticism the guttering of poetic liveliness, derided Macpherson's Ossian in 1818 because he is the bard of a god-depleted, ailing nature; Yeats's Oisin in 1889 has undergone rejuvenation. He wars, feasts and dances in mockery of 'Time and Fate and Chance', and his scorn for languor or fatigue is Yeats's dismissal of the enervation of literary late-coming.

The earlier romantics backed away guiltily from an imagination which would steal fire and re-create the world: Coleridge casts it out from the *Biographia*. Yeats has advanced beyond such scruples to declare, as he does in 'Meditations in Time of Civil War', that 'the daemonic rage / Imagined everything'. To imagine is to retrieve images silted away in the past or in the brain's lower depths, and their restoration is a conferring of sovereignty: Oisin prides himself on his 'angry king-remembering soul', and another poem calls forth 'queens that were imagined long ago'. Once he has trained the images in obedience to him, Yeats can make gifts of them, rewarding his friends with immortality. In 'Beautiful Lofty Things' he enumerates them as 'all the Olympians'. The promotion to godhead happens instantaneously, with despotic arbitrariness and favouritism, in the gap between two lines:

> . . . Maud Gonne at Howth station waiting a train,
> Pallas Athena in that straight back and arrogant head.

The power of the thing lies in its whimsical casualness. Yeats feels no need to labour over the divinising of loved ones, or philosophically to justify his partiality, like Coleridge with Hartley or Shelley with his psychic other halves, and therefore—in this superb completion of what the romantics, more hesitant in their competition with deity, commence—he circles back to the confidence of an earlier poetic time, reclaiming the honorific rights of patronage employed by the Renaissance maker: by Spenser immortalising Elizabeth Boyle or Donne doing likewise for Elizabeth Drury.

Yeats models his making on incarnation, addressing Christ as a compeer ('You can fashion everything / From nothing every day') but reminding him of his inferiority ('You have lacked articulate speech'); and in contrast to the chastely linguistic entry of eternity into time marked by Eliot when the Word condescends to the world, Yeats's first coming is a copulative union—the swan's ravishment of Leda, or the coupling recounted by lunatic Tom in *Words for Music Perhaps*:

> The stallion Eternity
> Mounted the mare of Time
> 'Gat the foal of the world.

Michael Robartes, catechising the dancer, instructs her in the palpability and carnality of symbols, which are, like the generative honey in 'Among School Children', offerings from one organism to another:

> Did God in portioning wine and bread
> Give man His thought or His mere body?

Yeats's ballerinas are Salomés gyrating more recklessly than Wilde's poised heroine will ever do. The bodies they agitate are god's means of manifesting himself. It follows, since to see a symbol is to clothe an archetype in flesh, that the poet can employ imagination in defiance of that mortal decline which overtakes romantic nature and menaces Yeats himself. Man has after all, he decides, created death; interment, as 'Under Ben Bulben' (with its preparations for Yeats's own death and resurrection) proposes, only stows corpses 'back in the human mind again', where they will germinate once more.

Again Yeats has, in his enunciation of a romantic faith, cyclically brought back the Renaissance. The grave-diggers at Ben Bulben are characters from *Hamlet*, unearthing a skull which the hero re-animates as Yorick, and the terse lyric 'Death' rehearses once more Donne's victory over the enemy in his sonnet, except that whereas Donne must content himself with outwitting death, syllogistically gabbling to get in the last word, Yeats can rely on the supine calm of a body which 'knows death to the bone', and thus in the sibillance of 'supersession of breath' can make music from a last gasp which, he insists, is voluntary. Where death supervenes, Yeats challenges it by his feats of imaginative resurrection. When, in 'In Memory of Major Robert Gregory', he remarks that 'all that come into my mind are dead', there is a newly vital metaphor in the phrase: these people actually come into Yeats's head, like spooks entering the medium, and will be accommodated there for eternity. His mind is the soil, the compost of a collective life, in which they are embedded: as close companions they are incorporated in him, 'a portion of my mind and life'.

Many of his greatest poems, like this one, are elegies, but always the remembering is unremorseful. Again in his completing of romanticism he has accomplished the revival of something older, now recalled to youth. The romantic poem knows itself to be an epitaph, the engraving of a experience lost or killed when written about; the Renaissance poem enjoys the deathlessness of art. Edward King may be dead, but Lycidas is not. That is why Milton's poem so disgusted Johnson, who already had something of the romantic sentiment about literature's mortality and the vanity of its protest against death. Yeatsian monuments—Parnell's, for which the builder has probably not been paid; Pollexfen's tomb of gray stone; his own epitaphs, carved on a stone at Thoor Ballylee or glowering at passers-by from limestone in Drumcliff churchyard—have no romantic despair. They are Renaissance renascences of the persons they memorialise.

Parnell in the 1913 poem revisits Dublin to inspect his effigy, before going back (for the time being) to sleep. The epitaph is the poem's ideal state for Yeats, because it consists of words incised or impressed into concise and runic unforgettability, and because by that act it effects the laid-out horizontal man's return to the rectitude—Maud's straight back, the haughtiness of comportment everywhere praised in Yeats—of the vertical. Impressionism to him means this im-pressing, chipping away at adamantine stone as when (entitling his volume of essays in 1918) he shapes an agate; and the cutting is a certification of enduring value, so that 'Parnell's Funeral' can describe the imaginative process as a mint:

> That woman, the Great Mother imaging,
> Cut out his heart. Some master of design
> Stamped boy and tree upon Sicilian coin.

Carved and incised, the tomb like the coin is the image's perpetuation. Yeats liked to think of poems as architecture, of the breath exhaled in 'Death' or by the 'breathless mouths' of 'Byzantium' congealed into a structural material, like bricks and mortar. He admired Arthur O'Shaughnessey's remark that poets 'built Nineveh with their sighing', and his own poet in *The Wind Among the Reeds* (1899) labours to build with his rhymes and sculpt forms in air. Even water, the romantic element of remissness on which Keats's name is only momentarily written and which Byron's Venetian Doge in *The Two Foscari* marries because it is the destructive welter of an inimical nature, can be formed and shaped like stone by Yeats. In 'Coole Park and Ballylee, 1931' he hardens it into the mould of a symbol: 'What's water but the generated soul?' In 1923 in 'Ancestral Houses' he allows a fountain to choose for its shower 'whatever shape it wills'.

This notion of meaning as indentation or inscription, sculpting form into significance, marks romanticism's change into symbolism. The romantic image is elusive, immaterial: a light that never was on sea or land. The Yeatsian symbol, on the contrary, embodies and emblematically proclaims its meaning. Will in Lawrence's *The Rainbow* hand-carves a butter-stamper which seals the churned squares with the device of a phoenix: to Anna, 'it seemed a new thing come to life. Every piece of butter became this strange, vital emblem.' The symbol here is an upraising into a third dimension, and a token, like Yeats's runes, of resurrection. Hopkins in the poems he wrote between 1876 and 1889 reads nature in this way, as a forge like that manned by his farrier Felix Randal (or like the imperial smithies of Yeats's Byzantium), where things are branded with divine import, 'charged'—as he says of the world—'with the grandeur of God'. The charge is an electric shock of vitality, a voltage of significance: Hopkins speaks of 'electrical horror' in 'The Wreck of the Deutschland', just as Dylan Thomas was to wire and electrocute romantic nature in referring to 'the force that through the green fuse drives the flower'. Charge at the same time means mission for Hopkins: reality's duty of manifesting symbolic purpose. The symbol is a thing's combustion. This is why in Hopkins objects flash or crackle into exegetical life. Dragonflies, kingfishers or windhovers are flames in flight, adazzle with meaning. The symbol is Heraclitean fire in one poem, 'shining from shook foil' in another. In romantic poems, symbols are only dimly intuited, half created and half perceived by Wordsworth at Tintern Abbey or Shelley at Mont Blanc; in Yeats, however, they are violently impressed on the objects he studies, and in Hopkins they are invested with the wounding trenchancy of stigmata, a 'fire of stress' which 'must be instressed', permitted to sear and letter flesh as a signal. The stress is a blazing, bleeding mark like the martyring strokes dealt to the nuns aboard the *Deutschland*; it doubles as a metrical infliction, when Hopkins's spearing accents—in, for instance, 'Off her once skéined stained véined variety'—single out words and jolt or jar them into emphatic profile.

Romanticism tends to pine unrequitedly for its ideal realms, doubting that it will ever arrive there. Tennyson's dying Arthur first says he is bound for Avilion then modestly retracts his confidence, wondering if indeed he will get there and acknowledging that his mind is clouded with a doubt: Tennyson is agnostic even about an imagined heaven of fantasy. Yeats dispenses with this timidity, and with the sad romantic postponement which—in compensation, as in Childe Roland's case—persuades itself that the journey not the arrival matters. He wills himself to Byzantium, and is there the moment he sets out.

Preliminary drafts for his 1927 poem about the holy city described the sailing, in the company of bronzed mariners; then Yeats cancelled the middle, to begin at the end. Yet that magniloquent end is present in the beginnings of Yeats's poetry, where Byzantium (in another demonstration of the continuity and the uncompromising consistency of his imagination) goes by other names. For Naschina in 1885 it is the 'lake-nurtured isle' of love, for Oisin it is the Island of Content, for Baile and Ailinu in 1903 it is the Land of the Living Heart, with its orchards of gem-stones. Forgael in *The Shadowy Waters* (1906) is sailing there: his destination is the place where the world ends and the mind is made unchanging by miracle and ecstasy. Nearer home, it is mapped in *The Rose* as the lake isle of Innisfree. Yeats's account of that apicultural garden allotment is often regretted as a specimen of the juvenile romanticism he forswore; but he became more not less romantic as he proceeded, and the qualities of this poem are those of the Byzantine pair—above all, a proud wilfulness ('I will arise.... And I shall have') and the temporal urgency of going 'now' to Innisfree. There is no vague elegiac gentility about the place, as in King Arthur's island-valley or John Betjeman's Leamington Spa. Yeats is as specific as Crusoe, or Kipling when he constructs his Vermont cabin, about the details of his housekeeping and his domestic economy. He is to have nine bean-rows exactly, and the bees are not there to make a muffled, wordless, Tennysonian music. The glade is to be loud with them. Yeats, when he recited the poem, positively boomed it. A fantasy would be whispered, permitting us to overhear it; Yeats makes the poem a public proclamation. Imagining

Innisfree 'while I stand on the roadway, or on the pavements grey', he resembles Whitman declaiming Shakespeare from the upper deck of a Broadway omnibus. One of his last poems, 'A Statesman's Holiday', rephrases Arthur's lament and voices it with a braggart's italicised resonance: like Arthur grieving over the old order, Yeats regrets the fall of great houses and the loss of friends; but whereas Arthur can only dimly dream of Avilion, Yeats bellows his 'foul old tune' in the poem's stanzaic refrains—'*Tall dames go walking in grass green Avalon.*' Despite his denial that he is a de Valéra or a King of Greece and his retreat from office to the noisy, unrespectable irresponsibility of song, Yeats is a statesman in his evocation of Avalon, for that realm is to be, like the solitude of Innisfree or the imperial despotism of Byzantium, an autocracy of imagination.

Byzantium is constituted by the same brazen music which resounds through Innisfree. Soul must 'clap its hands and sing, and louder sing'. There is also the bee-keeper's confident prescription of provisions in those salmon-falls and the mackerel-crowded seas. (Yeats argued that the Ireland Spenser despised and whose oppression he helped to contrive was, if he had only known it, his imagined Faeryland. Can he have been remembering here the indigenous landscape where *The Faerie Queene* ends, with the fair Shure and its thousand salmon?) The poem coerces reality. 'And therefore' in the second stanza is a magnificent non-sequitur, since Yeats has omitted the intermediary stages of the voyage: it is an edict which cannot be argued with. The first line shares this peremptory impatience. 'That is no country for old men' is an executive, exclusive declaration. Yeats's imperativeness qualifies him to supplant the city's 'drowsy Emperor'. He is the Kubla Khan whom Coleridge, seeking immunity by withdrawing from Kubla into the persona of the poet and then withdrawing even further into the frightened spectator of the poet, could never admit to being. Hence his hammering of the uprisen form from gold. This idea might have preciously aesthetic. Symons, anticipating Yeats's Grecian goldsmiths in 1893, compared Pater's writing 'in its minute elaboration' to 'goldsmith's work—so fine, so delicate is the handling of so delicate, so precious a material'. Yeats, however, emphasises brutality not finesse, and metrical clangour not the musical silence of Pater's intervals of listening. The purpose of the hammering is to make a noise and keep the Emperor from sleeping. Reverie here is forbidden.

Mythology was to Yeats, as it had been to Spenser, a warrant of poetic power, a coercion (more lordly and forceful in Yeats than in Spenser's looser, topographically indistinct Faeryland) of correspondences between divergent times and places: Yeats's enamelled, metallic tree is J. G. Frazer's many-branched anthropological blossomer, on whose 'golden bough' he determines to sing. Thus, in its different use of Frazer, Byzantium is a reproach to Eliot's waste land, and indeed to Frazer himself, who disparaged magic (in which Yeats believed) as faulty reasoning and saw it yielding at last to religion which in turn surrendered to the rationality of science. Yeats as poet is one of those divine kings whose priestly rites in Africa Frazer documented. By contrast, Eliot's Fisher King is a maimed and disinherited potentate, moping by the scummy Thames. Eliot could think of mythology only as critique, the past's judgement on the present (as he put it in his essay on *Ulysses*). Introducing his Oxford anthology of modern poetry in 1936, Yeats says that Eliot's generation considered that 'the past had deceived us: let us accept the worthless present', while Auden's generation, rejecting the present, too, awaited a revolutionary reckoning and meanwhile wrote 'the poetry of the future'. Yeats—for whom literary time was a continuum, who 'wrote as men had always written', and of the same subjects—finds these divisions of time futile. Mythology's service is to equalise all epochs, so he can sing simultaneously 'of what is past, or passing, or to come'.

Sequence mythologically becomes cycle. 'Whatever is begotten, born, and dies' is not Eliot's melancholy enumeration of 'birth, and copulation, and death', because body has its rebirth as soul, object its second coming as symbol, like the spectres Yeats summons on All Souls' Night in 1920. The second Byzantium poem in 1930 does not even need to attend that eventual cyclical return. This Byzantium has advanced beyond miry biology, the mythological insemination of Spenser's Garden of Adonis or Yeats's own impregnated Leda: it is a palace of art for the age of mechanical reproduction, where propagation—whether of 'blood-begotten spirits' or 'flames begotten of flame'—happens tirelessly and illimitably. The smithies installed there succeed to the thresher's flail which ravages and excites the earth in 'Kubla Khan' or the turbine Henry Adams worshipped, and they define Byzantium as a factory of imagery. The frenzy of self-remaking to which Yeats was to sentence himself in 'An Acre of Grass' is here conducted as if industrially: 'Those images that yet / Fresh images beget.' Metre, the truculent, obsessive stamped foot of imagination determined to get its own way (Blake 'beat upon the wall / Till truth obeyed his call'), is now the metabolism of the machine.

Yeats seems to punish his language into lyricism. His early poems describe their words as wrought, like the iron twisted into shape by Sheba in 'On Woman'. Sometimes the manipulative making is domestic handicraft: Dectora in *The Shadowy Waters* wants to knead the moon, Yeats himself in 'Adam's Curse' stitches and unravels verse. In Arcady, it is woodwork: the characters in 'Shepherd and Goatherd' cut out their rhymes on bark. Men in 'The Double Vision of Michael Robartes' and words in 'Coole Park, 1929' are made by pounding and beating, like the smelting and pummelling of steel into a sword. In Byzantium music is made by hammering, and Yeats delights in demonstrating how words can be compelled into one shape and then scourged and worried into the opposite. With its winding and unwinding, its 'complexities of fury' and 'furies of complexity', its 'image, man or shade' and 'man, more image than a shade', the poem is manufactured from recombinings and reversals, whose high-handedness with meaning almost does not matter. Thus Yeats could get away with first writing 'breathing mouths' then changing the phrase to its opposite, 'breathless mouths'; and, less concerned with precise identification than Coleridge's mariner when he sees the phantom ship, he can say of the spirit, 'I call it death-in-life and life-in-death.' The dialectical energy of language and its contrariness (which licenses opposites because, as Yeats says in his commentary on 'Parnell's Funeral', they are 'not negation, not refutation') permits both to be true. 'Byzantium' sounds like an anvil chorus. The music of its grand, perfect, audibly swaggering last line—'That dolphin-torn, that gong-tormented sea'—is a sonic vehemence, as orotund as gongs or as brassily barbarous as cymbals and almost, appropriately since the dolphins wound the sea they romp through, a vibrant pain to the ear.

Yeats is fond of saying that poetry raves, like the wind outside the Gore-Booth house in 1927 or the slut behind the till in 'The Circus Animals' Desertion'. It does so in Byzantium, in Crazy Jane's insouciant rant when reproved, '*Fol de rol, fol de rol*', or in the coital harangue of Solomon's witch, who speaks in tongues and 'howled, maiu-d, barked, brayed, belled, yelled, cried, crowed'. Mallarméan pure poetry approximates to bird-song, and in *The Shadowy Waters* Forgael solemnly tries to interpret the cries of gulls, gannets or divers. But it can just as well, in Yeats, imitate gruffer animal noises. In 'The Curse of Cromwell' he goes out to parley in the stable with 'the dogs and horses that understand my talk'. And most often, Yeats's purified dialect of poetry—in recollection of the unique English alliance between symbolism and nonsense—envies the eloquent inarticulacy of laughter. Already in *The Island of Statues* in 1885 the precious arcane knowledge the enchantress wants to purloin from Naschina is laughter, a secret denied to the fairies because 'it dwells alone on mortal lips'. A half-century later, Yeats marvels at the sage laugh-lines wrinkling the faces of his carved Chinamen.

He begins from aestheticism, which is consciously the enfeebled end of romanticism, but—as always—renews and humanly enlarges it. Fergus the poet-king, in quest of Druidic 'dreaming wisdom' in one of the dialogues from *The Rose*, describes himself adrift and fluent, a Pateresque river of impressions. Like the Gioconda, he can claim 'I have been many things', except that his apparitions have not been bodily but mere ephemera of atmosphere—'A green drop in the surge, a gleam of light / Upon a sword.' The policy of metamorphosing continues, though the method alters. Yeats becomes many things by dramatisation not dissolution, so that in 'The Phases of the Moon', included in the *Wild Swans at Coole* volume in 1919, he accuses himself of 'an extravagant style / . . . learnt from Pater', and now unlearned. Or rather he has his persona and surrogate Michael Robartes, into whom he has meanwhile remade himself, do the accusing of a sloughed self.

Here, too, Yeats has magnificently taken over an evasive device of aestheticism. His masks are a development from Wilde's attitudinising: a dialectical version of the Bunburying in *The Importance of Being Earnest*. Yet the perfection of the Wildean mask is its beatific blandness. Either there is nothing behind it—as is the case with Phipps the butler in *An Ideal Husband*, who is 'a mask with a manner', empty and therefore superciliously symbolic of 'the dominance of form'—or else it is a cosmetic varnish, like Dorian's picture, over putrefying flesh. The Yeatsian vizor, like that 'of burning gold / With emerald eyes' in 'The Mask', from the *Green Helmet* volume (1910), is the welder's safeguard: a protection against the ferocity of the heat directed at it and seething beneath it. So it is with the bronze head which, in one of Yeats's final poems, stands for Maud Gonne. The mask is what is supernatural in her, and what therefore outlasts her life. Wilde's masks deny drama, since his people are what they wear and what they say and have no interior to be interrogated; Yeats's are a means of ritually arming for it, like those of the Greek theatre, which contort themselves in a rictus of agony no human face could sustain for long. They are formulae for poetry as he defined it: provoked by the quarrel with himself. They are also a redefinition of lyric as drama, for they allow his characters to quarrel with a creator who has, in them, objectively got rid of emotions the lyric subjectively confesses.

Thus the presumption of 'The Phases of the Moon' is that Robartes and Aherne have, as Yeats said in a note, fallen out with their maker, whom they here upbraid. Aherne toys with the notion of ringing Yeats's bell and deceiving him by impersonating someone else. Robartes, who has been declared dead by Yeats 'to round his tale', prefers safely to stay so. Of course Yeats can never permit a character to free itself from him, as the dramatist can. His masks are the self's disguises, its invocation of opposites as he explains in 'Ego Dominus Tuus', or its cunning transference of responsibility—'Tom O'Roughley' attributes its cheery sacrilege to the wanton Tom, putting Yeats's words incongruously into his mouth and then returning to tip the wink by adding, after another stanza of defiance, 'Or something of that sort he said.' Wildean affectation multiplies the personality in a hall of mirrors, exponentiating illusions; though Yeats also argued, as he put it in 1900, that crude reality simply reflected 'as in multiplying mirrors' emotions reserved to poetic solitude, he aims the mirror away from himself and sets it to entrap and transmit, as in a burning-glass, a radiance otherwise unseeable, like that of Helen's blazing body in 'A Woman Homer Sung'.

The Wildean hero is resigned to dwelling in the prison of glassy reflections. Yeats's characters want to escape from it. Forgael, who believes that the gods breathe their dreams 'on the burnished mirror of the world' and then wipe it clean, frets to penetrate the dream, 'not . . . its image on the mirror!' Aibric tells him that 'while / We're in the body that's impossible.' But adoption of the mask permits Yeats to be a temporary tenant of another body, or—when he shuffles through the school-room grimacing at his own decrepitude—to wear his own as if it were someone else's. The Wildean alias (Bunbury or Ernest) is a

Yeatsian *alter ego*. Thus Wilde advises adhesion to the surface, warning those who go beneath it to read the symbol that they do so at their peril, because the symbol is both their incrimination and Wilde's; Yeats accuses himself of an exactly converse fault, ornamenting the surface rather than revealing the symbol:

> Players and painted stage took all my love,
> And not those things that they were emblems of.

Yeats's happy shepherd could be paraphrasing a Wildean theory of language when he says that 'Words alone are certain good.' But in Wilde that would be a counsel of despair—mockingly resilient in *The Importance of Being Earnest*, dispirited and lamely incapable of lyricism in the poem about the waltzers in the brothel where 'sometimes they seemed to try to sing'. In Yeats the statement is one of triumphant certainty (until, in one of his final poems, it is questioned by a mortifying echo which belies his verbal authority). Nevertheless, Yeats credits Wilde with his own deployment of words as power. He remembered him as 'essentially a man of action, . . . a writer by perversity and accident, [who] would have been more important as soldier or politician.' Words are ascertainment to Yeats because utterance is mastery, and he liked to think of Wilde's aphoristic conversation as a technique for the imposition of will. His rounded cadences seemed to have been 'written . . . all overnight with labour', massively deliberated.

He generously misreads Wilde's jesting nominalism, and at the same time revises the exhausting romantic pursuit of the image. Romantic poets exert themselves to attach significance to fleeting things—escaping birds or clouds, the hedonistic instants treasured by Browning's Bishop—and are always too late. Yeats confidently commands symbols, and manages them as if by appointment. Declaration, nomination, arrogation are the gestures of his poetry: 'I declare this tower is my symbol', he says as he moves in (Coleridge can only fearfully imagine such absolutism, and nervously gainsays it as he looks up at Wordsworth on his dread watch-tower), or else, with the predatoriness of the swan selecting Leda as its seminal vessel, he announces 'that girl I declare / A beautiful lofty thing.' Coole Park is positively ransacked to supply him with emblems for his own moods.

In the earlier poems, Yeats exercises this power as bewitchment. The lover in *The Wind Among the Reeds* complains that 'a man with a hazel wand'—Aengus, Master of Love, and also the magus Yeats—has changed him into a symbol, 'a hound with one red ear'. In the later poems, magic gives way to politics, and symbols are recruited by conscription not sorcery. The proclamation of the Irish Republic in 'Easter, 1916' provokes Yeats to rally a troop of his own, comprising friends (but unnamed, for enlistment in the poem is their relegation to the membership of archetypes) who are 'changed, changed utterly' by Yeats's appropriation of them. Rhetoric is militation, embattlement: Cuchulain in *The Rose* fights against the incoming tide, the martyrs of 1916 against the occupying British, and Yeats conceives of poetry as their weaponry. Thought, in one of the poems from *In the Seven Woods* (1904), is whittled into an arrow; Yeats exults in the 'rapturous music' of 'clashing . . . sword-blades'. He always imagines the poet to be a warrior, with 'a sword upstairs', and though in 'Reconciliation' he proposes hurling all those antique heraldic props—'helmets, crowns, and swords'—into the pit he makes no such renunciation, for the metaphor was actualised when in 1920 he was presented by Junzo Sato with a ceremonial Japanese sword. It takes over from Oisin's lettered blade, 'Whose shine / No centuries could dim.' Furnishing his tower, it serves as a trophy of changelessness, and in a later dialogue its razor-edge and its mirroring steel are brandished by the proud self to taunt the timorous, pacific soul.

Yeats's completion of romanticism here requires the reversal of its gradual generic declension—from epic to pastoral in Spenser, from epic to lyric in Wordsworth. The lyric to Yeats is shamingly unmartial, 'a little song made out of a moment of indolence'; he is ambitious to engage in 'some great epic made out of the dreams of one poet and of a hundred generations whose hands were never weary of the sword'. He stands as well against the long tendency of English poetry towards informality, even formlessness: the amorphousness which relaxes epic in Spenser and Wordsworth goes with a descent from knights to shepherds, a settling into the comfort of the mock-heroic, singing (as Cowper does in *The Task*) of upholstered sofas. Yeats on the contrary thinks of poetry as ennoblement, the elevation of life into rhyme as he says in 1931, or as escalation: his tower is 'raised rhyme upon rhyme', re-erecting from earth upwards that ladder let down from heaven for angelic errands in *Paradise Lost*.

Wielding symbols as armaments, Yeats is as much a clangorously violent and primitive poet as he is a modern, for he utters words as orders and sends them out like men the English will shoot down, whereas it is the modern poet's conviction that words are just impotent sounds—Coleridge's 'water, water everywhere' or his crackling onomatopoeic ice—or else charming, futile playthings: Auden, a virtuoso solver of crossword puzzles, used to eat his dinner enthroned on one or another volume of the *Oxford English Dictionary*. Systematising his symbols as if they were emblems, Yeats seems also less a romantic than a Renaissance poet, treating his art, like Sidney under the tutelage of Pugliano or distinguishing himself in the tournament, as equestrianism. He is 'mounted', he says, 'in that saddle Homer rode', and in *The King of the Great Clock Tower* he watches his tragic characters ride by. The horseman exists at an altitude: metaphor, too, for Yeats is a mount, a proud heightening. 'Processions that lack high stilts have nothing that catches the eye', he says in one of his last poems, calling himself a Daddy-long-legs stalking on fifteen-foot pins. He criticises the romantics for not putting their images on parade. Keats, he argues, is 'a fragmentary symbolist' who 'does not set his symbols in the great procession': the march-past Blake saluted in Chaucer's pilgrimage, which Yeats admired in the 'strange procession' of Shakespeare's histories, and which Nature choreographs to silence Mutabilitie; the trooping of Yeats's own mystic menagerie, those circus animals performing their pyrotechnical stunts.

A poet so monopolistic and so anachronistic—belonging to all times at once—could hardly be tolerated. His great successors, Eliot and Auden, must, to ensure their own modernity, declare him antedeluvian. He left on record his scepticism about them, calling their revolution 'stylistic only' and marginalising their poetry by considering it as satire. He told Stephen Spender in 1935 that his own spiritualism had been vanquished by 'the political era', and prophesied that this would lead in turn to 'an age dominated by the psychologists': an uncannily accurate foresight of Auden's poetic and intellectual development after 1939.

The poetic characters of Auden and Eliot revise their Yeatsian forebears. Yeats's Irish airman in 1918 is an aeronautical Alastor, or Shelley's cloud propellor-boosted. Indifferent to ideology, he rejoices in war because it offers him the chance of exhilarating death. By contrast, the aquiline 'helmeted airman' of Auden's poem 'Consider' in 1930 is an omniscient social conscience, looking down through the rifts in the clouds at a prostrate world awaiting rectification. The Magi in *Responsibilities* (1914) are myth-makers like Yeats himself, engineering rebirths and if necessary faking miracles. Unsatisfied by Calvary, they resume their quest, seeking once more 'the uncontrollable mystery on the bestial floor'. Eliot's in 'The Journey of the Magi' (1927) do not dabble in blood or divination. They are disgruntled tourists, complaining of the dirt and the high prices, adjudging the natal stable only 'satisfactory'. On their way to Bethlehem they have a symbolic preview of the crucifixion, in a valley with three trees and an inn where men dice for pieces of silver. The Yeatsian magi seek the perpetual rebirth which is the bequest of myth; Eliot's Magi understand the birth only as a preliminary to the curative death which they penitentially await.

Having accused Yeats of heresy in *After Strange Gods* (1934), Eliot went on to effect his posthumous conversion. He identified the ghost who admonishes him in the bombed London of his last quartet, 'Little Gidding' (1942), as the spectre of Yeats. That revenant extols to Eliot the 'refining fire / Where you must move in measure, like a dancer', counselling him by employing a Yeatsian emblem. But it is an emblem already reinterpreted by Eliot. The refining fire is purgatorial, and the ghost's persona derives from Yeats's play *Purgatory* (1939) which Eliot, delivering the first Yeats lecture at the Abbey Theatre in 1940, had called 'not very pleasant'. The reason for his distaste is its heresy: he 'cannot accept a purgatory in which there is no . . . Purgation.' That cauterising heat is here supplied, in despite of Yeats, by the incandescent planes which blitz the city, and Yeats himself is healed and purged by them.

Auden does not bother about Yeats's redemption but forgivingly lays him to rest in a poem written shortly after his death in 1939. 'In Memory of W. B. Yeats' denies its subject's faith in the effectuality of his art. 'Poetry', Auden declares, 'makes nothing happen', and—in its imagery of airports, Bourse, barometer, hospital and electric current—his poem admits the modern, temporal reality Yeats had valiantly held off. Auden notices yet tolerates Yeats's silliness. Poetry cannot alter history. All the same, Auden hints that its value resides in its very powerlessness: disenfranchised, it is uncorrupted by executive tampering, and is therefore precious to 'the free man'. The poet may no longer be, as he was for Yeats, a magus; he can still, however, be a magician, a solemnly playful linguistic virtuoso. Auden in his turn, rendering industrial modernity strange, takes over from Yeats (temporarily) the role of last romantic.

— 35 —

Epic, Romance and the Novel

The novel's initial premise in the eighteenth century is the mockery of epic, in the nineteenth the domestication of romance. But these ancestral genres, to which its novelty is averse, return to reconnect literature with its sources and to propose an alternative direction for the novel.

Consecrated to the private and the secret life, the novel had—to Mme de Staël in 1800—announced a feminisation of literature. From Jane Austen's comedies of courtship to George Eliot's moral scrutiny of her maidens choosing, from Austen's angry defence of the sorority of novelists to Virginia Woolf's contention that any woman is nicer and better than any man, that affiliation holds good. There is opposition, however, from novelists for whom the form's preoccupation with love and marriage is a weakness, and who lament its denial of heroism: it is a premise of realism that no man is a hero to his valet, or to the novelist who sees inside him. Is this not a betrayal of literature's epic powers—its fortifying of an individual life menaced by time, and of a society whose memory it is? Robert Louis Stevenson argues this way in *Virginibus Puerisque* (1881), suggesting that 'marriage, if comfortable, is not at all heroic', that it causes a slackening and degeneration of moral being. He cites as two of its casualties—and casualties, too, of the novel's middling reductiveness—the men in *Middlemarch*: Lydgate misallied with Rosamond, Ladislaw becalmed by the fireside with Dorothea. Don Quixote, he believes, was duty-bound to remain a bachelor. Otherwise he could not have followed 'the fine wildings of the . . . heart'. Those wildings are the episodic, irresponsible liberties of romance: what Jim Hawkins in Stevenson's *Treasure Island* (1883), referring to Captain Flint, describes as following the sea; or lighting out for the Territory, as Tom Sawyer does, to evade the repressive matriarchy of Aunt Sally.

By Stevenson and Mark Twain romance is equated with running away from home, and reassigned from the devotedly missionary knights of Malory, Spenser and Tennyson to prankish adolescents. Romance might be defined as epic for boys, a ceremony of initiation issuing in tribal membership. Harvey Cheyne in Kipling's *Captains Courageous* (1897), swept overboard from a luxury liner, is rescued by a fishing boat on which he spends the season in comradely toil, unlearning the pettish effeminacy engendered in him by society. His is a happy accident, and his fall symbolises the buoyancy of romance, which Stevenson calls 'the poetry of circumstance'—a serendipitous trust in whatever is to happen next, a relaxed passivity.

When there is no such assurance of a safety-net, when the leap is into the unknown or an immersion in the destructive element, catapulting oneself out of society into a sinking void, then Harvey's tumble becomes the jump of Conrad's Lord Jim in 1900 from the sinking *Patna*; and romance changes into epic, tragically aware of how a fragile human community needs to be held together by that force of will which is the faith of epic, like the friable hills of San Francisco—in Kipling's account in 1889—engineered into tense adhesion by the whirring underground wires which drive the cable-cars, or like Towson's rivets in *Heart of Darkness* in 1902. The hero of romance is a nimble high-diver, elated by 'deep soundings' as Stevenson says and confident of flotation; the hero of epic hangs above an abyss, and risks everything when he acts. All Conrad's characters have that precipitous terror: Nostromo above his bottomless gulf, Verloc in *The Secret Agent* (1907) edging warily through the embassy 'as if . . . surrounded by pitfalls', Castro in *Romance* (written with Ford Madox Hueffer) in 1903 questioning his own valour on the cliff, Marlow dreading the 'unknown depths' within Jim, the wife in *Almayer's Folly* (1895) wanting to jump overboard from the pirate vessel.

For the ancient epic hero, the trial was only of physical hardihood or moral fibre; for Conrad's men it is not a matter of monster-slaying but an existential challenge, confronting beasts which stalk social jungles—Conrad called the revolutionaries of *Under Western Eyes* apes in a terroristic wilderness—and recognising the infirmity of civilisation. The older epic ritually guaranteed the reliability of society, as the *Beowulf* poet does in describing the erection of the mead-hall. The novel, furnishing the world with realistic replicas, took that security for granted. Conrad perceives the conventionality of the delusion. The folly of his first hero, Almayer, is both architectural and novelistic: he stamps his foot to demonstrate the solidity of the house of fiction he has constructed among the Bornean undergrowth, even though his savage wife in her rages rips down the curtains to make sarongs and incinerates the furniture in order to cook rice.

Embarrassed by such atavism, Forster in *Aspects of the Novel* (1927) apologises for story-telling as a primitive relic, the parleying of cave-men round their camp fire, just as Almayer scorns Babalatchi's narrative as 'a tale for men that listen only half awake by the camp fire'. But literature begins with an oral spell for keeping darkness, demons and silence away, and Forster need not have been so dismissive, for there is a tragic moral here. Literature's epic valour lies in speaking out, raising its voice in defiance. Its protest fails, of course, in the echoing nullity of Forster's own Marabar or the unsonorous black tunnel of *Romance* where 'one's voice lost itself without resonance'. Writing is an even more doomed and ineffective defence against a world which cannot be hunted, trapped, known. Though in Kipling's story 'Regulus' (1908) the young trainees for imperial command are taught Latin as an exercise in warfare, learning words like pack-drill, Conrad's language-teacher in *Under Western Eyes* (1911) despairs in his 'wilderness of words', which he knows to be an enemy not an armament: 'words . . . are the great foes of reality.' The reversion to origins is an act of self-denial. Conrad and Kipling interrogate the nature of the literature they produce, analysing its means, gloomily reckoning its usefulness.

Forster's reference to primitivism is acute. This is an anachronistic withdrawal of the novel from its place in literary history, possible because Kipling the Anglo-Indian and Conrad the Pole are at an angle to that history, not even housed by the English language. The American emigrés in Kipling's 'An Habitation Enforced' (1905) find the English of the homeland unintelligible; Conrad wrote English with a calculated unidiomatic foreignness, as if mistranslating—Charles Gould's 'lecture of the letters' his father sends from Costaguana in *Nostromo* (1904) or 'the hour of oration' which is prayer not speech; the unacclimatised speech patterns of Stein or the Frenchman in Sydney in *Lord Jim*—because the guarded protocol of epic requires him to feel himself alienated from his medium, undeceived by its pretensions. Language is an importation to and an imposition on Costaguana. Conrad exposes its inauthenticity and its mismatch with reality by writing multilingually, lapsing into Spanish phrases or Italian when he reports on ethnic sectors of the country, Frenchifying his phraseology when describing the false dandyism of Decoud, noting Hirsch's mongrelising of Spanish and German and his ingratiation with his captors 'by calling them *hochwohlgeborene Herren*, which in itself sounded suspicious'. Nostromo's glamorous phoniness is betokened by the neologism which is his badge, his 'name that is properly no word'.

Language conserves its integrity for Kipling by dialectal secession. It limits itself to a tribe, which it exists, like the idiom of Anglo-Saxon epic, to rally: thus the contrast in his story 'The Wish House' (1924) between the ancient Sussex accent of the witchy crones with their 't's softened to 'd's and the affectedly elongated metropolitan vowels of the visiting nurse. Dialect serves as professional argot, the technical slang of a cadre, and as a weapon. Laughton O. Zigler in 'The Captive' (1902), whose 'speech betrayed his nationality', regionally restricts that nationality: more than an American, he is an Ohian; more even than that, he *is* his native town of Akron. And he metonymically lends his name to the weapons he invents and merchandises among the Boers, which express as well his spluttering, rat-a-tat voice: the Laughton-Zigler automatic two-inch field-gun and Laughtite the explosive. 'It's me', he says of the Zigler automatic. It is the ego automated, mounting guard on its tribal boundaries.

In Conrad, too, literature harks back to its beginnings in oral projection. His characters are voices: the booming rabble-rousing bass of Verloc, Decoud's shout of *'Gran' bestia!'*, the scolding monologue of the invisible *dame de compagnie* in *Under Western Eyes*, vociferating in either Russian, French or

German, Kurtz in *Heart of Darkness* who is to Marlow 'a voice . . . very little more than a voice . . .—this voice', just as Marlow to his auditors is a voice from the dusk on the yawl. Voice is the will's commandment, so that the first symptom of Razumov's moral collapse is the rasping of his unresonant, tindery throat. A Conrad story has value epically only if it is testimony orally relayed, because the telling bardically shares knowledge, rehearses memory, and cements society. Henry James hushed the woman at the party who was reciting to him the anecdote which became *The Spoils of Poynton*: he had to complete it silently and secretly. Conrad, however, must tell it aloud, so that Marlow repeats—in an epic ceremony—the things he has been told in Africa and the 'unspeakable secrets' he has not been told to a group of bondsmen who, at anchor in the Thames, represent the institutional managers of society, evacuated in a navigable bunker: among them are a lawyer, an accountant, and a company director.

The narrative act, creating solidarity, must be passed on indefinitely, so that *Heart of Darkness* is not Marlow's speech but the report of that speech by one of his companions. Literature has returned to its parliamentary past among Chaucer's cackling fowls and squabbling pilgrims, while at the same time it discerns a future where there will be only upraised, unintelligible voices with no moderator between them: Eliot attached an epigraph from *Heart of Darkness* to the first draft of his *Waste Land*. Disjoined from the narrative which gives it meaning, 'Mistah Kurtz—he dead' is uttered by one of Eliot's hollow, ownerless voices. Marlow's yarning has reassurance as its purpose, and this is what justifies Conrad's often-criticised rhetoric; the immense undulant sentences describing the voyage of the *Patna* are, as is the descending night, a practised benediction, a rite like a nursery rhyme for calming the world and inducing 'a marvellous stillness'. The voice of Marlow has an almost Orphic talent for creating placation, even complacency.

As well as a garrulous bard like Shakespeare's Gower, Marlow is a medieval scribe. This is how he describes himself, bent at his desk and hoping to soothe Jim by routinely writing letters. Kipling's 'The Eye of Allah' (1926) takes place in a medieval monastic scriptorium, and the scholar in his 'Dayspring Mishandled' (1928) studies the scribal copying of Chaucer manuscripts and rigs up an identity for each amanuensis by looking for quirks of spacing or penmanship. The medieval office survives in the India of *Kim* (1901): the letter-writer in the bazar is an inefficient tribal memory, a one-man 'bureau of misinformation'. The blind woman in '"They"' (1904), unable to read or write, resuscitates the old English tally of hazel twigs for doing her household accounts.

Lessing, expounding the shield of Achilles, ruled that the epic must know about its own means of production, and when—in their resumé of literature's early history, advancing from speech to script to print—Kipling and Conrad arrive at the stage of book-making, they dramatise writing as manufacture. The practical joker in 'Dayspring Mishandled' undertakes the forgery of a Chaucer poem as an industrial experiment, brewing an ink of hawthorn bark and wine ('a practically eternal stuff', epically stalwart), growing wheat in his garden and grinding it himself to enrich the formula, trying out birdlime, and whittling a medieval pen for himself. Kipling's *Something of Myself* in 1937 includes a salute to his own tools—deep-dyed black ink, custom-built blocks of off-white paper—and remembers his shift from hand-dipped Waverley nibs to a time-saving fountain pen as if it were a scriptorial equivalent of the industrial revolution. If the book's fabrication is an epic labour, so is its destruction. The heroine of Kipling's great story 'Mary Postgate' (1915) commemorates the young flier's death by setting ablaze a funeral pyre like Beowulf's, onto which she heaps the adventure stories and technical manuals which were his instructors in heroism. The fire is fuelled by 'Hentys, Marryats, Levers, Stevensons, Baroness Orczys': from the incineration of romance, epic is made.

Conrad is preoccupied in *Nostromo* with supplying his pamphleteers and journalists with the raw materials they need, since literature like minerals must be wrested from the earth. Decoud's newspaper is possible because 'a large consignment of paper' has arrived from America, the Monterist petition is scrawled on 'dirty-grayish rough paper (perhaps looted in some village store)', the Separationist proclamation is compromisingly scribbled on paper printed with the heavy letter-head of the mine administration, and the galleys of Don José Avellanos's history, printed on Decoud's press, are jeeringly published as litter, 'fired out as wads for trabucos loaded with handfuls of type, blown in the wind, trampled in the mud.' The politics of Costaguana are documentary: the characters have a superstitious faith in *pronunciamentos*, as if they can write (rather than, like Verloc, speaking) their wishes into law—Don Juste Lopez poses with his goose-quill over a blank sheet of paper, on which he intends to write an address to Montero; the chief of Sulaco transforms a bandit into a general on a piece of paper. Trusting less in literary instruments, the Russians of *Under Western Eyes* punish the paper which legalistically oppresses them—Razumov impales the sheet on which he has scribbled his creed, stabbing it to the wall—or erase it. Nihilism means the annihilation of history, precedent, print: under snow, Russia is 'a monstrous blank page' on which nothing has yet been inscribed. Or else it is a mess of charred, illegible print: the 'mere litter of blackened pages' which is the reward of Razumov's studies, the 'flimsy blackened pages', cabbalistically doodled on, of Haldin's letter. Politics in this novel eruptively disturbs the sedate habits of reading and writing. Razumov in his agitation takes up a book but after two lines 'lost his hold on the print' and thereby (because of the image of tenacity) his tenure of reality; the language teacher, transcribing Razumov's diary, takes up a pen 'ready for its office of setting down black on white' but holds it poised in the air, recognising its inadequacy as a recording angel.

The conundrum of the text in Conrad is its constant self-disqualifying, its reminders that it is bearing false witness. Kurtz manifests himself discursive-ly—'A voice! a voice!'—and also textually, writing seventeen pages of anthropological commentary to which he appends a murderous postscriptum, but neither mode succeeds in revealing him or articulating a horror which must remain symbolic: that is, emptily unspecified. Cipher is a stratagem for disguise, a conspiracy of signs. Marlow is a paranoid reader, imagining that Towson's book is in code when it is only in Russian. People, like texts, can circumvent reality by renominating themselves as symbols. This is the fradulence of the financier de Barral in *Chance* (1913), as papery a fiction as printed money: 'He was a mere sign, a portent. There was nothing in him.' His treasury resembles Conrad's genius as Forster, brilliantly but too critically, described it: a casket harbouring no jewel but a vapour.

The practice of writing in Conrad is an elision or cancelling of meanings, an abstract magic turning words into signposts leading nowhere beyond themselves. Haldin speaks in slangy code, conspiring with 'Another' against 'a certain person'. Conrad remarks that revolutionaries are compulsive name-changers, and he mocks their revisionism by reducing names to ignominy, having the language teacher appraise Razumov as 'nothing but a name', tagging other characters with an intriguing namelessness (Prince K——, General T——, Madame de S——), alliteratively nicknaming the thug Nikita Necator so as so supply him with the initials of nonentity: like Razumov sticking paper with his penknife, he signs his victims, leaving on them the stabbed signature N.N. Writing and revolution are both almost algebraically abstracted in *The Secret Agent*. Logos changes to logo: Verloc's identity is Δ. But the triangle's equilateral economy and purposiveness are contradicted by the idiotic scrawlings of Stevie, whose calligraphy makes diagrams of revolution and its meaninglessness: 'circles, circles; innumerable circles, concentric, eccentric.' They stand for chaos, random repetitiousness, not the completion of Browning's book-like ring. As if in agreement with her brother's cartoons of futility, Winnie throws the 'gold circlet' of her wedding-ring into the dust-bin.

Nostromo hints throughout at the fallacy of its own testimony. Conrad slyly boasts in his preface that he is the only person to have read Avellanos's massacred book: his pre-text is a fictional history, invented and then destroyed by himself. What passes for history in Costaguana turns out to be legend, and Conrad's initial chapter of exposition disputes at every point the veracity of what he is recounting. The account of the ghostly adventurers is a fable, quibblingly qualified—'tradition has it', or they 'are believed to be', or 'it could only have been'. Geography is just as much a matter of surmise. Punta Mala, seen from the gulf, appears not to exist. Azuera is 'what seems to be' a patch of mist. And the two impalpable regions have as their boundary an 'imaginary line' crossed—though still not seen—by ships. The truth can never be got at because it has already been falsified, linguistically inflated. Politics is a disease of language: the typographical portentousness called by Razumov 'Liberty with a capital. ... Liberty that means nothing precise'; the allegorical shadow-play of slogans which entitles Guzman Bento the Citizen Saviour of the Country or translates him into the vernacular as El Gobierno Supremo. Costaguana is a place where reality is subjected to an idealizing which transforms it into unreality. Decoud upbraids this habit in Charles Gould, who must falsify his activities into a fairy tale, yet Decoud has no purchase on a reality of his own and suffers from a cynicism which is the corrosive inverse of Gould's idealism: he 'lost all belief in the reality of his actions past and to come'. Nostromo culpably lives by and for a grandiose fiction. And Conrad implicates himself in the same collusive deceit—for if, as he admits, no one knows how Decoud dies, how can the novelist know? Is he not at the end of the novel perpetrating a legendary fraud like the one he subtly disparages at the beginning?

Conrad's texts are a paper chase of unconsecutive, misleading clues. Narrative travels in circumlocutory loops. Information about Barrios's coup does not cross from one seaboard to the other but is cabled to the United States, from where it ricochets back; a cable to Paris must pass through San Francisco and New York. These indirections are compounded by the digressive meanderings of the surrogate narrators whom Conrad must employ: the political history is completed long after the event by the pompous Captain Mitchell, and even then only incidentally, as he discharges his new duty as tour guide.

James disapproved of Conrad's collaborative narratives, and of *Chance* in particular; they implied a slight to James's own belief in the presidency of all-seeing consciousness, authorial and authoritative. *Chance* begins in the first person, but soon startlingly changes to the third. For Joyce in *A Portrait of the Artist as a Young Man*, such a transference is evolutionary: Stephen acclaims a similar advance from first to third person in the old ballad of 'Turpin Hero' as a growth beyond the lyric mode towards the dramatic. In Conrad, it stands for a baffling regression: how can any deposition be accredited if we do not know who is making it? Self-effacing omniscience is against the rules. The narrator must stand up and declare himself, so his involvement in and manipulation of the narrative can be handicapped. Conrad prefers narrative to be teamwork, an almost epic enlistment in a society of one's fellows, convened—as over Jim or Kurtz—to study the case of someone who has ejected himself from that society.

Suffering diaspora in space, Conrad's histories are also rearranged in time. His wilful time-shifts, jerkily anticipating events or omitting consequences, answer to his conviction that actions do not amass significance before the fact, in Hamlet-like meditation, but only after they are gratuitously committed. Jim jumps first, and later asks himself why he did so. Meaning is a posterior guess not an anterior motive, and it lies, as Marlow demonstrates in *Heart of*

Darkness, not inside an episode but outside and around it. The novels are a species of baffled inquest, like that in the Eastern port assigning blame for the incident of the *Patna*, or like the inquisition conducted by the secret police to which Haldin, even under torture, cannot or will not respond. *Chance* encourages its characters to act, then speculates on why they irrationally or ambiguously did so (in contrast with the almost mystic function of Jamesian consciousness which is, as in Maggie's management of the adultery in *The Golden Bowl*, to foresee and thus frustrate action, to ensure by the surveillance and control of minds from within that nothing will ever happen): Marlow demands 'Why this secrecy? Why did they elope?' or asks of little Fyne, 'Was he arguing, preaching, remonstrating?'

The fission of narrative goes with a sundering of the world into estranged, alien, unmatching objects. The secondhand furniture dealer in *The Secret Agent* keeps such a stock—'an unhappy, homeless couch, accompanied by two unrelated chairs', further disabled by being set outdoors in the alley where no one will sit on them. Conrad's most gruesomely forceful image for this disintegrativeness is the smithereens, carefully collated by Heat, which are the remnants of Stevie and of his possessions, 'a heap of mixed things, which seemed to have been collected in shambles and rag shops' or 'a heap of nameless fragments' spaded up in a stew of flesh, blood, gravel, bark and wood. Those mangled bits become in Eliot the rubbishy fall-out of iconoclasm: not Virginia Woolf's shower of innumerable atoms but the 'heap of broken images' which dissociatively furnish the waste land. Stevie's physical fate happens metaphorically to the other characters. Verloc is 'shaken morally to pieces', Winnie's personality is 'torn into two pieces'. Given this detonated, psychic sundering, the imperative of conduct is, as Verloc tells his wife, to 'pull yourself together'.

That is the interpreter's commandment, too, reassembling distracted bits and discerning relations between them. Flora says to Marlow at the end of *Chance*, 'Truth will out'; but it never comes out, in Conrad, of its own accord. It must be worked for, salvaged from the abyss of time (Mitchell's chronometer is stolen by the rebels, and Brierly in *Lord Jim* leaves his on the ship's rail before he jumps to death), retrieved at the source of that river in the Congo which flows in reverse 'to the earliest beginnings of the world', and its capture, like Kurtz's murderous gloss on his own text, is an epic discipline of enforcement, or what Kipling tersely calls 'executive capacity'. To interpret Kurtz would be to have exterminated him, which is why the story's moral courage and its contagious peril lies in its failure to do so. Marlow either cannot interpret the horror, or else, for Kurtz's fiancée, misinterprets it. In Razumov's case, the *a posteriori* interpreting of his life into meaning is a punishing frenzy: 'Write. Must write! He! Write!' he tells himself, or 'I must write—I must, indeed! I shall write—never fear.'

Technique is therefore for Conrad a matter of nervous rigour and self-control, impelled by the fear of chaos. The systematic attention to hinges, bolts or stanchions of Captain MacWhirr in *Typhoon* (1903) represents this grace and valour: he stands for and is named after what Forster in *A Passage to India* (1924) calls 'the whirring of action', mystically and also nauseously arrested at Marabar. The same prowess is exhibited by Winnie's 'methodical proceedings' as she lays the table. Winnie's concentration on the small tasks which are her defence against hysteria and also her refurbishment of her weapons (for among the implements she has to handle is the carving knife she uses to slay Verloc) is extolled by the masons in Kipling's 'In the Interest of the Brethren' (1918), who declare 'there's a procedure, a ritual, in all things' and love the sedative 'ritual of handling things'; and in Mary Postgate, unflappably waiting out the German's death-rattle, it becomes a homicidal skill. Mary's employer considers her 'deadly methodical'. The method is a talent for regimentation—Mary lays out gaudy socks and ties in a trooping of colours—and for extermination, delivering cart-loads of impedimenta to be burned in the destructor.

'Mary Postgate' is an epic counterpart to *Jacob's Room*: the boots, books and trinkets the warrior leaves behind are not belaboured for their absurd, insentient solidity, a mockery of the spirit which has flown; they are made to honour their owner by sharing his end in a ceremony of suttee at the bottom of the garden. Its heroine's revenge raises what Flaubert called the pitilessness of style to a military drill. Method in its deadly stricture provides Kipling with a formal alternative to Stevie's crazed, impotent circles. This is the straight line—the seventy-two miles of rail without a curve through the teak forest in 'Mrs Bathurst' (1904); the straight line through the upper pasture in 'An Habitation Enforced', suddenly and mysteriously kinked; the obedient course of the Atlantic traffic lanes beneath the aeroplane of the enforcers in 'As Easy as A.B.C.' (1912).

As the shortest distance between two points, the line is a Roman road, an avenue for power on the march, and as well a proviso of aesthetic geometry. It explains why the short story is Kipling's chosen form, and his epic answer to the novel. Novels are paradises of loose ends, encouraging detours. In Kipling there can be no such deflections. The monks in 'The Eye of Allah' have a holy dread of marginalia, the freaks and sports which congest in the illustrative borders of manuscripts and therefore 'stand outside the rational mind'; the gossiping women in 'The Wish House' have 'many ends, loose since last time, to be ravelled up'. Kipling conceives of writing almost as a police pro-blem—'The Church that was at Antioch' (1929) reviews the theological and linguistic strife of *Salomé* as an irritation to the occupying Roman garrison, one of whose functionaries remarks, 'religions are part of my office-work'—and only so long as the story is kept short can its orderliness and its security from invasion by extraneousness be guaranteed. Sooner or later, the straight line will have to warp into a curve. Kipling cannot tolerate the meandering topography of Sterne, which sketches the instinctive waywardness of novels. His reproof to it is the closure of a circuit, used by the aerial policemen of the A.B.C. fleet to quell the Chicago riots. They detain protestors inside the invisible, invincible barrier of a flying loop, where they are pinioned 'straining against nothing'. And they see London, known to them from their supercilious height as the Little Village, corseted inside a similar sanitary cordon, fitted 'inside her ring of girdling Main-Traffic lights—those eight fixed beams at Chatham, Tonbridge, Redhill, Dorking, Woking, St. Albans, Chipping Ongar, and Southend'. The metropolis, that ultimate fluid pudding or baggy monster which encouraged the amorphous expansiveness of the Victorian novel, has been cramped into the patrolled precinct of the short story.

It is interesting that Conrad should have been so exercised by the criticism that *Lord Jim* was a short story he had let get out of control. That, daringly, is what *Lord Jim*, in its refusal to be a novel, comes to resemble: an anecdote indefinitely extrapolated; an abbreviated epic of crisis and irrevocable action giving way to a protracted, leisurely, itinerant romance quest, which is its aftermath, and which can never be completed. Like Stein's hobby, romance is a chasing of butterflies. Its narrative principle is the aleatory one after which Conrad entitles *Chance*, his account of chivalric pursuit. John Kemp in *Romance* speaks of himself as being wafted into romance, and of having 'come to put my trust in accident'. The genre means irresponsibility, charmed disengagement from the need to choose or to act. Kemp shrugs off the claims of rival political factions, saying 'I was looking out for romance.' The novel's period is the Byronic one and Kemp encounters a professional colleague of the poetic extemporisers in 'Beppo', Manuel-del-Popolo Isturiz, 'an *improvisa-dor—an artist*', who rhapsodises on the twanging mandolin. Life, in romance, has a similar, providential unexpectedness.

Yet Conrad is aware that romance is the blithe offspring of a primordial epic, which John's father busies himself in writing. Adventure is a career of juvenility, what John calls, speaking of O'Brien's part in the Irish fiasco of 1798, 'the heroism of youth—of romance, in fact'; and that is why Marlow is careful to insist that *Chance* is 'not exactly a story for boys'. At the Casa Riego, John encounters 'vitality exhausted, . . . a body calcined, . . . romance turned into stone'. That petrification is fluent romance's reversion to the sturdy, defensive, stautesque integrity of epic. The same generic shifts are shrewdly calculated in *Nostromo*. It cannot be a novel, because Costaguana is no society and its people, as corrodedly unreal as the place they exploit, are not characters. It therefore pretends to be romance, and Conrad in his preface poses as its chevalier, sojourning in Sulaco in courtly worship of 'the "beautiful Antonia"'. But Decoud exposes the sentimentality of considering life as 'a moral romance', and Nostromo himself represents the folly and easy morality of adventurism, improvising his existence yet at the same time (when he appropriates the silver) seeing to it that he is rewarded. Stevenson's 'poetry of circumstance' is not, here, a buoyant comfort. Conrad paraphrases it as 'idiotic contingency', on whose mercy the characters rely: Decoud realises that he will perish and his project fail if Hirsch so much as coughs or sneezes. So after all the work is epic, as redefined for modernity by Shaw in 1898, in his exposition of Wagner's *Der Ring des Nibelungen*; it is epic industrialised, entrusting the manufacture of Achilles's sword to a factory like that of Wagner's Alberich. In ancient epic, man strengthens his encampment against marauding nature: Beowulf defending the hall, John Kemp clanging shut the gates of the Casa Riego. The modern epic, rather than maintaining an armed guard against nature, pillages it for profit. In Wagner's Nibelheim, at the marble quarries in Lucca visited by Gould and Emilia, and in Costaguana's silver mines, its subject is 'the tearing of the raw material of treasure from the earth': the economic invention and endowment of society.

Jim, too, temporises between romance and epic. Though he and his girl are 'knight and maiden', his more important duty is as a tribal warrior, palisading Patusan and mounting guns on the earth wall. Marlow is impatient with his romanticism and unable to comprehend its impractical idealism: being 'one of us', Jim had no business being romantic. From this irritable, affectionate relationship the entire complexity of the work, and its adjacency to the form of the novel, arise. Novelists are proprietorial, even predatory about their characters—James fusses over and dotes upon Hyacinth Robinson in a preface which is the account of a creative love-affair, Jane Austen monopolistically asserts that no one but herself will much like Emma. Conrad can never license this exhausting, all-knowing love. Character proudly protects its mystery from the assault of an inner, novelistic empathy. The language teacher's error is to make a novel from his redaction of Razumov's journal, and Razumov—sensing himself being made the old man's pet character—protests 'I am not a young man in a novel' and rejects the would-be novelist's presumption of his motives. It is too easy for the novelist to elect himself as god. In Conrad he must be, more arduously and improvingly, a man, with no power over his fellows but still with a duty to advise and assist them.

All of *Lord Jim* is a Jamesian preface about the relationship between novelist and character, except that Conrad, revising James, sees them as fraternal equals, war-comrades as Stein calls Doramin, and thus can investigate the ambiguities, inequity and final unsatisfactoriness of their contact. Marlow admits that, as novelist, he is Jim's entrepreneurial exploiter. He cannot remember Jim's 'very words', so supplies him with his own. Jim's recreation of a moment he can scarcely remember, over which he verbally prevaricates—'I had jumped . . . it seems', he says, or 'I . . . jumped', those innocuous dots opening up consequent abysses like Milton's enjambments—is seconded by Marlow's recreation of Jim. He adopts Jim as a character; gives him a character indeed (as the phrase used to be) when he writes a reference for him. The Jamesian arrogation of identity is at work: 'I make myself unreservedly responsible for you' says Marlow, who in the letter has characterised Jim as if he were 'an intimate friend'. But Jim will not surrender his volition to this novelistic embrace. Epically, he relies on his own deed and on his own death to rehabilitate himself and immortalise his name; romantically, he simply wanders off, 'preparing to leave', like Stein, for a destination which will always be mysterious. Despite his assumption of responsibility Marlow cannot follow him or understand him but must be content with mediating him, like the language teacher pondering the moral foreignness of Razumov. He might actually be said to have betrayed Jim, for he is unable to prevent his death and forbidden even to describe it, having to make do with Brown's narrative. The epic honour of *Lord Jim* requires that it fail to be a novel.

E. M. Forster arrives, more disablingly, at a conviction of the irreconcilability of the forms. The novel cannot be epically roused to militate against the way we live now; it colludes after all with a paltry, oppressive reality, which is why—after *A Passage to India*—Forster forswore it. For him, as in their different ways for H. G. Wells with his romances of scientific prediction and for Lawrence with his rainbows of resurrection, the novel rather than acquiescing in the reduced present imaginatively decrees the future. Forster's endings are millenial new beginnings: the salute to the child in *The Longest Journey*, the abounding hay crop in *Howards End*, Aziz's dream of Indian nationhood and racial union.

Forster said he stopped writing novels because the world had changed unrecognisably. In fact he gave up because the world refused to change in obedience to his expectations of it. Imagination cannot bring to pass the new world for which it longs; and Forster begins to doubt his own fitness for citizenship in that heroic community. His heroes, like Aziz and Fielding, prove incapable of altering obstructive reality, and in *Arctic Summer*—begun in 1911, then abandoned—Forster acknowledged that they are let down by his own timorousness. The stories he left incomplete collapse just when the heroes, and Forster himself, are required to declare themselves; or they subside into the helpless wishful thinking of pornography, daydreaming about a dawn of Whitmanesque sexual fraternity they cannot actualise.

Women must be excluded from the male broils of epic. Marlow in *Heart of Darkness*, obscuring the truth from Kurtz's Intended, argues that 'They—the women I mean—are out of it—should be out of it', and Captain Mitchell declares that it is not the place of sailors to marry. Forster's problem was his inability to enforce this prohibition. He resented the heterosexual tyranny which confined his subject matter to 'the love of men for women and vice versa', but lacked Hemingway's resoluteness in describing a world of solidarity and derring-do, of men without women. In a talk in 1910 on 'The Feminine Note in Literature' he argues that women judge and value themselves only in relation to another person (which means that they belong in novels, the form which fusses over these relationships and succumbs—as *Howards End* suspects—to the sloppiness they engender), while men, untrammelled by this emotional possessiveness, are loyal to 'an unembodied ideal': the grand impersonal folly of the epic quest. The example of this male ethic which Forster adduces is *Lord Jim*. The hero tests himself against his own austere goals, rather than exploring himself by commitment to a woman. Planning a novel the same year, Forster carefully barred the debilitating female: 'Plenty of young men and children in it, and adventure', he specified, 'but no love-making.' He follows the same course as Rupert Brooke, one of the models for Martin Whitby in *Arctic Summer*, who, shocked and repelled by Ka Cox's infidelity, rejected women and their novelistic intrigues to enrol, in 1914, as a warrior. *Arctic Summer* laments the obsolescence of such a figure, the epic combatant who scorns social effeminacy and proves himself—as another early story, 'Nottingham Lace', puts it—'fit for the battle', which is trumpetingly capitalised as Life.

Longing for the epic trial of valour, Whitby is stranded in a trite modernity which has declared that 'romance and adventure . . . must go'. He tries to revive these male ideals by befriending a young soldier called March, who is sleekly taking on that 'last edge of steel' that will armour him as an epic warfarer. March's brother is named Lance: an anthropoid weapon, a 'joyous knight of the sabre who clashes and roars'. The story's crisis is Lance's capitulation at Cambridge to the emasculating female. Convicted of a sexual transgression, he is disowned by his brother for offending against the creed of the phalanx, and shoots himself. Whitby and March locate in Milan a setting for epic exploits, a medieval castle 'tinged with Romance'. March saves Whitby's life; Whitby is mortified when a cinema fire reveals to him his own cowardice. He is the existential character Isherwood was to call the 'Truly Weak Man', sentencing himself to hardships to persuade himself—as Forster said of Jim—of his own worth, and *Arctic Summer* anticipates the professions which Auden and Isherwood, in their epic fables of the 1930s, selected as assays of their own infirmity. March spurns his family and takes to 'soldiering and mountaineering': beyond him lie Auden's aviators, the intrepid mountaineers on F6, or (in *Journey to a War*) the reporter venturing into the combat zone. Forster's men rejoice in the brotherhood of the locker-room. The March brothers confer in a bathroom dedicated to their exclusive use. But male communion is baffled by the snobbish apartness of the female. The men in 'Nottingham Lace' guiltily establish an accord, although 'one is never supposed to be acquainted until one's womenfolk have called.' These vaginally-dentated tyrants (Martin's wife 'loved to have something to bite on'), arbiters of Sawston, have even captured the heroic code and made it defer to them. Forster notes that March's male idealism has been fantasticated into futile 'chivalry towards women': the unmanned, dismounted warrior, no longer able to tussle with biological compeers, now opens doors for women or surrenders his seat to them in buses; militaristic, homoerotic epic droops into hagridden, heterosexual romance.

Maurice, written in 1913–14 and then suppressed, is about that generic declension and defeat. Maurice's fantasies are epically athletic. His prize Greek oration at school praises war for rendering you 'robust by exercising your limbs'. The epic is Nordic as much as classical: he sees the departing migrant ship as a Viking funeral. And he envisages mountaineering as a team of bonded males. In his desire for truth he wants 'to ascend, to stretch a hand up the mountainside until a hand catches it'. But epic must capitulate to romance and the knightly service of ladies. When Maurice confides his homosexuality to Dr Barry, he is decried as 'a disgrace to chivalry'. After this decline, the next stage in Forster's despairing recapitulation of literature's early history is exile to pastoral and acceptance of its quiet despair. *Maurice* intends its pastoral to be as apocalyptic as Lawrence's in *Lady Chatterley's Lover*: the form prophesies the dissolution of society, which is why Forster thought it unpublishable 'until my death or England's'. Failing to shake a society sustained by the novel, Forster sends Maurice and the gamekeeper Alec into hiding in nature, where they will live as woodcutters. Even that recourse was subsequently denied them: in 1960 Forster noted that England had razed its covert greenwood, leaving 'no forest or fell to escape to today', colonising and socialising the entire island.

The alternative now had to be invented—as the homosexual Arcady where Ralph and Tony, in another posthumously recovered story, will live 'the glorious unquestioning life of the body', or as Little Imber, a pastoral vengeance for men who, in Forster's future, have been virtually exterminated by rapacious women. A captive male, enslaved to propagation, teams with another man to devise a means of reproduction which bypasses the obnoxious female organs. Between them, in a pagan grove, they generate quantities of homosexual homunculi. 'Males', Forster concludes, 'had won.' Yet when he describes a society close to the blood-brotherhood of Conrad's navy or Kipling's team-games and engineering corps, in the ship's company of his libretto for Benjamin Britten's opera *Billy Budd* (1951), he acknowledges its impossibility. Melville's metaphysical parable twists into a thwarted triangular romance: Claggart cannot possess Billy's handsomeness, and so destroys him; Vere cannot utter his love for Billy, and so cannot save him. The ideal can survive, as for Whitby, only in a fiction. Forster's innocent pornography indulges doting hopes which expect no fruition. He accuses himself of lacking the courage to see that fiction through. Explaining why he gave up *Arctic Summer*, he charges himself, in the terms of his own epic, with a failure to act and achieve, a faltering of command: 'I had not settled what was going to happen.' The epic artefact is a mountain peak, and Forster—like Isherwood later in *Lions and Shadows*, allying his own evasive circumnavigations to the quest for a north-west passage—flunks the test of his own puissance with which it confronts him: he lacked the sense of 'a solid mass ahead, a mountain round or over or through which the story must somehow go'. His final comment is as moving as Birkin's insistence at the end of *Women in Love* on believing in that 'eternal union with a man too' which Ursula condemns as perversity. His twinned men, he says, could have got to the end of *Arctic Summer* as 'companions in defeat. But such an ending doesn't interest me.' Since the world had censored his fantasy and prevented it from coming true, he preferred to stop writing.

Forster's two great novels are written against themselves, in demarcation of the form's impotence or irrelevance. The subject of *Howard End* (1910) is the epic one of empire, the expanded arena of heroic action, but the novel with its 'feminine note' quits that field or denies knowledge of it. Ernst Schlegel is a refugee from Prussianism; his daughter Margaret declares 'an Empire bores me'. The novel's cult of introversion and emotional nuance relegates the doings of empire to background noise. Paul Wilcox carries the white man's burden in West Africa, Simpson's resounds with chat of cables to Uganda, a contingent of Anglo-Indian ladies turns out for Evie's wedding. Margaret, looking over the Wilcox house in Ducie Street, identifies the modern capitalist with the warriors and hunters of old, and sees the dining-room as an Anglo-Saxon banqueting-hall.

That epic has been renounced, and is recoverable only in the combative din of Beethoven's Fifth Symphony with its skirmish of giants and goblins; in its place is a shapeless modern version of romance—life as muddle not (as in epic) battle, a chaos of false clues and unconsecutive sign-posts, coincidental and unmanageable. Leonard Bast longs for adventure and worships 'Romance', yet can find it only in the books which crush the life out of him, just as for the Schlegels the German epic is now merely musical.

With the same lassitude which made him sigh over telling a story in his Cambridge lectures, Forster implies that the novelist must be a practical, managing Wilcox, and he undertakes the chores of the form with weary reluctance: he begins with a shrug, and leaves the expository plotting to Helen's letters. He has no patience with the novel's corporate solidity, or its Trollopean labour of verification—'facts, and facts, and empires of facts', in the Schlegel father's phrase. The form is an apparatus of, and is compromised by, the materialism of its society. It investigates that society's fabric—'Property, interest, etc.;'—and with its lumber of persons and freight of words is a too-capacious container, an item in 'the civilization of luggage'. Hence the centrality to it of a house and a squabble over inheritance: novels like heirlooms are devices for attaching ourselves to the earth and pretending to permanence on it; Mrs Wilcox's gift of Howards End to Margaret offends against the laws of property, just as her abrupt, dematerialising death offends against the laws of fiction, which must conscientiously persist in its illusion of life, not gratuitously break off.

Howards End sees the novel as a vain exercise in speculation and accumulation, allied with the property boom in London or the possessiveness of Mr Wilcox. Helen, in one of the work's many comic, exhilarated apocalypses, says 'in the end the world will be a desert of chairs and sofas . . . rolling through infinity with no one to sit upon them.' Virginia Woolf considers the same possibility—the tenantless furniture in the dead Jacob's room, Mr Ramsay's aerodynamic kitchen table—and is delighted by it, because people will have been reprieved from the dumb bulk of objects and exhaled as pure, bodiless consciousness: for her, it is a dream of the novel's abstraction from matter. To Forster, it signifies the novel's metaphysical deceit, its enchainment to a world imagined to be real because it can be seen and, briefly, owned. Crusoe's earnest fabrication is no longer a comfort.

A Passage to India also interprets the novel as on the one hand a mocking decline from epic, on the other an exporting of a provincial, irrelevant notion of reality: at once a parody and a fraud. Its epic sponsor is Whitman, from whom the title is excerpted. But Whitman's American dream of democratic brotherhood is baffled by Forster's India. Romance, too, is pilloried. Adela Quested is named after the chivalric quest and she seeks adventures, yet her crisis in the cave hardly qualifies as one. It exposes to her the irrelevance of mere happening, the mendacity of orderly narrative—which is why she so inexplicably withdraws her prosecution of Aziz.

The passage to India is also Virginia Woolf's voyage out, or to the lighthouse: a casting-off of tame, landed novelistic realism. India exposes the superfluity of the novel's punctilious discriminations. Its life is undifferentiated. There can be no novelistic innerness in a country where 'nothing's private', and where animals and insects—the wasp in the cloakroom, for instance—refuse to remain outdoors. 'India', as Ronny sees, 'isn't a drawing-room.' Individuality, so cherished by the novel, is an illusion in India. When Mrs Moore says she does not understand people but only knows whether she likes them or not, Aziz flatteringly calls her an oriental. The orientalising of the novel requires eventually the philosophical abolition of character, reduced by Christopher Isherwood in his mystical California to 'a single man': a plural mind impeded by bodily singularity. Mrs Moore sniffs at the notion of 'people's characters, as you call them': the identification of a person with the moral credentials inaccurately assigned to him.

It follows that the novel's cultivation and sanctifying of personal relationships cannot work, for 'the majority of living beings' is blithely indifferent to 'what the minority, which calls itself human, desires or decides'. If the individual is a falsity, then the actions that novels derive from him lose their meaning. Godbole finds the legalistic issue of Aziz's guilt—the outcome of plot, the definition of dramatic responsibility—to be an error of perception, since Adela could equally well be said to have violated herself: 'When evil occurs, it expresses the whole of the universe. Similarly when good occurs.'

Individual existence is a mere apportioning of fancy dress, employed as disguise by Aziz's friends when they resume 'their self-esteem and the qualities that distinguished them from each other', and realism caters to the itchy-fingered larceny of ignorant creatures, the inheritors of Crusoe, Moll Flanders and Dombey: Forster names 'the desire for possessions' as the destroyer of the heart. Robbed of these trappings, the derelict person is just a zone of consciousness like Prufrock or the intersecting of many unhoused, twittering minds like Eliot's hollow men. Fielding experiences this lucid insanity, feeling 'we exist not in ourselves, but in terms of each other's minds.' Forster demonstrates the flimsy construction and facile annihilation of thoughts which imagine themselves as beings by the casualness with which he extinguishes characters—Mrs Moore, the Rajah—as if they cease to exist when he, like a forgetful god, stops cogitating them. The parenthetical exterminations in *To the Lighthouse* announce the mercy of what Virginia Woolf called 'the death of the individual'. The same impromptu demises in Forster announce a diminution even of death. That occasion for etherising as spirit or flowing away as water, suicidally venerated by Woolf, simply proves to Forster the irrepressibility of our conceit, which invents tragedy to make our cessations significant. Adela learns that 'all these personal relations we try to live by are temporary. I used to feel death selected people, it is a notion one gets from novels.'

There can as a result be no narrative, and Forster's novel contains at its centre a cavity, a vacuity, harbouring a sound which robs language of value by its resistance to transliteration. The echo goads Adela to mania, and demeans literature to nonsense: '"Boum" is the sound as far as the human alphabet can express it, or "bou-oum", or "ou-boum,"—utterly dull.' With a mystical ennui, Forster sees the contrivances of narrative as specious lies about this stupefying nothingness. To conceal life's dullness, books exaggerate in the hope of proving it interesting and justifying their own existence. This was Schopenhauer's critique of novelistic narrative, and the reason for his approval of *Tristram Shandy*. Forster is abstinently faithful to this perception. Having learned from India the fatuity of character and the inconsequentiality of agitated, ineffective action, he resigns from literature, or perhaps espouses music, immaterial and indivisible, instead. His criticism describes the novel symphonically and hears as its end a reverberation in silence; in *A Passage to India* the Hindus prepare for God's birth with a musical din, unpunctuated because inextricable, battering 'individual clods' into the tumult of a collective life: 'The braying banging crooning melted into a single mass which trailed round the palace before joining the thunder.'

The disciplines of epic serve both Conrad and Kipling as conservative enforcements of order—Kurtz's policy of extermination in Africa, Inspector Heat's logical use of detection in London as a reassembly of a disintegrated society (just as he has meticulously pieced together the exploded corpse of

Stevie without missing 'a single piece as big as a postage-stamp'), Kim's apprenticeship in mensuration which levelly rules landscape out and subjugates to his pacing the 'great, grey, formless India' beyond the comprehension of padres and colonels. The lama has a spiritual and aerial overview of India, 'all Hind, from Ceylon ... to ... Suchzen'; onto Kim, astride his gun, devolves the responsibility of holding that unstable expanse together at ground level, first by running its errands as bazaar gossip and intelligencer, then by the scientific deployment of compasses and measuring-chains and the solemn game of politics. The lama urges him 'to abstain from action' and has himself given up its fidgetings: his presence is 'a perfect safeguard against consequences'. But Kim must toil on the exhausting wheel of action and reaction, and maintain the fiction of reality. Forster retires from that effort, announcing the so-called reality to be unmanageable and calling fiction's brave, Crusoesque bluff.

— 36 —
Renewing the Novel

Symons, in his essay on Mallarmé, declares that 'the age of epics is past'. Story-telling—the anxious constitutional activity of Conrad's narrators or Kipling's, reciting history and thus maintaining society—is obsolete, and has been replaced by the lyrical study of symbolist moments. The lyric, Symons believes, is the only legitimate literary kind, and all other forms must be subdued to it. 'The novel should be psychological', he says in an essay on Huysmans; and this means that it should be poetic. The process is one almost of religious conversion, overthrowing the novel's mercenariness—its fixation with 'the amorous and ambitious and money-making intelligence of the conscious and practical self'—to make it, like the symbol, a revelation of the soul. It must learn a mystic, meditative quietude: 'purged of the distraction of incident', it will be 'internalised to a complete liberty'. With epic eliminated, romance has been freed, as Henry James says in 'The Story in It' (a story which, in obedience to Symons's aesthetics, disdains to be a story at all), to become 'a sort of consciousness'. At the same time the novel is invaded by lyricism—saturated by poetry as Virginia Woolf says, adopting the word from James, who said he had chosen the form of his saturation. In James the dissolution of action frees consciousness; in Virginia Woolf it goes further, recording the discursiveness of unconsciousness; in D. H. Lawrence it unleashes the life of a surging subconsciousness.

The subjective adventure begins in Pater's *Marius the Epicurean* (1885), where the novel is overtaken by the hedonism—and, in preparation for the cerebral trials of James's people, the martyrdom—of consciousness. Marius defects from the busy world of the materialist novel: 'more given to contemplation than to action', he is 'an idealist, constructing the world for himself', oppressed by 'the reality, the tyrannous reality of things visible'. The Victorian novel had counselled conciliation with that reality and its unromantic Monday mornings. Marius acknowledges no reality except consciousness, which translates objects into symbolic shadows of themselves and life into a day-dream. His epiphany in the olive grove persuades him that the universe of matter is but the conjuration of 'one indeflectible mind, wherein he too became conscious', and once he sees through it—declaring it, as Virginia Woolf did, to be a semi-transparent envelope or a luminous halo—he has rendered it unreal, discerned it to be 'actually dissolving away around him'. The objects which remain are the imprisoning cases for souls. To view them as symbols, as Marius does when looking at the trees against the sky, is to free those spirits into the airy subjective amphitheatre which is the life of mind. The Wordsworthian life within us and abroad narrows to a tangential overlapping of intelligences, or a desperate savouring of elapsing sensation. Marius's Cyrenian philosophy of 'the "Ideal Now"' begets in him a retinal discipline which is the injunction of impressionism: 'to keep the eye clear'. His vow to 'miss no detail of this life of realised consciousness in the present' becomes the urgent avocation of Jamesian character. Strether in *The Ambassadors* (1903) entreats little Bilham to be one of those on whom nothing is lost.

After Christopher Newman undergoes conversion on the way to a meeting in Wall Street in *The American* (1876), James secedes from the epic tradition of American literature with its deer-slayers, whale-hunters and tree-fellers, just as he exiled himself from an America which was not 'the land of leisure', and which censured the novelist's reflective existence. He had modelled himself artistically on the tycoons who are the heroes of American naturalism— Dreiser's industrial magnates, or the Rothschilds, who sharpened James's 'desire to distinguish myself by personal achievement'—and justified his work to his family as an exercise in aggrandisement. When his brother objected to the slimness of *The Europeans* (1878), James signalled his intention to do 'something fat', and assessing receipts from *Confidence* (1880) he points out to his sister, 'I go on enlarging.' But the only power he permitted to himself or his characters was that of perception. The will has its triumph in understanding, not, like Dreiser's titans, in ownership.

Pater's Marius, resisting all creeds and dogmas, has the Jamesian mind, whose fineness no idea can violate. Yet increasingly James's subject is that mind's violation of the other intelligences it oversees, its extensions of capitalizing consciousness: the raids on sexual secrets made by the literary sleuth in *The Aspern Papers* (1888) who, despite his false visiting card and his disclosure of his true name to Miss Tina, remains anonymous because he is an unimpeded and unscrupulous subjectivity, a novelist with the freedom to intuit emotions and ransack drawers; the equally nameless governess in The *Turn of the Screw* (1898), whose rage to know is a power to conjure up (and to make others responsible for) the demons she has imagined; the definition in *The Sacred Fount* (1901) of voyeurism as a 'high application of intelligence' and a craft of symbolist decipherment, scrutinising 'psychologic signs'. Jamesian love is a consummation of mental command, a science of mind. For Dr Sloper in *Washington Square* (1880), who appraises his daughter and her young man as surfaces to be formulaically ruled by him, it is geometry; for Acton in *The Europeans*, disturbed by his feeling for the Baroness, it is algebra, which 'is saying a good deal; for [he] was extremely fond of mathematics'.

Since the form's purpose is the training and dilation of consciousness, novels are for James hermeneutic fables, schools of interpretative cunning. This is the subject of *What Maisie Knew* (1897). Maisie's acquisition of wisdom about the sexual perfidy of adults is her advance towards the novelist's omniscience: 'Oh yes, I know everything!' she can radiantly cry. The 'fierce light' trained on Maisie's parents by the divorce court is James's equivalent to the elucidation of George Eliot's mind on its progressive march—except that knowledge in James is not a positivist divinity, and can teach only the stoic helplessness of connoisseurship. When Olive in *The Bostonians* (1886) offers to show Basil evidence of human progress, he replies that 'the human race has got to bear its troubles'.

James's 1907 preface calls Maisie 'the infant mind'. His novel is about the abandonment of a romantic conception of infancy—Keats's young, greedy appetite, Wordsworth's graced idiot boy—and it conspires at Maisie's morally necessary corruption, ensuring that she 'not only felt it, but knew she felt it'. James himself is her satanic tutor, teasing her with his hints and tantalising the reader by the exclusiveness of his conspiracy with her: 'Oh decidedly I shall never get you to believe the number of things she saw and the number of secrets she discovered!' Romantic vision, adept at opening casements and projecting alternatives to the actual, is replaced by the conditioning constriction of mind, poetic freedom by novelistic necessity. James begins, in Maisie's literal chamber of maiden-thought, with the phantasmagoria which is romantic imagination. She stares at her unintelligible circumstances as at images in a magic-lantern show, or 'strange shadows dancing on a sheet'. Thereafter she graduates to the perilous valour of novelistic imagination, a power of clairvoyance enabling her to see the invisible—'such horrors!' as Mrs Wix shrills, speaking of the covert adulteries as if they were the ghosts at Bly in *The Turn of the Screw*—and to eavesdrop on the implicit, or the unspeakable. Maisie's aptitude at innuendo provokes Mrs Wix's ultimate, appalled compliment: 'You're too unspeakable! Do you know what we're talking about?'

Maisie is, in both the aesthetic and the necromantic senses, a medium, and James's question is whether she remains unsullied by the messages relayed through her—by, for instance, her father's commission to call her mother, on his behalf, a nasty horrid pig. Or does she herself invent the messages she passes on? Her father merely says an unspecified 'something'; it is Maisie who shockingly gives voice to it. Because Maisie's is an aesthetic education, it is represented mainly, like Stephen Dedalus's, as a process of language-learning; and what she comes to know, thanks to her vaunted mispronunciation of Glower Street or her solution of nonsensical coinages like Mrs Beale's 'thingumbob', is the untrustworthiness of words as insignia for things, or as deputies for persons. Hence her puzzlement about 'the monosyllable "he"', which in her mother's vocabulary used to have one reference only, but now has very many others. Her most instructive lesson in the arbitrary employment of words and their skill at concealment concerns entitlement. Her father tells her that his Countess's title is not English. Maisie wonders if it is French. No, he says, 'it's American'—which means non-existent, a hyperbolic fiction. Maisie's apparent non-sequitur admirably comprehends the case: 'Ah then of course she must be extremely rich.' Having learned English as if it were a foreign language, bemused by significations but guessing at inflection and nuance, Maisie goes on to try out her perceptual skills on French. At first her store of words consists 'mainly of the names of dishes'; then she realises, listening to a song, that she 'knew what "amour" meant too, and wondered if Mrs. Wix did.' What she knows is how different it is from the word 'love' which presumes to translate it. The height of her career is reached when, astonishingly, she begins to speak in tongues, rattling off an idiom she has not officially learned. Planning elopement to Paris with Sir Claude, 'she not only by illumination understood' his French dialogue with the porter, 'but fell into it with an active perfection', ordering the porter, *'Prenny, prenny. Oh prenny!'*

Innocence means an incapacity to discriminate truths from the falsehoods which allure her, like the 'little dead sister' who is not real but is therefore 'the more romantic'. The infant Maisie has books for a nursery. 'She was at the age for which all stories are true and all conceptions are stories', says James; later he notes, 'The child had been in thousands of stories.' When the protection of these romances is withdrawn, she is alerted to the chasms between words and deeds, novels and veracity. She perceives, as Wilde's Miss Prism would have it, what fiction means.

In *The Awkward Age* (1899), a French novel—as symbolically anonymous as the one studied by Dorian Gray—stands for a forbidden knowledge, seized, when she illicitly reads it, by Nanda. The novel is presumably by Zola, who is cited elsewhere by Vanderbank; it is a work, according to Mrs Brook, of 'abject, horrid, unredeemed vileness' about those sluices and gutters which are the sites of naturalism: 'people . . . sticking fast in their native mud.' *The Awkward Age* is James's critique of this besmirchment. It wings over the surface, as Mrs Brook says, rather than excavating beneath it; its imperatives are concealment not exposure, consecration not defamation. At the same time it dispenses with a lowering realism, for nothing in it is circumstantially, unequivocally real. Everything has been made mental and therefore symbolic, from adultery to food. 'Won't you eat something?' says Mrs Brook at tea. 'One of the nice little round ones?' We never discover what they are: even the cakes are conceptual.

James takes a society as seamily corrupt as any in Zola, but abstracts its sexual intrigues and petty thievery (as in the case of the £5 filched by Harold) as the topics of a disinterested symposium, whose disputants experiment in freeing talk, purging the tribal dialect and inspecting meanings, and fine one another for tawdry paradoxes. They have been reprieved from the need to make a living. Brookenham's employment is glossed with evasive vagueness: it is allegedly in 'Rivers and Lakes' and supplies him with 'twelve hundred—and lots of allowances and boats and things. To do to the work.' When Mr Longdon enquires, 'What *is* the work?' Vanderbank cannot say. The salary is a subsidy to idleness and an allowance to introspection. This is a society of decadent superfluity. The shiftless Harold is 'a born consumer'; Mitchy's affluent theory is that luxuries—'I don't literally need the big turquoise in my neck-tie'—are one's only necessities. Memories are sumptuary items. Vanderbank coffers his in a reliquary, wrapped in 'the gold paper of the mind'. Consciousness itself is consumptive. Nanda's colloquies with Mr Longdon are fuelled by cigarettes: smoke is their nimbus of cerebration. Domestic arrangements have vanished into the mind, like the kitchen implements in Virginia Woolf's *The Waves* (1931) shimmering in a haze as light robs them of identity and outline. Longdon refers to Vanderbank's 'intellectual board', with its congestion of inedible, discussable dishes; Mrs. Brook's guests require 'intellectual elbow-room'. The very furniture is an apparatus to think with. Vanderbank serves in Mrs Brook's drawing-room 'only as one of those queer extinguishers of fire in the corridors of hotels. He's just a bucket on a peg'; a symbolic decoy, that is. Soon the furniture will levitate, in a ballet of ideal categories. Mr Ramsay's philosophy in *To the Lighthouse* (1927) is imagined as 'a kitchen table . . . when you're not there', parked in a pear tree.

Like Pater's Aurelius, 'the man of mind' presiding in the 'empty house' of the head, James's contemplatives reside in a house of fiction which is inevitably haunted, prowled at twilight by 'the ghost of a dead thought'. Virginia Woolf's Mrs Ramsay enunciates rules for housekeeping in such a place. Shut the doors and open the windows, she orders the Swiss maid: the body's confinement to compartments is atoned for by the ventilation which frees the eye and the mind. In James's cranial architecture, though, a portal (through which Max Beerbohm's cartoon, positioning him at the key-hole, had him peep) can allow for the passage of secrets from one mind to the next, as when Mrs Brook 'opened an inch or two, for Vanderbank, the door of her dim radiance'. The next ground-plan of the house of fiction is made by Virginia Woolf, who calls it, in 'The Mark on the Wall' (1921)—a demolition of the novel's flimsy, epistemological furnishings, which fill up space in the hope of attesting to material reality—'a world not to be lived in'.

Dedicating his people to cogitation, James makes an intellectual aristocracy of them. They are, as they constantly remind each other, magnificoes; Mitchy's entertaining is 'princely'. Their gossip is promoted to a religious observance when they are called 'votaries of that temple of analysis' which is the Buckingham Crescent salon. At its most audacious, James's rhetoric sanctifies and deifies them. Only gods or their intercessors could possess such lofty, infallible consciousness. Aggie consequently is an angel (though grounded by an adjective which, having to be trebled, protests too much: 'a real, real, real one'), while her elders are Olympians. Lady Fanny hovers aloft, 'a great glorious pagan' or 'a great calm silver statue'; the Duchess swaggers 'like some brazen pagan goddess'; Mrs Brook, like Caesar imprinting his foot in the firmament, is 'a fixed star', resembling both the moon and Marble Arch; the dapper Van is 'Apollo in person'. It is their intelligence which qualifies them for heroism, just as Mrs Brook's foresight is a power of prophetic intervention. Redeploying partners at Mrs Grendon's, she 'pulled us down—just closing with each of the great columns in its turn—as Samson pulled down the temple'. For that temple, being an airy, analytic edifice, can be toppled and re-erected at will.

The Jamesian seminar here, the 'common consciousness' of shared intelligence, leads to the group minds of Virginia Woolf's novels—the eight young Ramsays, the six elective siblings of *The Waves*. Indeed Mitchy anticipates those random showers of innumerable atoms which are, in Virginia Woolf's view, the constituents of consciousness and of modern fiction, when he remarks that 'the saloon is now . . . but a collection of fortuitous atoms'. No charmed circle constrains them in Virginia Woolf; she must make art from an arrangement of the mind's haphazard, perhaps deranged, perceptual fall-out, and precariously plan social occasions—Mrs Dalloway's cocktails or Mrs Ramsay's dinner—as eucharistic meals of grace. Whereas the Jamesian great good place is a club, a place of conversation, the symposium in Virginia Woolf must do without dialogue and attune itself to silence. Though it is alleged that the characters in *The Waves* speak, they are eyes not voices, observers not articulators. Speech, being an aptitude of the individual, merely reminds them of their alienness. Louis will not utter because he is embarrassed by his Australian accent.

The Golden Bowl (1904) is a consummation of the change proclaimed by Arthur Symons. The novel becomes at once psychological and poetic, and does so by its transcendence of reality. Symons's rule prescribes an economic and aesthetic decadence: the superstructure's ignorance of the mercenary base on which it is raised. Reality means penny-pinching. Charlotte, who has 'only twopence in the world', proposes travelling by a penny omnibus, engages a penny chair in Hyde Park, intends to scavenge for bargains in the Baker Street bazaar, and haggles over the price of the golden bowl. Art, a concomitant of affluence and leisure which are (as Maggie says to her father) the languid attributes of gods, signifies pricelessness, or at least indifference to price: Maggie tells Amerigo, who has been purchased for her as a curio and an expensive rarity, 'I haven't the least idea what you cost.' James acknowledges the moral peril of a life conducted aesthetically. That freedom from want and from obligation to reality symbolised by art also prompts Amerigo's adultery. Acquired as an exhibit, 'the man's in a position in which he has nothing in life to do.' Maggie's response to this betrayal is, however, a fortifying of the imperturbable surface—Dorian's painted face—which is, in Wilde, art's safeguard against use. She copes formalistically. Mrs Assingham remarks that with Maggie 'the forms are two-thirds of conduct'. The same law of deportment, which is the triumph of manner over morals, serves in art: form regulates conduct; at its boldest it subdues, even abolishes content. By giving the appearance of not noticing or caring, Maggie makes Amerigo and Charlotte notice and care; by doing nothing, she mesmerically makes them do her bidding.

Its ambition of transcendence requires *The Golden Bowl* to be subtly contradictory. Maggie declares herself to be shrieking aloud in despair, yet she does so silently. Form again has muffled, annihilated content. It is a theatrical work, with a plot like one of Wilde's comedies of adultery, and it stage-manages expert coups and tableaux—Fanny smashing the bowl as Amerigo enters, Maggie embracing Charlotte as all the other characters arrive to witness her bravely histrionic act. Maggie, playing her self-scripted part, is constantly likened to an actress, or a ballerina executing a difficult step, or—at her most mentally acrobatic—to a 'little trapezist girl'. Charlotte and Amerigo belong in the libidinally darkened theatre of opera. When she appears in the upper window at Matcham and greets him in Italian, they play out a scene from *Don Giovanni*; Maggie sees them as a 'pair of operatic, of high Wagnerian lovers'.

This incipient drama is contradicted by the introversion of narrative and the placidity of consciousness. Maggie's skill is the prevention of drama. The novel is her form because in it nothing need be said, and nothing need happen (which, as Shaw's bored characters in *Heartbreak House* acknowledge when they lament 'nothing happens', is drama's death). So *The Golden Bowl* arranges theatrical crises and confrontations only to stifle them. Its dialogue is silent—the 'queer minute without words' when Amerigo and Charlotte are reunited, the 'wordless, wordless smile' of victory (requiring a doubled word to stand for wordlessness) which passes between Adam and Maggie. Terence in Virginia Woolf's *The Voyage Out* (1915) wants to write a novel consisting of 'the things people don't say'. James had already written it. When Amerigo returns from the excursion to Gloucester, Maggie is given a long, theatrically climactic speech of complaint and pleading. James first transcribes it, then denies that she has uttered it. His report of it is a précis of silence: 'Some such words as those were what *didn't* ring out.' Charlotte's ramble with Amerigo in Bloomsbury is defined as the occasion 'we're not to speak of'. Maggie's triumph—a credo for moral survival, and a theoretical defence of novels—is comprehensively stated by Fanny when she says, 'Nothing . . . *will* happen. Nothing *has* happened. Nothing *is* happening.'

As well as this cancellation of drama by novel, *The Golden Bowl* rehearses the novel's ancient absorption of epic in pastoral. It conceives of society as a Conradian jungle, pitted with abysses, where a military preparedness is advised. Hence Colonel Assingham's recollection of 'battalions, squadrons, tremendous cannonades', cavalry charges or 'the perpetual booming of guns', and his conscription, with his wife, for sentry duty. They solemnly memorise 'the soldiers' watchword at night'. The characters they serve are invested with power by James's honorific similes, which install them as the potentates of a new Renaissance. Verver is a latter-day pontiff, Charlotte a poisoning Borgia, Amerigo a voyaging adventurer rediscovering the new world first sighted by his ancestor. Yet despite this pomp and officiousness, which has Charlotte at the diplomatic reception being sought after '*en très-haut lieu*' by 'the greatest possible Personage', the novel domiciles its characters in a 'garden of thought', pacifically meditative. Adam's surname doubly evokes the spring, and he is often likened (although he is a tycoon) to a lamb; his innocence betokens to Amerigo an 'almost Arcadian optimism'. Maggie achieves the pastoralising of Bloomsbury, conceiving of the British Museum as a reflective enclave in landscape. She calls it 'the great Bloomsbury hive', its 'packed passages and cells' inhabited by 'flower-loving and honey-sipping' thinkers. And the image of the apiary recurs near the end to represent her nurturing and safekeeping of emotions in the pastoral cloister of the mind: 'clinging with her winged concentration to some deep cell of her heart, she stored away her hived tenderness as if she had gathered it all from flowers.'

Overcoming actuality, James manages the novel's sublimation. The bowl, for instance, begins as a collectible trinket, but is economically disqualified by its flaw, then shattered. Thereafter it is reconstituted as an image, and has a symbolic second coming. It signifies indeed a Grail: a chalice sacred to art, not faith. When Adam visits the dealer Gutermann-Suess at Brighton, a commercial transaction and the taking of tea are exalted into sacraments by 'the touch of some mystic rite of old Jewry'. The same hallowing happens to the sundered bowl. Fanny breaks it so that Maggie can, mentally, restore it, but as image not object, 'the golden bowl—as it was to have been. . . . The bowl with all happiness in it. The bowl without the crack.' When Maggie solders it by perceiving its uncorrupted, unearthly meaning, Fanny is able to have a vision of it, and the obscured verbal figure (as James calls it) hovers in air like the apparition of the Grail to a Tennysonain Knight. 'For Mrs. Assingham too the image had force, and the precious object shone before her again, reconstituted, plausible, presentable.'

The sublimatory skill of the characters resides in their images. Overstating, they can overcome their personal cases. Their aim is to arrive at a godly, aerial perspective on themselves. Maisie's knowingness, now sovereign, has reclaimed the sky. The judgement of vantage for supervision is of concern throughout the novel, since consciousness has come to mean perspective. Adam measures the perspectives of the park at Fawns, Maggie tracks Charlotte through its mazy vistas and perspectives, and Fanny's conversation trains the Colonel in perspectival vision and in mental leaps through space, forever testing him with 'a new view to jump to'. Fanny defines the novel's science of vision and its rule of sublime renunciation—like Millie enfolding with her grace a world she has quit in *The Wings of the Dove* (1902)—when she says 'you must have had things to be beyond them. It's a kind of law of perspective.' It is this perspective on Paris and youth and a lost paradise which Strether in *The Ambassadors* attains by returning to Massachusetts. Because consciousness is altitude (or at least, in Strether's case, marginal, horizontal distance), the imagery of *The Golden Bowl* is always vertiginous. It enables the characters to look down on themselves from a height. It sees Brighton perched on steep cliffs; Maggie refers to Amerigo's villa as 'the "perched" place' and to her father as the scaler of a dizzy peak; Charlotte, lent an extra hauteur by her 'high tiara', poses 'half way up the "monumental" staircase' at the Foreign Office.

Intelligence consists in possessing a head for heights and a vertical propulsiveness: Fanny's moral sense is hydraulic, like a lightning elevator in a skyscraper, and in conversation with Maggie she ascends 'with the whizz . . . of a rocket'. Amerigo's reference to Adam's fifteen-storey buildings is no accident, because James interprets this imagistic talent as an architectural experiment, raising pagodas or (in another of Maggie's figures) unsteady edifices of children's blocks, erecting formal contraptions in defiance of gravity: 'they had built strong and piled high.' In the year of *The Golden Bowl*'s publication James returned to New York, where he chided the new skyscrapers because they over-reached not to regain heaven but merely to maximise rents. Their height is commercial calculation, not a pinnacling of intelligence. The only building with the requisite mental eminence, and with the trust, shared by his characters, in imagery, ornament and art as a means of perfecting and upraising lowly nature—form's cancellation of function, which is Maggie's prescription for coping with life—has already been demolished. James, like Maggie reconstituting the bowl, restores it in memory. 'Wasn't it somehow', he asks of the old university building in Washington Square, 'with a desperate bravery, both castellated and gabled?'

James refines the acquisitiveness of his carpet-bagging characters by treating matter as spirit, possessions as art, emotions as mental attitudes. Virginia Woolf was bothered by the materiality of the novel, and saw descriptive narrative as an acquisitive impulse, validating the world by coveting it. After a visit to the Victoria and Albert Museum—which she is not able, like Maggie at the British Museum, to placate as thought—she wrote to her sister Vanessa Bell, 'I see I shall have to write a novel entirely about carpets, old silver, cut glass and furniture. The desire to describe becomes almost a torment; and also the covetousness to possess. I don't think this has much to do with their artistic value though.' The mode of abstraction she deployed against a world too harshly real was to empty it into what she calls, in one of the sketches from *Monday or Tuesday* (1921), 'an unwritten novel': a work containing nothing and no one except, as in James, spectral thoughts. Hence the deserted houses and vacated rooms which are her ideal settings—the mansion prowled by ghostly lovers in an early story, the Ramsay home abandoned to time, the room which is Jacob's abandoned bodily husk, the house in *The Waves* flooded by light, the frail stage-set of Poyns Hall stranded between the acts. The theoretical 'room of one's own' which is the territorial minimum of personal freedom has no view. Its tenant might be Isabella Tyson in 'The Lady in the Looking-Glass', whose 'mind was like her room', which is empty except for a mirror. Virginia Woolf punningly subtitles this piece 'A Reflection', referring both to the mirror's reflexivity and to the Pateresque commandment to steep the observed world in reflection. The mirror's bland mimesis is mistrusted: after all, it is untrue to reality, which it reverses. And when the process of mental reflection begins, that pretended reality retreats. Isabella's looking-glass is less the mirror which promenaded down the highway than the surreal refractor which hangs on Alice's wall.

Pater's impressionism emphasized the fluency of consciousness. For Jacob dabbling in his rock pool, for Mrs Swithin in *Between the Acts* (1941) staring into the lily pond, or for Mrs Dalloway plunging into London as if immersing herself, the mind's triumph is one of dissolution. The six subjects of *The Waves* merge as waves do. Connected as she was with the visual arts through her sister, Clive Bell and Roger Fry, Virginia Woolf introduces to the novel the opposed abstractions of contemporary painting: the drowning of reality by impressionism, the fracturing of reality into facets by cubism; impressionism's luminous halos and wraith-like transparencies against cubism's solid but sculpturally dissected objects; death and communion by water against the rocky irreducibility, 'stark and straight', of the lighthouse with its all-seeing eye.

To Virginia Woolf the impressionist—who called her sister a dolphin and Ottoline Morrell (Hermione in *Women in Love*) a dapper mackerel—society is an aquarium. Marius the Epicurean's 'purely material world, that close, impassable prison-wall' is a glass tank, a vitreous envelope; there is a visit to such an installation at Scarborough in *Jacob's Room*. Reality must undergo submergence in order, aqueously loosened, to become impression or symbol. The sea-change can happen lachrymosely, as when Mrs Flanders's tear makes the bay quiver, a mast bend 'like a wax candle in the sun' (the solar decomposition which is Dali's surrealism), and even convinces the lighthouse—the solidest of objects in the later novel—to wobble. At the same time a painter on the beach is representing her; his reduction of her to an abstract violet-black dab, like the 'angular essences' and diagrammatic blocks with which Lily Briscoe replaces people in *To the Lighthouse* or the architecture of squares and oblongs which the dance band constructs in *The Waves*, is a cubist perception, happening at the same time as her sorrowing impressionist welter.

Lily is proud that her art makes no attempt at human likeness. 'The symbolic outline . . . transcended the real figures.' Dipping things, Virginia Woolf's characters wash away their vexatious identity. It takes a downpour to make a community of the audience for the pageant in *Between the Acts*. The communion meal served by Mrs Ramsay is a stew, and the fruit dish presents its offerings as divers in deep seas like Pater's Gioconda, suggesting a Neptune's banquet fetched up from the ocean floor. The Elizabethan frost is a nightmare in *Orlando* (1928) because it contrives solidification—the fate of incarceration in the gross body which Neville in *The Waves*, 'weighed down by food', happily suffers, as opposed to the mystic freedom to send the mind out on expeditionary forays, like the 'airs, detached from the body of the wind' roaming through the Ramsay house—and even petrification, along with a frigid insensitivity. Thaw means the reversion to impressionist flux, to the tide described by Pater in the conclusion of *The Renaissance*. The Victorian policeman at Hyde Park Corner in *Orlando* stands for the interdict of authority, imposing a deathly stability. When his hand falls, and the sway of the eminent Victorians he upholds falters, the coagulated river of perception can rush on again: 'the stream became liquid; the massive conglomeration of splendid objects moved, dispersed, and disappeared into Piccadilly.' *Mrs Dalloway* seeks London's saturation in poetry, which means that the rooted, statuesque, institutional city is set aswim. Clarissa is a naiad. Her party dress is that of a silver-green mermaid, 'lolloping on the waves'. Escorting the Prime Minister through the crush, she is luring him and the pompously material world whose deputy he is into her lyrical drowning-pool. Peter Walsh sees London beautified by its merger in and with water: its foliage is that of a city under the waves. Metaphor equips objects with a bouyant capacity to negotiate these gulfs. A bus in Westminster seems, as Elizabeth Dalloway embarks, to spread sails for a voyage up Whitehall.·

This underwater abstracting implies a formal nihilism about the novel. Virginia Woolf dreams of the death of the individual (or, because it is the same thing, his elongation beyond himself and beyond the compartments of self and gender: this is the case of Orlando, living for centuries and—since a person consists in whimsical, immaterial, migratory mind—inhabiting now a male body, now a female one); the denigration of narrative (Bernard the novelist in *The Waves* confesses, 'I begin to doubt if there are stories'); the end of mimesis. In *To the Lighthouse* it is Mrs McNab the char who in the empty, thought-haunted house refurbishes that old fictional utensil the looking-glass, and, like Wilde's Caliban, grimaces at herself in it, not comprehending the abstract pronouncement that 'the mirror was broken'. At the same time, she exhumes the novel's past, dredging up from oblivion 'all the Waverley novels and a tea-set'. Minta Doyle has taken the precaution of leaving the third volume of *Middlemarch* on a train. Virginia Woolf called it, rather oppro-biously, a book for grown-up people, but her own work is lyrically unreconciled to the necessity of ageing: 'Why must they grow up and lose it all?' Mrs Ramsay asks of her brood. Like Wordsworthian infants, Virginia Woolf's people are members of nature, and of one another. To be individuals is their agony, and the sextet in *The Waves* laments the rending pain of separation. Against this bodily sundering, *The Waves* proposes an interpenetration of minds.

Light is the solvent here, just as in *Mrs. Dalloway* it atomises persons into atmospheres, allowing Clarissa to vaporise as 'mist between . . . people' and sending the sky-writing aeroplane on its looping trapeze, like thought, through the air. At noon, '*Light descending in floods dissolved the separate foliation into one green mould*': fission is overcome by affoliation, which is in human terms the affiliation of the six conjoined people. Through Septimus Smith, whose lunacy consists in a faith in the life of trees and the universality of mind and of love along with a scepticism about his own singleness and the reality it is manacled to, Virginia Woolf admits the madness of her method. Rezia, Septimus's wife, like the house-cleaning Mrs McNab, is a traditional novelistic functionary, trying to persuade him that 'they were "people" now' or, as they sit in Regent's Park, placing her hand 'with a tremendous weight on his knee' to anchor and therefore to realise him. Septimus kills himself rather than submit to the prescriptive therapy and insidious mind-control of the antique novel, which recommends—as Dr Holmes does, as if recollecting George Eliot's validation of the wider world and of a charitable extroversion—that he should 'take an interest in things outside himself'. Where characters do not volunteer to expire into pure consciousness, they are mercifully exterminated, so they can be reborn in the minds of others—Mrs Ramsay in Lily's, Percival (the athlete, activist and extrovert won over from the world of objects and empire to that of subjectivity and insubstantiality when he is killed) in the six friends who commemorate and consume him.

The parentheses within which the characters of *To the Lighthouse* abruptly die are the instruments of a novelistic euthanasia. Everything which happens in the novel is made to do so inside brackets—'(Jasper and Rose came in)'—because events are interstices, interruptions of a consciousness whose life is continuous and undifferentiated. The parenthesis puts a cordon around them. As capsules or containers, like those rock pools which Nancy scrutinises and (overcoming the insulation of personality) changes back into the sea, these typographical cells stand for the claustrophobia of being an individual. When they close shut they expunge the self in its solitary confinement, and thus set it free. Ideally they would be boxes with nothing inside them but thin air. *Orlando*, in one of its Sternean jokes, delights in the parenthesis as an eliminator: it frames an abstract blankness, in this case the meaninglessness of narrative duration. Orlando watches the seasons repeat themselves in a long sentence kept going by Virginia Woolf's beloved semi-colons, which she uses elsewhere as end-stoppings, marking off words from one another and thus accusing them of responsibility for our isolation and estrangement. At the end of this cycling, inconsequential review of chronology, Orlando reaches 'a conclusion which, one cannot help feeling, might have been reached more quickly by the simple statement that "Time passed" (here the exact amount could be indicated in brackets) and nothing whatever happened.'

The final phrase, for Virginia Woolf as for Maggie Verver, marks the triumphant achievement—the negative capability—of the novel. Virginia Woolf's last novel defines her form parenthetically, as an intermission: a novel is what happens between the acts of a play, when action is abated. The italic landscapes of *The Waves* are another typographical remonstrance to the novel and its staid, earth-bound language. As an abstractor, Virginia Woolf is concerned with shape-changing. This can mean the soft fluidity to which things in the house impressionistically succumb in *The Waves*; it can also cement the stricture of the Whitehall statues—Pitt, Chatham, Burke and Gladstone—who mobilise armies and sentence young men to death in *Jacob's Room*, and who represent the cubist world of objects at its most stupidly solid. She is concerned therefore as well with the form of words. *The Waves* is about the gap between the differentiated human world and the inextricability of nature, where separate objects and existences are rendered molten by light and made to commingle. Italic print corresponds to that refining of an adipose reality, the territory of Mr Bennett, Mrs Brown and Mrs McNab: it is literally expressive, compressing words and squeezing them closer in the hope of their merger, tilting them away from the vertical as if poising them for flight.

Consciousness in *The Waves* abstracts itself from the body by making pictures of thoughts. The images described by the characters are impressionist hazes (Bernard's ring, quivering in a loop of light) or else cubist blocks of flattened, non-referential pigment (Susan's 'slab of pale yellow' encountering 'a purple stripe'). In their world, saturation means elucidation—the lighthouse beam inspecting the empty house. Vexatious, singular human selves are in retreat. The technical bravura of *Jacob's Room* lies in its refusal to contain him. He impressionistically evanesces; behind him he leaves only the inert, unforthcoming cubes—a chair, some books—which he owned. Genius is a disappearing act, like Chittenden's in the Gare des Invalides, a resort to that bodilessness which impresses Virginia Woolf as a sovereign power when she sees 'a Royal hand attached to an invisible body' on the edge of the box at Covent Garden.

The novel's disconnected paragraphing affords Jacob lacunae in which to make himself scarce. At the same time as being impressionistic blanks, those pictures of an impalpable nothing which Hazlitt criticized in Turner, these empty spaces mark cubism's disintegration of the object into facets. It can only be known partially, from angles which afford inconsistent views. Instead of unifying Jacob and convincing his selves to team up as a person, Virginia Woolf fractures them like Picasso disassembling a face, and compartmentalises him. His room is one compartment, his cubicle at the British Museum another, the pigeon-hole where his walking-stick is stored a third. Each contains only an aspect. Though all the separate walled niches of the reading room comprise 'an enormous mind' (which is how Virginia Woolf, in contrast with Maggie Verver's pastoral subduing of it to rumination, describes the British Museum), that domed and cranial amalgam is 'beyond the power of any single mind to possess it'. And if a multicamerate mind remains less than the sum of its divided parts, then the same cubist rule vivisects the human body: 'In Evelina's shop off Shaftesbury Avenue the parts of a woman were shown separate.' Jacob dies opportunely, to escape the novelist who will nullify him by knowing him.

Towards the end he is ceasing to be a pictorial atmosphere or a discordant cubist puzzle and anthropomorphising himself once more. The human form he reassumes is sculptural: flesh hardened into stone (or, on the river in *Orlando*, kept at degree zero by ice). In Hyde Park he looks 'monolithic', his gaze unwavering. The novel begins to be overtaken by more or less mortuary monuments: the stiffened politicians, 'as smoothly sculptured as the policeman in Ludgate Circus', who make war, and the parliamentary elders on their plinths in Whitehall. At the Erechtheum Jacob senses their threat to him, when he feels 'These statues annulled things so!' Before the clubmen and Cabinet ministers can assign rank, character and manhood to him, conscripting him for that epic of citizenry and military service written by Kipling on what Virginia Woolf calls 'the other side', he wings away. The last exhibit placed in evidence about him is his shoes, items which, ever since Vincent van Gogh's painting of his boots, query the existence they are meant to found and ascertain. What business has a consciousness with footwear?

This dual abstraction seemed to D. H. Lawrence a blasphemy. In the introduction he wrote to his own paintings in 1929, he protests against the obliteration of the world by impressionism, and the splintering assault on it by cubism. Nature has been either etherised by light, rid of its substance and made to shimmer ecstatically as 'illusion, illusion, illusion', or else cracked and fissured as if by Epstein's rock-drill and strewn about (in the phrase Lawrence used of the cubists) as 'a chaos of lumps'. Both catastrophes happen to Jacob; indeed he might be what Lawrence calls, in his mockery of the aesthetics of symbolism and the jargon of Roger Fry and Clive Bell, 'the Holy Ghost of Significant Form'. Certainly the symbol means, to Virginia Woolf, the advent of a bogey. Jacob leaves his letters open as if he expected to return; Septimus does return inside Mrs Dalloway's consciousness, as Mrs Ramsay does in Lily's. The third section of *To the Lighthouse* summarises and completes the first section abstractly (when Lily steps back 'to get her canvas . . . into perspective') and thus spectrally, for its constituents are now conceptual phantoms. Cam, as if dead, looks back to the shore and sees it, too, as the undiscovered country, whose people are 'free like smoke, . . . to come and go like ghosts'.

Lawrence could be describing any Virginia Woolf novel when he says, objecting to the eminence of a form which to him is the answer to a romantic death-wish, 'Landscape is a background with the figures left out.' The writing of the novel is the expunging of those intrusive figures, allowing Lily to contemplate 'the empty places' which are the symbol's havens. In the great study of Hardy he wrote in 1914, Lawrence deplores the fatality of abstraction, and argues that 'whenever art . . . becomes perfect, it becomes a lie.' Though he has the same messianic ambitions for the novel as James and Virginia Woolf, wanting its saturation with a psychic poetry, he conceives of its future differently. Indeed he sees the Jamesian novel as the agent of an enfeebling socialisation, contending that 'man is the only creature who has deliberately tried to tame himself.' The novel, because it understands man solely as a social being, abets this sacrifice of vigour. In this respect Lawrence is closer to the Conradian epic, except that his jungles and hearts of darkness are our physiological thickets: he attends to 'cries far down in our forests of dark veins' and marks out 'a strange dark continent that we do not explore'. (Conrad's imperial geography maps the fundament when Mellors invades Lady Chatterley anally, and brings her to 'the very heart of the jungle of herself'.) He is averse as well to that aesthetic retrenchment which provoked Robert Louis Stevenson to say that James saw life as monstrous in its energetic riot and required art to be 'neat, finite . . . emasculate', and which persuades Virginia Woolf to dissever and sunder her texts, since only spots, moments, scraps and fragments are poetically redeemable.

Lawrence, who believed that 'we need more looseness. . . . an apparent formlessness' (as he said in a translation of Verga's *Cavalleria Rusticana*), returns to the novelistic shape of the Victorians—dynastic, epochal, forever in transit—because it is more apt for representing life as process and passage, and the rites which solemnise those 'places of passing over'. Lawrence speaks of the novel's carbonising (as against those diamantine metaphors which ornament the characters of James, causing the analytic Maggie to resemble 'a little pointed diamond' and making Adam dread being 'scratched by diamonds' which are carved angularities). Scorchingly, it is 'the one bright book of life', and its fire makes light as it reveals 'the changing rainbow of our living relationships'. Yet for all this inflammatory strife, Lawrence is the most devoutly traditional of novelists, growing back into the past as he comes through into the future.

Symbolism in him is not purchased, as by James's characters, for whom it is a prerogative of surfeit and indolence; it is excavated. The social novel remains on the earth's surface. *Sons and Lovers* (1911) begins there with its documentation of the collieries, but mines beneath that crust of convention, retrieving and accruing meaning as it goes, turning Morel the miner into a troglodyte or satyr who only ever washes to the waist and 'below . . . thinks [it] doesn't matter' and who laconically speaks of his initiation at work as when 'I went down'. The colliery serves Lawrence as a creative model, for he treats his rooted characters as geological deposits, disappearing underground. Hardening her heart, Mrs Morel crystallizes; Morel she scorns for having 'no grit'.

Novelistic process is a biological or chemical torment, exposing things to a burning fiery furnace where they will boil down—like Paul in his illness, when all the cells in his body rage to collapse—and be forged anew. Darkness does this to the landscape seen from Nottingham Castle, eroding form into undifferentiated, upheaving mass, a matrix of pain and struggle: an enwombing night, not the mere annihilation blotting out Giles and Isa at Poyns Hall.

A primitive industrial process again lies behind this combustible deforming of objects, not Virginia Woolf's dissipation of them as vapours, mists or gases: Morel smelting metal to mend boots or whittling straws into explosive fuses; Paul unstuffing the straw doll and incinerating it with paraffin on a brick altar, wickedly rejoicing as the wax drips and seethes. Realism is a brutalising system, forcing us to acknowledge only what Paul, miserable in the stocking manufacturer's office, calls 'the outside things'. William Morel is sickened, even maddened by this apprenticeship to the actual and external. Dying, he babbles of commercial consignments and devalued cargoes, like a demented Crusoe. By contrast with the infliction of realism, which possessively kills things, poetic metaphor starts them into life. Mrs Morel sees the cornshocks miraculously bowing, and when Mr Lievers claps his hands the field—as if in response to a thunderous creative fiat—'broke into motion' with startled, skipping rabbits.

Lawrence prescribes his own death for the individual: not the mind's escape from the body (the conundrum Jacob's friends puzzle over) but the mind's retraction into the body, the self's absorption by the species—like Paul 'almost unaware of [Clara] as a person: she was only to him then a woman', and a woman fused with him by the adhesion of mouths; or Paul vitally glorying in the brawl with Baxter because he is a virile challenge, rather than a personal enemy. Lawrence inscribes identity on limbs or faces, and demonstrates how our knowledge of each other is, at its profoundest, skin deep. Hence his descriptions of Paul's knitted brows, Miriam's 'pitiful, resigned arms', Baxter's slackening eyelids. Though the novel is about Paul's rage to be free of his parents, its creative wisdom and its traditionalism plead for reconcilement with them. Morel's job allegorically prefigures Lawrence's: the quest for carbon. And from Paul's anguished observation of his mother—the crow's-feet incised near her eyes, her knuckles swollen by hot water, the terrible stubborn clenching of her mouth against the death-cry that rends her—Lawrence learns another of the morals of his art. As sons and as lovers, we are flesh of the flesh of others; the novel exists to honour that derivation, being 'the highest exampe of subtle inter-relatedness'. It healingly reunites the family of man, and is familially embedded in a literary past which is its heritage.

The novel's resumption of that inheritance is the subject of *The Rainbow* (1915) and *Women in Love* (completed in 1917, published in 1920). *The Rainbow*'s research is into what Ursula, acknowledging her individual paltriness, feels to be 'the great past'. It is a genealogy for the novel, which, like

Anna when Tom marries Lensky's widow, is 'a child without parents'. Lawrence makes possible for it as for Tom a 'new birth', by recovering its ancestry. It begins in the 1840s as a Victorian novel: the man and towing horse crossing the sky in silhouette are characters from Hardy, and the arrival of the industrial canal and the railway are from George Eliot. But as its annals unfurl ahead, they also unfold behind, retrieving old, eternal narrative forms, inexhaustible as genes or genres, prior to the novel's novelty. Thus Tom remembers for Anna 'all the little nursery rhymes and childish songs that lay forgotten at the bottom of his brain'.

The ultimate kinship of all selves and their stories makes the novel a re-convoking of epic, as when 'the children lived the year of Christianity, the epic of the soul of mankind', epic because collective and eternally repetitious. This novel about dooming the real to be 'commonplace unreality' and transfiguring reality as vision at the sign of the rainbow finds a warrant for itself in the Bible, that text so universally prolific of meanings, the progenitor of all subsequent tales and the organ of figuration. As a creation myth, the Bible attains through its exegetes a perpetuity of re-creations. The interpretation of scripture is a constant subject in *The Rainbow*—Will studies emblematic systems, Ursula bothers about the literal truth of the Bible—because therein lies literature's means of equalling Tom Brangwen's urge 'to propagate himself'. Ursula consults Genesis, 'her favourite book' as it was Jane Eyre's, and reminds herself of its injunction to fructify and multiply. Novels began with the impudent misinterpretation of scripture: Shamela's text-tickling, Crusoe's use of his Bible as a guide to winning friends and influencing people above. What they desacralise, Lawrence consecrates anew by showing the Bible's acts forever re-enacted in daily human lives, and announcing incarnations within fertile human bodies. Will the wood-carver learns from Renaissance art because it is skilled in mythological revision and reincarnation, smuggling unregenerate classical spirits into the Christian sacraments, and Lawrence attempts the same synthesis. As well as a muddy midland Eden he invents a pagan Arcady where Ursula (though named, as the girl explains, after a saint) can also be a nymph, Miss Inger a Diana slick and chill from bathing, and Anthony Schofield a goat-god, like a Forsterian Pan. On this there overlaps yet another mythic terrain, Wagner's gloomy north, as opposed to those satyr-thronging southern groves: Gudrun is named after Gutrune from *Götterdämmerung*, so the fabling of the world's beginning in the garden is connected (in *Women in Love*, where the Wagnerism becomes more insistent) with that other fable of its end. And because this typology can extend indefinitely, the sacred denominations are allegorised all over again when the village boys nickname Ursula 'Urtler' and Gudrun 'Good-runner', proverbially mimicking Siegfried's pun when he asks in *Götterdämmerung* if those are good runes he reads in Gutrune's imploring eyes.

With its eternal returns—tidal, seasonal, annual—typology not only confers form on the novel's narrative but becomes a rhythmic habit of its prose. Lawrence is obsessively repetitious because his words catch feelings evolving and must say the same things over and over because each time they mean something new: the shudder or sick after-taste when Ursula stiffens 'in rejection, in rejection'; the pregnant pause which impregnates a glance with meaning when she 'looked at him—looked at him'; the dialectical working-through of contradictions when 'A great mood of humility came over her, and in this humility a bondaged sort of peace. She gave her limbs to the bondage, she loved the bondage, she called it peace.' Perhaps the most astonishing such sentence occurs in *Women in Love*, as Gudrun keeps watch over Gerald's father. It makes music from its varyings, and modulates (goading the cycle to begin again) into its opposite in its punning final word: 'For to realise this death that he was dying was a death beyond death, never to be borne.'

The most synoptic of books, the built scripture inscribing all stories in stone, is the cathedral, and it is Lawrence's self-image for *The Rainbow*. Will, who wants to visit all the cathedrals of England, takes Anna to Lincoln; Ursula sees Rouen with Skrebensky and gives it back all the 'majestic . . . stability' and 'splendid absoluteness' Monet, depicting it as an impressionist mirage, had robbed from it. The analogy of the cathedral achieves the work's anachronistic enlargement: at once Victorian (Will reads Ruskin, and *The Rainbow* is often closer to his mode of architectural epic than to any previous novels) and genuinely medieval, for Lawrence believes that the book is an ark containing, like the lists of Chaucer or Lydgate, all of life. Thus the cathedral's infinitude can be reconstructed inside frail paper walls, as it is when Will's book on Bamberg 'lay in his hands like a doorway', and can be made as well a biological sanctuary, a womb as bountifully seminal as the earth, or as scripture. Anna contains its arched futurity within herself: 'She was a door and a threshold.'

Though it is *The Rainbow*'s continuation, *Women in Love* has lost this unitary faith. It describes not a reborn eternity but a divisive, relative, fractious modernity, and its typology—the link backwards from George Eliot's 'maidens choosing' to Ursula's recollection of Genesis 'where the sons of God saw the daughters of men'; the synthetic pantheon wherein the Brangwen girls are sisters of Artemis while Gerald is branded for his fratricide as Cain and, simultaneously, a Nibelung, the loveless dwarf profiteering in his foul noctural kingdom—twists into parody. The characters play-act their progenitors, in the eurhythmic ballets for up-to-date nymphs choreographed by Hermione, or the gladiatorial ju-jitsu of Birkin and Gerald, limbering up for Homeric savagedom or Wagnerian blood-brotherhood. It is as cosmopolitan as *Daniel Deronda*, yet its traversal of Europe is a symptom of unreality and deracination. Its literary culture is immense—Birkin quotes Browning and argues about Jane Austen, Gudrun is likened to George Eliot's Hetty Sorrell, Turgenev is translated and *Paul et Virginie* cited—yet the texts it employs as prototypes amount to a library only, not a cathedral. The polyglot dialogues of Gudrun and Loerke talk through the entire history of art, discussing Goethe, Mozart, Rousseau, Schiller and Böcklin (among others), yet they recapitulate the chronology in order to end it. Instead of the medieval order which is both past and future in *The Rainbow*, they scorn the futurists and acclaim the primitive ('West African wooden figures, Aztec art'). Living through apocalypse, they are neurotically nostalgic for prehistory.

That disposition has its consequences for the novel's form. In contrast with the burgeoning of narrative as pedigree in *The Rainbow*'s biblical series of begettings, *Women in Love* fragments into anecdotes and analytic episodes, connected solely by their querulous modern demand for diversion. Hence the water-party or the soirées at the Pompadour, the trips to country houses or to Innsbruck. A predatory, dissatisfied humanity has overrun the world and subjugated nature; everything exists to be dissected, and Lawrence tires of the Jamesian symposium—all that 'TALKING' as he says, in angry capitals, in *Lady Chatterley's Lover* (1928). *Women in Love* revenges itself on an anthropomorphism which the novel institutionally props up. It is an attempt, like a tragic *Jacob's Room*, to write a novel without human beings. Its episodes are meditations on the otherness, the unknowability of birds, beasts and flowers, their instinctive existences immune to that novelistic consciousness extolled by Henry James—Mrs Salmon's chattering canaries, the shrill smug robin, Winifred's clawing rabbit, Gerald's stallion, Birkin's cats, the flagrant scarlet fuchsias. Or else it is about things, solid objects, not magicked into art as by James with his spoils of Poynton or atomised into ideas as by Virginia Woolf, but steadfastly attesting to a reality that puling mental humans cannot possess. Virginia Woolf sends Mr Ramsay's table to perch in the tree because it is an intellectual and therefore air-borne quantity; Birkin gives away the chair he buys at the market because he is unworthy of its worn, weathered materiality, and vows to live without furniture. He, not the chair, is the ghost. 'Your things are so lovely!' says Ursula of Birkin's tea-cups. There are excurses on gems, on an African fetish which is Lawrence's negroid Mona Lisa, a wooden woman with 'thousands of years of purely sensual, purely unspiritial knowledge behind her', and on clothes, those intimate caressing sheaths which confirm the body's sensory awareness. Birkin admires Gerald's caftan, and the sisters, in an enraptured, almost religious exchange, calling the coveted silk items 'jewels' and 'real lambs!', agree that 'one gets the greatest joy of all out of really lovely stockings.'

Renewing the novel means for Lawrence either annulling the people who—as he said of *A Passage to India*—so congest and trivialise it, or convincing them to be reborn. *Women in Love* begins with a social wedding, an alliance bolstering the actual, but ends with Birkin's demand for the impossible quartet of relationships which the world disallows. *Lady Chatterley's Lover*, Lawrence's last novel, his bravest and most tragically defeated, ascribes that refusal to the conservatism of a literature it cannot, after all, renew. It is about the failure to attain and hold to the internalised state of complete liberty of which Symons speaks.

Lawrence attempts that internality, even identifying narrative with that oldest of stories, coitus. He calls Michaelis's orgasm 'his crisis'. The word belongs to a theory of plot, where it is the Aristotelian critical moment; it doubles as a theory of lyrical intensification, since poetry was described by Mallarmé as the language of a state of crisis. Lawrence's language is in crisis here because of its desire to keep faith with this orgasmic condition. Yet how can it do so except by exhausting repetition? 'Rippling, rippling, rippling, like a flapping overlapping of soft flames . . . it was over too soon, too soon. . . . This was different, different.' The novel divides itself between this poetic exacerbation (setting words to compete with the coital ache of Wagner's chromaticism, Lawrence's obsession since 1912 in *The Trespasser*, whose hero Siegmund is a violinist in the orchestra at Covent Garden) and irate, prosaic editorialising about England and the industrial age. It comes to mistrust literary language, which has let it down. The sterilised Clifford's career as a *littérateur* is his badge of repression and of inauthentication. He is a voluntary exile even from his nativity in language, preferring French. He reads Racine and Proust, educates Mrs Bolton in saying '*j'adoube*' when they play chess, and chatters about Venice in slangy French. Against him, Mellors is a linguistic renegade, who knows French and German, can lard his conversation with Spanish and Latin tags, but reverts to the subterranean and unliterary idiom of Derbyshire dialect, giving Connie lessons in its pronunciation: he corrects her imitated 'Ay!' to 'Yi!'

Connie asks in her torment, 'Was it real? Was it real? . . . Was it real?' This is the rhetorical question of all fiction, to which modern novels mostly hope for an answer in the negative. Mr Surrogate the corrupt ideologue in Graham Greene's *It's a Battlefield* (1934) needs his abstract theory to counteract his dismayed disbelief 'that these things were real—Capitalism and Socialism', while Conder the journalist invents bogus existences for himself in fantasy and by seeing life metaphorically can make 'his discontent . . . as unreal as his world'. Connie's appeal is answered, much later, by Mellors, but then not in the obsolete language to which she clings. Stroking her 'two secret openings', he assures her, 'Th'art real, th'art real.'

At the same time as its splits off from a language too genteelly circumspect, the novel, assuming a duty to maintain a continuity with 'the old England' and 'connexion with the Elizabethans', recovers a literary tradition for itself. Mellors's dialect, being optional, is as much an artifice as the Greek of Sidney's Arcadian shepherds; shit, piss, arse and cunt are the vocables of an inverse poetic diction. When he twines forget-me-nots in Connie's pubic hair and adorns her mound of Venus, he is resurrecting the genital deities of Spenser's Garden of Adonis. The novel is, in fact, a pastoral—set not in a garden of thought like James's at Fawns or Virginia Woolf's at Kew but in an off-limits, carnal Eden. Clifford quotes a poetic simile likening violets to the lids of Juno's eyes. Though Connie rejects it, thinking the Elizabethans 'rather upholstered', her love for Mellors inducts her into an Elizabethan pleasance where godhead can be regained because sexual love is our mythic self-immortalising. She who at first is Persephone, ejected from hell into a cold spring, briefly but revocably becomes the rampant Venus of Shakespeare and Spenser. Mellors instructs a painter to portray them as 'Vulcan and Venus under the net of art. I used to be a blacksmith, before I was a game-keeper.'

The fall from this bodily joy, when it occurs, is a lapse into literature. The novel ends, as *Howards End* (reluctantly) begins, with a succession of letters. In Forster these are unwelcome emissaries of events, interrupting a meditative peace. Pressed to begin a novel by them, he is sentenced again to the world of telegrams and anger. In Lawrence the letters are a deadening epilogue, translating experience into literature. Clifford, who can only describe the return of Bertha Coutts to Mellors's bed in circumlocutory Latin or allude to Mellors's preference for <u>recondite</u> sexual postures by mentioning Cellini, rewrites the pastoral as mock-epic, archly dubbing Bertha 'the Venus of Stacks Gate' and her consort the Apollo of Tevershall. Mellors is captured by literature, reduced to a character: first Rabelais, next de Sade, then Don Rodrigo from the Spanish ballad. And he assents in the declension. The novel's final exhibit (unannounced by Lawrence, as if he had already given up in despair) is his letter to Connie, which admits the addictive routine of writing—'Now I can't even leave off writing to you'—and acknowledges language's origination in absence and incapacity: 'Well, so many words, because I can't touch you. If I could sleep with my arms around you, the ink could stay in the bottle.' The writer is the failed lover. No wonder T. S. Eliot so penitentially dissevered the man who suffers (or loves) from the mind which, disinterestedly, creates.

Though its last words are depressed, *Lady Chatterley's Lover* does contain a syllabus for a renewed, millenial literature. It comprises the works on Mellors's shelf in his hut, reviewed by Connie who is gratified to find 'he was a reader after all'. He has 'books about Bolshevik Russia, books of travel, a volume about the atom and the electron, another about the composition of the earth's core, and the causes of earthquakes: then a few novels: then three books on India.' All these books are significant for Lawrence, which is why he does not accord them titles. They exist in potential, and will have to be written by others. They sum up his effort to start revolution in the novel by treating it as a species of biology (in *The Rainbow's* account of psychic nucleolation), geology or physics, in succession to George Eliot's natural history; the documentation of travel refers both to his other effort to expatriate the novel, to rescue it from England with (as Gudrun says in Innsbruck) its dampening gloom and its compulsory socialisation, and to the hunted itinerancy of his own career with its residences in Italy, Australia, Mexico and the American south-west. In this register of <u>seditious</u> apocrypha only the 'few novels', on loan from a circulating library, seem <u>inapposite</u> and <u>supernumerary</u>.

37

The Waste Land
and the Wastobe Land

As an ultimate proof of English literature's continuity, there is no secession in it of the modern from the past. No period is more eclectically traditional than that of modernism: the contemporary means the simultaneous presence of all the past. Applied to literary history, the relativity theory turns temporal succession into spatial companionship. Forster sees all the novelists at a round table in the British Museum reading room, at work on books which amount to a single compendious book, just as Thomas Dekker in *A Knight's Conjuring* (1607) had described all the poets harboured together in the Fortunate Isles; T. S. Eliot can in 'East Coker' (1940) walk back into the writing of his remote ancestor Thomas Elyot by quoting his *Boke Named the Gouvernour* (1531), while Orlando lives through all of English literature from Shakespeare to Virginia Woolf and, constantly scribbling, recomposes it into a many-branching, exfoliating unity in her immense, organic, abundantly selling poem *The Oak Tree*. Bloom in *Ulysses* (1922) swiftly abridges that proliferation into a formula for endless recurrence: 'Past was is today. What now is will then tomorrow as now was be past yester.'

The time-zones of the *Four Quartets* turn this simultaneity of literary history into a spiritual problem. Krishna in 'The Dry Salvages' (1941) declares the future to be already the past, a premature state of nostalgia. This theory is Eliot's reconciliation to his complaint, in an essay of 1936, that Milton had anticipated and thus prevented what came after him. Now that the future is futureless, the poet must write backwards not forwards. This is an imperative of Krishna's mysticism, and of Eliot's own classicism, which sees each new work as an addition to the past. Against evolutionary notions, Eliot proposes that history is pattern, consisting of immutable 'timeless moments'. Instead of growth, its principle is that of figural re-enactment: it can be savingly 'renewed, transfigured, in another pattern', or else left to the perdition of disfigurement, like the bombed street in 'Little Gidding' (1942). Either way it is as ideally motionless as the Chinese jar in 'Burnt Norton' (1935).

Yeats contrived the same spatial recension of serial, literary time in the self-made zodiac of *A Vision*. In 1922 he assigned his predecessors and his contemporaries together to twenty-eight temperamental lunar phases, housing them all on a 'great wheel' which revolves through the heavens as fixedly and uneventfully as Eliot's jar. Creativity means truth to the horoscope as plotted by Yeats: Shakespeare meekly concurs with his astrological reading and is therefore 'the greatest of modern poets'; out of phase, Shelley takes to angry pamphleteering and Carlyle is fated by the constellations to raucous, rhetorical assertion, while under another configuration Shaw and Wells are condemned to the falsity of domineering intellect. At the system's centre is a moment as sacredly eternalised as a Joycean epiphany, or as Eliot's 'winter's afternoon, in a secluded chapel' blessed by light: of Phase Fifteen Yeats has 'no description except that this is a phase of complete beauty', to which all poetry tends or from which it declines.

If, in poetry, history is something to be redeemed, as it is by Yeats's astrology or Eliot's incarnation when it punctuates time, in the novel it need not be cancelled because it can be, all at once, contained. Virginia Woolf sends the novel's career into reverse in *Jacob's Room*. Dismissing the ponderously solid novels of the eminent Victorians, she writes one adhering to the procedures of their predecessors. 'The eighteenth century has its distinction', she notes of the panelling in Jacob's lodging. Jacob's 'mystic book' is *Tom Jones*. The novel which has always been praised for its account of a complete man, warts, unruly genitals and all, is adopted as a prototype in a novel which is its antithesis, being about a man so incomplete and fragmented that he is not there at all. In *Between the Acts*, where old Bartholemew contentedly reviews the laden book-shelves, Miss La Trobe is said to have 'the whole of English literature to choose from' for her pageant. Parodically restaging that literary past by cramping it into a single afternoon like Eliot at Little Gidding, Virginia Woolf also contradicts the pageant's jaunty evolution by unearthing ever deeper pasts which are insistently present. Poyns Hall is the lumber-room of the national museum, stocked with mid-Victorian furniture, boasting an indeterminately ancient arch ('Norman? Saxon?') and a barn locally thought to resemble a Greek temple. A guide book from 1833 is quoted, yet beyond that there are reports of 'the great eighteenth-century winter'.

Literature, like the house, is the heirloom of an extended family. (Dekker's Chaucer had installed Spenser in the chapel of Apollo and adopted him as a son; Milton relates himself to the same ancestry by telling Dryden that Spenser was his master—and by in turn making Dryden his disciple.) But though old Bart and Mrs Swithin are the remembering elders who maintain the literature—he reveres books as 'the treasured life-blood of immortal spirits' and poets as 'the legislators of mankind', she acknowledges writers as ancestors, 'the poets from whom we descend by way of the mind'—the novel senses the uprooting of this generative, collective life, and a return to an age which predates literature. Mrs Swithin's current reading is Wells's *Outline of History*. That is a work of cosmic optimism, and it is contradicted by her atavistic imagination. She re-sows rhododendron forests in Piccadilly, and re-merges 'the entire continent, not then . . . divided by a channel'. Wells's primitives, eventually supplanted by his hypernaturally lucid moon-men, have not been outgrown in *Between the Acts*. The name of the boy who delivers the fish is recorded in the Domesday Book, a local dowager is 'the indigenous, the prehistoric', and Giles, when he reverts to sulking infancy, regresses to savagery: 'He kicked—a flinty yellow stone, . . . edged as if cut by a savage for an arrow. A barbaric stone. . . . Stone-kicking was a child's game.'

Stephen declares in *Ulysses* that 'history is a nightmare from which I am trying to awake'. Joyce's previous works make their escape into nothingness: the deathly snow which ends *Dubliners* (1914), Stephen's disappearance at the end of *A Portrait of the Artist as a Young Man* (1916) into silence, exile and the aloofness of aesthetic deity. Instead of elimination, *Ulysses* proposes an affectionate inclusion. It begins and ends with benedictions of a nature the previous works deny: Mulligan's matutinal blessing of 'the tower, the countryside and the awaking mountains' leads at length to Molly's panting catalogue—'God of heaven theres nothing like nature the wild mountains then the sea and the waves rushing then the beautiful country with fields of oats and wheat and all kinds of things.' The muses of the history Stephen is employed to teach are 'the daughters of memory'. At the outset they dictate a dull rote-learning, in the catechistic lesson about the Romans, but the later catechism in Bloom's house is an invigorating trial of 'mnemotechnic', arguing the novel's aspiration to a total recall of human experience; and though the repetitions of the school-room are numbing—for Stephen's pupils history is 'a tale . . . too often heard'—that same principle, enunciated by Bloom on the beach when (remembering previous sappy Junes of wooing) he says 'History repeats itself', becomes the work's mythic solace.

Repetitiousness is the stability of history, whose motive, in Bloom's fantasies of courting, is love. The awakening from history is made possible by myth, and by love. At the lying-in hospital Bloom says that 'Force, hatred, history [are] not life for men and women'; they are 'the opposite of that that is really life'. Asked what that opposite condition is, he replies 'Love'. And his Christ-like redeeming love for the teeming, shoddy reality of the world sets off a mythic procreation, a swelling exponentiation, in the word itself: 'Love loves to love love.' Conjugation is copulation. Bloom rigs up an impromptu pedigree of concupiscence, which concludes that 'this person loves that other person because everybody loves somebody but God loves everybody.' Earlier he had thought the priest's welcoming of Dignam into paradise to be formulaic, unfelt because repetitious: 'Says that over everybody.' Now he knows that impartiality to be a human—as it is for Joyce a literary and linguistic—responsibility. The god with whom Stephen allies himself in *A Portrait* is a disdainful aesthete; the god thanked in the lying-in hospital as 'the Author of my days!' or invoked by Molly is a rampant creator, in homage to whom *Ulysses* not only encompasses the whole of creation but, like Spenser describing Genius's guardianship of the portal, describes the living we do before and after we are officially born—the embryo's development, the hanged man's erection.

Like Dickens, Joyce returns the novel to its patriarchal origins in

Shakespeare, present throughout *Ulysses* as a type of all-embracing goodness: Bloom thinks that Martin Cunningham, 'sympathetic human man', looks like Shakespeare. From tragicomedy issues the novel's friendly union of opposites. Chuckling on their way to Dignam's burial, Bloom, Dedalus and their fellows are Johnson's mourner and reveller combined, conjoining funeral and festivity. Behind the episode lies Shakespeare's situating of death within life. Bloom recollects Romeo's 'love among the tombstones', Hamlet's causerie with the gravediggers, and Antony's exhibition of Caesar's body, whose wounds are strident mouths with flapping tongues: all occasions when death, supposedly the tragic terminus, is lived through with a bold comic heroism and thus, as in Falstaff's resurrection at Shrewsbury, recovered from. This is myth's eternal return—to earth, when Bloom imagines the soil fattened by corpse manure, and to that cosy charnel of which Molly is trustee and where she salts away a banana: 'theyre all mad to get in there where they come out of.'

Ulysses restates at its beginning the predicament of infidel, disorderly reality with which nineteenth-century literature concludes. Mulligan, holding the mirror up to Stephen as Hamlet had held it up to nature, quotes 'the rage of Caliban at not seeing his face in the glass': realism is a disgruntled spoiling of romanticism. And like Wilde's Bosie, the despairing realist ends in the gutter, as a debased naturalist. Thus Mulligan places in evidence the snot-green nose-rag of the bard. But if romanticism has fallen from grace into realism and has then further sullied itself as naturalism, it can be restored as symbolism. Like Bloom pondering the wormy, pullulating graveyard, Stephen thinks the ground can be mined for archetypes: poets can 'wrest old images from the burial earth'.

In *A Portrait* the artistic symbol is literally a robbery from religion, which it seeks to supplant. The schoolboys who capture the monstrance know that 'God was not in it of course when they stole it.' Like the Grail in Tennyson, or in *Parsifal* or *The Golden Bowl*, the symbol has been relieved of religious duties so that it can fulfil new artistic ones. Beerbohm could therefore pertinently demand, in a cartoon, what Tennyson's knights were going to *do* with the chalice when they found it, since for them its value inhered in its uselessness. The Stephen of *Ulysses* cannot remain content with his earlier self's Dedalan flight from reality. The 'uncreated conscience' towards which he flees turns out to be the biological mystery and religious miracle he ponders, thinking about midwifery, as 'creation from nothing', when a child is hauled 'squealing'—for in Joyce, life is announced by sound and the nascence of language—'into life'. The real cannot be romantically elided, or naturalistically soiled and shamed. It must be accepted, and when it is it will be seen as a symbol, invested everywhere, even at its foulest or most trivial, with creative meaning. In this sense Joyce's vision and his procedures are medieval. Since the world is a supplementary scripture, literature need only take inventory of its contents, like Chaucer's Monk with his anthologies of tales or Lydgate with his tables;

and because words are the marvel of creation, literature can do no better than attempt a *summa* of them as well. The programme Stephen scholastically phrases as the 'ineluctable modality of the visible' has as its counterpart the infinite modulability of the audible. *Ulysses* is full of every possible sound the body can emit or imitate, from the bawled 'maaaaaa' of the baptised infant Bloom thinks of or the 'pa pa pa pa pa pa pa' of Cissy's baby to the agonised death-rattle of Stephen's mother and the apocalyptic 'Pwfungg!' of the expiring gas-jet; its vocabulary extends from a cancelled negative—when 'POST NO BILLS' is in part erased so the prohibition becomes a bountiful multiple, 'POST 110 PILLS'—to the simpering affirmatives of Mrs Breen with her 'Yes, yes, yes, yes, yes, yes, yes', or Molly's 'yes I said yes I will Yes.' Words exist, as the world does, to be both seen and heard. Like a medieval illustrator Joyce causes them to germinate by his decorative distortions of them: each page resembles the 'illuminated scroll of ancient Irish vellum' presented to Virag.

Looking with a horrified commiseration at the schoolboy Sargent who cannot do his sums, Stephen asks, 'Was that then real? The only true thing in life?' The child has been made real, made to signify, because a mother 'had loved him, borne him'. The phantasmagoria of Night-town proposes that nothing is real, everything the wish-fulfilling performance of a scenario devised by the id: hence Bloom's kinky playlets, and Stephen's therapeutic staging of *Hamlet*. The episode is in dramatic form because it sees the mind as a theatre of flickering shadows and psychic bogeys; a brothel where the subconscious is its own obliging procurer. As a novel, *Ulysses* has a mission different from this theatrical one of staging fantasies. It must, like Sargent's mother, endow things with reality by loving them. Its realism manifests appetency, even appetite.

The Hegelian 'totality of objects' catalogued by epic are here lip-lickingly edible—Bloom's sausages and his sweet citrus soap, the pungent mockturtle oxtail mulligatawny over which he mentally slavers and the green cheese he feeds on, Virag's fondness for gooseberry fool, Molly's meal of tender chicken, Boylan's experimental fondling of tomatoes, the onion-breathed shopman and the candied 'sugarsticky girl'. Bloom regurgitates a delicious moment of communion when he kisses Molly who, eating a seedcake, transfers its chewed mawkish pulp from her mouth to his. He has a dietary theory of literature, believing aestheticism to be a consequence of malnutrition (as he reflects in the case of A.E.'s apparently vegetarian companion). He is right, because language is an oral pleasure. Hence the cooing, warbling chorus of the kisses which flock round him in Night-town, and the mastication of words by the gross diners in the Burton restaurant who speak with their mouths full: 'I munched hum un thu Unchster Bunk un Munchday.'

Joyce's Dublin is real as Virginia Woolf's London refuses to be, because it can be smelled, tasted, apprehended by the body. She specifies in *Mrs Dalloway* that the rumour of a royal shopping exhibition passes down Bond

Street 'invisibly, inaudibly, like a cloud'. Impressionism hazily confounds sight and stifles speech. Yet though Bloom wonders, watching the blind stripling, at the 'queer idea of Dublin he must have', it is an accurate idea because he negotiates an olfactory city, as vividly present as the odour of lacerated nail fragments so relished by Bloom himself. Bloom realises that the blind man is oriented by 'sense of smell' and by tastes (which, as Proust discovered, are shortcuts to memory). He perceives Dublin exactly as the sand-blind Joyce did Trieste, Zurich and Paris: by the sensual alertness and avidity of imagination. Coincidences, the instigators of urban narrative, are corporeal encounters in Joyce, acts of samaritarism. When Bloom sees Parnell's brother pass by, he assumes there 'must be a corporation meeting today'. It was Mulligan who dressed his bee sting; and the tenuous 'connecting link' between Bloom and Stephen through Mrs Riordan is an umbilical tie, since Bloom has performed a 'special corporal work of mercy for her'. By contrast, because Virginia Woolf's characters wear the body unwillingly and consider it to be 'nothing at all', its coincidence with another has no empathetic or charitable virtue. Her London is a filmy web of vagrant minds. Lady Bruton's lunch guests are 'attached to her by a thin thread' which tautens and refines as they leave her until it snaps and she—unable to maintain its cohesion—falls uncaringly asleep. The collectivity of mind in Virginia Woolf depends on there being no bodily approximation; hence the cerebral interchange between Clarissa and Septimus, whom she never meets and who is in any case providentially dead.

Even when they are not physically entangled, Joyce's characters are consorting in and with the gregarious plenum of language. Garrulity is the ground of their society: at the hospital, 'discursiveness . . . seemed the only bond of union between tempers so divergent'. The omnipresent liveliness of the city is adept, like myth, at self-dissemination, and extols 'the bounty of increase'. Dublin throngs with stories, all wanting to be told at once. Only Stephen, in a reversion to *Dubliners*, practises the alienated, abbreviated, solitary form of the short story—like the one he constructs at Bloom's house, where a man and a woman, disconnected, read and write in a lonely hotel. Against the cellulation of the short story, the novel exults in populousness; against its shortness, in an epic longevity and in tireless longueurs. Bloom, looking at the stars, compares their eternity with the 'parenthesis of infinitesimal brevity' which is a human life. To have children is one means of self-prolongation; to speak or to write are others, for words in Joyce are a plentiful, budding family.

The metempsychosis which is a principle of mythic narrative, allowing the minds of the Homeric characters to commute into these Dubliners, is an unruly skill of language, too. It overtakes that word itself, when Molly takes it apart as 'met him pikehoses' or as 'met something with hoses in it': the pun is a transmigration of words, and a way of chewing and melding them, savouring them edibly and introducing them to opposites they might otherwise shun, as when Bloom dissolves Our Lady of Carmel in his mouth by thinking 'sweet náme too: carmel', caramelising the sacred place. Words have their own genetic laws of cross-breeding and perpetuation. Bloom's name, sacrificially slaughtered when he misreads 'Blood of the Lamb' as 'Bloo . . . Me?', or butchered by a misprint which inserts it in the newspaper as *L. Boom*, is healingly headlined by the typesetters, upraised to Bloomdom and to supremacy in 'the new Bloomusalem'. Or it can commingle and mate with Stephen's name, when they change into Stoom and Blephen. Since language is a family, a city, a world—an entire, abounding creation—Joyce instinctively anthropomorphises the alphabet. Bloom hears schoolchildren reciting it in a slurred, musical legato: 'Ahbeesee defegee kelomen opeecue rustyouvee double you.' (The sentence ends, reproductively, with duplication.) Later the men with sandwich-boards perform the roles of separate letters when they parade H.E.L.Y.'S. through the streets. When the 'S plods by, the apostrophe itself is apostrophised. A.E. is a pair of ambulant initials, and the rear admiral is attended by a serried troop of them—K.G., K.P., K.T., P.C., K.C.B., M.P., J.P. . . . and so on indefinitely. For Gerty, words send out sprouting tendrils like the illuminated capitals in medieval books: she dreams of 'Society with a big ess.' In the games of charades which Bloom recalls, people enact words, with the gymnastic double-jointedness of Erté's balletic alphabet. And even bodily emissions conform to the figurations of print. Bloom's urine emerges in the shape of a bifurcated Y. By contrast, the Woolfian alphabet is a march exclusively of mind, a relay of spindly capitals which decline to stand for anything in particular. Mr Ramsay has thought himself as far as Q but despairs of toiling on through the frigid wastes to R; no one ever gets as far as Z.

Ulysses attempts a demonstration of all the capacities of language. Swift in the *Tale of a Tub* had seen journalism as the mockery of literature by manufacture. Joyce at the newspaper office (Homer's cave of the winds) discerns the inadvertent poetry of the industry. The newspaper is a metaphor for the city: it compartmentalizes people in its paragraphs, yet also thrusts them into random collisions. As well, and again like the city, it requires the arcane, detective ingenuity of decipherment. Symbolist poems are written backwards; lines of type—like 'mangiD. kcirtaP.'—must be read backwards. This reversibility, as in Lenehan's twin palindrome 'Madam, I'm Adam. And Able was I ere I saw Elba', grants to language that power of infinite replication possessed by Yeats's multiplicity of imagistic mirrors. Ultimately Joyce dreams of a word which will be able, spreading in both directions at once, to circumnavigate the word thanks to its fertile self-compounding. Nationalgymnasiummuseumsanatoriumandsuspensoriumsordinaryprivatdocentgeneralhistoryspecialprofessordoctor Kriegfried Ueberallgemein is just about entitled to that engirdling universality; some of Joyce's astoundingly prolix sentences in the episode at the cabman's shelter seem, like Ulysses, to traverse the earth before limping home to the place from where they so long ago set out.

This athletic prowess of language enables Joyce to interpret journalism as a vocal art, like ancient epic poetry. The newspaper calls itself 'A GREAT DAILY ORGAN' and serves as a public mouth; print or typesetting (as Whitman realised, praising the 'many-cylinder'd steam printing-method' of the Hoe method) is an eugenic mechanising of propagation. Every copy it generates has its own life-cycle, commuting through 'various uses, thousand and one things' (like the migrant spirits of myth) to end as wrapping for meat, or as Bloom's means of wiping himself in the privy. Print garrulously seeks relief from its own silence. Bloom hears the paper-sorting machine saying 'sllt' and the door creaking: 'Doing its level best to speak. . . . Everything speaks in its own way', and elsewhere *Ulysses* describes the bardic barking of a red setter and has Lord Harry study 'a grammar of the bull's language'. The headlines which divide Joyce's sections or columns are an attempt, in their silent noise, to speak, and they find a voice in the newsboys who rush from the office to shout them throughout the city. Bloom's trade of advertising is also epically ennobled here. The ad is heroic broadcasting, the ego's thunder: 'There's a hurricane blowing', says the editor. Trying to place his notice, Bloom enters 'puffing'. The ad itself constitutes a puff, a modestly megaphonic version of what O'Madden Burke calls the 'divine afflatus', which is oratory. This inflation is a flatulent medical symptom when the hospital chapter writes Johnsonese: with their 'incipient ventripotence' and 'ovoblastic gestation', the sentences bulge into an hysterical pregnancy. Mulligan's ponderously jovial 'conceit' is both witticism and a physical conception like the embryos he delivers.

Mallarmé scorned what he described as a vulgarly journalistic style, and sought to win over language to the non-referential freedom of poetry. For Joyce, journalism is itself boldly poetic, and its redaction of days ('That was in eightyone, sixth of May' or 'Have you *Weekly Freeman* of 17 March?') serves to balance myth's attention to aeons. No kind of writing is excluded from Joyce's ample polity. Stenography, for instance, is welcome because it can keep up with the jottings of the subconscious mind, as in Bloom's dictation to himself of the letter to Martha: 'It is utterl imposs. Underline *imposs*. To write today. . . . In haste. Henry. Greek ee.'

The almost biological urge of words to find partners accounts for their incorporation in one another as portmanteaux. The crowd pursuing Bloom shrieks 'helterskelterpelterwelter': it is a compound and so is the word naming it, and so are the words it utters—'Stopabloom! Stopperrobber!' More discreetly, words implode and interpenetrate, as in the brand names of the products Bloom merchandises, Bacilikil for insect powder or Uwantit for a multipurpose pocket-knife. Hospitable to all things, Joyce's language groans with lists like that of the Cyclops's livestock. It enumerates the innumerable, as epic has always done, from Homer's ships to Crusoe's ledger (except in Milton, with his numberless devils).

For similar reasons it has an infinite tolerance of cliché, in which it venerates a proverbial wisdom. The cliché means an apparatus for duplication. Even repetition is an addition to its family. As well, in Flaubert's dictionary of *idées reçues*, it is an heirloom, a tribal heritage received from the past, like language itself. So Joyce treats the time-honoured adages from which the episode in the shelter near Butt's Bridge is made with the respect due to linguistic elders. These formulae have a gentle, experienced social tact, distending to occupy the silences of the taciturn Stephen: 'There ensued a somewhat lengthy pause.' While professing 'to cut a long story short', the cliché takes pains to keep it going, covering awkward interims. It is a spell for ensuring participation and concord, as in the succession of clichés Bloom employs to defuse the antagonism between England and Ireland. His worn customary phrases are a 'common parlance': like Johnsonian poetry, they command unanimity, echoed by every bosom; like the periodic syntax of James, for instance in the elaborate prevarications which lengthen the opening paragraph of *The Ambassadors*, they have a diplomatic finesse at avoidance.

Joyce also admires the industrious indefatigability of print, gathering and distributing information which would seem useless if it were not so archaeologically precious, enabling an object like the jar of Plumtree's potted meat to remember its provenance and to honour its maker, thanks to the loquacity of its label. Always Joyce indicates the humane purpose of language, which is indeed the defining talent of our humanity. Words are grown by and within our bodies, and when ventilated—by song, or by the gruff tornado of air resonated from the cave of citizen Cyclops's mouth—they are the breath of life. Hence the book's membrification of itself, assigning each chapter to the tutelage and patronage of a bodily part. The library is the abode of brain, the Cyclops's tavern of muscle, the lilting sirens enchant the ear while the Circean brothel confounds the locomotor apparatus. *Ulysses* anthropomorphises literary form, and thus its summary symbol of language and of itself is the flagrant Molly, the fleshly volume—'I in my skin'—who envelops it all, having engorged it. She worries, significantly, that 'my belly is a bit too big', but mostly marvels at 'what we have inside us'. What she has inside her is the world and its image, the book. She is the dormant genius of Joyce's language, the matrix of that generative faculty which is human speech, and she subliminally reunites all the idioms sundered at Babel. Reclaiming a sentence of Spanish from the depths she congratulates herself on her retentiveness: 'See I haven't forgotten it all I thought I had only for the grammar.'

Like the gladly promiscuous Molly, Joyce includes the many in order to demonstrate their oneness. It is the ambition of Spenser who also, in pursuance of it, 'writ no language' in particular but many; and is undone by Milton, who in revision of Spenser's union of all mythologies sought to establish the historicity of a single myth and the authority of a single language. *Ulysses* cannot only be a single-handed history of literature. It must at the same time act as a genealogy for all languages. Its imperative is not the dialectal purifying that Mallarmé passed on to Eliot, but amalgam. Like Bloom the Jew who is of no nation and therefore vagrantly of all, Joyce does not linguistically exile himself from English—like Haines the Englishman prattling Gaelic, revered by the milk-woman as 'a grand language' although she mistakes it for French, or like Lenahan adopting a French lingo to rail against the English—but punningly seeks its reunion with every other speech, making it, like music, international.

It is the lyricism of Italian which prompts Simon Dedalus to call it 'the only language'. Bloom knows that melody is a numerical system and can thus intuit the deep structure of all languages, for which he has a convivial, compounded name: 'Musemathematics.' (Pope's Mathesis in *The Dunciad* was not mad at all, but a musical prophetess.) Stephen espouses abstract alternatives to language, which threatens him because it inveigles him into kinship. Lynch says 'he likes dialectic, the universal language', and Stephen propounds his own scheme for compounding the senses, neither in the colour-organs and olfactory correspondences of Mallarmé nor in Wagner's operatic merger of all subordinate arts but in Yeats's plays for dancers, written in esperanto because they require no words: 'gesture, not music, not odours, would be a universal language.' Both modes are counsels of despair. Dialectic is a mechanism for contradiction and cancellation, the dance is a revoking of 'the gift of tongues'. Later, like Sterne's characters, Bloom and Stephen try to arrive at a *lingua franca* by exercises in translation. In a solemn exchange, Stephen writes down 'the Irish characters for gee, eh, dee, em' while Bloom draws 'the Hebrew characters ghimel, aleph, daleth'. Yet the fraternal offering is in vain because neither can speak the language he can write. Their knowledge is futilely 'theoretical, being confined to certain grammatical rules of accidence and syntax and practically excluding vocabulary': a dead language is one which cannot be vocalised. However, though they do not recognise it, they have already by the mutuality of their affection learned the universal language. Bloom calls song, in a cliché which is a precious truth, 'language of love'. Stephen asks his mother's ghost to impart to him, if she now knows it, 'the word known to all men', and subsequently answers his own question when he reflects, 'Love, yes. Word known to all men.'

He owes the revelation, and the ending of his quarrel with his mother, to the parental source of his own language in Shakespeare, for at that moment he is pondering *Pericles* and the natural magic of its deaths and rebirths by water, which restore to the hero the supposedly perished mother of Marina. Eliot assumed the character of Pericles in 'Marina' (1930). His poem is about the image as a revenant from the grave, the uprisen facsimile of something irretrievably lost, and Eliot's Pericles, resigning 'my speech for that unspoken', volunteers to join his daughter in death. But the Pericles of Joyce—who is both Bloom and Stephen—regains in life mother, wife and child. The image for Joyce's characters is not 'unsubstantial, reduced by a wind' to ghostliness as in Eliot; it bodes literal, miraculous resurrection. 'Will he not see reborn in her', asks Stephen, 'with the memory of his own youth added, another image?' The recognition heals Stephen. The same imagistic second coming is the wonder of *Ulysses* which, by remembering and reconciling itself with the tradition whose issue it is, rejuvenates that tradition.

The Waste Land (1922) is about its own poetic forebears; is indeed assembled or spelled (to use Eliot's first choice for the line about the shoring of fragments against our view) from them. Yet it reviews literary history as a cemetery, and rather than revivifying the past broods over its interment. Joyce sees history and literature endlessly and gleefully repeating themselves. Eliot appraises modernity as a dead end. Committing himself to that stilled, completed past—achieving the self-entombing which to him was the grave behest of classicism—he writes as if he were a ghost, like the man who says 'it seems that I have been a long time dead' in an early draft of *The Waste Land*, like Tiresias, or like Prufrock pretending to be Lazarus. He played patience, the game he also assigns to Edward in his play *The Cocktail Party* (1950), as a self-mortifying rite, the occupation of an aching and tedious eternity: he enjoyed the steady arrival at cancellation, when all cards are rendered null, because (as he told Auden) it was so like being dead.

The waste land is the devastated inheritance of culture, to which the present lays waste. Eliot's poem is about iconoclasm, idol-smashing. It purposely dissevers itself, then obstructs its own interpretative reassembling. It first exhibits a 'heap of broken images', which the soiled river nymphs fumble to reconnect with 'broken fingernails of dirty hands' and which are, for a moment only, arranged into the authoritarian statue of 'a broken Coriolanus'. Joyce punningly paraphrases this bone-yard in *Finnegans Wake* (1939) as 'the wastobe land'—the once and future kingdom of his own linguistic plenty—and saves Eliot from the morbid consequence of his vision by enrolling the waste land in a study of comparative mythology, which equates it with the pastorals it sought, vainly, to desecrate. It is 'a lottuse land, a luctuous land, Emeraldilluim, the peasant pastured.' Might not Eliot be, despite himself, the successor of the poet Stephen Dedalus refers to as 'Lawn Tennyson?'

Joyce's correction of Eliot is the more necessary because *The Waste Land* was prompted in part by Eliot's reading of the early sections of *Ulysses*—or rather by his misreading of them. For Eliot persisted in believing *Ulysses* to be an imposition of order and pattern, by its predestining use of myth, on an otherwise meaningless modern reality. This is Eliot's own aim, and is responsible for the process of attrition and deduction by which he makes poetry. But Joyce has a positive delight in disorder, and wants his work to contain everything and everyone, just as Eliot needs to feel (with the help of the

Occam's razor editorially wielded by Ezra Pound) that the poetry has excluded as much as possible, punished itself to attain what he calls at the end of the *Four Quartets*

> A condition of complete simplicity
> (Costing not less than everything).

Joyce's way is that of surfeit, Eliot's that of abstinence, and they are not the same. Even when Joyce orders himself, in the catechistic exam in *Ulysses*, to 'reduce Bloom . . . to a negligible negative irrational unreal quantity', he achieves his multiplication, as Bloom is geometrically expounded into a thronging company of other selves. Joycean reduction cannot help but be aggrandisement. Joyce's 'hugeness'—the honorofic title Bloom uses when worshipping his instructress in the brothel—is what James called the 'muchness' of the Victorians.

Pound is essential to *The Waste Land* because he is an agent of prevenience, a guardian like those forbidding angels in *The Cocktail Party*. Eliot needs the collaboration of a censor, whose function is that of the Shadow in 'The Hollow Men' (1925): scything interposition between idea and act, conceit and creation; a deathly interruptor and obliterator. Pound is to Eliot a conscience, a super-ego, saving him from surrender to his own poetic gift. He inserts the equivocations which keep Prufrock from presuming, or from eating a peach. Pound is the better maker because he assists Eliot in the poem's unmaking or miscarrying; yet the sacrifices he imposed were not enough to satisfy Eliot, who in 1923 told Ford Madox Ford there were about thirty good lines in the poem, and challenged him to locate them. Poundian deletion, unauthorised by Joyce, could only damage and puritanically disable *Ulysses*. For serial publication in 1918, Pound ventured to cut the account of Bloom at stool. The excision defeated the work's ambition of bodily wholeness, its desire to incorporate all of experience, from Bloom's defecation to Molly's aria-like fart, letting her wind (as she says in a rhyme) go free, from the fraternal urinating of Bloom and Stephen to the triggered ejaculations of Blazes Boylan.

Eliot's literary history is tragically dissociated, Joyce's comically continuous. Therefore where Eliot takes over images from Joyce, the borrowing—or, as Eliot guiltily volunteered to describe it in his theory of allusion as larceny, the theft—serves to demonstrate their imaginative difference. The mongrel that Stephen observes on the beach, clawing as if for 'something he buried there, his grandmother', becomes the dog that Eliot, simultaneously quoting from Webster, warns will dig up corpses. But necrophilia like the dog's is licensed in *Ulysses*, where even corpses are fecund (the hanged boy in the Night-town episode ejects 'gouts of sperm through his death clothes') and ghosts return, like Stephen's mother, to reprieve the living. Quoting is also, like the dog's frantic delving in the sand, a serendipitous scavenging for those found objects which are the surreal flotsam of language. In the linguistic underground of *Finnegans Wake*, Joyce finds in every word and phrase a crypt of quotation, which he restores to life. In Eliot, however, the act of quoting (of which *The Waste Land* so largely consists) is more than a theft: it is the robbery of a grave. Hence the carrion appetite of the hound in Webster's dirge. *The Waste Land* always associates its quoting with such grisly exhumations (parodies of resurrection), or with the aborting of life. Thus in 'The Burial of the Dead' with which the poem begins, he is disinterring Chaucer by ghoulishly echoing the Prologue to *The Canterbury Tales*. Chaucer's April gently engenders life, Eliot's cruelly disturbs an insentient hibernation which would much sooner remain dead. The Chaucerian society inseminated by that season is a vital, quarrelsome parliament; Eliot's is an echoic catacomb 'where the dead men lost their bones', resounding with ownerless voices like the anonymous witnesses overheard in the Hofgarten or the offstage reports of the sailor in the mast and the shepherd in the look-out from *Tristan und Isolde*.

A quote is a grieving reminiscence, like the obituary from *The Tempest*: 'I remember / Those are pearls that were his eyes.' The same song occurs to Stephen during his promenade on the beach, but Ariel's obituary for a father who is not dead at all and will be born again thanks to comedy instigates a meditation on our daily reawakening of the dead in thought—'God becomes man becomes fish. . . . Dead breaths I living breathe'—and on the benignity of 'seadeath' because it is reclamation by what Mulligan, looking at Dublin bay, calls 'our great sweet mother'. The virtues of water are profusely extolled in the catechism. Joyce praises 'its universality: its democratic equality . . .: its vastness . . .: its unplumbed profundity.' Bloom adores his ablutions because they are his commerce with this fluent female element. Stephen the hydrophobe protectively recoils from this common life, masculinely personifying the ocean and egotistically bottling it ('*Prix de Paris*: beware of imitations'), but all the same the rivery ubiquity of consciousness causes his thought to swim, later, into Bloom's head. Stephen's envy of the mildness of sea-change becomes Bloom's 'Drowning they say is pleasantest. See your whole life in a flash.'

Here, too, there is a complicated overlap with Eliot. Before Pound dissuaded him, he had attached to *The Waste Land* an epigraph from *Heart of Darkness* in which Kurtz, before twice crying 'The horror!', is assumed to have drowningly lived 'his life again, in every detail . . . during that supreme moment of complete knowledge'. The quotation is apposite, because Kurtz's own quoted last words are so unreliably, invitingly ambiguous. He cries 'in a whisper at some image'. What he says, in 'no more than a breath', is his failed attempt to translate the image into words, to formulate confessionally (like Eliot's equally guilty and evasive Hamlet) the 'objective correlative'. He therefore is the parent of Eliot's reluctant or repentant speakers—the man who cannot speak to the hyacinth girl, or the one accused by the neurotic woman in 'A Game of Chess' of never speaking. The untrustworthiness of Kurtz's own quote makes

Eliot shift, when choosing an epigraph for 'The Hollow Men', to a scornfully obituary quote about him: 'Mistah Kurtz—he dead.' Kurtz's dying renactment of desire, temptation and surrender is transferred to the poem's drowned man, Phlebas the Phoenician. But he, too, is deprived of that conciliatory retrospection which Bloom envies.

A death by water in Eliot is not immersion, like Bloom's bath in the 'gentle tepid stream', but abrasion. Crabs and lobsters (exoskeletally armed against the putrescence of flesh) scratch and nibble at Bleistein on the ocean floor. Prufrock thinks he 'should have been a pair of ragged claws / Scuttling across the floors of silent seas.' The witchy chorus in *Murder in the Cathedral* (1935) feeds on 'The living lobster, the crab, the oyster, the whelk and the prawn.' The mollusc is an invulnerable predator because it is desensitised by its shell, saved from the neurasthenia of human being. Prufrock aspires to that impermeability; so did the surrealists. Crustaceans are a recurrent image in Salvador Dali's art, admired for their solution to the horror of the organic. The work of the creatures which consume Bleistein is seconded by Pound, who wears away erosively at the account of Phlebas until all that is left of it is a postmortem. At first the sailor remembers a long literary past. He is both Dante's Ulysses and Tennyson's, at once the navigator of a watery limbo encountered in hell and the moody Victorian introvert to whom the deep moans; beyond them he is, like Bloom, Homer's Odysseus, for whom the sea—like the city—is a course of sorrows, testing the heart's endurance and the mind's adaptability. There are reminiscences in him of Coleridge's haunted mariner when he sees fiendish sirens in the cross-trees, and of Kipling's captains courageous when he turns into a fisherman settling down his dories in the eastern banks. But all that Eliot prompts Phlebas to remember, Pound causes him to forget. Hollowed, he can become a symbol.

The Waste Land is made by such mutilations. It sees pictorial iconography as a kind of butchery, wracking bodies into emblematic significance: the barbarous misuse of Philomel is one among 'other tales, from the old stumps and bloody ends of time' (a phrase confusingly telescoped by Pound). The fable is a carcase, violated over again by interpreters. Whereas mythology in *Ulysses* is seminally bountiful and lenient, encouraging the one to procreate the many and welcoming caricatures among its offspring—as when Bloom, the man with the thousand faces, contorts his features 'so as to resemble many historical personages'—in Eliot the myth is sterilely mocked by a litter of false births. Lil aborts a child with some pills supplied by a quack chemist. Eliot likewise aborts quotes, denying the literary past rebirth in the present by a vengeful prematureness, a deathly speeding-up of poetic development.

Thus in 'The Fire Sermon' a line from Marvell is interrupted before the winged chariot can arrive, and motor traffic announces itself instead; and the typist for whom fornication is something she is glad she has got over and done with has also abortively, wearily anticipated the quote from *The Vicar of*

Wakefield about fallen women which, before it can be completed, is replaced by a gramophone record. The gramophone is the dead automating of poetry. (Edward and Lavinia rely on it in *The Cocktail Party*, without liking music, as a respite from conversation and each other. Bloom by contrast has a scheme for making the gramophone a means of life's vocal resurrection: 'have a gramophone in every grave', enabling you to converse with defunct elders. The machine as he employs it would be properly a medium for garrulous, sociable spirits.)

The same fatal abridgement of a natural life-cycle happens with Eliot's two quotations from *Tristan* in 'The Burial of the Dead'. The first is the beginning of the opera: the sailor's chanting which taunts Isolde—a quote in Eliot has to be the aggravation, as by the dog's nails, of a wound—and provokes her rage against the abductor Tristan. There follows the unconsummated anecdote of the hyacinth girl. After it Eliot inserts the melancholy line of the shepherd who, at the end of *Tristan*, is watching for Isolde's return, and who reports that the sea is empty. Quoting from the recriminatory first act and the desolate, delirious third, Eliot has omitted the middle of *Tristan*, which describes the sensual rapture of the lovers: he has, once more, gouged out his source by his abbreviated extractions from it. In the lying-in hospital—his factory of foison, his Garden of Adonis—Joyce who is, like Bloom admiring his floating penis, 'father of thousands', allegorises such a contraceptive precaution. His history of evolving language has reached Bunyan, and he notes that the young roisterers have been supplied by Preservative with a stout shield of oxengut, a guard against Offspring, called Killchild. Mythology scatters seed with genial recklessness, like Mr Dedalus with his fifteen children or Mina Purefoy with her 'houseful of kids at home'; only allegory mistrustfully sheaths and wastes it.

In Joyce incarnation equals impregnation (eternity's reproduction of itself in time) which in turn equals quotation: the divine word, proclaimed by Stephen in Night-town, made manifest as flesh. Dixon in the hospital salutes 'a pregnant word' and, when Bloom conceives a child, appeals on his behalf 'in the name of the most sacred word our vocal organs have ever been called upon to speak'. The human race is the collective parent of a multitudinous issue, language. Rather than this biological miracle, quotation in Eliot means a nightmarish return from the dead. *The Waste Land* is a poem of spectres, which are reverberations or reminiscences, like the distant thunder and the funereal bells in the fifth section, and the quote is a word which will not stay in its grave: the ghost encountered near Saint Mary Woolnoth, the hooded figure 'who always walks beside you'. The poem's liturgical achievement is the undoing of incarnation and resurrection, when it proclaims that 'He who was living is now dead' and reneges on the Chaucerian spring by adding that 'We who were living are now dying.' Joycean naming is the gift of life in a word, as in his comic list of guests at the wedding of the forest ranger with Miss Fir Conifer of Pine Valley, all of whom are flowers, plants or trees, because language is our family tree. Eliot's names, acid in their exactitude, are the denial of life: all we know of Mrs Equitone, or of De Bailhache, Fresca and Mrs Cammel in 'Gerontion' (1919), is these tags attached to them which are the calling-cards of unreal selves. J. Alfred Prufrock is a suit of clothes incongruously outfitting a state of mind.

In Joyce as in Spenser, nature's reconquest of a lost wholeness leads to a fertile hermaphroditism. The impregnated Bloom is 'the new womanly man' and Molly 'wouldn't mind being a man and get up on a lovely woman'. Eliot's equivalent to these genitally composite parents is the withered androgyne Tiresias, 'old man with wrinkled dugs', and he, though he contains everyone else, is neutered by his exile from the poem and from the land of the living. He is, Eliot says, 'a mere spectator and not . . . a "character"'. But consciousness is always in Eliot a voyeur, the mind conducting surveillance of a body it has rendered impotent. This is his bequest from James: 'Portrait of a Lady' (1910) is his poetic analysis of the Jamesian novel, studying the novelist's subtly malicious, even murderous relationship with the character through whom he, at second hand, lives; Eliot's first title for 'A Game of Chess' was 'In the Cage', a reference both to Petronius's cell-bound sibyl and to her modern avatar, the telegraph girl in James's 1898 story, existing vicariously inside her wire cubicle.

Consciousness in Joyce is a hold-all. Molly wonders if Leopold is 'thinking of me or dreaming am I in it'. Everyone is in her dream, as in that of Earwicker in *Finnegans Wake*. Others, like the stranger to Dublin who questions her, have the same longing to find themselves within her where they began and belong: 'Who is in your mind now tell me who are you thinking of who is it tell me his name who tell me who.' Yet when the woman in *The Waste Land* makes the same demand—'What are you thinking of? What thinking? What?'—the reply is a negation: 'Nothing again nothing.' Another of Pound's salving deductions from the poem is what Eliot apologises for, inside inverted commas, as character. Eliot supplied the river nymphs with suburban biographies. Then he excised the details of a *petit-bourgeois* background, reducing character to voice—and to voice which is any case borrowed, since the nymphs babble the alliterative refrain of Wagner's Rhine-maidens, 'Weialala leia.' The mind's companionable collective in Joyce houses Everyman (addressed in the hospital episode) and makes room for his progeny in a processional which announces, in mutations of Earwicker's name, that Here Comes Everyone who Haveth Childers Everywhere: hence the thronging march-past for Bloom's investiture as monarch. There is in Eliot a traffic in memories which, being ownerless, are a soiled common property—thus in an early version the harried spouse in 'A Game of Chess' was permitted to 'remember / The hyacinth garden', although he is not in that section of the poem—but the consciousness of his people is at best a reading-list, a library of unassimilable influences. Orlando at least single-handedly writes English literature; Fresca, the first heroine of 'The Fire

Sermon', merely laxatively reads it, enlisting Richardson to ease her bowel movement and mixing Gibbon, Rossetti, Pater and Symonds with the *Daily Mirror* in a 'chaotic mish-mash potpourri'.

The most encyclopaedic being in Eliot is necessarily a dead man: the 'familiar compound ghost' whom he so movingly entreats in the blitzed London of 'Little Gidding', and who is both Dante's Virgil and Eliot's 'dead master' Yeats. Their conference as poets takes place either in the underworld, or among the ruins of a city which is a populous grave. The poet who in *The Waste Land* made a bulwark from his anthologising of fragments now in the *Four Quartets* signs on for emergency work as a fire-warden, and classically mans the battlement in 'a dead patrol'. The revenant here is also Hamlet's father, the bogey psychoanalytically and theologically demonstrated by Stephen in *Ulysses* to be Shakespeare himself: 'the Son striving to be atoned with the Father' is 'the Father [who] was Himself His own Son'. That atonement works in *Ulysses* to produce a concord of opposites, of sexes as well as generations. A male impersonator is playing *Hamlet* in Dublin, and Bloom wonders if he might have been a woman . . . which would certainly explain Ophelia's suicide. The comically incorrigible body has its own remedies for tragic distress. Masturbating on the strand, Bloom quotes Francisco's comment at the changing of the guard in *Hamlet*, 'For this relief much thanks.' No such bawdily reconciliatory healing can happen in Eliot. In 1919 he prepared for an Oedipal interpretation of *Hamlet*, arguing that the hero's baffled emotion for his mother does not, as if ashamed, adequately declare itself in the play. Eliot himself shares Hamlet's perplexity when he confronts Yeats. He is the son who inherits from the forbidding parent the onerous duty of poetry, and who is warned that he cannot rejuvenate the tradition but must grow old along with it. Enumerating the cold and bitter 'gifts reserved for age', Yeats instals Eliot in a pantheon which is at the same time a mausoleum.

By the time of the *Quartets*, Tiresias has been redefined as a sage classical elder, wise in 'the knowledge of dead secrets'. Eliot in *The Waste Land* refuses, however, to claim such omniscience for himself. So determined is he to represent the fracturing and agnosticism of consciousness, which cannot know itself and has no faith in its own statements (like Prufrock reproved by being told 'That is not what I meant at all'), that he appends to the poem a set of learned notes whose ironic purpose is to show how ignorant he is of his own work. He professes unfamiliarity with the Tarot pack, does not know the origins of the ballad about Mrs Porter, and has forgotten from which Antarctic memoir he got the tale of the supernumerary explorer, though he is pedantically specific about Canadian ornithology and the details of billing in the currant trade. As befits the classical scholar, who helpfully transcribes a passage from Ovid, he is a dolorous connoisseur of defunct things, even if they are sounds: when the poem describes the 'dead sound on the final stroke of nine' emitted by the Saint Mary Woolnoth clock, Eliot notes that it is 'A phenomenon which I have often noticed.' The poem begins by protesting at the re-arousal of memory when admixed with desire. It ends, in the notes, with the quietism of a pretended amnesia, unable to remember and therefore immune to desire.

Consciousness in Joyce, on the contrary, insists on total recall. This is the purpose of the penultimate chapter's catechism: an infallible cosmic mind (Joyce's) knows the answers to all questions, and can remember things—for instance the exact venues in which Bloom had previously pondered the outcome of the horse race—that the characters would have forgotten. When Joyce, mentioning the items of furniture in Bloom's parlour, instructs himself 'Describe them', he does not do so, like Bernard in *The Waves* with his mania for describing, to cause their evanescence into impressions; he wants to anchor, solidify and realise them, which means taking them into his creative care. The world he oversees is the sum of all things that exist, and his descriptive love must be shared out impartially between them all.

Because Joyce envisions literary history as a cycle, *Ulysses* can go through the declension of its genres secure in the awareness that parody is not debasement but humanisation, and what falls will irrepressibly rise again. It is forever rehearsing the change from epic to romance. At one moment O'Ryan bringing Alf a beaker of ale is accomplishing a blood-brotherly rite in the mead-hall; next he is a dapper Arthurian courtier, 'chivalrous Terence' proffering the 'nectarous beverage' to 'the soul of chivalry, in beauty akin to the immortals'. A similar law of literary evolution presses epic towards quixotic mock-epic, for instance when Bloom's bee-sting is described as a wound received from 'a horrible and dreadful dragon'. Beyond the mock-epic lies the humbled reality of the novel. Stephen's initial declaration seeks exemption from the arduous responsibilities of epic and romance: 'I'm not a hero.' Molly resents the aspersions cast on her by the lowly form of the novel, and rejects her ancestress in one of the first novels: 'I don't like books with a Molly in them like that one he brought me about the one from Flanders a whore always shoplifting.' Yet Joyce's benison to these people is the completion of the cycle which restores them to a forfeited grace and to heroism. He shows the Blooms and their elective son to be elementally equal to their Homeric prototypes, not shabby parodies. Epic, when Stephen explicates the genres in *A Portrait*, is a place from which to start. From its impersonality, a single lyrical self is salvaged; then that personal voice is dramatically extroverted and bestowed on others. When all these stages have been worked through and literature's history recapitulated, epic becomes, in *Ulysses*, the place to go home to. It begins, as the *Portrait* ends, with Stephen's refusal of his family (he will not kneel at his dying mother's request); it ends with his reclamation by the family as the Blooms conjoin to adopt him as their lodger.

The same cycles in *The Waste Land* mean defilement. The sacred texts Eliot cites are profaned when he quotes them. Both he and Joyce recur to the medieval figural method, like Stephen's pupil copying 'the unsteady symbols' from the board. But the symbol puts on flesh in Joyce, and is made real. *Ulysses* starts with Mulligan's consecration of his shaving bowl as a chalice. When Mr Deasy says that 'All history moves towards one great goal, the manifestation of God', Stephen answers 'That is God', referring to a noise in the street. That indeed is his divinity as an artist: he can sanctify the real by declaring it to be a symbol. Eliot accuses this process of being idle whimsy when he says in the notes to *The Waste Land*, 'the Man with Three Staves . . . I associate, quite arbitrarily, with the Fisher King.' Symbol-making is not <u>coadunative</u> or cohesive, as Coleridge thought, but just a <u>specious</u> pretence of correspondence.

Whereas the symbol is in Joyce a body—'This is my body', says Bloom in his bath, quoting from the mass—in Eliot it is a husk, a shell, scraped clean of meaning. He notes in 'Little Gidding' that

> We have taken from the defeated
> What they had to leave us—a symbol.

The figure in Eliot is therefore successively disfigured. That is the case with the foreshortened literary cycle in 'A Game of Chess'. The courtesan is first Shakespeare's Cleopatra on her barge, next Pope's trivial Belinda at her toilet-table, thereafter (when the scene changes to the pub and Lil is recommended to get a nice set of dentures) Swift's cartoon of Belinda as the self-disassembling harlot. Each parody is a gruesome modernisation of its predecessor, an iconographic plastic surgery: Lil's friend says she ought to be ashamed 'to look so antique'. Another smaller cycle puts Shakespeare through a jeering death and an unwelcome rebirth. The echo of Enobarbus's pentameters gets syncopated and caricaturally misspelled in 'that Shakespe-herian Rag'. (When Joyce misspells Shakespeare's name in *Finnegans Wake* he does so in tribute to his godly creativity, calling him Shapesphere, and to his common human goodness, calling him Shopkeeper. Stephen equates 'God, the Sun, Shakespeare, a commercial traveller', and takes the ordinariness of his name to prove the demotic fertility of language: 'Shakespeares were as common as Murphies.') After Eliot's jazzy attempt to revive antiquated Shakespeare, he returns once more as a ghostly voice from beyond when the chorus at closing-time—'Goonight Bill. Goonight Lou. Goonight May'—mingles with Ophelia's touchingly formal exit from the ribaldries of her mad scene: 'Good night, ladies, good night, sweet ladies, good night, good night.'

Ulysses continues Browning's liberation of language from literature, of noise and song from the rational exchanges of speech. It is a work of a clamorous, versatile onomatopoeia (which in Greek means word-making). It resounds with the sibillation of waves ('seesoo, hrss, rsseeiss, ooos'), the cat's ingratiating 'Mkgnao!', Molly's grunting 'Mn', the acoustic tinkle of her peeing or her sopranoish elongation of vowels in 'looooves' old sweet 'ssooooooong', Davy Byrne's yawning 'Iiiiiiiiiaaaaaaach!', the neologistic neighing of the horse which rewrites Swift as 'Hohohohohohoh!', or the muttered embarrassment of the confessional, overheard as 'And I schschschschschsch'. In Eliot such transliterations do not poetically enfranchise bodily functions and the nature of which they partake; they are systematic proofs of lyricism's absurdity, since what may sound melodious looks fatuous when written down—the cockerel's 'Co co rico', the nightingale's 'Jug jug', punningly reclaimed for lyrical sensuality by Joyce in *Finnegans Wake* when he hears the 'naughtingerls juckjucking benighth me'. Celia in *The Cocktail Party* hears Edward's voice as an insect's twittering: 'You might have made it by scraping your legs together— / Or however grasshoppers do it.'

Whereas Joyce's language has a rivery and mellifluous liquidity, as effluent as the personified Liffey in *Finnegans Wake* or as Molly with her seething internal tides (she feels the blood menstrually 'pouring out of me like the sea'), Eliot's idiom studies sparseness, aridity. A desert, whether it is the dusty hell under the red rock or the blank, blinding Antarctic or the 'zero summer' of 'Little Gidding', is the location best suited to a tragedy. Eliot accordingly subjects his words to a penitential dessication. T. E. Hulme had in *Speculations* (1924) identified classicism with dryness, characterising the romantic as messily fluid and vaporous. Eliot further identifies this parched condition with sanctity. The visionary lotus pool in 'Burnt Norton' has value because it is drained, a cavity of dried concrete. The only lyrical sound in *The Waste Land* is that, as Eliot phrases it in an early draft of 'The Fire Sermon', of the 'dry grass singing'. In 'Ash-Wednesday' (1930) the singing is done by whitened, marrow-gutted bones, the penitential left-overs of human being, and they are joined in their chirping by Celia's cicada. Joyce's characters are warblers because the tuned, exhaled air is the body's gratitude for the gift of life within it. When Simon Dedalus sings an aria from *Martha*, Bloom reflects on the 'long long breath he breath long life'. Stephen later delights him with the same tenor voice, 'the rarest of boons'. Hynes's 'highclass vocalism' stirs the saloon, and Molly relishes Ben Dollard's base barreltone. Eliot's language forbids this mitigation. Stravinsky, asked in 1961 why he had set no Eliot, said 'his words . . . do not need music' (though he did compose an exception to his rule when he made an anthem from the stanzas about the dove-like dive-bomber in 'Little Gidding').

As Harry in *The Family Reunion* (1939) sets off on his mission to the tropic of expiation, his military uncle tells him, 'You'll have to learn the language / And several dialects.' The preparation for santity is linguistic. 'Ash-Wednesday' prescribes a redemption for language which is an abstaining from poetry, a 'Speech without word and / Word of no speech.' That sacred word, which once spoke the world into existence, now cloisters itself in silence or dwells hermit-like, as 'Burnt Norton' discovers, in a desert.

Eliot had once praised Donne for rescuing poetry from its alliance with instrumental music. Though the title of the *Four Quartets* ventures a musical analogy, the poems, retraversing the history of poetry since Donne, confirm that refusal. Donne's composition of songs which cannot be sung is seconded by Keats's audition of music which remains unheard, played in Eliot's case by the breathless flute of the garden god (Pan deprived of his pipes) in 'Ash-Wednesday'. The time the poems redeem is that of literary history and they do so, with an honesty and austerity which are a holy rule, by denial, reviewing the alternatives the tradition contains only to renounce them. Their rhetoric is one of deprivation: a litany predicated on the successive nots which enforce the sacrifice in 'East Coker', or on the modest negation which begins 'The Dry Salvages' ('I do not know much about gods'), deadly recited in a limbo when there is 'nothing to think about', at last reaching as its termini 'nobody's funeral' or a 'meeting nowhere, no before and after'.

They are poems convinced that 'the poetry does not matter', and they prove themselves in good faith by writing flatly, in for instance the third section of 'East Coker', by adopting someone else's style as an exercise in self-abnegation—Yeats's at the end of the ghost's address, Donne's in the conceited allegory of the wounded surgeon—or by patient paraphrase of a source, in the commentary on Krishna. They punish themselves as they go along, each movement gainsaying its predecessor: 'That was a way of putting it—not very satisfactory.' And they are obsessively, aggravatedly repetitious. Eliot invites this charge only to convict himself of it thrice over:

> You say I am repeating
> Something I have said before. I shall say it again.
> Shall I say it again?

The repetitions are another kind of scourging. Eliot admits the fraudulence of poetry's concentration on lyrical instants. In the case of *The Waste Land* he engaged Pound or, jokingly, Ford to isolate the few poetic moments lost in the work. As edited by Pound, the poem is all climaxes—except that they are all anti-climactic. In the *Four Quartets* no editing occurs. Eliot insists on continuing between the revelatory instants, toiling through 'the waste sad time / Stretching before and after.' Writing is the occupation of an interim. 'The years of *l'entre deux guerres*' which he speaks of in 'East Coker' and says he has wasted are the years between Virginia Woolf's acts, and the disputed frontier between prose and poetry (or passion) across which Forster hopes connectingly to stretch in *Howards End*. Woolf and Forster both redeem the time by exalting its prose into poetry. Eliot chastens the poetry by causing its subsidence into expository prose.

Hence his discounting of his poetic predecessors. 'Burnt Norton' begins with a romantic lyric, set in the rose-garden or wonderland of English pastoral, planted with Blake's sunflower, glinting with Hopkins's kingfisher, alive with the laughing voices of Kipling's children from '"They"' absconded in the foliage. Yet the beauty of the thing is its disqualification, for 'The Dry

Salvages' decides that the lyric is a vain mimicry of incarnation. Apprehending the intersection of timelessness with time 'is an occupation for the saint', not for the poets; romanticism is sacrilege. 'East Coker' retreats from the romantics to the metaphysicals, whose intellectualism is an exegetical surgery, questioning the distempered organism, analysing feeling so as to effect its cure. Anesthesia, here and on the cerulean operating-table of Prufrock, is the prevention of the aesthetic, which means sensitivity. 'The Dry Salvages' takes advantage of its setting to correct the different heresy of American romanticism. The poem's Mississippi is Whitman's river, the lively flux which he sees coursing even down Broadway, but in Eliot it is regulated by the bell and—since its flotsam is the mess of history—must be ended or abandoned. As 'a problem confronting the builder of bridges', it defies Hart Crane's mythic engineering of integration in *The Bridge* (1930). Crane's messianic Brooklyn Bridge, rejoining man with the forfeited sky, was his answer to the despair and diaspora of *The Waste Land*, where 'London Bridge is falling down falling down falling down.' Crane's bridge imbibes the river through its 'choiring' girders. Eliot reminds him that nature cannot be sublimated by 'worshippers of the machine'. Yeats is introduced to be controverted. His 'refining fire' is not the scorching smithies of Byzantium but the frigid purgatory of the sterile infirmary in 'East Coker'. And when Eliot positions himself 'in the middle way' he is correcting Dante, who is ushered into other worlds when in the middle of his life's journey. Eliot must remain in middle age, and must content himself with the other middle way categorised by the rhetoricians: the mean style, unadapted to the heights.

Though 'Little Gidding' proposes 'an easy commerce of the old with the new', that is not what the *Four Quartets* achieve. The new censures the old; the old prohibits the new. Literary time has reached a stop, and Eliot can escape from the nightmares of history and of possession by poetry. Thereafter he either apologises for writing poetry, as in his dedication to his second wife (with whom he babbles 'the same thoughts without need of speech' or meaning, so that poetry is superfluous and perhaps also—publicising a private delight—improper), or writes pieces like the wartime 'Defence of the Islands' which, as he chastely notes, 'cannot pretend to be verse'.

38

Literature is a love-affair with language. The first long phase of English literature is about the language's triumph over its sense of vernacular inferiority. That imputation of lowly unworthiness suits Chaucer, who can make the native tongue the preserve of canny experience as against the authoritarian orthodoxy of Latin. English literature will free itself by flouting classical precedents: as an essay in his own ironic stratagems, Chaucer has the barnyard characters of the 'Nun's Priest's Tale' mistranslate the Latin tags they cite. At last, *Arcadia* and *Euphues* make these sleights unnecessary by saving English from the accusation of barbarianism, and evincing its infinite capacities. The Arcadian shepherds speak Greek, but they speak it in English. Milton, by making God speak English with a Latinate word-order, justifies the language itself as both classical and holy. But that confidence is once more unsettled by the romantics, for whom language is an impediment, misrepresenting feelings in words, best when marred, as by Wordsworth's burbling idiot boy. They transmit this unease to the novelists. The translation of muddled words back into musical silences or pictorial gestures is the obsession of Sterne's Yorick. Less nimble, Conrad's Marlow can only paraphrase the 'unspeakable', while Tom Brangwen in *The Rainbow* is frustrated by his 'unutterably silent' wife.

The translative activity—a symptom of language's romantic crisis as, in medieval literature, it announces the other crisis provoked by the classics—is a desperate matter in Lawrence. He brings together the medieval and the modern conscience about language: the fear that the letter disfigures a spirit which is in the first case scriptural, in the second mystically emotional. The courage of *The Rainbow* is its tormented admission of these difficulties. In the process it recites the early history of literature along with the history of the Brangwen clan. It grieves over the advance from speech to writing as a desacralising lapse. Tom is powerfully moved when Tennyson's 'Ulysses' or Shelley's 'Ode to the West Wind' are spoken; reading them, 'the very fact of the print' repels him, and causes him to hate books 'as if they were his enemies'. He has a similar revulsion from school exercises in composition, and is bullied by the Latin master, on whom he revenges himself by breaking his head with a slate. Though less violently iconoclastic, Eliot shares his dismay at 'the intolerable wrestle / With words and meanings.' When Tom formulaically addresses the Polish widow, she replies in 'a phrase of polite speech in a foreign language merely'. Yet all speech is in a foreign language: how can words render the behests of the body? Lawrence seeks not to purify tribal dialect but to defend it against purification.

Braithewaite rejoices when Anna answers one of his teasing questions in dialect. Her education, however, corrupts her. Like Conrad in *Nostromo* deliberately mistranslating French into English to show that language is no ground of community, Lawrence has her vacillate between languages. Her father mocks her distaste for his 'boozing in Ilkeston' by taunting her dialectally: 'What's wrong wi' Il'son?' To her mother, she has translated herself unreachably into French. She is irritated by 'a certain *gaucherie*, a gawkiness' (as Lawrence slangily translates it) in her, by her desire to seem 'a lofty demoiselle'. Her quarrel with her parents is linguistic; her love for them dispenses with language, in an intercourse which is 'wordless, intense and close'. The words which estrange her from them also alienate her from God. She learns Latin at school, and Lawrence transcribes several lines of the Ave Maria she memorises. But what thrills her is the unintelligibility of these verbal spells. Translated, they are reduced, and do not correspond to the spirit inhering in the rosary. Chaucer's pilgrimage seditiously forgets its spiritual symbolism and turns into a literal and literary journey. Langland calls off his pilgrimage because the same change, which he sees as a corruption, has overtaken it. Anna shares his outrage at literature's institutionalisation of spirit: at church, 'the *language* meant nothing to her: it seemed false. She hated to hear things expressed, put into words. . . . She tried to read. But again . . . the sense of the falsity of the spoken word put her off.' Hers is the medieval objection; in a later Brangwen generation, Ursula, who thrives at the Grammar School, has the modern literary consciousness, prizing symbols precisely because they are liberated from use and meaning. She trembles 'like a postulant when she wrote the Greek alphabet', adores a Latin verb because 'it meant something, though she did not know what it meant', and delights in the silly insipidity of her French exercise, *J'ai donné le pain à mon petit frère*. Like Lewis Carroll's characters, she knows that mathematics is the highest and most rarified state of symbolism. For her there is magic in the algebraic proposition that '$x^2 - y^2 = (x+y)(x-y)$'.

Education cannot harm Ursula since she continues to separate it from rational understanding. The symbol remains inviolate so long as it is unintelligible. By contrast, Joyce's Stephen Dedalus at school hungers to acquire and understand words, because they first locate him in the world and then enable him wilfully to subjugate it. He sees growth as the acquisition of linguistic powers. 'When would he be big like the fellows in poetry and rhetoric?' he wonders, and he shares an infirmary room with a bold 'fellow out of third of grammar' who instructs him in riddles and puns. The forbidden knowledge he seizes is of vocabulary: what, for instance, does smugging mean? Once mastered, language allows him to declare himself central to the universe, as in the little rhyme he writes on the flyleaf of his geography book. Joyce is therefore unperplexed by the linguistic obstruction of meaning and obfuscation of God which enrages Lawrence. Stephen learns that there are 'different names for God in all the different languages in the world', but is assured that God understands them all and is the same everywhere.

That faith exonerates language from the curse of Babel. Joyce's puns valiantly reunite English words with their divorced counterparts in other languages. Samuel Beckett believed that *Finnegans Wake* had invested English with the universality of medieval Latin.

Joyce and Lawrence have different solutions to the medieval problem of letter and spirit. For Joyce the letter is itself a spirit: words are to be worshipped. For Lawrence there must always be a disabling gulf between them. English literature grows in tandem with a series of translations from the Bible, extending from Wycliffe to the King James version, which work to make the spirit inhere in outlandish vernacular letters. Lawrence undoes this entire history by declaring that Will Brangwen 'did not care about the Bible, the written letter'. Refusing to accept it as fact, he wishes it away, taking 'that which was of value to him from the Written Word' and adding it to his own spirit. He untranslates the Bible, and unwrites the opprobiously written word. After him, like Langland abolishing the profane field full of folk, Birkin in *Women in Love* condemns a world which is hostile to spirit: 'Humanity doesn't embody the utterance of the incomprehensible any more. Humanity is a dead letter'—defunct because unable to transmit spirit's messages. Joyce, however, in *Ulysses* hails language's human gestation and literature's sacrament. In the lying-in hospital Stephen delivers himself of a parable: 'In woman's womb word is made flesh but in the spirit of the maker all flesh that passes becomes the word that shall not pass away.' In the brothel he restates this verbal cosmogeny: 'In the beginning was the word, in the end the world without end.'

The polysyllabic hubbub of *Finnegans Wake*, where language originates in the catarrhal rumble of a thunderclap—the babbling clatter of Humpty Dumpty's fall at the outset, the hundred-lettered, premonitory roar of Shem's pamphlet—seems to deny this articulacy of the logos. The mob in the tavern, accusing Earwicker, derides Stephen's gospel: 'In the buginning is the woid, in the muddle is the sound-dance and thereinoften you're in the unbewised again.' The word is voided; language is just a cry in the darkness. Shaun's romance with Iseult changes woman from the incubator of the word to its executioner, for she uses, absorbs and discards the prattling man: 'In the beginning was the gest . . ., for the end is with woman, flesh-without-word.' Shaun denounces as well the bogus scripture of Shem's letter, where spirit is dimmed and thus damned, where syllables pretend to be sibylline but are actually sillybillies and holiness is wholly holey: 'Every dimmed letter in it is a copy and not a few of the silbils and wholly words I can show you in my Kingdom of Heaven.' *Finnegans Wake* is aware of the manifold truancies of the text, and as a warning to itself casually mentions an act of scribicide, yet it is grateful for the sustaining nutriment of language, stored like the 'spadefuls of mounded food' Shaun feasts on, and for the impregnable haven of literature. Glugg, worsted in the children's games, determines on a literary exile, and ships out to an American promised land renamed, as the headquarters of his avocation, Pencylmania. There, in a synopsised paragraph, he writes *Ulysses* all over again.

The alphabet in *To the Lighthouse* is a tundra of haughty, skeletal initials, where the only destination is a zero. In *Finnegans Wake* those bleak letters which are Mr Ramsay's sign-posts interlink in a human chain binding us to the primal father, and they are forever intermarrying: 'A and aa ab ad abu abiad.' The *Abiad* might be the alphabet itself as an epic poem. The flower-maidens encircle Chuff in an alphabetic garland, spelling out RAYNBOW. And since we have made language the intimate accomplice of our loving, it is natural that words should mimic our sexuality and venture to engender on their own. Glugg, remembering when erotically tempted how useful a go-between a book was to Dante's Paolo, thinks 'letters be blowed'. It is not a dismissal but a fond hope that the letters may act as a spoor-bearing breeze, seeking out and enticing a co-respondent. This will be their semaphore: 'I is a femaline person. O, of provocative gender. U unisingular case.' Birkin, who egotistically wills humanity's annihilation, exempts himself from language's genitive energies and its alimenting of us. In a discussion of eating, he asks 'Why should every man decline the whole verb? First person singular is enough for me.' Joyce's conjugations are irresistibly conjugal, infinitively inquisitive. Hence the aspirated flurry of questions about the slamming of the door: 'When the h, who the hu, how the hue, where the huer?' That domestic explosion is the sound of doom, and the death it prophesies is an extermination of words. It recalls to Joyce the martial alliterativeness of Nordic epic with its consonantal tattoos. Vowels, which are the living breath in words and their musicality, rendered as a yawning musical scale when the children go to bed ('Ha he hi ho hu'), are suffocated. 'Gonn the gawds, Gunnar's gustspells' compress into a breathless Götterdämmerung, or 'gottrdmmrng'. In this guttural grumble, the word is disemvowelled. These are the edicts of the father; but the complementary genius of language is the mother, whose words are eloquently reassuring even when silent. The sleeping children are guarded by the iterated incantation 'Mummum': mum's the word for maternity and for peace.

During Joyce's account of the educational curriculum in the nursery, Iseult learns grammar from her gramma. Its rules are the tricks of her sexual witchery. The object in all her sentences is an erotic quarry; even if neuter, that object is made flagrantly human by being misspelled as 'nuder'. The wise ancient advises Iseult, in dealing with a young man, to 'take the dative with his oblative', and in a footnote supplies an example of this flirtatious mood ('I'd like his pink's cheek'). Above all, she counsels, 'mind your genderous towards his reflexives'. The reflex actions of the erectile body are the copulative commandments of language. Thus syntax is 'sintalks', subjunctives are underground or internal tunnels like those of the subway or like the conduits of the human body ('subjunctions'), Shem's arcane penmanship resembles Sanskrit which is a 'sinscript', and the mastery of words is a libertine career, rewarded by the attainment of a 'volupkabulary'. The very word for language is traced to its physiological source as 'lungorge'; when emitted from the organism it goes slumming with gusto as 'slanguage', or musically takes to the air as the 'pigeony linguish' in which Anna Livia tipatongues Earwicker during their love-making.

Language is as incontinently immortal as Finnegan. Puns, which are language's libido, incite small wakes inside words, rewriting mourning as festivity: funerals are 'funereels', a cemetery is a gourmand's 'Creamtartery'. If an entry in Johnson's dictionary isolates words in a singularity which Johnson felt Donne's poetry or Shakespeare's 'bodkin' had outraged, and at the same time etymologically studies the protracted death of classical antecedents, then Joyce is rewriting Johnson's lexicon. Words escape their separate cubicles, and instead of reckoning the mortality of Latin and the schism in its universality they cross-fertilise to renew the vernacular. Their compounding is fraternal, familial, communal: they 'reamalgamerge', are 'everintermutuomergent', and incorporate together all creatures of 'manorwombanborn'. Anna Livia's manifestoes are not content to be starchy paper but serve as sucking mammaries and misbehave festively when Joyce calls them her 'mamafesta'.

The polyglot pun, by causing these rampant alliances across linguistic frontiers, jokingly rebuilds Babel. Its esperanto doubles as a key to all mythologies, for it can reconcile creeds as easily as dialects. In Jaun's sermon, the dying Christ is coupled with the yogi Krishnamurti as 'Chris-na-Murty'. The universality forfeited by Latin has devolved upon opera, adopted by Joyce, like the pun, as an easy-going international language which crosses borders by subtitling its words with the emotional immediacy of music. *Finnegans Wake*, some of which Joyce recorded for the gramophone, sends literature's development from speech to script to print into reverse, returning to its beginnings in the puissance of the voice, or, as he puts it when Shaun speaks and sends the word off on its migratory adventures, the voce, vote and voise. Jaun's wooing of Swift's Vanessa resounds with an orchestral choir of twittering birds, and as Juan he toasts Iseult with a Verdian brindisi or 'brandisong', quoting also from Ottavio's 'me O treasauro' in *Don Giovanni*. Opera is the imperium of voice, as reverberant as those intermittent thunderclaps, as dulcet as Jaun's warbling. Joyce hears it as a sonic cataclysm, 'grand operoar', yet defers to it as the ultimate freeing of speech, for music has saved words from being merely verbal captions for things, has kept them vibrantly alive. Therefore, describing the crowd in the pub, he alters the free-shooter of Weber's *Der Freischütz* to a free speaker, or to a convocation of 'frayshouters'. Phonetic events become operatic personages. Shaun's inquisitors, punning on Wagner's Tristan's tantric encoding of himself as Tantris when he besieges Isolde, rattle off a sequence of mutable quibbles: 'Tantris, hattrick, tryst and parting, by vowelglide!' That last word disguises the Great Vowel Shift as another Wagnerian character, the singer and harpist Vogelweide from *Tannhäuser*.

Like love in *Ulysses*, an operatic word is ubiquitously at home in all languages, and Wagner's peripatetic knights have as their companion in *Finnegans Wake* the troubador of Verdi's *Il Trovatore*. What Kev's love-letters lack in truth they make up for in tunefulness: '*Se non é vero son trovatore*.' Taff expatriates the singer to Russia as 'Trovatorovitch' and accompanies himself on the balalaika. Taff transliterates the Count's aside in the opera, '*Io fremo*', as 'I frumble'; Juan, a lisping serenader, revises it as 'The froubadour! I fremble!' Between them, Wagner's crusaders and Verdi's balladeer attest to the musicality of Joyce, and to his medievalism. His aim, like those industrious collaters and anthologists Chaucer, Gower, Lydgate and Malory, is to tell all stories at once; he does so by making them overlap as puns, or by twining them together and tiering them as counterpoint.

The last ventures of such syncretism are Gower's opening-out of closed, climactic drama into ambling, digressive narrative in Shakespeare's *Pericles*, and Spenser's tally of all created things in *The Faerie Queene*. Shakespeare's Gower overcomes the limits of drama, whose ideal stage is a room from which there is no exit, by setting it afloat; Spenser's ambition of confluence leads him, with the same bold impossibility, to represent a wedding of two rivers. Joyce is as fluvial as they are. His element is 'those polyfizzyboisterous seas', which carry all people and all literature as their buoyant flotsam. Spenser has to equivocate geographically, trying to match the maps of his Faeryland with the world outside it. Joyce can relocate a single place everywhere by having it embark, making it drift through watery metamorphoses. Thus Tasmania, named at first Van Diemen's Land, is chosen by Glugg as the answer to one of the riddles, since it is the location of a coral pearl, and as 'Tossmania' is a nasty winter ailment which the Ondt in the fable thinks he has contracted.

The same universalising is the biological fund of the characters. Earwicker and Anna Livia are multiplied until they involve all other existences, which they in any case, in their couplings, have brought to birth. HCE is an omnipotent word, siring synonyms and pseudonyms by the thousand as it is magnified through the 'expending umniverse' of the work, littering the world with the letters which are his insignia and, like the scribbling Shem, 'letter from litter' begetting a literature. He wriggles inside other words and sprouts assertive capitals, as in 'HeCitEncy'; he is an empty vessel luxuriating in the sound it makes as 'Hircups Emptybolly'; he is breezily benign when 'Howe cools Eavybrolly'; speaking in tongues, he spouts Chinese as 'Hung Chung

Egglyfella'. His name offprints an entire language as he becomes an Everyman. At his sparest he is represented by a chemical formula, reactively marrying molecules: $H_2 C E_3$. Reduced further, he is further aggrandised in a runic talisman. The initial of his surname performs antics of its own, collapsing flat onto its back at the fall as ⌶, gesturing backwards in 'ancientest signlore' as ⴺ when Earwicker swears an oath at the Wellington monument. In his role as paterfamilias of the Doodles clan, his emblem bestrides the earth as ⊓, phallically three-legged.

His consort Anna Livia Plurabelle is a river, and she exists in a verbal state of flux. Mythology is riverine, a tributary sacred because subterranean, like Coleridge's Alph at Xanadu. Joyce names mythology for a stream, 'folkloire', and unlike Milton, who reproves the errant snakings of the river in Eden, permits it to diverge, revise its course and contradict itself: hence Shaun's public requests from him 'an esiop's foible'. The pluralising of Anna Livia makes her run backwards to the wellspring of Latin where she begins as 'appia lippia pluvaville', jubilantly conjugates her as it sings her praises ('Vivi vienne, little Annchen! Vielo Anna, high life!'), and orchestrates her as a choral hallelujah when, at the end of a Sanctus, she is heard as 'Anneliuia!' She courses through tenses and times as ebulliently as she floods spaces: 'Anna was, Livia is, Plurabelle's to be.' Like the primal word worshipped by Stephen, she extends from alpha to omega: 'as Anna was at the beginning lives yet and will return . . . rerising.' And she predates the immemorial deluge in her imper-sonation of Aunty Dilluvia. Her name progressively rewrites itself as life, the expansive sum total of creation. Liffey first wells into that global terrain to which the children address their Christmas telegram, 'this land of the livvey', and then transcribes itself as scripture in the testament which Shaun—paraph-rasing Lawrence's account of the novel as an inflamed tablet of spirit, a 'bright book of life'—calls his 'authordux Book of Lief'.

Like HCE and ALP with their literary litters, *Finnegans Wake* welcomes every literary work predating it as its offspring, not an ancestry of inhibiting precedent. Vico has replaced Comte as the theorist of literary history: the long march of mind curls itself into those wheeling gyres which turn somersaults in the curriculum and describe in the air a dizzy 'gyrotundo'. Joyce can therefore correct the historical despair of Tennyson's Arthur by attaching to it the regenerative prediction of myth: 'The old order changeth and lasts like the first.' The once and future king has his renaissance as an ignited word, an energetic verb of potentiality, introduced by Sanskrit benedictions when the *ricorso* begins: 'Archthuris coming! Be! Verb umprincipiant through the trancitive spaces!' Yet this medieval romance is no more than the second coming of the classical epic, and Joyce connects the birth of his new world with the calamity of the old, 'when Troysirs fall'. The tragedy has been reprieved by the pun as a lewd comic mishap. The mob of Earwicker's accusers, like poets from the compiler of the *Gest Hystoriale* to Milton contemplating an

Arthuriad, research their case against him by reviving the legendary half-truths of the matter of Britain, and elect a herald as their advocate: 'he'd be our chosen one in the matter of Brittas more than anarthur.' And before this alliance of ancients and moderns, classic and romantic, there is the Anglo-Saxon epic with its ceremonies for preserving art in a grave-mound, like *Beowulf* or the ship at Sutton Hoo. Yawn is questioned 'about this mound or barrow' and about a missing Norse vessel, 'a burial battell, the boat of millions of years'.

Joyce can rewrite the subsequent history of literature by the mere expedient of subversively misspelling it. Shelley's *Prometheus Unbound* had predicted the world's end in a blaze of light; it makes amends by sponsoring that world's regeneration when—as the twins spy on their parents making love—it is cited as 'Promiscuous Omebound'; and the terminal misery of Swift's satire, whose worst curse is to deny men their right to a death, is revised so as mythically to outwit death when, at the very end of the *Wake*, the senescent Struldbruggs mate with the snorting Houyhnhnms and the stallion of eternity mounts the mare of time: Anna Livia remembers Shaughnessy's mare being given 'the hillymount of her life. With her strulldeburgghers! Hnmn Hnmn!' Yeats's name, its meagre initials expansively spelled out like one of Joyce's earth-encircling compounds, spills over into the landscape in which, as a spirit, he resides: he undergoes a reconciliatory dissolution as 'Doubbllinnbbayyates', being given—with typical Joycean largesse—a double dose of consonants. Swift is monastically castigated with his own name when it is spelled as 'Swhipt', and Shaw splutters expletively as 'Pshaw'. Joyce's language evolves from the symbolist signing of Wildean aphorism, 'letting punplays pass for earnest', and the opaquer riddling of Jabberwocky. He pays tribute to the writers who have enabled him to rewrite literature by miswriting them. Wilde disperses into his own manifold Wiles, while the logician of nonsense covers with his 'Dadgerson's dodges' the malfeasances of his 'Lewd's carol'. Joyce's puns are a loving nicknaming, retroactively enlisting predecessors as offspring: he marvels at Shakespeare as Shikespower and pastorally pets him at Sheepskeer. By contrast Shaw makes use of Shakespeare's variously garbled spellings of his own name to conflate him with the rest of a literary history which Shaw does not familially grow into but—having reduced it to a single mongrelised word—casts off. Zoo in *Back to Methuselah*, speaking from the snooty distance of AD 3000, recalls 'an ancient writer whose name has come down to us in several forms, such as Shakespear, Shelley, Sheridan, and Shoddy'.

Finnegans Wake does not abruptly end the past, but ensures its continuation; it is innocent of the modernist conscience which agonises over the inadequacies of language because it has lost faith in the value of literature. That inquest of his own means is conducted by a writer who seems more technically conventional than Joyce but who is in fact much more of an imaginatively agnostic modern, Aldous Huxley.

Lecturing at Santa Barbara in 1959, Huxley recorded his admiration for the versatile intelligence of his grandfather T. H. Huxley, 'never happy unless he was doing three or four full-time jobs at once'. But the Victorian sage was dealing with a world where knowledge was humane and where literature could qualify as a humanist gospel. Aldous Huxley confronts a world of technical specialisms and of an engineered, chemically-induced spirituality, where literature has ceased to comprehend the nature anatomised by science and positively interferes with our advance (thanks to the mental technology of hallucenogenic drugs) to the enlightenment which Huxley called 'unstructured transpersonal consciousness'. Literature's mission to humanise has turned, for Huxley, into a metaphysical error. The anthropomorphism of novels deters us from the recognition of our own unreality and irrelevance. Satirically, Huxley assassinates the obsolete human person, resolving Webley's corpse in *Point Counter Point* (1928) into an exhalation of noxious gases; mystically, he causes that same creature psychedelically to vaporise, like the body tagged as William Asquith Farnaby in *Island* (1962) raying into a bright, vacant, visionary state of awareness. Humanity had made the universe a suburb. Huxley sought release from this 'all too human world' by discrediting its pet institution of literature. He could approve the novels of Lawrence and Joyce only because he saw in them, wrongly, an inductive science, examining psychological change under laboratory conditions. The Santa Barbara lectures deplore 'the story-telling faculty' as a misuse of intelligence, and account words a casualty of evolution, relics of a primitive need to colonise the world by naming its contents. Now science has shown that world to be 'refreshingly other', it is best described by numbers, formulae and equations.

Huxley has his own version of Joyce's translation of languages into companionability. Rivers in *The Genius and the Goddess* (1955) spells out the obscenest of four-letter words, 'L-o-v-e', and then translates it into 'the decent obscurity of the learned languages, *Agape, Caritas, Mahakaruna*'. Each migration further relieves it of its tawdry emotional meaning as the alibi for Ruth's execrable verses or for the 'official fiction' of the life someone has written of the novel's hero, the atomic physicist Maartens; it is voided at last as grace, a condition of selflessness averse to human fussing. We need, Rivers says, 'another set of words'—yet they are not to be Joyce's learned slang or Lawrence's growling dialect. 'Those still non-existent words' will be a technocratic jargon synthesising such neologisms as muco-spiritual, dermato-charity, mastonoetic and viscerosophy, reducing emotions to their 'physiological correlates' and unleashing minds from the glandular prison of bodies into 'non-material fields'. This will be a language able to register the cerebration of geniuses like Maartens and the instinctual hungering of goddesses like his wife Katy, who are the polarities of what Huxley's 1959 lectures entitled 'the human situation', and who are untranslatable by literature. Together they constitute a pair of classical deities domiciled in California, for 'the Olympians . . . were nothing but a pack of superhuman animals with miraculous powers.'

Rivers denounces poetry as a fraudulent chemistry, 'alchemy in reverse' turning 'the pure lyrics of experience . . . into the verbal equivalents of tripe and hogwash', and the novel as a narrative maundering, condemned to fail by the tense it chooses since it stumbles through the past looking for an enlightenment which exists not in memory but in immediate experience. Cancelling out Milton and Proust at once, he declares that 'Time Regained is Paradise Lost, and Time Lost is Paradise Regained.' Huxley saw man as an amphibian, perplexed between body and spirit. Literature will only arrive at the truth of man's state if it transforms itself into science. Thus Rivers, engaged by Maartens as a research assistant at Berkeley, foresees for the novel a future as physics—when he relativistically divides himself into 'me-then' and 'me-now', or draws in the air with the stem of his pipe a diagram of an erotic intrigue as the triangular intersection of 'three co-ordinates'—or as inorganic chemistry, when he analyses character and reality as liquid mixtures. The conventional world is '*café au lait*—fifty per cent skim milk and fifty per cent stale chicory', slopping psychophysical stimuli together with a quotient of recycled verbiage. Maartens by contrast has the constituents of a cocktail. Like a highball, he stirs together half a pint of fizzing intellectuality with 'a small jigger of immediate experience'.

Whereas Joyce punningly conflates Krishnamurti with Christ and thus makes him an ambassador of the serially reborn word, Huxley in one of the essays collected in *Adonis and the Alphabet* (1956) quotes Krishnamurti as a spokesman for a clarity which frees us from the known, from the ensnaring would-be realities sustained by literature, from Joyce's entropic cycles: 'organized group thought is merely repetitive'. Krishnamurti counsels silence. Huxley, following him, requires that literature defer to 'the non-verbal humanities'. He encourages the ghost to house itself in a machine, and ranks books with the domesticated genies of applied science. Bloom wants to use the gramophone to keep the dead—at least vocally—awake, and the new twelve-tube high-fidelity radio purchased for the tavern in *Finnegans Wake* is a battery-operated vocalist, equipped with 'a vitaltone speaker' and a magnetic coupling-system whose brand-name couples two composers of romantic songs, Bellini and Tosti. In Joyce the machine which transmits the voice revivifies literature. For Huxley, technology has abolished the printed book and summoned back the Homeric bard. The Hundred Great Books, he points out, have been recorded for the phonograph and 'can be listened to painlessly—at meals, while washing up, as a substitute for the evening paper'. This is not Joyce's 'history as her is harped', though Huxley does compare the talkative vinyl with the balladry of the medieval harpers; it is muzak.

If the Joycean word known in all languages must be analysed and redistilled in the laboratory, as it is by Rivers, then the congested Joycean everywhere, compressing the world into Dublin and environs, exists for Huxley only in the museum of universal history on the MGM backlot at Culver City where, he notes, distant locations abut and you walk from Romeo and Juliet's Verona to Tarzan's jungle and then, by way of Harun-al-Rashid's Araby, into the flimsy Meryton assembled for the film of *Pride and Prejudice* (1940) on which Huxley himself had worked.

Finnegans Wake expects perpetual renewal. However, the modernism which Joyce is often said to have inaugurated is no rollicking wake, and when *Finnegans Wake* is enlisted as a copy-book for that sombrely posthumous era, it is made to forego its comic jubilation. The moribund hero of Beckett's novel *Malone Dies* (1951) is a Finn who is impatient to die, and determined not to awake again. The loss of consciousness is not his merger with a collective unconsciousness but simply the mercy of coma, and no 'great loss' at that. Instead of the flooding life of Molly or Anna Livia, he experiences the guttering of the body's tides, which he calls 'gurgles of outflow'; instead of their dilation to enwomb everyone and everything, he suffers through the abdication of his extremities, which leave him to float off into the void. His twin sluices, penis and anus, vanish in different directions. If he were to stand up, he feels he would 'fill a considerable part of the universe'—but that enlargement is a prelude to annihilation, swelling into a vapid nothing. His gassy expansion goes with a shrivelled diminution. The sense of being so contracts that 'in the end I could almost be buried in a casket'.

Unlike Tim Finnegan in the ballad who is revived by the whisky or the giant Finn MacCool recumbent until he is ready to resume life, Beckett's characters are domiciled in the grave, like the urn-buried characters of *Play* (1963) or the fossilising Winnie in *Happy Days* (1961). Their artistry consists in the mortuary finesse with which they undertake their own interring. Narrative is their attempt to wear out time by imposing a routine on it, and they see it—like Malone occupying his last days by telling stories which lead, on purpose, nowhere—as a level horizon which will soon taper to a stop. Malone's little finger gropes ahead of his expending pencil across the page 'and gives warning, falling over the edge, that the end of the line is near'. The accomplished sentence is no exhilarating, heavenly 'sundance' but a sentence of death: language flattened into the straight line of the cardiograph when the heart-beat stops. Beckett's utterances are fatally linear, without Joyce's cyclical retour. If the recurrent pulse starts up again, like the chair in *Rockaby* (1981)—a mortal metronome, alive on the old woman's behalf—it is an artificial resuscitation. The sappy Joycean heroines have aged into terminal patients.

The epic, incremental generosity of Joyce's art alters to a grudging division and abbreviation of intolerable time: Malone reckons that a summation of his life will take him a quarter of an hour, and will consist, in contrast with Joyce's synopticon, of three stories only; Pozzo in *Waiting for Godot* (1955) manages an even more economical implosion by deciding 'one day we were born, one day we'll die, the same day, the same second'. Life is a waiting room, literature a penitential pastime. Malone writes himself to death, as the woman in *Rockaby* rocks herself there, and contemplating a pencil which he has sharpened at both ends is pleased to note that 'my lead is not inexhaustible'. He writes in an exercise-book ruled in squares for calculation because writing is the only exercise he is permitted, and because the grid is the page's cellulation and its fractionalising. Mental arithmetic—like the 'manipulation of concrete numbers' by Saposcat in one of Malone's stories—is a properly futile model for literature, its success consisting in arrival at a row of noughts. Technique equals subtraction, never Joyce's compounding additiveness. Joyce called the naturalism of *Dubliners* a style of 'scrupulous meanness'; Malone is a fanatical practitioner of that manner: 'scrupulous to the last, finical to a fault, that's Malone, all over.' By making Finn finical, Beckett ensures that it will all soon be over.

Joyce's polylingual music—the plurality of Anna Livia's tributaries—is synthesised as gibberish by Malone. He cannot decompose the 'volume of sound' into its constituents; all the world's noises merge as 'one vast continuous buzzing'. Joyce's vocal literature leads in Beckett to the voice's expiring abstraction from the body whose witness it once was. 'Loosen your talk-tapes' say the washerwomen in *Finnegans Wake*, wanting to swap gossip about Anna Livia as they scrub their dirty linen. But for Beckett's Krapp and for the woman in the rocking-chair, whose consciousnesses are a playback, the voice has been supererogated by a tape which is fixed, inflexible, looped like an endless purgatory. In *Not I* (1972) the voice belongs to no one, and babbles, spot-lit, from the wound of a bodiless mouth on a blacked-out stage. Billie Whitelaw, whose voice it was, remembers primally screaming as she oxygenated, blindfolded and mummified inside a hood.

Harold Pinter also resummons the voice from the grave in a play about a wake, and about Beckett's employment of drama as a last rite. Deborah in his *A Kind of Alaska*, heartbreakingly played by Judi Dench in 1982, has been comatose for twenty-nine years, a victim of sleeping-sickness. Awakened, she is a child's voice in a body which has outgrown and abandoned her. The voice cannot presume to own its experience, or even to comprehend itself. Thinking perhaps of Beckett's linguistic expatriation of himself (he writes in French, then translates back into English), Pinter has Deborah ask, 'What language am I speaking? I speak French, I know that. Is this French?' Like Malone discarding his tubular sex, she is the quizzical spectator of a body with its own automatic biological will. 'Where did you get those breasts?' she asks her sister, who can only reply, 'They came about.' And time—the torture of duration which is Pozzo's curse, and which makes Beckett abbreviate his plays to spasms, evacuations of breath—can also be withdrawn from, thanks to the relativity theory: 'Is the war still over?' Deborah enquires. Roused from her somnolence, she does not undergo mythic renewal but has to step back into the weary forced march of history. At first she believes she must be dead; once she understands she is alive, she sets about the long process of beginning to die.

While the Joycean voice suffers this extradition from the body, Joyce's language or languages, once so fluently compatible, turn into Newspeak, an exportable, international jargon. This is the official idiom of Orwell's Oceania in *Nineteen Eighty-Four* (1949). Orwell's theory of language tragically contradicts Joyce's: ahead he sees depletion not augmentation, and he treats contemporary politics as a systematic word-murder. The beasts in his *Animal Farm* (1945) dumbly delimit the human alphabet and its spectrum of possibility. One of the cart-horses cannot get beyond D, another memorises all the letters but cannot assemble words from them, the mare will learn only as many as are necessary to spell her own name, and the rest are stuck at A. Illiteracy equals for Orwell a forfeiture of human freedom. The enslavement of Oceania demands the systematic decimation of English: Syme the lexicographer in *Nineteen Eighty-Four* delights in 'the destruction of words', and admires Newspeak as 'the only language in the world whose vocabulary gets smaller every year'. Ampleforth ponders a similar paucity in verse: 'The whole history of English poetry has been determined', he believes, 'by the fact that the English language lacks rhymes.' Newspeak contrives an implosion of words in portmanteaux which, rather than ribaldly enriching significance as Joyce's do, narrow them to slogans, abbreviating them until they excite stock responses only and dispensing with that supplementary life of aura, echo and association, in which literature grows. The Orwellian B vocabulary was for him the diction of totalitarian politics, dependent on the taciturn, terrifying messages relayed by Nazi, Gestapo and Comintern; it has since become the idiom of corporate capitalism and of advertising. Ours is a world of neon-lit initials and acronyms, of language reduced to a denotative minimum: TV, VCR, CIA, AT&T, A&P where they watch their Ps and Qs, AM and FM, B12 and DC10 . . . the short-hand and stenography of a standardised consumerism; a concrete poetry of commodities.

In succession to Orwell, Anthony Burgess—an admirer and expositor of Joyce, who has even made an operatic adaptation of *Ulysses*—wrote *A Clockwork Orange* (1962) in the slangy lingo of the delinquent Alex. The coinages mock Joyce because they are not a research into the native sources of speech but an ersatz, as synthetic as the chemically tinctured potions in the milk bar, 'moloko . . . with vellocet or synthemesc or drencrom'. This is an argot for a post-literate age, where no one reads newspapers, people who borrow books from the Public Biblio are accounted degenerates, and everyone viddies everything, as Alex says, on the telly. Words as for Malone have been supplanted by noise, electronically amplified. Alex taunts enemies with expletive 'lip-music: brrrrzzzzrrrr.' His talk is the uprooting of English not, as Joyce hoped, its liquid re-marriage with neighbouring tongues, since it mongrelises a Russian vocabulary with American street-talk.

It remains for the composer John Cage to subject Joyce to a final mechanisation. The inexhaustibility of Joyce succumbs to modernist rote (Malone's 'What tedium'), his patterned recurrences to randomness. The sentence with its tail in its mouth, like 'riverrun', mystically whole, untwines and disperses. When Malone dozes while writing, 'the subject falls far from the verb and the object lands somewhere in the void'. Cage sees it as his modernist duty to assist this unmaking by rewriting or (as he put it when publishing his cut-up of the text in 1978) *Writing Through Finnegans Wake*. Whereas Joyce dreams of a sentence open-armed enough to carry all the words in the world, Cage, who considers syntax a military imposition, seeks the sentence's abolition. He writes through Joyce to effect 'a transition from a language without sentences . . . to a "language" having only letters and silence'. That non-referential 'language' will be music. Cage's nullification of sentence and meaning reorganises Joyce's text to be read vertically, like Chinese or like musical counterpoint. Haikus are extracted whose spine is a mesostic (an acrostic row running down the middle of the words, not marshalling initial letters) spelling out, over and over again, the name JAMES JOYCE. The aleatory is obsessively systematised: that is the formula of so-called post-modernism.

Since then, Cage has even more derangingly deconstructed the *Wake* in his *Muoyce*, recited by him at the Whitney Museum in New York in 1984. Now his modernist gift to it is the reduction of words to phonetic runes, chanted into a microphone. The text is pulverised into incomprehensibility, and the 'demilitarized' gobbledegook which results—'permienting hi himself then pass ahs c'—is intoned in lines whose timing is determined by random numbers generated for Cage by computers at the Bell Laboratories, and whose droned or muttered melodic arcs are improvised by him. Joyce, Cage fondly fancies, 'would have been delighted by what happens when intention is removed from the *Wake*'. Babel has collapsed into rubble again.

39

The Stages of Drama

Once the stage had contracted from an amphitheatral circle into a square room with a retractable fourth wall, drama was made to confine itself to the observation of what might happen in that room. Shaw complained that the only subject available to the dramatists of his time was social and sexual liaisons. The romantics evade the claustrophobia of the room by rendering its walls lyrically transparent: through them can be seen the astral transfigurations of *Prometheus Unbound*. The renewal of the drama proceeds by expanding the stage's cramped parlour or boudoir. In Hardy's *The Dynasts* (1903–8) and Shaw's *Back to Methuselah* (1921) it opens into the arena of history. Or else its secular living-room is reconsecrated, when Eliot writes a play for performance in a cathedral or in *The Family Reunion* brings the Aeschylean furies into the house. Eliot retains the social gatherings which are the occasions of the older drama—a cocktail party, for instance—but shows them to be solemn rites not frivolous entertainments.

If the stage cannot be made the site for mystery and miracle, it is vacated. In contrast with the congested decor of nineteenth-century dramaturgy, copiously substantialising the collapsible room, the director Peter Brook declares that the modicum of drama is an 'empty space'. Perhaps a desert, like that where Beckett's characters await Godot; perhaps, more clinically, it is the white box of tricks within which Brook in 1970 staged the flying circus of his *Midsummer Night's Dream*. At its most frugal, it is constituted each evening by the gipsy fortune-teller who, in Brook's *La Tragédie de Carmen* (1981), traces a ring in the sand and lights small bonfires around it to guard her occult zone.

Where the room remains, it is defined as a blind alley, and its inescapability becomes the subject of the play: the château in Sartre's *Les Sequestrés d'Altona* (1956), or the various locked and bolted cells which are the scenes of Pinter's drama—the mental asylum which is his suffocating, sound-proofed *Hothouse* (1958); the attic in *The Caretaker* (1960) where a pitched battle for precious *lebensraum* is acted out and housekeeping is warfare, so that Mick tries to evict Davies with the vacuum-cleaner; or the entrenched frontier of a Hampstead study which Pinter calls his *No Man's Land* (1975). When Hardy in *The Dynasts* scenically extemporises a cathedral inside the Louvre and then resolves it into 'a gigantic café', plants a tropical landscape inside Carlton House, and enjoins the rearrangement of the boxes and the levelling of interior doors in the opera house at Covent Garden, or when Shaw in *Man and*

Superman (1901–3) dissolves the Sierra Nevada into 'nothing: omnipresent nothing', using light as Adolphe Appia or Edward Gordon Craig prescribed to dematerialise the theatre, they are demonstrating that the stage can re-encompass the world, and restoring to it a Shakespearean amplitude—except that the wooden O is now a hole in space, and Hardy looks down at the world and its trivial skirmishes from mid-air, while Shaw looks back on it from the eternality of 'the year 31,920 A.D.'. For their successors, there is no such infinitude. Every Pinter stage is a cul-de-sac: one of his most fiendishly tortuous speeches, in *No Man's Land*, is about the impossibility of driving a car out of Bolsover Street in central London.

Hardy hybridly calls *The Dynasts* 'an epic-drama'. That is only one of its bold formal contradictions. Epically, its narrative disputes the right of history to see itself as drama, since events cannot be ascribed to the volition of single human actors but are the results of an impersonal, immanent necessity. The Commons debates the issue of whether France willed Napoléon's existence. Though he insists on behaving as if the world were his theatre, impatiently crowning himself and quarrelling (as Murat says) with clocks because they are not as expeditious as his wishes, history is not character in action, and nor is drama. Just as Sheridan prompts the Regent at Brighton, manipulating him like a ventriloquist's dummy, and just as Josephine is compelled to sign the severing parchments while pretending that it is her own supposedly free choice, so Napoléon is operated by an 'unmotived' Will outside him. Hardy begins not with decisive action by the character Shaw, in his own Napoleonic play in 1896, called a man of destiny, but with the parliamentary repealing of an Act. Decrès warns Napoléon against his tendency to behave like a dramatist, ascribing motives to actors.

Hardy's epic is a metaphysical reproof to the drama, because it transfers the responsibility for deeds to the 'ubiquitous urging' of a time-spirit, and abolishes the individual by eliminating 'the combatants as beings', representing them instead—as in the aerial perspective of Leipzig—as 'amorphous drifts, clouds and waves of conscious atoms'. Its protagonists are as immobilised as Hamlet: Metternich in Vienna observing Talleyrand, 'no muscle moving'; Wellington at Waterloo 'acting while discovering his intention to act'. Queen Louisa calls it a 'historied drama' which she first reads about and then has to perform in. Again her hybrid term covers an encounter of opposites: narrative recitation, foreordaining events in the recitatives of the recording angels with their books of fate, and the illusory independence of dramatic enactment.

That contrast sharpens into another between epic and pastoral. Tolstoy, writing about the same historical crisis, divides it between the epic embattlement of war and the pastoral repose of peace, and suggests that the novel can understand history only by indirection—by studying lives on its margin, like Natasha's, and ostracising the analysis of policy and strategy to an appendix. The conference of Napoléon and Alexander at Tilsit is not dramatised by Hardy, but mimed in dumb show, then overheard by an English spy. The same tactical avoidance converts bellicose epic into placid pastoral: as Nelson dies at Trafalgar, his captain, Hardy's namesake, touchingly remembers the Wessex landscape of his childhood.

The historical tragedy, relayed to remote Wessex, is re-enacted there as mythic mumming and as comic festivity. Napoléon, rumoured by the yokels to feast on babies, is burned by them in effigy, consumed by the nature he defies and ravages. For history is less an epic salute to human initiatives than a pastoral commiseration with earth's travails and grievances. When Napoléon's rant at Borodino dies away, Hardy eavesdrops on the silence, and 'the sputtering of the green wood fires, which . . . hold a conversation of their own'. He hears or sees the landscape beneath the battlefields. The cries from the plain at Leipzig resemble a rookery, and the armies along the Rhine writhe 'like scaly serpents'. At Waterloo the French troops, spreading out into their fighting-places, are metaphorically translated to rustic Wessex, 'their arms glittering like a display of cutlery at a hill-side fair'. Human agents are granted membership in the earth, and their history calligraphically writes upon that collective body (Leipzig seen from far above is a letter D) or alters its posture. Earth, anthropomorphised, is Hardy's protagonist. Mannheim at the junction of its two rivers resembles a human head pinioned in a cleft stick, and the map of Europe looks from the overworld like a debilitated Lear, 'a prone and emaciated figure' whose vertebrae are the Alps, the mountain-chains its starved ribs, its head sagging in despair towards the Spanish peninsula. The lowlands are a garment it is discarding, the sea its distressed bed of pain.

Drama must make do with puny individuals; Hardy's tragic hero is a continent in agony. And as well as studying the agitations and slumped exhaustion of its geological physique, he can render it transparent to expose its distraught nerves and febrile ganglia. He anatomises Austerlitz, baring the 'brain-like network of currents and ejections' which are the twitchings of the Immanent Will, and Napoléon as he prepares to invade Russia is seen to be a tissue of that filmy cerebellum.

The redundant individual is absorbed by a reborn Greek chorus, as Hardy's supervising Pities or (more boisterously) his rollicking boatmen singing a ballad about Trafalgar in a Wessex inn. The Shakespearean stage with its celestial painted ceiling and its infernal trap-door boxed the universe. Hardy opens up the infinite space of which Hamlet, trapped in his theatre, dreams. The two tiers of the Shakespearean plot are the vertically ranked orders of metaphysical existence. Thus while the parliamentarians are squabbling, 'the four Phantoms' (those choric spirits) slip into the stranger's gallery of the Commons to watch. The chamber has equipped itself with a perch for emigrants from supernature.

From this merger of Greek tragedy with Shakespearean history, Hardy makes a new kind of drama. Nietzsche believed Wagnerian opera was the rebirth of Greek tragedy, with music as the upsurgence of Dionysus and words as the rational decrees of Apollo. Shaw in the preface to *Back to Methuselah* sees Beethoven's Choral Symphony and Wagner's *Ring* as the prototypes for his own drama. To the enchantments of music, the Wagnerian theatre added the illusory hypnosis of light and (as in Shaw's scenic metamorphosis in the Sierra Nevada) of obliviating dark. The critic Hanslick said that the miracles of Bayreuth's *Ring* in 1876 were possible only because of electricity. The theatre is a mechanised magic. Hardy, too, makes drama from the invisible, perpetually transitional processes of music, and from the atmospheric altering of light. At Lobau his stage-directions insist that we observe something which cannot be seen, the birth-pangs of 'a huge event'. His only way of representing this is by electrifying the air: the twilight strains and quivers with suspense. During the ball in Brussels before Waterloo, the occasion of Jos's panic in *Vanity Fair*, Hardy directs that 'the air is ecstasizing', intensifying the sexual urgency of the dancers.

As Birnam Wood marches to Dunsinane, Shakespeare literalises a prophetic metaphor. But Hardy's is a theatre where the only actors are metaphors, and at Waterloo Napoléon and his marshals do battle against verbal and visual hallucinations, interpreting the advancing English as 'a darkly crawling, slug-like shape', a new-leafed wood, or 'the creeping shadow from a cloud'; this is a clairvoyant theatre, existing to be seen as much as to be heard. In South Wessex the burgesses rig up a dais on which they will entertain George III—the medieval or Elizabethan actor's platform. The king calls it 'but a stage, a type of all the world'. For Hardy it is too dwarfed a microcosm. The Spirit of the Years, listening to Napoléon speak at Ulm, transfers him to a more properly cosmic theatre, moving from the body strutting and fretting its hour upon the boards to the shadow (or idea) projected onto a screen which is a sky-cloth: '*we clearly sight him | Moved like a figure on a lantern-slide.*' The physical presence of the actor is dispensed with; he becomes a ghost conjured up by electricity. The dramatist is his projector: the Spirit's '*all-compelling crystal pane*'. The oracle in *Back to Methuselah* prophetically dilates herself thanks to 'a foolish picture . . . thrown on a cloud by a lantern'. When Edward Gordon Craig, envisioning, like Hardy, a theatre of mood and of musical kinesis, designed *Hamlet* for Stanislavsky in Moscow in 1912, he changed Elsinore from a castle of obtuse concreteness into an abstract cinema, airily building it of white screens on which Hamlet's thoughts could be shadowily imprinted. The scenery is moving inside the mind, and that is the most panoramic amphitheatre—and the most private viewing-booth—of all.

For Hardy, the disability of drama is its unity of place, overcome by his 'migratory Proskenion'. Its liability for Shaw is its unity of time. His evolutionary vitalism strains against the form's abbreviation. Life's imperative is to grow, to develop, which requires the elasticising of the play with its miserly allowance of two hours' existence. Adam and Eve in *Back to Methuselah* are tormented yet challenged by brevity. Adam tells the serpent that love is 'too short a word for so long a thing', and when Eve laments that the fatiguing trek of aspiration is 'too long a story', the serpent supplies her with a single verb—'to conceive'—which, conjugated, will unfold from itself all of human history. Shaw's project for infinitely extending human life demands the serial elongation of the play. Metabiology contrives a metadrama.

Even longer-winded than the *Ring*, *Methuselah* was designed for performance on five consecutive nights. It blithely bypasses *The Dynasts*, unearthing Napoleon in AD 3000 only to dispense with him, since he lacks foresight and specialises in extermination not the continuance of longevity. Shot by the oracle, he flees to the statue of Falstaff and gibbers prayerfully there. The fat knight is numbered by Shaw in the preface to *Man and Superman* among those 'instinctive temperaments' who are Shakespeare's comically unteachable characters. His colleagues include Coriolanus and Leontes, and he demonstrates (to Shaw) Shakespeare's failure as a dramatist: one, that is, who engineers change, using the play to mobilise history, like Stephen Poliakoff in the railway carriage where his play *Breaking the Silence* (1984) is set. But in *Methuselah* Falstaff is accorded a pastoral wisdom. His evasiveness ensures him a kind of eternity, and his statue was raised after the 1914–18 war, when statesmen discovered that cowardice might be the preservation of the world.

Methuselah cannot accept the temporal begrudgement of its form because it needs to rally a country whose impulses are as regressive as those of the Shakespearean comedians. Confucius in AD 2170 considers the English mind 'not an adult mind', and regrets that English civilisation is still in its infancy. The literary journeys on which that mind sets out do not arrive at their destinations, but double back to home base. Shaw recalls this tendency of the Chaucerian and the Sternean voyages in AD 3000 when the elderly gentleman tells Fusima that he has come to Galway 'on a pious pilgrimage'. She wonders if that is 'some new means of transport'. He insists that he refers to no machine, to 'a sentimental journey'. Keeping the play in motion is Shaw's remonstrance to the English lassitude which delays Chaucer's company and Yorick.

It is also his reproof to the cyclical repetitiousness, as he sees it, of Shakespearean comedy, seasonally recurring. The Festival Day in AD 31,920 rebukes the childish gambolling of Shakespeare's sheep-shearing, or his Christmas revels with their cakes and ale. Shakespeare's characters dance in comic settlement of their discords. That choreographing of drama seems, to Shaw's contemporaries, the mystic secret of the form: Wagner glossed Beethoven's Seventh Symphony as the apotheosis of the dance, and Craig in 1905 hailed Isadora Duncan as a muse whose cavortings showed that 'the Art of the Theatre has sprung from action—movement—dance'; Yeats's Old Man in *The Death of Cuchulain* (1939) wants to produce his play as a ballet, because 'when there are no words there is less to spoil.' All this Shaw's Ancient sagely refutes: 'Dancing is a very crude attempt to get into the rhythm of life', he tells the capering young gymnasts. Shaw gets into that rhythm verbally not athletically. His life-force, as exhibited by Tanner or Dudgeon in *The Devil's Disciple* (1897) or Higgins in *Pygmalion* (1912), is an untiring, ebulliently rhythmical talkativeness. Yeats's spirits brought him metaphors for poetry; the voices in *Saint Joan* (1923), as if from some aerial prompt-box, train the heroine in a rhetorical vehemence. The last words of Eve's ghost at the end of *Methuselah* quote Shakespeare's easy-going comic optimism: 'All's well.' But Shakespeare's Helena uses the proverb to cheer herself up, and Shaw thought her insistence proved that a happy ending was a delusion. From Eve it comes as biological achievement, rather than Helena's wistful hope. All is well because 'my clever ones have inherited the earth'. This is a species of divine comedy, culminating not in marriage—whereby Shakespearean couples, like Mirabell obtaining Millamant's acquiescence in child-bearing, attain a proxy immortality—but in the race's perpetuation.

That millenium re-educates the dramatist as a scientist. Pygmalion, mimicked by Higgins when he phonetically refashions Eliza, returns in his own person in *Methuselah*, having synthesised two human creatures in his laboratory. In his case as in Higgins's, the freedom of dramatic character, which licenses the Shakespearean actor to do whatever he wills, is a unique peril. The delight of Shakespeare in creating characters who elude or defy him is the horror of these Shavian dramatists: Eliza walks out on Higgins, Pygmalion's female mannequin bites him to death. Shaw's wish is for a character who will be his obedient creature, determined by him. As a god-like artificer, he is more of a martinet than either of his Pygmalions, inventing automata which respond instantly to his cues. Martellus denies that Pygmalion's figurines are alive because they must be operated by stimuli from without. Yet it is this mechanistic infallibility which makes them, for Pygmalion, such exemplary specimens. It qualifies them, too, as ideal Shavian actors, and their debut consists in a dance, stimulated by flattery and rewarded by applause. The laws of evolution are the rules of dramaturgy. This is the meaning of Joan's voices, contrivances of dramatic puppetry: they tell Joan what to do, and she in her turn tells the politicians what to do. Henry V achieves the capitulation of besieged Harfleur by orating at it; Joan raises the siege of Orleans by stirring up a wind. Her triumph is not a verbal and theatrical marvel only, like Henry's. The breeze which flaps the pennant, makes the page sneeze and sends the boats upstream is the onward-rushing breath of Shavian speech: the gusty volatility of his harangues.

Shakespeare, being so retrograde, has to be put through an evolutionary course in adaptive self-improvement. This is the service Shaw performs for the Roman plays in *Caesar and Cleopatra* (1889). Shakespeare's infirm Caesar is raised to godliness by Shaw, while Cleopatra is reduced to kittenish infancy. The play is about her Eliza-like education by Caesar, not her debauches with

Antony, who is another instinctive, priapic and gluttonous temperament, almost a Falstaff. Caesar allows him to be 'in excellent condition—considering how much he eats and drinks', and himself makes do with cerebral and abstemious diet of peacocks' brains and barley water. Though Cleopatra reveres Caesar she cannot love him, because he is a god and therefore cannot be hurt by her. Equally unwilling to gratify her sensually himself, he sends Antony to her. As a dramatist, he relies on the manipulability of his creations. Pygmalion's plastic figments can make love, because doing so is entirely a matter of stimuli and reflex actions. Caesar likewise incites desire in his Cleopatra, and manufactures Antony to satisfy it.

Apollodorus the amateur artist honours Caesar as a colleague. 'No longer . . . the conquering soldier', he is 'the creative poet-artist', one of the company of philosopher-kings listed by Shaw as his own predecessors in the *Man and Superman* preface. Caesar boasts that he practises war, peace, government and civilisation as arts. He is also expert at the polity of drama. He knows the dramatist to be an unmoved mover, who, like the fissiparous Lilith in *Methuselah*, brings to birth others to act on his behalf. In Shakespeare's play the Romans resent his pretension to deity and—vengefully but also lovingly—reclaim him for humanity by analysing his ailments. In Shaw's work, humanity is something to be superseded, and his Caesar has already done so. Cleopatra worships the immunity to feeling which offends the Shakespearean conspirators. Caesar converts Diderot's paradox of the actor into the paradox of the dramatist, studying stasis, leaving action and acting to his subordinates. His triumphs in the play are the things he does not do: he lets prisoners escape, refuses to read the intercepted letters from his enemies, will not use torture, and stands by while the Alexandrian library burns. He has arrived to the seventh degree of concentration sought by Shotover in *Heartbreak House* (1919), which is indifference. Thus he can even predict and perform his own death as if he were that absent god the dramatist, not a suffering character. When he tells Rufio, 'I have always disliked the idea of dying: I had rather be killed', he is encouraging the assassins in *Julius Caesar* to do him a favour.

Shaw endows Lear with the same comic sagacity in *Heartbreak House*. Yeats imagines a Lear whose tragic anguish is, as in the Nietzschean worship of Dionysus, a comic elation, and conflates him with a Sophoclean prototype in his version of *Oedipus at Colonus* (1934). The blinded king has wandered off, like Lear on the heath, as an 'old ragged, rambling beggarman'. He awaits his end patiently and is relieved rather than maddened by the 'prolonged loud thunder and abundant lightning' which announce it. Having passed beyond grief and rage, he expires with the serenity of Gloucester not like the protesting Lear, 'in a manner altogether wonderful'. He can graduate to a rejoicing comedy; Shaw's Lear has to be reprieved by comedy, and instructed in its evolutionary survivalism. The doughty Shotover has lasted to his Methuselah-like age because he has learned not to care, and can cope with his pelican daughters—flighty Hesione, officious Ariadne, and ingenuous Ellie, whom he spiritually adopts and at last marries—because he is aware that the natural term of the human parent's affection for its offspring is six years, which he has long since exceeded. Yet there is no sublime Yeatsian frenzy to him, and he unsentimentally paraphrases the wisdom of Gloucester, who learns that 'ripeness is all', by calling his serenity 'the sweetness of the fruit that is going rotten'. He is a brisk comic leveller, rather than a tragic brooder on the bare forked animal, and can tolerate the gatecrashing of strangers because at his age he makes no distinctions between his fellow-creatures. His salvation is that he does not take even his role of Lear seriously. In the same way Hector, romancing Ellie, is deliberately play-acting Othello ('only, of course, white, and very handsome') by inventing tales of the anthropophagi and imperial tiger-hunts, whereas Randall is not enough of a witty or sceptical comedian to know that his pose—again that of 'Ellie's favourite, Othello'—is entirely histrionic.

Shotover does not rely on the gods to send a meteorological apocalypse, like Lear's storm. Again, with the comic character's practicality, he brews it himself in an improvised lab, stockpiling dynamite so he can blow up the human race when sufficiently provoked. The extrusion from the house is not banishment to unaccommodated, niggardly nature but a camping-trip in Arden. Though Hector proposes, 'Let us all go out into the night and leave everything behind us', Ellis considerately offers Mangan the use of her waterproof to lie on. With the indestructibility and resilient cunning which are the biological safeguards of comedy, these characters outface the tragic 'promised end' as Shakespeare calls it, live through the bombardment, and have the temerity to hope that their destroyers will come again tomorrow, to challenge them with another ultimate stimulus.

Shaw is sanely unable to tolerate the prestige of tragedy. He hears the primal scream—Lear's reiterated 'howl'—as a comically indignant exclamation. He remarks in the *Methuselah* preface that a baby's bawling when it enters the world is what Shakespeare mistook for 'the most tragic and piteous of all sounds'. In fact, the infant is merely trying out its lungs and learning to breathe. From that yell will come *bel canto*, and from that the eloquent jabbering of Shavian language. 'Your flow of words is simply amazing' says the statue to Juan in *Man and Superman*. The melody of howling explains why Shaw, in quest of alternatives to the disgraced Shakespearean dramatic forms (for comedy now means a play about courtship, and tragedy has degenerated into a murder mystery), looks to the musical theatre.

Methuselah points to Mozart's *Magic Flute*, Beethoven's Ninth Symphony and Wagner's *Ring* as its predecessors; *Man and Superman* attempts to be *Don Giovanni* without the music. Its adherence to Mozart is a snub to Shakespeare: Shaw considers Juan a Hamlet more authentic than Shakespeare's hero, whose intellectual rebellion is halted when he is made to play the detective, just as

Burge in *Methuselah* turns the makeshift magus Prospero into Wagner's Wotan meditating on *das Ende* and, having quoted the speech about the great globe's dissolution, calls it 'good sound biology'. Shelley had already transformed *The Tempest*'s 'rough magic' into scientific revolution in his lyrical drama. Shaw, whose Juan is a 'Promethean foe of the gods', performs the feat over again in what he calls, in his debate with Ana, 'a universal melodrama'—melodrama meaning drama with music, and music being for Shaw the pulse of an irrepressible vitalism, heard in the racing exuberance of the overture to *Don Giovanni* or in the unappeased yearning of the prelude to *Tristan und Isolde*. Expect 'no human comedy', Juan tells Ana. Wilde had, with laughing nihilism, dehumanised that comedy in *The Importance of Being Earnest*; Shaw superhumanises it when he exports Ann and Jack to the inferno, expands them into archetypes or biological genii, and changes comedy of manners into opera.

But there is a problem to this reconstitution of the *Gesamtkunstwerk* (Wagner's reunion of all the arts), and this is that Shaw's would-be opera is attempting to outgrow music. For though Shaw laments Hamlet's marathon of palaver, having 'to talk at any cost through five acts', and though he knows that music's power is to turn conversation into a vigorous grace which, like Yeats's dance, has dispensed with words, he mistrusts that fickle transfiguring. The vitalism of music is if anything too rampant, too much like the undiscriminating sensual ferment of Don Giovanni or the Duke in Verdi's *Rigoletto*. Not responsible to words, music has a referential promiscuity which alarms Shaw in Verdi's *Falstaff*. The bibulous, gluttonous knight belongs, to Shaw's disconcertment, in opera. He commented in 1894 that music, 'absolutely unmoral', will lend itself to any emotion, 'base or lofty', and depicts 'Falstaff's carnal gloating over a cup of sack' as easily as the humanitarian strivings of the Ninth Symphony.

Therefore *Man and Superman* dares not entrust its philosophy to music. It decides instead on a dual insurance by prosaic explication, expounding Juan's ethic before the event in its 'epistle dedicatory' and after it by printing Tanner's manual for revolutionaries. Within the play it reforms Mozart's writhing, cavorting, minuetting and duelling physical creatures as talking heads. Hell is Shaw's heaven because, like the future predicted by the She-Ancient in *Methuselah*, it is a region of unimpeded thought: 'here we have no bodies', Juan tells Ana, so the rage of desire which exists between them in the opera, and which urges them to sing, is quelled. Music is rectified by being lamed. Mendoza's recitation on the musical name of Louisa is an aria deprived of music, and a lesson in the fatuity of lyricism. Where Mozart is quoted, Shaw's characters, whose prowess is in talking, mar him. The statue, a shrill counter-tenor, cannot give voice to the rumbling divine judgements of the Commendatore because Mozart set them for a bass, and the devil appropriates some verses of Giovanni's which he sings 'in a nasal operatic baritone', ruined by the French method of vocal production. Ana has chastely renounced music, which served to bait her man-trap. She played the spinet to advertise her accomplishments to potential suitors; now she is married to Ottavio, she leaves the instrument unopened. As compensation for losing her, and as an occupation of boring bachelordom, Ann sentences Tavy to 'go a good deal to the opera'. When Straker licentiously whistles his favourite aria, Tanner remembers an eighteenth-century critique of opera. What is too silly to be said can be sung, and what is too silly to be sung can be whistled. Tanner's objection, like Shaw's with *Falstaff*, is to the melodic elision of words: 'unfortunately your whistling . . . is unintelligible.'

Mozart's singers become rhetoricians, his libertine wastrels mechanics or scientists. Leporello, instead of functioning as Giovanni's factotum and procurer, is schooled in engineering and, as Straker, repairs Tanner's automobile. Max Frisch, extending Shaw's logic, thought that a Giovanni for the modern age should give up his research into nature's sexual secrets and (in tandem with Shelley's Prometheus) change his field to nuclear physics.

Having in *Man and Superman* and *Methuselah* adumbrated Wagner's art-work of the future, Shaw returns in *Saint Joan* to the native origins of drama in morality and miracle. Inevitably the project entails the refutation of Shakespeare, whose Joan in *Henry VI* is the victim of the dramatist's 'blackguardly scurrility' and subservience to patriotic propaganda. Shakespeare is charged with ignorance of the 'medieval atmosphere'. But Shaw, returning to the medieval dramatic forms, inculcates in them the same adaptation he has already imposed on Shakespeare. He modernises the religious drama, which means secularising it. His chronicle is a morality play which paradoxically juggles moral categories, deriding the craven nationalism of Shakespeare or refusing to represent the Inquisitor as an ogre, and a miracle play which withholds belief in miracles—except those wrought by and in the theatre, for Shaw understands Joan's visionary faculty as an aptitude of 'dramatic imagination', which is to him the same thing as 'the evolutionary appetite'. She is a dramatist who envisages an event and then foresightedly commands it to occur.

In *The Dynasts*, on the road from Smolensko, Hardy orders that 'endowed with enlarged powers of audition as of vision, we are struck by the mournful taciturnity' of the retreating army. The battleplans of Hardy's characters are also a matter of omniscient dramaturgy, or of busy stage-management. Like a director deploying extras, Nelson disperses Adair's marines and sends Burke below, while Weirother choreographs in advance the engagement at Austerlitz. It is the exercise of this bossy, executive skill which renders Joan, as Shaw says, 'unbearable'. Begging the question of veracity, the Archbishop of Rheims sees in her a persuasive actress, and defines her miracles as *coups de théâtre*, feats of legerdemain 'very wonderful to the people who witness them, and very simple to those who perform them'. A miracle is an act, designed to produce faith: it is a trickery innate to the theatre. The Inquisitor is a dramatist who, staging the ceremonial of interrogation, cannot get his actors to obey his directions. When he orders the Chaplain to sit, the insurrectionary player says he 'will NOT sit down'; when the Inquisitor wearily tells him in that case to remain standing, the Chaplain at once resumes his chair, declaring, 'I will NOT stand.' Joan provokes her own martyrdom by a reckless commandeering of the stage like the Chaplain's. At Rheims she acts the Archbishop off his own altar. In the epilogue, she proposes a return engagement, exploiting the theatre's daily routine of resurrection, like Falstaff dying and arranging to be born again on the field of Shrewsbury: 'shall I rise from the dead, and come back to you a living woman?' The believers who pray to her are aghast at the possibility, and beg her to remain quietly dead.

The model of Greek tragedy is as irrelevant to Shaw as that of Christian marvel with its scenic bemusements. It is the Archbishop's pedantry which makes him claim that 'the old Greek tragedy is arising among us' and interpret Joan's fate as 'the chastisement of hubris'. The theatre must evolve beyond mystification. Instead of miming the god's début in the world, it conducts an experiment under sealed, controlled conditions.

Yeats, however, reuniting mythologies, brings together in his plays the forms that Shaw dissociates and discounts. His adaptations of the Theban plays overlay Oedipus and Lear; On Baile's Strand (1904) joins classical tragedy with comic Shakespearean history. The predestined Cuchulain discovers that he has killed his own son, and rushes out to make war against the incoming tide. Yet lined up quaking on the bench with the Fool and the Blind Man, he is Lear between his fool and the eyeless, visionary Gloucester. And when he is offstage, the hall of tragic tribunal reverts to the tavern at Eastcheap, with the comedians squabbling over scraps of food and making plans to rob the ovens.

In The Resurrection (1931), Yeats fuses Christian miracle with the divine possession of the followers of Dionysus, who in Nietzsche's theory bring tragedy to birth. The Hebrew wonderingly presides over a magician's vanishing-act as Christ quits the tomb; the Greek cheers on a transvestite vaudeville which congests the street: 'My God! What a spectacle! In Alexandria a few men paint their lips vermilion.' Resurrection coincides with revelry because, as the tapping drums and clattering rattles announce, music is inciting tragedy to that gaiety Yeats sensed in Lear and Hamlet. The Greek boldly laughs at Calvary. The singing bacchante whom the god has invaded gilds his finger-nails, cross-dresses and wears a wig of gilded cords. The risen Christ, stalking though the theatre, relies on a mask not make-up. That shield for the face is worn also, grotesquely and extravagantly, by Yeats's Fool and the Blind Man in On Baile's Strand: the mask is the actor's announcement of his parity with God and of his pallid membership of the dead, his ghostly, spiritual exclusion of himself from humanity. When Yeats's characters retire behind those false faces they are, like Christ, ghoulishly immortalising themselves, and asserting the shamanistic sacredness of their profession. The mask achieves that severing of the head demanded by the Old Man in *The Death of Cuchulain*, or that mutilation of himself by Oedipus when he puts out his eyes and wanders to Colonus, 'a ragged man with a disfigured face'. Thus Yeats recovers the ancient source of drama: the staging of a sacrifice.

Because the Dionysian rites are, in the Nietzschean theory adopted by Wagner, the birthplace of opera, they are drama's means of verifying itself and of rooting itself again in music. Auden, writing (in collaboration with Chester Kallman) a libretto for Hans Werner Henze's *The Bassarids*, performed at Salzburg in 1966, adapts the *Bacchae* of Euripides so as to comment on this coupling of classical drama with romantic music.

In Auden's version, the classical tragedy analyses the fatalities of romanticism. The bacchants are children of a nature they trust—Agave sings an aria about the prohibited delights of Mount Cytheron, described by the librettists as Wordsworthian—but which is shown to be a ravening, maddening, destructive energy. Agave's god is not Wordsworth's with his mild-mannered, suburban pantheism. That safe, official, romantic credo is espoused by the trendy Tiresias, here costumed as an Anglican archdeacon of advanced views. Dionysus is the romantic as a decadent destroyer: he dresses like a Byronic rebel, and comports himself with the affected langour of Wilde. his worshippers are the army of modern, metropolitan savages, sexual and political terrorists incited by romanticism to break their chains—a rabble of bohemians in dirty dungarees with matted beards, or girls modelling their hair-dos on the sex-kitten Bardot.

This romantic frenzy twistedly parodies the classical theatre. The opera contains an intermezzo which ridicules the Greek gods, Romanising them in a playlet about their lecherous intrigues, and debauches the neoclassicism of the self-styled age of reason. On a rococo stage painted to resemble a landscape by Boucher, Agave and Autonoe squabble in rhyming couplets about a handsome guardsman. Agave is a smutty Venus drooling over a bashful Adonis. The giddy travesty of classical archetypes goes with a psychoanalytic reading of romantic mania. Auden defines the theatre as a fun-fair of extravagant, histrionic id. In the intermezzo 'what the audience see are Pentheus' repressed phantasies'. Dionysus is the romantic treachery that Pentheus disowns in himself: his conversion by the lithe, flirtatious god is a homosexual seduction. Pentheus emerges from it feminised. He borrows his mother's clothes to go spying on the bacchants. Yet the mother nature he submits to is a fiendish hag: Agave herself, reclaiming him, tears him to pieces. Auden's enchanting singer Dionysus is Shaw's Juan reviewed by an age in which romanticism had come to mean collective hysteria. The myth, in Auden's use of it, is (like the theatre itself) about the inescapability of our desires and compulsions.

When the drama reunites itself with myth, its imperative alters from action—what Shaw calls the 'law of change', which means that drama is the provocation of a climax, an irreversible process culminating in Nora's slamming of the door in Ibsen's *A Doll's House*, or the sound of axes felling Chekhov's cherry orchard—to re-enactment, since the play is the mystery seasonally and perpetually reborn. This is why Shaw's characters are so dismayed by Joan's offer to return. She is hinting that she might be something even more intolerable than a saint: a goddess. This cyclical logic changes Yeats's tragedies into regenerative comedies. As Oedipus at Colonus calmly abides a reminiscence of events in *King Oedipus* (1928), which are themselves already a replaying of that long-ago tragedy at the cross-roads, so Cuchulain in the play about his death has to perform over again the fight from *On Baile's Strand*. It is this which makes Yeats's purgatory (in the play Eliot found so doctrinally reprehensible) unpurgatorial, because it is a theatre of re-enactment where the Old Man and the Boy in every generation quarrel and murder each other and are reinvigorated by their violence, a renewal like that of the sexual act wherein—as the Old Man looks on—his mother and his drunken father conceive him.

The matriarch Maurya in J. M. Synge's *Riders to the Sea* (1905) is caught in a sequence of tragedies which can be foreseen but not prevented. She has lost five of her menfolk already to the devouring sea and will lose the last. Cathleen calls her 'an old woman with one thing and she saying it over'. The lives of Synge's peasants are already ritualised by repetition: they knead cake, spin at the wheel, work ropes into halters, and identify the drowned Michael by counting the stitches in a stocking. Tragedy finds in routine a bleak consolation. The bereaved women busy themselves with the formulaic procedures of burial, ordering a deep-dug grave and a coffin of white boards, laying out the dead son's clothes and sprinkling them with holy water, rhythmically keening. Colum wonders at the single omission. Maurya has not provided nails, despite 'all the coffins she's made already'. Their idioms suggest the completion latterly of events taking place on the instant—Cathleen says 'there's someone after crying out by the seashore'—and their theatrical comportment seeks to live down the mobility of action and gesture. Maurya is directed to move 'very slowly', and settling on her stool or kneeling she assumes postures in which she will be fixed for an eternity.

Because they have exiled action—spatially by setting their crises out of doors like Cuchulain's fight with the waves or Bartley's last ride by the water's edge, temporally by interpreting those crises as fatal recurrences of the past which will recur again in the future—the plays of Yeats and Synge are one-acters, in contrast with the necessary protractions of Hardy and Shaw: the drama is a brief excerpt from an unending story. Re-enactment is the priestly duty of Eliot's Becket, who declares, 'Whenever Mass is said, we re-enact the Passion and Death of Our Lord; and on this Christmas Day we do this in celebration of His Birth'. The officiating divine performs simultaneously a tragedy and a comedy. Administering the sacraments, he is Johnson's mourner and reveller in one.

But his is a theatre newly ordained. *Murder in the Cathedral* is a commentary on and a critique of *Saint Joan*, giving its four assassins speeches of glib Shavian exculpation. Joan's martyrdom is a political killing not, like Becket's, a trial of religious grace. Shaw takes care to secularise the stage. When Joan proposes that kings should donate their realms to God and reign as his bailiffs, Warwick sees through the appearance of theocracy: her notion is an attempt to disenfranchise the aristocracy and make the monarch the absolute power. The drama in recompense impertinently encroaches on sacred ground. At the inquisition, the page warns Warwick, 'this is an ecclesiastical court; and we are only the secular arm'. Shaw's dramatising of Joan abets the theatrical flair of her own imagination. Eliot by contrast preserves Becket's faith from the worldly temptation of drama. The most insidious danger he faces is that of playing the part of martyr in self-glorification. He is therefore on guard against action and acting, for martyrdom means patience (the card game which was Eliot's grimly funny rehearsal for extinction).

When Becket says that 'action is suffering/And suffering is acting', he rephrases Wordsworth's contrast between action's momentariness and suffering's quiet eternity in *The Borderers*. That is a romantic and mystic denial of drama, to which Eliot adds a theological objection of his own. Becket's position is exactly that of Hamlet, whose refusal to participate in the drama made the play (in Eliot's judgement) a failure. But though that abstention from theatrical derring-do may mean artistic defeat, it does ensure spiritual victory. The chorus of Canterbury women have their own way of forestalling it. They are excluded from dramatic motion—'for us, . . . there is no action,/But only to wait and to witness'—and they recite spells against its unsettling of Becket, repeating that 'we do not wish anything to happen'. Their protection is their impersonality, their populous, collective unconsciousness. They are the earth's memory. With their sensual anecdotes of feasts and their rural gossip, their brewing of beer and cider, they might be the spirits of Shakespearean pastoral—except that they do not urge comic renewal but a stricken fixity. Their advice is the undoing of action. They tell Thomas 'return, return to France./Return. Quickly. Quietly.' Their own language frustrates dramatic instrumentality by Maurya's spell-like 'saying it over', annulling words by multiplying them: 'grey the sky, grey grey grey'.

Eliot's defiance of the theatre contrasts with Jean Anouilh's acclimatisation of the saint to it in his own *Becket* (1958). Like Hal and Falstaff in the tavern treating kingship as a role and alternating between it, Anouilh's Becket and his Henry II are interchangeable virtuosi. Laurence Olivier demonstrated their adaptable versatility by first playing Becket in New York in 1960, then switching next year to Henry. The spiritual and secular realms are to them alike as arenas for performance. Henry taunts Becket by saying that what looks like morality in him is only aesthetics; Becket retorts that governing can be as amusing as a game of tennis. Their relationship is the scheming competitiveness of old troupers, jostling to monopolise the limelight. Thus Henry raises his son to kingship prematurely to cheat Becket of his episcopal right of anointing. Whereas Eliot's Becket fears drama as the meretricious enemy of faith, Anouilh's fears faith because it puts an end to drama, and is reluctant to be made archbishop because he may take the office too seriously—cease to play at it, and begin to believe in it. That, for him, would be the martyrdom. His histrionic defence is to dress up for his death and insist on performing it. Titivating himself in his vestments, he says, 'I must look my best today.'

Hamlet the reluctant actor, whose revenge on the world is to see it as a fraudulent theatre, remains an exemplar in Eliot's subsequent plays. His cursed mission to set the time to rights is Harry's confrontation of 'the world, which I cannot put in order' in *The Family Reunion*. Harry, like Hamlet, cannot find words to explain or objectify his predicament. Re-enactment is his trauma, the psychic performance of his fantasy. He feels 'no horror of my action', the murder he imagines he has committed, 'only . . . the repetition of it/Over and over'. At an angle to what passes for reality, he sees its sham: 'One had that part to play.' The other characters complain, too, of being miscast, and of the tacky scenery in front of which they must posture. The choric uncles and aunts admit to being shifty and embarrassed, like amateur actors with no parts assigned yet and costumed for the wrong play, while Agatha regrets that she and Mary have been relegated to 'watchers and waiters: not the easiest role'. The Mediterranean is a painted backdrop, Harry's wife likewise a prop ('A restless shivering painted shadow') or perhaps a cinematic chimera—for in contrast with Hardy's anticipation of the cinema as a speculum, Eliot sees it as a compounding of the theatre's fault, the more dangerous because its unreality so accurately and expensively reproduces the real. Bela Szogody's studio, Pan-Am-Eagle, studies a decayed English mansion in *The Cocktail Party* with a view to reifying it in California. Harry can at least lay hold of the policeman and attest, 'He *is* real.' Yet is he? The leaden constabulary clichés in which he talks mark Winchell as a theatrical caricature. The play he is lumpishly plodding through is *The Murder of Gonzago* (or Agatha Christie's tribute to it, *The Mousetrap*) not *Hamlet*.

In *The Cocktail Party* the drama, unable to be the correlative for a poetic state of mind and spirit, counsels omission and mystification. It begins with an anecdote about a tiger-hunt whose point Julia misses because the story has already been told before the play begins; later there are the spurious mysteries of Julia's lost glasses, Lavinia's absence and the non-existent aunt. The actors feel one another de-realising, de-solidifying into cinematic spectres. Peter experiences Celia's jilting of him as a fade-out 'into some other picture—/Like a film effect'. What they fret over as 'the real reality' is only a willed projection, like the cinema's electric phantoms. The Hamlet who treats these cases is now an elderly professional, doubling as psychiatrist and priest, efficacious because only vestigially present in this world of theatrical similitudes: Harcourt-Reilly is at first an 'unidentified guest', and his clinical speciality is people who have outgrown the social personality they wear, ceased to believe in it as Edward says, and who therefore feel themselves to be 'unfinished'. His analysis of the worldlings who are his patients introduces a new version of lyricism's romantic arrest of drama. In his clinic or confessional, character, 'stretched on the table', returns to the etherised passivity of consciousness in its twilight zone at the beginning of 'Prufrock'. Though Harcourt-Reilly refers to his surgical assistants as 'masked actors', the body they operate on is sufferingly, lyrically inert, having renounced (or, by the ether, been robbed of) dramatic agency. It is an objective correlative, but the subject to which it corresponded no longer exists.

> You're suddenly reduced to the status of an object—
> A living object, but no longer a person. . . .
> All there is of you is your body
> And the 'you' is withdrawn.

Since character has been unmade, its speech is an idle automatic twittering. Poetry must ignore that factitious chitchat and eavesdrop on silences. Reilly analyses Edward by studying 'what you do not say'. In Shakespeare, metaphor is the verbal miming or reminiscence of action: Macbeth and Othello are the images they use. But Eliot is bound to sever that connection, making the metaphors hint at an interior secret which has been abstracted from the stage, penitentially banished from this *agora* of gossip and alcoholic tippling. Harry will not countenance a dramatic language, because his truth is 'unspeakable,/Untranslatable'; Edward demurs when Reilly's 'figure of speech is somewhat . . . dramatic' and himself employs images as semaphore, a cryptic lyricism resisting dramatic explication: 'O God, what have I done? The python. The octopus.' The purpose of Eliot's poetic drama is to demonstrate the incompatibility of its twinned constituents.

He is theologically comforted by this formal inconsistency. Poetry teaches drama pacification—that of Becket's martyrdom, or Reilly's case supine on the couch. In the poetic drama of Auden and Isherwood the same condition emphasises the irreconcilability of their endeavours and rationalises the psychological division within themselves. Auden's moody, poetic choruses in *The Dog Beneath the Skin* (1935) diagnose the country as a sick-bay where actions ingrow and fester, a region of debilitation and ineffectuality, which renders irrelevant the energetic dramatic quest of Isherwood's Alan for the missing Francis (who is all the time accompanying him, dressed as his dog). The mountaineer Ransom in their *Ascent of F6* (1936) is Becket reinterpreted as an existential weakling, fitter for psychoanalysis than for canonisation. Ransom's mother taunts him with refusing 'the greatest action of his life' because of his hatred for his brother. Mountain-climbing is a dramatic career only to Mr A., who applauds the team for being 'prepared to risk their lives in action'. From that physical strife, the Abbot, like Eliot's tempter, offers Ransom relief, attempting to recruit him for the contemplative existence of the monastery; and like Eliot's heroes, Ransom inclines already to the listlessness of Hamlet, addressing to a skull unearthed on the peak a version of Hamlet's conversation with the remains of Yorick. But it is because Ransom so lacks the vigour and certainty of heroism that he must persevere, contriving his own destruction and employing the theatre as a zany vaudeville where his unfettered urges jazzily act themselves out.

The model of a sacred theatre is for Auden and Isherwood not Eliot's chanted liturgy but the cabaret, the form innate to Berlin where they lived during the 1930s, because it is a noisy Dionysia, an extravaganza of the unconscious, like that staged—and declared to be 'unbearably tragic'—at the Nineveh Hotel in Dog Beneath the Skin. The Dog is a compendium of theatres, all magicked into existence at the behest of the motive which one of the medical officers calls 'Phantasy Building': the brothel with its peep-shows, each 'resembling a theatre box-office'; the charade where Francis's dog's skin makes its debut; the masked fête where the villagers, like the characters in Volpone, mutate into animals. The Vicar, unlike Becket at Christmas, takes to the pulpit as to a stage, and during his sermon works himself into a frenzy: the histrionic is the hysterical. The infirmary of Paradise Park has ten theatres—but they are disinfected chambers for operating on the sick, not arenas for performance. In Auden's and Isherwood's melodrama On the Frontier (1938) the stage itself, that disputed room which is the social forum of nineteenth-century drama, schizophrenically splits. The border between warring Ostnia and Westland bifurcates it, and its two halves, though possessing the same fitments arranged in the same way, represent antagonistic cultures. The left-hand Westland sector of the room is austere and academic, the Ostnian, on the right, is plushly bourgeois and reactionary. The stage's lay-out rehearses the dualistic quota of political options.

Auden later turned to opera as the preserve of that human freedom traditionally exercised in drama: every high C accurately intoned was, he thought, proof positive of the unconditioned will. But in these early plays written with Isherwood, characters are obsessed psychic automata, and for this reason drama is pre-empted in them by machines. The Westland dictator has a loud-speaker for a face, and is exposed as 'not a man at all! He's a gramophone!' The choric suburbanites Mr and Mrs A. in F6 patiently listen to the dictation or dictatorship of a radio announcer, while in the room on the frontier a pair of wireless sets, one tuned into Ostnian and the other to Westlandian propaganda, jabber antiphonally at each other.

In contrast with Hardy's specular ambitions for the theatre, radio achieves the play's withdrawal from visibility and its reduction of actors to voices, of actions to words vibrating in thin air. Hence its importance as a medium for Beckett, or for Pinter, whose *Family Voices* (first broadcast in 1981, staged later) is an epistolary piece consisting of spoken letters: it prefers writing to enactment, silence to speech. One of its voices, sounding from the grave, is a father's admonishment to his son. He ends the play by declaring, 'I have so much to say to you. . . . What I have to say to you will never be said.' Pinter's *Victoria Station* (1982) is a play whose action consists in vocal relays on a radio linking an overseer in his control-booth and a befuddled taxi-driver. The controller is a god inefficiently directing the world *ex machina*. He talks into one machine, 'trying to make some sense of our lives' and putatively steers another, imagined machine: 'I'm a monk. . . . I lead a restricted life. I haven't got a choke and a gear lever in front of me. I haven't got a cooling system and four wheels.' The driver is a disoriented voice, not responding to instructions, ignorant of Victoria's whereabouts, scarcely knowing who he is. Though the circuit between directorial dramatist and delinquent actor has been closed, they still cannot communicate through it.

Victoria Station concludes in silence, darkness and stasis. The driver says 'No, I won't move' and, after a pause, 'I'll be here.' The lights go out in both the booth and the car. Though Craig thought theatre meant kinesis, and Shaw evolution, modern drama, controverting its own form, seeks arrival at immobility. Mazzini's requiem for dramatic activation in *Heartbreak House*—'Nothing happened . . . Nothing ever does happen . . . Nothing happens. . . . Nothing will happen', conjugating the verb only to ensure its impotence—becomes the frightened litany of Eliot's women of Canterbury who 'do not wish anything to happen', or the bored conviction of Mr and Mrs A. that 'nothing that matters will ever happen' and the chorus's 'Nothing is done, nothing is said' in *Dog Beneath the Skin*. It issues finally in the stoic capering of Estragon in *Waiting for Godot* (1955), keeping himself on the go because there's 'Nothing to be done'. Beckett's characters are stalled in a discussion of the theatre's structural laws and a review of its exhausted gambits. Vladimir tells the story of Christ because 'it'll pass the time'. Jean Paul Richter remarked on the brisk celerity of the drama, as opposed to the novel's leisurely deliberation. But Hamlet decelerated drama, and put on plays or engaged in bouts of deceptive acting in order to dissuade time, with its consequentiality and its retributiveness, from passing. The worst crime of which modern drama can convict him is effectuality: Tom Stoppard's demonstration in 1967 that because of him, *Rosencrantz and Guildenstern are Dead*.

With a beautiful severity of conscience, the attendants on Godot ensure that nothing happens because of them, and deny that their routines have sped time. When Pozzo and Lucky exit, Vladimir says 'that passed the time'. Estragon corrects him: 'It would have passed anyway.' Vladimir persists in his fallacy, which is the illusion of drama with its foreclosed Aristotelian unity: 'Yes, but not so rapidly'. The players are tired theatrical hacks, and they agree that what they are suffering through is 'worse than being at the theatre', or the circus or the music-hall. Pozzo apologises for the lapse in his rhetorical rant at nightfall, for his memory of his lines is defective. Still they trot out their depleted acts, singing, dancing, reciting and even, in the extremity of their tedium, performing each other, as when Vladimir and Estragon play at being Pozzo and Lucky. They are desperately reliant on their props to sustain them—their hats, the radish, the vaporizer, the boots, the tree. Estragon explains why: they must fasten on these things, and do bits of business with them, 'to give us the impression that we exist'. Vladimir, like a Prospero at the end of his tether, retaining his wand because it is a cripple's crutch, exhaustedly agrees: 'Yes, yes, we're magicians.'

That inability to die which is the comedian's salvation, when Falstaff falls at Shrewsbury or when Papageno in *The Magic Flute* farcically resolves on suicide, becomes the curse of Beckett's players, who cannot terminate their own game and find that it is impossible to hang yourself without a rope. At the end of each act of *Waiting for Godot*, Beckett intervenes to refuse the possibility of action. In the first, Estragon proposes that they should go and Vladimir says 'Yes, let's go'; in the second, the exchange is in the opposite direction; but in both a stage direction denies them mobility and sentences them to remain imprisoned in the theatre: '*They do not move.*' Procrastinating Hamlet has reached his quietus at last.

40

Symbols and Secrets

The symbolist poem is a verbal <u>philtre</u>, sedating the reason. That derangement happens systematically: the potion can be chemically formulated. Its mystery is as rationally contrived as a crossword puzzle or a detective story, and depends simply on the concealment or confusion of truth. During the 1930s, the romantic magician adopts a more inconspicuous and modern uniform, disguising himself as an engineer (in Auden's boyish fascination with mining technology, and his continuing delight in the poem as a contraption, the dottily useless appliance dreamed up by an inventor), perhaps as a medical student (like the young Isherwood, urged by Auden to handle his septic literary subjects with rubber gloves), sometimes as a flier or a photographer. Yet all the while he is manufacturing explosives, brewing narcotics, or spreading contagion. Isherwood admires film in *Prater Violet* (1945) because it resembles the saboteur's time-bomb, and Auden hints that poetry is a species of germ warfare, the poet's communication of his sickness. Behind the killer with his little case in 'Gare du Midi' (1938) who 'walks out briskly to infect a city' lies Auden's contention in a notebook in 1929 that infectious diseases signify 'the unconscious sense of unity between men': the poet's fatal vocation is to transmit the lesion which is love. Romantic symbolism has learned up-to-date-ness, studying new trades and allying itself with radical politics and with psychoanalysis. The poem's riddle is now the catchphrase which instigates a revolution, or the diagnosis which ascertains a spiritual malady.

Isherwood's Maurice in *The Memorial* (1932) is the poet as technician or as pyrotechnician, intimidating Eric by his conjuring tricks and his mechanical know-how, brandishing wires from the throttle-control of a motor-bike or explaining 'the proper adjustment of valve tappets and the engine timing'. This was to be the elderly Auden, the virtuoso of crabbed stanza forms and clerihews, the artful deployer of academic jargon and street slang. The activity remains romantically perilous, for the machine can betray you. Isherwood's flying Dutchman in *The Memorial*—a latter-day instalment of Shelley's Ariel or of Joyce's Icarus, who has 'invented a new type of aeroplane engine'—dies when a strut breaks. His machine side-slips and is 'burnt to a tangle of wires'. Equally volatile and equally dangerous is the express train from London to Scotland whose journey Auden described for the 1936 film *Night Mail*. It is an apocalyptic engine, snorting and steaming, whose cargo is a consignment of literature (in its primitive sense of letters). Auden speedily opens and inspects all the mail as if the human race had voided its testamentary secrets on the last day:

> The cold and official and the heart's outpouring,
> Clever, stupid, short and long,
> The typed and the printed and the spelt all wrong.

The poem's rhythmic acceleration is the machine's headlong rush, with the literary evidence against us that it has appropriated, to a collective judgement.

The illicit thrill of the poem is its violation of a taboo: its opening of our mail and its foreknowledge of our woes, our debts and the embarrassing intimacies confided to pink and violet paper. Auden's early poems tease and arouse because of their secretiveness. They are obscure in self-defence, sealed against that analysis of dreams which happens in *Night Mail*. The symbol is involuted for its own protection. Though these poems declare that it is time for the destruction of error, their own cabbalistic cunning lies in the creation of error, in their 'difficult images' (as Auden in 1927 calls them in 'No trenchant parting this') or 'unusual images' (in the 1929 poem 'On Sunday Walks') or in the signals which in 'Venus Will Now Say a Few Words' he points to as 'references in letters to a private joke'. Their scenarios—impromptu migrations to Cape Wrath, alpine views through a hotel's plate-glass window, the laying of railway-lines and the siting of dams—are excerpts from a narrative which cannot, for security reasons, be clarified.

In his contribution in 1932 to *An Outline for Boys and Girls and Their Parents*, Auden sees words as 'a bridge between a speaker and a listener'. The bridge's portage, like the night mail's, is meaning, conveyed by the speaker to the listener. But in the early poems that bridge is unconstructed, or else blown up. The spy in 'The Secret Agent' (1928) discovers that 'the bridges were unbuilt and trouble coming'. A poem must be cryptically concise, emblematically fretted, like Verloc's triangle or Stevie's whirling spirals, which have their counterparts in the psychological tests devised by the airman in Auden's *The Orators* (1931) for trapping enemies: a box of caged crosses, or two sympathetically adjacent circles. As in this trap baited by the airman, reading the poem is the interpreter's inadvertent betrayal, his collusion with a poet whose words are a psychosomatic guilt. Every imputation of meaning is a treason, like the anecdotes betraying a favourite colour in 'The Questioner Who Sits So Sly' or the friend's 'analysis of his own failure' in '1929'. The poems harbour their secrets like bodily exhalations or subcutaneous irritations: one has its terrorists couched 'in arm-pit secrecy', another is provoked into being by 'the intolerable neural itch'; *The Orators* includes an epistle to a wound which is an anal fissure. Auden's notorious disdain for hygiene—in contrast with the prim tidiness and surgical asepsis of Isherwood—is a proviso of his poetic integrity, guarding his private diseases and distresses. Back from

Berlin, he looks to Isherwood like 'an exceedingly dirty millionaire': the ruined millionaire who is Eliot's Christ in the *Four Quartets*?

Flesh, corruptible and frail, was Christ's camouflage. Kierkegaard's saviour appears shabbily costumed, as a broken-down Quixote, and goodness manifests itself to Herman Melville—in Auden's 1939 poem about him—as the ordinary, stammering seraph Billy Budd. Auden's creativity requires a similar incognito, a guise to supplement his obscuring words. The poet therefore chooses to be a spy, keeping his profession secret on pain of death, or a detective, quietly and patiently righting wrongs done to others. Auden prays in *The Orators* to private eyes like Sherlock Holmes and Hercule Poirot as deliverers.

The novelist also considers himself a cryptographer, garnering and relaying seditious information which, decoded, would be the self's and society's unmaking. Conrad's secret agent is less Verloc than the artist himself, who as a symbolist astutely plays a double game: he relays truths which, like Kurtz's last words, are protected by their unintelligibility; challenged, he will misinterpret them, as Marlow does when he lies to the Intended.

After Conrad, the analogy between the novelist and the expert at espionage is intimated by Somerset Maugham in the stories about the agent Ashenden which he began publishing in 1927. (Hitchcock filmed an adaptation of one of them in 1935 as *The Secret Agent*; when, the following year, he filmed the Conrad novel, he had to call it *Sabotage*.) Maugham's Ashenden originates from the novelist's own 'experiences in the Intelligence Department during the last war, . . . rearranged for the purposes of fiction'. Yet very little rearrangement is necessary, for the structure of his investigations is already that of a modern novel. Ashenden is in at the beginnings or the ends of operations, or is sometimes drafted to cope with a ⁻problem in the middle, but never sees a completed action. Maugham conservatively opined that a novel must have a beginning, middle and end, and in that order. Ashenden's activities school him in the different structural sleights of the avant-garde: his cases are like 'those modern novels that give you a number of unrelated episodes and expect you by piecing them together to construct in your mind a connected narrative'. The same enigmatic logic is a law for symbolist poetry, and despite Maugham's protest, Ashenden when deciphering a numerical cable wills himself into the mental state of the artist encoding experience and employing language to mystify, not to elucidate. 'His method was to abstract his mind from the sense till he had finished, since he had discovered that if you took notice of the words as they came along you often jumped to a conclusion and sometimes were led into error.'

The symbolist poet is a high priest, uttering esoterica. The novelist, according to the persona devised for himself by Isherwood, understands cipher as the malefactor's shifty, sympathetic effort to cover his guilt. His words are the sad muddle of an irredeemably fallen world, where the artist must learn to be a citizen—hence Kuno's coded letter to van Hoorn in *Mr Norris Changes Trains* (1935), at once deciphered by the police, or the suggestive missives telegraphed by Margot to Norris in what Frl. Schroeder believes to be 'a secret language. . . . Every word has a double meaning'; and though Isherwood is, as a novelist, the detective scrutineer of his characters, he is also, as the main character of those novels, a nervous fugitive from the vigilance of others, emissaries of a state which his art covertly defies. As William Bradshaw in *Mr Norris Changes Trains* he intrudes on Olga and 'for all she knew . . . might be a detective', yet in the street he squints rapidly right and left, afraid of being watched and followed. In *Goodbye to Berlin* (1939) he inspects the stains on Frl. Schroeder's rugs and wallpaper, silently extorting from her a confession of the small social crimes these marks memorialise, or takes careful note of Sally Bowles's grubby nicotine-stained hands. This is the voyeurism of the policeman, collecting the clues scattered or (in the case of Sally's soiled fingers) externalised by the guilty body. However, it is the novelist's humbling vocation to be, as Auden's poem in 1938 reminded Isherwood, 'among the Filthy filthy too', so included in the novel's incriminating exhibits is the much-sullied pair of baggy flannel pants, exposed when a cloakroom girl demands his overcoat, worn by Herr Issyvoo himself.

The moral nicety of Isherwood's novels is his accusation of himself: he is culprit not creator in them. Writing is his systematic disabling of himself, until he approximates to the nervy inauthenticity and failed authority of the character he calls in *Lions and Shadows* (1938) 'the truly weak man, the neurotic hero'. For Auden, a poem is a wound's suppuration, the secretion of a private fault; for Isherwood, a novel is a symptom of social ineptitude and anxiety-ridden exclusion. They write because they cannot, with the 'direct, reasonable' certainty of 'The Truly Strong Man', live. Their art is a maimed legacy of alienation.

Auden in the *Outline* explains language and literature as cries of pain for a world lost to us as soon as we become conscious of it, from which we are further estranged by our very imagining of it. The first speakers were self-admitted failures: hunters from whom the catch had got away. Later, every writer is an unrequited lover. The wisdom of his melancholy craft is to learn acceptance of his creation's infidelity to him, and it is this forgiveness Auden, in 1937, extends to the partner of a night in 'Lay your sleeping head, my love'. Isherwood's observing marks his ostracism. He is a victim of that emotional calamity in language treated by Auden in his essay on writing. Inflection means inclination: Auden quotes some Latin tags to show that if a man loves a dog, the dog is grammatically altered by being in that relation. Inevitably this affectionate agreement of words cannot last. Self-consciousness makes people, and especially writers, 'separate their thoughts and feelings from the things they are feeling and thinking about'. English is 'the least inflected language', the one which tries hardest to enforce its segregation of words and of existences (though Auden notes that it does permit some grudging instances of inflected reciprocation—'I love *him*. *He* loves *me*.').

Isherwood's language, bereft, exemplifies this law. In *Goodbye to Berlin* the novelist is an alien, 'in a foreign city, alone, far from home'; in *A Single Man* (1964) he is still known only as an outcast, deracinated and set down in the temporary, fickle ground of the Santa Monica slide area, bearing as well the extra, alien status of homosexuality in a community of heterosexual breeders like George's neighbours the Strunks. He forbids to himself the omniscience that the novelist can automatically assume. He has to guess that Frl. Schroeder is about fifty-five, cannot in his gullibility work out what Frl. Klost does for a living, and has to suffer Sally's lacerating analysis of him. And though he spends a creative lifetime on the study of his infirm solitariness, he cannot ever definitively know himself. The latest Isherwood has withdrawn, in his own view, to the inscrutability of a third person, the stranger he happens to be. This is how he refers to himself in *Christopher and His Kind* (1977) or *My Guru and His Disciple* (1980). William Bradshaw, dogged by the detective, now must put up with the worse incrimination of celebrity, which also entails entrapment, relegation to society's list of those whose existences it has co-opted for itself: Isherwood's journal *October*, written in 1979, ends with his discovery of himself doubly entered in an almanac, in ledgers of 'renowned homosexuals' and 'renowned religious converts', and when in the same month he is being drawn by Don Bachardy he screws his face into an unforthcoming mask and delights in his achieved inscrutability—'My old face is horrible with ill will. Most satisfactory.'

If the self is an inauthentic other, then the names it goes by are the aliases which cover a misdemeanour. The pseudonym of William Bradshaw, made up from Isherwood's vestigial middle names, is his forged card of identity. He is comically gratified when people misrepresent him by mispronouncing his name, like his landlady with her 'Herr Issyvoo', and he collaborates in the creative fraud by having his name printed in Chinese on a business card in *Journey to a War* (1939). Transliterated, it is a garbled phonetic cover for a being in camouflage: Y Hsiao Wu. It is additionally elided, with the systematic misunderstanding which is the logic of symbolism in both Auden and Isherwood, when the Chinese address him as Mr Y, or as Isherman.

Nicknaming may uncertify Isherwood, disputing the caption that family and society conventionally attach to him, but it secures him entry into another, absconded community—the group, the team, bonded together by the exchange of winks, knowing grins (like those which pass between Isherwood and Otto on Reugen in 1931, or between him and Schmidt when Norris introduces them) and boyishly heroic titles. The origins of a poem for Auden and of a novel for Isherwood are in this kind of fraternal conspiracy. The cadre of ruined boys in *The Orators* suspect one of their number because he is illicitly infatuated by 'verbal puzzles'. That engagement in linguistic intrigue is the start of a poetic career, just as the dexterity of the elderly Auden at solving crossword puzzles was a relaxed rehearsal of his skill at code-breaking. The airman in *The Orators* defines the poem as classified psychological information, top secret because incriminating: 'self-regard is the treating of news as a private poem', is nurtured by eavesdropping, and can be analysed as 'a sex-linked disease'. This gives the work of the young Auden its unique menace, a consequence of riddling, retentive obscurantism. The very texture of the verse is a verbal conspiracy: in the epilogue to *The Orators* the alliteration, the metrical urgency and the repetitions are language's team-work, a prosodic drill for arming the poem against the censorious invasion of interpreting reason. Rhythm is solidarity, cementing the phalanx of the poetic line. Auden defines it as 'what one word expects of one another'—that is, its duty.

Isherwood cannot rely on the existence of society, from which the neurotic hero is an outcast; as the capsules inside which his novels happen, he must invent conspiratorial cells. Generally these are infantile, or at least adolescent. The young Auden and Isherwood were Peter Pans suffering from a bad case of paranoia. (The aerial perspectives of Auden's aviator, 'THE AGENT OF . . . CENTRAL AWARENESS', are the surveillance conducted by that total awareness which is paranoia.) Auden's onanistic creator finds emotional safety in numbers, in membership of a like-minded and mutually supporting gang:

> Schoolboy, making lonely maps:
> Better do it with some chaps.

So it is with Isherwood's rallying of players for hockey, football and cricket as exercises in a defensive 'Narcissism and Claustrophobia' in *All the Conspirators* (1928), or the scrutiny of ordnance maps—the world deciphered from mid-air; paranoia as panorama—in the same novel. The characters of *The Memorial* take refuge in clubs, committees, naughty after-dark dives, cricket elevens and select school forms. These are the sanctuaries of the alien self, escaping from its family and eventually, when Auden and Isherwood left for America in 1939, from its country—for England is to them a hereditary ailment, and Isherwood's rejection of it is completed by his critical analysis of his parents in 1971 in *Kathleen and Frank*.

When at the end of *Goodbye to Berlin* the Nazis establish their command of the city, Isherwood interprets this as a reversion to a public-school régime of terror, enforced by arcane, jargon-ridden favouritisms: 'The newspapers are becoming more and more like copies of a school magazine.' Auden had claimed in 1934 to know all about fascism because he had lived as its subject when a pupil at public school. But despite the qualms of liberal conscience, the imagination exalts in the cabal of the bully-boys with their passwords and uniforms and epic companionability. Auden in 1966 disowned *The Orators*, considering it half-mad and declaring it to be written by someone he no longer recognised. That ploy safeguards the work, though, and actually pays wondering tribute to its vivid, enchanting, imaginative involuntariness.

Isherwood continues to seek out small, peripheral, occluded worlds, microbes to compensate for the novelists's forfeiture of society at large. Arnold Bennett's grand hotel in *Imperial Palace* (1930) is a city in miniature, a technological island moored in central London and resembling in its self-sufficiency one of those ocean liners which were known as navigable hotels. Visiting the control-room which regulates the place's micro-climate and its water-supply, the manager Evelyn Orcham is an omnipresent god superintending the workings of his cosmic machine; reviewing the foyer he is even more smugly demi-urgic—'he beheld the display and saw that it was good'. Isherwood's equivalent is the Viennese film studio of *Prater Violet*, which he compares to a palatial Renaissance court, containing an amplitude of existence, an extravagance of character and a flamboyance of manner expunged from the society outside. It is therefore the place where the novelist goes into hiding. And there he practises not Bennett's conservative regimentation of society, with Evelyn as benevolent dictator, but sedition: the director Bergman salutes the cinema as a relentless machine which, once set in motion, 'simply ripens to its inevitable explosion'.

To call yourself a camera is to adopt the spy's incognito. Now the film-maker has exchanged espionage for terrorism. The camera had always for Isherwood been capable of x-raying surfaces, enabling him to see circulation at Lady Klein's party in *The Memorial* as the rotation of granules in amoebae. That incisive vision—which attracts him to the glass-walled buildings of Berlin and to the naked bathers on Reugen or, later, on the beach at Santa Monica: heliotropic creatures flaunting a moral transparency—is a surgical inquisition of bodies. Allen the medical student in *All the Conspirators* wields a scalpel in the dissecting-room, and elsewhere deploys a symbolic surgeon's knife against 'vague words and dreamy thoughts'. The cinema flays faces, exposing the motives, registered in physiological quirks, beneath them. The doctor on Reugen boasts of knowing the degenerate Otto 'through and through', though Isherwood adds that he knows only his adenoids and tonsils.

The cinema is the perfection of such disinterested scrutiny, relentlessly stripping us of our illusions, like Isherwood denuding Sally. It is the form, for him, which institutionalises the analytic consciousness that Auden's airmen has from on high; and it develops gradually from a satirical sectioning of the body into a mystical shedding of that body, whose whims it demonstrates to be so absurdly motiveless, like the wanderings of Jeanne Moreau in Antonioni's film *La Notte*, much praised by Isherwood. Isherwood practised screenwriting as a Zen routine, learning from it how to abstain from the use of words and, as if in transcendental meditation, to organise silence. Sally wants work at Ufa, the Berlin film studio, and expects the movies to be a career of spiritual self-denial. Subsisting on cigarettes and Prairie Oysters, she will not eat because hunger makes her feel saintly; the bogus Rakowski, posing as an agent of MGM, possesses credibility because he wears camel-hair underpants, which 'might have belonged to John the Baptist'. Norris submitting himself to sexual flagellation and Baron von Pregnitz (in the same novel) 'torturing himself daily on an electric horse, a rowing-machine and a rotating massage belt' are Isherwood's first ascetics: trainees for a spiritual betterment catered to later in his career by the movies, which ponder the antics of bodies in order to study 'how actions look in relation to each other; how much space they occupy and how much time', by Vedanta, which teaches the body's dispensability, and by those Californian work-out salons where those who are still the body's prisoners are made to do aerobic penance.

Observation is a cool, neutral discipline in Isherwood. His characters are differentiated by an ocular iconography, which treats the eye as an unblinking lens. When William calls on Norris, he is fixed by the gaze of an eye (belonging to Schmidt) plugged into the peep-hole in the door. This is the private eye, a metonym for detection: the motto of the Pinkerton Agency, for which Dashiel Hammett was an operative, was a staring eye which boasted 'We never sleep.' Norris calls Schmidt's eye aquiline or vulture-like, and as a seer the camera-man is a colleague of the helmeted airman or the birds of prey he outsoars. Thus Graham Greene names his hired killer in *A Gun for Sale* (1936) Raven, and has him evade moral accountability and emotional susceptibility by photographing the world, which means to appraise it as a target. The novel begins with Greene's observation of the assassin, who is himself an observer: 'He looked like any other youngish man going home after his work.' When Raven reaches his victim's house, he reviews it para-photographically: 'His eyes, like little concealed cameras, photographed the room instantaneously.' That means minimal denotation, a checklist of 'the desk, the easy chair, the map on the wall, the door to the bedroom behind', not the loving, novelistic labour of description. In the bedroom the killer photographs a photograph, an image of a victim already brutalised as he will be one more time by this pitiless vision: 'His eyes again photographed the scene, the single bed, the wooden chair, the dusty chest of drawers, a photograph of a young Jew with a small scar on his chin as if he had been struck there with a club.'

Norris teaches his own eyes inscrutability, as if what lay behind them were the camera's mechanical intelligence only. 'Light-blue jellies', like shell-fish in a rock pool, they are not—when William looks into them—'mirrors to his soul'. Janin's eyes likewise are 'cold, prominent, rudely inquisitive', like protruding lenses. The Baron relies on the defensive shield of a rimless monocle, a lens apparently 'screwed into his . . . face by . . . some horrible surgical operation'. It gives him a bifocal face: the glazed eye can flash hostilely, returning the world's reflection, while the naked one squirms and shifts. When, exercising in his gym, he is caught without the armouring monocle, he appears spiritually stripped, 'his eyes . . . fixed in a short-sighted, visionary stare' like someone 'engaged in a private religious rite': is mysticism then myopia? Not to be defeated, William aims at him an eye which makes a microscopic survey of the confidential flesh, and deduces, with forensic acuity, that he has been exposing himself to artificial sunlight, because the skin around his nose is peeling. Norris ruefully congratulates William on the bland cruelty of his scrutiny: 'Nothing escapes your eye. Yet another of our domestic secrets is laid bare.'

The injunction of the '30s is to look—Auden's 'Look there!' in the last poem of his first volume, or his 'Look, stranger' in 1935, Orwell's 'Look at the factories' or 'Look at any bourgeois Socialist' or 'Look at any picture of a tramp in *Punch*' in *The Road to Wigan Pier* (1937): realism is a photographic fragmentation and indexation of the world, reckoning its contents as specimens. The habit gets into Orwell's punctuation, obliging him to segregate adjectives with supernumerary commas, isolating each word to make sure it does its proper job of inscribing meaning and culpability. In *Down and Out in Paris and London* (1933) he washes the hotel crockery in 'the hard, Paris water', or watches with revulsion the 'fat, pink fingers' of the cook fondling the food. Those commas are analytic dissectors: each word is a separate stain. Seeing is Orwell's solacing disengagement.

Verbal transcription enables him to detach himself from the squalor in which he is mired. When there is a murder under his window, he chooses to recall and record only the colour of the victim's blood, 'curiously purple, like wine'. The iniquity of impoverishment and the routine of documentation coincide. The down and out have resigned their freedom and independent will and can be assessed as objects; it is the alienating device of the documentor to see the self as another. Therefore, in the dolorous sequence of second-person sentences describing the hard work of being unemployed—'You go to the baker's. . . . You go to the greengrocer's. . . . You slink out of the shop', and so on with numbing indefiniteness—Orwell, like Isherwood investigating Issyvoo or Christopher, examines himself as someone who is not himself, an insentient statistic. Six francs a day cannot purchase individuality, and collectivising his own case by classing himself as 'you' Orwell is reduced to a common denominator of need. He has personally ratified his proposition that 'a human being is primarily a bag for putting food into'.

Documentary is writing at a meagre minimum, elected by Orwell because he cannot morally afford to write novels about the condition of society. Literature is a luxury commodity, catering to those 'other functions and faculties [which] may be more godlike' but which are consequent upon a full belly. Why, Orwell asks, don't the unemployed write? It is because they lack the comfort, solitude and peace of mind the task would require, and because their paralytic existence kills creative energy. Accordingly, Orwell's own book denies itself the liberating recourse of imagination. Novels tell palliative lies, like those mass-produced in the Fiction Department of *Nineteen Eighty-Four*. Documentary's demand, in the slogan of the Mass-Observation Movement started by Charles Madge and Tom Harrisson in 1937, is for 'less stories and more facts'. *The Road to Wigan Pier* cannot be a novel because the house of fiction is ravaged and unintelligible. In the tripe-shop where Orwell lodges, four people sleep in a befouled drawing-room furnished with a ghastly cross between a sideboard and a hall-stand. The den has the 'defiled impermanent look of rooms that are not serving their rightful purpose'.

Orwell disallows that mercantile realism which, from Crusoe to Dombey, described objects as a means of acquiring and securing them, and valued the affectionate use to which they had been put by human beings, like James Agee reverencing the faded denim of the share-croppers in his documentary *Let Us Now Praise Famous Men* (1941). Possession in Orwell's dispossessed world can only be the imprimatur of filth, the communication of disease. Mr Brooker has the 'peculiarly intimate, lingering manner of handling things' common to 'people with permanently dirty hands' and signs the slices of bread he cuts for the lodgers with a black thumb-print; for good measure he grips the full chamber-pot 'with his thumb well over the rim'. Narrative implies the existence of options, closed to those whose life is a plaintive repetition, a squalid, urban version of the routines of pastoral. 'The most dreadful thing about people like the Brookers', Orwell says, 'is the way they say the same things over and over again. It gives you the feeling that they are not real people at all.' He therefore abandons them, and the book which begins with the detailed density of a novel ends as social theory and political prophecy.

Orwell chides Lawrence for mythologising—which means fictionally aggrandising—the life of the proletariat. Lawrence's miners are soiled, dark gods. Orwell's are the serfs of an economic system, crawling and hacking and dying beneath the earth in order to subsidise the writer's idleness, so that even to look at them is, in Orwell's self-accusation, an offence: 'it is . . . humiliating to watch coal-miners working. It raises in you a momentary doubt about your own status as an "intellectual" and a superior person.'

This is the moral nausea of documentary in the '30s—its arraignment by what Heisenberg in the previous decade announced as the uncertainty principle. The observed now wounds the conscience of the observer. In Auden and Isherwood, too, observing grows more guiltily insecure throughout the decade. Already in *All the Conspirators* the bird-watching and shutter-bugging of Colonel Page are evidence of sexual mania, and in the airman's alphabet the observer is glossed as a peeper and a peerer, hauntedly watching the sky for signs of retribution. Auden associated the camera-man with the ornithologist, since both so adore the self that they contrive its elimination and invisibility, that way managing to manipulate others by spying on them. The headmaster in *The Orators* warns that only those boys unworthy of citizenship will take up the sly hobby of bird-watching, and in *The Prolific and the Devourer* (1939) Auden describes the apolitical man—Aristotle's idiot, now psychoanalysed as a misfit—as a solitary deviant, 'perhaps . . . a photographer or a bird-watcher or a radio mechanic'.

Auden shows photographic realism to be after all a romantically solipsistic dream or crime. This is why its method is so cunningly compromised and teased in the *Letters from Iceland* (1937) which Auden wrote with Louis MacNeice. Auden includes tips for photographers, explaining where Agfa and Kodak film can be bought in Reykjavik, tries replaying the journey as if it were film rushes, and expatiates on photography as '*the* democratic art' because it does away with technical skill and makes artistic merit a function of the choice of subject. It is a reproof to the exclusivity of art. Just as Agee's collaborator Walker Evans in 1931 declared photography to be an art in no need of operators, and one which therefore suited democratic America, so Auden contends in the Iceland letters that 'the only decent photographs are scientific ones and amateur snapshots'.

Outlandish though the claim may be, it is important as an argumentative tactic, because it enables Auden to mark down two kinds of artistic conceit (and in doing so to handicap himself, as the truly weak man should). Photography is Auden's rebuttal first of romanticism, with its self-glorifying Poets' Party. He does allow that the 'technical advances' of those poets were brilliant, but since then technique has been consigned to the care of the photographer's gadgetry. Secondly, photography announces his secession from Bloomsbury, with its impressionist and cubist variants of romanticism. In his letter to the painter William Coldstream, Auden affirms that 'We'd scrapped Significant Form, and voted for Subject.'

The democracy of the art prompts him to make a book which is an album, an assemblage of quotes, based on the principle of photographic compilation. He remarks about snapshots that you need a lot to make an effect: 'a single still is never very interesting by itself'. *Letters from Iceland* therefore anthologises snippets, in its 'Sheaves from Sagaland' or its compendia of German marching songs, lullabies and proverbs. It is made by the elegiac act of collecting which, like photography, seizes the present and converts it into the irrecoverable past. Auden pilfers from a landlady's postcard collection a diagram of the Icelandic mountains, carried off for reproduction in the book. He becomes simply the perceptions he appropriates, or the subjects in which he is interested. This is how he characterises himself in the fourth section of his interpolated 'Letter to Lord Byron'. His documentarism—'anonymous, observant, / A kind of lab-boy, or a civil servant'—enables him to revive a romantic dichotomy between the sublimity of ego and what Keats called negative capability, only now the engine of negation is the camera. He writes to Byron because of Byron's mobile, worldly disdain for everything represented by Wordsworth. Yet in selecting this exile as a pen-pal he enlists in the ranks of what Allen in *All the Conspirators*, referring to Baudelaire and Poe, calls a 'debased romanticism'. Byron is a part of all that he has met, Auden only of all he has snapped or, by petty larceny or confessed plagiarism, collected. He indicts himself for possessing a sickness he identified in a 1929 journal entry: there realism is seen as a neurotic anxiety of 'the jackdaw mind', collecting and filing away memorabilia 'against the reckoning day'.

By the time of *Journey to a War*, the photographer has been declared suspicious, and is penalised accordingly. There is a printed warning against cameras on the river boat to Canton; Auden has to pay $30 in customs duty on his when they arrive. The machine's own users begin to mistrust it. As they leave Wenchow for Shanghai, Isherwood comments that 'a cabin port-hole is a picture-frame', falsifying the view by retroactively arranging China into a postcard. The observer doubts the propriety of his own habit, and the probability of what he thinks he sees. The war-stricken country is to Isherwood a scene 'dream-like, unreal', and the hotel outside Kukiang is 'far, far too beautiful to be real'. What is being documented is a surreal alternation between boredom and frenzy. Visual anecdotes are absurd in their irrationality: a man is glimpsed riding a green horse (which turns out to be in camouflage). Nor can Auden's promise in 'Spain 1937' that tomorrow, after the revolutionary reckoning, there will be 'the photographing of ravens', be trusted. The eagle's aerial eye is as morally blind as those of the self-soliciting schoolboys in the bushes, or as Colonel Page closing in on his prey with his camera. On top of a mountain pass, Isherwood notes that the only neutral observer is an 'unjudging bird', which would survey this 'tiny, dead patch in the immense flowery field of luxuriant China' and take it to be 'the Bad Earth'. During their journey Auden and Isherwood meet a camera-man who, in his death-defying sorties as a reporter, evinces a heroism they shamingly lack: this is Robert Capa, a veteran of the Spanish Civil War, killed in 1954 by a land-mine while photographing the war in Indo-China for *Life*, and granted military honours by the French. Auden bluffingly apes Capa's aesthetic valour. Trying to wheedle passage into the combat-zone, he pretends that 'a journalist has his duty, like a soldier. It is sometimes necessary for him to go into danger.' The aviator, in *The Orators* an overseeing conscience, now conducts reconnaisance homicidally. As they are buzzed by Japanese fighter planes, Isherwood remembers stories about the murderous fancies of pilots who, annoyed by some insignificant speck below, will squander rounds of ammunition on eliminating it. Up in the air, the flier is an observer discharged from human responsibility to what he observes and annihilates.

Much later, after Isherwood's conversion to mysticism in California, the aerial view stands for a saintly renunciation of the earth. Stephen Monk looks down on the painted desert as he flies out of Los Angeles in *The World in the Evening* (1954) and is consoled by its callous indifference: it is 'a world fit only for hermits, reptiles and military manoeuvres'. In China, however, Isherwood is the grounded target of those exterminating angels with their torpedos, and shudders with fear. Auden mocks him by assuming the posture of that other documentary shootist, the photographer: he caught 'us unawares with his camera'.

Cecil Beaton, serving with the winged squadrons of the Royal Air Force in 1942, retained his faith in the omniscience of the flier, seen by him as an ersatz photographer. Beaton's airmen have attained, he says, 'a means of expression': their fighter planes are visionary cameras. But Rex Warner in his novel *The Aerodrome* (1941) imagines a state supervised by these aloof fascists, freed from time and space, for whom the Air Force is an anti-gravitational evangelism. The Air Vice-Marshal extols the beauty of their risk-taking existence, 'poised for a brief and dazzling flash of time between two annihilations'. This is the nervously ecstatic tempo of the photographer's life, too, enduring eternities of uneventfulness punctuated by those life-and-death instants when the shutter clicks: Henri Cartier-Bresson's decisive moments. The acquisition of wings means, for Warner's fascist corps, the repudiation of earthly emotional ballast. '"Parenthood", "ownership", "locality" are the words of those who stick in the mud of the past.' The observer is the uprooted alien, potentially the killer. Whereas the literary project of the '30s was observation, the next decade worries about a panoptic society where observing people is a means of controlling them. This is the nightmare of *Nineteen Eighty-Four*, with its omnipresent telescreens, its snooping policemen and its Big Brother, whose régime is founded on his censorious watching of its subjects. The lachrymose human eye has been supplanted by a coolly fishy lens, just as Winston's teeth are extracted and replaced by plastic choppers. The hectoring man in the canteen wears spectacles which 'because of the angle at which he was sitting . . . caught the light and presented . . . two blank discs instead of eyes'; Winston refers to him as 'the eyeless creature'. If observation is exposed as the policing of thought, then documentation in Orwell's novel admits its own fraudulence. It is Winston's job, by the destruction of newspapers and the rewriting of history after the event, to prove fictions true 'by documentary evidence'.

The end of *Goodbye to Berlin* tactfully renounces the passive record of phenomena made by Isherwood the camera from his window at the beginning. In the winter of 1932–3 he patrols the streets he had formerly looked down on, in company with the anti-Nazi Herr N. Though they are in the city, they are protected against it, for their language lessons take place in Herr N's closed car. Driving through another city, Arnold Bennett's Evelyn reflects that 'the interior of the car was the most private, the most secure room in all Paris'; the car serves Isherwood and his pupil as a mobile and defensively occluded 'camera obscura'. Inside it, N. takes photographs without an apparatus. Watching S.A. thugs forcing pedestrians off the pavement, he notes, 'One sees some queer sights in the streets nowadays.' Photography is not after all the mechanically impartial compilation of a dossier; it is a tragic art, subjecting the thing it treasures to loving embalmment, not brisk cancellation as by Greene's gunman Raven. Isherwood watches N. 'bend forward to the window and regard a building on a square with a mournful fixity, as if to impress its image upon his memory and to bid it good-bye'. The camera is an instrument for reverie, ritually pre-figuring the dying eye's farewell to the world. Its negatives are the ghostly tracery of our loss. What starts as a documentary cataloguing of the real ends as a romantic research of symbols.

Auden in 1969 avowed in a short poem 'I Am Not a Camera'. Isherwood outgrew the 1930s in California by studying sanctification, and made the camera do atonement by illuminating spirits: he prepared a treatment of the life of Buddha which MGM for a while planned to film. Auden, meanwhile, in New York, having abandoned Marxism for the Christian theology of Kierkegaard and Reinhold Niebuhr, concentrated on mortification, the humbling and chastening of the flesh. The camera, therefore, with its cult of physical delectation, came to seem impiously superficial. For it, people were nubile or grotesque exteriors, 'anatomical data', not souls capable of transfiguration. Auden from now on sets his poetry to sympathise with the hurt, redeemed interiors of those who are jostled anonymously in the city's lonely crowd, like the woman at the luncheon counter of 'In Schrafft's' (1947), shapeless, indeterminate, undistinguished, whose smile yet attests that a god has visited her and has been received, or like the fickle Chester Kallman, to whom Auden addressed a Christmas poem in 1941 electing him a saviour:

Because it is through you that God has chosen to show me my beatitude. . . .
As this morning I think of the Paradox of the Incarnation I think of you.

For a holy man of his own, an equivalent to Isherwood's swamis, the maturer and wiser Auden chose Shakespeare's Falstaff, canonised in *The Dyer's Hand* (1962) as one whose all-forgiving, dog-like devotion to the princely boy who rejects him is a sacrificial extremity of love, like Christ's remitting of mankind. The camera would see in Falstaff only a sagging, corpulent sack. But in 'Vespers', from 'Horae Canonicae' (1949–54), Auden's own 'Aquarian belly', which disqualifies him in Isherwood's physically fit Utopia, is the badge of his citizenship in Arcadia; and Falstaff in turn is repatriated to Eden in Windsor Forest by opera, the form which overhears the vocal plangency of souls and ignores the unwieldiness of corseted, perspiring bodies. Auden argues that the definitive Falstaff, the redeemed one, is Verdi's— who magnanimously pardons his persecutors and leads them in a celebration of the world's biological comedy—rather than Shakespeare's, left to die disconsolate. Falstaff's salvation by opera confirms what Auden believed to be the blessedness of music, not translating, like literature, across the sad gap between experience and image. Song is impartially generous, and in the 1938 poem 'The Composer' it calls no existence wrong and lavishes its forgiveness 'like a wine'. That vinous bounty recalls the tippling Falstaff, and also Christ's miracle at the wedding feast.

Casting off the personae of the 1930s, Auden grew to mistrust the camera because of its indelicacy about love. The cinema, he pointed out in a *Vogue* article in 1948, misrepresents love as an exchange between nubile bodies; opera knows it to be a communion of spirits, crying aloud for release from that flesh. The lovers in his 1969 poem therefore flinch from the rudeness of a mutual close-up by shutting their eyes before they kiss. What they are adoring is an idea not a face: the innocent infant inside Auden's alcoholic fat knight. Falstaff is Auden's saddest but also serenest and most uncomplainingly martyred character, and he knows that the poet's vocation is to love a world which will never reciprocate that feeling, to 'suffer dully', as Auden tells 'The Novelist' in 1938, 'all the wrongs of Man'. Isherwood finds self-contempt easy, because it is a mystic self-rejection. In *Lions and Shadows* he calls himself 'the public lavatory that anyone might flush', and in 1965 his Ramakrishna humbles his own caste-pride and acquires holiness by cleansing a privy. Auden more morosely sees it as his duty to submit to infection, since as he says in his journal in 1929, 'only body can be communicated' and love is that body's contagious disease. The poet heals us by volunteering to assume our sickness: he is the lover we make use of overnight and then, like Hal, discard. This is the tragedy of Falstaff, and also, thanks to Christian miracle, his comedy.

Auden saw poetry's origin in a scar or a bruise. Ireland hurts his Yeats into poetry, and his Rimbaud is 'made a poet' by the cold and burst pipes; whereas the composer can deal in sweet sounds, the poet's materials are 'images . . . that hurt', dragged from 'his living' as if from his innards. It is this which makes Auden—who urges Benjamin Britten in 'Underneath an abject willow' (1936) to put himself emotionally and sexually at risk—so great a love poet and such an expert on suffering. He admires the Dutch painters in 'Musée des Beaux Arts' (1938) for their Shakespearean understanding: our agony is excruciating but also laughable, as when Falstaff's demise is described by the hostess, and above all insignificant, for the reveller will never heed the mourner. Breughel's Icarus is Auden's revision of the hubristic aviator in *The Memorial*. The plunge to earth is a moral necessity not a mechanical lapse, and like Gloucester's suicidal leap from the cliff at Dover the tragic fall is a lesson in the body's comic reclamation by gravity. Hence the unique compound of the macabre and the grievingly compassionate in Auden's 1937 ballads (two of his finest poems) about the cancer-stricken Miss Gee and the messianic maniac Victor. The surgical unseaming of Miss Gee adheres to the precepts of Isherwood's clinical realism, yet flouts them by its angry arousal of feeling; the wife-killer Victor reverts when captured to a childish mildness, and having carved up Anna now occupies himself in remaking her as a woman of clay—perhaps that primeval statuette whose physique, in Auden's comment on the Venus of Willendorf, is the cuddly, motherly prototype of Falstaff's?

Auden's most lovingly sympathetic poems are those of 1938–9 to his fellow-artists, novitiates, like him, to sorrow, who return or renege on a gift of genius which is to them an infliction: Rimbaud reforming himself as an engineer, A. E. Housman as a crabbed classics don, Matthew Arnold as a jailor-faced inspector of schools, Edward Lear as a harmless, avuncular schizophrenic. Auden can understand their resignation, because their profession seems so heartbreakingly futile. Language's efforts are mocked by music, and by silence. The polysyllabic chatter of Oxford in his 1937 poem cannot regain the lyrical delight of the rooks imparadised or cradled in the college garden, which, like gurgling babies or musicians, 'still speak the language of feeling'; orotund, talkative Henry James is commemorated, in the poem Auden wrote in 1941 at his grave, by a taciturn stone. The artistic life faithfully lived extends the offering of love to a world which needs it (as Auden says in his elegy for Freud) but will not remember to be grateful. The poet is the prince's dog.

The runic secretiveness of Auden's early poems hints at psychological crimes, expressed as physical deformations. Symbol is symptom, announcing what a 1927 poem calls 'the secrecy beneath the skin'. In 1949 Auden returned to the subject of our gossiping traffic in secrets, but now the conspiracy is an announcement of love, which means 'to share a secret', and a pious capitulation to 'our Father . . . / From whom no secrets are hid.'

The same evolution occurs in the novels of Graham Greene, who raises the detective story to the status of a metaphysical fable. The novelist is God's spy, an interrogative father confessor. *The Power and the Glory* (1940) considers the ethics of Greene's own artistry, which presumes a godly knowledge and exacts from him a hard-won godly tolerance. The whisky priest cleanses those he confesses, but is himself left without the means of absolution. On the night before his execution he tries confusedly to confess himself, and can do so only by an act of novelistic imagination, inventing a colleague to quiz and analyse him. The policeman Scobie in *The Heart of the Matter* (1948) practises detection as a holy office, and sees as its paradoxical purpose the release, not the conviction, of malefactors. He says that 'a policeman should be the most forgiving person in the world'. With the exception, that is, of the novelist, whose privy insights into people load him with an onerous responsibility to them. Like a more conscientious Catherine Morland, Scobie reflects, as he searches Druce's bedroom, that our drawers contain humiliations, and 'petty vices' are 'tucked out of sight like a soiled handkerchief'. Ever since the eighteenth century, the novel has worried about the proximity of fiction to mendacity, and it is accused again by Greene of being a false or infidel consciousness. The Mission library outlaws the form because, as Mrs Bowles puts it, 'we are not teaching the children how to read in order that the~ can read—well, novels', and the fatuous Mrs Halifax reads 'the same novels over and over again without knowing it'.

Scobie himself reads romances which, like the westerns manufactured by Rollo Martins in *The Third Man* (1949), are at least unworldly, allegories of good's crusading combat with evil or of our quest for the buried treasure of our lost immortality. He cherishes a copy of *Allan Quatermain* awarded him as a school prize, notices an abridgement of *Ivanhoe* for use in schools on Harris's desk, and learns that the boy called Fisher has read *Treasure Island*. The novel anchors us in society; romance frees us from it for adventures which are, when deciphered, trials of the spirit, like Rollo's confrontation with his boyhood friend and metaphysical adversary, Harry Lime. Auden and Isherwood, collaborators in epics of mountaineering or romances of exploration, jettison the novel in China. They read *Guy Mannering* and *Framley Parsonage* on the train to Hankow, grudgingly admire 'Scott's skill in spinning out a story', but find Trollope dull because 'interested exclusively in money'. The novel's mercenariness troubles Scobie less than its fictional aversion to truth. Wilson, whose guilty secret is the poems he writes, accepts that 'his profession was to lie'. Devising narratives to conceal his adultery or faking a diary to provide an alibi for his suicide, Scobie must learn the same aesthetic craftiness, but his every instinct revolts against the telling of a lie. The cost to his integrity when he at last reconciles himself to doing so is his supreme sacrifice: he so loves the world that he consents to become a novelist for its sake. As in Auden's poem, the trader in secrets must surrender all his scavenged data to God, whose agent he is revealed to be. When Scobie dies, his wife laments that 'he hasn't any secrets left', and Wilson adds, 'his secrets were never very secret'.

The ageing Auden is less a father confessor than a Mater Dolorosa. He envies Falstaff's corpulence, arguing that old men are not only babes again (like the 'big baby', querulously in need of sleep, to whom Auden near the end of his life in 1972 wrote a lullaby): they are old women, puffy, pink-faced, shrill-voiced; nature has in them reunited opposites. Already in his letter to Byron, Auden remarks that he is daily growing more like his mother. Eventually he took to impersonating her, sagely referring to himself as a collective parent, 'your old mother'. The team-spirit of the '30s childishly yearns for this absolution in second childhood: the hotel in *Journey to a War* is prep school with a jolly, bossy headmaster as host, and in *Letters from Iceland* one of the imaginary schoolgirls, Hetty, writes to her friend Nancy and cements their secret society in fits of conspiratorial laughter—'What giggling, my dear!' The elderly, matriarchal Auden disciplines the world by loving it, not—like the aviators of the early poetry—by overseeing it, and makes no claim to a lofty immunity from fault. 'She mayn't be all She might be', Auden admitted, 'but She is *our* Mum', and she of course knows best. The absorbent rock of 'In Praise of Limestone' (1948) pleases him because it is geologically 'like Mother', shaped in 'rounded slopes' and nurturing its offspring of sons from the chuckling rivers which have their sources within its body; in the poems about his Austrian summer house, 'Thanksgiving for a Habitat' (1962–4), Auden plays the home-maker and provider, convening a family of friends and distributing its members throughout the establishment where he is den-mother.

He even took to declaiming Spender's 'I think continually of those who were truly great' (from *Preludes*, 1930–3) as 'Your old mother thinks continually of them that are truly great', and it is remarkable what a difference, and perhaps a moral improvement, his recitation made to the poem. Spender is callow, competitive, envying the 'lovely ambition' of those he admires and wants to equal. He imagines them to be, like him, Wordsworthian infants, writing out of their recollection of 'the soul's history' before birth. Auden, taking up the poem, changes it from the work of a young man to that of an old woman, who understands the eagerness of her juniors to inherit the world and can allow them to do so because hers is the womb which bore them and of which they sing. Fostering the brood of his own successors, Auden can bequeath himself to them, like his Yeats who, dying, 'became his admirers'.

The conspiracy of the '30s is that of youth against age. Isherwood keeps to his faith, and stays perpetually young by revising his past. In *Christopher and His Kind* he rewrites the evasive, anonymous Issyvoo as the blatantly intimate Christopher, inducts the alien into the freemasonry of his sexual fellows, and achieves his earlier self's rebirth as a gay militant of the 1970s. The later Auden knows that history cannot be altered, and that in memory we must suffer through it again and again in the hope of expiation. His revisions to poems or (in the case of 'Spain') excisions of them do not rewrite the past but express remorse for it, as when 'September 1, 1939' laments the errors of that 'low dishonest decade'. At last, Auden acquires the tolerant parental hindsight of time, which in a 1940 poem knows 'the price we have to pay' and reminds us (like mother) that 'I told you so'. The poet who identified England after he had left it with 'my own tongue' could expect kindness from a time which, however cruelly it was wearing him down,

> Worships language and forgives
> Everyone by whom it lives

—for language is the great work of time, the voluminous family of man presided over by mother. As he ages into the likeness of that symbolic parent, Auden makes his peace with history.

— 41 —
'Now and in England'

At the end so long a history, there is a temptation to declare finality and termination, and the literature of the last two generations encourages (or so it seems) this arrival at an ending. While the drama strains to instigate historical change in a society which has slowed complacently to a halt, the novel loses faith in history and in itself as an interpreter of the present. Its England, no longer a place whose reality can be trusted, is marginal, insignificant. Only by the jingoistic derision of abroad, which Kingsley Amis mocks in *I Like it Here* (1958) or *One Fat Englishman* (1963), can England be made to matter. Doris Lessing sees London in *In Pursuit of the English* (1960) as if from an extra-terrestrial's eyrie: her friend Rose inhabits a London constricted to the half-mile of streets where she feels safe, 'a . . . tunnel, shored against danger by habit' defensively introverting 'this terrible, frightening city'. Earth is a burrow. The novel advances into the air and into the future, submitting what Amis in his 1959 lectures on science fiction calls a report 'on Terran civilization'. There is even the rumour of a spaceship in the spa town of Iris Murdoch's *The Philosopher's Pupil* (1983).

The novel consequently maps an epilogue to England. Drama, too, in John Osborne's commentary on the demise of the music-hall in *The Entertainer* (1957), farewells an old England. The landscape tended by poetry in the same period is that of a little England, imperilled and not given long to live: Philip Larkin in 'Going, Going' describes the slovenly ruining of nature. Amis in his justification of science fiction quotes the classical rhetorician Scaliger, who says 'poetry represents things that are not'. Hence the novel's projections of the social hells which await us; hence, in Larkin, poetry's supposition of a blank, comfortless heaven which is important precisely because it is elsewhere. Literature appears determined to resign from the time and place made sacred by Eliot at Little Gidding, 'now and in England.'

Yet its predicted things to come are prevented from arriving by literature's retention and unending revaluation of its own past. The imagined futures or elsewheres are contributions to that past: deracinated Arcadys. Merely by continuing, history makes traditionalists of us all. The only dissent is amnesia. The more English literature anxiously and restlessly changes, the more it stays the same. Is nostalgia its only formula for revolution?

Though it began the English drama all over again in 1956, Osborne's *Look Back in Anger* is, as its title declares, a retrospective play. Its protagonist rails in remorse for an old England which has been lost, and is retrievable only in concerts of Vaughan Williams's music on the radio, or in a pastoral game-playing which restores childhood, with Alison as a squirrel and Jimmy as a bear or rabbit. Jimmy's recollection is not romantically tranquil, 'picking daffodils with Auntie Wordsworth'. It iconoclastically subsumes and consumes the past in living through it again. He specialises in soiling, defamatory parody. His Eliotic epic about the modern world is called 'The Cess Pool', and in one of his scathing vaudevilles he includes a lyric entitled 'She said she was called a little Gidding, but she was more like a gelding iron.' His society has unmanned him. He responds by imitating its two oldest kinds of heroic aggressors, the epic ruffian and the chivalric defender of faith. Alison imagines him going into battle against her genteel family 'with his axe swinging round his head' or, alternatively, as a 'knight in shining armour'. He is as well the modern mockery of the heroic prototype: a Tamburlaine giving to yelling and to blowing his own trumpet (left over from the days when he had a jazz band), whose armaments are not oaths or curses but polysyllables like 'pusillanimous'. And the barbarous loudmouth is additionally enfeebled by being made the colleague and contemporary of Shaw's impotent lecturers or Wilde's frivolous anarchists. The clue to Jimmy's Shavianism and to the pathos of his patter is the surname of his friend Hugh Tanner, whom he likens also to the poet Marchbanks from *Candida*; he taunts Helena by calling her Lady Bracknell and offering her a nonexistent cucumber sandwich.

Jimmy Porter belongs simultaneously in all periods of English literature. Alison believes him to be potentially another Shelley, and Helena hears in his harangues the rhetoric of the French Revolution. But even if he had been granted that romantic liberty, history would have conspired to weaken and cheapen him. Alison adds that 'He's what you'd call an Eminent Victorian. Slightly comic—in a way': the verbal terrorist transformed into a pompous wiseacre; the radical whose fury is the reflex of a regretful conservatism. Osborne eventually found for the dispossessed Jimmy a home in the past of English literature. The eighteenth century permits him, as it did Virginia Woolf's Jacob with his 'mystic book', to be a complete man. He is the embittered, impoverished relic of the character Osborne turned to in writing the film script for Tony Richardson's *Tom Jones* (1963). The sensual binges and oyster-guzzling of Albert Finney's Tom in Osborne's adaptation justify Jimmy as an instinctive innocent, 'escaping from everything' (as Alison says of their play-acting) by 'being animals'.

The traditionalism of our literature soon enough takes Jimmy Porter hostage. By now the angry young man is a grand old man, with a younger generation to venerate and imitate him. Thus Jimmy's slur on Wordsworth's daffodils prompts a similar rejection from Furry in Howard Brenton's *The Churchill Play* (1974). He rages about 'Bloody school. Bloody poetry bein' read at ye. Bloody daffodils wavin' in 'wind.' But in dismissing the past he confirms his affinity with it: he is after all virtually quoting Jimmy. And like Osborne's pastorally nostalgic hero, Furry upbraids Wordsworth only because—in the police state exhibited as England's future in *The Churchill Play*—his vision of a green and pleasant country is no longer true; he abuses the heritage because he has been disinherited.

Brenton returns to reinterpret the history perused by Jimmy in a play which derives its title from Furry's diatribe, *Bloody Poetry* (1984). Its characters are those romantic failed gods whom Alison identifies as Jimmy's ancestors: Shelley and Byron, here seen indulging themselves in Italian exile, remote from the revolutionary emergency of their age. The meaning of Furry's phrase has bifurcated. 'Bloody poetry' is a curse on the art as a frivolous, sensuous pastime, an excuse—as Shelley and Byron employ it—for neglecting political loyalties and personal duties; but poetry might justify itself if it became truly bloody, dirtied with the gore of action. Then it could win back its power to accuse and alter reality. To do so, it must give up the lyric and change into drama—specifically, of course, into Brenton's drama, issuing a violent challenge to its public. Art takes up again the arms which, throughout the entire history of English literature, it has been laying down: its function is to be one of what Brenton calls, in another play, the *Weapons of Happiness*.

For Osborne, drama is protest. Hence his choice of the first protestant as an examplar in his 1961 play, also for Albert Finney, *Luther*. His missionary urgency means that Osborne's plays increasingly turn into lectures. The loggia of the villa in the tropics in *West of Suez* (1971) is the talking-room of the well-made play, trying to keep history at bay but now menaced from all sides. The writer Wyatt Gillman, first played by Ralph Richardon, is Jimmy prematurely aged and ennobled, comprising the history of literature in personal reminiscence. He sports a hat he may have been given by Yeats or George Moore, remembers Rupert Brooke, quotes (and reincarnates) Johnson. He is an orthodox adherent to a dramatic and linguistic Lutheranism: the English genius resides for him in the King James Bible and Cranmer's Book of Common Prayer. Language elects him its prophet. When a crass interviewer asks him about the Gift of Tongues, he replies that he believes in 'pride of tongue'. Against him, Osborne aims the new verbiage of inarticulacy, in the obscene tirade of the drop-out Jed, whose rhetoric is lethal because it is the cue for Wyatt's murder. Osborne's characters stand guard over the polluted tribal dialect, so that their main dramatic activity is the ironically undramatic one of reading. Jimmy scans the Sunday papers, Robert in *West of Suez* performs the BBC programme listings, and *A Sense of Detachment* (1972) consists of a recitation from a brochure of scabrously pornographic novelettes, alternating with performances of lyrics by Yeats, Betjeman and Rod McKuen.

Because Osborne's England has betrayed its past, his drama travesties the history it summarises. The small island west of Suez is Prospero's absolute monarchy, now colonised by invading American tourists. The brownish servant Leroi is 'the geni of the island', Wyatt a Prospero deprived of his wand who plays the sage on television. Elsewhere he is referred to as a parlour Lear, put on trial by his four daughters.

The same disinheritance is implicit in *The Entertainer*, which cast Olivier as the lewd, down-at-heels music-hall comedian Archie Rice. The actor who had so rousingly cried God for England in the Old Vic's wartime production of *Henry V* takes on himself the country's post-war shame, exhibiting a peekaboo Britannia to a depleted public in a theatre jeeringly named The Empire. Archie's 'personal myth', as Osborne calls it, amounts to a pitiful talent for self-deception. The music hall, tawdry and near to extinction, signifies to Osborne an ancestral England of folk art. Within it, Archie goes through the motions of an act he no longer believes in. Osborne describes his deadpan manner as 'a comedian's technique' which absolves him from commitment to anyone or anything. The paradox of the comedian is his nullity, here close to despair. Archie's face is a mask, 'held open by a grin and dead behind the eyes'. His motto is his culpably indifferent 'Why should I care?'

After almost two decades, he is re-activated by Trevor Griffiths in *Comedians*, first performed in 1975, which mobilises the drama by invigorating the music hall. Griffiths's play is didactically set in a schoolroom, at an evening class for amateur comics; Eddie Waters, the tutor, corrects Osborne's elegiac prefatory note to *The Entertainer* when, listening to yet another stale whimsy, he asks, 'How can they say Music Hall is dead when jokes like that survive . . . down the ages?' Eddie is a radicalised Archie, who tells his pupils, in revision of Freud, that 'a true joke . . . has to do more than release tension, it has . . . to *change the situation*.' Drama is a rehearsal for retributive action, a warm-up and a work-out. One of the comedians includes some kung fu exercises in his routine, and explains (dressed as a bovver boy) that he needs a train to smash up. The class's practice at accelerating its patter fortifies the group's morale and prepares it for the fray. The communist Tagg in Griffiths's *The Party* (1973)—Olivier's last role on stage—defines revolution as dramaturgy in a tirade against the merely verbal weaponry of his intellectual comrades. Theory, he says, must prove itself on the muscles, and in the sweat of determined brows. Political tactics are the bold initiatives of dramatic action, 'the essential connective imperative' (as Tagg says) 'between past and future'. In Griffiths's *Real Dreams* (1984) these dialectical callisthenics, redefining drama as a communal engagement, yield to a spiritual limbering-up. This play, about a cell of guerillas in Cleveland in 1969, ends with a session of Tai Chi exercises.

Drama constitutes an agenda for social renewal. Henze's 1976 opera *We Come to the River*, for which Edward Bond supplied the text, was subtitled 'actions for music'. Unless conscripted to the purposes of revolution, the theatre is a region of decadent, defeatist feigning. In Bond's *The Woman* (1978) a playlet about Trojan politics is chimerically enacted inside Heros's head.

Priam's son rails at the war-hungry Hecuba by saying 'You bully people by acting! She treats this city as if it was on a stage.' His cue here is Hamlet's revulsion from the obscenity of impersonation and its elaborately bogus simulation of feeling: 'What's Hecuba to him or he to Hecuba?' Bond cancels the theatre's flattering reproduction of actuality. Hamlet's mirror held up to nature does not accuse people but enables them to admire themselves. Hecuba was long ago the Venus of Asia, and 'can still see it in the glass'; a bored watchman outside besieged Troy says that his vigil is 'like staring at the back of a mirror for five years', to which his companion rejoins, 'no loss in your case.' Rather than the realistic facsimile, Bond's drama resorts to the petrified formality of the classical mask, which delineates the skull beneath the skin. Masked, the actor has ceased to be a unique and sentient individual; he becomes instead a sacrificial offering, his face contorted into the grimacing rictus which denotes either tragedy or comedy. Hecuba married Priam when he was old, and thought she might be able to tell what he looked like in youth if she saw him asleep: 'But he looked', she reports, 'even older—as if a mask had been pushed through from underneath.' Later she herself vanishes behind this unfeeling façade. She, too, rejects the theatrical hysteria of Hamlet's Hecuba threatening the flames, and she discovers a valour in the dead, leering face worn by the entertainer, Archie Rice. After the murder of Astyanax, she blinds herself. No longer able to see, she becomes in exchange inscrutable. Like the Thane of Cawdor in *Macbeth*, she gives the lie to acting's physiognomic mimicry: there is no longer an art 'to find the mind's construction in the face'. Heros is maddened by her seizure of this power: 'You cover your eye. That's not rational. I look at the face that Priam kissed—and it's a mask. If I could see your eye I'd know if you lied.'

The theatre for Bond has lost its power to galvanise society, concentrating instead on individual fates. He reclaims that primal, community-convening force by working through the history of drama and revising its forms and genres as he goes. His early piece, *Saved* (1965), is about drama's origins in a ritual killing: it is a Greek tragedy set in the slums of south London, and in it the society's slaughtered scapegoat is a baby stoned to death in its pram. Though it is a tragedy, Bond refuses to treat it as such, which would mean the indulgence of self-pity, a validation of merely personal emotions. He calls it 'an Oedipus comedy'. Having staged the infanticide with brutal glee, he prescribes a course of healing. The play's last scene, almost a dumb show, studies the mending of a chair. The theatre unleashes the fury of a contagious madness, then—in this episode of play therapy—sets about administering a cure. Catharsis now consists in do-it-yourself carpentry. Bond returns to the birth of tragedy in *The Woman*, and again revises it. The *Oresteia* of Aeschylus is about the overthrow of matriarchy, and the transference of power from kin to state. Its masked male actors are the usurpers, even the assassins, of the women they portray. Bond disallows this repressive coup. *The Woman* conspires against a war-mongering patriarchy: Heros is providently felled by an alliance between Hecuba and Ismene.

After the Greeks, Bond does battle with Shakespeare. *Lear* (1971) is Bond's recension of a character to whom Shakespeare is not capable of doing justice. Lear is, Bond believes, 'the most radical of social critics', but his righteous rage is enfeebled by being passed off as madness. What ought to incite revolution lapses wastefully into a tragedy. Lear's insanity is his condemnation to ineffectiveness. Bond's Cordelia, trying to dissuade him from preaching to the disaffected, says that 'if you listened to everything your conscience told you you'd go mad'. Whereas the Shakespearean character renounces politics, Bond's Lear at first deploys power violently and autocratically and at last, instead of subsiding into acceptance, marshals opposition to that power. The play begins with him personally executing a worker whose negligence has interrupted work on a wall to fortify his demesne; it ends with him shot as he attempts to sabotage those ramparts himself. This is not the serenely uncaring Lear of Shaw in *Heartbreak House*, nor the domesticated lion of *West of Suez*. Resignation here means neutering, not the meditative calm of Shakespeare's Gloucester. 'In future', a councillor instructs Bond's Lear, 'you will not speak in public.' If the theatre is not used as a public address system, it is no better than a deluding dream. That is its vicious service to Lear's daughters, of whom he says 'They live in their own fantasies!' Fontanelle's consort had an actor pose for the photographs he included in his love-notes to her.

The calamity of Lear overtakes Shakespeare himself in Bond's play about his death, *Bingo* (1973). Here Shakespeare is ironically put on trial by a theory of tragedy which his own plays flout: his fatal flaw is his investment in the iniquitous social order against which Lear rails. Bond finds Shakespeare guilty of a seamy deal to enclose some common land in Stratford, evicting a populace of hereditary small-holders. The manoeuvre is Shakespeare's betrayal of Lear, for the land in question symbolises the heath which is his forum, the common space where truths can be brought into the open. Shakespeare's remorse disables drama. Mute and morose, he is beyond both acting and reacting. 'His movements and face express nothing', Bond directs. The histrionic reactions of others are just spurious theatre to him. When his wife wails and scratches outside the sick-room from which Shakespeare has excluded her, he notes that her hysteria is 'put on'. He denies himself the recourse of poetry, too. His disgusted monologue about a bear-baiting telegraphs details—'the chain. Dogs on three sides. Fur in the mouth'—rather than, in the oratorical manner of Lear, singing an aria. Suicide, Shakespeare's judgement on his own venality and pettiness, is attended by none of the tragic hero's special pleading. Hurriedly gobbling pills, Shakespeare reflects on the otioseness of this physical extinction. He has been dead since the play began.

Restoration (1981) is Bond's revision of that period's comedies, demonstrating their sexual intrigues to be persecution and colonisation by other means; and *Early Morning* (1968), about the lethal perversity of Queen Victoria, is his commentary on Victorian melodrama, here presented—in an orgy of fly-swatting, game-hunting, assassination and cannibalism—as a theatre of cruelty. Aggression, Bond argues in the preface to *Lear*, is a disease of the 'technosphere' in which we are unnaturally compelled to live. His theatre is that brutal place in little: a torture-chamber, like the mechanism which extracts Lear's eyes. *Early Morning* is the equivalent of a pillory. It places historical characters in the stocks, and pelts them for imaginary crimes. It is aware of the analogy between the theatre and the gallows, and validates the cynic's claim that if a public execution were announced outside during the performance of a tragedy, the play would instantly lose its audience. Bond's Victorians scramble for tickets to sold-out ceremonies of judicial murder. The Lord Chamberlain thinks hanging 'satisfies the people' and is 'something to live up to'. Howard Brenton's plays stage history as an obscene side-show, a spectator sport for the victors, like the savage Roman circuses. His Victorians at the Derby in *Epsom Downs* (1977) flog mounts which are naked, trussed and harnessed human beings; an imperial legionary in his *The Romans in Britain* (1980) celebrates the army's appropriation of a new colony by sodomising a young Briton.

Jimmy Porter was alarming because of the noise he made. In a literature where the poets tend not to speak out (as Arnold say of Gray) and the novelists, like Virginia Woolf's Terence, transcribe 'the things people don't say', he renews drama's function of vociferation. In succession to him David Hare in his 1975 play *Teeth 'n' Smiles*, set at a Cambridge graduation ball, lends that haranguing voice the assistance of a microphone and a violent percussive back-up: the lyrics of the rock singer Maggie are acid assaults on society.

After Maggie's electronically boosted eloquence come the imprecations of Susan in Hare's *Plenty* (1978), who says all the things about which society has decreed that we should be politely silent, naming Nasser, for instance, during the debacle of Suez. Ann snubs Jack Tanner by treating his expostulation as chit-chat: 'Go on talking.' Susan's husband is less temperate. 'Please can you stop', he screams, 'can you stop fucking talking for five fucking minutes on end?' Susan is an alienation effect on legs. She is also, to Hare, the spirit of drama. The form is about acting and about speaking out, which ought to be radical gestures. A dramatic action is a gratuitious act. It puzzles, startles, even appalls us, and in responding to it—for the character's action demands our reaction—we scrutinise our own values. Susan specialises in the bizarre initiatives which are the stuff of drama. She fires a gun at a lover, demolishes a drawing-room, insults the guests at a diplomatic reception. Her life is an exercise in that dialectical renovation after which Hare names the play he wrote in 1975 about the Chinese revolution, *Fanshen*. The word means overturning, an enforced remaking of oneself. It is the dramatic action as self-criticism and self-redemption. A woman achieves her 'fanshen' by casting off shyness and learning not to be afraid of making public declarations. To appear on stage is to stand up and be counted. The inert Hamlet of *Waiting for Godot* is now accused of shrinking from the political challenge. His query about being and not being serves as a motto for genteel stultification in Trevor Griffiths's television play *Country: 'A Tory Story'* (1981). Daisy asks Dollie why she gave up her career on stage. Dollie explains that she couldn't, unfortunately, act. Daisy lays down the conservative law on such matters: 'Ladies *don't* act. Ladies are.' One of the terrorists in Griffiths's *Real Dreams*, debating a raid on a supermarket, politically corrects the quietism of Hamlet, who considers only cerebral options and betrays the activism of drama by taking refuge in soliloquy: 'To do or not to do' is for Sandler the crucial question.

Tom Stoppard responds to this phrasing of the dramatic problem, also from inside a re-interpretation of *Hamlet*, with a nonchalant fatalism. The victims in his *Rosencrantz and Guildenstern are Dead* (1967) have no alternative but to consent to the dramatist's execution of them: nothing, despite Sandler, can be done. Stoppard writes out the antic randomness which makes Hamlet so dangerous an anarchist. His Rosencrantz and Guildenstern pass the time by tossing coins, yet in doing so they disprove the chanciness that Hamlet cunningly exploits. In eighty-five consecutive throws the coin comes up heads, and Rosencrantz wins every toss. Shakespeare might seem to have assigned identities to them arbitrarily and interchangeably, and his characters—when they stray into Stoppard's scenes—regularly mistake one for the other. Stoppard, however, outfits each with his own predestining traits: Guildenstern nervy and suspicious, Rosencrantz more easily deluded by the theatre's feignings. Thus he deprives them of the free will that Shakespearean characters enjoy, which is as well the radical recourse of Hare's people. All they know is that they have been sent for to Elsinore, or that they have been sent to England with Hamlet. They are pre-empted and coerced by Shakespeare's lines. The account Ophelia gives of Hamlet's dementia in Shakespeare here functions as a stage-direction. The Shakespearean text acquires oracular power. When Guildenstern demands to know who decides when a character dies, the player darkly replies '*Decides?* It is written.'

In Stoppard's theatre, society cannot be changed. That is the mistake of his Lenin in *Travesties* (1974), who, when he seizes the rostrum to agitate, reduces drama to diatribe. Performance in Stoppard is a patterned and beautifully pointless drill. It sports with this inefficacy in the philosophical gymnastics of *Jumpers* (1972) or in the intellectual cricket of Henry in *The Real Thing* (1982). The aesthetic integrity which is Henry's 'real thing' contradicts social reality, just as acting reneges on political activism. All he needs to do to defuse the protest in Brodie's anti-nuclear skit is to rewrite it as a better play. Adultery is rendered unreal by being played: Charlotte lost her virginity to the actor who was Giovanni to her Annabella in a British Council tour of *'Tis Pity She's a Whore*, and Annie succumbs to Billy while they are rehearsing the same play;

but when she diverges from Ford's script, addressing him by his real name and kissing him in earnest, the scene has to be called off. Charlotte at least did not surrender on stage. She waited, she insists, till they got back to the Zagreb boarding house.

In *Travesties*, too, the performance of a play within the play suffices to frustrate a political takeover of drama. The inset piece this time is *The Importance of Being Earnest*, performed in Zurich in 1918 by an amateur company whose business manager was James Joyce. In the same city at the same moment Lenin was awaiting his summons to Russia, and Tristan Tzara (co-opted for Wilde's play by Stoppard, who has him play John Worthing) was staging Dadaist outrages. Though Lenin prefers an art more bourgeois than the scarifying absurdism of Tzara, Dada is the revolution by other means. Against these manic confounders of the established past—among whose institutions is literature, terrorised when Tzara cuts up a Shakespeare sonnet—Stoppard adheres to Wilde, who 'may occasionally have been a little overdressed but . . . made up for it by being immensely uncommitted.' Wherever his characters slip into recitation from or rehearsal of Wilde, their adherence to the prior text marks their denial or witty denunciation of innovation. Henry Carr, an official of the British consulate, plays Algernon and in a revision of Wilde's first scene castigates his butler Bennett about the scandal of Bolshevism, complaining that the over-supply of spies makes it impossible to get a café table. The Wildean hero is languidly scornful of Lane's moral principles and social attitudes; Carr employs Algy's lines to discipline the fellow-travelling Bennett. Likewise he has, in a later scene, to defend Wilde against the accusation of political irrelevance by a Cecily who is Lenin's research assistant. Miss Prism in Wilde's play took care to keep Cecily uninformed about economics, and counselled omission of the chapter on the fall of the rupee. Stoppard's Cecily has studied it all the same, and uses it against her original creator, vilifying decadence and epigrams as 'a luxury only artists can afford'.

Though Joyce only managed the troupe's finances, Stoppard needs him—since he is the inviolate artist unperturbed by politics, who when asked 'What did you do in the Great War?' replies, 'I wrote *Ulysses*'—to deliver an authoritative rebuke to the revolutions in Russia and in the surrealist unconsciousness. He casts him, accordingly, as Lady Bracknell. His debate with Tzara about Dada corresponds to Lady Bracknell's interrogation of Jack, who is displeasing to her because he has no daddy and may be suspected, in a manner which recalls to her the worst excesses of the French Revolution (since the Russian one hasn't happened yet), of having mislaid him. This restitution of parental authority bases its delivery on the catechism from the penultimate chapter of *Ulysses*. Joyce, omniscient, asks the questions; Tzara, yielding to him by playing along with the format, obligingly answers them. So Stoppard's characters are on the one hand Wilde's dictatorial matron and the young man without a lineage or a respect for society, and on the other the Joycean father reconciled with a hitherto rebellious and straying son. Because both Wilde and Joyce are precedents, they can be cited, whenever Stoppard quotes or imitates them, to curb the present's secession from them, whether in politics or in art.

Differentiating his own drama from Chekhov's, which is emotional, Bond calls it a 'theatre of history'. The actors are to be history's midwives: 'our acting . . . is directed to the future. . . . The actors . . . become the illustrations of the story as well as the speakers of the text.' David Hare's drama more quizzically examines the mismatching of history and theatre. *A Map of the World* (1982) watches an historical confrontation being falsified and trivialised when a film is made about it. His television play about a wartime propaganda unit, *Licking Hitler* (1978), accuses its medium of the same duplicity. Diderot's actor can only mime feelings if he doesn't feel them. The propagandist is usually assumed to do without such dubiety, to believe fanatically in what he is saying. Yet Archie in *Licking Hitler* serves Allied purposes by pretending to espouse the Nazi cause. In his broadcasts to Germany, he defends the Führer against the quixotry of Rudolph Hess. As Hare's surrogate, he manufactures propaganda by devising plays. Two of his team are cast as German officers who, sending signals over short-wave radio, relax into scurrility about their leaders. The little scenario is played out nightly, with improvised sound effects, in front of the microphones. To further truth, Archie invents lies. Propaganda schools him in the production of meretricious entertainment, which he turns out in his post-war films. Susan in *Plenty* tries to dupe herself, for instance when telling the boy she has selected as her inseminator that she likes and then that she loves him, but she is not so expert at it as most of us—accomplished amateur actors—are. She relies on others to do her lying for her. When a man with whom she has been illicitly holidaying dies, she asks the British Embassy to inform his wife. The official inquires if she intends him to lie. She says, gravely and humorously, that she would prefer it if he did. Does the theatre, like polite society, require dishonesty of us? Anna in *Licking Hitler* drops out of society—and of the play, since her conversion occurs in a narrated epilogue and is not dramatised—because of 'the lying, the daily inveterate lying, the thirty-year-old deep corrosive national habit of lying'.

Hare's second television play, *Dreams of Leaving* (1980), recommends abdication from a theatre which is the native habitat of illusion and deception. The heroine is a chic, fake revolutionary, who sabotages the rigged art-market by stealing a lithograph from the gallery where she works. In her case the self-critique of the peasants in *Fanshen* is glib self-exposure: during one of her careers Caroline photographs whores and their clients in London brothels. Does her policy of abuse and indictment amount to anything more than a facile desire to shock? William, the young provincial journalist whom she teases, translates her wounding honesty into a casual permissiveness. At the end of the play he is seen ensconced among his mod. cons., at ease in television's consumer heaven, reporting that he and his wife 'keep an open marriage' because they believe their union 'is refreshed by affairs'. The truth-telling which Susan saw as a sacred duty now licenses a spendthrift promiscuity. Anna quits society; Caroline more drastically forswears language. Susan's mania is vehemently rhetorical, but when Caroline goes mad she lapses into hunched catatonia. Hare, as if mistrusting his own volubility, follows her example and deserts speech for the muteness of imagery. Caroline is characterised not by what she says but by how Kate Nelligan (for whom the parts of Anna, Susan and Caroline were written) looks, with her detached, frostily beautiful face, and by what she looks at.

Because Hare is questioning drama, changing its concern from character in action and in rallying speech to a static, silent contemplation of images, paintings are important tokens in *Dreams of Leaving*. When Caroline takes William on a tour of the gallery store-room, she pulls a Mondrian from a rack and disappears briefly behinds its diagram of rectilinear perfection. Nelligan in this play is not the prophetic voice of *Plenty* but an iconic face, alabaster and unyielding, as rigorously pure as the Mondrian. Her madness is abstractly expressionist. After the Mondrian, she produces a Rothko, and stares at it for a moment. 'They sort of float in space', she says of it. That is her own destination—unmoored from earth, weightlessly whirling through a void. Hare writes such abstractions into his script. Her face, when William quizzes her about herself, is indecipherable, sometimes invisible: at one point while they are talking she switches out the light and continues to speak in the darkness. The play's dream is of leaving more than the false gods which enthral William.

It is followed—in Hare's next work for television, *Saigon: Year of the Cat* (1983)—by an epic and collective dream of leaving. The Americans fleeing from Vietnam are refugees from drama, and all that remains of their occupancy is a series of images, intently specified in Hare's script, of places which have been voided, nullified: depopulated Saigon after the curfew, the deserted lounge of the Cercle Sportif, an apartment left to await the looters, a whole city clambering into helicopters on the US Embassy roof to be lifted up into Caroline's free-floating space. The staff of the Embassy meanwhile work overtime to shred the past before the withdrawal. How can drama keep up with history's mass-production of fictions and its mechanised erasure of them? Hare's *Pravda* (1985), written in collaboration with Brenton, rowdily rejoices, against its better judgement, in Fleet Street's output of untruths.

Drama rages to mobilise society; the novel traditionally wants to be a conspectus of that society—to contain, comprehend and thus to pardon. That ambition of comprehensiveness, dominant from Fielding's itinerant survey of England in *Tom Jones* to Lawrence's dynastic annals in *The Rainbow*, persists in Anthony Burgess's vast *Earthly Powers* (1980). The earthly power of the

[683]

novel is its sympathy with the human comedy. Hence the corollary between the novel-writing of one of Burgess's heroes, the octogenarian man of letters Toomey, and the unearthly powers of exorcism and miracle-working deployed by the other, the sainted Carlo Campanati.

Toomey remembers the entire century to date, and in doing so makes his literary predecessors his coevals. Dropping their names, gossiping about them or even impersonating them (when he registers at a Bloomsbury hotel as Henry M. James), he has competitively outdone them all. He is their inheritor and usurper, taking over Aldous Huxley's apartment in Albany when Huxley leaves for America in 1937, hanging his walls with photographs of Thomas Mann, Wells and Hemingway, seeking advice from Ford Madox Ford. His sliest encroachments are upon Eliot and Joyce, the century's mythologists. Eliot he reprimands, in a message relayed through Wyndham Lewis, for his misinterpretation of the Tarot pack in *The Waste Land*: 'a novelist could never get away with that sort of inattention to detail'. Joyce, his friend, is similarly trumped. The composer Domenico, who makes a Broadway musical from *Ulysses*, calls it 'the book of the century'. Is it that, or only the book of a day? Toomey was in Dublin on Bloomsday in 1904 and remembers it because he was seduced then by A.E., whose concurrent walk-on in *Ulysses* gives him 'an alibi which no appeal to history could break'. Writing himself into *Ulysses*, Toomey is also assuming the collective character of Eliot's Tiresias, foresuffering (as he remembers the loss of his virginity in that hotel room) all of the age's woes.

Not content with elbowing out Eliot and Joyce from creative primacy, Toomey additionally ventures to write—or at least to recite—the entire history of the literature which predates them. One of his plays anthologises the development of drama, following three characters through successive acts of Elizabethan tragedy, Restoration comedy, and Shavian debate, delivering them at last to the present. For Hollywood he prepares a treatment of King Arthur and the collapse of his chivalry, and has to explain to the baffled moguls that the legend is about 'Celtic Christianity fighting for its life against the Anglo-Saxons', whose barbarism turns out to be woefully contemporary. A producer wants to know 'Did they say *fuck* in those days?' Toomey wearily explains, 'It's a very old word. Anglo-Saxon.' Toomey's most extravagant feat is a bardic recital of English literature's plots from *Beowulf* and Chaucer to Henry James (who is himself with a vestigial middle initial), undertaken to entertain the man who drives him through the Australian desert from Darwin to Alice Springs. Of course he alleges he has written them all. His companion suspects him of having plagiarised *Paradise Lost*, but requests an encore of 'The Pardoner's Tale.'

These wholesale appropriations serve Toomey's celebration of literature, and of the language which makes it possible. *Earthly Powers* is as much a treatise on linguistics as a novel. Toomey is polygot, and universally learned about dialect, remarking on the kinship between Maltese and Moghrabi Arabic, listening to discourses on ethnology and linguistics, smiling at the provinciality of some French jurors at a film festival who claim to 'understand neither the Canadian French dialogue nor the English subtitles' of a Quebec entry. (Toomey knows that Québécois is 'only eighteenth-century Norman.') Joyce's search was for the word known in all languages. Toomey's virtuoso delight is in translating a being known in all languages into all of those languages one after the other as Deus, Allah, Bog, Jumala and Mungu. That being is the primal speaker, God, and Toomey acknowledges and revels in the artist's rivalry with this absent precursor and colleague.

Carlo's argument for the existence of deity presupposes Toomey's own art: 'There has to be a creator. This Creator created everything', as Toomey creates a whole literature during that journey through the outback. The book Toomey is most anxious to have written is Genesis because, as Domenico says, it describes 'the birth of language'. He therefore rewrites Genesis as homosexual heresy, and in doing so outdoes Shakespeare, who merely, with prophetic prematureness, sneaks his name into the Bible in Psalm 46, whereas 'I had actually written a book of it.' (Burgess, it should be remembered, has written novels about Moses, Christ and Shakespeare.) Local linguistic theogonies are glanced at. A Sikh taxi-driver tells Toomey how the Tamil tongue came about. One day God invented a world's worth of languages, and when a Tamil complained in dumb show that none had been assigned to him, God farted and gave him the rippling, rumbling emission as his means of utterance. Every writer has been graced by the Pentecostal Paraclete. What is the saint but an artist who attributes his involuntary power of speech to a celestial ventriloquist? Carlo, dying as the Pope, admits as much when in his last words he subtly transposes pronouns and, like a poet imbibing inspiration, says 'Lord hear my prayer and let thy cry come unto me.' Because Carlo's concern is 'marrying the speech of earth to that of heaven', he can draw on a divine or diabolical potency in words which are still spirits, as when he lapses into Neapolitan slang to curse and terrorise a Mafioso during a mass in Chicago. His papal project of ecumenism is possible only when a word is invented for it: 'Ecumenico' is 'the big word', and Toomey confesses that it 'was new to me, who had done little Greek'. But his linguistic eclecticism is a secular counterpart to Carlo's intended reunion of churches. His policy is one of linguistic exogamy, remarrying human tribes by collating their quarrelsome dialects. This is the reward of John Campion's anthropological research in Africa. He has ascertained, Toomey is assured, 'that there is a relation between linguistic structures and family constellations'.

Language makes a god of Toomey, and not an invisibly vocal one like Carlo's Holy Spirit but (to use the word he applies to Norman Douglas) an omnifutuant, Ovidian one. The history Toomey narrates is apparently a long desacralization. When he is visited by the archbishop who wants posthumously to prove Carlo a miracle-worker, he says, like Hazlitt reflecting on the death of a poetic god, 'The world was once all miracle. Then everything started to be explained.' His own profession, he adds, is an agnostic but credulous one: novelists 'lie for a living'. But Toomey's fictions are the sublimest earthly power of all, daily and man-made miracles. Though homosexual, he writes a novel of heterosexual passion 'to prove . . . the limitlessness of the creative artist's province'. When he proposes a libretto on the subject of Saint Nicholas, Domenico demurs because saints belong in oratorio not opera. Toomey will not accept the relegation. Opera is, thanks to its music, a bold sanctification of profane and secular existence; the novel, equally, is a gospel for humanists, their bright book of abounding life.

Iris Murdoch's novels are a courageously sustained, rigorously honest effort to secure the form's entitlement to this status as the guarantor of human freedom. They manage it, again, by revaluing literary history. Victorian novels were about the individual's engagement in society. Since then the form has polarised into an account either of solipsistic individuals who believe in no society, or of totalitarian societies which will permit no one to be an individual: into psychoanalysis or sociology. The novel describes either Isherwood's mystically solitary single man, or Orwell's politically regimented, mind-controlled Winston Smith. It is trapped in the mutually cancelling opposition over which Jake and Lefty argue in their debate on Marxism in *Under the Net* (1954). Is the person a self-sufficient consciousness, or a social being? Can he be both?

Bradley Pearson in *The Black Prince* (1973) blithely ignores the contemporary problem. His 'reading life . . . consists simply of the greatest English and Russian novels of the nineteenth century'. (And, it might be added, of Shakespeare, an honorary and ultimate novelist. *The Black Prince* is an explication of *Hamlet*. It rewrites the play as a novel, with Bradley as Shakespeare creating Julian as his character and his love. Creativity in the great novels, is, to Iris Murdoch, the miraculous generation of free-standing people with stubborn wills of their own like Hamlet's, let loose into a world which the god fondly leaves to its own devices.) Murdoch defines the difficulty in her 1953 study of Sartre. The novel must be saved from exclusive dominion by Freud on the one hand and Marx on the other. Existentialism professes to venerate our liberty to make ourselves up as we go along, with the bravado Murdoch so admires in Hamlet, yet its art denies that liberal permission. Roquentin in Sartre's *Nausée* is sickened by the world's haphazard contingency, and Jake is made jokingly to share this affliction when he remarks of a South London suburb that here 'contingency reaches the point of nausea'. The philosopher's theory is betrayed, in Sartre's case, by the novelist's practice, which is too ideologically prescriptive.

Under the Net is a brilliant reproach to Sartre, understanding existentialism as the accident-prone comedy of a dangling man, suspended (like Jake on the fire-escape) in mid-air, or thrashing to remain afloat (as when he boozily swims the Thames). Jake is expert at all existential balancing-acts: judo, tennis, dancing. He exercises his freedom as a sportive delight, at ease in a comic randomness, rather than dolefully confronting choice as a tragic burden like that humourless Hamlet, Roquentin. Jake wonders at his friend Dave's philosophical indifference to 'loose ends'. (Dave has a nauseously contingent address, off the Goldhawk Road.) What, however, is the novel but a paradise—as Henry James critically objects—of loose ends? Iris Murdoch associates the form with a derangedly funny, explosive volatility, and acclaims the chaos which James reproved in the Victorians. Her images for it in *Under the Net* are zig-zagging firecrackers, and Heisenberg's whirlingly busy electrons. Jake's career is a succession of farcically energetic episodes lapsing, at almost every chapter's end, into sleep.

This existentiaism in overdrive revives in the novel the antic disposition of Shakespearean comedy. Like the pirouetting Benedick in *Much Ado*, Jake believes man to be a giddy thing. Anticlassical and unclassifiable, the novel represents to Murdoch a special mental generosity, joyously open to experience. The wise man Hugo, manufacturer of skyrockets, 'noticed only details. He never classified.' This makes him, in Jake's view, 'almost completely truthful'. He possesses that 'whole truth' which Aldous Huxley argued that literature was seldom—except, perhaps, in novels—able to tell. The novel therefore has an affinity with goodness, the value declared to be sovereign by Murdoch in a 1967 lecture, because it opposes the psychological meodrama of romanticism with its sublime egomania. Goodness is meek, effaces itself, and compassionately accepts the arbitrary scheme of things. Its creations are characters like Shallow and Silence, Dostoyevsky's idiot or Tolstoy's Petya Rostov. Kierkegaard's good man was likely to appear in the shabby guise of a tax-collector. It is significant that Bradley in *The Black Prince* has been a functionary of the Inland Revenue, an anonymous exemplar of accountability. The sculptor Alexander in *A Severed Head* (1961) criticises the offence of modern art against the individual and his proper freedom. He finds it difficult to finish the head he is carving because 'we don't believe in human nature in the old Greek way any more. There is nothing between schematized symbols and caricature.'

Nevertheless there remains, for Iris Murdoch, a difficult gap between the moral theory of fiction and its imaginative practice. Hence her sympathy with her hero's analysis of Shakespeare in *The Black Prince*. Bradley judges *Hamlet* to be his greatest play, but suggests that it should not be, for only mediocre art countenances the writer's use of a character as his self-vindicating fantasy. *Hamlet* is Shakespeare's apology for the vanity of art, a 'self-castigation in the presence of the god'. Yet no one is more aware than Murdoch of the artist's temptation meddlingly to play god, like the Prospero (a theatrical director) in her 1978 novel *The Sea, The Sea*. Art finds contingency intolerable, and wants to manage it into formal containment. Eventually Jake's panorama of a London which, west of Earls Court, straggles off into chancy meaninglessness, is cordoned inside—and rendered necessary by—the map of the underground Circle Line travelled and talismanically studied by the hero of *A Word Child* (1975). As a philosopher, Murdoch has another qualm about her own artistic procedures. She inherits Plato's mistrust of imagination. Hugo takes charge of a company pledged to such tawdry fabling, Phantasifilms Ltd, which has 'decided that human beings were bad box office and started on [a] series of animal pictures'. In her 1976 lecture on Plato's parable of the reality of sunlight and the false glimmer of fire in the cave, Murdoch identifies television as that flickering illusion: art at its shoddiest. Her heroes succumb to imagination as to concupiscence. After he has refused the bribe, Jake, getting drunk in a Paris bar, fantasises about how he would have spent it, and sees himself ribaldly enjoying fame, power and the favours of women in a flat overlooking Hyde Park. He summons up in his reverie all the greedy compensations which artists, according to Freud, lavish on themselves in the worlds they imagine. When Bradley hears *Der Rosenkavalier* at Covent Garden, he is disgusted by the way Strauss's score acts as pander or procurer to him: '"music" for me was simply an occasion for personal fantasy, . . . the muck of my mind made audible.'

Murdoch calls Sartre a romantic rationalist. To rationalise romanticism means to realise it—penitentially transferring it, as the Victorians had done, from poetry to the unaccommodatingly actual novel. Reality for Jake is a hangover. Ordered to Paris and offered £30 as expenses, he considers this latest existential whimsy 'curiously unreal. Except for the thirty pounds. That was real; like the next morning object which proves that it wasn't all a dream.' The complexity in Murdoch's case is that part of her longs to be beguiled by the dream, while another part strives to fly from its enchantment. The romantic fantasist accepts a philosophical duty to unlearn romanticism (the conceit of Milton's Satan and of Kantian man, ragingly selfish and averse to goodness) and to outgrow fantasy.

The rescue in *The Unicorn* (1963) works through this long and agonising process of exorcism in literary history. Hannah is kept prisoner in a room of mirrors; Marian, hired to teach her, seeks to release her from a paralysing spell. The lesson she wants to administer is that of freedom. In her turn she is a pupil apprenticed to a philosopher, and studies Greek with Effie. Ensorcelled by an illusion, Hannah belongs in the first age of romance. She is the unicorn helplessly caged in the late fifteenth-century tapestry at the Cloisters in New York. When Denis says she is imprisoned, Marian replies, 'We're not living in the Middle Ages.' Denis corrects her: 'We are here.' Jamesie remarks that everyone in the novel's Celtic kingdom of witchcraft is 'related to the fairies', whose expulsion from the land by canting friars, when romance was first censoriously rationalised, the Wife of Bath complains of; Denis is a satyr. The mystery can be overturned if, as at the Renaissance, it is allegorised, interpreting the dream as an educative trial. This happens with the courtly love in *The Unicorn*. The worshipped beauty is promoted from an erotic to a spiritual value, and the salmon leaping from the pools are souls approaching God. Yet this symbolism, which assigns safely orthodox meanings to the romantic images, may be the most deluded romanticism of all. It is the novel's pragmatic, secular conviction that, thanks to it, 'the era of realism was beginning'. Hannah, however, complains that she has been made unreal by all those who, in the novel, think about her so obsessively. At last with the curses lifted, the mirrors shattered, Marian can depart for 'the real world'. Effie after the expurgation sees the case differently, and counsels advance from mere realism to a reality which can do without the deceptions of art. It was their folly falsely to deify Hannah, denying her humanity. The novel has been trumped up, as Effie puts it, as 'a fantasy of the spiritual life, a story, a tragedy'.

The fetishised Hannah turns later into the 'eidolon' impiously adored by Bradley. *The Black Prince* happens simultaneously in a conceptual heaven and on a ludicrous earth; it is at once an illumined theory of art and an uninhibited comic novel about the muddle and mayhem of living; severely rational, and irresistibly romantic. Bradley experiences love sometimes as enlightenment, and describes himself as Plato's 'cave-dweller emerging into the sun', sometimes as possession by a 'black Eros'. The twinned, inextricable emotions of the lover are the quarrelling motives of the artist. As a fleshly weakling, the artist creates in order to compel from others a complicity with his will. As a god, he creates, resignedly and sacrificially if he can, to set others free. One kind of art and love is represented by the indulged predatoriness of Strauss's opera, the other by the renunciation of control in Shakespeare, who in the sonnets permits his own loved ones to betray him and blesses them for doing so. This is the '*natural*, as it were Shakespearean felicity in the moral life'. It is one of Bradley's small dialectical achievements to win over Strauss's wily heroine to the altruistic Shakespearean ethic: he consoles himself for the loss of Julian by remembering the Marschallin's voluntary surrender of Oktavian.

Bradley's calamity is that the dual manias of love and art oblige him to be untrue to the nature of life. The good man, he says, will prefer truth to form and style. Is the artist then a reprobate? And love, too, raises idols of a perfection and irreproachable dignity which people may have in art, but never in life. The moral and theological norm of the novel censures Bradley's lyrical fervour and his operatic dramaturgy of desire: 'The novel is a comic form. Language is a comic form. . . . God, if He existed, would laugh at His creation.' The intensity of his love prevents him from making the kind of art he venerates. He is a Shakespeare who will not cut the umbilical cord attaching Hamlet to him, a novelist who cannot allow his world to be laughable and disobedient. Julian tells him that he has 'spoilt all the fantasy fun of your love by bringing it out into the real world'. At the beginning he scorned Priscilla's attempted suicide as 'pure fantasy'; at the end a series of insulting postscripts dismiss his own narrative as just that—a 'dream-story', or an Oedipal wish-fulfilment.

A Severed Head states the opposition between the morality of living and the brazen irresponsibility of artistic dream or nightmare as a warfare of theologies: Christian redeemers against dark gods; a religion of love against one which, when Honor Klein cleaves the air with her Samurai sword, emphasises power and the irrational regimenting of people by magic. Honor's sword means the same thing as Yeats's. It is the weapon of that ignoble savage, imagination. Palmer Anderson the analyst treats the psyche as a mechanism to be cleansed and repaired. His credo is 'We are civilized people.' His sister Honor the anthropologist despises 'civilized' behaviour, and that is precisely the source of her hold on the infatuated Martin. Palmer, though credited by Martin with possessing his own species of magic, may be guilty of profaning a goddess. The patron of psychiatry is Psyche, who is the bride of Cupid in Spenser's Garden of Adonis. Martin recalls the legend in which she was told that, if she kept silent about her consort's identity, the child she bore would be a god; if she told, she would bear a mortal. Does rationalising deconsecrate the secret deity which is romance?

Reality, Hannah's therapeutic reprieve from the madness of imagination, is—as Martin discovers in *A Severed Head*—no more than a pretence. He comes near to accusing the novel of propping up a world in which the ego can be comfortable. Antonia's aspiration to a communion of souls seems to him 'a metaphysic of the drawing-room': a devastating comment on the adulterous seminaries of Henry James. The Eastern sages admired by Bradley work for the 'destruction of the dreaming ego', and one of their techniques might be an auctioning off of the fitments which anchor Antonia's drawing-room. Iris Murdoch experiments with this dematerialisation in *Henry and Cato* (1976). Henry, revolted by 'the cornucopia of the American supermarket', returns to England to inherit an ancestral home which he sees as an encumbrance to the spirit and a snare to the self, now beguiled into playing the squire. The impedimenta of his house of fiction are ponderously solid, depressingly real—dusty busts of emperors, lamps made out of huge vases, massive chests of drawers, tables with brass rails, shaggy rugs. Henry plans to free himself by selling it all off. He learns from the priest Cato that 'what you call the funny world is the real world. It's where God is, where truth is.' Yet despite his nostalgia for a monastically emptied world elsewhere, Cato is abducted and held prisoner in a malodorous Plato's cave: a dank green dungeon where the graffiti on the wall, studied by the light of a candle, picture the origins of literature in the indestructible ego's assertion of itself and its claim to immortality. 'Cato's eyes . . . found themselves *reading*. There was a name, *Jeff Mitchell*, and a date. A crude drawing. Other names. . . . The whole wall was covered with names and dates.' And Henry, having rolled up the rugs, boxed the netsuke and filed away the Landseer sketches for consignment to the sale-room, changes his mind, gathers together again the materiality he had thought to abolish, decides not to vanish into the holy 'nowhere' of middle America, accepts the illusion of the family house he is 'stuck with', and even considers embellishing it with some new purchases of his own.

His repudiation and rehabilitation of the world are matched by the virtuousity of Iris Murdoch's own conjuring. She invents a supplementary set of existences just outside the novel, makes them in their absence as real as if they were present, and then, like Prospero with his insubstantial pageant, causes them to evaporate, all in demonstration of her own wizardry. Henry's former colleagues from St Louis, Russ and Bella, besiege him with telegrams, postcards and letters, then unaccountably disappear to Santa Cruz; and a crucial character in the plot, Giles Gosling—the borough architect, who designs the council estate to be built on the parkland Henry intends to give away—is constantly invoked, sometimes comes to call, yet never (materially, that is) appears: so compelling is Iris Murdoch's artistry that she can make us believe in characters she has not in fact created. This is fiction's most audacious and alarming bedevilment: Mrs Gamp's invention and assassination of Mrs Harris.

Is the novelist a benevolent but misguided sorcerer, his fictions uncompelling charms? Must the novel remain an ineffectual romance? This is the suggestion of Angus Wilson in *As If By Magic* (1973), and it is the fantasy of his agronomist Hamo, whose new rice will restore bounty to the depleted earth. Hamo is a deflated version of the Victorian novelist, gloating over the irrepressibility of his creation. 'Here's richness' might be his too-trusting motto. Anthony Powell's novelist X. Trapnel in *A Dance to the Music of Time* (1951–75) says 'a novelist's like a fortune-teller'. He can impart certain information only, and his predictions will not necessarily come true.

Whereas the Victorian novelist is a know-all, Powell's narrator Nick Jenkins models his art on two figures whose knowledge is either partial (having to be supplemented by hearsay) or arcane and unreliable: the seventeenth-century gossip John Aubrey, whose *Brief Lives* Powell has edited, and the same period's magus Robert Burton, from whom Powell derived the title of his first novel *Afternoon Men* (1931) and about whom Nick writes a book. Like Aubrey, Nick can only report tales about people whose motives he can never be sure of. Was Widmerpool, for instance, a Russian agent? Aubrey's speculations are complemented by Burton's spells, which are occult rumours—the mysteriously bleeding elderberries in the last novel of Powell's sequence, *Hearing Secret Harmonies*, or the dabbling of the alchemist Fenneau in what Nick calls 'the scholarly end of Magic'. Discerning patterns in a dance which seems random, guessing at a design, Nick is the gossip as soothsayer. As he watches the wheeling flight of birds, a temporal dance in the air to unheard music, he reflects that to the initiated among the ancients 'the sight would have been vaticinatory'. Powell's sequence coheres thanks to coincidences which titillate the gossip, because sooner or later everyone will be intertwined—probably erotically, as in the horned dance Gwinnett describes—with everyone else, but which are also spooky, telepathic wish-fulfilments: the guru Dr Trelawney (himself named after another famously unreliable gossip and fictionist, Trelawny, the friend and biographer of Byron and Shelley) calls these novelistic conjugations 'magic in action'. The dance is performed to no music dispensed in social formality, like that for the Highbury ball in *Emma*. It is sung to by the west wind and enacts the ascent of the 'liberated soul': 'hearing secret harmonies' is a quotation from another seventeenth-century alchemist, Thomas Vaughan. It is the dance of the rapt, naked cultists on midsummer night at the stumpy megaliths called the Devil's Fingers.

Powell's vast serial novel is not a solidifying of society, like the chronicles of Trollope or Balzac, for the world as Nick sees it is 'a fading mirage'; nor is its research into the past comparable with Proust's, for memory in Powell is a ghoulish resurrection of the dead, not an affair, as when Proust eats the cake, of sensual regurgitation. Gwinnett reports on a black mass whose 'idea was to summon up a dead man called Trelawney'. Harmony is Power, according to Murtlock's mysticism; but for Powell the novel's powers are unearthly.

Therefore at the same time as his sequence is extending forwards historically from the 1920s to the present, it is mythically reaching backwards through the layered pasts of English culture. The reappearances of characters are the reincarnations of seasonally dying and re-arisen gods. Scorpio Murtlock pops up in the newspapers each year like 'a vernal demigod'. Powell's people commune in memory, and what they have in common is the literature which is their psychological past, revived by them in the present. Moreland and Nick have, quite independently, been haunted since childhood by the description of Apollyon's advance in *The Pilgrim's Progress*. When Murtlock walks into the wedding in his blue robe, it is as the embodiment of this shared fantasy. When Widmerpool self-purgingly drops out, he turns into a figural replica of Ariosto's Orlando, about whom Nick has been reading. When Delavacquerie quotes Middleton's play *The Roaring Girl*, Nick comments that it 'sounds very contemporary': literature's history is a perpetuity of rebirths, an unending collective which atones for the brevity of single lives.

Powell's social rites are the past's successive returns to life. At the Royal Academy banquet, the Victorian era has its comeback. One of Nick's neighbours at the dinner is an actor, whose nightly business is reincarnation: last season he 'had performed a rather notable Shallow', endowing Shakespeare's moribund character with a renewed lease of life, and he 'was now playing in an Ibsen revival'. That particular magic coincidence effects another exhumation within Nick, for the Ibsen play stars Polly Duport, daughter of his long-ago mistress Jean. Gauntlett belongs at the beginning of the nineteenth century, with Scott's romantic antiquaries, happily resident in a haunted house and 'allowing himself archaisms of speech, regional turns of phrase, otherwise going out of circulation'. Gwinnett's academic interest in the Jacobeans introduces the seventeenth century into the present. He studies Trapnel as a vindictive, latter-day Tourneur, and interprets Murtlock's rites as a replaying of 'Tourneur's scene in the charnel house'. Gauntlett's phrases, out of circulation, cycle back in his speech; Scorpio's celebrants caper inside a 'sacred circle'. Within that precinct, everyone is enclosed. Nick points out to Gwinnett that another of his Jacobeans, the dramatist Beaumont, 'was a kind of first-cousin of my own old friend, Robert Burton'. Nick reads himself back into the Elizabethan Renaissance in Harrington's version of Ariosto, seeking an imaginative lineage for Burton, 'something of an Ariosto fan', then finds Orlando's journey to the moon replicated in his own present: he writes 'a year before the astronauts actually landed there'. In youth, Nick enacted the oldest and most immemorial historic role of all, dressing up to represent one of the Seven Deadly Sins at Stourwater in 1938. When, thirty years later, some of the performers from this Gothic charade regroup on a committee to award a book prize, Norman suggests they should make a myth from the pageant, seasonally reincarnating it: 'Do the Seven Deadly Sins in rotation. The book wins, which best enhances the sin-of-the-year.' Fiona, when she joins the Harmony cult, drifts back into a medieval mentality and looks like a T-shirted 'lady from the rubric of an illuminated Book of Hours'. Or is she, Nick wonders, cavorting in a Victorian illustration of that past, 'a Tennysonian-type Middle Age', with Rusty as an androgynous page and Henderson a down-and-out troubadour? A touch of genuine medievalism, however, is their bare and 'long unwashed' feet.

Powell's solemn dance, haltingly motorised in the rally of vintage cars in *Temporary Kings* (1973), ends in the present just at that symbolic literary instant when the medieval world is overtaken by the modern. Widmerpool dies jogging, disdaining Scorpio's injunction that 'to increase the speed would disrupt the Harmony'. His fatal breaking of ranks recalls Chesterton's elegiac comment on the inability of *The Canterbury Tales* (or of *Piers Plowman*) to continue: the Dance has given way to the Race, mythic ordinance to the scrambling competitiveness of history.

The novel warns of its withdrawal from responsibility for interpreting that history in three satires about hack academic practitioners of the historian's trade: Kingsley Amis's *Lucky Jim* (1954), Anthony Burgess's *The Wanting Seed* (1962), and Malcolm Bradbury's *The History Man* (1975).

Amis guys the self-deception of a period which fancied itself as a second instalment of the Elizabethan age. History is to him a fatuous lie, and in his drunken lecture Jim Dixon libels Merrie England as an unmerry hell. The fraud can only be maintained by a pedantic snobbery. By contrast with Waugh's Brideshead, where the age of faith glows still thanks to the lamp in the chapel, the odious Welch in Amis's novel does reverence to the past in amateur concerts of Renaissance music and in the ancestral 'breakfast technics' of his household, with chafing dishes to recall 'an earlier epoch'. The fiction is manufactured from 'frenzied fact-grubbing', like Jim's when he researches his article on fifteenth-century shipbuilding. The imposture to which he is a party provokes Jim to farcical arson. He burns his bed-sheets at the Welches' and razors the charred bits.

Thereafter, Amis's satire prescribes arrival at the terminus of history, in the geriatric apocalypse of *Ending Up* (1974); or else it refuses to allow history even to begin: in *The Alteration* (1976) he imagines a cosily timeless England where the Reformation and its eventual industrial consquences never happened. Now instead of radically and angrily rejecting history like Jim, Amis conservatively arrests it. Merrie England is perpetuated by castration. The novel is about the planned neutering of a choir-boy, to preserve his angelic voice. Is artistic impotence the cost of this denial of history? From now on in Amis, the fictional creator is let down by the dejected useless organ which is *Jake's Thing* (1978).

Burgess in *The Wanting Seed* announces the bankruptcy of the historical novel by assigning Tristram Foxe to teach in a school's Social Studies Department, where he looks back—from an overpopulated future where both fertility and artistic creativity are in official disrepute—on the disreputable cult of human perfectibility and liberal hope known as Pelagianism. It was, he explains, 'the British Heresy'—it sponsored the fecundity of English literature, in Chaucer, Spenser, Shakespeare and Dickens. Shakespeare in particular is accused of having been an over-prolific god, fostering 'unwanted life'. He is converted after the event to the age of zero population growth by being abbreviated: someone on the tube is reading *Dh Wks v Wlym Shkspr*. When history has been ended, so must literature be, for it is the generous fertile transmission of life. The Prime Minister disapproves of personification because it pretends things are alive. A statue is erected to T. S. Eliot, 'long-dead singer of infertility'. Yet literature and life prove irrepressible. Eliot's own words are quoted at him in contradiction of his prophylactic ethic by babes and infants. Beatrice-Joanna's illicitly conceived child burbles 'Da da da', taking over for its own purposes the rumble of the Upanishadian thunder from *The Waste Land*. And Burgess replenishes the race by keeping alive the festive, pullulant, Shakespearean vocabulary, using one of Othello's words to describe the new cult of flesh-eating, which goes along with the revival of mass and its consumption of divinity and gratifies a sacramental hunger for language. 'The New Year', he reports, 'commenced with stories of timid anthropophagy.'

Bradbury's history man is a radical sociologist who has abolished history and with it reality. His dissociation from the past leaves the novel adrift in a limbo where everything is fictitious, even (according to the author's note) the year 1972. Bradbury is writing a comic and inimitably English version of the *nouveau roman*, demonstrating the impossibility of creating fiction in a world which mistrusts its own factual substance. Howard Kirk denies that reality exists, and labours, by espousing leftist causes, to invent it. His dedication to a future of social vindication exiles him from the novel's recreative, remembering past-historic tense. He quotes Freud's definition of neurosis as 'an abnormal attachment to the past', and thrives in a provisional, impromptu present, the time-zone of Bradbury's narration. The contingent for Iris Murdoch is the trajectory of a zany, hilarious freedom: hence Hugo's fireworks, or the predicaments of *An Accidental Man* (1971). For Bradbury, it is less the prowess of existential self-invention than a slack, permissive courting of meaninglessness. A modern story is not, Howard explains, 'a tale with causes and motives' but 'a chapter of accidents'. It studies tropisms, the abutting of objects: 'a Henry and a window came into chance collision'. It is a cowardly fallacy of the Kirks to plot their lives, cramming their diaries in anticipation with 'many events'. Their entertaining is also a disablement of the novel. Whereas the novelist devises relationships between his characters, the Kirks, rearranging the furniture for a party, clear the way for interactions which are to be the encounters of atoms. They deny at the same time the purposiveness of drama. 'We're planning a bit of action', says Howard. 'No, not that kind of action. . . . An accidental party.' They are domestically opening up the aleatory arena which is the playground of modernism: this is to be the kind of party 'where you meet anyone and do anything'. Inside those parameters, as Howard's jargon calls them, novelistic attachments and alliances are disallowed. Howard can understand relationships only as exploitation. Though the person in conjunction with others may be trapped in political servitude, the person alone does not exist. 'How do you define a character?' Howard demands. 'How do you define a person? Except in a socio-psychological context.' Howard himself scarcely exists. He is, as Bradbury's title indicates, no more than a humbug-ridden, humanoid *Zeitgeist*, working through the available role-sets.

At Howard's university, literature has arrived at a condition like his own of utter, emptied relativity. His colleague Miss Callander is the high priestess of this interpretative trickery, rewriting the tale which Bradbury tells for Howard as a *nouveau roman* and treating it as a Jamesian study in 'the angle of vision'; she demonstrates that this technical adjustment can alter the nature of the story and the deserts of its protagonists. As practised by her, criticism is the engineered controversion of verbal truth. When Howard wonders how, to fend him off, she has managed to make the same Blake proverb mean two quite different things, she explains, 'I did it via the instrument of literary criticism.' Criticism collaborates in the denial of history.

It is a rule for the medieval cathedral-builders in William Golding's *The Spire* (1964) that 'if you are going up four hundred feet you will have to go down four hundred feet': Jocelin's skyscraper totters on a cliff of mud. Golding applies this same structural logic to the novel's evolution. If it is to project a future beyond history, it must dredge up a past before history; and it may discover that they are the same. Golding's narrative of Neanderthal man in *The*

Inheritors (1955) atavistically predates the novel. But its primeval ogres are the medieval apes or griffins clambering over Jocelin's cathedral, and also the modern boys who revert to savagery in *Lord of the Flies* (1954).

The Inheritors takes an epigraph from Wells's *Outline of History*, which Mrs Swithin is reading in *Between the Acts*, and which she uses as a spell to bring history to its end. Making art, for Golding, is itself a regression, belying man's belief in a progressive history. His boys on the island in *Lord of the Flies* invent art when they symbolically imagine, hunt and kill a pig. The same image-worship occurs when the creatures of *The Inheritors* 'have pictures'. Consciousness is for them visual not verbal, and therefore it is a summoning of bogeys not a rational articulation of thought. Lok is despised because he 'has a mouthful of words and no pictures'. The heads of Golding's cave-men are Plato's caves, flickering with illusions like Lok's 'pictures of having had a picture'. Golding describes his red beast's brows as 'great caverns where the eyes were hidden. . . . dark as though already the whole head was nothing but a skull'. Imagination is the *ignis fatuus* glinting in this cerebral gloom. As a visionary, Jocelin in *The Spire* retains a primitive susceptibility, and is maddened by it. He dreads art as witchcraft, imagery as a haunting. The power 'to re-create scenes that never happened'—source of the premonitory Neanderthal pictures—can only be explained by Jocelin as an aptitude of the devil. Despite his clerical vows, art dooms him to contemporaneity with Oa, Ha, Fa, Mal and Nil in *The Inheritors*: anger boils from 'some pit' inside him, and he sees the world as 'a filthy thing, a rising tide of muck'.

So it is with Kingsley Amis's Maurice in *The Green Man* (1969), a publican whose inn is planted in an England not jocosely ancient like Welch's but foully retrograde. The pub has existed since the Middle Ages, and is stalked by a seventeenth-century necromancer, with whom Maurice must do combat. His contest with a devil cannot be represented by the metaphysically timid, tamely secular form of the novel, and Maurice specifically rejects it. Maurice's bookshelves contain no novelists. He considers theirs a piffling art, rendering only a fraction of 'the total world' into whose abysses he is in danger of tumbling, and in a supermarket he buys a paperback of what appears to be *Lucky Jim* only to drop it in a rubbish basket, accusing it of 'the endemic unreality of all fiction' and shrugging, 'Oh well, what had I expected? The thing was a novel.'

Amis's malign, fair-haired seraph wishes he could, like a cosmic novelist, re-plot the world. But nobody 'has ever credited me with . . . the power . . . of abolishing historical fact'. Though tempted, like Swift's deity, to play practical jokes on his creation and satirically devise destruction, to ordain 'cosmic collisions' or set down a dinosaur in Piccadilly Circus, he must restrain himself from anticipating his plot's eventual outcome, which will be Armageddon.

What he calls 'this foreknowledge business' is, however, seized from him by the novelists. Victorian novels were habitually set some 'thirty years since', because the past is, as George Eliot says, less disturbed than the present, easier to contemplate; the contemporary historical novel is set, by contrast, in the future. The present is too easily ignorant. The novel wants to foreknow the worst. The drama seeks history's mobilising, like Trevor Griffiths wanting to change the situation. The novel cannot make that allowance of free will to its agents. Plot is a collective predestination. Thus Angus Wilson's *The Old Man at the Zoo* (1961) takes place in 1970–3, during and after a nuclear assault on London; L. P. Hartley's *Facial Justice* (1960) is set 'in the not very distant future, after the Third World War', which—in a future recalling Golding's past—leaves the world with a meagre population of cave-dwellers; Doris Lessing's *The Four-Gated City* (1969) is a narrative of the half-century, ending between 1995 and 2000 by which time, thanks to ecological catastrophe, the British Isles are tersely categorised as Destroyed Area II; and Anthony Burgess broadcasts in 1982 *The End of the World News*.

Wilson's novel begins with the report of God's death. The narrator, never having believed in his existence, does not heed the rumours. The fatality all the same has alarming consequences for novelists, who must take over from the absconded primal author and authority. This is their glorious opportunity, and at the same time their despair. If God does not exist, surmises a character in Dostoyevsky, then anything is possible. If God is dead, then the novel must fill in for the Bible. 'If no God', Burgess speculates in *The Wanting Seed*, 'there must at least be a pattern-making demiurge': that is, a human artist, the choreographer perhaps of the temporal dance as Powell describes it in *A Question of Upbringing* (1951), where 'human beings . . . [move] hand in hand in intricate measure'. But Powell mistrusts his own novelistic plotting of their steps, and wonders whether patterns are the tracery of 'seemingly meaningless gyrations'. Does God anthropomorphically conduct a minuet, or just make molecules arbitrarily orbit and spiral? In Iris Murdoch, as the unbelieving priest says in *The Time of the Angels* (1966), 'The death of God has set the angels free. And they are terrible'—seducers like Beautiful Joe in *Henry and Cato*. God has been dissipated into the angels who are his thoughts. Or gods have taken refuge in pictorial allegories, where they are embodied as human desires: Bronzino's reptilian Cupid in *The Nice and the Good* (1968), Titian's twin Venuses in *The Sacred and Profane Love Machine* (1974), Max Beckmann's tragically clown-faced Christ in *Henry and Cato*. In Doris Lessing, if there is no God there must at least be astronauts, who are angels on missions of scientific mercy. In Amis, God's retirement unleashes a devil, who is the avenging satirist; in Wilson, it frees the animals in the zoo, just as in Daphne du Maurier's 1952 story it uncages the birds. A giraffe in Regent's Park tramples its keeper to death in *The Old Men at the Zoo*. This uprising of the beasts predicts 'the obliteration of human creation'.

Wilson's is a congested England, afflicted by claustrophobia. London, to Forster so muddlingly infinite, makes Wilson's Carter feel confined. Overpopulation has driven the landscape into retreat, so that four regions have to be protected as nature's last stand, 'Zones of Scenic Beauty'. There are plans to found a wilderness on a gentrified estate, where in an Historic British Reserve deer, wolves, golden eagles and brown bears would reclaim the land: again the future strives to resurrect Golding's savage past. But the project is abandoned, and *The Times* opines that 'our island . . . is too small' to accommodate wild life. In this cramped, levelled world, the zoo is a microcosm and an ark, which gathers behind wire netting and puts on show the plenitude of a creation soon to be extinct. Bobby, hoping to restore a Victorian enjoyment of the zoo as an exotic, festive Eden, says 'we could be one of the last colourful places in England'. This refurbishment of the zoo stands for Wilson's project to revive the rampaging liveliness of the Victorian novel, celebrated in his criticism. His British Day at the Zoo is a Victorian pageant of Welch's Merrie England. A small world is installed in Regent's Park, with avenues radiating out to miniature continents and dioramas of the worlds elsewhere into which Victorian Britain overflowed—Stanley's Africa, Botany Bay, a Hudson Bay fur station, the jungles of the Raj. The occasion recalls the global bustle of nineteenth-century novels, and animates as well the ebullient circuses posed in tableaux in Victorian genre pictures: Jumbo the elephant is to participate in a spectacle modelled on 'Frith's famous painting'. Yet there is no retrieving this rowdy, quirky, optimistic heritage. Instead, after Britain capitulates to the pan-European bombs and agrees to federate, a European Day is staged to make official the ban on Englishness.

Hartley's New State in *Facial Justice* has expunged and ended history, ensuring that nothing of the past survives into the present. It has therefore stunted the novel. Wilson cannot bring back the colourful inequalities, the splendours and miseries, of Victorian England, so the only characters left to him are the imported fauna at the zoo—gazelles, llamas, lemurs and tapirs—or survivors from before the flood like Lord Godmanchester, soon to die out; Hartley's futuristic welfare state has set about cosmetically abolishing the quirks and quiddities of character which the novelist prizes. Its Equalisation (Faces) Centre impartially assigns new, blandly average looks to the conditioned citizens of wrecked England. Individuals have been reduced to human units whose quota of personality—averaging a niggardly $17\frac{1}{2}$ per-cent—is chemically adjusted. Faces are classified as Gamma+ or Beta−, and there is an array of numerical models to choose between when applying to have your physiognomy upgraded. The heroine Jael is Alpha, which is anti-social. 'How precious it was', she reflects, 'to be still herself!' Judith warns her not 'to show a marked Personal Preference. . . . It leads to inflammation of the ego'. Conversation between these plasticised clones is an exchange of safe catch-phrases. If you cannot supply the requisite cliché when challenged on the street by an inspector, you are liable to a fine. Typology assists the administrative typecasting of the populace. The Department of Criminal

Nomenclature obliges people to name themselves, as an instruction in humility, after biblical or classical murderers, relying on numbers as the single slight concession to idiosyncracy: Jael 97, Judith 91, Electra 94.

All dwellings have been rendered uniform and belong to the state, to disallow the notion of possession. The house of fiction is now illegal. Jael aspires to have a home. Joab asks, 'By aspiration do you mean a perpendicular or a horizontal movement of the mind?' Either is correct, so long as it is not upward, like Golding's spiring. A cathedral is indeed the last remnant of a world which dreamed heroically and sublimely of height. In the cratered dullness of East Anglia, where England's residual population of two million cowers, only the west tower of Ely Cathedral looms above ground. 'Piercing the heavens, [it] spoke another language' than the dictator's litany of levelness. Ely arouses a will which has been prohited. When Jael wants to go there (where she starts an ecstatic riot of worship), her brother worries that 'as a Failed Alpha you represent the Voluntary Principle.' Language has been democratised by governmental edict. Now all words are equal, and free from regimentation by grammar. Literature has as a result been frustrated, for it is the premium of an outlawed individuality. When Jael ironically reviews a concert she has attended and praises the incompetence of a soloist as 'evidence of our common humanity', flinching from the Ely-like 'pinnacle of excellence', she is annoyed by the feebleness of her writing. Then she realises that this is form's subservient matching with content: 'to be consistent with its own thesis [her essay] must be mediocre, or very bad indeed.'

Hartley's future is the present allegorised, just as 1984 is 1948 with its digits transposed. Len Deighton's *Bomber* (1970), set on a non-existent day in the past—31 June 1943, date of an ill-fated RAF raid on Germany—is about the future, and the novel's adjustment to things to come. Deighton's Cohen reproves historians who 'review the past as a series of errors leading to the perfect condition that is the present time', and warns that we should never forget the existence of future time. Hartley's mediocracy will outlaw literature; Deighton's new dispensation requires it to acquire new skills. He begins in prehistory, acknowledging the 'primitive fears' of the bomber crews and their trust in the primordial technology of witchcraft, linking the motorised, winged monsters above the airfield with their predecessors, 'the pterodactyls that are still found fossilized in the nearby chalk quarries'. The airmen entrust their lives to machines, which apparently have their own predatory volition. It is as if the plane decides to go on the mission to Germany, and just takes its crew along as passengers. The human reaction, in fear and awe of 'mechanical performance', is to undergo cybernetic mechanisation: Binty's sex-life is conducted on and maybe by his motor-bike.

Bomber trains the novel in the same scientific aptitudes. Deighton proposes that the best way to narrate the life-history of a crew is on a graph. Individual emotions are resolved into their physiological correlates. Fleming's terror is computed by his 'loss of peristalsis and gastric juice', the carbohydration of his blood and the wrinkling of his scrotum. But the body can no longer be relied upon as a determinant of character, since it is likely to be violently elided and collectivised: Kit's trunk is atomised by a shell, Jimmy is analytically liquidised into a puddle of viscerae, other bodies are glued to a road's surface by the heat of a blast, and when Sweet's plane crashes into Frau Kestern's farm his remains get intimately entangled with hers and those of the French soldier she had, at the time, been coupling with. Writing suffers the same mangled decomposition when Gerd Böll's letter to August Bach is run over by a lorry, torn by a fireman's boot, swallowed by a sewer and then coughed up in a froth of grey pulp from the nozzles of the hose. The qualifications for the novelist are from now on not those of emotional intuition or acquaintance with the human heart but the possession of technical data and a billion-dollar brain: Deighton reads instrument panels, deciphers cloud patterns, tracks anti-cyclones, measures the content of water particles in the air ('twenty thousand ... in every cubic inch') and navigates by triangulating velocities in a small feat of mental geometry. Then, in an afterword, he assigns his creativity to the care of a word-processor, and pays grateful tribute to the computer's 'memory coding', which has taken charge of history and is our up-to-date electronic Mnemosyne. 'This', he notes of *Bomber*, 'is perhaps the first book to be entirely recorded on magnetic tape for the I.B.M. 72IV.'

Deighton sees the novel's future as applied science. Doris Lessing demands its reformation as metaphysics. Anna Wulf in Lessing's *The Golden Notebook* (1962) plays a game of cosmic dilation, conceptually taking off from earth. She begins with the most insignificant items in a room, then progressively withdraws from them, further and further until she moves 'out into space' and reviews the diminished world revolving far beneath her. The two infinitudes, minute and immense, conjoin. Lessing equalises inner and outer space: 'we are investigating subatomic particles and the ... limits of the planetary system ... simultaneously', as she remarked in 1982. The universe is, after all, Hamlet's nutshell. Anna's game supplies Lessing with an imperative for the novel. *The Four-Gated City* begins in the rancid, realistic interior of a London fish-and-chip shop, and before it ends is observing London from an extreme vertical distance, 'as visitors from a space ship might'; it begins in the illusion-addicted England of the late 1940s, 'a country absorbed in myth', or in the even more spurious 'England' of Martha Quest's mother, remembered from her girlhood, and ends, after the destruction of Britain, with its emigration and reproduction elsewhere, in extra-territorial communities furnished by survivors—outside Nairobi, for instance—with the trappings of an archetypal Englishry, named 'Little England', 'Newest England', 'England Again': post-mortem sequels to a deceased country.

In *Bomber* the house of fiction implodes when a missile hits Voss's home. Digging through the flattened rubble, Gerd peels away 'the compressed layers that had once been storeys', descending through one floor after another until he arrives in the cellar. On a London bomb site, Martha Quest also archaeologically excavates an impacted house of fiction, stripping off thirteen separate skins of wall-paper, each the exiguous wrapping of a life now buried. This research through the tumulus of earth into which the novel's prehistory has sunk is countered by a mental ascent into the reclaimed sky, where the novel will have its future. Walking towards Notting Hill, Martha's body is an efficient machine on automatic pilot, her head 'a lighthouse or a radio set', beaming signals through the atmosphere. She is uncreated as a person, elucidated as an 'open-pored receptive being who hadn't a name', a transmitting-station of consciousness. Sex with Mark is a transfusion of febrile high energy from the mains; she is a candidate for analysis by one of Jimmy's machines which chart 'the human brain in terms of electric impulses'. The novel, like little England, must be outgrown. Mark betrays his fable of the heavenly city when he plans 'to turn it into a kind of novel'. Martha believes that what literature calls ' "life" had no place in that study', and is proud that it is ' "unreal".' Opposed to the realist blandishments of the novel, which renders the world covetable like the window-displays in the Oxford Street shops Martha wonders at, is the allegory of inner and outer spaces, where the world is analytically taken to pieces. Dr Lamb the psychiatrist is a figure from a morality play, wearing 'a mask which said "I am wisdom"', and it does not matter 'what he was personally'. The breakdown he induces in Martha and his insistence that she must kill the self is his benign pulverising of the false quantity the novel once knew as character. He is investigating her as if she were Lessing's sub-atomic particles.

Psychiatry, like Martha's casual sex with Jack, is, in the phrase Lessing uses of Jack's bordello-like consulting-room, 'a breakdown area'. The incest between Palmer and Honor Klein in *A Severed Head*, an intercourse of psychoanalysis and anthropology, has become a formula for generating a new breed of novel. The progeny of such unions, as Iris Murdoch's Martin learns from reading mythology, is often monstrous. But Murdoch's is the loose, baggy monster which is the Victorian novel, embodied as the marine creature in *The Sea, The Sea* and predicted by Loxias in *The Black Prince* when he says that artists create as if returning to the sea to spawn: 'The creator of form must suffer formlessness. Even risk dying of it'; Lessing's is not a revenant from past depths but a mutant visitor from the beyond, the product not of the subconscious sea but of the hyperintellectual sky.

In *Shikasta* (1979), the first of her galactic chronicle *Canopus in Argos: Archives*, Lessing lifts off from the England in which she arrived as a bemused colonial. Earth itself is a colonised planet now, policed by emissaries from outer space. Lessing's agent Johor looks back on Shikasta's 'century of destruction', our own twentieth century which was one long war with brief intermissions. Lessing herself can only see the realistic novel as a product of the small-minded, territorial squabbles which provoked that appalling combat. She leaves behind 'the petty fates of . . . individuals'. While Johor consults Proust in preparing his report on the troubled planet, he appraises him as 'sociologist and anthropologist', just as Lamb tells Martha, when she demands remedies for her crisis, 'you need a historian perhaps, or a sociologist'—never a novelist; the *History of Shikasta*, already in its three thousandth volume, studies not novelistic consciousness but the collective 'mentation' of these irrational earthlings.

However, this literary future is conceivable only as a circling-back to the remote past. The rulers from Canopus entrust information to a cadre of native story-tellers and song-makers who are forgetful and inefficient medieval bards, babbling of 'the far off times' and 'the great days', even though they are 'talking of no more than thirty years before'. Lessing's sacralisation of the lowly, literal novel operates by a longer feat of memory: her astral annals are modelled, she says, on the epic of sacred literature which is the Old Testament. Francis Coldridge in the *The Four-Gated City*, working to rehabilitate Africa in the late 1990s, complains that 'the human race has never had a memory', and that its history is a feeble substitute for it. That lack is made good by Francis's mother Lynda who, after becoming mercifully schizophrenic, has premonitory visions. This gift is Lessing's restitution and reversal of history: the novel's purpose, like Lynda's premonitions, is to remember the future before it happens.

L. P. Hartley in *The Go-Between* (1953) calls the past a foreign country, where they do things differently. Imaginatively expatriating England, novelists since the war render it foreign by writing either about its remote past like Golding, or about its future. The present requires what Kingsley Amis euphemises, in the case of the chorister's gelding, as an alteration. For Philip Larkin, reality itself is a foreign country: a yearning romantic elsewhere; a blazingly white and vacant symbolist nowhere.

Larkin's early prose poems are about an England in which reality has been suspended—and thus symbolically mystified—by the edicts of wartime emergency. John Kemp in *Jill* (1946) arrives at an arbitrary point in empty space which a railway porter alleges to be Oxford. The claim is unverifiable, because the name-plates on the platform have been removed. To baffle invaders, his native land has made an enigma of itself. His return journey to a blitzed Huddlesford has as its destination a place which may or may not still exist; his college cronies refuse to believe that it ever did so, claiming it to be a music-hall fiction. John himself is described by a teacher as a symbol best left undeciphered: 'one of those mysteries that are not worth solving.' He maintains the same attitude of hermeneutic disinterest towards his own experience. He leaves Huddlesford without seeing the parents he has come back to find; he incinerates the nonexistent Jill. He knows himself to be as illusory a fiction as the heroine of his nympholepsy. His teacher first invents him by encouraging him, and he receives identity as a disorienting gift of grace from without when his room-mate deigns to address him by his first name. Imagination enables him to be a foreigner to himself. When buying a bow-tie, he elaborately impersonates in fantasy the elegant Christopher. He turns to the composition of a novel because he wants to inhabit an existence other than his own. Like the first novelists, he is an epistolary forger, writing love-letters to a creature who is the self's projection onto another. The shame he feels when hearing himself 'referred to in the third person' is banished when he liberates that supernumerary person, its sex magically changed, for an independent career: 'He began writing about [Jill] in the third person.'

Jill is about creativity as our willed escape from actuality. Yet the dangerous triumph of John's creative effort is his invention of a being who is set free by his love for her, enabled to elude his control. Jill is less a character in a novel, authorised and anatomised and utterly known by the novelist, than the whimsically unreliable, playfully autonomous character of drama. She hints as much herself in an essay she reads, written by John on Minerva's behalf, about Shakespeare's difficulties with Shylock: the comic money-lender escapes from his creator and decides to be a tragic martyr. Or she is the even more ungraspable character of poetry, the romantic image or the symbol. John is paralysed by her 'habit . . . of appearing just at the moment when he was unable to follow her': she is Keats's *belle dame*, or his nightingale. This is imagination's tragedy. Ophelia was 'the more deceived' by it, and Keats, when the nightingale escapes, laments the 'deceiving elf' of fancy. Larkin's response thereafter is to congratulate himself on his disillusion; to be, as he puts it in the title of his 1955 volume of poems, *The Less Deceived*.

Katherine, the refugee of *A Girl in Winter* (1947), flinches from a reality in which she is an alien. At Dover, 'she did not want to land in this foreign country'. Everything in England is unintelligible, and she, too, with the symbolist's reverent instinct, propitiates the mystery by sparing it from analytic reason. She wonders what the posters saying 'Heat Wave' and 'Lunchtime Scores' mean, but refrains from asking. Nor can she 'break into the meaning' of Mr Anstey's aggrieved love-letter. The season abets her estrangement by crystallising things, icing and isolating them as images: 'the frost made everything stand alone and sparkle.' Winter's refrigeration is also an insurance against feeling, against the pain of John Kemp's or Ophelia's feverish vulnerability. Katherine is pleased when her hand is numbed by the water from the drinking-fountain; Miss Green whimperingly demands gas—'total anaesthetic'—when she has her tooth out. Denied a novelistic relationship with the society, Katherine instead apprehends it poetically. Appearances whose meaning is obscured become strangely or threateningly symbolic, like the 'dark, allusive conversation' of women leaning on counters in the shops. She experiences English, in a way the poet envies, as an idiom entirely new, idiosyncratic and intense. Mrs Fennel's unexceptional remark about the weather 'spoken as it was in a foreign language, came to Katherine with something of the impact of a line of poetry'.

Larkin's scruple as a poet is his exclusion of himself from experience with its sad, deceptive fulfillments. Like Katherine taken on her tour of an unknowable world or John in uninhabited Huddlesford, he is an exile in his own reality. It is this which makes such a grumpy unwilling romantic of him. Gazing in at the dance-hall in 'Reasons for Attendance' and imagining 'the wonderful feel of girls', he is Yeats's Keats with his face pressed to the window of the sweet-shop. Only by resigning himself to not living is he able to write. His charm is that he represents this sacrifice not as a solemn, hieratic vow, like Wordsworth or Yeats in their dread, absolutist watch-towers, but as a shuffling and pitiable incapacity: the missed chance of the Larkin in 'Annus Mirabilis', from the 1974 volume *High Windows*, who is just too late for sexual intercourse when it is invented in 1963. Larkin has said that deprivation is to him what daffodils were to Wordsworth. The remark is as affectionately dependent on the past it seems to dismiss as the sarcastic recollection of those same daffodils by Jimmy Porter or Brenton's Furry; it wryly claims kinship with Wordsworth rather than difference from him, because Wordsworth is already a poet habituated to loss, taking precautions against the time—soon to come—when he will be deprived even of the daffodils. Jill ends, remorsefully, in the flames; her successor in 'Lines on a young lady's photograph album', is saved from this immolation by the camera, which collects her in tranquility. At first, like John Kemp, Larkin wants her to be 'a real girl in a real place'. Then he reconciles himself to her protective sepulture in the album's unreality, and her relegation to the heaven of the past. Like Wordsworth's Lucy, the snapshot is the image as a souvenir. The same morbid service is performed sculpturally by the Arundel tomb in *The Whitsun Weddings* (1964): time transfigures the petrified couple, as the death-chamber of the camera does, into an untruth. Consciousness itself is an album of salvaged images. Larkin's interiors are cameras, sealed against the intrusion of a mortal truth—as perfected as Platonic ideas in the billboards of 'Essential Beauty', where 'in frames as large as rooms' the good life is proclaimed; more gloomily retentive in the mental theatres of 'The Old Fools', where senility is pictured as 'having lighted rooms/Inside your head, and people in them, acting.'

The poetry is made by privation, by emptying. Its spaces are austerely idyllic because they do not contain Larkin: 'Such attics cleared of me! Such absences!' Negative capability is in him a talent for self-negation. Katherine's desensitised winter turns into the obviated, abstracted settings of the poems, like the castle from which life has been evacuated at the end of Keats's *Eve of St Agnes*. In *The Less Deceived* these anywheres, locations like Coventry Station where nothing happens, are domestic nowheres, cubicles for solitude and cancellation—the 'special shell' of the disused chapel in 'Church Going', the 'bare and sun-scrubbed room' in 'Dry-Point', the 'squadron of empty cars' at the race-track in 'At Grass' or, most bleakly splendid in its phrasing, the 'desolate attic' into which the Victorian seducer spends himself in 'Deceptions'. The words Larkin treasures are those which no longer worry about possessing meaning or reference. Hence his morose affection for the 'scentless, weightless, strengthless, wholly/Untruthful' five syllables which are a girl's discarded maiden name, the appellation of an obsolete self. In *The Whitsun Weddings* Larkin's cells begin to resemble the airless tomb of the symbolist poem, locked and insulated against the live outdoors: the 'hired box' which was Mr Bleaney's allotment of space, the ambulances 'closed like confessionals', the humid carriage with its musty cushions which is the hearse from which Larkin looks out on a marrying world. In *High Windows* Keats's magic casements frame an infinite nothing. The sky pleases Larkin beause it is an ultimate insignificance, an empty space. Bathers in 'To the Sea' grasp 'at enormous air', above the vacated town in 'Livings' depends 'a big sky'. The Dutch scene in 'The Card-Players' is ominously roofed by 'starlessness', Larkin in 'Sad Steps' is outstared by 'the moon's cleanliness'. The lucent sky-scraping mortuary of the hospital in 'The Building' has a replica in the aerial architecture of cemented vapour: 'Cut Grass' looks up at a 'high-builded cloud', a memorial made from the life exhaled by the mown stalks.

The poems have their own palette of deprivation. Their recurrent tone is a desolating, blank whiteness, an absence of vital colour. White has always been a symbolist preference (along with the Hamlet-like costume of inky black monastically recommended to the dandy by Baudelaire), because it purges the world of significance. Théophile Gautier wrote a 'Symphonie en blanc majeur', and Robert Rauschenberg in 1951 made a series of white paintings which were scoured voids. But the Larkin who in his novels magics away England's reality and opens up the gelid blankness—an ice-age of emotion, with snowflakes accumulating into a burial mound and 'icefloes moving down a lightless channel of water'—which Katherine pictures at the end of *A Girl in Winter*, has in his poems, in compensation, found for the chilly homeless symbol a place in daily English reality.

Thus his whitely abstracted images are 'a wild white face' in a receding ambulance or, in 'Sympathy in White Major', the colourless potion of a gin and tonic, into which he drops four ice-cubes. The drink is his comical and actual English equivalent to the opium of the symbolists, or the mescalin of Huxley's California. Amis's tippling publican in *The Green Man* also boozes mystically: his cocktails grant him elevation of the spirit, and temporary release from the body. Larkin mixes for himself at the end of the day a concoction which provokes those correspondences between the senses and the arts relished by Mallarmé. His drink even makes music, when the ice chimes as it falls into the empty glass. The poem wryly acknowledges the gap between this intoxicating, obliterating whiteness, whose ice is a sliver from what 'The Old Fools' calls 'extinction's alp', and the different registration of the non-colour in society and in reality, where it is a sign of merely racial pedigree. Larkin in the glow of drink toasts himself as 'the whitest man I know', and at once adds that 'white is not my favourite colour'. The poem alcoholically formulates the symbol, then rejects it.

The radiant girl on the poster in 'Sunny Prestatyn' wears taut white satin, as mystical a costume as Tennyson's white samite. Again the symbol is jeeringly dethroned by actuality. Graffiti scribblers supply the ideal nymph with a lustfully itchy body, or stigmatise her with pen-knives. Then the paper is ripped across, leaving only 'some blue'. But that damage is her angelic ascent into the 'deep blue air' of 'High Windows'. The exotic colours of the symbolists, luxuriously evoked by Wilde's Salomé for instance, are in Larkin a synthetic unreality, chemically devising natureless fabrics for his fallen nymphs to wear. The Whitsun brides exchange whites for the 'lemons, mauves, and olive-ochres' of their going-away dresses, and in 'The Large Cool Store' they can shop for bri-nylon nighties tinted 'lemon, sapphire, moss-green'.

The symbolist rhetoric of annihilation acquires in Larkin a glumly English voice. His nearest approach to *néant* is a gruff taciturnity, which insists that there is 'Nothing to be said' or shrugs at the end of the elegy for Mr Bleaney 'I don't know.' He has a genius for linguistic begrudgement, making interiors tragic by stranding objects in a syntactic desuetude, denying them sentences to come alive in: thus, in 'Home is so Sad',

> Look at the pictures and the cutlery.
> The music in the piano stool. That vase.

Likewise the Baudelairean *poésie des départs* finds in Larkin its plaintively comic correlative—doing a bunk in the poem from *The Less Deceived* named after Baudelaire's phrase; taking off in a Comet from Heathrow airport in 'Naturally the Foundation will Bear Your Expenses'. Always, as in these propulsive leave-takings, the end of the poem mimes a small death. That is a romantic fear, and 'Forget What Did' concludes, like Keats's autumn poem with its migrating swallows, at the premonitory moment 'when the birds go'. In 'Going, Going' Larkin anticipates, as he surveys a greedily annexed and poisoned nature, all 'England gone'; but the venerable age of the attitude equips its nihilism with a ready-made consolation. Already in Chaucer and Spenser the native ground is unhallowed, and from Blake through Wordsworth to Ruskin and Hopkins poetry has complained of nature's destruction and of England's. There is an indigenous heartiness to Larkin's despair.

In the poetry of Ted Hughes, imperilled England is regained by excavation. The pond where the pike swims in his *Lupercal* (1960) is 'deep as England': a pool of collective unconsciousness. For Seamus Heaney, too, imagination roots itelf in a subsoil. The bogland of Heaney's Ireland is a mouldy humus of memory and a muddy well of earth's throttled speech. Hughes and Heaney have therefore both literally returned to the English poet's ancient identification with the husbandman, which made Langland allegorise the ploughman's vocation or Spenser represent himself as Colin Clout. Hughes farms in Devon in *Moortown* (1979), Heaney leaves Belfast for what he calls, in a collection also published in 1979, *Field Work* at Glanmore.

Their recurrence to husbandry happens at a moment when the English pastoral is being declared by others extinct, or exposed as a fraud. Barbara in Hare's *Saigon* remembers the indecent, damp greenness of England, with its cramping hedgerows and its crowded airlessness. Suffocated, she has had to leave. Ian McEwan gruesomely inters the pastoral in his 1978 novel *The Cement Garden*. It is by now an inorganic assemblage of bric-à-brac—a plaster statuette of Pan presides over a rockery and a dried pond in a south London yard—and is best paved over and repressed by concrete. The only pleasures permitted are arid ones, mockeries of the poet's marriage with nature. When Jack masturbates, his seed quickly dies and dries, crusting on the pavement. Cement is his weapon against the messy, bodily obscenity of nature, a constipation of vital process. Heroically, Jack exerts himself to solidify the earth, to block its uprising rivers of seepage and rot. Whatever is fluid in the novel is foul: McEwan's equivalents to Heaney's slurping articulate peat bog are Jack's oily integument of pustules, the slick goo of suntan lotion he smears over his sister, the green scum which grows on the crockery stowed under his bed, the custardy bowels of the frog he squashes, and the putrefying stench of his mother, announcing herself through the coffining layer of concrete. Even though he gives up washing and taking baths, Jack cannot abolish nature. The nightmare of this novel is, in McEwan's film *The Ploughman's Lunch* (1982), a mere cynical imposture. The eponymous meal, like the cement garden, symbolises England. It is supposedly a rustic repast. By eating bread and cheese, we can all pretend to be simple countryfolk. Actually no ploughman ever ate it. One of McEwan's soured journalists points out that it was invented only a few years ago, as a marketing ploy to get people to eat in pubs. The pastoral has been captured by the advertising agencies, latter-day mythographers.

As farmers and as archaeologists, Hughes and Heaney remain unregenerate romantics. In 'The Horses' from *The Hawk in the Rain* (1957) Hughes, confirming Larkin's comment, writes his own version of Wordsworth's poem about the daffodils: an anecdote of world-hatching energy—for the horses starting into life at dawn are an eruptive genesis, like the making of a poem—tranquillised for recollection 'in din of the crowded streets'. Hughes's jaguar is Blake's tiger reborn; his tomcat, fanged and blood-thirsty, derides the domestic pets of T. S. Eliot's Old Possum. The ultimate exhibit in his bestiary is the poet himself, the wild man in social captivity, described in one of the 1957 poems as 'the monster'. Hare calls his play *A Map of the World* because such a map, according to Wilde, would be worthless unless it contained a Utopia, and the dramatist's obligation is to marshal history's advance towards that future. Hughes's poetic maps can dispense with Utopias but must contain wildernesses and jungles, and he laments in 'Fourth of July' that 'the right maps have no monsters'. Here, like D. H. Lawrence, he sees the colonisation of America as the extinction of the irrational. He retains, however, his own biological cartography: a darkness still burns in the body's underworld, and in the blood. *Moortown* extends this primitive map-making by redrawing Prospero's island and returning it to the possession of Caliban's dam, Sycorax. The rational engineer with his wand and his white magic has, as his secret consort, the monster. Hughes's beasts all engage in their own proleptic writing. As the poet's fingers move on the blank pages, so the thought-fox neatly imprints the snow outside, and the gnats in *Wodwo* (1967) inscribe a scribbled lexicon on the air.

The sequence about the rearing of beef cattle in Devon sees the routines of farming as analogies for the parturition which agonisingly brings to birth—and then slaughters—a poem. More viscerally than earlier romantics, Hughes creates from a rending labour of the body. The words, placenta-like, are an extension from him. Therefore his poems about the miscarrying torments of the animals in his care: the lamb which 'could not get born', or the one which expires 'with the yellow birth mucus / still in his cardigan', the struggle of a calf from the gushing, puddled interior of its mother. 'February 17th' is about the romantic creator's killing of a brain-child, sentenced to die as soon as it is written down. Hughes slits the throat of a lamb and levers off the head to help it get born; he then has to reach in and drag the corpse out of the ewe. His Prometheus, in one of the poems developed from Peter Brook's ritual performance of *Orghast* at Shiraz in 1972, needs the vulture to assist his poetic re-creation of himself by tearing the liver from his body, for the predator gnawing at him teaches him what it is to possess that organ imitated by imagination, a womb. Theogony, the most audacious poetic feat, also happens in a byre. Hughes's Prometheus 'had resolved god / as a cow swallows its afterbirth'.

This research of the insides coincides with the exhuming of a past secreted in the earth. The bear in *Wodwo* digs 'through the wall of the Universe', and in *Remains of Elmet* (1979) the ancient Briton under the rock is buried with the bones of a sabre-tooth tiger. Hughes's poetry is an enforced unearthing, the Caesarean sectioning of nature. Elmet in Yorkshire was the last Celtic kingdom to fall before the advancing, rationalising Angles, and its defenders with the instinct of poets made their stand in a ditch; Hughes finds the glaciated valley to be a grave—of Celtic antiquities and of industrial wreckage ('old siftings of sewing machines and shuttles'), of tree-cenotaphs and of Emily Brontë, fatally embraced by the landscape—but also a womb, for he wishes a salutary decay on a derelict mill, saying

> Before these chimneys can flower again
> They must fall into the only future, the earth

and requesting for another Victorian ruin 'two minutes silence / In the childhood of earth'. His anchorage and grounding enable Hughes to extend backwards and downwards to the epic beginnings of literature, which long precede the pacified spirit of pastoral. The thistles in another *Wodwo* poem are a vengeful resurrection, their spikes an outgrowth from the 'splintered weapons and Icelandic frost . . . of a decayed Viking'; sawing bloodied horns off his cattle in *Moortown* and heaping up the severed parts, Hughes might himself be a Viking, carving from nature antlers to ornament a helmet.

His earth toughens, grows calloused and metallic. Like Wordsworth's it has a mineral stoicism. 'Below words', he listens for 'meanings that will not part from rock.' Heaney describes a nature softer, more spongily absorbent. Things in Hughes are gripped in the dead rigour of an iron or an ice age, like the frozen tractor in *Moortown*; things in Heaney are gobbled up by a ground which stores them as nourishment and is itself, as he says in *Door into the Dark* (1969), 'kind, black butter', yieldingly molten. Hughes seeks the skeleton, and imagines himself skinning a dead badger found on a Somerset road or hacking off its head and boiling it down 'to liberate his masterpiece skull'. The murder is preservative: 'I want him / to stay as he is.' Heaney has no need of such violence, or of the abbatoir which is Hughes's *Gaudete* (1977). His soggy moss is as adhesive, retentive and affectionate as memory.

Traditionally, the pastoral connotes a meditative inertia. Marvell's gardens are endangered by mowers. For Heaney, though, poetry is an agrarian labour, and in *Death of a Naturalist* (1966) he describes the pen as an implement for digging. The chore of blackberry-picking is another analogy for writing. The poet like the farm-hand dabbles in gore and mire: red ink from the berries stains his fingers. This is Heaney's commentary on the rapine of Wordsworth's nutting. Instead of his predecessor's assault on nature, Heaney describes a grateful feeding. Wordsworth's hands are guilty—is imagination a robbery from divinity, like Eve's of the apple?—while Heaney's are childishly reddened and sticky. The writer is a licensed, innocent mess-maker. In 'Churning Day', Heaney's reminiscence is of Keats: creativity is fermentation. Rural trades mime the discipline of poetry. The thatcher pins down his world as he staples sheaves, and the diviner's forked, twangling rod of hazel is the wand of a bucolic Prospero. The divination of water sources, though conducted 'without a word', exactly catches the poet's mystic access to a well of eloquence—the backyard pump which is Heaney's 'personal Helicon'—stored underground. A parched laconicism signals a critical seizure in language. Speech for Heaney's docker is 'clamped in the lips' vice', and the plunger in 'Rite of Spring' ices up, blocked in catatonia. Christ's miracle at Cana is interpreted by Heaney as a poetic feat, unleashing in a gush of words the 'water locked behind the taps'.

The bog's gift to Heaney is its damp, malleable volubility. It is an oral earth, 'the unstopped mouth/Of an urn' as he says in one of of the 1975 *Bog Poems*, and therefore, in its irrigating torrent of speech, a reply to the coolly silent vessel overheard by Keats. It is a nest for what the bog queen calls 'illiterate roots', but that very illiteracy ensures the backward growth of poetry from script to speech. Heaney's earth is succulently vocal. Wounding it with a spade, he hears the 'soft lips' of the gash mutter, and in one of the poems from *North* (1975) that labial orifice becomes the 'opened ground' of a woman's body when she gives birth. As a guzzling mouth and a ruminating maw, insatiably swallowing swords and caskets along with pats of butter, the quagmire is Heaney's medium of connection with language and with his predecessors who are also embroiled in it.

If Johnson, melancholically glossing Lichfield, understands etymology as a funeral, Heaney sees it as the lively organic plantation of a word, the resumption of that marriage to a thing or a place so grievously broken off in Auden's theory of writing. Thus in 'Beldberg', pondering 'Mossbawn,/A bogland name', he seeks the word's literal rooting—possible only if the word is illiterate, which means alive in speech not deceased in print—as 'a forked root in that ground'. He speaks of language as a sediment, in which we are collectively embedded, like the Elizabethan vocabulary in *Wintering Out* (1972) which 'beds us down' and makes the guttural Irish intermarry with and into the alliterative British Isles, or like the wedding ring 'bedded forever', interred while alive in flesh on the hand of the 'Mother of the Groom'.

Etymology is for Heaney an affair 'of roots and graftings', the applied science of the farmer. Speech advances into an era of primitive industry, employing the tongue as a factor, which melds the sound into what 'A New Song' describes as 'a vocable'. Phonetics, too, is in Heaney's understanding a recapitulation of his language's and his country's history. The vowel, emitted by an open mouth, is a licking, burbling spring from 'native haunts'. Ploughing, as the 'Glanmore Sonnets' in *Field Work* declare, is the opening of vowels in the ground. Vowels are also the gustatory pleasure of language, tickling the soft palate like the oysters Heaney sups and from which he imbibes 'verb, pure verb'; they are the salivation of 'soft-mouthed life', envied by Heaney's pike (so dissimilar from the same fish in Hughes, with its malevolent grin). While vowels are spawningly liquid and effusive, consonants are the dry delimitation of terrain, staking out demesnes and plosively sounding aggressive fanfares. Against the throaty gargling of the Celtic vowels, Heaney hears consonants as the march-past of an invading Anglo-Saxon army. Alliteration is language's military measure.

Rather than purifying speech, like Mallarmé and Eliot, Heaney muddies it. From this immersion derives his covenant with the entirety of a literary past inherited and tended, as if it were the land, by him. Therefore, when he remembers Hamlet, it is not as the moral novelist of Iris Murdoch, selflessly and with god-like generosity substantiating a dream and advancing from Bradley Pearson's 'fantasy world' to 'the real world' where we all must live, nor as the radically propulsive dramatist approved by Griffiths and restrained by Stoppard, revving up an inert society, but as a poet like himself, equally intimate with the nutritious soil, following as Heaney does 'a worm of thought/ . . . into the mud': in *North* he announces, 'I am Hamlet the Dane', handler of skulls, smeller of rot, jovial delver in graves, blathering about an Ophelia who has preceded him into the bog.

Heaney's sense of words as a fertilisation of nature enables him, like the Elizabethans, to restore to language its status as the indwelling spirit of place. He catches a chimerical glimpse of Spenser 'dreaming sunlight', and offers to Ireland the imaginative sanctification bestowed on England by Drayton's *Poly-Olbion* in his auditions of the vocal sites in *Wintering Out*: the hill of Anahorish with its 'soft-gradient/of consonant, vowel-meadow'; reedily guttural and gurgling Moyola; Toome with its 'soft blastings' inside the mouth, clearing an alluvial souterrain in the throat; Broag whose 'black *O*' tunnels into the cleaving murk of the river-bank. He digs back through the impasted strata of poetry, resuming its history—when he arrives at bedrock— within himself, just as he has absorbed the language into his own body. In an iambic twilight he proposes to his wife (who dismisses the notion) that they are latter-day versions of William and Dorothy Wordsworth. Asleep on the moss in Donegal, they impersonate Shakespeare's Lorenzo and Jessica, extradited from Belmont to a cold climate. Fishing, Heaney recites the angling lore of Izaak Walton; spearing rats with a pitch-fork, he asks over again the question which perplexed Shelley and Sidney: 'What is my apology for poetry?'

As a museum of archaeological and verbal treasures, the bog allows him congress with an even profounder buried past. Reflecting on the etymology of '*bān-hūs*', he resorts to the mead-hall of Bede, where the soul is a bird in transit fluttering lost in the roof; and raking through his dungeon of linguistic relics he comes upon an echo of bardic enunciation:

> The scop's
> twang, the iron
> flash of consonants

—the rallying alliterativeness of *Beowulf*, which instigates poetic speech in English. Earth constitutes for Heaney a vertical anthology of literature. The end, when it arrives, is a reunion at long last with the beginning.

Index